LEGAL PROBLEMS OF
INTERNATIONAL ECONOMIC RELATIONS

CASES, MATERIALS AND TEXT ON THE NATIONAL AND INTERNATIONAL REGULATION OF TRANSNATIONAL ECONOMIC RELATIONS

Fifth Edition

By

John H. Jackson
University Professor
Georgetown University Law Center

William J. Davey
Guy Raymond Jones Chair in Law
University of Illinois College of Law

Alan O. Sykes, Jr.
James and Patricia Kowal Professor of Law
Stanford University School of Law

AMERICAN CASEBOOK SERIES®

Mat #40360106

American Casebook Series and West Group are trademarks registered in the U.S. Patent and Trademark Office.

COPYRIGHT © 1986, 1995 WEST PUBLISHING CO.

© West, a Thomson business, 2002

© 2008 Thomson/West
      610 Opperman Drive
      St. Paul, MN 55123
      1–800–313–9378

Printed in the United States of America

ISBN: 978–0–314–16026–3

 *TEXT IS PRINTED ON 10% POST CONSUMER RECYCLED PAPER*

Preface to the Fifth Edition

In the preface to the First Edition of this Casebook, we said that "preparing a book on the subject of international economic regulation is like trying to describe the landscape by looking out the window of a moving train—events tend to move faster than one can describe them." Nothing could be more true in our experience as we prepared the Fifth Edition.

The breadth and scope of the subject matter has become almost overwhelming, and has posed great challenges to us, as well as our many colleagues in law teaching who teach from this book, and all of our students. The treaty framework of our subject has not greatly changed since the Third Edition—which described in detail the full results of the Uruguay Round and the creation of the World Trade Organization (WTO). However, since 1996 an amazingly rich and detailed jurisprudence has developed in the WTO, particularly through the 85 decisions of the new Appellate Body, which has put its stamp on the interpretation of a number of important GATT provisions (especially Articles III and XX), as well as several of the other WTO agreements (particularly, the Antidumping, Safeguards, SPS and Subsidies Agreements). It has been the goal of our work on the Fifth Edition to incorporate this jurisprudence into these teaching materials to the fullest extent possible and the new edition contains over 30 WTO decisions.

The basic theme of the previous editions—the impact of international economic interdependence and the struggle of legal institutions to cope with that circumstance—has been confirmed many times over, and is carried forward in this edition.

We have benefited from our own experiences in teaching with the previous editions. We have also benefited from the suggestions and criticisms of the many student and faculty users. The Uruguay Round expanded the subject, and to keep the book manageable, it will be easily seen that both the subtractions and the additions for this edition have been substantial. We do not claim the perfect balance between the myriad of competing desires of teachers and students of this subject, but we hope and expect that we have considerably improved the book with our efforts.

An important basic goal of all editions, however, needs to be repeated. It is very easy to tally up multiple dozens of subjects which a potential international legal practitioner would find useful when he or she begins to grapple with real world problems. We do not intend to offer a complete coverage of these dozens of subjects, nor even a substantial portion of them. We aim, instead, to offer the student, professor, or current practitioner, the means to achieve a basic understanding of the international economic system as it operates in real life, and as it is constrained or aided by a number of fundamental legal institutions, including national and international constitutional documents and processes. In doing this adequately, we have necessarily had to minimize the coverage of many other practical topics. In a number of cases, however, many of those topics have been covered in other courses in the curriculum.

Our goal for this book, and courses based upon it, is to penetrate deeply into subjects which can have great importance to the government or private practitioner, but which are essentially not covered in other law courses. In addition our goal is to build for the student a knowledge of the "foundations" of the legal system and institutions of international economic relations. This implies knowledge of the constituent international instruments and processes, and the ways those interact with the important national constituent instruments and processes.

The objective of this book is to look at the legal principles and processes as they affect decisions regarding international economic relations, whether the decisions be those of private citizens or enterprises, or government officials. Thus there is an integration of national regulation and international law, and to a much lesser extent private transaction law (which however is not emphasized in this course because it is often a part of or at least analogous to material learned in other courses). For example, United States constitutional and regulatory rules have an intimate and weighty connection and influence on the international rules of the WTO. One must study both to fully understand how they operate, because they interact.

Secondly, the emphasis is on trade in goods because this is generally at the center of international economic relations. However, we have expanded our treatment of the new topics added in the Uruguay Round negotiations, with particular focus on dispute settlement decisions in the intellectual property area and services. Nonetheless, it is our view that the principles learned in discussing trade in goods are almost always transferable to other economic relation subjects, e.g. the constitutional problems of division of governmental authority within a nation, the practicalities of negotiating new international rules, the "constitutional" status of international norms, the difficulties of international dispute settlement procedures, the particular weight of special interest groups and their influence compared with broader but more diffuse foreign policy objectives or the interests of the consumers, the operation of legislative bodies, the decision and voting processes of international organizations, the economic complexity of some of the rules and the difficulty of fact finding.

Thirdly, the emphasis of this book is on the legal processes in *context*, but the emphasis is on *law*. The context obviously includes difficult conceptual and empirical questions of economics and political science, of sociology, history and especially overall foreign policy. But the emphasis here is on those subjects which have developed relatively sophisticated *rule* systems. There are many important subjects which have not yet developed such rule systems, and while touched upon they have not been selected for extensive treatment. (A course in economics, or world politics, therefore, might involve quite a different selection.) For example, both export controls and problems of developing countries merit considerable policy attention. But rule systems or the influence of law on those subjects is not (yet) weighty. Both subjects are dealt with in this book, but the focus on the primary goal of understanding the operation of *law*, means that it is necessary to eschew some tempting elaborations of policy questions when they, as yet, depend so little on law. This does not foreclose, of course, the opportunity for a particular teacher to construct for his or her class a rule formulating exercise based on the current and temporary materials bearing on the policy issues. Nor does this reflect any view of the authors regarding the relative importance in a broader context of non-legal materials or information. It reflects our view that it is useful for law students to examine closely to what extent their particular skills and knowledge could contribute to solution of the myriad international economic problems.

Fourthly, a basic goal of these materials is to be sensitive to their use in the setting of the American law school curricula, so as to avoid unnecessary duplication of other courses, and to present to the student a coherent subject matter that is not likely to be obtained elsewhere. This is the reason, for example, for de-emphasizing private transaction law in this book, while focusing on government regulation. It is also a reason for minimizing duplication of material often included in either public or private (conflicts) international law. To a certain degree we see this course as a logical sequel to the course in public international law. However, this book is designed to accommodate the many students who take it without first having taken international law.

Fifthly, closely related to the previous "premise," is the notion that this course should be sensitive to the problems faced by practitioners—lawyers or officials, but should also offer the student something which he or she may never again (in practice) have the opportunity to get—namely, an opportunity to examine at length and in depth the overall operation of the "legal system" governing international economic affairs. The day to day problems faced by practitioners will quickly give the young lawyer experience in "how to do it," and great expertise on rather precise narrow topics. What is hard to obtain after leaving law school is the opportunity to spend a considerable amount of time achieving a comprehensive understanding of the total system and the interrelationships of its parts. This book emphasizes this comprehensive viewpoint.

Finally, so as to minimize the otherwise rapid obsolescence of both this book and students' learning, attention has been directed more toward the "constitutional" or fundamental aspects of the subject, eschewing too much concern with very recent "current events."

One last note. Many non-case materials are included. In particular, documents are important, and the supplement contains the text of key documents. Most chapters contain many queries or problems, and often these must be discussed in the context of the documents in the supplement. Consequently the class time needed for such discussion may be greater than would appear from the number of pages devoted to a topic. Often class discussion can center around the problems in the light of the material furnished, including the documents.

This book is designed primarily for a three-semester hour course (45 classroom hours) although it is clear that a course of such length cannot cover all of this book. A four-hour (60 classes) course would likely be both necessary (and sufficient) to complete all of this book. A shorter course is feasible with careful selection, as many of our users know.

JOHN H. JACKSON
WILLIAM J. DAVEY
ALAN O. SYKES

Washington, D.C.
Champaign, Illinois
Palo Alto, California

Acknowledgments

The fifth edition of this book has built considerably on the first four, and thus we continue to be in the debt of all those who contributed so much to them. As the book evolved into its fifth edition, we were particularly indebted to the comments and reactions received from teachers and students who used prior editions, in particular those who have taken our courses in international trade law at the University of Michigan Law School, the Georgetown University Law Center, the University of Illinois College of Law, the University of Chicago Law School, and the Stanford University School of Law. In addition, we are much indebted to our friends and colleagues, both within and without the legal profession, both here and abroad, who have patiently engaged in discussions with us and/or reviewed drafts of the manuscript covering some of the difficult issues raised in a book with such a broad scope as this one.

While it is not possible to name all of those who contributed significantly to our work and thinking in preparing this edition, a few individuals who have worked with us closely are particularly worthy of recognition. Professor Davey thanks his administrative assistant Sue Carrell, and Professor Sykes wishes to thank Stefania Fusco for invaluable research assistance.

*

Summary of Contents

Chapter 1. The Policies Underlying International Economic Relations

Chapter 2. An Introduction to the Economics of International Trade

Chapter 3. The United States Constitution and Regulation of International Economic Affairs

*

Table of Contents

Chapter 8. Border Measures I: Tariffs and Customs Rules

Chapter 9. Border Measures II: Quotas, Non–Tariff Barriers and Transparency

Chapter 22. Monetary Affairs and Trade Policy

Table of Cases

The principal cases are in bold type. Cases cited or discussed in the text are roman type. References are to pages. Cases cited in principal cases and within other quoted materials are not included.

Court Decisions (U.S. and European)

Table of WTO Decisions
(with Short Names and Full Cites)
(Principal cases are in bold)

Note: For the complete WTO document identifier, add to the document number "/R" for the panel report and "/AB/R" for the Appellate Body report. For compliance reports, add "W" to the foregoing for the first compliance reports and "W2" for the second.

Short Name	Full Case Title and Citation	Pages
Argentina—Footwear (EC)	**Argentina—Safeguard Measures on Imports of Footwear**, WT/DS121, adopted 12 January 2000	**705, 718, 722**
Argentina—Hides and Leather	Argentina—Measures Affecting the Export of Bovine Hides and Import of Finished Leather, WT/DS155 and Corr.1, adopted 16 February 2001	463
Argentina—Poultry Anti–Dumping Duties	Argentina—Definitive Anti–Dumping Duties on Poultry from Brazil, WT/DS241, adopted 19 May 2003	517
Australia—Automotive Leather II (Article 21.5—US)	Australia—Subsidies Provided to Producers and Exporters of Automotive Leather—Recourse to Article 21.5 of the DSU by the United States, WT/DS126, adopted 11 February 2000	906
Australia—Salmon	Australia—Measures Affecting Importation of Salmon, WT/DS18, adopted 6 November 1998	284, 332, 667
Brazil—Aircraft	**Brazil—Export Financing Programme for Aircraft**, WT/DS46, adopted 20 August 1999	284, 365, **888**
Brazil—Aircraft (Article 21.5—Canada) I & II	Brazil—Export Financing Programme for Aircraft—Recourse by Canada to Article 21.5 of the DSU, WT/DS46, adopted 4 August 2000 and 23 August 2001	894
Brazil—Retreaded Tires	Brazil—Measures Affecting Imports of Retreaded Tyres, WT/DS332, adopted 17 December 2007	599, 627, 643
Canada—Aircraft	**Canada—Measures Affecting the Export of Civilian Aircraft**, WT/DS70, adopted 20 August 1999	284, 365, **858**
Canada—Aircraft (Article 21.5—Brazil)	**Canada—Measures Affecting the Export of Civilian Aircraft—Recourse by Brazil to Article 21.5 of the DSU**, WT/DS70, adopted 4 August 2000	305, **884**, 894
Canada—Aircraft Credits and Guarantees	Canada—Export Credits and Loan Guarantees for Regional Aircraft, WT/DS222, adopted 19 February 2002	894
Canada—Aircraft Credits and Guarantees (Article 22.6—Canada)	Decision by the Arbitrators, Canada—Export Credits and Loan Guarantees for Regional Aircraft, WT/DS222/ARB, 17 February 2003	365
Canada—Autos	**Canada—Certain Measures Affecting the Automotive Industry**, WT/DS139, adopted 19 June 2000	**483**, 489, 515, 904, **959**
Canada—Dairy	Canada—Measures Affecting the Importation of Milk and the Exportation of Dairy Products, WT/DS103, adopted 27 October 1999	284, 384, 442, 907
Canada—Patent Term	Canada—Term of Patent Protection, WT/DS170, adopted 12 October 2000	1007
Canada—Periodicals	**Canada—Certain Measures Concerning Periodicals**, WT/DS31, adopted 30 July 1997	320, **966**
Canada—Pharmaceutical Patents	**Canada—Patent Protection of Pharmaceutical Products**, WT/DS114, adopted 7 April 2000	**1107**, 1034
Canada—Wheat Board	**Canada—Measures Relating to Exports of Wheat and Treatment of Imported Grain**, WT/DS276, adopted 27 September 2004	**449**
Chile—Alcoholic Beverages	Chile—Taxes on Alcoholic Beverages, WT/DS87, adopted 12 January 2000	561
Chile—Price Band System	**Chile—Price Band System and Safeguard Measures Relating to Certain Agricultural Products**, WT/DS207, adopted 23 October 2002	284, **436**
Dominican Republic—Import and Sale of Cigarettes	Dominican Republic—Measures Affecting the Importation and Internal Sale of Cigarettes, WT/DS302, adopted 19 May 2005	583, 605
EC—Approval and Marketing of Biotech Products	European Communities—Measures Affecting the Approval and Marketing of Biotech Products, WT/DS291, adopted 21 November 2006	668

Short Name	Full Case Title and Citation	Pages
Mexico—Telecoms	Mexico—Measures Affecting Telecommunications Services, WT/DS204, adopted 1 June 2004	970
Thailand—H—Beams	Thailand—Anti–Dumping Duties on Angles, Shapes and Sections of Iron or Non–Alloy Steel and H–Beams from Poland, WT/DS122, adopted 5 April 2001	824
Turkey—Rice	Turkey—Measures Affecting the Importation of Rice, WT/DS334, adopted 22 October 2007	443
Turkey—Textiles	**Turkey—Restrictions on Imports of Textile and Clothing Products**, WT/DS34, adopted 19 November 1999	279, 281, **506,** 746
US—1916 Act	United States—Anti–Dumping Act of 1916, WT/DS136, adopted 26 September 2000	284, 365, 804
US—Carbon Steel	United States—Countervailing Duties on Certain Corrosion–Resistant Carbon Steel Flat Products from Germany, WT/DS213, adopted 19 December 2002	779
US—Certain EC Products	United States—Import Measures on Certain Products from the European Communities, WT/DS165, adopted 10 January 2001	350
US—Continued Suspension	United States—Continued Suspension of Obligations in the EC—Hormones Dispute, WT/DS320 (on appeal as of June 2008)	669
US—Copyright	**United States—Section 110(5) of the US Copyright Act**, WT/DS160, adopted 27 July 2000	284, **1031**
US—Cotton	United States—Subsidies on Upland Cotton, WT/DS267, adopted 21 March 2005	321, 442, 907, 921
US—Cotton (Article 21.5—Brazil)	United States—Subsidies on Upland Cotton—Recourse to Article 21.5 of the DSU by Brazil, WT/DS267, adopted [24 June 2008]	907
US—Countervailing Measures on Certain EC Products	United States—Countervailing Measures Concerning Certain Products from the European Communities, WT/DS212, adopted 8 January 2003	284
US—Export Restraints	United States—Measures Treating Exports Restraints as Subsidies, WT/DS194, adopted 23 August 2001	862
US—FSC	**United States—Tax Treatment for "Foreign Sales Corporations"**, WT/DS108, adopted 20 March 2000	279, 280, 281, 284, **895**
US—FSC (Article 21.5—EC) I & II	United States—Tax Treatment for "Foreign Sales Corporations"—Recourse to Article 21.5 of the DSU by the European Communities, WT/DS108, adopted 29 January 2002 and 14 March 2006	903, 904
US—FSC (Article 22.6—US)	Decision by the Arbitrator, United States—Tax Treatment for "Foreign Sales Corporations", WT/DS108/ARB, 30 August 2002	365
US—Gambling	**United States—Measures Affecting the Cross–Border Supply of Gambling and Betting Services**, WT/DS285, adopted 20 April 2005	365, 366, 592, 599, 636, **972**
US—Gambling (Article 21.5—Antigua and Barbuda)	United States—Measures Affecting the Cross–Border Supply of Gambling and Betting Services—Recourse to Article 21.5 of the DSU by Antigua and Barbuda, WT/DS285, adopted 22 May 2007	990
US—Gambling (Article 22.6—US)	Decision by the Arbitrator, **United States—Measures Affecting the Cross–Border Supply of Gambling and Betting Services**, WT/DS285/ARB, 21 December 2007	**350,** 991
US—Gasoline	**United States—Standards for Reformulated and Conventional Gasoline**, WT/DS2, adopted 20 May 1996	280, 281, 315, 592, **606,** 626, 643
US—Helms Burton	United States—The Cuban Liberty and Democratic Solidarity Act, WT/DS39 (settled)	279
US—Hot–Rolled Steel	United States—Anti–Dumping Measures on Certain Hot–Rolled Steel Products from Japan, WT/DS184, adopted 23 August 2001	463, 778, 840
US—Lamb	**United States—Safeguard Measures on Imports of Fresh, Chilled or Frozen Lamb Meat from New Zealand and Australia**, WT/DS177, adopted 16 May 2001	325, **700, 712,** 720, **727,** 742
US—Lead and Bismuth II	**United States—Imposition of Countervailing Duties on Certain Hot–Rolled Lead and Bismuth Carbon Steel Products Originating in the United Kingdom**, WT/DS138, adopted 7 June 2000	335, **862**
US—OCTG Sunset Reviews	United States—Sunset Reviews of Anti–Dumping Measures on Oil Country Tubular Goods from Argentina, WT/DS268, adopted 17 December 2004	789
US—Offset Act (Byrd Amendment)	**United States—Continued Dumping and Subsidy Offset Act of 2000**, WT/DS217, adopted 27 January 2003	284, 365, **804**
US—Procurement	United States—Measure Affecting Government Procurement, WT/DS88 (settled)	589
US—Section 211 Appropriations Act	United States—Section 211 Omnibus Appropriations Act of 1998, WT/DS176, adopted 1 February 2002	1035
US—Section 301 Trade Act	United States—Sections 301–310 of the Trade Act of 1974, WT/DS152, adopted 27 January 2000	279, 304, 341
US—Shrimp	**United States—Import Prohibition of Certain Shrimp and Shrimp Products**, WT/DS58, adopted 6 November 1998	279, 281, 315, 335, 462, 592,

Table of GATT, NAFTA and CUSFTA Decisions

(Principal cases are in bold)

Table of U.S. Administrative Decisions

(Principal cases are in bold)

---

*

A Note on Style and Abbreviations

We have indicated deletions from quoted materials by asterisks, except that we have not indicated deletions of footnotes, citations or internal cross references. The following is a list of common abbreviations used in the book:

List of Common Abbreviations

AB	Appellate Body		EU	European Union
AD	Antidumping		FCN	Friendship Commerce and Navigation
ASP	American Selling Price			
BNA ITR	Bureau of National Affairs, International Trade Reporter—Current Reports		FOB	Free on Board
			GATS	General Agreement on Trade in Services
BOP	Balance of Payments		GATT	General Agreement on Tariffs and Trade
BTN	Brussels Tariff Nomenclature			
CAP	Common Agricultural Policy of the EU		GSP	Generalized System of Preferences
CIF	Cost, Insurance and Freight		HTS	Harmonized Tariff System
CIT	Court of International Trade		IBRD	International Bank for Reconstruction and Development ("World Bank")
Comecon	Council for Mutual Economic Assistance (Communist countries)			
			IMF	International Monetary Fund
COREPER	Committee of Permanent Representatives		ITA	International Trade Administration, U.S. Department of Commerce
CUSFTA	Canada-United States Free Trade Area		ITC	International Trade Commission (U.S. independent agency)
CVD	Countervailing duty(ies)			
DSU	Dispute Settlement Understanding		ITO	International Trade Organization
EC	European Community or European Communities		ITRD	Bureau of National Affairs International Trade Reporter—Decisions
E.C.R.	European Court Reports; Official Reports of the Court of Justice of the EC		LDC	Less Developed or Developing Countries
ECSC	European Coal and Steel Community		MAI	Multilateral Agreement on Investment (failed proposal)
EEA	European Economic Area			
EEC	European Economic Community		MFN	Most-Favored-Nation clause or treatment
EFTA	European Free Trade Association		MTN	Multilateral Trade Negotiations
Euratom	European Atomic Energy Community		NAFTA	North American Free Trade Area

xlix

NMEs	Nonmarket Economies	TRIPS	Trade-Related Intellectual Property Rights
NTB	Nontariff Barrier		
OECD	Organization for Economic Cooperation and Development	TRIMs	Trade-Related Investment Measures
OMA	Orderly Marketing Agreement	TEU	Treaty on European Union (known also as the Maastricht Treaty)
OTC	Organization for Trade Cooperation		
PPA	Protocol of Provisional Application of GATT	UNCITRAL	United Nations Commission on International Trade Law
PTA	Preferential Trade Agreement	UNIDROIT	International Institute for the Unification of Private Law
RTA	Regional Trade Agreement		
SPS	Sanitary and Phytosanitary	UNSITC	United Nations Standard International Trade Classification
SDR	Special Drawing Rights (in the IMF)	USITC	United States International Trade Commission (see ITC)
STC	State Trading Corporations		
STE	State Trading Enterprises		
STR	Special Trade Representative (U.S. Government)	USTR	United States Trade Representative (ex. Special Trade Representative (STR))
TEA	Trade Expansion Act of 1962 (U.S.)	VER	Voluntary Export Restraint
		VRA	Voluntary Restraint Agreement
		WTO	World Trade Organization

LEGAL PROBLEMS OF
INTERNATIONAL ECONOMIC RELATIONS

CASES, MATERIALS AND TEXT ON THE NATIONAL AND INTERNATIONAL REGULATION OF TRANSNATIONAL ECONOMIC RELATIONS

Fifth Edition

*

Chapter 1

THE POLICIES UNDERLYING INTERNATIONAL ECONOMIC RELATIONS

SECTION 1.1 INTERDEPENDENCE, GLOBALIZATION, AND THE CHANGING FUNDAMENTALS OF THE BRETTON WOODS SYSTEM

"Interdependence" may be overused, but it accurately describes our world today. Economic forces flow with great rapidity from one country to the next. Despite all the talk about sovereignty and independence, these concepts can mislead when applied to today's world economy. How "sovereign" is a country with an economy so dependent on trade with other countries that its government cannot readily affect the real domestic interest rate, implement its preferred tax policy, or establish an effective program of incentives for business or talented individuals? Many governments face such constraints today including, increasingly and inevitably, the government of the United States.

To a great extent, contemporary international economic interdependence can be attributed to the success of the institutions put in place just after World War II, what we call in this book the Bretton Woods System, which includes the IMF (International Monetary Fund) and GATT (the General Agreement on Tariffs and Trade). GATT was the engine for reducing tariff barriers to trade in goods, at least among the democratic market-oriented industrial countries. With the successful conclusion of the Uruguay Round of trade negotiations, the World Trade Organization (WTO) was created to replace GATT. The WTO system goes beyond the old GATT system to address trade in services, intellectual property, and other important areas previously outside its purview. Decreasing costs of transportation and communication have also played a profound role in increasing levels of trade and interdependence during the years since World War II.

With the decline of tariffs to near de minimis levels in developed countries, other much more complex barriers or distortions of trade have become relatively more important. Nontariff barriers are myriad, and

1

the ingenuity of man to invent new ones assures us that the problem of trade barriers will never go away.

One curious subject of interest to us in this book, and to practicing trade lawyers, is laws against "unfair" trade practices. In some cases trade may indeed be "unfair" by some intelligible standard, but in others the suspicion arises that practices are unfair only in the eyes of the import-competing industries that would like freedom from the challenges that competition can bring. Further, an increasing number of situations involve conflicts among contradictory economic, cultural and political goals across nations. Disputes about what is "unfair," therefore, often go to deep and fundamental differences of opinion about the appropriate economic role of governments.

Recent years have seen other issues bubble to the surface. The protestors at world economic summits of late, such as the 1999 WTO ministerial meeting in Seattle, urge that the globalization associated with the rise of the WTO poses a threat to the environment, to food safety, and even to human rights. Others complain that the governing bodies of the global economy—again most especially the WTO—are undemocratic and lacking in transparency. Whether or not these arguments have merit, they have clearly had an impact on political support for the WTO system, and on its likely agenda going forward.

There are innumerable other important and perplexing issues in international economic relations. Additional topics such as trade in services, competition policy, the environment and intellectual property, have become increasingly important to economic relations between nations.

We are also concerned in this book with the way that national legal systems interact with international legal rules and institutions. The process by which nations bind themselves to international agreements, for example, and the institutional structure of domestic institutions that implement rights and responsibilities under international law, are of deep practical and intellectual significance.

SECTION 1.2   OVERVIEW, PURPOSE AND STRUCTURE OF THE BOOK: REGULATORY APPROACH

The law of international economic relations has at least three levels of analysis. The first involves the private law of the transaction, which includes the contract and sales laws of the two nations involved, conflict of laws rules ("private international law"), insurance law, corporate law, maritime law and options for dispute resolution involving such matters. Because these subjects are treated in other basic law school courses, this book does not emphasize the private law of international transactions. Instead this book is focused on the next two components, which emphasize what could be termed regulatory activity, rather than transactions.

The second level of the law of international economic relations involves national government regulation of the activity. By this we mean the law of customs tariffs, export and import controls, quality and packaging standards, internal taxes (which may discriminate against foreign goods), special mixing or purchasing requirements (such as "Buy American" laws) and other regulatory matters. The purposes to be achieved by these laws are varied, often contradictory, and sometimes related to political pressures from special-interest groups at the expense of the nation as a whole.

The third and last component of the law of international economic relations is international law, or the law of international economic institutions. Typically, this body of law binds governments rather than private actors, yet its effects on private transactions can be profound, as much national legislation springs from it.

Chapters 1 through 7 of this book are designed to introduce these two critical components of the law of international economic relations, and to present an overall view of the "constitutional" working of the international legal system as it applies to international economic relations. Chapter 2 provides a brief introduction to policies underlying the broad system of regulation. Chapters 3 and 4 then turn to national government legal systems. The United States is the focus of a rather extended treatment in Chapter 3, partly because the book is designed for courses in that country, and also because the US economy is so important to the trading system. The European Union is the focus of Chapter 4. Chapters 5 through 7 then introduce the ground work for an understanding of the "international constitution" of the world trading system, with special attention paid to the WTO/GATT treaty structure and its dispute settlement system.

Chapters 8 through 18 take up the core substantive rules involved in the regulation of trade in products. Each chapter discusses one central regulatory technique or principle, relating the national law to the international rules and institutions. These chapters cover basic import restrictions—tariffs and quotas, most-favored-nation obligations and the free trade area exception to them, national treatment rules, the basic GATT exceptions for health and environment, the rules on product standards, safeguards and escape clauses, and finally laws designed to permit responses to "unfair" actions of governments or firms engaged in exporting.

These chapters should be viewed not only as an introduction to important trade policy issues, but as case studies of contemporary national and international legal rules relating to economic relations among nations. The legal principles explored in these chapters are possibly the most complex and refined of any international rules in existence today. How they operate (or fail to operate) in the face of modern economic, constitutional and other legal constraints is instructive beyond the details of the particular rules themselves.

To assist in understanding the overall structure of Chapter 8 through 18, the following outline suggests the relationships among the chapters, with an overall organization in five groups of subjects:

Group 1: Border Measures
Chapter 8: Tariffs/Customs; Chapter 9: Quotas, Non-tariff Barriers
Group 2: Non–Discrimination: MFN (Most Favored Nation)
Chapter 10: MFN; Chapter 11: Free Trade Areas & Customs Unions
Group 3: Non–Discrimination: National Treatment
Ch. 12: National Treatment; Ch. 13: Exceptions; Ch. 14: Product Standards
Group 4: Safeguards ("escape clause")
Ch. 15 Safeguards (major exception to liberal trade rules)
Group 5: "Unfair" Trade Rules
Ch. 16: Antidumping Duties; Ch. 17: Injury Test; Ch. 18 Subsidies & Countervailing Duties

We next turn to a series of other increasingly important subjects. In Chapters 19 and 20 we examine two newer subjects of regulation in the WTO/GATT system—intellectual property and services. Thereafter, in Chapters 21 to 23 we provide overview chapters concerning linkages between trade rules and other policies (human rights, labor standards and national security), monetary affairs and investment policies. The list could easily be longer, but space constraints preclude expanding it any further. Chapter 24 considers the special issues that arise for developing countries.

Finally, in Chapter 25, we step back from the mosaic of detail and try to develop some preliminary conclusions about the various national and international rules and institutions that can have such an important effect on the economic and even geo-political future of the world. Some readers may find that this chapter serves as much as an introduction as a conclusion, and may wish to review it now.

SECTION 1.3 GROWTH AND IMPORTANCE OF INTERNATIONAL TRADE

Trade between different areas of the world has occurred throughout history. Indeed, much of the world was discovered and explored by those seeking new trading opportunities—from the Phoenicians to Marco Polo to the Portuguese and Spanish explorers of the fifteenth and sixteenth centuries. The risks of trading expeditions in these times were great but they were viewed as worth taking in light of the potential profits.

In the "mercantilist" era, nations valued trade for the gold that it earned for the exporting nation and its citizens. To expand those earnings by gaining control of the sources of export commodities, as well as to secure export markets, European nations established colonies throughout the world. To maximize their earnings from trade, they often severely restricted imports. In the nineteenth century, however, in part due to economists who argued that gains from trade would be maximized if trade occurred without restrictions, nations began to reduce their import restrictions. The trend toward reduction was reversed in the 1870's, but the volume of trade continued to grow until World War I.

The period between World War I and World War II was a difficult time in the international economy. Increasing tariffs, particularly those enacted in the early 1930's by the Smoot–Hawley Tariff Act in the United States and comparable measures elsewhere, led to sharp declines in imports and exports. Many economic historians believe that these trade restrictions deepened the Great Depression significantly, although such claims are controversial and the effects of trade restrictions from country to country no doubt varied.[1]

Following World War II, many national leaders were convinced that it would be mutually advantageous—economically and otherwise—to promote international trade. This book is essentially a study of the institutions and structure that were put in place immediately after the war, as they have evolved to the present day. The focus will be on the central agreements of that structure—the World Trade Organization (WTO) charter and the General Agreement on Tariffs and Trade which it subsumed, better known as GATT. The principal goal of GATT, first signed in 1947, was to establish limitations on tariffs and to control the use of certain non-tariff barriers to trade. As a result of eight series of negotiations (called "rounds"), such as the Kennedy Round in the 1960's, the Tokyo Round in the 1970's, and the Uruguay Round in the 1980's and 1990's, significant reductions in tariffs have occurred. The history of tariff rates in the United States is shown in Table 1.1:[2]

Table 1.1

Ratio of Duties Collected to Dutiable Imports—United States

1821		45.0%
1831	(after Tariff of Abominations)	47.4
1841	(after Compromise Tariff)	34.6
1851	(after Walker Tariff)	26.6
1861	(after Tariff of 1857)	18.8
1871	(after Morrill and War tariffs)	44.0
1881		43.2
1891	(after McKinley Tariff)	46.5

1. The excerpt in Chapter 2 from Richard Cooper makes the argument that the Depression was compounded by trade wars. For a contrary view, see Barry J. Eichengreen, The Origins and Nature of the Great Slump Revisited, 45 Econ.Hist.Rev. 213 (1992); Barry J. Eichengreen, Did International Economic Forces Cause the Great Depression?, 6 Contemp.Pol. Issues 90 (1988).

2. Source: Bureau of the Census, Historical Statistics of the United States (various issues); and Department of Commerce, Statistical Abstract of the United States (1992); Peter Kenen, The International Economy 226 (1985); U.S. International Trade Commission, Value of U.S. Imports for Consumption, Duties Collected, and Ratio of Duties to Values, www.usitc.gov.

1901	(after Wilson–Gorman and Dingley tariffs)	49.8
1911	(after Payne–Aldrich Tariff)	41.3
1921	(after Underwood Tariff)	29.5
1931	(after Fordney–McCumber and Smoot–Hawley tariffs)	53.2
1941	(after Trade Agreements Act of 1934)	36.8
1951	(after formation of GATT)	12.3
1961		12.1
1971	(after Kennedy Round)	9.0
1981	(after Tokyo Round)	4.9
1991		5.1
2001		4.9
2006		4.5

From 1934 to 1952, i.e. from the time of the Smoot–Hawley tariff through the Reciprocal Trade Agreements Program to the initial implementation of GATT, average US tariffs on dutiable imports fell from 53% to 12.8%. Little reduction occurred in the next decade, but considerable further reductions occurred as a result of the Kennedy and Tokyo Rounds. Similar reductions have occurred in the tariff rates of other industrialized countries. The tariff cuts of the Uruguay Round reduce average tariffs for developed countries by another 38% and for developing countries by 24%.[3] If the average is calculated to include duty free imports as well, the average US tariff today is less than 2%.

Given the decline in protection that GATT initiated, it is no surprise that the period since the formation of GATT has witnessed significant increases in the volume of world trade. Between 1963 and 1973, world exports grew at a rate of approximately 8½% per year in volume. Even with the economic slowdown of the early 1980's, world exports grew at a rate of about 3% per year between 1973 and 1983. And, between 1983 and 1990, exports grew at a 6% rate. In each case, the growth in export volumes was at least 50% greater than the growth in total production during the same period.[4] That pattern continued and accelerated through the 1990's, with merchandise exports growing at a rate more than triple the rate of growth in merchandise production.[5] As a consequence, international trade has continued to grow more important to national economies. For the United States, the International Monetary Fund reported in 1992 that the combined total of imports and exports exceeded one trillion dollars for the first time. In the year 2000, that total was approaching $2 trillion, and in 2007 was above $2.6 trillion.

The degree of importance of trade to each country varies, of course, and one way to measure it is to compare the value of a country's exports with its total gross domestic product, as is done in Table 1.2.[6]

3. 11 BNA ITR 564 (1994); GATT, GATT Focus Newsletter, December 1993, at 6.

4. GATT, International Trade 1983/84, at 2 (Table 1) (1984); GATT, International Trade 1990/91, at 6 (Table 2) (1991).

5. WTO, International Trade Statistics 2000, available online at *http://www.wto. org/english/res_e/statis_toc_e.htm*;   The Economist, *Pocket World in Figures 2008 Edition* (Profile Books Ltd. 2006).

6. The OECD National Accounts 1960–97, Vol. 1, "Main aggregates" table for each

Table 1.2

**Exports of Goods and Services as a Percentage
of Gross Domestic Product**

(Measured at Current Prices)

Country	1960	2000
Australia	21.6	21.0
Canada	17.2	36.0
France	14.5	26.6
Germany	19.0	38.1
Japan	10.7	13.6
Netherlands	47.7	66.1
New Zealand	22.0	29.1
Sweden	22.8	44.9
Switzerland	29.3	44.5
Turkey	11.1	30.7
United Kingdom	20.9	28.3
United States	5.2	13.4

The increasing relative importance of world trade has meant that the economic welfare of one country is often tied closely to that of another. As we will see, this increasing interdependence of national economies has put strains on the WTO/GATT system, particularly during times of recession and slow economic growth.

SECTION 1.4   CHALLENGES AND POLICY TENSIONS OF CHANGING FUNDAMENTALS OF INTERNATIONAL LAW AND ECONOMIC RELATIONS

I feel about globalization a lot like I feel about the dawn. Generally speaking, I think it is a good thing that the sun comes up every morning. It does more good than harm. But even if I didn't much care for the dawn, there isn't much I could do about it. I didn't start globalization, I can't stop it—except at a huge cost to human development—and I'm not going to waste time trying. All I want to think about is how I can get the best out of this new system, and cushion the worst, for the most people.

—Thomas L. Friedman, The Lexus and the Olive Tree[1]

Certain policy tensions and puzzles often repeatedly occur in the materials and subjects of this book. Perhaps the most frequent of these is the basic tension about allocating decision making authority between sovereign nation-states or other entities (such as regional institutions) on the one hand and multilateral international organizations (such as

country, plus OECD Factbook 2007, Economic, Environmental and Social Statistics (for 2005 data), updated with http://dataweb.usitc.gov/prepared_reports.asp.

1. Thomas L. Friedman, The Lexus and the Olive Tree: Understanding Globalization xviii (Farrar, Straus, Giroux, 1999).

the WTO) on the other hand. One can see in the already huge jurisprudence of the WTO dispute settlement reports many examples of this tension.

The following paragraphs, drawn from published works,[2] address these and other similar issues, and may help the reader to be sensitively aware of these various examples as his or her attention moves through this book.

The last decade of the 20th Century and the first of the 21st Century may not be the most challenging period for the generally accepted assumptions of international law, but this period will certainly rank high on any such list. The growing depth and speed of change and adjustment required by globalization, accompanied by striking changes in government institutions, a remarkable increase in non-government activity and advocacy, an intense emphasis on market economic ideas and a backlash against them, have all chipped away at the relatively fragile (perhaps already crumbing) theoretical foundations of the international legal system as it has been generally accepted for centuries.

* * *

It is obvious to most observers of these subjects that the WTO, as surely the most intricate and profound legal component of international economic law, is deeply linked to general international law. Thus, it is not surprising that the WTO legal framework and the slightly more general framework of international economic law, cannot escape the many challenges and other conceptual problems about international law which are currently the subject of great academic and official government debate in many parts of the world. These debates are manifested in the recent meetings of major international law societies such as the American Society of International Law and its counterparts in other countries,[3] as well as in important governmental documents, reports, and activities, not the least of which include the wealth of writings, speeches, and other communications relating to the cosmic geopolitical controversies of the post September 11, 2001 years at the United Nations and elsewhere.[4] Questions being discussed include the legitimacy of many basic international law norms (especially those of customary internation-

---

2. This material is largely based on Chapter 1 of John H. Jackson, Sovereignty, the WTO, and Changing Fundamentals of International Law (Cambridge University Press, 2006), excerpt reprinted by permission of Cambridge University Press. This book is based partly on the Lauterpacht Lecture series delivered by Professor Jackson in November 2002.

3. Counterparts to the ASIL include the International Law Association (ILA), the British Institute of International & Comparative Law (BIICL), and various bar associations, such as the American Bar Asso-

ciations (ABA–International Section) and International Bar Association, Associations of the individual EU Member States and the European Bar Association CCBE (Council of Bars and Law Societies of Europe).

4. The literature for these debates and other commentary is voluminous. The pages of the *American Journal of International Law* illustrates some of the commentary, such as the agora on the Iraq invasion: *Agora: Future Implications of the Iraq Conflict*, 97 Am.J.Intl. 553 (2003).

al law), and the structure, efficacy, and creditability of important international institutions.

It is no surprise that international economic law (IEL), and the WTO in particular, is enmeshed in these broader issues of international law, but also that the subject of IEL, and its currently most important example, have practices and experiences that are extremely relevant to discussions in the broader context. Discussions probe the role of "sovereignty" concepts in the many tensions arising in the application of international norms which impinge, sometimes deeply, on nation-state government actions and responsibilities. These discussions also engage deep jurisprudential issues about the appropriate role of international juridical systems (such as the WTO dispute settlement procedures). Also subject to critical and disputed attention are issues of institutional structures, decision making, voting, criteria for membership, and obligation to perform the results of dispute resolution procedures. Many contemporary circumstances cast doubt on international legal "axioms," such as the role of the Vienna Convention on the Law of Treaties.

* * *

It is not claimed here that the thinking and concerns about international law are only recent, or that they are more aggravated now than they have been at any other time. History and other careful scholarship show various periods of momentous impact on international law by currents of thought,[5] some instigated by colossal events such as World War II. But in a less cataclysmic way, though nevertheless likely to be equally profound, current world trends of recent decades have required the traditional institutions and trends of thought about general international law to confront concepts and opinions about those institutions and thoughts which have been stimulated or caused by such actuality of the real world, and by thoughtful but often divergent reflections of participants and observers.[6]

* * *

In economic matters, equally momentous events and optimism were prevalent. The largest trade negotiation ever held (the GATT Uruguay Round (UR)), was winding to its April 1994 close, fostered by the United States and European Community. The UR results were nothing short of astonishing, extraordinarily fulfilling most of its agenda set at the 1986 Punta del Este launching conference. The results in some respects exceeded the original agenda, with the establishment of a new international organization—the World Trade Organization—to take over in 1995 for the troubled GATT (1948–1994). In a sense the new WTO

---

5. See, e.g., works cited in Jackson, supra note 2, ch. 1.1, n. 5 & ch. 2.

6. A few other important examples include: Louis Henkin, International Law: Politics and Values (Martinus Nijhoff Pub-

lishers, 1995); Oscar Schacter, International Law in Theory and Practice (Martinus Nijhoff Publishers, 1991); and Anne–Marie Slaughter, A New World Order (Princeton University Press, 2004).

completed the triad of institutions contemplated by the 1944 Bretton Woods Conference.[7]

Equally remarkable were the fundamental reforms made in the dispute settlement procedures which had evolved in the GATT. Central to these reforms was compulsory jurisdiction over all disputes arising under the UR "covered agreements," a totally new and unique Appellate Body and process, and virtually automatic adoption by the WTO of the dispute settlement reports, with not only an international law obligation to comply, but also a series of possible temporary "compensatory" measures designed to better induce such compliance.[8]

In this context also, international law (or international economic law) seemed ascendant and strongly reinforced by the rule-oriented procedures set forth in the UR treaty.

Throughout this period, and indeed throughout the last half century, the world has changed in ways that required new approaches and greater abilities to adjust. As the 20th century drew to a close, trouble began to cast longer shadows. The forces of globalization and interdependence posed increasing challenges to traditional concepts of nation-state actors in international affairs. International law, both in its general sense and the economic context, was profoundly tested.

* * *

Law at any level of government or human institution will forever be affected by the "facts on the ground;" namely the circumstances of the societies or institutions which both desperately need legal norms and legal institutions, but also feel constrained by them when they seem out of date or otherwise unable to cope with changing "facts on the ground." So it is no surprise that international law and institutions would be so challenged also.

* * *

One of the clear implications of the current circumstances is that nation-state governments are facing greater than ever difficulties in "governing," in the sense of offering policies which can be adopted at the nation state level, which have a reasonably good chance of "delivering" the benefits sought by constituents. If traditional barriers to risks spreading from one nation to another have been diminished through reduced costs and time for transport and communications, governments may try to use governmental barriers to reduce those risks. But as the world becomes more interdependent, the potential utility and effectiveness of those governmental barriers is increasing doubtful. Thus, there

---

7. The conference resulted in the Charters for the World Bank and the International Monetary Fund. The "Bretton Woods Conference" was officially called, "The United Nations Monetary and Financial Conference," held July 1–22, 1944. 44 nations met to negotiate the establishment of the IMF and World Bank. *See* United Nations Monetary and Financial Conference (Bretton Woods, N.H., July 1–22 1944), Proceedings and Documents 941 (U.S. Dep't of State Pub. No. 2866, 1948).

8. See Jackson, supra note 2, secs. 5.2 & 5.4.

should be inevitable pressures to turn to international cooperation of various sorts, often necessitating reliance on institutional mechanisms (e.g., international organizations), either existing or yet to be formed. However, the experience of some international institutions has not been satisfactory.[9]

When one adds to the mix the problem of weapons and the complexity of non-governmental actors (including terrorist actors), some of the older paradigms of international law increasingly appear antiquated and inappropriate. Can the system rely on state consent as the basis of all international norm legitimation? What about "rogue states?" What about the forces of the world market which often can ignore international legal norms when no effective "compliance pressures" seem to exist? Do the ancient and outdated concepts of Westphalian Sovereignty granting a state monarch power to do his will, regardless of its impact on his own citizens still apply? Can the large fictional notion of equality of nation-states really work when it operates in particular contexts with a different reality? What is the appropriate allocation of international institutional power among states with vast differences in population, natural resources, military force, and economic power?

Can treaties always solve the problems that the international legal system faces? To what degree can reliance be made on customary international law given its extreme ambiguity and indefiniteness in some cases? What is to be done about the "hold-out states" that refuse to recognize a developing customary norm and also refuse to sign a treaty?

Even as to treaties which have been adopted, is the international system constructed in a way that allows the treaties to operate efficiently, or does the often extremely difficult process for amendment render treaties so rigid that governments avoid them?

On a more detailed level, can the current rules about interpreting a treaty, such as those expressed in the Vienna Convention on the Law of Treaties as embodying customary international law, operate effectively in 21st century circumstances when major treaties with large memberships do not neatly fit into paradigms which seem to have derived from concepts associated with bilateral or small group membership treaties?

Can a strict rule of non-interference in a nation-state's "sovereignty" really work in a world that includes governments that have been willing to undertake horrible actions against their own citizens or against humanity? If not, what should external action on such governments entail, and what are appropriate limits to such action?

What legal entities should be considered as the appropriate beneficiaries of treaties or other international law? Clearly beneficiaries are not only governments. Which individuals should benefit? Which non-governmental organizations? What type of non-governmental enterpris-

9. See particularly Martin Wolf, Why Globalization Works 288–295 (Yale University Press, 2004).

es? Which should be considered deserving of legal operations for their benefit (e.g. market participants regarding WTO rules or individuals when rules should protect human rights)? In what situations should non-government actors be given privileges of participating in the formation and application of international law rules?

Examination of the extensively documented practice of the operation of international economic law reveals not only detailed experiences which bear on many of the questions posed above, but also provides analysis of some of those questions in greater depth and detail than can be found in any other sources.[10] It also reveals the necessity of an institutional framework for world markets to work successfully, and arguably establishes the rationale for a juridical (dispute settlement) type of institution as vitally important for such institutional framework. At least for economic activity based largely on market-oriented frameworks, a juridical system with at least modest precedent recognition is likely to be central to lower the "risk premium" for many international transactions. The WTO jurisprudence also demonstrates the importance of non-government beneficiaries of the rule-based system, particularly, the market participants.[11]

Some Selected Bibliography for Further Reading

WTO Trade Law and Policy

Won–Mog Choi, Like Products in International Trade Law–Towards a Consistent GATT/WTO Jurisprudence (Oxford University Press, 2003).

Douglas A. Irwin, Petros C. Mavroidis & Alan O. Sykes, The Genesis of the GATT (Cambridge University Press, 2008).

John H. Jackson, Sovereignty, the WTO, and Changing Fundamentals of International Law (Cambridge University Press, 2006).

John H. Jackson, The Jurisprudence of the GATT and the WTO: Insights on Treaty Law and Economic Relations (Cambridge University Press, 2000).

John H. Jackson, World Trade and the Law of GATT (Bobbs–Merrill Co. 1969). Classic work, very relevant.

John H. Jackson & Alan O. Sykes (eds.), Implementing the Uruguay Round (Clarendon Press, 1997).

Peter Sutherland et al., The Future of the WTO: Addressing Institutional Challenges in the New Millennium, Report by the Consultative Board to the Director–General Supachai Panitchpakdi, available at: http://www.wto.org/english/thewto_e/10anniv_e/future_wto_e.htm, last visited 14 Feb. 2008.

---

10. See discussion in Jackson, supra note 2, ch. 5. A prime example is the WTO *Shrimp-Turtle* case, discussed in sections 5.5 and 5.8.

11. See Jackson, supra note 2, ch. 4 (especially 4.2) & ch. 5 (especially 5.7).

Joel P. Trachtman, The International Economic Law Revolution and the Right to Regulate (Cameron May, 2005).

Peter van den Bossche, Law and Policy of the WTO (Cambridge University Press, 2006).

Foreign & International Law & International Relations

Ian Brownlie, Principles of Public International Law (Oxford University Press, 6th ed. 2003).

Abram Chayes & Antonia Handler Chayes, The New Sovereignty (Harvard University Press, 1995).

Jack L. Goldsmith & Eric A. Posner, The Limits of International Law (Oxford University Press, 2005).

John H. Jackson, Sovereignty, the WTO, and Changing Fundamentals of International Law (Cambridge University Press, 2006).

Harold Jacobson & Edith Brown Weiss (eds.), Engaging Countries: Strengthening Compliance With International Environmental Accords (MIT Press, 1998).

Joost Pauwelyn, Conflict of Norms in Public International Law: How WTO Law Relates to Other Rules of International Law (Cambridge University Press, 2003).

Chapter 2

AN INTRODUCTION TO THE ECONOMICS OF INTERNATIONAL TRADE

Although an understanding of the basic economic principles relating to international trade is not essential to a study of the law of international economic relations, some general exposure to those principles is helpful. Economists are not always in agreement on how these basic principles should be translated into policy, and their views are not always accepted in any event. Nonetheless, their views on the desirability of international trade and the effects of interferences with trade have played an important role in shaping the legal framework in which trade occurs. While much of the economics literature is too theoretical and technical for our purposes, the basic principles can be grasped by non-economists.[1] This section introduces a few of those principles, to which we will refer throughout the book, as well as a sampling of more advanced economic thought in the field of international trade. Here we consider 1) comparative advantage and gains from trade; 2) the effect of restraints on trade; 3) the validity of arguments in favor of trade restraints; and 4) the reasons for, or "political economy" of, trade restraints.

---

1. There are a number of useful textbooks and reference works on international trade. Less technically inclined readers may wish to consult the books excerpted in this chapter by Kindleberger and Kenen, as well as Thomas A. Pugel & Peter H. Lindert, International Economics (11th ed. 2000) and Paul R. Krugman & Maurice Obstfeld, International Economics: Theory and Policy (7th ed. 2005). More advanced treatments may be found in Avinash K. Dixit & Victor D. Norman, Theory of International Trade (1980); Jagdish N. Bhagwati, Arvind Panagariya & T.N. Srinivasan, Lectures on International Trade (2d ed. 1998); Robert C. Feenstra, Advanced International Trade (2004); the Handbook of International Economics, Volumes I, II (Ronald W. Jones & Peter B. Kenen eds., 1984); and the Handbook of International Economics, Volume III (Gene Grossman and Kenneth Rogoff eds., 1995). The "new trade theory," emphasizing imperfect competition and increasing returns, is discussed in Elhanan Helpman & Paul R. Krugman, Market Structure and Foreign Trade (1985); Elhanan Helpman & Paul R. Krugman, Trade Policy and Market Structure (1989); and in Paul R. Krugman, Rethinking International Trade (1990).

SECTION 2.1   COMPARATIVE ADVANTAGE AND GAINS FROM TRADE

Early economists embraced the "labor theory of value" as a way of understanding how prices are determined. The concept of comparative advantage developed during this early period, and thus relied at first on this now discarded theory of value. Nevertheless, the basic idea of comparative advantage survived, and is most easily exposited using the simplifying assumptions of these early economists. The following excerpt from Kindleberger recounts the development of the theory of comparative advantage, and indicates how it has survived into the modern period under more general assumptions.

CHARLES P. KINDLEBERGER, INTERNATIONAL ECONOMICS 17–21, 27, 33 (5th ed. 1973)[2]

LAW OF COMPARATIVE ADVANTAGE

The classical economists asked what goods would be traded between two countries because they thought the answer for trade between countries was different from that for trade within a country. Within a country, a region produces the goods it can make cheaper than other regions. The value of a commodity within a country, moreover, is determined by its labor content. If the product of a certain industry can be sold for more than the value of the labor it contains, additional labor will transfer into that industry from other occupations to earn the abnormal profits available there. Supply will expand until the price is brought down to the value of the labor it contains. Similarly, if a commodity sells for less than the worth of its labor, labor will move away into other lines until the gap is closed. The tendency of wages toward equality within a country results in prices of goods equal to their labor such as to equalize the return to labor in all occupations and regions. If wages are higher in California than in Massachusetts, labor will migrate to California. This will lower wages in California and raise them in Massachusetts, and the movement will continue until the return to labor is equated in the two regions. After labor has spread itself among several regions to equalize wages, these regions will produce and sell to each other what each region can make the cheapest. Its advantage in such commodities over other regions will be absolute. Therefore the theory of trade applicable to regions of a country is the theory of absolute advantage.

Classical economists thought that the labor theory of value valid in trade within a country cannot be applied between nations, since factors of production are immobile internationally. If wages are higher in the United States than in Britain, they stay higher, for migration cannot take place on a scale sufficient to eliminate discrepancies. Under these circumstances, the classical economists asked, what will the United States sell to Britain and Britain to America?

2. Reprinted by permission from International Economics, Fifth Edition, by Kindleberger (Homewood, IL: Richard D. Irwin, Inc., 1973).

Let us assume two countries and two commodities. If each country can produce one good cheaper (i.e., with less labor) than it can be produced in the other, as in the case of domestic trade, each will have an advantage in the production of one commodity and a disadvantage in the production of the other. Each country will then be anxious to export the commodity in which it has an advantage and import the commodity in which it has a disadvantage. The position is suggested in the following table, where wheat can be produced more cheaply in the United States and cloth more cheaply in Britain. The United States has an absolute advantage in wheat and an absolute disadvantage in cloth. It will export wheat and import cloth, which, with the numerical values given, may be assumed to exchange one for the other at something like the rate of one yard of cloth for one bushel of wheat:

Production of One Man in One Week

Product	In United States	In United Kingdom
Wheat	6 bushels	2 bushels
Cloth	2 yards	6 yards

But suppose that the labor content of both wheat and cloth is less in the United States than in Britain. Suppose that instead of merely 2 yards of cloth per week a man in the United States can produce 10. The position is then as follows:

Production of One Man in One Week

Product	In United States	In United Kingdom
Wheat	6 bushels	2 bushels
Cloth	10 yards	6 yards

It is evident that labor is more efficient in the United States than in the United Kingdom, and wages in the United States will be higher on that account. By assumption, however, migration will not take place to equalize wage rates.

Trade cannot now follow the decree of absolute advantage and a new principle is needed to take its place. This was developed by David Ricardo more than 150 years ago, in the law of comparative advantage. Ricardo observed that in cases similar to ours, while the United States had an absolute advantage over Britain in both wheat and cloth, it had a greater advantage in wheat than in cloth. He concluded that a country would export the product in which it had the greater advantage, or a comparative advantage, and import the commodity in which its advantage was less, or in which it had a comparative disadvantage. In this example the United States would export wheat and import cloth, even though it could produce cloth more efficiently than Britain.

The reasoning underlying this conclusion may be demonstrated arithmetically. Without international trade, wheat and cloth would exchange for one another in each country at their respective labor contents, which would differ as between the two countries. In the United States, 6 bushels of wheat, or one week's labor, would buy 10 yards of cloth. In Britain, by the same token, 6 bushels of wheat—three weeks' labor in the less productive country—would buy 18 yards of cloth. If the United States through trade can get more than 10 yards of cloth for 6 bushels of wheat (or more than 1⅔ yards of cloth per bushel of wheat), it will pay it to do so. It cannot hope to get more than 18 yards of cloth for 6 bushels of wheat (3 yards of cloth for a single bushel). This is the price which cloth producers in Britain can get without trade, and there is no reason for them to enter into foreign trade and be worse off.

Similarly, if Britain can get more than 2 bushels of wheat for 6 yards of cloth (more than one third of a bushel of wheat per yard of cloth), it will pay it to export cloth and buy wheat. But it cannot hope to get more than six tenths or three fifths of a bushel per yard—the American wheat farmers' price without trade.

For effective comparison, the prices should be quoted the same way. At any price for cloth cheaper than 10 yards (of cloth) for 6 bushels (of wheat), that is, for any more than 10 yards for 6 bushels, the United States will gain by shifting resources out of cloth into wheat and importing cloth. Similarly, at a price of cloth which would involve Britain giving up less than 18 yards for 6 bushels (equal to 6 yards for 2 bushels), it will pay Britain to move its labor out of wheat into cloth and import wheat in exchange for cloth rather than grow grain itself. Trade raises the price of wheat and lowers the price of cloth in the United States; it raises the price of cloth and lowers the price of wheat in Britain. Even when one country can produce both commodities more efficiently than another country, both can gain from specialization and exchange, provided that the efficiency advantage is greater in some commodity or commodities than in others.

On the basis of this type of demonstration, the classical economists concluded that international trade does not require offsetting absolute advantages but is possible where a comparative advantage exists. It goes without saying but must be said, as it is frequently forgotten, that a comparative advantage is always (and by definition) accompanied by a comparative disadvantage.

Production Possibilities Curves

The labor theory of value on which this analysis rested was subsequently rejected as invalid. The tendency for the return to labor to be equal throughout a country was seen by observation to be weak and faltering. Labor is not homogeneous. If there is an increase in the demand for barrels, the wages of coopers will rise above those of smiths, with whom they are not interchangeable. It became recognized that there is not one great class of labor with a single wage but a series of noncompeting groups among which the tendency to equalization of wages, at least in the short run, is weak or nonexistent.

A more fundamental objection, however, which would apply even if labor were homogeneous and commanded one price in a perfectly competitive market, is that goods are not produced by labor alone but by various combinations of all the factors of production: land, labor, and capital. To compare the labor content of two commodities—say, gasoline and textiles, or meat and shoes—gives an erroneous view of relative values. Gasoline production requires far more capital per unit of labor than textiles, and meat output more land than shoes. Variable proportions of factors in the production of different commodities make it impossible to use the labor theory of value, however qualified.

An escape from this impasse has been provided by Gottfried Haberler in the theory of opportunity costs. The cost of wheat in the long run is how much cloth a country has to give up to get additional units of wheat. It makes little difference whether the factors which leave the production of cloth are all suited to the output of wheat or not. The question is simply how much of one commodity must be given up to get more of the other.

The notion of opportunity cost is illustrated in international trade theory with production possibilities or transformation curves. Instead of saying that a week's labor will produce either 6 bushels of wheat or 10 yards of cloth, one says that all the factors of production can produce either 6 bushels of wheat or 10 yards of cloth per some appropriate unit of time, or some intermediate combination of them. In figure 2.1, where the vertical axis represents wheat and the horizontal axis cloth, the U.S. curve means that the resources of the United States, in the absence of foreign trade, can be used entirely to produce wheat, in which case 6 bushels (per capita per week) can be produced, exclusively for cloth, in which case output will consist of 10 yards per man-week, or some appropriate intermediate combination, such as 3 bushels of wheat and 5 yards of cloth. The production possibilities curve does not tell what will in fact be produced. More information is needed for this purpose, on the side of demand. It merely sets out what the possibilities are.

* * *

Factor Proportions

If international trade is based on differences in comparative costs, the curious student will proceed to the next question: What makes for differences in comparative costs? Why do the transformation curves of various countries differ?

The answer given to this question by Swedish economist Bertil Ohlin is two-fold: Different goods, he stated, require different factor inputs; and different countries have different factor endowments. If wheat is technologically best produced with lots of land relative to labor and capital, countries that have an abundance of land will be able to produce wheat cheaply. This is why Australia, Argentina, Canada, Minnesota, and the Ukraine export wheat. On the other hand, if cloth requires much labor relative to capital and land, countries that have an abundance of labor—Hong Kong, Japan, India—will have a comparative advantage in cloth manufacture and be able to export it.

* * *

Differences in comparative costs come about not only because of differences in factor endowments but also through specialization in different commodities. To a degree the choice of whether the United States or Britain specializes in one kind of an automobile or another, or this tractor or that, may be determined by historical accident. The fact is that, with each country specialized, a basis for trade exists, since each can produce one good cheaper than the other.

Notes

(1) As the reading from Kindleberger suggests, the principle of comparative advantage holds that nations trade because the amount of a good that must be sacrificed internally to produce a unit of another good varies across countries. The question as to why this tradeoff in production should vary need not be answered confidently before we can know that there are gains from trade. Nevertheless, the Kindleberger reading does suggest two of the traditional hypotheses about the sources of comparative advantage. Implicit in the old Ricardian model with labor as the only factor of production is one of them—some nations have access to superior technology, at least for the production of some things. The other hypothesis, mentioned explicitly by Kindleberger, is that countries are endowed with a different mix of "factors of production," such as unskilled labor, skilled labor, land and other natural resources. Because some goods require relatively more of these various factors to produce them, a nation that has them in abundant supply can have a comparative advantage in the production of a good even if all nations have access to the same technology.

A more recent and related idea is the "technology-gap" model of trade, often attributed to the late Raymond Vernon. The notion here is that some countries specialize in innovation and the introduction of new products, probably because of their greater scientific base and better educated work force (a factor endowment differential, although the "endowment" may be affected by social policy over time). Other nations specialize in imitation and mass production, which becomes possible after the production process is standardized and routinized: "The technological-gap theory makes use of the sequence of innovation and imitation, particularly as they affect exports. As a new product is developed in a country and becomes profitable in the domestic market, the innovating firm, which enjoys a temporary monopoly, has initially an easy access to foreign markets. * * * Later on, however, the profits of the innovating firm prompt imitation in other countries which may actually prove to have a comparative advantage in the production of the new commodity after the innovation is disseminated. * * * But as the innovating country loses, through imitation, its absolute advantage in one commodity, a new cycle of innovation imitation begins in another. Thus, the innovating country may continue to develop new products and may continue to have a temporary absolute advantage in products which are eventually more efficiently produced by other countries." Miltiades Chacoliades, International Trade Theory and Policy 305–06 (1978).[3]

(2) A rather different kind of argument to explain the pattern of trade relates to the possibility that trade may be driven by economies of scale. Suppose, for example, that two nations are identical in all relevant respects, but one of them somehow gets a "head start" in the production of a good that has substantial learning-by-doing economies. The nation with the head start may retain a cost advantage for a long time, or even indefinitely, and thus specialize in the production of the good for export. See Paul R. Krugman, Rethinking International Trade 152–82 (1990). Kindleberger hints at the possibility in the last paragraph of the excerpt, where he refers to patterns of trade that result from historical accident.

(3) The older theories of trade left little room for government action to affect comparative advantage or the pattern of specialization. The more modern theories, by contrast, suggest that the concept of "comparative advantage" itself may be fraught with confusion, because the pattern of trade that results in the end will reflect not only pre-existing "exogenous" differences among countries but also the results of governmental policies or chance. Likewise, they raise the possibility that government can deliberately create "comparative advantage" through subsidies for research and development, for specialized education, or for the establishment of particular industries subject to increasing returns to scale. The popular term for such government measures is "industrial policy." To be sure, the wisdom and efficacy of those policies is hotly disputed. We will not enter the fray, but will later consider whether industrial policy is somehow "unfair" and whether countries that do not employ it should want to and be able to restrict trade with those that do.

(4) The theory of comparative advantage developed under assumptions of perfect competition. Some of the implications of relaxing that assumption are explored below in the materials on strategic trade policy. If firms have monopoly power in a domestic market, however, one obvious consequence of trade is to constrain the ability of those firms to charge monopoly prices. Recent empirical evidence suggests that this effect can be quite important at times. See Levinson, Testing the Imports-as-Market–Discipline Hypothesis, 35 J.Intl.Econ. 1 (1993).

(5) The readings and comments to this point make no mention of exchange rates. In traditional economic models of trade, trade is always in balance and the exchange rate is an afterthought—indeed, money is not included formally, on the premise that exchange rates simply adjust to clear the market by balancing import expenditures with export earnings. Further, because the simple models are "static," there is no reason for the terms of the exchange between countries to fluctuate once trade has been opened and an equilibrium has been reached.

In reality, however, trade occurs with money, and the price of that money in terms of other currencies is variable. The fluctuation of exchange rates can have important effects upon the competitiveness of firms in

3. See also Edward Leamer, Sources of International Comparative Advantage (1984).

international markets. For some time, for example, the suggestion was made that the US dollar was "overvalued."[4] That is, it was asserted that the price of dollars relative to, say, yen, caused American goods to be "too expensive" in Japan and Japanese goods to be "too cheap" in the United States, resulting in a trade imbalance in favor of Japan. Such an imbalance is possible because when Americans buy yen in order to import from Japan, those abroad who sell the yen for dollars do not always use the dollars to buy goods and services from the United States. Instead, they may buy real estate, shares of stock, or other capital assets, among other things.

Turning the point on its head, when a country such as the United States becomes a relatively attractive place to invest—presumably because the real returns to those investments are expected to be relatively high—US exporters will suffer because the dollar will appreciate due to the demand for dollars for investment purposes. The same thing may happen because a trading partner has a comparatively high savings rate (like Japan). The United States then finances some of its imports by selling claims on capital assets rather than by selling its own goods and services in foreign markets. We will return in a later chapter to the question whether this deficit in the balance of trade should be viewed as a "problem" when we consider trade intervention for balance of payments purposes. At present, however, it suffices to note that because exchange rates do not automatically adjust to balance imports and exports, the teachings of comparative advantage models must be tempered by the realization that a country's international competitiveness may erode due to the appreciation of its currency.

SECTION 2.2   INTERFERENCE WITH FREE TRADE

Economist and Nobel Laureate Paul Samuelson once wrote, "[T]here is essentially only one argument for free trade or freer trade, but it is an exceedingly powerful one, namely: Free trade promotes a mutually profitable division of labor, greatly enhances the potential real national product of all nations, and makes possible higher standards of living all over the globe."[1] Put differently, Samuelson's claim is that free trade increases economic welfare, both for the world as a whole, and for each nation. In this section, we explore this claim in greater detail, including some of the new challenges to its correctness.

(A) EFFICIENCY VS. DISTRIBUTION

The gains from free trade to which Samuelson adverts, whether national or international, are *aggregate* gains. In other words, if one adds up the effect of a movement toward free trade on all affected parties—consumers, producers and government (the latter through its revenues)—the claim is that the net effect of a movement toward free

4. See, e.g., Rudiger Dornbusch, The Overvalued Dollar, Lloyds Bank Review, April, 1984, at 1–12; C. Fred Bergsten, The Villain is an Overvalued Dollar, *in* The United States in the World Economy: Se-lected Papers of C. Fred Bergsten 799–91 (1983).

1. Paul A. Samuelson, Economics 692 (9th ed. 1973).

trade is positive. For those familiar with concepts of producer and consumer surplus, the claim more precisely is that a movement toward free trade increases the sum of producer and consumer surplus in the economy, plus government revenue if it is not already redistributed and otherwise counted. These aggregate effects we term the "efficiency" consequences of trade policy.

Even if freer trade produces efficiency gains, that fact is entirely compatible with the possibility that a movement toward free trade may harm some individuals greatly. If the US textile, footwear or sugar markets were opened overnight to unfettered international competition, for example, many producers in those industries would no doubt soon go bankrupt, and many workers would lose their jobs. This has two important implications for thoughtful reflection about trade policy.

First, as a normative matter, the economist's argument for free trade is persuasive only if one supposes (a) that aggregate efficiency gains are a proper basis for evaluating the wisdom of policy irrespective of the changes in income distribution that may accompany them, or (b) that any unacceptable consequences of free trade for the income distribution are better addressed through alternative policy instruments. Even for those skeptical of the former position, the latter position may have much to commend it, though we are not able to dwell on it here.[2]

Second, as a positive matter, the fact that changes in trade policy produce gainers and losers explains the existence of political opposition to free trade. We return to these issues later.

(B) THE EFFICIENCY CASE FOR FREE TRADE AND THE CONSEQUENCES OF TARIFFS AND QUOTAS

The two most common types of restraints on imports are tariffs (a tax levied on imports at the time of importation, which usually has the effect of increasing the prices at which the imports are sold) and quotas (an upper limit on the quantity or value of imports allowed during a given time period).

Samuelson's argument above for free trade, and thus against the use of tariffs and quotas, is actually a trivial corollary of a well-know proposition in price theory often termed the first theorem of welfare economics: competitive markets, without externalities, are efficient, and interference with them is inefficient. To elaborate the idea with particular reference to trade, consider first the effects of a tariff. A tariff typically raises the price of an imported good because domestic sellers of that good now have an additional cost of production (the tariff) that

---

2. One of us has discussed the efficiency/distribution tension at length elsewhere, disputing many of the distribution arguments on their merits and developing the further argument that trade policy is a poor tool for redistribution in any event. See Alan O. Sykes, Countervailing Duty Law: An Economic Perspective, 89 Colum.L.Rev. 199, 209–13 (1989); Alan O. Sykes, Protectionism as a Safeguard: A Positive Analysis of the GATT Escape Clause with Normative Speculations, 58 U.Chi.L.Rev. 255, 269–72 (1991). See also Gary C. Hufbauer & Kimberly A. Elliot, Measuring the Costs of Protection in the United States (1993).

must be recouped. Domestic producers of goods that compete with the imported good will often be able to raise their prices as well because import competition is less of a constraint on their pricing policies. If so, domestic producers gain from the tariff. Just as clearly, domestic consumers lose from the need to pay higher prices. The government gains some revenue from the tariff. Samuelson's proposition can be restated as a claim that the sum of these effects is negative, and a geometric "proof" for a single market in a single importing country can be found in the following excerpt from Peter Kenen's textbook. Roughly speaking, the proof identifies two sources of net loss to an importing nation from a tariff: (1) the fact that some "marginal consumers" are priced out of the market by the higher price, so that their loss of consumer surplus is not recouped by any producer in the form of a higher price charged to them; and (2) the fact that the tariff induces domestic producers to expand their production of goods that compete with the imported good, consuming resources in the import-competing industry that could better be deployed elsewhere. The "proof" does rely implicitly on assumptions about the competitiveness of markets and the absence of externalities, and the implications of relaxing those assumptions are explored in the materials that follow.

PETER B. KENEN, THE INTERNATIONAL ECONOMY 17–19, 175–77 (1985)[3]

PRODUCTION, CONSUMPTION, AND TRADE IN A SINGLE COMMODITY

The effects of differences in relative costs cannot be examined by looking at markets one at a time. It is necessary to look at an entire national economy, and then compare it with another. Therefore, international economic analysis cannot make much use of standard partial-equilibrium price theory—of ordinary demand and supply curves. It must use general-equilibrium theory most of the time. Demand and supply curves can be used, however, to show how the opening of trade in a single commodity affects production and consumption in the domestic market, and they can be used to quantify the gains from trade.

Equilibrium Before Trade Is Opened

In Figure 2–1, the domestic demand curve for cameras is D_H, and the domestic supply curve is S_H. When there is no international trade in cameras, equilibrium will be established at E. The domestic price of a camera will be OP, domestic production will be OQ, and production will necessarily equal consumption. The diagram, however, says much more.

3. © 1985. Reprinted by permission of Prentice–Hall, Englewood Cliffs, New Jersey.

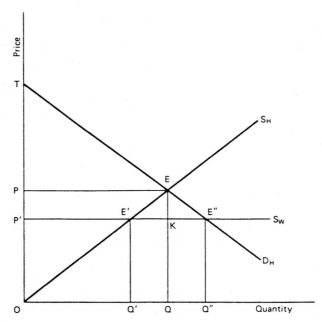

FIGURE 2-1

Effects of the Opening of Trade in the Market for a Single Good

Before trade is opened, the domestic price is OP, and the quantity OQ is produced to satisfy domestic demand. When trade is opened at the world price OP', domestic production falls to OQ', domestic consumption rises to OQ'', and the quantity $Q'Q''$ is imported to close the gap. The production effect is $Q'Q$, and the corresponding welfare gain is $E'KE$. The consumption effect is QQ'', and the corresponding welfare gain is $KE''E$.

When domestic markets are perfectly competitive, the supply curve is the sum of the marginal cost curves of domestic firms. Accordingly, the area under the supply curve measures the total cost of camera production. (Strictly speaking, it measures the total variable cost, but fixed cost plays no role in this analysis.) If OQ cameras are produced, total cost is given by the area of the triangle OQE. But total payments to producers (revenues) are given by the area of the rectangle $OQEP$. Therefore, the area of the triangle OEP serves as a measure of profit or *producer surplus*.

The area under the demand curve is meaningful, too. Under somewhat restrictive assumptions that need not detain us here, it measures the cash equivalent of the utility that consumers derive from their purchases of cameras. If OQ cameras are consumed, that cash equivalent is the area $OQET$. But consumers pay $OQEP$ for their cameras. Therefore, the area of the triangle PET serves as a measure of net benefit or *consumer surplus*.

Equilibrium After Trade Is Opened

Suppose now that trade in cameras is opened and that the world's supply curve is S_W. The world price of cameras, OP', is lower than the old domestic price, OP, and the world price must come to prevail in the domestic market if there are no transport costs or tariffs. Domestic firms will cut back production to OQ'. Domestic consumers will step up their purchases to OQ''. The gap between domestic demand and supply, $Q'Q''$, will be filled by imports.

What are the effects on economic welfare? Producer surplus will be $[OE'P']$. It will fall by $P'E'EP$. Consumer surplus will be $P'E''T$. It will rise by $P'E''EP$. As the increase in consumer surplus exceeds the decrease in producer surplus by $E'E''E$, consumers can compensate producers and come out ahead. The area $E'E''E$ measures the gain from the opening of trade in cameras. Note that it can be divided into two parts. The decrease in domestic output, $Q'Q$, contributes $E'KE$. This is the *production effect*. The increase in domestic purchases, QQ'', contributes $KE''E$. This is the *consumption effect*.

* * *

Effects of a Tariff With a Constant World Price

At the start of Chapter 2 [*see above*], we used a simple diagram to study the effects of trade in a single market. The same diagram can be used to study the principal effects of a tariff.

Effects in a Single Market

In Figure 8–1, the demand curve for cameras is D_H, and the domestic supply curve is S_H. If there is no trade at all, equilibrium will be established at E. If there is free trade and the foreign supply curve is S_W, equilibrium will be established at F. The domestic price will equal the world price, OP_1. Domestic consumption will be OC_1, domestic production will be OQ_1, and imports will be Q_1C_1 (equal to $F'F$).

Suppose that the importing country imposes a tariff at an ad valorem rate equal to P_1P_2/OP_1. As the foreign supply curve is perfectly elastic, the world price will stay at OP_1. But the domestic price will rise to OP_2. Domestic consumption will fall to OC_2, domestic production will rise to OQ_2, and imports will fall to Q_2C_2 (equal to $G'G$). The *consumption effect* of the tariff is C_1C_2. The *production effect* is Q_1Q_2 and is also called the *protective effect*. The two together measure the *restrictive effect*, the amount by which the tariff reduces import volume. The government collects P_1P_2 of tariff revenue on each imported camera, which means that it collects $G'GTT'$ in total tariff revenue. At this point in our work, we will assume that all such revenue is returned to households; the government reduces other taxes or raises transfer payments, so tariffs do not cut consumers' incomes.

What are the effects on economic welfare? Consumer surplus falls by P_1FTP_2. Producer surplus rises by $P_1F'T'P_2$. The difference is $F'FTT'$.

But $G'GTT'$ of this loss is offset by returning tariff revenue to households, so the net loss is reduced to $F'G'T'$ *plus* FGT. The area $F'G'T'$ is the welfare loss associated with the protective effect; the area FGT is the loss associated with the consumption effect. The total welfare loss is related to the restrictive effect of the tariff. * * *

Comparing Tariffs and Quotas

Figure 8–1 can be used to compare an import quota with an import tariff. Start again with free trade and suppose that the government imposes a quota that has the same restrictive effect as the tariff analyzed in Figure 8–1. It limits the volume of imports to Q_2C_2. The domestic price must rise to OP_2 to clear the domestic market. Domestic production will rise to OQ_2, imports will be Q_2C_2, and the two together will equal domestic consumption, which falls to OC_2. The consumption and protective effects of the quota are identical to those of the tariff when the two devices have identical restrictive effects.

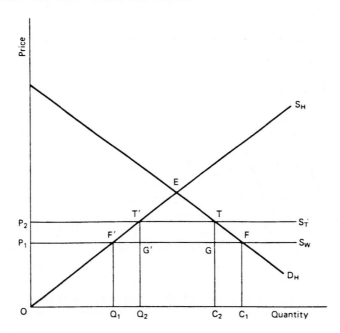

FIGURE   8-1

Effects of a Tariff in a Single Market

In the initial free-trade equilibrium, domestic consumers buy OC_1 at the price OP_1 determined by the foreign supply curve, S_W. Domestic producers supply OQ_1, and imports are Q_1C_1. An import tariff raises the domestic price to OP_2, so domestic consumers buy OC_2, domestic producers supply OQ_2, and imports are reduced to Q_2C_2. The consumption effect of the tariff is C_1C_2. The production (protective) effect is Q_1Q_2. The two together measure the restrictive effect. The government collects P_1P_2 of tariff revenue on each imported unit, or $G'GTT'$ in total tariff revenue.

There is, of course, one difference between the quota and the tariff. The tariff yields $G'GTT'$ in tariff revenue. The quota does not yield any. The revenue equivalent $G'GTT'$ goes as a windfall profit to importers standing at the head of the line when tickets are handed out. Under the assumption adopted previously, however, this difference is relatively unimportant. When the government returns its tariff revenue, consumers as a group get back what they pay out. When a quota is used instead of a tariff, importers collect what consumers pay out, but importers are consumers, too. Therefore, the welfare loss with the quota is $F'G'T'$ *plus* FGT, just as it was with the tariff.

The equivalence between a quota and a tariff can break down in two instances: when markets are not perfectly competitive and when the various demand and supply curves are subject to random shifts. Such random shifts need not affect the *expected* levels of production and consumption. Under a tariff, however, shifts in the foreign supply curve cause fluctuations in domestic output. Under a quota, they do not. (Furthermore, random fluctuations have different consequences for expected welfare under a tariff and under a quota.)

Notes

(1) The losses symbolized by $F'G'T'$ and FGT are sometimes referred to as "deadweight losses" of tariffs.

(2) In the case of quotas, it would be possible for the government establishing the quota to charge a fee for a license to use the quota, in which case it could recover some or all of the windfall profits of the importers.

(3) If a domestic industry is relatively concentrated, i.e. if only a few firms dominate the market, a quota could enable them to charge oligopolistic prices because no matter how high domestic prices rise, only a specified quantity of imports will be allowed to enter the country. More generally, there are other potentially important differences between tariffs and quotas in imperfectly competitive industries.

(4) If the aim of a quota or tariff is to protect the domestic industry, and it usually is, there is at least one other government action that could accomplish that result as well. If the government granted a subsidy to the domestic industry for each camera produced equal to P_2P_1, the domestic producers could afford to produce a quantity of cameras equal to Q_2 the same as if the P_1P_2/OP_1 tariff had been imposed. This would be true because their revenues would be the same as if the price were P_2 and they would therefore produce the amount associated with that price. Consumers would have the benefits of the free trade price of P_1. The government (and through taxes all citizens), of course, would have to pay for the subsidy. The taxes to raise the money for it would have their own distortions associated with them, and it is then an empirical question whether the subsidy would be better or worse from an efficiency standpoint. An argument for subsidy instead of protection, however, is that there are many ways to raise a given amount of revenue, and there is a decent chance that some method can be found that will be less damaging to the economy than trade protection. Whether the government

would have any incentive to find that less-distorting method if it exists, of course, is another matter.

(5) The complete argument against tariffs in the competitive case is in fact more complicated, because we have discussed only the effects on the market directly affected by the tariff (as does the excerpt above). In reality, a tariff reduces the demand for imports, and thus for the foreign exchange to buy them. The home currency appreciates as a consequence, and exports become more expensive to foreign purchasers. These effects must also be considered in a complete "general equilibrium" analysis of tariffs in an importing country. Attention to them, however, does not alter the conclusion that the sum of all the effects is adverse.

More broadly, an implication of the general equilibrium perspective is that a close linkage always exists between imports and exports. Because trade must "balance" in the long run (balanced trade is a standard assumption in general equilibrium models), any increase in exports will be matched by an increase in imports, and vice-versa, and of course any contraction in either of them will be matched as well.

(6) Various implications of a departure from the assumption of competition will be considered below, but one of them bears mention here and can significantly strengthen the case against tariffs. If a domestic industry is highly concentrated and able to exercise market power in the absence of free international competition, the elimination of tariffs can eliminate the distortions attributable to monopoly/oligopoly pricing. The major caveat relates to the strategic trade ideas in the next section.

(7) A further consideration is that significant resources may be expended in the pursuit of tariffs through the political process. Governments that are receptive to protectionist pressures, at least some of the time, encourage import-competing interests to lobby for protection. Likewise, interests that may be injured by protection will mobilize to resist it. These lobbying efforts are not costless, as anyone who has hired a Washington lobbying firm or who has bought a ticket to a Washington fundraiser can attest. An adamant commitment to free trade by a government, therefore, may have the additional benefit of discouraging such "rent-seeking behavior." (Of course, an adamant and credible commitment to *any* policy may do much the same thing, and the observation that the level of rent-seeking may be influenced by the prevailing policy in fact raises a host of subtle complications.)

(C) COMMON ARGUMENTS FOR TRADE RESTRICTIONS

The arguments for trade restrictions raised by the potential beneficiaries of them are numerous and varied. Most of the arguments have no foundation in economic analysis, although some are based on a belief that certain unrealistic assumptions underlie the economic analysis above. Interestingly, the arguments most often advanced in the press and in political circles tend to be the less persuasive, at least from the economic perspective. We begin with the arguments that, at least to us, appear quite unconvincing in general, and proceed to those that require more serious attention.

(1) Some Popular But Dubious Arguments

ALAN O. SYKES, COMPARATIVE ADVANTAGE AND THE NORMATIVE ECONOMICS OF INTERNATIONAL TRADE POLICY

1 J. Int'l Econ. L. 49, 68–70 (1998)[4]

SOME MISCONCEPTIONS ABOUT FREE TRADE

1. Trade and Jobs

Ross Perot's recent Presidential campaign in the United States devoted much energy to pressing the claim that trade liberalization—NAFTA in particular—would reduce the number of jobs in the American economy. NAFTA proponents responded with the claim that NAFTA would increase the number of jobs. This debate over the impact of trade on the number of jobs seems to resurface every time an important trade initiative arises.

To an economist, both sides of the debate ring hollow. Supply and demand in the labor market may be expected to balance in the long run just as it does in any other market, although transitory periods of disequilibrium may occur. The number of jobs in an economy will be determined by the labor supply and by the reservation wages of workers. A general decline in real wages may be expected to reduce the labor force somewhat as some workers exit to work in the home or to pursue leisure activities, and the reverse phenomenon may be expected if real wages rise. But absent a significant change in real wages economy wide, there is little reason to expect any significant change in the number of workers or jobs.

Incremental trade liberalization (such as that associated with NAFTA or the recent Uruguay Round) should not have much effect on real wages *on average*. To be sure, workers with specific human capital investments in import-competing industries can anticipate that their wages will fall with increased import competition, and the number of jobs in those industries will thus tend to decline. But workers in the export side of the economy will see increasing wages and employment opportunities as production shifts toward areas of greater comparative advantage. As a first order approximation, these effects may be expected to cancel out on average. Trade-related changes in the number of jobs, therefore, if any, are likely to be vastly smaller than other forces affecting job growth or loss such as the business cycle.

* * *

3. National Security and Self Sufficiency

Proponents of protectionist policies also appeal with some regularity to concerns about national security. Industries from steel to textiles to mining to agriculture can be heard to argue that their presence and

---

4.　Reprinted with permission.

prosperity is essential to the ability of the nation to prosecute a war effort successfully.

To be sure, war does require armaments and munitions, the soldiers must have uniforms and they must somehow be fed. But it hardly follows that a nation which may confront conditions of war must protect the industries that produce such items from decline in the face of foreign competition. Before arguments for protectionist policies based on national security can be taken seriously, a number of conditions must exist and a number of alternatives must be ruled out.

Many of the most important domestic productive facilities for national defense purposes will be supported in peacetime by government defense procurement—only where peacetime procurement is insufficient to support vital productive facilities do potential concerns about the contraction of domestic producers become important. Even then, the quantity of production of any particular good necessary to sustain a war effort and the domestic population during wartime may be considerably smaller than existing levels of domestic production. To take the case of steel in the United States, for example, the amount of production required for tanks, battleships and so on may be only a fraction of domestic capacity, and during large scale conflict other uses for steel such as new automobiles and new building construction can be put on hold. Only where import dependence would still exist at those reduced levels of domestic consumption need the analysis proceed any further.

The likelihood of imports becoming unavailable in wartime must then be carefully considered. For a nation like the United States, serious interruption of seaborne commercial traffic seems unlikely to occur for most goods or commodities in any scenario short of global conventional conflict on the scale of World War II. The probability of such conflict seems small at best in the nuclear age. Further, in the event of an interruption in seaborne traffic, adjacent trading partners may be able to take up much of the slack on many items (in the case of the United States, Canada to the North and Mexico to the South).

Where interruption of necessary imports seems a serious risk, the next issue is whether domestic capacity can be restored with reasonable dispatch. Even if an industry has closed down certain productive facilities that might be needed in wartime, it does not follow that those facilities cannot be reopened or rebuilt quickly enough to satisfy essential needs.

Finally, stockpiling during peacetime may well be a superior alternative to the protection of domestic capacity. Where the item in question is not perishable, a nation might be better off by buying up a supply of vital material at low prices in an open trading system than to burden itself over time with the high prices attendant on protectionism as a hedge against armed conflict. The funds tied up in a stockpile have some opportunity cost to be sure, but this cost can easily be smaller than the costs of excluding efficient foreign suppliers from the domestic market.

In the end, therefore, arguments for protectionism from the national security perspective require careful scrutiny and will rarely hold up to it.

(2) *Trade Restrictions to Address Domestic Distortions*

The efficiency argument for free trade, as noted, is a corollary of the principle that competitive markets, without externalities, are efficient. What if there are externalities?

ALAN V. DEARDORFF & ROBERT M. STERN, CURRENT ISSUES IN U.S. TRADE POLICIES: AN OVERVIEW[5]

"SECOND–BEST" ARGUMENTS FOR INTERVENTION

A crucial assumption underlying the classic gains-from-trade proposition is that everything within the domestic economy is working properly: all domestic markets are perfectly competitive, prices and wages adjust freely so that markets clear, and there are no externalities in production or consumption. If any of these conditions fails to hold, then there exists a domestic distortion and the first-best optimal results of free trade are no longer assured. Instead, the very distortionary effects that trade interventions are known to have could conceivably be used to offset the domestic distortion and make the economy better off.

* * *

Such use of trade intervention is said to be second best * * *. Because a tariff always distorts both producer and consumer behavior, while the externality in question concerns only one of these groups, a better policy is possible that addresses the original distortion more directly. * * *

The general principle is that trade intervention, by introducing two distortions rather than one, may succeed in solving one problem but only at the same time that it causes another. Trade policy is like doing acupuncture with a fork. No matter how carefully you insert one prong, the other is likely to do damage.

Such examples are rife in the theory of protection. The classic example is the infant-industry argument, where a tariff is said to protect a young industry while it learns to be efficient. The assumption here is that some market failure—such as an imperfection in the loan market or the impossibility of keeping new technical knowledge from being copied—makes it impossible for competitive firms to take advantage of what would otherwise be a profitable opportunity. A tariff or other import restriction can therefore be used temporarily to make the operation profitable even in the short run while the learning process is under way. Naturally, though, the success of such a policy depends crucially on a correct diagnosis of which industries really do offer the potential for such

5. U.S. Trade Policies in a Changing World Economy 15, 38–40 (Robert Stern ed., 1987). © 1987 by The Massachusetts Institute of Technology. Reprinted by permission of The MIT Press.

improvement over time. Also it may be difficult politically to remove protection once it has been put in place, even though this particular rationale for protection is explicitly temporary.

As in the case of the externality discussed above, the infant industry argument may be valid in the sense that a tariff may indeed be beneficial. But it is also true that some other policy would be superior. Once again a production subsidy, equal in size to the tariff, would yield exactly the same benefits to producers as the tariff, without causing the additional costly distortion of consumer choice. And even better might be a policy that subsidizes or guarantees loans to the industry, if the capital market was the real source of the distortion, or a policy that permits firms to appropriate technology if that was the problem. The general principle is simply that first best policies deal directly with the distortions involved, and distortions rarely involve the double effect on both producer and consumer choice that would be best addressed with trade intervention.

Many other arguments for intervention can similarly be traced to the presumption of a distortion somewhere in the domestic economy. Tariffs to protect "essential" industries, for example, depend on the private sector being unable to perceive or take advantage of the fact that these industries are essential, which often means that they confer social benefits on others in society. Tariffs to discourage consumption of undesirable goods similarly assume an undesirable social effect of such consumption, or else that consumers themselves have a distorted view of their own welfare. And finally, tariffs for employment and balance-of-payments purposes assume rather obviously that certain markets—labor and foreign exchange—are for some reason failing to adjust to equilibrium.

All of these arguments may be valid if the distortions on which they rest are correctly diagnosed, but once again they could be better dealt with by means of some other policies that deal more directly with the distortions in question.

(3) The "Optimal Tariff" Argument

The "proof" that tariffs and quotas reduce aggregate efficiency in an importing country, as noted, relied on "competitive assumptions." One of these assumptions is that the importing nation is a "price taker" in international markets, and cannot hope to lower the price that it pays for imports by restricting its purchases of them. If it can, it may be able to extract profits from foreign producers through appropriate tariff intervention.

ALAN V. DEARDORFF & ROBERT M. STERN, CURRENT ISSUES IN U.S. TRADE POLICIES: AN OVERVIEW[6]

NATIONAL MONOPOLY POWER AND THE OPTIMAL TARIFF

The idealized assumptions of the classic argument for free trade imply the optimality of free trade only for the world as a whole. For individual countries the optimality of free trade requires the additional assumption that the country is too small to have any influence, through its policies, over the prices at which it trades. Without that assumption it is well known that free trade is not optimal from a national perspective, and instead that there exists an optimal degree of trade intervention, known as the optimal tariff, that works by turning the country's terms of trade in its favor.

* * *

This argument is sometimes thought to require that the country in question be large, and therefore to apply only to such large industrialized countries as the U.S. However, the argument really applies to some extent to any country that is not insignificantly small. Furthermore, the size that is important is not the size of the country as a whole, but rather its share of world trade in markets in which it exports and imports. Since many countries tend to specialize their exports in a fairly small range of goods—exactly as trade theory predicts they should, incidentally—even quite small countries may have enough market power over the prices of their exports for the optimal tariff argument to apply.

The optimal tariff argument has the important feature that it involves a benefit for the intervening country only at the expense of the country's trading partners. Indeed, since free trade is known to be optimal for the world as a whole, it must be true that the rest of the world loses more than the tariff-levying country gains. Furthermore, the rest of the world, were it able to act collectively, would have the same sort of power over the terms of trade as does the original country and it is therefore quite inappropriate to think of a single country as levying an optimal tariff in isolation. The possibility that other countries may do the same, either in retaliation or simply because they too think they recognize an opportunity for gain, must surely be considered.

This feature of the optimal tariff argument—that it involves gain by one country at other countries' expense—is one that [is found] in some of the newer arguments for trade intervention. To address such arguments in a common framework, we will refer to such trade policies as being "exploitative intervention." Such policies typically are available to more than one, if not many, countries, each of which can have adverse effects on the others, and therefore require that strategic issues be

6. U.S. Trade Policies in a Changing World Economy 37–38 (Robert Stern ed., 1987). © 1987 by The Massachusetts Institute of Technology. Reprinted by permission of The MIT Press.

considered. Like other forms of exploitative intervention to be considered below, the optimal tariff argument is likely to find countries in the classic position of the Prisoners' Dilemma. That is, each country has available a policy that will benefit itself at the expense of others, but, if all countries simultaneously pursue that policy, all are likely to lose.

* * *

The appropriate policy * * * depends on what policies will be undertaken abroad, on how those policies may depend on the policies that we ourselves pursue or claim that we will pursue, and so forth. Thus exploitative intervention policies, even without the complications of imperfect competition, inevitably raise the complicated and perhaps unsolvable strategic issues.

Notes and Questions

(1) Just as nations may have market power with respect to their imports, so may they have market power in export markets. Governments can then assist their domestic industries in capturing monopoly profits from their foreign sales by limiting the quantity of exports with an export quota. Alternatively, the government can capture monopoly profits for itself through export taxes.

(2) There is little doubt that the United States has more monopoly power over its imports on average than most countries because of the size of its market. Likewise, small nations have little or no monopoly power, and cannot retaliate through their own optimal tariff measures if the United States tries to exploit its position. Are there other forms of "retaliation" that must be considered?

(4) Strategic Trade Policy and Its Extensions

The domestic distortion and optimal tariff analysis invokes national monopoly power and externalities to qualify, or at least refine, the efficiency case for free trade. The modern literature on "strategic trade policy" also relies on imperfect competition and externalities, but of a different sort.

PAUL R. KRUGMAN, IS FREE TRADE PASSÉ?[7]

The new view of international trade holds that trade is to an important degree driven by economies of scale rather than comparative advantage, and that international markets are typically imperfectly competitive. This new view has suggested two arguments against free trade, one of which is a wholly new idea, the other of which is an old idea given new force. The new idea is the *strategic trade policy* argument, which holds that government policy can tilt the terms of oligopolistic competition to shift excess returns from foreign to domestic firms. The old idea is that government policy should favor industries that yield *externalities*, especially generation of knowledge that firms cannot fully appropriate.

7. Journal of Economic Perspectives, Fall 1987, at 131–44. Reprinted with per-   mission of the American Economic Association.

Strategic Trade Policy

The strategic trade policy argument begins with the observation that in a world of increasing returns and imperfect competition, lucky firms in some industries may be able to earn returns higher than the opportunity costs of the resources they employ. For example, suppose that economies of scale are sufficiently large in some industry that there is only room for one profitable entrant in the world market as a whole; that is, if two firms were to enter they would both incur losses. Then whichever firm manages to establish itself in the industry will earn super-normal returns that will not be competed away.

A country can raise its national income at other countries' expense if it can somehow ensure that the lucky firm that gets to earn excess returns is domestic rather than foreign.

Suppose, then, that two countries are capable of producing a good. For concreteness, let the good be a 150–seat passenger aircraft, and call the "countries" America and Europe. Also, let there be one firm in each country that could produce the good: Boeing and Airbus, respectively.

To focus attention on the competition for excess returns, assume that neither America nor Europe has any domestic demand for the good, so that the good is intended solely for export; this allows us to identify producer surplus with the national interest. Also, assume that each firm faces only a binary choice, to produce or not to produce. Finally, assume that the market is profitable for either firm if it enters alone, unprofitable for both if both enter.

Given these assumptions, the game between Boeing and Airbus may be represented by a matrix like that shown in Table 1. Boeing's choices to produce (P) or not to produce (N) are represented by upper case letters, Airbus's corresponding choices by lower case letters. In each cell of the matrix, the lower left number represents Boeing's profit (over and above the normal return on capital), the upper right number represents Airbus's profit.

As the game is set up here, it does not have a unique outcome. To give it one, let us assume that Boeing has some kind of head start that allows it to commit itself to produce before Airbus's decision. Then in the absence of government intervention, the outcome will be Pn, in the upper right cell: Boeing will earn large profits, while deterring entry by Airbus.

Clearly Europe's government would like to change this outcome. The strategic trade policy point is that it can change the outcome if it is able to commit itself to subsidize Airbus, at a point before Boeing is committed to produce. Suppose that Europe's government can commit itself in advance to pay a subsidy of 10 to Airbus if it produces the plane, regardless of what Boeing does. Then the payoff matrix is shifted to that represented by Table 2. The result is to reverse the game's outcome.

Table 1

Hypothetical payoff matrix

		Airbus	
		p	n
Boeing	P	−5 −5	−5 100 0
	N	100 0	0 0

Table 2

Hypothetical payoff matrix after European subsidy

		Airbus	
		p	n
Boeing	P	5 −5	5 100 0
	N	110 0	0 0

Boeing now knows that even it if commits itself to produce, Airbus will still produce as well, and it will make losses. Thus Boeing will be induced not to produce, and the outcome will be Np instead of Pn. The surprising result will be that a subsidy of only 10 raises Airbus's profits from 0 to 110! Of this, 100 represents a transfer of excess returns from America to Europe, a gain in Europe's national income at America's expense.

The strategic trade policy argument thus shows that at least under some circumstances a government, by supporting its firms in international competition, can raise national welfare at another country's expense. The example just presented showed this goal being achieved via a subsidy, but other policies might also serve this purpose. In particular, when there is a significant domestic market for a good, protection of this market raises the profits of the domestic firm and lowers the profits of the foreign firm in the case where both enter; like an export subsidy, this can deter foreign entry and allow the domestic firm to capture the excess returns. As businessmen have always said, and as economists have usually denied, a protected domestic market can—under some circumstances!—promote rather than discourage exports, and possibly raise national income.

External Economies

There is nothing new about the idea that it may be desirable to deviate from free trade to encourage activities that yield positive external economies. The proposition that protection can be beneficial when an industry generates external economies is part of the conventional theory of trade policy. However, the rethinking of international trade theory has given at least the appearance of greater concreteness to the theoretical case for government intervention to promote external benefits.

It is possible to imagine bees-and-flowers examples in which externalities arise from some physical spillover between firms, but empirically the most plausible source of positive externalities is the inability of innovative firms to appropriate fully the knowledge they create. The presence of problems of appropriability is unmistakable in industries experiencing rapid technological progress, where firms routinely take each others' products apart to see how they work and how they were made.

* * *

External economies can now be identified with incomplete appropriability of the results of R & D, which immediately suggests that they are most likely to be found in industries where R & D is an especially large part of firms' costs. So by making tractable the modeling of a specific mechanism generating externalities, the new trade theory also seems to offer guidance on where these externalities are likely to be important.

The emphasis on external economies suggested by new trade theory is similar to the strategic trade policy argument in offering a reason for government targeting of particular sectors. However, the external economies argument differs in one important respect; policies to promote sectors yielding external economies need not affect other countries adversely. Whether the effect of one country's targeting of high-externality sectors on other countries is positive or negative depends on whether the scope of the externalities is national or international. There is a conflict of interest if knowledge spills over within a country but not between countries.

Critique of the New Interventionism

The positive economics of the new trade theory, with its conclusion that much trade reflects increasing returns and that many international markets are imperfectly competitive, has met with remarkably quick acceptance in the profession. The normative conclusion that this justifies a greater degree of government intervention in trade, however, has met with sharp criticism and opposition—not least from some of the creators of the new theory themselves.

Empirical Difficulties

The previous numerical example assumed that the European government knew the payoff matrix and knew how Boeing would respond to its policy. In reality, of course, even the best informed of governments will not know this much. Uncertainty is a feature of all economic policy, of course, but it is even greater when the key issue is how a policy will affect oligopolistic competition. The simple fact is that economists do not have reliable models of how oligopolists behave.

The externality argument for intervention runs up against the empirical problem of measuring external economies. By their nature, spillovers of knowledge are elusive and difficult to calculate; because they represent non-market linkages between firms, they do not leave a "paper trail" by which their spread can be traced. A combination of careful case study work and econometrics on the history of an industry may be able to identify significant external economies, but what we need for trade policy is an estimate of the future rather than the past. Will a dollar of R & D in the semiconductor industry convey ten cents worth of external benefits, or ten dollars? Nobody really knows.

By itself, the argument that making policy based on the new trade theory is an uncertain enterprise would only dictate caution and hard study, not inaction. When it is linked with the political economy concerns described below, however, it raises the question of whether the political risks associated with action outweigh any likely gains.

Entry

Suppose that a government is somehow able to overcome the empirical difficulties in formulating an interventionist trade policy. It may still not be able to raise national income if the benefits of its intervention are dissipated by entry of additional firms.

* * *

Suppose that external economies are associated with the manufacture of semiconductor chips, seemingly justifying a subsidy to chips production. If additional resources of labor and capital are supplied elastically to the industry, the external benefits of larger production will not be confined to the promoting country. Instead, they will be passed on to consumers around the world in the form of cheaper chips.

General Equilibrium

Even in a world characterized by increasing returns and imperfect competition, budget constraints still hold. A country cannot protect everything and subsidize everything. Thus interventionist policies to promote particular sectors, whether for strategic or externality reasons, must draw resources away from other sectors. This substantially raises the knowledge that a government must have to formulate interventions that do more good than harm.

Consider first the case of strategic trade policy. When a particular sector receives a subsidy, this gives firms in that sector a strategic advantage against foreign competitors. However, the resulting expansion of that sector will bid up the price of domestic resources to other sectors, putting home firms in these other sectors at a strategic disadvantage. Excess returns gained in the favored sector will thus be offset to at least some extent by returns lost elsewhere. If the government supports the wrong sector, the gain there will conceal a loss in overall national income. * * *

A similar point applies to externalities. Promoting one sector believed to yield valuable spillovers means drawing resources out of other sectors. Suppose that glamorous high-technology sectors yield less external benefit than the government thinks, and boring sectors more. Then a policy aimed at encouraging external economies may actually prove counterproductive. Again, the government needs to understand not only the targeted sector but the rest of the economy to know if a policy is justified.

* * *

Retaliation and Trade War

Strategic trade policy aimed at securing excess returns for domestic firms and support for industries that are believed to yield national benefits are both beggar-thy neighbor policies that raise income at the expense of other countries. A country that attempts to use such policies will probably provoke retaliation. In many (though not all) cases, a trade war between two interventionist governments will leave both countries worse off than if a hands-off approach were adopted by both.

Domestic Politics

Governments do not necessarily act in the national interest, especially when making detailed microeconomic interventions. Instead, they are influenced by interest group pressures. The kinds of interventions that new trade theory suggests can raise national income will typically raise the welfare of small, fortunate groups by large amounts, while imposing costs on larger, more diffuse groups. The result, as with any microeconomic policy, can easily be that excessive or misguided intervention takes place because the beneficiaries have more knowledge and influence than the losers.

LAURA D'ANDREA TYSON, WHO'S BASHING WHOM? TRADE CONFLICT IN HIGH TECHNOLOGY INDUSTRIES 10–11, 13 (1992)[8]

A dwindling number of economists and very few policymakers espouse the traditional free trade arguments as an overall prescription for US trade policy. Instead, a growing number of academic and policy economists are best described as moderate free traders: although they support the free trade ideal, they grudgingly concede that it is a long way off and conclude that unilateral measures to serve the national interest may be justified under some circumstances. * * *

Although I could easily hide behind the moderate free trade disguises described here, it would be disingenuous for me to do so. Unlike most free traders unilateral and moderate alike, I believe that what we as a

8. Reprinted by permission of the Institute for International Economics, Washington, DC.

nation make and what we trade matter. The composition of our production and trade does influence our economic well-being. Technology-intensive industries, in particular, make special contributions to the long-term health of the American economy. A dollar's worth of shoes may have the same effect on the trade balance as a dollar's worth of computers. But * * * the two do not have the same effect on employment, wages, labor skills, productivity, and research—all major determinants of our long-term economic health. In addition, because technology-intensive industries finance a disproportionate share of the nation's R & D spending, there is a strong presumption—supported by the evidence and the arguments * * * that they generate positive externalities for the rest of the economy. * * *

My trade policy agenda is a defensive one. I recommend that the nation's trade laws be used to deter or compensate for foreign practices that are not adequately regulated by existing multilateral rules. Unlike most traditional and even many moderate free traders, I am convinced that such practices can inflict substantial long-term injury on American producers. The case studies [in this book] provide compelling evidence of such injury. In addition I believe that, in pursuit of defensive objectives, US policymakers should be guided by the principle of selective reciprocity and motivated by the goal of opening foreign markets. Wherever possible, they should favor approaches that encourage trade and competition over those that discourage them.

As the case studies demonstrate, cautious activism in trade policy is not synonymous with protectionism. Indeed, both the cases and the global logic of high-technology industries indicate that protectionist measures, such as voluntary restraint agreements and price floors on imports, are at least as ineffective or counterproductive in such industries as they have proven to be elsewhere in the economy. * * * But cautious activism does sometimes violate the principles of nondiscrimination and diffuse reciprocity that remain the mainstays of US trade policy. Moreover, cautious activism does sometimes involve forceful unilateralism. And, as Moran notes, "Arm-twisting is hardly an attractive remedy compared to multilateral agreements founded upon mutual concessions."

All too often, however, the choice between self-serving unilateralism and cooperative multilateralism does not exist. Sometimes the only real choice is between inaction on the one hand and bilateral deals or unilateral action on the other. Under some circumstances the costs of inaction for American economic welfare are unacceptably high. We must not be hoodwinked by the soothing notion that, in the absence of US intervention, the fate of America's high-technology industries will be determined by market forces. Instead, they will be manipulated by the trade, regulatory, and industrial policies of our trading partners. Cautious activism has implications for domestic economic policy as well as for trade policy. A cautious activist supports general policy measures such as a more generous R & D tax credit and increases in public funding for civilian R & D and education—initiatives that would promote all of the nation's high-technology producers without singling out any one of them for special favor. But a cautious activist is willing to go further, recognizing that measures to support particular technologies or industries are sometimes warranted. To determine when such measures are required and what form they should take, the government needs an institutional capacity to monitor and respond to trends in global competition. Without such a capacity, America's policy has often been too little, too late. While we scramble to help our producers address crises that have been long in the making, both Japan and the European Community have forward-looking policies to nurture their high-technology industries. The American approach is no longer adequate, particularly at a time when cutbacks in defense R & D programs threaten to decimate public funding for science and technology unless new civilian programs are established to replace them.

Notes and Questions

(1) Laura Tyson, of course, was chair of the Council of Economic Advisors for a time during the Clinton administration. Her excerpt makes clear, as does Krugman's, that proponents of strategic trade policy advocate measures like subsidies and tax credits as often or more often than trade protection. This should remind you of the domestic distortions debate, and the problem of selecting the most efficient policy instrument for the job.

(2) Does Tyson have an adequate answer to Krugman's concerns about interventionism, such as the inability of government to know where to intervene, and the problem of capture by special interest groups?

(3) If high technology industries generate important positive externalities because of the research and development that goes on in them, why not let other countries subsidize it, and then free ride on the results? Is there any tension between the arguments above for the promotion of high-technology industries, and the popular sense that America does the research and Asia does the production?

(4) An important distinction to draw in thinking about trade intervention is between measures that benefit one country even though they reduce economic welfare globally, and measures that may enhance global as well as national welfare. Are you clear from the above materials as to which measures fall into each category? Would you expect nations acting together through a regime such as the WTO/GATT system to try and promise each other not to engage in the former sort of behavior, but to permit the latter?

(5) Distributional Considerations Again

DANI RODRIK, HAS GLOBALIZATION GONE TOO FAR? 4–7 (1997)[9]

I focus on three sources of tension between the global market and social stability and offer a brief overview of them here.

First, reduced barriers to trade and investment accentuate the asymmetry between groups that can cross international borders (either directly or indirectly, say through outsourcing) and those that cannot. In the first category are owners of capital, highly skilled workers, and many professionals, who are free to take their resources where they are most in demand. Unskilled and semiskilled workers and most middle managers belong in the second category. Putting the same point in more technical terms, globalization makes the demand for the services of individuals in the second category *more elastic*—that is, the services of large segments of the working population can be more easily substituted by the services of other people across national boundaries. Globalization therefore fundamentally transforms the employment relationship.

The fact that "workers" can be more easily substituted for each other across national boundaries undermines what many conceive to be a post-war social bargain between workers and employers, under which the former would receive a steady increase in wages and benefits in return for labor peace. This is because increased substitutability results in the following concrete consequences:

— Workers now have to pay a larger share of the cost of improvements in work conditions and benefits (that is, they bear a greater incidence of nonwage costs).

— They have to incur greater instability in earnings and hours worked in response to shocks to labor demand or labor productivity (that is, volatility and insecurity increase).

— Their bargaining power erodes, so they receive lower wages and benefits whenever bargaining is an element in setting the terms of employment.

These considerations have received insufficient attention in the recent academic literature on trade and wages, which has focused on the downward shift in demand for unskilled workers rather than the increase in the elasticity of that demand.

Second, globalization engenders conflicts within and between nations over domestic norms and the social institutions that embody them. As the technology for manufactured goods becomes standardized and diffused internationally, nations with very different sets of values, norms, institutions, and collective preferences begin to compete head on in markets for similar goods. And the spread of globalization creates opportunities for trade between countries at very different levels of development.

This is of no consequence under traditional multilateral trade policy of the WTO and the General Agreement on Tariffs and Trade (GATT): the "process" or "technology" through which goods are produced is immaterial, and so are the social institutions of the trading partners. Differences in national practices are treated just like differences in factor endowments or any other determinant of comparative advantage. However, introspection and empirical evidence both reveal that most people attach values to processes as well as outcomes. This is reflected in the norms that shape and constrain the domestic environment in which goods and services are produced—for example, workplace practices, legal rules, and social safety nets.

Trade becomes contentious when it unleashes forces that undermine the norms implicit in domestic practices. Many residents of advanced industrial countries are uncomfortable with the weakening of domestic institutions through the forces of trade, as when, for example, child labor in Honduras displaces workers in South Carolina or when pension benefits are cut in Europe in response to the requirements of the Maastricht treaty. This sense of unease is one way of interpreting the demands for "fair trade." Much of the discussion surrounding the "new" issues in trade policy—that is, labor standards, environment, competition policy, corruption—can be cast in this light of procedural fairness.

We cannot understand what is happening in these new areas until we take individual preferences for processes and the social arrangements that embody them seriously. In particular, by doing so we can start to make sense of people's uneasiness about the consequences of international economic integration and avoid the trap of automatically branding all concerned groups as self-interested protectionists. Indeed, since trade policy almost always has redistributive consequences (among sectors, income groups, and individuals), one cannot produce a principled defense of free trade without confronting the question of the fairness and legitimacy of the practices that generate these consequences. By the same token, one should not expect broad popular support for trade when trade involves exchanges that clash with (and erode) prevailing domestic social arrangements.

Third, globalization has made it exceedingly difficult for governments to provide social insurance—one of their central functions and one that has helped maintain social cohesion and domestic political support for ongoing liberalization throughout the postwar period. In essence, governments have used their fiscal powers to insulate domestic groups from excessive market risks, particularly those having an external origin. In fact, there is a striking correlation between an economy's exposure to foreign trade and the size of its welfare state. It is in the most open countries, such as Sweden, Denmark, and the Netherlands, that spending on income transfers has expanded the most. This is not to say that the government is the sole, or the best, provider of social insurance. The extended family, religious groups, and local communities often play similar roles. My point is that it is a hallmark of postwar period that governments in the advanced countries have been expected to provide such insurance.

At the present, however, international economic integration is taking place against the background of receding governments and diminished social obligations. The welfare state has been under attack for two decades. Moreover, the increasing mobility of capital has rendered an important segment of the tax base footloose, leaving governments with the unappetizing option of increasing tax rates disproportionately on labor income. Yet the need for social insurance for the vast majority of the population that remains internationally immobile has not diminished. If anything, this need has become greater as a consequence of increased integration. The question therefore is how the tension between globalization and the pressures for socialization of risk can be eased. If the tension is not managed intelligently and creatively, the danger is that the domestic consensus in favor of open markets will ultimately erode to the point where a generalized resurgence of protectionism becomes a serious possibility.

Each of these arguments points to an important weakness in the manner in which advanced societies are handling—or are equipped to handle—the consequences of globalization. Collectively, they point to what is perhaps the greatest risk of all, namely that the cumulative consequence of the tensions mentioned above will be the solidifying of a new set of class divisions—between those who prosper in the globalized economy and those who do not, between those who share its values, and those who would rather not, and between those who can diversify away its risks and those who cannot. This is not a pleasing prospect, even for individuals on the winning side of the divide who have little empathy for the other side. Social disintegration is not a spectator sport—those on the sidelines also get splashed with mud from the field. Ultimately, the deepening of social fissures can harm all.

JOSEPH E. STIGLITZ, MAKING GLOBALIZATION WORK 7–9[10]

THE TWO FACES OF GLOBALIZATION

In the early 1990s, globalization was greeted with euphoria. Capital flows to developing countries had increased sixfold in six years, from 1990 to 1996. The establishment of the World Trade Organization in 1995—a goal that had been sought for half a century—was to bring the semblance of a rule of law to international commerce. Everyone was supposed to be a winner—those in both the developed and the developing world. Globalization was to bring unprecedented prosperity to *all*.

No wonder then that the first major modern protest against globalization—which took place in Seattle in December 1999, at what was supposed to be the start of a new round of trade negotiations, leading to further liberalization—came as a surprise to the advocates of open markets. Globalization had succeeded in unifying people from around the world—against globalization. Factory workers in the United States saw their jobs being threatened by competition from China. Farmers in developing countries saw their jobs being threatened by the highly subsidized corn and other crops from the United States. Workers in Europe saw hard-fought-for job protections being assailed in the name of globalization. AIDS activists saw new trade agreements raising the prices of drugs to levels that were unaffordable in much of the world. Environmentalists felt that globalization undermined their decades-long struggle to establish regulations to preserve our natural heritage. Those who wanted to protect and develop their own cultural heritage saw too the intrusions of globalization. These protestors did not accept the argument that, economically at least, globalization would ultimately make everybody better off.

There have been many reports and commission devoted to the topic of globalization. I was involved in the World Commission on the Social Dimensions of Globalization, which was established in 2001 by the International Labor Organization (created in 1919 in Geneva to bring together government, business, and·labor).

* * *

The commission surveyed seventy-three countries around the world. Its conclusions were startling. In every region of the world except South Asia, the United States, and the European Union (EU), unemployment rates increased between 1990 and 2002. By the time the report was issued, global unemployment had reached a new high of 185.9 million. The commission also found that 59 percent of the world's people were living in countries with growing inequality, with only 5 percent in countries with declining inequality. Even in most of the developed countries, the rich were getting richer while the poor were often not even holding their own.

In short, globalization may have helped some countries—their GDP, the sum total of the goods and services produced, may have increased— but it had not helped most of the people even in these countries. The worry was that globalization might be creating rich countries with poor people.

Of course, those who are discontented with economic globalization generally do not object to the greater access to global markets or to the spread of global knowledge, which allows the developing world to take advantage of the discoveries and innovations made in developed countries. Rather, they raise five concerns:

- The rules of the game that governs globalization are unfair, specifically designed to benefit the advanced industrial countries. In fact, some recent changes are so unfair that they have made some of the poorest countries actually worse off.

- Globalization advances material values over other values, such as a concern for the environment or for life itself.

- The way globalization has been managed has taken away much of the developing countries' sovereignty, and their ability to make decision themselves in key areas that affect their citizens' well-being. In this sense, it has undermined democracy.

- While the advocates of globalization have claimed that everyone will benefit economically, there is plenty of evidence from both developing and developed countries that there are many losers in both.

- Perhaps most important, the economic system that has been pressed upon the developing countries—in some cases essentially forced upon them—is inappropriate and often grossly damaging. Globalization should not mean the Americanization of either economic policy or culture, but often it does—and that has caused resentment.

Notes and Questions

(1) In the readings by Rodrik and Stiglitz, to what extent are the objections to globalization grounded in the familiar tension between efficiency and distribution noted earlier, and to what extent are they grounded in something else? If the problem is one of growing inequality, where does the solution lie—at the global level or the national level?

(2) At this early stage of the course, students will have a hard time evaluating the merits of many arguments put forward by anti-globalization critics. Nevertheless, we think it useful at least to identify such lines of argument now. As you progress through subsequent chapters, consider what the basis might be for some of these claims, such as the notion that WTO rules are "unfair" to poorer countries, for example, or that they elevate material values over concerns for the environment and human life.

(3) How might globalization infringe "sovereignty?" If a nation voluntarily accedes to a treaty regime, can that regime meaningfully be said to intrude on that nation's sovereignty? In what other ways, if any, might globalization pose a threat to sovereignty?

(4) In the final excerpt of this section, Robert Lawrence, a former member of the President Clinton's Council of Economic Advisors, takes issue with some of the claims above, at least in so far as trade is said to be responsible for increasing income inequality in the Untied States.

ROBERT Z. LAWRENCE
THE GLOBALIZATION PARADOX: MORE TRADE LESS INEQUALITY[11]

It is fairly widely accepted that in the aggregate trade generates gains and promotes economic growth but it can also create winners and losers. In America's case, trade with developing countries is viewed as particularly problematic because it could put downward pressures on the earnings of lower-wage workers. And indeed, it is precisely this type of trade that has expanded especially rapidly over the past decade, partly because countries such as China and India have emerged as major global competitors and partly because the US has vigorously implemented Free Trade Agreements with Mexico (NAFTA) and other developing countries.

11. © VoxEu.org, September 4, 2007, reprinted with permission. These comments are based on the findings in Blue Collar Blues: Is Trade to Blame for Rising U.S. Income Inequality? (Washington, DC: Peterson Institute for International Economics, 2008).

Whereas most studies concluded that in the 1980s trade accounted for a relatively small share of the increase in US wage inequality, many now argue that the volume of trade has now grown to the point that much larger effects should be expected. For example, Paul Krugman recently wrote a Vox column making precisely this case.

It is true that by virtually all quantity and price indicators there were powerful globalisation forces operating during this period that might have been expected to increase wage inequality. Not only have imports from developing countries increased dramatically, but the relative prices of manufactured goods from these countries have declined steadily since the early 90s. Yet the big surprise is that over the past fifteen years wages of the least skilled Americans—the lowest 10 percent—have kept pace with the median. Moreover, since 1999, while real wage growth in general has been sluggish, most US relative wage and compensation measures indicate little evidence of increased inequality. This is true when workers are distinguished by skill, education, unionization, occupation and major sectors.

Apparently, the shocks from trade (or immigration) have not increased conventional wage inequality. This is surprising given the growing scale of the competition from low wage countries. There are two lines of explanation.

One is that the goods that the US imports are actually very sophisticated and produced in the US by relatively skilled workers. While it may cause displacement and could put downward pressure on wages generally, therefore, this competition does not increase wage inequality.

A second more benign view is that a significant amount of what America imports today is no longer produced domestically. Thus declining import prices simply yield consumer benefits but do not exert downward pressure on US wages nor cause dislocation of US workers. Paradoxically, globalisation is actually causing less inequality because specialisation is more advanced.

It appears that US trade today combines these two elements in proportions that are hard to disentangle, particularly at levels of disaggregation that allow for a sufficiently precise matching of products and the wages earned in producing them. At relatively high levels of aggregation the data indicate that manufactured imports overall, and even those from developing countries such as China, are concentrated in US manufacturing sectors which pay significantly higher than average US wages. This means that import displacement does not fall disproportionately on less skilled workers. While there has been considerable displacement from trade during this period, it has not increased wage inequality. At more disaggregated levels, however, the data suggests that goods imported from developing countries such as China are associated with relatively less skilled labor inputs and—judging by their unit values—qualitatively different from those produced by developed countries such as the US. This provides support for the view that much of this trade reflects more complete specialisation and as such does not result in either wage inequality or downward pressure on wages generally.

It will take more research to quantify the relative magnitudes of these two effects. Nonetheless, it does appear that over the past decade, US income inequality has continued to grow but not in a way that suggests trade with developing countries is the major reason. It's not the least skilled who have fallen behind but profits and the wages of the very richest Americans that have raced ahead.

SECTION 2.3   THE POLITICAL ECONOMY OF TRADE POLICY

The preceding materials are largely normative in their focus, addressing the question whether intervention is a good idea as a matter of economic policy. Another impressive body of economic thought addresses the positive aspects of trade policy, trying to explain the pattern of intervention that we actually observe, and to explain the extent of international cooperation over trade matters. We can only touch on these matters briefly.

The questions that one can address in this framework are virtually unlimited and, not surprisingly, many do not have satisfactory answers as yet. An essentially random sample of possible queries is: If all import-competing industries would like protection, other things being equal, why do only some industries get significant protection? If high technology industries are the ones that economic theory suggests *might* be appropriate to promote, why is protection usually greatest in declining industries such as steel and textiles? Are pressures for protection linked to the business cycle? Why did the European Common Market form when it did, and what explains who joined and who did not? Why does the WTO/GATT system have an unconditional most-favored-nation obligation built into much of it? Why do antidumping laws exist, and why does GATT tolerate them? To answer such questions, one must have a convincing explanation for how the political process operates in the trade policy arena.

(A) AN EARLY ACCOUNT: THE CONSERVATIVE SOCIAL WELFARE FUNCTION

W.M. CORDEN, TRADE POLICY AND ECONOMIC WELFARE 107–08 (1974)[11]

Let us now introduce the conservative social welfare function, a concept which seems particularly helpful for understanding actual trade policies of many countries. Put in its simplest form it includes the following income distribution target: any significant absolute reductions in real incomes of any significant section of the community should be

---

11. Reprinted by permission of Oxford University Press.

avoided. This is not quite the same as setting up the existing income distribution as the best, but comes close to it, and so can indeed be described as "conservative." In terms of welfare weights, increases in income are given relatively low weights and decreases very high weights.

The conservative social welfare function helps to explain the income maintenance motivation of so many tariffs in the past and the reluctance to reduce income maintenance tariffs even when it has become clear that the need for them is more than temporary. It can be regarded as expressing a number of ideas.

Firstly, it is "unfair" to allow anyone's real income to be reduced significantly—and especially if this is the result of deliberate policy decisions—unless there are very good reasons for this and it is more or less unavoidable.

Secondly, insofar as people are risk averters, everyone's real income is increased when it is known that a government will generally intervene to prevent sudden or large and unexpected income losses. The conservative social welfare function is part of a social insurance system.

Thirdly, social peace requires that no significant group's income shall fall if that of others is rising. Social peace might be regarded as a social good in itself or as a basis for political stability and hence perhaps economic development. And even if social peace does not depend on the maintenance of the incomes of the major classes in the community, the survival of a government may.

Finally, if a policy is directed at a certain target, such as protection of an industry or improving the balance of payments, most governments want to minimize the adverse by-product effects on sectional incomes so as not to be involved in political battles incidental to their main purpose.

Notes and Questions

Does the "conservative social welfare function" have any ethical appeal, or is it simply an effort to construct a positive explanation for observed policies? Is Corden implicitly saying that whatever we observe governments to be doing, it must be *defined* to be the maximization of social welfare? If Corden's construct is really just an attempt at explanation without normative overlay, how well does it work? Are all citizens treated equally in the degree of protection afforded against shocks to their incomes from import competition? Is comparable government protection afforded against loss of income due to domestic developments that lead companies to liquidate or to lay off workers? If not, can the conservative social welfare function provide an explanation?

(B) PUBLIC CHOICE THEORY AND ITS IMPLICATIONS

Corden wrote at a time when the modern theory of public choice was still relatively young. One of the central ideas of public choice is that political officials pursue their self interest, which often includes maximizing chances of reelection, maximizing campaign contributions, and the like (the theory has a distinct American bias given its origins, and detailed elaborations of how it would apply to non-democratic regimes are rare). As a general matter, this leads to the prediction that public officials will be more responsive to well-organized and well-financed interest groups that can mobilize votes, money, or both. It also suggests that governments will not maximize "social welfare" in any independent ethical sense.

With reference to trade policy, an immediate corollary is that consumer interests will often be poorly represented in policy formulation. The effects of most protectionist measures on the average consumer are quite modest, even though the aggregate effects are sizeable. Rarely will consumers mobilize to become involved with particular protectionist initiatives, therefore, because the gains to any one consumer are not worth the costs, and because each would like to free ride on the efforts of others. Producer groups, by contrast, will tend to organize quite well—the right government policy can be worth millions in profits.

Does this proposition lead to the prediction that all import-competing industries will receive considerable protection? The answer is no. Many industries are consumers of imported goods—the auto industry, for example, may utilize imported steel, imported electronics products, imported plastics, and so on. Such industries are hurt by protectionist measures that raise the costs of their inputs. Similarly, international capital is highly mobile. Many domestic companies earn substantial returns from their overseas operations. Protectionist initiatives can only damage those operations.

Moreover, the international consequences of protection must be considered. According to the general equilibrium theory of trade, restrictions on imports will lead to reduced exports over the long run, as trade must eventually balance. Moreover, new protectionist initiatives in one country may provoke direct retaliation in others—the response of other nations to the Smoot–Hawley tariff of the United States is illustrative. Hence, industries that rely on exports for much of their profits will have an incentive to oppose protectionist initiatives (the US agriculture lobby, for example, often testifies about fears of retaliation before Congress). The interests of exporters can be mobilized even more effectively when an opportunity arises for international cooperation to reduce trade barriers. Then, the failure to liberalize trade at home has immediate and certain consequences in scuttling an agreement that would give exporters greater access to foreign markets.

According to the public choice perspective, the battle over protectionist measures will be fought mainly between these competing producer interests. Those that buy the most tickets to fund raisers and are most persuasive in their promises to mobilize the vote will win out. This is not to say that consumer interests have no say in the matter whatsoever, or that every politician is a fully selfish individual with no high-minded principles on her agenda. But the basic producer-interest model has had considerable success as a positive matter, and is at least a useful starting point in answering questions about why things are the way they are.[2]

A further implication of the public choice perspective is that international agreements exist because they are politically beneficial to officials in their signatory governments, both initially and over time (otherwise, officials would benefit by causing their nations to drop out of them). Recent years have seen a great deal of work along these general lines.

(C) ELABORATING THE PUBLIC CHOICE PERSPECTIVE: MODERN THEORIES OF TRADE AGREEMENTS

Economists have developed two primary theories of international trade agreements over the past twenty years or so. These theories emphasize the terms of trade incentive for trade cooperation, and the role of cooperation in facilitating domestic political commitments. A small amount of work has also been done on the value of trade agreements in the presence of imperfect competition and increasing returns. Finally, some commentators have hinted that "economic" explanations for trade agreements should be set aside in favor of "political" explanations.

(1) The Terms of Trade Theory

The terms of trade theory holds that governments sign trade agreements to internalize a terms of trade externality between countries. Standard trade theory distinguishes between small countries, which cannot affect the prices of their exports and imports and therefore have no bargaining power vis-à-vis their trading partners, and large countries, which can choose trade taxes to maximize their own national incomes (by imposing an "optimal" tariff). In the case of large countries, Harry Johnson[3] noted that if two countries choose their optimal tariffs independently, that is, taking the policy of the other country as given, the resulting non-cooperative Nash equilibrium is inefficient. In essence, when each country imposes trade barriers in an attempt to manipulate the terms of trade to its own advantage, these actions tend to cancel each other out. The result of the higher trade barriers will be a much lower volume of trade with potentially little net change in the terms of trade, thereby leaving both countries potentially worse off than they would have been had they refrained from such policies.

The terms of trade externality arises from the *unilateral* nature of the tariff setting. Acting independently, countries may not be able to

---

2. Readers who wish to pursue the matter further might wish to consult Robert E. Baldwin, The Economics of the GATT, *in* Peter Oppenheimer (ed.), Issues in International Economics (1980); Robert E. Baldwin, The Political Economy of Protectionism, *in* Jagdish N. Bhagwati (ed.), Import Competition and Response (1982); Jagdish N. Bhagwati, Protectionism (1988); Ronald W. Jones & Anne O. Krueger (eds.), The Political Economy of International Trade (1990); Jagdish N. Bhagwati & Douglas A. Irwin (eds.), Political Economy and International Economics (1991); Robert Feenstra, Gene Grossman & Douglas Irwin (eds.), The Political Economy of Trade Policy: Papers in Honor of Jagdish Bhagwati (1996).

3. Harry G. Johnson, Optimum Tariffs and Retaliation, 21 Rev. Econ. Stud. 142 (1953–54).

avoid the inefficient equilibrium because, if one of them were to reduce its tariffs alone, the other country would still have a unilateral incentive to maintain its duties on exports from the tariff-reducing country. This logic was used by economists to demonstrate that countries can overcome this inefficient equilibrium by cooperating in binding agreements to reduce trade barriers.

One difficulty with the theory originally developed by Johnson was the assumption that the "objective function" of the government was to maximize national welfare. This assumption was at odds with much observed behavior in the trade arena, leading other economists to search for theories that rested on more realistic assumptions about government objective functions. Grossman and Helpman[4] developed a model of trade policy formation at the national level in a small country, in which political officials determine trade policy on the basis of an objective function that blends conventional national welfare with their own self interest in securing campaign contributions. The Grossman and Helpman model assumes that some industries are well organized to participate in the political process and some are not. The resulting political equilibrium then involves a mix of policies favoring organized interests that can deviate from the policies that would achieve national welfare maximization.

Grossman and Helpman then extended the analysis to consider two large countries whose actions influenced their terms of trade.[5] When acting unilaterally, each government is responsive only to its domestic interest groups, and thus the Nash equilibrium entails inefficiencies due to the international terms of trade externality. A trade agreement then has the potential to improve the welfare of both countries (as measured by their political objective functions) by addressing this externality problem. Because governments are not national welfare maximizers, however, the terms of a cooperative agreement may deviate significantly from the policies that conventional joint welfare maximization would require.

(2) The Domestic Political Commitment Theory

The commitment theory holds that GATT is a device allowing a government to avoid pressure from domestic interests (import-competing producers) to impose trade barriers. The political commitment theory differs fundamentally from the terms of trade theory in that there is no international externality associated with trade policy choices. Instead, trade agreements serve as a "hands-tying" mechanism that improves the bargaining position of each signatory government in relation to various domestic pressure groups. According to this approach, governments want to pursue a trade policy that will maximize national welfare, but special

---

4. Gene M. Grossman & Elhanan Helpman, Protection for Sale, 84 Am. Econ. Rev. 833 (1994).

5. Gene M. Grossman & Elhanan Helpman, Trade Wars and Trade Talks, 103 J. Pol. Econ. 675 (1995). See also Kyle Bagwell & Robert W. Staiger, The Economics of the World Trading System (MIT Press, 2002).

interests (import-competing producers) make it politically impossible for domestic authorities to implement such a policy. So the government signs a trade agreement with other countries to take trade policy out of the hands of domestic politicians (in, say, the legislature), increase the power of exporting interest groups, and raise the costs of returning to a policy of high tariffs.

This approach has been championed by Maggi and Rodriguez–Clare.[6] They focus on a small country (thereby ruling out terms of trade effects) in which factors of production are sector specific in the short-run but mobile in the long-run. Even if the government reaps some political benefits (from the specific factors) by imposing trade restrictions in the short-run, it may nevertheless wish to commit to a free trade agreement to avoid the economic distortion to resource allocation. In their framework, the speed of adjustment of factors over time between sectors, as well as the preferences of the government for campaign contributions over economic efficiency, determine the political outcome: the faster the adjustment and the more efficiency is valued, the more likely a government will prefer the improved allocation of resources as a result of trade agreements to the foregone rents from the political process by maintaining trade restrictions.

(3) Imperfect Competition

The "new trade theory" of the 1980's and 90's emphasized the implications of imperfect competition for international trade. It noted that trade and trade policy can have implications for the ability of firms with increasing returns to scale to reap scale economies, as well as for product variety that is valuable to consumers in a monopolistically competitive environment. Trade policy might also affect the ability of countries to benefit from certain positive externalities such as R & D spillovers that are limited in geographic scope (the Silicon Valley story). This thinking led numerous commentators to consider the possible virtues of "industrial policy" or "strategic trade policy" to promote the national interest in such industries, perhaps at the expense of other nations.

Such analysis may also offer insight into trade agreements. To the degree that nations pursue industrial policy in a manner that has negative externalities for other nations, the resulting noncooperative equilibrium will not be efficient. Trade agreements may then offer an opportunity to improve the situation.

A small amount of work has been done along these lines. Bagwell and Staiger[7] discuss the issue of subsidies in international trade. They note that nations granting subsidies for the purpose of increasing their

---

6. Giovanni Maggi & Andres Rodriguez–Clare, The Value of Trade Agreements in the Presence of Political Pressures, 106 J. Pol. Econ. 574 (1998).

7. Kyle Bagwell & Robert W. Staiger, The Economics of the World Trading System (MIT Press, 2002).

exports may in effect do so in competition with each other, and may thereby create a negative externality for other subsidizing governments. They may then wish to enter an agreement restricting subsidies, although such an agreement may not be in the interest of the trading community as a whole as it will impose negative externalities on the recipients of subsidies. Although their formal analysis focuses on a competitive model, they note that similar analysis would apply to governments that use subsidies in an effort to shift rents to themselves in imperfectly competitive industries.

Helpman and Krugman[8] consider tariffs in a model of monopolistic competition, in which consumers value product variety but firms have economies of scale (some initial fixed costs) that preclude maximal variety from being produced. They assume that governments are national income maximizers. Nations may have an incentive in such a model to use tariffs to stimulate consumption of domestically produced goods (the gain arising because their price is above their marginal cost in the monopolistically competitive equilibrium), a motivation that is distinct from (or in addition to) any desire to influence the terms of trade. When all nations do so, however, the resulting equilibrium will be inefficient, and room for cooperation arises. Helpman and Krugman note, however, that the use of tariffs to stimulate consumption of domestically produced goods is only a second-best policy, and that a consumption subsidy would dominate. If nations use their first best policy instruments, therefore, the sole motivation for tariffs in the Helpman–Krugman model is again simply to improve the terms of trade.

(4) Alternative "Political" Theories

Economists have long argued that a gap exists between the traditional welfare analysis of economists, and the political realities that animate trade agreements. Paul Krugman has remarked, for example, that "the optimal tariff argument plays almost no role in real-world trade disputes." Similarly, Robert Baldwin has noted that "economists tend to judge the rules of organizations such as the GATT on the basis of whether they promote economic efficiency, growth, and stability." Yet in Baldwin's view, "maximizing the collective economic welfare of individuals making up either a country or the world is, however, not the main policy objective of the GATT." Rather, "the broad objective is to help to maintain international political stability by establishing rules of 'good behavior' as well as mechanisms for settling disputes. . . ."

Do these comments by such distinguished trade economists suggest an alternative "political" theory of trade agreements, distinct from any of those set forth above? Might there be a sense in which trade agreements are not about the "terms of trade," for example, but instead are about "market access" and "political stability?"

---

8. Elhanan Helpman & Paul R. Krugman, Trade Policy and Market Structure (MIT Press, 1989).

The answer is somewhat unclear as a theoretical matter, even though the language of diplomats and trade negotiators rarely tracks the language of the economic theories outlined above. Unquestionably, trade negotiators seek better market access for their exporters. But why does market access matter to exporters? The obvious reason is that a lowering of trade barriers, and the attendant improvement in market access, will allow exporters to charge higher prices and make more money. By necessary implication, trade barriers affect the prices that exporters can command on world markets, the point that lies at the heart of the terms of trade theory.

Likewise, although diplomats may well have valued trade agreements for their potential to contribute to political stability, one must still ask why trade agreements were expected to generate political stability? Once again, the most plausible answer is that a reduction of trade barriers would stimulate exports and rearrange the pattern of production more in accordance with comparative advantage, thus enhancing the prosperity of nations. This rearrangement of the pattern of production would occur in response to the fact that as trade barriers declined, efficient exporters would find themselves able to make more money and would expand their operations.

Yet, one cannot rule out the possibility that there may be more to the "political" account than simply a restatement of the terms of trade rationale in different terms. In particular, the possibility arises that the formal terms of trade models represent government preferences in ways that do not fully capture what governments care about in practice. Such models exclude the possibility of internationally interdependent utilities, for example, which might explain certain government behavior that might be viewed as altruism (as toward developing countries). Likewise, there is some evidence at the outset of GATT that major players (such as the United States) cared directly about fostering prosperity among trading partners for the purpose of creating greater political stability in the world economy, and might have been willing to sacrifice its narrow national interest to some extent toward that end.

Notes and Questions

(1) With regard to international agreements, an interesting question arises as to what holds them together. If a nation decides to ignore its WTO obligations, for example, no army will attack it, and the most that aggrieved nations can do realistically is to ignore their own obligations in response (as "retaliation"). Thus, to the extent that WTO agreements are respected by their signatories, and we shall see that compliance with those obligations is remarkably high, it must be because nations (or, more accurately, the officials in power) could not benefit politically from cheating, or that they refrain out of fear that cheating will provoke retaliation that will more than wipe out the gains. The former possibility seems implausible as it is likely that many nations would find it advantageous to renege on some of their trade concessions if they thought other nations would ignore it. The second

hypothesis thus has more promise, and we will indeed focus intently on the retaliatory dimension in our studies of the WTO dispute resolution system.

(2) The alternative "political" theories of trade agreements must be understood to include the possibility that trade promotes world peace. This idea was evidently in the minds of many diplomats involved in the founding of GATT, as the next section indicates.

SECTION 2.4   FOREIGN POLICY GOALS AND INTERNATIONAL TRADE POLICY

As economists will quickly tell you, economic analysis is capable in principle of incorporating any consideration that affects the well being of any nation or the citizens of any nation. In practice, however, the economic perspective tends to emphasize issues that economic models can address readily. Other issues, however, may at times prove equally or more important.

(A) WAR AND PEACE

Probably the most important foreign policy goal related to international economic policy is the prevention of war. Many statesmen and scholars believe that modern history establishes a clear relationship between implementation of certain international economic policies and war. The importance of this relationship was particularly evident in the case of World War II.

RICHARD N. COOPER, TRADE POLICY AND FOREIGN POLICY[1]

The most disastrous single mistake any U.S. president has made in international relations was Herbert Hoover's signing of the Smoot–Hawley Tariff Act into law in June 1930. The sharp increase in U.S. tariffs, the apparent indifference of the U.S. authorities to the implications of their actions for foreigners, and the foreign retaliation that quickly followed, as threatened, helped convert what would have been otherwise a normal economic downturn into a major world depression. The sharp decline in foreign trade and economic activity in turn undermined the position of the moderates with respect to the nationalists in Japanese politics and paved the way for the electoral victory of the Nazis in Germany in 1932. Japan promptly invaded China in 1931, and the basis for World War II was laid.

Valuable lessons were learned from the Smoot–Hawley tariff experience by the foreign policy community: the threat of tariff retaliation is not always merely a bluff; tariffs do influence trade flows negatively; a decline in trade can depress national economies; economic depression

1. U.S. Trade Policies in a Changing World Economy 291–92 (Robert M. Stern ed., 1987). © 1987 by The Massachusetts Institute of Technology. Reprinted by permission of The MIT Press. See also John H. Jackson, World Trade and the Law of GATT ch. 2 (1969), particularly at 38ff.

provides fertile ground for politically radical nostrums; and political radicals often seek foreign (military) adventures to distract domestic attention away from their domestic economic failures. The seeds of World War II, in both the Far East and in Europe, were sown by Hoover's signing of the Smoot–Hawley tariff. * * *

DOUGLAS A. IRWIN, PETROS C. MAVROIDIS & ALAN O. SYKES, THE GENESIS OF THE GATT[2]

The most important political motivation for the GATT, for which the United States was prepared to make economic concessions, was world peace, in particular, the idea that flourishing trade reduces conflict among nations. The liberal argument that trade promotes peace goes back at least to the 18th century and is associated with Baron de Montesquieu and Immanuel Kant. The idea was later expounded by 19th-century liberal thinkers, such as Richard Cobden and John Stuart Mill.

[Roosevelt's Secretary of State] Cordell Hull enthusiastically embraced this view. As Hull wrote in 1934: "The truth is universally recognized that trade between nations is the greatest peace-maker and civilizer within human experience." The Roosevelt administration's program

> to secure trade agreements with the principal nations is the first step in a broad movement to increase international trade. Upon this program, rests largely my hope of insured peace and the fullest measure of prosperity.

Indeed, Hull envisioned the reciprocal-trade-agreements program in the 1930s as the first step in a worldwide campaign to restore political stability.

Was Hull correct in his view that international trade promotes peace and cooperation among nations? At the time, Hull was certainly perceived as being correct in the eyes of many. In 1945, he was awarded the Nobel Peace Prize for his efforts to promote international political and economic cooperation. In the opening public statements at the 1947 Geneva conference, there is much support for the view that economic cooperation would promote political cooperation. In particular, countries that had been directly involved in World War II, and that had suffered great material damage and casualties, saw the GATT as a part of a new era of international cooperation that would reduce the risks of war in the future. In the view of Baron van der Straten–Waillet (Belgium), the economic union between his country, the Netherlands, and Luxembourg offered an appropriate example of how economic nationalism can be defeated; it should be extrapolated to the world sphere. While acknowledging the leading role that the U.S. government was playing, he argued

2. Prepared for the American Law Institute Project on Principles of World Trade Law, © Cambridge University Press, 2008, reprinted with permission from Chapter 3. Footnotes omitted.

in favor of emulating at the world level his own country's experience. Wilgress (Canada) offered a similar view to that of the Benelux countries: he preached in favor of relaxing (to the extent necessary) one's national sovereignty in order to promote the common good. Philip (France) stressed the positive role that bilateral trade agreements could play, and argued in favor of ensuring that they coexist with ITO, since they share the same objective: to open up markets. Huysmans (Netherlands) urged the ITO to open up to enemies as well, since, in his view, the contribution to world peace would be increased as more and more joined the ranks of the ITO.

Sir Stafford Cripps (UK) started by stressing that "we all failed to appreciate sufficiently the direct relation between international economic policies and the danger of war." In his view, the GATT and ITO project demonstrated the will for international cooperation and the abandonment of dangerous unilateral policies. Finally, Wilcox (United States) emphasized the links between the GATT/ITO with the other Bretton Woods institutions, and the wider peace process. Echoing the spirit of Hull, he explained his government's view that the establishment of the world trading system was a major contribution to the new world order that nations would be jointly building in order to break with the past.

Is it true that trade fosters peace? There are several channels by which increased international trade or economic interdependence may reduce the chances of war and increase the likelihood of cooperation. The higher incomes that are associated with greater trade increase the opportunity cost of military conflict. * * * Trade also provides an alternative mechanism for extracting resources from other countries; goods can be acquired by mutually beneficial exchange rather than by military conquest. Thus, the fear of the potential economic consequences from the disruption of trade, and the reduced benefits of obtaining resources via military means, may deter some states from initiating a conflict.

Another channel by which trade can reduce the likelihood of war is by increasing communication across states. Recent theories of strategic bargaining suggest that war results from asymmetric information about states' interests and capabilities rather than calculations about the costliness of war itself. Economic interdependence provides more information across states, thereby promoting transparency and facilitating costly signaling, and thereby reducing asymmetries of information.

However, conflict theorists have also suggested that trade can increase conflict. As Morrow notes:

> current theory on the initiation and escalation of disputes casts doubt on the idea that trade prevents international conflict. If higher interdependence reduces a nation's resolve for war with its trading partners, the effect of interdependence on conflict is indeterminate. It could make the initiation and escalation of dispute more or less likely. Trade makes war less attractive to both parties, but

the target's lower willingness to fight makes coercion of the target easier and more attractive to the initiator.

Through this channel, Rowe suggests that globalization may have helped to cause World War I.

Given the different perspectives on the determinants of conflict and the role of trade in influencing them, the relationship between trade and conflict is an empirical question. * * * However, as with most empirical relationships, establishing definitive causality is extremely difficult. In this case, trade may promote peace, but peace certainly promotes trade, while the prospect of conflict reduces trade. Hence, states that are politically friendly are more likely to trade with one another, whereas trade may be low between states with a likelihood of conflict. This can account for the positive correlation between trade and peace, but in this case there is no causal relationship between trade and peace.

These empirical weaknesses have led researchers to believe that the relationship between trade and peace may be a contingent one that is mediated by various factors that can affect the strength of the relationship. For example, there is evidence that while trade inhibits conflict between democracies, autocracies are insulated from popular pressure and hence rising trade has no impact on their propensities to initiate military conflict. Furthermore, some studies find that economic interdependence reduces conflict between high-income countries but has little impact on conflict between low-income countries. One of the most robust empirical relationships in political science is that democracies tend not to fight one another, so to the extent that more trade promotes political liberalization, it may indirectly promote peace.

(B) OTHER FOREIGN POLICY GOALS

Not all foreign policy goals are aimed at, or even consistent with, promoting peace. Indeed, among the principal general foreign policy goals that affect international economic policies are the desire of one nation to strengthen its allies and to avoid strengthening its potential enemies and to convince (or to attempt to force) foreign countries to change their behavior or policies. For example, the United States has no doubt followed policies inconsistent with its economic self-interest, narrowly defined, in order to promote growth and economic strength in Western Europe and Japan. On the other hand, the United States maintains trade restrictions in respect of trade and other economic relations with countries such as North Korea and Iran. In the recent past use of trade restrictions designed to force policy changes has become more common. They are viewed as an acceptable alternative to the use of force, and while their effectiveness may often be questioned, they serve as a symbolic objection to the policies of the foreign state, thereby satisfying the domestic political need to do something to register such objections.

Chapter 3

THE UNITED STATES CONSTITUTION AND REGULATION OF INTERNATIONAL ECONOMIC AFFAIRS

SECTION 3.1 INTRODUCTION TO CHAPTERS 3 AND 4

In this and the next chapter, we begin our study of national governmental regulation of international trade. In addition to regulations that apply to purely domestic affairs, governments traditionally have exercised an additional measure of control, for a variety of political and economic policy reasons, over transactions with persons in foreign nations. Objectives of these controls could be the following: protecting the balance of payments and national reserves, influencing international political alignments, protecting domestic business from competition of foreign goods, preserving natural resources, enhancing national security, protecting the environment, etc. Chapters 3 and 4 examine some of the basic national constitutional problems that impinge on the way nations regulate their international trade. Later, we will examine in some detail the specifics of various regulations, such as tariffs, antidumping and countervailing duties, and a plethora of non-tariff barriers.

This chapter focuses on the problems faced in regulating international economic transactions under the US Constitution. The materials in this chapter are divided into five additional sections. Section 3.2 provides an overview of the constitutional division of powers in the United States between the President and Congress. Section 3.3 looks at the delegation of powers by Congress to the President and at the mosaic of legislation in the United States by which Congress has delegated extensive authority to the President in respect of international economic affairs, focusing especially on the series of trade acts which began with the 1934 Reciprocal Trade Agreements Act. In Section 3.4, we focus on US constitutional provisions that affect the negotiation and implementation of international agreements. We then turn in Section 3.5 to the role of the courts in reviewing Executive Branch action in this area. Finally, in Section 3.6, we consider problems related to the federal structure of the United States.

There are a number of very perplexing and relatively unanswered questions in US constitutional law relating to international affairs generally and international economic affairs in particular. Some introductory comments at the beginning of the sections below pose some of these questions. The following excerpt should assist the reader to appreciate the relationship of various questions to each other and help focus attention on how issues concerning international constitutional divisions of regulatory power have important impacts on practical day-to-day affairs.

Readers should be aware that during most of the last decade the United States public and government (especially the Supreme Court) have been engaged in a remarkably extensive debate and discussion about the distribution of powers in the US government. Particularly this has focused on the powers of the President, notably in the context of the threats of terrorism illustrated by the September 11, 2001 attack on New York City. These discussions and debates express great concern that national security worries will need new governmental approaches, but contrary concerns that these worries will result in overreaction that will greatly diminish the rights of citizens contrary to the centuries of jurisprudence developed under the US Bill of Rights in the US Constitution. Very little of this debate has addressed the effect and role of international economic relations, but it seems clear that the broader governmental debate about freedoms versus security, and powers of the presidency, is relevant to various forms of government power including economic activities such as trade. (See also Section 3.2 below)

In that regard, a poignant sentence in the Supreme Court 2004 majority opinion by then Justice Sandra Day O'Conner regarding presidential power in time of "war" is illustrative of possible evolution of power allocation thinking. She said in Hamdi v. Rumsfeld, "We have long since made clear that a state of war is not a blank check for the President when it comes to the rights of the nation's citizens."[1]

JOHN H. JACKSON, JEAN–VICTOR LOUIS & MITSUO MATSUSHITA, LAW AND WORLD ECONOMIC INTERDEPENDENCE[2]

* * * Immediately after World War II, several initiatives converged into a proposal to establish an International Trade Organization (ITO). After years of international negotiations, the 1948 draft Havana Charter was completed. This charter would have established an ITO to become the framework for international rules designed to prevent the kind of

1. Hamdi v. Rumsfeld, 542 U.S. 507, 536, 124 S.Ct. 2633 (2004).

2. From John H. Jackson, Jean–Victor Louis & Mitsuo Matsushita, Implementing the Tokyo Round: National Constitutions and International Economic Rules 1–2 (1984). Reprinted by permission of the authors.

destructive national government "beggar-thy-neighbor" policies many thought had contributed to the causes of the war. Despite these elaborate preparations, the effort to create an ITO ultimately failed (although an earlier effort to create monetary rules and a monetary fund—the IMF—had succeeded). The ITO effort failed largely because of the domestic constitutional and political structure of the country then economically preeminent—the United States. It failed despite the fact that the major leadership for the effort to create it had come from the United States itself. But this leadership was that of the executive branch or presidency in the United States. Under the US constitutional and legal requirements, for the government to formally accept the ITO charter, the executive branch had to get the approval of the US Congress, and this the Congress refused to give. In 1950 it was clear that it would be futile to continue trying to obtain this approval, and the ITO was stillborn.

At the same time as the efforts to create an ITO were occurring, another set of international economic rules was being drafted. These were embodied in an agreement entitled The General Agreement on Tariffs and Trade, commonly called the GATT. Unlike the ITO, the GATT did come into force, largely because particular laws at that time allowed the executive branch to commit the United States to the GATT obligations without further approval of Congress. In fact the GATT gradually had to fill the vacuum created by the ITO failure, and today it has come to play the central role in the international economic system as it relates to trade in goods. It plays this role uneasily, however, with a defective constitutional structure not designed to support it.

This sequence of events amply demonstrates the importance of national constitutional and legal constraints on the process of formulating, implementing, or changing international rules. The compartmentalization of legal processes into international on one hand and national on the other can lead to serious misunderstandings of the world today. In fact, that world is a complex intertwining of national and international legal, economic, and other constraints and forces. The current expression international interdependence, so apt and yet so trite, often conjures up an image of economic forces and influences, but the legal systems of nations have also become interdependent, not only among themselves but also with the international legal systems that now are influencing daily events.

* * *

The constitutional, governmental policy and structural questions considered here need not be viewed as unique to international economic relations. Many of the issues discussed come up in a large variety of subject areas, including many domestic subjects. The constant struggle between the President and Congress in the US Government conditions much of the national political life of the United States. The study of this struggle in this book can, therefore, also be viewed as sort of a "case study" of constitutional law and politics. One of the interesting (and for lawyers perplexing) aspects of this struggle is that relatively little of it gets to the courts, especially the Supreme Court. This is more so for international affairs, but the fact is that the daily strife often ends in accommodations and compromises, or stand-offs, which none of the parties to a particular contest want to test in the courts. * * * Fortunately, we have a few court opinions to help us find our way into the foyer of the subject, but often these opinions raise more questions than they resolve. The rest of the way is relatively uncharted, and recourse must be had to a variety of historical and legal documents as well as to general reporting about various incidents that are relevant.

CONSTITUTION OF THE UNITED STATES OF AMERICA

Excerpts Relevant to International Economic Relations

ARTICLE I

SECTION 8. The Congress shall have Power To lay and collect Taxes, Duties, Imposts and Excises, to pay the Debts and provide for the common Defence and general Welfare of the United States; but all Duties, Imposts and Excises shall be uniform throughout the United States;

To borrow Money on the credit of the United States;

To regulate Commerce with foreign Nations, and among the several States, and with the Indian Tribes;

* * *

To make all Laws which shall be necessary and proper for carrying into Execution the foregoing Powers, and all other Powers vested by this Constitution in the Government of the United States, or in any Department or Officer thereof.

* * *

SECTION 10. No State shall enter into any Treaty, Alliance, or Confederation; grant Letters of Marque and Reprisal; coin Money; emit Bills of Credit; make any Thing but gold and silver Coin a Tender in Payment of Debts; pass any Bill of Attainder, ex post facto Law, or Law impairing the Obligation of Contracts, or grant any Title of Nobility.

No State shall, without the Consent of the Congress, lay any Imposts or Duties on Imports or Exports, except what may be absolutely necessary for executing its inspection Laws: and the net Produce of all Duties and Imposts, laid by any State on Imports or Exports, shall be for the Use of the Treasury of the United States; and all such Laws shall be subject to the Revision and Control of the Congress.

No State shall, without the Consent of Congress, lay any Duty of Tonnage, keep Troops, or Ships of War in time of Peace, enter into any Agreement or Compact with another State, or with a foreign Power, or engage in War, unless actually invaded, or in such imminent Danger as will not admit of delay.

ARTICLE II

SECTION 1. The executive Power shall be vested in a President of the United States of America. He shall hold his Office during the Term of four Years * * *

* * *

SECTION 2. The President shall be Commander in Chief of the Army and Navy of the United States, and of the Militia of the several States. * * *

He shall have Power, by and with the Advice and Consent of the Senate, to make Treaties, provided two thirds of the Senators present concur; and he shall nominate, and by and with the Advice and Consent of the Senate, shall appoint Ambassadors, other public Ministers and Consuls, Judges of the supreme Court, and all other Officers of the United States, whose Appointments are not herein otherwise provided for, and which shall be established by Law; but the Congress may by Law vest the Appointment of such inferior Officers, as they think proper, in the President alone, in the Courts of Law, or in the Heads of Departments.

* * *

SECTION 3. He shall * * * receive Ambassadors and other public Ministers; he shall take care that the laws be faithfully executed.

* * *

ARTICLE III

* * *

SECTION 2. The judicial Power shall extend to all Cases, in Law and Equity, arising under this Constitution, and Laws of the United States, and Treaties made, or which shall be made, under their Authority;—to all Cases affecting Ambassadors, other public ministers and Consuls;—to all Cases of admiralty and maritime Jurisdiction. * * *

In all Cases affecting Ambassadors, other public Ministers and Consuls, and those in which a State shall be Party, the supreme Court shall have original Jurisdiction. In all the other Cases before mentioned, the supreme Court shall have appellate Jurisdiction, both as to Law and Fact, with such Exceptions, and under such Regulations as the Congress shall make.

* * *

ARTICLE VI

* * *

This Constitution, and the Laws of the United States which shall be made in Pursuance thereof; and all Treaties made, or which shall be made, under the Authority of the United States, shall be the supreme Law of the Land; and the Judges in every State shall be bound thereby, any Thing in the Constitution or Laws of any State to the Contrary notwithstanding.

SECTION 3.2 THE UNITED STATES CONSTITUTION AND INTERNATIONAL ECONOMIC RELATIONS

(A) INTRODUCTION

It is impossible to extricate the question of distribution of powers over foreign economic affairs from the general problem of distribution of powers over foreign affairs in United States governmental and constitutional practice. The reader is probably familiar with the broad themes of this story:[1] The great increase in Executive power during the 1930's and during and after World War II; the concern in the 1960's and early 1970's (particularly in relationship to the Vietnam War) that the Executive had become too strong; the revulsion at the disclosures of misuse of Executive power during the "Watergate" episode; and the ensuing struggle of Congress to restore some of its power in the international affairs area. However, in this book, and particularly this chapter, we endeavor to focus on the problem of international economic affairs, as opposed to foreign affairs generally.

There are some puzzling and very important questions involved in the issue of distribution of powers. For example, how can international negotiations, especially economic or trade negotiations, be carried on by a democracy such as the United States? Particularly when the Executive Branch is theoretically separate from the Legislative Branch, some important difficulties occur. It is perhaps impossible for Congress, as such, to negotiate economic subjects; its members are usually too beholden to particular parochial constituencies, and consequently have difficulty formulating overall negotiating positions and objectives that are in the broader national interest. In addition, who speaks for Congress? It is doubtful that even the duly constituted leadership of either House of Congress can speak for that House, much less for Congress as a whole, on international trade matters. Consequently, a foreign negotiator will not negotiate seriously with someone whom he feels cannot "deliver" on the commitments made. The Executive Branch is not quite in the same

---

1. See John E. Nowak & Ronald D. Rotunda, Constitutional Law 236–267 (7th ed. 2004); Louis Henkin, Constitutionalism, Democracy, and Foreign Affairs (1990); Laurence H. Tribe, American Constitutional Law 637–657 (3rd ed. 2000); The Tethered Presidency: Congressional Restraints on Executive Power (Thomas H. Franck ed., 1981); Thomas H. Franck & Edward Weisband, Foreign Policy by Congress (1979); Arthur M. Schlesinger, The Imperial Presidency (1973); Louis Henkin, Foreign Affairs and the Constitution (2nd ed. 1975); Francis O. Wilcox, Congress, the Executive and Foreign Policy (1971); Symposium on Presidential Power, 40 Law & Contemp. Prob. Nos. 2 & 3 (1976).

position. Generally, at least within the scope of the authority contained in the Executive Branch, whether by constitutional right or through statutory delegation by previous Act of Congress, the commitments of high officials negotiating on behalf of the United States can be formulated so as to represent the commitments of the President and the Executive Branch. Insofar as further legislation is necessary, however, there is a realm of uncertainty about the commitments, comparable to that described above for the Legislative Branch. Trading partners of the United States remember all too well commitments made during the course of the Kennedy Round of negotiations on tariffs and trade, which never came into effect because Congress never enacted the legislation required to implement them.

Consequently, the dilemma facing thoughtful students of international economic affairs in the United States today is that, on the one hand, there appears to be a need to limit or circumscribe the very extensive authority that has grown up in the Executive Branch over international economic affairs; on the other hand, it is not clear that the United States will be able to bargain effectively in international economic negotiations if such limitations are imposed. The Executive Branch appears to be the only viable agent for such negotiations, and the feebler its power, the less effective will be its negotiating ability, unless it can somehow persuade its trading partners that Congress is prepared to deliver on those commitments that require congressional action. We discuss how the United States has tried to address this problem in Section 3.3 below.

The discussion of presidential powers is therefore divided between this Section 3.2 ("inherent" powers) and Section 3.3. In Section 3.3, we return to presidential powers, but there in the context of the President's delegated powers under various statutes. There is not an easily defined distinction between the President's inherent powers and his delegated powers. The approach of the courts, or for that matter of Congress and the Presidency itself, towards delegated powers can be either broad or narrow. The philosophy of the *Curtiss–Wright* case, giving broad leeway to presidential inherent powers, would also lead to a broad approach with respect to statutory delegations. In Section 3.3(B) we give a brief overview of congressional powers, again a subject that recurs in later sections.

One broad question this leads to (probably unanswerable) is whether the President or Congress has generally implemented those policies that are in the best interests of the United States as a whole. For those who, like many economists (see Chapter 2), believe that a "liberal" or "freer" trade policy (allowing more imports) is in the best long-run interest of the United States as a whole, the question can be more specifically phrased: In general is the Presidency or Congress likely to be more protectionist?

More specifically, in considering the materials one can ask the following question: Was the *Curtiss–Wright* case correct (and was Justice

Sutherland's dicta correct)? What is the impact of *Youngstown* and *Dames & Moore* on Sutherland's view of presidential foreign affairs powers?

What exactly did the *Guy Capps* case stand for? Does the Court of Appeals opinion have any viability today? What could we expect federal courts to do today in the event of a court challenge to an international agreement entered into by the President concerning economic matters but without congressional participation? How far will the courts likely go to limit the President's foreign affairs activities because of a lack of statutory delegated powers? How viable today would a challenge to presidential actions be under the arguments used in the *Consumers Union* case?

Finally, there are some other questions: How does the existence of legislation make a difference to presidential power when the legislation does not explicitly authorize what the President wants to do? What is "preemption" by Congress? And, as to all these questions, should the answers differ in the context of foreign affairs as opposed to domestic affairs?

(B) THE PRESIDENT'S INHERENT FOREIGN AFFAIRS POWERS

UNITED STATES v. CURTISS–WRIGHT EXPORT CORP.

Supreme Court of the United States, 1936.
299 U.S. 304, 57 S.Ct. 216, 81 L.Ed. 255.

Mr. Justice Sutherland delivered the opinion of the Court.

On January 27, 1936, an indictment was returned in the court below, the first count of which charges that appellees, beginning with the 29th day of May, 1934, conspired to sell in the United States certain arms of war, namely fifteen machine guns, to Bolivia, a country then engaged in armed conflict in the Chaco, in violation of the Joint Resolution of Congress approved May 28, 1934, and the provisions of a proclamation issued on the same day by the President of the United States pursuant to authority conferred by § 1 of the resolution. In pursuance of the conspiracy, the commission of certain overt acts was alleged, details of which need not be stated. The Joint Resolution (c. 365, 48 Stat. 811) follows:

> *Resolved by the Senate and House of Representatives of the United States of America in Congress assembled*, That if the President finds that the prohibition of the sale of arms and munitions of war in the United States to those countries now engaged in armed conflict in the Chaco may contribute to the reestablishment of peace between those countries, and if after consultation with the governments of other American Republics and with their cooperation, as well as that of such other governments as he may deem necessary, he makes

proclamation to that effect, it shall be unlawful to sell, except under such limitations and exceptions as the President prescribes, any arms or munitions of war in any place in the United States to the countries now engaged in that armed conflict, or to any person, company, or association acting in the interest of either country, until otherwise ordered by the President or by Congress.

[The President proclaimed a prohibition on arms sales and the defendant violated the prohibition and was indicted. The lower court quashed the indictment and the United States appealed.]

Whether, if the Joint Resolution had related solely to internal affairs it would be open to the challenge that it constituted an unlawful delegation of legislative power to the Executive, we find it unnecessary to determine. The whole aim of the resolution is to affect a situation entirely external to the United States, and falling within the category of foreign affairs. The determination which we are called to make, therefore, is whether the Joint Resolution, as applied to that situation, is vulnerable to attack under the rule that forbids a delegation of the lawmaking power. * * *

It will contribute to the elucidation of the question if we first consider the differences between the powers of the federal government in respect of foreign or external affairs and those in respect of domestic or internal affairs. That there are differences between them, and that these differences are fundamental, may not be doubted.

The two classes of powers are different, both in respect of their origin and their nature. The broad statement that the federal government can exercise no powers except those specifically enumerated in the Constitution, and such implied powers as are necessary and proper to carry into effect the enumerated powers, is categorically true only in respect of our internal affairs. In that field, the primary purpose of the Constitution was to carve from the general mass of legislative powers *then possessed by the states* such portions as it was thought desirable to vest in the federal government, leaving those not included in the enumeration still in the states. Carter v. Carter Coal Co., 298 U.S. 238, 294, 56 S.Ct. 855, 865, 80 L.Ed. 1160. That this doctrine applies only to powers which the states had, is self evident. And since the states severally never possessed international powers, such powers could not have been carved from the mass of state powers but obviously were transmitted to the united states from some other source. During the colonial period, those powers were possessed exclusively by and were entirely under the control of the Crown. By the Declaration of Independence, "the Representatives of the United States of America" declared the United [not the several] Colonies to be free and independent states, and as such to have "full power to levy War, conclude Peace, contract Alliances, establish Commerce and to do all other Acts and Things which Independent States may of right do."

As a result of the separation from Great Britain by the colonies acting as a unit, the powers of external sovereignty passed from the

Crown not to the colonies severally, but to the colonies in their collective and corporate capacity as the United States of America. Even before the Declaration, the colonies were a unit in foreign affairs, acting through a common agency—namely the Continental Congress, composed of delegates from the thirteen colonies. That agency exercised the powers of war and peace, raised an army, created a navy, and finally adopted the Declaration of Independence. Rulers come and go; governments end and forms of government change; but sovereignty survives. A political society cannot endure without a supreme will somewhere. Sovereignty is never held in suspense. When, therefore, the external sovereignty of Great Britain in respect of the colonies ceased, it immediately passed to the Union.

* * *

It results that the investment of the federal government with the powers of external sovereignty did not depend upon the affirmative grants of the Constitution. The powers to declare and wage war, to conclude peace, to make treaties, to maintain diplomatic relations with other sovereignties, if they had never been mentioned in the Constitution, would have vested in the federal government as necessary concomitants of nationality. * * * As a member of the family of nations, the right and power of the United States in that field are equal to the right and power of the other members of the international family. Otherwise, the United States is not completely sovereign. * * *

* * *

* * * In this vast external realm, with its important, complicated, delicate and manifold problems, the President alone has the power to speak or listen as a representative of the nation. He makes treaties with the advice and consent of the Senate; but he alone negotiates. Into the field of negotiation the Senate cannot intrude; and Congress itself is powerless to invade it. As Marshall said in his great argument of March 7, 1800, in the House of Representatives, "The President is the sole organ of the nation in its external relations, and its sole representative with foreign nations." Annals, 6th Cong., col. 613. The Senate Committee on Foreign Relations at a very early day in our history (February 15, 1816), reported to the Senate, among other things, as follows:

> The President is the constitutional representative of the United States with regard to foreign nations. He manages our concerns with foreign nations and must necessarily be most competent to determine when, how, and upon what subjects negotiation may be urged with the greatest prospect of success. For his conduct he is responsible to the Constitution. The committee considers this responsibility the surest pledge for the faithful discharge of his duty. They think the interference of the Senate in the direction of foreign negotiations calculated to diminish that responsibility and thereby to impair the best security for the national safety. The nature of transactions with foreign nations, moreover, requires caution and unity of

design, and their success frequently depends on secrecy and dispatch.

U.S. Senate Reports, Committee on Foreign Relations, vol. 8, p. 24.

It is important to bear in mind that we are here dealing not alone with an authority vested in the President by an exertion of legislative power, but with such an authority plus the very delicate, plenary and exclusive power of the President as the sole organ of the federal government in the field of international relations—a power which does not require as a basis for its exercise an act of Congress, but which, of course, like every other governmental power, must be exercised in subordination to the applicable provisions of the Constitution. It is quite apparent that if, in the maintenance of our international relations, embarrassment—perhaps serious embarrassment—is to be avoided and success for our aims achieved, congressional legislation which is to be made effective through negotiation and inquiry within the international field must often accord to the President a degree of discretion and freedom from statutory restriction which would not be admissible were domestic affairs alone involved. Moreover, he, not Congress, has the better opportunity of knowing the conditions which prevail in foreign countries, and especially is this true in time of war. He has his confidential sources of information. He has his agents in the form of diplomatic, consular and other officials. Secrecy in respect of information gathered by them may be highly necessary, and the premature disclosure of it productive of harmful results. Indeed, so clearly is this true that the first President refused to accede to a request to lay before the House of Representatives the instructions, correspondence and documents relating to the negotiation of the Jay Treaty—a refusal the wisdom of which was recognized by the House itself and has never since been doubted. * * *

The marked difference between foreign affairs and domestic affairs in this respect is recognized by both houses of Congress in the very form of their requisitions for information from the executive departments. In the case of every department except the Department of State, the resolution *directs* the official to furnish the information. In the case of the State Department, dealing with foreign affairs, the President is *requested* to furnish the information "if not incompatible with the public interest." A statement that to furnish the information is not compatible with the public interest rarely, if ever, is questioned.

* * *

* * * A legislative practice such as we have here, evidenced not by only occasional instances, but marked by the movement of a steady stream for a century and a half of time, goes a long way in the direction of proving the presence of unassailable ground for the constitutionality of the practice, to be found in the origin and history of the power involved, or in its nature, or in both combined.

* * *

The judgment of the court below must be reversed and the cause remanded for further proceedings in accordance with the foregoing opinion.

Reversed.

MR. JUSTICE MCREYNOLDS does not agree. He is of the opinion that the court below reached the right conclusion and its judgment ought to be affirmed.

MR. JUSTICE STONE took no part in the consideration or decision of this case.

Notes

(1) A particularly strong criticism of the Sutherland view of history is found in Raoul Berger, The Presidential Monopoly of Foreign Relations, 71 Mich.L.Rev. 1 (1972), who states at 26–28:[2]

* * * The sole issue was whether this was an improper delegation, a question that might adequately have been answered under the *Field v. Clark* line of cases. But the aims of Justice Sutherland soared beyond this modest goal; he would launch a theory of inherent presidential power over foreign relations. To this end he confined the enumeration of powers doctrine to "domestic or internal affairs"; in foreign affairs, he explained, in terms recalling the descent of the Holy Ghost, "the external sovereignty of Great Britain * * * immediately passed to the Union." In this he was deceived. it hardly needs more than Madison's statement in *The Federalist No. 45*, that "[t]he powers delegated by the proposed Constitution are *few and defined* * * * [they] will be exercised principally on *external* objects, as war, peace, negotiation, and foreign commerce," to prove that the powers over *foreign relations* were enumerated and "defined." Deferring for a moment further comment on Sutherland's aberrant theory, let it be assumed that somehow the *nation* or Union obtained "inherent" powers over foreign relations, and it still needs to be shown how the power came to be vested *in the President*. For, as Justice Frankfurter pointed out, "the fact that power exists in the Government does not vest it in the President." * * *

McDougal and Lans, who relied heavily on these dicta, acknowledged that Sutherland's analysis "unquestionably involves certain metaphorical elements and considerable differences of opinion about historical facts," but concluded that he "may have been expressing a thought more profound than any involved in quarrels about the naming of powers." This is to conclude that Sutherland was right for the wrong reasons. Apparently the "profound" thought was the "important fact * * * that the imperatives of survival have required the Federal Government to exercise certain powers."

(2) In YOUNGSTOWN SHEET & TUBE CO. v. SAWYER, 343 U.S. 579, 72 S.Ct. 863, 96 L.Ed. 1153 (1952), the Supreme Court faced a challenge to the decision, during the Korean War, by President Truman to seize American steel mills in order to keep them open in face of a labor strike. In

2. Reprinted by permission of Raoul Berger.

the majority opinion, Justice Black noted that "[t]he President's power, if any, to issue the order must stem either from an act of Congress or from the Constitution itself." 343 U.S. at 585, 72 S.Ct. at 866. Since the Government did not rely on statutory authorization for the seizure, the issue was whether authority for the President's order could be found in some provisions of the Constitution. The Government argued that while there was no express power on which the President could rely, "presidential power should be implied from the aggregate of his powers under Article II of the Constitution. Particular reliance is placed on provisions in Article II which say that 'The executive Power shall be vested in a President . . .'; that 'he shall take Care that the laws be faithfully executed'; and that he 'shall be Commander in Chief of the Army and Navy of the United States.' " 343 U.S. at 587, 72 S.Ct. at 867. Justice Black concluded that none of these general provisions could justify the seizure of steel mills in the United States.

Justice Jackson wrote a concurring opinion which contained the following often-quoted passage (343 U.S. at 635–638, 72 S.Ct. at 870–871):

1) When the President acts pursuant to an express or implied authorization of Congress, his authority is at its maximum. * * *

2) When the President acts in absence of either a congressional grant or denial of authority, he can only rely upon his own independent powers, but there is a zone of twilight in which he and Congress may have concurrent authority, or in which its distribution is uncertain. Therefore, congressional inertia, indifference or quiescence may sometimes, at least as a practical matter, enable, if not invite, measures on independent presidential responsibility. * * *

3) When the President takes measures incompatible with the expressed or implied will of Congress, his power is at its lowest ebb, for then he can rely only upon his own constitutional powers minus any constitutional powers of Congress over the matter. Courts can sustain exclusive Presidential control in such a case only by disabling the Congress from acting upon the subject. Presidential claim to a power at once so conclusive and preclusive must be scrutinized with caution, for what is at stake is the equilibrium established by our constitutional system.

DAMES & MOORE v. REGAN, 453 U.S. 654, 101 S.Ct. 2972, 69 L.Ed.2d 918 (1981), is one of the few Supreme Court cases since the end of World War II that has touched on the question of inherent presidential powers in foreign affairs. It involved a challenge to President Carter's orders transferring certain blocked iranian assets under US jurisdiction, nullifying attachment orders previously obtained thereon and suspending claims against iran pending in US courts. The orders were issued as part of the agreement by which American hostages held in Iran were released. In upholding the transfer and nullification orders, Justice Rehnquist gave a broad reading to the scope of the authority delegated to the President by Congress. After reviewing what he considered to be congressional acquiescence in past cases where a President had negotiated the settlement of international claims, Justice Rehnquist Concluded: "in light of all of the foregoing—the inferences to be drawn from the character of the legislation Congress has enacted in the area, such as the International Emergency Economic Power Act (IEEPA) and the Hostage Act, and from the history of acquiescence in executive claims settlement—we conclude that the President was authorized to suspend pending claims." 453 U.S. at 686, 101 S.Ct. at 2990. The significance of this case is colored by the special factual setting in which it arose. The orders were necessary to implement the agreement under which the hostages were to be released. Given a more pedestrian factual situation, the Court might not have been so accommodating to the President.

(3) In UNITED STATES v. GUY W. CAPPS, INC., 204 F.2d 655 (4th Cir.1953), Chief Judge Parker refused to allow the United States to sue a company that had imported seed potatoes for planting purposes into the United States from Canada and had apparently resold them for food purposes. At the time, the US and Canadian governments had agreed that Canada would limit its potato exports to the US to seed potatoes and require all Canadian exporters to sign a contract to this effect. The suit by the United States government for damages as a third party beneficiary of the sales contract was based on this US–Canada agreement. Judge Parker concluded that the agreement between the US and Canada was improper because the President had not followed the statutory provisions established by Congress for imposing limits on agricultural imports. Those provisions included an investigation by the Tariff Commission. In Judge Parker's view (204 F.2d at 658–660):

> * * * We have little difficulty in seeing in the evidence breach of contract on the part of defendant and damage resulting to the United States from the breach. We think, however, that the executive agreement was void because it was not authorized by Congress and contravened provisions of a statute dealing with the very matter to which it related and * * * the contract relied on, which was based on the executive agreement, was unenforceable in the courts of the United States for like reason. We think, also, that no action can be maintained by the government to recover damages on account of what is essentially a breach of a trade regulation, in the absence of express authorization by Congress. The power to regulate foreign commerce is vested in Congress, not in the executive or the courts; and the executive may not exercise the power by entering into executive agreements and suing in the courts for damages resulting from breaches of contracts made on the basis of such agreements.

> In the Agricultural Act of 1948, Congress had legislated specifically with respect to the limitations which might be imposed on imports if it was thought that they would render ineffective or materially interfere with any program or operation undertaken pursuant to that act. * * *

> There was no pretense of complying with the requirements of this statute. * * *

> It is argued, however, that the validity of the executive agreement was not dependent upon the Act of Congress but was made pursuant to the inherent powers of the President under the Constitution. The answer is that * * * the power to regulate interstate and foreign commerce is not among the powers incident to the presidential office, but is expressly vested by the Constitution in the Congress. * * * In the recent case of Youngstown Sheet & Tube Co. v. Sawyer, 343 U.S. 579, 72 S.Ct. 863, 867, 96 L.Ed. 1153, * * * [t]he rule was well stated by Mr. Justice

Jackson in his concurring opinion * * * as follows: [quoting the third numbered paragraph of the concurrence, see note (2) above].

We think that whatever the power of the executive with respect to making executive trade agreements regulating foreign commerce in the absence of action by Congress, it is clear that the executive may not through entering into such an agreement avoid complying with a regulation prescribed by Congress. Imports from a foreign country are foreign commerce subject to regulation, so far as this country is concerned, by Congress alone. * * *

The case was affirmed by the US Supreme Court at 348 U.S. 296, 75 S.Ct. 326, 99 L.Ed. 329 (1955), but on completely different grounds. It dismissed the US complaint against the defendant, noting that there was no showing of bad faith, neglect or carelessness on the part of defendant, since its purchaser, the A & P grocery chain, also sold potatoes for seed purposes. In his book, SUPER CHIEF—Earl Warren and His Supreme Court—A Judicial Biography 165–66 (1983), Bernard Schwartz described the Supreme Court's approach in the *Guy Capps* case. According to Schwartz, it appears that most of the Court agreed with Chief Justice Warren that the President had the power to do what he did, but the Court apparently wanted to avoid a decision on that issue, which was a controversial one in Congress at the time. Schwartz quotes a memorandum from Justice Frankfurter to his colleagues that stated: "In order to avoid entanglement in the explosive issue * * * the whole Court exercised not a little astuteness to have the case go off on a different ground to such an extent that the fact that the power to make treaties and executive agreements was in issue was not even mentioned but was discreetly covered up by reference to 'other questions' which we said there was no occasion to consider."

CONSUMERS UNION OF U.S., INC. v. KISSINGER

United States Court of Appeals, District of Columbia, 1974.
506 F.2d 136, cert. denied, 421 U.S. 1004, 95 S.Ct. 2406, 44 L.Ed.2d 673 (1975).

[The US Court of Appeals upheld a judgment of the District Court that in negotiating voluntary export restraints undertaken by foreign producers to alleviate the domestic steel industry's problems in the 1960 and early 1970s, the Executive did not act in violation of Congress's foreign commerce powers under Article 1, Section 8, Clause 3 of the Constitution and of the laws relating to the regulation of foreign trade set forth in Title 19 of the U.S. Code, including Sections 301 and 352 of the Trade Expansion Act of 1962. In his opinion, Judge McGowan wrote:]

* * * State Department officials [had] entered into discussions that lasted from June to December, 1968, and resulted in letters being sent to the Secretary in which the Japanese and European producer associations stated their intentions to limit steel shipments to the United States to specified maximum tonnages for each of the years 1969, 1970 and 1971.[3]

---

3. [original note 4] The letters to the Secretary, dated December 23, 1968, were approvingly read by President Johnson after their receipt, and were transmitted by

* * * [E]xtensions, covering 1972 through 1974, were forthcoming in letters dated early in May, 1972, and announced by the President on May 6.

The two 1972 letters are substantially alike. Each states the signatories' intention to limit exports of steel products to the United States both in aggregate tonnages and, within such limits, in terms of product mix. Each represents that the signatories "hold themselves [itself] ready to consult with representatives of the United States Government on any problem or question that may arise with respect to this voluntary restraint undertaking" and expect the United States Government so to hold itself ready.[4] In addition, each states that its undertaking is based on the assumptions that (1) the effect will not be to place the signatories at a disadvantage relative to each other, (2) the United States will take no unilateral actions to restrict imports by the signatories to the United States, and (3) the representations do not violate United States or international laws.

* * *

* * * [N]othing in the process leading up to the voluntary undertaking or in the process of consultation under them differentiates what the Executive has done here from what all Presidents, and to a lesser extent all high executive officers, do when they admonish an industry with the express or implicit warning that action within their existing powers or enlarged powers to be sought, will be taken if a desired course is not followed voluntarily.

* * * From the comprehensive pattern of its legislation regulating trade and governing the circumstances under and procedures by which the President is authorized to act to limit imports, it appears quite likely that Congress has by statute occupied the field of enforceable import restrictions, if it did not, indeed, have exclusive possession thereof by the terms of Article 1 of the Constitution. There is no potential for conflict, however, between exclusive congressional regulation of foreign commerce—regulation enforced ultimately by halting violative importations at the border—and assurances of voluntary restraint given to the Executive. Nor is there any warrant for creating such a conflict by straining to endow the voluntary undertakings with legally binding effect, contrary to the manifest understanding of all concerned and indeed, to the manner in which departures from them have been treated.[5]

the Secretary on January 14, 1969, to the respective Chairmen of the Senate Finance Committee and the House Ways and Means Committee. The recipients thereupon issued a joint announcement welcoming the voluntary restraints and releasing the texts of the producers' and the Secretary's letters. No mandatory import quota legislation was recommended by the committee thereafter.

4. [original note 6] It is undisputed that "[i]n negotiating the arrangements and all

of their specific terms, the State Department officers explained to the foreign producers that they were being asked to make the requested commitments by the Executive Branch of the United States Government on the ground that they were in the national interest of the United States." JA 155a.

5. [original note 12] In 1969 the Japanese, and in 1972 all foreign producers, exported to the United States more steel or

Notes and Questions

(1) In his dissenting opinion in Consumers Union v. Kissinger, Judge Leventhal points at the economic effect of the voluntary restraints, "that parallels that of import quotas proclaimed by the President." Furthermore, he says, "(t)he arrangements are not unilateral announcements but the culmination of bilateral discussions that were not only participated in, but initiated by State Department officials. Although the final letters that embody the specific limitations are astutely couched in a litany of a 'voluntary restraint undertaking' on the part of the foreign steel producers, the circumstances are instinct with bilateral undertaking. * * * To say, as the majority opinion does, that the steel arrangements worked out by the President fall within inherent Presidential authority not preempted by Congress is to allow the circumvention of these procedural safeguards whenever that suits the Executive."

(2) Section 607 of the Trade Act of 1974 (Documents Supplement) contains a congressional grant of immunity from antitrust laws with respect to the voluntary arrangements on steel examined in this case. An interesting question is whether the procedures followed in this case could be used today in light of the escape clause provisions in the 1974 Act (Sections 201–204).

(3) So-called "voluntary export restraints" seemed to spread rapidly in the 1980's. There was considerable worry that these "grey area" measures were undermining the international regime of liberal trade. We will examine how the WTO Safeguards Agreement dealt with such measures in Chapter 15 infra.

SECTION 3.3   TRADE LEGISLATION IN THE UNITED STATES: PRESIDENT AND CONGRESS ACCOMMODATE

(A) INTRODUCTION

Although the President of the United States has only limited constitutional powers regarding the conduct of international economic relations, over the years Congress has delegated vast authorities to the President. These delegations, embodied in numerous statutes enacted over decades, often are so general or ambiguous as to give the President considerable freedom to act.

Subsection B will discuss delegation of international economic powers by Congress and the constitutional limitations on Congressional supervision of those delegated powers. Subsection C will discuss generally the delegated powers of the President and how they have been interpreted by the courts. Subsection D will briefly survey the history and substantive provisions of the "core" international trade legislation of the United States. Subsection E will then survey the US government structure for the conduct of international economic relations.

---

particular types of steel product than their undertakings contemplated. In no case were the "excess" goods denied entry into the United States. Rather, consultations were sought and the next year's voluntary quota reduced by the amount of the excess.

(B) CONGRESS AND CONTROL OF INTERNATIONAL ECONOMIC RELATIONS

The United States Constitution grants Congress the power "to lay and collect taxes, duties, imposts and excises," and "to regulate commerce with foreign nations and among the several states."[1] Congress is very conscious of its special role in international economic policy,[2] and even though the conduct of general foreign policy, particularly political and defense matters, may rest largely in the Executive Branch, when it comes to economic foreign policy, Congress does not hesitate to assert itself.

The basic dilemma, as stated before, is the problem of Congress exercising its power and control over international economic policy while accommodating the necessity of the United States acting and negotiating through spokesmen who have the authority to commit the United States.

Here we will look briefly at two constitutional issues that Congress must bear in mind in resolving its dilemma—the constitutional limits on delegation of legislative authority and the unconstitutionality of such congressional oversight devices as the legislative veto.

(1) The Constitution and Delegation of Authority by Congress

The general issue of the extent to which Congress may delegate its authority is sometimes thought to be largely an issue of the past. In the 1930's, several "New Deal" statutes were declared unconstitutional on these grounds.[3] Since that time, however, no statute has been invalidated for this reason by the Supreme Court, although Justice Brennan, in a concurring opinion dealing with the Subversive Activities Control Act of 1967, noted the danger of congressional delegation of power which allows "overbroad, unauthorized, and arbitrary application of criminal sanctions in an area of protected freedoms." In that opinion Justice Brennan felt that the statute was constitutionally insufficient because it "contains no meaningful standard" and no procedures to contest administrative designations under it.[4]

In the cases litigating the validity of the 1971 wage-price freeze, the courts sustained a broad congressional delegation of authority to the President to impose such controls. The challenged statute provided simply, "The President is authorized to issue such orders and regulations as he may deem appropriate to stabilize prices, rents, wages, and salaries at levels not less than those prevailing on May 25, 1970." In AMALGAMATED MEAT CUTTERS & BUTCHER WORKMEN OF NORTH AMERICA, AFL–CIO v. CONNALLY, 337 F.Supp. 737 (D.D.C. 1971), Judge Leventhal said (at 745):

1. U.S. Const. Art. I sec. 8, cls. 1, 3.

2. Senate Comm. on Finance, Trade Reform Act of 1974, S. Rep. No. 1298, 93d Cong., 2d Sess. 14 (1974).

3. John E. Nowak & Ronald D. Rotunda, Constitutional Law 177–185 (7th ed. 2004).

4. United States v. Robel, 389 U.S. 258, 272–73, 88 S.Ct. 419, 428, 19 L.Ed.2d 508 (1967).

* * * That officials may lawfully be given far greater authority than the power to recognize a triggering condition was recognized * * * in the famous Grimaud case where a unanimous Court "admitted that it is difficult to define the line which separates legislative power to make laws, from administrative authority to make regulations." There is no analytical difference, no difference in kind, between the legislative function—of prescribing rules for the future—that is exercised by the legislature or by the agency implementing the authority conferred by the legislature. The problem is one of limits.

* * * Congress is free to delegate legislative authority provided it has exercised "the essentials of the legislative function"—of determining the basic legislative policy and formulating a rule of conduct—held satisfied by "the rule, with penal sanctions, that prices shall not be greater than those fixed by maximum price regulations which conform to standards and will tend to further the policy which Congress has established." * * * The issue is whether the legislative description of the task assigned "sufficiently marks the field within which the Administrator is to act so that it may be known whether he has kept within it in compliance with the legislative will."

Note

The delegation issue has often arisen in the context of tariff and trade legislation, the classic case being Marshall Field & Co. v. Clark, 143 U.S. 649, 12 S.Ct. 495, 36 L.Ed. 294 (1892). In J.W. HAMPTON, JR., & CO. v. UNITED STATES, 276 U.S. 394, 48 S.Ct. 348, 72 L.Ed. 624 (1928), for instance, the Court upheld a statute saying, (at 409):

* * * If Congress shall lay down by legislative act an intelligible principle to which the person or body authorized to fix [customs duties on imported merchandise] is directed to conform, such legislative action is not a forbidden delegation of legislative power. If it is thought wise to vary the customs duties according to changing conditions of production at home and abroad, it may authorize the Chief Executive to carry out this purpose, with the advisory assistance of a Tariff Commission appointed under Congressional authority.

(2) Constitutional Limitations on Congressional Supervision of Delegated Powers

The fact that Congress has delegated power to act in an area to the President does not indicate that Congress has no interest in what the President does. Indeed, Congress carefully monitors presidential action through hearings and other means. One method developed by Congress to increase the effectiveness of its oversight procedures was the legislative or congressional veto. A typical congressional veto provision requires the President to report to Congress action taken pursuant to a delegated authority and permits Congress or one House thereof to veto or disallow the action within a certain time period. The use of such provisions was challenged in IMMIGRATION & NATURALIZATION SERVICE v.

CHADHA, 462 U.S. 919, 103 S.Ct. 2764, 77 L.Ed.2d 317 (1983), where the US Supreme Court, in an opinion by Chief Justice Burger, struck down a provision that authorized either House of Congress, by resolution, to invalidate a decision by the Attorney General, made pursuant to authority delegated by Congress, to allow a particular deportable alien to remain in the United States.

Such a "veto power", said the Court, is invalid because the decision is not taken by both Houses and is not presented to the President (thereby depriving him of his right to veto Congressional action, in which case a two-thirds vote in each House is required to enact the legislation). "Congress must abide by its delegation of authority until that delegation is legislatively altered or revoked." 462 U.S. at 955, 103 S.Ct. at 2786. In a dissenting opinion, Justice White stated that it was hard to understand why Congress may delegate legislative power, but may not reserve a check on that "legislative" power for itself. 462 U.S. at 986, 103 S.Ct. at 2802.

One particularly interesting alternative to the legislative veto is the so-called "fast track" procedure (described in Section (D) below), which has been used since 1979 to implement trade agreements into US law. Under this procedure the President is authorized to take a particular action (e.g., negotiate an agreement), but congressional approval is required to implement the results of the negotiation. Since the form of congressional approval is a statute that could be vetoed by the President, the concerns of *Chadha* would seem to be met. The fast track procedure resembles the legislative veto in that the President is delegated power to negotiate an agreement, but either House can "veto" the President's proposed agreement by not passing the nonamendable implementing legislation proposed by the President.

(C) THE PRESIDENT AND DELEGATED INTERNATIONAL ECONOMIC POWERS

The President has been delegated a considerable amount of "emergency" power over international economic affairs. Congress has struggled to find the appropriate line between giving the President too much discretion and yet giving him enough authority so he can be effective when necessary. In this brief overview we look first at some of these delegations, and then turn to powers contained in non-emergency trade legislation.

(1) The President's Emergency Powers

The National Emergencies Act, adopted by Congress in 1976, provided for the termination of most of the President's emergency powers.[5] Exempted from these termination provisions was the Trading With the Enemy Act (TWEA), originally enacted in 1917.[6] This Act has been used

---

5. Pub.L. No. 94–412, 90 Stat. 1255 (codified at 50 U.S.C.A. sec. 1601 et seq.). The Act contained legislative veto provisions that are probably unconstitutional in light of the *Chadha* decision discussed in Section 3.3(B) supra.

6. 50 U.S.C.A.App. sec. 1 et seq.

to regulate economic relations between the United States and a number of countries considered to be unfriendly, such as Cuba, North Korea, and Vietnam. It was also used from 1968 to 1974 to regulate foreign direct investment by US citizens.

In 1977, Congress adopted the International Emergency Economic Powers Act (IEEPA).[7] IEEPA restricted use of TWEA to time of war, and thus IEEPA is now the principal peacetime source of presidential emergency authority in international economic affairs.

IEEPA authorizes the President, if he declares a national emergency, inter alia, to regulate (a) foreign exchange transactions, (b) transfers or payments involving interests of a foreign country or national, and (c) property in which a foreign country or national has any interest, in order to deal with an unusual or extraordinary external threat to the national security, foreign policy or economy of the United States.[8]

(2) The President's Specific Delegated Powers

In addition to the "emergency" authority discussed above, there is a plethora of statutes that authorize regulation by the President of international economic relations.

Many of these that relate to trade will be mentioned or discussed in later chapters. They include subjects such as antidumping and countervailing duty legislation, Section 301 procedures, unfair trade practices, national security exceptions, and the Export Administration Act.

(3) Judicial Control of Delegated Authorities

The courts have generally treated the President kindly when interpreting his statutory powers. Since 1945, the US Supreme Court has never found the President to have exceeded his powers in the area of international economic relations (but only a few cases of this type have been considered by the Supreme Court). The Executive Branch has not fared as well in the lower federal courts, but, as is discussed in Section 3.5(C) infra, that is usually because the contested action involved application by lower ranking government officials of specific statutory standards established by Congress in a detailed regulatory scheme such as the antidumping legislation, as opposed to the exercise by the President or his officers of a more discretionary power.[9]

---

7. Pub.L. No. 95–223, title II, 91 Stat. 1626 (codified at 50 U.S.C.A. sec. 1701 et seq.). Congress permitted certain actions taken under TWEA—such as the regulations dealing with Cuba—to be renewed from time to time by the President. 50 U.S.C.A. sec. 1706(a)(2). The so-called grandfather powers under the TWEA were interpreted by the U.S. Supreme Court in Regan v. Wald, 468 U.S. 222, 104 S.Ct. 3026, 82 L.Ed.2d 171 (1984) (upholding President's right to revise regulations under grandfather powers). On IEEPA generally, see Lee R. Marks & John C. Grabow,

The President's Foreign Economic Powers after Dames & Moore v. Regan: Legislation by Acquiescence, 68 Cornell L.Rev. 68 (1982); Note, The International Emergency Economic Powers Act: A Congressional Attempt to Control Presidential Emergency Power, 96 Harv.L.Rev. 1102 (1982).

8. 50 U.S.C.A. secs. 1701, 1702(a)(1).

9. The major exceptions to this statement are the *Guy Capps* case, discussed in Section 3.2(B) supra, and the *Schmidt, Pritchard* case, discussed in this subsection.

A few significant cases which have struggled with delegated authorities to the President, and the degree of discretion or scope which would be allowed the President in implementing those authorities, include the following:

1) UNITED STATES v. SCHMIDT PRITCHARD & CO., 47 C.C.P.A. 152 (1960), cert. denied, 364 U.S. 919, 81 S.Ct. 283, 5 L.Ed.2d 259 (1960), this is one of the few cases that refused to uphold a Presidential trade action increasing duties. It held that the President was not authorized to increase duties on bicycles in an amount differing from that recommended by the Tariff Commission.

2) AIMCEE WHOLESALE CORP. v. UNITED STATES, 468 F.2d 202 (C.C.P.A.1972), upheld Presidential action increasing duties on bicycles, accepting that it was done pursuant to "renegotiation authority" under GATT Article XXVIII.

3) UNITED STATES v. YOSHIDA INTERNATIONAL, INC., 526 F.2d 560 (C.C.P.A.1975), reversing, 378 F.Supp. 1155 (C.C.P.A.1974), upheld the Presidential imposition of a "tariff surcharge" (generalized increase of tariffs on imported products) for balance of payments reasons, referring the broad wording of the Trading With the Enemy Act.

4) FEDERAL ENERGY ADMINISTRATION v. ALGONQUIN SNG, INC., 426 U.S. 548, 96 S.Ct. 2295, 49 L.Ed.2d 49 (1976). The Supreme Court upheld the Treasury Secretary's decision (under Presidential authority) to impose a substantial fee on oil product imports, because of broad statutory language authorizing the President to "adjust imports."

5) ZENITH RADIO CORP. v. UNITED STATES, 437 U.S. 443, 98 S.Ct. 2441, 57 L.Ed.2d 337 (1978). The Supreme Court upheld Treasury determinations not to assess countervailing duties to off-set certain alleged "subsidy practices" by the Japanese government on products shipped to the United States. The practice was remission of internal Japanese taxes on the products when they were exported, and the Supreme Court noted the historical interpretation of the countervailing duty law and the GATT rules which allowed such remission.

(4) Note: Statutes Governing the Administrative Process as It Relates to International Economic Relations

The extensive control over private transactions resulting from regulation of international economic affairs involves a number of questions also found in other areas of government economic regulation. There are several issues that promise to be peculiarly significant for the conduct of foreign affairs generally, and the problems of international economic regulation particularly. Essentially the question is whether foreign affairs issues should be exempted from "fair procedure" or similar statutes.

Some of the most significant statutes are listed below. The international trading system has not yet been extensively involved with most questions raised by these statutes, but there are phrases and texts in the

WTO agreements (especially the TBT Agreement, which regulates product standards), and portions of the Services Agreement (GATS), which could raise some interesting international law dimensions in respect of these questions.

(a) *The Administrative Procedure Act (APA)*, exempting "military and foreign affairs functions" from certain procedures;[10]

(b) *The National Environmental Policy Act (NEPA)* for which the courts have held that the failure of the USTR to prepare the required environmental impact statements cannot be challenged because under the trade laws there is no reviewable final agency action under the APA until the President submits the agreement to Congress for approval (since Presidential actions are not reviewable under the APA, this effectively precludes review of a decision not to prepare an impact statement);[11]

(c) *The Freedom of Information Act (FOIA)* (5 U.S.C.A. sec. 552(b)) that exempts certain matters to be kept secret in the interest of national defense or foreign policy, as well as trade secrets and commercial or financial information obtained from a person and designated privileged or confidential; and

(d) *The Federal Advisory Committee Act* (5 U.S.C.A. App. secs. 1–15), that contains elaborate provisions with respect to public access to meetings, minutes and documents of federal "advisory committees." In the area of international economic relations many advisory committees operate.[12] Certain provisions of the Act do not apply to trade advisory committees established under Section 135 of the Trade Act of 1974. 21 U.S.C.A. sec. 2155(f).

(D) THE UNITED STATES TRADE ACTS AND THE RECIPROCAL TRADE AGREEMENTS PROGRAM

(1) History of US Tariff Legislation

Professor F.W. Taussig, in his classic "The Tariff History of the United States" notes:[13]

> The early economic history of the United States may be divided into two periods. The first, which is in the main a continuation of the colonial period, lasted till about the year 1808; the embargo marks the beginning of the series of events which closed it. The second

---

10. See specifically Section 4 APA, 5 U.S.C.A. sec. 553(a)(1) (rule-making procedures); Section 5 APA, 5 U.S.C.A. sec. 554(a)(4) (adjudicatory procedures); Section 3 APA, 5 U.S.C.A. sec. 552(b)(1) (information supplying requirements). See also Mast Industries, Inc. v. Regan, 596 F.Supp. 1567 (CIT 1984).

11. Public Citizen v. USTR, 5 F.3d 549 (D.C.Cir.1993). In November 1999, President Clinton directed that a careful assessment and written review be made of the potential environmental impacts of major trade agreements. Executive Order 13141, 64 Fed.Reg. 63169 (implementing guidelines in 65 Fed.Reg. 77942).

12. S.Rep. No. 93–1298, 93d Cong., 2d Sess. (1974).

13. F. Taussig, The Tariff History of the United States 8 (8th ed. 1931). For other works on U.S. tariff history, see U.S. Senate, History of the Committee on Finance, 91st Cong., 2d Sess. 49 (S.Doc. No. 91–57, 1970).

began in 1808, and lasted through the generation following. It was during the second period that the most decided attempt was made to apply protection to young industries in the United States.

From a time in the 18th century, when the British colonies in North America were essentially required to import virtually all manufactured items, to the 1930's, the history of US tariffs is one of ups and downs, often related to domestic problems (such as the Civil War and the need for federal government revenues, a party overturn or some economic stress).

In describing the passage of the Tariff Act of 1930, the infamous Smoot–Hawley Tariff, Taussig goes on to note:[14]

> The difficulty, as already intimated, was mainly in our political system. The accepted procedure, not new in 1930 but then more firmly established than in previous years, deserves description. In each of the two committees which deal with the tariff—that on Ways and Means in the House and that on Finance in the Senate—the traditions and methods are ideal for log-rolling.

Since the Smoot–Hawley Tariff Act of 1930, thoughtful persons in Congress have recognized the difficulty of Congress' developing a tariff in the national interest. As one senator stated in 1934:[15]

> [O]ur experience in writing tariff legislation * * * has been discouraging. Trading between groups and sections is inevitable. Log-rolling is inevitable, and in its most pernicious form. We do not write a national tariff law. We jam together, through various unholy alliances and combinations, a potpourri or hodgepodge of section and local tariff rates, which often add to our troubles and increase world misery.

(2) The Reciprocal Trade Agreements Act of 1934

From this experience, and the leadership of Secretary of State Cordell Hull, Congress enacted the Reciprocal Trade Agreements Act of 1934, by which it delegated to the President the authority to negotiate international trade agreements for the reciprocal reduction of tariffs.

The language of the 1934 Act not only delegated negotiating authority to the President, but also gave the President authority to "proclaim" the resulting modifications of tariff and import restrictions, i.e. an implementing authority. This language, which has been included in every trade negotiating authority enacted since, was probably chosen for the original act more as a result of tradition and precedent than for any calculated purpose. As one of the authors has noted:[16]

14. Id. at 491.

15. 78 Cong.Rec. 10379 (1934) (remarks of Senator Cooper).

16. John H. Jackson, The General Agreement on Tariffs and Trade in United States Domestic Law, 66 Mich.L.Rev. 249, 283 (1967). Reprinted by permission of the Michigan Law Review Association.

As early as 1798, an act empowered the President to undertake commercial intercourse with a foreign country (France) and "to make proclamation thereof." This terminology was followed in a series of other international trade statutes during the ensuing century. The Supreme Court, in passing on the constitutionality of the delegation of power to the President under the Tariff Act of 1890, held that no "legislative power" was delegated because the President could only issue a proclamation based on particular findings of fact specified in the statute. Later tariff statutes reinforced this practice of establishing a proclamation power as the normal means for the President to implement tariff changes.

The Senate Report on the 1943 Act stated:[17]

Under the Trade Agreements Act changes in our tariff rates are made, so far as our domestic law is concerned, by the President's proclamation under the authority of the Trade Agreement Act. Changes in the tariff rates are not made by the agreements, per se.

The authority granted in the 1934 Act extended for a period of three years, and this authority was renewed for various periods in a series of subsequent acts.[18] The 1945 renewal of the Act was crucial because it was the foundation of the United States' acceptance of membership in GATT (discussed in Chapter 6). By the time of the 1945 Act, the United States had entered into 32 reciprocal trade agreements, all of them bilateral in nature.[19]

(3) The Trade Act of 1974

After the completion of the Kennedy Round of negotiations in 1967, there was considerable criticism in Congress of the results of that negotiation from the point of view of US domestic producers. When the trade agreements authority ran out on June 30, 1967, it was anticipated that it would be promptly renewed. However, protectionist pressure in the United States, reinforced by international economic problems that had arisen partly because of the Vietnam War, and partly because of the inflexibility of the Bretton Woods System (particularly as it involved fixed exchange rates), made the political climate difficult, to say the

---

17. S.Rep.No. 258, 78th Cong., 1st Sess. 47, 48 (1943).

18. Act of June 12, 1934, c. 474, 48 Stat. 943 (codified at 19 U.S.C.A. sec. 1351), as amended, Joint Resolution of March 1, 1937, c. 24, 50 Stat. 24 (three-year extension); Joint Resolution of April 12, 1940, c. 96, 54 Stat. 107 (three-year extension); Joint Resolution of June 7, 1943, c. 118, 57 Stat. 125 (two-year extension); Act of July 5, 1945, c. 269, sec. 1, 59 Stat. 410 (three-year extension); Act of June 26, 1948, c. 678, sec. 2, 62 Stat. 1053 (one-year extension); Act of September 26, 1949, c. 585, sec. 3, 63 Stat. 697 (three-year extension); Act of June 15, 1951, c. 141, sec. 2, 65 Stat. 72 (two-year extension); Act of August 7,

1953, c. 348, title I, sec. 101, 67 Stat. 472 (one-year extension); Act of July 1, 1954, c. 445, sec. 1, 68 Stat. 360 (one-year extension); Act of June 21, 1955, c. 169, sec. 2, 69 Stat. 162 (three-year extension); Act of August 20, 1958, Pub.L. No. 85–686, sec. 2, 72 Stat. 672 (four-year extension). Act of October 11, 1962, Pub. L. No. 87–794, 76 Stat. 872 (five-year extension and setting up also the provision of "Special Trade Representative"; further discussed in Subsection E below).

19. See Hearings on Extension of the Reciprocal Trade Agreements Act Before the House Comm. on Ways and Means, 79th Cong., 1st Sess. 38, 636, 932 (1948).

least, for a trade bill. It was not until the end of 1974 that it was renewed—the first significant gap in that authority since the original 1934 Act was passed.

Meanwhile, in May 1970, the President had established a Commission on International Trade and Investment Policy, known as the Williams Commission.[20] The Commission was composed of a number of businessmen, labor leaders and academics, and had a professional staff headed by an economist as executive director, Professor Isaiah Frank. It was perhaps the most comprehensive official commission for the study of United States international trade policy that had ever been organized. The Williams Commission reported in 1971, avoiding extremes, but generally reporting a need for further liberalization of United States trade, while protecting US trading interests from the shocks of surging imports and unfair activities from abroad. Most notable of its recommendations were probably those which advocated the renewal of tariff and trade agreements authority, and those which recommended a revision of the escape clause and adjustment assistance program so as to make these remedies more available.

The great significance of the Trade Act of 1974 existed not only in its renewal and revision of the traditional trade agreements authority, but also in a series of other titles dealing more or less comprehensively with United States relations with Communist countries, establishing a preferential tariff system for developing countries, and revising the rules bearing on United States law regarding imports affected by unfair foreign actions and portions of the law dealing with the escape clause and adjustment assistance. To a large extent it has been the framework for US trade policy since, although often amended.

(4) The 1974 Trade Act and the Fast Track

It is difficult to negotiate agreements on non-tariff barriers (NTBs). The problem facing Congress is how to place limitations on the authority to negotiate such agreements, without at the same time destroying the credibility of United States negotiators. In 1973 a trade bill allowing Congress to "veto" trade agreements within a 90 day period, was introduced by the administration and was basically accepted by the House. The Senate, however, at the height of the Watergate presidential crisis, was not willing to go this far. Recognizing, however, that the usual process of adoption of a statute had failed in previous attempts to implement international NTB agreements, it was willing to go along with a special set of rules, the key ingredients of which, in the eyes of some observers, were threefold: 1) preventing a committee or committee chairman from "bottling up" legislation so that it could not come to the floor for a vote; 2) providing for consideration in each House of the NTB agreement and implementing legislation without the possibility of amendment, since amendment would require returning to the interna-

---

20. Commission on International Trade and Investment Policy, United States Inter- national Economic Policy in an Interdependent World, Report (1971).

tional bargaining table and redoing the bargain which had already been agreed internationally; and 3) providing for limitation of debate on the floor of both Houses (to prevent a Senate filibuster, for example). This is called the "Fast Track".

The version adopted by the Senate was accepted by the House, and basically provided that NTB agreements and implementing statutes be rapidly considered by both Houses of Congress (within an overall time limit which is usually 90 days) under special procedures that satisfy the three criteria mentioned above.[21]

Other provisions of the 1974 Trade Act provided for extensive "pre-negotiation procedures" by which various sets of public hearings are to be held so that American citizens can comment on the possible effect of tariff reductions or NTB agreements before American negotiators are authorized to make concrete offers at the international bargaining table. Many of these procedures follow those which had been in effect for previous trade rounds, but in the 1974 Act there was an additional set of procedures relating to the establishment of particular economic sector negotiating advisory committees of private citizens or business representatives, having to do with major fields of manufacturing or agricultural endeavor (e.g., steel, chemicals, electronics, etc.)[22]

(5) The Trade Agreements Act of 1979

JOHN H. JACKSON, UNITED STATES LAW AND IMPLEMENTATION OF THE TOKYO ROUND NEGOTIATION[23]

For the United States to both accept and implement the major non-tariff agreements of the [Tokyo Round—MTN] required congressional approval, and under the Trade Act of 1974 this was to be accomplished by normal legislation, which, however, was to be considered by the Congress under the "fast-track" procedure described earlier. The interesting fashion in which the procedure turned out to operate is revealing for the United States governmental and confidential processes.

[The way the fast-track operated in fact in 1979, is somewhat surprisingly different from that which might seem suggested by the statutory language, particularly in giving the Congressional members and their staff persons (and lawyers) a much more significant role than was implied by the statute, as outlined in the paragraphs following below. Furthermore, although this may seem like "old history", in fact all subsequent uses of the fast track followed a practice very similar to the way in which it occurred in the first use in 1979, so there has been a

21. Trade Act of 1974, secs. 102, 151; 19 U.S.C.A. secs. 2112, 2191.

22. Id., secs. 131–35, 19 U.S.C.A. secs. 2151–2155.

23. From John H. Jackson, Jean–Victor Louis & Mitsuo Matsushita, Implementing the Tokyo Round: National Constitutions and International Economic Rules 162–168 (1984). Reprinted by permission of the author.

"precedent" or "practice" effect on the basic structure of the procedure. Similar fast-track language (sometimes called "Trade Promotion Authority" or "TPA") has been used in subsequent statutes providing trade negotiating authority to the President and has been used to implement many bilateral or other small regional free trade agreements. A visit to the web site for the US Trade Representative[24] lists more than 20 such agreements in effect or in process.]

Under the "fast-track" procedure, the President was required to notify the Congress ninety days before he signed any NTB agreements, and to consult with key congressional committees during that time. Congress had been kept informed generally throughout the course of the Tokyo Round negotiations, and key congressional committees had developed professional staff whose full time was devoted to following the course of the negotiations. When the President notified the Congress in early January 1979, about the tentative NTB agreements, his officials sent to the Congress detailed information about the status of the negotiations, including the tentative drafts of the various agreements that were contemplated. Anticipating this, congressional staff, in consultation with key senators and congressmen, had designed a procedure that closely paralleled the normal procedure followed in work on bills, except that in this case no bill had yet been introduced in the Congress.

When a committee of Congress begins to formally consider a bill that has been introduced and prepares that bill for report to the floor of the whole House, its session is often called a markup, indicating that the committee is marking up the bill with its proposed changes. The consultations with the executive branch during the ninety days before completion of the international agreements were called non-markup sessions, and followed very closely this type of procedure. One important difference was that the sessions were not open to the public.

The principal committees devoting time to this subject were the Senate Finance Committee and the House Ways and Means Committee (particularly the latter's Subcommittee on Trade). These committees met extensively with executive branch officials, including the trade negotiators, and on some subjects entered into detailed negotiations about the matters that should be included in a statute implementing the international agreements. Particularly close attention was given to antidumping and countervailing duty laws. Perhaps most surprising, the members of Congress informed the executive branch that they desired to have their own staff (including the legal staff of the House and the Senate), develop the actual text of the bill the President would introduce.

Further procedures also indicated the parallel with normal legislative processes. On certain issues the Ways and Means Committee and the Finance Committee did not agree, so they held a "non-conference" joint session at which they resolved their differences in order to present a united front to the executive branch. Throughout this process the

24. Trade Agreements Home, United States Trade Representative: http://www.   ustr.gov/Trade_Agreements/Section_Index. html (last visited March 03, 2008).

executive branch officials participated, influenced the deliberations, and were in a position of some bargaining power, since it was understood that it was the President's bill that would be ultimately introduced and that could not be amended afterward.

After the international agreements were initialed in Geneva, the executive branch prepared the bill that the President introduced to the Congress. Understanding the political realities, the President's officials took almost the exact text of the draft bill that had been prepared by the congressional committees and staff. The President then arranged to have the bill introduced in June 1979.

Once the bill had been introduced, the basic substantive work was over, since it could not be amended. Thus, from the point of view of the Congress, the consultation period, including the non-markup and the non-conference, that went on before the bill was introduced was crucial in shaping the bill so that it would gain enough support in both houses of Congress to be able to pass. Thus, after the bill was introduced the normal procedures for enacting legislation were a formality. To no one's surprise, the bill passed. What was surprising was the overwhelming vote in favor of the bill: 90 to 4 in the Senate, and 395 to 7 in the House.

One interesting development in these congressional procedures for approval of the MTN agreements was the involvement of foreign nation interests. Early in the ninety-day consultation procedures, * * * officials of the EEC realized * * * that the shape of the statute the Congress was formulating would have a profound effect on the practical implementation of the MTN agreements. Once the statute became US law, it would be hard to persuade the Congress to change it. * * * The fact that the United States procedures were moving faster than those of any other country would also be highly influential. Consequently, the EEC took the logical step: they hired professional (legal and economic) representation in Washington, D.C. to monitor as closely as possible what was going on in the congressional consultation with the executive branch officials. These representatives reported quickly and frequently to the EEC officials, and thus on certain issues EEC negotiators could raise questions with their American counterparts. If the EEC objected to a direction they saw the congressional-executive sessions taking, it could and did make it known that it would deem certain statutory formulations a breach of the international obligations assumed by both the EEC and the United States.

* * *

In all this extensive consultation between the executive branch and the Congress, with the tugging and compromising that inevitably goes on in the legislative process, the testimony of participants was that the congressional committees were responsive to executive branch objectives that nothing be included in the US statute that would require the United States to be in default of any of its international obligations under the MTN results. To confirm this observation, after the bill was forwarded to the Congress in final form there was an official statement by the EEC Commission to the effect that in the opinion of the EEC officials, on the whole, the bill reflected the spirit and the letter of the MTN agreements.

Several aspects of this procedure for enacting the Trade Agreements Act of 1979 are particularly interesting and potentially significant. At least in the first decade of fast track use, the Congress was evidently pleased with the procedure. The heavy involvement of the congressional committees in the drafting process gave the Congress confidence and a feeling of security that the executive branch was not trying to foist something upon Congress without giving it an opportunity to influence the results.

The Congress' satisfaction with the procedure is evidenced not only by statements in the committee reports and other legislative history, but more concretely by the fact that it extended by eight years the period prescribed for the procedure under the 1974 Act. In addition, in Section 3(c) of the 1979 Act the Congress adopted virtually the same procedure for amending US law implementing the MTN agreements when such amendments are necessary to fulfill a "requirement of, amendment to, or recommendation under such an agreement." * * * Thus, if an international disputes panel rules against the United States on a question of interpretation of an MTN agreement, and US law prevented the executive branch from implementing the international interpretation, this procedure could be followed to change US law.

The second interesting aspect of the procedures for enacting the 1979 act is a somewhat unusual problem concerning the techniques of interpreting it. Normally US courts are influenced in their interpretation of a statute by its legislative history. This history consists of, among other things, the committee hearings and debates, the committee reports, and statements on the floor of both houses while the bill was being considered. * * * Under the "fast-track" procedure, however, a bill was introduced by the executive branch and could not be amended. Thus the executive branch was in theory the draftsman, and its intent was arguably the intent of the draftsman. The executive branch sent to Congress, along with the drafted bill, a Statement of Administrative Action indicating its intentions in administering the new legislation. Thus this statement is an important part of the legislative history, and arguably is the definitive source of legislative intent. However, [the House Report] * * * stakes out a claim to be considered as a prime source of legislative history, just as it would normally be for other legislation. Moreover it also presents a view of the role of the Statement of Administrative Action, and notes that those statements "are not part of the bill and will not become part of US statutes. * * * They will not provide any new, independent legal authority for executive action."

Finally, the role of the MTN agreements themselves in the legislative history must be considered. As will be seen below, it is clear that the agreements do not themselves become US law, but the committee reports state, "This bill is drafted with the intent to permit US practice to be consistent with the obligations of the agreements, as the United States understands those obligations." Thus it seems fair to conclude that the trade agreements (and presumably their preparatory work) can be used as at least a secondary source of legislative history of the 1979 act when other sources fail to resolve an issue.

(6) The 1988 Trade Act and Fast Track

During the 1980's and early 1990's, there were two relatively major, general trade acts (1984 and 1988). The second of these addressed the participation of the United States in the Uruguay Round, and it provided for the use of fast track procedures to implement the result of the negotiations. As before, the tendency of Congress continued to be to specify that the international agreements that were ratified were not themselves "self-executing." The implementing bills for the United States–Israel, United States–Canada and the North American Free Trade Agreements, the latter which were negotiated under the 1988 Act, contained clauses in the implementing statutes addressing this issue and legislative history that reinforced that the statute itself would implement the international obligations, but the treaties would not be directly applicable as "statute-like" laws in US jurisprudence. In the United States–Canada and the North American Free Trade Agreement implementing statutes, additional attention was given to the role of the States and State law in a federal system (which will be examined in Section 3.6). The same was true for the Uruguay Round.

(7) Fast Track and the Uruguay Round Implementing Legislation

The following is a summary outline of the fast track procedure as applied to the Uruguay Round:[25]

1. General Authority: Usually in its authority for non-tariff barrier negotiations, the Congress specifies the possibility of using the fast track procedure, with a deadline date before which the proposed agreement must be signed for it to qualify for the fast track. There is also a procedure for notifying the Congress when the President intends to begin negotiations that would utilize the fast track.

2. Consultations with Congress: Generally, at least 90 calendar days before signing an international agreement (120 calendar days for the Uruguay Round under the 1993 extension of the fast track), the Executive must notify Congress of his intention to enter into an agreement. Usually the Executive will submit a reasonably complete draft of the agreement, so that Congress can appraise it and have its inputs. Congress will have hearings during this period. At the same time, or a little bit after the notification, various advisory committees to the negotiation must report.

---

25. Trade Act of 1974, sec. 151, 19 U.S.C.A. 2191, as amended, Omnibus Trade and Competitiveness Act of 1988, secs. 1102–1103, 19 U.S.C.A. secs. 2902–2903; Pub.L.No. 103–49, sec. 1, 107 Stat. 239 (1993) (adding 19 U.S.C.A. 2902(e)(Special Provisions Regarding Uruguay Round Trade Negotiations)).

3. The signing of the agreement must be before the statutory deadline date in order for the fast track to be available for the adoption of the implementing legislation.

4. After the signing, there has not in the past been any time limit within which the President must submit a Bill to the House and Senate. The practice has been for the Executive to consult extensively with Congress and then formulate a draft Bill. When the President finally submits the Bill, he can submit his own version recognizing that to deviate from the congressional desires will lose him votes in the process. Along with the implementing Bill, the President submits a "statement of administrative intent" which describes how he expects the legislation to be administered. This is an important part of the "legislative history" under this procedure.

5. As part of the rules of procedure of the House and Senate, the Bill is sometimes considered simultaneously and sometimes completing the House first (as the Constitution requires for a revenue Bill). The key characteristics of the procedure are as follows:

  1) The Bill may not be amended (this is perhaps the most important).

  2) Committees must discharge the Bill within 45 days, so they cannot bottle up the process.

  3) There must be a vote on the floor of each House within a certain number of days (e.g., 15 days after the Bill is reported) with limited debate in both Houses. (Thus, there can be no filibuster in the Senate.)

In general, there is a total time period of 60 legislative days unless a revenue Bill is involved, in which case it is 90 days. However, calendar days can amount to almost twice the amount of legislative days.

In the case of the Uruguay Round, the fast track authority in the 1988 Act expired in the summer of 1993 and had to be extended. Under the extension, notification had to be made to Congress under the required consultation period 120 days in advance of signing the agreement. The last date for signing the agreement was set at April 15, 1994. This meant that the Uruguay Round agreements needed to be sufficiently completed for notification to Congress (which is not a complete final draft) on December 15, 1993. This was achieved sufficiently for purposes of the statute and the congressional consultation period. Congress conducted hearings and extensive consultations during the first few months of 1994, and the Final Act of the Uruguay Round was signed in Morocco on April 15, 1994, thus qualifying for the fast track procedure.

After extensive discussions, the implementing legislation was introduced in September and adopted in December 1994. The Uruguay Round Agreements Act specifically provides that the agreements themselves do not prevail over any other US statute, and that they do not create private rights of action, and special provisions are made for the relationship of the Treaty text to state law. See the Document Supplement for Uruguay Round Agreements Act, sec. 102; 19 U.S.C.A. sec. 3532.

The text of Section 102 (a) (1), declaring that the Uruguay Round agreements do not themselves prevail over another US statute, is broadly identical to that of Section 3(a) of the 1979 Trade Agreements Act. Section 102(c)(1), limiting private rights of action, is broader than the corresponding provision of the 1979 Act (Section 3(f), 19 U.S.C.A. sec. 2504), but, since in both cases the agreements are non-self-executing, the effect is likely to be the same.[26]

In Section 6.7 we discuss the domestic law effect of the Uruguay Round agreements. Other notes regarding the 1994 Act occur throughout this book, and of course, the same is true for the effects of the agreement itself.

(8) *Fast Track after 1995*

After 1995, with the WTO in force, the WTO members began to contemplate a new round of negotiations, which as described in Section 6.5(D) has been much more problematical than before (and still not successful, as this is being written in Spring 2008.) Since the prior fast track authority had expired, it was understood that such a negotiation would need a new version of this statutory authority. However, Congress was much less favorable to such authority than it had previously been. After much debate and by a margin of only one vote in the House, Congress granted new authority to the President pursuant to the Trade Promotion Authority Act of 2002. The authority granted by the act— trade promotion authority or TPA—is similar to the fast track authority granted previously, but it was renamed because of the controversy surrounding the "fast track" procedures.

Under the TPA Act, the authority expired in 2005, although the act provided for a two-year extension if requested by the President and not disapproved by either House of Congress. The President made such a request and neither House disapproved, so the TPA authority was extended until the last day of June 2007. That date passed without the WTO negotiations being far enough along for there to be sufficient political support to extend it again (which would have required a new statute). Consequently, at the time this is being written in Spring 2008, no TPA or fast track procedure exists. Of course, the United States can negotiate without TPA or fast track authority, but other nations may not wish to negotiate in the context of normal Congressional procedures, which would not provide an up or down vote on the final negotiated package, making it vulnerable to amendment and maneuvers to delay.[27]

---

26. David Leebron, Implementation of the Uruguay Round Results in the United States, in John H. Jackson & Alan O. Sykes (eds.), Implementing the Uruguay Round 212 (1997).

27. Smith, Carolyn C. Trade Promotion Authority and Fast–Track Negotiating Authority for Trade Agreements: Major Votes Washington, D.C.: Congressional Research Service, 2006. Available at: http://fpc.state. gov/documents/organization/73937.pdf (last visited February 28, 2008).

Notes and Questions

(1) Fast track procedures have now been used to implement the results of two GATT rounds (the Tokyo Round and the Uruguay Round), as well as a considerable number of free trade agreements, including such controversial ones as the North American Free Trade Agreement (NAFTA) with Canada and Mexico and the Central America–Dominican Republic–United States Free Trade Agreement (CAFTA–DR). These procedures have been criticized by some, who argue that they are undemocratic. How could such an argument be constructed? Do you agree with it?

(2) Fast track procedures include (i) statutory components, which can only be changed by an amendment passed by both Houses of Congress and approved by the President and (ii) House and Senate rule components, which can be changed by either House acting alone. Thus, to work as intended, the procedures require at least a minimum degree of cooperation between the President and the congressional leadership. In 2008, disagreements between the White House and congressional leadership over the proposed Colombia–US FTA resulted in a House of Representatives' decision to modify the House rules on the timing of the consideration of that FTA. H.Res. 1092, passed April 10, 2008 (providing that sections 151(e)(1) and 151(f)(1) of the 1974 Trade Act will not apply to consideration of the implementing bill). While this was the first time the rules had been changed, such changes had been threatened in the past and had on at least one occasion influenced ongoing negotiations.

(E) THE STRUCTURE OF US GOVERNMENT FOR CONDUCT OF FOREIGN ECONOMIC RELATIONS

It is impossible to give the reader any fixed or precise "road-map" of decision-making and exercises of regulatory power in the Executive Branch of the United States, because these functions are constantly shifting and changing.[28] At the apex, of course, are the White House and the aides and assistants immediately surrounding the President. Each President tends to operate with these individuals in a different way, and so the lines of authority tend to shift from one President to the next, and indeed even during the term of office of a particular President. Some Presidents have designated one particular "assistant" through which all international economic matters will funnel to the President. Other Presidents have even designated a small "agency" in the White House to perform this coordinating function. Most Presidents have also utilized "Cabinet Committees" of various types, which meet and make recommendations to the President. The most significant agency for trade matters affiliated with the Office of the President is the US Trade Representative (USTR), which is described below.

28. A description of trade policy functions as of June 2005 is found in House Comm. on Ways & Means, Overview and Compilation of U.S. Trade Statutes 322–333, 109th Cong., 1st Sess. Comm. Print: WMCP: 109–4, (2005). It also contains a summary, as well as the text, of US trade laws. Much of the information of this subsection can also be found in the United States Government Manual. Other information has been obtained from interviews or from one of the author's general knowledge obtained from his work in Washington. In addition, there are many informative US Government agency websites, e.g. www.ustr.gov, www.usitc.gov, etc.

When one moves down from the apex of United States government policy formation and coordination, going beyond the borders of the Executive Office of the President, one finds considerably more stability in the allocation of functions relating to various statutory delegations of authority over international economic policy. These functions are widely dispersed among various governmental agencies or departments. Many of these agencies or departments have developed particular constituencies, with special interest in the regulatory measures, that lead the departments to guard their jurisdictions jealously. It is not surprising, therefore, that occasions will arise when the United States government will be taking actions through one department which are, or at least appear to be, inconsistent with actions taken by another department. Overall, it is quite easy to count over four dozen agencies in the Executive Branch with jurisdiction touching on international economic matters and over a dozen independent agencies or authorities with such concerns. Obviously included among these departments are the Department of State, the Department of Treasury, the Department of Commerce, the Department of Defense, and important sections of the Department of Agriculture and Department of Labor. One of the most important independent agencies is the United States International Trade Commission (ITC), formerly the United States Tariff Commission. Add to these the dozen and a half congressional committees and subcommittees giving attention to these matters and one can begin to appreciate the difficulty of originating and implementing a consistent overall international economic policy for the United States.

In the 1980's and early 1990's there have been a number of proposals to centralize and unify executive branch authority over international trade into a single department, sometimes called the "DITI" (Department of International Trade and Industry). These proposals have been very controversial. Some of them would merge the USTR with most of the current Commerce Department to create such new department. Some would even include the International Trade Commission in this department.[29]

As noted above, the most significant agency on trade matters in the Executive Branch is the Office of the United States Trade Representative (USTR). Originally entitled the Special Trade Representative (STR) in the 1962 Act which created this agency, its permanence was recognized by a change of name in a 1980 Presidential reorganization order. The 1974 Act had already elevated the head of this agency (always called the Trade Representative, with status of Ambassador Extraordinary and Plenipotentiary) to cabinet level.[30]

---

29. See 2 BNA Intl. Trade Rptr. 88, 421 (1985).

30. See Trade Expansion Act of 1962, Pub.L. No. 87–794, secs. 241–42, 76 Stat. 878 (codified in part at 19 U.S.C.A. sec. 1872); Trade Act of 1974, Pub.L. No. 93– 618, sec. 141, 88 Stat. 1999 (codified at 19 U.S.C.A. sec. 2171); Reorganization Plan No. 3 of 1979, 93 Stat. 1381; Executive Order No. 12188 of Jan. 2, 1980, 45 Fed. Reg. 989.

This agency is charged with negotiations with foreign nations on trade and a number of other economic matters, and coordinates much of the United States government policy formulation on such matters. Statutes have set up a group of inter-agency committees, and USTR officials are often charged, either by statute or presidential order, to chair such committees. The agency has always been small, however, usually numbering only slightly more than 150 professional level staff persons. It often relies on other agencies or departments for staff work, and receives help from persons detailed from other agencies.

The US government often works through inter-agency committees, and trade policy is no exception. There have been a series of trade committees at different levels, set up in statutes or regulations in connection with USTR, including the Trade Policy Staff Committee and the Trade Policy Review Group. Sometimes, Presidents have also utilized other White House coordinating committees or cabinet level groups for coordination—such as the National Economic Council.

Usually, a committee composed of mid-level officials of many departments and agencies drafts instructions and e-mails for US representatives abroad, prepares testimony and bills for Congress, etc. When agreement is not possible at this level, matters tend to be considered by an intermediate level supervising committee, on which representatives are usually from the Assistant Secretary level. Subsequently, the matters can go to a subcabinet or a cabinet level committee, and finally they can be referred to the President for his decision.

SECTION 3.4   INTERNATIONAL AGREEMENTS AND U.S. LAW

(A) INTRODUCTION—THE RELEVANT QUESTIONS

We turn in this section to an exploration of a series of key legal questions relating to international agreements in United States law, namely: (1) What is the legal authority of US officials, such as the President or his officers, to negotiate internationally with a view to entering into an international agreement? (2) What is the legal authority and procedure for US officials to accept an international agreement as a binding obligation of the United States under international law? and (3) What is the legal authority and procedure for implementing an international agreement in the domestic law of the United States? The second of these questions relates to so-called "treaty making" authority, although in the United States there are international agreements that are not called treaties. In the United States, the third question involves consideration of whether the agreement is "self-executing." In some other countries, the question is whether it has "direct effects" or is "directly applicable."[1]

As to the first of these questions, the generally accepted viewpoint is that the President and his officers can negotiate on any subject at any

---

1. See Section 4.3 infra.

time. This does not necessarily imply the authority to accept as binding the results of the negotiation. The negotiation will often be "ad referendum" with the understanding that the President will have to obtain authority to accept the agreement which results from the negotiation. The limits of this "pure negotiating" authority have not often been probed by the Courts or by Congress; the *Consumers Union* case, Section 3.2 supra, is perhaps the best available judicial discussion of this topic.

Of course, the authority to "negotiate" may be relatively useless if representatives of other countries feel that the President or his officers will not be able to obtain authority to accept the results of the negotiation. This is a question of "negotiation credibility" to which we have alluded and which we will discuss again. It should be noted that in other countries or legal systems, such as the European Union, executive officials may not even have the authority to negotiate. That is to say, before any discussions with foreign representatives that could be characterized as potentially leading to an international agreement can occur, there must be some sort of authorization procedure.[2]

It is useful to set the questions mentioned above and explored in this section in some depth, in the context of a series of questions more generally concerning making and implementing treaties. The following is one "inventory" of those questions, some of which do not trouble US law much; but others of which are very troublesome. The questions with an asterisk are those which arguably most concern US law but not all of those are discussed in this course (these questions are usually a central subject for general international law courses). Question 4 is the subject of sub-section B of this section; questions 6, 7 and 8 are dealt with in sub-section C.

VALIDITY UNDER U.S. CONSTITUTIONAL LAW

1.　The power to negotiate

2.　The power to "sign" (usually ad referendum, only to certify the text.)

*3.　The power to "accept" as binding international law obligation (often termed ratification)

*4.　The "validity" of the treaty under national (municipal) constitutional law. Cf. The validity under international law as a binding obligation.

IMPLEMENTING

*5.　The power to implement, carry out, the treaty obligations

*6.　Direct application of the treaty in domestic (municipal) law (or in the US "self-executing" or "statute like")

*7.　Invocability in municipal law (contrasted with "direct effect")

2.　See Section 4.4 infra.

*8. Hierarchy of norms in domestic law when treaty norm conflicts with other norms of municipal law.

ADMINISTERING

*9. The power to administer a treaty, which includes a series of issues such as:

— procedure to formally "ratify"

— power to interpret for domestic application and as a matter of international law

— power to represent the nation-state in treaty institutional procedures (bilateral or multilateral meetings, etc.)

— the power to "vote" in such procedures, the power to amend the treaty

— the power to terminate the treaty (on various grounds including the exercise of a treaty termination clause)

(B) POWER TO ENTER INTO INTERNATIONAL AGREEMENTS—EXECUTIVE AGREEMENTS AND THE PRESIDENT'S POWER

In US law a distinction is made between treaties and executive agreements. The Constitution requires the Senate to advise and consent by a two-thirds vote to the ratification of a treaty, but it makes no mention of executive agreements. In international law, no such distinction is made—both "treaties" and "executive agreements" are considered to be treaties as that term is used in international law. The use of this different terminology in the United States—unfortunately unavoidable now—is a source of some confusion.

In fact one can discern the following different types of international agreements under US law:

(1) Treaties, in the US constitutional sense, requiring advice and consent of two-thirds of the Senate.

(2) Congressional Executive Agreements previously authorized, where Congress has enacted legislation delegating to the President the authority to enter into an international agreement (example: typical trade agreements authority, such as section 101 of the Trade Act of 1974).

(3) Congressional Executive Agreements subsequently authorized, where after an agreement is negotiated, the President seeks authority from Congress to accept the agreement as a binding international obligation of the United States (example: Bretton Woods Agreements Act, 22 U.S.C.A. §§ 286–86x).

(4) Presidential Executive Agreements, sometimes termed "inherent" presidential agreements, where the President accepts an agreement as a binding obligation of the United States without any participation by Congress, on the basis of his "inherent" or constitu-

tional authority (examples: agreements on the disposition of armed forces in foreign countries under the Commander-in-Chief Clause).

(5) Treaty Executive Agreements, where a treaty approved by the Senate leaves certain details of implementation to be worked out by various governments at a later time, and may thus explicitly or implicitly authorize the President to enter into international agreements to accomplish such implementation. (The same could be said of authorizations contained in Congressional Executive Agreements.)

From the Executive Branch's point of view executive agreements are speedier and easier, and avoid the minority Senate veto (of one third, plus one) that could block a treaty. But from the point of view of Congress, of course, the presidential executive agreement threatens to diminish the congressional role in foreign affairs, thus risking direct domestic legal effects of self-executing agreements without congressional participation.

Some, like McDougal[3] argue that the broad powers of control over external relations that the Constitution has granted both to the President and to Congress would be meaningless if they did not "include the instrumental powers, first, to authorize the making of intergovernmental agreements and, secondly, to make these agreements the law of the land." McDougal argues that the practices of successive administrations have made executive agreements "appropriate instruments for handling many important aspects of our foreign relations." Resistance, he says, comes either from those who "fear what majority control may be able to achieve in an integrated, responsible foreign policy," from those defending the Senatorial prerogative, "upon an assumption often none too unconscious that the safety of the nation and the sanctity of the Constitution would be imperiled if one third of the Senate could not dictate the nation's foreign policy," or from those claiming that majority control would imperil minority interests.

On the other hand, the great increase in the use of executive agreements since the beginning of the Twentieth Century has been very worrisome to others who criticize unchecked Executive Branch power, particularly in light of Supreme Court decisions that held that executive agreements, as federal law, prevailed over inconsistent state law by reason of the Supremacy Clause. Raoul Berger points at the fact that executive agreements are not mentioned in the Constitution and at how the Framers "made clear beyond doubt that the specific objective of the treaty clause was to preclude the President, acting alone, from entering into international agreements."[4] Berger also points at the relatively recent nature of executive agreements and at the fact that in some cases they are even kept secret from the Senate and the general public. Citing

---

3. Myres McDougal and Asher Lans, Treaties and Congressional—Executive or Presidential Agreements: Interchangeable Instruments of National Policy, 54 Yale L.J. 181, 534 (1945), at 187–89.

4. Raoul Berger, The Presidential Monopoly of Foreign Relations, 71 Mich. L.Rev. 1, 33–37 (1972).

Kurland he asks: "Should the Constitution really be read to mean that by calling an agreement an executive agreement rather than a treaty, the obligation to secure Senate approval is dissolved?"

During the 1994 Congressional debate over the adoption of the Uruguay Round Agreements Act (to authorize the President to ratify and to implement the Uruguay Round treaty)[5] a challenge was raised to the constitutionality of the fast track procedure used for Congressional approval of the Act. The challenge argued that Senate advice and consent pursuant to the treaty clause was the only proper procedure for approval. This was refuted by a group of eminent scholars, and the Congress, including the Senate, overwhelmingly approved the Act in 1994 (in a post election "lame-duck" special session at the end of the year). In fact, the Senate vote was more than two-thirds, but the process used was the fast track procedure described earlier.[6]

Several challenges to fast track procedure have been brought to US courts, particular related to NAFTA, but so far none have succeeded. See, e.g., Made in the USA Foundation v. United States, 242 F.3d 1300 (11 Cir. 2001), cert. denied, 534 U.S. 1039, 122 S.Ct. 613, 151 L.Ed.2d 536 (2001) (issue of whether NAFTA was treaty requiring senate ratification under the treaty clause was nonjusticiable political question).

The following is a US Department of State document that was created to assist officials in deciding which "treaty making" procedure to use. Consider several questions: 1) Does this document really help? 2) Is this document really consistent with US constitutional practice? 3) Is there any constitutional constraint on the President when he or his officials are choosing between the Senate Treaty process and the Congressional statutory procedure?

U.S DEPT. OF STATE, FOREIGN AFFAIRS MANUAL, VOLUME 11, POLITICAL AFFAIRS, CIRCULAR NO. 175 ON THE NEGOTIATION AND CONCLUSION OF TREATIES AND OTHER INTERNATIONAL AGREEMENTS (2006)

Section 722 *GENERAL OBJECTIVES*
(CT:POL–44; 05–26–2006)

5. Interested students can find more detail on some of this congressional action in John H. Jackson, The World Trading System ch. 3 (2nd ed. 1997); and "The Great 1994 Sovereignty Debate" in John H. Jackson, The Jurisprudence of the GATT and the WTO: Insights on Treaty Law and Economic Relations (2000) (also published as: John H. Jackson, The Great 1994 Sovereignty Debate: United States Acceptance and Implementation of the Uruguay Round Results, 36 Colum.J.Transnatl.L. 157–88 (1997)).

6. Letter from Laurence Tribe to Senator Robert Byrd, July 19, 1994, and Memorandum of Law Re: Statutory Procedure for Approval of the Uruguay Round Trade Negotiations and the WTO, November 11, 1994. See the account of the 1994 Congressional action on the Uruguay Round Agreements in David W. Leebron, Implementation of the Uruguay Round Results in the United States, in Implementing the Uruguay Round (John H. Jackson & Alan Sykes eds. 1997), at 175–242 (especially pp. 179, 180, 204, and 205). See also Jackson, supra note 5, at Section 3.2.

The objectives [of these procedures] are:

(1) That the making of treaties and other international agreements for the United States is carried out within constitutional and other appropriate limits;

* * *

(4) That timely and appropriate consultation is had with congressional leaders and committees on treaties and other international agreements;

* * *

Section 723.3 *Considerations For Selecting Among Constitutionally Authorized Procedures*
(CT:POL–44; 05–26–2006)

In determining a question as to the procedure which should be followed for any particular international agreement, due consideration is given to the following factors along with [constitutional requirements]:

(1) The extent to which the agreement involves commitments or risks affecting the nation as a whole;

(2) Whether the agreement is intended to affect state laws;

(3) Whether the agreement can be given effect without the enactment of subsequent legislation by the Congress;

(4) Past US practice as to similar agreements;

(5) The preference of the Congress as to a particular type of agreement;

(6) The degree of formality desired for an agreement;

(7) The proposed duration of the agreement, the need for prompt conclusion of an agreement, and the desirability of concluding a routine or short-term agreement; and

(8) The general international practice as to similar agreements.

In determining whether any international agreement should be brought into force as a treaty or as an international agreement other than a treaty, the utmost care is to be exercised to avoid any invasion or compromise of the constitutional powers of the President, the Senate, and the Congress as a whole.

Section 723.4 *Questions As To Type Of Agreement To Be Used; Consultation With Congress*
(CT:POL–48; 09–25–2006)

* * *

c. Consultations on such questions will be held with congressional leaders and committees as may be appropriate.

Notes and Questions

Like two gladiators in a constitutional arena, Congress and the President are currently circling each other and probing to try to define what will be the appropriate relationship between them. Exactly what the division of power will ultimately be, or should be, is difficult to say. Consider some of the following problems.

(1) The General Agreement on Tariffs and Trade is an executive agreement which was accepted for the United States by the President in 1947 under the then existing Trade Agreements Act authority, which authorized the President

(a) To enter into foreign trade agreements * * *; and

(b) To proclaim such modifications of existing duties and other import restrictions * * * as are required or appropriate to carry out any [such] foreign trade agreement.[7]

Ever since, there have been questions raised whether the foregoing language authorized the President to enter into the General Agreement. We explore this issue in more detail in Section 6.7 infra.

(2) The 1967 Anti–Dumping Code, an agreement negotiated under GATT auspices in the Kennedy Round, was accepted by the President without explicit statutory authority, on the argument that it required changes only in administrative practices of the Executive Branch, which were within the delegated authority of that Branch. Is this an appropriate use of executive agreements? Does it matter whether the agreement requires changes in long established administrative practices, although the changes would not be inconsistent with any statute? Members of Congress have complained about Executive Branch changes in long established administrative practices, particularly when done to fulfill an executive agreement not approved by Congress. Indeed, as noted in Section 16.4 infra, Congress effectively forbade implementation of the Code. Later, under the Trade Act of 1974, a special procedure was set up for the approval of non-tariff barrier agreements, and in commenting on that procedure, the congressional reports make it abundantly clear that when such agreements change an established administrative practice (or regulation), they should be submitted for congressional approval.[8]

(3) The Organization for Economic Cooperation and Development is governed by a 1960 convention to which the United States is obligated as a treaty. Article 5 of that convention authorizes the Organization to take decisions that are binding on its members. It has been argued that, since the executive branch will be representing the United States in the Organization, the convention will operate to give the Executive power to agree on decisions in certain substantive fields. Abram Chayes, then Legal Adviser of the United States Department of State, however, stated: "This argument is based on the erroneous assumption that the convention in any way concerns itself with the distribution of powers within the

---

7. Reciprocal Trade Agreements Act of 1934 as amended. See Section 3.3 Note 18.

8. See, e.g., Senate Comm. on Finance, Trade Reform Act of 1974, S.Rep. No. 93–1298, 93d Cong., 2d Sess. 75 (1974).

United States or any other member state. * * * Under article 5 the Organization may take decisions, but the convention is silent as to the process by which a member nation, within its own internal system, arrives at the point where it may cast an effective vote in favor of a particular decision." A statement for the record added that "the power of the United States to cast a favorable vote and bind the United States in any particular case must be sought in a source outside the convention."[9] When the United States representative does not have the authority, under United States law, to bind the United States, he will either veto the decision, or abstain (thus permitting the decision to become binding as to other member countries) or approve, subject to compliance with US constitutional procedures.

(C) DOMESTIC LEGAL EFFECT AND IMPLEMENTATION OF INTERNATIONAL AGREEMENTS IN U.S. LAW[10]

The question of whether and to what extent a valid international agreement has domestic legal effects involves at least three sub-questions that courts and officials do not always clearly distinguish. (Note: If the agreement is not valid under US law, the next questions are irrelevant.) First, does the international agreement, or any part of it, have "direct applicability" or a "self-executing effect" in US law, so that at least some litigants in US courts are entitled to rely on its provisions, and courts must accept those provisions as applicable law?

The second question is whether a particular party to litigation can rely on a provision of an international agreement. This question is closely related to the first and often courts do not distinguish these two questions, but there can be a distinct difference between them. The second question concerns the "standing" of the party. Even if a provision of an international agreement is self-executing, is the particular party who claims the benefit of that provision a party entitled to make such a claim under that provision?

Third, there is a separate question of "hierarchy of norms." If the international agreement is inconsistent with a prior or subsequent federal or state statute or constitutional provision, which prevails?

In connection with these questions, the reader should remember the language of the United States Constitution quoted in this book at the end of Section 3.1, including the phrase "... all Treaties made, or which shall be made, under the Authority of the United States, shall be the supreme Law of the Land; ..."

9.   107 Cong.Rec. 4157 (1961); John H. Jackson, Status of Treaties in Domestic Legal Systems: A Policy Analysis, 86 Am. J.Intl.L. 310 (1992).

10.   John H. Jackson, The Jurisprudence of GATT & the WTO 310–340 (2000); John H. Jackson, United States of America, in The Effect of Treaties in Domestic Law 141 (Francis G. Jacobs & Shelley Roberts eds., 1987); Thomas Buergenthal, Self–Executing and Non–Self–Executing Treaties in National and International Law, 235 Recueil des Cours (1992–IV).

JOHN H. JACKSON, STATUS OF TREATIES IN DOMESTIC LEGAL SYSTEMS[11]

For those who have not had contact with the literature and practice of treaty effects in domestic law, let us first examine the broad outlines of the existing international situation with respect to the direct applicability of a treaty, using a simple paradigmatic hypothetical to illustrate it. Suppose nations M and D have entered into an international treaty that includes the following obligation:

> With respect to the right to own property within the territory of either contracting party (nation M or D), the citizens of the other contracting party shall have equal and nondiscriminatory treatment as compared to treatment received by the citizens of that contracting party within which the property is located.

The intent of this language is to equalize the property ownership rights of both countries' citizens within the territory of each contracting party, a traditional expression of "national treatment" obligations found in many bilateral and multilateral[12] treaties, although the subject of the obligation may differ widely.

In traditional explanations of the effect of treaties (going back a century or more), a distinction is made between "monist" and "dualist" states.[13] This terminology has been criticized, and clearly it is too "dichotomous" in flavor, since there are various degrees of direct application of treaties, to say nothing of the considerable confusion about it. Nevertheless, even though not precise, these terms are used and may help to demonstrate the major alternative approaches.

Let us assume that State M is considered "monist" and state D is considered "dualist," and in each state a citizen of the other has been refused rights to own property by the national government even though that state's citizens possess those rights. What is the national legal situation?

Traditionally, the "monist" state's legal system is considered to include international treaties to which M is obligated. Thus, a citizen of D can sue as an individual in the courts of M to require that he be treated in accordance with the treaty standard.[14]

---

11. Reproduced with permission from 86 AJIL 310, 313–315 (1992), © The American Society of International Law.

12. [original note 16] For example, The General Agreement on Tariffs and Trade (GATT), Article III; and many treaties of friendship, commerce, and navigation. * * *

13. [original note 18] [See, e.g., I. Brownlie, Principles of Public International Law (5th ed. 1990); Sasse, The Common Market: Between International & Municipal Law, 75 Yale L.J. 695 (1966).] The author is aware that some writers tend to down play this terminology, or feel that it is unnecessary. See, e.g., the descriptions of such views in McDougal, The Impact of International Law upon National Law: A Policy–Oriented Perspective, 4 S. Dakota L.Rev. 25, 28, 31 (1959). Nevertheless, as a matter of empirical observation, court opinions, national officials and authors do use this terminology, at least in some jurisdictions. See, e.g., I. Brownlie, supra, Chapter II; Meinhard Hilf, Rights, Institutions and Impact of International Law According to the German Basic Law 177 (1987).

14. [original note 19] It is assumed in this article that aliens or citizens of the relevant foreign nation have access to the courts of a domestic legal system.

On the other hand, the term "dualist" has been used to describe the contrary result in state D. In a dualist state, international treaties are part of a separate legal system from that of the domestic law (hence a "dual" system). Therefore, a treaty is not part of the domestic law, at least not directly. Without further facts, a citizen of M who is refused the property ownership privilege in D that D's citizen has there, has no way to sue in the courts of D because those courts apply the law of D, which does not include the rule expressed in the treaty (at least not yet). The citizen of M's only recourse is to persuade his own government to use diplomatic means to encourage D to honor its obligation and assure him equal property ownership rights.

It is generally said that for the treaty rule to operate in the domestic legal system of a dualist state, there must be an "act of transformation," that is, a government action by that state incorporating the treaty norm into its domestic law.[15] This may be a statute duly enacted by the parliament that uses all or part of the treaty language and incorporates it as a statutory matter into domestic law.[16] Sometimes such a statute may paraphrase the treaty language, or "clarify" or elaborate the treaty language. In all these cases, the domestic law is that of the act of transformation, but the treaty language usually has "relevance" in interpreting the statutory language, under various theories of the domestic jurisprudence.[17] Other legal instruments can also serve as an act of transformation, including a regulation of an administrative body (if its authority so permits), and possibly even an action or decision of a court or tribunal (again, depending on the authority of the tribunal.)[18]

---

15. [original note 20] When an international treaty does not have direct effect in the domestic law system, but it is necessary to provide domestic rules to carry out the international treaty, in many cases such rules can be provided by an "act of transformation," such as a statute, which incorporates the treaty, or most of the treaty language, and makes that language through this statute a part of the domestic legal system.

16. [original note 21] In many cases, the statute which operates as the act of transformation also authorizes the appropriate government officials to "accept" or ratify the treaty itself. For example, see the U.S. Trade Agreements Act of 1979, Pub. L. No. 96–39, 93 Stat. 144 (1979), especially § 3 Relationship of Trade Agreements to United States Law, and relevant legislative history. See J. Jackson, The World Trading System: Law and Policy of International Economic Relations 97 (2nd ed. 1997); Frowein, Federal Republic of Germany, in The Effect of Treaties in Domestic Law 63, 66 (F. Jacobs & S. Roberts eds., 1987).

17. [original note 22] See e.g., American Law Institute, Restatement of the Law (Third), Foreign Relations Law of the United States § 114 (1987) (which reads, "Where fairly possible, a United States statute is to be construed so as not to conflict with international law, or with an international agreement of the United States"). See also J. Jackson, The World Trading System: Law and Policy of International Economic Relations 95–96 (2nd. Ed 1997); J. Jackson, J.-V. Louis & M. Matsushita, Implementing the Tokyo Round: National Constitutions and International Economic Rules 167 (1984). See generally The Effect of Treaties in Domestic Law (F. Jacobs & S. Roberts eds., 1987).

18. [original note 23] For example, (although probably rare) a court might be delegated authority to issue a device that would apply a treaty, perhaps on a petition for mandamus. This situation is to be distinguished from a court's deciding that a treaty is directly applicable in a particular case.

(1) Self–Executing International Agreements

The question of whether a treaty has direct domestic law effect is, under United States law (in contrast to the law of a number of foreign nations), a question of whether the treaty is "self-executing" and purports directly by its own terms to give rights to individual citizens, rather than simply imposing the international legal obligation upon the national government to effectuate those rights. One classic case is Sei Fujii v. State of California, 38 Cal.2d 718, 242 P.2d 617 (1952), which held that certain provisions of the United Nations Charter were not self-executing. The California court said (242 P.2d at 620–22), "it must appear that the framers of the treaty intended to prescribe a rule that, standing alone, would be enforceable in the courts" and concluded that the United Nations Charter "pledges the various countries to cooperate" and "represents a moral commitment," but that the provisions at issue "were not intended to supersede existing domestic legislation."

If the provisions of an international agreement are not self-executing, and if implementation of the agreement requires some changes in domestic US law (not always the case), then some additional action by government bodies will be necessary. This raises the question of authority to implement an agreement. A number of different forms of implementation are possible. Congress may enact a statute that will implement the agreement or the President or other officials may have authority to implement the agreement by issuing or changing regulations.

Sometimes the question of "self-executing" is made a subject of understanding between the Executive Branch and the Senate during the treaty ratification process. For example, the 1962 International Coffee Agreement was ratified after Senate approval,[19] but the Senate record notes understandings between the Senate and the Executive Branch (which were crucial for obtaining Senate approval) that the treaty would not be self-executing.[20]

How does a court determine when an international agreement is self-executing? What sort of language in the agreement itself does it look to? If the language of the agreement is ambiguous, what other sources will a court address? Intent of the draftsmen as expressed in the "preparatory work" for the agreement? Is the issue of any appropriate concern to the foreign parties, or is it solely a US constitutional law question? If the latter, would US courts look primarily or solely to the intentions expressed by the US negotiators? Would that category be deemed to include Congressmen or Senators? Suppose the Senate, in its advice and consent, expressed its view that an international agreement was not self-executing as drafted, should that view prevail? Suppose it is clear from the record that the Senate advice to favor ratification was premised on the belief that the agreement was not self-executing, is that determinative? (We will have occasion to consider in Chapter 6 the

19. International Coffee Agreement Act of 1965, Pub. L. No. 89–23, 79 Stat. 112 (codified at 19 U.S.C.A. sec. 1356a et seq.)

20. 109 Cong. Rec. 1926 (1963).

question of whether the General Agreement on Tariffs and Trade is a self-executing agreement.)[21]

On March 25, 2008, the US Supreme Court in Medellin v. Texas, ___ U.S. ___, 128 S.Ct. 1346, ___ L.Ed.2d ___ (2008) issued an opinion (6 to 3) in a complex case that could have profound effects on the questions discussed above and elsewhere in this and other chapters of this book, concerning the issue of self-executing treaties (or what some nations term "direct application" of treaties). The case involved the Vienna Convention on Consular Relations which requires parties (including the United States) to notify a citizen of a foreign nation arrested by a party government, that he is entitled to contact the consulate of the foreign nation of which he is a citizen. The US state of Texas made arrests and tried Mexican citizens for murder, and issued a death sentence including to a prisoner named Medellin, without notifying the accused as required. The International Court of Justice in a case brought by Mexico ruled the Mexican nationals were entitled to review and reconsideration of their state-court convictions and sentences in the US. The Mexican national brought a case in Texas to require the ICJ ruling to be carried out.

Despite a memorandum from the US President ordering the State of Texas to comply, the US Supreme Court (in an opinion by Chief Justice Roberts joined by four other justices, with a concurring opinion by Justice Stevens) affirmed the State court's decision not to do so. The Supreme Court's opinion held that the ICJ ruling did not have domestic legal effect in the United States, and so was not binding on the State of Texas. The opinion extensively discussed the relationship of international treaties and international tribunal rulings and indicated that for such rulings to be directly applied in the US required a high degree of clarity that such application was intended by the treaty, or by an act of Congress which so applied the treaty. A strong dissenting opinion by Justice Breyer (joined by Justices Souter and Ginsburg) noted a long series of precedents deemed by the dissenters to require a result contrary to the majority and set forth a series of other arguments why such a rigorous requirement of clarity should not be imposed. The language of the opinion could clearly have implications for other subjects, such as trade and international economic law. There will soon be elaborate literature to explore the implications of the opinion.

DETLEV F. VAGTS, THE UNITED STATES AND ITS TREATIES: OBSERVANCE AND BREACH[22]

It is generally agreed that some treaties of the United States are not self-executing, that is, that they cannot be enforced by the courts

21. Regarding how U.S. courts have evaluated whether a treaty is to be treated as self-executing, as described in John H. Jackson, The Jurisprudence of the GATT and the WTO: Insights on Treaty Law and Economic Relations ch. 17 (2000), based on

John H. Jackson, United States, in Francis G. Jacobs & Shelley Roberts (eds.), The Effect of Treaties in Domestic Law ch. 8 (1987).

22. 95 Am.J.Intl.L. 313, 321 (April 2001).

without further action by Congress. Which treaties are and which treaties are not self-executing is less clear.[23] Constitutionally, some treaties cannot be self-executing, most notably those that obligate the United States to pay money to a foreign state or to foreign parties, an obligation that cannot be carried out save by statute.[24] It has also been stated, though with less clear foundation, that a treaty cannot create criminal law.[25] Certain treaties have been found to be non-self-executing because the Senate clearly expressed such an intention or it can be implied. For present purposes, it suffices that there is a category of treaties that the United States is obligated to make domestically effective, although it has not done so.

CARLOS MANUEL VÁZQUEZ, THE FOUR DOCTRINES OF SELF–EXECUTING TREATIES[26]

The distinction between self-executing and non-self-executing treaties has particularly confounded the lower courts, whose decisions on the issue have produced a body of law that can only be described as being in a state of disarray. Much of the problem is the result of sloppy reasoning and careless use of precedent. For example, the Ninth Circuit recently dismissed a treaty argument out of hand with a simple citation to a Supreme Court footnote stating that a different provision of the treaty was not "self-executing."[27] (As noted, it is well accepted that certain provisions of a treaty may be self-executing while others are not.) But even the courts that have been somewhat more conscientious in attempting to classify treaties according to Chief Justice Marshall's distinction have been confounded by the unusual hybrid domestic/international nature of the distinction. Unfortunately, they have had little guidance from the Supreme Court, which has not said more than a sentence or two about the distinction in any case for nearly a century.

* * *

If integrity is to be restored in to this area of the law, the courts must recognize that the terms "self-executing" and "non-self-executing" do not have a unique meaning with respect to treaties. In examining "self-execution" arguments, the courts should therefore carefully consider the precise reason that the particular treaties before them are claimed

---

23. [original note 66] For recent controversial writing on the topic, see John C. Yoo, "Globalism and the Constitution: Treaties, Non–Self-Execution, and the Original Understanding," 99 Colum. L. Rev. 1955 (1999); Martin S. Flaherty, "History Right? Historical Scholarship, Original Understanding, and Treaties as 'Supreme Law of the Land,'" id., at 2095; Carlos Manuel Vázquez, "Laughing at Treaties," id. at 2154; John C. Yoo, "Treaties and Public Lawmaking: A Textual and Structural Defense of Non–Self-Execution," id. at 2218.

24. [original note 67] U.S. Const. Art. I, sec. 9.

25. [original note 68] The Over the Top, 5 F.2d 838, 843 (D.Conn.1925).

26. 89 Am.J.Intl.L. 695, 722–23 (October 1995).

27. [original note 136] See United States v. Aguilar, 883 F.2d 662, 680 (9th Cir.1989), cert. denied, 498 U.S. 1046, 111 S.Ct. 751, 112 L.Ed.2d 771 (1991).

to be judicially unenforceable, and in deciding the issue they should rely only on precedents involving that issue. Finally, and most importantly, the courts should decide the issue in full cognizance of the central role that the Constitution assigns to them in the enforcement of treaties.

————

In connection with trade agreements, the US Congress has been increasingly explicit about its desire that the agreements themselves not be self-executing. Section 102 of the implementing legislation for the Uruguay Round Agreements is a clear example of this.[28] Similar language can be found in implementing statutes relating to US free trade agreements with Israel, Canada and Canada/Mexico in the North American Free Trade Agreement.[29] See Section 6.7 infra.

Although a treaty is sometimes not self-executing or "directly applicable," it is a serious mistake to assume that the treaty is therefore irrelevant. Such a treaty does not have "statute-like" status and will not have its own text directly applied in a case, but the treaty nevertheless has some serious impacts and effects (despite some misguided federal court opinion language in that regard). The following are some (but not all) of those effects:

1) The jurisprudence of the US courts generally follows the idea that if any ambiguity exists in a statute which a court is interpreting, and one option is consistent with US international obligations and others are not, the court should choose the option which makes the US statute consistent (thus avoiding a US breach of its treaty obligations.) This was established by the *Charming Betsy* case early in US constitutional history, and is a principle enunciated in the Restatement of Foreign Relations Law.[30] In US courts recently, there have been a number of challenges to the use of *"Charming Betsy"* consistency principles, and some courts have refused to apply it in certain contexts. In particular, there has been noted a tension between *Charming Betsy*, and the *Chevron* case (See Section 3.5(C), below), which has led at least a few courts to rule in trade law contexts that *Chevron* (deference to the US government administrative agency concerned) should trump *Charming Betsy*. Question: Is the consistency principle required by international law as "good faith" application of a treaty (or other international rules)?

28. Uruguay Round Agreements Act, sec. 102; Pub. L. No. 103–182, § 102, 107 Stat. 2057, 2062 (1993) (codified at 19 U.S.C.A. sec. 3312); David W. Leebron, Implementation of the Uruguay Round Results in the United States, in John H. Jackson & Alan O. Sykes (eds.), Implementing the Uruguay Round 175, 211–218 (1997).

29. Uruguay Round Agreements Act, sec. 102; Pub.L.No. 103–182, sec. 102, 107 Stat. 2057, 2062 (1993) (codified at 19 U.S.C.A. sec. 3312) (NAFTA); Pub.L.No. 100–449, sec. 102, 102 Stat. 1851, 1853

(1988) (codified in note to 19 U.S.C.A. sec. 2112) (Canada); Pub.L.No. 99–47, sec. 5, 99 Stat. 82, 83 (1985) (codified in note to 19 U.S.C.A. sec. 2112) (Israel).

30. See American Law Institute, Restatement of the Law 3rd, Foreign Relations Law of the United States, Section 114 (1986). That section's notes cite the case of Murray v. Schooner Charming Betsy, 6 U.S. (2 Cranch) 64, 2 L.Ed. 208 (1804). See also the discussion above in this section 3.4 (C).

2) Sometimes a statute incorporates treaty language by reference, e.g., the statute says "the provisions of article X of the Treaty of Y shall apply in this case."

3) Sometimes a statute requires US officials or others to do their duty "consistent with Treaty X" or "consistent with Article 5 of Treaty X."

4) The legislative history of the statute may clearly or impliedly indicate that the purpose of the statute is to implement US obligations under a treaty. This gives legislative history weight to an interpretation choice which pursues this goal. In the 1994 Act implementing the Uruguay Round agreement, the statute itself says that the Congress "approves" the Statement of Administrative Action made by the President as required by the Fast Track procedure, and this seems to even strengthen the concept of choosing treaty consistency in some cases.

5) Treaty language may be deemed to articulate policies which the treaty parties including the United States have accepted, and those policies maybe used to help interpret a statute.

6) The existence of treaties accepted by the US may be indication of "federal preemption" of a subject matter, preventing state contrary action.[31]

7) So called soft law "rules", such as advisory or voluntary or moral obligations, could influence legal situations.

8) The *PLO* case (see subsection 3 below, and footnote 35.) The case stated (by US lower court decision) a very strong presumption in favor of the consistency principle, suggesting that it would be overcome only by very explicit indications by the legislature that it was intended that the US government would act inconsistently with its international obligations.

An additional question may arise in the *Charming Betsy* (consistency principle) approach, as to what is the international law rule to which consistency in domestic statute interpretation is called for? For example, is the decision of an international tribunal, such as the WTO Appellate Body, a statement of "international law"?

(2) An Individual's Right to Invoke International Agreements; Standing

Even if an international agreement is self-executing, it remains to determine if a particular individual is entitled to invoke the agreement's provisions.[32] In other words, does that individual have "standing?" For example, an international agreement may be self-executing in that federal government officials have authority to implement its provisions in their daily official tasks (e.g., apply a particular tariff to Company A,

---

31. See Bethlehem Steel Corp. v. Board of Commissions, described in Note 2 following the *Crosby* case in Section 3.6.

32. See generally Lori F. Damrosch, Louis Henkin, Richard C. Pugh, Oscar Schachter & Hans Smit, International Law: Cases and Materials 396–401 (4th ed. 2001).

or restrain the exports of Company B). On the other hand, a particular challenger (e.g., Company X) may not be sufficiently affected by the provision for the courts to grant it the right to invoke it.

A case that touches on these subjects is Diggs v. Richardson, 555 F.2d 848 (D.C.Cir.1976). This case concerned a United Nations Security Council Resolution calling upon U.N. members to have no dealings with South Africa that impliedly recognized the legality of its continued occupation of Namibia. Plaintiffs argued that the resolution was self-executing and that US government officials had violated its terms. The US government argued that Security Council resolutions are not legally binding, that the resolution at issue was not self-executing, that plaintiffs lacked standing and that the case concerned a political question not appropriate for judicial resolution. The Court of Appeals affirmed the dismissal of the case by the lower court (555 f.2d at 851), "on the ground, related to the issue of standing, but analytically distinct, that even assuming there is an international obligation that is binding on the United States—a point we do not in any way reach on the merits—the U.N. resolution underlying that obligation does not confer rights on the citizens of the United States that are enforceable in court in the absence of implementing legislation."

(3) *Hierarchy of Norms: Which Rules Take Precedence?*

If faced with a conflict between state and federal law or between an international agreement and a statute, a court must try to reconcile the opposing provisions. In doing so, a court should normally try to construe a statute so it does not conflict with international law or an international agreement of the United States.[33] If it is unable to do so, then it must decide which is superior. In the United States, federal law prevails over state law (see Section 3.6 below). Federal statutes and international agreements are deemed to be of the same rank, and thus generally it is considered that the later in time will prevail, at least in the case of treaties.[34]

In an interesting case concerning a US statute which prohibited certain foreign organizations (such as the Palestine Liberation Organization) from having offices in the US, including prohibition of an office permitted by the United Nations and thus arguably falling under a treaty provision binding the US, a federal district court "reconciled" the treaty provision with the statute by saying in effect that the statute did not explicitly say the Congress intended to violate its treaty obligations so the words of the statute which seemed clearly to mandate closing the PLO office, were not applied to do so. The case was not appealed by the Executive Branch (which had originally opposed the statutory clause).

---

33. American Law Institute, Restatement of the Law (Third), Foreign Relations Law of the United States sec. 114 (1987) [hereinafter Restatement].

34. Restatement, supra note 33, sec. 115. See, e.g. the Guy Capps case discussed in Section 3.2 supra; Swearingen v. United States, 565 F.Supp. 1019 (D.Colo.1983); Note, Superceding Statutory Law by Sole Executive Agreement: An Analysis of the American Law Institute's Shift in Position, 23 Va.J.Intl.L 671 (1983).

Thus it is not likely that this approach will be deemed to significantly influence future court cases, but the principle of requiring the Congress to be "super explicit" when they intend to act inconsistently with an international agreement, is an interesting approach with some merit.[35]

The following materials consider (a) whether the Treaty–Making Power expands federal constitutional authority, and (b) the position of executive agreements vis-à-vis state law.

(a) The Treaty Power and Domestic Legal Effect

The reader probably recalls the United States Supreme Court case of MISSOURI v. HOLLAND, 252 U.S. 416, 40 S.Ct. 382, 64 L.Ed. 641 (1920), which held that a valid treaty (with Canada relating to migratory birds) must prevail over state law, even if a United States federal statute on the subject might be considered an unconstitutional interference with state power in the absence of a treaty. Justice Holmes said in this case:[36]

> * * * Acts of Congress are the supreme law of the land only when made in pursuance of the Constitution, while treaties are declared to be so when made under the authority of the United States. It is open to question whether the authority of the United States means more than the formal acts prescribed to make the convention. We do not mean to imply that there are no qualifications to the treaty-making power; but they must be ascertained in a different way. It is obvious that there may be matters of the sharpest exigency for the national well-being that an act of Congress could not deal with but that a treaty followed by such an act could, and it is not lightly to be assumed that, in matters requiring national action, "a power which must belong to and somewhere reside in every civilized government" is not to be found.

Subsequent cases suggest some limitations on the treaty-making power, such as constitutional civil liberties limitations (see Reid v. Covert, 354 U.S. 1, 77 S.Ct. 1222, 1 L.Ed.2d 1148 (1957)), and matters of "purely domestic concern," such as the right to provide for the development of the United States share of the waters of the Niagara River, reserved to Congress in a 1950 Treaty with Canada. Power Authority of New York v. Federal Power Commission, 247 F.2d 538 (D.C.Cir.1957).

(b) Executive Agreements and Domestic Legal Effect

In UNITED STATES v. BELMONT, 301 U.S. 324, 57 S.Ct. 758, 81 L.Ed. 1134 (1937), the United States Supreme Court was confronted with President Roosevelt's decision to grant diplomatic recognition to the Union of Soviet Socialist Republics in exchange for, inter alia, the assignment to the US government of assets owned by a Russian corporation and located in the United States. The corporation had been nation-

---

35. United States v. Palestine Liberation Organization, 695 F.Supp. 1456 (S.D.N.Y.1988). See reference at John H. Jackson, Status of Treaties in Domestic Legal Systems, in The Jurisprudence of the GATT and the WTO: Insights on Treaty Law and Economic Relations ch. 18 (esp. p. 357 n. 118) (2000).

36. 252 U.S. at 433, 40 S.Ct. at 383.

alized by the Soviet government. In a challenge to the title of the United States to the assets, the Court stated that "(t)he recognition, establishment of diplomatic relations, the assignment, and agreements with respect thereto, were all parts of one transaction, resulting in an international compact between the two governments." It continued by affirming that the actions fell within the President's powers over external affairs and that the advice and consent of the Senate was not required as in the case of treaties.

The Court then observed that, "although this might not be a treaty requiring ratification by the Senate, it was a compact negotiated and proclaimed under the authority of the President, and as such was a 'treaty' within the meaning of the Circuit Court of Appeals Act, the construction of which might be reviewed upon direct appeal to this court."

"Plainly," continued the Court, "the external powers of the United States are to be exercised without regard to state laws or policies. The supremacy of a treaty in this respect has been recognized from the beginning. Mr. Madison, in the Virginia Convention, said that if a treaty does not supersede existing state laws, as far as they contravene its operation, the treaty would be ineffective. 'To counteract it by the supremacy of the state laws, would bring on the Union the just charge of national perfidy, and involve us in war.' * * * And while this rule in respect of treaties is established by the express language of cl. 2, Art. VI, of the Constitution, the same rule would result in the case of all international compacts and agreements from the very fact that complete power over international affairs is in the national government and is not and cannot be subject to any curtailment or interference on the part of the several states. Compare United States v. Curtiss–Wright Export Corp., 299 U.S. 304, 316 et seq., 57 S.Ct. 216, 81 L.Ed. 255." 301 U.S. at 330–331, 57 S.Ct. at 760–761.

Note

See also United States v. Pink, 315 U.S. 203, 62 S.Ct. 552, 86 L.Ed. 796 (1942).

SECTION 3.5   THE COURTS AND FOREIGN RELATIONS

(A) INTRODUCTION

The cases in the previous sections of this chapter suggest considerable hesitancy on the part of the courts to "second-guess" the President in his conduct of foreign affairs. As Professor Henkin has written "[F]oreign affairs make a difference. The courts are less willing to curb the political branches and have even developed doctrines of special deference to them. They have asserted judicial power to develop doctrines to safeguard the national interest in international relations against both judicial interference and invasion by the States.''[1]

One example of hesitancy by the federal courts to intrude into foreign affairs is the Act of State doctrine under which courts in the United States generally decline to examine the validity of acts of a governmental nature taken by a foreign sovereign government within its own territory. This doctrine has been held by the Supreme Court to be a matter of federal law, and therefore must be applied by state courts.[2] Although the Supreme Court has recognized that there may be exceptions to the doctrine, its hesitancy to intrude into foreign affairs is highlighted by the fact that the principal exception to the Act of State doctrine was created by Congress in reaction to the *Sabbatino* decision.[3] Similarly in the area of sovereign immunity (the general principle that a sovereign government cannot be sued without its consent), it has been Congress and not the courts that has taken the lead in expanding the jurisdiction of US courts into areas that those courts had been hesitant to enter.[4] These two topics are treated extensively in most international law casebooks and will not be examined here.[5]

In this section, we will look first at a leading Supreme Court case, where the Court goes out of its way to avoid reviewing action taken by a regulatory agency because the President had the final say over the agency's ultimate decision. We will then briefly look at how federal courts have reviewed a variety of executive decisions taken under the various statutes regulating international trade.

The reader will recall the note near the beginning of this chapter that draws attention to the extensive discussions and debate in the US about issues regarding the allocation of authority among the US separate powers (legislature, executive, courts, states). Much of this debate has also been related to the relationship of international law to domestic law in the US. Although most of this heated debate involves subjects of security related to human rights, and is not directly relevant to international economic matters, nevertheless the principles enunciated could quite often have relevance to decisions or measures involving international economic relations.

---

1. Louis Henkin, Foreign Affairs and the Constitution 206 (2nd ed. 1975).

2. Banco Nacional de Cuba v. Sabbatino, 376 U.S. 398, 84 S.Ct. 923, 11 L.E.2d 804 (1964).

3. 322 U.S.C.A. sec. 2370(e)(2). This exception, created by the so-called Second Hickenlooper Amendment, provides that a U.S. court shall not invoke the Act of State doctrine in cases of expropriation that are illegal under principles of international law unless the President suggests to the court that the doctrine should be applied.

4. See Foreign Sovereign Immunities Act of 1976, Pub.L.No. 94–583, 90 Stat. 2891.

5. See, e.g., William W. Bishop, International Law 659–700, 876–99 (3rd ed. 1971); Barry E. Carter & Phillip R. Trimble, International Law 595–708 (1999); Henry J. Steiner, Detlev F. Vagts & Harold H. Koh, Transnational Legal Problems: Material and Text 753–819 (4th ed. 1994).

(B) JUDICIAL REVIEW AND FOREIGN AFFAIRS

CHICAGO & SOUTHERN AIR LINES, INC. v. WATERMAN S.S. CORP.

Supreme Court of the United States, 1948.
333 U.S. 103, 68 S.Ct. 431, 92 L.Ed. 568.

MR. JUSTICE JACKSON delivered the opinion of the Court.

[By a five to four decision, the Supreme Court reversed a Court of Appeals decision and dismissed the petition of an airline company (Waterman) which was protesting the award of an international air route (between the US and a foreign country) to Chicago and Southern.]

Congress has set up a comprehensive scheme for regulation of common carriers by air. Many statutory provisions apply indifferently whether the carrier is a foreign air carrier or a citizen air carrier, and whether the carriage involved is "interstate air commerce," "overseas air commerce" or "foreign air commerce," each being appropriately defined. 49 U.S.C. § 401(20), 49 U.S.C.A. § 401(20). All air carriers by similar procedures must obtain from the [Civil Aeronautics Board (CAB)] certificates of convenience and necessity by showing a public interest in establishment of the route and the applicant's ability to serve it. But when a foreign carrier asks for any permit, or a citizen carrier applies for a certificate to engage in any overseas or foreign air transportation, a copy of the application must be transmitted to the President before hearing; and any decision, either to grant or to deny, must be submitted to the President before publication and is unconditionally subject to the President's approval. Also the statute subjects to judicial review "any order, affirmative or negative, issued by the Board under this Act, except any order in respect of any foreign air carrier subject to the approval of the President as provided in section 801 of this Act." It grants no express exemption to an order such as the one before us, which concerns a citizen carrier but which must have Presidential approval because it involves overseas and foreign air transportation. The question is whether an exemption is to be implied.

This Court long has held that statutes which employ broad terms to confer power of judicial review are not always to be read literally. Where Congress has authorized review of "any order" or used other equally inclusive terms, courts have declined the opportunity to magnify their jurisdiction, by self-denying constructions which do not subject to judicial control orders which, from their nature, from the context of the Act, or from the relation of judicial power to the subject-matter, are inappropriate for review.

* * *

* * * That aerial navigation routes and bases should be prudently correlated with facilities and plans for our own national defenses and raise new problems in conduct of foreign relations, is a fact of common knowledge. Congressional hearings and debates extending over several sessions and departmental studies of many years show that the legislative and administrative processes have proceeded in full recognition of these facts.

* * *

[W]hen a foreign carrier seeks to engage in public carriage over the territory or waters of this country, or any carrier seeks the sponsorship of this Government to engage in overseas or foreign air transportation, Congress has completely inverted the usual administrative process. Instead of acting independently of executive control, the agency is then subordinated to it. Instead of its order serving as a final disposition of the application, its force is exhausted when it serves as a recommendation to the President. Instead of being handed down to the parties as the conclusion of the administrative process, it must be submitted to the President, before publication even can take place. Nor is the President's control of the ultimate decision a mere right of veto. It is not alone issuance of such authorizations that are subject to his approval, but denial, transfer, amendment, cancellation or suspension, as well. And likewise subject to his approval are the terms, conditions and limitations of the order. 49 U.S.C. § 601, 49 U.S.C.A. § 601. Thus, Presidential control is not limited to a negative but is a positive and detailed control over the Board's decisions, unparalleled in the history of American administrative bodies.

Congress may of course delegate very large grants of its power over foreign commerce to the President. The President also possesses in his own right certain powers conferred by the Constitution on him as Commander-in-Chief and as the Nation's organ in foreign affairs. For present purposes, the order draws vitality from either or both sources. Legislative and Executive powers are pooled obviously to the end that commercial strategic and diplomatic interests of the country may be coordinated and advanced without collision or deadlock between agencies.

* * *

In this case, submission of the Board's decision was made to the President, who disapproved certain portions of it and advised the Board of the changes which he required. The Board complied and submitted a revised order and opinion which the President approved. Only then were they made public, and that which was made public and which is before us is only the final order and opinion containing the President's amendments and bearing his approval. Only at that stage was review sought and only then could it be pursued * * *.

While the changes made at direction of the President may be identified, the reasons therefore are not disclosed beyond the statement that "because of certain factors relating to our broad national welfare and other matters for which the Chief Executive has special responsibility, he has reached conclusions which require" changes in the Board's opinion.

The court below considered, and we think quite rightly, that it could not review such provisions of the order as resulted from Presidential direction. The President, both as Commander-in-Chief and as the Nation's organ for foreign affairs, has available intelligence services whose reports neither are nor ought to be published to the world. It would be intolerable that courts, without the relevant information, should review and perhaps nullify actions of the Executive taken on information properly held secret. Nor can courts sit in camera in order to be taken into executive confidences. But even if courts could require full disclosure, the very nature of executive decisions as to foreign policy is political, not judicial. Such decisions are wholly confided by our Constitution to the political departments of the government, Executive and Legislative. They are delicate, complex and involve large elements of prophecy. They are and should be undertaken only by those directly responsible to the people whose welfare they advance or imperil. They are decisions of a kind for which the Judiciary has neither aptitude, facilities nor responsibility and have long been held to belong in the domain of political power not subject to judicial intrusion or inquiry. We therefore agree that whatever of this order emanates from the President is not susceptible of review by the Judicial Department.

* * *

* * * The dilemma faced by those who demand judicial review of the Board's order is that, before Presidential approval, it is not a final determination even of the Board's ultimate action, and after Presidential approval, the whole order, both in what is approved without change, as well as in amendments which he directs, derives its vitality from the exercise of unreviewable Presidential discretion.

* * *

MR. JUSTICE DOUGLAS, with whom MR. JUSTICE BLACK, MR. JUSTICE REED and MR. JUSTICE RUTLEDGE concur, dissenting.

Notes and Questions

(1) The dissent in the foregoing case did not question the non-reviewability of the President's action. Rather, it argued that orders of the Board should be reviewable, because "[t]hose orders can be reviewed without any reference to any conduct by the President, for that part of the orders which is the work of the Board is plainly identifiable." The dissenters believed that such limited review would ensure that the Board had acted within the limits of its authority.

(2) In HAIG v. AGEE, 453 U.S. 280, 101 S.Ct. 2766, 69 L.Ed.2d 640 (1981), the Supreme Court upheld State Department regulations applied to revoke the passport of an American citizen who was engaged in a campaign to expose the identities of agents of the Central Intelligence Agency. In so doing, it stated (453 U.S. at 290–292, 101 S.Ct. at 2773–74):

The [1926] Passport Act does not in so many words confer upon the Secretary a power to revoke a passport. Nor, for that matter, does it expressly authorize denials of passport applications. Neither, however, does any statute expressly limit those powers. It is beyond dispute that the Secretary has the power to deny a passport for reasons not specified in the statutes. * * * Particularly in light of the "broad rule-making authority granted in the [1926] Act," Zemel [v. Rusk], 381 U.S., at 12, 85 S.Ct., at 1278 [1965], a consistent administrative construction of that statute must be followed by the courts " 'unless there are compelling indications that it is wrong.' "This is especially so in the areas of foreign policy and national security, where congressional silence is not to be equated with congressional disapproval. * * * Applying these considerations to statutory construction, the Zemel Court observed:

> [B]ecause of the changeable and explosive nature of contemporary international relations, and the fact that the Executive is immediately privy to information which cannot be swiftly presented to, evaluated by, and acted upon by the legislature, Congress—in giving the Executive authority over matters of foreign affairs—must of necessity paint with a brush broader than that it customarily wields in domestic areas.

The opinion by Chief Justice Burger in this 7–2 decision was issued three days before Dames & Moore v. Regan, discussed in Section 3.2(B) supra.

(3) Are the policy reasons for deference to presidential discretion when exercised in the area of foreign affairs persuasive? Do these reasons adequately provide a rationale for distinguishing between foreign and domestic affairs as to the degree of judicial review that is appropriate? Do any of the reasons stated as applying to foreign affairs also apply to domestic affairs? If the world continues on a course of greater and greater economic (and other) interdependence, and more of everyone's affairs become intertwined with international transactions or policies, will a policy of greater deference to executive prerogative in foreign affairs cause serious inroads into the US constitutional system of checks and balances? Of protection of individual citizen rights?

(4) The February 1, 1977 issue of Forbes magazine at page 23, described the procedure for presidential determinations under § 801 of the Federal Aviation Act as "a political cesspool," in reporting on an application by Delta Airlines for a transatlantic route from London to Atlanta and Texas which had been recommended by the CAB, but sent back by President Ford for a new analysis. The Forbes article suggested that the President's action may have been politically motivated because the outgoing administration was "piqued at the South, which voted for Carter." The article concludes: "If there is a moral to this, it is that Section 801 causes more trouble than it is worth. The State Department negotiates landing rights with other countries; by itself the CAB should decide which US carriers fly under them. Other regulators—in international banking and telecommunications, for example—deal with foreign policy issues." (The CAB no longer exists; its functions were taken over by the Department of Transportation.)

(5) In UNITED STATES v. ALVAREZ–MACHAIN, 504 U.S. 655, 112 S.Ct. 2188, 119 L.Ed.2d 441 (1992), the Court refused to deny US courts jurisdiction to try a Mexican citizen who was kidnapped in Mexico through activity allegedly induced by the United States government officials and

brought to the United States and arrested for conspiracy to murder a US Drug Enforcement Agent. The Supreme Court, with three dissents, upheld the arrest and concluded that an extradition treaty did not prevent it. At one point in the majority opinion, the Court said (112 S.Ct. at 2196):

> Respondent and his amici may be correct that respondent's abduction was "shocking," Tr. of Oral Arg. 40, and that it may be in violation of general international law principles. Mexico has protested the abduction of respondent through diplomatic notes, App. 33–38, and the decision of whether respondent should be returned to Mexico, as a matter outside of the Treaty, is a matter for the Executive Branch.

In a footnote the Court comments on "the advantage of the diplomatic approach to the resolution of difficulties between two sovereign nations, as opposed to unilateral action by the Courts of one nation." 504 U.S. at 669, 112 S.Ct. at 2196 n.16.

(C) JUDICIAL REVIEW OF ADMINISTRATIVE ACTION: THE PROBLEM OF STANDARD OF REVIEW

STEPHEN P. CROLEY & JOHN H. JACKSON, WTO DISPUTE PROCEDURES, STANDARD OF REVIEW, AND DEFERENCE TO NATIONAL GOVERNMENTS[6]

Until fairly recently, and broadly speaking, reviewing courts exercised considerable deference with respect to agencies' "factual" determinations, and accorded less deference to agencies' "legal" decisions.[7] This two-tiered approach reflected a familiar division of function between the separate branches of government, according to which agencies were to handle the more or less "technical" aspects of statutory implementation, while courts were to ensure that agencies exercised their authority within the boundaries of the law. This bifurcated approach also followed the US Administrative Procedure Act's direction for courts to "decide all relevant questions of law,"[8] which itself reflected traditional understandings of the proper roles of courts and agencies. Traditionally, judicial deference to agencies' legal determinations required special justification, whereas deference to factual determinations did not. That general rule was altered, however, in 1984, when the US Supreme Court handed its decision in Chevron U.S.A. v. Natural Resources Defense Council, Inc.,[9] in which the Court articulated a new standard of review for agencies' interpretations of law—the *Chevron* doctrine.

THE CHEVRON DOCTRINE

Courts applying the *Chevron* doctrine face to sequential questions, often referred to as "step one" and "step two" of *Chevron*. First: Has

---

6. Reproduced with permission from 90 AJIL 193, 202–204 (1996). The American Society of International Law.

7. [original note 38] See, e.g., FTC v. Gratz, 253 U.S. 421, 427, 40 S.Ct. 572, 64 L.Ed. 993 (1920).

8. [original note 39] 5 U.S.C. § 706 (1988).

9. [original note 40] 467 U.S. 837, 104 S.Ct. 2778, 81 L.Ed.2d 694 (1984).

Congress "directly spoken to the precise question at issue,"[10] or is the statute interpreted by the agency "silent or ambiguous"?[11] To answer this question, the reviewing court applies the "traditional tools of statutory construction."[12] If upon applying those traditional tools, the reviewing court concludes that Congress has indeed spoken to the precise issue in question, then "that is the end of the matter";[13] the court will hold the agency faithful to Congress's will, as unambiguously expressed in the statute.[14]

If the court concludes instead that the statute is "silent or ambiguous" with respect to the interpretive question at issue, then the reviewing court proceeds to a second question—step two: Is the agency's interpretation of the statute a "reasonable" or "permissible" one?[15] If the court determines that the agency's interpretation is not reasonable, then the court will defer to the agency's interpretation, even if—and this is the bite of the *Chevron* doctrine—the agency's interpretation is not one the court would have adopted had it considered the question on its own.[16]

* * *

According to many US administrative law scholars, the *Chevron* doctrine constituted a significant shift of power from courts to the agencies.[17] * * * [T]he shift is commonly justified by reference to some of the most important principles underlying US administrative government—expertise, accountability and administrative efficiency.

Note

Professor Thomas Merrill has observed that in practice, the effects of the *Chevron* decision on judicial treatment of administrative decisions appears to have been limited:[18]

10. [original note 42] Id. at 842.

11. [original note 43] Id. at 843.

12. [original note 44] Id. n.9; see also K Mart Corp. v. Cartier, Inc., 486 U.S. 281, 300, 108 S.Ct. 1811, 100 L.Ed.2d 313 (1988) (Brennan, J. concurring); NLRB v. United Food & Commercial Workers Union, Local 23, 484 U.S. 112, 123, 108 S.Ct. 413, 98 L.Ed.2d 429 (1987); INS v. Cardoza–Fonseca, 480 U.S. 421, 446, 107 S.Ct. 1207, 94 L.Ed.2d 434 (1987).

13. [original note 45] Chevron, 467 U.S. at 842.

14. [original note 46] For examples of lower courts' invocation of step one of the Chevron doctrine, see, e.g., Skandalis v. Rowe, 14 F.3d 173, 178–79 (2d Cir.1994); Sweet Home Chapter of Communities for a Great Oregon v. Babbitt, 17 F.3d 1463, 1464 (D.C.Cir.1994), rev'd on other grounds, 515 U.S. 687, 115 S.Ct. 2407, 132 L.Ed.2d 597 (1995); Satellite Broadcasting & Communications Ass'n of Am. v. Oman, 17 F.3d 344, 348 (11th Cir.), cert. denied, 513 U.S. 823, 115 S.Ct. 88, 130 L.Ed.2d 40 (1994).

15. [original note 47] Chevron, 467 U.S. at 842–44.

16. [original note 48] Id. At 843 n. 11 ("The court need not conclude that the agency construction was the only one it permissibly could have adopted to uphold the construction, or even the reading the court would have reached if the question initially had arisen in a judicial proceeding.") (citations omitted).

17. [original note 51] See, e.g., Davis & Pierce, [Administrative Law Treatise], sec. 3.3 [3d ed. 1984].

18. Thomas W. Merrill, Judicial Deference to Executive Precedent, 101 Yale L.J. 969, 982–985 (1992). Reprinted by permission of the Yale Law Journal and Fred B. Rothman & Company from The Yale Law Journal, vol. 101, pp. 969–1041.

* * * First, it is clear that *Chevron* [was] often ignored by the Supreme Court [in the years following the decision].

* * *

Second, although *Chevron* is generally regarded as directing that courts give greater deference to executive interpretations, there is no discernible relationship between the application of the *Chevron* framework and greater acceptance of the executive view. Indeed, cases applying *Chevron* have on the whole produced fewer affirmances of executive interpretations than those that do not follow *Chevron*.

* * *

Third, * * * the emergence of *Chevron* has caused a decline in reliance on the traditional contextual factors for determining whether deference is appropriate.

(D) FEDERAL COURT REVIEW OF ADMINISTRATIVE TRADE ACTIONS

(1) The Court of International Trade[19]

Most litigation involving international trade statutes in the United States now occurs in the Court of International Trade (CIT). The CIT was formerly known as the Customs Court. It received its new name in a 1980 statute that also significantly expanded its jurisdiction.[20] The CIT is a court of nine judges, no more than five of whom may belong to any one political party. It is based in New York City. Its decisions are appealable to the US Court of Appeals for the Federal Circuit and ultimately to the Supreme Court.

The CIT has exclusive jurisdiction under 28 U.S.C.A. section 1581 over appeals or actions involving (a) denials of protests by the US Customs Service, (b) challenges by US competitors of import classification decisions, (c) antidumping and countervailing duty cases, (d) trade adjustment assistance to workers, firms and communities, (e) country of origin determinations, (f) disputes over the confidentiality of information submitted to the International Trade Commission, (g) customshouse brokers' licenses, (h) challenges by importers of classification decisions and (i) the United States as a defendant that arise out of any law providing for revenues from imports; tariffs, duties, fees or other taxes

19. See generally William J. Davey, The United States Court of International Trade and the Court of Appeals for the Federal Circuit, in Adjudication of International Trade Disputes in International and National Economic Law 297–322 (Ernst-Ulrich Petersmann & Günther Jaenicke eds., 1992).

20. Customs Courts Act of 1980, Pub.L. No. 96–417, 94 Stat. 1727. The exclusive jurisdiction of the Court of International Trade was made broader in 1980 in part to avoid the problem of conflicting decisions on trade issues arising in the District Courts. Prior to the 1980 Act, there was confusion as to the extent of the Customs Court's exclusive jurisdiction and some parties preferred to litigate in District Courts because the limited powers of the Customs Court often meant they could not obtain what they viewed as appropriate relief (e.g., injunctions). See H.Rep. No. 96–1235, 96th Cong., 2d Sess. 19 (1980). See generally Recent Developments, The Customs Courts Act of 1980, 13 Law & Poly.Intl.Bus. 281 (1981).

on imports; and embargoes or quantitative restrictions on imports (other than those imposed for public health and safety reasons).[21] It also has jurisdiction under 28 U.S.C.A. section 1582 over civil actions by the United States to recover duties, penalties and customs bonds. The 1980 Act in general greatly expanded access to the CIT to include most persons with a real interest in challenging or defending a trade-related action.[22]

The scope of review in the CIT depends on the type of action brought. A trial "de novo" is held in actions brought by the United States under section 1582 and in cases where jurisdiction is based on section 1581, category (a), (b), (e), (f) or (g) of the preceding paragraph.[23] In antidumping and countervailing duty cases, certain government actions are reviewed to determine if they were arbitrary, capricious, an abuse of discretion or unlawful; while others are reviewed to determine if they were supported by substantial evidence in the agency record or unlawful.[24] In some antidumping or countervailing duty cases, the courts have been very intrusive in altering administrative actions. In trade adjustment assistance cases, the determinations of the agency are considered conclusive if supported by substantial evidence in the record, but the CIT has the authority for good cause shown to order the agency to take further evidence.[25] In other actions, the CIT's review is made pursuant to the Administrative Procedure Act, which generally establishes a substantial-evidence standard for agency action taken on a record and an arbitrary-capricious standard for other agency action.[26]

(2) Judicial Review in International Trade Cases

This somewhat complex structure of review for international trade actions taken by the Executive Branch largely reflects a desire by Congress to limit Executive discretion under certain trade statutes. Given the opportunity, private litigants quickly began to challenge Executive action more frequently. Indeed, challenges of preliminary decisions in antidumping and countervailing duty cases became so burdensome that Congress limited them in 1984.[27] We will consider recent CIT and Federal Circuit decisions in some detail when we examine the various US trade statutes in later parts of this book. Here we will only try to give a flavor of the scrutiny provided by the CIT and the Federal Circuit and of how it seems to vary depending on the nature of the challenged action.

Escape Clause. MAPLE LEAF FISH CO. v. UNITED STATES, 762 F.2d 86 (Fed.Cir.1985), arose under the so-called escape clause. The issue

---

21. There is an exception to the CIT's jurisdiction for imports of obscene materials.

22. See 28 U.S.C.A. sec. 2631.

23. 28 U.S.C.A. sec. 2640(a).

24. 28 U.S.C.A. sec. 2640(b); 19 U.S.C.A. sec. 1516a.

25. 28 U.S.C.A. sec. 2640(c); 19 U.S.C.A. sec. 2395(b).

26. 28 U.S.C.A. sec. 2640(d); 5 U.S.C.A. sec. 706.

27. Trade and Tariff Act of 1984, sec. 623 (elimination of interlocutory appeals), Pub.L. No. 98–573, 98 Stat. 2948, amending 19 U.S.C.A. sec. 1516a.

was the standard of review to be applied to a challenge to the President's decision to order import relief measures after the International Trade Commission (ITC) had found that the US prepared and preserved mushroom industry was being injured by imports of those products. The Court ruled (762 F.2d at 89):

> The critical element is that the area of the "escape clause" legislation undoubtedly involves the President and his close relationship to foreign affairs, our nation's connections with other countries, and the external ramifications of international trade. More than that, Congress has vested the President with very broad discretion and choice as to what he decides to do affirmatively, or even whether he should do anything. * * *

> In international trade controversies of this highly discretionary kind—involving the President and foreign affairs—this court and its predecessors have often reiterated the very limited role of reviewing courts. For a court to interpose, there has to be clear misconstruction of the governing statute, a significant procedural violation, or action outside delegated authority. On the other hand, "[t]he President's findings of fact and the motivations for his action are not subject to review."

Multifiber Arrangement. In upholding action taken by the Executive Branch in respect of limitations on textile imports against challenges alleging statutory, administrative and constitutional defects, the Court of Appeals for the Federal Circuit stated:

> We accentuate, again, that legislation conferring upon the President discretion to regulate foreign commerce involves, and is reinforced and augmented by, the President's constitutional power to oversee the political side of foreign affairs. In the area of international trade, "intimately involved in foreign affairs," "congressional authorizations of presidential power should be given a broad construction and not 'hemmed in' or 'cabined, cribbed, confined' by anxious judicial blinders."

AMERICAN ASSN. OF EXPORTERS & IMPORTERS—TEXTILE & APPAREL GROUP v. UNITED STATES, 751 F.2d 1239, 1248 (Fed.Cir. 1985).

Adjustment Assistance. In KATUNICH v. DONOVAN, 594 F.Supp. 744 (CIT 1984), an appeal of the Secretary of Labor's decision to refuse to grant benefits under the Trade Act of 1974, the CIT stated (594 F.Supp. at 753):

> In light of the Secretary's admission that "1980 would have been a better year for the present analysis," it was incumbent upon the Secretary to make a greater effort to obtain the required information. The record does not reveal any efforts made by the Secretary to obtain the necessary information for a meaningful evaluation of plaintiffs' petition.

Summary. If any conclusion can be drawn from the foregoing, it would seem to be that where courts are dealing with detailed statutory provisions, with legislative history that indicates dissatisfaction with past administration of those laws, such as the antidumping and countervailing duty laws, they are willing to exercise serious oversight of Executive Branch actions on the grounds that Congress has specified in some detail what rights it wishes to be protected. On the other hand, where courts are dealing with broad grants of power to the President or ministerial actions involving Customs administration, they are unlikely to second guess the Executive Branch.

(3) Costs of Judicial Review

The large increase in trade-related cases brought in the federal courts in the last few years has caused some to wonder if the costs of judicial review of complex administrative procedures are too high. One of the authors of this book has contrasted the benefits of the present system—promotion of open, informed, consistent decision-making by trade officials, giving every interested party a "day in court" and thereby promoting acceptance of decisions—with the costs—the risk of creating inflexible rules, unjustified harassment of weaker parties, large fees payable to lawyers and economists. His conclusions are set out in Chapter 25. As we analyze the operation of the many US trade laws, the reader should attempt to form a view of whether the costs would seem to outweigh the apparent benefits.

(4) Scope of International "Judicial" Review

In recent years the question of the standard of review for an international dispute settlement panel, such as those in the GATT or the new WTO dispute settlement systems, has been more prominent. It was even a major issue in the final weeks of negotiation of the Uruguay Round in December 1993. This matter will be taken up in Chapter 7 when we deal with WTO dispute settlement.

SECTION 3.6   FEDERAL–STATE RELATIONS AND INTERNATIONAL ECONOMIC REGULATION

(A) INTRODUCTION

The United States has a federal form of government under its Constitution. A constitutional US federal law overrides an inconsistent state law, although the Constitution places some limits on the powers of Congress and the federal government. The division of powers between the federal government and the state governments involves several important questions involved here.

First, what constitutional limits are there on the federal government, due to the federal structure of the United States? (It can plausibly be argued there are none, at least as to foreign affairs, although there clearly are political constraints resulting from a federal structure.) Second, the reverse question is what constitutional constraints are there on state government exercise of power, especially when that exercise affects international economic affairs (as almost everything does today)? This requires examination of several subordinate situations, such as: a) the case where the federal government has established a rule that conflicts with state law, and b) the case where there is no federal rule. Finally, it is useful to examine the evolution of cooperative mechanisms for state participation in federal activities regarding international economic relations.

The questions that remain troublesome in the area of federal–state relations concern the power of the states to regulate and tax foreign commerce. The Constitution authorizes the federal government to regulate such commerce, but what state power exists when the federal government has not acted or prohibited state action? The cases in this section have been selected to highlight important issues of federal–state relations as applied to international trade, such as:

(A) Can states ever regulate goods imported from a foreign country? Or exports to be sent to a foreign country? If they are not preempted, how far can they go? Are the tests of the limits on state power over interstate commerce also to be applied to foreign commerce, or will different tests be used?

(B) To what degree can states tax imports from another country? Tax foreign companies?

(C) Is there any limit on what the federal government can do by way of preventing state government actions which affect foreign commerce? Do these limits vary depending on whether imports or exports are involved? Do they apply to services as well as goods?

These questions cannot all be answered definitively, but the materials in the following sub-sections will provide some insights. We will return to some of these issues later in the book.

(B) FEDERAL CONSTRAINTS ON FEDERAL POWERS TO REGULATE AND MAKE TREATIES CONCERNING INTERNATIONAL ECONOMIC RELATIONS

JOHN H. JACKSON, UNITED STATES LAW AND IMPLEMENTATION OF THE TOKYO ROUND NEGOTIATION[1]

Since the structure of the US government under its Constitution is federal in nature—that is, it consists not only of a central government but also of state governments that have considerable independent authority and sovereignty—it might be thought that the division of powers

---

1. From John H. Jackson, Jean—Victor Louis & Mitsuo Matsushita, Implementing the Tokyo Round: National Constitutions and International Economic Rules 142–143 (1984). Reprinted by permission of the author.

between the federal and state governments would be an important constraint on the scope of federal government action in the area of foreign affairs.

There has been a long and extraordinarily detailed history of constitutional evolution and accommodation between state powers and the federal powers. * * * Furthermore, in domestic affairs, the evolution of US constitutional law has been generally in the direction of concentrating power in the federal government. It is reasonably well established today that the federal government has supremacy, if it chooses to exercise it, over almost all issues that have any commercial overtones.

* * *

In foreign affairs, there is virtually no Supreme Court opinion that rules against the exercise of federal power on the grounds that it conflicts with state power, as long as the exercise of federal power was itself otherwise constitutional. Thus, although the Supreme Court has held that state powers sometimes prevail over international treaties (such as in the offshore oil cases), the basis for this decision was itself an exercise of federal power, namely an Act of Congress.

The courts and federal authorities can rely on a number of clauses in the Constitution in arguing that the exercise of federal power will prevail over state power in the areas of foreign relations. Such clauses include the commerce clause, the supremacy clause, the treaty clause, and clauses on presidential power, including his power to receive ambassadors, and his authority as Commander in Chief.

Notes and Questions

(1) In 1976, the Supreme Court (in a 5–4 decision) placed some limits on the power of the federal government to regulate state and local governments in National League of Cities v. Usery, 426 U.S. 833, 96 S.Ct. 2465, 49 L.Ed.2d 245 (1976), where it held that certain provisions of the Fair Labor Standards Act could not be applied to state and local government employees. The Court ruled essentially that the federal government could not impair the attributes of state sovereignty by regulating the wages of state employees and thereby interfering with the integral governmental functions of states. That case was overruled in a 5–4 decision in 1985. Garcia v. San Antonio Metropolitan Transit Authority, 469 U.S. 528, 105 S.Ct. 1005, 83 L.Ed.2d 1016 (1985). It remains to be seen whether the Court, as predicted by one dissenter, will reverse itself again soon.

In NEW YORK v. UNITED STATES, 505 U.S. 144, 112 S.Ct. 2408, 120 L.Ed.2d 120 (1992), the Supreme Court expressly declined to reconsider the holding in *Garcia*. In discussing the ability of the federal government to influence State regulatory decisions, the Court wrote (505 U.S. at 167, 112 S.Ct. at 2423–2424):

First, under Congress' spending power, "Congress may attach conditions on the receipt of federal funds." * * *

Second, where Congress has the authority to regulate private activity under the Commerce Clause, we have recognized Congress' power to offer States the choice of regulating that activity according to federal standards or having state law preempted by federal regulation. * * *

* * *

By contrast, where the Federal Government compels States to regulate, [such compulsion is invalid].

(2) In Section 3.4(C)(3) we previously noted the case of Missouri v. Holland, 252 U.S. 416, 40 S.Ct. 382, 64 L.Ed. 641 (1920), in which the Court held that the federal government's powers vis-a-vis the states could be enlarged by the conclusion of an international agreement or treaty. Does this mean that the federal government can effectively regulate on matters (if any) otherwise reserved to states if it first enters into a treaty on the subject?

(C) STATE REGULATION AND FOREIGN COMMERCE

(1) Introduction

Considerably more US federal court activity has concerned constitutional limits on state regulation which affects foreign commerce. First, where the federal government has acted in a particular area, by a statute, treaty or otherwise, several different situations can be analyzed: the case of a direct and explicit clash between the federal and the state law; and a situation where the federal government has acted but the clash between federal and state law is only implicit (a situation analyzed under the "preemption doctrine"). Second, where the federal government has not acted at all, the "dormant commerce clause" and related questions are raised.

(2) Federal Action and Federal Rules that Clash With State Rules

Notes and Questions

(1) In Section 3.4(C)(3), we discussed the general problems of "hierarchy of norms," i.e. which of two clashing rules should prevail. Here we face that question in the context of a federal-state conflict, but regarding not only international agreements but other federal law making (statute, regulation, etc.). The Restatement notes, "Since any treaty or other international agreement of the United States, and any rule of customary international law, is federal law * * *, it supersedes inconsistent State law or policy whether adopted earlier or later."[2]

(2) The issue of preemption is usually framed as follows: Although there may not be a direct clash between some federal rule and a state rule, if there is sufficient federal government regulatory and rule making activity that a court could imply that the federal government intended to exclude state action, i.e., to "preempt the field," then no state action concerning the particular subject matters would be valid. The most

2. American Law Institute, Restatement of the Law (Third), Foreign Relations Law of the United States, sec. 115 comment e (1987).

important case in this respect is Crosby v. National Foreign Trade Council.

CROSBY v. NATIONAL FOREIGN TRADE COUNCIL

Supreme Court of the United States, 2000.
530 U.S. 363, 120 S.Ct. 2288, 147 L.Ed.2d 352.

JUSTICE SOUTER delivered the opinion of the Court.

* * *

In June 1996, Massachusetts adopted an "Act Regulating State Contracts with Companies Doing Business with or in Burma (Myanmar)," 1996 Mass. Acts 239, ch. 130 (codified at Mass. Gen. Laws secs. 7:22G–7:22M, 40 F. 1/2 (1997)). The Statute generally bars state entities from buying goods or services from any person (defined to include a business organization) identified on a "restricted purchase list" of those doing business with Burma. * * *

* * *

[Three months later,] Congress passed a statute imposing a set of mandatory and conditional sanctions on Burma. See Foreign Operations, Export Financing, and Related Programs Appropriations Act, 1997, sec. 570, 110 Stat. 3009–166 to 3009–167 (enacted by the Omnibus Consolidated Appropriations Act, 1997, sec. 101(c), 110 Stat. 3009–121 to 3009–172). * * *

[The federal Act] imposes three sanctions directly on Burma. [First,] it bans all aid to the Burmese government except for humanitarian assistance, counternarcotics efforts, and promotion of human rights and democracy. The statute instructs United States representatives to international financial institutions to vote against loans or other assistance to or from Burma, and it provides that no entry visa shall be issued to any Burmese government official unless required by treaty or to staff the Burmese mission to the United Nations. These restrictions are to remain in effect "[u]ntil such time as the President determines and certifies to Congress that Burma has made measurable and substantial progress in improving human rights practices and implementing democratic government." Sec. 570(a).

Second, the federal Act authorizes the President to impose further sanctions subject to certain conditions. Sec. 570(b). * * *

Third, the statute directs the President to work to develop "a comprehensive, multilateral strategy to bring democracy to and improve human rights practices and the quality of life in Burma." Sec. 570(c). * * *

[A] fourth section requires the President to report periodically to certain congressional committee chairmen on the progress toward democratization and better living conditions in Burma as well as on the development of the required strategy. Sec. 570(d). And [a] fifth part

* * * authorizes the President "to waive, temporarily or permanently, any sanction [under the federal act] . . . if he determines and certifies to Congress that the application of such sanction would be contrary to the national security interests of the United States." Sec. 570(e).

* * *

Respondent National Foreign Trade Council is a nonprofit corporation representing companies engaged in foreign commerce; 34 of its members were on the Massachusetts restricted purchase list in 1998. Three withdrew from Burma after the passage of the state Act, and one member had its bid for a procurement contract increased by 10 percent under the provision of the state law allowing acceptance of a low bid from a listed bidder only if the next-to-lowest bid is more than 10 percent higher.

[Previously,] the Council filed suit in the United States District Court for the District of Massachusetts, seeking declaratory and injunctive relief against the petitioner state officials charged with administering and enforcing the state Act. The Council argued that the state law unconstitutionally infringed on the federal foreign affairs power, violated the Foreign Commerce Clause, and was preempted by the federal Act. * * * [T]he District Court permanently enjoined enforcement of the state Act, holding that it "unconstitutionally impinge[d] on the federal government's exclusive authority to regulate foreign affairs."

The United States Court of Appeals for the First Circuit affirmed on three independent grounds. It found the state Act unconstitutionally interfered with the foreign affairs power of the National Government under Zschernig v. Miller, 389 U.S. 429, 88 S.Ct. 664, 19 L.Ed.2d 683 (1968); violated the dormant Foreign Commerce Clause, U.S. Const. Art. I, sec. 8, cl. 3; and was preempted by the congressional Burma Act.

* * *

A fundamental principle of the Constitution is that Congress has the power to preempt state law. Even without an express provision for preemption, we have found that state law must yield to a congressional Act in at least two circumstances. When Congress intends federal law to "occupy the field," state law in that area is preempted. And even if Congress has not occupied the field, state law is naturally preempted to the extent of any conflict with a federal statute. We will find preemption where it is impossible for a private party to comply with both state law and federal law, and where "under the circumstances of [a] particular case, [the challenged state law] stands as an obstacle to the accomplishment and execution of the full purposes and objectives of Congress." Hines v. Davidowitz, 312 U.S. 52, at 67, 61 S.Ct. 399, 85 L.Ed. 581 (1941). What is a sufficient obstacle is a matter of judgment, to be informed by examining the federal statute as a whole and identifying its purpose and intended effects. * * *

[W]e see the state Burma law as an obstacle to the accomplishment of Congress's full objectives under the federal Act. We find that the state law undermines the intended purpose and "natural effect" of at least three provisions of the federal Act. * * *

First, Congress clearly intended the federal act to provide the President with flexible and effective authority over economic sanctions against Burma. Although Congress immediately put in place a set of initial sanctions, * * * it authorized the President to terminate any and all of those measures upon determining and certifying that there had been progress in human rights and democracy in Burma. It invested the President with the further power to ban new investment by United States persons, dependent only on specific Presidential findings of repression in Burma. And, most significantly, Congress empowered the President "to waive, temporarily or permanently, any sanction [under the federal act] . . . if he determines and certifies to Congress that the application of such sanction would be contrary to the national security interests of the United States."

* * * [T]he statute has placed the President in a position with as much discretion to exercise economic leverage against Burma, with an eye toward national security, as our law will admit. And it is just this plenitude of Executive authority that we think controls the issue of preemption here. The President has been given this authority not just to make a political statement but to achieve a political result. It is simply implausible that Congress would have gone to such lengths to empower the President if it had been willing to compromise his effectiveness by deference to every provision of state statute or local ordinance that might, if enforced, blunt the consequences of discretionary Presidential action.

And that is just what the Massachusetts Burma law would do in imposing a different system of economic pressure against the Burmese political regime. * * * [T]he state statute penalizes some private action that the federal Act * * * may allow, and pulls levers of influence that the federal Act does not reach. But the point here is that the state sanctions are immediate and perpetual, there being no termination provision. This unyielding application undermines the President's intended statutory authority by making it impossible for him to restrain fully the coercive power of the national economy when he may choose to take the discretionary action open to him * * *. Quite simply, if the Massachusetts law is enforceable the President has less to offer and less economic and diplomatic leverage as a consequence. * * * It thus "stands as an obstacle to the accomplishment and execution of the full purposes and objectives of Congress."

[Second,] Congress manifestly intended to limit economic pressure against the Burmese Government to a specific range. * * * Congress's calibrated Burma policy is a deliberate effort "to steer a middle path."

The State has set a different course, and its statute conflicts with federal law at a number of points by penalizing individuals and conduct that Congress has explicitly exempted or excluded from sanctions. [The Court furthermore points at differences in the scope of subject matter addressed by the ban and the class of companies at which the acts are aimed.]

The conflicts are not rendered irrelevant by the State's argument that there is no real conflict between the statutes because they share the same goals and because some companies may comply with both sets of restrictions. The fact of a common end hardly neutralizes conflicting means, and the fact that some companies may be able to comply with both sets of sanctions does not mean that the state Act is not at odds with achievement of the federal decision about the right degree of pressure to employ. * * * Sanctions are drawn not only to bar what they prohibit but to allow what they permit, and the inconsistency of sanctions here undermines the congressional calibration of force.

Finally, the state Act is at odds with the President's intended authority to speak for the United States among the world's nations in developing a "comprehensive, multilateral strategy to bring democracy to and improve human rights practices and the quality of life in Burma." * * * As with Congress's explicit delegation to the President of power over economic sanctions, Congress's express command to the President to take the initiative for the United States among the international community invested him with the maximum authority of the National Government, cf. Youngstown Sheet & Tube Co., 343 U.S., at 635, 72 S.Ct. 863, in harmony with the President's own constitutional powers. * * *

Again, the state Act undermines the President's capacity, in this instance for effective diplomacy. It is not merely that the differences between the state and federal Acts in scope and type of sanctions threaten to complicate discussions; they compromise the very capacity of the President to speak for the Nation with one voice in dealing with other governments. * * *

* * *

The State's remaining argument * * * contends that the failure of Congress to preempt the state Act demonstrates implicit permission. * * *

The argument is unconvincing on more than one level. A failure to provide preemption expressly may reflect nothing more than the settled character of implied preemption doctrine that courts will dependably apply, and in any event, the existence of conflict cognizable under the Supremacy Clause does not depend on express congressional recognition that federal and state law may conflict. Hines, 312 U.S., at 67, 61 S.Ct. 399. The State's interference of congressional intent is unwarranted here, therefore, simply because the silence of Congress is ambiguous.

Notes

(1) Although the Supreme Court affirmed the judgment of the Court of Appeals, we will see in the following note that it did so not on the same broad grounds used by that court, but limited itself to applying ordinary

preemption rules. This narrow scope has been read by many to be at least a partial victory over the exceptional and much broader approach of the so-called dormant foreign affairs doctrine. Professor Vázquez, on the other hand, has argued that the case was in fact not a narrow decision.[3] "(E)ven though the Court said that its decision was based on a straightforward application of 'settled ... implied preemption doctrine,' the brand of pre-emption analysis the Court engaged in was anything but ordinary. Indeed, the *Crosby* version of preemption analysis is subject to the very same sorts of objections that *Zschernig's* critics have leveled at the Dormant Foreign Affairs doctrine. Moreover, if the case were taken as a model for deciding issues of preemption in purely domestic cases, it would be anything but narrow. The decision would be narrow only if it its approach to preemption were confined to suits implicating foreign relations. But then the Court's holding would begin to resemble a decision on dormant foreign affairs grounds." And in fact Professor Vázquez argues that *Crosby's* approach to preemption would have yielded the same conclusion even if there had been no federal Burma law.

(2) As noted above, the Court of Appeals in the *Crosby* case, in National Foreign Trade Council v. Natsios, 181 F.3d 38 (1st Cir. 1999), delivered a much more elaborate opinion, which included inter alia the following language:

> The Constitution's foreign affairs provisions have been long understood to stand for the principle that power over foreign affairs is vested exclusively in the federal government. James Madison commented that "if we are to be one nation in any respect, it clearly ought to be in respect to other nations." The Federalist No. 42, at 302 (James Madison); see also id. at 303 (noting that the Articles of Confederation, by failing to contain any "provision for the case of offences against the law of nations," left "it in the power of any indiscreet member to embroil the Confederacy with foreign nations"). Alexander Hamilton, discussing state regulation of foreign commerce, noted that
>
> > the interfering and unneighborly regulations of some States, contrary to the true spirit of the Union, have, in different instances, given just cause of umbrage and complaint to others, and it is to be feared that examples of this nature, if not restrained by a national control, would be multiplied and extended till they became not less serious sources of animosity and discord than injurious impediments to the intercourse between the different parts of the Confederacy.
>
> Id. No. 22, at 192 (Alexander Hamilton); see also id. No. 45, at 328 (James Madison) (stating that "the powers delegated by the proposed Constitution to the federal government are few and defined," and "will be exercised principally on external objects, as war, peace, negotiation, and foreign commerce"). Justice Taney echoed Madison's and Hamilton's views in Holmes v. Jennison, 39 U.S. (14 Pet.) 540, 10 L.Ed. 579 (1840), commenting that "it was one of the main objects of the Constitution to make us, so far as regarded our foreign relations, one people, and one nation." Id. at 575 (Opinion Of Taney, J.).

---

3. Carlos Manuel Vázquez, Whither Zschernig?, 46 Vill.L.Rev. 1259 (2001).

Indeed, the Supreme Court has long held that "power over external affairs is not shared by the States; it is vested in the national government exclusively." United States v. Pink, 315 U.S. 203, 233, 62 S.Ct. 552, 86 L.Ed. 796 (1942). In the Chinese Exclusion case, for example, the Court commented that "for local interests the several States of the Union exist, but for national purposes, embracing our relations with foreign nationals, we are but one people, one nation, one power." Chae Chan Ping v. United States, 130 U.S. 581, 606, 9 S.Ct. 623, 32 L.Ed. 1068 (1889). In Hines v. Davidowitz, 312 U.S. 52, 61 S.Ct. 399, 85 L.Ed. 581 (1941), the Court stated that "our system of government is such that the interest of the cities, counties and states, no less than the interest of the people of the whole nation, imperatively requires that federal power in the field affecting foreign relations be left entirely free from local interference." Id. at 63; see also United States v. Belmont, 301 U.S. 324, 57 S.Ct. 758, 331, 81 L.Ed. 1134 (1937). ("In respect of our foreign relations generally, state lines disappear."). As the Court explained in United States v. Curtiss–Wright Export Corp., 299 U.S. 304, 57 S.Ct. 216, 81 L.Ed. 255, (1936), when it comes to foreign affairs, the powers of the federal government are not limited: "the broad statement that the federal government can exercise no powers except those specifically enumerated in the Constitution, and such implied powers as are necessary and proper to carry into effect the enumerated powers, is categorically true only in respect of our internal affairs." Id. at 315–16.

Federal dominion over foreign affairs does not mean that there is no role for the states. A limited role is granted by the Constitution. See Restatement (Third) of Foreign Relations Law of the United States sec. 201 reporters' note 9 (commenting that "under the United States Constitution, a State of the United States may make compacts or agreements with a foreign power with the consent of Congress (Article I, Section 10, clause 2), but such agreements are limited in scope and subject matter" and that "[a] State may make some agreements with foreign governments without the consent of Congress so long as they do not impinge upon the authority or the foreign relations of the United States"). * * * As one learned commentator explains, some degree of state involvement in foreign affairs is inevitable: "in the governance of their affairs, states have variously and inevitably impinged on U.S. foreign relations." L. Henkin, Foreign Affairs and the United States Constitution 162 (2d ed. 1996).

* * *

* * * There is a threshold level of involvement in and impact on foreign affairs which the states may not exceed. As Zschernig stated:

> The several States, of course, have traditionally regulated the descent and distribution of estates. But those regulations must give way if they impair the effective exercise of the Nation's foreign policy. Where those laws conflict with a treaty, they must bow to the superior federal policy. Yet, even in absence of a treaty, a State's policy may disturb foreign relations.

389 U.S. at 440–41 (emphasis added) (citations omitted). Zschernig did not hold, as Massachusetts argues, that a sufficiently strong state interest could make lawful an otherwise impermissible intrusion into the federal government's foreign affairs power.

* * *

* * * The Massachusetts law presents a threat of embarrassment to the country's conduct of foreign relations regarding Burma, and in particular to the strategy that the Congress and the President have chosen to exercise. That significant potential for embarrassment, together with the other factors [discussed previously], drives the conclusion that the Massachusetts Burma Law has more than an "incidental or indirect effect" and so is an impermissible intrusion into the foreign affairs power of the national government.

* * *

* * * The importance of the federal government's ability to speak with one voice on foreign affairs does not mean that Congress must act, or that the states can never act, in a particular area. See 512 U.S. at 329. As the Court commented in Wardair Canada, Inc. v. Florida Department of Revenue, 477 U.S. 1, 106 S.Ct. 2369, 91 L.Ed.2d 1 (1986), * * * "The Federal Government is entitled in its wisdom to act to permit the states varying degrees of regulatory authority.... We never suggested in [*Japan Line*] or in any other [case] that the foreign commerce clause insists that the federal government speak with any particular voice." Id. at 12–13 (emphasis in original).

* * *

The Supreme Court has repeatedly suggested that state regulations that touch on foreign commerce receive a greater degree of scrutiny than do regulations that affect only domestic commerce. See South–Central Timber, 467 U.S. at 96; Reeves, 447 U.S. at 437 n.9; Japan Line, 441 U.S. at 448 (noting that "there is evidence that the Founders intended the scope of the foreign commerce power to be ... greater" than that of the domestic commerce power). * * *

* * *

* * * Supreme Court decisions under the Foreign Commerce Clause have made it clear that state laws that are designed to limit trade with a specific foreign nation are precisely one type of law that the Foreign Commerce Clause is designed to prevent. In *Container Corp.*, the Supreme Court stated that state legislation that relates to foreign policy questions violates the Foreign Commerce Clause "if it either implicates foreign policy issues which must be left to the Federal Government or violates a clear federal directive." Container Corp., 463 U.S. at 194 (emphasis in original); see also Japan Line, 441 U.S. at 448–49 (stating that "foreign commerce is preeminently a matter of national concern" and noting that "the need for federal uniformity is no less paramount in ascertaining the negative implication of Congress' power to 'regulate Commerce with foreign Nations' under the Commerce Clause"). "If state action touching foreign commerce is to be allowed, it must be shown not to affect national concerns to any significant degree, a far more difficult task than in the case of interstate commerce." Tribe, American Constitutional Law sec. 6–21, at 469. * * *

* * *

* * * Supreme Court decisions * * * make clear that a state law can violate the dormant Foreign Commerce Clause by impeding the federal government's ability to "speak with one voice" in foreign affairs, because such state action harms "federal uniformity in an area where federal uniformity is essential." Japan Line, 441 U.S. at 448–49; see also Container Corp., 463 U.S. at 193.

* * *

* * * Where, as here, the federal government has acted in an area of unique federal concern and has crafted a balanced, tailored approach to an issue, and the state law threatens to upset that balance, the state law is preempted. Under the Supremacy Clause, the Massachusetts Burma Law is unconstitutional. Cf. Missouri v. Holland, 252 U.S. 416, 40 S.Ct. 382, 64 L.Ed. 641 (1920).

* * * The conduct of this nation's foreign affairs cannot be effectively managed on behalf of all of the nation's citizens if each of the many state and local governments pursues its own foreign policy. Absent express congressional authorization, Massachusetts cannot set the nation's foreign policy.

Consider the differences in approach of the Court of Appeals and of the US Supreme Court. What is the significance of this difference in terms of future impact on the issues of allocating state and federal powers concerning foreign affairs activity? Why do you suppose the US Supreme Court (unanimous opinion but two justices concurring) was so terse and constrained in its opinion?

(3) In Bethlehem Steel Corporation. v. Board of Commissioners, 276 Cal.App.2d 221, 80 Cal.Rptr. 800 (1969), the Court of Appeals of the Second District reviewed the California Buy American Act (Govt. Code Secs. 4300–4305), requiring that contracts for the construction of public works or the purchase of materials for public use be awarded only to persons who will agree to use or supply materials which have been manufactured in the United States, substantially all from materials produced in the United States.

Citing United States v. Pink, 315 U.S. 203, 232, 62 S.Ct. 552, 566, 86 L.Ed. 796, the court noted that "these are delicate matters. If state action could defeat or alter our foreign policy, serious consequences might ensue. The nation as a whole would be held to answer if a State created difficulties with a foreign power."

As to the argument that until such time as the federal government acts, either by conflicting legislation or international agreement, state legislation is unobjectionable, the court replied, citing Hines v. Davidowitz, 312 U.S. 52, 63, 61 S.Ct. 399, 402, 85 L.Ed. 581, that

[O]ur system of government is such that the interest of the cities, counties and states, no less than the interest of the people of the whole nation, "imperatively requires that federal power in the field affecting foreign relations be left entirely free from local interference." To permit state legislation to concurrently operate in this sphere would very certainly "imperil the amicable relations between governments and vex the peace of nations." (Oetjen v. Central Leather Co., 246 U.S. 297, 304, 38 S.Ct. 309, 311, 62 L.Ed. 726; see Ricaud v. American Metal Co., 246 U.S. 304, 308–310, 38 S.Ct. 312, 62 L.Ed. 733.)

The court had stated earlier in its opinion:

Only the federal government can fix the rules of fair competition when such competition is on an international basis. Foreign trade is properly a subject of national concern, not state regulation. State regulation can only impede, not foster, national trade policies. The problems of trade expansion or non-expansion are national in scope, and properly should be national in scope in their resolution. The fact that international trade forms the basis of this country's foreign relations is amply demonstrated by the following. At the present time the United States is a party to commercial treaties with 38 foreign nations. In addition, there are tax treaties presently in effect between the United States and 31 countries. The United States is a party to many other international treaties and agreements regulating, directly and indirectly, its commercial relations with the rest of the world. See, for example, the General Agreement on Tariffs and Trade; The United Nations Charter; The International Monetary Fund Agreement of 1945. * * * Certainly, such problems are beyond the purview of the State of California. As stated in United States v. Pink, supra, 315 U.S. 203, 232, 62 S.Ct. 552, 566, 86 L.Ed. 796: "These are delicate matters. If state action could defeat or alter our foreign policy, serious consequences might ensue. The nation as a whole would be held to answer if a state created difficulties with a foreign power."

The court concluded that the California Buy American Act was an unconstitutional intrusion into an exclusive federal domain. The case was not appealed to the California Supreme Court.

(4) In U.S. v. Locke, 529 U.S. 89, 120 S.Ct. 1135, 146 L.Ed.2d 69 (2000) The Supreme Court unanimously struck down several state regulations governing Washington state waters used by oil tankers coming from the Pacific ocean and either destined to American or Canadian ports. The Court acknowledged the international aspects of the case, noting also the United States' argument that international agreements would have "pre-emptive force over the state regulations in question." The Court, however, concluded that it was not necessary to deal with that issue, "because the state regulations * * * are pre-empted by federal statute and regulations." At 102. Later, the Court does bring back international obligations through a back door by stating that "(a) state law in this area [in which Congress had acted] * * * would frustrate the congressional desire of achieving uniform, international standards." At 110.

(5) In Gerling Global Reinsurance Corp. of America v. Harry W. Low, Commissioner of Insurance of the State of California, 240 F.3d 739 (9th Cir. 2001), the Court of Appeals found that, although California's Holocaust Victim Insurance Relief Act (HVIRA) indirectly affected foreign commerce by

possibly requiring a company related to a California company to search for information, it did not impede the federal government's ability to speak with "one voice" in matters affecting foreign commerce. West's Ann. Cal. Ins. Code secs. 13800–13807. In fact, Congress had spoken affirmatively in the domain of Holocaust-era insurance policies by issuing the Holocaust Assets Commission Act and had therefore, at least implicitly, encouraged state laws such as the HVIRA. U.S. Holocaust Assets Commission Act of 1998, sec. 2, 22 U.S.C.A. sec. 1621 note. The federal government's power in the domain of foreign affairs, said the court, is not mentioned in the text of the Constitution, but can be derived from the structure of the constitution and the nature of federalism.

(3) When the Federal Government Has Not Acted or Almost Not Acted (Dormant Commerce Clause)

TUPMAN THURLOW COMPANY v. MOSS

United States District Court, M.D. Tennessee, Nashville Division, 1966.
252 F.Supp. 641.

PER CURIAM.

[The Tennessee Labeling Act] challenged in this proceeding * * * requires that any person selling or offering for sale in the State of Tennessee any meats or meat foods which are the products of any foreign country to the United States "shall so identify each product and its foreign origin." If * * * labeling is not feasible, it is provided that "a conspicuous sign in lieu of the label shall be displayed near the stock or display of the product." If foreign meats are combined with domestically produced meat into one product, the product shall be so labeled. In the event preservatives of any kind are used in any packaged meat product, the preservative shall be identified, along with the quantity used, and clearly displayed on any such package.

* * *

The Plaintiff, a New York board meat importer, alleges that the passage of the Labeling Act has caused plaintiff's Tennessee customers to refuse to purchase its imported meat, thus for all practical purposes destroying the Tennessee market for its direct sales.

* * * While the Commerce Clause as construed by the Supreme Court does not prohibit all state regulatory measures affecting interstate commerce, the Supreme Court has invariably outlawed those state restrictions which unduly and unreasonably burden or restrain interstate commerce when evaluated in terms of legitimate state or local interests, or those state restrictions and regulations which unreasonably discriminate against such commerce. * * *

The burdensome and discriminatory character of the present legislation can scarcely admit of doubt when it is considered in the light of the pertinent facts. In sweeping terms the Labeling Act requires that "each quarter of each carcass, each carton, each retail package, or individually packaged item shall be plainly identified with a brand or label stating that it is a foreign product and naming the country of its origin." * * * The evidence discloses that manufacturers and processors of meatfoods and products, such as wieners, bologna, hamburgers, baby foods, and other products, customarily, use foreign and domestic meats indiscriminately without any effort to keep the one separate from the other. The Labeling Act would require such products to be labeled to show the fact of co-mingling and the country in which the foreign meat had its origin. It would be necessary for Tennessee handlers of plaintiff's meat or meat products to keep track of or trace the origin of such meat, purchased either directly or through wholesalers or manufacturers, in order that the ultimate product sold to consumers in the State of Tennessee could be identified and labeled with the country of origin, or labeled in such way as to indicate that foreign and domestic meats both had been used. That these requirements of labeling are exceedingly burdensome is self-evident. * * *

* * * It is insisted that for almost a century states have been enacting legislation pursuant to their police power, with the approval of the Supreme Court, to protect citizens from being deceived or misled in their purchase of commodities, especially foods and food products, at retail.

In seeking to answer the question how consumers in Tennessee are misled by the sale of meat in that state which was originally imported, defendants point to the fact that the plaintiff's imported meat is frozen in the country of origin[, but usually sold as a fresh processed product, thereby deceiving consumers into believing the product was never frozen].

[However] there is no evidence that food products, such as those referred to by the defendants, are supposed by a consumer to be a fresh product, in the sense that the meat content has never been frozen. Nor is there any evidence that such products are generally offered for sale or represented to the public as fresh products. But whether these assumptions by the defendants are correct or not, it is difficult to see how the Labeling Act could have been designed to protect the consumer from deception, when the same protection is not afforded him in purchasing the same products which have been manufactured from frozen domestic meat. * * *

* * * The present labeling requirement, in contrast, would do nothing except inform the public that a meat product had its origin in a foreign country without conveying any information as to its nature, quality or quantity. In addition, as noted, it imposes substantial burdens upon meat and meat products of foreign origin without imposing the same burdens upon meat and meat products of domestic origin.

It is further insisted by the defendants that the present legislation does not offend the Commerce Clause because it operates only on goods which have come to rest in Tennessee so as to become part of the common property of the state. The cases cited by the defendants involving the "come to rest" and original package doctrines, merely recognize, because of the nexus with the state thus established, the power of the state to impose taxes or regulations upon those foreign goods which are designed to compete in the domestic market. Conceding that the imported meats in the present case are designed to compete in the domestic market, and that the state therefore has the power to regulate, it remains evident that the state may do so only if the regulations apply equally to foreign and domestic meats, and thus make possible equal competition in the domestic market.

* * *

In accordance with this opinion a form of judgment will be submitted declaring the Labeling Act * * * to be in conflict with the Commerce Clause and therefore void, and permanently enjoining the State Commissioner of Agriculture and the State Chemist and Director of Foods Division, Department of Agriculture, from enforcing the provisions of [the Act].

Note

In PORTLAND PIPE LINE CORP. v. ENVIRONMENTAL IMPROVEMENT COMMISSION, 307 A.2d 1 (Me.1973), the Supreme Court of Maine upheld a complex state regulatory enactment designed to fix responsibility and compensation for oil spills occurring in Maine waters. The State regulation imposed an annual license fee per barrel of oil transferred over coastal waters of the state. This fee was used to create a revolving fund to cover clean-up costs of spills, and research and development concerning environmental damage due to the transfer of oil in those waters.

Among the many challenges to the state regulation were a challenge based on the US constitutional clause (Article I, Section 10, Clause 2) that prohibits states (without consent of Congress) from laying imposts or duties on imports or exports, "except what may be absolutely necessary for executing * * * Inspection Laws," and a challenge based on the Commerce Clause.

The Court rejected the Import–Export Clause challenge on two grounds (307 A.2d at 36):

> * * * First, the license fee is not imposed "on Imports or Exports." Because the transfer fee is imposed on an activity related to the importation of oil [i.e., off-loading] *rather than on the property imported*, the fee is not sufficiently direct to be "on Imports" under Article I, Section 10, Clause 2.

> Second, the license fee is not a duty or impost since the overall effect of the Act is the establishment of a regulatory scheme for controlling oil pollution which is essentially to protect the public interest and affords benefits to those subject to the license fee.

The plaintiff's Commerce Clause challenge included the argument that this state regulation imposed excessive burdens on interstate commerce. In rejecting to this argument, the Court wrote (307 A.2d at 37–39):

Included in the ''just share'' of state tax burdens imposed on interstate commerce is the cost of preventing and remedying harm caused by a danger inherent in the interstate commerce being taxed.

[The Court then applies a three-part test concluding: (1) that the tax does not discriminate against interstate and foreign commerce because the fee is also imposed upon transfers resulting from intrastate shipment; (2) that the license fee reflects ''a fair if imperfect approximation'' of the conduct which gives rise to the danger against which the Act seeks to guard; and (3) that plaintiffs have failed to sustain their burden of proving that the license fees collected are ''excessive'' in relation to the costs incurred by the taxing authorities. The Court therefore concludes that it cannot find that the $4,000,000 limit of the Fund is irrational in light of the catastrophic damages which may be cause by an oil spill.]

(D) ILLUSTRATIVE U.S. COURT CASES

US law regarding federal constitutional norms affecting the allocation of authority between the federal government and state governments is very extensive, with over two centuries of cases and practices, sometimes difficult to reconcile with each other.

The following is a list of a few cases which have special relevance to international trade subjects, to provide a bit of ''flavor'' about this jurisprudence.

(1) **Japan Line, Ltd. v. County of Los Angeles**, 441 U. S. 434, 441 U.S. 434, 99 S.Ct. 1813, 60 L.Ed.2d 336 (1979): The US Supreme Court reversed a California Supreme Court opinion upholding state taxation on cargo containers owned by foreign entities for use in international commerce. The US Supreme Court held such tax invalid as imposing risk of double taxation on instrumentalities of foreign commerce as well as impairing federal uniformity in a matter of international concern.

(2) **Itel Containers Int'l v. Huddleston**, 507 U.S. 60, 113 S.Ct. 1095, 122 L.Ed.2d 421 (1993): The US Supreme Court upheld Tennessee sales tax on proceeds from the lease of shipping containers delivered in Tennessee, rejecting an argument that the tax was preempted by international agreements, because the court found no explicit federal policy to preempt when the tax was not expressly prohibited by the applicable international agreements.

(3) **Container Corp. v. Franchise Tax Bd.**, 463 U.S. 159, 103 S.Ct. 2933, 77 L.Ed.2d 545 (1983): US Supreme Court upheld the so-called unitary tax applied by California to the income of corporations doing business in the state. The tax was based on the proportion of a corporation's total payroll, property and sales that are in California.

(4) **Xerox Corp. v. County of Harris**, 459 U.S. 145, 103 S.Ct. 523, 74 L.Ed.2d 323 (1982): US Supreme Court disallowed local property taxation of goods manufactured in Mexico, shipped to the US and held in customs bonded warehouse awaiting shipment to Latin America. In **R.J. Reynolds Tobacco Co. v. Durham County**, 479 U.S. 130, 107 S.Ct. 499, 93 L.Ed.2d 449 (1986), the Court upheld a state property tax

applied to tobacco imported by Reynolds and held in bond for aging. In another case, **Michelin Tire Corp. v. Wages**, 423 U.S. 276, 96 S.Ct. 535, 46 L.Ed.2d, 495 (1976) the Court ruled that imports could be taxed once they were no longer in transit.

(5) **South-Central Timber v. Wunnicke**, 467 U.S. 82, 104 S.Ct. 2237, 81 L.Ed.2d 71, (1984): The US Supreme Court held that if a state is acting as a market participant rather than as a market regulator, then the dormant commerce clause places no limitation on its activities. Alaska proposed to sell timber from state lands, but to require that the purchaser partially process the timber prior to shipping it out of Alaska. The court held that if the state was only acting to sell its owned product, it could be all right, but once it tried to restrict downstream activity, it could not avail itself of the market participant doctrine.

(6) **K.S.B. Technical Sales Corp. v. North Jersey Dist. Water Supply Comm'n**, 75 N.J. 272, 381 A.2d 774 (1977): New Jersey Supreme Court upheld a state "Buy American" statute which applied to purchase of water supply service equipment, noting that GATT applies, but has an exception in Article III, paragraph 8 for government purchases.

(7) **Trojan Tech., Inc. v. Pennsylvania**, 916 F.2d 903, 911 (3d Cir. 1990): Federal circuit court upheld an act which directed Pennsylvania state agencies to require use of only US made steel in public works projects.

(8) **Lucchino v. Brazil**, 82 Pa.Cmwlth. 406, 476 A.2d 1369 (1984): A state court upheld a state statute that banned the purchase by state government agencies of steel, iron, and aluminum products imported from countries which in turn discriminate against such products made in Pennsylvania. It found evidence that defendant countries had so discriminated.

Question

Do you think the courts would rule differently after the case of *Crosby v. National Foreign Trade Council* was decided?

(E) STATE COOPERATION AND CONSULTATION IN U.S. INTERNATIONAL ECONOMIC AFFAIRS

The following is a note prepared for this book in 1994, by Professor Schaefer who during the Uruguay Round negotiation and application, was personally involved in the procedures developed for federal-state cooperation and coordination regarding trade obligations which could have effects on state law of US sub-federal government agencies and entities. While some of the numbers have changed, the authors felt it was useful to the readers to repeat this short text explanation of an interesting federalism example under international economic relations and obligations. One example of several changes since the note was written is that now the number of US states committed to the Uruguay Round plurilateral treaty text on Government Procurement is 39.

MATTHEW SCHAEFER, NOTE ON STATE INVOLVEMENT IN TRADE NEGOTIATIONS, THE DEVELOPMENT OF TRADE AGREEMENT IMPLEMENTING LEGISLATION, AND THE ADMINISTRATION OF TRADE AGREEMENTS (JANUARY 18, 1994)[4]

Trade agreements are increasingly impacting sub-national governments. The reason for the increased impact is at least two-fold. First, there is an increased emphasis on binding sub-national governments to obligations within international trade agreements. Second, the enlarged scope of trade agreements includes areas in which sub-national governments exercise jurisdiction. For instance, the Uruguay Round negotiations will bring trade-in-services under rules of the world trading system for the first time. The U.S. states as well as sub-national governments in other nations are very active in regulating service industries, including professional and financial services. With this stated, it is important to note that devices are still used by which some existing practices of sub-national governments are exempted from international trade obligations. The North American Free Trade Agreement (NAFTA), for example, allows existing state and provincial measures that would otherwise violate the obligations of the services, financial services and investment chapters to be "grandfathered" if the measures are identified within a year or two.

While U.S. state government policy-makers have long realized the importance of trade agreements in economic terms, they have recently placed an enhanced emphasis on understanding, and sometimes attempting to limit, the potential legislative and regulatory constraints of such agreements. In response to these potential constraints, the U.S. states have sought continued input into U.S. trade negotiations, increased involvement in the development of implementing legislation for trade agreements, and a larger role in the administration of trade agreements for state-related matters.

The mechanism by which states give formal input in the negotiation of trade agreements is the Intergovernmental Policy Advisory Committee (IGPAC). IGPAC has a statutory basis originally dating to the 1974 Trade Act. Currently, IGPAC has 30 members, including 14 State Governors, 5 state legislative representatives, a state environmental secretary and a state agriculture commissioner. The IGPAC meets periodically throughout trade negotiations with U.S. trade negotiators to receive updates on the status of negotiations and to give advice on how negotiations should proceed. The IGPAC is required to submit a report on negotiations thirty days after the President notifies Congress of his intent to enter into a trade agreement. Such reports give an assessment by IGPAC of the proposed agreement.

---

4. Matthew Schaefer, International Trade Consultant to the National Governor's Association and the Western Governor's Association (1994). This note was prepared at the request of Professor Jackson for inclusion in this book.

The large number of component units within the U.S. federation makes participation of all 50 states within the IGPAC forum difficult as a practical matter. Thus, many state associations in which all 50 states are represented, such as the National Governors' Association and the National Council of State Legislatures, have adopted policy resolutions on trade negotiations and transmitted the policy to the Administration. In some instances, however, state input has been given on a more ad hoc basis. For instance, IGPAC was not reconvened for the NAFTA supplemental negotiations on labor and environment. Instead, interested state Governors monitored the negotiations and sent letters expressing their views on the negotiations.

Therefore, state input in trade negotiations is generally limited to advice (i.e. the states have no veto power or binding advisory capacity). The one exception lies in the area of government procurement negotiations. The U.S. approach has been to bind the states to obligations within the renegotiated GATT Government Procurement Code on a voluntary basis only (despite the fact that U.S. negotiators believed as early as the Tokyo Round that they would have the constitutional authority to bind the states without their consent). While the U.S. is strongly seeking commitments from all 50 states to bind some of their procurement to the rules of the renegotiated Code, the final decision on whether to make a commitment and the extent of the commitment is a decision for each state to make on a voluntary basis. As of December 15, 1993, the United States Trade Representative had received voluntary commitments from 24 states to bind some or all of their procurement.

IGPAC reports and policy resolutions of the state associations contain recommendations for the implementing legislation of trade agreements as well. The number and depth of state recommendations for implementing legislation was greater than ever before for the implementing package of the NAFTA. One central element of the National Governors' Association and Western Governors' Association policy resolutions was a recommendation to ensure meaningful state participation in future dispute settlement cases and in the activities of committees established by NAFTA for the purpose of harmonizing standards. Additionally, the Governors sought to improve communications between the federal and state governments on trade matters.

Dispute settlement became a concern because of a 1992 GATT panel decision ruling that measures in over 40 states relating to alcoholic and malt beverages violated the GATT. The states believed that the informal consultation process during that dispute was insufficient. The states were interested in the work of the committees established under NAFTA because of a concern that harmonization efforts between the three countries would diminish the flexibility of states to set different standards. While any recommendations of the committees would be nonbinding in the sense that further Congressional or Executive action would be necessary to implement them, such recommendations could provide the impetus for preemptive federal action.

The exact nature and extent of state participation and federal-state consultations with respect to the administration of NAFTA was worked out over many months of discussion between representatives of the Governors, the Congress, and the Office of the United States Trade Representative (USTR). The final results of the NAFTA implementing package established a new process for federal-state communication on trade. As directed by the NAFTA package, the USTR has named a "NAFTA Coordinator for State Matters." The coordinator is responsible for disseminating information to the states on relevant matters including dispute settlement cases affecting the states and committee activities addressing matters within the concurrent or exclusive jurisdiction of the states. The coordinator will cooperate with other federal agencies to ensure all relevant information is transmitted to the states. In return, the Governors have agreed to select a single point of contact within each of their states for NAFTA trade matters. The new communication system will reduce problems that have occurred in the past, such as the federal government sending surveys on trade related matters to the wrong state agency or official.

The NAFTA implementing legislation also requires the USTR to involve states "to the greatest extent practicable at each stage of the development of U.S. positions regarding [state-related] matters that will be addressed by committees, subcommittees or working groups established under the Agreement or through dispute settlement processes provided for under the Agreement." The legislation notes that the state involvement will include involvement through appropriate representatives of the States. The accompanying statement of administrative action clarifies that state representatives will be allowed to participate in federal agency preparations for committee activities and dispute settlement cases affecting their interests but will act only as observers at actual committee meetings and panel hearings, unless a more active role is determined to be appropriate.

The NAFTA implementing bill is the first time states have been granted a guaranteed right to be informed and participate in trade matters affecting the states. It represents an accommodation to the new realities of trade agreements, specifically the increased impact that trade agreements have on the states. It is likely that the NAFTA implementing package will serve as a model with appropriate modifications and additions for the Uruguay Round implementing package and future trade agreement implementing bills.

Notes and Questions

(1) The NAFTA implementing legislation referred to in the foregoing excerpt is section 102(b)(2) of the North America Free Trade Agreement Implementation Act, Pub. L. No. 103–182, 107 Stat. 2057 (1993) (codified at U.S.C.A. sec. 3312).

(2) Are the procedures described in the foregoing note adequate? If you were a Governor, would you want additional rights for States? Of what kind?

Chapter 4

INTERNATIONAL ECONOMIC REGULATION IN THE EUROPEAN UNION

SECTION 4.1 INTRODUCTION

This book emphasizes problems of US law, partly because of its expected audience but also because the United States plays such a major role in the world trading regime. Although space and time prevent exploring the legal systems of other major trading nations in any great depth, this chapter should assist the reader in understanding how some of the problems we explored in Chapter 3 are handled in the European Union (EU), which is the world's largest trading entity. Further, detailed information on how other WTO members formulate and implement trade policy can be found in the Trade Policy Reviews conducted of all WTO members by the WTO Trade Policy Review Body and available on the WTO website.

In Chapter 3, we saw that the ability of the United States to engage effectively in trade negotiations was very much affected by the constitutional division of powers between the President and Congress and between the federal government and the states. It may also be affected by the relative openness of the US legislative process and the degree to which individuals have access to the courts to challenge state or federal actions that are allegedly inconsistent with US international obligations. The other members of the world trading system also must deal with splits in authority between different constituent elements of their governments and with judicial systems with rules that differ from those applicable in US courts.

In studying the materials in this chapter, the reader should focus on the following questions:

(1) How have the different institutional conflicts present in the United States and the EU affected the formation of international economic law in the past and how might they affect the scope and results of future negotiations on changes in such law?

(2) Does the possibility of an individual challenging government acts as inconsistent with international economic law (or the lack of such a possibility) mean that international agreements will be adhered to more (or less) faithfully?

(3) What implications should the answers to these questions have in constructing institutions and norms of international economic law?

(4) Which entities of the government structure have the authority to regulate international trade?

(5) What is the relationship between parliamentary institutions, executive organizations, and the judiciary, in this regard?

(6) What special problems do federal states or customs unions have with the authority of the central government over external trade matters?

(7) What bodies in a country or union have the power to enter into an international agreement?

(8) What is the legal effect of such an agreement in the country or union?

(9) In which cases does such an agreement prevail over other internal law, or not?

The materials in this chapter will not answer all these questions, but these questions have motivated the selection and emphasis of those materials.

SECTION 4.2 INTRODUCTION TO THE EUROPEAN UNION[1]

We study the European Union in part because it is one of the key players in international trade negotiations. As important, we examine it because it is a fascinating exercise in "nation" building, two aspects of which have considerable importance for the international system. The first is the way in which it has removed barriers to trade among its member states; the second is the role of effective dispute settlement and treaty enforcement in the process of economic integration. The international community is not about to engage in the degree of economic integration that characterizes the EU today, but the EU's experience in reducing trade barriers and improving compliance with agreements through dispute settlement mechanisms provides lessons of obvious relevance and importance. We begin in this section by describing the activities and sketching the institutions of the EU. Then, we consider the relationship of EU law to member state law, followed by a examination of the respective external relations powers of the Union and its

---

1. For further references on the European Union and the issues treated in this section, see George A. Bermann, Roger J. Goebel, William J. Davey & Eleanor M. Fox, Cases and Materials on European Union Law (2d ed. 2002). This section is based in part on William J. Davey, European Integration: Reflections on Its Limits and Effects, 1 Indiana J. Global Legal Studies 185 (1993).

member states and the position of international agreements under EU law. We conclude with a broad perspective on the economic integration of Europe generally.

The genesis of the European Union (EU) was the European Coal and Steel Community (ECSC), which was established in 1952. It was followed by the 1957 Treaty of Rome, which established the European Economic Community (EEC).[2] The EEC was often referred to initially as the European Common Market and more recently as the European Community or EC. As of November 1993, the Maastricht Treaty on European Union (TEU) came into force, creating a European Union, one component of which is the EC. From that point on, it became common to use the terms European Union or EU generally, even when referring to matters that technically concerned the EC. In this chapter, we will follow that usage, although it is worth noting that almost all of the activities of the EU (as used in the foregoing broad sense) are in fact conducted pursuant to the EC Treaty and it is the EC that is a member of the WTO.

The original members of the EEC were Belgium, France, Italy, Luxembourg, the Netherlands and West Germany. They were joined in 1973 by Denmark, Ireland and the United Kingdom, in 1981 by Greece, in 1986 by Portugal and Spain, and in 1995 by Austria, Finland and Sweden. Ten countries joined in 2004—Cyprus, the Czech Republic, Estonia, Hungary, Latvia, Lithuania, Malta, Poland, the Slovak Republic and Slovenia. With the accession of Bulgaria and Romania in 2007, there are now 27 EU member states. The EU is currently negotiating accession with Croatia, the Former Yugoslav Republic of Macedonia and Turkey. In Western Europe, only Iceland, Norway and Switzerland are not EU members and their economies are closely integrated with the EU through various agreements.

The principal objective of the Treaty of Rome was the creation of a common market among its member states. More specifically, the Treaty provided for the elimination of barriers to the free movement of goods, workers, services and capital among the member states and the establishment of a common tariff and commercial policy towards non-members. To facilitate these measures, the Treaty also provided for common policies in agriculture, competition (antitrust matters) and transportation and for the harmonization of member state laws generally to the extent required for the proper functioning of the common market. As a result, there is important EU legislation in such fields as the environment, worker and consumer protection, gender equality, corporate law and securities regulation, and taxation.

It took some time for the EU to create a true internal market in goods, labor, services and capital. By 1968, duties on trade in goods

---

2. There have been a number of significant amendments to the original EEC Treaty (now formally the EC Treaty), and its provisions have been renumbered. The most convenient source for the currently effective version of the treaty is the Europa website: europa.eu.

between the member states had been eliminated. However, for much of the 1970s and early 1980s, relatively little progress was made at the legislative level because of the inability of the Council to reach consensus on many Commission proposals. Indeed, during this period it was largely through expansive Court of Justice decisions that continued progress was made towards realizing the internal market goal. The Court ruled, for example, that normally a good lawfully marketed in one member state could be marketed in the others, notwithstanding local restrictions that purported to limit such marketing possibilities. While this ruling could be used by individuals to challenge many indirect member state restrictions on intra-Community trade, it was not a panacea for the creation of the internal market. By its nature, the Court's role was limited to striking down member state barriers to trade. It could not force adoption of positive legislation needed to complete the internal market.

In 1985, inspired by a Commission White Paper on the completion of the internal market, the member states agreed upon amendments to the basic treaties in the Single European Act, which came into force in 1987. The Single European Act set December 31, 1992, as a goal for completion of the internal market. The Act helped make that goal realistic by amending the legislative process so that a form of super majority voting, instead of unanimity, was made the rule for adoption of most measures necessary to complete the internal market. Spurred on by studies showing the great economic costs imposed on the EU by the lack of an internal market, 95% of the 1992 internal market program was agreed to on schedule at the Community level, with 80% implementation at the member state level.

As a result, the EU has come close to creating a completely free and open internal market amongst its member states. Goods move freely, and so do workers. Where professional qualifications are an issue, there are rules on recognition of diplomas and so on. Services can be provided freely throughout the Community. Where they are regulated (such as insurance and banking), there are Community rules indicating which member state is allowed to regulate which service providers and on what types of substantive regulations may be imposed. As importantly, where divergent member state laws could have impeded the flow of goods from one member to another (e.g., different rules on labeling), the Community has often acted to adopt a single, community-wide rule.

The Maastricht Treaty created the status of European citizenship and under the Schengen Agreement among most EU members, travelers are no longer subject to border controls within most of the EU. The Maastricht Treaty also laid the groundwork for closer coordination of economic policies and ultimately resulted in the creation of the European Central Bank and, on January 1, 2002, the physical substitution of the "Euro" (€) for the national currencies of Austria, Belgium, Finland, France, Germany, Greece, Ireland, Italy, Luxembourg, the Netherlands, Portugal and Spain. Slovenia joined the Euro zone in 2007.

In addition to removing trade barriers, there are several other significant trade-related aspects of Community integration. First, market integration sharply highlights disparities in regional wealth and the trade-related consequences that may result therefrom. Richer countries will be concerned about possible job losses to poorer regions where wage rates are lower and environmental rules less strictly enforced; poorer countries will feel entitled to assistance in implementing common policies proposed by richer countries or may simply insist on such help as a price for supporting new Community initiatives. Accordingly, the Community has adopted mechanisms to reduce these disparities by transferring wealth from the richer member states to the poorer ones. Second, market integration necessitates the adoption of joint policies with respect to subsidization of industry. These policies include (i) limits on the rights of individual member states to subsidize local producers, which would distort trade patterns in the internal market and lead to wasteful competitive subsidization, and (ii) adoption of common strategies of increasing overall community wealth through government action, whether this be coordinated infrastructure developments or joint aid to specific industries. The Community over time has become more and more active in pursuing such policies.

The EU has a unique institutional structure.[3] There are five important institutions: The Commission, the Council, the European Council, the European Parliament and the Court of Justice. The Commission, which is based in Brussels, was designed to be the most "European" of the institutions. It is headed by a President (chosen by the member states, but subject to approval by Parliament), with each commissioner being responsible for a particular part of the Commission's work. Commissioners are appointed for five-year terms as independent persons and not as representatives of particular governments. As of 2008, a national of each member was on the Commission, but the overall number of Commissioners is expected to be reduced in the future.

The Commission is the executive arm of the EU. It is charged with ensuring that the treaties are observed and that the decisions of the institutions are faithfully implemented. The Council has delegated extensive powers to the Commission to enable it to administer programs and enforce rules. The Commission also plays an important role in the legislative process. Generally, the Council may act only on a Commission proposal and may amend it only by unanimous vote, even if adoption of the proposal would normally require only a "qualified majority." (This power has been reduced in the later stages of the codecision procedure described below.) To finance its numerous programs, which in 2007 necessitated a budget of over 115 billion euros (approximately $180 billion), the EU relies mainly on its share of member state value added tax revenue, an amount from each member state based upon it gross domestic product, customs revenue and agricultural levies. The vast

3. The institutional structure will change in important details when the 2007   Treaty of Lisbon is ratified.

majority of the budget is spent on agricultural programs and regional aid.

The *Council*, also based in Brussels, is composed of one representative from each member state. The actual membership of the Council varies depending on the issue before it—national transport ministers discuss transport issues; national agricultural ministers consider agricultural questions. The more important issues are handled by the general affairs council, which consists of the foreign ministers of the member states. The Council is the principal legislative body of the EU, although as noted below, the power of the European Parliament over legislation has grown significantly over time. The Council voting structure depends on which particular power under which of the treaties it is exercising. In some cases each member state has one vote and a simple majority prevails; in other cases a super or "qualified" majority is required; and in still other cases, unanimity is required. When a qualified majority is required, the member states are assigned different numbers of votes, roughly based on their relative populations.

The *European Council* is the name given to summit meetings of member state leaders. At meetings of the European Council, the leaders discuss and often decide upon the direction of EU policy. Their decisions are later implemented by member state representatives in the Council. These meetings occur at least twice a year.

The *European Parliament* is based in Strasbourg. Its members are directly elected by the voters of the various EU states, with the number of each state's seats allocated in rough proportion to the state's population. With respect to the Union legislative process, the Parliament initially had only the right to give non-binding advice on proposed legislation. More recently, it has gained considerable additional powers. In 1987, pursuant to the Single European Act, the consultation requirement was considerably strengthened by the addition of the so-called cooperation procedure. Although the Parliament's views could ultimately be ignored, the voting rules made it more difficult to do so in some cases. Under the Maastricht Treaty, effective in 1993, Parliament gained so-called codecision powers in certain areas. These powers mean that Parliament can effectively veto adoption of legislation, although it still lacks the power to initiate legislation. The range of legislation subject to the codecision procedure was significantly expanded by the 1998 Amsterdam Treaty and even further expanded by 2000 Nice Treaty. As a result, codecision has become the process applicable to most legislation, although the Parliament's powers in some areas—particularly agriculture and the common commercial policy—remain relatively limited. However, under these recent amendments, Parliament has also gained powers in the field of external relations, where its approval is needed for certain types of international agreements (although not for simple commercial policy agreements). Parliament constantly seeks to expand its powers and influence, and it is likely that there will be further expansions of its power in the future, although some member states are leery of giving Parliament power at their expense. Others, however, feel that the Union suffers from a "democracy deficit" because Union institutions are too isolated from Union citizens. In their view, expanding the powers of Parliament would help to solve this problem.

The *Court of Justice* (sitting at Luxembourg) is one of the most interesting, and from a juridical point of view, most impressive institutions of the European Union. There are 27 judges, assisted by 8 Advocates General, who recommend decisions to the court in cases assigned to them. The Court has established a remarkable record over the last half century. Its work has on the whole enhanced both the unity and the central powers of the EU institutions. An American lawyer is struck by some of the parallels between Court of Justice case developments and those of the United States Supreme Court.[4] In effect, the European Community operates within a system of judicial review (court power to annul unconstitutional acts) which is both very similar to that of the United States and very different from the judicial systems in some of the major EU member states. Given the relatively subordinate role of the judiciary in many European government systems, it is striking to find such a strong judicial role played in the EU structure.

Under the provisions of the EC Treaty, the Commission or a member state may sue another member state in the Court for failing to fulfill an EC obligation. Likewise, the Commission, the Council or a member state can ask the Court to review acts of the Council or Commission for violations of the Treaty or EC rules, for lack of competence, for infringement of essential procedural requirements or for misuse of powers. They may also sue the Commission or Council for failure to act when required. In addition, when certain Community acts that are of direct and individual concern to a person are at issue, that person may bring an action challenging such acts. Finally, and of particular importance, a party litigant in the court of a member state may be able, in asserting the applicability of EC law, to obtain a Court of Justice ruling on that issue by requesting the member state court to refer the EC law issue to the Court of Justice. If there is no appeal of the member state court's decision in the case, that court is required to refer the EC law issue to the Court of Justice.

Pursuant to the SEA, a Court of First Instance was created. It initially was given jurisdiction over appeals of Commission competition law decisions and labor cases, with a right of appeal to the Court of Justice. As of 1994, it was given initial jurisdiction of all claims by individuals challenging EC acts. Labor cases are now handled by the Civil Service Tribunal.

Often, issues of EU law can and will be brought to the Court of Justice. To a remarkable degree, then, one observes that much activity in the EU is conducted with reference to the fact of its ultimate challengeability in the Court. In short, lawyers are important, their

---

4. For an informed discussion of such parallels, see Courts and Free Markets (T. Sandalow & E. Stein eds., 1982).

expertise is growing, and possibly so also is their influence (although Europe, especially the Continent, has traditionally been less influenced by lawyers, private or public, than the United States has been). In connection with the EU's exercise of powers relating to international economic power, then, EU law can be expected to have considerable importance.

From the perspective of international economic relations, two questions concerning the EU are of particular importance: (1) To what extent is legislation or other action taken by the EU enforced in the individual member states, i.e. the relation of EU law to national law? (2) What powers does the EU have in the realm of international economic affairs and to what extent does it share them with the member states? We will look at each of these issues in turn.

SECTION 4.3   THE FORCE OF EU LAW IN THE MEMBER STATES

One of the more interesting questions presented by the European Union is the relationship of EU law to member state law. What is the status of the EC Treaty under member state law? Of other EU acts? What happens when there is a conflict? Who decides which law prevails? In reviewing the following material the student should consider how the issues discussed in Sections 3.4 (International Agreements and US Law) and 3.6 (Federal–State Relations) would be resolved in the EU.

VAN GEND & LOOS v. NEDERLANDSE ADMINISTRATIE DER BELASTINGEN

Court of Justice of the European Communities, Case 26/62.
[1963] ECR 1.

[The Court of Justice was asked in an Article 234 reference whether former Article 12[1] of the EC Treaty had direct effects within the territory of a Member State, i.e. whether nationals of a State could, on the basis of Article 12, lay claim to individual rights that national courts had to protect. In this particular case, the issue was whether they could challenge in national court an alleged tariff increase on the ground that it violated Article 12. The Court responded as follows:]

To ascertain whether the provisions of an international treaty extend so far in their effects it is necessary to consider the spirit, the general scheme and the wording of those provisions.

The objective of the EEC Treaty, which is to establish a Common Market, the functioning of which is of direct concern to interested

---

1. Article 12 was a transitional provision designed to prevent tariff increases of any kind during the period when tariffs between the member states were being phased out. It provided: "Member States shall refrain from introducing between themselves any new customs duties on imports or exports or any charges having equivalent effect, and from increasing those which they already apply in their trade with each other."

parties in the Community, implies that this Treaty is more than an agreement which merely creates mutual obligations between the contracting states. This view is confirmed by the preamble to the Treaty which refers not only to governments but to peoples. It is also confirmed more specifically by the establishment of institutions endowed with sovereign rights, the exercise of which affects Member States and also their citizens. * * *

In addition the task assigned to the Court of Justice under Article [234], the object of which is to secure uniform interpretation of the Treaty by national courts and tribunals, confirms that the states have acknowledged that Community law has an authority which can be invoked by their nationals before those courts and tribunals.

The conclusion to be drawn from this is that the Community constitutes a new legal order of international law for the benefit of which the states have limited their sovereign rights, albeit within limited fields, and the subjects of which comprise not only Member States but also their nationals. Independently of the legislation of Member States, Community law therefore not only imposes obligations on individuals but is also intended to confer upon them rights which become part of their legal heritage. These rights arise not only where they are expressly granted by the Treaty, but also by reason of obligations which the Treaty imposes in a clearly defined way upon individuals as well as upon the Member States and upon the institutions of the Community.

* * *

The wording of Article 12 contains a clear and unconditional prohibition which is not a positive but a negative obligation. This obligation, moreover, is not qualified by a reservation on the part of states which would make its implementation conditional upon a positive legislative measure enacted under national law. The very nature of this prohibition makes it ideally adapted to produce direct effects in the legal relationship between Member States and their subjects.

* * *

It follows from the foregoing considerations that, according to the spirit, the general scheme and the wording of the Treaty, Article 12 must be interpreted as producing direct effects and creating individual rights which national courts must protect.

AMMINISTRAZIONE DELLE FINANZE DELLO STATO v. SIMMENTHAL S.P.A.

Court of Justice of the European Communities, Case 106/77.
[1978] ECR 629.

[An Italian beef importer brought an action in Italian court to recover certain veterinary and public health inspection fees it had been required to pay when importing beef from France. The Court of Justice had previously ruled that the fees violated Article [28] on the free movement of goods. Under Italian law only the Italian Constitutional Court could declare an Italian statute invalid. One of the questions asked by the lower Italian court in this Article [234] reference was whether Community law required that the lower court be able to take such action and order repayment of the fees. The Court of Justice answered:]

[I]n accordance with the principle of the precedence of Community law, the relationship between provisions of the Treaty and directly applicable measures of the institutions on the one hand and the national law of the Member States on the other is such that those provisions and measures not only by their entry into force render automatically inapplicable any conflicting provision of current national law but—in so far as they are an integral part of, and take precedence in, the legal order applicable in the territory of each of the Member States—also preclude the valid adoption of new national legislative measures to the extent to which they would be incompatible with Community provisions.

Indeed any recognition that national legislative measures which encroach upon the field within which the Community exercises its legislative power or which are otherwise incompatible with the provisions of Community law had any legal effect would amount to a corresponding denial of the effectiveness of obligations undertaken unconditionally and irrevocably by Member States pursuant to the Treaty and would thus imperil the very foundations of the Community.

The same conclusion emerges from the structure of Article [234]. * * *

The effectiveness of that provision would be impaired if the national court were prevented from forthwith applying Community law in accordance with the decision or the case-law of the Court.

It follows from the foregoing that every national court must, in a case within its jurisdiction, apply Community law in its entirety and protect rights which the latter confers on individuals and must accordingly set aside any provision of national law which may conflict with it, whether prior or subsequent to the Community rule.

Accordingly any provision of a national legal system and any legislative, administrative or judicial practice which might impair the effectiveness of Community law by withholding from the national court having jurisdiction to apply such law the power to do everything necessary at the moment of its application to set aside national legislative provisions which might prevent Community rules from having full force and effect are incompatible with those requirements which are the very essence of Community law.

Notes and Questions

(1) *Van Gend & Loos* sets forth the Court of Justice's classic formulation of the nature of the EU: "A new legal order * * * for the benefit of which the states have limited their sovereign rights * * * and the subjects of which comprise not only Member States but also their nationals." This

viewpoint gives the Court great power and discretion since a new legal order may well require the Court to formulate new legal principles and rules.

(2) An issue similar to that in *Simmenthal II* arose in The Queen v. Secretary of State for Transport ex parte Factortame Ltd., Case C–213/89, [1990] ECR I–2433. In a case challenging an Act of Parliament as violating the EC Treaty, a U.K. trial court concluded that the plaintiffs would prevail on the merits and would suffer irreparable damage if interim relief were denied. It thereupon issued a preliminary injunction enjoining enforcement of the Act. The appeals court reversed on the ground that under U.K. constitutional tradition, a court may not enjoin an Act of Parliament. The House of Lords then asked the Court of Justice whether Community law required an English court to grant preliminary injunctive relief in such a case. Relying on *Simmenthal II*, the Court answered that "Community law must be interpreted as meaning that a national court which, in a case before it concerning Community law, considers that the sole obstacle which precludes it from granting interim relief is a rule of national law must set aside that rule."

(3) One of the legal instruments used by the EU is the directive. A directive requires the member states to adopt legislation that conforms to the terms of the directive within a certain period of time. Directives have been used frequently, particularly to require harmonization of member state rules on matters affecting trade among the member states (e.g., environmental and consumer protection measures). In cases where a member state has failed to act within the specified time limit, the Court of Justice has ruled that provisions of the directive may have direct effect if the conditions specified in *van Gend & Loos* are met. See, e.g., Van Duyn v. Home Office, Case 41/74, [1974] ECR 1337. It has also ruled that individuals harmed by the failure of a member state to implement a directive have to be given a right of action for damages against the member state in certain circumstances. Francovich v. Italy, Case C–6/90, [1991] ECR I–5357. Such rulings obviously put pressure on the member states to implement directives promptly.

(4) The conclusion that EU law is supreme raises many of the same questions that arise in the US in respect of federal-state relations. For example, to what extent does EU legislation preempt a field, so as to preclude member state legislation? The Court of Justice has not hesitated to find that member state legislation has been preempted. However, the recent amendments to the EC Treaty (the SEA and TEU) introduced the concept of "subsidiarity" to EU law:

> In areas which do not fall within its exclusive competence, the Community shall take action, in accordance with the principle of subsidiarity, only if and insofar as the objectives of the proposed action cannot be sufficiently achieved by the Member States and can therefore, by reason of the scale or effects of the proposed action, be better achieved by the Community.

EC Treaty, art. 5. This concept, combined with new provisions explicitly authorizing member states to impose stricter rules in certain areas (e.g., environment, consumer protection), so long as they are not otherwise inconsistent with the Treaty (EC Treaty, arts. 176, 153(f)), represents an interesting attempt to take local concerns into account in a federal system. Whether it will be given meaningful content remains to be seen.

A second example of preemption is raised by the following question: To what extent are member states prevented from applying local standards (e.g., health, safety, etc.) to bar entry of goods from other member states, assuming that those standards do not conflict with positive EU legislation? This question raises issues such as those found in so-called Dormant Commerce Clause cases under the US Constitution. We touched on this issue in Section 3.6.

(5) Consider to what extent the supremacy of EU law over national law might allow member state governments to implement unpopular programs opposed by national legislatures by not vigorously opposing such programs in EU institutions. What could a national legislature do to prevent this? This lack of accountability has given rise to discussion of whether there is a ''democracy deficit'' in the EU and, as noted in the prior subsection, motivates many of those who want to give more power to the European Parliament, so that there will be more popular control of EU institutions.

(6) Generally, over time the courts of the EU member states have accepted that EU law prevails over inconsistent national law, although German courts continue to claim that they could rule otherwise in certain circumstances. More specifically, the German Constitutional Court indicated early on that it reserved the right to review EU acts for consistency with the basic rights guaranteed in the German Constitution, but more recently it has decided that so long as the Court of Justice recognizes the existence of fundamental basic rights as a component of EU law, which it does, the German court will not undertake such a review. The German court expressly reserves the right to do so, however, and it expressed a variant of this view most recently in 1993 in upholding the TEU against a claim that it violated the German Constitution. Brunner v. European Union Treaty, [1994] 1 CMLR 57, 89. It was initially expected that the United Kingdom would have difficulty accepting the primacy of EU law because of the traditional sovereign rights of Parliament. But to date, that has not seemed to be a problem. See generally George A. Bermann, Roger J. Goebel, William J. Davey & Eleanor M. Fox, European Union Law ch. 8 (2d ed. 2002).

SECTION 4.4   THE UNION'S POWER IN EXTERNAL COMMERCIAL RELATIONS

In this section we focus on the Union's power in external commercial relations. This power derives from Article 133 of the EC Treaty, which provides in part:

1. The common commercial policy shall be based on uniform principles, particularly in regard to changes in tariff rates, the conclusion of tariff and trade agreements, the achievement of uniformity in measures of liberalization, export policy and measures to protect trade such as those to be taken in event of dumping or subsidies.

2. The Commission shall submit proposals to the Council for implementing the common commercial policy.

3. Where agreements with one or more States or international organizations need to be negotiated, the Commission shall make recommendations to the Council, which shall authorize the Commission to open the necessary negotiations. * * *

The Commission shall conduct these negotiations in consultation with a special committee appointed by the Council to assist the Commission in this task and within the framework of such directives as the Council may issue to it. * * *

The EU negotiates trade agreements with third countries as follows: First, the Commission holds preliminary talks with the country concerned. If successful, the Commission recommends to the Council that formal negotiations be opened. If the Council agrees, it authorizes the Commission to negotiate along the lines of a specific mandate. The Commission then proceeds to negotiate the agreement under the watchful eye of a special committee composed of member state representatives (called the Article 133 Committee). If the negotiations succeed, the Commission initials the results on behalf of the EU and presents the results to the Council, which has the ultimate authority to approve or reject any agreement. The Council acts by qualified majority under Article 133. Parliamentary approval of Article 133 agreements is normally not formally required.

(A) SCOPE AND EXCLUSIVITY OF THE COMMON COMMERCIAL POLICY

OPINION 1/94

(World Trade Organization—WTO).
[1994] ECR–I 5267.

[The Community's Explicit External Powers]

The Commission's main contention is that the conclusion of both GATS [the WTO's General Agreement on Trade in Services] and TRIPS [the WTO Agreement on Trade–Related Aspects of Intellectual Property] falls within the exclusive competence conferred on the Community in commercial policy matters by Article [133] of the EC Treaty. That point of view has been vigorously disputed * * * by the Council, by the Member States * * * and by the European Parliament. * * *

As regards [services other than transport], it should be recalled at the outset that in Opinion 1/75 the Court * * * held that "the field of common commercial policy, and more particularly that of export policy, necessarily covers systems of aid for exports and more particularly measures concerning credits for the financing of local costs linked to export operations." The local costs in question concerned expenses incurred for the supply of both goods and services. Nevertheless, the Court recognized the exclusive competence of the Community, without drawing a distinction between goods and services.

In its Opinion 1/78, the Court rejected an interpretation of Article [133] "the effect of which would be to restrict the common commercial policy to the use of instruments intended to have an effect only on the traditional aspects of external trade." On the contrary, it considered that "the question of external trade must be governed from a wide point of view," as is confirmed by "the fact that the enumeration in Article [133] of the subjects covered by commercial policy ... is conceived as a non-exhaustive enumeration."

The Commission points out in its request for an opinion that in certain developed countries the services sector has become the dominant sector of the economy and that the global economy has been undergoing fundamental structural changes. The trend is for basic industry to be transferred to developing countries, whilst the developed economies have tended to become, in the main, exporters of services and of goods with a high value-added content. The Court notes that this trend is borne out by the WTO Agreement and its annexes, which were the subject of a single process of negotiation covering both goods and services.

Having regard to this trend in international trade, it follows from the open nature of the common commercial policy, within the meaning of the Treaty, that trade in services cannot immediately, and as a matter of principle, be excluded from the scope of Article [133], as some of the Governments which have submitted observations contend.

In order to make that conclusion more specific, however, one must take into account the definition of trade in services given in GATS in order to see whether the overall scheme of the Treaty is not such as to limit the extent to which trade in services can be included within Article [133].

Under Article I(2) of GATS trade in services is defined, for the purposes of that agreement, as comprising four modes of supply of services: (1) cross-frontier supplies not involving any movement of persons; (2) consumption abroad, which entails the movement of the consumer into the territory of the WTO member country in which the supplier is established; (3) commercial presence, i.e. the presence of a subsidiary or branch in the territory of the WTO member country in which the service is to be rendered; (4) the presence of natural persons from a WTO member country, enabling a supplier from one member country to supply services within the territory of any other member country.

As regards cross-frontier supplies, the service is rendered by a supplier established in one country to a consumer residing in another. The supplier does not move to the consumer's country; nor, conversely, does the consumer move to the supplier's country. That situation is, therefore, not unlike trade in goods, which is unquestionably covered by the common commercial policy within the meaning of the Treaty. There is thus no particular reason why such a supply should not fall within the concept of the common commercial policy.

The same cannot be said of the other three modes of supply of services covered by GATS, namely, consumption abroad, commercial presence and the presence of natural persons.

As regards natural persons, it is clear from Article 3 of the Treaty, which distinguishes between "a common commercial policy" in paragraph (b) and "measures concerning the entry and movement of persons" in paragraph (d), that the treatment of nationals of non-member countries on crossing the external frontiers of Member States cannot be regarded as falling within the common commercial policy. More generally, the existence in the Treaty of specific chapters on the free movement of natural and legal persons shows that those matters do not fall within the common commercial policy.

It follows that the modes of supply of services referred to by GATS as "consumption abroad," "commercial presence" and the "presence of natural persons" are not covered by the common commercial policy.

* * *

[As to the TRIPS Agreement, the] Commission's argument in support of its contention that the Community has exclusive competence under Article [133] is essentially that the rules concerning intellectual property rights are closely linked to trade in the products and services to which they apply.

It should be noted, first that Section 4 of Part III of TRIPS, which concerns the means of enforcement of intellectual property rights, contains specific rules as to measures to be applied at border crossing points. * * * Since measures of that type can be adopted autonomously by the Community institutions on the basis of Article [133] of the EC Treaty, it is for the Community alone to conclude international agreements on such matters.

However, as regards matters other than the provisions of TRIPS on the release into free circulation of counterfeit goods, the Commission's arguments cannot be accepted. [Although the Court conceded that there is a connection between intellectual property rights and trade in goods, it noted that is not enough to bring such rights them within the scope of Article 133, especially since they affect internal trade just as much as, if not more than, international trade. Moreover, the Court noted that while Articles 94, 95 and 308 provide a basis for harmonizing national laws on intellectual property, the decision-making rules under those articles differ from those applicable under Article 133.]

If the Community were to be recognized as having exclusive competence to enter into agreements with non-member countries to harmonize the protection of intellectual property and, at the same time, to achieve harmonization at Community level, the Community institutions would be able to escape the internal constraints to which they are subject in relation to procedures and to rules as to voting.

* * *

[The Community's Implied External Powers]

In the event of the Court rejecting its main contention that the Community has exclusive competence pursuant to Article [133], the

Commission maintains in the alternative that the Community's exclusive competence to conclude GATS and TRIPS flows implicitly from the provisions of the Treaty establishing its internal competence, or from the existence of legislative acts of the institutions giving effect to that internal competence, or else from the need to enter into international commitments with a view to achieving an internal Community objective. The Commission also argues that, even if the Community does not have adequate powers on the basis of specific provisions of the Treaty or legislative acts of the institutions, it has exclusive competence by virtue of Articles [95 and 308] of the Treaty. The Council and the Member States which have submitted observations acknowledge that the Community has certain powers, but deny that they are exclusive.

With particular regard to GATS, the Commission cites three possible sources for exclusive external competence on the part of the Community: the powers conferred on the Community institutions by the Treaty at internal level, the need to conclude the agreement in order to achieve a Community objective, and, lastly, Articles [95 and 308].

The Commission argues, first, that there is no area or specific provision in GATS in respect of which the Community does not have corresponding powers to adopt measures at internal level. According to the Commission, those powers are set out in the chapters on the right of establishment, freedom to provide services and transport. Exclusive external competence flows from those internal powers.

That argument must be rejected.

It was on the basis of Article [71(1)(a)] which, as regards that part of a journey which takes place on Community territory, also concerns transport from or to non-member countries, that the Court held in *ERTA* that the "powers of the Community extend to relationships arising from international law, and hence involve the need in the sphere in question for agreements with the third countries concerned."

However, even in the field of transport, the Community's exclusive external competence does not automatically flow from its power to lay down rules at internal level. As the Court pointed out in *ERTA*, the Member States, whether acting individually or collectively, only lose their right to assume obligations with non-member countries as and when common rules which could be affected by those obligations come into being. Only insofar as common rules have been established at internal level does the external competence of the Community become exclusive. However, not all transport matters are already covered by common rules.

The Commission asserted at the hearing that the Member States' continuing freedom to conduct an external policy based on bilateral agreements with nonmember countries will inevitably lead to distortions in the flow of services and will progressively undermine the internal market. * * *

In reply to that argument, suffice it to say that there is nothing in the Treaty which prevents the institutions from arranging, in the common rules laid down by them, concerted action in relation to non-member countries or from prescribing the approach to be taken by the Member States in their external dealings. * * *

* * *

Unlike the chapter on transport, the chapters on the right of establishment and on freedom to provide services do not contain any provision expressly extending the competence of the Community to "relationships arising from international law." As has rightly been observed by the Council and most of the Member States which have submitted observations, the sole objective of those chapters is to secure the right of establishment and freedom to provide services for nationals of Member States. They contain no provisions on the problem of the first establishment of nationals of non-member countries and the rules governing their access to self-employed activities. One cannot therefore infer from those chapters that the Community has exclusive competence to conclude an agreement with non-member countries to liberalize first establishment and access to service markets, other than those which are the subject of cross-border supplies within the meaning of GATS, which are covered by Article [133].

Referring to Opinion 1/76, the Commission submits, second, that the Community's exclusive external competence is not confined to cases in which use has already been made of internal powers to adopt measures for the attainment of common policies. Whenever Community law has conferred on the institutions internal powers for the purposes of attaining specific objectives, the international competence of the Community implicitly flows, according to the Commission, from those provisions. It is enough that the Community's participation in the international agreement is necessary for the attainment of one of the objectives of the Community.

The Commission puts forward here both internal and external reasons to justify participation by the Community, and by the Community alone, in the conclusion of GATS and TRIPS. At [the] internal level, the Commission maintains that, without such participation, the coherence of the internal market would be impaired. At [the] external level, the European Community cannot allow itself to remain inactive on the international stage: the need for the conclusion of the WTO Agreement and its annexes, reflecting a global approach to international trade (embracing goods, services and intellectual property), is not in dispute.

That application of Opinion 1/76 to GATS cannot be accepted.

Opinion 1/76 related to an issue different from that arising from GATS. It concerned rationalization of the economic situation in the inland waterways sector in the Rhine and Moselle basins, and throughout all the Netherlands inland waterways and the German inland waterways linked to the Rhine basin, by elimination of short-term overcapacity. It was not possible to achieve that objective by the establishment of autonomous common rules, because of the traditional participation of vessels from Switzerland in navigation on the waterways in question. It was necessary, therefore, to bring Switzerland into the scheme envisaged by means of an international agreement. Similarly, in the context of conservation of the resources of the seas, the restriction, by means of internal legislative measures, of fishing on the high seas by vessels flying the flag of a Member State would hardly be effective if the same restrictions were not to apply to vessels flying the flag of a nonmember country bordering on the same seas. It is understandable, therefore, that external powers may be exercised, and thus become exclusive, without any internal legislation having first been adopted.

That is not the situation in the sphere of services: attainment of freedom of establishment and freedom to provide services for nationals of the Member States is not inextricably linked to the treatment to be afforded in the Community to nationals of non-member countries or in non-member countries to nationals of Member States of the Community.

Third, the Commission refers to Articles [95 and 308] of the Treaty as the basis of exclusive external competence.

As regards Article [95], it is undeniable that, where harmonizing powers have been exercised, the harmonization measures thus adopted may limit, or even remove, the freedom of the Member States to negotiate with non-member countries. However, an internal power to harmonize which has not been exercised in a specific field cannot confer exclusive external competence in that field on the Community.

Article [308], which enables the Community to cope with any insufficiency in the powers conferred on it, expressly or by implication, for the achievement of its objectives, cannot in itself vest exclusive competence in the Community at international level. Save where internal powers can only be effectively exercised at the same time as external powers, internal competence can give rise to exclusive external competence only if it is exercised. This applies a fortiori to Article [308].

* * *

Whenever the Community has included in its internal legislative acts provisions relating to the treatment of nationals of non-member countries or expressly conferred on its institutions powers to negotiate with non-member countries, it acquires exclusive external competence in the spheres covered by those acts.

The same applies in any event, even in the absence of any express provision authorizing its institutions to negotiate with non-member countries, where the Community has achieved complete harmonization of the rules governing access to a self-employed activity, because the common rules thus adopted could be affected within the meaning of *ERTA* if the Member States retained freedom to negotiate with non-member countries.

That is not the case in all service sectors, however, as the Commission has itself acknowledged.

It follows that competence to conclude GATS is shared between the Community and the Member States.

[The Commission raised arguments similar to the foregoing in respect of the TRIPS Agreement. The Court rejected them for the same reasons set out above in respect of GATS.]

At the hearing, the Commission drew the Court's attention to the problems which would arise, as regards the administration of the agreements, if the Community and the Member States were recognized as sharing competence to participate in the conclusion of the GATS and TRIPS agreements. While it is true that, in the negotiation of the agreements, the procedure under Article [133] of the Treaty prevailed subject to certain very minor adjustments, the Member States will, in the context of the WTO, undoubtedly seek to express their views individually on matters falling within their competence whenever no consensus has been found. Furthermore, interminable discussions will ensue to determine whether a given matter falls within the competence of the Community, so that the Community mechanisms laid down by the relevant provisions of the Treaty will apply, or whether it is within the competence of the Member States, in which case the consensus rule will operate. The Community's unity of action vis-à-vis the rest of the world will thus be undermined and its negotiating power greatly weakened.

In response to that concern, which is quite legitimate, it must be stressed, first, that any problems which may arise in implementation of the WTO Agreement and its annexes as regards the coordination necessary to ensure unity of action where the Community and the Member States participate jointly cannot modify the answer to the question of competence, that being a prior issue. As the Council has pointed out, resolution of the issue of the allocation of competence cannot depend on problems which may possibly arise in administration of the agreements.

Next, where it is apparent that the subject-matter of an agreement or convention falls in part within the competence of the Community and in part within that of the Member States, it is essential to ensure close cooperation between the Member States and the Community institutions, both in the process of negotiation and conclusion and in the fulfillment of the commitments entered into. That obligation to cooperate flows from the requirement of unity in the international representation of the Community.

The duty to cooperate is all the more imperative in the case of agreements such as those annexed to the WTO Agreement, which are inextricably interlinked, and in view of the cross-retaliation measures established by the [WTO] Dispute Settlement Understanding. Thus, in the absence of close cooperation, where a Member State, duly authorized within its sphere of competence to take cross-retaliation measures, considered that they would be ineffective if taken in the fields covered by GATS or TRIPS, it would not, under Community law, be empowered to retaliate in the area of trade in goods, since that is an area which on any view falls within the exclusive competence of the Community under Article [133] of the Treaty. Conversely, if the Community were given the right to retaliate in the sector of goods but found itself incapable of exercising that right, it would, in the absence of close cooperation, find itself unable, in law, to retaliate in the areas covered by GATS or TRIPS, those being within the competence of the Member States.

Notes and Questions

(1) The Court also ruled that the EU had the exclusive power to conclude the GATT-related agreements on trade in goods, including products subject to the ECSC and Euratom Treaties, and that Article 133 was a sufficient basis for such action, even in respect of the agreements on agriculture and sanitary and phytosanitary measures. In this regard, the Court stated: "The objective of the [WTO] Agreement on Agriculture is to establish, on a worldwide basis, a fair and market-oriented agricultural trading system (see the preamble to that Agreement). The fact that commitments entered into under that Agreement require internal measures to be adopted on the basis of Article [37] of the Treaty does not prevent the international commitments themselves from being entered into pursuant to Article [133] alone." The 2000 Nice Treaty expanded the scope of Article 133 to cover agreements covering trade in services and the commercial aspects of intellectual property, subject to certain limitations, such as unanimity requirements in some cases.

(2) How does the general foreign relations power of the European Union compare with that of the United States federal government? How do its foreign commercial powers compare? Is there an "implied powers doctrine" in the European Union?

(B) IMPLEMENTATION OF THE COMMON COMMERCIAL POLICY

At the base of the common commercial policy is the common tariff, known as the Combined Nomenclature (CN), that classifies and establishes tariff rates for all products imported into the EU. It is supplemented by the Taric, the integrated EU tariff, which is used for statistical reporting and which incorporates special import provisions not included in the CN. The EU has entered into numerous preferential agreements that provide for duty-free entry of (or reduced duties on) goods originating in a country entitled to the preference and otherwise satisfying the terms of the applicable agreement. The EU has such agreements with most European and Mediterranean countries and most developing countries, some of which are described in the next subsection.

Pursuant to Article 133, rules for imports have been adopted, under which restrictions may be imposed on imports causing injury to an EU industry. In addition, the EU has adopted procedures pursuant to which antidumping duties may be imposed upon dumped products and countervailing duties may be imposed upon subsidized products. See Chapters 16–18 infra. It has also adopted procedures allowing imposition of duties or quotas or the suspension or withdrawal of trade concessions in response to injurious illicit commercial practices of other nations.

Notes and Questions

(1) As a negotiator for the United States, how would you satisfy yourself that an EU negotiating team consisting of Commission officials was authorized to negotiate pursuant to Article 133(3)? To enter into a particular agreement? Is the involvement of the Article 133 Committee sufficient protection? One of the French objections to the 1992 EU–US agreement on agricultural trade matters was that the Commission had exceeded its negotiating mandate. The French objections ultimately led to changes in the agreement.

(2) If the Council (consisting of member state representatives) has to approve any agreement negotiated by the Commission, and if the Article 133 Committee (also consisting of member state representatives) oversees negotiations, why does it matter whether the member states participate directly in negotiations?

(3) In terms of implementing controversial international trade policies, would you say that it is easier, harder, or no different, to do in the EU than in the United States?

(C) INTERNAL LEGAL EFFECT OF INTERNATIONAL AGREE-MENTS UNDER EU LAW

The Court of Justice has held that international agreements form part of the EU legal system and that, in some cases, they may be invoked by individuals in member state courts, just as provisions of the EC Treaty may be invoked under *van Gend & Loos*. Under the Court's cases, a provision of an international agreement concluded by the EU may have direct effect if the provision sets forth an unconditional obligation that is central to the purpose of the agreement. Hauptzollamt Mainz v. C.A. Kupferberg & Cie., Case 104/81, [1982] ECR 3641. The Court has limited the scope of the *Kupferberg* holding for trade agreements, however, by also ruling that even if a provision in an EU trade agreement is identical to one in the EC Treaty, the provision in the trade agreement may not be interpreted as broadly as the EC Treaty provision if the purposes of the two treaties are different (e.g., creating a free trade area as opposed to creating an internal market with sovereign institutions). See, e.g, Polydor Ltd. v. Harlequin Records Shop Ltd., Case 270/80, [1982] ECR 329; European Economic Area, Opinion 1/91, [1991] ECR I–6079.

In International Fruit Co. v. Produktschap, Cases 21–24/72, [1972] ECR 1219, 1227–1228, the Court of Justice considered whether GATT Article XI, which bans the use of quotas, had direct effect. It concluded that it did not because of what might be called the various loopholes in GATT. With the creation of the WTO and its stricter disciplines and binding dispute settlement system, the question arose again. In PORTU-GUESE REPUBLIC v. COUNCIL, Case C–149/96, [1998] ECR I–7379, Portugal challenged the decision implementing a textiles agreement with

India and Pakistan on grounds that it violated WTO rules, as well as certain rules and principles of Community law. As to the possibility of giving direct effect to WTO rules, the Court stated (paras. 36–48):

> While it is true that the WTO agreements, as the Portuguese Government observes, differ significantly from the provisions of GATT 1947, in particular by reason of the strengthening of the system of safeguards and the mechanism for resolving disputes, the system resulting from those agreements nevertheless accords considerable importance to negotiation between the parties.

> [Noting WTO provisions dealing with failures to implement dispute settlement rulings, which include the possibility of negotiations over compensation on a temporary basis pending implementation, the Court stated that] to require the judicial organs to refrain from applying the rules of domestic law which are inconsistent with the WTO agreements would have the consequence of depriving the legislative or executive organs of the contracting parties of the possibility afforded by Article 22 of [the Dispute Settlement Understanding] of entering into negotiated arrangements even on a temporary basis.

* * *

> As regards, more particularly, the application of the WTO agreements in the Community legal order, it must be noted that, according to its preamble, the agreement establishing the WTO, including the annexes, is still founded, like GATT 1947, on the principle of negotiations with a view to "entering into reciprocal and mutually advantageous arrangements" and is thus distinguished, from the viewpoint of the Community, from the agreements concluded between the Community and non-member countries which introduce a certain asymmetry of obligations, or create special relations of integration with the Community, such as the agreement which the Court was required to interpret in *Kupferberg*.

> It is common ground, moreover, that some of the contracting parties, which are among the most important commercial partners of the Community, have concluded from the subject-matter and purpose of the WTO agreements that they are not among the rules applicable by their judicial organs when reviewing the legality of their rules of domestic law.

> Admittedly, the fact that the courts of one of the parties consider that some of the provisions of the agreement concluded by the Community are of direct application whereas the courts of the other party do not recognize such direct application is not in itself such as to constitute a lack of reciprocity in the implementation of the agreement.

> However, the lack of reciprocity in that regard on the part of the Community's trading partners, in relation to the WTO agreements which are based on reciprocal and mutually advantageous arrange-

ments and which must ipso facto be distinguished from agreements concluded by the Community, * * * may lead to disuniform application of the WTO rules.

To accept that the role of ensuring that those rules comply with Community law devolves directly on the Community judicature would deprive the legislative or executive organs of the Community of the scope for maneuver enjoyed by their counterparts in the Community's trading partners.

It follows from all those considerations that, having regard to their nature and structure, the WTO agreements are not in principle among the rules in the light of which the Court is to review the legality of measures adopted by the Community institutions.

Notes and Questions

(1) In the ECJ's view, the fact that the WTO dispute settlement system has formally ruled that Community legislation is incompatible with WTO rules does not change the situation. Leon van Parys NV v. BIRB, Case C–377/02, [2005] ECR I–1465. For WTO issues that are not yet within the realm of the EU, the ECJ has ruled that it is a matter of national law as to whether to give WTO rules direct effect. Merck Genericos v. Merck & Co., Case C–431/05, Judgment of September 11, 2007.

(2) The foregoing opinion is of particular interest because of its characterization of GATT and the WTO Dispute Settlement Understanding, which are the major subjects of this book. As you read the rest of the materials in the book, consider whether the Court's characterization is apt. The Court of Justice did recognize in the *Portuguese Republic* case, at paragraph 49, as it has elsewhere that:

> [W]here the Community intended to implement a particular obligation assumed in the context of the WTO, or where the Community measure refers expressly to the precise provisions of the WTO agreements, [then] it is [appropriate] for the Court to review the legality of the Community measure in question in the light of the WTO rules.

In a subsequent case, the Court elaborated on this point as follows:

> 2. The procedural requirements of Article 50 of the TRIPS Agreement, and in particular Article 50(6), are not such as to create rights upon which individuals may rely directly before the Community courts and the courts of the Member States. Nevertheless, where the judicial authorities are called upon to apply national rules with a view to ordering provisional measures for the protection of intellectual property rights falling within a field to which the TRIPS Agreement applies and in respect of which the Community has already legislated, they are required to do so as far as possible in the light of the wording and purpose of Article 50(6) of the TRIPS Agreement, taking account, more particularly, of all the circumstances of the case before them, so as to ensure that a balance is struck between the competing rights and obligations of the intellectual property right holder and of the defendant.

Schieving–Nijstad v. Groeneveld, Case C–89–99, [2001] ECR I–5851 (answer to question 2). See also Petrotub SA v. Council, Case 76/00, 2003 ECR I–79.

(3) The EU institutions may be held liable for non-contractual damages that they have caused to individuals. Attempts to hold the institutions liable for harm caused by actions that had later been found to violate WTO rules have not been successful so far. See, e.g., FIAMM v. Council, T69–00, Court of First Instance Judgment of December 14, 2005, appeal pending as of January 2008.

(4) Notwithstanding the foregoing cases, the ECJ does seem to be influenced by WTO decisions. See, e.g., F.T.S. International BV v. Belasting-dienst–Douane West, Case C–310/06, Judgment of July 18, 2007 (same result as WTO reports on classification of salted chicken cuts–see Section 7.4(C) infra); Ikea Wholesale Ltd v. Commissioners of Customs and Excise, Case C–351/04, Judgment of September 27, 2007 (same result on permissibility of "zeroing", see Chapter 16 infra).

(5) How do the decisions in *International Fruit* and *Portuguese Republic* on the direct effect of the WTO agreements compare to the US decisions discussed in Section 3.4 supra on self-executing international agreements and standing?

(6) Assuming that a treaty concluded by the EU was found to have direct effects, how would a conflict between the treaty and the Treaty of Rome be resolved? The treaty and prior EC legislation? The treaty and subsequent EC legislation? The treaty and a member state constitution? The treaty and prior member state legislation? The treaty and subsequent member state legislation?

SECTION 4.5   THE FUTURE ECONOMIC AND POLITICAL INTEGRATION OF EUROPE

The wide range of EU activities has inevitably raised questions of how closely integrated politically the EU should become. Although the EU treaties focus on economic matters, it has been understood from the beginning that some of their framers viewed them as having the longer range objective of European political union. Indeed, the very title of the Treaty on European Union indicated that the EU member states are moving toward a closer political relationship. Nonetheless, the question of how much and how fast the EU should evolve toward political union has remained controversial. A further step toward closer union—the proposed Constitutional Treaty—was effectively abandoned after Dutch and French voters rejected it in 2005, although many of its provisions were carried over into the Lisbon Treaty, which was signed in December 2007 but has not yet been ratified. The longstanding debate over whether the current EU member states should "deepen" their relationship before undertaking to "widen" the Union was resolved in favor of widening with the 12 accessions in 2004–2007 (although current applicants—especially Turkey—may find the accession process to be lengthy). Whether a Union of 27 members will find it difficult to deepen its relationship remains to be seen. In that regard, it is worth noting that in some areas, such as the adoption of the Euro and the abolition of internal border controls, greater integration has been undertaken by a subset of Union members and the treaties contain provisions that enable that to be done in other areas.

WILLIAM J. DAVEY, EUROPEAN INTEGRATION: REFLECTIONS ON ITS LIMITS AND EFFECTS[1]

E. *Lessons From European Economic Integration*

The recent history of Europe presents a textbook study of how economic integration proceeds. In particular, it suggests (i) that there are certain criteria that must be met before it is possible to move from one level of economic integration to the next and (ii) that there may be basic sociopolitical factors that limit the economic integration process.

1. *Requirements for Integration*

The experience of the EC suggests that there are at least two basic requirements for successful market integration to occur. First, there must be institutions with meaningful powers that have integration as one of their fundamental goals. In this connection, there needs to be both an institution that affirmatively promotes market integration and one that effectively enforces the integrating rules that are adopted. Second, there must be some minimum degree of commonality of interests (economic, environmental, social, etc.) among the countries that are attempting to integrate their markets. In the case of the EC, both of these requirements have been met.

Much of the success of the EC can be attributed to the existence of formal institutions at the European level that have pressed the case for further integration and that have taken steps to encourage and enforce integration. In particular, the Commission has served throughout most of the EC's history as a pro-market-integration force. Even when progress toward the single market was slow, the Commission continued to push for it. The actions of the Commission must be compared to the actions of the member states, acting individually or through the Council. By and large, the member states have often opposed expansive interpretations of the EC Treaty, and in particular the powers of the Community and the supremacy of Community law. They also tend to reflect parochial national interests in decisionmaking. This has not been true of all member states all of the time, but even the member states that on a general level have endorsed a strong and expanding Community have often opposed strength in the Community in specific cases when issues of particular concern to them were at stake. Thus, the existence of an institution like the Commission that has integration as a primary goal would seem to be a virtual prerequisite to market integration. Without

1. 1 Ind. J. Global Leg. Studies 185, 190–193 (1993). This and other excerpts from this publication in this chapter are reprinted with the permission of the Indiana Journal of Global Legal Studies.

such an institution, the natural tendencies of nations to resist incursions on their sovereignty (or detriments to groups in their populations) will greatly retard progress toward integration. This conclusion is underlined by the EC–EFTA experience, where the lack of meaningful institutions was viewed as a hindrance to integration. The EEA Agreement represents an improvement over the cooperation based on the EC–EFTA free trade agreements, but it does not provide for the transfer of any sovereign powers to EEA institutions and does not limit the power of decision of the parties. Intensification of integration in simple free trade areas may be expected to proceed slowly.

As important as effective institutions are as a driving force for integration, there is also a need for an institution to ensure that the rules providing for integration are enforced. In the case of the EC, the European Court of Justice (ECJ) has played a critical role in that regard. From its early decisions that established the right of individuals to invoke Community law in national courts, and the supremacy of Community rules over national rules, to far-reaching decisions striking down disguised barriers to trade, the ECJ has played a critical role in the integration process. It seems clear that integration would have proceeded at a much slower pace, but for the ECJ. In most of its path-breaking decisions, the member states (or some of them) were opposed to the position taken by the ECJ. Yet, they ultimately accepted the decisions, suggesting that their opposition was not fundamental, but that some institutional mechanism to overcome it was required. The ECJ has proved to be effective in that role.

The second requirement for market integration is a certain degree of commonality between participants in the market. This is not to say that countries have to be at identical levels of economic development with similar views on economic, environmental and social issues generally. But there is a need to have some degree of congruence. In the case of the EC, there is variance in the levels of development of the various member states which has caused problems. But, as noted above, they have been reduced through the provision of substantial aid from the richer countries to the poorer ones. Without such a process, one can wonder whether the Community would have integrated to the extent that it has, since there probably would have been more serious disputes over many issues. In particular, the use of mutual recognition as a market-unifying principle, both by the Court and in Community legislation, would have been much more restricted if the member states varied too widely in their approaches to regulating markets. As important, the free movement of workers, which is a fundamental part of an integrated market, is unlikely to be accepted if there are significant variations in the wealth of the constituent members since such variation will likely lead to significant, and potentially socially destabilizing, migration.

2. The Limitations on Integration

The EC is already having to confront the question of whether there are natural limits on economic or market integration. In essence these potential limits seem to stem from a lack of a commonly accepted agreement between the various member states as to what policies need to be integrated in order to achieve an optimal level of market integration, while respecting national sovereignty. The lack of agreement appears at two levels: disagreements over the need to harmonize certain policies at all; and disagreements about what is the proper balance between harmonization and the rights of individual member states (or subdivisions thereof) to make their own, independent decisions on matters directly affecting them.

An example of a basic policy disagreement over the need for integration of a specific policy would be the UK decision to eschew monetary union and the social policy provisions to which others agreed at Maastricht. As the number of member states expands, such differences may be expected to occur more often. Fear of such a result has animated those who argue that the current Community should be "deepened" before it is "widened." * * * [I]t seems that the forces in favor of widening the Community first have won. Time will tell whether in fact a widened Community will be a less integrated one.

The second type of disagreement presents more fundamental problems and may arise even if there is fairly broad agreement on the general outlines of all major policies among the member states. This type of disagreement stems from the desire of local communities to have some say over matters that affect their quality of life directly. It is not about the desirability of eliminating "red tape" at borders or standardizing essentially mechanical details, such as the characteristics of basic products, but rather about such topics as the appropriate level of environmental protection. For example, all member states may agree on the need to regulate air pollution, but one or more may feel that it wants stricter standards than the ones to which the others are willing to agree. The current debate over "subsidiarity" highlights this problem. As discussed below, drawing the line between what should be regulated at the Community level and what may be done at the local level will probably preoccupy the Community in the coming years and will serve as a limit on further integration.

The process of European integration is instructive for those thinking about the future of the globalization process in the world at large, both economically and otherwise. Much of the globalization process is driven by factors beyond the control of governments, but the European experience suggests that such factors alone are not enough to maintain momentum toward a truly integrated global economy. It suggests, in particular, that the process needs institutions to push it forward and that even with relatively strong institutions, there are fundamental limits on the process imposed by desires for local autonomy over certain issues. On a practical level, it suggests that further integration of the world economy of the sort epitomized by GATT's Uruguay Round agenda may only be practical if combined with stronger institutions for rulemaking and improved dispute settlement procedures for rule enforcement. But such changes are precisely those that are strenuously opposed by groups seeking local autonomy. These factors suggest that the process of globalization may proceed more slowly in the near future than it has in the recent past.

Chapter 5

INTERNATIONAL LAW AND IN-TERNATIONAL ECONOMIC RELATIONS

SECTION 5.1 INTRODUCTION: WHAT IS INTERNATIONAL LAW AND WHY DO NATIONS UTILIZE IT?

(A) INTERNATIONAL LAW AND INTERNATIONAL ECONOMIC LAW

Previous chapters have developed fundamental economic concepts, presented the basics of international sales transactions and explored important aspects of national government regulation. In this and the next two chapters, we introduce the basics of international law, which operates as the "constitution" for international economic relations.[1] To better understand this law, it is important to become acquainted with some of the fundamental concepts of international law and to understand the context of the more specialized international law relating to economic affairs. The latter topic includes both "international economic law" and "international economic organizations." These topics are discussed in the present chapter. In the next two chapters, we introduce other crucial aspects of this "constitution." Chapter 6 examines the most important institution in the world trading system, the World Trade Organization (WTO). Chapter 7 discusses the dispute settlement system that is so significant and so central to this international "constitution."

(B) INTERNATIONAL LAW

This book cannot, of course, consider very deeply the many aspects and complex facets of international law.[2] Some readers will have devel-

1. See generally John H. Jackson, The World Trading System (2nd ed. 1997); John H. Jackson, Sovereignty, the WTO, and Changing Fundamentals of International Law (2006).

2. For additional materials, see Lori F. Damrosch et al, International Law: Cases and Materials (4th ed. 2001); Barry E. Carter & Phillip R. Trimble, International Law (4th ed. 2003); Ian Brownlie, Principles of

171

oped knowledge of that subject elsewhere. However, for readers who have not had such opportunity, the next section has been designed to introduce some of the basic concepts of international law. The later sections will focus more particularly on international economic law and the landscape of international economic institutions and organizations.

When considering international law, the reader might reflect on the following questions or propositions:

1) What is the theoretical basis for international law rules and the obligation to follow them?

2) Sources of international law have often been divided into so-called "customary international law" norms, and "conventional" or "treaty" norms (treaties are sometimes called "conventions"). It is important to understand the distinction between these and the interplay between them. International economic law tends to focus on treaty law, since arguably there are very few substantive customary international law norms for economic behavior.

3) What are the important aspects of treaty law? The Vienna Convention on the Law of Treaties (1980), parts of which reflect rules of customary international law, is particularly relevant. For example, its treaty interpretation rules are very important.

4) An important question is the relationship of international treaties to domestic law. This question was taken up for the United States in Chapter 3 and for the EU in Chapter 4, but the relationship varies from country to country and constitution to constitution. We can only touch on that relation in this chapter, but in considering trade policy questions in later chapters, we often encounter issues about this relationship.

5) Sometimes it is hard for common law students and practitioners to understand that international law does not have a strict "stare decisis" precedent system. Like in many other legal systems in the world, courts or tribunals do not feel as strongly obligated to follow prior precedent as would be the case in common law systems. Nevertheless, precedent plays an important persuasive role, as will be seen throughout this book.

6) Traditional international law has been deemed to provide rules that govern relationships between governments. Thus, the basic origin of international law suggests a very small role for individuals or private firms. Governments enter into a treaty, or invoke a dispute settlement process. When individuals or private firms have a grievance against a foreign government, typically they must go to their own government and try to persuade their government to provide "diplomatic protection" in the sense of carrying their case forward to an international forum. This can be quite confusing at times. Increasingly this different legal status

Public International Law (6th ed. 2003); Henry J. Steiner, Detlev F. Vagts & Harold H. Koh, Transnational Legal Problems: Materials and Text (4th ed. 1994); Gillian Triggs, International Law: Contemporary Principles and Practices (2006).

for governments as compared to individuals or firms is being broken down.

7) The role of the individual under international law, both as a legal entity obligated to obey international law norms and as a legal entity benefited by international law norms (such as human rights rules), has been evolving. This evolution has been particularly rapid since World War II and it is now generally accepted that individuals do have a certain international legal status.

8) These various trends also relate to the question of "public participation" in international law processes. With the increasing attention for globalization and its impact on society, many international procedures and organizations have been criticized because they operate under diplomatic practices where only governments have access to information, the right to bring procedures or the right to participate in meetings. This is being strongly challenged in a number of countries by interest groups and academics who criticize the antidemocratic character of globalization and of these diplomatic traditions in international organizations.

(C) BASIC THEORY OF INTERNATIONAL OBLIGATIONS AND POLICIES SUPPORTING A "RULE BASED" SYSTEM

Why do or should nations follow international obligations? The "theory of international law" has long been a subject for extensive discussion and writings. A few extracts should suggest the flavor, and further references are suggested in this footnote.[3]

LOUIS HENKIN, HOW NATIONS BEHAVE, LAW AND FOREIGN POLICY 47 (2d. 1979)

It is probably the case that almost all nations observe almost all principles of international law and almost all of their obligations almost all of the time.

OSCAR SCHACHTER, TOWARDS A THEORY OF INTERNATIONAL OBLIGATIONS[4]

* * * As a subject, the "foundation of obligation" is as old as international law itself; it had a prominent place in the seminal treatises

3. Interested readers may also want to see: Thomas M. Franck, Fairness in International Law and Institutions (1998); Rosalyn Higgins, Problems & Process: International Law and How We Use It (1995); Abram Chayes and Antonia Handler Chayes, The New Sovereignty: Compliance With International Regulatory Agreements (1998); Louis Henkin, International Law: Politics and Values (1995); Oscar Schachter, International Law in Theory and Practice (1991); Jack Goldsmith and Eric Posner, The Limits of International Law (2006); John Murray, The United States and the Rule of Law in International Affairs (2004); Rosalyn Higgins, Problems and Processes: International Law and How We Use It (1995).

4. From The Effectiveness of International Decisions (Papers and proceedings of a conference of the American Society of International Law) 9, 9–12, 30–31 (Steven M. Schwebel ed., 1971). Reprinted by permission of A.W. Sijthoff International Publishing Co. N.V., Leyden.

of the founding fathers—Suarez, Vittoria, Grotius, Pufendorf et al.—and it remained a central issue in the great controversies of the nineteenth century. In our century it has had a lesser place; it was largely overtaken by the discussion of "sources" and evidence, centered around Article 38 of the Statute of the International Court. Although subordinated, it was not neglected and each of the leading scholars of the twentieth century found himself impelled to advance a fresh analysis. No single theory has received general agreement and sometimes it seems as though there are as many theories or at least formulations as there are scholars. We can list at least a baker's dozen of "candidates" which have been put forward as the basis (or as one of the bases) of obligation in international law:

(i) Consent of states

(ii) Customary practice

(iii) A sense of "rightness"—the juridical conscience

(iv) Natural law or natural reason

(v) Social necessity

(vi) The will of the international community (the "consensus" of the international community)

(vii) Direct (or "stigmatic") intuition

(viii) Common purposes of the participants

(ix) Effectiveness

(x) Sanctions

(xi) "Systemic" goals

(xii) Shared expectations as to authority

(xiii) Rules of recognition

On looking at this wide array of ideas concerning the "true" or "correct" basis of obligation in international law it may be wondered, on the one hand, whether the choice of a "basis" has any great practical significance and, on the other, whether the diversity of opinion does not reveal a radical weakness in the conceptual structure of international law.

For some pragmatically-inclined international lawyers, the issue is not likely to be regarded as important. As long as the obligation itself—the legal norm or prescription—can be identified in one of the so-called formal sources—treaty or custom or in general principles of law—it seems to matter little what the underlying basis of the obligation may be. It is, therefore, understandable that most contemporary treatises and textbooks on international law pass quickly and lightly over the problem of the "foundation." Like the chaplain's opening prayer at public meetings, it has little effect on what is said afterwards. The practical international lawyer is supposed to be concerned not with the foundation of obligation but with the so-called "sources," formal and material.

But this is more easily said than done. Somehow conceptions as to the basis of obligation arise time and again, and not only in theoretical discussion about the binding force of international law. They come up in concrete controversies as to whether a rule of law has emerged or has been terminated; whether an event is a violation or a precedent; and whether practice under a treaty is accepted as law. They are involved in dealing with situations in which solemn declarations, couched in legal terminology, are adopted by official bodies which have no formal authority to lay down prescriptive rules. They come up when there is substantial variance between what is preached and what is practiced; or when consensus (or expectations) are limited in geographical terms or in duration. These are not, of course, new problems and over the years they have been the subject of much jurisprudential writing. But in the last few years the general problem has assumed a new dimension. The peculiar features of contemporary international society have generated considerable normative activity without at the same time involving commensurate use of the formal procedures for international "legislation" and adjudication.

It may be useful to recall the main factors which have emerged in international life in the last few years to give enhanced importance to problems of indeterminacy of obligation.

First, there has been the much-discussed "quasi-legislative" activity by the General Assembly and other United Nations bodies purporting to lay down, expressly or by implication, requirements of State conduct or to terminate or modify existing requirements.

Second, there has been a recognition of so-called "rules of the game," based on implicit understandings or unilateral actions and acquiescence. This has been a notable feature of Great Power behavior in regard to their use of armed force.

Third, there have been the social revolutions which have overturned traditional orders and have challenged the assumptions on which prior conceptions of authority were based.

Fourth, the growing interdependence of States—especially in economic and technological activities—has vastly increased patterns of cooperation and reciprocal behavior which have not been institutionalized in the traditional modes of lawmaking.

Fifth, the increased "permeability" of national States has resulted in a diminishing barrier between matters of international concern and those of domestic jurisdiction. Related to this is the fact that the United Nations Charter—particularly its articles relating to respect for human rights and self-determination of peoples—has brought domestic activities before collective organs for appraisal on the basis of international criteria.

Sixth, the expansion of science and technology with international impact both beneficial and harmful has given rise to informal means of setting standards and exercising supervision without entering into tight and tidy legal instruments.

The mere statement of these trends indicates how extensive and far-reaching are normative processes which cannot easily be placed into the categories of treaty and customary law, at least as these terms have been applied traditionally. Lawyers are made uncomfortable by this and they ceaselessly endeavor to pour the new wine into the old bottles and to market it under the time-honored labels. They will treat many of the cases as problems of treaty interpretation; others will be dealt with on the assumptions applicable to traditional customary law. But when we examine the arguments and the grounds for decision, we find more frequently than not that the test of whether a "binding" rule exists or should be applied will involve basic jurisprudential assumptions. Even the International Court of Justice, which is governed expressly by Article 38 of its Statute as to the sources of law, has demonstrated time and again that in their deliberative process the judges have had to look to theory to evaluate practice.

* * *

By way of conclusion I shall anticipate some objections to the main tenor of my thesis and offer a brief defense.

First there is the criticism of those who will consider that "legal obligation" may be dissolved by having it depend on expectations, perceptions and probable compliance. In their view "legality like virtue is not a matter of degree" and while we may have compassion we should have no uncertainty when the fallen damsel has indeed fallen. But actually most of us will view virtue as a matter of degree and we should recognize that legal obligation—whether national or international—also may involve "degrees" and that it will depend on attitudes, expectations and compliance. True, these factors will in turn depend on law. The circularity is there, but it is not vicious; it simply takes account of interactions and influences. To be sure, at a given point one may have to decide in a concrete context whether or not an obligation exists (this can also be stated in operational terms) and that judgment will have to be made on the basis of the relevant variables. The more serious risk is to live in a "make-believe" world where the "law is always the law" and as a consequence in cynical reaction to reject a large body of normative phenomena that are actually operative in international behavior. To impose hard-and-fast categories on a world filled with indeterminacies and circularities can only result in a pseudo-realism which does justice neither to our experience nor to our higher purposes.

A second objection may come from those who believe that diverse political and cultural determinants preclude any truly international obligations in today's world. But this is a question of empirical fact, not of *a priori* judgment, and, as we indicated above, our experience provides enough evidence to indicate that divergent systems and beliefs exhibit concordances on a wide array of international norms. We have ample proof that mankind shares common characteristics and needs and its efforts to satisfy those needs provide a realistic basis for an international normative structure. In our view the specific features of that structure must be identified and validated in terms of shared expectations and attitudes, rather than in trans-empirical terms.

JOHN H. JACKSON, WORLD TRADE AND THE LAW OF GATT 757, 760, 763 (1969)[5]

Departures from legal norms always occur in a legal system, to one degree or another. There is nothing unique about GATT or international legal norms in this respect. Many domestic laws fall into disuse or are abused. There is usually a price to be paid, however, for the widespread existence of practice that is inconsistent with the legal obligations. The price is not always easy to measure, but often the phrase "disrespect for the law" is used as a shorthand expression for it. The existence of practice that is inconsistent with legal rules, particularly when such divergent practice results in profit of one kind or another, usually increases the incentive for other departures from the rule and, therefore, the number of other departures. Consequently, one of the values of a legal rule—the enhancement of stability and predictability—is lost. Of course the practice of departing from legal rules can be limited to specific types of rules, and this can support an argument that the "custom" is itself a norm that now assists attainment of the goals of the legal system. But there are two detriments associated with such "customary" norms. First, the customary norms are usually less well-defined than legislated or agreed norms and therefore promote activity that is less stable and less predictable. Secondly, and perhaps more serious, when the customary activity is directly inconsistent with the legal norm, there are conflicting signals emitted in the prediction process and there is a danger that the custom of departing from the legal rule will encourage (or at least not discourage) departures from other legal rules.

* * *

Thus it can be seen that a variety of techniques have been utilized in GATT to achieve some of the basic objectives of the international community with respect to international trade and commerce. The four mentioned above can be summarized as: (1) legal norms, backed by a complaint or a dispute-settling procedure; (2) elaborate discussion and consultation, with a view to alerting other nations to future national policies; (3) the use of Working Parties, subcommittees, and discussions in plenary sessions to bring moral force upon countries to conform their individual national policies and practices to either the legal norms or the stated objectives of GATT; and (4) the use of negotiation and bargaining

---

5. From World Trade and the Law of GATT by John H. Jackson, copyright 1969, by the Bobbs Merrill Company, Inc. Reprinted by permission. All rights reserved.

as a means to formulate new obligations and to settle differences about old obligations.

One of the features in GATT—and most likely a feature in many international organizations and institutions today—that makes it more complex to evaluate the degree of "compliance" with the existing legal norms is the confusion and ambiguity that exists about the nature of some of those norms. Some of these norms can be separated into two groups. One group might be labeled "norms of obligations" while another group may be labeled "norms of aspiration." This dichotomy touches a basic problem of legal philosophy that exists in domestic law also. It requires elaboration.

Norms of obligations can be used to designate those legal norms toward which the attitude is that a person or country should feel obligated to follow. This feeling of obligation may stem from an idea of moral duty or a pragmatic recognition of consequences that might follow if the norm is broken but, in either case, the term designates more than just a "statement of purpose or objective."

A "norm of aspiration," on the other hand, can be used to designate a mode of conduct that everyone thinks is desirable, but toward which there is no feeling of obligation. Nations generally feel obligated to fulfill their treaty agreements. But when an international body votes a "recommendation," even if a nation voted in favor of the recommendation, it may not feel obligated to carry out that recommendation.

* * *

This somewhat elaborate discussion leads to the following point: there is a danger in mixing "norms of obligation" in the same instrument with "norms of aspiration," when the distinction between the two is not clearly signaled to the participants of that instrument. The danger is that some countries will consider a particular phrase to be a "norm of obligation" while others will consider the same phrase to be a "norm of aspiration." This can lead to tensions and disputes in international affairs and it can also be very misleading to particular participants in the institution. When many countries follow certain international obligations, the premium (in terms of economic reward) to a country that decides to depart from that obligation may be even greater than it would have been had there been no obligation at all. Just as in domestic society when the production or sale of an opiate drug is prohibited, the profit to be realized by successful evasion of that prohibition is immensely greater than would be the case if there were no prohibition at all. In certain circumstances, the same may be true in international economic relations. Another side of the same coin is the fact that certain activities that are inconsistent with an international legal norm have a greater chance of succeeding when other nations are inhibited from retaliation by the existence of that or other similar norms.

STATEMENT OF GATT DIRECTOR–GENERAL ARTHUR DUNKEL[6]

[I]nternational economic policy commitments, in the form of agreed rules, have far-reaching domestic effects, indeed effects so important that they are indispensable for democratic governance. They are the element which secures the ultimate coordination and mutual compatibility of the purely domestic economic policies. They form the basis from which the government can arbitrate and secure an equitable and efficient balance between the diverse domestic interests: producers vs consumers, export industries vs import-competing industries, between particular narrowly defined industries. Last but not least, only a firm commitment to international rules makes possible the all-important reconciliation, which I have already alluded to, of the necessary balance on the production side and on the financial side of the national economy.

I am still convinced that it is in the national interest of every trading nation to abide by the rules, which were accepted as valid for good times and bad, and to frame their internal policies accordingly. One of the major benefits of international disciplines is that they offer equal opportunities and require comparable sacrifices from all the countries involved in international competition. Those who believe in the open trading system must recognize and accept the need to correct those rigidities in their economic and social systems which obstruct the process of continuing adjustment on which economic growth depends.* * *

JOHN H. JACKSON, SOVEREIGNTY, THE WTO, AND CHANGING FUNDAMENTALS OF INTERNATIONAL LAW[7]

Persons who have the misfortune of tangling deeply with the logic and sources of international law generally, know well the extensive history and literature of the subject, embracing the Greeks and Romans and, more recently, eminent philosophers including Kant, Austin, Kelsen, Stone, and many more in recent decades.[8] These and others realize how, in some cases, a rigorous pursuit of the "holy grails" of universal truths can end in a recognition of "universal uncertainties." Indeed some of this phenomenon is an attribute of legal philosophy generally, with its many rich avenues of discourse and some remarkable contributions to understanding. To some extent, international law is but a subsubject of the broader explorations of questions such as "what is law?" and numerous other jurisprudential main and side streets. An interesting question, not to be considered in depth here, is whether there is

6. Address in Hamburg, West Germany. GATT Press Release No. 1312, March 5, 1982.

7. John H. Jackson, Sovereignty, the WTO, and Changing Fundamentals of International Law 32–33 (Cambridge University Press, 2006).

8. For an overview of the history of international law, see Arthur Nussbaum, A Concise History of the Law of Nations (Macmillan, rev. ed. 1954); David J. Bederman, International Law in Antiquity (Cambridge University Press, 2001).

something about international law that renders these explorations "different in kind" and not just "different in degree." The complexity of multi-levels of power, legitimacy, monopolies of force or lacks thereof, perhaps suggest some such difference.

In that light, and recognizing the limited goal of this chapter, a number of questions about international law can be mentioned (but only as a sample of a broader terrain.) Here are some:

(1) What is the source of international law?

(2) Related to (1) what are the elements of legitimacy for international law norms?

(3) To what degree are those two questions related to and dependent on the concept of sovereignty (a concept under considerable criticism which Chapter 3 will overview)?

(4) What is the role of empirical observation (sometimes logically related to a concept termed "induction") in attempts to answer the questions above?

(5) How should "compliance" with the norms affect some of these questions, and if (as would be maintained in this work) compliance is a key to effectiveness of norms, what sort of practices might enhance the degree of compliance with international law norms?

(6) How do disciplines such as international relations (political science), and economics relate to these questions?

These and other questions are constant challenges to the broad subject of international law (and to law generally), but the goal here is to focus more particularly on the effects of "globalization" on these and other questions as related to activity we can list under the phrase "international economic law" or, more particularly, the WTO. In other words, what are the actual or potential effects (including long-term effects) of the phenomena outlined in the previous section on international law in general and international economic law (as part of international law) in particular?

SECTION 5.2   CERTAIN FUNDAMENTALS OF INTERNATIONAL LAW

(A) SOURCES: CUSTOM OR TREATIES?

Traditionally, the sources of international law have been enumerated similarly to the list found in Article 38 of the Statute of the International Court of Justice:[1]

Article 38.—1. The Court, whose function is to decide in accordance with international law such disputes as are submitted to it, shall apply:

1. Statute of the International Court of Justice, annexed to the Charter of the United Nations; signed at San Francisco, June 26, 1945; entered into force for the United States on Oct. 24, 1945 (59 Stat. 1031, 1055; TS 993; 3 Bevans 1153).

a. international conventions, whether general or particular, establishing rules expressly recognized by the contesting states;

b. international custom, as evidence of a general practice accepted as law;

c. the general principles of law recognized by civilized nations;

d. subject to the provisions of Article 59, judicial decisions and the teachings of the most highly qualified publicists of the various nations, as subsidiary means for the determination of rules of law.

2. This provision shall not prejudice the power of the Court to decide a case ex aequo et bono, if the parties agree thereto.

Yet it is generally recognized that rules or standards which effectively influence international action do not always fall within the above categories. The problem of recognizing the development of a new rule from the sources listed is often formidable.

JOHN H. JACKSON, THE WORLD TRADING SYSTEM 26–27 (2nd Ed. 1997)[2]

Sources of international law can generally be divided into "customary" or "conventional." The latter term refers to treaties, which are often termed "conventions." Customary international law is defined as rules of national behavior that can be ascertained from the practice of nations when such practice reveals that nations are acting under a sense of legal obligation (opinio juris). Unfortunately, customary international law norms are quite often ambiguous and controversial. On many propositions of customary international law, scholars and practitioners disagree not only about their meaning but even about their existence. The traditional doctrines of establishing a norm of customary international law leave a great deal of room for such controversy.

(B) CUSTOMARY NORMS OF INTERNATIONAL LAW: WHAT ARE THEY?

AMERICAN LAW INSTITUTE, RESTATEMENT OF THE LAW (THIRD), FOREIGN RELATIONS LAW OF THE UNITED STATES, § 102 COMMENT B (1987)[3]

* * * "Practice of states" * * * includes diplomatic acts and instructions as well as public measures and other governmental acts and

---

2. © 1997 by The Massachusetts Institute of Technology. Reprinted with permission of The MIT Press.

3. This and other excerpts from this publication in this chapter are reprinted by permission of the American Law Institute.

official statements of policy, whether they are unilateral or undertaken in cooperation with other states * * *. Inaction may constitute state practice, as when a state acquiesces in acts of another state that affect its legal rights. The practice necessary to create customary law may be of comparatively short duration, but * * * it must be "general and consistent." A practice can be general even if it is not universally followed; there is no precise formula to indicate how widespread a practice must be, but it should reflect wide acceptance among the states particularly involved in the relevant activity. Failure of a significant number of important states to adopt a practice can prevent a principle from becoming general customary law though it might become "particular customary law" for the participating states. * * * A principle of customary law is not binding on a state that declares its dissent from the principle during its development.

In a book entitled "The Concept of Custom in International Law," Professor D'Amato notes the "tremendous amount of disagreement among scholars and publicists over the rules of customary international law,"[4] and Professor Byers has written that,[5]

> Unlike treaty rules, which result from formal negotiation and explicit acceptance, rules of customary international law arise out of frequently ambiguous combinations of behavioural regularity and expressed or inferred acknowledgments of legality. Despite (or perhaps because of) their informal origins, rules of customary international law provide substantive content to many areas of international law, as well as the procedural framework within which most rules of international law, including treaty rules, develop, exist and change.

Villiger notes:[6]

> Customary and treaty rules may exert a strong influence on each other. Non-identical rules of one source can modify rules of the other, or cause them to pass from use. Identical rules can parallel each other and assist in their mutual interpretation and ascertainment. * * * Clearly, if the rules of one source may bear in such a manner on the other, this results in a considerable relativization of the sources with regard to one another * * * Nevertheless, a relativization does not mean that customary law and treaties lose their independence or individuality, because otherwise such interactions as the customary modification of treaties would not be conceivable

4. Anthony A. D'Amato, The Concept of Custom in International Law 5 (1971).

5. Michael Byers, Custom, Power and the Power of Rules 3 (1999).

6. Mark E. Villiger, Customary International Law and Treaties: A Manual on the Theory and Practice of the Interpretation of Sources (2nd ed. 1997).

in the first place. The different conditions of the formation and existence of each source are the very cause for these processes.

IAN BROWNLIE, PRINCIPLES OF
PUBLIC INTERNATIONAL
LAW (5TH ED. 1998)[7]

Opinio juris et necessitatis. The Statute of the International Court refers to "a general practice accepted as law." Brierly speaks of recognition by states of a certain practice "as obligatory," and Hudson requires a "conception that the practice is required by, or consistent with, prevailing international law." Some writers do not consider this psychological element to be a requirement for the formation of custom, but it is in fact a necessary ingredient. The sense of legal obligation, as opposed to motives of courtesy, fairness, or morality, is real enough, and the practice of states recognizes a distinction between obligation and usage. The essential problem is surely one of proof, and especially the incidence of the burden of proof.

(C) TREATIES

MARK E. VILLIGER, CUSTOMARY INTERNATIONAL
LAW AND TREATIES 57–58 (2nd Ed. 1997)

Does international law provide for any superiority of rules of one source, namely customary law or treaties, which necessarily override rules of the other, regardless of origin, content, or duration of validity? * * * The silence in Article 38 [Statute of the International Court of Justice] as to a hierarchy of sources accurately reflects the structure of the international legal order to which an *a priori* hierarchy of the sources is an alien concept. The reason for this is that customary law and treaties are autonomous sources. * * * Some authors have given the different explanation that customary law and treaties must be independent because they can stimulate and influence each other.

JOHN H. JACKSON, SOVEREIGNTY,
THE WTO, AND CHANGING FUNDAMENTALS
OF INTERNATIONAL LAW[8]

A critical factor in treaty law is the institutional setting in which the treaty will operate, particularly as to the institutional structure for interpreting and applying the treaty. The existence in such structure of a juridical body is extremely influential on various attributes of the treaty,

---

7. This and other excerpts from this publication in this chapter are reprinted with permission of the Clarendon Press, Oxford. This material appears in the sixth edition (2003) at page 8.

8. John H. Jackson, Sovereignty, the WTO, and Changing Fundamentals of International Law, sec. 2.3, at 45 (Cambridge University Press, 2006).

including interpretation techniques, compliance effectiveness, evolutionary change, development of practice, filling of treaty gaps (ambiguities or lacunae), and so on. Sections 2.5 and 6.6 will return to this question of juridical institutions.

Combining a number of the variety dimensions discussed above, leads into questions of how a treaty application may change over time. If the membership is small, it may permit of fairly efficient changes by amending or renegotiating the treaty. But if the membership is large, like the WTO or many other organizations with well over 100 parties, the amending clauses in the treaty structure are often not usable because of super-majority requirements and/or other political or practical constraints. This can lead to "treaty rigidity" which can be recognized in a large number of important current international law institutions including the United Nations, the Bretton Woods group (the IMF and the World Bank), and of course the WTO. When there is treaty rigidity in organizations which have to cope with constant and accelerating change of circumstances (such as the globalized economy), a very serious question arises as to how such institution can or should cope with change. This becomes essentially a "constitutional" question, although many diplomats abhor (or are frightened by) the term "constitutional."

Perhaps the most important source of international obligation and the one which writers tend to think is most often followed, treaties, nevertheless, pose a series of difficult questions. The basic "core" principle is "pacta sunt servanda." But how are treaties formed? Who do they bind? How are they changed? What effect do they have on domestic law of nations that are parties to the treaty? How are treaties terminated? How are they interpreted? Various attempts have been made to codify or systematize rules relating to these questions, the most prominent for the United States being the American Law Institute 1987 Restatement (Third) of the Foreign Relations Law of the United States, and the U.N. International Law Commission Convention on the Law of Treaties, put in final form at a conference at Vienna in 1969.[9] The Convention came into force in 1980. The United States has not ratified it, but considers many of its provisions to be rules of customary international law.

9. The Vienna Convention on the Law of Treaties, with annex, done at Vienna, 23 May, 1969 (text: UNGA U.N. Doc. A/Conf. 39/27, May 23, 1969; see also U.N. Conf. on the Law of Treaties, UNGA U.N. Docs. A/Conf. 39/1–28). See also Ian M. Sinclair, The Vienna Convention on the Law of Treaties (2d ed. 1984); T.O. Elias, The Mod- ern Law of Treaties (1974); Shabtai Rosenne, The Law of Treaties: A Guide to the Legislative History of the Vienna Convention (1970). The Restatement (Third) closely follows the Vienna Convention. See American Law Institute, Restatement of the Law (Third), Foreign Relations of the United States, secs. 301–339 (1987).

VIENNA CONVENTION ON THE LAW OF TREATIES

Article 26. Pacta Sunt Servanda

Every treaty in force is binding upon the parties to it and must be performed by them in good faith.

Article 27. Internal Law and Observance of Treaties

A party may not invoke the provisions of its internal law as justification for its failure to perform a treaty. This rule is without prejudice to article 46.

* * *

Article 31. General Rule of Interpretation

1.   A treaty shall be interpreted in good faith in accordance with the ordinary meaning to be given to the terms of the treaty in their context and in the light of its object and purpose.

2.   The context for the purpose of the interpretation of a treaty shall comprise, in addition to the text, including its preamble and annexes:

(a) any agreement relating to the treaty which was made between all the parties in connection with the conclusion of the treaty;

(b) any instrument which was made by one or more parties in connection with the conclusion of the treaty and accepted by the other parties as an instrument related to the treaty.

3.   There shall be taken into account, together with the context:

(a) any subsequent agreement between the parties regarding the interpretation of the treaty or the application of its provisions;

(b) any subsequent practice in the application of the treaty which establishes the agreement of the parties regarding its interpretation;

(c) any relevant rules of international law applicable in the relations between the parties.

4.   A special meaning shall be given to a term if it is established that the parties so intended.

Article 32. Supplementary Means of Interpretation

Recourse may be had to supplementary means of interpretation, including the preparatory work of the treaty and the circumstances of its conclusion, in order to confirm the meaning resulting from the application of article 31, or to determine the meaning when the interpretation according to article 31:

(a) leaves the meaning ambiguous or obscure; or

(b) leads to a result which is manifestly absurd or unreasonable.

ARTICLE 33. INTERPRETATION OF TREATIES AUTHENTICATED
IN TWO OR MORE LANGUAGES

1. When a treaty has been authenticated in two or more languages, the text is equally authoritative in each language, unless the treaty provides or the parties agree that, in case of divergence, a particular text shall prevail.

* * *

ARTICLE 34. GENERAL RULE REGARDING THIRD STATES

A treaty does not create either obligations or rights for a third State without its consent.

* * *

ARTICLE 46. PROVISIONS OF INTERNAL LAW REGARDING
COMPETENCE TO CONCLUDE TREATIES

1. A State may not invoke the fact that its consent to be bound by a treaty has been expressed in violation of a provision of its internal law regarding competence to conclude treaties as invalidating its consent unless that violation was manifest and concerned a rule of its internal law of fundamental importance.

2. A violation is manifest if it would be objectively evident to any State conducting itself in the matter in accordance with normal practice and in good faith.

* * *

ARTICLE 60. TERMINATION OR SUSPENSION OF THE OPERATION
OF A TREATY AS A CONSEQUENCE OF ITS BREACH

1. A material breach of a bilateral treaty by one of the parties entitles the other to invoke the breach as a ground for terminating the treaty or suspending its operation in whole or in part.

2. A material breach of a multilateral treaty by one of the parties entitles:

(a) the other parties by unanimous agreement to suspend the operation of the treaty in whole or in part or to terminate it either:

(i) in the relations between themselves and the defaulting State, or

(ii) as between all the parties;

(b) a party specially affected by the breach to invoke it as a ground for suspending the operation of the treaty in whole or in part in the relations between itself and the defaulting State;

(c) any party other than the defaulting State to invoke the breach as a ground for suspending the operation of the treaty in whole or in part with respect to itself if the treaty is of such a character that a material breach of its provisions by one party radically changes the position of every party with respect to the further performance of its obligations under the treaty.

3.   A material breach of a treaty, for the purposes of this article, consists in:

(a) a repudiation of the treaty not sanctioned by the present Convention; or

(b) the violation of a provision essential to the accomplishment of the object or purpose of the treaty.

* * *

ARTICLE 62. FUNDAMENTAL CHANGE OF CIRCUMSTANCES

1.   A fundamental change of circumstances which has occurred with regard to those existing at the time of the conclusion of a treaty, and which was not foreseen by the parties, may not be invoked as a ground for terminating or withdrawing from the treaty unless:

(a) the existence of those circumstances constituted an essential basis of the consent of the parties to be bound by the treaty; and

(b) the effect of the change is radically to transform the extent of obligations still to be performed under the treaty.

* * *

ARTICLE 64. EMERGENCE OF A NEW PEREMPTORY NORM
OF GENERAL INTERNATIONAL LAW (JUS COGENS)

If a new peremptory norm of general international law emerges, any existing treaty which is in conflict with that norm becomes void and terminates.

JOHN H. JACKSON, SOVEREIGNTY, THE WTO, AND CHANGING FUNDAMENTALS OF INTERNATIONAL LAW[10]

In fact, as observers and practitioners of international law relating to treaties know well, there are a very large number of interpretive techniques. There is no attempt in this brief overview to inventory all of them, but most lists of treaty interpretive techniques would include the items set forth in the footnote.[11] Readers will certainly recognize that

10. John H. Jackson, Sovereignty, the WTO, and Changing Fundamentals of International Law 183–184 (Cambridge University Press, 2006).

11. The following are treaty interpretation concepts or approaches possibly relevant: priority to text and plain meaning; attention to the intent of the drafts persons; preparatory work (sometimes termed legislative history); the object and purpose of the agreement; a doctrine that no clause in a treaty should be without some impact, and therefore, the treaty should be interpreted to implement each treaty clause; questions of when there is conflict between different parts of a treaty, and how to define conflict, and whether the different treaty provisions can be reconciled; prior

some, but not all, of these treaty interpretation techniques are embodied in the language of the VCLT, and they will recall that the VCLT is not applicable "as such" in many situations, particularly regarding large multilateral organizations, because the VCLT has not been ratified by many of the members. This is particularly true of the WTO.[12] Although not applicable as a treaty, the language of the VCLT nevertheless has been widely accepted as expressing the customary international law of treaties, at least as to interpretation, and, therefore, it is often referred to in contexts where it does not strictly apply as a treaty. This is certainly the case in the WTO (and in GATT before it), where panels have, on several important occasions, quoted extensively from the VCLT, particularly as to interpretation in Articles 31 and 32, as noted earlier in this chapter.

However, there is room for rethinking the application and adequacy of the VCLT regarding treaty interpretation. It can be questioned whether that treaty, in many instances, seems more suited to application to bilateral treaty situations (or at least small group situations) than to large on-going, multilateral treaties. These large multilateral treaties have aspects resembling more a constitution than a bilateral contract.

(D) SOVEREIGNTY, SOVEREIGN EQUALITY AND THE PROBLEM OF VOTING

IAN BROWNLIE, PRINCIPLES OF PUBLIC INTERNATIONAL LAW 289
(5th Ed. 1998) (6th Ed. at 287)

The sovereignty and equality of states represent the basic constitutional doctrine of the law of nations, which governs a community

---

practice over time, or practice under the agreement; teleological interpretation; evolutionary interpretation; realist school of interpretation, focusing on the juridical preferences of the individuals who are the judges; a broader general policy motivation for interpreting the text (or interpreting the treaty relatively unconstrained by the text); standards of review (degree of deference to the nation state); situations where the text seems to imply further aspects of the treaty obligations not necessarily explicitly mentioned; general obligation of good faith in treaty implementation; reasonably expectations of the parties to the treaty; mandate to be guided by the decisions and dispute reports of other organizations or predecessor organizations (such as GATT); rules on burden of proof using presumptions and ideas about shifting burden of proof; notions of balancing some of the interpretation techniques by consideration of non-trade policies; ideas of interpreting a treaty in the direction of multilateralism rather than unilateralism.

12. The WTO Member states who have *not* ratified the VCLT, are: Angola, Antigua & Barbuda, Bahrain, Bangladesh, Belize, Benin, Bolivia, Botswana, Brazil, Brunei, Burkina Faso, Burundi, Cambodia, Chad, Côte d'Ivoire, Djibouti, Dominica, Dominican Republic, El Salvador, Fiji, France, Gambia, Ghana, Grenada, Guinea, Guinea Bissau, Guyana, Hong Kong, Iceland, India, Indonesia, Ireland, Israel, Jordan, Kenya, Macao, Madagascar, Maldives, Mauritania, Namibia, Nepal, Nicaragua, Norway, Pakistan, Papua New Guinea, Qatar, Romania, Saint Kitts and Nevis, Saint Lucia, Sierra Leone, Singapore, South Africa, Sri Lanka, Swaziland, Taipei, Thailand, Trinidad & Tobago, Turkey, Uganda, United Arab Emirates, United States, Venezuela, Zambia, and Zimbabwe. *See* the current list of countries that have ratified the Vienna Convention, available at http://untreaty.un.org (by subscription), visited February 20, 2008.

consisting primarily of states having a uniform legal personality. If international law exists, then the dynamics of state sovereignty can be expressed in terms of law, and, as states are equal and have legal personality, sovereignty is in a major aspect a relation to other states (and to organizations of states) defined by law. The principal corollaries of the sovereignty and equality of states are: (1) a jurisdiction, prima facie exclusive, over a territory and the permanent population living there; (2) a duty of non-intervention in the area of exclusive jurisdiction of other states; and (3) the dependence of obligations arising from customary law and treaties on the consent of the obligor.

LOUIS HENKIN, THE MYTHOLOGY OF SOVEREIGNTY[13]

1.   Talk of "sovereignty" is heavy in the political air, often polluting it.

2.   "Sovereignty" sometimes subsumes—and conceals—important values. It is used to express the essential quality of a state, the basic entity, abstract but real, of the international political systems. "Sovereignty" is used to describe the autonomy of states and the need for state consent to make law and build institutions. "Sovereignty" is used to justify and define the "privacy" of states, their political independence and territorial integrity; their right and the rights of their peoples to be let alone and to go their own way.

But sovereignty has also grown a mythology of state grandeur and aggrandizement that misconceives the concept and clouds what is authentic and worthy in it, a mythology that is often empty and sometimes destructive of human values.

3.   For example: Sometimes—a half century after the UN Charter!—we still hear that a sovereign state cannot give up its sovereignty right to go to war, or to act in self-defense or in defense of other "vital interests," as it sees them. Often we still hear that a sovereign state cannot agree to be bound by particular international norms—e.g., on human rights, or on economic integration (as in Europe). Even more often, sovereignty has been invoked to resist "intrusive" measures to monitor compliance with international obligations—human rights commitments or arms control agreements.

4.   It is time to bring sovereignty down to earth; to examine, analyze, reconceive the concept, cut it down to size, break out its normative content, repackage it, perhaps even rename it.

* * *

9.   I do not insist that in international life there should necessarily be more rather than less governance. Minimal international governance means greater autonomy and privacy for states and societies, which are

---

13. Reproduced with permission from ASIL Newsletter (March–May 1993), at 1 &   6. © The American Society of International Law.

important values in international as in national life. But excessive international governance does not loom as a great threat; international law and institutions are still primitive. More international regulation generally and stronger international institutions may come with the enlightenment that comes with democracy in national societies, but for now, surely, there is need for effective international governance at least for maintaining international peace and to prevent genocide and other massive, gross violations of human rights.

* * *

11.   Away with the "S" word!

STEPHEN D. KRASNER, SOVEREIGNTY: ORGANIZED HYPOCRISY[14]

This muddle in part reflects the fact that the term "sovereignty" has been used in different ways, and in part it reveals the failure to recognize that the norms and rules of any international institutional system, including the sovereign state system, will have limited influence and always be subject to challenge because of logical contradictions (nonintervention versus promoting democracy, for instance), the absence of any institutional arrangement for authoritatively resolving conflicts (the definition of an international system), power asymmetries among principal actors, notably states, and the differing incentives confronting individual rulers.

* * *

The term sovereignty has been used in four different ways—international legal sovereignty, Westphalian sovereignty, domestic sovereignty, and interdependence sovereignty. International legal sovereignty refers to the practices associated with mutual recognition, usually between territorial entities that have formal juridical independence. Wesphalian sovereignty refers to political organization based on the exclusion of external actors from authority structures within a given territory. Domestic sovereignty refers to the formal organization of political authority within the state and the ability of public authorities to regulate the flow of information, ideas, goods, people, pollutants, or capital across the borders of their state. * * *

Organized hypocrisy is the normal state of affairs.

————————

Readers may find it interesting and amusing to read the 1648 Treaty of Westphalia (often said to be the origin of nation-state sovereignty

14. Reprinted from Stephen D. Krasner,   (Princeton University Press, 1999).
Sovereignty: Organized   Hypocrisy   3–9

concepts). This can be found on the World Wide Web by searching for "Treaty of Westphalia."

JOHN H. JACKSON, SOVEREIGNTY, THE WTO, AND CHANGING FUNDAMENTALS OF INTERNATIONAL LAW[15]

In broad brush, it is possible to see the antiquated definition of sovereignty that should be relegated as something like the notion of a nation-states supreme absolute power and authority over its subjects and territory, unfettered by any higher law or rule (except perhaps ethical or religious standards) unless the nation-state consents in an individual and meaningful way. It could be characterized as the nation-state's power (embodied in the Prince?) to violate virgins, chop off heads, arbitrarily confiscate property, and indulge in all sorts of other excessive and inappropriate actions.

No sensible person would agree that such an antiquated version of sovereignty exists at all in today's world. A multitude of treaties and customary international law norms impose international legal constraints (at least) that circumscribe extreme forms of arbitrary actions on even a sovereign's own citizens.

But then what does sovereignty, as practically used today, signify? Here we can consider a tentative hypothesis: most (but not all) of the time when sovereignty is used in current policy debates it really refers to questions about the allocation of power; normally government decision-making power. That is, when a party argues that the US should not accept a treaty because to do so would take away US sovereignty, what the party most often really means is that he or she believes a certain set of decisions should, as a matter of good government policy, be made at the nation-state (US) level and not at an international level.[16] Another way to put it, is to ask whether a certain governmental decision should be made in Geneva, Washington DC, Sacramento, Berkeley, or even a smaller sub-national or sub-federal unit of government. Or, when focusing on Europe, should a decision be taken in Geneva, Brussels, Berlin, Bavaria, Munich, or a smaller unit?[17]

Question

A question to consider in relation to the WTO: Is full nation-state sovereignty a requirement of membership in the WTO? See Section 6.6 and WTO Articles XI, XII, and XIII.

---

15. John H. Jackson, Sovereignty, the WTO, and Changing Fundamentals of International Law 71–72 (Cambridge University Press, 2006).

16. The author previously articulated these concepts in John H. Jackson, The Jurisprudence of the GATT and the WTO: Insights on Treaty Law and Economic Relations (Cambridge University Press, 2000),

at 369. "Power" is used here similarly to the phrase "effective" or "legitimate authority," although these terms could be subject to considerable additional discussion.

17. John H. Jackson, *Sovereignty— Modern: A New Approach to an Outdated Concept,* 97 Am.J.Intl.L. 782–802 (2003).

One of the more perplexing questions of current international economic affairs is the problem of the appropriate structure for voting in international organizations. There are strong proponents for equal voting, "one nation—one vote," and equally strong proponents for other systems. The following excerpts may suggest some of the policies involved in connection with this question, but they do not convey the intensity with which various views are held.

ROBERT A. KLEIN, SOVEREIGN EQUALITY AMONG STATES: THE HISTORY OF AN IDEA[18]

The resolutions of the United Nations are theoretically capable of expressing the general will of its members. The claim to legitimacy, however, is wide open to question. There is a gross disproportion between voting power and real power. The smallest and financially weakest states, representing a minority of the total population in the organization, possess a majority of the votes. Paying a fractional share of the assessments of the organization, they are able to outvote those paying the highest rates. At budget time, when expenditures for the coming year come up for approval, the major powers, paying two-thirds of all UN costs, feel the full impact of majority rule. They find themselves chosen to foot the bill for projects which they voted against and which the majority, by themselves could never afford.

[According to Klein, this often leads to injustices and irresponsible behavior. As an example he points at the reasoning of the General Assembly with regard to Gibraltar.] In 1713 Spain transferred the rock to Britain under the terms of the Treaty of Utrecht. In recent years Spain has contested before the appropriate organs of the United Nations the ancient cession of its territory. A 1966 resolution of the General Assembly invited the two parties to start negotiations and both accepted. [Great Britain, however, found that it] could not simply transfer one population to the rule of another country without regard to the opinions and desires of the people concerned. [The British Government therefore organized a referendum. According to the United Nations and Spain, however] the matter did not involve a colonial situation but the territorial integrity of Spain. The fate of the Gibraltarians was a matter to be determined solely by bilateral negotiations between the British and Spanish governments.

Britain, nevertheless, held the referendum. Forty-four voters chose to be affiliated with Spain; over 12,000 elected to remain under British rule. In spite of this overwhelming expression the General Assembly sought to nullify the result. Resolution 2429 XXIII declared the continuation of the colonial situation in Gibraltar incompatible with the purposes of the Charter and previous Assembly resolutions. Britain was given a deadline: to end its rule by 1 October 1969.

18. Reprinted from Sovereign Equality Among States: The History of an Idea, at 148–149, by Robert A. Klein, by permission of the University of Toronto Press© University of Toronto Press 1974.

That day has long since come and gone. Neither Spain nor Britain has changed its position. The UN is powerless to enforce its resolution. Spain and Britain have resumed bilateral talks. But the contradictory levels of meaning embodied in the idea of equality and its corollary, the principle of self-determination, stand exposed.

Questions

How do these issues relate to the question which States should have a permanent seat on the U.N. Security Council, or how the relative size of the Member States of the European Union should be reflected in the weight of their vote in the EU Council and the number of seats they have in the European Parliament? Are these issues also comparable to those related to the representational characters of the House of Representatives and the Senate in the American constitutional system? How should these issues affect governing principles of international economic organizations?

HENRY G. SCHERMERS & NIELS BLOKKER, INTERNATIONAL INSTITUTIONAL LAW: UNITY WITHIN DIVERSITY §§ 795–797 (3rd Rev. Ed. 1995)[19]

B.   Weighted Voting

(i) Desirability

Several systems of weighted voting have been considered in order to compensate the inequality of Members.[20] The main argument in favor of this procedure is one of equality. It is unfair for the interests of a large population to be set aside in favor of the interests of two or three other populations which, even when combined, are smaller.

Another argument for weighted voting is its mitigating effect on "trading" with votes. In systems where votes are not weighted, states which have votes but no substantial interests may vote in favor of a proposal in order to gain support for other proposals instead of basing their vote on the issue involved. The effect of such abuses is decreased by giving States relatively fewer votes in matters in which they are not directly interested.

The main problem of weighted voting is the criterion on which extra weight should be given. Should it be population, national income, power, or some other criterion?

19. © 1995, 1997, 1999 Kluwer Law International. This and other excerpts from this work in this chapter are reprinted with the kind permission from Kluwer International.

20. [original note 135] Catharine Senf Manno, Selective Weighted Voting in the UN General Assembly, 20 Int.Org. (1966), pp. 37–62, and further literature quoted there (p. 37); Carol Barret and Hanna Newcombe, Weighted Voting in International Organizations, Peace Research Reviews, April 1968; Joseph Gold, Weighted Voting Power: Some Limits and Some Problems, 68 AJIL (1974), pp. 687–708; F.K. Listerm Decision–Making Strategies for International Organizations: The IMF Model (1989).

As a rule, the size of the population seems the most suitable factor, but in several fields this does not seem appropriate. States like China and India, which would thus obtain the greatest voting strength, have limited interest in foreign trade, air navigation, or safety at sea, which are of great importance to smaller States such as the Netherlands and Norway.

Several other criteria have also been considered. Voting power proportional to financial contribution unduly favors the richer States (contributions are based on financial capacity, rather than on the interests involved). Furthermore, this weighting may create problems if the decisions are so important that States would be prepared to pay larger contributions in order to obtain extra votes.

* * *

Only when the interests involved are specific and isolated from other interests is it relatively easy to find a key for a weighted voting system. If an organization covers many different interests, the use of a weighted voting formula might be considered only for some isolated subject matters and either a non-weighted or a differently weighted voting system for other subjects. This will inevitably lead to problems in defining to which category a particular question belongs, and although clear preliminary definitions may limit such problems, they can never be entirely excluded.

(E) ROLE OF PRECEDENT

STATUTE OF THE INTERNATIONAL COURT OF JUSTICE (1945)

ARTICLE 59

The decision of the Court has no binding force except between the parties and in respect of that particular case.

IAN BROWNLIE, PRINCIPLES OF PUBLIC INTERNATIONAL LAW 21 (5th Ed. 1998)

Strictly speaking, the Court does not observe a doctrine of precedent, but strives nevertheless to maintain judicial consistency.

JOHN H. JACKSON, SOVEREIGNTY, THE WTO, AND CHANGING FUNDAMENTALS OF INTERNATIONAL LAW[21]

a) Precedent: Many flavors of a complex concept

Too often some observers and commentators (publicists) have tended to discuss the use of precedent in judicial decision-making as involv-

---

21. John H. Jackson, Sovereignty, the WTO, and Changing Fundamentals of International Law 173–175 (Cambridge University Press, 2006).

ing a dichotomous choice. They talk about it in terms of whether there is the principle of *stare decisis*, or not. Like many dichotomous analyses, this is deeply flawed.[22] Actually, when one begins to examine the real world, and looks at comparisons between various legal systems, it is quickly apparent that there are a number of different approaches to the underlying problem. That underlying problem is the question of how much influence a prior decision of a judicial body should have when considering new cases.

Stare decisis is a concept generally applied only in common law jurisdictions of the world, which is to say those jurisdictions that derive their legal system, at least in a major proportion, from that of England. *Stare decisis* is a rather strong form of "precedent," and sometimes the terms are used interchangeably. Nevertheless, there are many jurisdictions of the world, both at the nation-state level, above and below (including, generally, international law juridical systems), which use a degree of precedent in their deliberations. This degree of precedent can vary from one system to another, and sometimes can vary within the same system, depending on the nature of different groupings of cases. Often, it is said that European continental legal systems are not based on *stare decisis* and, some would even say, are not based on a precedent system, because, arguably, the courts are supposed to work from a statutory or codified set of norms directly, without being unduly tilted by prior cases. There is even some historical practice that tended to forbid judges from citing or relying on precedent.[23] Yet when, in today's world, contemporary court reports are examined, it is often the case that there is at least reference made to prior cases, and many people generally believe that the prior cases have a considerable impact. To some extent, observation of human behavior suggests a desire for consistency, and with respect to certain societal goals, particularly in the economic area, a degree of predictability and stability, has important impacts on the success of economic and other societal structures.

22. See Raj Bhala, The Myth About Stare Decisis and International Trade Law (Part One of a Trilogy), American University International Law Review 14 (1999): 845; Raj Bhala, The Precedent Setters: De Facto Stare Decisis in WTO Adjudication (Part Two of a Trilogy), Florida State University Journal of Transnational Law & Policy 9 (1999): 1; Raj Bhala, The Power of the Past: Towards De Jure Stare Decisis in WTO Adjudication (Part Three of a Trilogy), George Washington International Law Review (2001): 873. See also Zhu Lanye, The Effects of the WTO Dispute Settlement Panel and Appellate Body Reports: Is the Dispute Settlement Body Resolving Specific Disputes Only or Making Precedent at the Same Time?, Temple International and Comparative Law Journal 17 (2003): 221.

23. This was based on the Montesquieu concept of a strict separation of powers, see Zenon Bankowski et al., Rationales for Precedent, *in* Interpreting Precedents: A Comparative Study, D. Neil MacCormick & Robert S. Summers, eds. (Ashgate/Dartmouth, 1997): 481, 482. For today's use of precedents in French law, see Article 5 of the French Civil Code which declares "it is prohibited for judges to decide by way of general provisions and rules on the cases that are brought before them." Article 455 of the Code of Civil Procedure requires a judgment to be motivated; a decision making exclusive reference to a precedent has been considered a violation of the motivation requirement, *see* Michel Troper & Christophe Grzegorczyk, Precedent in France, in Interpreting Precedents, id, at 103, 115.

But there are also clearly some legal institutions, perhaps more on the order of administrative agencies that disdain recognition of prior cases, and feel no inhibitions about doing so.

Thus, it seems clear that the word precedent has a broad application, which, in some contexts, could include the phrase *stare decisis*, but in many other contexts, such as in international tribunals, or in continental European law, does not mean *stare decisis*, but instead refers to a different form of utilization of prior cases in current case considerations. This distinction has been raised in discussions with respect to the European Court of Justice (ECJ), which sits in Luxembourg. Upon examination, it is quite clear that it is not *stare decisis* in the sense of court operations either in England, other common law countries, or the United States and its Supreme Court. There is, however, some commentary that there is something of a convergence going on in judicial affairs among these different legal systems.[24]

Nevertheless, there remains a distinction. It is not easy to get to the core of that distinction, but perhaps the discussion of the US Supreme Court in *Planned Parenthood v. Casey*,[25] is most revealing, when Justice Stevens indicates in his separate opinion, that he feels constrained by the precedent of *Roe v. Wade*,[26] such that, although he might have preferred to vote differently in *Planned Parenthood*, he felt an obligation to follow the precedent that was established by *Roe v. Wade*. By way of contrast, in the ECJ one can see situations where, without any apparent constraint by precedent, the Court endeavors to undertake to change a conclusion that they have adopted in some previous cases. Recently, one of the Advocate Generals, in his presentation to the ECJ, explicitly urged the Court to take that approach and the Court, in its judgment, noted a need to reconsider the older judgment.[27] Consequently, there is some "daylight" between the concepts of *stare decisis*, and the concept of even fairly strong use of precedent, as arguably occurs in the European Court of Justice, and probably elsewhere.

In addition, other legal systems in Europe may in fact have a somewhat softer approach to precedent than does the ECJ. It is also

---

24. John Henry Merryman, The Loneliness of the Comparative Lawyer and Other Essays in Foreign and Comparative Law (Kluwer Law International, 1999), at 17–52; Mathias Reimann, The Progress and Failure of Comparative Law in the Second Half of the Twentieth Century, American Journal of Comparative Law 50 (2002): 671.

25. Planned Parenthood of Southeastern Pa. v. Casey, 505 U.S. 833, 112 S.Ct. 2791, 120 L.Ed.2d 674 (1992).

26. Roe v. Wade, 410 U.S. 113, 93 S.Ct. 705, 35 L.Ed.2d 147 (1973).

27. SA CNL–SUCAL NV v. HAG GF AG, Case C–10/89, 1990 E.C.R., I–3711, at para. 10. In this judgment, the court held: "the Court believes it necessary to reconsid-

er the interpretation given in that judgment in the light of the case-law which has developed with regard to the relationship between industrial and commercial property and the general rules of the Treaty, particularly in the sphere of the free movement of goods," Opinion of the Advocate General, para. 67, p. 3749. Regarding the ECJ approach to precedent, see L. Neville Brown & Tom Kennedy, The Court of Justice of the European Communities, 5th ed. (Sweet & Maxwell, 2000), at 368; Alec Stone Sweet & Margaret McCown, Discretion and Precedent in European Law, in Judicial Discretion in European Perspective, Ola Wiklund, ed. (Kluwer Law International 2003): 84, 109.

interesting to note that the ECJ has been applying concepts of judicial review, which enable them to declare void ("annul") legal documents deriving from the European Commission or Council, as violating the basic treaty structure. In short, they find some of those other legal measures unconstitutional, even though, in the legal systems of many EU member states, there appears to be no doctrine of judicial review that strong.[28]

International tribunals surely do not follow *stare decisis*. The Statute of the International Court of Justice (ICJ) states, in Article 59: "The decision of the Court has no binding force except between the parties and in respect of that particular case."[29] Likewise, the general perception under international law is that, although there is a precedential effect that seems to be operating de facto and in practice, there is certainly not *stare decisis*, and in some cases, not a very strong precedent effect.

Taking all of this into account, as well as a number of other examples in the world and in the literature, it seems that a better approach to the word precedent is to view it as a multi-layered concept, or at least having a number of different approaches of different flavors. Perhaps the most stringent precedent effect is *stare decisis*, although even that is, in some cases, perhaps arguably in the United States and in the United Kingdom, less stringent than it was some decades ago. The ECJ is clearly following an approach of considerable deference to its own prior cases. It thus might be considered the next level away from *stare decisis*. Likewise, the International Court of Justice appears to relish citations of its prior cases. One can identify other legal systems that actually give even less deference and, therefore, might be considered to be another step down the ladder of a precedent rigor index. There could be a number of other gradations and, in particular towards the bottom, there could simply be an attitude that the juridical body or administrative tribunal would simply look at or take into account the reasoning of prior cases, but feel under no particular obligation to follow those cases or be very consistent with them. Of course, in the background of all of this is the extensive jurisprudential literature (particularly in the United States) that notes that courts have a number of different ways to get around, or avoid, the rigor of *stare decisis*, such as by distinguishing a case, or other interpretive techniques.[30]

28.   See Walter van Gerven, The European Union:ÊA Polity of States and Peoples (Stanford University Press, 2005), at especially Chapters 2 and 3.ÊFor the example of France, see Didier Maus, The Birth of Judicial Review of Legislation in France, *in* Constitutional Justice under Old Constitutions, Eivind Smith, ed. (Kluwer Law International 1995): 113. For the example of the United Kingdom, see William Wade, British Restriction of Judicial Review—Europe to the Rescue, *in* Judicial Review in International Perspective, Mads Andenas, ed. (Kluwer Law International, 2000): 267. On the Dutch system of limited judicial review, see Tim Koopmans, Courts and Political Institutions–A Comparative View (Cambridge University Press, 2003), at 76.

29.   Statute of the International Court of Justice, June 26, 1945, 59 Stat. 1031, T.S. No. 993, entered into effect 24 Oct. 1945.

30.   See Henry M. Hart & Albert M. Sacks, The Legal Process: Basic Problems in the Making and Application of Law, tentative ed., (Cambridge Mass., Harvard University, 1958), at 1348; H.L.A. Hart, The Concept of Law (Clarendon Press, 1961), at

(F) STATE RESPONSIBILITY

JAMES CRAWFORD, THE INTERNATIONAL LAW COMMISSION'S ARTICLES ON STATE RESPONSIBILITY: INTRODUCTION, TEXT AND COMMENTARIES (2002)[31]

ARTICLE 1—RESPONSIBILITY OF A STATE
for its INTERNATIONALLY WRONGFUL ACTS

Every internationally wrongful act of a State entails the international responsibility of that State.

ARTICLE 31—REPARATION

1.   The responsible State is under an obligation to make full repatriation for the injury caused by the internationally wrongful act.

ARTICLE 34—FORMS OF REPARATION

Full reparation for the injury caused by the internationally wrongful act shall take the form of restitution, compensation and satisfaction, either singly or in combination, in accordance with the provisions of this Chapter.

HENRY J. STEINER, DETLEV F. VAGTS & HAROLD H. KOH, TRANSNATIONAL LEGAL PROBLEMS: MATERIALS AND TEXT 338 (4th Ed. 1994)

The growth of the law of state responsibility reflected the more intense identification of the individual (or later, the corporation) with his country that accompanied the nationalistic trends of the 18th to early 20th centuries. That growth would not have taken place but for Western colonialism and economic imperialism which reached their zenith during this period. Transnational business operations centered in Europe, and later in the United States as well, penetrated Asia, Africa and Latin America. Thus security of the person and property of a national inevitably became a concern of his government. That concern manifested itself in the vigorous assertion of diplomatic protection and in the enhanced activity of arbitral tribunals. Often the arbitrations occurred under the pressure of actual or threatened military force by the aggrieved nations particularly in Latin America.

WILLIAM W. BISHOP JR., INTERNATIONAL LAW: CASES AND MATERIALS 742 (3rd Ed. 1971)

What happens procedurally is that a national of state A who feels himself wronged by state B takes the matter up with the foreign office of

131–132; Interpreting Precedents, supra note 23.   **31.** Cambridge University Press, 2002, at 61, 67.

his own country. If state A, the claimant's government, believes there has been a violation of international law by state B, it may, if it considers it desirable to do so, take the matter up through diplomatic channels with the foreign office of state B. A settlement may be reached at this stage, after presentation of the claim internationally and some negotiation; both foreign offices may agree that the claim is not good under international legal standards, or the respondent state may admit liability and make reparation. If the two states cannot agree, the claim may be submitted to arbitration, or held until enough claims have accumulated between the two states for them to create an arbitral claims commission, or dealt with as part of a lump sum settlement, often followed by adjudication before a national tribunal such as the Foreign Claims Settlement Commission of the United States.

(G) THE INDIVIDUAL AND INTERNATIONAL LAW

IAN BROWNLIE, PRINCIPLES OF PUBLIC INTERNATIONAL LAW 584–585 (5th Ed. 1998)

* * * [T]o say the individual is, or is not, a 'subject' of international law is, in either case, to say too much and to beg a great many questions. The individual does not bear responsibility for breaches of obligations imposed by the customary law of nations because most of these obligations can only rest on states and governments, and, further, he cannot bring international claims. Yet there is no rule that the individual cannot have some degree of legal personality, and he has such personality for certain purposes. Thus the individual as such is responsible for crimes against peace and humanity and for war crimes. Treaties may confer procedural capacity on individuals before international tribunals. It is not helpful therefore to pose the question as one of legal personality in all aspects or not at all. The problem, it is suggested, responds to an empirical approach. Although there is no rule that individuals cannot have procedural capacity before international jurisdictions, the assumption of the classical law that only states have procedural capacity is still dominant and affects the content of most treaties providing for the settlement of disputes which raise questions of state responsibility, in spite of the fact that frequently claims presented are in respect of the losses suffered by individuals and private corporations.

NORTH AMERICAN FREE TRADE AGREEMENT, CHAPTER ELEVEN: INVESTMENT

ARTICLE 1101

Scope and Coverage

1. This Chapter applies to measures adopted or maintained by a Party relating to: (a) investors of another Party; (b) investments of

investors of another Party in the Territory of the Party; and (c) with respect to Articles 1106 and 1114, all investments in the Territory of the Party.

* * *

ARTICLE 1116

Claim by an Investor of a Party on Its Own Behalf

1. An investor of a Party may submit to arbitration under this Section a claim that another Party has breached an obligation under: (a) Section A or Article 1503(2) (State Enterprises), or (b) Article 1502(3)(a) (Monopolies and State Enterprises) where the monopoly has acted in a manner inconsistent with the Party's obligations under Section A, and that the investor has incurred a loss or damage by reason of, or arising out of, that breach.

———

Furthermore, individual states have substantial discretion in defining the rights of individuals to enforce international law. For example, states may grant rights to individuals which they may enforce directly. Alternatively, a state may provide a remedy under its domestic law to give effect to a rule of international law. In some cases, an individual or corporation may enter into an agreement with a foreign state by the terms of which disputes arising out of the agreement are to be decided according to principles of international law.

(H) EFFECTIVENESS AND SANCTIONS

HENRY G. SCHERMERS & NIELS BLOKKER, INTERNATIONAL INSTITUTIONAL LAW §§ 1451–1517, 1549–1550 (3rd Rev. Ed. 1995)

The constitutions of most international organizations provide for some degree of coercion, but not for severe sanctions. This coercion can be introduced in cases where there is a major breach of obligations, but sometimes its use is restricted to particular situations, such as the non-payment of contributions. * * *

In some cases, the general congress may only impose specific sanctions. These sanctions usually deprive members of rights or privileges which result from their participation in the organization. * * * In other organizations, possible sanctions are not specified: the organization is empowered to take any coercive measures which it deems appropriate. * * *

Two general questions are relevant: (1) May international organizations impose sanctions on members which have violated obligations other than those contained in the constitutions of the organization? (2) May sanctions be taken which are not provided for in the constitution of the organization? A strict interpretation of powers would suggest a negative answer to both questions. An international organization's task is limited. It has no power to act beyond the field attributed to it. Expediency would also suggest a negative answer, at least to the first question. A delegation of meteorologists to a meeting of the WMO, for example, must decide whether WMO members fulfill their obligations under the WMO constitution. They may not be the most suitable people to judge whether a certain state is an aggressor or has violated basic principles of international law. On the other hand, international organizations are not isolated units: they form part of a general international structure and therefore should abide by the rules of that structure.

[Professors Schermers and Blokker discuss a number of possible sanctions, including:]

(a) Suspension of voting rights, which they say "is mainly used as sanction for the non-payment of financial contributions."

(b) Suspension of representation.

(c) Suspension of services of the organization: they cite particularly cases where the International Monetary Fund may declare a member ineligible to use its resources noting the following cases:

   (1) If a Member fails to fulfill any of its obligations under the constitution.

   (2) When the Fund is of the opinion that a Member is using its resources in a manner contrary to its purposes.

   (3) If a Member fails to exercise appropriate control to prevent the use of the Fund's resources to meet a large or sustained outflow of capital.

(d) Suspension of rights and privileges of membership.

(e) Expulsion from specific organs: They note: "(n)o constitutions provide for expulsion from particular organs as a sanction, but a member normally has no constitutional right to participate in an organ, apart from the general congress."

(f) Expulsion from the organization.

(g) Sanctions through other organizations:

Expulsion from some organizations automatically leads to ejection from others. Thus, states expelled from the UN cease to be members of UNESCO, states expelled from the International Monetary Fund cease to be members of the World Bank, states that are no longer members of the World Bank cease to be members of the IFC (International Finance Corporation) and the IDA (International Development Organization).

(h) Economic sanctions.

(i) Forces of international organizations and military enforcement: they note principally the practice of the United Nations.

(j) Other sanctions.

(k) Sanctions against individuals: publicity, warning, withdrawal of support and, most importantly, fines.

Note

We will explore some of the foregoing issues raised in this section—such as voting and sanctions—in the remainder of this chapter and in the two following chapters in the context of the International Monetary Fund and the WTO/GATT system.

SECTION 5.3 INTERNATIONAL ECONOMIC LAW

(A) INTRODUCTION

JOHN H. JACKSON, THE WORLD TRADING SYSTEM 25–26 (2d Ed. 1997)[1]

In recent years one has increasingly heard references to "international economic law."[2] Unfortunately, this phrase is not well defined. Scholars and practitioners have differing ideas about the meaning of this term. Some would have it cast a very wide net, and embrace almost any aspect of international law that relates to any sort of economic matter. Considered broadly, almost all international law could be called international economic law, because almost every aspect of international relations touches in one way or another on economics. Indeed, it can be argued from the latter observation that there cannot be any separate subject denominated as international economic law. A more restrained definition of international economic law, however, would embrace trade, investment, and services when they are involved in transactions that cross national borders, and those subjects that involve the establishment on national territory of economic activity of persons or firms originating from outside that territory.

* * *

Two unfortunate bifurcations of the subject of international economic law exist, however. One is the distinction between monetary and trade affairs. Given that both are, in a sense, "two sides of the same coin," a degree of artificiality separates them as topics. Yet international organizations, national governments, and even university departments tend to indulge in the same separation; and given that the whole world cannot

---

1. © 1997 by The Massachusetts Institute of Technology. Reprinted with permission of The MIT Press.

2. See Pieter VerLoren van Themaat, The Changing Structure of International Economic Law (1981). See also John H. Jackson, "Economic Law, International" in Encyclopedia of Public International Law (1985); Dominique Carreau et al, Droit In-

ternational Economique (1990); Paolo Picone and Giorgio Sacerdoti, Diritto Internazionale Della Economia (1982); John H. Jackson, International Economic Law: Reflections on the "Boiler Room" of International Relations, 10 American University Journal of International Law and Policy, no. 2 (Winter 1995), 595.

be studied at once, there is great practical value in taking up the trade questions separately.

An even less fortunate distinction of subject matter is often made between international and domestic rules. This book will not indulge in that separation. In fact, the domestic and international rules and legal institutions of economic affairs are inextricably intertwined. It is not possible to understand the real operation of either of these sets of rules in isolation from the other. The national rules (especially constitutional rules) have had enormous influence on the international institutions and rules. Likewise the reverse influence can often be observed.

(B) INTERNATIONAL CUSTOMARY LAW AND ECONOMIC BE-HAVIOR

When we search for customary norms of international law that relate to economic transactions, there is precious little to be found apart from the extensive developments on expropriation of property. There are, however, many international law norms that, although not focused on economic affairs, nevertheless have considerable importance to them. The basic norm of "Pacta Sunt Servanda"—the rule that treaties must be followed in good faith—is a foundation for treaty-based law (which is very important to economic regulation). The general subject of treatment of aliens, of which expropriation of property is a part, is also highly relevant to economic interaction among nations. Even international norms on human rights have been increasingly injected into discussions and negotiations on economic affairs. But let us try to ascertain what, if any, customary international norms exist specifically for economic affairs.

GEORG SCHAWZENBERGER, THE PRINCIPLES AND STANDARDS OF INTERNATIONAL ECONOMIC LAW[3]

I. THE FORMS OF INTERNATIONAL ECONOMIC LAW

Compared with the other two law-creating processes of international law—international customary law and the general principles of law recognized by civilized nations—the emphasis in International Economic Law is on treaties.

a. Treaties

The economic interest of States made short work of natural-law fallacies. Writers have asserted freedom of commerce or navigation as natural rights and deduced such rights from any first principles they cared to adopt as the starting points of their arguments. Yet, unless they were quick to reduce their claims to imperfect rights, they merely served

3. 117 Recueil des Cours 1, 12, 14 (1966–I). Reprinted by permission of the   Hague Academy of International Law.

to lend a spurious respectability to untenable claims. This was what happened when, in 1824, an ill-advised United States Secretary of State relied for evidence of the absolute right of freedom of navigation on the River St. Lawrence, on natural law in general and Grotius, Pufendorf, Wolff and Vattel, in particular. All that his British counterpart had to do was to take him at his word and raise the issue of reciprocal British privileges on navigable rivers in the United States not covered by British treaty rights.

* * *

b.   International Customary Law

In relative significance, international customary law lags behind treaties in International Economic Law. Even so, it fulfills three important functions:

1.   It provides the background against which consensual international economic law must be construed.

2.   In its rules on international responsibility and warfare on land and at sea, international customary law provides the bulk of the rules governing the laws of international economic torts and economic warfare.

3.   By the treaties and parallel national practices to which, in an evolution extending over nearly a millennium, International Economic Law has given rise, it has made two major contributions to international law at large. By way of generalization of rules originally limited to foreign merchants, it has laid the foundations for the rules of general international customary law on the freedom of the seas in times of peace and war, and for the rule on the minimum standard for the treatment of foreign nationals.

The growth of the rules on the exhaustion of local remedies, denial of justice, the outlawry of piracy jure gentium, and the transformation of the right of shipwreck into the law of salvage are further illustrations of the contributions made by International Economic Law to general international customary law.

GEORG SCHWARZENBERGER, EQUALITY AND DISCRIMINATION IN INTERNATIONAL ECONOMIC LAW[4]

* * * In the absence of bilateral and multilateral treaty obligations to the contrary, international law does not ordain economic equality between States nor between their subjects. Economic sovereignty reigns supreme. It is for each subject of international law to decide for itself whether and, if so, in which form, it desires to grant equal treatment to

---

4. 25 Yearbook of World Affairs 163,   of Stevens & Sons, Ltd., London.
163 (1971). Reprinted with the permission

other States and their subjects or give privileged treatment to some and discriminate against others.

Sometimes it is claimed that the principle of "non-discrimination", often termed the "Most–Favored–Nation" obligation, is a norm of customary international law, a question to which we will return in Chapter 10. In addition, in the international discourse of today there is often argument over whether there exists in international law some general obligation to assist developing countries in their efforts to make economic progress. Some of these ideas have been incorporated into treaty-based law (such as Part IV of GATT, or resolutions of the United Nations Conference on Trade and Development), so it may no longer be necessary to base such arguments solely on customary law. Again these are subjects to which later chapters, particularly Chapter 24, return.

(C) ECONOMIC TREATIES

No attempt will be made here to canvass or catalogue the myriad of bilateral economic treaties. Perhaps most important of these are "BITs" (bilateral investment treaties), "FCN" (Friendship–Commerce–Navigation) treaties, "Economic Cooperation Agreements,"[5] the various treaties for the avoidance of multiple taxation, a long line of "commercial treaties" dealing with tariffs and customs matters (often superseded by modern multilateral agreements), and particular commercial treaties dealing with a specific product group (e.g., textiles or meat).[6] Many bilateral treaties deal with taxation, and other more specialized subjects of economic regulation.

The brief materials that follow should help to lend perspective to materials in the rest of this book that focus on modern multilateral agreements as a source of international regulatory obligation.

ERIC V. YOUNGQUIST, UNITED STATES COMMERCIAL TREATIES: THEIR ROLE IN FOREIGN ECONOMIC POLICY[7]

FUNCTIONS OF THE FCN TREATY

As its title suggests, the traditional friendship, commerce and navigation treaty is designed to establish an agreed framework within which mutually beneficial economic relations between two countries can take

---

5. See, e.g., US–China Accord on Industrial and Technological Cooperation, signed and entered into force, January 12, 1984.

6. See, e.g., US Dept. of State, Treaties in Force (A list of Treaties and Other International Agreements of the United States in Force).

7. Reprinted from Studies in Law and Economic Development, Vol. II, study no. 1, at 72, 73–76, George Washington University International Law Society (May, 1967). Reprinted by Permission of the George Washington University International Law Society. "Studies in Law and Economic Development" continues as the Journal of International Law and Economics.

place, creating a basic accord governing day-to-day intercourse between them. It is bilateral, rather than multilateral in nature. Such a treaty is "one of the most familiar instruments known to diplomatic tradition" and probably the simplest type of general agreement with meaningful provisions available in United States treaty practice. It sets forth the terms upon which trade and shipping are conducted, and governs the rights of individuals and firms from one state living, doing business, or owning property within the jurisdiction of the other state. * * *

* * *

The commercial treaty occupied a central foreign policy role during the formative years of the Republic. It served both as a symbol of peaceful relations and a protector of vital commercial interests. In a world of exclusively bilateral relations, it was virtually the sole instrument for important peacetime agreements between nations. The history of this country's foreign economic policy is written in the negotiations on commercial treaties.

* * *

THE MODERN FCN TREATY PROGRAM—1945 TO PRESENT

After World War II, as after the First World War, the United States decided to revise the FCN treaty and employ it in a program aimed at modernizing its commercial treaty relations with other countries.

* * *

These postwar FCN treaties retained many of the traditional provisions of the older treaties. They differed from their predecessors primarily in that they placed greater emphasis on the right of establishment and promotion of private foreign investment, as opposed to trade and shipping, which were the areas of greatest concern in negotiation of earlier FCN treaties. This change in emphasis was a direct reflection of the increased foreign investment role of American business firms after World War II as well as the fact that, after 1934, the trade promotion aspects of commercial treaties had largely been taken over by the reciprocal trade agreements program, and that the General Agreement on Tariffs and Trade (GATT) provided the principal forum for negotiating tariff adjustment and furthering trade promotion objectives after World War II. * * *

KENNETH J. VANDEVELDE, U.S. BILATERAL INVESTMENT TREATIES: THE SECOND WAVE[8]

* * * By 1967, however, there appeared to be no other countries willing to conclude a U.S. FCN treaty. Accordingly, the FCN program expired in the mid–1960s.

---

8. 14 Mich.J.Intl.L. 621, 624–626 (1993). Reprinted with permission of the Michigan Journal of International Law.

At the very time the U.S. FCN program was drawing to a close, several European States were enjoying considerable success negotiating bilateral investment protection agreements which differed from the U.S. FCNs in that they were devoted exclusively to investment protection. After repeated calls from Congress and the U.S. business community for a U.S. investment treaty program similar to the European programs, the State Department decided in 1977 to launch the U.S. BIT program.

The BIT program, as it was conceived in the mid–1970s, had a number of purposes. One of the most important, at least in the minds of the early proponents of these treaties, was to counter the claim made during the 1970s by many developing countries that customary international law no longer required that expropriation be accompanied by prompt, adequate, and effective compensation, if indeed it ever had. This claim was embodied most visibly in the U.N. General Assembly's adoption in 1974 of the Charter of Economic Rights and Duties of States (CERDS), which had provided that compensation for expropriation was to be measured by the law of the expropriating State. That is, the CERDS seemed not only to challenge the standard of prompt, adequate, and effective compensation, but to assume that there was no international minimum standard at all. The United States hoped to create a network of bilateral treaties embracing the prompt, adequate, and effective standard that would counter assertions that State practice no longer supported that standard.

A second purpose was to protect existing stocks of investment owned by U.S. nationals and companies in the territory of other States. U.S. BIT negotiators, at least at the inception of the program, did not consider the promotion of future investment to be a goal of the BITs. The promotion of investment in particular countries would have been inconsistent with the U.S. policy of letting the market direct investment flows and could have raised opposition to these treaties on the part of labor groups concerned about the loss of jobs. Even had the promotion of foreign investment been a goal of the program, U.S. negotiators saw no evidence that a BIT actually would result in increased investment in a particular country. Rather, investment decisions were based on numerous factors—such as political stability, the availability of low wage labor or natural resources, the development of the infrastructure, the size of the domestic market, and the legal climate—very few of which were addressed by a BIT.

A third purpose of the BITs was to depoliticize investment disputes. Traditionally, the remedies available to an investor whose investment was expropriated or otherwise injured by actions of the host State depended upon the involvement of the investor's government in the dispute. This resulted in the U.S. government's routine involvement in disputes between individual investors and foreign States, which inevitably complicated the conduct of foreign policy. The BITs were intended to establish legal remedies for investment disputes that would not necessitate the involvement of the investor's own government.

Note

As of February 2008, the United States was a party to 40 BITs.[9] A number of other BITs had been negotiated and signed, but not yet ratified. Worldwide 2,573 BITs had been negotiated at the end of the 2006.[10]

SECTION 5.4   THE BRETTON WOODS SYSTEM AND WORLD ECONOMIC RELATIONS

At the core of contemporary international regulation of economic relations is a group of institutions and multilateral international agreements which can be termed the "Bretton Woods System." There are numerous other institutions and agreements besides those that are generally considered part of the Bretton Woods System, and the next section of this book will take up some of those other institutions. However, to understand international regulation of economic relations, it is essential initially to study the Bretton Woods System, comprising the International Monetary Fund (IMF), the International Bank for Reconstruction and Development (IBRD—the "World Bank") and the General Agreement on Tariffs and Trade (GATT). These institutions and agreements were developed during a series of conferences beginning near the end of World War II, extending to the end of the 1940's. In 1944, the Bretton Woods conference itself was held at Bretton Woods, New Hampshire, in the United States. This conference developed the institutions and agreements on the financial side of economic relations, namely the IMF and IBRD. The General Agreement, however, was developed in a series of conferences beginning in the Fall of 1946, and extending to mid–1948.[1] In this section our focus is on the IMF; in the next chapter we study GATT and its successor—the World Trade Organization (WTO).

9. List of US Bilateral Investment Treaties, Office of Investment Affairs (IFD/OIA), Bureau of Economic and Business Affairs, US Dept. of State, November 1, 2000, http://www.state.gov/www/issues/economic/ bilateral.htm (visited April 17, 2001), and Bilateral Investment Treaties and Related Agreements, US Department of State, http://www.state.gov/e/eeb/ifd/c644.htm (visited February 20, 2008).

10. UNCTAD, Recent Developments in International Investment Agreements (2006—June 2007), UNCTAD/WEB/ ITE/IIA/2007/6, http://www.unctad.org/en/ docs/webiteiia20076_en.pdf (last visited February 21, 2008).

1. See generally The International Monetary Fund, 1945–1965 (J. Keith Horsefield ed., 3 vols. 1969); IMF, The International Monetary Fund 1966–1971 (1984); Edward S. Mason & Robert E. Asher, The World Bank Since Bretton Woods (1973); Roberto Lavalle, Le Banque Mondiale et ses Filiales (1972); Richard N. Gardner, Sterling–Dollar Diplomacy (new expanded ed. with rev. intro. 1980).

GERALD M. MEIER, THE BRETTON WOODS AGREEMENT—25 YEARS AFTER[2]

I. THE BRETTON WOODS SYSTEM AS A CODE OF INTERNATIONAL ECONOMIC CONDUCT

The term "Bretton Woods system" incorporates the GATT as well as the IMF and World Bank, because the Bretton Woods Conference looked forward to the creation of an ancillary institution that would reduce obstacles to international trade and give effect to the principle of multilateral nondiscriminatory trade. Although the initial plans for the Havana Charter and the creation of an International Trade Organization were not carried out, the GATT emerged as a multilateral agreement embodying commercial policy provisions essentially similar to the Havana Charter chapter on commercial policy. While the IMF was intended to repair the disintegration that had befallen the international monetary system prior to the War, and the World Bank was designed to stimulate and support foreign investment, which had declined to insignificant amounts, the GATT was intended to reverse the protectionist and discriminatory trade practices that had multiplied during the pre-war depression years. The Fund and GATT were to collaborate on exchange policies and trade policies. In combination, the Fund, the Bank, and GATT were designed to help the advanced industrial countries achieve the multiple objectives of full employment, freer and expanding trade, and stable exchange rates. * * *

* * *

A. The Uneasy Triangle

The overriding international economic policy question for most nations has been whether they can attain simultaneously the multiple objectives of high levels of employment (as stated in article I of the Fund Agreement), trade liberalization (as proposed by GATT), and balance-of-payments equilibrium with stable exchange rates (as proposed by the IMF). To the extent that these objectives conflict, some policy tradeoffs must occur.

In their efforts to achieve full employment, countries have often resorted to import restrictions. Even though international trade theory would label the advocacy of trade restrictions in order to promote full employment as a "non-argument" or as a "third, fourth, or "best" " policy measure, governmental policies have often in reality had this neomercantilistic aspect. The pursuit of full employment also can entail balance-of-payments disequilibrium or departure from the condition of a fixed exchange rate. As a country undertakes expansionary domestic measures to achieve full employment, it is probable that its imports will increase and/or its exports fall so much that a deficit arises in the country's international payments balance. Some tradeoff must then occur between full employment and balance-of-payments equilibrium

---

2. 39 Stanford L.Rev. 235, 237, 245–246 (1971). Reprinted by permission of the Board of Trustees of the Leland Stanford Junior University.

with stable exchange rates, or between full employment and trade liberalization. Finally, if a balance-of-payments deficit arises, the country will likely attempt to remedy the situation either by undertaking measures that restrict employment and contract income, in order to reduce imports and stimulate exports, or by imposing trade restrictions.

When confronted by these policy conflicts, most governments have allowed the objective of full employment to dominate national economic policy making even at the cost of a retreat from trade liberalization or pressure on their balance of payments. The central challenge to the operation of the Bretton Woods system has therefore been how to allow nations to pursue their domestic economic objectives without having to forgo the gains from trade or suffer balance-of-payments disequilibrium.

In Chapter 22, we will take a more detailed look at the relationship of international trade and international monetary policies. In this subsection, however, a few of the basic constitutional and structural aspects of the International Monetary Fund (known as the IMF or simply the Fund) will be taken up, so that these can be compared and contrasted with other institutions (such as GATT and the WTO), and so that we will have an overall view with which to approach some of the problems concerning the "constitutional" questions of international economic law. For example, it is important to know in this connection, what are the necessary steps (both internationally and nationally) that must be taken in order to amend the IMF Articles of Agreement. In addition, it is important to know who has the definitive authority to interpret the IMF articles, how decisions are made, what are the voting rules and practices and what procedures exist for dispute resolution and sanctions.

The United States has participated in the IMF (and other Bretton–Woods institutions, such as the World Bank), under the authority of the Bretton–Woods Agreements Act of 1945, as amended.[3] Several salient provisions of that act are as follows:

BRETTON WOODS AGREEMENT ACT[4]

Sec. 4(b)(4). Whenever, under the Articles of Agreement of the Fund or the Articles of Agreement of the Bank, the approval, consent or agreement of the United States is required before an act may be done by the respective institutions, the decision as to whether such approval, consent, or agreement, shall be given or refused shall (to the extent such decision is not prohibited by section 5 of this Act) be made by the Council [a group consisting of the Secretaries of State, Treasury and Commerce, the Chairman of the Board of Governors of the Federal Reserve System, the President of the Export–Import Bank and a repre-

---

3. 22 U.S.C.A. secs. 286–86gg.

4. As amended, secs. 4(b)(4), 5, 26; 22 U.S.C.A. secs. 286b(b)(4), 286c, 286e–6.

sentative of the President], under the general direction of the President. No governor, executive director, or alternate representing the United States shall vote in favor of any waiver of condition under article V, section 4, or in favor of any declaration of the United States dollar as a scarce currency under article VII, section 3, of the Articles of Agreement of the Fund, without prior approval of the Council.

Sec. 5. Unless Congress by law authorizes such action, neither the President nor any person or agency shall on behalf of the United States (a) request or consent to any change in the quota of the United States under article III, section 2(a), of the Articles of Agreement of the Fund; (b) propose a par value for the United States dollar under paragraph 2, paragraph 4, or paragraph 10 of schedule C of the Articles of Agreement of the Fund; (c) propose any change in the par value of the United States dollar under paragraph 6 of schedule C of the Articles of Agreement of the Fund, or approve any general change in par values under paragraph 11 of schedule C; (d) subscribe to additional shares of stock under article II, section 3, of the Articles of Agreement of the Bank; (e) accept any amendment under article XXVIII of the Articles of Agreement of the Fund or article VIII of the Bank; (f) make any loan to the Fund or the Bank or (g) approve either the disposition of more than 25 million ounces of Fund gold for the benefit of the Trust Fund established by the Fund on May 6, 1976, or the establishment of any additional trust fund whereby resources of the International Monetary Fund would be used for the special benefit of a single member, or of a particular segment of the membership, of the Fund. Unless Congress by law authorizes such action, no governor or alternate appointed to represent the United States shall vote for an increase of capital stock of the Bank under article II, section 2, of the Articles of Agreement of the Bank, if such increase involves an increased subscription on the part of the United States. Neither the President nor any person or agency shall, on behalf of the United States, consent to any borrowing (other than a borrowing from a foreign government or other official public source) by the Fund of funds denominated in United States dollars, unless the Secretary of the Treasury transmits a notice of such proposed borrowing to both Houses of the Congress at least 60 days prior to the date on which such borrowing is scheduled to occur.

Sec. 26. The United States Governor of the Fund is directed to vote against the establishment of a Council authorized under Article XII, Section 1 of the Fund Articles of Agreement as amended, if under any circumstances the United States' vote in the Council would be less than its vote in the Fund.

Congress has attempted to keep control of US participation in the IMF in other ways as well. For example, the US representative is to work against any extension of assistance to a country whose government harbors terrorists, 22 U.S.C.A. sec. 286e–11, and to seek to assure that no IMF decision will undermine the US policy regarding comparable treatment of public and private creditors. 22 U.S.C.A sec. 286e–8. In 1983, Congress adopted numerous directives to the Executive Branch as to what policies it should espouse and when it should consult with senior Members of Congress in respect of the IMF. See Pub.L.No. 98–181, title 8, 97 Stat. 1267. One addition requires the US representative to work to have the IMF, as a condition of extending financial assistance, obtain the beneficiary's agreement to eliminate unfair trade and investment practices that the U. Trade Representative determines to be deleterious to the international trading system. 22 U.S.C.A. sec. 286gg(b).

The IMF Articles of Agreement establish an elaborate institutional structure, with a Board of Governors, an Executive Board, Managing Director and staff of international civil servants. Notable is the importance of the weighted voting system (also a feature in the World Bank). The IMF establishes a system of quotas determining how much each member must contribute to the capital of the IMF, and voting is largely determined by the percentage of the quota total allocated to each member.

Under this system the United States has slightly more than 15% of the total votes allocated. Other countries with significant voting rights include Japan with about 6% of the allocated voting rights and three European Union members—Germany, France and the UK—with voting rights of about 6%, 5% and 5% each. These EU members together can cast approximately 16% of the allocated votes, again more than 15%. These are crucial numbers, because approval of amendments to the charter and quota changes requires not only a super majority of members for amendments (three-fifths) but also approval by those holding at least 85% of the voting power. Therefore a voting member or group with over 15% of the voting rights has an effective veto over amendments and quota changes.

In addition, since the US vote must conform to the US statutes controlling US IMF membership (as can be seen in the text above of the Bretton Woods Agreements Act of 1945 as amended from time to time), it is the case that currently the US Congress controls the veto power of the US in the IMF (and World Bank.)

The IMF Article XXIX establishes a procedure for resolving disputes, with submittal to the Executive Board for a decision. While not as "legalistic" as the WTO system, it nevertheless has been utilized for some cases, and has potential for broader use (subject to the diplomatic politics of the organization). Likewise there is provision in the IMF Charter for "sanctions" such as ineligibility to have access to certain rights (such as drawing funds), or even forced withdrawal from the fund.[5]

5. International Monetary Fund Pamphlet Series No. 37, at 18–19 (David D. Driscoll ed., 4th ed. 1984); IMF Executive Directors and Voting Power, March 19, 2001, http://www.imf.org/external/np/sec/memdir/eds.htm (visited 20 February 2008); See also Joseph Gold, Interpretation: The IMF and International Law 115–16 (1996);

Joseph Gold, Some Characteristics of Operation—The Avoidance of Sanctions, from Horsefield, supra note 28, vol. II, at 578; See generally Union of International Associations (ed.), Yearbook of International Organizations (published annually); Marcel A.G. van Meerheaghe, International Economic Institutions (1992); Bernard Colas, Global economic co-operation: a guide to agreements and organizations (2nd ed. 2000); Michel Bélanger, Institutions économiques internationales: la mondialisation économique et ses limites (6th ed. 1997).

Chapter 6

THE LEGAL STRUCTURE OF THE WTO/GATT SYSTEM

SECTION 6.1 INTRODUCTION: THE NEW WORLD TRADING SYSTEM[1]

The end of the eight-year Uruguay Round of trade negotiations in 1994 brought a profound change in the legal structure of the institutions for international trade. Since 1947, the General Agreement on Tariffs and Trade (the General Agreement or GATT) was the principal international multilateral treaty for trade, although technically it was only in force "provisionally." In theory, the General Agreement did not establish an "organization," although in practice GATT operated like one. The Uruguay Round resulted in the creation of a new and better defined international organization and treaty structure—a World Trade Organization (WTO)—to carry forward GATT's work. Some have suggested that this is the most significant result of the Uruguay Round, and that it

---

1. See generally John H. Jackson, World Trade and the Law of GATT (1969); John H. Jackson, The World Trading System (2nd ed. 1997); John H. Jackson, Restructuring the GATT System (1990); William J. Davey, The WTO/GATT World Trading System: An Overview, in Pierre Pescatore, William J. Davey & Andreas F. Lowenfeld, Handbook of GATT Dispute Settlement (1994); Dominique Carreau et al., Droit International Economique (3d ed. 1990); John H. Jackson, The Jurisprudence of GATT and the WTO (2000); Kenneth W. Dam, The GATT: Law and International Economic Organization (1970); Thiébaut Flory, L'Organization Mondial du Commerce: Droit International et Substantiel (1999); Robert E. Hudec, Enforcing International Trade Law (1993); Robert E. Hudec, The GATT Legal System and World Trade Diplomacy (1975); Robert E. Hudec, Essays on the Nature of International and Trade Law (1999); Pierre Lortie, Economic Integration and the Law of GATT (1975); Edmond McGovern, International Trade Regulation

(3rd ed. 1999); The GATT Uruguay Round: A Negotiating History: 1986–1992 (Terence P. Stewart ed., 1993); Pieter Verloren van Themaat, The Changing Structure of International Economic Law (1981); Executive Branch GATT Studies, Nos. 1–13, Senate Comm. on Finance, Subcomm. on International Trade, 93d Cong., 1st Sess. (Compilation of 1973 Studies prepared by the Executive Branch: Comm. Print, March 1974). GATT published an annual report entitled "GATT Activities In 19___." It also published a compilation of Basic Instruments and Selected Documents (BISD), which includes the major actions taken by the GATT contracting parties. See also GATT, Analytical Index (6th ed. 1994), a provision-by-provision analysis of the General Agreement that cites relevant GATT actions interpreting and applying each of them, and GATT, Status of Legal Instruments (looseleaf). The WTO publishes an annual report, volumes of "Dispute Settlement Reports" and a loose leaf WTO Status of Legal Instruments.

214

is part of a series of circumstances (including economic integration in Europe and North America) that may be the most profound change in international economic institutions since the Bretton Woods Conference of 1944.

The institutional reforms of the Uruguay Round include not only the WTO, but also substantial revisions of the dispute settlement procedures, which will be taken up in the next chapter. In this chapter, we will explore the history and characteristics of GATT, as predecessor (and still the existing treaty source for substantive norms) to the WTO. We will then examine the WTO itself, and follow this with explorations of certain institutional questions, such as membership and decision making, provisions for future trade negotiation rounds and the domestic law effect of the GATT, WTO and related treaties. Before doing this, however, a brief overview of the treaty structure may assist readers to better understand the material that follows. (The reader should examine the structure of these treaties in the Documents Supplement, as he or she reads the brief description that follows.)

The General Agreement is a treaty that deals almost entirely with trade in products. The Uruguay Round for the first time has produced a comparable treaty for trade in services (broadly defined) and a new treaty dealing with intellectual property. These three treaties form the core and bulk of the substantive international rules that will be administered by the WTO. What do these treaties provide?

GATT 1947 & 1994: The General Agreement on Tariffs and Trade, completed in late 1947 and amended and embellished with a variety of treaty instruments (about 200), provides an important "code" of rules applying to government actions which regulate international trade. The basic purpose of the General Agreement is to constrain governments from imposing or continuing a variety of measures that restrain or distort international trade. Such measures include tariffs, quotas, internal taxes and regulations which discriminate against imports, subsidy and dumping practices, state trading, as well as customs procedures and a plethora of other "non-tariff measures" that discourage trade. The basic objective of the rules is to "liberalize trade" so that the market can work to achieve the policy goals outlined in Chapters 1 and 2. An additional and very important rule is the "MFN" or Most Favored Nation Clause of Article I, which provides that government import or export regulations should not discriminate between other countries' products. Likewise Article III establishes the "national treatment" obligation of non-discrimination against imports. Article II establishes that the tariff limits expressed in each contracting party's "schedule of concessions" shall not be exceeded. The thrust of the General Agreement is to channel all "border protection" against imports into tariffs, and provide for agreements for tariff reductions, which are "bound" in the schedules and reinforced by Article II rules and the rest of the agreement.

The General Agreement also has a number of exceptions, such as those for national security, health and morals, safeguards or escape clauses (for temporary restraint of imports), free trade agreements, and the like.

Annex 1A to the WTO Agreement incorporates a document labeled GATT 1994 which is essentially GATT 1947 as amended and changed through the Uruguay Round, along with all the ancillary agreements pertaining to trade in goods.

GATS: The General Agreement on Trade in Services resulted from negotiations in the Uruguay Round on one of the "new subjects." The word "services" embraces more than a hundred different service sectors, such as banking, tourism, communications, medical, legal, insurance, brokerage, transport, etc. Many of these sectors are difficult and complex to regulate. The policy makers of the 1980's felt that global economic trends were making services an ever larger portion of international and national markets, thus necessitating some type of multilateral rule structure comparable to that for goods, in order to inhibit a growing tendency of governments to limit competition with restrictions and protectionist measures. The trade negotiators naturally tended to use analogies to GATT rules to try to regulate services, although sometimes the analogies did not work too well. Nevertheless, the GATS agreement has counterpart provisions to MFN and national treatment. It also has a system of "schedules of concessions." The GATS, however, also includes rules on competition and monopoly policy (antitrust). It contains exceptions clauses similar to GATT's on health and morals, and national security. It also includes clauses on "transparency," calling for openness and publication of information affecting traders.

TRIPS: The Agreement on Trade–Related Aspects of Intellectual Property Rights is designed to provide rules requiring governments to ensure a certain minimum level of protection for patents, copyrights, industrial designs, trademarks, business secrets and similar matters. It incorporates provisions of some of the major intellectual property treaties (such as the Berne Convention concerning copyrights and the Paris Convention on patents). One of the major goals of proponents of this agreement was to add a measure of "enforceability" through a GATT-type dispute settlement system to intellectual property norms. Rules included in this agreement also require governments to provide civil and administrative procedures and remedies for rights-holders to pursue. This agreement also has clauses concerning MFN treatment, national treatment and transparency, as well as exceptions for national security.

Added to these three major substantive agreements, are the WTO Charter itself, an understanding on dispute settlement provisions, a "Trade Policy Review Mechanism," and an annex with two so-called "plurilateral agreements" (there were originally four in 1995, but two of them—the dairy and meat agreements—are no longer in effect). A chart showing the relationship follows:

WTO CHARTER

Annex 1: Multilateral Agreements
        Annex 1A: GATT 1994 (including agreements on trade in goods, understandings and the Marrakesh Protocol)
        Annex 1B: GATS
        Annex 1C: TRIPS
Annex 2: Dispute Settlement Rules
Annex 3: Trade Policy Review Mechanism
Annex 4: Plurilateral Agreements (optional)
        Annex 4A: Civil Aircraft
        Annex 4B: Government Procurement

By adhering to the WTO Charter, countries become subject to all of the annexed agreements, except the plurilateral agreements, adherence to which is optional. There are also, as part of the April 1994 Final Act that established the WTO structure, an assortment of appended Ministerial Decisions, Declarations, Understandings and Recommendations.

SECTION 6.2 GATT AND ITS TROUBLED HISTORY[1]

(A) GATT'S ORIGINS AND "BIRTH DEFECTS"[2]

National leaders never intended for GATT to become the central international trade organization. The original idea was to create a broader international organization to be named the "International Trade Organization" (ITO), but history was not kind to that idea.

The initiatives towards the development of a GATT and an ITO began during World War II and came principally from the United States. Two strands of American economic policy converged to encourage these initiatives. The first strand was the general "Reciprocal Trade Agreements" program of the United States, originating with the 1934 Act that enabled the President to negotiate mutual reductions of tariffs. Weaknesses of the bilateral approach became apparent, however, and a multilateral approach seemed to offer some solutions for those weaknesses.

A second strand of American policy recognized the role of international economic affairs in causing World War II and sought to prevent a reoccurrence of such an event. It was recognized by American policy makers that organizations to regulate national practices affecting inter-

---

1. See John H. Jackson, World Trade and the Law of GATT (1969); Richard N. Gardner, Sterling–Dollar Diplomacy (new expanded ed. with rev. introd. 1980).

2. See Jackson, supra note 1, ch. 2; Gardner, supra note 1; William A. Brown, Jr., The United States and the Restoration of World Trade (1950); Clair Wilcox, A Charter for World Trade (1949); William Diebold, The End of the I.T.O. (Essays in International Finance No. 16, Princeton University, 1952).

national monetary flows, as well as trade, would be needed, and in 1944 a monetary conference was held at Bretton Woods.

In 1945 Congress again extended the Reciprocal Trade Agreements Act.[3] Late in that year, the United States Department of State invited a number of other nations to enter into multinational negotiations for the reduction of tariffs. At about the same time the United Nations was beginning its work, and the UN Economic and Social Council (ECOSOC) was established. At the first ECOSOC meeting in February 1946, the United States introduced a resolution, which was adopted, calling for the convening of a "United Nations Conference on Trade and Employment" with the purpose of drafting a charter for an international trade organization.[4]

The first preparatory committee for this effort convened in the Fall of 1946 in London, to consider a "Suggested Charter for an International Trade Organization" drafted by the United States government.[5] Following this meeting, a drafting subcommittee met at Lake Success, New York, early in 1947,[6] and then the full preparatory conference convened again in Geneva from April to October, 1947.[7] At this conference, the multilateral tariff negotiations were conducted, in addition to the continuing work on a draft charter for the ITO that was to be concluded at the Havana conference during the early part of 1948.

The General Agreement on Tariffs and Trade (GATT) was drafted at the Geneva conference, simultaneously with the tariff negotiations and the work on the ITO charter. The basic idea for the General Agreement was that it would be an agreement to embody the results of the tariff negotiations, but that it would also include some of the general protective clauses that would prevent evasion of the tariff commitments. It was not contemplated that GATT would be an organization; indeed, when early drafts of the General Agreement included terminology that suggested an organization, these were intensely criticized in hearings before US congressional committees on the grounds that the President had no authority to accept international organization membership for the United States without congressional approval.[8] It was understood that an ITO charter would be submitted to Congress (or to the Senate) for approval. The tariff agreements (including the General Agreement) were being negotiated under the authority of the Reciprocal Trade

3. An Act to Extend the Authority of the President Under section 350 of the Tariff Act of 1930, 79th Cong. 1st Sess., 59 Stat. 410 (1945).

4. US State Dept. Press Release, Dec. 16, 1945, reproduced in 13 Dept. State Bull. 970 (1945); 1 U.N. ECOSOC Res. 13, U.N. Doc. E/22 (1946); see Jackson, supra note 1, sec. 2.2.

5. See London Report, First Session of the Preparatory Committee (1946); U.N. Doc. EPCT/CII/1–66 (1946).

6. See New York Report, U.N. Doc. EPCT/34 (1947); U.N. Doc. EPCT/C.6/W.58 (1947).

7. See U.N. Docs. EPCT/A/SR/1–43; EPCT/B/SR/1–33 (1947); U.N. Doc. EPCT/TAC/SR. 1–28 (1947).

8. See Hearings on the Trade Agreements Act and the Proposed ITO Before the House Ways and Means Comm., 80th Cong. 1st Sess. (1947); Hearings on Operation of the Trade Agreements Act and Proposed ITO Before the Senate Finance Comm., 80th Cong. 1st Sess. (1947).

Agreements Act extension of 1945. However, the General Agreement was intended to be a subsidiary agreement under the ITO charter, and to depend upon the ITO charter and the ITO secretariat for servicing and enforcement. Indeed, most of its general clauses were drawn from comparable clauses drafted for the ITO, and it was understood that most of these clauses would be changed to conform to the corresponding version of the ITO charter that emerged from the later Havana conference.[9]

The United States tariff agreements authority was going to expire in the middle of 1948, and it was obvious that an ITO charter would not be in effect by then. Partly for these reasons, the United States and other countries desired to have the General Agreement accepted and implemented as soon as possible. Because some countries would require parliamentary action in order to accept many of GATT's general clauses, the General Agreement itself was not applied. Instead, a "Protocol of Provisional Application" (PPA) was signed in late 1947, by the twenty-two original members of GATT, and this protocol became effective on January 1, 1948.[10] It was only through this protocol that the General Agreement was applied. Originally it was thought that after the ITO charter came into force, the Protocol of Provisional Application would fall by the wayside, and the General Agreement would be applied definitively.

The Havana conference in early 1948 completed the draft charter of the ITO, but since the United States was the strongest economy in the post-war world, and since the initiative for an agreement came from the United States, other countries waited to see if the United States would accept the ITO. The ITO was several times submitted to Congress and extensive hearings were held upon it, but by the late 1940's the enthusiasm of international cooperation that prevailed immediately after World War II had faded, and the composition of Congress had shifted to a stance less liberal on trade matters and less internationally oriented. Recognizing the inevitable, in December 1950, the Executive Branch announced that it would not re-submit the ITO charter to Congress for approval, so for all practical purposes the ITO charter was dead.[11]

The death of the ITO meant that GATT was, by default, the central organization for coordinating national policies on international trade. By now somewhat enlarged by additional members, the GATT countries recognized that the General Agreement was ill-suited to perform the role that had been thrust upon it. Consequently it was decided to overhaul it and establish a small organization to operate it, to be known as the Organization for Trade Cooperation (OTC). The ninth session of the Contracting Parties of GATT (October 1954 to May 1955) was the

9. See Jackson, supra note 1, sec. 2.4.

10. Protocol of Provisional Application to the General Agreement on Tariffs and Trade, Oct. 30, 1947, 61 Stat. pts. 5, 6,

TIAS No. 1700, 55 UNTS 308; see also Jackson, supra note 1, sec. 3.2.

11. See Diebold, supra note 2; Jackson, supra note 1, sec. 2.5.

"review session" at which a number of amendments to GATT were prepared and a draft charter for the OTC completed.[12]

The OTC charter met the same fate as the earlier ITO charter. Congress would not accept it.[13] A number of the amendments to the General Agreement, however, were ultimately brought into force, accepted for the United States under the authority of the then current Trade Agreements Act. Subsequently, it was amended only once, with the 1964 amendments to add Part IV relating to developing countries.[14]

One legacy of this troubled history has been a long festering quarrel in the United States over the "legality" of GATT, a subject that we take up below in Section 6.7.

GATT's troubled history explains why the nation participants in GATT were not called "members," but instead were called "contracting parties." This terminology tends to down play the notion of "organization."

When the Uruguay Round commenced, it was possible to list a number of serious problems facing GATT, most of which could be traced to "birth defects" dating from this troubled history of its origins:

1) GATT application was controversial, flawed and still "provisional," although the GATT rules did apply as binding international treaty obligations. Grandfather rights still existed, even though they were originally intended to be temporary. A number of other institutional problems stemmed from this basic treaty structure, including the difficulty of the amendment process, its uncertain relationship to domestic laws, the lack of a unified dispute settlement procedure, questions of membership and the ill-defined powers of the contracting parties.

2) The amending provisions of the General Agreement were such that it was considered nearly impossible to amend it. The delay required by the treaty acceptance process, the difficulty of obtaining the required number of acceptances, the shift in bargaining power involved under the amending procedure in the context of a large membership and the fact that even when an amendment is effective it would not apply to countries which did not accept it, were all reasons why the amending procedure had fallen into disuse. This caused a certain rigidity and inability to develop rules to accommodate the many new developments in international trade and other economic interdependence subjects. One result was the development of an elaborate system of "side agreements or codes," which created additional problems.

3) A key problem was the relationship to GATT of these many side agreements, which in most cases were stand-alone treaties, but which were intimately linked to the GATT treaty structure itself. It was

---

12. See GATT, 3d Supp. BISD (1955); Agreement on the Organization for Trade Cooperation, GATT Doc. Final Act, 9th Session; see also Jackson, supra note 1, sec. 2.5.

13. See Jackson, supra note 1, at 51.

14. Id., sec. 3.4. and Appendix C, at 888–897, list of GATT Protocols and Agreements. See GATT, Status of Legal Instruments.

unclear in some circumstances what this relationship was and whether an obligation contained in a side agreement would prevail over one contained in the General Agreement or vice versa. In any event, since the side agreements tended to have a series of separate procedures for various matters including dispute settlement, there was a certain inefficiency in the potential "forum shopping." Side agreements bound only governments that accepted them, and the opportunity for countries to pick and choose led to "GATT a la carte."

4) The relationship of the GATT treaty system to domestic law in a variety of GATT member countries was very murky. This might have existed in any event, regardless of the basic treaty structure, since national legal systems differ so widely. Nevertheless, it seemed that some more attention could be given to the possibility of certain international treaty obligations with respect to how the trade and economic rules should be implemented domestically. More attention has been given to this question in recent years, sometimes under the rubric "transparency." It should be noted that the General Agreement itself has several clauses (e.g., Article X) that are related to transparency, dealing with publication and administration of trade regulations.

5) There were a number of troublesome problems with respect to membership, or "contracting party status," in the GATT system. There were various ways by which a nation could become a "member" of GATT or one of the side agreements. In some cases, membership could be obtained by a territory that did not have full independent international sovereignty. In certain cases, former colonies could be sponsored for membership and enter GATT with very little substantive commitment, reducing the "terrain of reciprocity," and leading to criticisms of unfairness. The General Agreement had an "opt out" clause (Article XXXV) by which individual GATT contracting parties could opt out of a GATT relationship with other parties, at one time only (when one of them originally enters GATT). Furthermore, there were a number of instances where there was an effective "opt out" at a later time, with murky legal results. Article XXI with an exception for "national security" purposes is related to this issue.

6) The powers of the contracting parties defined in the General Agreement were very ambiguous. Indeed, they were so broad that they could be the subject of abuse (although they have not been so abused). There were a number of unsettled and disquieting issues, such as the power of the contracting parties to interpret the General Agreement and the relationship of actions of the contracting parties to some of the side agreements. Furthermore, the decision making process left much to be desired. The so-called "consensus approach," which had evolved to ameliorate some of the problems of a one-nation one-vote structure, had slowed the decision making process and made it hard to confront difficult issues. The GATT Council had been created out of whole cloth by resolution of the contracting parties, and had been delegated almost all of their powers, but had no treaty status.

7) The dispute settlement processes of GATT were one of the more intriguing institutional developments of the institution. The treaty language was very sparse indeed, but many decades of practice had resulted in a considerable amount of exegesis. A Tokyo Round "understanding" elaborated and formalized many of the dispute settlement procedures that had developed in the early decades of GATT practice.

8) Finally, there was a long festering problem with respect to the relationship of GATT to the other Bretton Woods institutions, particularly the International Monetary Fund and the World Bank.

(B) THE GATT LEGAL STRUCTURE

The General Agreement, including the remarkably detailed commitments on tariffs that comprise the "Tariff Schedules," fills many volumes of treaty text. The "General Articles" of General Agreement comprise the basic trade policy commitments. These articles, now numbering thirty-eight and covering seventy pages of text (see Documents Supplement), contain a number of detailed rules and obligations designed generally to prevent nations from pursuing "beggar-thy-neighbor" trade policies which would be self-defeating if emulated by other nations. GATT is not a single agreement, but is a series of over two hundred agreements, protocols, proces-verbaux, etc.[15] Some of these protocols are amendments to the text of the general articles, while many are corrections or revisions (in the light of renegotiations) of the tariff schedules.

As noted above, the beginning point for understanding the GATT obligations is Article II, relating to the tariff schedules, in which each country commits to limit its tariffs on particular items to the level it negotiated. Many of the remaining GATT obligations are designed in large part to reinforce the basic tariff obligations. In addition, there are two broad non-discrimination obligations: (i) Article I contains the "Most Favored Nation" clause, which effectively prohibits discrimination amongst other parties in respect of imports or exports, and (ii) Article III contains the national treatment obligation, which specifies that imports shall be treated no worse than domestically produced goods under internal taxation or regulatory measures.

In addition to obligations, however, the General Agreement contains a large number of exceptions. It has been said that the agreement is "riddled with exceptions," and that "a lawyer could drive a four-horse team through any obligation that anybody had." The exceptions include those for escape clause actions against injurious and increasing imports; for balance of payments problems; for customs unions and free trade areas; for health and conservation measures; and for national security.

The General Agreement, central as it was to international trade regulation from 1948 to 1994, was never itself applied definitively. Rather, it was applied by the "Protocol of Provisional Application"

---

15. See Jackson, supra note 1, ch. 3.

(PPA), signed October 30, 1947, the key paragraphs of which reads as follows:[16]

PROTOCOL OF PROVISIONAL APPLICATION OF THE GENERAL AGREEMENT ON TARIFFS AND TRADE

1. [Australia, Belgium, Canada, France, Luxembourg, the Netherlands, the United Kingdom and the United States] undertake, provided that this protocol shall have been signed on behalf of all the foregoing Governments not later than 15 November 1947, to apply provisionally on and after 1 January 1948:

> (a) Parts I and III of the General Agreement on Tariffs and Trade, and

> (b) Part II of that Agreement to the fullest extent not inconsistent with existing legislation.

2. The foregoing Governments shall make effective such provisional application of the General Agreement, in respect of any of their territories other than their metropolitan territories, on or after 1 January 1948, upon the expiration of thirty days from the day on which notice of such application is received by the Secretary–General of the United Nations.

* * *

5. Any Government applying this Protocol shall be free to withdraw such application, and such withdrawal shall take effect upon the expiration of sixty days from the day on which written notice of such withdrawal is received by the Secretary–General of the United Nations.

———————

Each time a country later became a party to GATT, it did so under a protocol with essentially the same terms (but different dates) or through a procedure by which it was deemed to come within such a protocol.[17] While GATT Article XXXI allowed a country to withdraw from GATT after six months' notice, the PPA shortened that notice period to sixty days.

The most important clause of the PPA, however, was the "existing legislation clause" of paragraph 1(b), the clause giving rise to what are known as "grandfather rights." Those grandfather rights were a source of difficulties, acrimony and dispute throughout the existence of GATT.

---

16. Protocol of Provisional Application of the General Agreement on Tariffs and Trade, Oct. 30, 1947, 61 Stat. pts. 5, 6, TIAS No. 1700, 55 UNTS 308; see also Jackson, supra note 1, sec. 3.2.

17. See Jackson, supra note 1, secs. 3.2, 4.4.

Early practice in GATT established that in order for a grandfather right to be invocable by a party, the existing legislation must be "mandatory." This follows from the history of GATT that the principal reason for the PPA was to provide an opportunity for countries to accept the General Agreement provisionally without having to submit it to their parliamentary approval procedures. Thus, if the executive had the authority to conform governmental measures to GATT obligations, it was argued, there should be no "existing legislation exception."

Although grandfather rights have had a troubled history in GATT, in later years they became less and less important, partly because many of them have withered away. One of the features of the WTO Charter is that it definitively put to rest the open-ended concept of grandfather rights. However, one GATT grandfather right was perpetuated in the WTO Charter's definition of GATT 1994 (the US Jones Act).

SECTION 6.3 THE WORLD TRADE ORGANIZATION[1]

(A) ORIGINS OF THE NEW CHARTER

Although there was substantial realization that GATT was handicapped in many ways because of the circumstances surrounding its origins, there was no indication during the 1980's and during the preparations for the Uruguay Round negotiations that there would be a proposal for a new organization during the round. There seemed to be a fear that such a proposal would attract too much opposition, especially in the US Congress, which had twice before struck down such proposals in the trade area. The agenda and negotiating structure that resulted from the ministerial meeting launching the new round at Punta del Este, Uruguay, in September 1986, did not include any indication that a new charter would be considered. It did include a negotiating topic on, and a group charged with considering, the "Future of the GATT System" (the

---

1. The published literature about the WTO is very extensive, with Amazon.com listing 1,411 items!! (last visited February 20, 2008). The following is a list of a few prominent selected works for interested readers. John H. Jackson, Sovereignty, the WTO, and Changing Fundamentals of International Law (2006); Peter Sutherland et al., The Future of the WTO: Addressing Institutional Challenges in the New Millennium, Report by the Consultative Board to the Director–General Supachai Panitchpakdi, available at: http://www.wto.org/english/thewto_e/10anniv_e/future_wto_e.htm; Peter van den Bossche, Law and Policy of the WTO (2006); Ernst–Ulrich Petersmann (ed.), Reforming the World Trading System (2005); Peter Gallagher, Patrick Low & Andrew L. Stoler, Managing the Challenges of WTO Participation: 45 Case Studies (2005); Yasuhei Taniguchi, Alan Yanovich & Jan Bohanes (eds.), The WTO in the Twenty–First Century: Dispute Settlement, Negotiations, and Regionalism in Asia (2007); Giorgio Sacerdoti, Alan Yanovich & Jan Bohanes (eds.), The WTO at Ten: The Contribution of the Dispute Settlement System (2006); Andreas F. Lowenfeld, International Economic Law (2002); Mitsuo Matsushita, Thomas J. Schoenbaum & Petros C. Mavroidis, The World Trade Organization: Law, Practice, and Policy (2d ed. 2006); Merit E. Janow, Victoria Donaldson & Alan Yanovich (eds.), The WTO: Governance Dispute Settlement and Developing Countries (2008). Additional bibliographic material on the WTO can be found at the web site for the Georgetown Institute of International Economic Law, at www.iiel.org. For older materials and items more focused on GATT, see Section 6.1 supra, n. 1.

acronym "FOGS" was considered appropriate). The FOGS group, however, focused on GATT's relationship to the monetary part of the Bretton Woods system and on designing the new Trade Policy Review Mechanism (TPRM). It did not attempt more ambitious restructuring of the international trade institutions. A separate negotiating group was assigned the task of revising the dispute settlement procedures.

Only later did the ideas for a new organization begin to emerge. The Government of Canada first put forth a formal proposal (in May of 1990) for a WTO—World Trade Organization. Later that year, the European Union indicated it favored a similar organization, but preferred the name MTO—Multilateral Trade Organization. At the December 1990 Brussels Ministerial Meeting (which resulted in an impasse), the draft documents only mentioned the possibility of future exploration of a new organization.

After regrouping from the Brussels impasse, the then GATT Director–General, Arthur Dunkel, spurred the negotiators to produce in December 1991 a complete rough draft of the negotiation results, pasting together tentative texts of the entire package (with many holes and text in square brackets indicating unresolved matters). In this draft, for the first time, the world saw a draft charter for a new organization—an MTO. During 1992 and 1993 the negotiators worked on this draft in the face of various objections, particularly from the United States, to revise it and make it more acceptable. Finally, in the final hours of the December 1993 negotiations, there was agreement (including the United States) to a charter proposal, but the name was changed back to WTO, as it now stands. This proposal was then finalized in Morocco in April 1994, and submitted to governments for ratification.

It is important to realize that the WTO is not the ITO (the 1948 International Trade Organization.) The ITO Charter included five sizeable chapters filled with substantive rules concerning international economic behavior, plus a chapter with an elaborate set of institutional clauses. The WTO Charter by comparison, is a "mini-charter," relatively spare regarding institutional measures and containing no substantive rules, although large texts of such matter are included in annexes. This overall structure of the WTO is itself significant. It suggests a spirit of flexibility, which allows for texts to be added or subtracted over time and for the evolution of institutions necessary for implementation of the rules.

(B) THE STRUCTURE OF THE WTO

The WTO Charter is confined to institutional measures. Unlike the General Agreement, it clearly establishes an international organization, endows it with legal personality, and supports it with the traditional treaty organizational clauses regarding "privileges and immunities," secretariat, director-general, budgetary provisions and explicit authority to develop relations with other inter-government organizations and, important to some interests, non-government organizations. The charter prohibits staff of the secretariat from seeking or accepting instructions from any government "or any other authority external to the WTO."

Most significantly, the charter explicitly outlines four important annexes that technically contain thousands of pages of substantive rules. Indeed it is reported that the total "package" of the text of the Uruguay Round results weighs 385 pounds and consists of over 26,000 pages, including annexes and schedules.

The annex structure is important; the different annexes have different purposes and different legal impacts:

Annex 1 contains the "Multilateral Agreements," which comprise the bulk of the Uruguay Round results and which are all "mandatory," in the sense that these texts impose binding obligations on all members of the WTO. This reinforces the single package idea of the negotiators, departing from the Tokyo Round approach of "pick and choose" side texts, or "GATT a la carte." As outlined above, the Annex 1 texts include the following:

Annex 1A consists of GATT 1994, which includes the revised General Agreement with new understandings, side agreements on 12 topics ranging from agriculture to preshipment inspection, and the vast "schedules of tariff concessions" that make up the large bulk of pages in the official treaty text. The schedule for each of the major trading countries, the United States, Japan and the European Union, constitutes a volume of printed tariff listings. There are a number of "side agreements," some originating from the Tokyo Round results (as revised in the Uruguay Round). These are as follows:

Agriculture (see Section 9.3(A) infra)

Application of Sanitary and Phytosanitary Measures (Section 14.2)

Textiles and Clothing (Section 9.3 (B))

Technical Barriers to Trade (Standards) (Section 14.3)

Trade–Related Investment Measures (TRIMs) (Section 12.3)

Implementation of Article VI of GATT 1994 (Dumping) (Chapters 16–17)

Implementation of Article VII of GATT 1994 (Valuation) (Section 8.3(C))

Preshipment Inspection

Rules of Origin (Section 8.3(D))

Import Licensing Procedures (Section 9.2)

Subsidies and Countervailing Measures (Chapters 17–18)

Safeguards (Chapter 15)

Annex 1B consists of the General Agreement on Trade in Services (GATS), which also incorporates a series of schedules of concessions (Chapter 19).

Annex 1C consists of the Agreement on Trade–Related Aspects of Intellectual Property (TRIPS) (Chapter 20).

Annex 2 has the dispute settlement rules, which are obligatory on all members, and which form (for the first time) a unitary dispute settlement mechanism covering all the agreements listed in Annex 1, Annex 2 and Annex 4 (i.e., all but the TPRM procedures) (Chapter 7).

Annex 3 establishes the Trade Policy Review Mechanism (TPRM), by which the WTO will review the overall trade policies of each member on a periodic and regular basis, and report on those policies. The approach is not supposed to be "legalistic," and questions of consistency with WTO and Annex obligations are not the focus; rather the focus is the general impact of the trade policies, both on the country being examined and on its trading partners.

Annex 4 contains the four agreements that are "optional," termed "plurilateral agreements." This is a slight departure from the single package ideal, but the agreements included tend to be either targeted to a few industrial countries, or to be more "hortatory" in nature without real legal impact. The four agreements deal with government procurement (see Section 12.5 infra), trade in civil aircraft, bovine meat and dairy products. The latter two have been terminated. Clearly this annex, which may be added to, leaves open some important flexibility for the WTO to evolve and redirect its attention and institutional support for important new subjects that may emerge during the next few decades.

(C) GOVERNING STRUCTURE

The governing structure of the WTO follows some of the GATT 1947 model, but departs from it substantially. At the top there is a "Ministerial Conference," which meets not less often than every two years. Next there is not one, but four "Councils." The "General Council" has overall supervisory authority, including responsibility for carrying out the functions of the Ministerial Conference between Ministerial Conference sessions. The General Council schedules five or so regular meetings a year, but it also meets additionally as required by events. In addition, however, there is a Council for each of the Annex 1 agreements, thus:

Council for Trade in Goods

Council for Trade in Services, and

Council for Trade–Related Aspects of Intellectual Property Rights

A "Dispute Settlement Body" (DSB) is established to supervise and implement the dispute settlement rules in Annex 2. The General Council is authorized to perform the DSB tasks. Likewise there is a TPRM Body for the Trade Policy Review Mechanism.

(D) LEGAL CONTINUITY AND EFFECTS

There is strong indication in various parts of the WTO Charter to promote a sense of legal and practice continuity with GATT. Except as otherwise provided, the WTO shall "be guided by the decisions, procedures and customary practices followed by [GATT 1947]." Art. XVI:1. The secretariat of the GATT 1947 became the WTO secretariat.

An interesting new clause is included in the WTO Charter, which reads:

> Each Member shall ensure the conformity of its laws, regulations and administrative procedures with its obligations as provided in the annexed Agreements. Art. XVI:4.

More on this subject can be found at Section 6.7 below.

(E) APPRAISING THE NEW CHARTER

JOHN H. JACKSON, TESTIMONY BEFORE THE SENATE FINANCE COMMITTEE, MARCH 23, 1994

First, the WTO essentially will continue the GATT institutional ideas and many of its practices, in a form better understood by the public, media, government officials and lawyers. To some small extent, a number of the GATT "birth defects" are overcome in the WTO. The WTO Charter (XVI:1) expressly states the intention to be guided by GATT practices, decisions, and procedures to the extent feasible.

Second, the WTO structure offers some important advantages for assisting the effective implementation of the Uruguay Round. For example, a "new GATT 1994" is created and thus countries effectively withdraw from the old GATT and become members of the new GATT. This procedure avoids the constraints of the amending clause of the old GATT that might make it quite difficult to bring the Uruguay Round into legal force.

Third, the WTO ties together the various texts developed in the Uruguay Round and reinforces the "single package" idea of the negotiators, namely, that countries accepting the Uruguay Round must accept the entire package (with a few exceptions).

Fourth, another important aspect of the WTO structure is that it facilitates the extension of the institutional structure (GATT-like) to the new subjects negotiated in the Uruguay Round, particularly services and intellectual property. Without some kind of legal mechanism such as the WTO, this would have been quite difficult to do since the GATT itself only applies to goods. The new GATT structure separates the institutional concepts from the substantive rules. The GATT 1994 will remain a substantive agreement (with many of the amendments and improvements developed throughout its history, including in the Uruguay Round.) The WTO has a broader context.

Fifth, similarly the WTO will be able to apply a unified dispute settlement mechanism, and the Trade Policy Review Mechanism to all of the subjects of the Uruguay Round, for all nations who become members.

Sixth, the WTO Charter offers considerably better opportunities for the future evolution and development of the institutional structure for international trade cooperation. Even though the WTO Charter is minimalist, the fact that there is provision for explicit legal status, and the traditional organizational privileges and immunities to improve the efficiency of an organization helps in this regard. With the WTO focusing on the institutional side, it also offers more flexibility for future inclusion of new negotiated rules or measures which can assist nations to face the constantly emerging problems of world economics. For example, already mentioned for such attention are environmental policies and competition policies.

There is some confusion about the effect of a WTO and its actions on US law. It is almost certain to be the case (as Congress has provided in recent trade agreements) that the WTO and the Uruguay Round treaties will not be self-executing in US law. Thus they do not automatically become part of US law. Nor do the results of panel dispute settlement procedures automatically become part of US law. Instead the US must implement the international obligations or the result of a panel report, often through legislation adopted by the Congress. In a case where the US feels it is so important to deviate from the international norms that it is willing to do so knowing that it may be acting inconsistently with its international obligations, the US government still has that power under its constitutional system. This can be an important constraint if matters go seriously wrong. It should not be lightly used of course. In addition, it should also be noted that governments as members of the WTO have the right to withdraw from the WTO with six months notice (XV:1). Again, this is a drastic action that would not likely be taken, but it does provide some checks and balances to the overall system.

THE SUTHERLAND REPORT (2004)[2]

34. The inception of the WTO reflected a recognition by the overwhelming majority of states that exist today that the process of trade liberalization and increasing economic interdependence required an institutional and constitutional base going beyond that provided imperfectly by the GATT. This was particularly necessary because the Uruguay Round had greatly expanded the ambit of traditional trade negotiations into new and sensitive areas of domestic economic policy-making.

* * *

51. However, it is clear that there is a need to continue creating and legitimizing structures that influence globalization and that is the

---

2. Peter Sutherland et al., The Future of the WTO: Addressing Institutional Challenges in the New Millennium, Report by the Consultative Board to the Director–General Supachai Panitchpakdi, available at: http://www.wto.org/english/thewto_e/10 anniv_e/future_wto_e.htm, The membership of this Consultative Board were Peter Sutherland, Jagdish Bhagwati, Kwesi Botchwey, Niall Fitzgerald, Koichi Hamada, John H. Jackson, Celso Lafer and Thierry de Montbrial.

role for the WTO that we seek to improve. The WTO system is a significantly more complicated system than was the GATT. At the same time principles like non-discrimination through the most-favoured-nation (MFN) rule are now replete with so many exceptions and derivations that there is a need to stand back to review where we have reached (see Chapter II). The WTO now provides so many examples of instruments that can be used to accelerate or brake the process of market opening that there is a clear need to access them and to ensure that they are appropriate, necessary and effective.

* * *

54. The notions of "fairness" and "a level playing field" are subject to much abuse for domestic political purposes. Fairness and evenness tend to be in the eye of the beholder, especially when commercial interests are at stake. However, the WTO is the only global institution that has attempted (with reasonable success) to create a set of rules for trade that have reflected concern for the interests of the poorer countries; the rules reflecting the economic understandings of the time. True, there are still tasks to be accomplished, such as the removal of agricultural subsidies in the rich countries and the lowering of industrial tariffs in the poor countries. But these have been very much on the agenda of successive multilateral trade negotiations—not least, the Doha Round.

* * *

CONCLUSIONS

* * *

5. The WTO has competences and powers that were previously the monopoly of states. Ultimately what counts is whether the balance between some loss of "policy space" at the national level and the advantages of cooperation and the rule of law at the multilateral level is good or bad. The Consultative Board's view is that it is already a positive for all WTO Members and will be increasingly so in the future.

SECTION 6.4   DECISION–MAKING IN GATT AND THE WTO

Since GATT was not viewed as an organization, it is not surprising that the General Agreement had little in it about decision making. Article XXV called for one-nation one-vote and decision by a majority of votes cast, unless otherwise provided. The language reads:

1. Representatives of the contracting parties shall meet from time to time for the purpose of giving effect to those provisions of this Agreement which involve joint action and, generally, with a view to facilitating the operation and furthering the objectives of this Agreement. Wherever reference is made in this Agreement to the con-

tracting parties acting jointly they are designated as the CON-
TRACTING PARTIES.

This language is remarkably broad. Although cautiously utilized (at least
in the early years), it was the basis for much GATT activity. For the
United States, for instance, this language posed a danger. First, the
United States could have been outvoted in a GATT with over 120
members, over two-thirds of which were developing countries, and over
half of which were formally associated in one status or another with the
European Union. Second, a nation's vote is cast by the Executive Branch
of its government, and for the United States (and possibly other countries as well) an Executive decision to vote for a measure could result in
its acceptance of a binding international obligation, without participation
of its Legislative Branch. In practice, however, this was probably not a
realistic danger, since the preparatory work, the failure of the ITO and
OTC, the criticism of Congress, and the worry over voting strength, led
the Contracting Parties to be cautious in voting additional obligations.
Moreover, a short withdrawal notice period and the relative ease of
breaching obligations have also been sources of caution. Most efforts in
GATT got accomplished through a process of negotiation and compromise, with varying degrees of formality and a tacit understanding that
agreement was necessary among countries with important economic
influence.

One important question of the scope of authority under Article XXV
was whether the Contracting Parties had the power to make definitive
interpretations of the General Agreement, binding on all members. For
example, the Contracting Parties, in a decision of 9 August, 1949, ruled:[1]

> The reduction of the rate of duty on a product, provided for in a
> schedule to the General Agreement, below the rate set forth therein,
> does not require unanimous consent of the Contracting Parties.

From time to time, various working groups or panels of GATT have
reported their interpretations of the General Agreement, and these
reports have been "adopted" by the Contracting Parties. In addition,
once in a while the chairman of the Contracting Parties has made an
"interpretative ruling," and no objection has been raised in the Contracting Parties' meeting.[2]

The General Agreement also had measures specifying the procedure
and votes for amending the agreement and for waivers.

The WTO Charter substantially changes all of this and contains an
elaborate matrix of decision making procedures, with important constraints around them. Basically there are five different techniques for
making decisions or formulating new or amended rules of trade policy in
the WTO Charter: decisions on various matters, "interpretations," waivers, amendments to the agreements, and, finally, negotiation of new

---

1. GATT, II BISD 11 (1952); see also
John H. Jackson, World Trade and the Law
of GATT 21 (1969).

2. See GATT, II BISD 12 (1952) (Ruling
by the Chairman on 24 August 1948).

agreements. The following chart summarizes the provisions. Examination of the WTO Charter provisions in the Documents Supplement will reveal even more complexity!

WTO DECISION MAKING

ORDINARY DECISIONS: ARTICLE IX:1

The WTO Charter specifies that the GATT practice of decision making by consensus is to be continued for the WTO Ministerial Conference (MC) and General Council (GC), but when consensus cannot be achieved, decisions will be made on the basis of the majority of votes cast, with each member having one vote, unless otherwise provided.

INTERPRETATIONS: ARTICLE IX:2

The MC and GC have exclusive authority to adopt interpretations of the WTO Charter and the Multilateral Trade Agreements. Interpretations of the Annex 1 agreements are to be based on a recommendation of the Council for that agreement and require an affirmative vote from three-quarters of the overall WTO membership. Interpretations are not to be used to undermine Article X's amendment procedures.

WAIVERS: ARTICLE IX:3

The MC may waive an obligation under the WTO Charter and the Annex 1 Multilateral Trade Agreements. If consensus cannot be reached, the grant of a waiver requires an affirmative vote of three-quarters of the overall WTO membership. In the case of Annex 1 agreements, the waiver request is to be submitted to the relevant Council (e.g., Goods, Services or TRIPS), which will submit a report to the MC. Article IX:4 provides that any waiver granted shall specify the exceptional circumstances justifying it and a termination date. Waivers are subject to annual MC review.

AMENDMENTS: ARTICLE X

Amendments to the WTO Charter and the Annex 1 Multilateral Trade Agreements may be proposed to the MC by members or Councils. If consensus cannot be reached, the approval of an amendment for submission to the members requires a two-thirds vote of the overall WTO membership. Generally, amendments come into force on acceptance by two-thirds of the members. If it has been determined that the amendment will not affect member rights and obligations, it comes into force for all members at that time. Otherwise, amendments come into force only for those members accepting them, unless by a three-quarters vote of the overall WTO membership, it is decided that if a member does not accept the amendment it shall be free to withdraw or remain a member with permission of the MC. (In the case of GATS, amendments to certain provisions come into force on a two-thirds vote. For the other provisions, they come into effect for those approving them, but are subject to the same three-quarters vote procedure.)

Amendments to certain rules take effect only upon acceptance by all members: WTO decision making and amendment rules (Arts. IX, X); GATT Arts. I (MFN) & II (Tariff Schedules); GATS Art. II:1 (MFN); TRIPS Art. 4 (MFN).

Amendments to Annexes 2 (Dispute Settlement) & 3 (TPRM) can be made by MC action alone (without member acceptance), but for Annex 2, approval must be by consensus. Art. X:8

NEGOTIATING OTHER AGREEMENTS: ARTICLE III:2

The WTO is to provide a forum for negotiations on agreements contained in its annexes. It may also provide a forum for other negotiations on trade relations and a framework for the implementation of the results of such negotiations, by decision of the MC.

ANNEX 4: PLURILATERAL AGREEMENTS

Decision making and amendments under these agreements is governed by the rules contained in each agreement. (Arts. IX:5, X:10) The MC may add trade agreements to Annex 4 by consensus; it may delete agreements from Annex 4 on the request of the members party to the agreement. Art. X:9.

In addition, it is important to understand the potential of the dispute settlement procedures, and the panel and Appellate Body reports that result (the subject of the next chapter), on the change or evolution of the trade rules.

In GATT there was some worry about waivers being used as a sort of "easy track" substitute for amendments. Some GATT documents discussed this problem,[3] but the practice of GATT was rather relaxed on this point. The WTO Charter stiffens considerably the rules regarding waivers and makes explicit the power of the organization to terminate waivers (an issue of some contention in GATT.) See Article IX:3.

Likewise in GATT there was concern about the amending rules (contained in Article XXX). The unanimity required for certain amendments had never been achieved, and the requirement otherwise of two-thirds (but not binding on hold-outs) was increasingly difficult to fulfill as the number of GATT contracting parties increased. This difficulty was a major factor in the Tokyo Round negotiations, leading the participants to utilize "side" codes or agreements on a number of GATT subjects as a way to avoid the need for amendments. But these codes only bound governments which accepted them, and in the Uruguay Round it was decided that a "single package" approach should be followed, so that all governments that became members of the WTO would be obligated to accept almost all of the agreements and rules. The whole package itself was accepted as a totally new treaty, thus avoiding the GATT amending procedure (and probably resulting in technical withdrawals from the old

---

3. GATT Doc. L/403, 7th Sept. 1955.

GATT). The amending rules of this new package are somewhat similar to the GATT rules, so it is possible that the inconveniences of the GATT rules will continue to be a problem. However, the WTO rules do have some areas of greater flexibility for changing trade rules.

THE SUTHERLAND REPORT (2004)[4]

280.　Certainly, the most dramatic solution to the troublesome system of decision-making in the WTO would be to look again at the consensus rule. Voting is provided for in the Marrakesh Agreement with specific majorities required for specific situations. However, the practice of decision-making by consensus in the WTO has been, so far, to the exclusion of voting. Consensus was also the norm in the GATT, although voting was used, for instance in the case of new accessions and for waivers.

* * *

283.　On the other hand, there are also disadvantages to the consensus system of decision-making. As the number of Members grows larger and larger (now 148, perhaps going to 170 or more), it becomes harder and harder to implement needed measures that require decisions, even when there is a vast majority of the Members that desire a measure. The consensus requirement can result in the majority's will being blocked by even one country. If the measure involved a fundamental change, such difficulty would probably be worthwhile, as adding a measure of "constitutional stability" to the organization. But often there are non-fundamental measures at stake, some of which are just fine-tuning to keep the rules abreast of changing economic and other circumstances.

SECTION 6.5　TRADE NEGOTIATING ROUNDS

(A) OVERVIEW

One of the more important roles that GATT has played during the last four decades has been its sponsorship of a series of major multinational trade negotiations. So far there have been eight such trade negotiating "rounds." The rounds are summarized by the following chart:[1]

---

4. Peter Sutherland et. al., The Future of the WTO: Addressing Institutional Challenges in the New Millennium, Report by the Consultative Board to the Director–General Supachai Panitchpakdi, available at: http://www.wto.org/english/thewto_e/10 anniv_e/future_wto_e.htm.

1. For the first five rounds, see Gerard Curzon, Multilateral Commercial Diplomacy 81 (1965). For the Kennedy Round, see John W. Evans, The Kennedy Round in American Trade Policy 281 (1971). For the Tokyo Round, see GATT, The Tokyo Round of Trade Negotiations: Report by the Director–General of GATT 118 (1979) and GATT, The Tokyo Round of Trade Negotiations: Supplementary Report by the Director–General of GATT 6 (1980) (collectively, the GATT Tokyo Round Reports). For the Uruguay Round generally, see The GATT Uruguay Round: A Negotiating History: 1986–1992 (Terence P. Stewart ed., 1993).

	Countries Participating	Trade Affected
1. Geneva, Switzerland 1947	23	$10 Billion
2. Annecy, France 1948	33	Unavailable
3. Torquay, England 1950	34	Unavailable
4. Geneva 1956	22	$2.5 Billion
5. "Dillon Round," Geneva 1960–61	45	$4.9 Billion
6. "Kennedy Round," Geneva 1964–67	48	$40 Billion
7. "Tokyo Round," Geneva 1973–1979	99	$155 Billion
8. "Uruguay Round," Geneva 1986–94	120 +	$3.7 Trillion

The first five of these rounds focused on negotiations for the reduction of tariffs. As it turned out, the sixth round also focused on tariffs, although one of the expressed goals for the round was to deal significantly with non-tariff barriers. The seventh round was predominantly concerned with non-tariff measures, although considerable attention was still given to tariff reductions. (The negotiation procedures and problems concerning tariffs will be discussed in Chapter 8.) Finally, the Uruguay Round continued detailed work on many non-tariff measures, but greatly expanded the scope of the trading system by adding services and intellectual property subjects, and, as previously indicated, created a significant new institution. Preliminary estimates of the trade affected by the Uruguay Round include $2.7 trillion for goods, plus approximately $1 trillion for services.

From the time that the new WTO organization came into being (Jan. 1 1995) this organization has endeavored to launch and complete a new round of negotiations (the ninth of the ongoing system, or the first under the WTO), but success has been difficult, as will be discussed at the end of this section.

(B) TOKYO ROUND (1973–1979)

JOHN H. JACKSON, RESTRUCTURING THE GATT SYSTEM 26–29 (1990)[2]

In [the Tokyo MTN] round non-tariff in addition to tariff measures were addressed extensively for the first time. Except for the original drafting of the GATT itself, the MTN results may well be the most far-reaching and substantively important product of the seven major trade rounds. The MTN results included, in addition to tariff reduction protocols, nine special agreements, and four "understandings," dealing with subjects as follows:

---

2. Reprinted by permission of The Royal Institute of International Affairs. Restructuring the GATT System was published by Pinter for the Royal Institute of Interna-tional Affairs, London. It was published in North America for the RIIA by the Council on Foreign Relations Press, New York.

Agreements on:

1) Technical Barriers to Trade

2) Government Procurement

3) Interpretation and Application of Articles VI, XVI & XXIII (Subsidies)

4) Arrangement Regarding Bovine Meat

5) International Dairy Arrangement

6) Implementation of Article VII (Custom Valuation)

7) Import Licensing Procedures

8) Trade in Civil Aircraft

9) Implementation of Article VI (Anti–Dumping duties)

Understandings on:

1) Differential and More Favorable Treatment, Reciprocity and Fuller Participation of Developing Countries

2) Declaration on Trade Measures Taken for Balance-of-Payments Purposes

3) Safeguard Action for Development Purposes

4) Understanding Regarding Notification, Consultation, Dispute Settlement and Surveillance

The overall impact of these results was to substantially broaden the scope of coverage of the GATT system.

The legal status of these various agreements and understandings, however, was not always clear. The nine agreements are drafted as "stand-alone" treaties, each with signatory clauses, and in most cases with institutional measures which include a committee of signatories with certain powers, and a dispute settlement mechanism (part of the "Balkanization" mentioned earlier.) Of these agreements, seven have sufficiently precise obligations to be called "codes." The others tend to confine their terms to the development of consultation mechanisms, statements of objectives, and only a few weak provisions which actually provide binding obligations. In one case, an agreement has been sufficiently troubled that the United States and some other signatories have formally withdrawn from it.

The "understandings," have a much more ambiguous status. These instruments mostly express goals or very general obligations, or (in the case of dispute settlement) describe procedures which arguably were already followed. These are not signed as independent agreements. The CONTRACTING PARTIES in November 1979, adopted these understandings. The implication of some of the provisions in these understandings is such as to suggest a "waiver" from other GATT obligations, while other provisions elaborate procedures in the manner in which a "decision" under GATT Article XXV might do. The understanding regarding dispute settlement, has been extremely important, since the GATT treaty provisions on this subject are so slim. This understanding (which, however, has a number of ambiguities) has provided a reasonably definitive account of the practice which had developed over the decades of GATT activity.

As "stand-alone" treaties, the "codes" obligate only those nations which sign and ratify them. A number of questions can then be raised about the legal relationship of these codes to the GATT itself. First, in theory, GATT parties which do not sign the agreements are not bound by them, and no provision of a "code" can alter their GATT rights. Since the GATT obligations include the most-favored-nation clause, however, if a code provides treatment for the trade of any other code signatory which is more favorable than that provided in GATT, such treatment is arguably required to benefit a GATT member which has not signed the code. The GATT CONTRACTING PARTIES in November 1979 adopted a decision which takes this position. However, some codes may not fall within the terms of the GATT MFN clause, for example, Government Procurement.

Some of the "codes" have titles which relate them to the GATT, such as the "Agreement on Implementation of Article VI," and another on "Interpretation and Application of" several GATT Articles. Again, non-signatories can argue that they are in no way bound by such codes. However, if these codes can be deemed to be "practice" of the GATT contracting parties, they could themselves be evidence of evolving interpretation of the GATT language itself. This could be especially true if further practice in GATT develops, without protest from non-signatories of the codes, which follows a code interpretation. In these ways GATT parties who have not signed a code may find that they effectively become obligated to code terms which "interpret" the GATT.

(C) URUGUAY ROUND (1986–1994)

Much of the preceding parts of this chapter present the results of the Uruguay Round. It is an extraordinarily broad and detailed product that resulted in an overhaul of the entire GATT system, embracing over 50 separate texts brought into one single package through the WTO charter. The following is one illustrative comment about that round:

STATEMENT OF GATT DIRECTOR–GENERAL PETER SUTHERLAND[3]

In every sense, the Uruguay Round is a global negotiation with a global result. For the first time, a negotiation under the auspices of GATT has covered virtually every sector of world trade. For the first time too, participation has been global. Indeed, perhaps the most significant feature about this negotiation has been the large number of developing countries taking part, and taking part actively. Their contribution to the Round has been a vital one, reflecting the importance of the multilateral system in creating and maintaining opportunities for sustainable development.

3. GATT, News of the Uruguay Round, NUR 081, Dec. 21, 1993, at 2.

Important new areas of the world economy have been brought under multilateral disciplines. The General Agreement on Trade in Services provides for a new set of multilateral rules for the conduct of services trade. It simultaneously creates a framework for a continuing process of liberalization. These rules take account of the particular features of trade in services and are based on fundamental principles of non-discrimination and national treatment. The outlook for job creation in this fast growing and dynamic sector, which accounts for over 60 percent of world production, is now better than ever.

* * *

The results on market access for goods represent a major milestone in the history of the GATT. Tariffs are expected to have been reduced by around 40 percent. Of equally far reaching importance is the substantial rise in security in the world trading system by virtue of the large increase in tariff bindings, not only but especially by developing countries, many of whom have undertaken wide-ranging economic reforms in recent years intended to achieve fuller integration with world markets. And if we factor in comprehensive tariffication of the measures affecting trade in agriculture, over 95 percent of world merchandise products will now be secured by tariff bindings, representing an enormous advance in predictability and stability of trading operations.

(D) NEGOTIATIONS UNDER THE WTO

At the end of the Uruguay Round there was considerable speculation about the prospects for another, ninth, round. Many observers expressed the view that the era of "rounds" was over, that the world could no longer wait for ten or more years between rounds to solve pressing and fast changing problems of international economic relations, and that rounds were so cumbersome and hard to manage that they should give way to other techniques of negotiation and rule making for the international trading system.

On the other hand, some of the advantages of rounds continued to be pointed out. For example, a round often provides more "trading material," in the sense that different nations have different objectives and may be more willing to yield in certain areas, if there are other relatively unrelated matters which attract them to an overall package. In addition, world leaders are more likely to become directly and personally involved in a "large package" negotiation than one that merely involves small bits of rather technical material.

In the late 1990's important agreements on telecommunications and financial services were successfully negotiated in the context of the services agreement. But the attempt to launch a ninth round of multilateral trade negotiations at the WTO Ministerial Meeting in Seattle in December 1999 failed after a week in which street protests caught global media attention. The events in Seattle have been described in terms of an "inside problem," and an "outside problem." The "inside problem" was what was really going on in the negotiations and the disagreement among Members over a wide array of old and new issues (agriculture, the position of developing countries, the question of which new issues to deal with and whether to launch a full new round or deal with different issues one at a time, etc.). The "outside problems" were the demonstrations, the tensions involved with that and the organization of NGOs and public participation. These relate to issues of "transparency" and "participation" in dispute settlement, negotiations and decision-making mechanisms.

After the failure at Seattle, the next (fourth) Ministerial Meeting was held in November 2001 at Doha, the capital of the Middle Eastern nation of Qatar. (This happened to occur only a couple of months after the 9–11 attack on New York City.) This meeting resolved to pursue an ambitious trade negotiating agenda which appeared reasonably optimistic—the so-called Doha Development Agenda. However at the fifth Ministerial Meeting in September 2003 in Cancun, Mexico, the process met strong resistance, especially from developing countries. Attempts since to reinvigorate the negotiations continued with a Ministerial Meeting in Hong Kong in December 2005, followed by various spurts of negotiating activity. By early 2008, the efforts seemed to be stalled, and many observers doubted that any success was possible until after the November US elections. Consequently, as this is written (February 2008) it is very hard to predict whether there will be any successful results from the Doha negotiations in the near term.

As usual, the major contested issues concern (i) agricultural subsidies and market access and (ii) the so-called NAMA (non-agricultural market access) negotiations in goods and services. Broadly speaking, developing countries want the US and the EU to cut subsidies and provide more access under item (i), while the US and the EU want more from the developing world under item (ii). There are, of course, other controversial issues under discussion as well, such as anti-dumping rules. It has been pointed out that delay in completing, or even the collapse of, the negotiations will not prevent the continuation of other WTO activities, such as dispute settlement. Indeed, with stalemate in the negotiations, the dispute settlement process is likely to be even more important, with more nations bringing issues to the dispute settlement system because they are unable to resolve the issues otherwise.

SECTION 6.6   ACCESSION AND MEMBERSHIP

(A) INTRODUCTION AND GATT HISTORY

In this section we will discuss the process by which a country can become a Member of the WTO. After a brief overview of the procedures that existed under the original GATT, subsection B will discuss the procedures for accession to the WTO and how they differ from those under the old GATT. In section C we will look at the possibilities that exist to "opt-out" of WTO commitments with other Members at the time of accession. Finally section D will look more specifically at the accession of the People's Republic of China to the WTO. We will also look at the problems under US law related to the granting of Permanent Normal Trade Relations status to China.

Following the fiction that GATT was not an organization, its participating nations or customs territories were called "Contracting Parties," and not "members." The WTO Charter changed this. The new charter designates participants as "Members." A bit of the GATT history on accession is relevant, however, because it clearly influences the interpretations and practices under the WTO Charter. Indeed, the process of negotiating accession remains largely the same.

There were basically two ways by which a country could become a contracting party to the General Agreement on Tariffs and Trade (other than as an original signatory to the Protocol of Provisional Application). Article XXXIII specified the "normal" procedure for membership. This article required a decision of two-thirds majority of the existing contracting parties, and accession to GATT on terms "to be agreed between such government and the CONTRACTING PARTIES." The article, however, only hints at the most important prerequisite to becoming a member through this procedure—the "ticket of admission" required from the acceding country by way of trade and tariff commitments negotiated at the time of entry.

Suppose, for example, an industrialized country wished to join GATT. The existing members of GATT, through previous tariff and trade negotiating rounds, had each committed themselves not only to the general provisions of the Agreement, but in most cases to extensive and detailed tariff commitments contained in a schedule for each country. For a new country to enter GATT without agreeing to comparable tariffs would allow it to obtain a "free ride" in receiving the previously negotiated concessions of the existing members. Consequently, the existing members appropriately desired a negotiation with the applicant country, which must result in the applicant agreeing to a series of tariff concessions that the existing members feel are reciprocally balanced to those commitments that they have already made in GATT. Often this negotiation has been held in the context of a general trade or tariff round. For example, Japan negotiated for entry during the 1955 Geneva Round.

A first step for membership may be no more than to obtain "observer status" for the applicant. Following this, there may be a declaration by the Contracting Parties of special commercial relationships, often providing that existing GATT parties will extend GATT treatment, including MFN, to the new participant, if the new participant reciprocates. Sometimes such a declaration is called a declaration of "provisional accession" and it results in "de facto" application of the General Agreement. Finally, a protocol for accession itself will be negotiated and after the necessary decision by the Contracting Parties, will be open for signature (although as soon as the applicant country signs, the protocol becomes effective under its terms, since the Contracting Parties' vote is acceptance for GATT). The process suggests that the Contracting Parties acting jointly have legal personality under international law, enabling them to enter into an international agreement directly with the country.

A second way by which countries could become GATT parties was through "sponsorship" under Article XXVI:5(c). This paragraph applied primarily to countries that had become independent after having been ruled by a GATT Contracting Party that had applied the General Agreement to the territory in question. The first country to accede under these provisions was Indonesia in 1950, and over the years, many other nations became contracting parties by this route. It was generally agreed that the sponsored new member would apply the General Agreement as its parent sponsor was applying it on the date of sponsorship, including the "grandfather" clauses of the Protocol of Provisional Application or similar accession protocol.

Most significantly, a sponsored country did not need to negotiate a "ticket of admission." If the parent country had negotiated a separate schedule on behalf of the territory that had become a country, the commitments in that tariff schedule would become the schedule of the newly independent country in GATT. In practice, the separate schedules for colonial territories were very brief, often containing only a few tariff commitments. In some cases, there were no such tariff schedules at all. Thus, this meant that some parties had no schedule, i.e. no tariff commitments in GATT.[1] As noted earlier, this was raised fairness problems in the eyes of some.

(B) MEMBERSHIP AND ACCESSION TO THE WTO

One of the achievements of the WTO in its short life is its continuing attraction of new members. With a total membership now (March 2008) reaching 153 (if two pending accessions are completed with ratification). This compares to the membership at the beginning of the WTO on January 1, 1995, which was 76. In addition, 29 countries are negotiating for membership, including most importantly, Russia.

Articles XI and XII of the WTO Charter state the requirements for membership of and accession to the WTO. It is generally assumed that countries that accede to the WTO as new Members will also have to comply with the requirements that Article XI sets out for the original Members. It is interesting to note, however, that the Charter does not specifically require this.

Article XI

ORIGINAL MEMBERSHIP

1.   The contracting parties to GATT 1947 as of the date of entry into force of this Agreement, and the European Communities, which accept this Agreement and the Multilateral Trade Agreements and

---

1.   See generally John H. Jackson, World Trade and the Law of GATT secs. 4.5, 10.1 (1969).

for which Schedules of Concessions and Commitments are annexed to GATT 1994 and for which Specific Commitments are annexed to GATS shall become original Members of the WTO.

2.   The least-developed countries recognized as such by the United Nations will only be required to undertake commitments and concessions to the extent consistent with their individual development, financial and trade needs or their administrative and institutional capabilities.

Article XII

ACCESSION

1.   Any State or separate customs territory possessing full autonomy in the conduct of its external commercial relations and of the other matters provided for in this Agreement and the Multilateral Trade Agreements may accede to this Agreement, on terms to be agreed between it and the WTO. Such accession shall apply to this Agreement and the Multilateral Trade Agreements annexed thereto.

2.   Decisions on accession shall be taken by the Ministerial Conference. This Ministerial Conference shall approve the agreement on the terms of accession by a two-thirds majority of the Members of the WTO.

3.   Accession to a Plurilateral Trade Agreement shall be governed by the provisions of that Agreement.

It can be seen that some of the GATT concepts have been carried over, such as the "ticket of admission," and "independent customs territory" status. There is, however, no provision in the WTO Charter comparable to GATT Article XXVI providing for easy accession by sponsorship of a former colonial mother country. All WTO Members, both original Members and those seeking accession, are expected to have tariff and service schedules, even if they contain relatively few meaningful commitments. The phrase in Article XII "on terms to be agreed" is obviously crucial and GATT procedures and practice have clearly influenced the direction taken in the WTO.

Often the initial approach of a potential applicant for WTO membership is a request to become an observer. When a country or separate customs territory decides that it wants to become a Member of the WTO it submits a communication to the Director General of the WTO indicating its desire to accede to the WTO under Article XII. This communication is then circulated to all Members and the General Council can decide to establish a Working Party. The Applicant is then required to submit a Memorandum describing in detail its foreign trade regime, its rules, regulations, and economic policies related to international trade in goods, services, and intellectual property rights, as well as certain economic statistics. The Secretariat can provide technical assistance. The Memorandum is sent to the Secretariat and circulated to all Members who are invited to submit questions. The Working Party will then start discussions with the Applicant about the Memorandum, the questions submitted by Members, and the changes that may be needed in its trade regime. When these consultations have sufficiently advanced, members may initiate bilateral accession negotiations on market access for goods and services and on the other terms to be agreed. When the Working Party and the bilateral negotiations have been concluded, a Schedule of Concessions and Commitments to GATT 1994 and a Schedule of Specific Commitments to the GATS will be prepared. These will then be reviewed multilaterally and annexed to the Protocol of Accession, of which they become an integral part. The Protocol of Accession contains the terms of accession agreed by the Applicant and the members of the Working Party. The Working Party must approve a report that includes the draft Protocol. In the WTO this approval has generally been by "consensus." This Protocol of Accession is submitted to the General Council or Ministerial Conference together with a summary of the Working Party's discussions and a draft Decision. A two-thirds majority in the General Council is required for adoption of the Protocol. The Protocol of Accession will enter into force thirty days after the Applicant has signed or, if parliamentary approval is required, after it has deposited the Instrument of Ratification.

(C) NON–APPLICATION

When GATT was negotiated, the original text required a unanimous decision to accept a new Contracting Party. After the 1948 Havana Conference, however, this provision was changed to a two-thirds majority. Nevertheless, it was felt that no country should be forced to accept a trade agreement with another country without its own decision to do so. For that reason a "non-application" or "opt-out" provision was added to the Agreement. Thus, Article XXXV of GATT was designed to allow, on a one-time availability basis, an option to either a newly acceding state or any existing Contracting Party, to table a notification that as between the acceding state and that existing Contracting Party, the Agreement would not apply, even after the accession. Often political considerations enter into the decision to opt out of a trading relationship, as suggested by the past invocation of the option by India and Pakistan against South Africa. The most extensive set of "opt out" invocations were those exercised by a number of countries against Japan at the time Japan entered GATT in the middle of the 1950's. Subsequently, most of those countries withdrew their Article XXXV invocation, often after individual bilateral negotiations with the government of Japan resulting from special commitments. This "opt-out" or "non-application" provision has been used under the GATT approximately eighty-six times (most of these invocations have subsequently been withdrawn).[2]

Article XIII of the WTO Charter is an updated version of Article XXXV of GATT. It states:

2. See Analytical Index: Guide to GATT Law and Practice, Geneva 1995, p. 1034.

Article XIII

NON–APPLICATION OF MULTILATERAL TRADE AGREEMENTS BETWEEN PARTICULAR MEMBERS

1. This Agreement and the Multilateral Trade Agreements in Annexes 1 and 2 shall not apply as between any Member and any other Member if either of the Members, at the time either becomes a Member, does not consent to such application.

2. Paragraph 1 may be invoked between original Members of the WTO which were contracting parties to GATT 1947 only where Article XXXV of that Agreement had been invoked earlier and was effective as between those contracting parties at the time of entry into force for them of this Agreement.

3. Paragraph 1 shall apply between a Member and another Member which has acceded under Article XII only if the Member not consenting to the application has so notified the Ministerial Conference before the approval of the agreement on the terms of accession by the Ministerial Conference.

4. The Ministerial Conference may review the operation of this Article in particular cases at the request of any Member and make appropriate recommendations.

5. Non-application of a Plurilateral Trade Agreement between parties to that Agreement shall be governed by the provisions of that Agreement.

Article XIII of the WTO is largely a continuation of GATT Article XXXV. In contrast to GATT 1947 Article XXXV, however, Article XIII of the WTO Charter no longer contains a provision requiring that the opt-out possibility applies between two Members only if they have not entered into tariff negotiations. Article XIII also differs from the old system in that it explicitly requires notification to the Ministerial Conference. The United States has invoked WTO Article XIII several times in respect of former Communist regimes, including a "carried over" case from GATT Article XXXV, but has withdrawn its invocation once Congress has approved permanent normal trading relations status for the country. See Section 10.3(C) infra.

(D) CHINA'S ACCESSION TO THE WTO

The potential accession and integration of China to the WTO is one of the most important challenges and opportunities for the WTO and its Members. China's accession differs in scope and in political implications from the normal process of accession, but nevertheless provides a clear example of how accession works in practice.

China was one of the original 1948 GATT Contracting Parties, but the government representing China at GATT, the "Nationalist Chinese" or Taiwan, withdrew China from GATT in 1950. Over time the PRC government assumed China's seat in many international organizations, including the United Nations and the International Monetary Fund. In more recent years, the PRC joined the Multifiber Arrangement associated with GATT, and became an observer at GATT. Some argue that the withdrawal of China from GATT was attempted by a government that was not in control, and therefore was not effective. However, several counterarguments have been made, such as China's decade-long absence from GATT. It was nevertheless agreed that for the PRC's "re-entry" into GATT the accession procedures would be used. When the Uruguay Round terminated GATT 1947 and created the WTO, it was clear that the WTO accession procedures would apply.

Nicholas Lardy has indicated a number of reasons why WTO accession is of great importance to China, the United States, and the world trading system in general.[3] He observes that China has become a major player in international investment and trade but that it needs to be further integrated into the global economic system. China's leaders, he says, have staked their legitimacy on their ability to create economic growth. Continued economic growth has thus become a sine qua non to stay in power. Especially after the Asian crisis, many Chinese leaders have seen globalization of production as the only viable alternative, and, indeed, one that China could benefit from. Chinese leadership has also started to realize that further integration into the world economy requires development of a market economy. WTO membership will oblige China to comply with the rules of the world trade system. Reform-minded Chinese leaders can use the WTO obligations as a lever to complete transition to a market-oriented economy.

China's accession, says Lardy, is also of great importance to the United States and the world trading system in general. For many years, China has been the single largest country outside the trading system. China's WTO membership will also greatly increase the possibilities for foreign direct investment in the Chinese market (telecommunications, distribution, financial services) and will increase market access and leads to the availability of lower cost imports for consumers in the United States. Further economic integration may also make China a "more constructive participant" in new trade negotiation rounds. The increased ability to achieve economic reform and liberalization will allow China to meet the needs and expectations of its population, will create greater stability, and will be beneficial to the rest of the world too. Better economic conditions may, in the long term, also lead to a more pluralistic political system, and will likely "lead to stronger trade and investment ties between China and Taiwan that may contribute to a gradual reduction of tensions between the two."

A substantial barrier to overcome for China's WTO accession in the United States was parts of the 1974 Trade Act relating to trade relations with communist countries (so called Non–Market Economies or NMEs).[4]

---

3. See for a more complete overview of his views: Nicholas R. Lardy, Issues in China's WTO Accession, Congressional Testimony, US–China Security Review Commission, May 9, 2001.

4. See generally Sylvia A. Rhodes & John H. Jackson, United States Law and China's WTO Accession Process, 2 JIEL 497–510 (1999).

Under these statutes, the United States cannot grant MFN treatment (or as it has been termed in US law since 1998 "normal trade relations") to products of an NME that denies its citizens the right to emigrate, or imposes sanctions on emigration.[5] Section 402 of the Trade Act of 1974, the so-called Jackson–Vanik Amendment, allows the President to waive these requirements, subject to annual review.[6] Although the United States and the PRC entered into a bilateral trade agreement in 1979, the PRC was subject to this annual review process. In light of China's WTO accession, several arguments were made that it was important for the United States to allow Permanent Normal Trade Relations (PNTR) with China. The most important was that it would ensure compliance with the WTO requirement of "unconditional most favored nation treatment," and would ensure that the United States reap the full benefits of China's WTO accession.[7] In September 2000 the US Congress passed a bill giving the President the right to decide, after accession of the PRC to the WTO, that trade relations with China will no longer be subject to annual review and will be granted MFN treatment on a permanent basis.

China's membership was finally WTO approved at the November 2001 Doha Ministerial Meeting, and became final 30 days later by Chinese ratification. Some fears of the impact of China membership on the WTO have generally not been realized, but a number of issues (mostly expected) have arisen about the China–WTO relationship, particularly because of tensions between different economic systems.

SECTION 6.7 EFFECT OF THE WTO/GATT AGREEMENTS ON DOMESTIC LAW

This section deals more specifically with WTO treaty application in the United States, since that has some unique features. The general topic of treaty application and effects in US law has already been treated more extensively in Section 3.4 supra.

(A) THE GENERAL AGREEMENT IN U.S. LAW

A final issue to consider is that there are vast differences among nations about how they approach the issue of "direct application" of treaties in their domestic law. Here we treat the question from a US perspective. This material relates to matters taken up in Chapter 3, but here we focus particularly on the General Agreement on Tariffs and Trade and the WTO Charter.

The General Agreement was an executive agreement entered into by the President of the United States. Because Congress never explicitly

---

5. Trade Act of 1974 secs. 401ff., 19 U.S.C.A. secs. 2431ff. (West 1980 and Supp. 1999).

6. Trade Act of 1974 secs. 402.

7. See for an overview of arguments John H. Jackson, Letter to US Representatives Jim Kolbe, Cal Dooley, Robert Matsui and David Dreier, March 21, 2000, Inside US Trade vol. 18, no. 14, April 7, 2000.

approved it, questions have been raised from time to time as to whether the President had the authority to enter into it and as to its status in domestic US law, i.e. is it a self-executing agreement and did it apply to the states?[1] When the WTO entered into force on January 1, 1995, some of these questions became moot. The GATT text is now part of Annex 1 to the WTO and no longer has a separate legal status. This history, however, still has context significance and illustrates some of the issues of treaty application in US law.

As to the question of GATT's self-executing nature, one of the authors has argued that although the General Agreement itself was to be self-executing, application under the Protocol of Provisional Application is not self-executing. Nevertheless, under statutory authority giving the President the power to "proclaim" trade agreements,[2] if the President had the authority to enter into the General Agreement, he had the authority to make it part of United States domestic law, which he did for all except Part IV, which was added in the 1960's.

As to the more basic question of whether the President exceeded his powers under his trade agreements authority when he entered into the General Agreement, consider the following:

JOHN H. JACKSON, THE GENERAL AGREEMENT ON TARIFFS AND TRADE IN UNITED STATES DOMESTIC LAW[3]

From examining the text of the [trade agreements authority], one can see that it places no explicit hurdle against multilateral trade agreements. Furthermore, it was stressed in testimony before the congressional committee that the 1947 GATT negotiations would in reality be "bilateral," as before, with the results of the many bilateral negotiations simply drawn together in one instrument, for the sake of convenience. Even an opposing Congressman commented that merely because the result was one instrument signed by all, did not in itself mean that the President had exceeded his statutory authority. Thus, one can conclude that GATT does not go beyond the statutory authority merely because of its multilateral nature.

A more serious statutory assault on GATT is the argument that specific provisions of GATT exceed the authority delegated to the President by the Trade Agreements Act. Careful analysis is required to evaluate this argument, but to discuss each clause of GATT here would be tedious and lengthy. Appendix A outlines the sources, if the reader wishes to pursue the matter as to any specific article of GATT. Without reference to specific GATT provisions, however, the arguments for the

---

1. In Section 3.4 supra, we dealt generally with the problems in US law of international agreements, both in respect of how they are properly accepted by the United States as binding agreements and their application as domestic law.

2. See discussion in Section 3.4(C) supra.

3. 66 Mich.L.Rev. 249, 294 (1967). This and other excerpts from this publication in this chapter are reprinted by permission of the Michigan Law Review Association.

statutory validity of our adherence to GATT can be summarized as follows: (1) the language of the Statute can be read to permit United States entry into GATT, since it authorizes "trade agreements" either without explicit limitation or with limitations that can be interpreted not to preclude an agreement such as GATT; (2) the legislative history shows that provisions such as those in GATT were contemplated by Congress; (3) prior trade agreements known to Congress had provisions like those of GATT, thus further evidencing congressional intent; (4) later actions of Congress can be taken as recognizing or accepting GATT; and (5) several court cases, while not directly litigating the validity of GATT, have resulted in decisions and opinions that necessarily imply its validity.

In the early years of GATT, congressional antagonism led Congress on at least one occasion to specify in a statute that "no trade agreement * * * shall be applied in a manner inconsistent with the requirements of this section."[4] In extensions of the trade agreements authority in 1953, 1954, 1955 and 1958, Congress inserted a clause which read, "the enactment of this Act shall not be construed to determine or indicate the approval or disapproval by the Congress of the Executive Agreements known as the General Agreement on Tariffs and Trade."[5] In the Trade Act of 1974, Congress for the first time explicitly provided authority to appropriate funds to meet the US obligation to contribute to the GATT budget. (Prior to that action the President had used other funding sources under his control, such as his contingency funds, but always reported to Congress on his action.) The 1974 statutory clause (Section 121(d)) reads (still somewhat begrudgingly!): "This authorization does not imply approval or disapproval by the Congress of *all* articles of the General Agreement on Tariffs and Trade" (emphasis supplied).

It would seem that an issue like this, after such a long history of recognition by the US government of the validity and binding nature of GATT, would be laid to rest. Yet in a 1983 report by the House Commerce Committee concerning a proposal for a "domestic content" requirement on automobiles sold in the United States, the Committee stated: "GATT is an executive agreement, never ratified by the Senate under the Constitution."[6] A footnote to the statement reads as follows:

> The American Law Division of the Congressional Research Service (CRS) in a June 6, 1983 memorandum commented on the legal nature of GATT and said:

> Some ambiguity surrounds the precise legal nature of the General Agreement on Tariffs and Trade (GATT). GATT came into force for

---

4. 65 Stat. 75 (1951).

5. 72 Stat. 673 (1958); 69 Stat. 162 (1955); 68 Stat. 360 (1954); 67 Stat. 472 (1953).

6. H.Rep. No. 98–287, 98th Cong., 1st Sess., part I, at 22 (1983).

the United States on January 1, 1948, pursuant to a protocol of Provisional Application to which the United States agreed to (sic) by way of an executive agreement. Some courts apparently refuse to give full legal effect to GATT since Congress never ratified it. See, e.g., Sneaker Circus, Inc. v. Carter, 457 F.Supp. 771, (E.D.N.Y.1978), aff'd 614 F.2d 1290 (2d Cir.1979).

The Conference Report (H.Rept. No. 93–1644, December 19, 1974, p. 27) concerning the Trade Act of 1974 notes a provision was added to section 121 of the Act stating that the authorization of appropriations for payment by the United States of its share of expenses to GATT "does not imply approval or disapproval by the Congress of all articles of the GATT."

The footnote is somewhat misleading. The Second Circuit did not find it necessary to address this issue in *Sneaker Circus*. In the lower court, Judge Costantino had stated, "Plaintiff's claim that the President's action violated the General Agreement on Tariffs and Trade * * * is likewise without merit, since Congress has never ratified GATT," 457 F.Supp. at 795, citing United States v. Yoshida Intl., Inc., 526 F.2d 560, 575 n. 22 (C.C.P.A.1975). (The *Yoshida* court did not hold that the General Agreement was not a binding international agreement.) Judge Costantino's statement seems to be directly inconsistent with the Supreme Court's holding in the *Belmont* case, discussed in Section 3.4 supra. He went on to note, however, that "Even if GATT were applicable," its provisions were complied with. Id.

In any event, having made the above quoted statement, the Committee did not claim that the General Agreement was an invalid agreement, but rather went on to argue that the proposal was consistent with it. The fact that the Committee felt it necessary to argue that the proposal was GATT consistent is itself very interesting to the question of appraising GATT's effectiveness.

The authors are aware of no US state or federal court which held the General Agreement not to be a binding international agreement for the United States, and many cases have applied GATT rules.[7] The situation as to the agreements resulting from the GATT-sponsored Tokyo Round negotiation was entirely different, as discussed below, and of course the WTO and Uruguay Round texts have a different status now.

A more complicated issue was the extent to which GATT rules could be used to defend or attack an administrative agency's interpretation of US law. Of course, if there is a direct conflict between a US statute and the general agreement, the US statute controls. But what if there is no direct conflict? What was the relevance of the GATT rules in interpreting the US statute? Consider the following excerpt from Suramerica De

---

7. See e.g., Baldwin–Lima–Hamilton Corp. v. Superior Court, 208 Cal.App.2d 803, 25 Cal.Rptr. 798 (1962); Bethlehem Steel Corp. v. Board of Commrs., 276 Cal. App.2d 221, 80 Cal.Rptr. 800 (1969) (Section 3.6 supra); Territory of Hawaii v. Ho, 41 Hawai'i 565 (1957) (Section 12.4 infra).

Aleaciones Laminadas, C.A. v. United States, 966 F.2d 660, 667–668 (Fed.Cir.1992):

> [E]ven if we were convinced that Commerce's interpretation [of the US statutory requirements for filing an antidumping investigation] conflicts with the GATT, which we are not, the GATT is not controlling. While we acknowledge Congress's interest in complying with U.S. responsibilities under the GATT, we are bound not by what we think Congress should or perhaps wanted to do, but by what Congress in fact did. The GATT does not trump domestic legislation; if the statutory provisions at issue here are inconsistent with the GATT, it is a matter for Congress to decide and remedy.

Questions

Do you agree? Is the court's approach consistent with the Restatement (Third) of the Foreign Relations Law of the United States (1987), § 114, which states, "Where fairly possible, a United States statute is to be construed so as not to conflict with international law or with an international agreement of the United States?" Other courts discussing this issue include Mississippi Poultry Assn., Inc. v. Madigan, 992 F.2d 1359 (5th Cir.1993) (affd. en banc); Footwear Distributors & Retailers of America v. United States, 852 F.Supp. 1078 (CIT 1994).

(B) THE GENERAL AGREEMENT AND STATE LAWS

There is, however, a perplexing question of international law effect the relation of GATT and WTO obligations to state laws in the United States. This stems from the language of GATT Article XXIV, paragraph 12, which reads:

> 12.   Each contracting party shall take such reasonable measures as may be available to it to ensure observance of the provisions of this Agreement by the regional and local governments and authorities within its territory.

The following 1967 extract may help to focus the issues presented by this paragraph.

JOHN H. JACKSON, THE GENERAL AGREEMENT ON TARIFFS AND TRADE IN UNITED STATES DOMESTIC LAW[8]

Simple and straightforward as it appears, this language contains an ambiguity that has an important impact on the domestic law application of GATT. The opposing interpretations can be expressed as follows:

(A) The language does not change the binding application of GATT to political subdivisions, but it recognizes that in a federal system certain matters are legally within the power of subdivisions and beyond the control of the central government. In such a case, the central govern-

---

8. Supra note 3, at 302–304.

ment is not in breach of its international obligations when a subdivision violates GATT, as long as the central government does everything within its power to ensure local observance of GATT.

(B) On the contrary, this language indicates that GATT was not intended to apply as a matter of law against local subdivisions at all, and even when the central government has legal power to require local observance of GATT, it is not obligated under GATT to do so, but merely to take "reasonable measures."

If the second interpretation is correct, then GATT cannot be invoked as a matter of law in any state proceeding involving state law. This precise issue has risen in several cases, including a very recent California case. The unanimous conclusion of the courts thus far has been that GATT does apply to and override state or territorial law. However, the State Department took the contrary position in a letter to the Hawaii Territorial Supreme Court in the earliest of these cases. This letter, signed by the then State Department Legal Advisor, Herman Phleger, referring to Article XXIV:12, stated:

> This provision * * * has always been interpreted as preventing the General Agreement from overriding legislation of political subdivisions of contracting parties inconsistent with the provisions of the Agreement; by placing upon contracting parties the obligation to take reasonable measures to obtain observance of the Agreement by such subdivisions, the parties indicated that as a matter of law the General Agreement did not override such laws. * * * In light of the provisions of paragraph 12 of Article XXIV * * * the reliance by the Supreme Court of the Territory on Article VI, clause 2 of the United States Constitution to invalidate the legislation would appear to have been based on a misconception of the General Agreement and of its effect on the legislation of the parties to it * * * It is suggested that you might desire to request a rehearing of the case on the basis that the particular constitutional grounds relied on are not appropriate in view of paragraph 12 of Article XXIV.

This letter is consistent with the testimony of a State Department official in hearings before a Senate Committee in 1949, one-and-one-half years after GATT was signed. * * *

The actual drafting history of GATT, however, leaves one with a somewhat different impression. The language of Article XXIV:12 was drawn directly from an identical provision that was in the draft ITO Charter at the time the GATT draft was formulated.

What, then, can be concluded from the preparatory history of Article XXIV:12? The fragments of that history that were recorded suggest that this clause was intended to apply only to the situation in which the central government did not have the constitutional power to control the subsidiary governments. Australia and other countries made reference to this situation. The United States delegate did likewise, adding his tentative judgment that the United States did not find itself in this circumstance. Thus, it can be argued that the interpretation which was presented at the outset of this section is the correct one, despite the opposing view expressed in the 1949 Senate Finance Committee hearings.

In the Uruguay Round, this situation was addressed by the adoption of an understanding on Article XXIV:12. It provides:

ARTICLE XXIV:12

13.   Each Member is fully responsible under the GATT 1994 for the observance of all provisions of the GATT 1994, and shall take such reasonable measures as may be available to it to ensure such observance by regional and local governments and authorities within its territory.

14.   The provisions of Articles XXII and XXIII of the GATT 1994 as elaborated and applied by the Understanding on Rules and Procedures Governing the Settlement of Disputes may be invoked in respect of measures affecting its observance taken by regional or local governments or authorities within the territory of a Member. When the Dispute Settlement Body has ruled that a provision of the GATT 1994 has not been observed, the responsible Member shall take such reasonable measures as may be available to it to ensure its observance. The provisions relating to compensation and suspension of concessions or other obligations apply in cases where it has not been possible to secure such observance.

15.   Each Member undertakes to accord sympathetic consideration to and afford adequate opportunity for consultation regarding any representations made by another Member concerning measures affecting the operation of the GATT 1994 taken within the territory of the former.

Does this clarify the issues raised above?

(C) IMPLEMENTATION OF THE URUGUAY ROUND

The Uruguay Round Agreements are not self-executing and thus have no direct "statute-like" effect in US law, although the agreements can and should have an indirect effect on US courts and officials when they interpret provisions of US law.

DAVID W. LEEBRON, IMPLEMENTATION OF THE URUGUAY ROUND RESULTS IN THE UNITED STATES[9]

In short, the Uruguay Round Agreements themselves are unlikely to be directly applied in any proceeding other than a proceeding brought by

9. Reprinted from John H. Jackson & Alan O. Sykes (eds.), Implementing the Uruguay Round 212–214 (1997).

the United States for the purpose of enforcing obligations under the agreements. To the extent that the agreements are fully implemented by the statutory language, this is not a matter of concern, but many aspects of the agreement were not explicitly implemented by the legislation. The agreements, including authoritative interpretations by the WTO or decisions of dispute settlement panels, might still be applied either by a court to resolve ambiguities in the language of a statute or by administrative agencies in promulgating rules and regulations. But such applications could not lead to an interpretive result that was contrary to any clearly expressed intent of Congress.

These restrictive aspects of United States implementation are consistent with United States practice since the Tokyo Round. What is newer is the attempt to circumscribe the effect of the statute itself. Generally speaking, statutes later in time take precedence over both earlier statutes and treaties. Although every effort will be made to construe statutes in order to avoid conflicts, implementation of the language and purpose of the later statute will prevail when two statutes cannot be reconciled. A critical question is how broadly a statute should be interpreted when it arguably conflicts with previous legislation. This was a matter of considerable concern in the implementation of the Uruguay Round Agreements, particularly regarding environmental protection and product standards. Congress included provisions intended to limit the potential effects of not only the Uruguay Round Agreements, but also the implementing legislation itself. Section 102(a)(2) of the URAA provides:

Construction.—Nothing In This Act Shall Be Construed

(A) To amend or modify any law of the United States, including any law relating to—

(i) the protection of human, animal, or plant life or health,

(ii) the protection of the environment, or

(iii) worker safety, or

(B) To limit any authority conferred under any law of the United States, including Section 301 of the Trade Act of 1974, Unless specifically provided for in this Act.

The effect of this provision is to greatly limit the extent to which the Act may be interpreted as altering laws (which for this purpose include administrative regulations). * * * If any statutes of the United States not specified in the implementing legislation need to be amended to conform to the Uruguay Round Agreements (whether as a result of dispute settlement or a voluntary determination by the United States), the normal legislative process would have to be followed.

Note on U.S. Participation in the WTO

As already noted in Section 3.6 supra, the 1994 Uruguay Round Agreements Act provides that US federal law prevails over a Uruguay Round agreement in event of a conflict, section 102(a), and that Uruguay Round agreements prevail over state law, but only in actions brought by the US government. Section 102(b)(2). In addition, under the Act no person (except the United States) has a cause of action or defense under any Uruguay Round agreement by virtue of congressional approval thereof, nor may any person challenge a federal, state or local law or action or inaction on the grounds that it is inconsistent with a Uruguay Round agreement, nor may a private party rely on the results of an action brought by the federal government. Section 102(c). The Statement of Administrative Action that accompanied the bill also stresses that the agreements are not self-executing.

In addition, the Act provides for much closer congressional oversight of US WTO/GATT participation than in the past. It establishes a number of reporting and congressional consultation requirements (i.e., with the Ways and Means and Finance Committees), particularly in respect of WTO decision making and dispute settlement. Sections 122, 123, 127. In particular, the Act provides that the United States shall work for continuation in the WTO of the GATT practice of decision making by consensus, section 122(a), and for increased transparency in the WTO in general. Section 126. It also provides for five-year reviews of US participation. Section 125.

Chapter 7

DISPUTE SETTLEMENT

SECTION 7.1 INTRODUCTION

(A) INTRODUCTION

The WTO's dispute settlement system has been called its crown jewel. Yet much of the controversy surrounding the WTO has arisen as a result of dispute settlement decisions on controversial issues. Since it is through the system that the WTO's rules are elaborated and given meaning and since lawyers are intimately involved in its operation, it is particularly appropriate to undertake a detailed examination of the system in this chapter. We begin with a discussion of whether a legalistic/adjudicative/rules-oriented approach or a pragmatic/negotiation-based/power-oriented approach is the best way to resolve trade disputes in the WTO system. After a detailed examination of how the WTO's Dispute Settlement Understanding operates in practice, we then consider a number of key issues that have arisen, such as: What sort of claims may be brought? How are those claims evaluated? What remedies are available? How are conflicting norms resolved? What rights do non-governments have?

(B) GOALS AND METHODS

A fundamental question that arises in constructing and evaluating dispute settlement systems at the international level is whether the systems should be primarily designed to adjudicate disputes or to mediate them. If mediation is the goal, then a dispute settlement system must emphasize methods designed to encourage the contending parties to negotiate a solution to their dispute. If adjudication is the goal, then a system must be able to apply the relevant rules consistently and ensure that the decisions produced by the system are implemented. As noted in Section 7.2, the GATT system became more and more adjudicative over the years, culminating in the court-like WTO system. Not everyone is convinced that this evolution has been desirable. The following materials present somewhat different viewpoints.

WILLIAM J. DAVEY, DISPUTE SETTLEMENT IN GATT[1]

What are the goals of GATT dispute settlement, and would they be better achieved by emphasizing adjudication or negotiation?

1. GOALS OF GATT DISPUTE SETTLEMENT

* * *

In the case of an alleged rule violation, the principal goal of a dispute settlement system is to stop the violation. Even if the dispute settlement system cannot compel compliance with the rule, and even if compliance without compulsion is unlikely, a lesser goal—such as achieving compliance with a watered-down version of the rule—or a goal that ignores the rule altogether would undermine the rule, and by implication all other GATT rules. GATT rules would become meaningless. So as long as there are agreed-upon rules, their enforcement must be the principal goal of the dispute settlement system. This conclusion suggests that in determining whether the GATT dispute settlement system should be more or less adjudicative in nature, the issue is whether a more adjudicative system would promote greater compliance with GATT rules.

* * *

2. ADJUDICATION OR NEGOTIATION

One result of emphasizing adjudication in the GATT dispute settlement system would likely be an increase in the number of cases considered by panels. While an emphasis on adjudication is not inconsistent with negotiated resolution of trade disputes, participants believing that attempts at a negotiated solution had failed would naturally request a dispute settlement panel. The existence of this possibility means that parties would probably abandon attempts at negotiated solutions more quickly than under a system where negotiation was the only alternative. Critics of the adjudication model argue that such increased use would poison the atmosphere within the GATT system to the eventual detriment of all parties, and that it could lead to the collapse of GATT, particularly if so-called "wrong" cases are brought. Proponents argue that it would increase overall compliance with GATT rules to the general benefit of all. These contentions are explored below.

a. *Poisoning the Atmosphere*

Critics of the adjudication model claim that it will promote conflict and contentiousness in an organization that must promote negotiated solutions to achieve its goals. The need to promote negotiated solutions is said to exist because even if a panel report vindicated the complaining party, there is no guarantee that the other party will correct its viola-

---

1. 11 Fordham Intl.L.J. 51, 67–78 Fordham International Law Journal. (1987). Reprinted with permission of the

tion. Thus, obtaining the other party's compliance with the violated GATT rule will necessarily be the subject of negotiations as to the exact form and timing of compliance. Since such diplomatic contracts will almost always be required, the legalistic approach is viewed as counter-productive because it poisons the atmosphere in which those contacts take place. Moreover, economic relations between the contending parties may deteriorate generally as positions in the dispute harden and bad feelings spill over into other areas.

It is difficult to analyze this criticism. Whether or not the atmosphere between two parties had been poisoned cannot objectively be determined by examining tangible evidence. If the atmosphere has been tainted, it is because one or both of the parties has deemed it so. One can evaluate, however, some of the reasons that are given as causes of a poisoned atmosphere.

First, it is suggested that the publicity associated with use of the dispute settlement system will make it more difficult to resolve the dispute. Publicity may embarrass the respondent by publicly labeling it a wrongdoer, thereby causing it to become intransigent. To the extent that positions taken by the parties become public, it becomes more difficult for them to modify these positions without appearing to back down. This situation impedes settlement of the dispute because neither side wants to appear to lose. These arguments seem rather weak because trade disputes are not secret. Even if they are handled through negotiations, one side will argue publicly that the other side has done something wrong. In addition, general positions on the issues will usually become known, at least to those who have an interest in the dispute.

Second, it is suggested that the filing of a complaint is a contentious act in itself, which will worsen relations. The weight of this argument would seem to depend on how frequently the dispute settlement system is used. If it is used only infrequently and only a few parties ever lose, initiation of a complaint would be something of a slap in the face. The ignominy of a loss would also loom larger. But to the extent that there are many cases, and the major trading nations are both winners and losers, this argument loses whatever force it had. So long as the dispute settlement system is viewed as a mechanism for resolving the myriad disputes, both major and minor, that arise between ninety-odd countries on a reasonably regular basis, there should be no poisoning of the atmosphere. As use grows, the system will be viewed as a normal part of the relationships between countries.

Third, it can be argued that a complaint will lead the respondent in that case to bring an action against the original complainant on other grounds. If this occurs, it will increase the number of disputes the system must handle, but that in itself is not undesirable. Indeed, if more complaints lead to a higher level of compliance with GATT rules, it would be beneficial. It could be argued, however, that more cases will result in more unresolved disputes, which could adversely affect GATT's prestige. For example, an increase in the number of disputes between two parties could make resolution of any one dispute more difficult if its resolution is tied to resolution of all others. While this may occur, it would occur in a system emphasizing negotiation as well. In any event, the tying together of different issues is not necessarily a negative result. Disputes that cannot be solved individually may be disposed of as part of a global solution. By indicating which party is in the right on the individual disputes, the dispute settlement system can play an important role in pushing the ultimate global settlement toward compliance with GATT rules. If the disputes are left entirely to negotiations, it is less clear that there would be any factor pushing the solution toward that suggested by the GATT rules.

All in all, the argument that an adjudicative system will poison the atmosphere of GATT is not compelling. Moreover, it is arguable that such a system will improve the atmosphere of GATT. Emphasis on negotiation is likely to lead some countries to use their relative political and economic strength to take advantage of weaker countries, a situation fundamentally incompatible with a system that stresses rules. Rules tend to treat everyone in the same fashion. Negotiated settlements tend to favor the party with the best negotiating position, which often will be the more economically powerful party. This is probably why smaller countries often support a legalistic system, as they perceive that they will be treated more fairly under such a system. As such, it can be argued that an adjudicative approach would improve the atmosphere of GATT by stressing fairness.

b. Wrong Cases

A second objection made to be a legalistic system is that it will result in what Professor Hudec has called "wrong" cases being brought into the system. A wrong case is a dispute the resolution of which undermines the GATT trading system. Several kinds of wrong cases have been suggested.

First, there is the case where a country has violated the rules of the General Agreement, but has done so unavoidably. Typically such violation would occur because of domestic pressures that the government cannot ignore. It is argued that condemning that government for violating the General Agreement in such circumstances is both unfair and inappropriate. It is considered unfair because the government is perceived to have no choice but to do what it did. It is considered inappropriate because the domestic political pressures will prevent the government from correcting the situation.

This sort of wrong case is not likely to damage GATT. The argument that it will seems to be based on a criminal law analogy. This analogy holds that an adverse decision by a dispute settlement panel is wrong and unfair because such decision is tantamount to convicting the respondent of a criminal act that it did not intend and could not prevent. This analogy is, however, inappropriate. Even assuming that the respondent really could not prevent the violation and did not intend it, a violation occurred. Since the General Agreement contains a negotiated balance of obligations, it is difficult to see why one country that has upset that balance should be able to do so without any offsetting penalty. While it might be inappropriate to punish a government that was helpless to prevent the violation, it does seem appropriate to put pressure on the government to correct the violation and, perhaps, to award relief to those countries adversely affected by the violation. Surely there is nothing unfair about such an outcome. Moreover, such action is appropriate since it will likely promote compliance with GATT rules. In particular, it may help respondent's government counteract domestic pressures if that government can honestly argue that condemnation by GATT is likely and retaliation by trading partners is possible. To the extent that such an argument is successful, compliance with the General Agreement will be improved. In short, in some cases noncompliance may be inevitable, but there would be more compliance if GATT condemned rule violations than if GATT ignored them.

The second example of a wrong case is one that is initiated in respect of an issue on which the GATT community has either not yet reached a consensus or on which past consensus has broken down. In such a case it is unthinkable that both parties will accept the panel's decision, whatever it may be. Examples of such cases would include those challenging agricultural trade practices, such as those of the EC, the 1962 Uruguayan complaint against numerous developed country import restrictions, and the US complaint against EC tax systems in the DISC case.

Cases such as these undeniably put strains on the GATT system. The panel reports may generate considerable controversy, especially if they uphold the complainant's position. Moreover, the strains endure in time, as these cases are likely to remain unresolved for years. The critical point to remember, however, is that GATT has survived these wrong cases. Indeed, the United States and the EC have resolved a number of agricultural disputes through GATT, and the Uruguayan complaint, while not achieving what Uruguay sought, did lead to some reduced import restrictions. Thus, the "wrong" cases that GATT has faced so far might better be viewed as difficult cases that sorely tested the system, but that did not damage it.

What about the future possibility of wrong cases such as these? An adjudicative model of dispute settlement allows parties to push for interpretations of rules that are not commonly agreed upon. The risk exists in any system, but in a legalistic system it is more serious because the system guarantees that the party pressing the claim can obtain a decision, whereas in a system based on negotiated solutions the claim is never seriously considered. But does guaranteeing consideration of such claims undermine GATT. To begin with, it is quite possible that the panel will reject the controversial interpretation, particularly if it is novel. Even if the claim is accepted, several points are worth noting. First, the fact that it is accepted suggests that there is some basis for it. Second, if all of the contracting parties—or at least two-thirds of them—

agreed that compliance with the panel decision should not be required, they could grant a waiver of the obligation at issue. Third, so long as there is the possibility that the GATT Council must approve a panel report, an outlandish complaint leading to an unacceptable result seems remote. Nonetheless, it must be conceded that a profusion of wrong cases such as those mentioned above might weaken GATT.

c.   Compliance With GATT Rules

The principal argument in favor of a relatively more legalistic system is that it would better promote compliance with GATT rules than would a negotiation/consensus system.

An adjudicative system would promote compliance with GATT rules in two ways. First, it would discourage infractions of GATT rules. To the extent that countries know that they will be called to account if they violate the rules, they will be less likely to do so because the perceived cost of a violation will rise. In a more legalistic system the cost may include counteraction that negates any benefits from violating the rules. Further costs involve being labeled as a rule violator, a status that in and of itself imposes some cost, particularly in future negotiations over trade issues. Thus, to the extent that an adverse dispute panel decision is anticipated, countries will hesitate to violate the rules. Indeed, domestic political pressures may be directed elsewhere when the government can make a case against noncompliance with GATT. By contrast, in a negotiation/consensus system, the only cost may be unpleasant diplomatic exchanges, a negligible cost compared to the domestic political and economic benefits obtained by violating the rules.

Second, to the extent that an adjudicative approach produces more panel decisions, compliance with GATT rules will improve simply because panel decisions tend to be implemented, if not immediately, then over time. In general there has been an excellent, though admittedly at times slow, record of compliance with dispute settlement decisions that have been adopted by the Council. So long as most decisions are respected, adherence to the rules under a legalistic system will be better than in a negotiation/consensus system.

Furthermore, even if one party initially refuses to comply with a dispute settlement decision, that decision will affect the relative negotiating positions of the two contending parties. At the very least, the loser will suffer embarrassment. Moreover, that nation will have to justify its noncompliance with the panel decision. Such noncompliance, having been sanctioned, must be dealt with in other areas which are the subject of negotiations. In these other areas, as well as in negotiations directly on the subject matter of the dispute, the winner will gain leverage from having its positions vindicated by the panel report.

Thus, all other things being equal, it is likely that compliance with panel decisions will be increased and adherence to GATT rules better served by a more legalistic system. With an increase in the number of decisions, the obligations of GATT members will become clearer and better defined. Thus, the increased compliance with GATT rules will be compliance with more precisely defined rules.

JOHN H. JACKSON, THE WORLD TRADING SYSTEM 109–111 (2d ed. 1997)[2]

POWER-ORIENTED DIPLOMACY CONTRASTED WITH RULE-ORIENTED DIPLOMACY

One way to explore the questions raised above is to compare two techniques of modern diplomacy: a "rule-oriented" technique and a "power-oriented" technique. This perhaps puts the issue in too simple a dichotomy (because in practice the observable international institutions and legal systems involve some mixture of both), but it is nevertheless a useful way to examine the policy issues involved. This dichotomy can be explained as follows:

In broad perspective one can roughly divide the various techniques for the peaceful settlement of international disputes into two types: settlement by negotiation and agreement with reference (explicitly or implicitly) to relative power status of the parties; or settlement by negotiation or decision with reference to norms or rules to which both parties have previously agreed.

For example, countries A and B have a trade dispute regarding B's treatment of imports from A to B of widgets. The first technique mentioned would involve a negotiation between A and B by which the most powerful of the two would have the advantage. Foreign aid, military maneuvers, or import restrictions on other key goods by way of retaliation would figure in the negotiation. A small country would hesitate to challenge a large one on whom its trade depends. Implicit or explicit threats (e.g., to impose quantitative restrictions on some other product) would be a major part of the technique employed. Domestic political influences would probably play a greater part in the approach of the respective negotiators in this system, particularly on the negotiator for the more powerful party.

On the other hand, the second suggested technique—reference to agreed rules—would see the negotiators arguing about the application of the rule (e.g., was B obligated under a treaty to allow free entry of A's goods in question?). During the process of negotiating a settlement it would be necessary for the parties to understand that an unsettled dispute would ultimately be resolved by impartial third-party judgments based on the rules so that the negotiators would be negotiating with reference to the respective predictions as to the outcome of those judgments and not with reference to potential retaliation or actions exercising power of one or more of the parties to the dispute.

In both techniques negotiation and private settlement of disputes is the dominant mechanism for resolving differences; but the key is the

2. © 1997 by The Massachusetts Institute of Technology. Reprinted by permission of The MIT Press.

perception of the participants as to what are the "bargaining chips." Insofar as agreed rules for governing the economic relations between the parties exist, a system which predicates negotiation on the implementation of those rules would seem for a number of reasons to be preferred. The mere existence of the rules, however, is not enough. When the issue is the application or interpretation of those rules (rather than the formulation of new rules), it is necessary for the parties to believe that if their negotiations reach an impasse the settlement mechanisms which take over for the parties will be designed to apply fairly or to interpret the rules. If no such system exists, then the parties are left basically to rely upon their respective "power positions," tempered (it is hoped) by the good will and good faith of the more powerful party (cognizant of its long-range interests).

All diplomacy, and indeed all government, involves a mixture of these techniques. To a large degree, the history of civilization may be described as a gradual evolution from a power-oriented approach, in the state of nature, towards a rule-oriented approach. However, never is the extreme in either case reached. In modern Western democracies, as we know them, power continues to play a major role, particularly political power of voter acceptance, but also to a lesser degree economic power such as that of labor unions or large corporations. However, these governments have passed far along the scale toward a rule-oriented approach, and generally have an elaborate legal system involving court procedures and a monopoly of force, through a police and a military, to ensure the rules will be followed. The US government has indeed proceeded far in this direction, as the resignation of a recent president demonstrates. When one looks at the history of England over the last thousand years, I think that the evolutionary hypothesis from power to rule can be supported. And more recently, when one looks at the evolution of the EC, one is struck by the evolution toward a system that is remarkably elaborate in its rule structure, effectuated through a court of justice, albeit without a monopoly of force.

In international affairs, a strong argument can be made that to a certain extent this same evolution must occur, even though currently it has not progressed very far. The initiatives of the World War II and immediate postwar periods toward developing international institutions are part of this evolution, but as is true in most evolutions there have been setbacks, and mistakes have been made. Likewise when one focuses on international economic policy, we find that the dichotomy between power-oriented diplomacy and rule-oriented diplomacy can be seen. We have tried to develop rules, in the context of the International Monetary Fund and the GATT. The success has been varied.

Nevertheless, a particularly strong argument exists for pursuing gradually and consistently the progress of international economic affairs toward a rule-oriented approach. Apart from the advantages which accrue generally to international affairs through a rule-oriented approach—less reliance on raw power, and the temptation to exercise it or flex one's muscles, which can get out of hand; a fairer break for the smaller countries, or at least a perception of greater fairness; the development of agreed procedures to achieve the necessary compromises—in economic affairs there are additional reasons.

Economic affairs tend (at least in peace time) to affect more citizens directly than may political and military affairs. Particularly as the world becomes more economically interdependent, more and more private citizens find their jobs, their businesses, and their quality of life affected if not controlled by forces from outside their country's boundaries. Thus they are more affected by the economic policy pursued by their own country on their behalf. In addition, the relationships become increasingly complex—to the point of being incomprehensible to even the brilliant human mind. As a result, citizens assert themselves, at least within a democracy, and require their representatives and government officials to respond to their needs and their perceived complaints. The result of this is increasing citizen participation, and more parliamentary or congressional participation in the processes of international economic policy, thus restricting the degree of power and discretion which the executive possesses.

This makes international negotiations and bargaining increasingly difficult. However, if citizens are going to make their demands heard and influential, a "power-oriented" negotiating process (often requiring secrecy, and executive discretion so as to be able to formulate and implement the necessary compromises) becomes more difficult, if not impossible. Consequently, the only appropriate way to turn seems to be toward a rule-oriented system, whereby the various citizens, parliaments, executives and international organizations will all have their inputs, arriving tortuously to a rule—which, however, when established will enable business and other decentralized decision makers to rely upon the stability and predictability of governmental activity in relation to the rule.

Notes and Questions

(1) There are, of course, other goals of dispute settlement systems than rule enforcement and the achievement of mutually acceptable solutions. Among such other goals are fairness, efficiency, consistency and predictability. Are there other goals that should be considered? As you read the materials in this chapter, you should consider how effectively the WTO dispute settlement system achieves all of these goals.

(2) The existence of an adjudicative model does not rule out the possibility of negotiated settlements. We will see that the many WTO disputes are in fact settled without resort to formal proceedings. Nonetheless, some observers have been concerned that the WTO might become too litigious. For example, in February 2001, three former Directors–General of GATT/WTO issued the following joint statement:

Having discussed together the political, public and economic environment in which the multilateral trading system is currently functioning we wish to make a number of observations, to express certain concerns and to present several suggestions.

* * *

We are struck by the very high level of trade dispute settlement cases being handled in the WTO. In one sense, this is a sign of the success and effectiveness of the new system which emerged from the Uruguay Round. It is notable that developing countries are making increased use of the system as complainants. Our concern is that the dispute settlement system is being used as a means of filling out gaps in the WTO system; first, where rules and disciplines have not been put in place by its member governments or, second, are the subject of differences of interpretation. In other words, there is an excessive resort to litigation as a substitute for negotiation. This trend is dangerous in itself. The obligations which WTO members assume are properly for the member governments themselves to negotiate. The issue is still more concerning given certain public perceptions that the process of dispute settlement in the WTO is over-secret and over-powerful.

* * *

Dispute settlement is one of the great successes of the WTO. Yet the current burden of cases is probably too heavy. Again, it is a matter of perception. But the WTO cannot be known solely for its judicial prowess, still less for the number of times its members are given clearance to retaliate where dispute findings are not implemented satisfactorily. It is unfortunate if the first option for governments seeking to put right trade grievances is resort to the WTO dispute settlement process. The better route—and it should be the first option—must always be good faith consultation and direct bilateral negotiation. Above all, the spate of disputes and the large overhang of retaliatory actions—actual or threatened—between the United States and the European Union is one of the most troublesome barriers to securing leadership from the WTO's two biggest beneficiaries. The new US Administration should make it a priority to work with the EU to resolve the outstanding transatlantic differences. We believe that all WTO members—but the EU and US in particular—must exercise the utmost restraint in their recourse to the dispute settlement system. Litigation in trade matters is not, and must not become, an automatic alternative to negotiation.

Joint statement of February 1, 2001 by former GATT/WTO Directors–General Arthur Dunkel (1980–1993), Peter Sutherland (1993–1995) and Renato Ruggiero (1995–1999). At the time of their statement, there was a concern that part of the difficulty in starting the negotiating round now known as the Doha Development Agenda was caused by a failure of the EU and the US to work together because of pending dispute settlement cases.

(3) The WTO Dispute Settlement Understanding (see Documents Supplement) states in Article 3(2), "The dispute settlement system of the WTO is a central element in providing security and predictability to the multilater-

al trading system." Former GATT Director–General Arthur Dunkel once noted:[3]

> International economic policy commitments, in the form of agreed rules, have far-reaching domestic effect. * * * They are the element which secures the ultimate co-ordination and mutual compatibility of the purely domestic economic policies. They form the basis from which the government can arbitrate and secure an equitable and efficient balance between the diverse domestic interests: producers v. consumers, export industries v. import-competing industries.

In the same vein, they also allow planning by private parties.

(4) Does Professor Davey dismiss too easily the problems of using adjudicative methods to solve disputes among sovereign states? For example, for the adjudicative approach to work, nations must generally follow the decisions. What if they do not? In particular, what if the most powerful nation does not? Professor Hudec, a leading scholar on GATT dispute settlement, has expressed concern that the Uruguay Round reforms, which adopt and even go beyond those suggested by Professor Davey for making the system more adjudicative, may be the "worst of all worlds." He writes:

> [The reforms] will assert the authority of GATT law more forcefully, but if the major GATT countries are not ready to change their behavior, these stronger demands will only produce more visible and dramatic legal failures. And if that were to happen, the credibility of GATT legal obligations would almost certainly plunge.[4]

Professor Hudec conditions his fears by noting that a successful Uruguay Round, with substantive agreements that do not paper over disputes as happened in the Tokyo Round, would reduce the likelihood of a dispute settlement failure. He further notes that a failure to strengthen significantly the dispute settlement system in the Uruguay Round might undermine its past successes. These successes have raised expectations that if not met would have "an extremely discouraging impact for a long time to come."[5]

One of the main reasons for Professor Hudec's concern is his view of US behavior in GATT dispute settlement cases in the late 1980's and 1990's. During this period, the US exercised its power to delay and, in some cases, block the adoption of panel reports by the GATT Council (or Code committee) and failed to implement promptly certain adopted panel reports. If the US attitude persists, what effect would that have on the WTO dispute settlement system? Is that possibility reason enough to raise doubts about the desirability of the adjudicative approach? As you read the next section, consider whether there is evidence to date that the WTO reforms went too far in adopting an adjudicative approach. As we will see in Section 7.3(B) infra, implementation of DSB recommendations has sometimes been slow, but in general has occurred. Whether that record will be maintained remains to be seen.

---

3. GATT/1312 (Mar. 5, 1982).

4. Robert E. Hudec, Enforcing International Trade Law 364 (1993). See generally Eric A. Posner & John C. Yoo, Judicial Independence in International Tribunals, 93 Calif.L.Rev. 1 (2005).

5. Hudec, supra note 4, at 365. For Professor Hudec's evaluation of the new system after three years, see Robert E. Hudec, The New WTO Dispute Settlement Procedure: An Overview of the First Three Years, 8 Minn. J. Global Trade 1 (1999).

(5) The problems of non-compliance would be exacerbated to the extent that a dispute settlement system produces results that state parties believe impose obligations beyond those to which they agreed. Given this consideration, should those charged with dispute settlement be more conservative in interpreting international obligations than national courts may be in interpreting national statutes? In particular, should international dispute settlement bodies be hesitant to adopt expansive interpretations of vague rules, even if such interpretations are consistent with broadly worded objectives of an agreement? In the international arena, is it rather the province of negotiators to refine obligations? After all, international agreements are consensual arrangements entered into by sovereigns. We will explore this and related issues in Section 7.4(D) infra.

(6) Should individuals have the right to invoke the WTO dispute settlement system? Would it lead to stricter enforcement of international rules because affected individuals could be counted upon to try to enforce their rights where governments might not for a variety of political or other reasons? Would such a possibility cause governments to hesitate to enter into broad commitments?[6] To date, there seems to have been little interest among most WTO members in allowing private party involvement in dispute settlement proceedings, even as observers. We will explore this and related issues in Section 7.4(E) infra. We will see in Chapter 11 that private parties are involved in certain of the dispute settlement mechanisms of the US–Canada and North American Free Trade Agreements. For example, private parties have the right to appeal administrative decisions in antidumping and countervailing duty matters to binational panels, where they brief and argue their positions. In addition, private parties may demand third-party arbitration of investment disputes with NAFTA governments (see Chapter 23 infra), and they have limited rights to cause the initiation of enforcement reviews under the NAFTA environmental side agreement.[7]

SECTION 7.2   DISPUTE SETTLEMENT IN THE GATT SYSTEM

There are 19 clauses in the General Agreement which obligate GATT parties to consult in specific instances.[1] These provisions cover such varied subjects as customs valuation and invocation of the Escape Clause. Likewise, there are sprinkled throughout the General Agreement at least seven different provisions for compensatory withdrawal or suspension of concessions.

While Article XXIII is GATT's principal dispute settlement provision, it contains very little procedural detail. Consequently, the GATT parties had to improvise and develop procedures through practice over the years. Initially, the Contracting Parties considered disputes at their regular meetings. In some cases, working parties were used. A working

---

6. See Jackson, supra note 2, at 187.

7. See North American Agreement on Environmental Cooperation, arts. 14(1), 15(4).

1. This paragraph is based on John H. Jackson, World Trade and the Law of GATT, sec. 8.2, at 164 (1969).

party is understood in the GATT context to mean a body whose members are "nations," so that each nation may send a representative of its own choice. In the 1950's, largely as a result of the influence of then GATT Director–General Eric Wyndham–White, it became the practice to use panels to consider disputes. A panel is composed of individuals acting in their individual capacities, and not as national representatives. Interestingly, this shift early on in GATT's history shows a desire in GATT to emphasize adjudication by independent decision makers as opposed to negotiated settlements of differences by national representatives. The panel members, usually three in number, were in fact often chosen from available national representatives to GATT. Their reports were then (usually) adopted by consensus in the GATT Council.

The procedures used in the GATT system were codified in a 1979 Tokyo Round understanding.[2] There were also two further declarations on dispute settlement in the mid 1980's[3] and then a series of improvements agreed upon at the Uruguay Round midterm review session in 1989.[4] These procedures were largely carried over in the WTO procedures.

The GATT system experienced some problems with delays and failures to adopt reports because of blocking tactics by losing parties that prevented a consensus in the GATT Council. We will see how the WTO system addresses those problems in the next section. Generally, however, the GATT dispute settlement system can be viewed as relatively successful. Many disputes were settled without resort to the panel procedures. Indeed, only about 40% of the disputes resulted in a panel report adopted by the Council.[5] As to the results of the system, Professor Hudec concluded in his comprehensive study that of the 139 complaints through 1989 that he found to have been valid, conceded as valid, settled or withdrawn despite their probable validity, the complaining party received full satisfaction in 60% of the cases and partial satisfaction in another 29%.[6] This success rate—almost 90%—is extremely high. Few, if any, international dispute settlement systems can claim such success rates over a similarly long time period.

SECTION 7.3   THE WTO DISPUTE SETTLEMENT UNDERSTANDING

The WTO Agreement provides that one of the principal functions of the WTO is the administration of the Understanding on Rules and Procedures Governing the Settlement of Disputes, which is Annex 2 to

2. Understanding Regarding Notification, Consultation, Dispute Settlement and Surveillance, 26th Supp. BISD 210 (1980).

3. 1982 Ministerial Declaration on Dispute Settlement Procedures, 29th Supp. BISD 13 (1983); 1984 Action on Dispute Settlement Procedures, 31st Supp. BISD 9 (1985).

4. 1989 Improvements to the GATT Dispute Settlement Rules and Procedures, 36th Supp. BISD 61 (1990).

5. Robert E. Hudec, Enforcing International Trade Law 375–83 (1993).

6. Id. at 285–87.

the WTO Agreement and which is set out in the Documents Supplement. Indeed, the Dispute Settlement Understanding (DSU) states that the dispute settlement system "is a central element in providing security and predictability to the multilateral trading system" (art. 3.2). The DSU sets forth a comprehensive statement of dispute settlement rules and, while it builds on the past GATT practices, it makes several fundamental changes in the operation of the system. The DSU is administered by the Dispute Settlement Body (DSB), which is the WTO General Council acting in a specialized role under a separate chair. The DSU regulates dispute settlement under all covered WTO agreements, although under some agreements special rules and procedures will be applicable.[1]

The general philosophy of WTO dispute settlement is set out in Article 3 of the DSU. Among the principles that are enshrined in that article are the following:

First, it is recognized that the system serves to preserve the rights and obligations of Members and to clarify the existing provisions of the WTO agreements in accordance with the customary rules of interpretation of public international law. In this regard, it is also noted that the prompt settlement of disputes is essential to the functioning of the WTO and the maintenance of a proper balance between the rights and obligations of WTO Members.

Second, it is agreed that the results of the dispute settlement process cannot add to or diminish the rights and obligations provided in the WTO agreements. In this regard, the DSU explicitly notes the right of Members to seek authoritative interpretation of provisions pursuant to Article IX of the WTO Agreement, which itself provides that it is the exclusive means for interpreting the WTO Agreement.

Third, several provisions highlight that the aim of dispute settlement is to secure a positive solution to a dispute and that a solution that is acceptable to the parties and consistent with the WTO agreements is clearly to be preferred.

Fourth, although the DSU provides for the eventuality of non-compliance, it is explicitly stated in DSU Article 3.7 that "the first objective of the dispute settlement mechanism is usually to secure the withdrawal of the measures concerned if these are found to be inconsistent with the provisions of any of the covered agreements". Retaliatory action is described as the last resort.

---

1. Appendix 2 to the Dispute Settlement Understanding lists the special or additional dispute settlement rules and procedures. There are special rules, in particular, under the Antidumping and Subsidies Agreements. The DSU explicitly provides that the DSB Chair may decide what rules and procedures to follow when there is a dispute. DSU, art. 1.2. This unification of dispute settlement procedures eliminated forum shopping, which was a problem after the Tokyo Round because many Tokyo Round agreements had their own dispute settlement procedures, under the control of each agreement's supervisory body. See John H. Jackson, GATT Machinery and the Tokyo Round Agreements, *in* William Cline (ed.), Trade Policy in the 1980s, at 159, 185–87 (1983).

(A) THE DSU PROCEDURES[2]

There are four major phases of WTO dispute settlement: First, the parties must attempt to resolve their differences through consultations. Second, if that fails, the complaining party may demand that a panel of independent experts be established to rule on the dispute. Third, and new under the DSU, is the possibility of an appeal by any party to the dispute to the Appellate Body. Finally, if the complaining party succeeds, the DSB is charged with monitoring the implementation of its recommendations. If the recommendations are not implemented, the possibility of negotiated compensation or authorization to withdraw concessions arises. The following materials describe the issues relevant at each of these stages, with particular emphasis on how the DSU deals with them, and, in particular, on the innovations it introduced compared to the GATT system.

(1) Consultations

The requirement that disputing parties consult with a view toward satisfactorily adjusting the matter is contained in Article XXIII itself. The hope is that the parties will resolve their dispute without having to invoke the formal dispute settlement procedures. The rules regarding consultations are set out in article 4 of the DSU. The manner in which the consultations are conducted is up to the parties. The DSU has no rules on consultations beyond that they are to be entered into in good faith and are to be held within 30 days of a request. During the consultations, both parties try to learn more about the facts and the legal arguments of the other party. Despite the fact that the structure of consultations is undefined and there are no rules for conducting them, a significant number of cases end at the consultations stage (either through settlements or abandonment of a case). If consultations fail to settle a dispute within 60 days after the request therefor, the complaining party may request the establishment of a panel. Art. 4.7. In fact, consultations often go on for more than 60 days.

(2) Panel Process

Under the DSU, the right of a party to have a panel established is clearly set out in article 6.1. If consultations fail to resolve a dispute within the 60–day time frame specified in article 4, a complainant may insist on the establishment of a panel and, at the meeting following that at which the request first appears on the DSB's agenda, the DSB is required to establish a panel unless there is a consensus in the DSB not to establish a panel. Since the complaining party may prevent the formation of this "reverse" consensus, there is effectively a right to have a panel established. This is in contrast to the GATT system. Although

---

2. This section is based in part on William J. Davey, The WTO Dispute Settlement System, *in* Gary P. Sampson & W. Bradnee Chambers (eds.), Trade, Environment and the Millennium 119–142 (United Nations University Press 1999) (2d ed. 2001); see also David Palmeter & Petros C. Mavroidis, Dispute Settlement in the World Trade Organization: Practice and Procedure (2d ed. 2004).

persistent complainants virtually always succeeded in getting the GATT Council to establish a panel, their success sometimes came only after long periods of delay.

(a) Setting up the panel

Once a panel is established, it is necessary to select the three individuals who will serve as panelists. DSU article 8 provides for the Secretariat to propose potential panel members to the parties, who are not to object except for compelling reasons. In practice, parties are relatively free to reject proposed panelists, but if the parties do not agree on panel members within 20 days of establishment, any party may request the WTO Director–General to appoint the panel on his or her own authority. Art. 8.7. In recent years, the Director–General has appointed some members of considerably more than one-half of the panels composed.

Article 8.1 of the DSU provides that panels shall be composed of

"well-qualified governmental and/or non-governmental individuals, including persons who have served on or presented a case to a panel, served as a representative of a Member or of a contracting party to GATT 1947 or as a representative to the Council or Committee of any covered agreement or its predecessor agreement, or in the Secretariat, taught or published on international trade law or policy, or served as a senior trade policy official of a Member."

These criteria could be roughly summarized as establishing three categories of panelists: government officials (current or former), former Secretariat officials and trade academics or lawyers. It is specifically provided that panelists shall not be nationals of parties or third parties, absent agreement of the parties. It is also specified that in a case involving a developing country, one panelist must be from a developing country (if requested). Of the individuals actually chosen for panel service, it appears that the vast majority (over 80%) are current or former government officials.

The DSU provides that panelists serve in their individual capacities and that Members shall not give them instructions or seek to influence them. In addition, the DSB has adopted rules of conduct applicable to participants in the WTO dispute settlement system. The rules require that panelists "be independent and impartial, shall avoid direct or indirect conflicts of interest and shall respect the confidentiality of proceedings." To ensure compliance with the rules, such persons are to disclose "the existence or development of any interest, relationship or matter that person could reasonably be expected to know and that is likely to affect, or give rise to justifiable doubts as to, that person's independence or impartiality." Disputing parties have the right to raise an alleged material violation of the rules, which if upheld, would lead to the replacement of the challenged individual.[3]

---

3. WT/DSB/RC/1. See generally Gabrielle Marceau, Rules on Ethics for the New World Trade Organization Dispute Settlement Mechanism, Journal of World Trade, vol. 32, no. 3, June 1998, at 57.

(b) The task of panels

The DSU provides in article 7.1 for standard terms of reference (absent agreement to the contrary). The standard terms direct a panel "To examine, in the light of the relevant provisions in (name of the covered agreement/s cited by the parties to the dispute), the matter referred to the DSB by (name of party) in document DS/ ... and to make such findings as will assist the DSB in making the recommendations or in giving the rulings provided for in that/those agreement/s." The Appellate Body has emphasized in its rulings that panels may not stray beyond their terms of reference. In practice, the document mentioned above will be the panel request made pursuant to article 6.2, which requires that the request "specify the measures at issue and provide a brief summary of the legal basis of the complaint sufficient to present the problem clearly." There are often extensive, but usually unsuccessful, arguments that the second requirement has not been met.[4]

More generally, DSU article 11 provides that a panel shall make an objective assessment of the matter before it, including an objective assessment of the facts of the case and the applicability of and conformity with the relevant WTO agreements. In the *EC Hormones* case (see Chapter 14 infra), the Appellate Body elaborated on this requirement as follows (para. 133):

> [W]hen may a panel be regarded as having failed to discharge its duty under Article 11 of the DSU to make an objective assessment of the facts before it? Clearly, not every error in the appreciation of the evidence (although it may give rise to a question of law) may be characterized as a failure to make an objective assessment of the facts. In the present appeal, the European Communities repeatedly claims that the Panel disregarded or distorted or misrepresented the evidence submitted by the European Communities and even the opinions expressed by the Panel's own expert advisors. The duty to make an objective assessment of the facts is, among other things, an obligation to consider the evidence presented to a panel and to make factual findings on the basis of that evidence. The deliberate disregard of, or refusal to consider, the evidence submitted to a panel is incompatible with a panel's duty to make an objective assessment of the facts. The wilful distortion or misrepresentation of the evidence put before a panel is similarly inconsistent with an objective assessment of the facts. "Disregard" and "distortion" and "misrepresentation" of the evidence, in their ordinary signification in judicial and quasi-judicial processes, imply not simply an error of judgment in the appreciation of evidence but rather an egregious error that calls into question the good faith of a panel. A claim that a panel

4. See William J. Davey, WTO Dispute Settlement: Segregating the Useful Political Aspects and Avoiding "Over-legalization", *in* Marco Bronckers & Reinhard Quick (eds.), New Directions in International Economic Law: Essays in Honor of Professor John H. Jackson 291–307 (2000).

disregarded or distorted the evidence submitted to it is, in effect, a claim that the panel, to a greater or lesser degree, denied the party submitting the evidence fundamental fairness, or what in many jurisdictions is known as due process of law or natural justice.

While the Appellate Body found some instances where it concluded that the panel's representations of its experts' view were not accurate, it found that the EC failed to establish a violation of article 11.

(c) Panel procedures

A panel normally meets with the parties shortly after its selection to set its working procedures and time schedule. The DSU's standard proposed timetable for panels makes provision for two meetings between the panel and the parties to discuss the substantive issues in the case. Each meeting is preceded by the filing of written submissions. The DSU permits other WTO members to intervene as third parties and present arguments to the first meeting of the panel. While panel and Appellate Body proceedings have traditionally not been open to the public, since 2005 several panel meetings have been open to the public pursuant to the agreement of the parties. A party is free to choose the members of its delegation to hearings. Thus, parties may be assisted, and often are, by private counsel.

Among the most fundamental issues that arise in assessing a complaint is the assignment of the burden of proof. Generally speaking, the decisions of the Appellate Body have held that the burden of proof rests upon the party who asserts the affirmative of a particular claim or defense. If that party adduces sufficient evidence to raise a presumption that what is claimed is true, then the burden shifts to the other party to rebut the presumption. The Appellate Body has also spoken in terms of the need for a claimant to establish a *prima facie* case.

In GATT dispute settlement, it was often the case that factual issues were not that important. The basic issue was typically whether a particular governmental measure violated GATT rules. To date, comparatively more WTO disputes have involved disputed factual issues. In order to establish facts, panels normally ask oral and written questions to which the parties are expected to respond. The parties often bring experts versed in the relevant field to panel meetings. Some parties have submitted affidavit evidence to establish facts. By and large, the fact-finding procedures of panels are relatively less sophisticated than those of national courts, although it can be expected that more sophisticated fact-finding techniques will develop as the need for fact-finding becomes more acute.

One area in which panels have already become more sophisticated is in the use of experts in scientific matters. In this regard, the DSU provides that if a panel deems it appropriate, it may consult either individual experts or form an expert review group to advise it on technical and scientific issues. Panels have consulted multiple experts on an individual basis in cases arising under the SPS Agreement (see

Chapter 14), in one case involving health issues and in one case involving environmental issues. In each case, the panel asked the parties to suggest possible experts and sought information from the relevant international scientific agency. The parties were also invited to comment on the questions that the panel proposed to ask the experts. Following receipt of the experts' answers, the parties had the opportunity to comment in writing on the answers and an "experts' meeting" was held at which the panel and the parties could question the experts.

One basic issue faced by panels is what sort of standard of review should be applied in reviewing challenged measures. Of course, in some cases that issue is not particularly significant. The only issue is whether the measure violates a WTO rule. But in an increasing number of cases, the assessment of a measure's consistency with WTO rules involves an assessment of the justification for a measure, for example, of whether a measure is "necessary" within the terms of an exception contained GATT Article XX or whether a measure is "based on" or rationally related to a risk assessment in the case of an SPS (health) measure. In such a case, to what extent should a panel or the Appellate Body defer to the challenged government's assessment of necessity or rationality? The DSU gives no guidance on this issue beyond directing panels to make an objective assessment of the matter before them. This is obviously a key issue and we consider it in detail below in Section 7.4(D).

After hearings and deliberations, the panel prepares a report detailing its conclusions. Traditionally, the panel has submitted its description of the dispute and of the parties' arguments to the parties for comment. Under the DSU, panels are required to submit an interim report containing their legal analysis for comment as well. Art. 15. Appendix 3 of the DSU specifies time limits for implementations of the various stages in the panel process. Those time limits suggest that the panel report should normally be issued within six to nine months of the establishment of the panel. In practice, cases typically take much more time than that.

(d) Consideration and adoption of panel reports

Under GATT dispute settlement practice prior to conclusion of the Uruguay Round, after a panel issued its report, it was considered for adoption by the GATT Council. Traditionally, decisions in the Council were made by consensus, which meant that any party—including the losing party—could prevent the Council from adopting a panel report. If unadopted, a report would represent only the view of the individual panel members. While parties did not often permanently block adoption of reports, some reports were never adopted (even when the underlying dispute was resolved) and others were adopted only after months of delay. Many commentators felt that this was a major failing in what was otherwise a fairly successful GATT dispute settlement system. Indeed, it is difficult to explain to someone new to the subject why the losing party by itself should be able to prevent adoption of a panel report.

The DSU fundamentally changed this procedure. It eliminates the possibility of blockage by providing in article 16 that a panel report shall be adopted unless there is an appeal (see below) or a "reverse consensus," i.e., a consensus *not* to adopt the report. This switch from requiring a consensus for adoption to requiring a consensus to block adoption is a very significant change. It appears that it was adopted in hopes that it would satisfy US complaints about weaknesses in the GATT system and thereby result in the United States using the system in the future instead of taking unilateral action as it had done sometimes in the past. Basically, other GATT parties were willing to make the change as a way to rein in US unilateralism in trade matters. Indeed, article 23.1 of the DSU requires WTO members to use the WTO dispute settlement system exclusively if they "seek the redress of a violation of obligations or other nullification or impairment of benefits under the covered agreements." We will consider the effect of this provision on US law and practice in Section 7.4(F), where we examine so-called Section 301 of the US Trade Act of 1974, as amended.

(3) *The Appellate Body*

The change in the consensus rule described above was paired with the introduction of a right to appeal a panel decision. The DSU creates a standing Appellate Body with seven members, appointed for four-year terms and representative of WTO membership. Only one reappointment is permitted. The Appellate Body is authorized to draw up its own working procedures, in consultation with the Chairman of the DSB and the Director–General. These procedures regulate the operation of the Appellate Body and process by which appeals are made and considered. They are available at the WTO website.

The Appellate Body hears appeals of panel reports in divisions of three, although its rules provide for the division hearing a case to exchange views with the other four Appellate Body members before the division finalizes its report. The members of the division that hears a particular appeal are selected by a secret procedure that is based on randomness, unpredictability and the opportunity for all members to serve without regard to national origin. The Appellate Body is required to issue its report within 60 (at most 90) days from the date of the appeal, and its report is to be adopted automatically by the DSB within 30 days, absent consensus to the contrary (as explained above). The appealed panel report is also adopted at that time, as modified by the Appellate Body report.

The Appellate Body's review is limited to issues of law and legal interpretation developed by the panel. However, the Appellate Body has taken a broad view of its power to review panel decisions. It has the express power to reverse, modify or affirm panel decisions, but the DSU does not include a possibility of remanding a case to a panel. Partly as a consequence, the Appellate Body has adopted the practice, where possible in light of a panel's factual findings, of completing the analysis of particular issues in order to resolve cases where it has significantly modified a panel's reasoning. This avoids requiring a party to start the whole proceeding over as a result of those modifications. It has been proposed in the Doha negotiations that the Appellate Body be given remand authority. There seems to be broad agreement that this should be done, but there is not yet agreement over the details of how to do it.

Although the Appellate Body has never articulated a standard of review that it will apply on appeals of panel reports, it has engaged in fairly intensive review of such reports. In doing so, it has in general left its stamp clearly on most areas of WTO law. Indeed, in respect of GATT Articles III and XX, and the SPS, Safeguards and Subsidies Agreements, the Appellate Body jurisprudence is particularly rich and far-reaching. While strict notions of "stare decisis" do not apply in the WTO, it is clear that prior cases do play an important role in dispute settlement, especially those considered to be well-reasoned and persuasive. Indeed, the Appellate Body noted early on that adopted GATT panel reports created "legitimate expectations" that similar matters would be handled similarly, and both panels and the Appellate Body frequently support their decisions by extensive citation and quotation of prior decisions. Thus, it is appropriate to speak of the Appellate Body's effect on "WTO law".

Generally speaking, the Appellate Body tends to rely heavily on close textual interpretation of the WTO provisions at issue, stressing that a treaty interpreter must look to the ordinary meaning of the relevant terms, in their context and in light of the object and purpose of the relevant agreement (a requirement of Article 31 of the Vienna Convention of the Law of Treaties) and must not interpret provisions so as to render them devoid of meaning. The Appellate Body has expressed the need to respect due process and procedural rights of Members in the dispute settlement process, but by and large it has recognized considerable discretion on the part of panels, which has led it in the end to reject most procedural/due process challenges. On the whole, it is difficult to characterize the Appellate Body as being more or less deferential to WTO member discretion than panels. While it has significantly cut back on the scope of panel rulings in some cases, it has significantly expanded the scope of liability in others.

(4) Implementation and Suspension of Concessions

If it is found that a complaint is justified, the panel/Appellate Body report typically recommends that the offending member cease its violation of WTO rules, normally by bringing the offending measure into conformity with its obligations. After it adopts a report, the DSB monitors whether or not its recommendations are implemented. The DSU requires a losing respondent to indicate what actions it plans to take to implement the panel's recommendations. If immediate implementation is impracticable, then implementation is required within a reasonable period of time. Art. 21.3. The reasonable period of time is normally set by agreement of the contending parties, or, absent agreement, by arbitration, typically by a member of the Appellate Body. Normally, the period is not to exceed 15 months; a range of 8–10 months is average.

If the recommendations are not implemented, the prevailing party is entitled to seek compensation from the non-complying member or request DSB authority to suspend concessions previously made to that member (sometimes referred to as "retaliation"). Art. 22.1. In this regard, the DSU modifies past GATT practice. Article XXIII permitted GATT contracting parties to authorize the prevailing party to retaliate if the losing party failed to end its violation of GATT rules. Such authorization was granted only once, however, and that was in 1955 to allow the Netherlands to suspend concessions made to the United States in a case involving GATT-inconsistent US quotas on Dutch agricultural products. The Netherlands apparently never utilized the authorization. Attempts to obtain authorizations in the 1980's failed because of the consensus rule, with the target country opposing the authorization. Now, under the DSU, suspension of concessions is to be authorized automatically in the absence of implementation or compensation, absent a consensus in the DSB to the contrary. Art. 22.6. There are specific arbitration procedures for determining the level of such a suspension if no agreement can be reached.

The DSU provides: "Prompt compliance with recommendations or rulings of the DSB is essential in order to ensure the effective resolution of disputes to the benefit of all Members" (art. 21.1). The DSB will normally recommend the withdrawal of any measure found to be inconsistent with a member's obligations, and the DSU explicitly provides that withdrawal of a nonconforming measure is preferred to compensation or suspension of concessions. Art. 22.1. Compensation and suspensions of concessions are viewed as "temporary measures," to be used when a report is not implemented in a reasonable time. The preference for withdrawal is also found in the WTO Agreement itself, where Article XVI:4 provides that "[e]ach Member shall ensure the conformity of its laws, regulations and administrative procedures with its obligations as provided in the annexed Agreements." Thus, there would appear to be an international law obligation to implement recommendations to withdraw inconsistent measures.

The application of the foregoing procedures on implementation and retaliation has been controversial. We will discuss why and other related issues in respect of remedies in Section 7.5 infra.

(5) *Research and Citation of WTO Reports*

WTO dispute settlement panel and Appellate Body reports are made available to the public on the WTO website (www.wto.org) on the same day that they are circulated to the WTO membership. Each dispute is assigned a DS number and all WTO documents related to the dispute are filed under that number. E.g., WT/DS1/1 et seq, WT/DS2/1 et seq. The Appellate Body has assigned standardized short names to all disputes (e.g., "US Gasoline" for "United States—Standards for Reformulated and Conventional Gasoline"). We give the full name and citation, including the date of adoption of the report by the DSB, when we excerpt portions of a report. We often use only the short names of the cases in other references. The tables in the front of the casebook include a list of short case names, with the full citation given for the cases.

Notes and Questions

(1) In 1987, Professor Davey summarized the principal complaints about the GATT dispute system as follows: (i) disuse, (ii) delays in the establishment of panels, (iii) delays in appointing panel members, (iv) delays in the completion of panel reports; (v) uncertain quality and neutrality of panelists and panel reports, (vi) blocked panel reports and (vii) non implementation of panel reports.[5] These problems were epitomized by the so-called *DISC* case, involving an EC challenge to a US tax law and a counter-challenge by the US against the tax rules of several European countries. Over a year elapsed between the start of consultations and the decision to establish a panel, and roughly two and one-half years passed before the panelists were selected. While the panel reports were issued promptly, their quality and content were severely criticized and they lingered on the Council's agenda for several years before action was finally taken.[6] The problem of disuse (only 38 complaints made in the 1960's and 1970's combined) disappeared in the 1980's (115 complaints).[7] As to the other problems, how does the DSU deal with each of them? Does more need to be done?

(2) The Uruguay Round changes have not received universal acclaim. Perhaps the most serious concern raised is the one raised at the end of Section 7.1—if a major economic power (such as the United States, the EU or Japan) refuses to comply with adverse panel or Appellate Body decisions, will the WTO dispute settlement system collapse? In addition, more specific concerns have been raised. Will the existence of the Appellate Body reduce the prestige of panel service and the quality of panel reports? Who will serve on the seven-person Appellate Body? Will they view their role more as mediators or as judges? If the former, what will be the effect on the dispute settlement system? Will the right of appeal increase delays? Will the opportunity of the parties to comment on the legal reasoning of the panel in its draft report cause panels to be too solicitous of the parties' positions? Will the reforms dilute the positive role that the Secretariat's legal staff played in improving the quality of panel reports? Given the experience since 1995, how would you evaluate these concerns?

5. William J. Davey, Dispute Settlement in GATT, 11 Fordham J.Intl.L. 51, 81–89 (1987). See also US Int'l Trade Comm'n, Pub. No. 1793, Review of the Effectiveness of Trade Dispute Settlement Under the GATT and the Tokyo Round Agreements (1985).

6. See John H. Jackson, The Jurisprudence of International Trade: The *DISC* Case in GATT, 72 Am.J.Intl.L. 747 (1978).

7. Robert E. Hudec, Enforcing International Trade Law 590–608 (1993).

(3) As noted above, one of the complaints about the GATT dispute settlement system arose from the effect of the consensus rule—the ability of the losing party to block adoption of the panel report. While this practice can certainly be criticized, it is worth remembering that the consensus rule provided GATT panel reports with political legitimacy—the organization adopted the panel reports without objection. Automatic adoption removes this political cover. Will that in itself reduce the legitimacy, and therefore the effectiveness, of the dispute settlement system? Will the existence of the Appellate Body provide an adequate substitute for adoption by consensus? There were other proposals to deal with the blockage problem. The principal one was the "consensus minus two" solution, which would not allow the parties to the dispute to block adoption of the panel report. Would that change have been better than automatic adoption? How could the system prevent the blocking of adoption by proxies (i.e., parties not directly involved in the dispute but willing to "represent" the losing party and block consensus, perhaps because of interests similar to the losing party or simply as a favor)?

(4) Note the provisions that govern a dispute arising under GATT Articles VI, XIX or XXVIII, and note that in each of these cases reaction by the aggrieved nation (with countervailing duties to a subsidy, with compensatory import restraints to an escape clause action and with compensatory withdrawal of tariff bindings to a prior withdrawal) requires no international permission, i.e. it can be effected unilaterally, if necessary. Compare these provisions with the DSU. If your country took an action which could be interpreted as either an escape clause action or a violation of a GATT binding (nullification and impairment), would you prefer a construction of the action as a violation, or as the exercise of a right under Article XIX? Which would most likely result in counter-response from the other side? Is there an anomaly in a situation which "rewards" violations compared to exercise of rights?

(5) Could monopoly or cartel practices give rise to an Article XXIII complaint? One GATT report suggested that such practices should not be the basis of such a complaint, because it was "dangerous" to use Article XXIII in these circumstances.[8] Why? Are there any definable boundaries to the use of the dispute settlement procedures?

(6) The DSU provides for other alternatives than formal dispute settlement if parties cannot resolve their disputes. Article 5 includes provisions on good offices, conciliation and mediation, and provides specifically that the Director–General may offer to provide such services in an effort to assist members in resolving disputes. These informal methods may be used in addition to or in lieu of the panel process. As of 2007, these alternative procedures had almost never been used, although in July 2001 the Director–General urged WTO members to consider using them.

---

8. GATT, 9th Supp. BISD 172 (1961); see John H. Jackson, World Trade and the Law of GATT 181 (1969).

(B) THE OPERATION OF THE WTO DISPUTE SETTLEMENT SYSTEM: 1995–2007

WILLIAM J. DAVEY, THE WTO DISPUTE SETTLEMENT SYSTEM: THE FIRST TEN YEARS[9]

A.   The First Five Years (1995–1999)

1.   General Trends

The first ten years' operation of the WTO dispute settlement system can be divided usefully into two parts. The first half of that period—from 1995 through 1999—was characterized by extensive use of the system by the United States initially, and later by the EU. While there was a wide range of disputes, this period was especially notable for carryover cases from the days of GATT and a focus on implementation of Uruguay Round results, particularly in respect of the TRIPS Agreement. For example, there were 185 consultation requests made from 1995 through 1999 involving 125 disputes [related consultation requests are counted as involving one dispute]. The United States initiated 60 consultation requests (involving 43 disputes), or about one-third of the disputes. Indeed, in the first three years, the United States initiated 35% of the consultation requests made. During the first five years, the EC initiated 47 consultation requests (involving 44 disputes), also about one-third of the disputes. Interestingly, the EC initiated 31% of the consultation requests in the last three years of the period (1997–1999), compared to only 11% in the first two years of the period (1995–1996). Of the other WTO members, Canada was also relatively active in the first two years, initiating 8 consultation requests (12.5%).

Probably the most noteworthy characteristic of WTO dispute settlement in its early years was the large number of very controversial cases involving systemic issues or specific fact situations that were carried over from the GATT system. Examples would include the *EC–Bananas* case, the *EC–Hormones* case, the *Japan–Film* case, the *US–Shrimp* case, the *US–Helms–Burton* case, the *Turkey–Textiles* case, the *India–Quantitative Restrictions* case, the *US–Section 301* case and, in a matter decided just after the end of the period, the *US–FSC* case. These cases all involved the US and/or EC and raised very sensitive and controversial issues. Except for the *Bananas* and the *FSC* cases, the disputes did not directly involve great amounts of trade, but they were nonetheless considered very important for symbolic reasons. Fortunately for the system, it managed to defuse these cases—the US lost the *Film* case and the EC lost the *Section 301* case and neither appealed, perhaps because in each case the losing party won some useful points; the *Helms-Burton* case was informally settled on the day the first written submission was due to be received by the panel. The *Turkey Textiles* and *India QR* cases disturbed some members for systemic reasons, but the actual results of the cases did not result in serious implementation difficulties for either respondent. In *Shrimp*, the US lost, but while the case was controversial, the Appellate Body report was welcomed by many as making the WTO

---

9.   8 JIEL 17, 17–25, 45–48 (2005). Reprinted with permission.

more environmentally friendly. The *Bananas* case presented the most difficult implementation problem because of a US–EC dispute over how to interpret the DSU. Indeed, that dispute came close to destroying the system in its relative infancy, but it was ultimately finessed, and an agreement on implementation was reached in 2001. * * * Of this early group of cases, only *Hormones* and *FSC* remained unimplemented for substantial periods of time and both have been subject to the imposition of retaliatory measures. Even as to those two, progress is being made on implementation. US legislation that came into force on 1 January 2005 is designed to implement the *FSC* decision and the EC claims that it implemented the *Hormones* decision by conducting a new risk assessment and adopting a new measure based on that assessment in 2003. The EC removed its sanctions relating to the *FSC* case when the new legislation came into effect, although it has initiated a new compliance panel proceeding challenging certain transitional aspects of the new legislation [Note: Those aspects were repealed promptly by Congress.] The US and Canada do not accept that the EC has implemented the *Hormones* report and their sanctions remain in place. The EC has initiated new panel proceedings with a view to challenging those sanctions as no longer justified, [which was pending as of the end of 2007].

Overall, the WTO dispute settlement system seemed to survive these controversial cases reasonably well, although it must be conceded that some of the WTO Members directly involved in the specific cases were somewhat embittered at certain results.

In addition, as noted above, the first five years were also noteworthy for the concern of some WTO members for implementation of the TRIPS Agreement. Indeed, this was one of the principal goals of the US in this period, as evidenced by the fact that it initiated 11 disputes under the TRIPS Agreement, most of which were settled without panel action. The EC was also active under the TRIPS Agreement in this period, having initiated five cases (two of which followed on similar US requests).

2. The Appellate Body

The most noteworthy single development in the first five years of WTO dispute settlement was the flowering of the Appellate Body. The role it would play in the WTO system was quickly put to the test as the first 12 panel reports were appealed. From the outset, the Appellate Body established itself as an activist tribunal. It modified 10 of the reports, effectively reversing one of them. In its review of panel reports, the Appellate Body did not focus on whether it approved of the result in general terms as some appellate tribunals do, but rather it closely examined the reasoning and wording of the panel reports, and it did not hesitate to modify reasoning or wording with which it disagreed.

The first appeal (*US Gasoline*) was noteworthy in that the Appellate Body stressed the need to focus on the exact words of the relevant treaty text and to apply the rules of the Vienna Convention on the Law of Treaties in order to interpret the WTO agreements. Moreover, in that appeal, which involved a successful challenge by Venezuela and Brazil of a US environmental measure, the Appellate Body first evinced a concern with ensuring that governments have adequate discretion to take what they view as necessary environmental measures, assuming of course that they meet GATT's nondiscrimination requirements. Thus, while the US failed to convince the Appellate Body that it met those requirements, it did obtain a decision that it considered to be more environmental-friendly.

The role of the Appellate Body in handling the six controversial cases discussed above that were appealed is quite instructive. The six cases involved commercial issues (*Bananas* and *FSC*), institutional issues (*India QR* and *Turkey Textiles*) and environmental/health issues (*Hormones* and *Shrimp*). In the cases involving commercial issues, the Appellate Body applied the rules relatively strictly. Indeed, in the *Bananas* case, the panel had ruled in the EC's favor on one of the two major issues in the case by interpreting a waiver obtained by the EC that explicitly permitted banana tariff preferences as also covering quota preferences. The Appellate Body—emphasizing the text of the waiver— reversed that part of the panel report. In the two institutional cases, the Appellate Body took a broad view of the jurisdiction of the WTO dispute settlement system—effectively ruling that it was competent to consider the justification of balance-of-payments measures and to decide on whether a free trade area or customs union was consistent with GATT Article XXIV.

In contrast, in the two environmental/health cases, the Appellate Body reports interpreted the relevant agreements so as to increase governmental discretion. In the *Hormones* case, the Appellate Body made a number of statements suggesting that the SPS Agreement should be interpreted so as to afford discretion to governments, such as by invoking the *in dubio mitius* principle and noting that although SPS measures are to be science-based, governments were not required to follow mainstream scientific opinion. In the *Shrimp* case, it built upon the *Gasoline* case in giving breadth to the exception in GATT Article XX(g) for measures related to the conservation of exhaustible natural resources. While it ultimately did not reverse the panels' findings of violations in the two cases, its criticisms of the strict approach taken by the panels, as well as the general tone and some of the specific language in its reports, were welcomed by those concerned that trade rules not override environmental measures.

The WTO dispute settlement system survived its first five years in good shape. It was used frequently by WTO members and it had successfully handled a number of very controversial cases. While members had complaints about individuals cases, they all stated their general satisfaction with the system in the course of the 1998–1999 DSU review in which it was agreed that only some fine-tuning of the system was needed.

B. The Second Five Years (2000–2004)

The second five years of the WTO dispute settlement system * * * were marked by a noticeable decline in consultation requests—a total of 127 requests, involving 94 disputes, through June 30, 2004, as opposed to 185 requests in the first five years, involving 125 disputes. More significantly, the US and the EC no longer were as dominant as complainants in the system. In the 2000–2004 period, the US filed 18 consultation requests involving 18 disputes (19% of disputes) and the EC filed 15 consultation requests, involving 15 disputes (16% of disputes). There was a noticeable drop in US and EC consultation requests after 2000. If 2000 is excluded, the share of the US would fall to 15% and that of the EC to 12%. This fall-off in activity is particularly noteworthy compared to the first five years.

In contrast, developing country use of the system increased dramatically. Indeed, it is striking to consider the evolution in the use of the WTO dispute settlement system by developing countries. In the first five years of the system's existence, developing countries initiated by themselves roughly one-quarter of the consultation requests. In the four and one-half years from 2000 to June 2004, developing countries initiated 62% of the consultation requests—more than doubling their relative share of initiations. Brazil has been particularly active, initiating 9 consultation requests. Thus, in the last few years developing countries have become more frequent users of WTO dispute settlement, both in absolute and relative terms. Interestingly, the majority of those cases have involved developing country respondents. That is to say, developing countries seem to have found the WTO dispute settlement system to be a useful mechanism to deal with a wide range of trade disputes—using it not only against developed countries, but also in their trading relations with other developing countries. Of particular note is the way in which Latin American countries have made extensive use of the system in their dealings with other. The importance of this development cannot be overemphasized because it has been argued since the beginning of the WTO that the WTO dispute settlement mechanism is too complicated for developing countries to make effective use of. Yet, in the last few years, at least some of them have become the major users of the system and seem to be able to use it effectively—in terms of settling their own trade disputes with each other.

As to the type of case brought, the number of trade remedy cases has significantly increased, as compared to the first few years, especially in respect of cases brought against US trade remedy measures and pursued through panel proceedings. Indeed, in terms of controversy, the WTO dispute settlement system has been controversial in recent times mainly because of the very critical reaction in Washington to US losses in these trade remedy cases.

A second type of controversial case became significant at the end of the first decade. This type of case involved challenges, mainly by developing countries, to certain policies of the US and the EC—witness India's somewhat successful challenge to the EC's GSP scheme, a multiparty challenge led by Brazil to the EC sugar program, a Brazilian challenge to

US cotton subsidies and a challenge by the US and others to the EC's biotech approval regime. These cases, and a few others, seemed aimed in part at influencing the ongoing Doha Development Agenda negotiations. That is to say that some members are trying to improve their negotiating position through victories in dispute settlement—a not unexpected development. * * *

At the end of its first decade, the WTO dispute settlement system still seems to be operating well. Indeed, much of the initial controversy surrounding the system has receded, except in Washington where it has undoubtedly risen because of concerns about the system's treatment of challenges to US trade remedy cases.

* * *

III.   The Record in Settling Disputes

The aim of the WTO dispute settlement system is the resolution of trade-related disputes between WTO members. As the Dispute Settlement Understanding makes clear, in cases where a violation is found, removal of the inconsistent measure is the goal. Otherwise, a mutually agreed solution is the preferred result. In any case, prompt settlement is said to be essential. In considering how the system has performed in meeting these goals, I will examine those cases started with a consultation request prior to July 1, 2002. I do not include the more recent consultations requests because so many of them involve pending cases.

A.   Disposition of Consultation Requests

Of the 181 disputes started with a consultation request prior to July 1, 2002, there are 107 disputes that either did not result in an adopted panel report or are not now pending before an active panel. It appears that they were resolved as follows:

Settled, after panel established	18
Settled, with notification to DSB	26
Settled, without notification	20
Dropped (for legal, political, commercial reasons)	24
Dropped (trade remedy measure not imposed/removed/expired)	15
Pending	4

* * * [I]t appears that most disputes are settled or become moot because the measure complained of ceases to exist. There do not appear to be many, if any, requests that are simply forgotten or that are not pursued because of power imbalances or otherwise.

B.   Implementation of Panel Reports

Of the 181 disputes started with a consultation request prior to July 1, 2002, there are 74 disputes where panels have been established and have reported or are actively working. Of those, six are pending cases, where no report has been issued or the reasonable period of time for implementation has not expired. Of the remaining 68 disputes where reports have been adopted, the complainant lost in 10 of them, such that no implementation was required. Of the 58 other disputes, there has been implementation in 48. That leaves 10 disputes where there has been no implementation or a disagreement between the parties over implementation. That suggests a successful implementation rate of 83%. It should be mentioned, however, that there have been a number of cases, now resolved, where there were long-running disputes over implementation. Examples of such cases would include the *EC Bananas*, *Australia Salmon* and *Canada Dairy* cases. Moreover, the record of successful implementation must also be tempered by the fact that in some cases, the complaining parties have accepted what they have claimed was less than full implementation. Nonetheless, for an international system of dispute settlement in which any case may be brought, this is an impressive record.

It is worth noting, however, that the record of the WTO system is comparable to that of the GATT system, where Hudec found similar success rates—60% full satisfaction; 29% partial satisfaction—over the 42–year period from 1948 to 1989. One might ask—if the record is no different, was the adoption of what is clearly a more complex system worthwhile. In that regard, it is worth remembering that one of the major complaints about the GATT system was that the need for consensus meant that difficult cases were not brought to the system for resolution and that the GATT system's success rate fell significantly in its last few years of operation.

Notes and Questions

(1) The number of consultation requests declined in the 2005–2007 period, averaging only about 15 per year, although panels and the Appellate Body have remained relatively busy, dealing with cases started in the past. For example, 10 panel reports and 5 Appellate Body reports were adopted in 2007. Recent statistics on panel and Appellate Body activity are most easily found in the annual reports of the Appellate Body, which are available on the WTO website. The 2007 report indicates that through 2007, there have been 132 panel reports and 83 Appellate Body reports adopted.

(2) Of the ten cases mentioned in the foregoing article where there had been no implementation, four had been implemented as of January 1, 2008 (*Japan–Apples*; *US–FSC*; *US–1916 Act*; *US–Offset (Byrd Amendment)*, although there were disputed transitional issues still at issue in the latter two cases); one was before a WTO panel where implementation was an issue (*EC–Hormones*); and implementation in one was partially still being contested, although formal proceedings had not been commenced (*US–CVDs on EC Products*). The four remaining, admitted cases of non-implementation were *Brazil–Aircraft*; *Canada–Aircraft*; *Chile–Price Band* and *US–Copyright*. Of course, as these older cases are gradually implemented or become irrelevant, other cases of non-implementation have occurred. The issues surrounding implementation and retaliation for non-implementation are considered in Section 7.5.

(3) At the conclusion of the Uruguay Round negotiations, it was decided that the new WTO dispute settlement rules and procedures should be reviewed before January 1, 1999. Although many proposals and comments were made in the review process, it appeared that in the main most Members were generally satisfied with the operation of the dispute settlement system. At the end of the review, no action was taken to revise the DSU. At the 2001 Doha Ministerial, it was agreed to have negotiations on DSU reform, with a target of reaching agreement by May 2003. The chair of the DSU reform negotiating session circulated a chairman's draft in May 2003, including those proposals on which he thought agreement could be reached. However, it was not possible to obtain agreement on that draft. Since then, the negotiations have continued. According to a 2007 report on the negotiations, the following topics were then under discussion: proposals relating to compensation and suspension of concessions, flexibility and Member-control, panel composition, post-retaliation, remand, sequencing (the Article 21–22 relationship), special and differential treatment, strictly confidential information, third-party rights, time-savings and transparency. We discuss several of these reform proposals in Sections 7.4 and 7.5.

SECTION 7.4   CRITICAL ISSUES IN WTO DISPUTE SETTLEMENT

In this section, we will consider a number of critical issues that have arisen in respect of WTO dispute settlement. We have had to be quite selective in choosing these issues, as the subject of WTO dispute settlement could now support a course by itself. The six issues we will examine are (i) the concept of nullification or impairment in GATT Article XXIII, both in violation and non-violation cases; (ii) the definition of challengeable "measures"; (iii) the methods used to interpret the WTO agreements; (iv) how to ensure the proper balance between political and judicial power, with specific consideration of the appropriate standard of review to be applied to government measures and techniques of judicial restraint; (v) transparency and participation of developing members and non-members; and (vi) the problem of unilateralism. Section 7.5 will deal with implementation issues, examining how retaliatory measures are applied and considering whether the remedies for WTO violations are adequate.

(A) GATT ARTICLE XXIII AND THE CONCEPT OF NULLIFICATION AND IMPAIRMENT

As in the case of the GATT dispute settlement system, the wording and structure of GATT Article XXIII play an important role in the WTO system. The other WTO agreements either expressly incorporate Article XXIII as the standard for dispute settlement or contain a provision very similar to it. In addition, DSU Article 3.1 provides: "Members affirm their adherence to the principles for the management of disputes heretofore applied under Article XXII and XXIII of GATT 1947."

A careful look at Article XXIII reveals a number of troublesome and peculiar characteristics. In fact (as one of the authors has written elsewhere), the draftsmen of the General Agreement had at least three objectives in mind for Article XXIII, and it is not likely that those objectives are consistent one with another.[1] The first objective was that Articles XXII (a general provision on consultations) and XXIII were to be the framework of a dispute settlement procedure, stressing the general obligation to consult on any matter relating to GATT. The second objective was that Article XXIII would play an important role in obtaining compliance with the GATT obligations. The customary international law analogy of *retorsion* was used. A third goal for these provisions of GATT was to establish a means for ensuring continued "reciprocity and balance of concessions" in the face of changing circumstances. This third goal is more in the nature of an "escape clause" or "changed circumstances" provision.

The structure of Article XXIII is complex. In order to prevail under the terms of Article XXIII, a complainant must show that either

(i) benefits accruing to it under the General Agreement are being nullified or impaired; or

(ii) the attainment of an objective of the General Agreement is being impeded.

GATT disputes have virtually always turned on whether benefits have been nullified or impaired, with the result that the meaning of the second quoted phrase is unclear.

In addition, the complainant must show that such nullification or impairment (or impedance of objective) is a result of:

(i) a breach of obligation by the respondent contracting party;

(ii) the application of any measure by the respondent contracting party, whether it conflicts with the General Agreement or not; or

(iii) the existence of any other situation.

Under the language of Article XXIII, as traditionally interpreted, a violation of the General Agreement was by itself neither sufficient nor necessary to entitle a party to relief. Over time, however, more emphasis in the dispute settlement process has been placed on whether a violation of the General Agreement has been shown.

For example, in 1962, Uruguay brought an Article XXIII complaint against a broad range of trade restrictions it alleged were maintained by 15 industrialized GATT parties. In deciding how it would handle the complaint, the panel noted the following:[2]

In cases where there is a clear infringement of the provisions of the General Agreement, or in other words, where measures are applied in conflict with the provisions of GATT and are not permitted under the terms of the relevant protocol under which the GATT is applied

---

1. John H. Jackson, World Trade and the Law of GATT 167–69 (1969).

2. Uruguayan Recourse to Article XXIII, 11th Supp. BISD 95, 100 (Panel report adopted Nov. 16, 1962).

by the contracting party, the action would, *prima facie*, constitute a case of nullification or impairment and would *ipso facto* require consideration of whether the circumstances are serious enough to justify the authorization of suspension of concessions.

The *prima facie* concept was also applied in situations involving quotas or domestic subsidies on products subject to agreed upon tariff limitations (i.e., tariffs bound under Article II, see Section 8.2 infra).[3]

In this section, we examine how the concept of nullification or impairment is treated in the DSU and in WTO cases. Since the rules and the cases differentiate between cases based on Article XXIII:1(a)—claims that a party failed to "carry out its obligations" (violation cases) and (ii) those based on Article XXIII:1(b)—claims involving no alleged violation (nonviolation cases), we will consider first dispute settlement rules particularly relevant to violation cases and then those applied to nonviolation cases.

(1) Nullification or Impairment in Violation Cases

By far the most common claim raised in GATT and WTO dispute settlement is that one party has violated its GATT/WTO obligations. The evolution of the nullification or impairment concept in violation cases (see below for discussion of non-violation cases) is quite interesting. As noted above, Article XXIII, by its terms, in a violation case, requires both a violation ("failure * * * to carry out its obligations") and that a "benefit accruing to [the complaining party] directly or indirectly under the Agreement is being nullified or impaired."[4] In early violation cases, the panel turned to the issue of nullification or impairment after finding a GATT violation. For example, in *Italian Discrimination Against Imported Agricultural Machinery*, see Section 12.2 infra, the panel noted that it "considered whether [the violation] had caused injury to the United Kingdom's commercial interests, and whether such an injury represented an impairment of benefits."[5] But in the *Uruguayan* case, as noted above, the concept of *prima facie* nullification or impairment was introduced.

UNITED STATES—TAXES ON PETROLEUM AND CERTAIN IMPORTED SUBSTANCES
34th Supp. BISD 136 (1988).
Panel Report adopted June 17, 1987.

[Certain US legislation, known as the Superfund Act, deals with the cleanup of hazardous waste sites. The Act imposed a tax of 8.2 cents per barrel on domestic crude oil received at a US refinery and a tax of 11.7 cents per barrel for petroleum products entered into the US for con-

---

3. See generally Jackson, supra note 1, at 182.

4. In lieu of nullification or impairment, relief under Article XXIII would also be available if it were established that "the

attainment of an objective of the Agreement is being impeded." No adopted panel reports have turned on this issue.

5. 7th Supp. BISD 60, 65 (Panel report adopted Oct. 23, 1958).

sumption, use or warehousing. It was effectively conceded by the US that the tax violated the national treatment requirement of GATT Article III:2. Instead, the main US contention was that] the tax differential was so small that its trade effects were minimal or nil and that the tax differential—whether it conformed to Article III:2, first sentence, or not—did not nullify or impair benefits accruing to Canada, the EEC and Mexico under the General Agreement. Canada, the EEC and Mexico considered this defence to be neither legally valid nor factually correct.
* * *

5.1.3 Under Article XXIII of the General Agreement contracting parties may bring complaints, inter alia, if they consider that benefits accruing to them under that Agreement are nullified or impaired. According to established GATT practice, described in the Annex to the 1979 Understanding on dispute settlement, "where there is an infringement of the obligations assumed under the General Agreement, the action is considered prima facie to constitute a case of nullification or impairment" (BISD 26S/216). The question raised by the case before the Panel is whether the presumption that a measure inconsistent with the General Agreement causes a nullification or impairment of benefits accruing under that Agreement is an absolute or a rebuttable presumption and, if rebuttable, whether a demonstration that a measure inconsistent with Article III:2, first sentence, has no or insignificant effects on trade is a sufficient rebuttal.

* * *

5.1.6 The Panel examined how the CONTRACTING PARTIES have reacted in previous cases to claims that a measure inconsistent with the General Agreement had no adverse impact and therefore did not nullify or impair benefits accruing under the General Agreement to the contracting party that had brought the complaint. The Panel noted such claims had been made in a number of cases but that there was no case in the history of the GATT in which a contracting party had successfully rebutted the presumption that a measure infringing obligations causes nullification and impairment. * * *

5.1.7 The Panel concluded from its review of the above and other cases that, while the CONTRACTING PARTIES had not explicitly decided whether the presumption that illegal measures cause nullification or impairment could be rebutted, the presumption had in practice operated as an irrefutable presumption.

5.1.8 The Panel then examined whether—even assuming that the presumption could be regarded as rebuttable in the present case—a demonstration that the trade effects of the tax differential were insignificant would constitute a proof that the benefits accruing to Canada, the EEC and Mexico under Article III:2, first sentence, had not been nullified or impaired.

5.1.9 An acceptance of the argument that measures which have only an insignificant effect on the volume of exports do not nullify or impair benefits accruing under Article III:2, first sentence, implies that the basic rationale of this provision—the benefit it generates for the contracting parties—is to protect expectations on export volumes. That, however, is not the case. Article III:2, first sentence, obliges contracting parties to establish certain competitive conditions for imported products in relation to domestic products. Unlike some other provisions in the General Agreement, it does not refer to trade effects. The majority of the members of the Working Party on the "Brazilian Internal Taxes" therefore correctly concluded that the provisions of Article III:2, first sentence, "were equally applicable, whether imports from other contracting parties were substantial, small or non-existent" (BISD Vol. II/185). The Working Party also concluded that "a contracting party was bound by the provisions of Article III whether or not the contracting party in question had undertaken tariff commitments in respect of the goods concerned" (BISD Vol. II/182), in other words, the benefits under Article III accrue independent of whether there is a negotiated expectation of market access or not. Moreover, it is conceivable that a tax consistent with the national treatment principle (for instance, a high but non-discriminatory excise tax) has a more severe impact on the exports of other contracting parties than a tax that violates that principle (for instance a very low but discriminatory tax). The case before the Panel illustrates this point: the United States could bring the tax on petroleum in conformity with Article III:2, first sentence, by raising the tax on domestic products, by lowering the tax on imported products or by fixing a new common tax rate for both imported and domestic products. Each of these solutions would have different trade results, and it is therefore logically not possible to determine the difference in trade impact between the present tax and one consistent with Article III:2, first sentence, and hence to determine the trade impact resulting from the non-observance of that provision. For these reasons, Article III:2, first sentence, cannot be interpreted to protect expectations on export volumes; it protects expectations on the competitive relationship between imported and domestic products. A change in the competitive relationship contrary to that provision must consequently be regarded ipso facto as a nullification or impairment of benefits accruing under the General Agreement. A demonstration that a measure inconsistent with Article III:2, first sentence, has no or insignificant effects would therefore in the view of the Panel not be a sufficient demonstration that the benefits accruing under that provision had not been nullified or impaired even if such a rebuttal were in principle permitted.

* * *

Notes and Questions

(1) The DSU provides in article 3.8:

In cases where there is an infringement of the obligations assumed under a covered agreement, the action is considered *prima facie* to constitute a case of nullification or impairment. This means that there is normally a presumption that a breach of the rules has an adverse impact on other Members parties to that covered agreement, and in such cases, it shall be up to the Member against whom the complaint has been brought to rebut the charge.

Both sentences appeared in the 1979 Understanding, but not together. In the panel's view, in the 1979 Understanding, the second sentence followed a sentence discussing when consideration should be given to authorizing retaliatory action. As such, the panel did not consider it to be directly on point as to whether it was appropriate to find nullification or impairment for purposes of a recommendation to bring an offending measure into compliance with GATT obligations. Does the new position of this sentence in the DSU affect the panel's reasoning? In WTO practice to date, panel reports usually contain a single sentence in the concluding section that cites article 3.8 and notes that in light of the violation found, benefits accruing to the complaining member have been nullified or impaired.

(2) Do you agree with the analysis in the *Superfund* case? As a policy matter, if a violation in fact has no trade impact, why should the offending party have to correct it?

(3) Suppose a party prevails in a dispute settlement proceeding without showing any trade effects of a violation. If the other party fails to implement the DSB's recommendation to withdraw the nonconforming measure, and no agreement on compensation can be reached between the parties, is the prevailing party entitled to suspend concessions? In what amount? See DSU, art. 22.4 ("The level of the suspension of concessions or other obligations * * * shall be equivalent to the level of nullification or impairment."). These issues are treated in Section 7.5 infra.

(4) The evolution of the need to establish nullification or impairment in GATT dispute settlement is a fascinating study in international rule making. In GATT, a system of case-by-case decision making gradually elaborated the sparse language of Article XXIII into a complex set of rules, which in time were ratified by inclusion in the DSU (and in its predecessor decisions on dispute settlement). This is a "bottom up" approach that is quite different than the "top down" procedure that normally might be expected in the international context.

(2) Nullification or Impairment in Nonviolation Cases

As we have already noted, the vast majority of GATT dispute settlement panel decisions have involved alleged violations of the General Agreement, but from the very early years of GATT, there have been occasional cases claiming nullification or impairment of benefits arising out of actions that are not claimed to be GATT violations. Since the formation of the WTO, such claims have occasionally arisen, but thus far the Appellate Body has not had occasion to examine Article XXIII:1(b) in any detail. The excerpts from the following case examine some of the key issues that arise in non-violation cases.

JAPAN—MEASURES AFFECTING CONSUMER PHOTOGRAPHIC FILM AND PAPER

WT/DS44/R.
Panel Report adopted April 22, 1998.

[The United States claimed that through the application of three broad categories of import liberalization "countermeasures" the Japanese Government for more than 30 years had inhibited the distribution and sale of imported consumer photographic film and paper in Japan. These three categories of measures included: (1) distribution measures, which allegedly encouraged and facilitated the creation of a market structure for photographic film and paper in which imports were excluded from traditional distribution channels; (2) restrictions on large retail stores, which allegedly restricted the growth of an alternative distribution channel for imported film; and (3) promotion measures, which allegedly disadvantaged imports by restricting the use of sales promotion techniques. The United States alleged, inter alia, that the above measures, individually and collectively, nullified or impaired benefits accruing to the United States within the meaning of GATT Article XXIII:1(b). The underlying factual dispute was too complex to be considered here, but the following excerpt examines the rationale for nonviolation claims and lays out the basic elements of such a claim. The panel ultimately rejected the US claim and the US did not appeal.]

10.35 The underlying purpose of Article XXIII:1(b) was cogently explained by the panel on *EEC—Oilseeds*:

"The idea underlying [the provisions of Article XXIII:1(b)] is that the improved competitive opportunities that can legitimately be expected from a tariff concession can be frustrated not only by measures proscribed by the General Agreement but also by measures consistent with that Agreement. In order to encourage contracting parties to make tariff concessions they must therefore be given a right of redress when a reciprocal concession is impaired by another contracting party as a result of the application of any measure, whether or not it conflicts with the General Agreement".

* * *

"The Panel considered that the main value of a tariff concession is that it provides an assurance of better market access through improved price competition. Contracting parties negotiate tariff concessions primarily to obtain that advantage. They must therefore be assumed to base their tariff negotiations on the expectation that the price effect of the tariff concessions will not be systematically offset. If no right of redress were given to them in such a case they would be reluctant to make tariff concessions and the General Agreement would no longer be useful as a legal framework for incorporating the results of trade negotiations".[6]

Clearly, the safeguarding of the process and the results of negotiating reciprocal tariff concessions under Article II is fundamental to the balance of rights and obligations to which all WTO Members subscribe.

10.36 Although the non-violation remedy is an important and accepted tool of WTO/GATT dispute settlement and has been "on the books" for almost 50 years, we note that there have only been eight cases in which panels or working parties have substantively considered Article XXIII:1(b) claims. This suggests that both the GATT contracting parties and WTO Members have approached this remedy with caution and, indeed, have treated it as an exceptional instrument of dispute settlement. We note in this regard that both the European Communities and the United States in the *EEC—Oilseeds* case, and the two parties in this case, have confirmed that the non-violation nullification or impairment remedy should be approached with caution and treated as an exceptional concept. The reason for this caution is straightforward. Members negotiate the rules that they agree to follow and only exceptionally would expect to be challenged for actions not in contravention of those rules.

* * *

10.38 In GATT jurisprudence, most of the cases of non-violation nullification or impairment have dealt with situations where a GATT-consistent domestic subsidy for the producer of a product has been introduced or modified following the grant of a tariff concession on that product. The instant case presents a different sort of non-violation claim. At the outset, however, we wish to make clear that we do not *a priori* consider it inappropriate to apply the Article XXIII:1(b) remedy to other governmental actions, such as those designed to strengthen the competitiveness of certain distribution or industrial sectors through non-financial assistance. Whether assistance is financial or non-financial, direct or indirect, does not determine whether its effect may offset the expected result of tariff negotiations. Thus, a Member's industrial policy, pursuing the goal of increasing efficiency in a sector, could in some circumstances upset the competitive relationship in the market place between domestic and imported products in a way that could give rise to a cause of action under Article XXIII:1(b). In the context of a Member's distribution system, for example, it is conceivable that measures that do not infringe GATT rules could be implemented in a manner that effectively results in a disproportionate impact on market conditions for imported products. In this regard, however, we must also bear in mind that tariff concessions have never been viewed as creating a guarantee of trade volumes, but rather, as explained below, as creating expectations as to competitive relationships.

* * *

6. [original note 1202] *EEC—Oilseeds*, adopted on 25 January 1990, BISD 37S/86, 128–129, paras. 144, 148.

10.41 We now return to our more detailed examination of the scope of Article XXIII:1(b). Article XXIII:1(b) provides in relevant part:

"If any Member should consider that any *benefit* accruing to it directly or indirectly under this Agreement is being *nullified or impaired* ... as the result of ... (b) the *application* by another Member of any *measure*, whether or not it conflicts with the provisions of this Agreement ..." (emphasis added).

The text of Article XXIII:1(b) establishes three elements that a complaining party must demonstrate in order to make out a cognizable claim under Article XXIII:1(b): (1) application of a measure by a WTO Member; (2) a benefit accruing under the relevant agreement; and (3) nullification or impairment of the benefit as the result of the application of the measure. We shall proceed with our analysis by considering in turn each of these three elements.

(a) APPLICATION OF A MEASURE

* * *

10.43 The ordinary meaning of *measure* as it is used in Article XXIII:1(b) certainly encompasses a law or regulation enacted by a government. But in our view, it is broader than that and includes other governmental actions short of legally enforceable enactments. * * *

10.44 In Japan, it is accepted that the government sometimes acts through what is referred to as administrative guidance. In such a case, the company receiving guidance from the Government of Japan may not be legally bound to act in accordance with it, but compliance may be expected in light of the power of the government and a system of government incentives and disincentives arising from the wide array of government activities and involvement in the Japanese economy. As noted by the parties, administrative guidance in Japan takes various forms. Japan, for example, refers to what it calls "regulatory administrative guidance", which it concedes effectively substitutes for formal government action. It also refers to promotional administrative guidance, where companies are urged to do things that are in their interest to do in any event. In Japan's view, this sort of guidance should not be assimilated to a measure in the sense of Article XXIII:1(b). * * *

10.45 Our review of GATT jurisprudence, particularly the panel report on *Japan—Semi-conductors*, teaches that where administrative guidance creates incentives or disincentives largely dependent upon governmental action for private parties to act in a particular manner, it may be considered a governmental measure. In that case, the panel found that although a measure was not mandatory, it could be considered a *restriction* subject to Article XI:1 because

"sufficient incentives or disincentives existed for non-mandatory measures to take effect ... [and] the operation of the measures ... was essentially dependent on Government action or intervention [because in such a case] the measures would be operating in a manner equivalent to mandatory requirements such that the difference between the measures and mandatory requirements was only one of form and not of substance . . .".[7]

* * *

10.49   * * * In our view, a government policy or action need not necessarily have a substantially binding or compulsory nature for it to entail a likelihood of compliance by private actors in a way so as to nullify or impair legitimately expected benefits within the purview of Article XXIII:1(b). Indeed, it is clear that non-binding actions, which include sufficient incentives or disincentives for private parties to act in a particular manner, can potentially have adverse effects on competitive conditions of market access. For example, a number of non-violation cases have involved subsidies, receipt of which requires only voluntary compliance with eligibility criteria. Moreover, we also consider it conceivable, in cases where there is a high degree of cooperation and collaboration between government and business, e.g., where there is substantial reliance on administrative guidance and other more informal forms of government–business cooperation, that even non-binding, hortatory wording in a government statement of policy could have a similar effect on private actors to a legally binding measure or what Japan refers to as regulatory administrative guidance. Consequently, we believe we should be open to a broad definition of the term *measure* for purposes of Article XXIII:1(b), which considers whether or not a non-binding government action has an effect similar to a binding one.

10.50   We reach this conclusion in considering the purpose of Article XXIII:1(b), which is to protect the balance of concessions under GATT by providing a means to redress government actions not otherwise regulated by GATT rules that nonetheless nullify or impair a Member's legitimate expectations of benefits from tariff negotiations. To achieve this purpose, in our view, it is important that the kinds of government actions considered to be measures covered by Article XXIII:1(b) should not be defined in an unduly restrictive manner. Otherwise, there is the risk of cases, in which governments have been involved one way or another in the nullification or impairment of benefits, that will not be redressable under Article XXIII:1(b), thereby preventing the achievement of its purpose. We would stress, however, that giving a broad definition to *measure* does not expand the scope of the Article XXIII:1(b) remedy because it remains incumbent on the complaining Member to clearly demonstrate how the measure at issue results in or causes nullification or impairment of benefits, and as explained below, in the final analysis the responding Member's government is only responsible for what it has itself caused.

* * *

(ii) Governmental versus private actions

10.52   As the WTO Agreement is an international agreement, in respect of which only national governments and separate customs terri-

---

7. [original note 1211] *Japan—Semiconductors*, BISD 35S/116, 155.

tories are directly subject to obligations, it follows by implication that the term *measure* in Article XXIII:1(b) and Article 26.1 of the DSU, as elsewhere in the WTO Agreement, refers only to policies or actions of governments, not those of private parties. But while this "truth" may not be open to question, there have been a number of trade disputes in relation to which panels have been faced with making sometimes difficult judgments as to the extent to which what appear on their face to be private actions may nonetheless be attributable to a government because of some governmental connection to or endorsement of those actions.

* * *

10.56   These past GATT cases demonstrate that the fact that an action is taken by private parties does not rule out the possibility that it may be deemed to be governmental if there is sufficient government involvement with it. It is difficult to establish bright-line rules in this regard, however. Thus, that possibility will need to be examined on a case-by-case basis.

* * *

(b) BENEFIT ACCRUING UNDER THE GATT

10.61   The second required element which must be considered to establish a case of non-violation nullification or impairment under Article XXIII:1(b) is the existence of a benefit accruing to a WTO Member under the relevant agreement (in this case, GATT 1994). In all but one of the past GATT cases dealing with Article XXIII:1(b) claims, the claimed benefit has been that of legitimate expectations of improved market-access opportunities arising out of relevant tariff concessions. This same set of GATT precedents suggests that for expectations to be legitimate, they must take into account all measures of the party making the concession that could have been reasonably anticipated at the time of the concession. * * *

10.62   In the particular case before us, the question of legitimate expectations of benefits accruing to the United States is complicated by the fact that the United States is claiming to have had expectations of improved market access benefits in respect of four different products (each under a different tariff line), granted during three successive rounds of multilateral trade negotiations. This claim raises two general issues. First, may the benefits legitimately expected by a Member derive from successive rounds of tariff negotiations? [The panel answered this question in the affirmative, based in part on the WTO Agreement's definition of GATT 1994 and in part on past GATT cases.] Second, what factors should be considered to determine if a Member should have reasonably anticipated measures that it claims nullified or impaired benefits?

* * *

10.72   The text of Article XXIII:1(b) simply refers to "a benefit accruing, directly or indirectly, under this Agreement" and does not further define or explain what benefits are referred to. Past GATT panel reports have considered that such benefits include those that a Member reasonably expects to obtain from a tariff negotiation.

10.76   [After reviewing those materials, the panel continued:] As suggested by the 1961 report, in order for expectations of a benefit to be legitimate, the challenged measures must not have been reasonably anticipated at the time the tariff concession was negotiated. If the measures were anticipated, a Member could not have had a legitimate expectation of improved market access to the extent of the impairment caused by these measures.

10.77   Thus, under Article XXIII:1(b), the United States may only claim impairment of benefits related to improved market access conditions flowing from relevant tariff concessions by Japan to the extent that the United States could not have reasonably anticipated that such benefits would be offset by the subsequent application of a measure by the Government of Japan. * * *

* * *

10.79   We consider that the issue of reasonable anticipation should be approached in respect of specific "measures" in light of the following guidelines. First, in the case of measures shown by the United States to have been introduced subsequent to the conclusion of the tariff negotiations at issue, it is our view that the United States has raised a presumption that it should not be held to have anticipated these measures and it is then for Japan to rebut that presumption. Such a rebuttal might be made, for example, by establishing that the measure at issue is so clearly contemplated in an earlier measure that the United States should be held to have anticipated it. However, there must be a clear connection shown. In our view, it is not sufficient to claim that a *specific* measure should have been anticipated because it is consistent with or a continuation of a past *general* government policy. As in the *EEC—Oilseeds* case, we do not believe that it would be appropriate to charge the United States with having reasonably anticipated all GATT-consistent measures, such as "measures" to improve what Japan describes as the inefficient Japanese distribution sector. Indeed, if a Member were held to anticipate all GATT-consistent measures, a non-violation claim would not be possible. Nor do we consider that as a general rule the United States should have reasonably anticipated Japanese measures that are similar to measures in other Members' markets. In each such instance, the issue of reasonable anticipation needs to be addressed on a case-by-case basis.

10.80   Second, in the case of measures shown by Japan to have been introduced prior to the conclusion of the tariff negotiations at issue, it is our view that Japan has raised a presumption that the United States should be held to have anticipated those measures and it is for the United States to rebut that presumption. In this connection, it is our view that the United States is charged with knowledge of Japanese government measures as of the date of their publication. We realize that knowledge of a measure's existence is not equivalent to understanding the impact of the measure on a specific product market. For example, a vague measure could be given substance through enforcement policies that are initially unexpected or later changed significantly. However, where the United States claims that it did not know of a measure's relevance to market access conditions in respect of film or paper, we would expect the United States to clearly demonstrate why initially it could not have reasonably anticipated the effect of an existing measure on the film or paper market and when it did realize the effect. * * *

* * *

(c) NULLIFICATION OR IMPAIRMENT OF BENEFIT: CAUSALITY

10.82   The third required element of a non-violation claim under Article XXIII:1(b) is that the benefit accruing to the WTO Member (e.g., improved market access from tariff concessions) is *nullified or impaired as the result of* the application of a measure by another WTO Member. In other words, it must be demonstrated that the competitive position of the imported products subject to and benefitting from a relevant market access (tariff) concession is being *upset by* ("nullified or impaired ... as the result of") the application of a measure not reasonably anticipated. The equation of "nullification or impairment" with "upsetting the competitive relationship" established between domestic and imported products as a result of tariff concessions has been consistently used by GATT panels examining non-violation complaints. For example, the *EEC—Oilseeds* panel, in describing its findings, stated that it had "found ... that the subsidies concerned had impaired the tariff concession because they *upset the competitive relationship between domestic and imported oilseeds*, not because of any effect on trade flows".[8] The same language was used in the *Australian Subsidy* and *Germany—Sardines* cases. Thus, in this case, it is up to the United States to prove that the governmental measures that it cites have upset the competitive relationship between domestic and imported photographic film and paper in Japan to the detriment of imports. In other words, the United States must show a clear correlation between the measures and the adverse effect on the relevant competitive relationships.

10.83   We consider that this third element—causality—may be one of the more factually complex areas of our examination. In this connection, we note that in the three prior non-violation cases in which panels found that the complaining parties had failed to provide a detailed justification to support their claims, the issue turned primarily on the lack of evidence of causality. * * *

Notes and Questions

(1) There have been two additional WTO cases where nonviolation claims have figured prominently. In *Korea—Government Procurement*, the

8. [original note 1241] Follow-up on the   114–115, para. 77 (emphasis added).
Panel Report, *EEC—Oilseeds*, BISD 39S/91,

US claimed that the Government Procurement Agreement covered the contracts let for the construction of the new Seoul airport at Inchon and, in the alternative, that if the contracts were not covered, then its legitimate expectations that they would be had been nullified or impaired. The US lost both claims and did not appeal. The case is noteworthy for its discussion of the relationship of WTO and international law, and, in particular, for the suggestion that the nonviolation rules are a development of the *pacta sunt servanda* principle of international law. In *EC—Asbestos*, the principal claims were violation claims and are discussed in Chapters 12 and 13, but there was also a non-violation claim, which was rejected. The case raised the question of whether a WTO member could have legitimate expectations that were nullified or impaired by the adoption of a health measure justified under the GATT Article XX(b). While such a claim would seem to be difficult to establish, the Appellate Body ruled that it was conceivable (although Canada had failed to establish its claim in that case).

(2) The only successful nonviolation claim since the early 1950's arose out of EU duty-free tariff bindings on oilseeds made in 1962. In a case brought by the United States, the US claimed that subsequent to making this binding, the EU adopted agricultural support programs that created an incentive to produce oilseeds in the EU that impaired benefits it could reasonably expect to accrue to it under the tariff concessions for oilseeds. The essential EU defense was that it is not legitimate to expect the absence of production subsidies even after the grant of a tariff concession because GATT Articles III:8(b) and XVI:1 explicitly recognize the right of parties to grant production subsidies. The panel rejected that argument. It also noted:

> 148.   * * * At issue in the case before it are product-specific subsidies that protect producers completely from the movement of prices for imports and thereby prevent tariff concessions from having any impact on the competitive relationship between domestic and imported oilseeds. The Panel considered that the main value of a tariff concession is that it provides an assurance of better market access through improved price competition. Contracting parties negotiate tariff concessions primarily to obtain that advantage. They must therefore be assumed to base their tariff negotiations on the expectation that the price effect of the tariff concessions will not be systematically offset. * * *

> 150.   * * * The Panel noted that the CONTRACTING PARTIES have consistently interpreted the basic provisions of the General Agreement on restrictive trade measures as provisions establishing conditions of competition. * * * [I]n the tariff negotiations in the framework of GATT, contracting parties seek tariff concessions in the hope of expanding their exports, but the commitments they exchange in such negotiations are commitments on conditions of competition for trade, not on volumes of trade.

> 151.   * * * The approach of the CONTRACTING PARTIES reflects the fact that governments can often not predict with precision what the impact of their interventions on import volumes will be. * * * The provisions of Article XXIII:1(b) could therefore in practice hardly be applied if a contracting party claiming nullification or impairment had

to demonstrate not only that an adverse change in competition has taken place but also that the change has resulted in a decline in imports.

EEC—Payments and Subsidies Paid to Processors and Producers of Oilseeds and Related Animal–Feed Proteins, 37th Supp. BISD 86, adopted on January 25, 1990.

(3) There were two cases from the early 1950's that accepted the legitimacy of non-violation complaints. In one case, Chile complained when Australia changed its policy on subsidizing fertilizer so as to remove the subsidy on the type of fertilizer that Chile had been exporting to Australia, while maintaining it on the type of fertilizer produced domestically. The Australian Subsidy on Ammonium Sulphate, II BISD 188 (1952) (Working party report adopted April 3, 1950). Chile claimed that this action nullified or impaired the tariff concession on fertilizer that it had obtained from Australia, and the working party agreed (II BISD at 193):

> It was agreed that such impairment would exist if the action of the Australian Government which resulted in upsetting the competitive relationship between [the two fertilizers] could not reasonably have been anticipated by the Chilean Government, taking into consideration all pertinent circumstances and the provisions of the General Agreement, at the time it negotiated the duty-free binding on [the fertilizer that it produced].

In another case, which is discussed in Section 10.2 infra, Norway successfully brought a complaint protesting a German change in tariff rates on products that had formerly been treated the same, with the result that relatively higher tariffs were imposed on the Norwegian product compared to competing products from other countries. Treatment by Germany of Imports of Sardines, 1st Supp. BISD 53 (1953) (Panel report adopted Oct. 31, 1952).

(4) Despite the long history of nonviolation claims, they remain controversial. In the Chile–Australia case, the Australian representative made the following statement in response to the decision:

> In view of * * * the fact that the working party has also found that the Australian subsidy on ammonium sulphate [fertilizer] is completely in accordance with the provisions of the Agreement including the provisions specifically relating to subsidies, Australia cannot consider it a sound argument that what a country might now say was its reasonable expectation three years ago in respect of a particular tariff concession should be the determining factor in establishing the existence of impairment in terms of Article XXIII. If it were accepted by the CONTRACTING PARTIES, then this interpretation of Article XXIII would require a complete re-examination of the principles on which Australia (and, we had supposed, all other countries) had hitherto granted tariff concessions. The history and practice of tariff negotiations show clearly that if a country seeking a tariff concession on a product desires to assure itself of a certain treatment for that product in a field apart from rates of duty *and to an extent going further than is provided for in the various articles of the General Agreement,* the objective sought must be a matter for negotiation in addition to the actual negotiation respecting the rates of duty to be applied.

If this were not so, and if an expectation (no matter how reasonable) which has never been expressed, discussed or attached to a tariff agreement as a condition is interpreted in the light of the arguments adduced in the report of the working party, then tariff concessions and the binding of a rate of duty would be extremely hazardous commitments and would only be entered into after an exhaustive survey of the whole field of substitute or competitive products and detailed analyses of probable future needs of a particular economy.

Do you agree? Are cases like this, which do not involve alleged violations of rules, appropriate for consideration in a dispute settlement system? Or do they present differences over policy issues that ought to resolved through negotiation of applicable rules? What problems may arise if policy disputes are adjudicated in a dispute settlement system?

(5) How does the DSU deal with nonviolation complaints under Article XXIII:1(b)? Examine DSU, art. 26.1. Are there any differences in the procedures to be followed or the remedies available under article 26.1 cases compared to regular cases? The Agreement on Trade–Related Aspects of Intellectual Property Rights provides that complaints based on Article XXI-II:1(b) and (c) will not be permitted for five years and during that time the governing body shall consider whether such complaints are to be allowed. TRIPS Agreement, art. 64. (The TRIPS Council has not taken any decision on the subject.) The General Agreement on Trade in Services allows for certain of such complaints. See GATS, art. XXIII:3.

(6) There have been no GATT or WTO decisions that have recognized nullification or impairment resulting from a complaint based on Article XXIII:1(c). How does the DSU treat such complaints? See DSU, art. 26.2.

(7) Is "nullification or impairment" a useful concept on which to base dispute settlement? Why not always require a breach of obligations? Isn't the nullification or impairment concept more compatible with negotiated dispute settlement as opposed to adjudication? It does allow consideration of problems that the rules fail to cover. But with only one adopted panel report recognizing such a situation since 1952, one can argue that it does not fill a pressing need. Moreover, nullification or impairment seems to be based on the idea that there is a reciprocal balance of concessions that should be maintained. Yet after almost 50 years of negotiations on an ever-broadening range of issues in the WTO, that idea of broad-based reciprocity may not be meaningful. One could argue that what is more important is that the agreed-upon rules are obeyed, and that if they are not, then offsetting compensation is afforded to balance the effect of the rule violations. On the other hand, can you see why negotiators might feel more comfortable entering into commitments with one another given the existence of the nonviolation rule?

(B) WHAT MEASURES MAY BE CHALLENGED?

The DSU requires that requests for consultations (art. 4.4) and establishment of panels (art. 6.2) identify the measures at issue. The DSU also provides that if a panel finds that there has been a violation of the rules, it is required to recommend that the measure at issue be brought into conformity with the rules. Art. 19.2. These and other DSU provisions have resulted in considerable attention being paid to the concept of "challengeable measure".

UNITED STATES—MEASURES RELATING TO ZEROING AND SUNSET REVIEWS

WT/DS322/AB/R.
Appellate Body Report adopted January 23, 2007.

[This case involved a challenge to an antidumping duty. The rules for applying such duties are examined in Chapter 16. At issue here is a practice known as "zeroing", which is a controversial technique for calculating average levels of dumping.]

73.   The measures challenged by Japan before the Panel were the "zeroing procedures" and the "standard zeroing line", [which refers to a specific line of computer programming code used by the US antidumping authority, which is the Department of Commerce (USDOC), when it develops a specific computer program to calculate a margin of dumping in a particular anti-dumping proceeding]. Japan claimed before the Panel that these "measures" were, as such, inconsistent with various provisions of the Anti–Dumping Agreement and the GATT 1994 * * *.

74.   The Panel first reviewed the nature and scope of "measures" that may be subject to "as such" challenges in WTO dispute settlement. The Panel recalled [several prior Appellate Body rulings: First,] "[i]n principle, any act or omission attributable to a WTO Member can be a 'measure' of that Member for purposes of WTO dispute settlement proceedings." [Second,] measures that can be subject to WTO dispute settlement include not only acts applying a law in a specific situation, but also "acts setting forth rules or norms that are intended to have general and prospective application." [Third,] that, in principle, there is no bar to "non-mandatory measures" being challenged as such.

75.   For purposes of determining the existence of such a rule or norm, the Panel recalled the Appellate Body's finding, in *US—Zeroing (EC)*, that a "panel must not lightly assume the existence of a 'rule or norm' constituting a measure of general and prospective application, especially when it is not expressed in the form of a written document", and that, when a challenge is brought against such a rule or norm, "a complaining party must clearly establish, through arguments and supporting evidence, at least that the alleged 'rule or norm' is attributable to the responding Member; its precise content; and indeed, that it does have general and prospective application." * * *

* * *

82.   * * * Article 11 of the DSU requires panels "to take account of the evidence put before them and forbids them to wilfully disregard or distort such evidence." Moreover, panels must not "make affirmative findings that lack a basis in the evidence contained in the panel record." Provided that a panel's assessment of evidence remains within these

parameters, the Appellate Body will not interfere with the findings of the panel.

83. The evidence before the Panel in this case included model computer programs used by the USDOC that serve as a basis for programs used in specific original investigations and periodic reviews. These programs include an instruction to apply zeroing through the "standard zeroing line". The Panel also had evidence before it regarding the application of the zeroing procedures in 16 different anti-dumping proceedings, including four original investigations, one new shipper review, and 11 periodic reviews.

84. Although the Panel did not consider the "standard zeroing line" to be a measure in itself, it found that zeroing has been a "constant feature of [the] US [Department of Commerce]'s practice for a considerable period of time". The Panel further found that the "standard zeroing line" "has been included in the vast majority of computer program[s] used by [the] USDOC to calculate margins of dumping ... and [even] where the line has not been included, [the] USDOC has used other methods to exclude export prices higher than the normal value from the numerator of the weighted average margin of dumping." In addition, the Panel noted that the United States had "not identified a single case in which a decision was taken to provide such an offset."

85. Moreover, the Panel observed that the evidence before it "shows that what is at issue goes beyond the simple repetition of the application of a certain methodology to specific cases." According to the Panel, "[t]he manner in which [the] USDOC's use of zeroing has been characterized in statements by [the] USDOC [and] other United States' agencies and courts ... confirms that [the] USDOC's consistent application of zeroing reflects a deliberate policy." For the Panel, the USDOC "has repeatedly stated that '[it does] not allow' export sales at prices above normal value to offset dumping margins on other export sales, has referred to its 'practice' or 'methodology' of not providing for offsets for non-dumped sales, has pointed out that the United States Court of Appeals for the Federal Circuit has ruled that the 'zeroing practice' ... is a reasonable interpretation of the law, that the US Congress was aware of [the] USDOC's methodology when it adopted the Uruguay Round Agreements Act, and that not granting an offset for non-dumped sales 'has consistently been an integral part of the [US-DOC]'s [W–W] analysis'." The Panel added that "the United States Department of Justice has stated that the USDOC 'has consistently applied its practice of treating non-dumped sales as sales with a margin of zero since the implementation of the [Uruguay Round Agreements Act]' and has referred to [the] USDOC's 'long-standing methodology' and to 'the zeroing practice, which has been followed for at least 20 years' and which 'predated the passage of the latest major amendment of the Anti-dumping law'." Finally, the Panel noted that the "United States Court of International Trade has stated that '[the USDOC's]

zeroing methodology in its calculation of dumping margins is grounded in long-standing practice'."

* * *

88.   In sum, we agree with the Panel's understanding of the Appellate Body's previous jurisprudence and the manner in which the Panel framed the question before it. We also consider that the Panel had sufficient evidence before it to conclude that the "zeroing procedures" under different comparison methodologies, and in different stages of anti-dumping proceedings, do not correspond to separate rules or norms, but simply reflect different manifestations of a single rule or norm. The Panel also examined ample evidence regarding the precise content of this rule or norm, its nature as a measure of general and prospective application, and its attribution to the United States. In our view, the Panel properly assessed this evidence. We therefore disagree with the United States that the Panel did not assess objectively the issue of whether a single rule or norm exists by virtue of which the USDOC applies zeroing "regardless of the basis upon which export price and normal value are compared and regardless of the type of proceeding in which margins are calculated."

Notes and Questions

(1) It is always possible to challenge the specific application of a measure (e.g., a specific antidumping duty) as being inconsistent with WTO rules, but parties often wish to challenge the measure "as such" so that the DSB's recommendation will require modification of the basic underlying measure (e.g., in this case, the US practice of zeroing). If an "as such" challenge is not possible, it may be necessary to bring a case each time that a measure is applied.

(2) The Appellate Body mentions at the end of paragraph 74 that in principle it is possible to bring an "as such" challenge to non-mandatory measures. This somewhat obscure reference concerns what is known as the mandatory-discretionary distinction, which dates from the days of GATT. A GATT panel once stated that:

> panels had consistently ruled that legislation which mandated action inconsistent with the General Agreement could be challenged as such, whereas legislation which merely gave the discretion to the executive authority of a contracting party to act inconsistently with the General Agreement could not be challenged as such; only the actual application of such legislation inconsistent with the General Agreement could be subject to challenge.

United States—Measures Affecting the Importation, Internal Sale and Use of Tobacco, 41st Supp. BISD 131, para. 118, adopted October 4, 1994. For example, a specific subsidy grant may be found to violate the SCM Agreement's ban on export subsidies, but can the general law under which such a subsidy was granted also be challenged, assuming that it effectively permits, but does not require, the grant of illegal export subsidies? Panels have continued to recognize the distinction, although the Appellate Body has never explicitly endorsed it. Can an argument be fashioned that a discretionary power to violate WTO rules could in itself be a violation of those rules because of the nature of the obligation contained in those rules? For example, what if the obligation were to not threaten to do something? Is Article XVI:4 of the WTO Agreement relevant to this issue? The mandatory-discretionary distinction was considered in the *US Section 301* case, which was a challenge to a US law authorizing USTR to investigate and to take retaliatory action against foreign trade practices that were found by USTR to be unfair. Once an investigation was opened, the statute required USTR to take certain actions by certain dates. The EC argued that these require-ments meant the US was in violation of DSU article 23.1, which requires WTO members to use and abide by the results of WTO dispute settlement procedures when they seek redress of WTO claims. The US conceded that the Section 301 procedures applied to WTO claims, but argued that USTR had sufficient discretion to ensure that the US would use and abide by the results of WTO dispute settlement. The panel's approach was as follows:

> 7.53   Despite the centrality of [the mandatory-discretionary distinction] in the submissions of both parties, we believe that resolving the dispute as to which type of legislation, *in abstract*, is capable of violating WTO obligations is not germane to the resolution of the type of claims before us. In our view the appropriate method in cases such as this is to examine with care the nature of the WTO obligation at issue and to evaluate the measure in question in the light of such examination. The question is then whether, on the correct interpretation of the specific WTO obligation at issue, only mandatory or also discretionary national laws are prohibited. We do not accept the legal logic that there has to be one fast and hard rule covering all domestic legislation. After all, is it so implausible that the framers of the WTO Agreement, in their wisdom, would have crafted some obligations which would render illegal even discretionary legislation and crafted other obligations prohibiting only mandatory legislation? Whether or not Section 304 violates Article 23 depends, thus, first and foremost on the precise obligations contained in Article 23.

* * *

> 7.59   The text of Article 23.1 is simple enough: Members are obligated generally to (a) have recourse to and (b) abide by DSU rules and procedures. These rules and procedures include most specifically in Article 23.2(a) a prohibition on making a unilateral determination of inconsistency prior to exhaustion of DSU proceedings. As a plain textual matter, therefore, could it not be said that statutory language of a Member specifically authorizing a determination of inconsistency prior to exhaustion of DSU procedures violates the ordinary meaning of Members' obligations under Article 23?

> 7.60   Put differently, cannot the raw text of Articles 23.2(a) and 23.1 be read as constituting a mutual promise among WTO members giving each other a guarantee enshrined in an international legal obligation, that certain specific conduct will not take place? Does not the text of Article 23.1 in particular suggest that this promise has been breached and the guarantee compromised when a Member puts in place legisla-tion which explicitly allows it to do that which it promised not to do?

7.61   On this reading, the very discretion granted under Section 304, which under the US argument absolves the legislation, is what, in our eyes, creates the presumptive violation. The statutory language which gives the USTR this discretion on its face precludes the US from abiding by its obligations under the WTO. In each and every case when a determination is made whilst DSU proceedings are not yet exhausted, Members locked in a dispute with the US will be subject to a mandatory determination by the USTR under a statute which explicitly puts them in that very danger which Article 23 was intended to remove.

The panel ultimately concluded that the US had made commitments to apply the Section 301 procedures consistently with WTO rules, including DSU article 23.1, and accordingly rejected the EC challenge. Each side claimed victory—the US because it technically won; the EC because the US had firmly committed always to use WTO procedures before retaliating—and neither appealed. Section 301, unilateralism and DSU article 23 are considered in more detail in Section 7.4(F) infra.

(3) Article 6.2 of the DSU requires that a request for panel establishment "identify the specific measures at issue and provide a brief summary of the legal basis of the complaint sufficient to present the problem clearly". Pursuant to DSU article 7 and practice, the panel request effectively establishes a panel's terms of reference. In deciding whether the requirements of article 6.2 have been met, the Appellate Body has focused on their due process rationale, that is to ensure that a respondent has adequate notice of what it must defend. Consequently, respondents have found it difficult to challenge claims by arguing that the panel request was insufficient, especially if they are unable to show prejudice. In practice, a panel request that specifies a measure is typically held to include various closely related measures (e.g., implementing measures, successive measures). Article 6.2 also presents the question of how much legal argument must be included in a panel request. Often, panel requests simply identify a measure and assert that it violates a list of specific WTO provisions. Is that sufficient for purposes of article 6.2? From the cases, it seems that if the provision listed is specific enough in that it encompasses one basic obligation, the mere listing will be deemed to present the problem clearly. Of course, if a provision is not listed specifically, no claim may be based on it.

(4) An additional problem in defining what constitutes a challengeable measure and what claims may be made against it arises under DSU article 21.5, which applies to disputes arising out of "measures taken to comply" with DSB recommendations. Article 21.5 proceedings are typically somewhat faster than regular panel proceedings, so they are preferred by frustrated complainants asserting non-implementation of DSB recommendations. As to how broadly the availability of article 21.5 proceedings should be, the Appellate Body has noted (*Canada–Aircraft (Article 21.5–Brazil)*, para. 41):

> [I]n carrying out its review under Article 21.5 of the DSU, a panel is not confined to examining the "measures taken to comply" from the perspective of the claims, arguments and factual circumstances that related to the measure that was the subject of the original proceedings. Although these may have some relevance in proceedings under Article 21.5 of the DSU, Article 21.5 proceedings involve, in principle, not the

original measure, but rather a new and different measure which was not before the original panel. * * * It is natural, therefore, that the claims, arguments and factual circumstances which are pertinent to the "measure taken to comply" will not, necessarily, be the same as those which were pertinent in the original dispute. Indeed, the utility of the review envisaged under Article 21.5 of the DSU would be seriously undermined if a panel were restricted to examining the new measure from the perspective of the claims, arguments and factual circumstances that related to the original measure, because an Article 21.5 panel would then be unable to examine fully the "consistency with a covered agreement of the measures taken to comply", as required by Article 21.5 of the DSU.

(5) The difficulty of defining what constitutes a challengeable measure arises in other contexts as well. For example, can private actions be challenged? See *Japan Film*, paras. 10.52–10.56, quoted in Section 7.4(A) supra. Does a measure have to be legally binding to be challengeable? See *Japan Semiconductors*, quoted in Section 9.2 infra.

(C) INTERPRETATION OF WTO AGREEMENTS

(1) *The Vienna Convention on the Law of Treaties*

DSU article 3.2 provides that the dispute settlement system serves to "clarify the existing provisions of [the WTO] agreements in accordance with the customary rules of interpretation of public international law". The Appellate Body has ruled that those rules are found in articles 31 and 32 of the Vienna Convention on the Law of Treaties. In Section 5.2(C) supra, we considered the Vienna Convention in general. In this section, we consider how the Appellate Body has used those rules in interpreting WTO obligations and consider some other sources that may aid in interpretation. In addition, we examine the idea of precedent in WTO dispute settlement and consider the interpretation problems raised by conflicting norms.

VIENNA CONVENTION ON THE LAW OF TREATIES

Signed 23 May 1969, entered into force 27 January 1980.

ARTICLE 31—GENERAL RULE OF INTERPRETATION

1. A treaty shall be interpreted in good faith in accordance with the ordinary meaning to be given to the terms of the treaty in their context and in the light of its object and purpose.

2. The context for the purpose of the interpretation of a treaty shall comprise, in addition to the text, including its preamble and annexes:

> (a) any agreement relating to the treaty which was made between all the parties in connexion with the conclusion of the treaty;

> (b) any instrument which was made by one or more parties in connexion with the conclusion of the treaty and accepted by the other parties as an instrument related to the treaty.

3.   There shall be taken into account, together with the context:

(a) any subsequent agreement between the parties regarding the interpretation of the treaty or the application of its provisions;

(b) any subsequent practice in the application of the treaty which establishes the agreement of the parties regarding its interpretation;

(c) any relevant rules of international law applicable in the relations between the parties.

4.   A special meaning shall be given to a term if it is established that the parties so intended.

ARTICLE 32—SUPPLEMENTARY MEANS OF INTERPRETATION

Recourse may be had to supplementary means of interpretation, including the preparatory work of the treaty and the circumstances of its conclusion, in order to confirm the meaning resulting from the application of article 31, or to determine the meaning when the interpretation according to article 31: (a) leaves the meaning ambiguous or obscure; or (b) leads to a result which is manifestly absurd or unreasonable.

———

As indicated in the list in Section 5.2(C) supra, not all WTO members are parties to the Vienna Convention. Indeed, the United States has not ratified it. It is generally accepted, however, that articles 31 and 32 do represent the "customary rules of interpretation of public international law" referred to in DSU article 3.2.

There are many questions raised by these rules. Where does one look for the ordinary meaning of terms? When "parties" are referred to in the VCLT, does it mean *all* parties? If not, which parties? Are there limits on what can be used as supplementary means of interpretation? The following case discusses many of these issues in the setting of a tariff classification dispute.

EUROPEAN COMMUNITIES—CUSTOMS CLASSIFICATION OF FROZEN BONELESS CHICKEN CUTS

WT/DS269/AB/R.
Appellate Body Report adopted September 27, 2005.

[Brazil and Thailand export frozen boneless chicken cuts with a salt content of 1.2%—3% to the EC. The dispute centered on whether the chicken cuts in question should be classified under tariff heading 02.10, which applies to "meat * * *, salted, in brine, dried or smoked". The frozen chicken cuts at issue clearly qualified as meat that had been salted. The basic issue in the case was whether they had been sufficiently "salted". The EC argued that heading 2.10 was limited to products that had been "deeply and homogenously impregnated with a level of salt sufficient to ensure long-term preservation". The level of salt content in the Brazilian and Thai chicken cuts was admittedly not sufficient to ensure long-term preservation.]

VII.   INTERPRETATION OF THE EC SCHEDULE IN THE LIGHT
OF ARTICLE 31 OF THE VIENNA CONVENTION

A.   *The Ordinary Meaning of the Term "Salted" in Heading 02.10 of the EC Schedule*

172.   The Panel divided its analysis of the "ordinary meaning", pursuant to Article 31(1) of the Vienna Convention, into two parts. First, the Panel examined the "ordinary meaning of the term 'salted' in subheading 0210.90.20"; in this part of its analysis, the Panel examined, exclusively, dictionary definitions of the term "to salt", finding that "the ordinary meaning of the term 'salted' includes to season, to add salt, to flavour with salt, to treat, to cure or to preserve". Secondly, in a section entitled "Factual context for the consideration of the ordinary meaning", the Panel examined three aspects, namely, the "products covered by the concession contained in heading 02.10"; the "flavour, texture, [and] other physical properties" of the products; and "preservation".

173.   The Panel concluded that "in essence, the ordinary meaning of the term 'salted' when considered in its factual context indicates that the character of a product has been altered through the addition of salt." The Panel further found that "there is nothing in the range of meanings comprising the ordinary meaning of the term 'salted' that indicates that chicken to which salt has been added is not covered by the concession contained in heading 02.10." At the same time, the Panel held that the ordinary meaning of the term "salted" was not dispositive of the question whether or not the specific products at issue were covered by the concession in heading 02.10.

* * *

175.   * * * The Appellate Body has observed that dictionaries are a "useful starting point" for the analysis of "ordinary meaning" of a treaty term, but they are not necessarily dispositive. The ordinary meaning of a treaty term must be ascertained according to the particular circumstances of each case. Importantly, the ordinary meaning of a treaty term must be seen in the light of the intention of the parties "as expressed in the words used by them against the light of the surrounding circumstances".

176.   * * * [T]here is no reference in the Vienna Convention to "factual context" as a separate analytical step under Article 31. * * * The Panel's consideration of these elements [listed in para. 172] under "ordinary meaning" of the term "salted" complemented its analysis of the dictionary definitions of that term. * * * [E]ven if * * * these elements are not to be considered under "ordinary meaning", they certainly could be considered under "context". Interpretation pursuant to the customary rules codified in Article 31 of the Vienna Convention is ultimately a holistic exercise that should not be mechanically subdivided

into rigid components. Considering particular surrounding circumstances under the rubric of "ordinary meaning" or "in the light of its context" would not, in our view, change the outcome of treaty interpretation. Therefore, we find no error in the Panel's interpretive approach.

* * *

B. *"Context"*

189. In interpreting the term "salted" in its context, pursuant to Article 31(2) of the Vienna Convention, the Panel considered "the terms of relevant aspects of the EC Schedule", namely, the "other terms" contained in heading 02.10, the structure of Chapter 2 of the EC Schedule, as well as "other parts of the EC Schedule". The Panel then proceeded to consider whether there are any other agreements or instruments that qualify as "context" under Article 31(2) of the Vienna Convention; in that category, the Panel examined the Harmonized System [discussed in Casebook Section 8.3] as well as the Schedules of WTO Members other than the European Communities. [The Panel then concluded that an examination of the context of the term "salted" did not alter its findings on the ordinary meaning of the term and did not indicate that heading 02.10 is necessarily characterized by a notion of long-term preservation.]

* * *

195. The Harmonized System is not, formally, part of the WTO Agreement, as it has not been incorporated, in whole or in part, into that Agreement. Nevertheless, the concept of "context", under Article 31, is not limited to the treaty text—namely, the WTO Agreement—but may also extend to "any agreement relating to the treaty which was made between all the parties in connection with the conclusion of the treaty", within the meaning of Article 31(2)(a) of the Vienna Convention, and to "any instrument which was made by one or more parties in connection with the conclusion of the treaty and accepted by the other parties as an instrument related to the treaty", within the meaning of Article 31(2)(b) of the Vienna Convention. Moreover, should the criteria in Article 31(3)(c) be fulfilled, the Harmonized System may qualify as a "relevant rule[] of international law applicable in the relations between the parties".

196. The Panel noted that the membership of the Harmonized System is "extremely broad" and includes the "vast majority of WTO Members". The Panel also pointed out, and no participant to this proceeding contested, that "the [Harmonized System] was used as a basis for the preparation of the Uruguay Round GATT schedules". * * * [After noting other connections between GATT/WTO and the Harmonized System, the Appellate Body concluded that "there was broad consensus among the GATT Contracting Parties to use the Harmonized System as the basis for their WTO Schedules" and that "this consensus constitutes an 'agreement' between WTO Members 'relating to' the WTO Agreement that was 'made in connection with the conclusion of'

that Agreement, within the meaning of Article 31(2)(a).'' Accordingly, the Appellate Body considered the Harmonized System to be relevant for interpreting WTO tariff commitments.]

* * *

210.   [In considering context, we now] turn to the terms other than "salted" in heading 02.10.

* * *

212.   [W]e are not convinced that the terms "dried, in brine and smoked" refer exclusively to the concept of "preservation". We note that the dictionary meaning of the term "to dry" is, in relevant part, "to remove the moisture from by wiping, evaporation, draining; preserve (food, etc.) by the removal of its natural moisture"; in turn, the dictionary meaning of the term "to smoke" is to "dry or cure (meat, fish, etc.) by exposure to smoke". The ordinary meanings of these terms suggest that the relevant processes can be applied to meat in various ways and degrees of intensity, thereby producing different effects on the meat, effects that may or may not place the meat in a state of "preservation". Nor are we persuaded by the European Communities' argument that the terms "dried" and "smoked", in the present context, "concern [exclusively] means to preserve". It is clear from the evidence on the record that, while the processes mentioned in heading 02.10—"salted, dried, in brine and smoked"—may include the notion of "preservation", these processes are also used extensively to confer special characteristics on meat products. Similar reasoning may also be valid with respect to the term "smoked".

* * *

[In further considering context, the Appellate Body referred to the Explanatory Note to heading 02.10 of the Harmonized System, which provides: "This heading applies to all kinds of meat and edible meat offal which have been *prepared* as described in the heading, other than pig fat, free of lean meat, and poultry fat, not rendered or otherwise extracted (heading 02.09)." (emphasis added) It also considered the Chapter Note to Chapter 16, which excludes from Chapter 16 products that are "prepared or preserved" by the processes specified, inter alia, in Chapter 2.]

225.   We also agree with Brazil and Thailand that the Explanatory Note to heading 02.10—which refers to meat that has been "prepared", but does not mention "preserved"—suggests that heading 02.10 is characterized by the notion of "preparation". Brazil and Thailand argue that products subject to one of the processes referred to in heading 02.10, but not necessarily placed in a state of "preservation" by application of these processes, would fall under heading 02.10. Such a conclusion, therefore, would preclude a reading of the term "salted" as suggested by the European Communities, namely, as referring exclusively to meat that has been "salted" so as to place the meat in a state of

"preservation". The reading suggested by Brazil and Thailand would appear to be supported by the fact that other Notes to the Harmonized System (most importantly, the Chapter Note to Chapter 16) use the terms "prepared", "preserved", and "preservation", suggesting that the use of the term "prepared" alone, without reference to "preserved", in the Explanatory Note to heading 02.10, is not inadvertent.

* * *

229.   As a result, we conclude that the Harmonized System and the relevant Chapter and Explanatory Notes thereto do not support the view that heading 02.10 is characterised exclusively by the concept of preservation. * * *

IX.   OBJECT AND PURPOSE

A. *Object and Purpose of the Treaty or of a Particular Treaty Provision*

238.   We begin our analysis with the question whether the Panel incorrectly distinguished between the object and purpose of the treaty and that of its individual provisions. It is well accepted that the use of the singular word "its" preceding the term "object and purpose" in Article 31(1) of the Vienna Convention indicates that the term refers to the treaty as a whole; had the term "object and purpose" been preceded by the word "their", the use of the plural would have indicated a reference to particular "treaty terms". Thus, the term "its object and purpose" makes it clear that the starting point for ascertaining "object and purpose" is the treaty itself, in its entirety. At the same time, we do not believe that Article 31(1) excludes taking into account the object and purpose of particular treaty terms, if doing so assists the interpreter in determining the treaty's object and purpose on the whole. We do not see why it would be necessary to divorce a treaty's object and purpose from the object and purpose of specific treaty provisions, or vice versa. To the extent that one can speak of the "object and purpose of a treaty provision", it will be informed by, and will be in consonance with, the object and purpose of the entire treaty of which it is but a component.

239.   Having said this, we caution against interpreting WTO law in the light of the purported "object and purpose" of specific provisions, paragraphs or subparagraphs of the WTO agreements, or tariff headings in Schedules, in isolation from the object and purpose of the treaty on the whole. Even if, arguendo, one could rely on the specific "object and purpose" of heading 02.10 in isolation, we would share the Panel's view that "one Member's unilateral object and purpose for the conclusion of a tariff commitment cannot form the basis" for an interpretation of that commitment, because interpretation in the light of Articles 31 and 32 of the Vienna Convention must focus on ascertaining the common intentions of the parties.

X.   SUBSEQUENT PRACTICE

251.   The European Communities appeals the Panel's finding that the European Communities' practice, between 1996 and 2002, of classifying the products at issue under heading 02.10 amounts to "subsequent

practice" within the meaning of Article 31(3)(b) of the Vienna Convention * * *.

* * *

254.   This issue raises the following questions: (i) what may qualify as "practice"? [and] (ii) how does one establish the agreement of the parties who have not engaged in the practice at issue? * * *

A.   *What May Qualify as Practice?*

255.   At the outset, we observe that "subsequent practice" in the application of a treaty may be an important element in treaty interpretation because "it constitutes objective evidence of the understanding of the parties as to the meaning of the treaty".

* * *

257.   In *US–Gambling*, the Appellate Body clarified that establishing "subsequent practice" within the meaning of Article 31(3)(b) involves two elements:

> . . . (i) there must be a common, consistent, discernible pattern of acts or pronouncements; *and* (ii) those acts or pronouncements must imply *agreement* on the interpretation of the relevant provision. (original emphasis)

258.   The Panel considered that the main question in the case at hand was whether "common" and "concordant" practice "necessarily means that all WTO Members must have engaged in a particular practice in order for it to qualify as 'subsequent practice' . . . or whether the practice of a sub-set of the entire WTO-membership, including the practice of one Member only, may suffice." The Panel noted that the International Law Commission ("ILC") had stated that:

> The [original text of Article 31(3)(b) of the Vienna Convention] spoke of a practice which "establishes the understanding of all the parties". By omitting the word "all" [in the final text], the Commission did not intend to change the rule. It considered that the phrase "the understanding of the parties" necessarily means the "parties as a whole". It omitted the word "all" merely to avoid any possible *misconception that every party must individually have engaged in the practice where it suffices that it should have accepted the practice.* (emphasis added)

The Panel inferred from this statement that "it is not necessary to show that all signatories to a treaty must have engaged in a particular practice in order for it to qualify as subsequent practice under Article 31(3)(b)". Rather, "it may be sufficient to show that all parties to the treaty have accepted the relevant practice."

259.   We share the Panel's view that not each and every party must have engaged in a particular practice for it to qualify as a "common" and "concordant" practice. Nevertheless, practice by some, but not all parties is obviously not of the same order as practice by only one, or very

few parties. To our mind, it would be difficult to establish a "concordant, common and discernible pattern" on the basis of acts or pronouncements of one, or very few parties to a multilateral treaty, such as the WTO Agreement. We acknowledge, however, that, if only some WTO Members have actually traded or classified products under a given heading, this circumstance may reduce the availability of such "acts and pronouncements" for purposes of determining the existence of "subsequent practice" within the meaning of Article 31(3)(b).

B. *How Does One Establish Agreement of Parties that Have Not Engaged in a Practice?*

[As to how to establish agreement of parties that have not engaged in a practice, the Panel held that WTO Members that did not "protest" the EC's classification practice from 1996 to 2002 could be presumed to have accepted it.]

281. We * * * have misgivings about deducing, without further inquiry, agreement with a practice from a party's "lack of reaction". We do not exclude that, in specific situations, the "lack of reaction" or silence by a particular treaty party may, in the light of attendant circumstances, be understood as acceptance of the practice of other treaty parties. Such situations may occur when a party that has not engaged in a practice has become or has been made aware of the practice of other parties (for example, by means of notification or by virtue of participation in a forum where it is discussed), but does not react to it. However, we disagree with the Panel that "lack of protest" against one Member's classification practice by other WTO Members may be understood, on its own, as establishing agreement with that practice by those other Members. Therefore, the fact that Brazil and Thailand, having actually exported the products at issue, may have accepted the European Communities' import classification practice under heading 02.10, is not dispositive of whether other Members with actual or potential trade interests have also accepted that practice. We, therefore, disagree with the Panel that "subsequent practice" under Article 31(3)(b) has been established by virtue of the fact that the Panel "[had] not been provided any evidence to indicate that WTO Members protested against the EC classification practice in question from 1996—2002".

XI. INTERPRETATION OF THE EC SCHEDULE IN THE LIGHT OF ARTICLE 32 OF THE VIENNA CONVENTION

282. We begin our analysis by pointing out that the means of interpretation listed in Article 32 are supplementary means to be resorted to when interpretation in the light of Article 31 leaves the meaning of a treaty provision ambiguous or obscure, or, in order to confirm the meaning resulting from the application of the interpretation methods listed in Article 31. * * *

283. We stress, moreover, that Article 32 does not define exhaustively the supplementary means of interpretation to which an interpreter may have recourse. It states only that they include the preparatory work of the treaty and the circumstances of its conclusion. Thus, an interpret-

er has a certain flexibility in considering relevant supplementary means in a given case so as to assist in ascertaining the common intentions of the parties.

[In discussing issues raised concerning what could be considered circumstances of a treaty's conclusion, the Appellate Body noted that (i) "not only 'multilateral' sources, but also 'unilateral' acts, instruments, or statements of individual negotiating parties may be useful in ascertaining 'the reality of the situation which the parties wished to regulate by means of the treaty' and, ultimately, for discerning the common intentions of the parties" (para. 289); (ii) "the precise date of conclusion of a treaty should not be confused with the circumstances that were prevailing at that point in time. Events, acts, and instruments may form part of the 'historical background against which the treaty was negotiated', even when these circumstances predate the point in time when the treaty is concluded, but continue to influence or reflect the common intentions of the parties at the time of conclusion" (para. 293); (iii) "[a]s far as an act or instrument originating from an individual party may be considered to be a circumstance under Article 32 for ascertaining the parties' intentions, we consider that the fact that this act or instrument was officially published, and has been publicly available so that any interested party could have acquired knowledge of it, appears to be enough. Of course, proof of actual knowledge will increase the degree of relevance of a circumstance for interpretation" (para. 297) and (iv) "judgments of domestic courts are not, in principle, excluded from consideration as 'circumstances of the conclusion' of a treaty if they would be of assistance in ascertaining the common intentions of the parties for purposes of interpretation under Article 32. It is necessary to point out, however, that judgments deal basically with a specific dispute and have, by their very nature, less relevance than legislative acts of general application (although judgments may have some precedential effect in certain legal systems)" (para. 309).]

310.   Having discussed the concept of "circumstances of the conclusion of a treaty" within the meaning of Article 32, we turn to reviewing the Panel's findings determining the relevance, for interpreting the term "salted" in the tariff commitment under heading 02.10, of the customs classification legislation, practice, and court judgments of the European Communities (namely, EC Regulation 535/94, the *Dinter* and *Gausepohl* judgments of the ECJ, certain Explanatory Notes to the Combined Nomenclature, and classification practice prior and subsequent to the conclusion of the EC Schedule). We then review whether the elements of the European Communities' law and practice examined by the Panel qualify as supplementary means of interpretation under Article 32 and support the Panel's conclusion with respect to the meaning of the term "salted" in the tariff commitment under heading 02.10.

[The Appellate Body modified certain aspects of the panel's analysis of these issues, but upheld its basic conclusion that these supplementary means of interpretation confirmed that the product at issue should be classified under heading 02.10.]

Notes and Questions

(1) In its initial reports, the Appellate Body relied quite heavily on dictionaries and, in particular, *The New Shorter Oxford English Dictionary*. More recently, its approach has been somewhat more nuanced, as indicated in paragraph 175 of the foregoing case.

(2) The *Chicken Cuts* case contains an extensive discussion of many of the issues that might arise in applying the rules of interpretation of the Vienna Convention. There are, of course, additional issues. For example, in deciding on the ordinary meaning of a term in a WTO agreement, would it be appropriate to look at how that term is defined in other treaties? What if all WTO members are not party to that other treaty? What if not all parties to the dispute are not party to that other treaty? In *US Shrimp* (excerpted in Chapter 13), the Appellate Body made such use of other treaties, even though some of the parties to the dispute had not signed or ratified them. Was that appropriate? Is it different than looking at various dictionaries to divine ordinary meaning?

(3) In interpreting WTO agreements, one obvious possible source of inspiration and guidance would be public international law. Is it appropriate for the Appellate Body to look to international law for answers? Or would that potentially violate the directive in DSU article 3.2 that dispute settlement should not add to or diminish the rights and obligations contained in the WTO agreements? In *US Gasoline*, the Appellate Body noted that the directive in article 3.2 "reflects a measure of recognition that the General Agreement is not to be read in clinical isolation from public international law". See Section 13.4 infra. In *US Shrimp* (para. 158), it stated: "[O]ur task here is to interpret the language of [GATT Article XX], seeking additional interpretative guidance, as appropriate, from the general principles of international law" and cited article 31(3)(c) of the Vienna Convention. In light of DSU article 3 and its emphasis that dispute settlement not change the rights and obligations of WTO members as expressed in the covered agreements, the United States has expressed concern in the DSU reform negotiations about the use of international law principles in WTO dispute settlement. TN/DS/W/82 (October 24, 2005). Do share such concern?

(2) The Role of Precedent

We have previously considered the role of precedent in general in Section 5.2(E) and that material should be reviewed before reading the following case.

UNITED STATES—FINAL ANTI–DUMPING MEASURES ON STAINLESS STEEL FROM MEXICO

WT/DS244/R.
Panel Report subject to appeal and modification.

[This case involved a challenge to an antidumping duty. The rules for applying such duties are examined in Chapter 16. At issue here is a practice known as "zeroing", which is a controversial technique for calculating average levels of dumping.]

7.101 We recall that this is not the first case in the WTO in which simple zeroing in periodic reviews has been challenged. The WTO-consistency of simple zeroing in periodic reviews was questioned before the panels in *US–Zeroing (EC)* and *US–Zeroing (Japan)*. In both cases, the panels found this practice not to be inconsistent with the obligations set out in the relevant provisions cited by the complaining parties. We also recall that the Appellate Body reversed the decisions of both panels and found simple zeroing in periodic reviews to be WTO-inconsistent.

7.102   We recall that we are not, strictly speaking, bound by previous Appellate Body or panel decisions that have addressed the same issue, *i.e.* simple zeroing in periodic reviews, which is before us in these proceedings. There is no provision in the DSU that requires WTO panels to follow the findings of previous panels or the Appellate Body on the same issues brought before them. In principle, a panel or Appellate Body decision only binds the parties to the relevant dispute. Certain provisions of the DSU, in our view, support this proposition. According to Article 19.2 of the DSU, for example, "[i]n accordance with paragraph 2 of Article 3, in their findings and recommendations, the panel and Appellate Body cannot add to or diminish the rights and obligations provided in the covered agreements". In the same vein, Article 3.2 of the DSU provides that "[r]ecommendations and rulings of the DSB cannot add to or diminish the rights and obligations provided in the covered agreements".

7.103   We also note, however, the Appellate Body's pronouncement, in *Japan–Alcoholic Beverages II*, regarding the impact of adopted panel reports for future panels dealing with similar issues. The Appellate Body opined:

> "Adopted panel reports are an important part of the GATT *acquis*. They are often considered by subsequent panels. They create legitimate expectations among WTO Members, and, therefore, should be taken into account where they are relevant to any dispute. However, they are not binding, except with respect to resolving the particular dispute between the parties to that dispute. In short, their character and their legal status have not been changed by the coming into force of the *WTO Agreement.*"

7.104   The above excerpt indicates that, although adopted panel reports only bind the parties to the dispute that they concern, the Appellate Body expects future panels to take them into account to the extent that the issues before them are similar to those addressed by previous panels. In *US–Shrimp (Article 21.5–Malaysia)*, the Appellate Body reiterated its findings in *Japan–Alcoholic Beverages II* and held that the same analysis applies to adopted Appellate Body reports. The Appellate Body clearly stated that the panel in the implementation proceedings under Article 21.5 of the DSU in *US–Shrimp (Article 21.5–Malaysia)* did not err in following the interpretative guidance provided by the Appellate Body in the original proceedings. To the contrary, the Appellate Body expected the panel to do so. More recently in *US–Oil Country Tubular Goods Sunset Reviews*, the Appellate Body opined that "following the Appellate Body's conclusions in earlier disputes is not only appropriate, but is what would be expected from panels, especially where the issues are the same''.

7.105   This indicates that even though the DSU does not require WTO panels to follow adopted panel or Appellate Body reports, the Appellate Body *de facto* expects them to do so to the extent that the legal issues addressed are similar. We also note, however, that the panel in *US–Zeroing (Japan)*, while recognizing the need to provide security and predictability to the multilateral trading system through the development of a consistent line of jurisprudence on similar legal issues, drew attention to the provisions of Articles 11 and 3.2 of the DSU and implied that the concern over the preservation of a consistent line of jurisprudence should not override a panel's task to carry out an objective examination of the matter before it through an interpretation of the relevant treaty provisions in accordance with the customary rules of interpretation of public international law. We also share the concern raised by the panel in *US–Zeroing (Japan)* regarding WTO panels' obligation to carry out an objective examination of the matter referred to them by the DSB.

7.106   After a careful consideration of the matters discussed above, we have decided that we have no option but to respectfully disagree with the line of reasoning developed by the Appellate Body regarding the WTO-consistency of simple zeroing in periodic reviews. We are cognizant of the fact that in two previous cases, *US–Zeroing (EC)* and *US–Zeroing (Japan)*, the decisions of panels that found simple zeroing in periodic reviews to be WTO-consistent were reversed by the Appellate Body and that our reasoning set out below is very similar to these panel decisions. In light of our obligation under Article 11 of the DSU to carry out an objective examination of the matter referred to us by the DSB, however, we have felt compelled to depart from the Appellate Body's approach for the reasons explained below.

Notes and Questions

(1) The panel was reversed, of course. In doing so, the Appellate Body had occasion to express its views on the obligation of a panel to follow Appellate Body decisions, as follows:

> 160.   Dispute settlement practice demonstrates that WTO Members attach significance to reasoning provided in previous panel and Appellate Body reports. Adopted panel and Appellate Body reports are often cited by parties in support of legal arguments in dispute settlement proceedings, and are relied upon by panels and the Appellate Body in subsequent disputes. In addition, when enacting or modifying laws and national regulations pertaining to international trade matters, WTO Members take into account the legal interpretation of the covered agreements developed in adopted panel and Appellate Body reports. Thus, the legal interpretation embodied in adopted panel and Appellate Body reports becomes part and parcel of the *acquis* of the WTO dispute settlement system. Ensuring "security and predictability" in the dispute settlement system, as contemplated in Article 3.2 of the DSU, implies

that, absent cogent reasons, an adjudicatory body will resolve the same legal question in the same way in a subsequent case.

161. In the hierarchical structure contemplated in the DSU, panels and the Appellate Body have distinct roles to play. * * * The creation of the Appellate Body by WTO Members to review legal interpretations developed by panels shows that Members recognized the importance of consistency and stability in the interpretation of their rights and obligations under the covered agreements. This is essential to promote "security and predictability" in the dispute settlement system, and to ensure the "prompt settlement" of disputes. The Panel's failure to follow previously adopted Appellate Body reports addressing the same issues undermines the development of a coherent and predictable body of jurisprudence clarifying Members' rights and obligations under the covered agreements as contemplated under the DSU. Clarification, as envisaged in Article 3.2 of the DSU, elucidates the scope and meaning of the provisions of the covered agreements in accordance with customary rules of interpretation of public international law. While the application of a provision may be regarded as confined to the context in which it takes place, the relevance of clarification contained in adopted Appellate Body reports is not limited to the application of a particular provision in a specific case.

162. We are deeply concerned about the Panel's decision to depart from well-established Appellate Body jurisprudence clarifying the interpretation of the same legal issues. The Panel's approach has serious implications for the proper functioning of the WTO dispute settlement system, as explained above. Nevertheless, we consider that the Panel's failure flowed, in essence, from its misguided understanding of the legal provisions at issue. Since we have corrected the Panel's erroneous legal interpretation and have reversed all of the Panel's findings and conclusions that have been appealed, we do not, in this case, make an additional finding that the Panel also failed to discharge its duties under Article 11 of the DSU.

WT/DS344/AB/R, adopted May 20, 2008. Do you agree? What can a panel do if it disagrees strongly with Appellate Body precedent?

(2) The Appellate Body defines the WTO *acquis* as including adopted panel reports in paragraph 160. Would you expect the Appellate Body to accord any deference to an adopted, but unappealed panel report?

(3) The Appellate Body's zeroing jurisprudence has been quite controversial, in part because it initially seemed to have difficulty in coming up with a clear, consistent rationale for its decisions. But given that Appellate Body has now seemed to have decided upon a rationale, is the panel's action at all appropriate? Would your answer be different, if there had not been a prior panel report on the same issue (*US–Zeroing (Japan)*) that had rejected the Appellate Body's ruling and been reversed? As noted in Section 5.2(E) supra, cases decided by the International Court of Justice are not viewed as creating binding precedent. Should that be relevant for WTO practice?

(4) A new Appellate Body member took office at the end of 2006, with two other new members assuming their duties at the end of 2007 and two more in the Spring of 2008. Should this large-scale shift of membership play

a role in a panel's decision to follow Appellate Body precedent? Interestingly, one of the new members of the Appellate Body was a panelist in *US–Zeroing (Japan)*.

(5) How can panelists square their DSU Article 11 obligation to make an objective assessment with Appellate Body decisions that they believe are wrong?

(3) Conflicts of Norms[9]

Given the wide scope of the WTO agreements and the fact that they were often negotiated in separate negotiating groups, it seems inevitable that there may be overlapping or even conflicting obligations in some cases. While the agreements themselves provide some means for resolving potential conflicts, others potential conflicts are not dealt with at all.

The WTO Agreement provides in Article XVI:3 that in the event of a conflict between it and any of the other WTO agreements, the WTO Agreement prevails. In the event of a conflict between GATT 1994 and any of the other Annex 1A agreements (i.e., the other agreements on trade in goods), the provisions of the other agreement prevail. WTO Agreement, Annex 1A, general interpretative note. There are no provisions, however, that deal generally with conflicts between the various agreements on trade in goods, although there are specific provisions in certain cases. For example, the Agriculture Agreement provides that GATT 1994 and the other Annex 1A agreements are subject to it (art. 21.1). There are also no general provisions dealing with conflicts involving the agreements on services (GATS) or intellectual property (TRIPS Agreement).

Under the general rules of public international law on conflicts, a treaty interpreter should attempt to interpret the relevant agreements so that there is no conflict, i.e., so that the agreements are compatible. However, as regards treaties having incompatible provisions, the relation of treaties between the same parties and with overlapping provisions is primarily a matter of interpretation, aided by presumptions. First, it is to be presumed that a later treaty prevails over an earlier treaty concerning the same subject matter. Second, a treaty may provide expressly that it is to prevail over subsequent incompatible treaties. These principles are not very pertinent for resolving the relationship between GATT, GATS and the TRIPS Agreement or between the various Annex 1A agreements. All agreements within the WTO framework have been concluded as a single treaty and at the same time—including GATT 1994—which renders the later-in-time rule inapposite. To some extent, the principle of effective treaty interpretation may be useful in avoiding incompatibilities between obligations provided for in the various WTO agreements.

9. This section draws extensively upon William J. Davey & Werner Zdouc, The Triangle of TRIPS, GATT and GATS, in Thomas Cottier & Petros C. Mavroidis (eds.), Intellectual Property: Trade, Competition and Sustainable Development 53–84 (2003).

WTO panels have had to define the notion of conflict for purposes of applying the General Interpretative Note to Annex 1A, which provides that in the event of a conflict between GATT 1994 and the other agreements on trade in goods, the other agreements prevail. In *EC Bananas III,* the panel concluded that the national treatment and MFN clauses of GATT 1994 and provisions of the TRIMs Agreement and the Agreement on Import Licensing Procedures (Licensing Agreement) could simultaneously apply to the same measure, i.e., the EC regime on the importation, sale and distribution of bananas. In dicta, the panel developed a broad notion of "conflict" between obligations contained in GATT 1994 and those provided for in the other Annex 1A agreements. It presumed such a conflict to exist not only in a situation where one agreement explicitly mandates what another agreement explicitly prohibits, but also in a situation where one agreement explicitly permits what another explicitly forbids. The panel acknowledged that in the latter case a Member could comply with both rules by not resorting to the right conferred by the permissive rule in order not to violate the prohibitive rule. However, it deemed such a result to be contrary to the principle of effective treaty interpretation because no meaning would be given to the permissive rule which would become entirely redundant. The panel gave the example of quantitative restrictions permitted by the safeguard provisions of the Agreement on Textiles and Clothing (ATC) which on their face are incompatible with the general prohibition of quantitative restrictions in Article XI of GATT.

In the *Indonesia Autos* case, the panel adopted a narrower notion of what constitutes a conflict than had the *Bananas* panel, essentially concluding that a conflict in the meaning of the Note to Annex 1A exists only in cases where one rule explicitly prohibits what another rule explicitly requires a Member to do. It is unclear, however, whether—as a result of this narrower notion of conflict—that panel would have answered differently the hypothetical posed by the *Bananas* panel, i.e., the relation between a prohibitive and a permissive rule. Given the *Indonesia Autos* panel's reliance in general on the principle of effective treaty interpretation, it is probably more appropriate to assume that this panel would have reached a conclusion similar to that of the *Bananas* panel. However, it would probably have reached that conclusion without labeling the relationship between a prohibitive and a permissive rule a situation of conflict, but it would likely have reasoned that effective treaty interpretation required it to give meaning to the conditional derogation under the safeguards clause of the ATC notwithstanding the general prohibition of quotas under GATT.

Notes and Questions

(1) Are you satisfied that the foregoing cases dealing with conflicts adequately address the issues? How broadly should the term "conflict" be defined? The issue of conflicts between GATT and GATS arose in *Canada Periodicals* and *EC Bananas III.* It is further explored in Chapter 19.

(2) How should a conflict between an obligation in a WTO agreement and a non-WTO-related agreement be analyzed? Consider the principles outlined above and article 31 of the Vienna Convention on the Law of Treaties. See Sections 11.3 and 13.6 infra (considering NAFTA and MEAs, respectively).

(D) BALANCING POLITICAL AND JUDICIAL POWER: STANDARDS OF REVIEW AND TECHNIQUES OF JUDICIAL RESTRAINT

The decisions of the dispute settlement system are adopted automatically, as long as there is not a consensus against adoption. In comparison, decisions by other WTO bodies are traditionally taken by a positive consensus in favor of a proposal. This difference means that it may be very difficult, if not impossible, for the WTO General Council to change an interpretation of a WTO agreement by a panel or the Appellate Body, even if there is widespread dissatisfaction with the interpretation amongst the WTO membership. For example, as discussed in Section 7.4(E)(2), the Appellate Body has ruled that it has the power to accept amicus submissions from individuals and entities that are not WTO members, such as non-governmental organizations. The Appellate Body decisions on amicus submissions have been harshly criticized by many WTO members in meetings of the WTO General Council and the DSB. Yet, as long as even one member supports the decisions, it is not possible to achieve a consensus to change them.

One can ask if this power imbalance is worrisome. As we will see in the remainder of the casebook, some dispute settlement cases have involved very controversial issues and it is highly probable that there will additional controversial cases in the future. Moreover, to the extent that the Doha negotiations remain stalled or achieve only limited results, WTO members may be tempted to use the dispute settlement system to try to achieve what has eluded them in negotiations. Indeed, as noted in Section 7.3(B), there have a number of cases brought in recent years that may have been designed to affect the negotiations, such as the *US Cotton* and *EC Sugar* cases. Do these possibilities suggest that panels and the Appellate Body should exercise judicial restraint to a greater degree than national courts, whose decisions on statutory and even constitutional interpretations are more easily changed by national legislatures?

In this subsection we examine the standard of review that the Appellate Body has used to evaluate government measures and actions. One can ask if it is appropriately deferential. We then consider a number of techniques of judicial restraint.

(1) WTO Rules on Standard of Review[10]

One of the more difficult problems faced in recent years by the WTO dispute settlement system is the choice of appropriate standards of

---

10. Generally on this subject see, Steven P. Croley & John H. Jackson, WTO Dispute Procedures, Standard of Review, and Deference to National Governments, 90 Am. J.Intl.L. 193 (1996), revised version in John H. Jackson, The Jurisprudence of GATT and the WTO, ch. 11 (2000).

review. The issue arises when the panel must review a national statute or administrative action where the issue is whether a specified standard contained in the WTO rules has been met. To take concrete examples, how much deference should a panel give to the decision of a national antidumping authority that the facts presented demonstrate material injury to domestic industry? How much deference should be given to a national health authority's decision to adopt a national safety standard that is stricter than an existing internationally accepted standard, where the national authority argues that its standard is appropriate given the state of (or lack of) scientific knowledge? In each of these cases, the basic question is whether the panel may (or should) reassess the facts presented to the national decisionmaker to determine if the panel agrees that they meet the WTO rule. Similar issues arise in national court review of administrative agency action. See Section 3.5 supra.

This problem had already arisen frequently in antidumping cases considered by panels established under the 1979 Antidumping Code. In large part as a result of concerns raised by the United States, the WTO Antidumping Agreement provides in article 17.6 that

> (i) in its assessment of the facts of the matter, the panel shall determine whether the [national antidumping] authorities establishment of the facts was proper and whether their evaluation of those facts was unbiased and objective. If the establishment of the facts was proper and the evaluation was unbiased and objective, even though the panel might have reached a different conclusion, the evaluation shall not be overturned;

> (ii) the panel shall interpret the relevant provisions of the [Antidumping] Agreement in accordance with customary rules of interpretation of public international law. Where the panel finds that a relevant provision of the Agreement admits of more than one permissible interpretation, the panel shall find the authorities' measure to be in conformity with the Agreement if it rests upon one of those permissible interpretations.

Do you think that this provision effectively prevents panels from second-guessing factual determinations of national authorities? If so, do you think it is appropriate? What does the second clause mean? What are the customary rules? How often would you expect panels to decide that the agreement could be interpreted in several different ways? It is worth noting that in the national context, respecting administrative discretion on the interpretation of a rule does not necessarily lead to inconsistent application of a rule, so long as the agency acts on a consistent basis. But on the international level, allowing different interpretations of a WTO agreement by national authorities means that there is no consistency because there is no longer one international rule. What other standards might be used to control panel discretion? Thus far, the Appellate Body has never recognized more than one permissible interpretation of a provision.

On the general issue of the standard of review in WTO cases, the Appellate Body had the following to say in the *EC Hormones* case (discussed in Section 14.2 infra):

114.   The first point that must be made in this connection, is that the SPS Agreement itself is silent on the matter of an appropriate standard of review for panels deciding upon SPS measures of a Member. Nor are there provisions in the DSU or any of the covered agreements (other than [Article 17.6(i) of] the Anti–Dumping Agreement) prescribing a particular standard of review. * * * Textually, Article 17.6(i) is specific to the Anti–Dumping Agreement.

115.   The standard of review appropriately applicable in proceedings under the SPS Agreement, of course, must reflect the balance established in that Agreement between the jurisdictional competences conceded by the Members to the WTO and the jurisdictional competences retained by the Members for themselves. To adopt a standard of review not clearly rooted in the text of the SPS Agreement itself, may well amount to changing that finely drawn balance; and neither a panel nor the Appellate Body is authorized to do that.

116.   We do not mean, however, to suggest that there is at present no standard of review applicable to the determination and assessment of the facts in proceedings under the SPS Agreement or under other covered agreements. In our view, Article 11 of the DSU bears directly on this matter and, in effect, articulates with great succinctness but with sufficient clarity the appropriate standard of review for panels in respect of both the ascertainment of facts and the legal characterization of such facts under the relevant agreements. Article 11 reads thus:

> * * * [A] panel should make *an objective assessment of the matter before it*, including an *objective assessment of the facts* of the case and the *applicability of and conformity with the relevant covered agreements,* * * * (italics by Appellate Body)

117.   So far as fact-finding by panels is concerned, their activities are always constrained by the mandate of Article 11 of the DSU: the applicable standard is neither *de novo* review as such, nor "total deference", but rather the "objective assessment of the facts". Many panels have in the past refused to undertake *de novo* review, wisely, since under current practice and systems, they are in any case poorly suited to engage in such a review. On the other hand, "total deference to the findings of the national authorities", it has been well said, "could not ensure an 'objective assessment' as foreseen by Article 11 of the DSU".

118.   In so far as legal questions are concerned—that is, consistency or inconsistency of a Member's measure with the provisions of the applicable agreement—a standard not found in the text of the SPS

Agreement itself cannot absolve a panel (or the Appellate Body) from the duty to apply the customary rules of interpretation of public international law. It may be noted that the European Communities refrained from suggesting that Article 17.6 of the Anti–Dumping Agreement in its entirety was applicable to the present case. Nevertheless, it is appropriate to stress that here again Article 11 of the DSU is directly on point, requiring a panel to "make an objective assessment of the matter before it, including an objective assessment of the facts of the case and the applicability of and conformity with the relevant covered agreements . . .".

119. We consider, therefore, that the issue of failure to apply an appropriate standard of review, raised by the European Communities, resolves itself into the issue of whether or not the Panel, in making the above and other findings referred to and appealed by the European Communities, had made an "objective assessment of the matter before it, including *an objective assessment of the facts . . .*". This particular issue is addressed (in substantial detail) below. Here, however, we uphold the findings of the Panel appealed by the European Communities upon the ground of failure to apply either a "deferential reasonableness standard" or the standard of review set out in Article 17.6(i) of the Anti-Dumping Agreement.

Notes and Questions

(1) To say that DSU article 11 provides the appropriate standard of review is only a starting point. The next question is how does one perform an objective assessment of the facts? So far, the Appellate Body has seemed to suggest that in matters involving health, governments should be afforded considerable discretion in their decisions on what protections are needed. For example, in the *EC Hormones* case, the Appellate Body noted (para. 194):

> [R]esponsible and representative governments tend to base their legislative and administrative measures on "mainstream" scientific opinion. In other cases, equally responsible and representative governments may act in good faith on the basis of what, at a given time, may be a divergent opinion coming from qualified and respected sources. By itself, this does not necessarily signal the absence of a reasonable relationship between the SPS measure and the risk assessment, especially where the risk involved is life-threatening in character and is perceived to constitute a clear and imminent threat to public health and safety.

In another part of the *Hormones* report, the Appellate Body stated: "We cannot lightly assume that sovereign states intended to impose upon themselves the more onerous, rather than the less burdensome obligation by mandating conformity or compliance with such standards, guidelines and recommendations. To sustain such an assumption and to warrant such a far-reaching interpretation, treaty language far more specific and compelling than that found in Article 3 of the SPS Agreement would be necessary." In a footnote it then referred to the principle of *in dubio mitius,* which it explained as follows: " 'The principle * * * applies in interpreting treaties, in deference to the sovereignty of states. If the meaning of a term is ambiguous, that meaning is to be preferred which is less onerous to the party assuming an obligation * * * ' " (para. 165 & n. 154, quoting R. Jennings & A. Watts (eds.), Oppenheim's International Law (9th ed. 1992))."

Similarly in the *EC Asbestos* case (see Section13.2 infra), the Appellate Body accorded considerable deference to France's decision on the level of protection needed to halt the spread of asbestos-related health risks:[11]

174.   In our view, France could not reasonably be expected to employ *any* alternative measure if that measure would involve a continuation of the very risk that the Decree seeks to "halt". Such an alternative measure would, in effect, prevent France from achieving its chosen level of health protection. * * *

178.   * * * In justifying a measure under Article XX(b) of the GATT 1994, a Member may also rely, in good faith, on scientific sources which, at that time, may represent a divergent, but qualified and respected, opinion. A Member is not obliged, in setting health policy, automatically to follow what, at a given time, may constitute a majority scientific opinion. * * *

In contrast, in trade-remedy cases, the Appellate Body has not been as deferential. For example, in *US Lamb*, the Appellate Body described the requirements of DSU article 11 in a safeguards case (see Chapter 15 infra) as follows:

103.   * * * [A]n "objective assessment" of a claim under Article 4.2(a) of the Agreement on Safeguards has, in principle, two elements. First, a panel must review whether competent authorities have evaluated *all relevant factors*, and, second, a panel must review whether the authorities have provided a *reasoned and adequate explanation* of how the facts support their determination. Thus, the panel's objective assessment involves a *formal* aspect and a *substantive* aspect. The formal aspect is whether the competent authorities have evaluated "all relevant factors". The substantive aspect is whether the competent authorities have given a reasoned and adequate explanation for their determination.

104.   This dual character of a panel's review is mandated by the nature of the specific obligations that Article 4.2 of the Agreement on Safeguards imposes on competent authorities. Under Article 4.2(a), competent authorities must, as a formal matter, evaluate "all relevant factors". However, that evaluation is not simply a matter of form, and the list of relevant factors to be evaluated is not a mere "check list". Under Article 4.2(a), competent authorities must conduct a substantive evaluation of "the '*bearing*', or the '*influence*' or '*effect*' " or "*impact*" that the relevant factors have on the "situation of [the] domestic industry". (emphasis added) By conducting such a substantive evaluation of the relevant factors, competent authorities are able to make a proper overall determination, *inter alia*, as to whether the domestic industry is seriously injured or is threatened with such injury as defined in the Agreement.

---

11.   Other examples are cited in John H. Jackson, Dispute Settlement and the WTO: Emerging Problems, 1 JIEL 329, 342 n.29 (1998), including the following statement in *US Gasoline*: "WTO Members have a large measure of autonomy to determine their own policies on the environment (including its relationship with trade), their environmental objectives and the environmental legislation they enact and implement."

105. It follows that the precise nature of the examination to be conducted by a panel, in reviewing a claim under Article 4.2 of the Agreement on Safeguards, stems, in part, from the panel's obligation to make an "objective assessment of the matter" under Article 11 of the DSU and, in part, from the obligations imposed by Article 4.2, to the extent that those obligations are part of the claim. Thus, as with any claim under the provisions of a covered agreement, panels are required to examine, in accordance with Article 11 of the DSU, whether the Member has complied with the obligations imposed by the particular provisions identified in the claim. By examining whether the explanation given by the competent authorities in their published report is reasoned and adequate, panels can determine whether those authorities have acted consistently with the obligations imposed by Article 4.2 of the Agreement on Safeguards.

106. We wish to emphasize that, although panels are not entitled to conduct a *de novo* review of the evidence, nor to *substitute* their own conclusions for those of the competent authorities, this does *not* mean that panels must simply *accept* the conclusions of the competent authorities. To the contrary, in our view, in examining a claim under Article 4.2(a), <u>a panel can assess whether the competent authorities' explanation for its determination is reasoned and adequate *only* if the panel critically examines that explanation, in depth, and in the light of the facts before the panel. Panels must, therefore, review whether the competent authorities' explanation fully addresses the nature, and, especially, the complexities, of the data, and responds to other plausible interpretations of that data. A panel must find, in particular, that an explanation is not reasoned, or is not adequate, if some *alternative explanation* of the facts is plausible, and if the competent authorities' explanation does not seem adequate in the light of that alternative explanation.</u> Thus, in making an "objective assessment" of a claim under Article 4.2(a), panels must be open to the possibility that the explanation given by the competent authorities is not reasoned or adequate.

How does the text we have underlined compare to the approach followed in *Hormones* and *Asbestos*? Are there reasons to have a stricter standard of review in trade-remedy cases, as opposed to health-related cases?

(2) The Canada–United States Free Trade Agreement and the North American Free Trade Agreement each established a mechanism for panel review of administrative decisions in antidumping and countervailing duty cases. A decision by a panel may be brought before an extraordinary challenge committee on the grounds, inter alia, that the panel applied an inappropriate standard of review. To date, the challenge committees have hesitated to second-guess the panel decisions, even where they have indicated that the panel had probably misapplied the applicable standard of review. One such case is excerpted in Chapter 11 infra.

(2) Techniques of Judicial Restraint

WILLIAM J. DAVEY, HAS THE WTO DISPUTE SETTLEMENT SYSTEM EXCEEDED ITS AUTHORITY?[12]

To date, I do not believe that the results of WTO dispute settlement evidence to any substantial degree over-reaching by the Appellate Body or panels so as to impose new obligations on Members or to limit inappropriately the discretion of Member government policy-making. * * *

* * * However, I have also noted a few examples (and there are more) where language in a specific case is capable of broad interpretation in the future. Thus, to the extent that it is believed that the WTO system has been too intrusive or might be in the future, it is appropriate to consider whether the WTO dispute settlement system should make greater use of what I term "issue-avoidance" techniques.[13] Over time, courts have developed a variety of such techniques to dispose of cases or issues within cases where a decision seems unnecessary, inappropriate or perhaps simply too controversial. Among the techniques used are

— limitations on the parties who may bring an action (e.g., "standing" or legal interest requirements);

— restrictions limiting the time at which an action may be brought (e.g., categorizing actions as too late (mootness) or too early (ripeness or failure to exhaust other remedies));

— categorization of actions as inappropriate for judicial consideration (e.g., political questions, *non liquet*); and

— exercise of judicial economy so as avoid considering issues (e.g., strict interpretation of terms of reference; resolution of only necessary issues).

Readers familiar with WTO/GATT dispute settlement case-law will recognize that panels and the Appellate Body have considered all of these issues: (i) standing—*Bananas*; (ii) mootness—*Indonesia Autos*; (iii) ripeness—*Section 301*; (iv) exhaustion—*US Salmon* (GATT Antidumping Code); (v) political-judicial balance—*India QR*; (vi) non-liquet—*Coconuts, EEC Wheat Flour Export Subsidies* (Tokyo Round Subsidies Code); (vii) terms of reference—*Bananas, India Patents I, Korea Dairy*; and (viii) judicial economy—*Wool Shirts, Salmon*. In this section, I will consider the US and international law rules in respect of these techniques and then consider whether the right balance has been struck by the WTO dispute settlement system in using them in the mentioned and other similar cases.

12. 4 JIEL 79, 96–110 (2001). Reprinted with permission.

13. [original note 24] See also Jeffrey L. Dunoff, The Death of the Trade Regime,

European Journal of International Law, vol. 10, no. 4, at 733, 757–760.

A. STANDING OR LEGAL INTEREST

The issue considered under the heading of "standing" is whether the complaining party is entitled to have the court decide the merits of the dispute. Or, put another way, whether the complainant has a legal interest that a court will protect.

* * *

In WTO dispute settlement, the issue of standing or legal interest was presented in the *Bananas* case. The EC argued that the panel should reject the US claims made in respect of GATT 1994 because the US did not export bananas and thus had no legal interest in claims related to trade in bananas as goods. The panel noted that there is no explicit requirement in the DSU that a complaining party must have a legal interest in order to bring a case. It also noted that GATT rules were concerned with competitive opportunities and that the US did produce bananas. Moreover, the US market was affected indirectly by the EC import regime for bananas. In the panel's view, a potential trading interest and a Member's interest in a determination of rights and obligations under the various WTO agreements were each sufficient.

On appeal, the Appellate Body noted that the case-law of the International Court of Justice did not indicate that there was a general international law rule that a party must have a legal interest to bring a case. In turning to the wording of GATT Article XXIII, the Appellate Body stressed that it provided that "If any *Member should consider* that any benefit accruing to it is being nullified or impaired ...", the Member is permitted to initiate consultations and thereafter dispute settlement proceedings. It also noted the language of DSU Article 3.7, which requires Members to exercise judgment in deciding whether to bring cases. For the Appellate Body, these provisions suggest that it is largely up to the WTO Member concerned to decide for itself whether it wishes to start an action and whether it will be fruitful.

In addition, the Appellate Body noted that the US did in fact have a potential export interest in bananas as a producer and that the internal market of the United States could be affected by the EC regime. It noted its agreement with the panel that

> "with increased interdependence of the global economy ... Members have a greater stake in enforcing WTO rules than in the past since any deviation from the negotiated balance of rights and obligations is more likely than ever to affect them, directly or indirectly."

Finally, it noted that the GATT claims were closely related to the GATS claims and that there was no question that the US had a right to bring the GATS claims.

From the foregoing, it would appear that a standing or legal interest requirement does not exist under the DSU. However, the Appellate Body concluded its discussion of standing in *Bananas* by stating that while the above mentioned factors taken together were enough to give the US the right to bring claims under GATT in that case, that did not mean that "one or more of the factors we noted in this case would necessarily be dispositive in another case". There have been no other cases to date, so the meaning of the Appellate Body's remark remains uncertain.

It is instructive to consider whether the factors cited as supporting the doctrine of standing in the US are relevant for WTO dispute settlement. The requirements under US law of redressable injury caused by the respondent arise from the US constitutional limitation of federal court jurisdiction to "cases" and "controversies". These requirements are not relevant to WTO dispute settlement since the DSU does not require injury to be shown (nullification or impairment is presumed if a rule violation is established) and redress in the form of a recommendation to bring a measure into conformity with WTO rules is always available. The other three factors, based on prudential concerns, do not seem relevant to WTO dispute settlement either. The rights asserted in WTO dispute settlement are by their nature the rights of a Member. Thus, the rules against third-party standing and generalized grievances seem inappropriate and the requirement that a plaintiff must be within the zone of interests protected by a statute is always met. Moreover, to the extent that the WTO Agreement represents a balance struck by all Members, the general concern about intermeddling does not seem applicable to the WTO. Thus, in my view, there does not seem to be a need to have a standing requirement in WTO dispute settlement proceedings.

* * *

D. EXHAUSTION OF AVAILABLE REMEDIES/ABSTENTION

The requirement that a plaintiff exhaust available remedies (i.e., more appropriate remedies available in another forum) is a device to provide for orderly consideration of issues. It is designed in part to ensure the use of the more appropriate tribunal to decide cases.

* * *

A requirement to exhaust national remedies would too often be tantamount to denying effective enforcement of WTO obligations for too long a period of time and would not seem to be an appropriate mechanism for avoiding difficult issues.

E. POLITICAL-JUDICIAL BALANCE

In the United States, the US Supreme Court has developed the so-called political question doctrine, which it invokes to avoid decisions in certain cases that have political ramifications. Of course, any court decision may have such ramifications, but the political question doctrine is designed to avoid decisions by the court that would bring it into conflict with politics. As expressed in *Baker v. Carr*:

> "Prominent on the surface of any case held to involve a political question is found a textually demonstrable commitment of the issue to a coordinate political department; or a lack of judicially discover-

able and manageable standards for resolving it; or the impossibility of deciding without an initial policy determination of a kind clearly for nonjudicial discretion; or the impossibility of a court's undertaking independent resolution without expressing lack of respect due coordinate branches of government; or an unusual need for unquestioning adherence to a political decision already made; or the potentiality of embarrassment from multifarious departments on one question."[14]

While commentators have viewed these criteria of limited use, the Court has often quoted this language. In practical terms, the Court has declined to rule, inter alia, on whether a state has a republican form of government as required by Article IV(4) of the US Constitution, on matters related to congressional governance, on the process for ratifying constitutional amendments and on some matters related to foreign policy. Its decisions are not that consistent, however, and counterexamples in the above categories may be found.

The ICJ has generally not accepted arguments that it should decline to rule on an issue because it is a political question. Rather, it has noted that many disputes have political ramifications, but that is not an excuse not to examine the legal issues presented.

As noted in Part I of this paper, in the GATT/WTO context, a political-question type issue has arisen in respect of whether certain matters arising under the balance-of-payments exceptions in GATT Articles XII and XVIII:B and under the regional trade rules of Article XXIV should be subject to review by panels and the Appellate Body. Generally, I conclude above that in considering the issue of balance within the WTO system, it is important that panels and the Appellate Body do not create rules that cause them to reject cases on *a priori* grounds. To do so risks upsetting the balance of rights and obligations among Members. The fundamental purpose of the dispute settlement system is to provide security and predictability to the multilateral trading system. It cannot do that if certain obligations are viewed as too political to be reviewed in dispute settlement. It may well be that panels and the Appellate Body should defer to a Member's decision in a specific case (e.g., where the issue of whether a measure meets the terms of an exception is a close one), but that does not mean that the dispute settlement system should not consider the claims in the first instance.

I would take this position even in cases where the respondent invokes GATT Article XXI—the national security exception. Of course, given the wording of Article XXI ("any action which *it considers* necessary"), I would expect panels and the Appellate Body to afford considerable discretion to the Member invoking that exception. Nonetheless, the possibility of dispute settlement review to prevent abusive invocations is appropriate.

14. [original note 51] 369 U.S. 186, 217 (1962).

F. Non liquet

A *non liquet* occurs when a judicial body decides not to rule on a case because the law is not clear or, put another way, there is a gap in the law. As so formulated, it is not an issue-avoidance technique found in US constitutional law, although it is not all that dissimilar to certain techniques discussed herein. The authorization to the ICJ to use general principles of international law as a source of law has been viewed as an attempt to prevent the use of *non liquet* by the ICJ.

The prime example of *non liquet* in GATT dispute settlement was the unadopted panel report in *EEC Wheat Flour Export Subsidies*, where in a somewhat confusing panel report, the panel, inter alia, noted an absence of legal certainty as to the meaning of the Tokyo Round Subsidies Code. That panel report is generally viewed as unsatisfactory.

* * *

Generally speaking, I think that *non liquet* is and should be a disfavored judicial technique. The WTO dispute settlement system is typically asked if a measure violates one or more of the covered agreements. Normally, the Appellate Body and panels should be able to answer that question using standard treaty interpretation methods. If a complainant is unable to establish a violation of an agreement, it will simply lose for that reason. Thus, I think that *non liquet* is not a technique that WTO dispute settlement should embrace.

* * *

H. Judicial Economy

GATT and WTO panels have traditionally ruled only on those claims of a party that must be addressed in order to resolve the matter at issue. Thus, if an aspect of a measure has been found to violate one GATT provision, panels have typically not considered whether it violates another provision as well. This practice, referred to as judicial economy, has been approved by the Appellate Body, although it has not always been followed.

There are essentially two pressures that have caused panels not to exercise as much judicial economy as they could. First, the advent of intensive appellate review has caused some panels to consider additional issues so as to provide alternative bases for findings that will increase the chance that their basic decision will be upheld or so as to enable the Appellate Body to have more of a record of factual determinations in the event it decides to "complete the analysis" in respect of an issue not dealt with by the panel.

Second, the Appellate Body has stated that panels should not exercise judicial economy to the extent that only a partial resolution of the matter results. In its words:

"A panel has to address those claims on which a finding is necessary in order to enable the DSB to make sufficiently precise recommendations and rulings so as to allow for prompt compliance by a Member with those recommendations and rulings 'in order to ensure effective resolution of dispute to the benefit of all Members' (quoting DSU Article 21.1).

In this case, for the Panel to make findings concerning violation of Article 5.1 * * *, without also making findings under Articles 5.5 and 5.6, would not enable the DSB to make sufficiently precise recommendations and rulings so as to allow for compliance by Australia with its obligations under the SPS Agreement, in order to ensure the effective resolution of this dispute with Canada. An SPS measure, which is brought into consistency with Article 5.1, may still be inconsistent with either Article 5.5 or Article 5.6, or with both."[15]

It is unclear how this guidance should be interpreted. It could be read to reject the very notion of judicial economy since more information about what would comply with an agreement would always be useful for implementation purposes.

As a general matter, I think that judicial economy is an appropriate technique for panels to use to avoid controversial issues. If a measure can be found to be inconsistent with WTO rules without addressing a difficult issue in the case, panels should not hesitate to avoid the difficult issue. Perhaps the issue will arise again, but perhaps it will not.

It should be noted that it is evident from the discussion of the exercise of judicial economy—in the argument sections of panel reports, in the interim review process and in the Appellate Body—that parties are often frustrated by the exercise of judicial economy. This is understandable, as a party may have devoted considerable time and effort to make a whole range of arguments and feel quite frustrated if many of them are not even considered. In my view, however, if the panel accepts one of a party's theories as to why a measure is WTO-inconsistent, that should be sufficient, particularly where the additional arguments may be difficult or controversial. For me, if anything, panels should probably be more willing to exercise judicial economy than they seem to be nowadays.

I. SCOPE OF APPELLATE REVIEW AND APPELLATE JUDICIAL ECONOMY

The Appellate Body has never articulated a standard of review to apply to its consideration of appeals. While DSU Article 17.12 provides that the Appellate Body shall "address each of the issues raised", it would seem that the Appellate Body has the flexibility of exercising judicial economy as well. It can simply say that having addressed certain issues, the remaining issues do not need to be considered separately. That statement, in itself, "addresses" the remaining issues.

To date, the Appellate Body does not seem to have exercised much judicial economy, except when it has declared that appealed issues are factual in nature and therefore beyond its purview. * * * For me, the

---

15. [original note 62] Appellate Body Report, *Salmon*, paras. 223–224.

Appellate Body could appropriately deal with more issues on the basis of judicial economy.

Conclusion

In general, I do not believe that the Appellate Body and panels have over-reached in the various reports adopted through September 25, 2000, in the WTO dispute settlement system, except perhaps in the few, relatively minor, matters mentioned at the end of Part I. In respect of issue-avoidance techniques, I think that over time the WTO system could profitably make more use of such techniques in respect of the timing of consideration of issues (mootness and ripeness) and the exercise of judicial economy. This is particularly true in the case of the Appellate Body in respect of mootness and judicial economy. The one caveat has been noted in connection with the discussion of judicial economy—it is necessary to have clear standards as to when these techniques will be used, so as to avoid having some Members believe that they have been unfairly treated differently than other Members.

Notes and Questions

(1) Does Professor Davey reach the right balance on which of these avoidance techniques should be used?

(2) In reading its decisions in some of the more controversial cases to date in Chapters 13 and 14 (such as the *Asbestos, Gasoline, Shrimp* and *Hormones* cases), consider whether the Appellate Body has generally acted in a way so as to afford considerable discretion to WTO members and in tune with prevailing political sentiments in at least the major powers in the WTO.

(3) The Appellate Body has ruled that it and panels have the power to accept amicus submissions from non-WTO members. As noted in next subsection, most WTO members disagree with this ruling, but they have not been able to change it. Should such member opposition influence the Appellate Body in its rulings?

(4) If the consensus rule is to be maintained, what other mechanisms might be used to enable the WTO membership to give effective feedback to dispute settlement decisions. The Sutherland Report[16] suggested the following:

> 251. A more constructive approach might be to occasionally select particular findings for in-depth analysis by a reasonably impartial, special expert group of the DSB, so as to provide a measured report of constructive criticism for the information of the WTO system, including the Appellate Body and panels. Such a report could be presented to the DSB for information, or conceivably could be adopted by the DSB. In an extreme case, perhaps the report could go so far as to recommend that the DSB and General Council take measures under Article IX of the [WTO Agreement], for a "definitive interpretation" of the treaty text.

16. Peter Sutherland et al., The Future of the WTO: Addressing Institutional Challenges in the New Millennium, Report by the Consultative Board to the Director– General Supachai Panitchpakdi, available at: http://www.wto.org/english/thewto_e/10 anniv_e/future_wto_e.htm.

252. Even a report presented or adopted for information only could have an important effect on the thinking of the Appellate Body members and the panelists for future cases. However, it would be important that these not have an impact on the instant case.

Would this be a useful reform? The US has proposed in the Doha negotiations that the parties to a dispute be given the power jointly to delete findings from panel reports prior to its circulation and that the DSB be given the power to partially adopt reports. These changes would enhance member control of dispute settlement outcomes. Would such changes be desirable? Effective?

(5) Concerns over judicial activism and political/judicial imbalance inevitably raise questions about the desirability of a more adjudicative, rules-based system, an issue we explored in Section 7.1. Do these concerns alter your view on that issue.

(E) TRANSPARENCY AND PARTICIPATION

One of the more controversial issues faced by the WTO dispute settlement system is how to deal with complaints by non-governmental organizations (NGOs) and others that the system lacks transparency and does not permit sufficient access for non-members. Indeed, there are also complaints from developing WTO members that they are not able to participate effectively in WTO dispute settlement.

(1) Transparency

Currently, panel and Appellate Body proceedings are usually closed to the public. Only the parties and, to a limited extent, third parties may attend the proceedings. The parties and third parties may make public their own submissions to a panel or the Appellate Body, but they are not required to do so. For parties who do not make their submissions public, the DSU requires them, on request, to provide a non-confidential summary that could be made public (art. 18.2). In practice, such summaries are often very brief and prepared only after considerable delay. The arguments of the parties and third parties are described in great detail in (or even attached to) panel reports and are summarized relatively concisely in Appellate Body reports. Since panel and Appellate Body reports (and all other WTO documents relating to specific disputes) are issued as unrestricted documents and placed on the WTO website on the same day as their distribution to WTO members, the parties' arguments become known in due course.

The United States has proposed that dispute settlement proceedings be open to the public and that submissions be made public when filed with the WTO. Should the WTO dispute settlement system adopt such or similar transparency rules? What are the advantages and disadvantages of more transparency? In that regard, what is the practice of other national and international tribunals—are their proceedings public? When are party submissions made public?

A number of WTO members—including the US and the EU—make their submissions public, but most do not. Starting in 2005, the US and the EU have agreed to open panel meetings to the public in a number of cases in which they have been the principal parties. This has been done with the agreement of all of the parties and the panels. Is this consistent with the DSU? Consider DSU articles 14 and 18 and the Appendix 3 working procedures. Could the Appellate Body open its hearings? Consider DSU article 17.10.

(2) Participation of Non-members

Even more controversial than transparency, is the proposal by the United States that non-parties should be permitted to make amicus curiae ("friend-of-the-court") submissions to panels and the Appellate Body. When the US proposals were discussed in the review of the DSU conducted in 1998–1999, there was considerable opposition to them. Many developing country Members view the WTO system as exclusively intergovernmental in nature and hesitate to open it in any way to non-governments. In their view, if an NGO wants to make an argument to a panel, it should convince one of the parties to make it, and if no party makes the argument, those members would view that as evidence that the argument is not meritorious. Moreover, they view such openness as favoring the positions espoused by western, developed country NGOs, which they view as likely not to be in their interest. Others argue that the credibility of the system would be much enhanced if it were more open and that openness would have no significant disadvantages.

While the DSU review was ongoing, the Appellate Body ruled that panels have the right to accept non-requested submissions from non-parties (such as NGOs).[17] It reversed a panel report that had concluded that while panels had the right to "seek" information under DSU article 13.1, they did not have the power to accept information that had not been sought. The Appellate Body criticized the panel for reading article 13 "in too literal a manner" (para. 107). The Appellate Body also ruled, however, that the panel's decision in that case to call the submissions to the attention of the parties and ask if the parties wished to adopt all or part of them was an appropriate exercise of its discretion.

Notwithstanding considerable criticism of the foregoing decision, the Appellate Body later ruled that it also had the power to accept amicus submissions, even though its working procedures and the DSU provisions applicable to it contained no provision like article 13.[18] Later, in the *EC Asbestos* case, the Appellate Body announced specific procedures for considering whether to accept amicus submissions in that case. That decision was harshly criticized in a special General Council meeting called to discuss the issue. Minutes of General Council of 22 November 2000, WT/GC/38 (Dec. 12, 2000).

Notes and Questions

(1) Should the WTO dispute settlement system permit amicus submissions? What are the advantages and disadvantages of doing so? In that regard, what is the practice of other national and international tribunals?

---

17. *US Shrimp*, paras. 99–110.

18. *US Lead and Bismuth Steel II*, paras. 139–142.

(2) One concern is that panels will be deluged with amicus submissions. Do you think that is likely? How might the problem be minimized?

(3) There is a concern that parties will not know on which, if any, amicus arguments or facts a panel or the Appellate Body intends to rely, and therefore will not be in a position to respond appropriately. What procedures could be devised to address this concern?

(4) Given popular fears of globalization and the WTO's connection therewith, could increased transparency and participation rights in dispute settlement play an important role in increasing the credibility of the WTO in a way that may be essential to ensure the future effectiveness of the WTO itself, as well as the dispute settlement system?

(5) Should there be disclosure rules for NGOs wishing to submit amicus briefs so that their sources of financial support and ties to interested parties are known?

(6) See generally Gabrielle Marceau and Matthew Stilwell, Practical Suggestions for *amicus curiae* Briefs before WTO Adjudicating Bodies, 4 JIEL 155–187 (2001).

(3) Participation of Developing Country Members

One difficult problem facing the WTO system is how to integrate developing countries into the system. This problem is discussed generally in Chapter 24 infra, but it is a particular problem in respect of dispute settlement. In 1962, Uruguay brought a series of complaints in GATT against 15 developed countries, alleging that dozens of practices by those countries had restricted Uruguayan export opportunities and thereby nullified and impaired its benefits under the General Agreement. The complaint was viewed more as an attempt to call attention to the problems of developing countries than as an attempt to obtain specific relief for Uruguay. Nonetheless, the whole process demonstrated that small countries have basic problems in trying to invoke the dispute settlement system, particularly when they need to collect extensive information to support complicated legal arguments. While smaller countries are undoubted better off by having WTO rules limiting the freedom of developed countries to impose trade restrictions than they would be in the absence of such rules, they clearly are not as able to use the dispute settlement system as developed countries to enforce WTO rules. This disparity is particularly evident when the question of suspending concessions is considered. Such an action by a large, powerful country against the trade of a small, developing country could be devastating, but retaliation by a small country against a large one may go virtually unnoticed in the large country and may even be counterproductive to the interests of the smaller country.

In 1965 and 1966 a GATT Committee on Legal and Institutional Framework created an Ad Hoc Group on Legal Amendments to consider proposals to amend Article XXIII. Such proposals included the provision of financial compensation to a developing country damaged by actions violating GATT, the automatic release of a developing country from GATT obligations toward an offending developed GATT member and a provision for collective GATT action against an offending party.[19] A procedure for developing country complaints was adopted as a GATT decision in 1966,[20] providing for time limits and heavy reliance on mediation by the Director–General of GATT, but the proposals mentioned above were not adopted. The special procedures were invoked only infrequently; they were, however, carried over into the DSU. They have not been invoked in the WTO.

The DSU has a number of provisions applicable to developing or least developed countries. They include, inter alia, provisions on consultations (arts. 4.10, 12.10), panel composition and procedures (arts. 8.10, 12.11), implementation (Arts. 21.2, 21.7), assistance and training (art. 27) and least developed countries (art. 24).

Notes and Questions

(1) One can argue that the effectiveness of rules favoring developing countries may vary depending on their precision. For example, one can compare the requirement that a panel in a case involving a developing country and a developed country must have a panelist from a developing country if the developing country requests (DSU art. 8.10) with the requirement in DSU article 21.2 that "[p]articular attention should be paid to matters affecting the interests of developing country Members with respect to measures which have been subject to dispute settlement". The first provision is clear and easy to apply. What does the second provision mean? Who is supposed to do this? What does "particular attention" require? How would you characterize the existing provisions favoring developing countries in terms of their actual usefulness?

(2) What additional rules do you think should apply to dispute settlement matters involving developing countries? In considering the ability of developing countries to use the DSU effectively, it would seem that smaller and poorer developing countries face three particular problems: (i) identifying potential cases, (ii) the high cost of employing private lawyers to handle their cases and (iii) the inability to use retaliatory measures to pressure defaulting developed countries to implement WTO obligations. What DSU changes might help to alleviate these problems? We examine the question of remedies more generally in Section 7.5 infra.

(3) In 2001, several developed and developing countries established the Advisory Centre on WTO Law (ACWL) as an intergovernmental organization to provide low-cost legal services and training to developing countries in respect of WTO matters. It has been quite active. See www.acwl.ch for information on its activities. What else should be done to address the problems of developing countries in this area?

(4) For additional information on developing country participation in WTO dispute settlement, see William J. Davey, "The WTO Dispute Settlement System: How have Developing Countries Fared?", Illinois Public Law Research Paper No. 05–17, available at http://ssrn.com/abstract=862804,

19. GATT, 14th Supp. BISD 139 (1969).

20. Procedures under Art. XXIII, Decision of 5th April, 1966, GATT, 14th Supp.

BISD 18 (1966); see also, Robert E. Hudec, The GATT Legal System and World Trade Diplomacy, chs. 18 22 (1975).

and Gregory Shaffer, The Challenges of WTO Law: Strategies for Developing Country Adaptation, 5 World Trade Review 177 (July 2006).

(F) UNILATERALISM AND THE DSU

Prior to and during the Uruguay Round negotiations, the subject of unilateralism—especially US unilateralism—was a major topic of concern to many countries. One specific US statute—Section 301 of the US Trade Act of 1974—was particularly controversial because it was used by the United States Trade Representative to take retaliatory action against foreign trade practices that it deemed to be "unfair." Indeed, many believe that the existence of Section 301 was the catalyst for the creation of the WTO dispute resolution system. Now that disputants can no longer block the process from going forward, the United States can no longer claim a need for self help when violations arise. And because WTO commitments are much broader than those of the GATT (including services and intellectual property, for example), it is much harder to argue that gaps in international law justify unilateral measures. In this section, we trace the history and operation of Section 301 and then analyze the extent to which DSU article 23 precludes unilateral action by WTO members.

(1) A Short Note on the History of Section 301

In 1962, partly because of the dissatisfaction of Congress with the way in which the Executive Branch had responded to citizen complaints against foreign government actions affecting international trade, Congress granted certain explicit powers to the President, authorizing retaliation with trade measures against certain foreign government actions.[21] This statute was replaced and considerably expanded by title III of the Trade Act of 1974, and particularly Section 301 thereof, which granted similar powers to the President. The Act also provided explicit procedures under which US citizens could petition the US government for action against harmful foreign government activities.

Under Section 301, USTR may initiate investigations upon petition or upon its own initiative. Most cases result from petitions. After a petition is filed, USTR decides within 45 days whether or not to "initiate" the investigation. Reasonably tight time limits apply for the completion of investigations, although USTR may extend the time by a number of months in "complicated" cases. The investigations are quite informal, but the petitioner and other interested parties (including the foreign government respondent) are afforded an opportunity to present their views.

Since 1988 the statute has had two tracks—Section 301(a) governing unfair practices that require "mandatory" action, and Section 301(b) governing cases that permit "discretionary" action. Section 301(a) applies to any foreign government practice that "violates, or is inconsistent with ... or otherwise denies benefits to the United States" under a

---

21. Trade Expansion Act of 1962, sec. 252, Pub.L. No. 87–794, 75 Stat. 879.

trade agreement, or "is in violation of, or inconsistent with" other international legal rights of the United States and "burdens or restricts United States Commerce." After initiating an investigation pursuant to Section 301(a), USTR must request informal consultations with the country in question. If these consultations do not yield a satisfactory solution, USTR may then invoke formal dispute resolution under the procedures set forth in the agreement at issue. No later than eighteen months after the initiation of the case, whether or not the international dispute resolution process has concluded, USTR must make a determination whether the practice in question violates the legal rights of the United States. If that determination is affirmative, USTR must simultaneously determine what action to take in response to the practice. No retaliatory action is necessary if the international dispute resolution process finds against the United States, if the foreign government agrees to conform its practice to the US view of its international obligations, or if the foreign government provides the United States with satisfactory compensation for the violation in the form of trade concessions on other goods or services. Otherwise, retaliation is "mandatory," though "subject to the specific direction, if any, of the President." Absent an agreement on modification of the challenged practice or compensation, the statute provides a range of retaliatory options, including duties or other restrictions upon exports of goods or services from the country under investigation. These sanctions must "be devised so as to affect goods or services of the foreign country in an amount that is equivalent in value to the burden being imposed by that country on US commerce."

Foreign government practices that do not violate Section 301(a) may nevertheless violate Section 301(b) if they are "unreasonable" or "discriminatory," and also "burden or restrict United States commerce." An "unreasonable" act is defined as one that is "unfair and inequitable." The statute provides a non-exhaustive list of examples of unreasonable acts, including denial of "market opportunities" or "opportunities for the establishment of an enterprise," failure to protect intellectual property rights, export targeting, toleration of anticompetitive practices by private firms, and denial of worker rights. The statute offers no comprehensive definition of "discriminatory" acts. It does indicate, however, that such acts include a denial of most-favored-nation or national treatment in "appropriate" cases involving goods, services, or investment. Retaliation in these cases is discretionary.

In 1984, Section 301 was amended to require that the Executive Branch produce an annual "National Trade Estimates" (NTE) report to identify important barriers to US exports on a country-by-country basis. Under the "Super 301" procedures added in 1988, which were in force for only a few years, USTR was required to use the NTE report to identify "priority practices, including major barriers and trade distorting practices, the elimination of which are likely to have the most significant potential to increase United States exports." It was also required to identify "priority foreign countries" and then initiate Section 301 investigations of each priority practice by each priority country.

Implementation of the "Super 301" provision began with USTR's identification, on May 26, 1989, of six priority practices by three priority countries. Three of the identified practices were Japanese: exclusionary government procurement practices in the supercomputer sector which barred foreign suppliers, a ban on procurement by the government of foreign-made satellites, and technical barriers affecting the import of forest products into Japan. Two of the identified practices were by India: one relating to investment restrictions, and the other to impediments to insurance sales. The last was an import licensing scheme administered by Brazil. A Section 301 investigation of each was initiated in June of 1989. Each country reacted angrily. Japan stated repeatedly, for example, that it would not negotiate under the threat of retaliation. But over the next year, Japan and the United States entered agreements settling each of the cases. Brazil settled its case by agreeing to remove a number of quantitative restrictions. The disputes with India were resolved by an agreement to negotiate over services and investment policy during the Uruguay Round.

The wisdom of Section 301 has been hotly debated. Critics labeled it a form of "aggressive unilateralism," with the United States seen as unjustifiably taking the law into its own hands. Objections were made to the fact that the United States could unilaterally decide whether its rights were violated and to the fact that the United States at times retaliated against practices that were indisputably legal under international law. Defenders of Section 301 argued that if it was used wisely, it was a reasonable self-help measure in the face of ineffective GATT dispute resolution as well as the broad gaps in the coverage of GATT commitments.[22] Further, it was noted that Section 301 provides to the Executive Branch authority over trade policy that ordinarily resides with the Congress, and thus puts the US President on a par with other world leaders whose constitutional systems already afford them much latitude in the formulation of trade policy.

Nowadays, although Section 301 remains on the books, it now bears little connection to "unilateralism" as a practical matter. Rather, it provides a vehicle whereby private industry can petition the government to take cases to the WTO, and it provides the Executive Branch with the statutory authority to implement WTO-authorized retaliatory sanctions. In the past decade, it has not been much used by private industry.

(2) Unilateralism and DSU Article 23

DSU article 23.1 requires that when WTO members "seek redress of a [WTO obligation], they shall have recourse to, and abide by, the rules and procedures of the [DSU]". Article 23.2 more specifically requires any determinations of WTO violations and imposition of retaliatory measures in respect thereof be in accordance with the DSU. Because Section 301

---

22. For a flavor of some of the debate, see Aggressive Unilateralism (Jagdish Bhagwati & Hugh Patrick eds. 1989); Alan O. Sykes, Constructive Unilateral Threats in International Commercial Relations: The Limited Case for Section 301, 23 L. & Pol. Intl.Bus. 263 (1992).

appears to require USTR to take retaliatory action in investigations of alleged WTO rule violations on the basis of a timetable that may require such action before WTO dispute settlement proceedings on the issue have been completed, the EU challenged Section 301 as a violation of DSU article 23. The WTO panel in *US Section 301* found on a provisional basis that Section 301 did appear to violate article 23, but ultimately concluded that it did not violate article 23 because of US commitments to use Section 301 consistently with article 23. Those commitments were found in statement made by the Executive Branch to Congress in connection with the approval of the WTO agreements and were reaffirmed by the US in statements made by the US to the panel. Neither side appealed. The US claimed victory because it was not required to change Section 301; the EU claimed victory because the panel report made it clear that it would be a violation of DSU article 23 for the US to act unilaterally. In any event, Section 301 is no longer a focus of attention.

It remains somewhat unclear, however, what DSU article 23.1 prohibits. For example, if WTO members X and Y are involved in a dispute, could they agree to suspend panel proceedings and refer the matter to non-WTO mediators? If the EU believes that Korea has violated its WTO obligations in respect of subsidies to shipbuilders, may the EU initiate a WTO case against Korea alleging that violation and simultaneously adopt its own program of subsidies for its shipbuilders in an attempt to cause Korea to change its policies? Or would the latter action violate article 23?

EUROPEAN COMMUNITIES—MEASURES AFFECTING TRADE IN COMMERCIAL VESSELS

WT/DS301/R.
Panel Report adopted June 20, 2005.

[According to Korea, the dispute arose "from an attempt by the European Communities to take the law into its own hands". It notes that the EC believed that Korea had subsidized Korean shipyards so as to cause "adverse effects" and "serious prejudice" to the EC and its shipbuilding industry. According to Korea, the EC explicitly adopted a two-track strategy to challenge the alleged Korean subsidies. First, it made a determination of subsidization and unilaterally implemented countermeasures against Korea under the so-called Temporary Defensive Mechanism ("TDM"), an EC Council Regulation. Second, it initiated a WTO dispute settlement proceeding against Korea in which it alleged that the Korean subsidies violated the SCM Agreement. In response, Korea initiated this WTO proceeding, in which it alleged that the TDM countermeasures violated, inter alia, DSU article 23.]

7.187   The obligation in Article 23.1 to have recourse to (and abide by) the rules and procedures of the DSU applies "when Members seek the redress of a violation of obligations or other nullification or impairment of benefits under the covered agreements or an impediment to the attainment of any objective of the covered agreements". Thus, an essential element in the interpretation of the scope of this obligation is the meaning of "seek the redress of a violation ..."

7.188 The phrase "seek the redress of a violation ..." implies that one necessary condition of the application of Article 23.1 of the DSU is that a Member acts in response to what it considers to be conduct of another Member that is in violation of that Member's obligations. In the words of the Panel in *US—Section 301*, a decision by a Member to "seek the redress of a violation ..." means that "in its preliminary view, there may be a WTO inconsistency". The Panel in *US—Certain EC Products* referred to this aspect of "seek the redress of a violation ..." as action "because of a perceived (or WTO determined) WTO violation" and "action in response to what [a WTO Member] views as a WTO violation". We agree with this approach.

7.189 [T]he Panel notes the definition of "redress" in the New Shorter Oxford English Dictionary:

"1. Reparation of or compensation for a wrong or consequent loss. 2(a). Remedy for or relief from some trouble; assistance, aid, help. (b) (obsolete) Correction or reformation of something wrong. 3(a) A means of redress; an amendment, an improvement. (b) (obsolete) A person who or thing which affords redress. 4. The act of redressing; correction or amendment of a thing, state, etc."

The fact that "redress" can mean "reparation of" or "compensation for" a wrong or consequent loss but also "remedy for" or "relief from" some trouble suggests that "the redress of a violation ..." within the meaning of Article 23.1 of the DSU can take various forms. One obvious modality of "redress" of a violation that a Member will "seek" is action by another Member to bring itself into conformity with its obligations by removing a WTO-inconsistent measure, but "redress" includes other possible "remedies", such as compensation or suspension of concessions or obligations. Therefore, to "seek the redress of a violation ..." may include but is not limited to a suspension of concessions or obligations. As observed by the Panel in *US—Certain EC Products,* the phrase "seek the redress of a violation ..." in the context of Article 23.1 of the DSU can be defined rather broadly as a "reaction against another Member, because of a perceived (or WTO determined) WTO violation, with a view to remedying the situation".

7.190 In interpreting the phrase "seek the redress of a violation ...", the Panel must also take into account as one relevant contextual element the fact that this phrase appears in a clause contained in an article designed explicitly with a view to "strengthening the multilateral system". These words must therefore be given a meaning consistent with that stated objective. Another relevant element of the context of the phrase "seek the redress of a violation ..." in Article 23.1 is that the DSU clearly provides for different types of "remedy". In the Panel's view, an interpretation of Article 23.1 in light of the objective of Article 23 and its context in the DSU suggests that it must apply to any act whereby a Member seeks to obtain unilaterally results that can be achieved via the remedies of the DSU through means other than recourse to the DSU. If Members were free to attempt to seek the redress of a violation by trying to achieve unilaterally what could be obtained through the DSU, it is difficult to see how the obligation to have recourse to the DSU could contribute to the "strengthening of the multilateral system".

7.191   In this regard, the Panel considers that the obligation "to have recourse" to the DSU is necessarily of an exclusive character. * * *

* * *

7.194   We note in this respect * * * the Panel Report in *US— Section 301* * * *:

"Article 23.1 is not concerned only with specific instances of violation. It prescribes a general duty of a dual nature. First, it imposes on all Members to 'have recourse to' the multilateral process set out in the DSU when they seek the redress of a WTO inconsistency. In these circumstances, Members have to have recourse to the DSU dispute settlement system to the exclusion of any other system, *in particular a system of unilateral enforcement of WTO rights and obligations*. This, what one could call 'exclusive dispute resolution clause', is an important new element of Members' rights and obligations under the DSU." * * *

7.195   To summarize, based on an interpretation of Article 23.1 in light of the ordinary meaning of its terms and in light of its context and object and purpose, and having regard to the reasoning of the Appellate Body and panels in previous disputes concerning Article 23, we consider that the requirement "to have recourse to" the DSU when Members "seek the redress of a violation ..." is * * * violated not only when Members submit a dispute concerning rights and obligations under the WTO Agreement to an international dispute settlement body outside the WTO framework but also when Members act unilaterally to seek to obtain the results that can be achieved through the remedies of the DSU. * * *

7.196   [T]he Panel considers that Article 23.1 must be interpreted to mean that Members may not seek to obtain results that can be achieved through the remedies of the DSU by means other than recourse to the DSU. * * * [T]he phrase "seek the redress of a violation ..." covers any act of a Member in response to what it considers to be a violation of a WTO obligation by another Member whereby the first Member attempts to restore the balance of rights and obligations by seeking the removal of the WTO-inconsistent measure, by seeking compensation from the other Member, or by suspending concessions or obligations under the WTO Agreement in relation to that Member. In the case of actionable subsidies, seeking the removal of the WTO-inconsistent measure includes seeking the removal by the subsidizing Member of the adverse effects of the subsidy. In our view, any unilateral attempt to obtain these results would be a violation of Article 23.1 of the DSU.

7.197 [H]owever, the concept of "seeking the redress of a violation" does not encompass the situation where a Member takes actions to compensate or attenuate the harm caused to actors within the aggrieved Member as a result of the allegedly WTO-consistent action, provided those actions are not designed to influence the conduct of the Member taking the allegedly WTO-inconsistent action, as outlined in the preceding paragraph. Thus, for example, trade adjustment assistance provided to help companies or workers affected by an allegedly WTO-inconsistent quantitative restriction to shift into other economic activities may be a response to WTO-inconsistent behaviour but would not constitute "seeking redress". This type of palliative action might address the harm caused to particular actors within a WTO Member by an alleged WTO violation but it is not designed to restore the balance of rights and obligations between Members.

* * *

7.208 In light of its conclusion above, the Panel must now proceed to a factual assessment to determine, in light of its interpretation of Article 23.1, whether the European Communities, by adopting the TDM Regulation [granting subsidies to EU shipbuilders], sought the redress of a violation by Korea of its obligations under the WTO Agreement without having recourse to the DSU. * * *

Did the European Communities act in response to what it considered to be a violation by Korea of its obligations under the WTO Agreement?

* * *

7.210 On its face, the TDM Regulation does not indicate that it is designed as a response to a violation by Korea of its obligations under the WTO Agreement. * * * Nevertheless, the Panel considers that the TDM Regulation reflects an allegation of WTO-inconsistent conduct.

7.211 The TDM Regulation uses terminology that is intimately connected with the provisions of Articles 5 and 6 of the SCM Agreement. The third Recital observes that a temporary defensive mechanism should be authorized for limited market segments and for a short and limited period only, "as an exceptional and temporary measure, and in order to assist Community shipyards in those segments that have suffered adverse effects in the form of material injury and serious prejudice caused by unfair Korean competition". Article 2(2) allows for the extension of the Regulation to LNG carriers if the Commission gives notice that it confirms that "[the] Community industry has suffered material injury and serious prejudice in this market segment caused by unfair Korean practices". The Regulation was proposed by the Commission when [a Commission] investigation * * * had produced evidence that subsidies granted by Korea were causing adverse effects within the meaning of the SCM Agreement to certain segments of the Community shipbuilding industry. We note that in explaining the background to the proposed

TDM mechanism, the European Commission stated in July 2001 that this proposal "follows a Commission investigation which found evidence of substantial subsidies that are incompatible with the WTO rules". When the Commission issued its first report on the results of this investigation, it stated publicly that "substantial subsidies have been granted to Korean shipyards through both export and domestic programmes which contravene the WTO's 1994 Subsidies Agreement." These factors demonstrate a clear factual link between the adoption of the TDM Regulation and the findings of WTO-inconsistent conduct by Korea. In the Panel's view, the application of Article 23.1 of the DSU is not limited to cases involving an explicit allegation of WTO-inconsistent conduct.

7.212   The Panel recalls its observation above that when a Member seeks "the redress of a violation ..." it has necessarily arrived at a "preliminary view" that a violation has occurred. The Panel agrees with the remark of the Panel in *US—Section 301* that such a preliminary view is distinct from a "determination" within the meaning of Article 23.2(a) of the DSU. The evidence before us indicates that the TDM Regulation was based on factual findings that clearly amounted to at least a "preliminary view" that Korea had committed breaches of its obligations under the SCM Agreement. It is not necessary to ascertain whether or not these findings, as contained in the reports submitted by the European Commission to the Advisory Committee, qualify as determinations within the meaning of Article 23.2(a) of the DSU.

7.213   The Panel also notes that the TDM Regulation is specifically directed against Korea. Article 2(1) of the Regulation provides that:

"Subject to paragraphs 2 to 6, direct aid in support of contracts for the building of container ships, product and chemical tankers as well as LNG carriers shall be considered compatible with the common market when there has been competition for the contract from a Korean shipyard offering a lower price."

The possibility to provide contract-related operating aid is confined to precisely those segments of the Community shipbuilding industry found by the European Communities to have suffered adverse effects of "unfair *Korean* competition" or "unfair *Korean* practices" and such aid may be provided only in cases where there has been competition for a particular contract from a *Korean* shipyard offering a lower price. The temporal application of the TDM Regulation depends upon the initiation and resolution or suspension of a WTO dispute settlement proceeding brought by the European Communities against *Korea*. The focus on Korea is also evident in that the introductory Recitals motivate the adoption of the Regulation by referring to Korea's alleged non-implementation of the Agreed Minutes relating to world shipbuilding and to the adverse effects on certain segments of the Community shipbuilding industry caused by "unfair Korean competition" or "unfair Korean practices". The fact that the Regulation singles out Korea in its manner of operation and its motivation demonstrates that the Regulation is "a reaction by a Member against another Member".

7.214   In light of these considerations, the Panel is satisfied that by adopting the TDM Regulation the European Communities acted in response to what it considered to be a violation by Korea of its obligations under the WTO Agreement.

Did the European Communities seek to restore the balance of rights and obligations?

7.215   With regard to whether the TDM Regulation is a unilateral act whereby the European Communities sought to restore the WTO balance of rights and obligations by seeking removal of Korea's allegedly WTO-inconsistent measure (or its effects), the Panel considers the following factors particularly relevant.

7.216   A key element of the design and structure of the TDM Regulation is that its application is explicitly limited to contracts signed during a period determined by the initiation and resolution or suspension of a WTO dispute settlement proceeding against Korea. * * * The fact that once the WTO dispute settlement case is resolved or suspended the TDM mechanism ceases to apply suggests that this mechanism serves to seek the same type of redress as the WTO dispute settlement case. The Panel recalls in this respect that the WTO dispute settlement case and the TDM Regulation are closely linked elements of the European Communities' "twin-track" strategy to deal with unfair Korean practices in the shipbuilding sector.

7.217   Thus, when the Commission submitted its first report on [its investigation], it stated the following in a press release:

> "Further to the adoption of its fourth report on the state of the EU shipbuilding industry last week, the Commission today approved the strategy it will propose to the Council of Ministers on 14/15 May, in order to address the persistent problems posed to the European shipbuilding industry by unfair trade practices by Korean shipyards. The investigation * * * has established that substantial subsidies have been granted to Korean shipyards through both export and domestic programmes which contravene the WTO's 1994 Subsidies Agreement. On this basis, the Commission will recommend that the matter be taken before the WTO through the initiation of a dispute settlement procedure by 30 June unless an amicable solution can be reached in the interim period. *In parallel, the Commission will propose accompanying measures in the form of a temporary support mechanism to European shipyards for the market segments considerably injured by unfair Korean trade practices and for the period required for the conclusion of the WTO procedure. Its entering into force will be simultaneous with the effective start of the WTO action.*"

In July 2001, when the Commission submitted a formal proposal to the Council, it issued a press release which stated:

"The Commission today adopted a proposal for a Council Regulation which would put in place a temporary defensive mechanism for European shipbuilding. *The proposal is one element of the Commission's two-part strategy against unfair Korean practices in this sector* and will cover the market segments that are considerably injured by these practices. It comes after a series of negotiations between the Commission and Korea, which failed to produce an agreement that would restore normal trading conditions. *The proposal is an accompanying measure to dispute settlement proceedings against Korea, which will be initiated in the WTO as soon as the Council expresses its favourable position on the temporary defensive mechanism. ...*

The proposal for a defensive temporary support mechanism follows a Commission investigation which found evidence of substantial subsidies that are incompatible with the WTO rules. Despite a series of negotiations between the Commission and the Korean Government, no amicable solution has yet been achieved. *Accordingly, the Commission has instigated its two part strategy for fighting these unfair practices: proposing a temporary defensive mechanism and the initiation of dispute settlement proceedings.*

The proposal for the temporary defensive mechanism is limited to those market segments in which the Commission investigation found that EU industry had been considerably injured by unfair Korean trade practices, namely container ships and product and chemical tankers.

* * *

7.219   [T]he simple fact that a Member responds to a perceived WTO violation by seeking to compensate or attenuate the harm caused to actors within the Member resulting from an alleged violation does not in itself represent "seeking redress" provided the action is not designed to restore the (perceived) balance of rights and obligations between the Members. Thus, if the European Communities had simply reinstituted in 2002 its former system authorizing member State aid to shipbuilding, such an action would likely not raise issues under DSU Article 23. However, in the view of the Panel, the TDM Regulation goes beyond a measure whereby the European Communities seeks to compensate or to attenuate the harm resulting from an alleged violation by Korea of its obligations under the SCM Agreement. The TDM Regulation, by its design and structure, is explicitly tied to WTO dispute settlement. That tie is confirmed by the Commission statements quoted above. In our view, the TDM Regulation operates directly and exclusively to alter the conditions of competition between Korean and Community shipyards in respect of individual transactions and is clearly designed to restore the balance of rights and obligations by inducing Korea to remove the alleged WTO-inconsistent measure.

7.220   In light of all the above factors, the Panel considers that the European Communities has sought unilaterally to achieve results that Article 23.1 requires to be sought through recourse to the DSU. By adopting the TDM Regulation, the European Communities acted in response to what it considered to be a violation by Korea of its obligations under the WTO Agreement and sought to restore the balance of rights and obligations by inducing Korea to remove the alleged WTO-inconsistent measure. * * *

7.221 Since it is undisputed that the European Communities adopted the TDM Regulation without having recourse to the DSU, the Panel concludes that by adopting the TDM Regulation the European Communities acted inconsistently with Article 23.1 of the DSU.

Notes and Questions

(1) The panel report was not appealed. The TDM Regulation expired in March 2005.

(2) Would the panel's reasoning apply if the EC measure at issue had been a suspension of the right of Korean commercial aircraft to land at EC airports?

(3) Suppose the TDM Regulation as described above had been implemented but without any explicit mention at all of the dispute with Korea. In other words, suppose that it had simply been presented as an aid program for European shipbuilders. Could a violation of Article 23.1 still be found? If not, does that suggest that governments may be able to take unilateral actions against WTO violations as long as they are discreet in how they present those actions?

SECTION 7.5 IMPLEMENTATION AND RETALIATION PROCEDURES AND REMEDIES

If DSB recommendations are not implemented, the prevailing party is entitled to seek compensation from the non-complying member and, if no compensation is agreed, to request DSB authority to suspend concessions previously made to that member (sometimes referred to as "retaliation"). Art. 22.1 The suspension of obligations normally occurs in respect of obligations of the same sort as were found to be violated, although cross-retaliation is permitted in certain circumstances. Under DSU article 22.6, suspension of concessions is to be authorized automatically in the absence of implementation or compensation, absent a consensus in the DSB to the contrary. There are specific arbitration procedures for determining the level of such a suspension and the appropriateness of cross-retaliation if no agreement on those issues can be reached. In this section we consider three issues: the problems caused by certain ambiguities in the text of DSU articles 21 and 22; the approach of arbitrators in determining the appropriate level of retaliation and whether there should be remedies other than retaliation available for non-implementation.

(A) AMBIGUITIES IN DSU ARTICLES 21 AND 22

The operation of the DSU's provisions on determining implementation and authorizing retaliation has been quite controversial because of certain ambiguities in the provisions of articles 21 and 22 of the DSU. The relevant provisions are:

> Article 21.5, which provides that "[w]here there is a disagreement as to the existence or consistency with a covered agreement of measures taken to comply with [DSB recommendations] such dispute shall be decided through recourse to these dispute settlement procedures, including wherever possible resort to the original panel;" and

> Article 22.2, which provides that "[i]f the Member concerned fails to bring the measure found to be inconsistent with a covered agreement into compliance therewith * * * within the reasonable period of time" and "[i]f no satisfactory compensation has been agreed to within 20 days after the date of the expiry of the reasonable period of time", the prevailing party "may request authorization from the DSB to suspend * * * concessions * * * ."

> Pursuant to article 22.6, "[w]hen the situation described in paragraph 2 occurs, the DSB, upon request, shall grant authorization to suspend concessions or other obligations within 30 days of the expiry of the reasonable period of time unless the DSB decides by consensus to reject the request."

In the *EC Bananas III* case, the US requested the DSB to authorize it to suspend concessions because the EC had failed to implement the DSB recommendations in the case. The EC argued that since it disputed whether its implementing measure was consistent with WTO rules, there had to be a determination under article 21.5 that its implementation measure was WTO inconsistent, before suspension of concessions could be authorized. The US responded that article 22 did not impose such a condition and that, as a practical matter, it would lose the right to have suspension of concessions approved by reverse consensus if its request were not acted upon within 30 days of the expiration of the reasonable period of time. In that regard, it noted that an article 21.5 panel would never be able to issue its report within such a timeframe.

Ultimately, after a week-long DSB meeting and much controversy, the US request was ruled to be in order. The EC then requested an arbitration under article 22.6 to determine the level of suspension, which is required by article 22.4 to be "equivalent to the level of nullification or impairment". The arbitrators were the members of the original panel, who were contemporaneously conducting an article 21.5 proceeding brought a few weeks earlier by Ecuador (one of the original complainants with the US). They simultaneously ruled in *both* matters that the EC implementing measures were not WTO-consistent and in the arbitration set the level of suspension at $191 million (as opposed to the US request of $520 million). The rulings were issued within the article 21.5 timeframe of 90 days, but not within the 30 day timeframe specified for the arbitration. At the end of that 30 day period, the US unilaterally imposed sanctions in an amount of $520 million (which it later reduced to $191 million). The EC initiated a panel proceeding, which reached the obvious conclusion that the unilateral US action violated various rules, including article 23 of the DSU. United States—Import Measures on Certain Products from the European Communities, WT/DS165R & AB/R, adopted January 10, 2001.

In subsequent cases, parties have generally agreed that both the 21.5 and arbitration procedures will be commenced promptly after the end of the expiry of the reasonable period of time, but that the arbitration will be suspended until the 21.5 panel rules (and typically until any appeal has been concluded). The requirement in article 22.6 that the DSB act within 30 days of the expiration of the reasonable period of time does not apply once an arbitration is requested. In such a case, article 22.7 simply provides for DSB action under reverse consensus rules following the receipt of the arbitrator's report, without specifying any time limit for action. The concurrent initiation of both article 21.5 and 22.6 proceedings thus avoids the US concern in *Bananas* that it would lose its right to a reverse consensus decision under article 22.6 if it first had to go to an article 21.5 panel. A proposal to clarify articles 21 and 22 so as to establish a sequence of procedures such as that now typically agreed to garnered substantial support immediately prior to the Seattle ministerial conference in 1999, but has never been adopted. The issue is still under negotiation.

Notes and Questions

(1) As of January 1, 2008, there had been 22 article 21.5 reports adopted, with several cases at various stages in the panel process. Does this suggest that some WTO members are taking questionable implementation measures as a way to postpone full compliance?

(2) After retaliation is authorized, how can a member demonstrate that it has come into compliance and have the retaliatory measures removed? The issue arose in the *Hormones* case. See Section 14.2, note 8.

(B) SETTING THE LEVEL OF RETALIATION

UNITED STATES—MEASURES AFFECTING THE CROSS–BORDER SUPPLY OF GAMBLING AND BETTING SERVICES

WT/DS285/ARB.
Decision by the Arbitrator, issued December 21, 2007.

[This arbitration arose out of a case brought by Antigua against the United States, in which it successfully claimed that the US had failed to live up to the commitments in its GATS schedule for the cross-border supply of gambling services, e.g., via the internet. The US invoked GATS Article XIV(a)'s exception for measures necessary to protect public morals or maintain public order. While the Appellate Body found that the challenged US measures could be justified under Article XIV(a), it also found that they did not comply with the terms of the chapeau to Article XIV. The chapeau specifies that the exceptions are available only for measures that "are not applied in a manner which would constitute a means of arbitrary or unjustifiable discrimination between countries where like conditions prevail". The Appellate Body concluded that the United States engaged in arbitrary discrimination because it permitted interstate, but not cross-border, gambling in respect of horseracing. The substantive issues in the case are discussed in detail in Chapter 19.]

2.2   In this proceeding, the United States challenges two distinct aspects of the request by Antigua for the suspension of certain obligations under the covered agreements. First, it challenges the level of suspension that Antigua seeks an authorization for (i.e. the figure of US$3.443 billion as the level of nullification or impairment of benefits accruing to Antigua). Secondly, the United States also challenges the choice of the sectors and agreement in which Antigua is proposing to carry out the suspension (i.e. certain obligations under the GATS and under the TRIPS Agreement). The Arbitrator therefore has two distinct determinations to make in these proceedings.

* * *

2.4   Article 22.4 of the DSU provides that "[t]he level of the suspension of concessions or other obligations authorized by the DSB shall be equivalent to the level of nullification or impairment". Article 22.6 further provides that "if the Member concerned objects to the level of suspension proposed . . ., the matter shall be referred to arbitration".

2.5   * * * Article 22.7 provides that "[t]he arbitrator acting pursuant to paragraph 6 (. . .) shall determine whether the level of such suspension is equivalent to the level of nullification or impairment (. .)". The DSU provides no further detail how exactly such equivalence might be established. * * *

* * *

2.8   This means that it is necessary to determine what this level of nullification or impairment of benefits is, in order to compare it to the requested level of suspension. Further, past arbitrators have also considered that, if they determined that the proposed level is not equivalent to the level of nullification or impairment as required by the DSU, then it was also their duty to estimate the level of suspension that they considered to be equivalent to the impairment suffered, with a view to contributing to the objective of prompt and positive settlement of disputes embodied in the DSU. This is also what the United States is asking the Arbitrator to do in this dispute.

* * *

2.22   [A]lthough the DSU provides no specific guidance on the allocation of burden of proof in arbitral proceedings under Article 22.6 * * *, previous arbitrators acting pursuant to Article 22.6 * * * have consistently determined that, as noted by both parties, the burden of proving that the requirements of the DSU have not been met rests on the party challenging the proposed level of suspension. This was first expressed as follows by the arbitrators in *EC–Hormones*:

"WTO Members, as sovereign entities, can be presumed to act in conformity with their WTO obligations. A party claiming that a Member has acted inconsistently with WTO rules bears the burden of proving that inconsistency. The act at issue here is the Canadian proposal to suspend concessions. The WTO rule in question is Article 22.4 prescribing that the level of suspension be equivalent to the level of nullification and impairment. The EC challenges the conformity of the Canadian proposal with the said WTO rule. It is thus for the EC to prove that the Canadian proposal is inconsistent with Article 22.4. * * *

2.23   This means that it is for the United States, in this dispute, to demonstrate in the first instance that the amount in which Antigua seeks to suspend concessions or other obligations is not equivalent to the level of nullification or impairment of benefits accruing to it.

* * *

2.25   [However,] both parties, including Antigua, have a duty to collaborate in the establishment of the relevant facts. It is in consideration of these elements that we requested Antigua to provide a Methodology Paper explaining how it arrived at its proposed level of suspension at the beginning of these proceedings.

* * *

III. ASSESSMENT OF THE PROPOSED LEVEL OF SUSPENSION

B. APPROACH OF THE ARBITRATOR

3.11   In this instance, we are therefore required to determine whether the amount of US$3.443 billion proposed by Antigua is equivalent to the level of nullification or impairment of benefits accruing to Antigua. As has been noted by previous arbitrators, for that purpose, we must first determine what the level of nullification or impairment of benefits accruing to Antigua is.

3.12   Antigua's proposed level of suspension is based on an assessment of the annual amount of trade that it considers that it has lost, as a result of the maintenance of the inconsistent US measures beyond the end of the reasonable period of time for implementation. To calculate the level of such lost trade, Antigua relies on a counterfactual scenario intended to reflect what the situation would have been, if the United States had complied with the DSB recommendations and rulings.

* * *

3.15   Although the parties are in agreement on the suitability of this general approach, the United States disagrees both with the counterfactual upon which Antigua has based its calculations and with the data used by Antigua to then estimate the level of its lost exports under that counterfactual. The threshold issue of the choice of counterfactual has a crucial bearing on subsequent steps in the determination of the level of nullification or impairment of benefits, as it effectively determines the basis on which subsequent calculations are to be made. We will therefore consider this issue first, before turning to the actual calculation of the level of nullification.

C.   Choice of Counterfactual

3.16   * * * Antigua has based its calculation of the level of nullification or impairment it has suffered on a counterfactual under which the United States would open to Antiguan operators the United States market for remote gambling without restriction. Antigua considers that, based on the "full" nature of the commitment made by the United States in its GATS schedule, as well as the findings by the original panel and the Appellate Body that this commitment requires the United States to provide market access to all services within the applicable sector, Antigua has a legitimate right to expect that the United States will comply with that commitment. Antigua further considers that it is completely reasonable for it to assume that the United States will observe its obligations under the "express language of the GATS that requires it to provide Antiguan service providers with full market access to consumers in the United States".

3.17   The United States disagrees with the key assumption underlying Antigua's counterfactual, namely that the United States would be assumed to have complied with its obligations by allowing Antiguan operators to provide unrestricted access to cross-border remote gambling and betting services to United States consumers. The United States considers that this scenario is "extraordinarily unrealistic and thus does not form the basis for a useful counterfactual in this arbitration". The United States considers this assumption to have no factual or legal basis and argues that Antigua's proposed scenario entirely ignores the context of this dispute, including the fact that the United States severely restricts, rather than promotes, internet gambling.

* * *

1.   Assessment of Antigua's proposed counterfactual

3.23   [T]he burden rests upon the United States to demonstrate that the level of suspension proposed by Antigua is not equivalent to the level of nullification or impairment of benefits it has suffered as a result of the continued application of the inconsistent US measures. For that purpose, it would not be sufficient, in our view, for the United States to simply identify the existence of alternative possible means of compliance, other than that envisaged by Antigua in its counterfactual. Rather, for the United States to succeed in its challenge, it must persuade us that the particular scenario identified by Antigua as the basis for its counterfactual is not such as to accurately reflect the level of nullification or impairment of benefits accruing to Antigua under the GATS as a result of the continued application by the United States of inconsistent measures.

3.24   We do not disagree with the United States that a WTO Member generally has the discretion to determine the means through which it will comply with adverse DSB rulings, provided that such means are consistent with the WTO covered agreements. However, this does not, in our view, imply that the Member concerned has the freedom to decide, for the purposes of a determination under Article 22.7 of the DSU, among a range of potential measures that it might have taken in order to comply with such rulings, which one should form the basis of the arbitrator's assessment. Our mandate under Article 22.7 of the DSU is to determine whether the level of suspension proposed by Antigua is "equivalent" to the level of nullification or impairment of its benefits. Our starting point, in this determination, must be Antigua's proposed level of suspension. In determining whether this proposed level is "equivalent", we must take care to ensure that the level of suspension is neither reduced to a level lower than the level of nullification or impairment of benefits accruing to the complaining party, such as to adversely affect that party's rights, nor exceeds the level of nullification or impairment of benefits, such that it would become punitive. This is the key consideration that must, in our view, guide our assessment of the US challenge to Antigua's choice of counterfactual.

* * *

3.26   We do not consider that the proposed counterfactual must necessarily reflect the "most likely" scenario of compliance by the Member concerned. By nature, a counterfactual represents a hypothetical scenario and thus there may be, in any given case, a degree of uncertainty as to what exact form compliance might have taken, had it occurred. The Member concerned may have had a range of WTO-consistent options at its disposal to choose from to ensure compliance. It is not for us to speculate on what might have been the "most likely" such scenario.

3.27   Nonetheless, the counterfactual should, in our view, reflect at least a plausible or "reasonable" compliance scenario. A counterfactual that would assume a compliance scenario that leads to an implausibly high level of nullification or impairment of benefits would lead to a suspension in excess of the level of nullification or impairment actually suffered. Conversely, a counterfactual that would underestimate the level of benefits accruing to the complaining party would risk leading to an unwarranted reduction of the level of suspension below the level that that complaining party is entitled to seek, namely "equivalence".

* * *

3.36   We note that the findings of the Appellate Body contain an initial finding that the measures at issue (three federal laws) are inconsistent with Article XVI of the GATS, followed by findings that these same measures are "necessary to protect public morals or maintain public order" within the meaning of paragraph (a) of Article XIV, but that the United States ultimately "has not established that these measures satisfy the requirements of the chapeau" of that provision.

* * *

3.40 Antigua's proposed counterfactual assumes that, as of 3 April 2006 (the end of the reasonable period of time for implementation), the United States would have granted it unrestricted access to its remote gambling market. As Antigua itself notes, it is based on an assumption, by Antigua, that it was entitled to "ignore" the United States invocation of Article XIV of the GATS in the underlying proceedings. The United States objects that this is an "extraordinarily unrealistic" scenario. * * *

3.41 In considering this question, we * * * note * * * that the United States has consistently asserted a public morals and public order policy both in the original proceedings and again in the compliance proceedings as a basis for maintaining restrictions on access to the United States remote gambling market. The United States has thus asserted this policy objective before and beyond the end of the reasonable period of time, which is the date at which the counterfactual situation is assumed to start.

3.42 We further note that the Appellate Body found that US measures restricting access to the remote gambling market were "necessary" within the meaning of Article XIV of the GATS for the protection of public morals and public order * * *.

3.43 In light of these elements, we consider that Antigua's assumption that it could simply "ignore" the failed US defence under Article XIV of the GATS, and that the United States would comply with the rulings by providing unrestricted access to all sectors of its remote gambling market for Antiguan operators, was not reasonable, taking into account the particular circumstances of this dispute.

* * *

3.46 * * * [W]hile Article 3.7 of the DSU does provide that the objective of dispute settlement proceedings is usually the withdrawal of the inconsistent measures, we do not read this provision to mean that this is in all cases the only possible outcome in disputes where a violation of one of the covered agreements has been found. The recommendations of the DSB to the United States in this dispute require it to bring its measures into compliance with the GATS. This did not necessarily require it to "withdraw" the measures by removing entirely the restrictions it maintained on remote gambling and betting services. We note in this respect that the "concept of compliance or implementation prescribed in the DSU" has been described by arbitrators mandated under Article 21.3(c) of the DSU to determine the reasonable period of time for implementation as "the withdrawal or modification of a measure, the establishment or application of which by a Member of the WTO constituted the violation of a provision of a covered agreement". Indeed, we note that Antigua itself appears to agree that a total prohibition on remote gambling and betting services (that is, no market access at all) would in fact also constitute a form of compliance by the United States in this dispute.

* * *

2.   Alternative counterfactual

3.50   Having determined that the counterfactual used by Antigua to estimate the benefits accruing to it in this dispute did not accurately reflect such benefits, we must now determine what would constitute a reasonable counterfactual, in the circumstances of this dispute.

3.51   * * * [A] reasonable counterfactual for the purposes of this dispute would have to take into account the US public policy objective of protecting public morals and public order.

3.52–3.53 [Excluding the scenario of] a complete prohibition on the provision of remote gambling services in the United States, [which] neither party has suggested, * * * [t] he other alternative scenario that has been presented to us is that identified by the United States, which assumes that the United States would provide unrestricted market access for remote gambling and betting services only in respect of horseracing gambling and betting.

* * *

3.56   [W]e are mindful that our mandate in these proceedings is not to determine the consistency with the WTO covered agreements of hypothetical compliance measures. We also note that, as we have stated above, whether the scenario at issue is the "most likely", as described by the United States, is not pertinent as such in our determination. Rather, as determined above, we must assess whether the proposed scenario could constitute a "plausible" or "reasonable" compliance scenario, in the circumstances of the dispute, for the purposes of calculating the level of nullification or impairment of benefits accruing to Antigua in the dispute.

3.57   We first observe [that] the specific aspect of the United States' measures that was found to lead to an arbitrary discrimination within the meaning of the chapeau of Article XIV of the GATS was the treatment of remote gambling and betting in respect of horseracing. This was the sole basis upon which the Appellate Body determined that the US measures were not justified under Article XIV of the GATS. * * *

3.58   In these circumstances, * * * we do not find it unreasonable to assume that compliance might have been achieved through the removal of this specific source of discrimination identified by the Appellate Body, that ultimately led the measures to be found not to be justified under Article XIV of the GATS. We also do not find it unreasonable to assume, in the circumstances of the dispute, that it may have been possible for the United States to remove such discrimination by opening access to remote gambling on horseracing for foreign providers. We also note that this is the only segment of the market that is currently already open to domestic providers, so that an extension of this access to foreign providers would seem to require only limited adjustments to the current situation.

3.59 In making this determination, we do not make any specific finding or determination as to the exact circumstances under which such opening might take place and what specific conditions might be required for the United States to justify, under the terms of Article XIV of the GATS, such a distinction between the treatment of remote gambling on horseracing and other forms of remote gambling. Rather, we are assuming that a range of implementation options might exist for the United States, not necessarily limited to total prohibition or total opening of its market to remote gambling services.

* * *

3. SEPARATE OPINION

3.62 One of the arbitrators is unable to agree with the [above] analysis and conclusions * * *. In the view of this arbitrator, it was not unreasonable for Antigua to assume, in the circumstances of this case, a counterfactual scenario under which the United States would provide unrestricted access to its remote gambling and betting market.

3.63 In the view of this arbitrator, it is appropriate to refer, as a starting point, to the findings and conclusions of the panel and the Appellate Body in this case. Specifically, the Appellate Body has determined that, although the three federal laws at issue are measures "necessary to protect public morals or public order", the United States had not demonstrated that they were applied in accordance with the requirements of the chapeau of Article XIV of the GATS.

3.64 The Appellate Body made this determination "in light of" only one specific discrimination that it identified in the application of the measures. However, this does not necessarily imply, as the United States suggests, that the specific problem found with the US measure at issue was restricted to the "limited issue of the regulation of remote gambling on horse racing". Rather, the overall conclusion of the Appellate Body was that the measures at issue (rather than simply the discriminatory treatment provided in respect of horseracing) were, as a result, not justified under Article XIV of the GATS. * * *

* * *

3.67 [I]t is not clear that the alternative counterfactual scenario envisaged by the United States, which involves a partial opening of a limited segment of the market, constitutes a more reasonable assumption in the circumstances of the case [than Antigua's scenario]. In particular, assuming, for the sake of argument, that such a scenario would constitute compliance with the recommendations and rulings of the DSB in this case (something that is not within our mandate to determine), it is not clear how the United States proposes to reconcile the protection of public morals or public order with the opening of one segment of the market (horseracing).

3.68   In light of the above, this arbitrator is not persuaded that the United States has demonstrated that Antigua's proposed counterfactual was unreasonable in the circumstances of the case.

3.69   This does not imply, however, that this scenario would constitute the only way in which the United States could have complied with these recommendations and rulings. As noted above, Members are free to choose the WTO-consistent means by which they will comply with DSB rulings, and there may be a number of ways in which the United States could have complied, and still could comply, with the rulings in this case. Nor does this determination imply that US policy objectives should not be taken into account. On the contrary, this arbitrator agrees with the determination of the majority that a reasonable counterfactual must take into account the US policy objectives. In that sense, nothing would require the US to abandon its objective of protecting public morals or public order, under Article XIV(a) of the GATS, in implementing, in the future, the recommendations and rulings of the DSB. Indeed, it is quite conceivable that the United States could have found ways in which to address these concerns while protecting such interests. Other WTO Members have chosen to open their market to remote gambling, and it would not be reasonable to assume that such Members do not also have similar policy objectives.

3.70   This arbitrator also notes Antigua's argument that the objective of inducing compliance with the rulings of the DSB is to be taken into account in the Arbitrator's assessment of Antigua's counterfactual. In the view of this arbitrator, the objective of inducing compliance cannot lead to suspension being authorized in excess of equivalence with the level of nullification or impairment of benefits, as foreseen in Article 22.6 of the DSU, and this must remain the benchmark against which the proposed level of suspension is assessed. At the same time, however, in a situation where different means of compliance might form the basis of a counterfactual in order to determine the level of nullification or impairment of benefits, the complaining party would not be prevented from selecting a counterfactual that may lead to a higher level of nullification or impairment than others, provided that such counterfactual is reasonable.

3.71   It should be borne in mind, in this respect, that the Member concerned has had the opportunity to comply with the rulings at issue, and that the very reason for the existence of countermeasures under the DSU is to induce compliance with the covered agreement that has not taken place within the period foreseen in the DSU. In these circumstances, the complainant is by necessity obliged to make certain assumptions as to how compliance might have taken place. * * *

* * *

D.   Calculation of the Level of Nullification

3.74   In light of our determinations above, we now proceed with an assessment of the exports "lost" by Antigua on the basis of a counterfactual under which the United States would have provided unrestricted market access to Antiguan operators only in respect of horseracing gambling and betting.

* * *

3.   Approach of the Arbitrator

3.172   [T]he approaches by both parties are radically different in terms of both the underlying data and the methodology used to determine Antigua's counterfactual levels of exports of remote gambling services to the United States. Both parties have made a number of valid arguments criticizing key aspects of the approach proposed by the other party. We feel unable to rely on the approach used by Antigua, as laid out in its methodology paper, in calculating the requested amount of countermeasures. At the same time, the approach put forward by the United States does not represent a convincing alternative either.

3.173   We, therefore, have no choice but to adopt our own approach. In so doing, we feel we are on shaky grounds solidly laid by the parties. The data is surrounded by a degree of uncertainty. For most variables, the data consists of proxies for what needs to be measured, and observations are too few to allow for a proper econometric analysis. Certain data that we have requested and that, to some extent, could have remedied this situation has not been provided. On methodological questions, parties, in a number of respects, have retained their extreme positions and have failed to propose alternative solutions that would have taken into account the exchange of arguments.

3.174   Hence, we are left with preciously little information and guidance. Nevertheless, we will attempt to stay as closely to the approaches proposed by parties as possible and to make a maximum use of the limited information base we were given, in particular to carry out some sensitivity analysis in support of our main approach. We will broadly follow the spirit of Antigua's original approach. * * *

3.175   In view of the non-reporting of remote gambling services data by Antigua and the consequent non-inclusion of such information in the relevant categories of the services trade statistics compiled by the ECCB [Eastern Caribbean Central Bank]/IMF/WTO, we are left with no real alternative to the GBGC [Global Betting and Gaming Consultants— a private gambling consulting group] data for a time series of Antigua's revenues from remote gambling. We have to assume that such revenues indeed constitute exports, i.e. that the domestic market in Antigua is negligible and that the allocation of revenues to various jurisdictions has been done according to the actual location of operations. On the basis of some of the additional information provided, we can check whether the order of magnitude of the GBGC data is not out of line with other statistics. Notably, we will calculate an average of revenues per employee using the public company data provided by Antigua. Another interesting point of comparison would have been an estimation of total revenues on the basis of the 2001 wage bill in Antigua's remote gambling sector, but, unfortunately, we were not provided with any evidence as to the average share of wages in total revenues.

3.176   We note that the GBGC data on Antigua's annual remote gambling revenues for the years 1999–2006 from the October 2007 release of the Quarterly eGaming Statistics Report has been significantly revised downwards, especially for the years before 2002, compared to the data of the May release, which was used by Antigua in its methodology paper. Given GBGC's own corrections, we feel, of course, compelled to use the most recent update of the data. We also recall that these figures constitute Antigua's global revenues and that no information on bilateral exports of gambling services from Antigua to the United States has been provided. However, Antigua provides some anecdotal evidence that the US share in Antigua's total revenues from remote gambling should be around 80 per cent. In the absence of better information and of any indication about how this share has developed over time, we feel that the most we can do is to reduce the GBGC time series of Antiguan remote gambling revenues by 20 per cent to obtain an estimate of its revenues from the United States and to do at least some justice to our impression that the United States indeed represents the dominant market for Antigua.

3.177   Like Antigua (in two of its three models) and the United States, we take the 2001–2002 period as the turning point when the US measures began to affect Antiguan exports of remote gambling services to the United States. Following the basic idea of Antigua's constant revenue methodology, we calculate the difference between Antigua's 2001 revenues and its actual revenues in each year 2002 to 2006. From these numbers, we determine the average annual revenue loss in the US market for Antigua to be about $304 million, according to the GBGC data.

* * *

3.179   As stated above, we use the information on revenues per employee from public listed companies as well as the data on employment in the remote gambling sector provided by Antigua to conduct a rough test of the order of magnitude of Antigua's remote gambling revenues. The data for seven publicly listed companies (three of which are licensed in Antigua) was taken from annual reports and is available for the years 2001 (for some companies 2002, 2003 or 2004) to 2006. Taking the average over those years gives an annual value of about $446,000/employee, and $447,000/employee if extreme values are removed. Multiplying the former value by the difference between the number of employees in 2001 and the number of employees in each year 2002 to 2006 (adjusted for the assumed 80 per cent US market share) and taking the average over those years results in an average annual revenue loss of about $196 million.

[Thus, the arbitrators took as their starting point, a level of nullification or impairment of between $196 million and $304 million in lost revenues to Antigua. They then made a number of adjustments.

First, they noted that compared to other suppliers of remote gambling services in the Americas, who would have been similarly affected by the US measures, Antigua lost relatively more of its global market share in the 2002–2006 period. Hence the arbitrators adjusted the above figures to reflect Antigua's decline in market share. The result was a range of $128 million to $164 million in lost revenue.

Second, the arbitrators noted that the worldwide share of horseracing in all gambling activities is about 11 percent. Taking 11 percent of the above revenue loss estimates resulted in a new range of lost revenue of between $14 million and $18 million.

Third, the arbitrators made adjustments for growth in the horseracing segment of the remote gambling market over time, i.e. from 2001, when the US measures were found to have started to affect Antigua, until April 2006, the expiration of the reasonable time for US implementation. The adjustment led to an increase in the estimate of revenue loss to between $18 million and $23 million.]

3.188   Taking account of the data uncertainties we have discussed earlier, we have decided to take the average of the two figures * * *. Averaging and rounding to the next full million results in an amount of US$21 million.

3.189   We therefore find that the annual level of nullification or impairment of benefits accruing to Antigua is US $21 million.

IV. PRINCIPLES AND PROCEDURES OF ARTICLE 22.3 OF THE DSU

[Article 22.3 of the DSU provides: "In considering what concessions or other obligations to suspend, the complaining party shall apply the following principles and procedures:

   (a) the general principle is that the complaining party should first seek to suspend concessions or other obligations with respect to the same sector(s) as that in which the panel or Appellate Body has found a violation or other nullification or impairment;

   (b) if that party considers that it is not practicable or effective to suspend concessions or other obligations with respect to the same sector(s), it may seek to suspend concessions or other obligations in other sectors under the same agreement;

   (c) if that party considers that it is not practicable or effective to suspend concessions or other obligations with respect to other sectors under the same agreement, and that the circumstances are serious enough, it may seek to suspend concessions or other obligations under another covered agreement;"]

4.2 In its request, Antigua states that, in considering what concessions and obligations to suspend, it applied the principles and procedures set forth in Article 22.3 of the DSU, and makes its request pursuant to Articles 22.3(b) and (c). Antigua notes that is a developing country with a population of approximately 80,000, and that with a combined land-mass of only 442 square kilometres, Antigua is by far the smallest WTO Member to have made a request for the suspension of concessions under Article 22 of the DSU and realises the difficulty of providing effective countermeasures against the world's dominant economy. Antigua argues that its natural resources are negligible and as a result not only are the country's exports limited (approximately US$4.4 million annually to the United States) but Antigua is required to import a substantial amount of the goods and services needed and used by the people of the country. Antigua submits that on an annual basis, approximately 48.9 per cent of these imported goods and services come from single source providers located in the United States. The imposition of additional import duties on products imported from the United States or restrictions imposed on the provision of services from the United States by Antigua will, in Antigua's view, have a disproportionate adverse impact on Antigua by making these products and services materially more expensive to the citizens of the country. * * *

* * *

4.4 Antigua also considers that the suspension of concessions and other obligations corresponding to a value of US$3.443 billion and wholly applied to the importation of services from the United States is neither practicable nor effective for various reasons. First, Antigua and Barbuda made no commitments under the sector at issue in this dispute * * *. Second, with respect to most of the other services covered by Antigua's [GATS] Schedule, suspension of concessions in the form of higher duties, tariffs, fees or other restrictions would have a disproportionate impact on the economy of Antigua and little or no impact on the United States. Third, even if Antigua were to rely exclusively on a suspension of concessions under the GATS, it would clearly not be able to recover the full amount of nullification and impairment caused by the inconsistent measures.

4.5 Additionally, in Antigua's view, the United States' continued non-compliance renders the circumstances serious enough, within the meaning of Article 22.3(c) of the DSU, to justify the imposition of appropriate countermeasures under other covered agreements, given that Antigua's gaming industry will continue to suffer serious losses, the government of Antigua will be deprived of critical revenue, the people of Antigua will be enjoined from participating in much needed employment and the overall economy of the nation will continue to suffer adverse effects for such time as the United States does not withdraw the measures at issue in this dispute or remove their adverse effects.

* * *

4.18 [Following the arbitrators in the *EC–Bananas III (Ecuador)* case, we believe] that the principles and procedures set forth in Article 22.3 of the DSU, which require the complaining party to make certain determinations, imply "a margin of appreciation" for the complaining party in making these determinations. At the same time, Article 22.3 sets out specific principles and procedures, that the complaining party must follow, and we understand the role of the arbitrator acting pursuant to Article 22.7 of the DSU to involve a review of whether those principles and procedures have been followed. * * * [T]his includes a determination "whether the complaining party in question has considered the necessary facts objectively" and also "whether, on the basis of these facts, it could plausibly arrive at the conclusion that it was not practicable or effective to seek suspension within the same sector under the same agreements, or only under another agreement provided that the circumstances were serious enough".

* * *

4.84 [A]n examination of the "practicability" of an alternative suspension concerns the question whether such an alternative is available for application in practice as well as suited for being used in a particular case. [T]he thrust of the "effectiveness" criterion empowers the party seeking suspension to ensure that the impact of that suspension is strong and has the desired result, namely to induce compliance by the Member which fails to bring WTO-inconsistent measures into compliance with DSB recommendations and rulings within a reasonable period of time.

* * *

4.89 To the extent that it relates to the suspension of obligations under the GATS, Antigua's concern that, as a small import-dependent economy, it could suffer an adverse impact from such suspension, is in our view pertinent to an assessment of whether suspension is practicable or effective. Specifically, we consider that these circumstances have the potential to affect significantly the effectiveness of the proposed suspension.

* * *

4.99 Overall, in light of all these elements, we consider that Antigua has provided sufficient elements in support of its determination, to satisfy us that it has considered objectively the relevant elements and that it could plausibly, on the basis of these elements, reach the conclusion that it was not practicable or effective to suspend concessions or other obligations with respect to "other sectors" under the GATS. By contrast, the United States has not * * * persuaded us that there are services sectors in which Antigua could suspend concessions or other obligations practicably or effectively.

* * *

4.109   In order to demonstrate the seriousness of the circumstances in this case, Antigua [cites the factors set out in paragraphs 4.2–4.5 above].

* * *

4.113   In our view, it was reasonable for Antigua to determine, in light of the elements it highlights, that the circumstances are "serious enough" within the meaning of Article 22.3(c). Specifically, in our view, the various considerations highlighted by Antigua are such as to exacerbate the difficulties in finding a way to suspend concessions or other obligations in a practicable or effective manner under the GATS.

4.114   We note in this respect that the extremely unbalanced nature of the trading relations between the parties makes it all the more difficult for Antigua to find a way of ensuring the effectiveness of a suspension of concessions or other obligations against the United States under the same agreement. We also note that the heavy reliance of Antigua's economy on the very sectors that would be candidates for retaliation under the GATS increases the likelihood that an adverse impact would arise for Antigua itself, including for low-wage workers.

* * *

4.116   In light of these elements, we find that Antigua could plausibly make a determination that "the circumstances are serious enough", within the meaning of Article 22.3(c).

* * *

4.119   Accordingly, we find that Antigua may seek to suspend obligations under the TRIPS Agreement.

[The arbitrator then noted that it would be incumbent on Antigua to ensure that, in applying such suspension, it does not exceed the authorized level. Moreover, it noted that the United States may have recourse to the appropriate dispute settlement procedures in the event that it considers that the level of concessions or other obligations suspended by Antigua exceeds the level of nullification or impairment the arbitrator determined for purposes of the award].

Notes and Questions

(1) The procedural and substantive aspects of the *Gambling* case are dealt with in detail in Chapter 19. In an attempt to resolve the case, the US withdrew the GATS concession at issue and attempted to negotiation compensation arrangements with other interested WTO members. It reached settlements with several of them, but not with Antigua.

(2) The *Gambling* arbitration illustrates some of the problems with establishing the level of nullification or impairment. Can you think of a less speculative way to do so than by using counterfactuals? Are you satisfied with the majority's reasoning on why the counterfactual it chose was the appropriate one? Does the majority adequately respond to the dissenting

view? Did the arbitrators make the appropriate adjustments when they refined the counterfactual?

(3) As of January 1, 2008, there had been article 22 arbitrations in 8 cases—*EC Bananas III, EC Hormones, Brazil Aircraft Subsidies, US FSC, US 1916 Act, Canada Aircraft, US Offset (Byrd Amendment)* and *US Gambling*—and others were pending. In each case (except *Gambling*, which was decided only in December 2007, and *US 1916 Act*), the DSB authorized suspension of concessions and concessions were suspended, except in the two aircraft cases. As of January 1, 2008, concessions were still suspended in *EC Hormones* and *US Offset*. In Chapter 21, we consider an historical study of the use of sanctions to achieve economic and political goals that questions whether sanctions are all that effective. In the WTO context, however, compliance has occurred in most of the relatively few cases where retaliatory measures have been imposed to date, although it is not clear how important those measures were in causing compliance.

(4) There have been three arbitrations under article 4.10 of the SCM Agreement. Article 4.10 provides for "appropriate countermeasures", while article 22.4 of the DSU provides for suspension of concessions in an amount equal to the level of nullification or impairment. What should be the practical effect of this difference in wording in specific cases? In the three article 4.10 arbitrations, the basis used by the arbitrators for the counter-measures was the amount of the subsidy. That approach was essentially agreed upon in the *Brazil Air* and *FSC* cases, and was used in the *Canada Aircraft* case after the arbitrators concluded that Brazil had not been able to defend a calculation based on the trade effects of the subsidy. The arbitrators in *Canada Aircraft* noted, however, that the use of the amount of the subsidy was not mandatory in export subsidy cases. They used the amount of the subsidy in the *Canada Aircraft* case because Canada conceded in that case that a level of countermeasures based on the amount of the subsidy, subject to adjustment, was appropriate. In fact, Canada proposed that the level of countermeasures be set at considerably below the amount of the subsidy because it had acted in good faith in granting export credits that were only later determined to be export subsidies. The arbitrators rejected that argument, noting that it was clear on the basis of an adopted panel report that when the subsidies were granted Canada's basic defense in the case was not valid. The arbitrators ultimately concluded that increasing the amount of the subsidy remaining to be paid by 20% would produce a level of appropriate countermeasures of approximately $250 million. In doing so, it took into account Canada's statement that it did not intend to stop providing the prohibited subsidy. In terms of trade effect, the original aircraft order was valued at $1.68 billion and 63 of the 75 planes (84%) involved had yet to be delivered as of the expiration of the time set for implementation. Thus, the trade effect yet to be felt as of that time was approximately $1.4 billion and the level of countermeasures amounted to about 17.5% of that trade effect.

(5) In the *US FSC* case, the EC was authorized to take countermeasures in respect of the total amount of the US subsidy, although presumably that subsidy had negative effects on the trade of other WTO Members as well. Was that appropriate? Suppose a second WTO Member had brought a successful action against the US in respect of the same subsidy as was at

issue in the *FSC* case. How would the right to take countermeasures be divided between the EC and the other WTO Member? The US objected very strongly to this part of the arbitrators' decision. What is your view? In the *Byrd* arbitrations, the level of suspension was limited in the first instance to the amount of duties distributed by the US related to exports from the suspending country. That amount was further reduced by the arbitrators to reflect their assessment of the actual trade impact of the US non-implementation.

(6) Article 22.3 of the DSU deals with the issue of "cross-retaliation", i.e. retaliation in one sector of trade for a violation of the rules in another sector. For purposes of article 22.3, all goods agreements are viewed as involving one sector, while GATS and TRIPS are subdivided by principal sectors, in the case of services, and by type of intellectual property right, in the case of TRIPS. Generally, suspension of concessions is to take place within the same sector as the violation. However, as detailed in *US Gambling*, in specified circumstances, suspension may be authorized in a different sector under the same agreement or under different agreements. In light of the *Gambling* decision, how difficult would say it is to establish the right to retaliate under a different agreement? Note that article 22.3 does not require an assessment of whether retaliation under another agreement would be practical or effective. Does that make sense? In the Uruguay Round negotiations, the possibility of cross-retaliation was controversial, in particular because developing countries worried that they would be the target of retaliatory measures in the goods area for violations of the TRIPS Agreement. In fact, the only instances to date of cross-retaliation involved the opposite situation. In both the *Gambling* case and in respect of Ecuador in the *Bananas* case, developing countries sought authorization to suspend concessions under the TRIPS Agreement.

(7) What is/are the purpose(s) of authorizing countermeasures or suspension of concessions? The two purposes commonly cited are (i) to induce compliance with the recommendations of the DSB and (ii) to rebalance the imbalance in concessions caused by the violation of WTO rules by one WTO member. The former purpose suggests that there is a WTO-based obligation to comply with WTO rules. Some would argue, however, that WTO members have a choice—to comply or accept suspension of concessions. Of course, as a practical matter, such a choice exists since the WTO has no means to force changes in a member's laws. But does the WTO Agreement recognize such a choice? Consider, inter alia, article 16.4 of the WTO Agreement and articles 3.7 and 22.8 of the DSU. Some commentators argue that if the goal of sanctions were really to "induce compliance," then sanctions would be set at a level designed to make violations clearly unattractive to the violator. By choosing the standard of "equivalent harm" to measure retaliation instead, a degree of similarity arises between the WTO system and the concept of expectation damages in contract law, which are set at a level that compensates the aggrieved party for the harm suffered but no more. Is that analogy convincing? Is it plausible that the equivalence principle serves to facilitate "efficient breach" of WTO obligations, i.e., that it permits members to buy out of compliance when the costs of compliance to them in political terms are excessively high? For an argument along these lines, see Warren F. Schwartz & Alan O. Sykes, The Economic Structure of Renegotiation and Dispute

Resolution in the World Trade Organization, 31 Journal of Legal Studies S179 (2002).

(8) It should be noted that under GATT Article XXIII suspensions were *not* limited to compensatory amounts (as compared to punitive amounts) and were not limited to actions by a nation which had been harmed. Theoretically, a "sanction" could authorize suspensions of concessions by many, if not all, members. The DSU effectively precludes this since it limits suspensions to those that have "invoked the dispute settlement procedures" (art. 22.2) and provides that the level of suspension "shall be equivalent to the level of the nullification or impairment." DSU art. 22.4.

(C) IMPROVING WTO REMEDIES

The WTO dispute settlement system generally provides only a prospective remedy for a violation. The defaulting member is required to bring the non-conforming measure into compliance with its obligations within a reasonable period of time. If it does so, it is not penalized in any way. If it fails to do so, the WTO system relies on retaliatory measures imposed by the prevailing party as the ultimate remedy for noncompliance. Although the system has a very good compliance record (see Section 7.3(B) supra), critics often question whether these remedies are adequate. In this section, we examine problems that arise from reliance on prospective relief and retaliation and consider other possible approaches.

NORWAY—PROCUREMENT OF TOLL COLLECTION EQUIPMENT FOR THE CITY OF TRONDHEIM

40th Supp. BISD 319.
Panel Report adopted May 13, 1992 by the Committee
on Government Procurement.

[This case arose under the Government Procurement Code, which is described in Section 12.5 infra. The panel concluded that Norway had violated the Code because the City of Trondheim had not instituted an open bidding procedure in respect of its procurement of certain highway toll collection equipment. The following part of the decision deals with the appropriate remedy for this violation.]

4.17   The panel then turned its attention to the recommendations that the United States had requested it to make. In regard to the United States' request that the Panel recommend that Norway take the necessary measures to bring its practices into compliance with the Agreement with regard to the Trondheim procurement, the Panel noted that all the acts of non-compliance alleged by the United States were acts that had taken place in the past. The only way mentioned during the Panel's proceedings that Norway could bring the Trondheim procurement into line with its obligations under the Agreement would be by annulling the contract and recommencing the procurement process. The Panel did not consider it appropriate to make such a recommendation. Recommendations of this nature had not been within customary practice in dispute settlement under the GATT system and the drafters of the Agreement on Government Procurement had not made specific provision that such recommendation be within the task assigned to panels under standard terms of reference. Moreover, the Panel considered that in the case under examination such a recommendation might be disproportionate, involving waste of resources and possible damage to the interests of third parties.

4.18   The United States had further requested the Panel to recommend that Norway negotiate a mutually satisfactory solution with the United States that took into account the lost opportunities in the procurement of United States' companies, including Amtech. Finally, the United States had requested the Panel to recommend that, in the event that the proposed negotiation did not yield a mutually satisfactory result, the Committee be prepared to authorize the United States to withdraw benefits under the Agreement from Norway with respect to opportunities to bid of equal value to the Trondheim contract. * * *

4.19   In examining these requests, the Panel first noted that, as instructed in its terms of reference, it had given Norway and the United States full opportunity to develop a mutually satisfactory solution. The Panel also noted that nothing prevented the two governments from negotiating at any time a mutually satisfactory solution that took into account the lost opportunities of United States' suppliers, provided such solution was consistent with their obligations under this and other GATT agreements. The issue was whether the Panel should recommend this and further recommend that the Committee be prepared to authorize the withdrawal of benefits under the Agreement from Norway if such a solution were not negotiated.

* * *

4.21   [Beyond noting that the US was somewhat inconsistent in its requests to the Panel], the Panel observed that, under the GATT, it was customary for panels to make findings regarding conformity with the General Agreement and to recommend that any measures found inconsistent with the General Agreement be terminated or brought into conformity from the time that the recommendation was adopted. The provision of compensation had been resorted to only if the immediate withdrawal of the measure was impracticable and as a temporary measure pending the withdrawal of the measures which were inconsistent with the General Agreement. Questions relating to compensation or withdrawal of benefits had been dealt with in a stage of the dispute settlement procedure subsequent to the adoption of panel reports.

4.22   * * * [T]he Panel noted the argument of the United States that, because benefits accruing under the Agreement were primarily in respect of events (the opportunity to bid), rather than in respect of trade flows, and because government procurement by its very nature left considerable latitude for entities to act inconsistently with obligations under the Agreement in respect of those events even without rules or procedures inconsistent with those required by the Agreement, standard panel recommendations requiring an offending Party to bring its rules and practices into conformity would, in many cases, not by themselves constitute a sufficient remedy and would not provide a sufficient deterrent effect.

4.23 In considering this argument, the Panel was of the view that situations of the type described by the United States were not unique to government procurement. Considerable trade damage could be caused in other areas by an administrative decision without there necessarily being any GATT inconsistent legislation, for example in the areas of discretionary licensing, technical regulations, sanitary and phytosanitary measures, and subsidies. Moreover, there had been cases where a temporary measure contested before the GATT had been lifted before a Panel had been able to report.

4.24 The Panel also believed that, in cases concerning a particular past action, a panel finding of non-compliance would be of significance for the successful party: where the interpretation of the Agreement was in dispute, panel findings, once adopted by the Committee, would constitute guidance for future implementation of the Agreement by Parties.

4.25 Moreover, the Panel was not aware of any basis in the Agreement on Government Procurement for panels to adopt, with regard to the issues under consideration, a practice different from that customary under the General Agreement, at least in the absence of special terms of reference from the Committee.

4.26 In the light of the above, the Panel did not consider that it would be appropriate for it to [make the recommendation requested by the United States].

Notes and Questions

(1) Did the United States receive adequate redress in the *Trondheim* case? If the DSU had been in effect, would the US have had a better argument for broader relief?

(2) Suppose that a panel concludes that a country has inappropriately applied antidumping duties to imports from a complainant. Would it be appropriate to recommend that the duties be refunded? This occurred in New Zealand—Imports of Electrical Transformers from Finland, 32nd Supp. BISD 55 (1986) (Panel report adopted July 18, 1985), but the United States blocked adoption of a panel report to the Antidumping Committee that recommended that the US reimburse such duties in a case involving certain Swedish steel exports to the US. The US has argued that the proposed recommendation was "of an extraordinary retroactive and specific nature." GATT Activities 1992, at 40.

(3) Under the DSU, one 21.5 panel recommended that a government, which had granted an WTO-inconsistent export subsidy, could "withdraw the subsidy" as required by article 4.7 of the Subsidies Agreement only by obtaining full repayment. The result was quite controversial and heavily criticized at the DSB meeting at which the panel report was adopted. (There was no appeal because of a prior agreement that neither side would appeal

the panel report.) Australia—Subsidies Provided to Producers and Exporters of Automotive Leather, WT/DS126/RW, adopted February 11, 2000.

(4) Does providing only prospective relief mean that WTO members in effect have a license to violate the rules without consequences for the two to three year period that it takes for the dispute settlement process to progress from consultation to the end of the reasonable period of time? Would some of the possible changes discussed in the following article be useful?

WILLIAM J. DAVEY, REMEDIES IN WTO DISPUTE SETTLEMENT (2001 UPDATED)

In considering remedies in the WTO system, it is important to recall that the existing remedies are prospective—whether in the form of compensation or retaliation. In addition, it is important to consider their two principal aims—to restore the balance of concessions that was upset when one member violated its obligations (a temporary aim since compliance is the preferred result); and to give that member an incentive to comply. The current problem with achieving the first aim—rebalancing—is that if retaliation is authorized, rebalancing takes place at a lower level of trade liberalization than had been agreed to. It would be desirable if a remedy could be devised that would not lead to less liberalization overall. One could consider monetary payments or requiring the payment of compensation through a reduction in other tariffs or trade restrictions maintained by the non-complying Member.[1]

In respect of the second aim—incentive to comply—there are two issues—timing and level of compensation or retaliation. At present, because remedies are prospective, there is an incentive initially to delay the time at which point they might be implemented, such as by seeking a long reasonable period of time for implementation and then forcing the victor to go through an article 21.5 panel (and Appellate Body) compliance proceeding. Moreover, if the threat of retaliation does not work, it is possible that the actual existence of retaliation will become viewed as the status quo and a long-term solution, even though the WTO rules in theory require compliance. This fear that retaliation will lose effect over time explains in part the US desire to implement the so-called carousel provision, by which the products targeted by retaliatory action would change on a regular basis once retaliation is authorized. A preferable solution may be to create incentives for early compliance, such as by providing that any retaliation will be calculated from a date prior to the date set for implementation or by providing for increasing retaliation over time.

These issues will require careful thought. While retaliation seems to work when threatened by a large country against a smaller one, and has worked as between two large countries, it may not be an effective

---

1. See Joost Pauwelyn, Enforcement and Countermeasures in the WTO, 94 Am. J.Intl.L. 335 (2000).

remedy for a small country (even if it can target sensitive large country sectors such as copyright holders). Moreover, the *Hormones* case shows that it is not always effective between the large players. Its inefficacy and the unfavorable position in which it leaves developing countries may soon combine to create a serious credibility problem for the system that must be confronted.

In considering how to improve WTO remedies, it will be necessary to consider whether there are other forms of remedies beyond compensation and retaliation that might be more effective. One possibility would be the payment of fines or damages. One obvious problem would be the disparity in fine-paying ability among WTO members. Any such system would have to be designed to avoid the possibility that rich members could effectively buy their way out of obligations in a way not available to the poor members. One alternative would be to tie the amount of fines to the size of the member's economy, or otherwise provide for a sliding scale that would minimize "discrimination" against poor members. To avoid the perception that the payment of fines is simply an alternative to compliance, the fines could be assessed annually (or on some other periodic basis) and could be increased over time. Such a system could serve as a method of rebalancing if the fines are paid to the member owed compliance and could promote prompter compliance if the fines are increased over time. While a system of fines or monetary compensation has not been discussed in detail in the past, it seems to have become a more realistic possibility in recent years. For example, the most recently negotiated US free trade agreements provide that a defaulting party can elect to pay monetary compensation in lieu of being subject to trade retaliation. Such an approach would be perhaps more attractive to developing countries if they were given the right to demand monetary compensation in the event of non-implementation of DSB recommendations.

A different sort of alternative would be to suspend certain WTO rights for the period of time that a member is not in compliance with its obligations. There are a wide variety of rights or benefits that might be suspended: voting rights, participation rights in meetings, technical cooperation, dispute settlement rights. Given the lack of voting in the WTO, suspension of voting rights would not seem to be an alternative. The limitation of participation rights might be difficult to define—it would not be in the interest of the WTO or its members to exclude one member from trade liberalization negotiations. Suspension of technical cooperation could also be self-defeating since it is usually concerned with implementation issues, and in any event, it would be applicable only to developing countries. The most promising area in which to consider suspension of rights would be in respect of dispute settlement. If a member refuses to comply with the results of dispute settlement when it loses, simple notions of fairness would argue that it should not be able to invoke the system against others. It would be necessary to define the rights to be suspended: at a minimum, five rights are easily identified— the right to request consultations, the right to request a panel, the right to request authority to suspend concessions, the right to participate as a third party and the right to participate in DSB meetings. It would be possible to create a scheme that would phase-in a loss of the foregoing rights over time.

Notes and Questions

(1) Which of the foregoing ideas seems to be most plausible—in terms of likely effectiveness and acceptance by WTO members?

(2) What others remedies might be considered? What remedies are typically available to aggrieved countries under public international law? As to the latter issue, the International Law Commission's Articles on State Responsibility provide that a State responsible for a wrongful act must (i) cease the act if it is continuing (art. 30) and (ii) make full reparation for the injury caused by the act (art. 31). Should the WTO dispute settlement system provide for such a remedy? Why should the WTO system differ from the international law standard in this regard? See generally James Crawford, The International Law Commission's Articles on State Responsibility: Introduction, Text and Commentaries (2002).

Chapter 8

BORDER MEASURES I: TARIFFS AND CUSTOMS RULES

SECTION 8.1 INTRODUCTION

(A) REGULATORY PRINCIPLES AND IMPORT RESTRAINTS: THE CORE OF THE SYSTEM

So far, we have examined the international economic system and its institutions in a general way, focusing on fundamental and institutional legal questions. The next chapters are structured vertically, that is to say, a functional subject is explored through both the national and international level, with the focus upon WTO rules and U.S. law.

The next 11 chapters deal with the most fundamental aspects of regulation of international economic relations. Any person involved with international trade policy, whether in government or in private life, will find that discourse generally assumes a knowledge of these topics. These subjects are essentially legal in the sense that they embody rules and principles similar to those found in legal systems, and there is a comparatively high degree of consensus and compliance with the rules.

The starting point—Chapter 8—is an examination of tariffs—the basic import restraint—and national customs laws related to tariffs. Chapter 9 considers quotas and other non-tariff barriers. Chapter 10 deals with the most-favored-nation (MFN) obligation, while Chapter 11 examines the far reaching exception from MFN treatment for free trade areas and customs unions. Then, in Chapter 12, we examine the national treatment obligation. The MFN and national treatment obligations are probably the two most fundamental principles of international trade regulation. Chapter 13 analyzes certain exceptions to those fundamental principles, looking in particular at the question of how environmental and health concerns are treated. Chapter 14 then considers the special problems of product standards, which are the subject of two WTO agreements. Chapter 15 looks at the problem of safeguards, which are measures taken to protect domestic industry from injurious foreign competition. The so-called Escape Clause permits safeguards in certain situations, thereby providing some flexibility in the rules. Chapters 16 to 18 introduce the problems raised when foreign exporters or countries use unfair export methods to the detriment of importing country producers. In particular, we examine two such methods—dumping and subsidies—and how they are controlled by international and national rules.

(B) INTRODUCTION TO CHAPTERS 8 AND 9

We began in Chapter 2 with an overview of the economic theories that underlie international economic policies. We have seen how the view that free trade is desirable and reduces the likelihood of armed conflict played a central role in the establishment of GATT. Throughout the rest of the book, the reader will see how the factors introduced in Chapter 2 have affected the creation of the international rules and national practices under them. In particular, we will see how the WTO rules enshrine the basic principles of free international trade, but at the same time allow exceptions to them, particularly in cases where imports are viewed as unfairly traded or as injurious to local industry, and we will see played out time and again the struggle between advocates of a broader national interest—free trade—and those defending the interests of a particular industry.

At the time that General Agreement on Tariffs and Trade was drafted in 1947, four techniques were considered to be the primary governmental methods of import restraint:[1] the tariff, the quota, subsidies and state trading enterprises. The basic and most prominent of these is the tariff, which is a tax imposed at the border on imported goods. Generally there are three types of tariffs: ad valorem, specific and mixed. An ad valorem tariff is a tax set as a percentage of the value of the imported goods. Thus, if a product valued at $100 were subject to a 10% ad valorem tariff, $10.00 would be due upon importation. A specific tariff is a flat charge per unit or quantity of goods, such as $1.00 per ton. A mixed tariff combines these two concepts, such as 5 cents per pound plus 10% of value. There are also "tariff quotas," which provide a different tariff rate depending upon the amount already imported into a country. For instance, a tariff quota might provide that the first 1,000,-000 tons of an imported product would be subject to a tariff of 10%, with all additional imports subject to a 20% tariff. As discussed in Chapter 2, the amount of a tariff is a cost of business to the importer that must be recovered when the good is sold in the importing country. Since domestically produced goods are not subject to the tariff, the domestic producer often may charge a higher price for its goods than it could in the absence of a tariff. In this sense tariffs protect domestic industries from foreign competition.

While tariffs are the most common import restraint, the quota or quantitative restriction is the most prominent of the plethora of nontariff barriers (NTBs) through which countries can restrain imports. A quota specifies the quantity of a particular good that a country will allow to be imported during a specified time period. The quota may be global,

---

1. See generally John H. Jackson, World Trade and the Law of GATT 305–08, 625–38 (1969).

in the sense that it expresses the total amount that can be imported from all sources; or it may be divided into country quotas that specify import limits on goods from specific countries (e.g., 1000 widgets each year from Japan, 500 from Taiwan, etc.). Quotas will be analyzed in more detail in Chapter 9 infra.

A subsidy can be used as a protective device if it is granted for the domestic production of goods, so that such goods can be priced lower in the domestic market than the comparable imported goods. Consequently, in contrast to tariffs and quotas, which result in higher prices, subsidies lead to lower prices, thereby favoring the consumer (at the expense of the taxpayer, of course). If sufficiently subsidized, domestic goods might be sold at a price so low as to drive all imports out of the domestic market, and therefore no imports would occur. WTO rules on subsidies are explained in Chapter 18.

State trading enterprises can also be used to restrict imports. They operate as follows: The government decrees that a particular corporation (usually government-owned) shall be the only entity allowed to import a certain type of commodity (such as tobacco or steel). The state trading corporation will then purchase goods abroad and resell them on the domestic market in competition with domestically produced goods. The degree of protection that this device affords will depend upon the mark-up which the state trading corporation imposes on the goods. If it purchases a product for $100 and resells it on the domestic market for $200, it has imposed a 100% mark-up. This can operate similarly to a 100% tariff, and reduces the demand for imported goods in competition with domestic goods. A state trading corporation can also use its purchases and sales to have the effect of a quota. For example, it may simply refuse to purchase more than a specified amount of foreign goods for domestic resale, thereby limiting the quantity of imports to that amount. GATT rules on state trading are examined in Chapter 9.

The GATT approach to these four basic protective devices differs considerably. Basically, GATT prefers the tariff, as do international economists generally. Tariffs, it is argued, are more visible, capture for the government much of the "monopoly profit" which they create, do not need licensing to administer, do not require government funds (in contrast to a subsidy), and give only a limited amount of protection, so that if a foreign-based industry is efficient enough, it will still be able to export to the tariff-imposing country. GATT therefore permits tariffs and if a country has not agreed to a limit on its tariff for a particular product, it is permitted under GATT rules to impose any tariff it wishes. Another advantage of tariffs is that tariff reduction is relatively easy to negotiate and the GATT structure provides for multilateral, international negotiations on the level of individual tariffs. In Section 8.2 we consider the basic GATT obligations in respect of tariffs. In Section 8.3 we look at tariffs from the national perspective, which essentially involves consideration of the basic issues of customs law.

In comparison, quotas are thought to entail the risk of government corruption in the licensing process. They also tend to conceal from the public the degree and cost of the protection being afforded domestic producers. Moreover, unless quota rights are sold, which is rarely the case, the extra profits that they yield go to the foreign seller, instead of the government, as would be the case with a tariff. On the other hand, quotas facilitate economic planning since the precise amount of imports can be predicted, which is not the case with tariffs. Nonetheless, as discussed in Chapter 9, GATT rules prohibit the use of quotas (with certain specified exceptions). WTO/GATT rules also limit the use of subsidies or state trading for restraining imports.

Beyond the basic four protective devices discussed above, there are many other nontariff barriers (NTBs) and we will have occasion to examine them throughout the book, particularly in Chapter 9.

SECTION 8.2   GATT TARIFF COMMITMENTS: THE BINDINGS

When it was negotiated in 1947, the basic purpose of the General Agreement on Tariffs and Trade was to cut tariffs significantly and to protect those cuts from indirect evasion through discriminatory internal taxes or other measures. After the failure of the International Trade Organization ratification process (described in Chapter 6), GATT assumed a broader role in regulating international trade than originally intended. Nonetheless, the negotiation and enforcement of tariff commitments has remained central to GATT. In this section, we trace the history of tariff negotiations in GATT and examine the basic GATT rules applicable to tariff commitments: the bindings made under Article II and the various tariff renegotiation provisions.

(A) GATT TARIFF NEGOTIATIONS

The various rounds of GATT negotiations have been previously described generally in Chapter 6; here we focus on tariff negotiations. In all trade negotiation rounds, a first important step has been the establishment of a tariff negotiations committee, consisting of a representative from each of the countries which are participating in the negotiations. Often countries that were not GATT Contracting Parties participated in GATT tariff negotiations, usually in anticipation of joining GATT. If such a country did not become a GATT party, it typically agreed to observe certain GATT-based rules so as to guarantee its tariff concessions.[1]

(1) The Early Years (1947–1961)

The first five tariff negotiating rounds were conducted under procedures following generally those established by the first round and can be summarized as follows: the first step was for each country to submit a

---

1. See Protocol of Bulgaria, GATT, 26th Supp. BISD 189 (1980).

"request list" on which it detailed for every other participant the concessions (specified product by product) which it desired the other country to make. Thus, if the United States felt that it had a potential for shipping aircraft to the United Kingdom, it would ask the United Kingdom for a tariff commitment on aircraft which would likely permit more U.S. sales of aircraft to the United Kingdom.

Next, each country would analyze the requests submitted to it and prepare an "offer list," which would indicate what tariff concessions it was willing to make in exchange for obtaining favorable treatment on its requests. Each of the request and offer lists would be furnished to every country participating in the negotiation.

A third step was a series of bilateral conferences between negotiating countries to begin to develop the bargain between them. The objective was to obtain concessions roughly equivalent in value to those that a country gave up. In general, offers on particular products would be extended to the country which was the "principal supplier" of that product to the offering country. Thus, if country X imported bicycles from countries A, B and C, with A supplying 60%, B supplying 30%, and C supplying 10%; then X would make its tariff offer to A, which supplied most of the bicycles and would stand to benefit most from a concession. Nevertheless, once A and X had come to a tentative agreement, then X would begin negotiating with B with respect to the same concession, trying to obtain from B some reciprocal concessions for the advantage B would automatically obtain under the MFN clause by the concession X was willing to extend to A.

Gradually, toward the end of this process, more and more concessions would fall into place and third party benefits would be reciprocated as the circle of bilateral negotiations was extended. Finally, all countries would finalize their offer lists. At this point, each country would have to evaluate the total concessions of all the other participants in the negotiations, to see whether it felt that as a whole they were equivalent in value to the concessions which it was giving. If it felt this was not the case, it would then notify the other participants that it was withdrawing some of its offers to remove the imbalance. Needless to say, a withdrawal could create a ripple effect of counter withdrawals, which could extend through the entire negotiation and destroy the results obtained so far. This stage of the negotiation has been accompanied with a considerable amount of bluff, tension, late night sessions and a certain amount of mediation by the secretariat.

By the time of the "Dillon Round" (1960–61), the item-by-item approach to tariff negotiations proved extraordinarily cumbersome. The technical problem of dealing with thousands of specific products was formidable enough. The process was further complicated, however, because the European Community, one of the main participants, had to negotiate internally in order to establish a common position among its six member states before it could negotiate on an item in GATT. Thus, it became almost impossible to make progress in the negotiations.

(2) The Kennedy Round (1963–1967)[2]

The difficulties in negotiating tariff cuts in the Dillon Round led the GATT Contracting Parties to conclude that it would be necessary for future tariff negotiating rounds to establish new procedures, and, in particular, it was decided to utilize a "linear technique" for negotiating tariff reductions. The precise negotiating rules implementing such a technique for the Kennedy Round were agreed upon in May 1964.[3] Basically, the rules called for offers of a 50% cut in tariffs as a "working hypothesis," except for most agricultural products. Countries then tabled "exceptions lists," specifying the products that they wished exempted from these general tariff cuts. The negotiations then focused principally upon the exceptions lists.

Several developed countries (Australia, Canada, South Africa and New Zealand) and all of the developing countries were exempted from making offers based on the linear technique. The four developed countries asked for an exemption because they depended heavily upon agriculture and raw material exports. Since these products were generally not included in the linear offers, if these countries were required to offer 50% tariff cuts on industrial products, they felt that they could not hope to achieve reciprocal concessions from other developed countries. As for the developing countries, they argued that under Part IV of GATT (added in 1964) they were not expected to offer reciprocal concessions in GATT trade negotiations and should therefore not be required to make the linear offer,[4] although they desired industrialized country 50% offers to include products of special interest to them.

Just before U.S. negotiating authority ran out on June 30, 1967, the Kennedy Round participants completed their agreements. The tariff reductions were substantial. The main industrialized countries—the EU, Japan, Sweden, Switzerland, the United Kingdom and the United States—made concessions on imports valued at $32 billion. Duty reductions affected 70% of these countries' dutiable imports, and the majority of these reductions were of 50% or more.

(3) The Tokyo Round Tariff Negotiations[5]

The Tokyo Round was supposed to focus on nontariff barriers, and in fact it did. However, the tariff negotiations, especially in the early years of the negotiation, remained very significant. Some have observed that this may have been due to the momentum of bureaucratic habits.

---

2. See generally John W. Evans, The Kennedy Round in American Trade Policy (1971); John H. Jackson, World Trade and the Law of GATT, sec. 10.5 (1969); Kenneth W. Dam, The GATT: Law and International Economic Organization 68–77 (1970).

3. GATT, 12th Supp. BISD 47, para. A4 (1964); GATT, 13th Supp. BISD 109–10 para. A (1965). See Dam, supra note 2, at 69–70; Evans, supra note 2, at 184–202; Jackson, supra note 2, at 223–27.

4. GATT, Art. XXXVI:8; GATT, Annex I, Ad Art. XXXVI:8.

5. See generally GATT, The Tokyo Round of Trade Negotiations: Report by the Director–General of GATT (1979); GATT, The Tokyo Round of Trade Negotiations: Supplementary Report by the Director–General of GATT (1980); Gilbert R. Winham, International Trade and the Tokyo Round Negotiation (1986).

Others suggested that during periods when the overall negotiation was largely stalled, the continuation of detailed and often mathematical talks about tariffs provided the continuity or "glue" which held the negotiation together, by providing a joint sense of purpose and movement, and a focus for lower level officials to continue their activities, thus maintaining the governmental structure necessary to accomplish the intense work that would come when the overall negotiation began to move forward.

In the case of the United States, the Trade Act of 1974 contained the tariff negotiating authority for the Tokyo Round. Initial proposals for the Act would have given the Executive unlimited tariff negotiating authority. Partly because of the "Watergate" climate and a weak (and perhaps disinterested) Executive, the tariff authority that finally emerged in the Trade Act allowed a 60% cut in any tariff existing on January 1, 1975, with provision for abolition of tariffs which on that date were not more than 5% ad valorem. Arguably this was extensive: One can compare it with the 50% tariff authority of the 1962 Act. On the other hand, by 1975 industrialized country tariff levels were generally between 8% and 9%, so that a 60% cut meant about a 5 percentage point reduction in tariff levels, while in previous negotiations a 50% cut could give an average reduction of 6 percentage points or more. Furthermore, given the swings in exchange rates in the early 1970's (as much as 20% in the dollar's relation to other currencies), exchange rate swings could have many times the influence of the authorized tariff rate changes under the 1974 Trade Act.

One of the serious controversies to be addressed in the Tokyo Round tariff negotiations was the so-called "disparities issue," which first arose in the Kennedy Round.[6] In the 1960's the European Union had implemented a common external tariff, which tended to be the average of the tariffs of its member states. As a result, it was a more uniform tariff without the "peaks and valleys" often found in a traditional national tariff schedule, such as the U.S. schedule. The EU argued that a 50% reduction in peak tariffs would not have an equivalent trade effect to a 50% reduction in its flatter tariff. For example, halving a 40% tariff would result in a 20% tariff, which would still offer considerable protection against imports. On the other hand, if a 20% tariff were cut in half, the resulting 10% tariff might not suffice to inhibit greatly increased imports.

This issue was resolved in the Tokyo Round by an agreement to use an algebraic formula—the so-called Swiss formula—for the initial tariff reduction offers. A variant of the following formula was used: $Z = (A$ times $X)$ divided by $(A + X)$; with X representing the initial rate of import duty applied, A a coefficient to be agreed upon, and Z the

6. See A.H.M. Albregts & A.J.W. van de Gevel, Negotiating Techniques and Issues in the Kennedy Round, in Economic Relations After the Kennedy Round 20, 23–31 (Frans A.M. Alting von Geusau ed., 1969); Thomas B. Curtis & John R. Vastine, Jr., The Kennedy Round and the Future of American Trade 82–91 (1971); Dam, supra note 2, at 73–76; Evans, supra note 2, at 186–200.

resulting reduced rate of duty.[7] Under this formula, if A were set at 16, then a 10% duty would be reduced to 6.15% (a cut of 38.5%), while a 20% duty would be reduced to 8.88% (a cut of 55.6%). In fact, there were considerable variations in the way this formula was applied, but it generally led to significant tariff cuts. The EU, Austria, Canada, Finland, Japan, Norway, Sweden, Switzerland and the United States agreed to reduce their weighted average tariffs on industrial products from 7.0% to 4.7% (10.4% to 6.4% based on simple tariff averages). In addition, the use of the tariff-cutting formula reduced the differences in their tariff levels by 25%, measured by standard deviation of national averages.[8]

(4) The Uruguay Round Tariff Negotiations (1986–1994)[9]

Like the Tokyo Round, the Uruguay Round was intended to focus on nontariff issues, but as in all GATT negotiating rounds, there were significant negotiations on tariffs. As in the Tokyo Round, the U.S. President was authorized to make 50% cuts in U.S. tariffs, with the proviso that tariffs of under 5% could be reduced to zero.[10]

Initially, the Uruguay Round had a tariff negotiating subgroup, as well as a number of other subgroups dealing with market access issues relating to specific products, such as tropical products and agriculture. The 1988 midterm review session in Montreal (which was completed in Geneva in April 1989) reached an agreement to cut tariffs on tropical products, an issue of particular interest to developing countries.

The Uruguay Round negotiations were later reorganized and one negotiating group was given a broad range of market access issues including tariffs. There were considerable difficulties in agreeing on an approach to tariff reduction—with the United States pushing for negotiations on an item-by-item basis, and many other countries arguing for a formula approach of the type used in the Tokyo Round. Ultimately, both were used. In the end, the GATT Secretariat reported on April 12, 1994, that implementation of the Uruguay Round tariff commitments would result in an overall decrease of 38% in average developed country tariffs (from 6.3% to 3.9%). In addition, there would be an increase in the number of industrial products receiving duty-free treatment in developed countries from 20% to 43%.

The round also resulted in a significant increase in the number of tariff lines "bound" under Article II. In the case of developed countries, the increase was from 78% to 99%; in the case of developing countries, it was from 22% to 72%; and in the case of countries in transition, it was from 73% to 98%.

7. See GATT, The Tokyo Round of Multilateral Trade Negotiations: Report by the Director–General of GATT 46–48 (1979).

8. GATT, The Tokyo Round of Multilateral Trade Negotiations, Supplementary Report by the Director–General of GATT 3–7 (1980).

9. See generally John Croome, Reshaping the World Trading System: A History of the Uruguay Round (2d ed. 1999)(written for the WTO); The GATT Uruguay Round: A Negotiating History (1986–1992) (Terence P. Stewart ed., 1993).

10. Omnibus Trade and Competitiveness Act of 1988, sec. 1102(a), 19 U.S.C.A. sec. 2902(a).

(5) Tariff Negotiations in the WTO

In 1996, there were WTO negotiations in respect of tariffs on information technology products, and at the Singapore Ministerial Meeting at the end of 1996, a significant number of WTO Members agreed to eliminate tariffs on such products. While not all members trading such products joined in the agreement, there was a "critical mass" that did agree.

In 2001, the Doha Development Agenda negotiations were launched, with non-agricultural tariff negotiations being a significant component of the overall negotiations. The negotiations are ongoing as of January 1, 2008, and are part of the so-called NAMA (non-agricultural market access) negotiations. It seems likely that a simple Swiss formula (see the Tokyo Round above) will be used, with different coefficients for developed and developing countries. There is not yet agreement on what those coefficients will be and the extent to which exceptions and flexibilities will be permitted, particularly for various groups of developing countries and new members. There are also a number of sectoral negotiations aimed at getting a critical mass of WTO members to agree to eliminate all tariffs on certain product groups. The Doha mandate called for reducing or eliminating tariff peaks, high tariffs and tariff escalation.

(6) Problems of Tariff Negotiations

There are two particular problems that stand out in tariff negotiations.[11] First, the MFN obligation, providing for a generalization of each nation's concessions to all other GATT members, tends to restrain willingness to make offers and concessions, particularly if some participants are dragging their feet. A foot dragger, whose offered concessions are relatively meager, stands to gain from the free ride effect of MFN if the other countries go ahead despite the foot dragging. The formula cuts described above are intended to reduce this problem, but to the extent that the full participation of smaller countries is often not crucial to the deals struck by the major trading nations, these smaller countries may evade the full effect of the formula through invocation of comparatively extensive exceptions or, in nonformula negotiations, through limited offers.

How would you expect the extent of free riding to be affected, if at all, by the choice of negotiating method for tariff cutting, for example, between item-by-item cuts or formula reductions? Are there other negotiation techniques that would reduce the likelihood of free riding? Despite the obvious interest of these questions, we have found no studies reaching firm conclusions on these issues.

A second difficulty arises from the reciprocity principle. While economists may believe that unilateral tariff cuts benefit a country's economy in the long run (see Chapter 1), tariff negotiations under GATT's auspices have typically been carried out with the objective in each participant's mind of gaining tariff concessions from others to match

---

11. See Jackson, supra note 2, at 240–248.

those that it makes itself. However, it is extremely difficult to measure the trade effects of tariff changes because the necessary information (e.g., price elasticities of the relevant products) is often nonexistent or unreliable and because many other unpredictable, nontariff related events (such as exchange rate shifts) may have much more important price effects than tariff cuts. The only easily available measure of tariff cuts is to multiply the tariff reduction times a recent year's import value figure. Thus, if a tariff is reduced from 20% to 10% and the total imports of the product were valued at $1 million in a recent year, the value of the reduction for purposes of comparing it to other reductions is 10% of $1 million or $100,000. Obviously, this measure is extremely imprecise.

Despite these problems, the notion of reciprocity has had enormous political impact. The idea of achieving equivalent concessions in tariff reductions appeals to laymen and politicians as "fair" and has helped to achieve the great reductions of tariffs that have occurred in the last 50 years. Perhaps reciprocity can be termed a "useful myth," but it would be nice if some new principles with comparable political appeal could be discovered. Perhaps a concept of "sector harmonization" will serve some of these functions. Such an approach was followed in the Tokyo Round agreement on civil aircraft, which provided for duty-free treatment for civil aircraft and engines and their parts.[12] In the Uruguay Round, a number of major trading nations agreed to eliminate tariffs on many pharmaceutical and chemical products, and as noted above, in 1996, a significant number of WTO Members agreed to eliminate tariffs on information technology products.

(B) THE OBLIGATION TO LIMIT TARIFFS

The central obligation of the General Agreement on Tariffs and Trade is that in Article II, which requires nations to limit their tariffs on particular goods to a specified maximum.[13] The current GATT tariff commitments or "bindings," as they are often called, are the result of eight major rounds of negotiation. They are contained in country-by-country schedules which are appended to the General Agreement and incorporated into it by reference in Article II. Each contracting party's schedule is, of course, different. A nation's GATT tariff schedule may differ from its national tariff schedule, in that the GATT schedule specifies the maximum tariff which can be applied for each product listed. The national tariff schedule, on the other hand, sets the actual rate applied by that country for each product. For products which are not on its GATT schedule, a country may charge any tariff it pleases. For products which are listed on the GATT schedule, it may charge a tariff below the GATT maximum, if it so desires. If it charges a tariff in excess of the GATT maximum, however, it is violating its GATT obligations,

---

12. Agreement on Trade in Civil Aircraft, GATT, 26th Supp. BISD 162 (1980).

13. See Jackson, supra note 2, at 201–211. See also Richard E. Caves & Ronald W. Jones, World Trade and Payments 281–86 (1973); Gerard Curzon, Multilateral Commercial Diplomacy 70–123 (1965); Dam, supra note 2, at 17, 18, 25–55.

unless a GATT exception applies, such as Article VI (antidumping and countervailing duties) or Article XIX (the Escape Clause).

There are a number of significant legal problems raised by the Article II obligation.[14] The GATT obligations relating to a tariff commitment can be divided into two groups. The first group consists of those obligations which relate specifically to a tariff binding and are triggered by the existence of that tariff binding on the GATT schedule. A second group of obligations consists of the more general GATT obligations (a sort of "code of good conduct for trade policy"), which relate not only to the treatment of goods that are listed on a schedule, but to all goods. These latter obligations (such as obligations on the use of quotas or national treatment obligations relating to internal taxation and regulations) have as one of their purposes the prevention of evasion of the GATT tariff bindings. Since the objective of obtaining a binding is to gain market access and since nontariff barriers inhibit such access, any NTB is, to a certain extent, an evasion of the GATT tariff bindings. Thus, all GATT rules limiting NTBs serve to protect the Article II bindings.

The group of obligations in the General Agreement which relate more directly to the tariff bindings and are generally limited to goods that are listed on the GATT tariff schedule, include the following:

(1) The tariff maximum or ceiling, as expressed in the schedule (see Article II:1 which obligates treatment "no less favorable" than that specified in the schedule).

(2) Other provisions of Article II designed to protect the value of the concession from encroachment by other governmental measures, such as "other charges," new methods of valuing goods, reclassification of goods (see Article II:3 & 5) and currency revaluations (Article II:6). See Section 8.3 infra.

(3) Limits on the protection against imports of a particular product which can be afforded by the use of an import monopoly (Article II:4). See Chapter 9 infra.

(4) A GATT interpretation that new subsidies granted on products covered in a nation's schedule, after the schedule has been negotiated, shall be considered a "prima facie nullification" for purposes of complaints under Article XXIII. See Section 7.4(A)(2) supra.

It should be emphasized that the GATT obligation refers to goods "which are the products of territories of other contracting parties." Thus if A and B are GATT parties and C is not, a company in A cannot buy products from C, ship them to B, and demand the GATT schedule treatment so long as the goods retain their C origin. See Section 8.3(D) infra.

---

14. For a discussion of these and other legal problems, see J. Jackson, supra note 2, at 211–217.

Notes and Questions

(1) There have been a number of WTO disputes concerning the interpretation of tariff and other schedules. One such case was the *EC–Chicken Cuts* case, excerpted in Section 7.4(C)(1) supra. In EUROPEAN COMMUNITIES–CUSTOMS CLASSIFICATION OF CERTAIN COMPUTER EQUIPMENT, WT/DS62, 67 & 68/AB/R, adopted by the DSB on June 22, 1998, the Appellate Body noted:

84. * * * Tariff concessions provided for in a Member's Schedule—the interpretation of which is at issue here—are reciprocal and result from a mutually-advantageous negotiation between importing and exporting Members. A Schedule is made an integral part of the GATT 1994 by Article II:7 of the GATT 1994. Therefore, the concessions provided for in that Schedule are part of the terms of the treaty. As such, the only rules which may be applied in interpreting the meaning of a concession are the general rules of treaty interpretation set out in the Vienna Convention.

In applying the rules of the Vienna Convention, the Appellate Body noted that it would be relevant in tariff classification cases to examine the Harmonised System and its Explanatory Notes, as well as decisions taken by the Harmonised System Committee of the World Customs Organization (see Section 8.3(B)(1) infra). The Appellate Body rejected the panel's position that the legitimate expectations of the exporting party were of particular relevance, at least insofar as violation cases were concerned. In its view:

109. * * * Tariff negotiations are a process of reciprocal demands and concessions, of "give and take". It is only normal that importing Members define their offers (and their ensuing obligations) in terms which suit their needs. On the other hand, exporting Members have to ensure that their corresponding rights are described in such a manner in the Schedules of importing Members that their export interests, as agreed in the negotiations, are guaranteed. There was a special arrangement made for this in the Uruguay Round. For this purpose, a process of verification of tariff schedules took place from 15 February through 25 March 1994, which allowed Uruguay Round participants to check and control, through consultations with their negotiating partners, the scope and definition of tariff concessions. Indeed, the fact that Members' Schedules are an integral part of the GATT 1994 indicates that, while each Schedule represents the tariff commitments made by *one* Member, they represent a common agreement among *all* Members.

110. * * * We consider that any clarification of the scope of tariff concessions that may be required during the negotiations is a task for all interested parties.

See also Canada—Measures Affecting the Importation of Milk and the Exportation of Dairy Products, WT/DS103 & 113/AB/R, paras. 125–143, adopted by the DSB on October 27, 1999.

(2) What happens when a new product is developed? Can a GATT tariff binding ever cover a product that did not exist when the binding was made? What if the new product is very similar, at least in some respects, to a

product that it is subject to a tariff binding? To take an actual case,[15] if Greece had bound a specific tariff rate on records (e.g., x drachmas per record), could it apply a higher rate to long-playing records on the grounds that such records did not exist at the time it made the binding, that long-playing records contained up to five times the volume of recordings of conventional records and that they were lighter and made of different material than conventional records? Would it matter that other countries distinguished between long-playing and conventional records? If the Greek binding had been set as an ad valorem duty, would this problem have arisen?

The GATT Contracting Parties did not definitively resolve this dispute. In the course of their consideration of it, they requested an advisory opinion from the Customs Co-operation Council, the body responsible for the Brussels Tariff Nomenclature (BTN), which at the time was the basis on which many countries classified goods for tariff purposes. See Section 8.3(B) infra. Although the Council declined to give such an opinion, it noted the BTN principle that "[g]oods not falling within any heading of the Nomenclature shall be classified under the heading appropriate to the goods to which they are most akin," but also noted that this principle did not apply if a tariff classification contained a residual heading, i.e., "other articles not elsewhere specified." Despite the lack of a resolution of the dispute, one of the co-authors of this book has concluded that "it seems that several principles are accepted by most contracting parties: (1) new products must be deemed within bound Schedule items where the description clearly covers them; (2) reference will be made to the national law of the party whose Schedule is under dispute to determine the principles of classification; but the national law is not determinative."[16]

(3) The two foregoing notes involved disputes over the scope of a GATT tariff binding. An analogous problem arises when a WTO member claims that under the MFN clause one of its products should receive the same favorable tariff treatment as a similar product from another country. See the *SPF Dimension Lumber* and *Spanish Coffee* cases, excerpted in Section 10.2 infra.

(4) What arguments might an adversely affected WTO member make in response to an unanticipated classification change, even if a technical violation of the tariff concession does not occur? See the *German Sardines* case, excerpted in Section 10.2 infra.

(5) Article II:2(c) provides that Article II tariff bindings do not prevent a party from imposing a fee or other charge "commensurate with the cost of services provided." Article VIII provides that import fees "shall be limited in amount to the approximate cost of services rendered" and shall not represent indirect protection or taxation. These provisions would clearly permit a party to impose a reasonable fee for a necessary health or safety-related inspection of imported goods. Would they permit a country to impose a fee designed to recover the entire cost of its customs service? The United States claimed that they did, and in 1986 it attempted to do so by imposing a customs user fee of 0.22% (reduced to 0.17% in subsequent years). Under the

---

15. Greek Increase In Bound Duty, Report by the Group of Experts, GATT Doc. L/580 (Nov. 9, 1956).

16. Jackson, supra note 2, at 214.

U.S. system, an import valued at $1 million would have to pay a $1700 fee, while one valued at $1000 would be charged $1.70. Are these fees commensurate with the cost of services rendered? A GATT panel concluded they were not because there was no demonstrable relation between the fee and the cost of processing *specific* transactions. The panel felt that the phrase "cost of services rendered" meant the "approximate cost of customs processing for the individual entry in question." U.S. Customs User Fee, GATT, 35th Supp. BISD 245, 290 (Panel report adopted Feb. 2, 1988). The panel also ruled that certain costs of the U.S. Customs Service could not be recovered because they were not services rendered in connection with dutiable imports. The United States revised its fee structure so that the 0.17% fee was subject to a $21 minimum and $400 maximum (slightly more for manual entries).[17] Given the panel's decision as described above, does this new fee comply with Articles II and VIII? Based on the wording of these two articles, do you think that the panel correctly concluded that the articles applied to a general fee like the U.S. user fee (as opposed to finding that they applied only to fees for special services not generally provided, such as health inspections)?

(6) Article II:1(b) provides that duties shall not exceed those set forth in a party's Schedule, "subject to the terms, conditions and qualifications set forth in that Schedule." Does the quoted language allow a party to make a duty rate subject to terms that would otherwise violate the General Agreement? For example, could a quota scheme that would normally violate Articles XI and XIII be saved by being expressed as a condition to a tariff rate under Article II? See U.S. Restrictions on Imports of Sugar, GATT, 36th Supp. BISD 331 (Panel report adopted June 22, 1990)(no). Accord, European Communities—Regime for the Importation, Sale and Distribution of Bananas, WT/DS27/R, paras. 7.112–7.118, adopted by the DSB on September 25, 1997.

(C) RENEGOTIATION OF TARIFF BINDINGS

Although the tariff binding is an obligation to limit the tariff on a particular product to the maximum listed in the tariff binding, the General Agreement contains a number of provisions that give considerable flexibility to this commitment.[18] These provisions are basically of two types: provisions that enable tariff bindings to be suspended temporarily and provisions that enable a particular tariff binding to be changed permanently. The first type is more appropriately the subject of discussion of GATT exceptions such as the Escape Clause (Chapter 15), retaliation-sanction type provisions of Article XXIII (Chapter 7), and provisions for waivers (Chapter 6). The second type of provision, however, deals with the procedures for negotiating and renegotiating the permanent schedule of obligations themselves. Although the great bulk of tariff reductions are negotiated during one or another of the so-called rounds described in Section (A), GATT is in fact the locus of more or less

---

17. Customs and Trade Act of 1990, sec. 111, 104 Stat. 635.

18. See generally Anwarul Hoda, Tariff Negotiations and Renegotiations Under the GATT and the WTO: Procedures and Practices (2001); Jackson, supra note 2, at 229–238.

continuous tariff negotiations. For example, a particular binding accepted by a nation during the Uruguay Round may later prove (due to changing circumstances or changing political context in the obligated nation) to be impractical or too onerous for the nation to follow. There are provisions in the General Agreement whereby that nation is entitled to reopen the matter and substitute other commitments in place of the one which it now desires to remove. In fact, a full survey of all the various types of changes which can be accomplished, as well as the techniques for obtaining new bindings, would include the following:

NEW NEGOTIATIONS

1) Bindings resulting from a negotiating "round" (Article XXVIII bis).

2) Negotiations for the accession of new members (WTO Article XIII) (described in Chapter 6).

3) Various other negotiations not specifically authorized by the General Agreement. Nations may, of course, negotiate with any other nation on an ad hoc basis for the reduction of tariff maximums below GATT scheduled rates. These negotiations need not be conducted in the context of GATT, but if any member of the negotiation is a WTO member, it is obligated under the MFN clause of GATT Article I to generalize the treatment promised. While these ad hoc bindings may or may not be included in the GATT schedules, they nevertheless will affect the trade of all WTO members.

RENEGOTIATIONS, MODIFICATIONS, RECTIFICATIONS

1) Reopening every three years (Article XXVIII:1).

2) Special circumstance renegotiations (Article XXVIII:4).

3) Reserved renegotiations (Article XXVIII:5).

4) Compensatory renegotiations due to formation of a customs union or free trade area (Article XXIV:6).

5) Renegotiations by developing countries (Article XVIII:7).

6) Withdrawal of concessions initially negotiated with a country that fails to become or ceases to be a GATT party (Article XXVII).

7) Rectifications (corrections of mistakes and other minor changes).

This is not the place to discuss each of these articles in detail, but a brief summary of several of the renegotiation provisions may assist the reader in understanding the GATT system.

Originally, the General Agreement was negotiated with the idea that tariff concessions would extend for only a three-year period, after which they would be renewed or modified. Article XXVIII embodied this principle by authorizing, after a three-year period, any nation to withdraw any concession or binding. If a binding were withdrawn, however, then the countries with whom the original binding had been negotiated or other countries which were major beneficiaries of the obligated tariff treatment, were entitled either to make reciprocal compensatory withdrawals of their own or to obtain from the withdrawing party substitute concessions of equivalent value. Article XXVIII details some of the procedures by which these renegotiations would occur. Subsequently, it was amended so that it specified that this "reopener" would occur every three years from January 1, 1958. At the time of the reopener, some WTO members have followed the practice of reserving rights to reopen beyond the technical time limit period provided in Article XXVIII.

Another important renegotiation provision is that which pertains to the formation of a customs union or free trade area.[19] Under Article XXIV, groups of nations can, under certain circumstances, join together into a customs union or free trade area and depart from the most-favored-nation obligation to the extent necessary to give duty-free treatment to other members of the customs union or free trade area. We discuss Article XXIV in Chapter 11 infra. In the case of a customs union, a common external tariff is substituted for the individual national tariffs of the members, and when this is done it is very likely that some of the tariffs of the common external tariff will be higher than some individual GATT tariff bindings made by members of the union. When this occurs, Article XXIV, paragraph 6, provides that "the procedure set forth in Article XXVIII shall apply." Unfortunately, the Article XXVIII description of procedures is quite skeletal and a number of difficult problems arise when these procedures are applied to the customs union case. Two important rounds of GATT negotiations have occurred in connection with these types of rights, both in the context of the development of the European Union.

The EC Treaty provided for a staged development of a common external tariff (CXT) and the elimination of separate national tariffs. Since the CXT tended to be an average of EU member state tariffs, whenever the lowest EU member state tariff on a product was bound in GATT and was raised above the binding to the EU average, renegotiation rights arose in non-EU countries. Most of the renegotiations concerned with the development of the EU occurred simultaneously with and as part of the Kennedy Round. One of the features of these renegotiations was the withdrawal by the EU of most GATT bindings on agricultural goods, particularly grains, since it was developing a common agricultural policy (CAP), with provision for high and variable tariffs, which would be inconsistent with those bindings. Since the United States was by then a major exporter of agricultural goods, particularly grains, to the EU it was seriously concerned with the loss of its trading rights and the imbalance in such rights that would allegedly ensue between the United States and the EU. Two particular disputes arose out of those renegotiation procedures: one called the "Chicken War," and the other called the "Standstill on Grain Rights."

The Chicken War[20] occurred when, after a dramatic increase in the export of U.S. frozen poultry and poultry parts to EU countries, the EU

19. See generally Jackson, supra note 2, at 575–623.

20. Dam, supra note 2, at 87–88; Evans, supra note 2, at 173–180; L. Thomas Gallo-

took action under its CAP to limit imports of these goods, thereby contravening a GATT binding. The matter was treated by the United States as a withdrawal of a concession on the part of several European countries, and the United States asserted its renegotiation rights under Article XXVIII. Since the EU was unprepared to grant the United States satisfactory substitute concessions, the United States indicated that it would withdraw concessions equivalent in value to the trade it lost because of the EU policy. The negotiations broke down, however, on the question of what was the value of the trade loss. Article XXVIII is not very satisfactory in the case of a breakdown of negotiations, since unilateral responses by each negotiating party could draw counter-responses and escalate the conflict. Recognizing the need for some kind of arbitral procedure to prevent such escalation, the Director–General of GATT, Eric Wyndham–White, was induced to suggest the appointment of a special panel composed of representatives from nondisputants, which would be charged with determining the precise issue of the amount of the trading rights which the United States had lost. This panel received briefs and oral arguments from both sides, the United States arguing that its trading rights had a value considerably more than that which the EU was willing to recognize. The panel came to a determination of that value somewhat in between,[21] and the United States and the EU agreed to abide by that determination. The United States then proceeded to withdraw its own concessions on brandy, trucks, starch and dextrin.[22] Since withdrawals under Article XXVIII are designed to be on an MFN basis, the United States had to choose products which were mostly supplied by EU countries, so that its withdrawal would hopefully only affect the export trade of those countries. Nevertheless, one country which was hurt by the "fall-out effect" of these withdrawals was Spain, and subsequently a lawsuit was brought in U.S. courts arguing that the President did not have authority to make the withdrawals in the manner in which he did.[23] The withdrawals did not result in a change in EU policies.

The grains rights problem was also very difficult. Again, the problem was that the CAP called for the withdrawal of EU member state concessions on the importation of grains, which had mostly been with the United States. Because no satisfactory resolution of the matter could be obtained during the Kennedy Round, the EU and the United States agreed to extend the grains rights to the United States until such time at some future negotiation when the United States would be able to "cash in" its rights.[24]

---

way, Star Industries Inc. v. United States: Sequel to the Chicken War, 6 Intl.Lawyer 48, 49–52 (1972); Herman Walker, Dispute Settlement: The Chicken War, 58 Am. J.Intl.L. 671 (1964).

21. GATT Doc. L/2088 (1963); reprinted in 3 Intl. Legal Materials 116 (1964).

22. Presidential Proclamation No. 3564, 28 Fed.Reg. 13247 (1963).

23. United States v. Star Industries, Inc., 462 F.2d 557 (C.C.P.A.1972), cert. denied, 409 U.S. 1076, 93 S.Ct. 678, 34 L.Ed.2d 663 (1972), sustained the President's authority.

24. See Agreements between United States and EEC of March 7, 1962, relating to grains and to wheat. 13 UST 958 & 960, TIAS Nos. 5034 and 5035. See also Agree-

Another important round of customs unions renegotiation occurred when the EU was enlarged by the admission to membership of the United Kingdom, Denmark and Ireland. The treaty of enlargement became effective January 1, 1973, with the extension of the common external tariff to the new members' markets. Once again a series of GATT bindings that had been in effect for those new members was withdrawn. An elaborate negotiation took place, which was called the "Twenty-four-Six" negotiation (GATT Article XXIV:6).

Initially the EU argued that the tariff reductions that the three acceding countries were implementing far outweighed the tariff increases involved in their joining the EU and that no other adjustments were necessary. The U.S. position was that it should be compensated for the loss of the lower tariff rates in the three acceding countries. In particular, the United States was unwilling to accept reduced industrial tariffs as an offset to loss of market access in the agricultural area. In 1974, the dispute was settled after the EU agreed, inter alia, to increase U.S. market access for tobacco, oranges and grapefruits, kraft paper, photographic film, non-agricultural tractors, excavating machinery, diesel and marine engines and outboard motors, engine additives, measuring instruments, pumps, plywood and other items.[25]

The accessions of Greece to the EU in 1981 and of Austria, Finland and Sweden in 1995 occurred without causing any major problems in EU–U.S. trade relations. The accession of Spain and Portugal in 1986 again raised the issue of how the United States was to be compensated for its loss of agricultural markets. The dispute was resolved in the Uruguay Round.[26] The US and the EU agreed in 2006 on appropriate compensation for the 2004 expansion of the EU, which added 10 new member states.

SECTION 8.3 CUSTOMS LAW

(A) INTRODUCTION

Customs law is a very detailed and specialized subject. It is important for the general study of trade policy, however, to understand certain of its basic principles because customs rules can be manipulated to have a significant impact on international trade flows. The rules we will examine concern the three determinations that customs officials must make in order to administer tariffs and quotas. First, they must classify the goods, identifying them under one of the categories in the tariff schedule. (Are they handkerchiefs or scarves? Shoes or sandals?) Second, the goods must be valued so that the ad valorem tariff rate can be

ment between the EEC and the United States entered into June 30, 1969, suspending agreements of March 7, 1962, relating to quality wheat and other grains. 20 UST 2864, TIAS No. 6761, 723 UNTS 411.

25. See Trade Agreement between the United States and the European Community, 10 Weekly Comp.Pres.Doc. 366 (1974).

26. Office of the U.S. Trade Representative, 1994 National Trade Estimate Report on Foreign Trade Barriers 73–74.

applied. Third, the origin of the goods must be determined so that it is possible to apply the appropriate tariff rate within the specific category. Only after those steps are completed, can customs officials specify the exact amount of tariff due on imported goods.

After a brief description of the few GATT rules that are applicable to tariff administration and an overview of U.S. customs procedures, we will examine the three issues mentioned above: classification, valuation and origin. In each case, we will first discuss the applicable international rules and then look at national (mainly U.S.) practice.

A number of GATT articles (particularly Articles VII through X) impose some international standards on the customs procedures followed by GATT parties. For example, Article X requires that customs laws and regulations be published promptly and that a tribunal be available to hear appeals from decisions by customs officials. As we saw in the preceding section (the *U.S. Customs User Fee* case), Article VIII limits the fees, formalities and penalties that can be imposed on imported products. Article IX limits the use of origin marking requirements, in particular by requiring MFN treatment, while Article VII deals with valuation of goods, a subject also dealt with in Tokyo and Uruguay Round agreements and to which we return below. In addition, Article V provides for freedom of transit for goods.

One important subject in the Doha negotiations is trade facilitation. The aim of the trade facilitation negotiations is to clarify and improve GATT Articles V, VIII and X "with a view to further expediting the movement, release and clearance of goods, including goods in transit". Any resulting agreement could affect many national agencies, such as those responsible for health and safety, food inspection, import licensing, tax collection, quality inspection and enforcement, and their policies would have to be coordinated in order to ensure compliance with the agreement. To that end, the negotiations are also intended to result in enhanced technical assistance and support for capacity building so that developing countries can undertake obligations within this area that are not beyond their means.

The administration of tariffs varies from country to country. Since our focus is on U.S. rules, we start with an overview of U.S. customs law.[1] When foreign goods reach the United States, they must be either formally entered into the United States at a port of entry or held in a bonded facility pending later entry or re-export.[2] Entry may be accomplished by the consignee (importer), its authorized regular employee or its agent.[3] After entry has been filed, the port director of customs will designate representative quantities for examination by customs officials,

---

1. The basic laws affecting customs are codified in 19 U.S.C.A., and the rules and regulations of Customs and Border Protection (formerly known as the Customs Service) are collected in 19 C.F.R.

2. Merchandise may also be imported by mail. See 19 CFR pt. 145 (2007).

3. Entry may also be made by the exporter or his agent in the United States. For regulations pertaining to the entry of merchandise, see 19 CFR pts. 141–43 (2007).

make an estimate of duties for deposit and release the bulk under bond. The examination is necessary to determine the classification, value and origin of the goods for duty assessment and to ensure that country of origin or other special marking requirements have been met, that no prohibited articles are present, that the shipment has been correctly invoiced and that no quantitative discrepancies exist. It is also at this time that a number of health and safety regulations are applied. Likewise in some cases there are quotas on the amount of goods which can be imported and customs officials, usually in conjunction with a licensing system, administer these quotas.

The final determination of the rate and amount of duty is termed "liquidation." The importer is notified of any variance from the estimate deposited; any increase must be paid, and any excess is automatically refunded (except for de minimis amounts). If the importer wishes to contest the liquidation, it must file a protest with the appropriate customs office to secure an administrative review. If the protest is denied and all assessed duties have been paid, the denial may be appealed to the Court of International Trade (CIT), which has exclusive jurisdiction over all such actions and which is headquartered in New York City. Appeals from the CIT go to the Court of Appeals for the Federal Circuit.

(B) CLASSIFICATION

The problem of classifying goods for customs purposes is a difficult one. So long as tariffs vary by product, it is necessary to have a system of categorizing every conceivable tradable good. At the same time, this system must be simple enough that it can be applied consistently by hundreds of customs inspectors to thousands of transactions daily. In this section, we examine first the international system that has been designed for the classification of goods and then turn to a number of classification issues that have arisen under U.S. law.

(1) International Rules: The Harmonized System

The desirability of a uniform, internationally accepted classification system has long been recognized.[4] It would ease international trade flows and tariff negotiations and make international trade statistics more reliable and useful. Following World War II a European Customs Union Study Group was established in Brussels and it developed a classification system variously known as the Brussels Tariff Nomenclature (BTN) and the Customs Cooperation Council Nomenclature. As part of its efforts, the Customs Cooperation Council (CCC) was established,[5] with one of its major purposes being to assume responsibility for supervising the application and interpretation of the Nomenclature. Over time, all major GATT members made the Nomenclature the basis of their customs

---

4. For the history of efforts to develop a uniform classification system, see Howard L. Friedenberg, The Development of a Uniform International Tariff Nomenclature: From 1853 to 1967 with Emphasis on the

Brussels Tariff Nomenclature (U.S. Tariff Commn., TC Pub.No. 237, 1968).

5. 22 UST 320, TIAS No. 7063, 157 UNTS 129.

tariffs, with the exception of the United States and Canada, and by 1967, three-quarters of the free-world's exports and imports were classified according to the Nomenclature for tariff purposes.[6]

The United States joined the CCC in 1970, but it did not adopt the Nomenclature, partly on the grounds that it had become outmoded and that a better and more modern classification system was needed. Subsequently, the CCC developed, with U.S. participation, the Harmonized Commodity Description and Coding System (the Harmonized System), which entered into force on January 1, 1988.[7] The United States adopted the Harmonized System, effective January 1, 1989.

There is another international classification system, which is utilized by the United Nations for reporting of trade statistics and which is entitled "Standard International Trade Classification" (SITC).[8] The Harmonized System is based in part on the SITC.

Notes and Questions

(1) The Harmonized System Committee meets regularly, under the auspices of the CCC, also known now as the World Customs Organization (WCO), to consider specific classification problems and disputes and to review the operation of the Harmonized System and update it and the explanatory notes as necessary, acting by consensus. The U.S. implementing legislation authorizes the President, upon recommendation of the U.S. International Trade Commission, to proclaim modifications to the U.S. tariff schedule to reflect changes in the Harmonized System. The changes are to be substantially rate neutral and must be reported to Congress prior to taking effect.[9]

(2) GATT contains no specific rules on customs classification, except that Article II:5 provides for negotiations "with a view to a compensatory adjustment" when a tariff classification ruling prevents implementation of a negotiated concession. As noted in Section 8.2, GATT tariff schedules are interpreted under normal treaty interpretation rules.

(3) Classification issues have arisen in two other important contexts in GATT. One early GATT case recognized that a legitimate tariff reclassification could nullify or impair the reasonable anticipation of a party, giving rise to a claim for compensation under Article XXIII. In addition, there have been GATT cases involving claims that a classification system denied MFN treatment to the complaining country's products by classifying them differently than essentially the same products from other countries. These cases are analyzed in Section 10.2 infra.

6. Customs Cooperation Council, The Activities of the Council (July, 1967 to June, 1969) 28 (1970).

7. International Convention on the Harmonized Commodity Description and Coding System, done at Brussels on June 14, 1983, and the Protocol thereto, done at Brussels on June 24, 1986. 1035 UNTS 3; KAV 2260.

8. Department of Economic and Social Affairs, Statistical Office of the United Nations, Series M, No. 34, Standard International Trade Classification, Revised (1961); Revision 2 (1975); Revision 3 (1986).

9. 19 U.S.C.A. secs. 3005–3006.

(2) *Classification Under U.S. Law*

The currently effective Harmonized Tariff Schedule of the United States (HTS or HTSUS), which is based upon the CCC's Harmonized System, came into effect on January 1, 1989.[10] According to the U.S. International Trade Commission, "the most noteworthy observation [about the implementation of the HTS] is the overall absence of complaints from the private sector."[11] It noted that the administrative agencies involved in customs administration welcomed the HTS because it provided better statistical data on trade that was more comparable to the data of U.S. trading partners and because it simplified the classification process (see Note 8 below).

The HTS contains around ten thousand 8–digit tariff lines. It is published annually by the United States International Trade Commission. The classification rules used to determine under which subdivision a product falls are complex. We will not attempt to cover these rules in a comprehensive fashion, but the following materials should give the reader a flavor of the issues involved in classification disputes.

HARMONIZED TARIFF SCHEDULE of the United States (1994)—Supplement 1

Annotated for Statistical Reporting Purposes

Heading/ Subheading	Stat. Suffix	Article Description	Units of Quantity	Rates of Duty 1 General	Rates of Duty 1 Special	2
8512		Electrical lighting or signaling equipment (excluding articles of heading 8539), windshield wipers, defrosters and demisters, of a kind used for cycles or motor vehicles; parts thereof:				
8512.10		Lighting or visual signaling equipment of a kind used on bicycles:				
8512.10.20	00	Lighting equipment	X	7.6%	Free (A, E, IL, J, MX) 3% (CA)	45%
8512.10.40	00	Visual signaling equipment . .	X	2.7%	Free (A, E, IL, J, MX) 1% (CA)	35%
8512.20		Other lighting or visual signaling equipment:				
8512.20.20		Lighting equipment	. . . .	Free		25%
	40	For the vehicles of subheading 8701.20 or heading 8702, 8703, 8704, 8705 or 8711	X			
	80	Other	X			
8512.20.40		Visual signaling equipment . .	. . . .	2.7%	Free (A, B, E, IL, J, MX) 1% (CA) [1]	35%
	40	For the vehicles of subheading 8701.20 or heading 8702, 8703, 8704, 8705 or 8711	X			
	80	Other	X			
8512.30.00		Sound signaling equipment	. . . .	2.7%	Free (A, B, E, IL, J, MX) 1% (CA) [1,2]	35%
	20	Horns	X			
	40	Other	X			

10. 19 U.S.C.A. sec. 1202.

11. U.S. Intl. Trade Commn., Investigation No. 332–274, at v (USITC Pub. 2296, June 1990).

Heading/ Subheading	Stat. Suffix	Article Description	Units of Quantity	Rates of Duty 1 General	Rates of Duty 1 Special	2
8512.40		Windshield wipers, defrosters and demisters:				
8512.40.20	00	Defrosters and demisters	X	3.9%	Free (A, E, IL, J, MX) 1.5% (CA) 2	35%
8512.40.40	00	Windshield wipers	X	3.1%	Free (A, B, E, IL, J, MX) 1.2% (CA)2	25%
8512.90		Parts:				
8512.90.20	00	Of signaling equipment	X	2.7%	Free (A, B, E, IL, J, MX) 1% (CA) 1	35%
		Of lighting equipment:				
8512.90.40	00	Of a kind used on bicycles	X	7.6%	Free (A, E, IL, J, MX) 3% (CA)	45%
8512.90.60	00	Other	X	Free		25%
8512.90.70	00	Of defrosters and demisters	X	3.9%	Free (A, E, IL, J, MX) 1.5% (CA) 2	35%
8512.90.90	00	Other	X	3.1%	Free (A, B, E, IL, J, MX) 1.2% (CA) 2	25%
8513		Portable electric lamps designed to function by their own source of energy (for example, dry batteries, storage batteries, magnetos), other than lighting equipment of heading 8512; parts thereof:				
8513.10		Lamps:				
8513.10.20	00	Flashlights	No	25%	Free (A, E, IL, J, MX) 10% (CA)	35%
8513.10.40	00	Other	No	6.9%	Free (A, E, IL, J, MX) 2.7% (CA)	40%
8513.90		Parts:				
8513.90.20	00	Of flashlights	X	25%	Free (A, E, IL, J, MX) 10% (CA)	35%
8513.90.40	00	Other	X	6.9%	Free (A, E, IL, J, MX) 2.7% (CA)	40%

1 See subheading 9905.85.56.
2 See subheading 9905.00.00.

Note the detail of the classification and the fine gradations in tariff rates between what might be viewed as similar goods (e.g., signaling devices for vehicles or miscellaneous auto parts). The above excerpt applied immediately before implementation of the Uruguay Round tariff reductions. Over time, tariff negotiations tend to lead to reduced and more standardized tariff rates. For example, as of 2001, after implementation of the Uruguay Round reductions, the items under heading 8512 were all subject to a column 1 duty of 2.5%, except for lighting equipment and parts (0%) and visual signaling equipment for bikes (2.7%). The rates under heading 8513 had been reduced by half.

The schedule has three columns, each with different tariff rates. The tariff rate applied depends upon the origin or source of the goods. Column 1 of the U.S. tariff indicates the general or "normal trade relations" rate, formerly known as the "MFN" rate. It is the rate applied to imports from countries receiving most-favored-nation treatment from the United States (see Chapter 10). Column 2 shows the "statutory rate," which is the rate imposed by the Smoot–Hawley Tariff Act of 1930,[12] as amended from time to time. The column 2 rate is applied to products from countries which do not receive normal (MFN)

12. Ch. 497, 46 Stat. 590 (1930), codified in 19 U.S.C.A. secs. 1202–1677k.

or special treatment.[13] Finally, there is a third column—the Special column. The rates in that column apply mainly to imports from countries who are beneficiaries of a U.S. tariff preference.[14] Generally, when a preferential arrangement is fully implemented, goods benefiting from it are admitted duty free. The beneficiaries of U.S. preferences include its free trade agreement partners: Australia, Bahrain, Canada, Chile, Dominican Republic, El Salvador, Guatemala, Honduras, Israel, Jordan, Mexico, Morocco, Nicaragua and Singapore, each of which has entered into a free trade agreement with the United States; most African, Caribbean and Andean countries (see Section 24.3(B) infra); and those countries which qualify for the U.S. Generalized System of Preferences (GSP) scheme, also discussed in Section 24.3(B) below.

Conceivably, a country could have many more columns in its tariff schedule. If it did not grant MFN treatment to other nations, it could have a tariff schedule with as many columns as there are nations with whom it trades. Obviously, this would be a very complex system to administer, and the origin of goods could be very critical in terms of the rate actually applied. Thus, questions of how to ascertain the true origin of goods (and prevent fraud) would loom large.

HARMONIZED TARIFF SCHEDULE OF THE UNITED STATES (2008)(REV. 1)

GENERAL RULES OF INTERPRETATION

Classification of goods in the tariff schedule shall be governed by the following principles:

1. The table of contents, alphabetical index, and titles of sections, chapters and sub-chapters are provided for ease of reference only; for legal purposes, classification shall be determined according to the terms of the headings and any relative section or chapter notes and, provided such headings or notes do not otherwise require, according to the following provisions:

2. (a) Any reference in a heading to an article shall be taken to include a reference to that article incomplete or unfinished, provided that, as entered, the incomplete or unfinished article has the essential character of the complete or finished article. It shall also include a reference to that article complete or finished (or failing to be classified as complete or finished by virtue of this rule), entered unassembled or disassembled.

13. Only Cuba and North Korea fell into this category as of January 2008. U.S. Harmonized Tariff Schedule (2008), General Note 3(b).

14. The letters in the Special column in the excerpted tariff schedule refer to the following preferences: A = GSP beneficiaries; CA = Canada; E = Caribbean Basin Economic Recovery Act beneficiaries; IL = Israel; J = Andean Trade Preferences Act beneficiaries; MX=Mexico. In the 2001 Schedule, D = African Growth and Opportunity Act beneficiaries and R = U.S.-Caribbean Basin Trade Partnership Act beneficiaries. As of 2008, there were four classes of industrial products that receive special treatment: civil aircraft under the GATT agreement on civil aircraft (indicated by C); certain Canadian automotive products and motor vehicles under the Automotive Products Trade Act (B); certain pharmaceuticals (K); and certain intermediate chemicals for dyes (L).

(b) Any reference in a heading to a material or substance shall be taken to include a reference to mixtures or combinations of that material or substance with other materials or substances. Any reference to goods of a given material or substance shall be taken to include a reference to goods consisting wholly or partly of such material or substance. The classification of goods consisting of more than one material or substance shall be according to the principles of rule 3.

3. When, by application of rule 2(b) or for any other reason, goods are, *prima facie*, classifiable under two or more headings, classification shall be effected as follows:

(a) The heading which provides the most specific description shall be preferred to headings providing a more general description. However, when two or more headings each refer to part only of the materials or substances contained in mixed or composite goods or to part only of the items in a set put up for retail sale, those headings are to be regarded as equally specific in relation to those goods, even if one of them gives a more complete or precise description of the goods.

(b) Mixtures, composite goods consisting of different materials or made up of different components, and goods put up in sets for retail sale, which cannot be classified by reference to 3(a), shall be classified as if they consisted of the material or component which gives them their essential character, insofar as this criterion is applicable.

(c) When goods cannot be classified by reference to 3(a) or 3(b), they shall be classified under the heading which occurs last in numerical order among those which equally merit consideration.

4. Goods which cannot be classified in accordance with the above rules shall be classified under the heading appropriate to the goods to which they are most akin.

* * *

6. For legal purposes, the classification of goods in the subheadings of a heading shall be determined according to the terms of those subheadings and any related subheading notes, and, mutatis mutandis, to the above rules, on the understanding that only subheadings at the same level are comparable. For the purposes of this rule, the relative section, chapter and subchapter notes also apply, unless the context otherwise requires.

ADDITIONAL U.S. RULES OF INTERPRETATION

1. In the absence of special language or context which otherwise requires—

   (a) a tariff classification controlled by use (other than actual use) is to be determined in accordance with the use in the United States at, or immediately prior to, the date of importation, of goods of that class or kind to which the imported goods belong, and the controlling use is the principal use;

   (b) a tariff classification controlled by the actual use to which the imported goods are put in the United States is satisfied only if such use is intended at the time of importation, the goods are so used and proof thereof is furnished within 3 years after the date the goods are entered;

   (c) a provision for parts of an article covers products solely or principally used as a part of such articles but a provision for "parts" or "parts and accessories" shall not prevail over a specific provision for such part or accessory; * * *

CONAIR CORP. v. U.S.

Court of International Trade.
Slip Op. 05–95 (Aug. 12, 2005).

Conair challenges the classification of its tabletop fountains by the United States Customs Service under the Harmonized Tariff Schedule of the United States (2000). Customs classified the tabletop fountains ("Serenity Ponds") under HTSUS subheading 3926.40.00 as "Other articles of plastics and articles of other materials of headings 3901 to 3914 ... Statuettes and other ornamental articles," subject to a tariff rate of 5.3%. Conair argues that the merchandise is properly classifiable under HTSUS subheading 8413.70.2004 as "Pumps for liquids, whether or not fitted with a measuring device; liquid elevators; part thereof; ... Other centrifugal pumps ... Other ... Submersible pumps," subject to no tariff.

* * *

* * * The parties agree that the Serenity Ponds: (A) are designed to create a tranquil atmosphere at home or in the office, (B) are intended to appeal to the consumer's visual and auditory senses, and (C) are comprised of: (1) a water reservoir or base; (2) an electric, submersible, centrifugal pump that sits in the base; (3) plastic tubing; (4) a power cord; and (5) various objects, such as simulated rocks, simulated bamboo, natural polished stones, through which and/or over which pumped water flows.

* * *

In a classification dispute, the court begins its analysis with [General Rule of Interpretation] GRI 1. If the proper classification cannot be determined by reference to GRI 1, it becomes necessary to refer to the succeeding GRIs in numerical order. * * *

In determining the proper classification, the Court may also refer to the Explanatory Notes, which constitute the World Customs Organization's official interpretation of the HTSUS. The Explanatory Notes, although not legally binding, are intended to clarify the scope of HTSUS subheadings and to offer guidance in interpreting [the] subheadings. Therefore, close textual analysis of the language of the headings and the accompanying explanatory notes is required in order to determine the proper classification of merchandise.

Conair argues that the subject tabletop fountains operate by pumping liquid water, which produces the sound of flowing water. This movement of water is made possible solely by means of a pump for liquids. Based on these statements, Conair contends that the Serenity Ponds are *prima facie* classifiable within HTSUS Heading 8413 by application of GRI 1. In making its claim, Conair insists that HTSUS Heading 8413 is an *eo nomine* provision[15] that covers an article in all its forms. Thus, for Conair, even though the Serenity Ponds consist of more parts than merely the pump, the subject merchandise answers only to the terms of Heading 8413 and is *prima facie*, described therein.

Conair further maintains that since the Serenity Ponds are *prima facie* classifiable under HTSUS Heading 8413, the Chapter Notes preclude them from being classified under Customs' chosen Heading 3926. This is because note 2(p) to Chapter 39 HTSUS states that Chapter 39 "does not cover: . . . Articles of Section XVI (machines and mechanical or electrical appliances)." Therefore, Conair urges the conclusion that, since the Serenity Ponds are *prima facie* classifiable under Chapter 84, the Chapter Notes provide that the Serenity Ponds may not be classified under Chapter 39.

* * *

The court finds that, although Conair is correct in its assertion that the pumps are *prima facie* classifiable under HTSUS Heading 8413, it is incorrect in claiming that classification may be resolved by reliance upon GRI 1. Each Serenity Pond consists of a pump, a decorative sculpture made of plastic (e.g. simulated rocks or bamboo), and natural stones. While the pumps themselves are properly classified under Heading 8413, the remaining parts of the Serenity Ponds are appropriately classified elsewhere. Because each component, when considered individually, is *prima facie* classifiable under a different HTSUS heading, reliance on GRI 1 is inappropriate. Therefore, it becomes necessary to refer to the succeeding GRIs in numerical order.

* * * [T]he Government states that GRI 2, insofar as relevant here, provides in subsection (b) that classification of goods consisting of more

---

15. An *eo nomine* designation is "one which describes [a] commodity by a specific name, usually one well known to commerce." * * *

than one material or substance must be determined according to the principles of GRI 3. The court agrees with this analysis.

The Government is also correct in its contention that * * * reference to the first sentence of GRI 3(a) does not end the inquiry. That sentence, incorporating the concept of "relative specificity," is inapplicable in the present case because it comes into play when a good, as a whole, is *prima facie* classifiable under two or more headings. Here, the Serenity Ponds are made up of parts or components each of which is *prima facie* classifiable under a different heading. The second sentence of GRI 3(a) provides that where "two or more headings each refer to part only of the materials or substances contained in mixed or composite goods ... those headings are to be regarded as equally specific in relation to those goods, even if one of them gives a more complete or precise description of the goods." * * *

In cases such as the present one, where classification pursuant to GRI 3(a) is not possible, the concept of "essential character" found in GRI 3(b) may direct the court to the proper resolution. * * * [I]n order to determine the essential character of composite merchandise under the TSUS, this Court has sought to determine which component is indispensable to the merchandise. * * * In weighing the multiple factors that may be present in any one case, the court must also be cognizant that the factor which determines essential character will vary as between different kinds of goods. It may, for example, be determined by the nature of the material or component, its bulk, quantity, weight or value, or by the role of a constituent material in relation to the use of the goods.

The parties disagree as to which component imparts the essential character of the Serenity Ponds. The Government contends that the plastic decorative sculpture, i.e., the simulated rocks or the plastic bamboo, is the component which imparts the essential character. In support of this conclusion, the Government observes that each style of fountain is named separately and can be distinguished from the others based on differences in the design of the plastic components. In other words, for the Government, the essential nature of each Serenity Pond results from the individual plastic sculpture that differentiates each style of the merchandise from the other models. Next, the Government points out that the pump is not visible to the consumer and, therefore, plays no significant part in creating the visual or decorative value of the article. * * * Finally the Government states that a view of the imported fountain can be enjoyed by an observer even when the pump is not in operation.

Conair disputes the Government's contention and asserts that the essential character of the Serenity Ponds is imparted by the pump: While the appearance of the fountain's contoured plastic may be one factor in a consumer's determination as to which model of Serenity Pond to buy, the decision to buy a Serenity Pond in the first place is based entirely on the presence of the submersible pump and its ability to generate the sound of flowing water. Indeed, it is difficult to imagine that a consumer would buy an article advertised as a "fountain," ... if the article could not produce flowing water.

* * *

* * * In reaching the ultimate question, the court finds that the Serenity Ponds' essential character is imparted by the pump. The parties agree that the Serenity Ponds are designed to create a tranquil atmosphere at home or in the office, and that they are intended to appeal to the visual and auditory senses of the consumer. To the extent that the Serenity Ponds succeed in creating this tranquil atmosphere, it is necessarily the water flowing over the simulated landscape that stimulates the visual and auditory senses. Indeed, any appeal to the auditory senses is present only when the pump is transporting water to the top of the Serenity Pond, thus allowing it to flow over the simulated rocks.

This conclusion is borne out by an examination of the Serenity Ponds themselves. * * * This examination leads to the conclusion that consumers would not purchase the Serenity Ponds for the purpose of enjoying the visual aspects of the plastic sculpture. It is only when the pump is running and the water is flowing that the Serenity Ponds could be said to have any "visual or auditory" appeal or create anything approaching "a tranquil atmosphere." That is, the water flowing over the sculptured plastic rocks gives them a more attractive look and also produces the sound of flowing water. Although the pump may not be visible, it is nonetheless indispensable to making the merchandise "what it is."

The direction given in the Explanatory Note to GRI 3(b) favors the court's conclusion. "The factor which determines essential character will vary as between different kinds of goods. It may, for example, be determined by ... *the role of a constituent material in relation to the use of the goods.*" Explanatory Note, Rule 3(b) (VIII) (emphasis added). The pump's role in relation to the use of the Serenity Ponds is essential. While the plastic component contributes to the manner in which the water flows, and thus to the Serenity Ponds' auditory and visual appeal, without the pump the water doesn't flow at all. Therefore, it is the pump that is essential to the use of the goods. Thus, as it is the pump that imparts each Serenity Pond its essential character, in accordance with GRI 3(b) the Serenity Ponds are properly classified as if they consisted of that component.

Notes and Questions

(1) In one of its rare classification opinion, the U.S. Supreme Court recently held that ruling letters issued by the Customs Service are not entitled to so-called *Chevron* deference when challenged in court. United States v. Mead Corp., 533 U.S. 218, 121 S.Ct. 2164, 150 L.Ed.2d 292 (2001).

(2) An interesting EU case, E.I. DU PONT DE NEMOURS INC. v. COMMISSIONERS OF CUSTOMS & EXCISE, Case 234/81, [1982] ECR 3515, involved the classification of the Du Pont product Corian, which

resembles marble in appearance, but consists by weight of about two-thirds aluminum hydroxide obtained from bauxite ore and one-third polymethyl methacrylate, an artificial plastic material. Should Corian be classified as artificial stone (heading 68.11) or a methacrylic polymer (heading 39.02)? Consider General Rule 2(b), excerpted above. The EC Court of Justice ruled that since Corian contained a material specified in heading 39.02, it was prima facie classifiable there under General Rule 2(b). (This rule could not be applied to classify Corian as an ore or as aluminum hydroxide, because the relevant notes excluded ores submitted to a chemical process and included aluminum hydroxide only as a separate element or chemically defined compound, which was not true in the case of Corian). As to the possibility of the artificial stone heading, the Court ruled:

> There is no universally accepted interpretation of [the] concept [of artificial stone] in either trade or scientific circles, although the prevailing view is that "artificial stone contains natural stone."

> * * * According to [the Explanatory] Notes, "artificial stone is an imitation of natural stone usually obtained by agglomerating pieces of natural stone, crushed or powdered natural stone * * * with lime or cement or other binders (e.g., artificial plastic material)."

> It was submitted by Du Pont * * * that the word "usually" * * * implies that there may be exceptions * * *. That argument cannot be accepted, however, for the position of the word "usually", which precedes the words "by agglomerating" and not the words "powdered natural stone", indicates in fact that an exception might be made at most to allow for the possibility of using a manufacturing process other than the agglomeration of binders with powdered natural stone, but not for the case where no natural stone is used.

The Court concluded that even if Corian were prima facie classifiable as artificial stone, Rule 3 would dictate the choice of heading 39.02 over heading 68.11. Do you see why? The Court relied on Rule 3(a), not 3(c).

(3) How would you classify a stereo component system including the following five components, with their respective values indicated separately in deutsche marks:

compact disc player (DM 164)

amplifier (DM 173.50)

tuner (DM 124)

double cassette recorder (DM 179)

record player (DM 55)?

Assume your choices are:

(1) 8519 9910—other sound-producing apparatus with laser optical reading systems (based on CD player);

(2) 8527—radio reception apparatus (based on tuner);

(3) 8519 3900—record player, or

(4) 8520 3190—double cassette player.

What result under Rule 3? The German Federal Supreme Finance Court concluded that Rules 3a and 3b were not helpful, leaving Rule 3c as determinative. In re Import of a Compact Disc Player, [1993] 1 CMLR 780 (Case VII K 2/91, Bundes-finanzhof, June 2, 1992). Note that the system had originally been classified as a CD player, which meant that it was subject to antidumping duties.

(4) One of the more controversial trade issues between the United States and Japan in 1992–1993 was whether minivans should be classified as trucks or cars. As noted in Section 8.2, as a result of the Chicken War, the U.S. raised its MFN tariff on trucks, and it remains at 25%, while the MFN tariff on cars is 2.5%. Although the increased tariff was designed to "punish" Germany, its effect in recent years has been to limit Japanese exports of trucks to the United States. Under the HTSUS, the choice for classifying minivans is between heading 8703 (Motor cars and other motor vehicles principally designed for the transport of persons)("cars") and heading 8704 (motor vehicles for the transport of goods)("trucks"). The U.S. has long classified as minivans as cars,[16] but after Treasury Department officials overruled a Customs Service decision to reclassify them as trucks, that decision was criticized by then presidential candidate Bill Clinton. Assuming there are no helpful notes, under which heading do you think minivans should be classified? Why? What information would be relevant to your decision? Would it matter if minivans were more closely related to trucks than cars as to some (or most) basic engineering factors? That minivans were subject to lower environmental and safety standards than regular passenger cars? That the auto industry reports minivan sales under the general heading of "light truck" sales? See Marubeni America Corp. v. United States, 821 F.Supp. 1521 (CIT 1993) (two-door sport utility vehicles should be classified as cars; key issue is whether they are for the purpose of transporting passengers or goods; rejects other factors such as those listed above). If the U.S. reclassifies minivans as trucks, what claims might Japan bring in the WTO? Who would likely prevail?

(5) Assume your client wants to import educational construction kits into the United States. The kits are designed for teenage children and consist of instructions and materials by which a small (and not very durable) electronic speedometer can be constructed, suitable for attaching to a bicycle or automobile. Assuming that only the asterisked tariff classifications are relevant, what duty will be imposed on the kits?

Tariff Heading	Article Description	Duty
8712.00	Bicycles and other cycles * * *	
8714.00	Parts * * * of vehicles of headings 8711 to 8713	
8714.99	Other	
*8714.99.80	Other	10%
9029	Revolution counters, * * *, speedometers	
9029.20	Speedometers and tachometers * * *	
*9029.20.20	Bicycle speedometers	6%
*9029.20.40	Other speedometers * * *	Free

16. It appears that the punitive tariff on trucks, which dates from 1963, was not intended to apply to the Volkswagen "box- on-wheels" station wagon, which arguably is a predecessor of today's minivans. See N.Y.Times, Jan. 7, 1964, at 39, col 4.

Tariff Heading	Article Description	Duty
9029.90	Parts and accessories	
*9029.90.40	Of bicycle speedometers	6%
*9029.90.80	Other	Free
9503	Other toys; reduced-sized ("scale") models * * *	
*9503.20.00	Reduced-size ("scale") model assembly kits, whether or not working models	Free
9503.30.00	Other construction sets and constructional toys	Free

The former U.S. tariff schedules contained a note to the effect that toys were articles chiefly used for the amusement of children or adults. Would this note be helpful in classifying the kits? In terms of strategy, the best rate is "other speedometers" while the worst is "bicycle speedometers." What is the danger of arguing for the "other speedometers" rate?

(6) Should "bicycle-type" speedometers, suitable for use on bicycles, but in fact used primarily on exercisers, be classified in the speedometers heading under the subheading "Bicycle speedometers and parts thereof" or "Other"? See Additional U.S. Rules excerpted above; Stewart–Warner Corp. v. United States, 748 F.2d 663 (Fed.Cir.1984)(based on chief use, should be "other").

(7) Which General Rule would you rely upon to classify a box containing several major elements of a tape recorder and the necessary parts to assemble it? What if some of the elements were imported separately?

(8) The Harmonized System approach to classification differs from the old U.S. system in a number of ways. Probably the most important changes are that (i) the old U.S. system often focused on use, while the HS attempts to classify goods according to their essential character; and (ii) the change in the case of textiles from classification on the basis of the fiber of chief value to the fiber of chief weight. In each case, the aim is to reduce uncertainty by reducing disputes over actual use or value. (The concept of use, of course, has not been eliminated. See Notes 5 and 6 above.)

(9) Classification is important only as long as tariff rates vary by product. Why are they likely to do so?

(C) VALUATION

Most tariffs are ad valorem, which means that the value of the goods subject to them must be ascertained in order to calculate the amount of tariff due. In this section, we describe the detailed valuation rules agreed upon in the Tokyo Round's Customs Valuation Code, which were largely left unchanged in the Uruguay Round, and then examine how U.S. courts have applied those rules.

(1) The GATT Customs Valuation Code

Prior to the Tokyo Round (1979), customs valuation was a controversial issue. Although GATT Article VII regulated valuation to some degree, it was not adequate. Indeed, an examination of the interpretative notes to Article VII demonstrates the wide disparities in practices that were permitted by Article VII. The U.S. system for valuation of goods for customs purposes, which benefited from the grandfather provisions of the Protocol of Provisional Application, was so complex and cumbersome that it was deemed to be a non-tariff barrier by many trading nations.[17] For its part, the United States objected to the imprecise and unpredictable valuation practices of many other countries. This dissatisfaction led to the negotiation in the Tokyo Round of a GATT Customs Valuation Code.[18] The background and the results of the negotiations are described in the Senate Report on the Trade Agreements Act of 1979.

SENATE REPORT 96–249

96th Cong., 1st Sess. 108–10 (1979).

The basis and complexity of customs valuation systems used throughout the world vary considerably. Some systems, such as the Brussels Definition of Value (BDV) used by the European Communities (EC) and most of the countries in the world, employ a "notional" standard for valuation purposes. Under this system, the customs value of an imported product is the price at which that product would be sold if the actual transaction in question were a perfectly competitive transaction. Adjustments to the actual value to reach the ideal value are made, and such adjustments are often criticized as arbitrary and almost always increase the value and, therefore, the tariff liability. Other customs valuation systems, such as the U.S. system, use a "positive" standard, where customs value is usually the price at which goods are sold in the actual transaction. In certain circumstances, such systems also provide for alternative definitions of value for use in those cases where the price cannot be used. Still other systems assess customs duties primarily on the basis of national or official values which are arbitrary and are used to increase duties collected and/or to protect domestic industries, or primarily on the basis of the domestic selling price of the goods in the country of exportation. Other aspects of customs valuation systems making for complexity and controversy include: The existence in some systems of numerous alternative definitions of value; complex laws and administrative regulations making it difficult to easily predict the amount of duty that will be owed; the absence of requirements and procedures for review of valuation decisions; and the absence of published administrative regulations and decisions.

Against this background, negotiations in the [Tokyo Round] on an international set of rules for customs valuation took place with the active participation of the major industrialized countries and many of the developing countries.

* * *

17. The former U.S. valuation system is described and contrasted with those of other countries in U.S. Tariff Commn., Customs Valuation (TC Pub.No. 180, 1966).

18. Agreement on Implementation of Article VII & Protocol, GATT, 26th Supp. BISD 116 (1980).

Summary of the Agreement

Methods of Customs Valuation.—The Customs Valuation Agreement establishes five alternative methods of customs valuation. Each is summarized briefly below in the order in which it would be applied.

1. *The transaction value of the imported goods*, i.e., the price actually paid or payable for the goods with adjustments for certain specified costs, charges, and expenses which are incurred but not reflected in the price actually paid or payable for the goods (including selling commissions, container costs, packing costs, certain royalties and licenses fees, and assists) (article 1 of the agreement).

2. If the transaction value of the imports cannot be determined or used, then the *transaction value of identical goods* sold for export to the same country, and exported at or about the same time as the imported goods (article 2 of the agreement).

3. If the transaction value of identical goods cannot be determined, then the *transaction value of similar goods* sold for export to the same country and exported at or about the same time as the imported goods (article 3 of the agreement).

4. If customs value cannot be determined by looking to transaction value, then the *deductive* value or *computed* value, as the importer chooses. The *deductive* value for the imported goods is determined by the price at which the imported goods, or identical or similar imported goods, are sold in the greatest aggregate quantity to unrelated persons in the country of importation in the same condition as imported (or after further processing), with deductions for commissions or profit, general expenses, transport and insurance costs, customs duties and certain other costs, charges and expenses incurred as a result of reselling the goods. (Article 5 of the agreement.)

5. The *computed value* of the imported goods, determined by summing the cost of producing the article in the country of exportation, an amount for general expense and profit, and the cost or value of all other expenses necessary to reflect the valuation option (i.e., f.o.b. or c.i.f.) chosen by the signatory. (Article 6 of the Agreement.)

In those rare instances where a value cannot be determined under any of the valuation methods described above, the agreement provides that "the value shall be determined using reasonable means consistent with the principles and general provisions of this code...." The customs values determined under this residual method "should be based to the greatest possible extent on previously determined customs values." Several valuation methods are specifically precluded from being used as a basis for determining customs value, including methods such as the American selling price (ASP) and foreign value methods currently used in the United States.

Circumstances Under Which the Transaction Value Will Not Be Used. The most significant circumstance under the agreement which would result in the transaction value not being used is when the transaction in question is between related parties. If the buyer and seller are related, the transaction value may not be used unless an examination of the circumstances surrounding the sale demonstrates that such relationship did not influence the price, or the importer demonstrates that the transaction value closely approximates one of several other enumerated values, subject to other criteria of the agreement.

Notes and Questions

(1) The Valuation Code was not significantly changed in the Uruguay Round. See Documents Supplement for the WTO Customs Valuation Agreement.

(2) Despite the special provisions designed to ease adherence to the Valuation Code by developing countries, many did not join. The principal reasons given were problems in respect of training customs personnel, determining proper procedures to apply the agreement, loss of revenue, providing guidance to importers and preparation of the necessary laws and regulations.[19] While all WTO members are required to accept the WTO Customs Valuation Agreement, many developing countries postponed implementation for five or more years. As of 2006, no WTO members were still postponing implementation, but over 50 members had not yet notified their valuation rules to the WTO as required. WTO, 2007 Annual Report, at 27.

(3) The Committee on Customs Valuation established by the Code reported in 1983 that experience in the first year "indicated that, in line with the Agreement's objectives, the vast majority of customs entries were being valued on the basis of transaction value."[20] The Committee has studied a couple of areas where interpretative difficulties have arisen under the Code, including the proper valuation of computer software and the treatment of interest charges in cases of deferred payment.[21]

(4) For more information on the Code, see Saul L. Sherman & Hinrich Glashoff, Customs Valuation: Commentary on the GATT Customs Valuation Code (1988).

(2) U.S. Valuation Rules

The Customs Valuation Code was implemented into U.S. law by title II of the Trade Agreements Act of 1979 (See Documents Supplement, Tariff Act of 1930, sec. 402; 19 U.S.C.A. sec. 1401a).[22] It is generally

---

19. Report of the Committee on Customs Valuation, GATT, 30th Supp. BISD 56, 61 (1984).

20. Id., at 59. A study by the U.S. Customs Service found that over 94% of entries in the ports examined were made on the basis of transaction value. U.S. General Accounting Office, New U.S. Valuation System for Imported Products is Better and Easier to Administer (Report No. B–201765, 1982).

21. Reports of the Committee on Customs Valuation, GATT, 31st Supp. BISD

273, 274 (1985). As a result of a committee decision on software, the EU determined not to include the value of the software in determining the value of goods containing software. Council Regulation 1055/85, [1985] Eur.Comm.O.J. No. L 112/50.

22. Pub.L. No. 96–39, 93 Stat. 144 (codified at 19 U.S.C.A. sec. 1401a). See Edward J. Hayward & Julie Long, Comparative Views of U.S. Customs Valuation Issues in light of the U.S. Customs Modernization Act, 5 Minn. J. Global Trade 311 (1996).

perceived in the United States that valuation disputes have declined with implementation of the Code.[23]

GENERRA SPORTSWEAR CO. v. UNITED STATES

United States Court of Appeals, Federal Circuit, 1990.
905 F.2d 377.

MAYER, CIRCUIT JUDGE:

Generra Sportswear Company of Seattle, Washington, contracted to purchase 595 women's 100% cotton knit blouses from Bagutta Garment Ltd. of Hong Kong at a price of $6.00 each. Bagutta agreed to obtain Type A Transfer quota for category 338/339 at $0.95 per unit.[24] Bagutta obtained quota for the shipment from LCL Manufacturer Co., Ltd. of Hong Kong at $1.28 per unit,[25] the cost of quota having gone up since Bagutta received Generra's purchase order.

The issue on this appeal, whether the quota charges were properly included in transaction value, is a matter of statutory construction. * * *

[B]ecause section 1401a(b) does not precisely address whether or not quota payments may be included in transaction value, we determine whether the appraisal was based on a permissible construction of the statute. Customs' interpretation will be accepted if it is "sufficiently reasonable." Unless it is clear that Congress' intent was to the contrary, courts normally defer to the agency's construction of the statutory scheme it administers.

We think Customs' construction of section 1401a(b), that transaction value may include quota charges, is permissible. It is reasonable to conclude that these charges were part of the "price actually paid or payable," defined in subsection 1401a(b)(4)(A) as "the total payment ... made, or to be made, for imported merchandise by the buyer to, or for the benefit of, the seller." The total payment from Generra to Bagutta was $6.95 per unit. The term "total payment" is all-inclusive. If Congress had intended to exclude quota payments from transaction value, it could have included them among the explicit exclusions enumerated in section 1401a(b)(3).

It is not important that the buyer itself did not pay the seller for the quota charges; the payment was made on behalf of Generra by its Hong Kong buying agent. Further, Generra admits that the "question whether or not the seller benefitted from the quota payment is a non-issue in this case." When the payment is made to the seller, it is not necessary to get

---

23. Munford P. Hall, II, Value's Greatest Hits (and Misses): A Complete History of Judicial Decisions Concerning Value Under the Trade Agreements Act of 1979—Volume I, 25 L. & Poly.Intl.Bus. 51, 67 (1993).

24. [original note 2] As a means of complying with voluntary restraint agreements with the United States, Hong Kong requires that an export license be obtained for each shipment for export. * * *

25. [original note 3] An exporter can obtain an export license by purchasing quota from another party. * * *

into whether the seller benefitted; the statute is written in the alternative: "to, or for the benefit of, the seller." 19 U.S.C. sec. 1401a(b)(4)(A).

The thrust of Generra's argument, and the essence of the trial court's reasoning, is that the quota payment was not "for imported merchandise." * * *

Accepting the stipulated fact that $0.95 of the total payment to Bagutta was for quota charges, it was reasonable for customs to conclude that the entire payment was "for imported merchandise" within the meaning of subsection 1401a(B)(4)(A). A permissible construction of the term "for imported merchandise" does not restrict which components of the total payment may be included in transaction value. Congress did not intend for the Customs Service to engage in extensive fact-finding to determine whether separate charges, all resulting in payments to the seller in connection with the purchase of imported merchandise, are for the merchandise or for something else. As we said in Moss Mfg. Co. v. United States, 896 F.2d 535, 539 (Fed.Cir.1990), the "straightforward approach [of section 1401a(B)] is no doubt intended to enhance the efficiency of Customs' appraisal procedure; it would be frustrated were we to parse the statutory language in the manner, and require Customs to engage in the formidable fact-finding task, envisioned by [appellant]."

As long as the quota payment was made to the seller in exchange for merchandise sold for export to the United States, the payment properly may be included in transaction value, even if the payment represents something other than the per se value of the goods. The focus of transaction value is the actual transaction between the buyer and the seller; if quota payments were transferred by the buyer to the seller, they are part of transaction value. That transaction value may encompass items other than the pure cost of the imported merchandise is reflected in section 1401a(b)(3), governing exclusions from transaction value. If excludable costs or charges are not identified separately from the price actually paid or payable, they are included in transaction value.

It was not necessary for the Customs Service to find that the quota charge was imposed as a condition of sale before considering it part of the "price actually paid or payable" under subsection 1401a(b)(4)(A). Nothing in the statute requires that. On the other hand, that a foreign seller must obtain quota before he can export goods to the United States reasonably indicates that quota payments are part of the "price actually paid or payable for the merchandise when sold for exportation to the United States." 19 U.S.C. sec. 1401a(b)(1).

That was the case here. Bagutta applied for an export license from the Hong Kong Department of Trade before shipping the blouses to Generra; the license form required Bagutta to name the quota holder, the quota reference and the quantity being shipped in quota units. The export license accompanied the goods out of Hong Kong as proof that Bagutta had quota for the shipment. Indeed, if quota were not a prerequisite to exportation, one wonders why Bagutta paid more than the contract price for quota, taking a loss, or even agreed to obtain quota in the first place.

Notes and Questions

(1) The EC Court of Justice reached the opposite result in a similar case under the EC regulation implementing the GATT Code, Ospig Textilgesellschaft KG W. Alhers v. Hauptzollamt Bremen–Ost, Case 7/83, [1984] ECR 609, as had the Court of Customs and Patent Appeals under prior U.S. law. United States v. Getz Bros. & Co., 55 C.C.P.A. 11 (1967). Do you agree with the Court's result? Should it matter that the identical product sold for the same price may be valued differently, depending on the cost of the quota rights? That the seller of the product may not benefit from the quota charge payment? Is the court right to ask only who paid how much to whom? To stress the need for simplicity?

(2) Suppose a Hong Kong business contracts with a U.S. client to supply a made-to-measure suit that it will purchase in Hong Kong and deliver to the client in the United States. On entry of the suit into the United States, should it be valued at the price paid by the Hong Kong business or the price its client will pay to the Hong Kong business? Review the wording of Section 402(b)(1) of the Tariff Act of 1930, 19 U.S.C.A. sec. 1401a(b)(1). When is this merchandise "sold for exportation to the United States?" See E.C. McAfee Co. v. United States, 842 F.2d 314 (Fed.Cir.1988)(value is price paid by middleman). Accord, Nissho Iwai American Corp. v. United States, 982 F.2d 505 (Fed.Cir.1992)(Japanese subway cars). How could you argue that this result is not consistent with *Generra Sportswear*? US Customs and Border Protection has proposed to override these results by rule, but the change had not been adopted as of January 2008.

(3) The rules on valuation are very technical. Suppose a company commits to buy a certain number of units of a product per year for import at $100 per unit, with the proviso that if it fails to do so, the price of each unit actually bought will be adjusted upwards. Is the additional price part of the value for duty assessment purposes? If instead the contract provides for liquidated damages in specified amounts for a failure to fulfill the purchase commitment, in the event of a shortfall would the damages be part of the value for duty assessment purposes? See United States v. Ford Motor Co., 463 F.3d 1267, 1283–84 (Fed. Cir. 2006).

(4) Notice that the value of any "assist" is added to the transaction value (see the definition in Section 402(h), 19 U.S.C.A. sec. 1401a(h)), as is any royalty or license fee related to the imported goods that the buyer is required to pay "as a condition of the sale of the imported merchandise." Tariff Act of 1930, sec. 402(b)(1)(C)-(D), 19 U.S.C.A. sec. 1401a(b)(1)(C)-(D).

(5) Your client wishes to ascertain the likely duty to be assessed on a product, made by its European parent, that it plans to import into the United States for resale. The normal duty rate for the product is 10% and the stated CIF invoice price is $1000. Shipping costs are $50, insurance $10 and packing $5. In addition, your client pays certain royalties to its parent on each resale. Your client has not been doing well financially and the parent has allowed it to defer inter-company payments indefinitely and such

amounts are now between 30 and 90 days past due. Discuss the problems that might arise in determining the applicable duty amount.

(6) The United States has always utilized an FOB method of valuation for customs purposes, whereas most of its trading partners use CIF.[26] This, of course, means that a 10% tariff applied by the United States produces less revenue and is less of a trade barrier than a 10% tariff applied by a country using CIF valuation—the difference being equal basically to 10% of the shipping and insurance costs, a fact negotiators must keep in mind when discussing reciprocal tariff concessions.

It has been argued that it would be unconstitutional for the United States to use CIF prices for customs valuation.[27] The constitutional provisions at issue are Article I, section 8, clause 1, and section 9, clause 6, which read, respectively:

> The Congress shall have power to lay and collect taxes, duties, imposts, and excises, * * * but all duties, imposts, and excises shall be uniform throughout the United States.

> No preference shall be given by any regulation of commerce or revenue to the ports of one state over those of another * * *.

It can be argued that CIF valuation would mean that identical goods, sold for the same price (excluding freight and insurance) would be taxed in different amounts on entry into the United States, thereby violating the uniformity clause. Similarly, CIF valuation would give a preference to U.S. ports closer to the port of dispatch. (Of course, if the cost of bringing goods to the United States is properly considered as part of their value, then FOB valuation leads to nonuniformity and gives a preference to distant ports.) What do you think of this constitutional argument? At the time this issue was discussed during the Tokyo Round, the chairman of the Senate Finance Committee was from Louisiana. Which system favors New Orleans?

(7) The U.S. valuation law prior to 1979 was a pastiche of provisions, some perpetuated from prior laws by special interest lobbying with Congress. No less than nine different standards were applied, depending on the product or circumstance. The most controversial standard was the American Selling Price (ASP) rule, which derived from the Tariff Act of 1922,[28] and which provided that where the statutory tariff did not equalize the difference between foreign and domestic costs of production, the President could change the valuation basis of the article to the ASP. The ASP was defined as the usual wholesale price, including preparation

---

26. An FOB price is the price at the point of shipment for the goods only, while a CIF price is the price for the goods plus an amount covering transportation and insurance to a specified destination. See Section 2.2(B)(2) supra. The relevant U.S. statute is Tariff Act of 1930, sec. 402(b)(4)(A), 19 U.S.C.A. sec. 1401a(b)(4)(A) (dutiable value excludes "any costs, charges, or expenses incurred for transportation, insur-

ance, and related services incident to the international shipment of the merchandise" to the United States).

27. This issue is discussed in U.S. Tariff Commission, Customs Valuation, Report to Senate Comm. on Finance, 93d Cong., 1st Sess. 83–86 (Comm.Print 1973).

28. Act of Sept. 21, 1922, ch. 356, sec. 315, 42 Stat. 941.

for shipping, at which an article manufactured in the United States was freely offered for sale. Prior to the Tokyo Round, the rule was applied to benzenoid chemicals, certain rubber-soled footwear, certain canned clams, and low-value wool-knit gloves. Although in 1969 less than one percent of United States imports were subject to the ASP rule,[29] the effect where applied was considerable. According to a Tariff Commission study of ASP imports in 1964, a 20% duty on some chemicals and footwear was the equivalent of up to 58% at normal customs value.[30]

The ASP method of customs valuation was not consistent with Article VII of GATT. Because ASP was law prior to GATT, however, it benefited from the "grandfather" clause of the Protocol of Provisional Application.[31] During the Kennedy Round of trade negotiations, an agreement was reached whereby the United States would eliminate ASP in exchange for certain European and Japanese concessions (mainly tariff reductions on chemicals and a French agreement to change their method of taxing automobiles so that United States auto exports would be more competitive in the French market). This agreement required approval by the U.S. Congress, which was never given. After several extensions of the deadline for acceptance of the agreement and in the face of congressional inaction, European parties to the agreement indicated in 1972 that they were not prepared to accept a further extension, and the agreement lapsed. The ASP system was eliminated when the United States implemented the Customs Valuation Code as described above. Its only importance today is that it is remembered by U.S. trading partners as a particularly objectionable nontariff barrier, one which the President agreed to eliminate in the Kennedy Round, but was unable to do so because of congressional inaction.

(D) RULES OF ORIGIN

Once goods have been classified and valued, it is necessary to determine their origin so that the proper tariff rate may be applied. Origin determinations would be unnecessary if tariffs were applied on a uniform, most-favored-nation basis, but increasingly nations have entered into preferential trading arrangements, such as free trade areas, customs unions and various programs favoring developing countries. The result has been that origin problems have become more significant in recent years. Moreover, origin determinations have become increasingly necessary to the administration of other non-tariff trade laws: origin-marking requirements, quota administration and application of anti-dumping and countervailing duties. The problems of determining origin have been compounded by recent trends toward global sourcing and multinational manufacturing, where different stages in manufacturing are performed in different countries, in part to take advantage of lower costs, but also in some cases with an eye toward establishing favorable

29. U.S. Tariff Commn., Customs Valuation: Report to the Senate Comm. on Finance, 93d Cong., 1st Sess. 71 (Comm.Print 1973).

30. U.S. Tariff Commission, Trade Barriers, pt. II, vol. 6, at 193 n. 1 (TC Pub.No. 665, 1974).

31. See Section 6.2(B) supra.

origin. Here we will consider briefly the international rules on origin and then consider how origin rules are typically applied.

(1) The International Rules on Origin

The General Agreement does not treat origin rules per se, although origin marking rules are dealt with in Article IX, which most fundamentally requires MFN treatment. Art. IX:1. The other provisions of Article IX are aimed at minimizing the use of origin marking requirements to hinder trade. For example, countries are to allow origin to be marked at the time of importation (if practicable) and in a way that is not too costly or damaging to the imported product. In addition, there have been various reports and recommendations on origin in GATT.[32] Prior to the Uruguay Round, the principal international agreement dealing with origin issues was the Kyoto Convention, which establishes only very general rules relating to origin.[33]

The Uruguay Round negotiations resulted in a WTO Agreement on Rules of Origin. The agreement calls for the harmonization of non-preferential origin rules through a work program to be undertaken by the WTO Committee on Rules of Origin and the World Customs Organization (WCO). Article 2 of the agreement contains a number of general rules that are applicable to non-preferential origin rules until such time as the harmonization work program is completed. For example, such rules are to be clearly defined; they are not to be used as instruments to pursue trade objectives; they are not by themselves to create restrictive, distorting or disruptive effects on international trade; the rules applicable to imports and exports are not to be more stringent that those applicable for determining domestic origin; they are to be based on positive standards (specification of what is required to achieve origin, not what is insufficient); and certain procedural rights are to be respected. After the harmonization program is completed, Article 3 of the agreement provides that origin rules are to apply equally for all purposes (i.e., for MFN purposes, antidumping and countervailing duty purposes, safeguard purposes, origin marking purposes and any discriminatory quotas or tariffs, as well as for government procurement and trade statistics purposes) and that generally the "last substantial transformation" standard shall be used to determine origin. That standard may be implemented through the use of such criteria as change in tariff heading, value added or completion of specific processes. The agreement is mainly concerned with non-preferential origin rules, but an annex contains a declaration on preferential rules, which requires, inter alia, that such rules be clearly defined and based on positive standards. The text of the agreement is in the Documents Supplement. As of January 2008, negotiations on non-preferential origin rules were continuing.

---

32. John H. Jackson, World Trade and the Law of GATT, sec. 17.8 (1969); see also the GATT reports published in: GATT, 1st Supp. BISD 100 (1953); GATT, 2d Supp. BISD 53 (1954); GATT, 5th Supp. BISD 33, 102 (1957).

33. International Convention on the Simplification and Harmonization of Customs Procedures, done at Kyoto May 18, 1973, entered into force Sept. 25, 1974, for the United States, Jan. 28 1984 (subject to reservations). KAV 2259.

(2) The Application of Origin Rules

The application of origin rules is a complex subject. At the outset, it should be clear that a product made in country A and transshipped via country B to country X is unlikely to be considered to have originated in B when it arrives in X. The difficult question arises when work is performed on a product in two (or more) countries. To take the prior example, how much must be done in B to give the product B origin? If B is the beneficiary of a preferential tariff, should the origin rule be different?

SUPERIOR WIRE v. UNITED STATES

United States Court of International Trade, 1987.
669 F.Supp. 472, affd., 867 F.2d 1409 (Fed.Cir.1989).

RESTANI, JUDGE:

[Superior began importing wire rod from Spain into Canada in 1984 following the imposition of preliminary antidumping and countervailing duties on wire rod imported from Spain into the United States. In a newly-established wire drawing facility in Canada, Superior drew the wire rod into wire before shipping the wire to its wire mesh operation in Michigan. It claimed Canada as the country of origin instead of Spain. Superior's practice continued after the United States entered into a Voluntary Restraint Agreement (VRA) with Spain covering wire and wire rod. In 1987, the Customs Service refused entry to Superior's imports of drawn wire from Canada on the grounds that they were of Spanish origin and lacked the proper certificates that would permit entry under the Spanish VRA.

The process by which rod is drawn into wire is as follows: The rod is uncoiled, cleaned and coated with a lubricant/rust preventative. The rod is then typically drawn through two dies. "The final result is a substantially stronger product, which is also cleaner, smoother, 'less springy,' less ductile, and cross-sectionally more uniform. Seventy percent of the wire imported by [Superior] is intended for use in making wire mesh for concrete sewer pipe reinforcement. * * * The sizes of rod imported produce a range of sizes of wire, but the physical properties of the rod limit the range of sizes of wire which may be effectively or economically produced from a particular size of rod. * * * [T]he chemical content of the rod and the cooling processes used in its manufacture determine the properties that the wire will have after drawing. * * * [T]he value added in terms of cost of the drawing process is about fifteen percent."]

The court now turns to the fundamental question of whether under generally applicable precedent a substantial transformation of the wire rod from Spain occurs when it becomes wire, so as to make the wire a product of Canada, and thus not subject to VRA restrictions. The basic test cited by the parties was set forth in a drawback case, Anheuser–Busch Brewing Ass'n v. United States, 207 U.S. 556, 562 (1908), which held that a product would be considered the manufacture or product of the United States if it was transformed into a new and different article "having a distinctive name, character or use." The test has been applied in various situations. * * *

Although all recent cases cite the *Anheuser–Busch* test, they apply it differently, and modify it somewhat. A name change, for example, is not always considered determinative. Therefore, although it is clear that a name change from "wire rod" to "wire" occurred here, this fact is not necessarily determinative. It may support, however, a finding of substantial transformation, as it did in Ferrostaal [Metals Corp. v. United States, 664 F.Supp. 535 (CIT 1987) (galvanizing of steel sheet effected substantial transformation)]. Likewise the change in tariff classification which occurred here is not dispositive, although it also may be supportive.

In recent years the courts have concentrated on change in use or character, finding various subsidiary tests appropriate depending on the situation at hand. An inquiry that is sometimes treated as a type of cross-check or additional factor to be considered in substantial transformation cases is whether significant value is added or costs are incurred by the process at issue. See United States v. Murray, 621 F.2d 1163 (1st Cir.1980) (blending of glues added no significant value). In National Juice [Prod. Assn. v. United States, 628 F.Supp. 978 (CIT 1986), which involved dilution of concentrated juice], values of between one and eight percent were not found to be significant. In Uniroyal v. United States, 542 F.Supp. 1026 (CIT 1982) (addition of outer sole did not substantially transform shoe upper under marking laws), no percentage was specified, but the cost of the alleged transformation was deemed insignificant. In *Ferrostaal*, on the other hand, a value, attributable to the transformation of at least thirty-six to nearly fifty percent of the value of the heat treated steel, reinforced the court's conclusion that galvanizing and annealing steel constituted a substantial transformation.

A value added test has appeal in many situations because it brings a common sense approach to a fundamental test that may not be easily applied to some products. The fifteen percent added value figure for the wire standing alone does not pull in either direction, but related concepts, including the amount of labor required to accomplish the change and the capital investment required relative to that required to produce the entire article, are also relevant to a determination of whether the change involves minor processing. Minimal processing is part of the factual background of cases such as *Murray, National Juice* and *Uniroyal*, all of which involve findings of no substantial transformation. The differences in capital investment and labor needed in the production of wire rod versus wire are enormous. Comparing only the production of wire from wire rod, versus the production of wire rod from billet, it becomes apparent that the processing performed in Canada is a minor finishing step which may be accomplished easily anywhere with a minimal amount of effort and investment. By itself such analysis may not provide the entire answer as to whether a substantial transformation has taken place, but it should comprise part of the analysis in a case involving the type of products and processes at issue here.

Turning to past precedent, the court observes that cases dealing with substantial transformations are very product specific and are often distinguishable on that basis, rather than by their statutory underpinnings. It is difficult to generalize from cases involving combinations of articles to those that involve processing of a single material. In addition, it is frequently difficult to take concepts applicable to products such as textiles and apply them to combinations of liquids or fabrication of steel articles. To determine whether the goods at hand are substantially transformed for purposes of VRA enforcement, the court should examine cases involving processing of metal objects without combination or assembly operations. Torrington Co. v. United States, 764 F.2d 1563 (1985) is one such case. As indicated, it involved the manufacture of needles in a beneficiary developing country [i.e., a country benefiting from the U.S. Generalized System of Preferences (GSP) for developing countries, which provides duty-free treatment to qualifying imports]. In the first stage of production of needles, a wire is straightened, cut, beveled, and drawn to form a needle blank. The blank is only useful in the needle-making process. In the next stage, an eye is struck into the needle, a groove is made for thread, and the needle is finished by various processes, including hardening, sharpening, and polishing. The *Torrington* court found that in order for plaintiff to prevail under the GSP statute, two substantial transformations were necessary; the court found both the first and second stages to be substantial transformations.

The second stage of processing discussed in the *Torrington* case involved a transformation from producers' to consumers' goods. * * * Although some of the processes involved here are the same as those involved in the second phase of *Torrington*, there is no clear change from producers' to consumers' goods. Wire rod is primarily intended for wire production, which, in turn, is primarily intended to be used for making wire mesh for concrete pipe reinforcement.

The processes involved in the first stage of *Torrington* are closer to the ones involved here. In fact, the *Torrington* court cited in support of its holding a Treasury Decision involving use of dies to draw plate steel into a cup-shaped rear engine housing. Two factors distinguish this aspect of *Torrington* from the case at hand. First, once the needle blanks were drawn they were fit for only one purpose; the raw material was then destined for one end use. This type of transformation does not occur when wire rod is drawn into wire. The composition of the wire rod determines what uses the wire may have. Although the steel and wire industries may have different names for the products, wire rod and wire may be viewed as different stages of the same product. The difference in stages may be important for tariff purposes but it is not determinative here. In contrast, the *Torrington* court stated, "the initial wire is a raw material and possesses nothing in its character which indicated either the swages [blanks] or the final product." Here, the wire rod dictates the final form of the finished wire. Second, the court cannot escape the statutory basis of the *Torrington* opinion. Apart from direct references to the purpose of the GSP already mentioned, the court also noted, " * * *

Torrington Portuguesa could do no more than it already does in the production of needles. In these circumstances we think Congress intended the GSP statute to apply."

The engine housing decision cited by *Torrington* also differs from the case at hand. Like the wire to needle blank change, the product was transformed from basic steel into a part with a unique destiny. In addition, the decision noted the involvement of a series of dies. Essentially only two die passes are involved here. The wire emerges stronger and rounder after the passes, but the wire loses a few other advantages, such as greater ductility, in the process. It looks much the same. Its strength characteristic, which is important to its end use, is altered, but the parameters of the strength increase was metallurgically predetermined in the creation of the steel billet and very specifically through the fabrication of the wire rod. Under these circumstances the court does not find a significant change in use or character to have occurred.

The court should also mention here the *Ferrostaal* case. The hot-dipped galvanizing processes involved there, which involved substantial chemical changes, were different from the cold drawing processes involved here. Although, applying broader analytical concepts, the changes in use and character were not greatly different from those involved here, the value added was significant. It appears that a larger capital investment, as well as possibly significant labor, was required to accomplish the transformation in *Ferrostaal*. Taken together these differences are sufficient to distinguish *Ferrostaal* from the case at hand.

Here only the change in name test is clearly met, and such a change has rarely been dispositive. No transformation from producers' to consumers' goods took place; no change from a product suitable for many uses to one with more limited uses took place; no complicated or expensive processing occurred, and only relatively small value was added. Overall, the court views the transformation from wire rod to wire to be minor rather than substantial. Accordingly, the country of origin of the wire must be considered Spain rather than Canada.

Notes and Questions

(1) The *Superior Wire* decision mentions many of the tests used for origin purposes. Although the court focused on the substantial transformation test, it also considered the impact of (i) a change in four-digit tariff heading, a test used in U.S. and EU free trade area agreements (subject to many exceptions) and (ii) the value added in the claimed country of origin, a standard which is also used extensively in preferential agreements, sometimes as a fall-back provision applicable when there has been no change in tariff heading. There are also special origin rules for certain products that specify in detail the processes that must have been performed on the product in a country in order to obtain origin. For example, the U.S. has special origin rules generally applicable to textile products.[34] Given the *Anheuser–Busch* test—transformation into a new article having a distinctive name,

34. 3719 CFR sec. 102.21 (2007).

character or use—was it appropriate for the court to consider the value added in Canada? How relevant is that to determining whether the three *Anheuser–Busch* criteria have been met?

(2) The purpose of the U.S. GSP scheme is to promote trade, while the purpose of a steel VRA is to limit trade. Should these different purposes influence origin decisions? Do you think that the district court in *Superior Wire* was in fact influenced by these purposes? Are you convinced by the court's distinction of *Torrington* in *Superior Wire*? In affirming the *Superior Wire* decision, the Federal Circuit noted that "[o]ur decision, should, therefore, not be understood to entirely rule out consideration of the context in which a country of origin determination must be made." 867 F.2d at 1415 n.2. For a fascinating description of the evolution of CIT and Federal Circuit thinking on this issue, see N. David Palmeter, Rules of Origin in the United States, in Rules of Origin in International Trade: A Comparative Study 27, 37–42 (Edwin Vermulst, Jacques Bourgeois & Paul Waer eds., 1994).

(3) Origin rules impact trade and investment decisions. Obviously, they are used to determine origin for applying the appropriate duty rate and other customs rules. As such, in order to gain favorable origin treatment, particularly where value-added rules apply, an exporter may choose to purchase components of its products from suppliers whose goods will help meet the value-added requirement. For example, in order to meet the 62.5% value-added requirement for automobiles under NAFTA, auto assemblers in NAFTA have an incentive to buy NAFTA origin parts so they will more easily meet NAFTA's preferential origin requirements when they export their autos to the other NAFTA members. Similarly, auto part makers may choose to locate their plants where their customers will most benefit from origin rules. When there is some doubt as to whether origin rules can be satisfied, the rules promote investment in the largest market in the free trade area. Do you see why? NAFTA origin rules are explored in Section 11.3(C) infra.

Nonpreferential origin rules may also influence the location and scope of plants built to supply particular markets, especially when the aim is to create origin so as to avoid duties (whether regular, antidumping or countervailing), quotas or other restrictive trade measures. See generally Rules of Origin in International Trade: A Comparative Study (Edwin Vermulst, Jacques Bourgeois & Paul Waer eds., 1994).

(4) Under the U.S. origin rules for GSP treatment, which affords duty-free entry to certain products of developing countries, the product (1) must be transported directly to the United States from the country of origin and (2) the sum of (a) the cost or value of the materials produced in the beneficiary country plus (b) the direct costs of processing operations performed in such country must not be less than 35% of the value of the product when imported into the United States.[35] Under certain circumstances groups of countries may count as one under these rules,

35. 19 CFR sec. 10.171–.178 (2007).

e.g., some or all of the Andean nations, the ASEAN nations and members of the Caribbean Common Market.[36]

As evidenced by the discussion of the *Torrington* case in *Superior Wire*, the phrase "materials produced in the beneficiary country" includes products manufactured there out of inputs from third countries. One of the difficult determinations that must be made under the GSP and other similar value-added origin tests is whether an input from a third country has been substantially transformed into an intermediate product, which then counts as a beneficiary country product for the value-added test when it is incorporated into the exported product. In *Torrington*, the court found that wire had been transformed into an intermediate product—needle blanks or swages—and permitted the value of the swages to count toward meeting the 35% test for value added in Portugal even though they were made of imported, non-Portuguese wire. Despite the *Torrington result*, courts often find that an intermediate product has not been produced if all of the processing takes place within a single plant. See, e.g., F.F. Zuniga v. United States, 996 F.2d 1203 (Fed.Cir.1993); Azteca Milling Co. v. United States, 890 F.2d 1150 (Fed.Cir.1989).

Similar problems arose under the U.S.-Canada Free Trade Agreement (FTA). In one controversial case, a Japanese automobile maker (Honda) exported automobile engines to Canada after assembly and some manufacture in the U.S.[37] The engines were installed in automobiles in Canada, and Honda then exported the autos to the U.S. The engines contained a substantial component of U.S. materials and labor and were treated as originating in the U.S. by Canadian authorities on their export to Canada. Nonetheless, U.S. Customs treated them as non-U.S. parts for FTA origin rule purposes when the completed cars were exported from Canada to the United States. For reasons that are too technical to explore here, the U.S. authorities took a different and much stricter view of how to interpret the FTA origin rules than had the Canadians. As a consequence, the automobiles failed (barely) to meet the 50% value-added test specified in the FTA and were subject to the MFN duty on automobiles, rather than being admitted duty free under the FTA. The U.S. and Canada agreed to settle their dispute over the Honda case by using the special origin rules for automobiles in the North American Free Trade Agreement. NAFTA, art. 403. Under those rules, the value on importation of all non-NAFTA origin components will be subtracted from the net cost to see if the 62.5% value-added threshold for automobiles is met. Thus, imported components will not count towards the value-added requirement, even if they have been manufactured into intermediate products. NAFTA, art. 403(1). For goods not subject to the special rules for autos, imported products manufactured into intermediate products would count toward NAFTA origin, just as

---

36. HTS, Headnote 4(a).

37. See David Palmeter, The Honda Decision: Rules of Origin Turned Upside Down, CCH Free Trade Law Reports, The Free Trade Observer, No. 32A (June 1992); Frédéric P. Cantin & Andreas F. Lowenfeld, Rules of Origin, The Canada–U.S. FTA, and the Honda Case, 87 Am.J.Intl.L. 375 (1993).

the needle blanks did in the *Torrington* case. NAFTA, art. 402(4). Why not apply the NAFTA auto origin rule generally and never count imported components to determine if a value-added threshold has been met? See Section 11.3(C) infra.

(5) Assume that a New Zealand owned, but Soviet registered fishing boat catches fish known as New Zealand Hoki in New Zealand's exclusive economic zone or EEZ (i.e., within 200 miles of New Zealand) but outside New Zealand's traditional territorial waters (i.e., beyond 12 miles of New Zealand). Assume further that the fish are beheaded, de-tailed, eviscerated and frozen on the boat and then landed and stored in New Zealand. Then assume that the fish are sent to South Korea for skinning, boning, trimming, glazing and packaging. Should the fish package be marked as a product of the Soviet Union, New Zealand or South Korea? In a case involving these facts, the U.S. Customs Service initially claimed that under the U.S. origin marking statute, 19 U.S.C.A. sec. 1304(a), the fish were a product of the Soviet Union since they were caught on the high seas by a Soviet boat. The exporter claimed they were a product of New Zealand since they were caught in New Zealand territory. The court rejected the latter argument on the grounds that the EEZ could not be considered New Zealand territory under international law, even though New Zealand had preferential rights to resources in its EEZ. The court would have concluded that the fish were a Soviet product except that it found that the fish were substantially transformed in South Korea where they arrived as "headed and gutted" Hoki and left as "individually quick frozen fillets." Koru North America v. United States, 701 F.Supp. 229 (CIT 1988). As a fish consumer, would you find it helpful to read that these fish were a product of South Korea?

(6) The goal of customs law is to establish simple rules that can be consistently applied. In light of the foregoing materials, how close would you say that U.S. origin rules come in meeting this standard? How precise and predictable is the substantial transformation test? What about a change of tariff heading test? Does it take adequate account of the concerns underlying origin rules? Recall that under that test the wire in *Superior Wire* would have had Canadian origin. Would a value added test be sufficiently precise? Or do the problems in Note 4 above suggest that it also is an inadequate solution? In addition to the problems discussed there, there are difficulties in deciding what non-material and non-labor costs should be counted in determining the value added in each jurisdiction.

(E) OTHER CUSTOMS ISSUES

There are two additional areas of U.S. Customs Law that may be of particular interest: special rules to assist exports and enforcement issues.

(1) Export Promotion: Foreign Trade Zones and Drawback

The aim of customs law is to tax goods that enter the United States for consumption. To the extent goods are not going to be used in the United States, no duty is applied. The simplest example of this principle is embodied in the rules on transit; goods passing through the United States on the way to another destination are not subject to duties.[38] In fact, such goods may even be stored and/or processed in the United States in special bonded customs warehouses.[39]

More complex are rules designed to promote U.S. exports. For example, under the foreign trade zone rules goods may enter a designated foreign trade zone in the United States without payment of duty, be processed and then exported.[40] If the resultant product is "exported" to the United States, duty is assessed on the new product, although arrangements may be made so that duties are assessed on the basis of the amount of the imported goods used in the product sold in the United States.

Similarly, since the aim of the customs law is to tax imported goods consumed in the United States, if imported goods are incorporated in a product that is exported from the United States, there are rules that permit 99% of the duties paid on the incorporated product to be recovered.[41] These so-called drawback rules are also designed to promote the United States as a place for manufacture of export goods. The rules for drawback are procedurally complex and any company hoping to avail itself of the rules should make sure it has complied in all respects in advance of exportation. Special rules on "substitution" are designed to allow drawback on a pro rata basis in the situation where domestic-origin and foreign-origin components are used in producing merchandise. Under these rules, if a foreign-origin component was used in a domestically sold item and a like domestic-origin component was used in an exported item, drawback would still be allowed.

Finally, another rule that is designed to promote U.S. manufacturing provides that the value for duty purposes of imported goods assembled abroad of U.S. components is reduced by the value of the U.S. components.[42] This provision provides some incentive for U.S. manufacturers to keep at least part of their production processes in the United States.

(2) Customs Law Enforcement

Section 592 of the Tariff Act of 1930 provides that no person shall enter merchandise into the United States by means of a document or statement that is material and false or by means of an omission that is material.[43] Penalties for this civil violation range from the value of the

---

38. See generally 19 U.S.C.A. secs. 1551–65; 19 CFR secs. 18.1–18.45 (2007). Of course, care is taken to exclude the possibility that the goods will be consumed or used in the United States without payment of duty. For example, goods in transit must generally be entered with the customs authorities, transported by bonded carrier and checked out of the United States. See 19 CFR secs. 18.20–18.22 (2007).

39. See generally 19 CFR secs. 19.1–19.49 (2007).

40. See generally 19 U.S.C.A. secs. 81a–81u; 19 CFR secs. 146.0–146.96 (2007).

41. See generally 19 U.S.C.A. sec. 1313; 19 CFR secs. 191.0–191.195 (2007).

42. 19 CFR secs. 10.11–10.26 (2007).

43. 19 U.S.C.A. sec. 1592(a)(1). Clerical errors or factual mistakes are not considered violations unless they are part of a

merchandise in the case of fraud to the lesser of that amount or twice the duties of which the United States is or may be deprived in the case of negligence.[44]

Prior to 1978, the penalty provisions of the U.S. law, which provided for forfeiture in all cases of violation, were claimed to be in violation of GATT Article VIII, paragraph 3, which prohibits substantial penalties for minor breaches.[45]

---

pattern of negligence. 19 U.S.C.A. sec. 1592(a)(2).

44. 19 U.S.C.A. sec. 1592(c). If the violation did not affect the assessment of duties, the penalty for negligence may be 20% of the value. The penalties for gross negligence are twice those for negligence (i.e. four times the duties/40% of the value).

45. See American Bar Assn., Section of Intl.Law, Report to the House of Delegates 2–3 (1975) to accompany resolution on section 502 adopted at the August 1975 meeting.

Chapter 9

BORDER MEASURES II: QUOTAS, NON–TARIFF BARRIERS AND TRANSPARENCY

SECTION 9.1   INTRODUCTION

Tariffs are the preferred trade barrier under the GATT rules, as we saw in Chapter 8, while quotas and other non-tariff barriers (NTBs) are disfavored. The economic effects of quotas have already been described in the Appendix to Chapter 1. In Section 9.2, we will see that GATT rules generally ban the use of quotas on imports and exports. That ban has not always been easy to implement, however, so we will have occasion to examine certain formal and "informal" exceptions whereby the use of quotas and similar measures was permitted or tolerated. In particular, we will look in Section 9.3 at the history and current use of quotas and similar measures in the areas of textiles and clothing, and in agriculture. One of the principal achievements of the Uruguay Round was the agreement to convert quotas and other non-tariff barriers on agricultural products to tariffs. We will evaluate the extent to which the use of such non-tariff barriers has been effectively limited. In Section 9.4, we will examine GATT rules on state trading, a mechanism that may be used by governments to duplicate the effect of tariffs and quotas. While the rules on state trading are underdeveloped, they have been clarified to some extent in WTO dispute settlement. Finally, in Section 9.5, we will consider more generally the WTO's approach to transparency and good governance, which is often useful in combating NTBs.

SECTION 9.2   ARTICLE XI

Article XI is commonly described as GATT's quota prohibition, but it is far broader than that. It provides as follows:

1.   No prohibitions or restrictions other than duties, taxes or other charges, whether made effective through quotas, import or export licenses or other measures shall be instituted or maintained by any contracting party on the importation of any product of the territory of any other contracting party or on the exportation or sale for

export of any product destined for the territory of any other contracting party. (Emphasis added.)

The broad sweep of this provision underscores the basic philosophy of the General Agreement in respect of import restraints. Such restraints are to be in the form of tariffs, and maximum tariff levels are to be negotiated by the contracting parties. Article XI bans other forms of import restraints, and once imported goods are admitted to a country, Article III generally prohibits the application to them of discriminatory internal taxes or other regulatory measures.

Probably the most difficult interpretative issue presented by Article XI is defining its scope. By its wording, it applies to all import restrictions "other than duties, taxes or other charges." Obviously, Article XI prohibits straightforward quotas on imports. But to what extent does it cover other measures that adversely affect imports? For example, does it apply to minimum import price requirements or to investment-related performance requirements? How "mandatory" must a government policy be in order to fall within the prohibition?

JAPAN—TRADE IN SEMI–CONDUCTORS
GATT Panel Report adopted May 4, 1988.
35th Supp. BISD 116 (1989).

[In the mid–1980's, there was considerable friction between the United States and Japan over trade in semi-conductors, which resulted in the initiation of antidumping investigations and a Section 301 investigation of Japanese exports of semi-conductors. Following protracted negotiations, the U.S. and Japan formally concluded an Arrangement concerning Trade in Semi–Conductor Products (the "Arrangement") on September 2, 1986. Under the Arrangement, the U.S. unfair trade investigations were suspended in return for Japanese commitments to expand foreign access to the Japanese semi-conductor market and to prevent dumping. The arrangement was challenged by the EEC, which was afraid that it would lead to adverse effects in its market (e.g., through increased exports of semi-conductors to the EEC at low prices).]

99. [After concluding the Arrangement,] the Japanese Government:

— requested Japanese producers and exporters of semi-conductors covered by the Arrangement not to export semi-conductors at prices below company-specific costs [i.e., not to dump, see Chapter 16 infra];

— collected data on company and product-specific costs from producers; introduced a statutory requirement, reinforced by penal servitude not exceeding six months or a fine not exceeding Y 200,000, for exporters of semi-conductors to report data on export prices;

— systematically monitored company and product-specific cost and export price data on semi-conductors which were sold for export to certain contracting parties other than the United States;

— instituted quarterly supply and demand forecasts and communicated to manufacturers its concern about the need to accommodate their production levels to the forecasts as compiled by MITI [Ministry of International Trade and Investment].

[Initially the cost and export price data were examined in connection with the decision on whether to issue an export license under Japan's COCOM regulations. Later, the examination of the data and the COCOM screening process were administratively separated. (COCOM was the international arrangement under which high tech exports to the former Soviet bloc were controlled by the U.S. and its Cold War allies.)]

* * *

102.   The Panel understood the main contentions of the parties to the dispute on the consistency of the measures set out in paragraph 99 with Article XI:1 of the General Agreement to be the following. The EEC considered that such measures constituted restrictions on the sale for export of semi-conductors at prices below company-specific costs through measures other than duties, taxes or charges within the meaning of Article XI:1. Japan contended that there were no governmental measures limiting the right of Japanese producers and exporters to export semi-conductors at any price they wished. The Government's measures to avoid sales at dumping prices were not legally binding and therefore did not fall under Article XI:1. Exports were limited by private enterprises in their own self-interest and such private action was outside the purview of Article XI:1.

103.   As for the export approval system, the EEC [asked the Panel to examine] the delays in the issuing of export licenses resulting from the monitoring of costs and export prices. The EEC considered that these delays constituted restrictions on exportation made effective through export licenses within the meaning of Article XI:1. Japan maintained that the delays in the granting of export licenses resulting from the monitoring of costs and export prices had occurred for purely administrative reasons and did not constitute restrictions within the meaning of Article XI:1, since no export license had ever been denied for reasons related to export pricing.

104.   The Panel examined the parties' contentions in the light of Article XI:1 * * *. The Panel noted that [the wording of Article XI:1] was comprehensive: it applied to all measures instituted or maintained by a contracting party prohibiting or restricting the importation, exportation or sale for export of products other than measures that take the form of duties, taxes or other charges.

105.   The Panel noted that the CONTRACTING PARTIES had decided in a previous case that the import regulation allowing the import of a product in principle, but not below a minimum price level, constituted a restriction on importation within the meaning of Article XI:1. The Panel considered that the principle applied in that case to restrictions on

imports of goods below certain prices was equally applicable to restrictions on exports below certain prices.

106. The Panel then examined the contention of the Japanese Government that the measures complained of were not restrictions within the meaning of Article XI:1 because they were not legally binding or mandatory. In this respect the Panel noted that Article XI:1, unlike other provisions of the General Agreement, did not refer to laws or regulations but more broadly to measures. This wording indicated clearly that any measure instituted or maintained by a contracting party which restricted the exportation or sale for export of products was covered by this provision, irrespective of the legal status of the measure.

107. Having reached this finding on the basis of the wording and purpose of the provision, the Panel looked for precedents that might be of further assistance to it on this point. It noted that the CONTRACTING PARTIES had addressed a case relating to the interpretation of Article XI:2(c) in the report of the Panel on "Japan—Restrictions on Imports of Certain Agricultural Products." [BISD 35S/163 (1989)] Under Article XI:2(c) import restrictions might be imposed if they were necessary to the enforcement of "governmental measures" restricting domestic supplies. The complaining party argued in the earlier panel proceedings that some of the measures which Japan had described as governmental measures were in fact "only an appeal for private measures to be taken voluntarily by private parties" and could therefore not justify the import restrictions. Japan replied that "to the extent that governmental measures were effective, it was irrelevant whether or not the measures were mandatory and statutory," that the governmental measures "were effectively enforced by detailed directives and instructions to local governments and/or farmers' organizations" and that "such centralized and mutually collaborative structure of policy implementation was the crux of government enforcement in Japan." The Panel which examined that case had noted that "the practice of 'administrative guidance' played an important role" in the enforcement of the Japanese supply restrictions, that this practice was "a traditional tool of Japanese government policy based on consensus and peer pressure" and that administrative guidance in the special circumstances prevailing in Japan could therefore be regarded as a governmental measure enforcing supply restrictions. The Panel recognized the differences between Article XI:1 and Article XI:2(c) and the fact that the previous case was not the same in all respects as the case before it, but noted that the earlier case supported its finding that it was not necessarily the legal status of the measure which was decisive in determining whether or not it fell under Article XI:1.

108. The Panel recognized that not all non-mandatory requests could be regarded as measures within the meaning of Article XI:1. Government-industry relations varied from country to country, from industry to industry, and from case to case and were influenced by many factors. There was thus a wide spectrum of government involvement ranging from, for instance, direct government orders to occasional gov-

ernment consultations with advisory committees. The task of the Panel was to determine whether the measures taken in this case would be such as to constitute a contravention of Article XI.

109. In order to determine this, the Panel considered that it needed to be satisfied on two essential criteria. First, there were reasonable grounds to believe that sufficient incentives or disincentives existed for non-mandatory measures to take effect. Second, the operation of the measures to restrict export of semi-conductors at prices below company-specific costs was essentially dependent on Government action or intervention. The Panel considered each of these two criteria in turn. The Panel considered that if these two criteria were met, the measures would be operating in a manner equivalent to mandatory requirements such that the difference between the measures and mandatory requirements was only one of form and not of substance, and that there could be therefore no doubt that they fell within the range of measures covered by Article XI:1.

[The Panel concluded, *inter alia*, that at least by April 1987, producers and exporters in Japan knew that the Japanese Government had made an undertaking to the United States to stop dumping, and that a failure by the Government to fulfil the commitment would have adverse consequences for Japan. They also knew that the Government had the fullest information available to identify any producers or exporters selling at prices below costs.]

111. The Panel considered that, in the above circumstances, the Japanese Government's measures did not need to be legally binding to take effect, as there were reasonable grounds to believe that there were sufficient incentives or disincentives for Japanese producers and exporters to conform. * * *

[The Panel then considered the second criterion—whether the measures were essentially dependent on the Government. In its analysis, the Panel cited Government descriptions of its role, the extensive monitoring scheme and collection of information on costs and export prices, and the government forecasts of supply and demand.]

116. * * * [Finally,] the Panel noted that Japan had stated in the proceedings of the Panel that "although monitoring by MITI was limited in scope, it was still meaningful because MITI represented a neutral and objective figure overseeing the entire industry while taking into account costs and prices among competing companies in Japan. Monitoring also helped to stamp out suspicion among companies that others were cheating or resorting to dumping." Japan had further stated that "if the semiconductor manufacturers were to pursue their own profits and ignore MITI's concern, the whole dumping prevention mechanism would collapse," and that "the administration presents (firms) with objective facts and considerations and others that are usually not obtainable by one firm alone." The Panel considered that these statements concerning the way in which the Government exercised its authority were a further

confirmation of the fact that the Government's involvement was essential to the prevention of sales below company-specific costs.

117. All these factors led the Panel to conclude that an administrative structure had been created by the Government of Japan which operated to exert maximum possible pressure on the private sector to cease exporting at prices below company-specific costs. This was exercised through such measures as repeated direct requests by MITI, combined with the statutory requirement for exporters to submit information on export prices, the systematic monitoring of company and product-specific costs and export prices and the institution of the supply and demand forecasts mechanism and its utilization in a manner to directly influence the behavior of private companies. These measures operated furthermore to facilitate strong peer pressure to comply with requests by MITI and at the same time to foster a climate of uncertainty as to the circumstances under which their exports could take place. The Panel considered that the complex of measures exhibited the rationale as well as the essential elements of a formal system of export control. The only distinction in this case was the absence of formal legally binding obligations in respect of exportation or sale for export of semi-conductors. However, the Panel concluded that this amounted to a difference in form rather than substance because the measures were operated in a manner equivalent to mandatory requirements. The Panel concluded that the complex of measures constituted a coherent system restricting the sale for export of monitored semi-conductors at prices below company-specific costs to markets other that the United States, inconsistent with Article XI:1.

118. The Panel then reverted to the issue raised by the EEC concerning the delays of up to three months in the issuing of export licenses that had resulted from the monitoring of costs and export prices of semi-conductors destined for contracting parties other than the United States. It examined whether the measures taken by Japan constituted restrictions on exportation or sale for export within the meaning of Article XI:1. It noted that the CONTRACTING PARTIES had found in a previous case that automatic licensing did not constitute a restriction within the meaning of Article XI:1 and that an import license issued on the fifth working day following the day on which the license application was lodged could be deemed to have been automatically granted. The Panel recognized that the above applied to import licenses but it considered that the standard applicable to import licenses should, by analogy, be applied also to export licenses because it saw no reason that would justify the application of a different standard. The Panel therefore found that export licensing practices by Japan, leading to delays of up to three months in the issuing of licenses for semi-conductors destined for contracting parties other than the United States, had been non-automatic and constituted restrictions on the exportation of such products inconsistent with Article XI:1.

[The Panel also concluded that the violation could not be excused by Article VI relating to dumping, since that article only authorized action by importing countries.]

Notes and Questions

(1) The *Japanese Semi-conductor* case is important because of its analysis of how GATT rules apply to voluntary export restraints. We examine such restraints in Chapter 15, which deals with the Escape Clause (Article XIX) and safeguard measures generally.

(2) In a 1999 case, *India—Quantitative Restrictions on Imports of Agricultural, Textile and Industrial Products*, WT/DS90/R, adopted September 22, 1999, a panel found that certain Indian measures—discretionary (non-automatic) import licensing systems; canalization of certain imports through government agencies; and a system allowing imports of certain products only by actual users, which precluded imports of consumer goods by wholesalers or retailers—violated Article XI:1. India had notified the measures as quantitative restrictions, but claimed that they were permitted for balance-of-payments reasons. This defense was rejected, as explained in Chapter 22.

(3) Related to the question of what sort of measure is a governmental measure is the question of how to deal with actions taken by state trading companies. Consider the Interpretative Note Ad Articles XI–XIV & XVIII, which provides that the terms "import restrictions" and "export restrictions" in those articles include restrictions made effective through state-trading operations. We discuss the problems associated with state trading companies in Section 9.4.

(4) Article XI speaks of "prohibitions or restrictions * * * *on the importation* of any product." Does this phrase include measures that are applied after importation if those measures deter or effectively prevent the import of products by making it difficult or impossible to sell them? In this regard, is there any significance to the difference in wording in Article XI between the phrase dealing with "importation" and that dealing with "exportation or sale for export".

In 1984, a GATT panel analyzed Canadian practices whereby foreign companies were permitted to invest in manufacturing plants in Canada only if they undertook that those plants would purchase inputs and other goods of Canadian origin in preference to imported goods. In response to a U.S. argument that this practice violated Article XI, the panel responded:[1]

> The Panel shares the view of Canada that the General Agreement distinguishes between measures affecting the "importation" of products, which are regulated in Article XI:1, and those affecting "imported products," which are dealt with in Article III. If Article XI:1 were interpreted broadly to cover also internal requirements, Article III would be partly superfluous. Moreover, the exceptions to Article XI:1, in particular those contained in Article XI:2, would also apply to internal requirements restricting imports, which would be contrary to the basic aim of Article III. The Panel did not find, either in the drafting history

---

1. Canada—Administration of the Foreign Investment Review Act, GATT, 30th   Supp. BISD 140, para. 5.14 (Panel report adopted Feb. 7, 1984).

of the General Agreement or in previous cases examined by the CONTRACTING PARTIES, any evidence justifying such an interpretation of Article XI.

The Uruguay Round on Trade–Related Investment Measures (TRIMs) provides that it violates Article XI:1 for a government to (i) restrict imports by an enterprise, either generally or by reference to its exports, or (ii) restrict exports, either in terms of specific products, in terms of volume or value of products, or in terms of a proportion of its local production. TRIMs Agreement, Annex, Illustrative List, para. 2. See Documents Supplement. We will consider in Chapter 12 how Article III deals with restrictions on imported products and with trade-related investment measures. In that regard, consider whether the division in the TRIMs Agreement between the measures that are deemed to violate Article III:4 and those that violate Article XI:1 supports the panel's distinction. The TRIMs Agreement is examined in Chapter 23.

(5) The Interpretative Note Ad Article III provides that an internal tax or regulation that is applied to imported and domestic products and is collected or enforced in the case of the imported product at the border is nevertheless to be regarded as an internal tax or regulation subject to Article III. Does this note support the distinction made by the panel in Note 4 above or does it mean only that Article III applies, without implying anything about the application of Article XI? In practice, GATT and WTO panels have tended to examine non-state trading measures applying to both imported and domestic products under Article III and not Article XI, but the issue is often not discussed, so the precise relationship of the two articles remains somewhat unclear.

(6) Assuming that an exception to Article XI:1 applies, must quotas be utilized consistently with the MFN obligation of Article I? Is it consistent with MFN treatment to allocate quota shares among WTO members? See Article XIII.

(7) When quotas are imposed, a licensing system is often used to determine who has the right to import under the quota. One of the Tokyo Round agreements was the Agreement on Import Licensing Procedures.[2] The basic provision of the Agreement—Article 1(3)—calls for the rules for import licensing procedures to be "neutral in application and administered in a fair and equitable manner." Article 1 of the Agreement requires the relevant rules and changes to them and the products to which they apply to be published promptly. It calls for forms and procedures to be kept "simple," and bans refusals of applications for minor documentation errors. It also provides that importations shall not be refused for minor deviations in value, weight or quantity from the licensed amount. Additional provisions in Article 3 require that all persons meeting the importing country's legal requirements be eligible to apply for licenses. In allocating licenses, consideration is to be given to an applicant's past performance and to ensuring a reasonable distribution of licenses to new importers, particularly those importing products from the least developed countries or developing countries. The provisions of the Agreement are essentially designed to prevent licensing procedures from constituting trade barriers in themselves. The

---

2. GATT, 26th Supp. BISD 154 (1980).

Agreement was modified in the Uruguay Round, but the above-mentioned basic provisions were carried forward.

(8) GATT rules and the Import Licensing Agreement do not mandate how quotas are to be allocated among individual suppliers (as opposed to countries). Under the general US rules on quota procedures, the United States in theory allocates quotas on a first-come, first-served basis, which involves some risk for an exporter since the goods may arrive at US customs just as the quota has been filled. See 19 CFR sec. 132 (2007). In fact, the US often relies on special arrangements with exporting countries, rather than these general rules. As we saw in the *Generra* and *Superior Wire* cases in the preceding chapter, entry to the United States was contingent on presentation of a document issued by the exporting country. One interesting development in US law with respect to quotas was the authorization in the 1988 Trade Act of the use of auctions to distribute quotas. One of the principal criticisms of quotas has been that they allow the foreign supplier to capture monopoly profits in the form of higher, scarcity-induced prices in the importing countries (compared to tariffs, which would have a similar effect, but benefit the government through higher tax collections). The sales of quota rights by auction would allow the government to capture these monopoly profits. Would the auction of quota rights be permissible under GATT rules? Consider Articles II and VIII.

(9) In the EC Treaty, Article 28 [formerly 30] provides: "Quantitative restrictions on imports and all measures having equivalent effect shall * * * be prohibited between Member States." Is this broader, narrower or the same as GATT Article XI:1? The EC Court of Justice initially gave Article 28 a much broader reading than the GATT panel gave Article XI:1 in the *Canadian Foreign Investment* case quoted above. In Procureur du Roi v. Dassonville, Case 8/74, [1974] ECR 837, the Court stated:

> All trading rules enacted by the Member States which are capable of hindering, directly or indirectly, actually or potentially, intra-Community trade are to be considered as measures having an effect equivalent to quantitative restrictions.

This broad reading of Article 28 has led the Court of Justice to uphold challenges to many Member States measures. See George A. Bermann et al., European Community Law ch. 13 (2d ed. 2002). Is Article XI:1 capable of supporting a similarly broad reading? Should it be given one? In recent years, the Court of Justice has cut back on its expansive reading of Article 28. Keck & Mithouard, Cases C–267 & 268/91, 1993 ECR–I 6097.

A Note on Export Controls

International trade policy and rules tend to focus on market access issues, with the goal of reducing import restrictions. However, exports are mentioned in GATT in at least 13 clauses and are related to obligations in several others.[3] The most significant obligations in GATT relating to treat-

---

3. See generally Michael Rom, Export Controls in GATT, 18 J.World Trade L. 125 (1984). GATT Art. I (MFN), para. 1; Art. VI (antidumping), paras. 1, 5, 6(b), 7(a); Art. VIII (fees and formalities), paras. 1, 4; Art. IX (marks of origin), para. 2; Art. X (publication), para. 1; Art. XI (quantitative restrictions), paras. 1, 2; Art. XIII (nondiscriminatory administration of quantitative restrictions), paras. 1, 5; Art. XVI (subsi-

ment of exports are the most-favored-nation treatment obligation of Article I, and the ban on prohibitions and quantitative restrictions of Article XI, which applies to exports as well as imports. Problems stemming from export promotion activities, such as subsidies, will be treated in Chapter 18. Of course, GATT clauses that apply generally to customs procedures, in many cases apply to those procedures affecting exports as well as imports.[4] The basic problem with GATT obligations relating to exports, however, stems from two facts: 1) There is no GATT obligation against the use of export taxes or fees; and 2) the exception to the GATT obligations restraining use of export restrictions are quite broad.

While Article XI prohibits export restrictions, in paragraph 2(a) it provides an exception for restrictions "temporarily applied to prevent or relieve critical shortages of foodstuffs or other products essential to the exporting contracting party." Article XX provides two broad and vague exceptions for restrictions on exports "necessary to ensure essential quantities of such materials to a domestic processing industry during periods when the domestic price of such materials is held below the world price as part of a government stabilization plan," (Art. XX(i)) and restrictions "essential to the acquisition or distribution of products in general or local short supply," provided that an equitable share principle is followed. Art XX(j). With these exceptions, a WTO member has considerable discretion to apply export restrictions. In the cases where it feels restrained by GATT rules from using quantitative restrictions, it can, of course, utilize export taxes or fees.

There have been relatively few complaints in GATT/WTO about export restrictions.[5] In 1949, Czechoslovakia brought a complaint against the United States in respect of controls that the US had imposed on exports to Czechoslovakia, arguing that the US controls discriminated against Czechoslovakia. The US controls were part of the national security measures imposed by the US on trade with the Soviet Bloc during the Cold War. The Contracting Parties, however, formally decided that the United States had not "failed to carry out its obligations under the Agreement through its administration of the issue of export licenses." The principal recent case on export controls was the *Japanese Semiconductor* case, excerpted above.

In the 1970's, many countries became concerned about export restrictions, particularly on oil as a result of the Arab oil embargo on the US and the Netherlands, but also on other commodities as a result of the US export restrictions on soybeans imposed in 1973 to relieve domestic shortages. These concerns resulted in negotiations on the subject of access to supplies of raw materials and finished goods in the Tokyo Round. These negotiations were difficult because they raised questions concerning national sovereignty over natural resources. The only result was an understanding that the GATT export provisions should be reassessed in the near future.[6] Except for

dies), Section B; Art. XX (general exceptions), paras. (i), (j); see John H. Jackson, World Trade and the Law of GATT 497–506 (1969).

4. See, e.g., GATT Arts. VIII and IX: (9).

5. See Frieder Roessler, GATT and Access to Supplies, 9 J.World Trade L. 25, 30 (1975).

6. See GATT, The Tokyo Round of Multilateral Trade Negotiations: Report by the Director–General of GATT 152 (1979).

negotiations on safeguards, export controls were not a significant issue in the Uruguay Round. It is worth noting, however, that in recent years, there has been increased concern over regulating exports of waste or domestically-banned products.[7]

The potential for future disputes over export controls should not be underemphasized, however. They figured prominently in the relationships between nations prior to World War II and arguably were one of the causes, or at least a trigger, of the outbreak of that war in the Pacific.[8]

In the case of the United States, the Constitution prohibits export taxes, but the United States imposes other export restrictions. The Department of Commerce's Bureau of Industry and Security (BIS) regulates the export and re-export of items for national security, nonproliferation, foreign policy, and short supply reasons under the Export Administration Regulations (EAR). 15 CFR 730–774 (2007). These regulations are often called "dual use" regulations, which highlights the fact that they are particularly concerned with items that can be used for both military and commercial applications. A relatively small percentage of total exports and re-exports requires the submission of a license application to BIS. License requirements and approval policies vary depending upon an item's technical characteristics, the destination, the end use, and the end user. Generally, the products that require licenses are those incorporating or involved in the production of high technology products. The State Department controls exports of weapons and military related items on the US Munitions List. In addition, the United States participates in various multilateral groups to coordinate export controls on arms, dual-use items, missile technology and items relevant to controlling the proliferation of nuclear, chemical and biological weapons. It is important to bear in mind that other US regulations may restrict export transactions with certain countries, such as those subject to general economic sanctions implemented by the President under the International Emergency Economic Powers Act. We discuss sanctions for political and national security purposes in Chapter 21 infra.

SECTION 9.3 EXCEPTIONS TO ARTICLE XI

The General Agreement contains two important exceptions to the quota ban in Article XI:1. First, Article XI:2 permits the use of (a) export restrictions to relieve critical shortages, (b) import and export restrictions necessary to apply certain commodity standards and (c) import restrictions to enforce certain government agricultural programs. Second, Articles XII and XVIII permit the use of quotas in the event of balance-of-payments problems. In addition, in practice many GATT parties have historically used quotas or similar measures to restrict imports of clothing and textile products and of agricultural products

---

7. For an overview of US rules and policies, see http://www.epa.gov/compliance/ monitoring/programs/rcra/importexport. html (visited Janaury 23, 2008).

8. James H. Herzog, Closing the Open Door: American–Japanese Diplomatic Nego-

tiations 1936–1941, at 92–101, 163–86, Naval Inst. Press (1973); Herbert Feis, The Road to Pearl Harbor: The Coming of the War Between the United States and Japan 107–09, 205–08, 267–70 (1950).

(other than under Article XI:2). As described below, one of the most important achievements of the Uruguay Round was to make those products effectively subject to the disciplines of Article XI:1. In this section, we look briefly at the use of quotas and similar measures to restrict imports of agricultural and clothing and textiles products and consider a recent WTO case on agricultural restrictions. The balance-of-payments exception is analyzed in Chapter 22.

(A) AGRICULTURAL PRODUCTS

Historically, GATT rules were not rigorously applied to agricultural trade, on either the import or export side.[1] As for agricultural imports, the United States obtained a waiver from the Article XI quota ban for certain of its agricultural programs in 1955.[2] Although few other formal waivers were granted in respect of agricultural products, other countries sometimes acted as if they viewed the US waiver as generally applicable. This lack of discipline was also exemplified by the agricultural trade policies of the European Community. In constructing its Common Agricultural Policy (CAP), the EC unbound most of its tariffs on agricultural products, which meant that it was free to charge any import duty it wished on those products. In fact, the EC often implemented the CAP by using variable levies, which were flexible import charges set (and adjusted regularly) so as to make imported agricultural products more expensive than the comparable EC product. They effectively kept imports out of the European market. Developing countries often claimed authority to impose quotas on agricultural products pursuant to the balance-of-payments exception. While GATT panel decisions in the late 1970's and 1980's strictly enforced the agricultural exceptions in Article XI:2, the import restrictions applied by the US, the EC and developing countries were not challenged (and may not have been challengeable) under Article XI. One of the main issues in the Uruguay Round was how to re-establish GATT disciplines on agricultural trade.

In the Uruguay Round Agreement on Agriculture, WTO members agreed to convert their nontariff import restrictions on agricultural products to tariffs and not to use such restrictions in the future except pursuant to the Agreement's special safeguard provisions and certain exceptions.[3] The initial tariffs have been set to approximate the current level of protection, but are to be reduced by 36% over a six-year period (24% over 10 years for developing countries). Current market access is to be maintained and certain minimum market access is to be provided if current access is less than three percent of domestic production (rising to five percent over the implementation period).[4] As a result of the tariffica-

---

1. See generally Davey, The Rules for Agricultural Trade in GATT, in M. Honma, A. Shimizu & H. Funatsu (eds.), GATT and Trade Liberalization in Agriculture (1993).

2. Decision of March 5, 1955, 3rd Supp. BISD 32.

3. WTO Agreement on Agriculture, art. 4(2).

4. GATT Focus, December 1993, at 6.

tion commitment, the exceptions for agricultural programs in Article XI:2 are of little importance today.

Agricultural trade flows are often affected by national subsidies paid to farmers. These subsidies may result in a significant expansion in production of agricultural products, which causes pressures to restrict competing imports and to subsidize exports to get rid of surpluses. In the Uruguay Round Agreement on Agriculture, developed WTO members agreed to cut certain specified domestic subsidies by 20% over the specified implementation period.[5] One aim of the agreement is to promote the use of subsidies that do not promote production or distort trade flows, such as those aim at only income support for farmers.[6]

Article XVI:3 of the General Agreement was designed to limit export subsidies on primary products. It did not ban them, but provided that they should not be used to obtain a "more than equitable share of world export trade" in a product, a concept that was refined in the Tokyo Round Subsidies Code.[7] In practice, however, the use of export subsidies on primary products was not effectively controlled by the "equitable share" language. While one early, pre-Subsidies Code GATT decision suggested that this standard could be used to control effectively the use of export subsidies,[8] a later decision by a panel appointed under the Subsidies Code essentially concluded that the language was too imprecise to be applied to world wheat trade.[9] The panel was criticized by some for having abdicated its responsibility, and its report was never adopted by the Subsidies Code governing committee, the body responsible for dispute settlement under the Subsidies Code. Indeed, one result of the decision was that dispute settlement under the Subsidies Code broke down completely during the 1980's as one or more signatories blocked the adoption of all subsequent panel reports issued under the Code's dispute settlement provisions during that time period.

The Uruguay Round Agreement on Agriculture takes a different approach to controlling agricultural export subsidies. It requires that they be reduced over the implementation period, compared to a 1986–1990 base period, by 36% in terms of value and by 21% in respect of the volume of exports benefiting from them.[10] (The WTO Subsidies Agreement now bans the use of export subsidies, but it is explicitly made subject to the Agreement on Agriculture.)

5. GATT Focus, December 1993, at 7.

6. See WTO Agreement on Agriculture, annex 2.

7. Agreement on Interpretation and Application of Articles VI, XVI and XXIII of the General Agreement on Tariffs and Trade (the Subsidies Code), art. 10; 26th Supp. BISD 56, 69.

8. French Assistance to Exports of Wheat and Wheat Flour, 7th Supp. BISD 46; see also European Communities—Refunds on Exports of Sugar, 26th Supp. BISD 290; European Communities—Re-

funds on Exports of Sugar—Complaint by Brazil, 27th Supp. BISD 69.

9. European Economic Community—Subsidies on Exports of Wheat Flour, GATT Doc. SCM/42. See 31st Supp. BISD 259. The text of the report can be found in 18 BNA U.S. Export Weekly 899–916 (1983).

10. WTO Agreement on Agriculture, art. 9(2)(b)(iv). For developing countries, the respective percentages are 24% and 14%.

CHILE—PRICE BAND SYSTEM AND SAFEGUARD MEASURES RELATING TO CERTAIN AGRICULTURAL PRODUCTS

WT/DS207/AB/R.
Appellate Body Report adopted October 23, 2002.

[Chile's price band system is a mechanism for setting the duty payable on importation of certain agricultural products. The duty applied consists of two components: (i) an ad valorem duty and (ii) a specific price band duty that is determined for each importation by comparing a reference price with the upper or lower threshold of a price band. The price bands are determined annually. The upper and lower thresholds for each price band are based on five years of average monthly prices for the product on US markets (adjusted for international inflation and excluding extreme values, i.e. the highest 25% and lowest 25% of the prices are excluded). The lowest and highest non-excluded prices are used as the threshold prices, adjusted for import costs so as convert them to c.i.f. prices. The reference price for each product is determined weekly and is the lowest f.o.b. price in any foreign "market of concern" during the previous week. It applies in respect of products that are shipped in that week. The specific duty is levied on each shipment of a product subject to the price band system. It is determined by comparing the applicable weekly reference price with the upper and lower thresholds applicable to the product:

> If the reference price falls between the upper and lower thresholds, no specific duty is levied.

> If the weekly reference price is higher than the upper threshold, no specific duty is assessed. Instead, a rebate equal to the difference is granted, up to the amount of the ad valorem duty.

> If the weekly reference price falls below the lower threshold, a specific duty equal to the difference between the reference price and the lower threshold is levied, but the total of the ad valorem duty and the specific duty are not in any case permitted to exceed Chile's WTO tariff binding of 31.5% on the products at issue.]

VIII.   Article 4.2 of the Agreement on Agriculture

192.   Argentina argued before the Panel that Chile's price band system is a measure "of the kind which has been required to be converted into ordinary customs duties" and which, by the terms of Article 4.2 of the Agreement on Agriculture, Members are required not to "maintain". Argentina claimed that, in maintaining the price band system, Chile is acting inconsistently with Article 4.2.

* * *

196.   [T]he preamble to the Agreement on Agriculture states that an objective of that Agreement is "to establish a fair and market-oriented agricultural trading system", and to initiate a reform process

"through the negotiation of commitments on support and protection and through the establishment of strengthened and more operationally effective GATT rules and disciplines". The preamble further states that, to achieve this objective, it is necessary to provide for reductions in protection, "resulting in correcting and preventing restrictions and distortions in world agricultural markets," through achieving "specific binding commitments," inter alia, in the area of market access.

* * *

200.   [Article 4] is the main provision of Part III of the Agreement on Agriculture. As its title indicates, Article 4 deals with "Market Access". During the course of the Uruguay Round, negotiators identified certain border measures which have in common that they restrict the volume or distort the price of imports of agricultural products. The negotiators decided that these border measures should be converted into ordinary customs duties, with a view to ensuring enhanced market access for such imports. Thus, they envisioned that ordinary customs duties would, in principle, become the only form of border protection. As ordinary customs duties are more transparent and more easily quantifiable than non-tariff barriers, they are also more easily compared between trading partners, and thus the maximum amount of such duties can be more easily reduced in future multilateral trade negotiations. The Uruguay Round negotiators agreed that market access would be improved—both in the short term and in the long term—through bindings and reductions of tariffs and minimum access requirements, which were to be recorded in Members' Schedules.

201.   Thus, Article 4 of the Agreement on Agriculture is appropriately viewed as the legal vehicle for requiring the conversion into ordinary customs duties of certain market access barriers affecting imports of agricultural products. Article 4 provides, in its entirety:

Market Access

1.   Market access concessions contained in Schedules relate to bindings and reductions of tariffs, and to other market-access commitments as specified therein.

2.   Members shall not maintain, resort to, or revert to any measures of the kind which have been required to be converted into ordinary customs duties[1], except as otherwise provided for in Article 5 and Annex 5.

---

[1]These measures include quantitative import restrictions, variable import levies, minimum import prices, discretionary import licensing, non-tariff measures maintained through state-trading enterprises, voluntary export restraints, and similar border measures other than ordinary customs duties, whether or not the measures are maintained under country-specific derogations from the provisions of GATT 1947, but not measures maintained under balance-of-

payments provisions or under other general, non-agriculture-specific provisions of GATT 1994 or of the other Multilateral Trade Agreements in Annex 1A to the WTO Agreement.

* * *

212. [T]he obligation in Article 4.2 not to "maintain, resort to, or revert to any measures of the kind which have been required to be converted into ordinary customs duties" applies from the date of the entry into force of the WTO Agreement—regardless of whether or not a Member converted any such measures into ordinary customs duties before the conclusion of the Uruguay Round. The mere fact that no trading partner of a Member singled out a specific "measure of the kind" by the end of the Uruguay Round by requesting that it be converted into ordinary customs duties, does not mean that such a measure enjoys immunity from challenge in WTO dispute settlement. The obligation "not [to] maintain" such measures underscores that Members must not continue to apply measures covered by Article 4.2 from the date of entry into force of the WTO Agreement.

* * *

215. * * * Chile has argued that the duties resulting from Chile's price band system are "ordinary customs duties". Chile maintains also that its price band system is not a measure of the kind which has been required to be converted, but is rather a system for determining the level of ordinary customs duties that will be applied between zero and the bound rate. * * *

216. * * * The application of a "variable import levy", or a "minimum import price", as the terms are used in footnote 1, can result in the levying of a specific duty equal to the difference between a reference price and a target price, or minimum price. These resulting levies or specific duties take the same form as ordinary customs duties. However, the mere fact that a duty imposed on an import at the border is in the same form as an ordinary customs duty, does not mean that it is not a "variable import levy" or a "minimum import price". Clearly, as measures listed in footnote 1, "variable import levies" and "minimum import prices" had to be converted into ordinary customs duties by the end of the Uruguay Round. The mere fact that such measures result in the payment of duties does not exonerate a Member from the requirement not to maintain, resort to, or revert to those measures.

* * *

227. [A]ll of the border measures listed in footnote 1 have in common the object and effect of restricting the volumes, and distorting the prices, of imports of agricultural products in ways different from the ways that ordinary customs duties do. Moreover, all of these measures have in common also that they disconnect domestic prices from international price developments, and thus impede the transmission of world market prices to the domestic market. However, even if Chile's price

band system were to share these common characteristics with all of these border measures, it would not be sufficient to make that system a "similar border measure" within the meaning of footnote 1. There must be something more. To be "similar", Chile's price band system—in its specific factual configuration—must have, to recall the dictionary definitions we mentioned, sufficient "resemblance or likeness to", or be "of the same nature or kind" as, at least one of the specific categories of measures listed in footnote 1.

* * *

232. We begin with the interpretation of "variable import levies". In examining the ordinary meaning of the term "variable import levies" as it appears in footnote 1, we note that a "levy" is a duty, tax, charge, or other exaction usually imposed or raised by legal execution or process. An "import" levy is, of course, a duty assessed upon importation. A levy is "variable" when it is "liable to vary". This feature alone, however, is not conclusive as to what constitutes a "variable import levy" within the meaning of footnote 1. An "ordinary customs duty" could also fit this description. A Member may, fully in accordance with Article II of the GATT 1994, exact a duty upon importation and periodically change the rate at which it applies that duty (provided the changed rates remain below the tariff rates bound in the Member's Schedule). * * *

233. To determine what kind of variability makes an import levy a "variable import levy", we turn to the immediate context of the other words in footnote 1. The term "variable import levies" appears after the introductory phrase "[t]hese measures include". Article 4.2—to which the footnote is attached—also speaks of "measures". This suggests that at least one feature of "variable import levies" is the fact that the measure itself—as a mechanism—must impose the variability of the duties. Variability is inherent in a measure if the measure incorporates a scheme or formula that causes and ensures that levies change automatically and continuously. Ordinary customs duties, by contrast, are subject to discrete changes in applied tariff rates that occur independently, and unrelated to such an underlying scheme or formula. * * *

234. However, in our view, the presence of a formula causing automatic and continuous variability of duties is a necessary, but by no means a sufficient, condition for a particular measure to be a "variable import levy" within the meaning of footnote 1. "Variable import levies" have additional features that undermine the object and purpose of Article 4, which is to achieve improved market access conditions for imports of agricultural products by permitting only the application of ordinary customs duties. These additional features include a lack of transparency and a lack of predictability in the level of duties that will result from such measures. This lack of transparency and this lack of predictability are liable to restrict the volume of imports. As Argentina points out, an exporter is less likely to ship to a market if that exporter does not know and cannot reasonably predict what the amount of duties will be. This lack of transparency and predictability will also contribute

to distorting the prices of imports by impeding the transmission of international prices to the domestic market.

* * *

246. [As to whether Chile's price band system effectively disconnects the domestic market from international price developments, in] our view—even though Chile's price bands are set in relation to world prices from a past five-year period—Chile's price band system can still have the effect of impeding the transmission of international price developments to the domestic market in a way similar to that of other categories of prohibited measures listed in footnote 1. There are factors other than world market prices that are relevant to the assessment of Chile's price bands. The prices that represent the highest 25 per cent as well as the lowest 25 per cent of the world prices from the past five years are discarded [as extreme values] in selecting the "highest and lowest f.o.b. prices" for the determination of Chile's annual price bands. Furthermore, we place considerable importance on the intransparent and unpredictable way in which the "highest and lowest f.o.b. prices" that have been selected are converted to a c.i.f. basis by adding "import costs". As Chile concedes, no published legislation or regulation sets out how these "import costs" are calculated.

247. In addition to the lack of transparency and the lack of predictability that are inherent in how Chile's price bands are established, we see similar shortcomings in the way the other essential element of Chile's price band system—the reference price—is determined. As we have explained, the duties resulting from Chile's price band system are equal to the difference between the price band thresholds and the reference price. Chile sets the reference price on a weekly basis, and it does so in a way that is neither transparent nor predictable.

* * *

249. Under Chile's price band system, the price used to set the weekly reference price is the lowest f.o.b. price observed, at the time of embarkation, in any foreign "market of concern" to Chile for "qualities of products actually liable to be imported to Chile". No Chilean legislation or regulation specifies how the international "markets of concern" and the "qualities of concern" are selected. Thus, it is not by any means certain that the weekly reference price is representative of the current world market price. Moreover, the weekly reference price used under Chile's price band system is certainly not representative of an average of current lowest prices found in all markets of concern. As a result, the process of selecting the reference price is not transparent, and it is not predictable for traders.

250. Furthermore, under Chile's system, the same weekly reference price applies to imports of all goods falling within the same product category, regardless of the origin of the goods, and regardless of the transaction value of the shipment. Moreover, unlike with the five-year average monthly prices used in the calculation of Chile's annual price

bands, the lowest "market of concern" price used to determine the weekly reference price is not adjusted for "import costs", and thus is not converted from an f.o.b. basis to a c.i.f. basis. This is likely to inflate the amount of specific duties applied under Chile's price band system, because these duties are imposed in an amount equal to the difference between Chile's annual price band thresholds, which are based on higher c.i.f. prices, and Chile's weekly reference prices, which are based on lower f.o.b. prices. Therefore, the way in which Chile's weekly reference prices are determined contributes to giving Chile's price band system the effect of impeding the transmission of international price developments to Chile's market.

251.   Consequently, even if were to assume, for the moment, that one feature of Chile's price band system is not similar to the features of "variable import levies" and "minimum import prices" because the thresholds of Chile's price bands vary in relation to—albeit historic—world market prices rather than domestic target prices, this would not change our overall assessment of Chile's price band system. This is because specific duties resulting from Chile's price band system are equal to the difference between two parameters—the annual price band thresholds and the weekly reference prices applicable to the shipment in question. Therefore, continuing with our hypothesis, even if we were to assume that one of the two parameters—Chile's annual price band thresholds—does not distort the transmission of world market prices to Chile's market, it would nevertheless remain that the other parameter—Chile's weekly reference prices—is liable to distort—if not disconnect—that transmission by virtue of the way it is determined on a weekly basis. Consequently, even in such a hypothetical case, the duties resulting from Chile's price band system, which are equal to the difference between these two parameters, would not transmit world market price developments to Chile's market in the same way as "ordinary customs duties".

252.   Thus, although there are some dissimilarities between Chile's price band system and the features of "minimum import prices" and "variable import levies" we have identified earlier, the way Chile's system is designed, and the way it operates in its overall nature, are sufficiently "similar" to the features of both of those two categories of prohibited measures to make Chile's price band system—in its particular features—a "similar border measure" within the meaning of footnote 1 to Article 4.2.

* * *

259.   The fact that duties resulting from Chile's price band system are "capped" at 31.5 per cent ad valorem merely reduces the extent of the trade distortions in that system by reducing the extent to which those duties fluctuate. It does not, however, eliminate those distortions. Moreover, the cap does not eliminate the lack of transparency, or the lack of predictability, in the fluctuation of the duties resulting from Chile's price band system. Thus, the fact that Chile's price band system

is subject to a "cap" may be said to make this system less inconsistent with Article 4.2. But this is not enough. Article 4.2 not only prohibits "similar border measures" from being applied to some products, or to some shipments of some products with low transaction values, or the imposition of duties on some products in an amount beyond the level of a bound tariff rate. Article 4.2 prohibits the application of such "similar border measures" to all products in all cases.

Notes and Questions

(1) Argentina later claimed that Chile had failed to bring its system into conformity with WTO rules and initiated an article 21.5 compliance proceeding. It ultimately prevailed and the compliance panel and Appellate Body reports were adopted May 22, 2007. No settlement had been reported as of January 2008.

(2) In its classic form, a variable levy is calculated with reference to domestic prices and applied so as to make imports more expensive than domestic supplies. Does Chile's price band system operate that way? Should that difference matter in analyzing its consistency with article 4.2?

(3) What changes might Chile make to its system so as to meet the Appellate Body's concerns as expressed in paragraphs 246–251? In particular, if the system were more transparent in its operation, would it be WTO-consistent? Or are variability and lack of predictability the fatal flaws?

(4) Would WTO rules preclude Chile from changing its industrial tariffs weekly in an unpredictable manner so long as it did not exceed its tariff bindings? For WTO rules on transparency, which might be relevant, see Section 9.5 infra.

(5) In addition to the *Price Band* case, there have been several other major cases that have arisen under the WTO Agreement on Agriculture. While they are too technical for inclusion here, we note the major issues considered. The cases include:

(i) the *Canada Dairy* cases, in which Canada's supply management system for dairy products was found to violate the Agreement on Agriculture because it provided export subsidies in excess of Canada's commitments. The original case and the compliance proceedings were important for their discussion of the definition of export subsidy under article 9.1(c)—payments financed by virtue of governmental action;

(ii) the *US Cotton* case, a very complex factual and legal case, in which the US was found to have exceeded its subsidy commitments under the Agreement on Agriculture in certain respects and to have violated the export subsidy prohibition of the Subsidies Agreement and caused serious prejudice to Brazil under that Agreement in certain circumstances. The case is of particular interest because of its analysis of the so-called peace clause (article 13 of the Agreement on Agriculture), export credits and the relationship of articles 10.1 and 10.2 of the Agreement (this issue provoked a dissent by an Appellate Body member), and the definition of decoupled income support (green box subsidies);

(iii) the *EC Sugar* case, in which the EC was found to have exceeded its export subsidy commitments. The key issues involved the interpretation of a qualifying footnote in the EC schedule, which was found to have no effect, and article 9.1(c); and

(iv) the *Turkey Rice* case, which involved what was determined to be a discretionary licensing system.

There may be more agricultural cases in the future as the so-called peace clause (article 13), which restricted the possibility of challenging certain agricultural measures, has now expired.

(6) The Agreement on Agriculture provided for further negotiations on agricultural trade, which started in 2000 and which are now part of the Doha negotiations. As was true in the Uruguay Round, the negotiations have been very difficult and are viewed as the key to reaching a comprehensive result in the overall negotiations. The position of the negotiations as of the beginning of 2008 is briefly summarized in Section 6.5(D) supra.

(B) CLOTHING AND TEXTILE PRODUCTS

International trade in textile and clothing products has historically been subject to extensive government regulation.[11] The regulation has sometimes been direct through the application of quotas and sometimes indirect through voluntary export restraints, the first of which was obtained from Japan by the United States in 1936. Following World War II, most European countries restricted textile imports through the use of controls justified by balance-of-payments concerns. As that justification became untenable, negotiations in GATT resulted in a series of agreements that effectively exempted textile and clothing products from the Article XI quota ban. The initial agreement was the Short–Term Arrangement Regarding International Trade in Textiles (the STA), which was in force from October 1961 until September 1962. It was replaced by the Long–Term Arrangement Regarding International Trade in Cotton Textiles (the LTA), which was in force from 1962 to 1973. Thereafter, the so-called Multifibre Arrangement (MFA) regulated such trade. The MFA was modified from time to time, but remained in effect when the WTO Agreement came into force in 1995. Over time, the MFA came to cover a much broader range of textiles than cotton textiles. It permitted the use of safeguard mechanisms in certain defined circumstances, but provided for the growth over time in the quotas imposed on textile and clothing imports. Developing countries were particularly dissatisfied with this treatment of clothing and textile products and the issue of bringing GATT disciplines back into this sector was a major one in the Uruguay Round.

The WTO Agreement on Textiles and Clothing (ATC) provided for the gradual reintegration of textile and clothing products into the General Agreement, so that they will in the future be subject to normal GATT rules. As a first step, article 2 of the ATC required that

11. See generally GATT Secretariat Study, Textiles and Clothing in the World Economy (1984).

[on January 1, 1995], each Member shall integrate into GATT 1994 products which accounted for not less than 16 per cent of the total volume of the Member's 1990 imports of the products in the Annex, in terms of [Harmonized System] lines or categories. The products to be integrated shall encompass products from each of the following four groups: tops and yarns, fabrics, made-up textile products, and clothing.

An additional 17 per cent were to be reintegrated at the beginning of 1998; 18 per cent at the beginning of 2002 and the rest (49 per cent) at the beginning of 2005. Under article 6 of the ATC, once textile and clothing products were reintegrated Article XIX, as interpreted by the Safeguards Agreement, would be the applicable safeguard provision. See Chapter 15 supra.

Developing countries were quite dissatisfied with the implementation of the ATC by the US, the EU and Canada. While the first one-third of tariff lines, as defined above, were reintegrated on schedule, in fact there were few restrictions imposed on products falling under those lines. Thus, there was little practical liberalization. Moreover, while quotas on textiles and apparel products were eliminated as of January 1, 2005, as required by the agreement, there was great concern among many developing countries that the elimination of the quotas would not benefit them, but would rather redound primarily to the benefit of China. Based on early import figures, it appears that there was a significant increase in Chinese exports to the EU and the US. In order to forestall formal safeguard action permitted under the Chinese accession protocol, China announced the imposition of an export tax. This was seen as insufficient in the EU, and as of June 2005, the EU persuaded China to agree to limit its exports of certain textile products through 2007. Subsequently, in November 2005, China agreed to limit certain textile exports to the US for three years (2006–2008).

SECTION 9.4   STATE TRADING

(A) THE INTERFACE PROBLEM

A basic structural assumption of the General Agreement is an international, free market system for trading. Many GATT rules make sense only in the context of such a market system.[1] They restrict the types of regulations which governments can impose on international traders, but do not purport to regulate the traders themselves. If the government is the trader or controls the trader, the rules may be ineffective since decisions ostensibly made independently by the trader may in fact reflect actions of the government.

This problem can be seen in a number of different contexts. For example, how can the GATT Article XI rule against use of quantitative restrictions—one of the basic principles of the General Agreement—be

---

1. See generally Interface One (Don Wallace et al. eds., 1980).

applied effectively where a government agency or a government-controlled company determines import and export levels through its purchasing and sales decisions? Even more basic, how can negotiations over tariff levels—one of the essential subjects of GATT negotiations—be meaningful if import levels are determined not by tariffs and prices, but rather by economic plans or decisions of government-controlled import monopolies? The following hypothetical situation illustrates this problem.

Let us assume that country M, a market economy country, and country S, a state trading country, are both members of the WTO. The General Agreement limits the use of quantitative restrictions on the importation of goods in Article XI, and provides for negotiation leading to tariff bindings under Article II that restrict the level of tariffs that a country can impose on its imports from other GATT members. Suppose countries M and S have negotiated between themselves and M has promised to bind its tariff on bicycles and widgets at no more than 10%. Suppose S has agreed to bind its tariffs on automobiles and gadgets at no more than 8% and 12%, respectively. In the case of M, private traders will send goods to M, with the confidence that they will be able to import them without incurring more than a 10% tariff charge. They can price their goods accordingly and proceed to import goods. If the tariff has been higher previously, the lower price allowed by the lower tariff should result in an increase in imports.

In the case of S, however, importing is accomplished only through a state trading monopoly, which is regulated by the government and pursues its import plans according to the economic plan of the country (and other foreign policy considerations). If the state trading monopoly can decide, as a matter of enterprise decision, to import no more than a given quantity of automobiles or gadgets, or to import those only from country A or B, rather than M, the fact that S's tariff on M's automobiles and gadgets has been lowered would not necessarily result in an increase of imports. If the import monopoly has complete discretion in determining the sales price of the imports, it may offset the effect of a tariff reduction by raising prices. Consequently, M may not receive reciprocal benefits for its trade concessions to S. S can sell more goods to M, through M's private traders; but M cannot sell more goods to S, if S's state trading agency has simply decided not to purchase more goods or to maintain prior retail prices.

In an oversimplified form, this hypothetical situation illustrates the major problem of establishing trade relations between nonmarket economies on the one hand, and the industrialized free market economies on the other. As the number of nonmarket economies has fallen dramatically since the disintegration of the Soviet bloc at the end of the 1980's, these concerns have lessened, but they are still relevant when the WTO admits to membership a country whose economy has a significant nonmarket component. Moreover, the same problem arises, albeit to a lesser degree, in relations between market economies wherever state trading monopolies exist. The problem described above is not the only one. Other GATT rules can be applied to nonmarket economies only with great difficulty. For example, the dumping rules require comparing export prices of a product to its normal value in the home market. But in a nonmarket economy there is no freely determined price in that economy to which the export price can be compared. Similarly, how can the rules against subsidies be applied when government control so permeates an economy that either everything or nothing can be considered a subsidy?

In the next section, we review Articles XVII and II:4—the GATT provisions dealing with state trading and nonmarket economies. You should consider whether these provisions adequately address the problems raised in the foregoing paragraphs. In particular, consider whether they are sufficient to deal with the problems that would be presented by the accession to the WTO of countries still in transition to market economy status.

(B) GATT REGULATION OF STATE TRADING[2]

(1) *State Trading Enterprises Defined*

The principal GATT provision regulating state trading is Article XVII, which applies to state trading enterprises.[3] Exactly what enterprises are covered by Article XVII? By its terms, Article XVII applies to "State enterprises" and enterprises to which a party has granted "exclusive or special privileges." These terms have been further refined through various GATT actions. For example, the 1994 Understanding on Article XVII adopts the following "working definition" of state trading enterprises:

> Governmental and non-governmental enterprises, including marketing boards, which have been granted exclusive or special rights or privileges, including statutory or constitutional powers, in the exercise of which they influence through their purchases or sales the level or direction of imports or exports.

More recently, the WTO has adopted an illustrative list:

ILLUSTRATIVE LIST OF RELATIONSHIPS BETWEEN GOVERNMENTS AND STATE TRADING ENTERPRISES AND THE KINDS OF ACTIVITIES ENGAGED IN BY THESE ENTERPRISES

(Adopted by the WTO Goods Council on October 15, 1999).

I. INTRODUCTORY COMMENTS

1. [This Illustrative List] is based on the Article XVII notifications made since 1980.

2. See generally Thomas Cottier & Petros C. Mavroidis, eds., State Trading in the Twenty–First Century (1998); John H. Jackson, World Trade and the Law of GATT, ch. 14 (1969); M.M. Kostecki, East–West Trade and the GATT System (1978); Edmond M. Ianni, The International Treatment of State Trading, 16 J. World Trade L. 480 (1982); Eliza R. Patterson, Improving GATT Rules for Non–Market Economies, 20 J. World Trade L. 185 (1986).

3. William J. Davey, Article XVII GATT: An Overview, in Cottier & Mavroidis, supra note 2, at 17.

2. The List * * * is based on a catalogue of those relationships and entities which have been previously included in notifications and, as such, reflects examples of relationships with governments and activities which various individual Members considered relevant in their notification of state trading enterprises. * * *

* * *

III. RELATIONSHIPS WITH GOVERNMENT

8. The following types of relationships between enterprises and governments should be considered as possible indications of the existence of a state trading enterprise. * * *

The enterprise[4] which is granted exclusive or special rights or privileges in the exercise of which it influences through its purchases or sales the level or direction of imports or exports * * * purchases or sells a given product or group of products, either directly or indirectly through third parties under contract or transfer of right; and one or more of the following applies:

(i) the enterprise is specially authorized or mandated by the government to do one or more of the following:

—control and/or conduct import or export operations;

—distribute imports;

—control domestic production, processing, or distribution.

(ii) all or part of the enterprise's activities are supported by government in one or more of the following ways, and the support afforded is specific or more favourable to the enterprise and not generally available to other entities, or is not warranted by purely commercial considerations:

—budget allocations;

—interest rate/tax concessions;

—guarantees (e.g. for loans or against business failure);

—revenue from the collection of tariffs;

—preferential access to foreign exchange;

—any off-budget support or assistance.

IV. ACTIVITIES ENGAGED IN BY STATE TRADING ENTERPRISES

9. The following activities are of the kind which might be engaged in by a state trading enterprise. An enterprise might engage in one or more of these activities, which can be directly related to importation,

4. [original note] Not included are entities, or government Ministries, that have only regulatory authority in areas relevant to international trade.

exportation, or the trade regime, or which can be related to trade in an indirect way. * * *

(a) Controls or conducts imports or exports;

(b) Administers multilaterally or bilaterally agreed quotas, tariff quotas or other restraint arrangements, or other import or export regulations;

(c) Issues licences/permits for importation or exportation;

(d) Determines domestic sales prices of imports.

(e) Enforces the statutory requirements of an agricultural marketing scheme and/or stabilization arrangement;

The following activities were included in some notifications:

(i) Authorizes or manages domestic production and/or processing of domestic production;

(ii) Determines the purchase price and/or sales price of domestic production;

(iii) Manages domestic distribution of domestic production and/or imports;

(iv) Undertakes purchases and sales of domestic production based on pre-determined floor and ceiling prices (intervention purchases/sales);

(v) Issues credit guarantees for producers, processors, exporters, or importers;

(vi) Engages in export- and support-related activities such as storage, shipping, processing, packaging, and insurance;

(vii) Controls or conducts marketing or distribution of processed products through subsidiaries or joint ventures in import markets;

(viii) Exercises quality control functions for imports or domestic production, including for export;

(ix) Engages in promotional activities for exports and/or domestic consumption;

(x) Procures and maintains emergency stocks of certain strategic and/or agricultural goods;

(xi) Negotiates or administers long-term bilateral contracts (including government-to-government) for exports and/or imports;

(xii) Undertakes purchases or sales necessary to fulfill contractual obligations entered into by the government.

Notes and Questions

Often, it is clear whether an enterprise falls within Article XVII's definition. But there are difficult issues raised by some cases. For example, does the existence of some right to control some (perhaps peripheral) aspect of importation or exportation result in state-trading-enterprise status? Is every government agency with some control over imports or exports covered? How would you answer those questions in light of the foregoing materials?

(2) *Article XVII*

Article XVII imposes both notification and substantive obligations in respect of state trading enterprises (STEs). First, Article XVII:4(a), as interpreted by GATT practice and the 1994 Understanding on Article XVII, requires notification of STEs. These notifications are designed to provide transparency in trade matters—one of GATT's basic goals. When the existence of such enterprises and their activities are revealed, other members are able to consider whether and how they are affected by them so that they may take appropriate measures.

More significantly, Article XVII regulates the activities of STEs, although its rules have not generally been considered to be very stringent. Under Article XVII:1(a), WTO members undertake that if they maintain an STE, that enterprise shall act in a manner consistent with GATT's general principles of nondiscriminatory treatment. This requirement is explained in Article XVII:1(b) to mean that such enterprises will make purchases and sales solely on the basis of commercial considerations.

CANADA—MEASURES RELATING TO EXPORTS OF WHEAT AND TREATMENT OF IMPORTED GRAIN

WT/DS276/AB/R.
Appellate Body Report, adopted September 27, 2004.

[The United States asserted that the Canadian Wheat Board Export Regime (the "CWB Export Regime") is inconsistent with Canada's GATT obligations because it results in the CWB making export sales that are not in accordance with the principles of subparagraphs (a) or (b) of Article XVII:1. The United States defined the CWB Export Regime as consisting of three elements: the CWB legal framework, which is the Canadian Wheat Board Act; the exclusive and special privileges granted to the CWB by the government of Canada; and certain actions of Canada and the CWB relating to the sale of wheat for export. The privileges referred to include: the CWB's exclusive right to purchase and sell Western Canadian wheat for export and for domestic human consumption; its right to set, subject to government approval, the initial price paid to farmers upon delivery of the wheat; and the Canadian government's guarantee of this initial payment, of the CWB's borrowing and of the CWB's credit sales to foreign buyers. The "actions" that are part of the measure as defined by the United States included Canada's alleged failure to exercise its authority to oversee the CWB, its approval of the CWB's borrowing plan and guarantee of the CWB's borrowing and credit sales, and the approval and guarantee by Canada of the initial payments made to farmers upon delivering Western Canadian wheat to the CWB;

as well as the CWB's sales of wheat destined for export on allegedly discriminatory or non-commercial terms.

The essence of the US claim under Article XVII was that the foregoing privileges gave the CWB more flexibility as to pricing and other sales terms than private entities enjoyed, which enabled and encouraged the CWB to offer non-commercial sales terms in violation of Article XVII:1(a) and to discriminate in its sales between export markets and between its home market and export markets in violation of Article XVII:1(b). The panel rejected the claim. In upholding the panel's findings on appeal, the Appellate Body dealt with two important issues in respect of the interpretation of Article XVII:1—first, the relationship of subparagraphs (a) and (b); second, the meaning of the phrase "solely in accordance with commercial considerations" in subparagraph (b).]

IV.   Relationship Between Subparagraphs (a) and (b) of Article XVII:1 of the GATT 1994

85.   Subparagraph (a) of Article XVII:1 contains a number of different elements, including both an acknowledgement and an obligation. It recognizes that Members may establish or maintain State enterprises or grant exclusive or special privileges to private enterprises, but requires that, if they do so, such enterprises must, when they are involved in certain types of transactions ("purchases or sales involving either imports or exports"), comply with a specific requirement. That requirement is to act consistently with certain principles contained in the GATT 1994 ("general principles of non-discriminatory treatment ... for governmental measures affecting imports or exports by private traders"). Subparagraph (a) seeks to ensure that a Member cannot, through the creation or maintenance of a State enterprise or the grant of exclusive or special privileges to any enterprise, engage in or facilitate conduct that would be condemned as discriminatory under the GATT 1994 if such conduct were undertaken directly by the Member itself. In other words, subparagraph (a) is an "anti-circumvention" provision.

* * *

89.   [T]he question we are asked to consider is how subparagraph (a) relates to subparagraph (b) of Article XVII:1. In our view, the answer to that inquiry is not found in the text of subparagraph (a). Rather, the words that bear most directly on the relationship between the first two paragraphs of Article XVII:1 are found in the opening phrase of subparagraph (b), which states that the "provisions of subparagraph (a) of this paragraph *shall be understood to require* that such enterprises shall ...". (emphasis added) This phrase makes it abundantly clear that the remainder of subparagraph (b) is dependent upon the content of subparagraph (a), and operates to clarify the scope of the requirement not to discriminate in subparagraph (a). * * *

90.   Subparagraph (b) also refers to "such enterprises", which can mean only the STEs defined in subparagraph (a). In addition, subpara-

graph (b) twice refers to "such purchases or sales". It is clear that the word "such" in this phrase must refer to the purchases and sales identified in subparagraph (a), namely the "purchases or sales [of STEs] involving either imports or exports". Thus, the word "such" in subparagraph (b) confirms the link between the two subparagraphs, and ties the content of subparagraph (b) back to subparagraph (a).

91. Having examined the text of subparagraphs (a) and (b) of Article XVII:1, it is our view that subparagraph (b), by defining and clarifying the requirement in subparagraph (a), is dependent upon, rather than separate and independent from, subparagraph (a). [The Appellate Body then concluded that the context of these provisions confirmed its view.]

* * *

110. [T]he two subparagraphs of Article XVII:1 are closely interrelated. As we have said, a panel faced with a claim of inconsistency with Article XVII:1(a) and (b) will, in most if not all cases, need to analyze and apply both provisions in order to assess the consistency of the measure at issue. Subparagraph (b) sets forth two specific conditions with which an STE must comply if allegedly discriminatory conduct falling, prima facie, within the scope of subparagraph (a) is to be found consistent with Article XVII:1. Yet, in order to know whether the conditions in (b) are satisfied, a panel must know what constitutes the conduct alleged to be inconsistent with the principles of non-discriminatory treatment in the GATT 1994. A panel will need to identify at least the differential treatment at issue. The outcome of an assessment under subparagraph (b) of whether the differential treatment is consistent with commercial considerations may depend, in part, upon whether the alleged discrimination relates to pricing, quality, or conditions of sale, and whether it is discrimination between export markets or some other form of discrimination.

111. It follows that, logically, a panel cannot assess whether particular practices of an allegedly discriminatory nature accord with commercial considerations without first identifying the key elements of the alleged discrimination. We emphasize that we are not suggesting that panels are always obliged to make specific factual and legal findings with respect to each element of a claim of discrimination under subparagraph (a) before undertaking any analysis under subparagraph (b). Rather, because a panel's analysis and application of subparagraph (b) to the facts of the case is, like subparagraph (b) itself, dependent on the obligation set forth in subparagraph (a), panels must identify the differential treatment alleged to be discriminatory under subparagraph (a) in order to ensure that they are undertaking a proper inquiry under subparagraph (b).

* * *

V.   INTERPRETATION OF SUBPARAGRAPH (B) OF
ARTICLE XVII:1 OF THE GATT 1994

A.   Making Purchases and Sales Solely in Accordance
with Commercial Considerations

137.   Before the Panel, the United States argued that the first
clause of subparagraph (b) must be interpreted as prohibiting STEs from
using their exclusive or special privileges to the disadvantage of "commercial actors". * * *

* * *

145.   [O]ur interpretation of the relationship between subparagraphs (a) and (b) of Article XVII:1 necessarily implies that the scope of
the inquiry to be undertaken under subparagraph (b) must be governed
by the principles of subparagraph (a). In other words, a panel inquiring
whether an STE has acted solely in accordance with commercial considerations must undertake this inquiry with respect to the market(s) in
which the STE is alleged to be engaging in discriminatory conduct.
Subparagraph (b) does not give panels a mandate to engage in a broader
inquiry into whether, in the abstract, STEs are acting "commercially".
The disciplines of Article XVII:1 are aimed at preventing certain types of
discriminatory behaviour. We see no basis for interpreting that provision
as imposing comprehensive competition-law-type obligations on STEs, as
the United States would have us do.

146.   Before leaving this issue, we refer to an additional argument
advanced by the United States. The United States observes that Article
XVII recognizes the risk that STEs with special privileges may be able to
use those privileges to the disadvantage of commercial actors in a given
market. According to the United States, to eliminate that risk, Article
XVII:1(b), therefore, constrains STEs to act "solely in accordance with
commercial considerations." For the United States, because commercial
actors naturally conduct their business on the basis of commercial
considerations, the first clause of Article XVII:1(b) necessarily must
prevent an STE from using its privileges in a way that creates serious
obstacles to trade and disadvantages such commercial actors. The United
States emphasizes that the Panel's interpretation, that the first clause of
subparagraph (b) does not prohibit STEs from using their privileges,
must be wrong because it "permits STEs to use their special privileges
to the full extent possible, even if this causes discrimination or other
serious obstacles to trade" and that "[t]his is no discipline at all".

* * *

148.   The Panel found that it could not accept the United States'
position for two main reasons. First, it was not supported by the text of
subparagraph (b) itself. Rather:

> ... the only constraint the first clause of subparagraph (b) imposes
> on the use by export STEs of their exclusive or special privileges is
> that these privileges must not be used to make sales which are not

driven exclusively by "commercial considerations" as we understand that term. Whether particular sales by an export STE are driven exclusively by commercial considerations must be assessed in light of the specific circumstances surrounding these sales, including the nature and extent of competition in the relevant market.

149. We agree with this statement by the Panel, and observe that it does not imply, as the United States suggests, that Article XVII:1 contains "no discipline at all". In fact, the Panel's approach emphasizes that whether an STE is in compliance with the disciplines in Article XVII:1 must be assessed by means of a market-based analysis, rather than simply by determining whether an STE has used the privileges that it has been granted. In arguing that Article XVII:1(b) must be interpreted as prohibiting STEs from using their exclusive or special privileges to the disadvantage of "commercial actors", the United States appears to construe Article XVII:1(b) as requiring STEs to act not only as commercial actors in the marketplace, but as virtuous commercial actors, by tying their own hands. We do not see how such an interpretation can be reconciled with an analysis of "commercial considerations" based on market forces. In other words, we cannot accept that the first clause of subparagraph (b) would, as a general rule, require STEs to refrain from using the privileges and advantages that they enjoy because such use might "disadvantage" private enterprises. STEs, like private enterprises, are entitled to exploit the advantages they may enjoy to their economic benefit. Article XVII:1(b) merely prohibits STEs from making purchases or sales on the basis of non-commercial considerations.

150. Moreover, we see force in the second reason that the Panel gave for rejecting the purposive interpretation put forward by the United States: that such an interpretation, which attributes a very broad scope to Article XVII:1, takes no account of the disciplines that apply to the behaviour of STEs elsewhere in the covered agreements. The Panel referred, in this regard, to the provisions of the SCM Agreement, Article VI of the GATT 1994 and the Agreement on Implementation of Article VI of the General Agreement on Tariffs and Trade 1994, and the Agreement on Agriculture.

* * *

Notes and Questions

(1) In the *Wheat Board* case, the panel found that certain Canadian treatment of imported grain violated GATT Article III. Its Article III findings were not appealed.

(2) Are you satisfied with the Appellate Body's response to the US argument in paragraph 148 that the result in the *Wheat Board* case means that Article XVII:1 contains "no discipline at all"?

(3) Although the issue was lurking in the case, the Appellate Body was not asked to rule on the scope of the nondiscrimination requirement in Article XVII:1(1) and, in particular, on whether it includes some sort of national treatment obligation. In that regard, Professor Jackson has conclud-

ed that a modified or relaxed form of the most-favored-nation obligation seems to be the general thrust of Article XVII:[5]

> The preparatory work reflects that the words "general principles of nondiscriminatory treatment" were inserted in Article XVII, paragraph 1(a), at Geneva (1947) in order to allay the doubt that " 'commercial principles' [in Article XVII, paragraph 1(b)] meant that exactly the same price would have to exist in different markets." Thus it appears that what is meant by "nondiscriminatory treatment" is a Most–Favored–Nation principle tempered by "commercial considerations," such as those listed in Article XVII, paragraph 1(b). The obligation in this paragraph also requires that adequate opportunity be granted to the other contracting parties' enterprises to compete "in accordance with customary business practice," which the draftsmen understood was "intended to cover business practices customary in the respective line of trade."

It can be argued that the preparatory work for the drafting of the General Agreement seems to limit the scope of Article XVII:1's nondiscriminatory treatment obligation to an MFN obligation and indicates that it was not intended to require also a national treatment standard. Thus, under that reading of Article XVII, the enterprise would be entitled to discriminate between domestic and foreign products in its purchases or its sales, as long as it does so on an MFN basis.[6] To date, GATT dispute settlement panels have not explicitly endorsed the limitation of Article XVII to MFN treatment, but one panel indicated that it "saw great force in [the] argument that only the most-favoured-nation and not the national treatment obligations fall within the general principles referred to in Article XVII:1(a)."[7] Do you think that Article XVII imposes a national treatment obligation as one of the commercial considerations that state trading enterprises are supposed to follow? Should it?

(4) GATT panels have applied Article III to the activities of state trading enterprises. In a case involving a Canadian provincial requirement that required imported beer to be transported to retail sales outlets by the provincial liquor authority, the panel found that Article III:4 had been violated because (i) domestically produced beer could be delivered by the brewer or other private haulers to retail outlets without provincial involvement and (ii) Canada could not show that the treatment of imported beer in this regard was not less favorable than the treatment of domestically produced beer.[8]

---

5. Jackson, supra note 2, at 346.

6. The General Agreement on Trade in Services (see Chapter 19 supra) requires WTO members to ensure that any monopoly service provider does not act in a manner inconsistent with their obligations under GATS Article II (MFN) and their specific commitments. GATS, art. VIII:1.

7. Canada—Administration of the Foreign Investment Review Act, 30th Supp.

BISD 140, 163 (Panel report adopted Feb. 7, 1984).

8. Canada—Import, Distribution and Sale of Certain Alcoholic Drinks by Provincial Marketing Agencies, 39th Supp. BISD 27, 77–80 (Panel report adopted Feb. 18, 1992). See also Canada—Import, Distribution and Sale of Alcoholic Drinks by Canadian Provincial Marketing Agencies, 35th Supp. BISD 37, 90 (Panel report adopted Mar. 22, 1988).

(5) An important interpretative note to the General Agreement explicitly provides that the term "quantitative restrictions," which restrictions are prohibited or governed by Articles XI through XIV and Article XVIII of GATT, includes restrictions "made effective through state trading operations."[9] Thus, import restrictions that would violate Article XI if imposed by a government cannot be made effective through the use of import monopolies.[10]

(3) Article II:4

GATT Article II, paragraph 4, relating to import monopolies, adds another obligation in respect of import monopolies, which normally would be state trading enterprises (although the converse is not necessarily true). Article II:4 provides that if a product is subject to a GATT tariff binding in the schedule of a country, the country may not evade that binding through the use of an import monopoly to provide protection in excess of that provided for in the schedule. A note to this provision provides that it will be applied in light of the provisions of Article 31 of the Havana Charter. The provision has been interpreted by several GATT panels, including two dealing with complaints about Canadian provincial liquor authorities, which have import monopolies. These complaints alleged, inter alia, that the Canadian authorities marked up the cost prices of imported alcoholic beverages more than they did the comparable prices of domestic beverages. The panel concluded in the first such case that[11]

> [M]ark-ups which were higher on imported than on like domestic alcoholic beverages (differential mark-ups) could only be justified under Article II:4, to the extent that they represented additional costs necessarily associated with marketing of the imported products, * * * [and] that the burden would be on Canada if it wished to claim that additional costs were necessarily associated with marketing of the imported products.

The panel rejected the Canadian argument that the differential mark-ups could be justified on the grounds that they represented a policy of revenue maximization, which charged higher mark-ups on imports in order to exploit the lower price elasticities for premium imported products. As so interpreted, Article II:4 represents a significant constraint on the pricing policies of import monopolies that deal with bound products. Article 31.5 of the Havana Charter also restricted the ability of import monopolies to restrict the volume of imports. It provided that such monopolies shall "import and offer for sale such quantities of the

---

9. GATT Annex I, Note ad Articles XI, XII, XIII, XIV and XVIII; see Jackson, supra note 2, at 348.

10. Japan—Restrictions on Imports of Certain Agricultural Products, 35th Supp. BISD 163, 229 (Panel report adopted Mar. 22, 1988).

11. Canada—Import, Distribution and Sale of Alcoholic Drinks by Canadian Pro-

vincial Marketing Agencies, 35th Supp. BISD 37, 88 (Panel report adopted Mar. 22, 1988). See also Canada—Import, Distribution and Sale of Certain Alcoholic Drinks by Provincial Marketing Agencies, 39th Supp. BISD 27 (Panel report adopted Feb. 22, 1992).

product as will be sufficient to satisfy full domestic demand for the imported product [subject to any rationing rules then in effect]." Article II:4 only applies to import monopolies, not to state trading enterprises generally.

Notes and Questions

(1) In light of the foregoing description of the GATT rules on state trading, how effectively would you say that they deal with the interface problems outlined at the beginning of this section?

(2) As noted earlier, the Uruguay Round negotiations produced an Understanding on Article XVII, which is reproduced in the Documents Supplement. To what extent did the understanding strengthen GATT regulation of state trading enterprises? What additional changes in GATT rules would you propose?

SECTION 9.5   TRANSPARENCY AND PROPER ADMINISTRATION[1]

(A) TRANSPARENCY

(1) In General

Transparency is particularly important for three reasons. First, the underlying goal of the WTO, as expressed in the preamble to the WTO Agreement, is to expand international trade so as to improve the world's economic condition. In order for traders to engage in cross-border transactions, which typically involve risks beyond those incurred in domestic transactions, they need to be able to find out what rules are applicable in the foreign territory. They need this information to assess the economics of a transaction (e.g., what tariff will be charged, what internal taxes must be paid) and whether their goods can be traded (e.g., are they subject to quantitative restrictions or technical standards). If they cannot find out such information, or if that information is difficult or expensive to come by, then trade is less likely to occur. Potential traders also need assurance that the applicable rules will be fairly and impartially applied. Thus, the WTO's basic rules on transparency are fundamentally important to its goal of promoting international trade.

Second, the transparency rules are also important for rule enforcement. The WTO system is often referred to as a rule-based trading system, in which WTO members make market access commitments and undertake to regulate international trade pursuant to specific rules. Transparency requirements facilitate rule enforcement by helping members verify that other members are living up to their basic WTO

---

1. This subsection is drawn from William J. Davey, GATT Article X: Transparency and Proper Administration, a paper presented at Conference on Implications for Chinese Administrative Law of China's Accession to the WTO, Shanghai, China, July 27–29, 2001, a modified version of which was published in William J. Davey, Enforcing World Trade Rules: Essays on WTO Dispute Settlement and GATT Obligations ch. 9 (2006).

obligations. This reinforces member confidence in the WTO system and facilitates future negotiations to the extent that members believe that WTO commitments are actually implemented.

Third, the transparency rules help combat the use of non-tariff barriers. As soon as the international system establishes restraints or regulations on particular protective devices, government officials and human ingenuity seem able to turn up some other measures to accomplish at least part of their protective purposes. That process can be blunted if such measures must be published in advance of their application and notified to the WTO for discussion.

(2) WTO Transparency Rules

The basic GATT rule on transparency is Article X:1. It requires prompt publication of government measures of general application related to broad categories of topics related to international trade. Indeed, the measures covered by Article X:1 are generally similar to the measures covered by GATT Articles I and III (the most-favored-nation and national treatment clauses), which have a rather broad scope of application. Similarly broad publication requirements are also found in the General Agreement on Trade in Services (GATS) and the Agreement on Trade–Related Aspects of Intellectual Property Rights (TRIPS Agreement). For example, GATS Article III:1 provides that: "Each Member shall publish promptly and, except in emergency situations, at the latest by the time of their entry into force, all relevant measures of general application which pertain to or affect the operation of this Agreement." Since GATS applies to measures "affecting trade in services", this is also a broad commitment. GATS Article III:4 has a requirement for establishment of "enquiry points" where members can find out information about a member's laws, regulations and administrative guidelines related to trade in services.

Almost all other WTO agreements contain provisions on transparency as well.[2] Measures regulated by an agreement (and, in some cases, proposed measures) typically must be notified. These notifications are circulated to the WTO membership. As a result, questions about notified measures (or failures to notify) may be raised in many WTO committees. Indeed, WTO committees spend extensive amounts of time reviewing notifications. In that process, WTO members may ask notifying members to explain how certain measures operate in practice and how they

---

2. An incomplete list would include, e.g., GATT Article XIII; Agreement on Sanitary and Phytosanitary Measures (SPS Agreement), art. 7 & Annex B (publication, enquiry points and notification); Agreement on Technical Barriers to Trade, arts. 2.9–2.12 (notification and publication), 10 (enquiry points); Agreement on Trade–Related Investment Measures, art 6 (transparency); Agreement on Implementation of Article VI of GATT 1994 (Antidumping Agreement), art. 12 (public notice); Agreement on Imple- mentation of Article VII of GATT 1994 (Customs Valuation Agreement), art. 12 (publication); Agreement on Preshipment Inspection, art. 2.5–2.8 (publication and enquiry points); Agreement on Import Licensing Procedures, arts. 1.4, 3.3 (publication); Agreement on Subsidies and Countervailing Measures (SCM Agreement), art. 22 (public notice); Safeguards Agreement, art. 3.1 (publication). See generally Marrakech Ministerial Declaration on Notification Procedures of 15 April 1994.

comply with WTO rules. As such, they are an important, albeit indirect, means of promoting compliance with WTO obligations. The discussions in these reviews also generally serve a valuable education and clarification function, as they allow the membership to express its views on the meaning of many WTO obligations.

Another important part of the WTO's transparency regime is the Trade Policy Review Mechanism, pursuant to which the trade policies of all WTO members are reviewed on a periodic basis (ranging from every two years for the four largest trading entities to every six or so years for the least active members). The review process is in itself a transparency exercise, since it aims to describe and analyze all aspects of a member's trade regime. That review process includes consideration of how the member meets its transparency obligations.

(3) WTO Transparency Rules in Dispute Settlement

There are two issues that have arisen in GATT/WTO dispute settlement as to the interpretation of publication requirements. First, there is the question of timing—at what point in time must publication occur? Second, what types of measures must be published?

On the timing issue, Article X was discussed by the panel and Appellate Body in the *US Underwear* case.[3] In that case, the United States had imposed restrictions on imports of underwear from Costa Rica. The measure putting the restriction into force was published on June 23, 1995, and it was provided that the measure applied for the 12–month period following March 27, 1995. The proposal for the measure had been published on April 21, 1995. In the panel's view, to the extent that the measure restricted imports during a period prior to publication of the proposal, it was in violation of Article X's publication requirement. On appeal, the Appellate Body noted:

> Article X:2 ... may be seen to embody a principle of fundamental importance—that of promoting full disclosure of governmental acts affecting Members and private persons and enterprises, whether of domestic or foreign nationality. The relevant policy principle is widely known as the principle of transparency and has obviously due process dimensions. The essential implication is that Members, and other persons affected, or likely to be affected, by governmental measures imposing restraints, requirements and other burdens, should have a reasonable opportunity to acquire authentic information about such measures and accordingly to protect and adjust their activities or alternatively to seek modification of such measures.[4]

The Appellate Body, however, viewed the issue in the case at hand to be controlled by the Agreement on Textiles and Clothing, which in its view

3. United States—Restrictions on Imports of Cotton and Man–Made Fibre Underwear, WT/DS24/R & WT/DS24/AB/R, adopted February 21, 1997 ("US–Underwear").

4. US—Underwear, WT/DS24/AB/R, p. 21.

did not permit retrospective application of a restraint measure at all, i.e. it could not apply to periods prior to June 23, 1995.

As to the scope of publication requirement, this issue arose in a case involving the SPS Agreement, which requires publication of SPS measures.[5] The issue in the case was whether certain guidelines developed by the relevant Japanese government agency were subject to the publication requirement. Japan argued that the guidelines did not need to be published because they were not enforceable regulations and that, in any event, they were available on request. The panel rejected these arguments, citing GATT practice to the effect that a non-mandatory government measure is also subject to WTO provisions in the event compliance with the measure is necessary to obtain an advantage from the government. The Appellate Body upheld the panel, noting that the object and purpose of the publication requirement is to "enhance transparency" and the scope of the requirement should be interpreted in light of that object and purpose.[6]

More generally, it should be noted that the WTO agreements that permit imposition of safeguards and antidumping and countervailing duties, have various detailed notification and publication requirements that apply at various stages of the investigatory process and in respect of implementation of measures. Panels and the Appellate Body have been relatively strict in enforcing these rules.

(B) PROPER ADMINISTRATION

EUROPEAN COMMUNITIES—SELECTED CUSTOMS MATTERS

WT/DS315/AB/R.
Appellate Body Report adopted December 11, 2006.

[A panel was established to consider a complaint by the United States that the European Communities' system of customs administration violated GATT Articles X:3(a) and X:3(b). The US claimed that the EC administered its customs law in a non-uniform manner, in violation of Article X:3(a). The US presented various instances of alleged non-uniform administration of EC customs law to illustrate that the EC system as a whole was inconsistent with the requirements of Article X:3(a). In addition, the US claimed that the EC did not provide for the prompt review and correction of administrative actions relating to customs matters as required by Article X:3(b). The panel rejected the US claims except to the extent that it found that the EC had violated Article X:3(a) in three specific cases involving tariff classification and customs valuation. On appeal, the Appellate Body reversed several aspects of the panel report, including the finding of an Article X:3(a) violation in two of

---

5. Japan—Measures Affecting Agricultural Products, WT/DS76R & WT/DS76/AB/R, adopted March 19, 1999 ("Japan–Agricultural Products").

6. Japan—Agricultural Products, WT/DS76/AB/R, para. 106.

the three above-mentioned cases. Of particular interest to the general interpretation of Article X were the following paragraphs in the Appellate Body report.]

V. Claims Regarding Article X:3(a) of the GATT 1994

196. We begin our analysis by recalling the text of Article X:3(a) of the GATT 1994:

> Each Member shall administer in a uniform, impartial and reasonable manner all its laws, regulations, decisions and rulings of the kind described in paragraph 1 of this Article.

* * *

199. Thus, [in prior cases] the Appellate Body distinguished between, on the one hand, the laws, regulations, judicial decisions, and administrative rulings of general application set out in Article X:1 of the GATT 1994 and, on the other hand, the administration of these legal instruments. The Appellate Body reasoned that, as Article X:3(a) establishes disciplines on the administration of the legal instruments of the kind described in Article X:1, claims concerning the substantive content of these Article X:1 legal instruments fall outside the scope of Article X:3(a). The statements of the Appellate Body * * * do not exclude, however, the possibility of challenging under Article X:3(a) the substantive content of a legal instrument that regulates the administration of a legal instrument of the kind described in Article X:1. Under Article X:3(a), a distinction must be made between the legal instrument being administered and the legal instrument that regulates the application or implementation of that instrument. While the substantive content of the legal instrument being administered is not challengeable under Article X:3(a), we see no reason why a legal instrument that regulates the application or implementation of that instrument cannot be examined under Article X:3(a) if it is alleged to lead to a lack of uniform, impartial, or reasonable administration of that legal instrument.

200. This distinction has implications for the type of evidence required to support a claim of a violation of Article X:3(a). If a WTO Member challenges under Article X:3(a) the substantive content of a legal instrument that regulates the administration of a legal instrument of the kind described in Article X:1, it will have to prove that this instrument necessarily leads to a lack of uniform, impartial, or reasonable administration. It is not sufficient for the complainant merely to cite the provisions of that legal instrument. The complainant must discharge the burden of substantiating how and why those provisions necessarily lead to impermissible administration of the legal instrument of the kind described in Article X:1.

* * *

VI.   The Panel's Interpretation of Article X:3(b) of the GATT 1994

298.   * * * We agree with the Panel that what is required by Article X:3(b) is that "the decisions of judicial, arbitral or administrative tribunals and procedures for the prompt review and correction of administrative action must govern the practice of the agency whose action was the subject of review by a tribunal or procedure in a particular case." Article X:3(b) leaves the specific structure of the review mechanism to the discretion of the Member concerned. Therefore, "such agencies" may encompass more or fewer agencies depending on the structure of the review mechanism. However, we do not see why the jurisdiction of a review tribunal or procedure and the binding effect of a review decision of that tribunal would always or necessarily have to extend to all agencies of a Member.

299.   In addition, we recall that Article X:3(b) relates to first instance review and contemplates the possibility of appeals to bodies of "superior jurisdiction" as well as the seeking of "a review of the matter" by a centralized agency. This would also suggest that the first instance review required by that provision need not necessarily cover the entire territory of a WTO Member.

300.   Accordingly, we are of the view that it does not follow from the ordinary meaning of Article X:3(b) that decisions of judicial, arbitral, or administrative tribunals or procedures for first instance review and correction of administrative action relating to customs matters must govern the practice of all the agencies entrusted with administrative enforcement throughout the territory of a WTO Member.

301.   We address next the question whether context suggests otherwise. We consider that Article X:3(a) of the GATT 1994 is relevant as context. The Panel, however, noted that Article X:3(b) of the GATT 1994 does not contain an express textual link to the obligation of uniform administration of customs laws in Article X:3(a). The Panel contrasted this with Article X:3(c) of the GATT 1994, which explicitly cross-references Article X:3(b). Against this background, the Panel considered that it was not possible to infer that the drafters of the GATT 1994 intended the obligation of Article X:3(b) to be read as simultaneously requiring uniform administration in accordance with Article X:3(a). In the Panel's view, this would amount to "merging different requirements that are currently contained in separate sub-paragraphs of Article X". We see no reason to disagree with the Panel's interpretation. We are also of the view that the requirement of "uniformity" contained in Article X:3(a) does not imply that under Article X:3(b) decisions of review tribunals must govern the practice of all agencies entrusted with customs enforcement throughout the territory of a WTO Member. Article X:3(a) requires, inter alia, uniformity of administration. In contrast, Article X:3(b) relates to the review and correction of administrative action by independent mechanisms.

302.   Finally, turning briefly to the treaty's object and purpose, we note the Panel's view that the due process objective underlying Article

X:3(b) is that "a trader who has been adversely affected by a decision of an administrative agency has the ability to have that adverse decision reviewed." We believe this due process objective is not undermined even if first instance review decisions do not govern the practice of all the agencies entrusted with customs enforcement throughout the territory of a WTO Member, so long as there is a possibility of an independent review and correction of the administrative action of every agency.

303.   For these reasons, we are of the view that Article X:3(b) of the GATT 1994 requires a WTO Member to establish and maintain independent mechanisms for prompt review and correction of administrative action in the area of customs administration. However, neither text nor context nor the object and purpose of this Article require that the decisions emanating from such first instance review must govern the practice of all agencies entrusted with administrative enforcement throughout the territory of a particular WTO Member.

Notes and Questions

(1) One tantalizing question that is raised by Article X is whether it requires, at least within the scope of its application, a certain standard of administrative due process or what might be called regulatory good governance. Is there language in the excerpt from the *EC Customs* case that could be used to support such an argument? In that regard, it is worth noting that, in connection with its analysis of the meaning of arbitrary discrimination as used in the chapeau to Article XX, the Appellate Body in *US Shrimp* opined that Article X:3, which was not directly at issue in the case, establishes "minimum standards for transparency and procedural fairness".[7] It found that the US procedures at issue, which it described as non-transparent and *ex parte*, and which did not provide for notice of the denial of an application, nor of the reasons therefor, nor of the possibility of an appeal, were all "contrary to the spirit, if not the letter, of Article X:3". The *US Shrimp* case is discussed in Chapter 13.

(2) Two WTO panel reports in antidumping cases have elaborated on the scope of the uniformity requirement in Article X:3(a). In *US—Stainless Steel from Korea*, Korea argued that the US had changed established practices in an antidumping investigation without an adequate explanation, thereby violating the uniformity and reasonableness requirements of Article X:3(a). The panel questioned the appropriateness of Korea's argument as in its view Article X should not be invoked to argue that a WTO member has violated its own domestic rules. It added, however, that the uniform administration obligation required "uniformity of treatment in respect of persons similarly situated". While it found no violation of this standard, the way in which it formulated the standard is itself of considerable interest.[8] It did stress, however, that

---

7.   United States—Import Prohibitions on Certain Shrimp and Shrimp Products, WT/DS58/AB/R, para. 183, adopted November 6, 1998.

8.   United States—Anti–Dumping Measures on Stainless Steel Plate in Coils and

Stainless Steel Sheet and Strip from Korea, WT/DS179/R, paras. 6.50–6.54, adopted February 1, 2001. The case was not appealed.

the uniformity requirement "cannot be understood to require identical results where relevant facts differ." Factual differences may often be present, but one can imagine cases where the panel's formulation of Article X:3's meaning might arise.

Similar issues arose in the *US—Hot–Rolled Steel from Japan* case. There Japan argued that the US had acted inconsistently with its past practice. The panel took a somewhat narrower view of the scope of Article X than had the *Korea Stainless* panel. The *Japan Steel* panel agreed that Article X was not an appropriate mechanism for ensuring that national administrative authorities conformed to national rules. It also noted that it would be hesitant to conclude that a practice consistent with the WTO Antidumping Agreement was in violation of GATT Article X. Further, it suggested that showing one case of non-uniform application of domestic law might not be sufficient to establish a violation of Article X, but rather that it would be necessary to show a pattern of such behavior that had a significant impact on the overall administration of the law and not simply the outcome of one case.[9]

(3) There has not been much consideration in dispute settlement cases of the meaning of Article X:3(a)'s requirement of "reasonable and impartial" administration. However, the issue was explored in the *Argentina—Hides* case. In that case, Argentina's hide export rules permitted a representative of the Argentine tanning industry to participate in export clearance procedures for hides, thereby giving the industry access to information about the activities of its suppliers. The EC claimed that the industry would use the information to advance its own interests at the expense of exporters since the industry had an interest in and a history of trying to restrict hide exports so as to increase the domestic supply of hides so as to reduce the prices that the tanning industry had to pay for hides. The panel found that Article X's reasonableness and impartiality requirements were violated by allowing such participation since it permitted a competing industry to obtain confidential business information, such as commercially sensitive pricing information.[10]

(4) China's Protocol of Accession to the WTO (WT/L/342 (23 Nov. 2001)) includes the following provisions:

> 2(A)2. China shall apply and administer in a uniform, impartial and reasonable manner all its laws, regulations and other measures of the central government as well as local regulations, rules and other measures issued or applied at the sub-national level (collectively referred to as "laws, regulations and other measures") pertaining to or affecting trade in goods, services, trade-related aspects of intellectual property rights ("TRIPS") or the control of foreign exchange.

9. United States—Anti–Dumping Measures on Certain Hot–Rolled Steel Products from Japan, WT/DS184/R, paras. 7.267–7.268, adopted by the DSB on August 24, 2001. The Article X issues were not appealed.

10. Argentina—Measures Affecting the Export of Bovine Hides and the Import of Finished Leather, WT/DS155/R, paras. 11.86–11.101, adopted February 16, 2001. The case was not appealed.

2(C)1. China undertakes that only those laws, regulations and other measures pertaining to or affecting trade in goods, services, TRIPS or the control of foreign exchange that are published and readily available to other WTO Members, individuals and enterprises, shall be enforced.

2(D)(1). China shall establish, or designate, and maintain tribunals, contact points and procedures for the prompt review of all administrative actions relating to the implementation of laws, regulations, judicial decisions and administrative rulings of general application referred to in Article X:1 of the GATT 1994, Article VI of the GATS and the relevant provisions of the TRIPS Agreement. Such tribunals shall be impartial and independent of the agency entrusted with administrative enforcement and shall not have any substantial interest in the outcome of the matter.

2(D)2. Review procedures shall include the opportunity for appeal, without penalty, by individuals or enterprises affected by any administrative action subject to review. If the initial right of appeal is to an administrative body, there shall in all cases be the opportunity to choose to appeal the decision to a judicial body.

How much broader are China's commitments than those required of WTO members generally under GATT Article X? Compare the scope of the "uniform administration requirement" in the Protocol with that of Article X:3(a), which is defined by Article X:1. Do the provisions of the China Protocol create certain minimum standards of regulatory good governance? Is it appropriate to impose stricter requirements on acceding members?

Review Problems for Chapters 8 and 9

Assume that Atlonia and Bugslavia are members of the WTO, while Xonia is not. Atlonia's schedule contains the following binding:

Handkerchiefs, cotton . . . 10%

This concession was negotiated at the most recent round of negotiations, partly pursuant to a request of a country named "Categorica" which at the time was the second largest exporter of handkerchiefs to Atlonia. The largest exporter to Atlonia at that time was "Dominata." Today, the largest two exporters of handkerchiefs to Atlonia are "Exportonia" (first), and "Factonia" (second.) All these countries are members of the WTO.

Bugslavia ships products to Atlonia, and the following cases arise. In each case indicate whether the Atlonia practice is consistent with GATT or not. (Refer to the GATT agreement in the Documents Supplement.)

(1) A tariff is imposed on the imports of cotton handkerchiefs produced in Bugslavia at the rate of:

(a) 12%.

(b) 8%.

(c) Specific rate of one drachma, and the handkerchiefs are valued at 8 drachmas each.

(d) Same, except value is 12 drachmas each.

(2) Imports are of handkerchiefs made of 50% cotton and 50% synthetic fiber; tariff imposed is 20%.

(3) Besides the tariff, a customs administration fee of 1 drachma per handkerchief is imposed, and mandatory import entry invoice forms are sold for 1 drachma each.

(4) All textile imports are valued by the highest price found for like goods in any market of the world.

(5) Textile imports are valued by applying Atlonia production cost factors, using standard Atlonia collective bargaining labor wage rates.

(6) All imports are valued for customs purposes as if their value included the standard Atlonia 10% domestic sales tax applied to all goods, domestic or foreign.

(7) After the binding was negotiated, Atlonia granted to its domestic textile industry an accelerated income tax depreciation rate for new capital expenses by that industry.

(8) Atlonia maintains a state trading monopoly for textile imports and imported handkerchiefs are sold at a 40% mark-up, after they have cleared customs and paid duty.

(9) Atlonia abolishes its state trading monopoly, but establishes an import quota for handkerchiefs at 1 million units per year. (Past imports have never exceeded 700,000 units per year.)

(10) A Bugslavia firm buys handkerchiefs from Xonia and ships them to Atlonia for resale. A tariff of 20% is imposed.

(11) On compact disc players, Atlonia has made no GATT binding. Atlonia now charges a tariff of 10% on imports of this product, but is developing a domestic industry to produce such players. It wishes to exclude imports of these products and consults you, its lawyer, about ways to accomplish this. Advise on the relative merits of the following proposals:

    (a) Impose a ban on imports of the product.

    (b) Subsidize with direct government grant equal to 50% of the cost of producing each item.

    (c) Raise the tariff from 10% to 100%.

    (d) Raise the tariff to 1000%.

    (e) Raise the tariff to 50% ad valorem, but provide that imported CD players shall be valued for customs purposes equal to the average price charged in the domestic market for domestically produced CD players.

    (f) Impose a requirement that imported CD players be stored in a warehouse for one year after importation, before resale.

(12) Suppose Atlonia had bound its tariff on CD players at 50%. Would that cause you to change your advice on the alternatives listed in (11)?

(13) Suppose its GATT binding of 50% were on "CD players," and Atlonia now decided to change its domestic tariff schedule to appear as follows:

CD Players:

Portable 100%

All other 50%

Could Atlonia do this without being in contravention of GATT rules?

(14) Some other techniques for Atlonia to consider (discussed in later chapters):

(a) Leave the tariff at 10%, but impose an internal excise sales tax of 50% which is waived on domestically produced goods.

(b) Require the exchange rate to be used in purchases of CD players to allow one-half the amount of Atlonia currency per unit of foreign currency.

(c) Require importers to deposit with an Atlonia bank an amount equal to the value of CD player imports, such amount to be refundable after six months (but with no interest).

(d) Allow imports of CD players only from countries which import a like amount of such product from Atlonia.

(e) Allow imports of CD players only from countries which themselves have a zero tariff on imports of CD players.

(15) If Atlonia decides to withdraw its tariff binding on handkerchiefs, what procedures in the WTO does it face? Which WTO members will have "negotiating" rights?

(16) If, at a new negotiation, Atlonia is prepared to reduce its tariff on silk handkerchiefs from 20% to 10%, and has recently been importing one million units of this product from Bugslavia, two million from Categorica, and three million from Dominata, all at a wholesale customs entry valuation of the equivalent of $1.00 per unit (before tariff), what value of concessions is Atlonia entitled to ask from each of these countries? How should one measure the value of a concession?

Chapter 10

NONDISCRIMINATION AND THE MOST–FAVORED– NATION CLAUSE

SECTION 10.1 INTRODUCTION[1]

(A) THE POLICIES UNDERLYING THE MFN PRINCIPLE

"The unconditional most-favored-nation (MFN) provision is the cornerstone of the international trade rules embodied in the General Agreement on Tariffs and Trade (GATT). The basic rationale for MFN is that if every country observes the principle, all countries will benefit in the long run through the resulting more efficient use of resources. Furthermore, if the principle is observed, there is less likelihood of trade disputes."[2]

1. For references on MFN in addition to those excerpted in this chapter, see generally John H. Jackson, World Trade and the Law of GATT ch. 11 (1969); Thomas Cottier & Petros C. Mavroidis (eds.), Regulatory Barriers and the Principle of Non–Discrimination in World Trade Law (2000); John H. Jackson, The World Trading System ch. 6 (2d ed. 1997); John H. Jackson, Equality and Discrimination in International Economic Law (XI): The General Agreement on Tariffs and Trade, Brit.Yb.World Aff. 1983, at 224 (1983); Warren Schwartz & Alan O. Sykes, Toward a Positive Theory of the Most Favored Nation Obligation and its Exceptions in the WTO/GATT System, 16 Int'l Rev. L. & Econ. 27 (1996); Warren Schwartz & Alan O. Sykes, Most Favored Nation Obligations in International Trade, New Palgrave Dictionary of Economics and the Law, Vol. 2 660 (Peter Newman ed. 1998); League of Nations Economic Comm., Equality of Treatment in the Present State of International Commercial Relations: The Most–Favoured–Nation Clause, L.N.Doc.C. 379, M. 250. 1936 II.B.; Gardner Patterson, Discrimination in International Trade: The Policy Issues, 1945–1965 (1966); Richard C.

Snyder, The Most–Favored–Nation Clause: An Analysis with Particular Reference to Recent Treaty Practice and Tariffs (1948); Hector Gros Espiell, The Most–Favoured–Nation Clause, 5 J. World Trade L. 29 (1971); Theodore C. Sorensen, Most Favored and Less Favorite Nations, 52 Foreign Affairs 273 (1974). In the context of the Tokyo Round, see Gary C. Hufbauer, J. Sheldon Erb & H.P. Starr, The GATT Codes and the Unconditional Most-Favored–Nation Principle, 12 Law & Poly. Intl.Bus. 59 (1980); Report of the International Law Commission on it Thirtieth Session, Draft Articles on Most–Favoured–Nation Clauses and Commentary, in Yearbook of the International Law Commission 1978, at 8–73 (Vol. 2, pt. 2, 1979) (U.N.Doc. A/CN.4/SER.A/1978/Add. 1 (Part 2)).

2. Executive Branch GATT Studies, No. 9, The Most–Favored–Nation Provision, at 133, Subcomm. on International Trade, Senate Comm. on Finance, 93d Cong., 2d Sess. (Compilation of 1973 studies prepared by the Executive Branch: Comm.Print 1974).

The importance of the most-favored-nation principle has been further underscored by GATT economists who have noted five significant benefits flowing from the principle.[3]

First, "[f]rom the economic viewpoint, [the MFN principle] ensures that each country will satisfy its total import needs from the most efficient sources of supply, allowing the operation of comparative advantage." If a country's tariff rates on a product vary and a higher rate is applied to the nearest or most efficient producer, then that producer may not be able to compete in the country's market, raising prices and costs in that market and reducing efficiency worldwide.

Second, "[f]rom the trade policy viewpoint, the MFN commitment protects the value of bilateral concessions and 'spreads security around' by making them the basis for a multilateral system." Because MFN treatment generalizes market-opening measures, it is a positive force for multilateral trade liberalization. It can be expected that more liberalization will be achieved with MFN than without. This is of great importance because without MFN, discrimination leads inevitably to more discrimination and all suffer, even if discrimination sometimes appears to be in the short-run interest of the discriminating country.

Third, "[f]rom the international-political viewpoint, the commitment to the MFN clause mobilizes the power of the large countries behind the main interest and aspiration of the small ones which is to be treated equally. It represents the only way to realize the ideal of sovereign equality of nations; in more practical terms, it guarantees the access of newcomers into international markets." This result may significantly reduce international tensions because those nations denied special trade advantages will resent it, and the more special advantages that are created, the more disputes that can be expected.

Fourth, "[f]rom the domestic-political viewpoint, the MFN commitment makes for more straightforward and transparent policies and for greater simplicity of administration of protection." For example, with general MFN treatment, special origin rules would be unnecessary.

Fifth, "[u]ltimately, the unconditional MFN commitment is of a constitutional significance. It serves as the safe constraint on the delegated discretionary powers of the executive branch in trade matters." If a government has a strong commitment to an MFN policy, special interests will be less likely to try to obtain and even less likely to get special discriminatory trade measures. Thus, trade generally will be freer of government interference.

There are, of course, some problems that arise from general application of the MFN principle. In particular, as discussed below and as we saw in Section 8.2, some countries, particularly smaller ones, may drag their feet in reducing tariffs and attempt to free-ride on the MFN principle. This complicates tariff negotiations, although the use of general tariff-cutting formulas may limit the scope of this problem.

---

3. GATT Focus, Sept.–Oct. 1984, at 3.

MFN has sometimes been described as the "central" policy of GATT and the post World War II trading system. Certainly it is one of the central policies, and the fact that it is Article I of General Agreement reinforces that position. Indeed, the "existing legislation" exception of the GATT 1947's Protocol of Provisional Application did not apply to Part I of the General Agreement, which includes Article I (as well as the tariff concessions article, Article II, discussed in Chapter 8).

The MFN principle of non-discrimination (one of GATT's two major non-discrimination principles, the other being the national treatment principle, taken up in Chapter 12), has been the center of considerable discussion and controversy in recent years. In this introductory section, after a description of the history of MFN, we consider whether there is any MFN obligation in customary international law, apart from treaty obligation. In Section 10.2, we look at the operation of the GATT MFN clause, examining the GATT and WTO decisions that have interpreted its scope and the major GATT-authorized exceptions to MFN treatment.

We conclude this chapter with an examination of US legislative approaches to the MFN principle, where we will find examples of support for the principle, but also derogations from it. In this connection, we consider the results of the Tokyo and Uruguay Rounds and the related US implementing legislation.

Despite its centrality in the WTO/GATT system, some question the future of the MFN rule as a fundamental principle of international trade agreements. They note that the MFN principle is now being eroded rapidly by the extensive use of exceptions to it and by various bilateral arrangements between nations which depart from the spirit if not the letter of the MFN obligations. In Chapter 11, we examine the most significant MFN exception—that for customs unions and free trade areas. In Chapter 24, we will explore the Generalized System of Preferences, which is designed to aid developing countries, but which is a departure from MFN.

Apart from exceptions to the MFN clause, there are some policy problems with the MFN principle itself.

JOHN H. JACKSON, THE WORLD TRADING SYSTEM 160–62 (2d ed. 1997)[4]

A second set of counterarguments stresses the risk of a unilateral unconditional MFN approach. These are the "foot-dragger" and "free-rider" arguments. To negotiate a general rule applicable to all nations in a system that stresses unanimity and consensus often means that a hold-out nation can prevent agreement or cause its provisions to be reduced to the least common denominator. This can greatly inhibit needed improvement in substantive or procedural rules.

On the other hand, for like-minded nations to go ahead with reforms and agreements without the "foot dragger," but to grant (as unconditional MFN requires) all the benefits of the new approach to the non-agreeing parties, gives the latter unreciprocated benefits without any of the obligations. This furnishes an incentive to nations to stay out of the agreement. This is what led the United States to require nations to accept the Subsidies Code obligations as a condition to receiving beneficial US treatment in countervailing duty cases (as specified in the Tokyo Round code).

* * *

CONDITIONAL AND UNCONDITIONAL MFN; CODE CONDITIONALITY

Under conditional MFN, when country A grants a privilege to country C while owing MFN to country B, then country A must grant the equivalent privilege to B—but only after B has given A some reciprocal privilege to "pay for it."

Under unconditional MFN, in the case above A must grant the equivalent privilege to country B without receiving anything in return from B. The United States pursued a "conditional MFN" policy prior to World War I, although many other major nations had by that time moved to an unconditional approach. The United States changed to an unconditional policy in 1923.

Several arguments are often voiced in preference of the unconditional approach over the conditional. In the first place, it is very difficult to negotiate for reciprocal concessions from a third-party beneficiary of benefits. When A grants to C a privilege, and B knows that MFN obligations require that privilege to go to B also, albeit after "payment," there is not a very strong incentive for B to be forthcoming in a bargaining process with A. Such negotiations can generate more rancor and trouble than they are worth. Second, unconditional MFN can help spread trade liberalization faster, given that any concession by a particular country is generalized to apply very broadly. The GATT MFN clause is clearly unconditional.

A different type of MFN concept has arisen in connection with various "codes," or side agreements on trade matters, negotiated in the Tokyo Round. In some of these codes, certain code members have taken the position that the benefits of code treatment would only be granted to nations that became members of the code (or at least reciprocated with code treatment). Thus, if A, B, and C belonged to a code which calls for an "injury" test requirement before countervailing duties can be applied to imports, A could argue that it need not give such "test" to the imports from X, which was not a code member. Sometimes this has been called "conditional MFN," but in fact it is not the same as the traditional "conditional MFN" concept, since it does not require a particular negotiation of reciprocal benefits. Instead, the code itself defines the nature of the reciprocity that is owed in order to receive the advantage of this type of MFN. The advantage of "code conditionality" is that it creates an incentive for other nations to join a code and submit to its discipline. If a general MFN obligation (e.g., in GATT) required all code nations to grant the favorable code treatment to nations that did not become code members, there would be substantially less incentive for such nations to join. They can take a "free-rider" approach, and claim the benefits without having to incur the discipline of code membership.

———————

Two of the Tokyo Round agreements, and the US statute implementing three of the Tokyo Round agreements, seemed to limit the benefits of those agreements to the countries which assumed the obligations of the particular agreement, a sort of "agreement" or "code" conditional MFN. See Section 10.3. In considering the materials below, the reader should keep in mind the difference between traditional conditional MFN and code conditional MFN. Under the WTO Agreement, there are now only two plurilateral agreements with limited membership—the revised Government Procurement Agreement and the Tokyo Round Civil Aircraft Agreement.

(B) THE HISTORY OF MFN

THE MOST–FAVORED–NATION PROVISION, EXECUTIVE BRANCH GATT STUDIES, No. 9, 133–35 (1973)[5]

HISTORY

The concept embodied in the MFN clause has been traced to the 12th century, although the phrase "most-favored-nation" did not appear until the end of the 17th century. The emergence of the MFN provision is largely attributable to the growth of world commerce in the 15th and 16th centuries. At that time England and Holland were competing with Spain and Portugal, and the French and the Scandinavians were challenging the Hanseatic League and the Italian Republics. Each country, seeking maximum advantage for its trade, found itself compelled to grant concessions in return. The role of the MFN provision was to link commercial treaties through time and between states. At first, the MFN provision applied to concessions granted only to specified states, but gradually the clause became generalized to apply to concessions granted to all countries.

The trend toward wide use of the MFN clause necessarily coincided with the decline of mercantilism. The mercantilist view that in any commercial exchange one nation wins and the other loses does not mix with the concept of reciprocal arrangements implicit in the MFN principle.

5. Subcomm. on Intl. Trade, Senate Comm. on Finance, 93d Cong., 2d Sess. (Compilation of 1973 studies prepared by the Executive Branch: Comm. Print 1974).

The unconditional form of the MFN clause—guaranteed equal treatment without requiring directly reciprocal compensation—was used exclusively until the late 18th century. In fact, conditional MFN—equal treatment conditional upon adequate compensation—was inaugurated in 1778 by the United States. During the first half of the 19th century, the conditional form was common in treaties in Europe and elsewhere. The wave of liberalism that swept Europe in the second half of the 19th century brought a return to use of the unconditional MFN clause in keeping with the free trade sentiment of the time. While European countries ultimately returned to the unconditional form, the United States was consistent until 1923 in its adherence to the conditional form. It should be noted, however, that in practice only a limited amount of United States trade was affected by reciprocal treaties involving conditional MFN. The United States consistently applied a single-schedule tariff to imports from all countries. Reciprocal treaties granting reductions from the general tariff rates were few in number at any given time.

The United States began granting conditional MFN with its first treaty after independence, the United States–France treaty of 1778. Article II provided that, "The Most Christian King and the United States engage mutually not to grant any particular favor to other nations in respect of commerce and navigation, which shall not immediately become common to the other party, who shall enjoy the same favor, Freely, If The Compensation Was Freely Made, Or On Allowing The Same Compensation, If The Concession Was Conditional" (caps added). Similar provisions in treaties with Prussia (1785) and Sweden (1793) served to establish the "American interpretation" that special favors must be specifically bought.

The position of the United States as a newcomer to world commerce largely accounts for its novel interpretation of the MFN clause. With the colonial ties to the British Empire broken, the United States had difficulty establishing an equal footing for trade with other nations. France and Spain, as well as Britain, attempted to exclude the Americans from trading with their overseas possessions. At the same time, these countries sought to penetrate the American market. Given European reluctance to grant initial reciprocity, the United States policy was to establish high duties and grant access to the American market only in return for access to markets controlled by Europe. Under the circumstances then prevailing the conditional MFN clause enabled the United States to maximize its bargaining leverage by offering no gratuitous access privileges.

The American principle of conditional MFN had a growing effect on commercial policy abroad, reaching its peak roughly between 1830 and 1860. The year 1810 marked the first conditional MFN clause in a treaty between European states (Great Britain and Portugal). In 1824 the clause was introduced to South America, where it remained dominant for the next 25 years. Of all European states, England was the most consistent in adhering to the unconditional MFN form through the first half of the 19th century, although the conditional clause was not uncommon in its treaties during that period.

Beginning with the Cobden treaty between France and England in 1860, the unconditional form of the MFN clause again prevailed in European commercial treaties. The benefits of the Cobden treaty were conditionally extended to other countries by France and unconditionally extended to others by England. It soon became apparent to England that under this arrangement the balance of advantages was in favor of France. To compensate for this, England launched a successful drive to conclude unconditional MFN treaties with other countries. The unconditional MFN clause was used exclusively in Europe after that time, in spite of a return to protectionism on the Continent after 1875.

While the United States and Europe were consistent in following their respective interpretations of the MFN clause during the latter 19th century, practice in other parts of the trading world varied. In South and Central America, for example, both forms of the clause were used with no clear-cut pattern, although the conditional form was used consistently in treaties between American states. Japan also used both forms.

The divergent interpretations of the MFN principle during the late 19th century were largely a manifestation of the economic relationship between the United States and Europe. World War I altered this relationship dramatically. Following the war, the United States no longer stood to Europe as an underdeveloped nation, dependent upon Europe for industrial goods and capital, content to export to Europe its raw materials. American products were now much in demand in Europe and American capital financed European factories. Therefore, in the 1920's United States policy changed, reflecting its broader and more important export interests. By offering complete and continuous nondiscriminatory treatment the United States sought to obtain the same treatment from other countries, thus reducing discrimination against United States exports.

JOHN H. JACKSON, WORLD TRADE AND THE LAW OF GATT 250–251 (1969)[6]

One of Wilson's fourteen points in 1918 urged "the establishment of an equality of trade conditions among all the nations consenting to the Peace," which was explained to mean "whatever tariff any nation might deem necessary for its own economic service, be that tariff high or low, it should apply equally to all foreign nations." The League of Nations Covenant likewise mentioned the goal of "equitable treatment for the commerce of all members" and the 1919 peace treaties contained MFN clauses. The League occupied itself with various economic and financial matters, but one prominent topic was MFN, on which the League prepared a series of reports and studies.

6. From World Trade and the Law of GATT, by John H. Jackson, copyright 1969, by The Bobbs–Merrill Company Inc. Reprinted by permission. All Rights reserved.

In 1936, the League published a study that included legal language for a recommended MFN clause, as well as a discussion of various problems, ambiguities, and policy questions of scope. At the same time, as chronicled elsewhere, international trade in the interwar period was breaking down and a variety of trade barriers were spreading from nation to nation. In 1930, the United States enacted the infamous Smoot–Hawley tariff and one reaction that has been attributed to this act was the introduction of a preferential trade system for the British Commonwealth. In 1934, the United States accepted Cordell Hull's reciprocal trade agreement program but, although MFN clauses were universally included in the trade agreements negotiated pursuant to that act, the treaties with Commonwealth nations excepted the Commonwealth preferences from MFN operation.

One of the prime post-World War II objectives of the United States was the dismantling of trade preferences, especially the Commonwealth system. The details of the clash between United States and British policy and public opinion in this respect are set forth in Richard Gardner's book Sterling–Dollar Diplomacy. The United States' preoccupation with Commonwealth preferences was so intense that an administrative spokesman told Congress in 1947 that eliminating these preferences was almost a sine qua non of success at the Geneva Conference. Failure to achieve this result has been blamed as one of the causes for the failure of the United States to accept the Havana Charter, thus causing the ITO to fail to materialize.

(C) THE NONDISCRIMINATION OBLIGATION IN CUSTOMARY INTERNATIONAL LAW

From time to time it is argued that countries are obligated under customary international law to extend nondiscriminatory treatment to other nations. Prior to World War I, there was no such obligation. As summarized by Professor Georg Schwarzenberger, customary law of the time recognized that:[7] "Freedom of commerce is a purely optional pattern of international economic law. As distinct from freedom of trade, it is compatible with monopoly of trade, preferential treatment and equality of treatment for foreign commerce. * * * The most important [optional standards for equality of commerce] are the standards of most-favoured-nation, national, identical and equitable treatment."

In the 1950's, some East European scholars argued that the United Nations principle of state equality applied to international commercial relations, thereby prohibiting the discrimination to which these countries were then subject.[8] These scholars stressed the noncommercial aspects of nondiscrimination, such as the promotion of friendly relations between states. Western scholars generally rejected that view, express-

7. Georg Schwarzenberger, Equality and Discrimination in International Economic Law (I), 25 Yearbook of World Affairs 163, 164–65 (1971). Reprinted by permission of Stevens and Sons Ltd., London.

8. This debate is ably described in John N. Hazard, Editorial Comment: Commercial Discrimination and International Law, 52 Am.J.Intl.L. 495 (1958).

ing, inter alia, the difficulty of applying traditional international commercial considerations to state trading countries at all.[9]

In 1978, the United Nations International Law Commission concluded its work on 30 draft articles on most-favored-nation clauses and recommended to the U.N. General Assembly that U.N. member states should conclude a convention based on those articles.[10] The articles specifically provide that MFN treatment is treaty-based.[11]

SECTION 10.2   THE MOST FAVORED NATION OBLIGATION IN GATT

(A) INTRODUCTION

In this section we explore the MFN obligations in the General Agreement on Tariffs and Trade. We first consider the scope and meaning of GATT Article I, and then we examine the exceptions to the MFN obligation. The problems at the end illustrate the complexity and variety of legal questions which can arise in connection with MFN obligations.

The GATT MFN article is a fundamental and central obligation of international trade policy, but it is not without interpretive problems, as its drafters realized.[1] The most difficult issues concern the scope of the clause's coverage. In the first instance, the clause applies to customs duties and any other import or export charges, the methods of levying them, all rules and formalities in connection with importation or exportation, and internal taxation and sales regulations. Second, the clause requires that any advantage granted in respect of these matters in respect of one product must be granted to the like product from other parties.

Three definitional issues are obvious. First, what are rules and formalities in connection with importation and exportation? What are import or export charges? Second, what is an advantage? Third, what is a like product? We explore these issues in the following materials and in the problems at the end of this section.

In discussing the scope of the MFN requirement of Article I, it must be kept in mind that many other provisions of the General Agreement have nondiscrimination requirements similar to Article I. Thus, the fact that an action taken by a contracting party does not fall within the scope of Article I, does not mean that discrimination will be permitted. For example, as we discuss below, there are nondiscrimination requirements

9. See generally Martin Domke & John N. Hazard, State Trading and the Most–Favored–Nation Clause, 52 Am.J.Intl.L. 55 (1958).

10. See Report of the International Law Commission, supra note 1, at 16. For a description of an earlier UN project relevant to this issue, see Piet Hein Houben, Principles of International Law Concerning Friendly Relations and Co-operation Among States, 61 Am.J.Intl.L. 703, 722–23 (1967).

11. Report of the International Law Commission, supra note 1, at 25 (Art. 8).

1. See generally John H. Jackson, World Trade and the Law of GATT (1969), ch. 11, note particularly sec. 11.2 discussing the drafter's views.

in Articles XIII (quota administration) and XX (general exceptions). Other MFN or nondiscrimination clauses include: Article IV(b) (cinema films); Article III:7 (international mixing requirements); Article V:2, 5 & 6 (transit of goods); Article IX:1 (marks of origin); Article XVII:1 (state trading); and Article XVIII:20 (measures to assist economic development).[2] There are, however, provisions of the General Agreement that authorize general nonobservance of Article I, such as the customs union and free trade area exception of Article XXIV, and GATT practices that do likewise, such as the authorization of discrimination in tariff matters in favor of developing countries.

(B) THE SCOPE OF THE MFN OBLIGATION

The general scope of the MFN obligation was discussed by the Appellate Body in EUROPEAN COMMUNITIES—REGIME FOR THE IMPORTATION, SALE AND DISTRIBUTION OF BANANAS, WT/DS27/AB/R, adopted by the DSB on September 25, 1997. In that case the EC argued that there were two separate EC import regimes for bananas, the preferential regime for traditional ACP bananas and the *erga omnes* regime for all other imports of bananas. According to the EC, the non-discrimination obligations of Articles I:1, X:3(a) and XIII of the GATT 1994 and Article 1.3 of the Licensing Agreement, applied only within each of these separate regimes. In response, the Appellate Body stated:

> 190. The issue here is not whether the European Communities is correct in stating that two separate import regimes exist for bananas, but whether the existence of two, or more, separate EC import regimes is of any relevance for the application of the non-discrimination provisions of the GATT 1994 and the other Annex 1A agreements. The essence of the non-discrimination obligations is that like products should be treated equally, irrespective of their origin. As no participant disputes that all bananas are like products, the non-discrimination provisions apply to all imports of bananas, irrespective of whether and how a Member categorizes or subdivides these imports for administrative or other reasons. If, by choosing a different legal basis for imposing import restrictions, or by applying different tariff rates, a Member could avoid the application of the non-discrimination provisions to the imports of like products from different Members, the object and purpose of the non-discrimination provisions would be defeated. It would be very easy for a Member to circumvent the non-discrimination provisions of the GATT 1994 and the other Annex 1A agreements, if these provisions apply only within regulatory regimes established by that Member.

> 191. Non-discrimination obligations apply to all imports of like products, except when these obligations are specifically waived or are otherwise not applicable as a result of the operation of specific provisions of the GATT 1994, such as Article XXIV. In the present case, the non-discrimination obligations of the GATT 1994, specifi-

2. See id. at 255.

cally Articles I:1 and XIII, apply fully to all imported bananas irrespective of their origin, except to the extent that these obligations are waived. * * *

The difficult cases involving Article I:1 issues have tended to be of two types: First, there have been cases where the key issue is the likeness of the products at issue for tariff purposes. Second, there have been cases where the grant of favorable tariff treatment to products imported by specific importers is alleged to result in de facto discrimination against the like products from some other WTO members. In this section, we will examine examples of both types of cases.

(1) The Concept of Like Product for Tariff Purposes

JAPAN—TARIFF ON IMPORT OF SPRUCE–PINE–FIR (SPF) DIMENSION LUMBER

GATT Panel Report adopted July 19, 1989.
36th Supp. BISD 167 (1990).

[Canada complained that Japan's tariffs on certain lumber cut to specified dimensions ("dimension lumber") violated the most-favored-nation clause of Article I. Lumber of some species of coniferous trees was tariff-free; lumber of other species was dutiable at 8%.]

5.4   According to Canada, Article I:1 required Japan to accord also to SPF dimension lumber the advantage of the zero tariff granted by Japan * * * to planed and sanded lumber of "other" coniferous trees * * *.

5.5   The Panel noted that the tariff classification * * * had been established autonomously by Japan, with negotiation.

* * *

5.7   In view of analysing the factual situation submitted to it under its terms of reference, the Panel had first to consider the legal framework in which the Canadian complaint had been raised. In substance, Canada complains of the fact that Japan had arranged its tariff classification in such a way that a considerable part of Canadian exports of SPF dimension lumber to Japan was submitted to a customs duty of 8 per cent, whereas other comparable types of dimension lumber enjoy the advantage of a zero-tariff duty. The Panel considered it impossible to appreciate fully the Canadian complaint if it had not in a preliminary way clarified the bearing of some principles of the GATT-system in relation to tariff structure and tariff classification.

5.8   The Panel noted in this respect that the General Agreement left wide discretion to the contracting parties in relation to the structure of national tariffs and the classification of goods in the framework of such structure [citing the *Spanish Coffee* case, which follows this case]. The adoption of the Harmonized System, to which both Canada and Japan have adhered, had brought about a large measure of harmonization in the field of customs classification of goods, but this system did not entail any obligation as to the ultimate detail in the respective tariff classifications. Indeed, the nomenclature has been on purpose structured in such a way that it leaves room for further specifications.

5.9   The Panel was of the opinion that, under these conditions, a tariff classification going beyond the Harmonized System's structure is a legitimate means of adapting the tariff scheme to each contracting party's trade policy interests, comprising both its protection needs and its requirements for the purposes of tariff and trade negotiations. It must however be borne in mind that such differentiations may lend themselves to abuse, insofar as they may serve to circumscribe tariff advantages in such a way that they are conducive to discrimination among like products originating in different contracting parties. A contracting party prejudiced by such action may request therefore that its own exports be treated as "like products" in spite of the fact that they might find themselves excluded by the differentiations retained in the importing country's tariff.

5.10   Tariff differentiations being basically a legitimate means of trade policy, a contracting party which claims to be prejudiced by such practice bears the burden of establishing that such tariff arrangement has been diverted from its normal purpose so as to become a means of discrimination in international trade. Such complaints have to be examined in considering simultaneously the internal protection interest involved in a given tariff specification, as well as its actual or potential influence on the pattern of imports from different extraneous sources. The Canadian complaint and the defense of Japan will have to be viewed in the light of these requirements.

5.11   "Dimension lumber" as understood by Canada is defined by its presentation in a standard form of measurements, quality-grading and finishing. It appears from the information provided by Canada that this type of lumber is largely used in platform-house construction in Canada as well as in the United States and that it has found also widespread use in Japan, is testified by the existence of a Japanese technical standard known under the name of "JAS 600".

5.12   Japan objected to this claim on different grounds. Japan explained that dimension lumber was only one particular type of lumber among many other possible presentations and that house-building is only one of the many possible uses of this particular kind of lumber. From the legal point of view, Japan contended that the concept of "dimension lumber" is not used either in any internationally accepted tariff classification, or in the Japanese tariff classification. In accordance with the Harmonized System, [the Japanese tariff heading at issue] embraces all types of coniferous wood "sawn or chipped lengthwise ... exceeding 6mm". Apart from the thickness and the grade of finishing, customs treatment of lumber according to the Japanese Tariff was determined exclusively on the basis of a distinction established between certain biological genera or species. Dimension lumber was therefore not identified as a particular category in the framework of the Japanese tariff classification.

5.13 The Panel considered that the tariffs referred to by the General Agreement are, quite evidently, those of the individual contracting parties. This was inherent in the system of the Agreement and appeared also in the current practice of tariff negotiations, the subject matter of which were the national tariffs of the individual contracting parties. It followed that, if a claim of likeness was raised by a contracting party in relation to the tariff treatment of its goods on importation by some other contracting party, such a claim should be based on the classification of the latter, i.e. the importing country's tariff.

5.14 The Panel noted in this respect that "dimension lumber" as defined by Canada was a concept extraneous to the Japanese Tariff. It was a standard applied by the Canadian industry which appeared to have some equivalent in the United States and in Japan itself, but it could not be considered for that reason alone as a category for tariff classification purposes, nor did it belong to any internationally accepted customs classification. The Panel concluded therefore that reliance by Canada on the concept of dimension lumber was not an appropriate basis for establishing "likeness" of products under Article I:1 of the General Agreement.

5.15 At the same time, the Panel felt unable to examine the Canadian complaint in a broader context, as Canada had declared expressly that the issue before the Panel should not be confused by broadening the scope of the Panel's examination beyond "dimension lumber" to planed lumber generally. Canada's complaint was limited to the specific product known in North America, and also in Japan, as dimension lumber. Canada did not contend that different lumber species per se should be considered like products, regardless of the product-form they might take. Thus there appeared to be no basis for examining the issue raised by Canada in the general context of the Japanese tariff classification.

SPAIN—TARIFF TREATMENT OF UNROASTED COFFEE

GATT Panel Report adopted June 11, 1981.
28th Supp. BISD 102 (1982).

[Prior to 1979, Spain had classified all unroasted, non-decaffeinated coffee under one tariff heading. In 1979, Spain subdivided its classification for such coffee into five parts, to three of which a 7% duty was applied and to two of which no duty was applied. Brazil, which was the principal supplier of the type of coffee subjected to duty, complained in GATT and a panel was established to consider the dispute. The Spanish tariff was not bound under GATT Article II.]

4.6 The Panel examined all arguments that had been advanced during the proceedings for the justification of a different tariff treatment for various groups and types of unroasted coffee. It noted that these arguments mainly related to organoleptic differences resulting from geographical factors, cultivation methods, the processing of the beans, and the genetic factor. The Panel did not consider that such differences were sufficient reason to allow for a different tariff treatment. It pointed out that it was not unusual in the case of agricultural products that the taste and aroma of the end-product would differ because of one or several of the above-mentioned factors.

4.7   The Panel furthermore found relevant to its examination of the matter that unroasted coffee was mainly, if not exclusively, sold in the form of blends, combining various types of coffee, and that coffee in its end-use, was universally regarded as a well-defined and single product intended for drinking.

4.8   The Panel noted that no other contracting party applied its tariff régime in respect of unroasted, non-decaffeinated coffee in such a way that different types of coffee were subject to different tariff rates.

4.9   In the light of the foregoing, the Panel concluded that unroasted, non-decaffeinated coffee beans * * * should be considered as "like products" within the meaning of Article I:1.

4.10   The Panel further noted that Brazil exported to Spain mainly "unwashed Arabica" and also Robusta coffee which were both presently charged with higher duties than that applied to "mild" coffee. Since these were considered to be "like products", the Panel concluded that the tariff régime as presently applied by Spain was discriminatory vis-à-vis unroasted coffee originating in Brazil.

Notes and Questions

(1) The concept of like products is a crucial one for the MFN clause of Article I:1. The same or similar language appears in other GATT provisions as well. For example, as we will see in Chapter 12, the obligation to provide national treatment under Article III is limited in part to like products. Under the provisions of Article VI, contracting parties are permitted to impose antidumping or countervailing duties on dumped or subsidized imports that materially injure domestic producers of the like product. The Escape Clause of Article XIX allows parties to restrict imports when the imports seriously injure a domestic industry producing like or directly competitive products.

It is agreed that the term "like product" should not necessarily be interpreted the same way in each of these provisions, and we will consider cases in several chapters dealing with these definitions. But how should the definition of the term vary from clause to clause? Since both Articles I and III are basic antidiscrimination provisions at the heart of the General Agreement, it can be argued that the term should be construed broadly in those articles, so as to strike down discriminatory measures wherever possible. On the other hand, it can be argued that the term should be interpreted most narrowly in the case of Article VI, since that article establishes an exception to general GATT rules. However, the Article VI exception exists because it is felt by many that dumped and subsidized imports are unfair, suggesting a broader interpretation perhaps. We will revisit the definition of like product in later chapters when we discuss the foregoing provisions.

(2) Would you characterize the *SPF* interpretation of the term like product as narrow or broad? What about the interpretation given in the *Spanish Coffee* case? Are they consistent? If not, which do you think was the preferable interpretation? In that connection, are you persuaded, as the *Spanish Coffee* panel seemed to be, that coffee is coffee? Does the market recognize any differences in types of coffee?

(3) The MFN clause has been characterized as an antidiscrimination provision. Do you think that the discrimination challenged in *SPF* and *Spanish Coffee* was the type of discrimination that the clause was designed to combat? Or should countries be free to classify products as finely as they wish for tariff purposes? How does the GATT principle, discussed in Section 8.1, that import protection should be afforded principally by tariffs relate to this issue?

(4) Historically, one impact of MFN on tariff negotiations is to encourage the use of narrower and narrower classifications of goods, as negotiating countries try to limit the benefit of a tariff binding to the nation with whom it is negotiating, preventing "free-rider" benefits to third parties. Thus if A and B both export brandy to the United States, and the United States wishes to reciprocate concessions made by A but not B, then the fact (if true) that most of A's brandy is high priced and most of B's brandy is low priced, will suggest to the United States that its "concession" to A should be only on high priced brandy and not on all brandy. The classic example of this technique was the product description contained in the Swiss–German Treaty of 1904, reducing German tariffs on the importation of "large dapple mountain cattle or brown cattle reared at a spot at least 300 metres above sea level and having at least one month's grazing each year at a spot at least 800 metres above sea level."[3]

What limits are there (or should there be) on such attempts to distinguish what on the surface appear to be identical products (i.e. brandy or cows)? Must there be some structural difference in the products? Is it enough that identical products were produced under different conditions? Sold at different prices?

———————

What other arguments, not based on Article I, might be raised under Article XXIII to challenge a discriminatory tariff classification? Consider the following GATT panel report.

TREATMENT BY GERMANY OF IMPORTS OF SARDINES
GATT Panel Report adopted October 31, 1952.
1st Supp. BISD 53 (1953).

[In 1951, the Federal Republic of Germany began imposing an import duty of 14 per cent on preparations of clupea pilchardus as

———————

3. See Gerard Curzon, *Multilateral Commercial Diplomacy: The General Agreement on Tariffs and Trade and Its Impact* on National Commercial Policies and Techniques 60 & n. 1 (1965).

compared with a duty of 20 per cent for clupea harengus and 25 per cent for clupea sprattus. The products were also treated differently in respect of internal taxes and quantitative restrictions. Although the parties disputed whether these three products were "like products" for the purposes of Articles I and XIII, the panel did not decide that issue. It simply noted that the history of the negotiations suggested that the parties had not considered them to be like products. The panel did consider, however, whether in the absence of a violation of Articles I and XIII, Norway's anticipated benefits under the General Agreement had been nullified or impaired.]

16. The Panel * * * agreed that such impairment would exist if the action of the German Government, which resulted in upsetting the competitive relationship between preparations of clupea pilchardus and preparations of the other varieties of the clupeoid family could not reasonably have been anticipated by the Norwegian Government at the time it negotiated for tariff reductions on preparations of clupea sprattus and clupea harengus. The Panel concluded that the Government of Norway had reason to assume, during these negotiations that preparations of the type of clupeae in which they were interested would not be less favourably treated than other preparations of the same family and that this situation would not be modified by unilateral action of the German Government. In reaching this conclusion, the Panel was influenced in particular by the following circumstances:

(a) the products of the various varieties of clupeae are closely related and are considered by many interested parties as directly competitive;

(b) that both parties agreed that the question of the equality of treatment was discussed in the course of the Torquay negotiations; and

(c) although no conclusive evidence was produced as to the scope and tenor of the assurances or statements which may have been given or made in the course of these discussions, it is reasonable to assume that the Norwegian delegation in assessing the value of the concessions offered by Germany regarding preparations of clupeae and in offering counter concessions, had taken into account the advantages resulting from the continuation of the system of equality which had prevailed ever since 1925.

17. As the measures taken by the German Government have nullified the validity of the assumptions which governed the attitude of the Norwegian delegation and substantially reduced the value of the concessions obtained by Norway, the Panel found that the Norwegian Government is justified in claiming that it had suffered an impairment of a benefit accruing to it under the General Agreement.

18.   In the light of the considerations set out above, the Panel suggests to the CONTRACTING PARTIES that it would be appropriate for the CONTRACTING PARTIES to make a recommendation to Germany and Norway in accordance with the first sentence of paragraph 2 of Article XXIII. This recommendation should aim at restoring, as far as practicable, the competitive relationship which existed at the time when the Norwegian Government negotiated at Torquay and which that Government could reasonably expect to be continued.

Notes and Questions

(1)   Do think that there was adequate evidence to show that Norway met the requirements for establishing a "non-violation" claim under the Article XXIII? Non-violation claims are discussed generally in Section 7.4(A) supra.

(2)   The GATT MFN clause applies only "to any product," and thus does not apply to services or consular rights and business establishment. An important policy question faced in the Uruguay Round was whether and to what extent a GATT Article I-type MFN obligation should be included in an agreement on trade in services. See Chapter 19 infra. The same issue arose in respect of the TRIPS Agreement. See Chapter 20 infra.

(2) The Breadth of the MFN Obligation

CANADA—CERTAIN MEASURES AFFECTING THE AUTOMOTIVE INDUSTRY

WT/DS139 & 142/AB/R.
Appellate Body Report adopted June 19, 2000.

7.   The Canadian measure at issue in this appeal is duty-free treatment provided to imports of automobiles, buses and specified commercial vehicles ("motor vehicles") by certain manufacturers under the Customs Tariff, the Motor Vehicles Tariff Order, 1998 (the "MVTO 1998") and the Special Remission Orders (the "SROs"). The conditions under which eligibility for the import duty exemption is determined are set out in the MVTO 1998, the SROs and certain Letters of Undertaking (the "Letters").

8.   The MVTO 1998 has its origins in the Agreement Concerning Automotive Products Between the Government of Canada and the Government of the United States of America (the "Auto Pact"), which was implemented domestically in Canada [in 1965].

9.   Under the MVTO 1998, the import duty exemption is available to manufacturers of motor vehicles on imports "from any country entitled to the Most–Favoured–Nation Tariff", if the manufacturer meets the following three conditions: (1) it must have produced in Canada, during the designated "base year", motor vehicles of the class imported; (2) the ratio of the net sales value of the vehicles *produced in Canada* to the net sales value of all vehicles of that class *sold* for consumption *in Canada* in the period of importation must be "equal to or higher than" the ratio in the "base year", and the ratio shall not in

any case be lower than 75:100 (the "ratio requirements"); and (3) the amount of Canadian value added in the manufacturer's local production of motor vehicles must be "equal to or greater than" the amount of Canadian value added in the local production of motor vehicles of that class during the "base year" (the "CVA requirements").

10.   The Panel found that, as a matter of fact, the average ratio requirements applicable to the MVTO 1998 beneficiaries are "as a general rule" 95:100 for automobiles, and "at least" 75:100 for buses and specified commercial vehicles.

11.   The MVTO 1998 states that the CVA used by a particular manufacturer shall be calculated based on the "aggregate" of certain listed costs of production, which are, broadly speaking:

— the cost of parts produced in Canada and of materials of Canadian origin that are incorporated in the motor vehicles;

— transportation costs;

— labour costs incurred in Canada;

— manufacturing overhead expenses incurred in Canada;

— general and administrative expenses incurred in Canada that are attributable to the production of motor vehicles;

— depreciation in respect of machinery and permanent plant equipment located in Canada that is attributable to the production of motor vehicles; and

— a capital cost allowance for land and buildings in Canada that are used in the production of motor vehicles.

12.   Through the SROs, Canada has also designated certain other companies, in addition to those qualifying under the MVTO 1998, as eligible to import motor vehicles duty-free. Canada promulgated the SROs under the authority of the Financial Administration Act for certain companies that had not met the original conditions of the MVTO 1965. The SROs entitle motor vehicles imported by these companies to receive the import duty exemption as long as they meet certain designated conditions. Specifically, the SROs provide for the remission of duties on imports of motor vehicles where conditions relating to certain specified production-to-sales ratio requirements and CVA requirements are fulfilled.

13.   With respect to the actual ratio and CVA requirements under the SROs, each SRO sets out specific ratio and CVA requirements to be met by the company receiving the SRO. For ratio requirements, the SROs issued before 1977 set the production-to-sales ratios at 75:100. Since then, almost all SROs have set ratios at 100:100. For CVA, requirements under the SROs range from 40 to 60 per cent, as follows.

14.   In accordance with its obligations under the CUSFTA [Canada–United States Free Trade Agreement], since 1989, Canada has not designated any additional manufacturers to be eligible for the import duty exemption under the MVTO 1998, nor has Canada promulgated any

new SROs. Also, the MVTO 1998 specifically excludes vehicles imported by a manufacturer which did not qualify before 1 January 1988. Thus, the list of manufacturers eligible for the import duty exemption is closed.

* * *

69.   On appeal, the issue before us is whether the import duty exemption accorded by this measure is consistent with Canada's obligations under Article I:1 of the GATT 1994. We are confronted with the daunting task of interpreting certain aspects of the "most-favoured-nation" ("MFN") principle that has long been a cornerstone of the GATT and is one of the pillars of the WTO trading system.

70.   In examining the measure in issue, we note that the import duty exemption is afforded by Canada to imports of some, but not all, motor vehicles. We observe, first of all, that the Canadian Customs Tariff provides that a motor vehicle normally enters Canada at an MFN tariff rate of 6.1 per cent. This is also the bound *ad valorem* rate in Canada's WTO Schedule of Concessions. The MVTO 1998 and the SROs modify this rate by providing the import duty exemption for motor vehicles imported by certain manufacturers meeting certain ratio requirements and CVA requirements. The MVTO 1998 accords the import duty exemption in the form of a "reduced rate of customs duty", established in the amended Canadian Customs Tariff as "free". The SROs accord the import duty exemption in the form of a full duty "remission".

71.   Although the measure on its face imposes no formal restriction on the *origin* of the imported motor vehicle, the Panel found that, in practice, major automotive firms in Canada import only their own make of motor vehicle and those of related companies. Thus, according to the Panel,

> General Motors in Canada imports only GM motor vehicles and those of its affiliates; Ford in Canada imports only Ford motor vehicles and those of its affiliates; the same is true of Chrysler and of Volvo. These four companies all have qualified as beneficiaries of the import duty exemption. In contrast, other motor vehicle companies in Canada, such as Toyota, Nissan, Honda, Mazda, Subaru, Hyundai, Volkswagen and BMW, all of which also import motor vehicles only from related companies, do not benefit from the import duty exemption.

72.   Therefore, the Panel considered that, in practice, a motor vehicle imported into Canada is granted the "advantage" of the import duty exemption only if it originates in one of a small number of countries in which an exporter of motor vehicles is affiliated with a manufacturer/importer in Canada that has been designated as eligible to import motor vehicles duty-free under the MVTO 1998 or under an SRO.

73.   Since 1989, no manufacturer not already benefiting from the import duty exemption on motor vehicles has been able to qualify under the MVTO 1998 or under an SRO. The list of manufacturers eligible for

the import duty exemption was closed by Canada in 1989 in fulfilment of Canada's obligations under the CUSFTA.

74. Thus, in sum, while the Canadian Customs Tariff normally allows a motor vehicle to enter Canada at the MFN duty rate of 6.1 per cent, the same motor vehicle has the "advantage" of entering Canada duty-free when imported by a designated manufacturer under the MVTO 1998 or under the SROs.

75. In determining whether this measure is consistent with Article I:1 of the GATT 1994, we begin our analysis, as always, by examining the words of the treaty. Article I:1 states, in pertinent part:

> With respect to customs duties and charges of any kind imposed on or in connection with importation or exportation ... *any* advantage, favour, privilege or immunity granted by any Member to any product originating in or destined for any other country shall be accorded *immediately and unconditionally* to the like product originating in or destined for the territories of *all other Members*. (emphasis added)

76. The applicability of certain elements of Article I:1 is not in dispute in this case. First, the parties do not dispute that the import duty exemption is an "advantage, favour, privilege or immunity granted by any Member to any product". Second, it is not disputed that some, but not all, motor vehicles imported from certain Members are accorded the import duty exemption, while some, but not all, like motor vehicles imported from certain other Members are not. Third, the Panel's interpretation that the term "unconditionally" refers to advantages conditioned on the "situation or conduct" of exporting countries has not been appealed.

77. One main issue remains in dispute: has the import duty exemption, accorded by the measure to motor vehicles originating in some countries, in which affiliates of certain designated manufacturers under the measure are present, also been accorded to like motor vehicles from all other Members, in accordance with Article I:1 of the GATT 1994?

78. In approaching this question, we observe first that the words of Article I:1 do not restrict its scope only to cases in which the failure to accord an "advantage" to like products of all other Members appears on the face of the measure, or can be demonstrated on the basis of the words of the measure. Neither the words *"de jure"* nor *"de facto"* appear in Article I:1. Nevertheless, we observe that Article I:1 does not cover only "in law", or *de jure*, discrimination. As several GATT panel reports confirmed, Article I:1 covers also "in fact", or *de facto*, discrimination.[4] Like the Panel, we cannot accept Canada's argument that

---

4. [original note 70] We note, though, that the measures examined in those reports differed from the measure in this case. Two of those reports dealt with "like" product issues: *Spain–Tariff Treatment of Unroasted Coffee; Japan–Tariff on Imports* *of Spruce, Pine, Fir (SPF) Dimension Lumber*. In this case, as we have noted, there is no dispute that the motor vehicles subject to the import duty exemption are "like" products. Furthermore, two other reports dealt with measures which, on their face,

Article I:1 does not apply to measures which, on their face, are "origin-neutral".

79.   We note next that Article I:1 requires that *"any advantage, favour, privilege or immunity granted by any Member to any product* originating in or destined for any other country shall be accorded immediately and unconditionally to the like product originating in or destined for the territories of *all other Members."* (emphasis added) The words of Article I:1 refer not to some advantages granted "with respect to" the subjects that fall within the defined scope of the Article, but to *"any advantage"*; not to *some* products, but to *"any product"*; and not to like products from some other Members, but to like products originating in or destined for *"all other"* Members.

80.   We note also the Panel's conclusion that, in practice, a motor vehicle imported into Canada is granted the "advantage" of the import duty exemption only if it originates in one of a small number of countries in which an exporter of motor vehicles is affiliated with a manufacturer/importer in Canada that has been designated as eligible to import motor vehicles duty-free under the MVTO 1998 or under an SRO.

81.   Thus, from both the text of the measure and the Panel's conclusions about the practical operation of the measure, it is apparent to us that "[w]ith respect to customs duties ... imposed on or in connection with importation ...," Canada has granted an "advantage" to some products from some Members that Canada has not "accorded immediately and unconditionally" to "like" products "originating in or destined for the territories of *all other Members."* (emphasis added) And this, we conclude, is not consistent with Canada's obligations under Article I:1 of the GATT 1994.

82.   The context of Article I:1 within the GATT 1994 supports this conclusion. Apart from Article I:1, several "MFN-type" clauses dealing with varied matters are contained in the GATT 1994. The very existence of these other clauses demonstrates the pervasive character of the MFN principle of non-discrimination.

83.   The drafters also wrote various exceptions to the MFN principle into the GATT 1947 which remain in the GATT 1994. Canada invoked one such exception before the Panel, relating to customs unions and free trade areas under Article XXIV. This justification was rejected by the Panel, and the Panel's findings on Article XXIV were not appealed by Canada. Canada has invoked no other provision of the GATT 1994, or of any other covered agreement, that would justify the inconsistency of the import duty exemption with Article I:1 of the GATT 1994.

discriminated on a strict "origin" basis, so that, at any given time, either every product, or no product, of a particular origin was accorded an advantage. See panel report, *Belgian Family Allowances*, G/32, adopted 7 November 1952, BISD 1S/59; panel report, *European Economic Community–Imports of Beef from Canada*, L/5099, adopted 10 March 1981, BISD 28S/92. In this case, motor vehicles imported into Canada are not disadvantaged in that same sense.

84. The object and purpose of Article I:1 supports our interpretation. That object and purpose is to prohibit discrimination among like products originating in or destined for different countries. The prohibition of discrimination in Article I:1 also serves as an incentive for concessions, negotiated reciprocally, to be extended to all other Members on an MFN basis.

85. The measure maintained by Canada accords the import duty exemption to certain motor vehicles entering Canada from certain countries. These privileged motor vehicles are imported by a limited number of designated manufacturers who are required to meet certain performance conditions. In practice, this measure does not accord the same import duty exemption immediately and unconditionally to like motor vehicles of *all* other Members, as required under Article I:1 of the GATT 1994. The advantage of the import duty exemption is accorded to some motor vehicles originating in certain countries without being accorded to like motor vehicles from *all* other Members. Accordingly, we find that this measure is not consistent with Canada's obligations under Article I:1 of the GATT 1994.

86. We, therefore, uphold the Panel's conclusion that Canada acts inconsistently with Article I:1 of the GATT 1994 by according the advantage of the import duty exemption to motor vehicles originating in certain countries, pursuant to the MVTO 1998 and the SROs, which advantage is not accorded immediately and unconditionally to like products originating in the territories of all other WTO Members.

Notes and Questions

(1) INDONESIA—CERTAIN MEASURES AFFECTING THE AUTOMOTIVE INDUSTRY, WT/DS54, 55, 59 & 64/R, adopted by the DSB on July 23, 1998 (not appealed), involved a challenge by Japan, the EC and the US to certain exemptions from Indonesian customs duties and internal taxes, which were alleged to be conditional and available *de facto* only to imports of motor vehicles from Korea but not to imports of like products from other WTO Members. The Indonesian measure at issue benefited imports by PT PTN, a private Indonesian company, of certain cars ("National Cars") made for it by Kia, a Korean company. The panel rejected Indonesia's argument that a private-sector choice, not government direction, was the reason why there were imports from Korea and that such a private choice was not within the scope of Article I. In the view of the panel:

14.143 * * * The GATT case law is clear to the effect that any such advantage (here tax and customs duty benefits) cannot be made conditional on any criteria that is not related to the imported product itself. [The panel cited *Belgian Family Allowances*, 1st Supp. BISD 59 (Panel report adopted November 7, 1952), involving a Belgian charge levied on purchases by public authorities that was applicable depending on whether products originated in a country that had a system of family allowances meeting certain criteria].

* * *

14.145 Indeed, it appears that the design and structure of the [challenged Indonesian measure] is such as to allow situations where another Member's like product to a National Car imported by PT PTN from Korea will be subject to much higher duties and sales taxes than those imposed on such National Cars. * * * The distinction as to whether one product is subject to 0% duty and the other one is subject to 200% duty * * * depends on whether or not PT TPN had made a "deal" with that exporting company to produce that National Car, and is covered by the authorization of June 1996 with specifications that correspond to those of the Kia car produced only in Korea. In the GATT/WTO, the right of Members cannot be made dependent upon, conditional on or even affected by, any private contractual obligations in place. The existence of these conditions is inconsistent with the provisions of Article I:1 which provides that tax and customs duty benefits accorded to products of one Member (here on Korean products) be accorded to imported like products from other Members "immediately and unconditionally".

The finding of a violation by the panel in *Indonesia–Autos* does not seem to depend on a showing of *de facto* discrimination, but rather only on the fact that some autos from Korea received more favorable tariff treatment than like autos from the complainants. The panel in *Canada–Autos* rejected this broad interpretation of Article I. In its view, the use of the word "unconditionally" in Article I:1 did not mean that the availability of a tariff rate could not be made subject to conditions, but rather that such conditions could not result in *de facto* discrimination. WT/DS139 & 142/R, paras. 10.18–10.30. The Appellate Body report does not explicitly address this issue. In your view, which panel report correctly interprets Article I:1? Could Article XVII have been invoked in these cases? The subsidy issues in the *Indonesia Autos* case are examined in Section 18.2(E) infra.

(2) How narrowly should like products be defined in a case like *Canada–Autos*? In United States—Denial of Most–Favored–Nation Treatment as to Non-rubber Footwear From Brazil, 39th Supp. BISD 128 (1993), adopted June 19, 1992, Brazil complained that the procedures under which US countervailing duties were revoked (i.e., terminated) violated the most-favored-nation clause of Article I. It claimed that the US applied different rules to goods imported under the US Generalized System of Preferences (GSP) than were applied to Brazilian imports. In its examination, the panel noted that the GSP products to which the allegedly more favorable procedures had actually been applied (industrial fasteners, industrial lime, automotive glass) were not like the product to which the less favorable procedures had been applied in the case of Brazil (non-rubber footwear). However, the panel noted that Brazil not only claimed that the application of these two procedures in concrete cases was inconsistent with Article I:1 of the General Agreement but also that the US rules themselves were inconsistent with that provision. As such, it noted that the products to which one rule accords advantages were therefore in principle the same products to which the other rule denies the advantages. Was the panel's application of "like product" consistent with those of the prior cases in this section?

(3) Because Article I's MFN obligation applies to internal taxes and sales regulations subject to Article III's national treatment obligation, the scope of the MFN obligation depends in part on the scope of Article III.

(C) GATT AND THE MFN EXCEPTIONS

The most significant GATT exceptions to MFN are found in two Articles related in one way or another to the issue of preferential trade arrangements. These are Article I:2 dealing with tariff preferences in force when the General Agreement was drafted and Article XXIV which allows for the formation of customs unions and free trade areas.

Article I:2 has become less significant over the years as the number of colonies declined drastically and the related colonial preferences largely disappeared. In practical terms, however, these preferences have effectively been replaced and vastly expanded under the so-called Generalized System of Preferences (GSP). This system was instituted under a 10 year GATT waiver obtained in 1971 by various industrial countries for the benefit of developing countries. Since the Tokyo Round, the GSP preferences have been maintained under the authority of the so-called Enabling Clause, which was adopted by the Contracting Parties at the conclusion of the Tokyo Round. See Decision of the Contracting Parties of Nov. 28, 1979, on Differential and More Favourable Treatment, Reciprocity and Fuller Participation of Developing Countries, 26th Supp. BISD 203 (1980). There is considerable controversy over the adequacy and desirability of developing country preferences. We will explore these issues in detail in Chapter 24.

Traditionally there has been an exception to MFN obligations for border traffic and limited regional arrangements, and so when GATT was drafted it was natural to include such an exception in GATT Article XXIV. It was generally thought that a customs union or free trade area, whereby associated countries eliminated barriers on each other's trade, would be a further step towards general trade liberalization and therefore should be permitted, at least as long as the preferential arrangement did not harm the trade of nonmembers. As we will see in Chapter 11, the economic desirability of such arrangements is now questioned by some. We will also examine in Chapter 11 the detailed conditions that customs unions and free trade areas must meet under Article XXIV.

There are also a few, less important exceptions to the General Agreement's preference for nondiscriminatory treatment. For example, Article VI allows imposition of countervailing and antidumping duties on subsidized exports or imports sold at less than domestic prices, resulting in injury to domestic industries. Article XIV permits discrimination in certain cases in the application of quotas justified on balance of payments grounds. Article XIX permits a country affected by another country's invocation of the Escape Clause to suspend concessions it had made to that country. Under Article XXI, deviations from MFN are permitted for national security reasons. Paragraph 2 of Article XXIII allows a country to be authorized to suspend concessions made to another contracting party that has nullified or impaired its benefits under the General Agreement.

(D) PROBLEMS

A, B and C are nations which are members of the WTO. X, Y and Z are nations which do not belong to the WTO, but A and X have a bilateral agreement in which each extends MFN to the other as to tariff duties.

(1) A charges a 10% tariff on bicycles from B. C, X and Y also export bicycles to A; what rate are they entitled to?

(2) X charges a 5% tariff on clock radios from Y. What rate are such products from A, B and Z entitled to when imported into X?

(3) A's GATT binding for toy clocks is 10%. Its custom bureau currently charges 5% tariff on toy clocks from Y. What rate should be applied by A to toy clocks from B, C and X?

(4) A's GATT binding for FM radios is 5%, but A's customs bureau is charging a 10% tariff pursuant to a statute just passed by its Parliament. What recourse do importers of FM radios from B, X or Y have against A? What procedures can be followed?

(5) A charges a tariff of 5% on motorcycle imports, and in addition imposes a quota on motorcycles from B, while prohibiting motorcycle imports from C, X and Y altogether. What rights have B, C, X and Y?

(6) A charges a 5% tariff on imports of autos which weigh less than 2000 pounds; a 20% tariff on other autos. B and X produce only autos weighing less than 2000 pounds; C and Y produce only autos heavier than that. What are the rights of C and Y?

(7) A charges a 5% tariff on imports of autos which operate on less than 20 miles per gallon; a 20% tariff on the rest. B and X autos use less than 20 miles per gallon; C and Y autos more. What are the rights of C and Y?

(8) A charges a 5% tariff on imports of autos without shatter-proof glass; but 20% for autos equipped with shatter-proof glass. A has a large domestic industry which produces shatter-proof glass, and so does B. B sells such glass to its own auto makers and to those of X, both of whom export autos to A. Do B and X have a valid complaint?

(9) A charges a 5% tariff on automobiles from countries with average auto industry wage rates over $4.00 per hour; 20% for autos from other countries. B and X auto wage rates are under $4.00 per hour, C and Y rates are over that amount. Do B and X have a valid complaint?

(10) A charges a 5% tariff on textile imports from countries with a per capita gross national product less than $1000 per year; a 20% tariff on the rest. C and Z are textile exporting countries with per capita annual GNP less than $1000. Do B, X and Y have any recourse?

(11) B imports hand-crafted baskets from Y in bulk lots of 1000, repackages them individually, and exports them to A. A's GATT binding on baskets is 10% but it charges a 30% tariff on these basket imports. Can B complain?

(12) A normally charges 5%, its GATT binding, on imports of cooking pans. Under a national countervailing duty law, its officials have determined that B's grants of low interest "development loans" to the cooking pan industry, for encouraging exports, are "subsidies" and consequently A imposes a countervailing duty of another 10% on pots and pans produced in B. C, X and Y have similar programs of government export encouraging loans and their cooking pan industries, as well as their basket weaving industries, benefit. However, A does not impose countervailing duties on either cooking pans or baskets from C, X or Y. Does B have a valid complaint?

(13) B's countervailing duty law exempts all imports from countries which have per capita annual GNP of less than $1000. Does A or Y have a valid complaint?

(14) Suppose B's countervailing duty law exemption were not explicit, but merely a "practice" of its officials?

(15) C, a developing country, exports bauxite (for aluminum production). It imposes: a) a ban on bauxite exports to A; b) a 50% export tax on exports of bauxite to X and Y, but not Z or B. What rights do A, X and Y have?

SECTION 10.3   THE MOST FAVORED NATION OBLIGATION IN UNITED STATES LAW

(A) THE TRADE ACT OF 1974

United States law specifies MFN treatment for most imports. Section 126(a) of the Trade Act of 1974 requires (unless otherwise provided by law) "any duty or other import restriction or duty-free treatment proclaimed in carrying out any trade agreement under this [Act] shall apply to products of all foreign countries, whether imported directly or indirectly."[1] For tariff purposes, the only countries that did not receive such treatment as of January 2008 were Cuba and North Korea. U.S. Harmonized Tariff Schedule (2008), General Note 3(b).

Today, the major exceptions to the above rule are (i) the Generalized System of Preferences for developing countries, created by title V of the 1974 Act and described in Chapter 24; (ii) similar, but more extensive, preferences for African, Caribbean and Andean countries under specific legislation described in Chapter 24; and (iii) the various US free trade agreements described in Section 11.3.

---

1.   19 U.S.C.A. sec. 2136. By its terms, section 126(a) only applied to duties or restrictions proclaimed in implementing the Tokyo Round agreements, which includes most of those now in force, but its effect has been extended to apply to the results of the Uruguay Round. Omnibus Trade and Competitiveness Act of 1988, sec. 1105(a)(codified at 19 U.S.C.A. sec. 2904). This policy predates the 1974 Act. For example, Section 251 of the 1962 Trade Expansion Act required that trade agreements concessions negotiated with one country be automatically extended to all others—whether or not an international commitment such as the GATT would entitle others to such concessions—so long as the recipient did not discriminate against US trade. Pub.L.No. 87–794, 76 Stat. 872 (1962).

Several other provisions of the 1974 Act permit departures from MFN treatment, most notably the balance-of-payments (BOP) authority (Section 122(a)(2)) and the revised retaliatory authority (originally Sections 301–302, now Sections 301–310).

(B) U.S. IMPLEMENTATION OF THE TOKYO AND URUGUAY ROUND AGREEMENTS AND MFN

As has been discussed previously, the Tokyo Round resulted in a whole series of side agreements on various trade issues. Generally, these agreements had procedural and governance provisions that gave a voice only to signatories. In that sense, even if the tangible benefits of the agreements accrued to all GATT members because of GATT's MFN requirements, nonsignatory members of GATT were treated differently. Much more significantly, two of the side agreements—the Subsidies Code and the Government Procurement Code—only obligated the parties thereto to apply the provisions of the Code to other parties.[2]

In implementing the Subsidies Code and the Government Procurement Code, as well as the Standards Code,[3] the US Trade Agreements Act of 1979 provided that the benefits of each of the three codes were to be available only to other parties of the code in question, and, in the case of the Subsidies Code, only to parties who had assumed obligations to the United States which were substantially equivalent to US obligations under the Code, which excluded some developing country parties to the Code.[4]

Notes and Questions

(1) An interesting question is whether the GATT MFN obligations could have been interpreted to require the United States to apply the rules of the Subsidies Code to nonsignatories who were GATT members and to signatories that the United States believed had not fully implemented the Code. Nonapplication by the United States would have meant that a Code party would not have been entitled to an injury determination before countervailing duties were imposed on its exports to the US. Not requiring such a determination would have made it far more likely that duties would be imposed. In the early 1980's, the United States refused to apply the Code to India on the grounds that even though India was a Code signatory, it had not undertaken the same obligations that the US had undertaken in the Code. India claimed that the United States had violated its basic obligations under Article I of GATT and invoked the GATT dispute settlement procedures. India later dropped its complaint when the United States announced that it would apply the Code to India.[5] Would India have won if its dispute

---

2. Agreement on Interpretation and Implementation of Article VI, XVI and XXIII, art. 1, GATT, 26th Supp. BISD 56, 57 (1980); Agreement on Government Procurement, art. II(1), GATT, 26th Supp. BISD 33, 35 (1980).

3. Agreement on Technical Barriers to Trade, GATT, 26th Supp. BISD 8 (1980).

4. Trade Agreements Act of 1979, secs. 101, 301, 422, 19 U.S.C.A. secs. 1671(a), 2511, 2552.

5. 46 Fed.Reg. 48391 (1981). An Indian representative at GATT stated to the Committee on Subsidies that Indian legislation did not contain provisions in conflict with the Subsidies Code and that it would com-

with the United States had been considered by a GATT panel? The issue in the Indian case was complicated by the fact that the old US countervailing duty law benefited from the existing legislation exception of the Protocol of Provisional Application.

(2) Under the WTO, parties that join the WTO must adhere to all of the various annexed agreements, with the exception of those dealing with government procurement and civil aircraft. As a result, the MFN problems presented by the Tokyo Round side agreements, all of which had limited memberships, did not arise in implementation of the Uruguay Round results. These problems could resurface, however, if the conclusion of the Doha negotiations results in new plurilateral agreements.

(3) For the most part, the US still limits the benefits of the Government Procurement Agreement to other parties to that agreement.[6] Does that practice violate Article I of GATT? Consider GATT Articles III:8 and XVII:1 in framing an answer. Could an MFN clause in a typical FCN agreement be invoked to claim MFN treatment in government procurement matters? For example, the U.S.-German Friendship, Commerce and Navigation Treaty of October 29, 1954, 7 U.S.T. 1839, TIAS 3593, provides in Article XVII:2 that

> [e]ach party shall accord to the nationals, companies and commerce of the other Party fair and equitable treatment, as compared with that accorded to the nationals, companies and commerce of any third country, with respect to: (a) the governmental purchase of supplies; (b) the awarding of concessions and other government contracts * * *.

Could the United States discriminate against Germany in the area of government procurement? Would the "fair and equitable" language allow such discrimination so long as Germany had not made concessions on government procurement similar to those made by the favored country? In 1993, Germany took the position, over EU protests, that this clause prohibited Germany from discriminating against US companies in certain procurement matters, even though there was an EC directive requiring such discrimination.[7]

(C) THE UNITED STATES AND COMMUNIST COUNTRIES

During the Cold War, the United States restricted its trade with Communist countries. In the case of exports, those countries were the main target of US export controls based on national security concerns and a frequent target of controls based on general foreign policy reasons. In the case of imports, the United States generally did not provide MFN treatment to imports from Communist countries, did not allow them to benefit from the US GSP program, and enacted a number of statutes (e.g., the antidumping laws and section 406 of the 1974 Trade Act) that provided means to restrict Communist country imports on the basis of more easily met standards than applicable to imports in general. This disparate treatment is becoming less significant as the United States

ply with the Code if it took countervailing action. GATT, 28th Supp. BISD 28 (1982). See also GATT, 29th Supp. BISD 113 (1983) (report of settlement).

6. Trade Agreements Act of 1979, sec. 301, 19 U.S.C.A. sec. 2511(b).

7. 10 BNA Intl. Trade Rptr. 974 (1993).

normalizes its relations with ex-Communist countries. Accordingly, in this section we will describe only briefly the history and current status of US controls on imports from Communist countries.

The United States extended most-favored-nation treatment to the Soviet Union in 1937.[8] However, in 1951 Congress directed that MFN treatment be withdrawn from all countries controlled or dominated by the World Communist movement.[9] In 1972, the United States entered into a trade agreement with the Soviet Union, which provided that Soviet exports to the United States were to receive MFN treatment.[10] The President proposed approval of the MFN agreement as part of the general trade bill introduced in 1973, which eventually was adopted as the Trade Act of 1974. The provisions dealing with MFN and Communist countries were the most controversial in the proposed legislation. The controversy centered on the extent to which the United States should use the prospect of granting MFN treatment to the Soviet Union as a lever to extract Soviet policy changes in other areas, and, in particular, the expansion of emigration opportunities for Soviet citizens.

As enacted, title IV of the Trade Act of 1974—known as the Jackson–Vanik provision, after its sponsors—(i) required that the President continue to deny MFN treatment to those countries not then receiving it,[11] (ii) established a procedure by which MFN treatment could be granted to such countries in the future,[12] and (iii) established a special procedure for limiting imports from Communist countries if the imports caused market disruption.[13] The Trade Act constituted a congressional rejection of granting MFN treatment to the Soviet Union and the 1972 trade agreement never came into effect.

The 1974 Trade Act tied the President's power to enter into commercial agreements with a Communist country and to grant MFN treatment to such country to the emigration rules of that country. The Act also provided, however, that the President could annually waive the free-emigration rule in certain circumstances. To prevent presidential misuse of the waiver power, the Act provided for the possibility of congressional disapproval of waivers granted by the President.

For the next twenty years, the result of these waiver procedures and other trade measures taken for foreign policy reasons was an ever changing US policy toward these countries. While most ex-Communist countries now receive MFN treatment, some do not have permanent MFN status and are still subject to the Jackson–Vanik provisions. In the case of China, the annual process was particularly controversial, although MFN status has continued in effect since first extended in 1979.

8. Presidential Proclamation, 50 Stat. 1619 (1937).

9. Pub.L.No. 49, Ch. 139, sec. 5, 65 Stat. 73 (1951).

10. U.S.-U.S.S.R. Agreement Regarding Trade, with annexes and exchange of letters; signed at Washington, 18 Oct. 1972. For reasons made clear in the text of this section, this agreement failed to enter into force.

11. Trade Act of 1974, sec. 401; 19 U.S.C.A. sec. 2431.

12. Trade Act of 1974, secs. 402–405; 19 U.S.C.A. secs. 2432–35.

13. Trade Act of 1974, sec. 406; 19 U.S.C.A. sec. 2436.

Indeed, the term "most-favored-nation treatment" was changed to "normal trade relations", to prevent critics from claiming that China was getting particularly favorable treatment as a most favored nation.[14] In 2000, Congress approved permanent normal trade relations status for China, conditional on its accession to the WTO.[15]

Notes and Questions

(1) Why is MFN treatment important? Without MFN treatment, what chance do a country's exports have in the US market?

(2) If you were advising a business client about the long term stability of trade relations between the United States and any of the countries subject to the annual waiver process, what would you advise?

(3) The general wisdom of linking trade policy to other policies, such as human rights, worker rights or arms sales, is discussed in Chapter 21.

---

14. Pub. L. 105–201, sec. 5003(b)(2), July 22, 1998, 112 Stat. 685, 789, substituted "normal trade relations" for "most-favored-nation treatment" wherever appearing in Section 402 of the 1974 Trade Act.

15. Pub. L. 106–286, October 10, 2000, 114 Stat. 880.

Chapter 11

FREE TRADE AREAS AND
CUSTOMS UNIONS

SECTION 11.1 INTRODUCTION

(A) THE GROWTH OF PREFERENTIAL TRADE ARRANGE-
MENTS

In Chapter 10, we introduced the most favored nation concept and its important exceptions. The most important of all has proven to be the Article XXIV exception for customs unions and free trade areas, so important that we treat it in a separate chapter. Many of these arrangements are regional in scope, but increasingly, preferential trading arrangements (PTAs) are being created between far flung trading partners (e.g., the United States and Israel).

Arrangements that reduce or eliminate trade barriers between two or more political units while maintaining barriers against imports from outside regions date back to the 19th century.[1] Customs unions, as they were generally called, were established by means of treaties or agreements between and among the various states of the German, Austrian and British empires. In the first half of the 20th century, before the establishment of GATT, there were customs unions between European, African and South American states. Since the formation of GATT, PTAs have continued to multiply and flourish.

Western Europe has the European Union (EU), formerly known as the European Economic Community (EEC), the European Free Trade Area (EFTA) and the European Economic Area (EEA). See Section 4.2 supra. The United States has entered numerous free trade agreements in recent years, the most important being the North American Free Trade Agreement (NAFTA) with Canada and Mexico. See Section 11.4 for more information on US participation in PTAs. In South America, MERCO-SUR and the Andean Community span many of the major trading nations, with a prospect of a potential union between them to create the Union of South American Nations. The Association of Southeast Asian Nations (ASEAN) includes most of the Southeast Asian economies.

---

1. See J. Viner, The Customs Union Issue (1950).

Other arrangements abound. It also bears noting that many nations are parties to multiple PTAs—the United States, Chile and Mexico are notable examples.

(B) THE CONSEQUENCES OF PREFERENTIAL TRADE ARRANGEMENTS

The trend toward regional integration has uncertain consequences for the world trading system. Economists divide the consequences of preferential trading arrangements into two categories—"trade creation" and "trade diversion."[2] Trade creation refers to the expansion of trade with efficient suppliers inside the customs union or free trade area. Trade diversion refers to a shift in trade from efficient suppliers outside the PTA to inefficient suppliers inside it, driven by the desire to take advantage of trade preferences.

For example, suppose that prior to NAFTA, the United States imports significant quantities of winter vegetables from Mexico because Mexico produces them efficiently and transport costs are low. After NAFTA, tariffs on these goods fall, and imports rise. The usual argument for gains from trade should apply, and both countries will benefit from this liberalization of trade—trade creation. By contrast, suppose that prior to NAFTA, the United States imports large quantities of textile products from India. And suppose that after NAFTA, investors establish textile factories in Mexico to produce for the US market solely because Mexico enjoys preferential access to the United States and is able to outcompete India for that reason. From the global perspective, specialization on the basis of comparative advantage has now been distorted—trade diversion. The consequences are particularly severe from India's perspective, as its exports contract due to the diversion of textile trade to Mexico. Even the United States may be worse off because of the diversion of trade. US consumers gain to be sure, but the US government has lost tariff revenue on imports from India, and it is possible that the loss in tariff revenue may exceed the gains to consumers. Some further considerations are developed in the following excerpts.

PAUL R. KRUGMAN, IS BILATERALISM BAD?[3]

As a general source of concern, however, the risk of trade diversion seems a weak point. It shows that under certain circumstances a

---

2. See generally J. Meade, The Theory of Customs Unions (1955); T. Scitovsky, Economic Theory and Western European Integration (1958); Lipsey, The Theory of Customs Unions: A General Survey, in R. Caves and H. Johnson (eds.), A.E.A. Readings in International Economics, Vol. XI (1968); B. Balassa, The Theory of Economic Integration (1961); J. Vanek, General Equilibrium of International Discrimination: The Case of Customs Unions, Harvard Economic Studies, Vol. CXXIII (1965); M. Krauss (ed.), The Economics of Integration (1973); A. El–Algraa & A. Jones, Theory of Customs Unions (1981); Paul R. Krugman & Maurice Obstfeld, International Economics ch. 9 (6th ed. 2003).

3. From International Trade and Trade Policy 9 (E. Helpman & A Razia, eds., 1991). Copyright © 1991 by the Massachusetts Institute of Technology. Reprinted with permission of the MIT Press.

customs union could be a mistake—but this is true of many economic policies, and policy concern based on the possibility of wide spread stupidity by governments may be realistic though not very interesting. Also, while a customs union with a *given* external tariff may be harmful to the members, a customs union that adjusts its tariff optimally is always beneficial; while optimal adjustment may be unlikely in practice, again this seems to reduce the concern over bilateralism to a fear that governments will make mistakes.

The point that a customs union is always potentially beneficial to its members has been made formally by Kemp and Wan. It may be useful to state the point informally. Suppose that two countries that happen to have the same tariff rate form a customs union. If they did not alter their external tariff rate, the increased trade within the union would represent a mixture of trade creation and trade diversion. Since the trade diversion would be harmful while the trade creation would be beneficial, the overall welfare effect would be ambiguous. (There may also be a terms of trade effect, to which we return below). The Kemp–Wan point, however, is that by adjusting the external tariff, the members of a customs union can always ensure a gain. Specifically, by reducing the tariff to the point at which external trade remains at its preunion level, the countries can ensure that there is no trade diversion. Also, since at this reduced tariff rate the offer to the rest of the world would be unchanged, the terms of trade of the customs union would also remain the same. So the welfare effect of a customs union that lowers its external tariff enough to prevent trade diversion is unambiguously positive. Now, in general, the customs union may choose to have a different tariff level than this; but if it does so, it is because this other tariff level yields still higher welfare. Thus a customs union is always potentially beneficial.

So far as good. But the last point—that a customs union may choose a tariff rate that is different from the one that leaves external trade at its preunion level—raises a potential negative possibility. The reason is that almost surely the optimal tariff rate for the customs union will be higher than this constant-trade level because the customs union will want to take advantage of its size to improve its terms of trade. Indeed, we may expect as a general presumption that a customs union, being a larger unit with more market power than any of its constituent members, will have an optimal external tariff that is higher than the preunion tariff rates of the member nations. Thus while our proof of potential gains relies on the hypothetical case of a customs union that does not lead to any trade diversion, in fact a customs union ordinarily will choose policies that do lead to trade diversion.

But this means that the formation of a customs union, while necessarily beneficial to the members, will certainly be harmful to the rest of the world and may reduce the welfare of the world as a whole (if such a measure can be defined).

Now let us return to the concern over bilateral and regional trading arrangements. One way to rationalize the concern of the trade negotiation professionals is the following: They fear that there may be a Prisoner's Dilemma at work in the formation of trading blocs. Imagine a world consisting of four countries, A, B, C, and D. Let A and B form a customs union; then other things equal they will be better off. However, they will have an incentive to improve their terms of trade by maintaining an external tariff that induces trade diversion—indeed, probably an external tariff that is higher than either of them would have on their own—and which therefore leaves C and D worse off. Similarly, C and D will be better off, other things equal, if they form a customs union, but their optimal external tariff will similarly induce trade diversion in the effort to achieve improved terms of trade. What could happen is that the resulting tariff war will induce enough trade diversion to leave everyone worse off than if they had not formed the customs unions.

ROBERT Z. LAWRENCE, EMERGING REGIONAL ARRANGEMENTS: BUILDING BLOCKS OR STUMBLING BLOCKS?[4]

The major regional initiatives currently under way are more likely to represent the building blocks of an integrated world economy than stumbling blocks which prevent its emergence. To be sure, there are risks that these initiatives could go astray. But the forces initiating these developments are the very opposite of protectionism. They represent positive, integrative responses to the pressures exerted by globalization. If accompanied by parallel progress at the GATT, regionalization could be a potent mechanism for freeing world trade and investment and harmonizing national institutional practices.

Growth. One key benefit to the rest of the world comes from the impact of regional arrangements in stimulating growth and thus demand for extra-regional exports. These growth effects stem from several sources. One is the income effect of the gains from trade. Secondly, such increased income induces increased investment. For example, Richard Baldwin estimates that the removal of trade and other internal barriers to trade and investment within Europe as a part of the Single Market will stimulate sufficient increases in investment to produce "dynamic" growth effects that will be greater than the "static" efficiency gains: up to a 10 per cent increase in total output, as compared to the 4.5 per cent figure (for static gains alone) estimated in the official Cecchini report prepared for the Commission.

External barriers. Open regional blocs can actually promote and facilitate external liberalization, that is, trade with parties outside blocs. On the political front, regions might be more willing to agree to liberalization than individual countries. The postwar experience with the EC is

4. From Finance and the International   Reprinted with permission.
Economy 23 (Richard O'Brien, ed., 1991).

heartening. Increased European integration after the Treaty of Rome was quite compatible with the lowering of Europe's external barriers. Gary Hufbauer, for example, has argued that the Kennedy Round of trade negotiations would not have occurred in the absence of the EC. "France and Italy, in particular, would have strongly resisted making any trade concessions in the 1960s, and Germany would not have made trade concessions in isolation from its continental partners." With the noteworthy exception of agriculture, therefore (an exception for which the EC was not solely to blame), increased regional integration among the original six members of the EC was associated with extensive participation in multilateral tariff reductions. Indeed the formation of the EEC was an important impulse for the Kennedy Round.

The European experience also demonstrates that excluded countries have stronger incentives to liberalize in a system with emerging regional arrangements. Instead of the fragmentation process some fear, an expansionary dynamic is likely. The prospects (indeed, the actuality) that major trading partners could move into arrangements from which they are excluded could well drive countries to join regional liberalization schemes.

Motivation. * * * The motive for completing the internal market [in Europe] is not to secure the European market for European producers by providing them preferential access, but instead to facilitate the free movement of goods, services, labour and capital throughout the Community. The EC Single Market initiative reflects the recognition that as the European economies became increasingly integrated, it was necessary to move beyond simply removing border barriers to achieve a much deeper degree of integration. To be sure, there is the hope that a larger market will improve European efficiency, but enhanced competition is precisely the mechanism by which the gains from trade are achieved.

Moreover deeper integration within Europe will facilitate trade with the rest of the world. A common set of standards, for example, makes it easier for all who wish to sell in Europe—not just insiders. A tough set of rules which inhibits governments from subsidizing domestic firms aids all their competitors, not only those located in the European Community. Once the larger European economies are committed to allow the free flow of resources within Europe, they will no longer be able to ensure each has a national champion in every industry, located within its territories. This undermining of the nationalist sentiments which drives much of the protectionism in the larger European countries will benefit outsiders. In addition, some of the mechanisms developed by the EC to deal with national diversity could serve as a model for further integration between the EC and its trading partners.

Despite theoretical uncertainty about the consequences of preferential arrangements, empirical economists often argue that existing regional arrangements tend to have positive economic effects for their members and no more than minimal adverse effects on the rest of the world. With particular regard to NAFTA, surveys of some of the empirical work may be found in North American Free Trade: Assessing the Impact (N. Lustig, B. Bosworth & R. Lawrence eds., Brookings, 1992) and G. Hufbauer & J. Schott, North American Free Trade: Issues and Recommendations (Inst. for Intl. Econ. 1992). See also K. Clausing, Trade Creation and Trade Diversion in the Canada–US Free Trade Agreement, 34 Can.J.Econ. 677 (2001). The evidence is somewhat mixed, however, and studies can be found that identify significant losses to non-member nations. See W. Chang & L. Winters, How Regional Blocks Affect Excluded Countries: The Price Effects of MERCOSUR, 92 Am.Econ.Rev. 889 (2002).

Finally, although the normative theory and consequences of regional arrangements have received considerable attention, less attention has been devoted to positive questions such as what determines when regional arrangements are formed, what determines who joins, and what determines whether the arrangement is a customs union or a free trade area. For an early effort to address some of these issues, see Johnson, An Economic Theory of Protectionism, Tariff Bargaining, and the Formation of Customs Unions, 73 J.Pol.Econ. 256 (1965).

Notes and Questions

(1) Krugman's concern is that regional arrangements may try to take advantage of their enhanced "monopoly power" in trade to raise their external tariffs to the "optimal" level—recall the discussion of the optimal tariff in Chapter 2. Putting aside the question whether governments in practice are motivated by the pursuit of the optimal tariff, look at Article XXIV to see whether governments can in fact do so under GATT. Suppose first that the arrangement is a customs union—what constraints are apparent in the text? What if it is a free trade area?

(2) In response to Lawrence's optimism, is there a danger that regional arrangements will create new interest groups as a result of trade diversion whose economic survival depends upon the maintenance of trade preferences? And if so, to what extent will those interest groups impede multilateral liberalization over the long haul?

(3) There is an increasing sense that WTO negotiations have become more unwieldy with the passage of time due to the growth in the membership (151 countries at this writing) and the expanded scope of WTO obligations. The proliferation of preferential arrangements probably reflects at least in part a sense that trade deals are easier to accomplish within the smaller numbers involved in negotiations of a PTA. The open question, aptly framed by Lawrence as the "building block" versus "stumbling block" issue, is whether the various PTAs will represent the end of the negotiating process, or the beginning of a newer and somewhat more consolidated multilateral process. At this writing, multilateral negotiations appear largely stalled while PTA negotiations seem to be flourishing. We leave to the reader whether any inference about the long-term picture can be drawn from the current state of affairs.

(4) Which type of PTA seems more likely to create significant trade diversion on average—a regional arrangement among close neighbors, or an arrangement between two distant countries?

SECTION 11.2 THE ARTICLE XXIV EXCEPTION

(A) HISTORY OF ARTICLE XXIV

JOHN H. JACKSON, WORLD TRADE AND THE LAW OF GATT 576–77 (1969)[1]

* * * The GATT draftsmen * * * termed the regional exception a "standard clause in all commercial treaties." By custom as well as explicit provision, certain regional arrangements had long been considered as an exception to the Most–Favored–Nation clause in commercial treaties. But regional arrangements had posed a difficult dilemma for commercial treaty draftsmen because of the danger of diluting the Most–Favored–Nation clause. * * *

* * * One of the major purposes that the United States sought to accomplish through GATT and the ITO was the dismantlement of trading preferences, especially the Commonwealth preferences. Yet even the United States recognized the legitimacy of an exception for customs unions. The original United States draft included clauses excepting such arrangements from Most–Favored–Nation and other obligations. But the problem was how to define such exception without opening the door to the introduction of all preferential systems under the guise of a customs union. The United States draft solution to this danger was to define a customs union to be the arrangement where "all tariffs and other restrictive regulations of commerce as between the ... members of the union are substantially eliminated" and where a uniform external tariff and regulation system exists for the union. In addition, the United States draft required that the common external tariff and regulation "shall not on the whole be higher or more stringent than the average level of the duties and regulations of commerce applicable in the constituent territories prior to the formation of such union." The United States representative explained this as follows: "Customs unions are desirable, provided that they [do] not cause any disadvantage to outside countries, in comparison with their trade before the customs union [was] effected."

Delegates from other nations at the 1946–1947 preparatory conferences urged, however, that a period of transition to form a customs

1. Copyright 1969, by The Bobbs–Merrill Company Inc. Reprinted by Permission. All rights reserved. See also John H. Jackson, The World Trading System 141 (1989); John H. Jackson, Regional Trade Blocs and GATT, 16 The World Economy 121 (1993); Uster, The MFN Customs Union Exception, 15 J. World Trade L. 377 (1981); J. Allen, The European Common Market and the GATT (1960); P. Lortie, Economic Integration and the Law of GATT (1975); V. Curzon, The Essentials of Economic Integration: Lessons of EFTA Experience (1974); Dam, Regional Economic Arrangements and the GATT: The Legacy of a Misconception, 30 U.Chi.L.Rev. 615 (1963).

union be allowed. The United States agreed that an "interim period" was reasonable, but "only after it had been definitely agreed to establish such a customs union." Ultimately, the Geneva draft ITO and the original GATT contained clauses incorporating these suggestions.

Although both customs unions and free trade areas in principle require the elimination of substantially all trade impediments between their members, in practice matters have worked out differently. A large number of regional associations have claimed the GATT Article XXIV exception, although arguably only a very few could really qualify. Yet even in questionable cases the preference system has been tolerated, and legal arguments have been ignored or resulted in a standoff without resolution. We consider below the extent to which the new WTO dispute settlement system has changed this situation.

(B) THE REQUIREMENTS OF ARTICLE XXIV

The Article XXIV MFN exception for trade groupings applies to three types of associations:

(1) A free trade area (defined in Article XXIV, paragraph 8(b), as an association of nations that eliminates barriers to imports from members on "substantially all" trade among them).

(2) A customs union (defined in Article XXIV, paragraph 8(a), as an association of nations that eliminates barriers to imports from members on "substantially all" trade among them and that further puts in place a common level of external tariffs for imports from nonmembers).

(3) An interim agreement leading to one of the above within a "reasonable period of time."

Among the issues that arise in its application and implementation are:[2]

(i) What is a "reasonable time" for an interim agreement to become a customs union or free trade area under paragraph 5?

(ii) What is "substantially all" trade under paragraph 8 and what "other restrictive regulations of commerce" must be eliminated ?

(iii) What does it take for imports to qualify as originating from a member state, i.e., what are the rules of origin and does Article XXIV place any constraints upon them?

(iv) With respect to a customs union, how does one ensure under paragraph 5 that tariffs and other barriers to trade with the customs union are "not on the whole * * * higher or more restrictive than the general incidence of the duties and regulations of commerce applicable in the constituent territories prior to the formation of such union," as required by Article XXIV(5)(a)?

---

2. See generally Jackson, supra note 1, ch. 24, especially secs. 24.6, 24.7, 24.8.

Under the old GATT system, these questions were never given clear answers. The compatibility of a free trade area or customs union agreement with the provisions of Article XXIV would be examined by a working party, which reported its findings and discussion to the Contracting Parties. These reports would discuss the relevant issues, but would not reach firm conclusions. Although numerous customs union and free-trade area agreements were considered by GATT, few were approved by any formal action by the Contracting Parties.[3] For example, despite extensive discussions, the GATT Contracting Parties never took a position on the EEC or its three enlargements, a fact highlighted in 1983 when the compatibility with Article XXIV of Greece's accession was the subject of an inconclusive working party report.[4] Indeed, in November 1992, it was stated at a GATT Council meeting that "over fifty previous working parties on individual customs unions or free-trade areas had been unable to reach unanimous conclusions as to the GATT consistency of those agreements. On the other hand, no such agreements had been disapproved explicitly."[5]

The new WTO Understanding on the Interpretation of Article XXIV of the General Agreement on Tariffs and Trade 1994 provides greater guidance on some issues. For example, Paragraph 3 provides that "[t]he 'reasonable length of time' (allowed for an interim agreement to produce a completed customs union or free trade area)* * * should exceed 10 years only in exceptional cases." It remains to be seen how frequently exceptional cases will be found. The Understanding also provides in Paragraph 10 that if an interim agreement does "not include a plan and schedule, contrary to paragraph 5(c) of Article XXIV, the working party in its report shall recommend such a plan and schedule."

At the Doha ministerial, WTO members "agree[d] to negotiations aimed at clarifying and improving disciplines and procedures under the existing WTO provisions applying to regional trade agreements." Doha Declaration, para. 29. As a result of the negotiations, a new "transparency mechanism" was adopted by the General Council. It provides for early notification of such agreements to the WTO and that members will examine notified agreements on the basis of a factual presentation made by the WTO secretariat. WT/L/671 (Dec. 18, 2006).

More fundamentally, a controversial issue in the GATT was whether the compatibility of an arrangement with Article XXIV could be raised in dispute settlement proceedings, particularly in cases where the working party examination had been completed and no action had been taken by the Contracting Parties. This question was discussed at some length in connection with a US challenge to the EU's trading arrangements with a number of Mediterranean countries in the early 1980's. Although the panel established to consider the case found that US benefits under the

3. See generally WTO, Regionalism and the World Trading System (1995).

4. GATT, 30th Supp. BISD 168–90 (1984).

5. GATT, Analytical Index 760 (6th ed. 1994).

General Agreement had been nullified or impaired, the report was never adopted.[6] The Uruguay Round Understanding on Article XXIV seeks to resolve this issue:

> 12. The provisions of Articles XXII and XXIII of GATT 1994 * * * may be invoked with respect to any matters arising from the application of those provisions of Article XXIV relating to customs unions, free-trade areas or interim agreements leading to the formation of a customs union or free-trade area.

The most prominent WTO dispute to date concerning what might be characterized as a regional trading arrangement was the *Bananas* case,[7] involving preferential treatment by the European Union of banana imports from certain countries. Because the preferences were ostensibly authorized by a waiver granted in relation to the Lomé Convention, however, the legal issues there involved the interpretation of the Convention and the waiver. The EU did not claim that Article XXIV was applicable. Article XXIV issues did arise to a great extent, however, in a lesser known case involving a dispute between India and Turkey over Turkey's textile imports policy following its entry into a customs union agreement with the European Union.

TURKEY—RESTRICTIONS ON IMPORTS OF TEXTILE AND CLOTHING PRODUCTS
WT/DS34/AB/R.
Appellate Body Report adopted November 19, 1999.

2. On 6 March 1995, the Turkey–EC Association Council adopted Decision 1/95, which sets out the rules for implementing the final phase of the customs union between Turkey and the European Communities. Article 12(2) of this Decision states:

> In conformity with the requirements of Article XXIV of the GATT Turkey will apply as from the entry into force of this Decision, substantially the same commercial policy as the Community in the textile sector including the agreements or arrangements on trade in textile and clothing.

In order to apply what it considered to be "substantially the same commercial policy" as the European Communities on trade in textiles and clothing, Turkey introduced, as of 1 January 1996, quantitative restrictions on imports from India on 19 categories of textile and clothing products.

3. The Panel considered claims by India that the quantitative restrictions introduced by Turkey were inconsistent with Articles XI and XIII of the GATT 1994, and Article 2.4 of the Agreement on Textiles and Clothing (the "*ATC*"). In the Panel Report, circulated on 31 May 1999,

---

6. See GATT, GATT Activities 1983, at 42–43; GATT, GATT Activities 1984, at 36–38.

7. European Communities–Regime for the Importation, Sale and Distribution of Bananas, WT/DS27.

the Panel reached the conclusion that the quantitative restrictions were inconsistent with the provisions of Articles XI and XIII of the GATT 1994 and consequently with those of Article 2.4 of the *ATC*, and rejected Turkey's defence that the introduction of any such otherwise GATT/ WTO incompatible import restrictions is permitted by Article XXIV of the GATT 1994.

* * *

41.   * * * The issue raised by Turkey in this appeal is whether these quantitative restrictions are nevertheless justified by Article XXIV of the GATT 1994.

42.   In examining Turkey's defence that Article XXIV of the GATT 1994 allowed Turkey to adopt the quantitative restrictions at issue in this appeal, the Panel looked, first, at Article XXIV:5(a) and, then, at Article XXIV:8(a) of the GATT 1994. The Panel examined the ordinary meaning of the terms of these provisions, in their context and in the light of the object and purpose of the *WTO Agreement*. The Panel reached the following conclusions:

> With regard to the specific relationship between, in the case before us, Article XXIV and Articles XI and XIII (and Article 2.4 of the ATC), we consider that the wording of Article XXIV does not authorize a departure from the obligations contained in Articles XI and XIII of GATT and Article 2.4 of the ATC.

* * *

> [Paragraphs 5 and 8 of Article XXIV] do not . . . address any specific measures that may or may not be adopted on the formation of a customs union and importantly they do not authorize violations of Articles XI and XIII, and Article 2.4 of the ATC. . . . We draw the conclusion that even on the occasion of the formation of a customs union, Members cannot impose otherwise incompatible quantitative restrictions.

Consequently, the Panel rejected Turkey's defence that Article XXIV justifies the introduction of the quantitative restrictions at issue. Turkey appeals the Panel's interpretation of Article XXIV.

43.   We note that, in its findings, the Panel referred to the chapeau of paragraph 5 of Article XXIV only in a passing and perfunctory way. The chapeau of paragraph 5 is not central to the Panel's analysis, which focuses instead primarily on paragraph 5(a) and paragraph 8(a). However, we believe that the chapeau of paragraph 5 of Article XXIV is the key provision for resolving the issue before us in this appeal. In relevant part, it reads:

> Accordingly, the provisions of this Agreement *shall not prevent*, as between the territories of contracting parties, *the formation of a customs union* . . . ; *Provided* that: . . . (emphasis added)

44.   To determine the meaning and significance of the chapeau of paragraph 5, we must look at the text of the chapeau, and its context,

which, for our purposes here, we consider to be paragraph 4 of Article XXIV.

45.   First, in examining the text of the chapeau to establish its ordinary meaning, we note that the chapeau states that the provisions of the GATT 1994 *"shall not prevent"* the formation of a customs union. We read this to mean that the provisions of the GATT 1994 *shall not make impossible* the formation of a customs union. Thus, the chapeau makes it clear that Article XXIV may, under certain conditions, justify the adoption of a measure which is inconsistent with certain other GATT provisions, and may be invoked as a possible "defence" to a finding of inconsistency.[8]

46.   Second, in examining the text of the chapeau, we observe also that it states that the provisions of the GATT 1994 shall not prevent *"the formation of a customs union"*. This wording indicates that Article XXIV can justify the adoption of a measure which is inconsistent with certain other GATT provisions only if the measure is introduced upon the formation of a customs union, and only to the extent that the formation of the customs union would be prevented if the introduction of the measure were not allowed.

47.   It follows necessarily that the text of the chapeau of paragraph 5 of Article XXIV cannot be interpreted without reference to the definition of a "customs union". This definition is found in paragraph 8(a) of Article XXIV, which states, in relevant part:

> A customs union shall be understood to mean the substitution of a single customs territory for two or more customs territories, so that
>
> (i) duties and other restrictive regulations of commerce (except, where necessary, those permitted under Articles XI, XII, XIII, XIV, XV and XX) are eliminated with respect to *substantially all the trade* between the constituent territories of the union or at least with respect to substantially all the trade in products originating in such territories, and,
>
> (ii) . . . *substantially the same* duties and other regulations of commerce are applied by each of the members of the union to the trade of territories not included in the union. (emphasis added)

48.   Sub-paragraph 8(a)(i) of Article XXIV establishes the standard for the *internal trade* between constituent members in order to satisfy the definition of a "customs union". It requires the constituent members of a customs union to eliminate "duties and other restrictive regulations of commerce" with respect to "substantially all the trade" between

---

8.   [original note 13] * * * The chapeau of paragraph 5 refers only to the provisions of the GATT 1994. It does not refer to the provisions of the *ATC*. However, Article 2.4 of the *ATC* provides that "[n]o new restrictions . . . shall be introduced *except under* the provisions of this Agreement or *relevant GATT 1994 provisions*." (emphasis added)

In this way, Article XXIV of the GATT 1994 is incorporated in the *ATC* and may be invoked as a defence to a claim of inconsistency with Article 2.4 of the *ATC*, provided that the conditions set forth in Article XXIV for the availability of this defence are met.

them. Neither the GATT CONTRACTING PARTIES nor the WTO Members have ever reached an agreement on the interpretation of the term "substantially" in this provision. It is clear, though, that "substantially all the trade" is not the same as *all* the trade, and also that "substantially all the trade" is something considerably more than merely *some* of the trade. We note also that the terms of sub-paragraph 8(a)(i) provide that members of a customs union may maintain, where necessary, in their internal trade, certain restrictive regulations of commerce that are otherwise permitted under Articles XI through XV and under Article XX of the GATT 1994. Thus, we agree with the Panel that the terms of sub-paragraph 8(a)(i) offer "some flexibility" to the constituent members of a customs union when liberalizing their internal trade in accordance with this sub-paragraph. Yet we caution that the degree of "flexibility" that sub-paragraph 8(a)(i) allows is limited by the requirement that "duties and other restrictive regulations of commerce" be "eliminated with respect to substantially all" internal trade.

49. Sub-paragraph 8(a)(ii) establishes the standard for the trade of constituent members *with third countries* in order to satisfy the definition of a "customs union". It requires the constituent members of a customs union to apply "substantially the same" duties and other regulations of commerce to external trade with third countries. The constituent members of a customs union are thus required to apply a common external trade regime, relating to both duties and other regulations of commerce. However, sub-paragraph 8(a)(ii) does *not* require each constituent member of a customs union to apply *the same* duties and other regulations of commerce as other constituent members with respect to trade with third countries; instead, it requires that *substantially the same* duties and other regulations of commerce shall be applied. We agree with the Panel that:

> [t]he ordinary meaning of the term "substantially" in the context of sub-paragraph 8(a) appears to provide for both qualitative and quantitative components. The expression "substantially the same duties and other regulations of commerce are applied by each of the Members of the [customs] union" would appear to encompass both quantitative and qualitative elements, the quantitative aspect more emphasized in relation to duties.

50. We also believe that the Panel was correct in its statement that the terms of sub-paragraph 8(a)(ii), and, in particular, the phrase "substantially the same" offer a certain degree of "flexibility" to the constituent members of a customs union in "the creation of a common commercial policy." Here too we would caution that this "flexibility" is limited. It must not be forgotten that the word "substantially" qualifies the words "the same". Therefore, in our view, something closely approximating "sameness" is required by Article XXIV:8(a)(ii). * * *

51. Third, in examining the text of the chapeau of Article XXIV:5, we note that the chapeau states that the provisions of the GATT 1994 shall not prevent the formation of a customs union *"Provided that"*. The

phrase *"provided that"* is an essential element of the text of the chapeau. In this respect, for purposes of a "customs union", the relevant proviso is set out immediately following the chapeau, in Article XXIV:5(a). It reads in relevant part:

> with respect to a customs union ..., the duties and other regulations of commerce imposed at the institution of any such union ... in respect of trade with contracting parties not parties to such union ... shall not on the whole be higher or more restrictive than the general incidence of the duties and regulations of commerce applicable in the constituent territories prior to the formation of such union ... ;

52. Given this proviso, Article XXIV can, in our view, only be invoked as a defence to a finding that a measure is inconsistent with certain GATT provisions to the extent that the measure is introduced upon the formation of a customs union which meets the requirement in sub-paragraph 5(a) of Article XXIV relating to the "duties and other regulations of commerce" applied by the constituent members of the customs union to trade with third countries.

53. With respect to "duties", Article XXIV:5(a) requires that the duties applied by the constituent members of the customs union *after* the formation of the customs union "shall *not* on the whole be *higher* ... than the *general incidence*" of the duties that were applied by each of the constituent members before the formation of the customs union. Paragraph 2 of the *Understanding on Article XXIV* requires that the evaluation under Article XXIV:5(a) of the *general incidence of the duties* applied before and after the formation of a customs union "shall ... be based upon an overall assessment of weighted average tariff rates and of customs duties collected." Before the agreement on this Understanding, there were different views among the GATT Contracting Parties as to whether one should consider, when applying the test of Article XXIV:5(a), the *bound* rates of duty or the *applied* rates of duty. This issue has been resolved by paragraph 2 of the *Understanding on Article XXIV*, which clearly states that the *applied* rate of duty must be used.

54. With respect to "other regulations of commerce", Article XXIV:5(a) requires that those applied by the constituent members *after* the formation of the customs union "shall *not* on the whole be ... *more restrictive* than the *general incidence*" of the regulations of commerce that were applied by each of the constituent members *before* the formation of the customs union. Paragraph 2 of the *Understanding on Article XXIV* explicitly recognizes that the quantification and aggregation of regulations of commerce other than duties may be difficult, and, therefore, states that "for the purpose of the overall assessment of the incidence of other regulations of commerce for which quantification and aggregation are difficult, the examination of individual measures, regulations, products covered and trade flows affected may be required."

55.   We agree with the Panel that the terms of Article XXIV:5(a), as elaborated and clarified by paragraph 2 of the *Understanding on Article XXIV*, provide:

> . . . that the effects of the resulting trade measures and policies of the new regional agreement shall not be more trade restrictive, overall, than were the constituent countries' previous trade policies.

and we also agree that this is:

> an "economic" test for assessing whether a specific customs union is compatible with Article XXIV.

56.   The text of the chapeau of paragraph 5 must also be interpreted in its context. In our view, paragraph 4 of Article XXIV constitutes an important element of the context of the chapeau of paragraph 5. The chapeau of paragraph 5 of Article XXIV begins with the word "accordingly", which can only be read to refer to paragraph 4 of Article XXIV, which immediately precedes the chapeau. Paragraph 4 states:

> The contracting parties recognize the desirability of increasing freedom of trade by the development, through voluntary agreements, of closer integration between the economies of the countries parties to such agreements. They also recognize that the purpose of a customs union or of a free-trade area should be to facilitate trade between the constituent territories and not to raise barriers to the trade of other contracting parties with such territories.

57.   According to paragraph 4, the purpose of a customs union is "to facilitate trade" between the constituent members and "not to raise barriers to the trade" with third countries. This objective demands that a balance be struck by the constituent members of a customs union. A customs union should facilitate trade within the customs union, but it should *not* do so in a way that raises barriers to trade with third countries. We note that the *Understanding on Article XXIV* explicitly reaffirms this purpose of a customs union, and states that in the formation or enlargement of a customs union, the constituent members should "to the greatest possible extent avoid creating adverse affects on the trade of other Members". Paragraph 4 contains purposive, and not operative, language. It does not set forth a separate obligation itself but, rather, sets forth the overriding and pervasive purpose for Article XXIV which is manifested in operative language in the specific obligations that are found elsewhere in Article XXIV. Thus, the purpose set forth in paragraph 4 informs the other relevant paragraphs of Article XXIV, including the chapeau of paragraph 5. For this reason, the chapeau of paragraph 5, and the conditions set forth therein for establishing the availability of a defence under Article XXIV, must be interpreted in the light of the purpose of customs unions set forth in paragraph 4. The chapeau cannot be interpreted correctly without constant reference to this purpose.

58.   Accordingly, on the basis of this analysis of the text and the context of the chapeau of paragraph 5 of Article XXIV, we are of the view

that Article XXIV may justify a measure which is inconsistent with certain other GATT provisions. However, in a case involving the formation of a customs union, this "defence" is available only when two conditions are fulfilled. First, the party claiming the benefit of this defence must demonstrate that the measure at issue is introduced upon the formation of a customs union that fully meets the requirements of sub-paragraphs 8(a) and 5(a) of Article XXIV. And, second, that party must demonstrate that the formation of that customs union would be prevented if it were not allowed to introduce the measure at issue. Again, *both* these conditions must be met to have the benefit of the defence under Article XXIV.

59.   We would expect a panel, when examining such a measure, to require a party to establish that both of these conditions have been fulfilled. It may not always be possible to determine whether the second of the two conditions has been fulfilled without initially determining whether the first condition has been fulfilled. In other words, it may not always be possible to determine whether not applying a measure would prevent the formation of a customs union without first determining whether there *is* a customs union. In this case, the Panel simply assumed, for the sake of argument, that the first of these two conditions was met and focused its attention on the second condition.

60.   More specifically, with respect to the first condition, the Panel, in this case, did not address the question of whether the regional trade arrangement between Turkey and the European Communities is, in fact, a "customs union" which meets the requirements of paragraphs 8(a) and 5(a) of Article XXIV. The Panel maintained that "it is arguable" that panels do not have jurisdiction to assess the overall compatibility of a customs union with the requirements of Article XXIV. We are not called upon in this appeal to address this issue, but we note in this respect our ruling in *India–Quantitative Restrictions on Imports of Agricultural, Textile and Industrial Products* [affirming] the jurisdiction of panels to review the justification of balance-of-payments restrictions under Article XVIII:B of the GATT 1994. The Panel also considered that, on the basis of the principle of judicial economy, it was not necessary to assess the compatibility of the regional trade arrangement between Turkey and the European Communities with Article XXIV in order to address the claims of India. Based on this reasoning, the Panel assumed *arguendo* that the arrangement between Turkey and the European Communities is compatible with the requirements of Article XXIV:8(a) and 5(a) and limited its examination to the question of whether Turkey was permitted to introduce the quantitative restrictions at issue. The assumption by the Panel that the agreement between Turkey and the European Communities is a "customs union" within the meaning of Article XXIV was not appealed. Therefore, the issue of whether this arrangement meets the requirements of paragraphs 8(a) and 5(a) of Article XXIV is not before us.

61.   With respect to the second condition that must be met to have the benefit of the defence under Article XXIV, Turkey asserts that had it not introduced the quantitative restrictions on textile and clothing

products from India that are at issue, the European Communities would have "exclud[ed] these products from free trade within the Turkey/EC customs union". According to Turkey, the European Communities would have done so in order to prevent trade diversion. Turkey's exports of these products accounted for 40 per cent of Turkey's total exports to the European Communities. Turkey expresses strong doubts about whether the requirement of Article XXIV:8(a)(i) that duties and other restrictive regulations of commerce be eliminated with respect to "substantially all trade" between Turkey and the European Communities could be met if 40 per cent of Turkey's total exports to the European Communities were excluded. In this way, Turkey argues that, unless it is allowed to introduce quantitative restrictions on textile and clothing products from India, it would be prevented from meeting the requirements of Article XXIV:8(a)(i) and, thus, would be prevented from forming a customs union with the European Communities.

62.　We agree with the Panel that had Turkey not adopted the same quantitative restrictions that are applied by the European Communities, this would not have prevented Turkey and the European Communities from meeting the requirements of sub-paragraph 8(a)(i) of Article XXIV, and consequently from forming a customs union. We recall our conclusion that the terms of sub-paragraph 8(a)(i) offer some—though limited—flexibility to the constituent members of a customs union when liberalizing their internal trade. As the Panel observed, there are other alternatives available to Turkey and the European Communities to prevent any possible diversion of trade, while at the same time meeting the requirements of sub-paragraph 8(a)(i). For example, Turkey could adopt rules of origin for textile and clothing products that would allow the European Communities to distinguish between those textile and clothing products originating in Turkey, which would enjoy free access to the European Communities under the terms of the customs union, *and* those textile and clothing products originating in third countries, including India. In fact, we note that Turkey and the European Communities themselves appear to have recognized that rules of origin could be applied to deal with any possible trade diversion. Article 12(3) of Decision 1/95 of the EC–Turkey Association Council, which sets out the rules for implementing the final phase of the customs union between Turkey and the European Communities, specifically provides for the possibility of applying a system of certificates of origin. A system of certificates of origin would have been a reasonable alternative until the quantitative restrictions applied by the European Communities are required to be terminated under the provisions of the *ATC*. Yet no use was made of this possibility to avoid trade diversion. Turkey preferred instead to introduce the quantitative restrictions at issue.

63.　For this reason, we conclude that Turkey was not, in fact, required to apply the quantitative restrictions at issue in this appeal in order to form a customs union with the European Communities. Therefore, Turkey has not fulfilled the second of the two necessary conditions that must be fulfilled to be entitled to the benefit of the defence under

Article XXIV. Turkey has not demonstrated that the formation of a customs union between Turkey and the European Communities would be prevented if it were not allowed to adopt these quantitative restrictions. Thus, the defence afforded by Article XXIV under certain conditions is not available to Turkey in this case, and Article XXIV does not justify the adoption by Turkey of these quantitative restrictions.

64. For the reasons set out in this report, the Appellate Body concludes that the Panel erred in its legal reasoning by focusing on subparagraphs 8(a) and 5(a) and by failing to recognize the crucial role of the chapeau of paragraph 5 in the interpretation of Article XXIV of the GATT 1994, but upholds the Panel's conclusion that Article XXIV does not allow Turkey to adopt, upon the formation of a customs union with the European Communities, quantitative restrictions on imports of 19 categories of textile and clothing products which were found to be inconsistent with Articles XI and XIII of the GATT 1994 and Article 2.4 of the *ATC*.

65. We wish to point out that we make no finding on the issue of whether quantitative restrictions found to be inconsistent with Article XI and Article XIII of the GATT 1994 will *ever* be justified by Article XXIV. We find only that the quantitative restrictions at issue in the appeal in this case were not so justified. Likewise, we make no finding either on many other issues that may arise under Article XXIV. The resolution of those other issues must await another day. We do not believe it necessary to find more than we have found here to fulfill our responsibilities under the DSU in deciding this case.

66. The Appellate Body recommends that the DSB request that Turkey bring its measures which the Panel found to be inconsistent with Articles XI and XIII of the GATT 1994 and Article 2.4 of the *ATC* into conformity with its obligations under these agreements.

Notes and Questions

(1) To what extent has the Article XXIV exception been limited by the Appellate Body's opinion in *Turkey Textiles*, particularly its reading of the chapeau of paragraph 5 (see paragraph 46 of the report)? Consider the following case: Countries A and B enter into a customs union, abolishing tariffs on, say, 98% of all trade between the two countries. Some years later, they propose to abolish the tariffs on the remaining 2% of trade. A third country, C, complains to the WTO that the further tariff reductions, which are not extended to goods imported into the customs union from C, violate Article I of GATT and cannot be justified under Article XXIV because the further tariff reductions are not introduced at the time of the formation of the customs union, and are plainly not necessary to make the formation of the customs union possible. Does C prevail? Sensible?

(2) Note the Appellate Body's view that Article XXIV is a defense and that the respondent must establish that it fully meets the requirements of Article XXIV:8 (paragraphs 58–60). How will panels decide if those requirements are met? If there are doubts, does the respondent lose? If so, does this case suggest that Article XXIV will likely be interpreted strictly in the

future, despite the longstanding tolerance by GATT/WTO members of a very loose interpretation? Is it appropriate for the dispute settlement system to implement that change, as opposed to the political organs of the WTO? Recall the discussion in Section 7.4(D) supra.

(3) Does the Appellate Body offer much guidance regarding the phrase "substantially all" trade? The European Union once urged 80% of all trade as a benchmark[9]—would that standard pass muster? Is there a principled way to give content to the "substantially all" requirement? Can that be done without a convincing theory of why it is there in the first place? Why should the GATT Contracting Parties have viewed small departures from the MFN obligation as unacceptable, yet have been willing to allow quite massive departures as long as they satisfy the "substantially all" criterion?

(4) The *Wheat Gluten* case in Section 15.3 examines the rules of the Safeguards Agreement that are applicable to the use of safeguards by a member of a free trade area. A thoughtful discussion of that set of issues, with useful implications for the broader questions raised here, is J. Pauwelyn, The Puzzle of WTO Safeguards and Regional Trade Agreements, 7 JIEL 109 (2004).

(5) In *Canada Autos*, Canada granted duty exemptions to certain imported automobiles imported by companies who satisfied certain "ratio requirements" and "Canadian value added requirements." Essentially, these requirements meant that if a manufacturer had sufficient domestic manufacturing facilities in Canada, it could benefit from the exemption but not otherwise. The effect was to favor certain automakers with substantial Canadian productive facilities. The scheme had first been put in place as part of the US–Canada Auto Pact in 1965, settling a trade dispute in automotive products, and had been modified and extended through additional agreements up through 1998. A panel ruled (and the Appellate Body affirmed) that the scheme violated, *inter alia*, the most-favored nation obligation of GATT Article I (General Motors vehicles could be imported at a lower duty rate than BMW vehicles, for example). In its defense, Canada argued before the panel that most (although not all) of the vehicles benefiting from the exemption came from the United States or Mexico, and hence that the exemption could be justified as an exception to the Article I obligation pursuant to Article XXIV as a *de facto* part of NAFTA. What do you think of Canada's argument? See the Panel Report, paras. 10.51–10.57.

(6) An interesting further issue arises for nations that use tariffs as an important source of government revenue—what if the elimination of trade barriers in the pursuit of a customs union or free trade area might impair the ability of the government to raise needed revenues? Should there be an exception to the requirement that duties be eliminated on "substantially all" trade for "non-protective revenue duties?" See European Economic Community—Agreement of Association With Malta, Working Party Report adopted on May 29, 1972. GATT, 19th Supp. BISD 94–95 (1973).

(7) Customs unions and free trade areas with developing countries raise still further issues regarding the ability of developing nations to invoke GATT exceptions for infant industry protection, and so on, when to do so

---

9. GATT, 6th Supp. BISD 70, 99 (1958).

might mean that they have failed to eliminate barriers on "substantially all" trade. There is an additional question whether preferential arrangements with developing nations are to be classified as arrangements subject to Article XXIV, or mere preferences for developing country exports permitted by other GATT provisions or decisions. See European Economic Community—Association Agreements With African and Malagasy States and Overseas Countries and Territories, Working Party Report adopted on April 4, 1966. GATT, 14th Supp. BISD 100–06 (1966). For the conclusions of the Contracting Parties adopted on the same date, see id., at 22.

(8) Departures from the most-favored-nation principle, including customs unions and free trade areas, necessitate rules of origin to determine whether or not imported merchandise is entitled to preferential treatment. Often, the origin of a good is obvious, as when it is produced entirely within the borders of a single exporting nation. But when a finished good has been through several stages of processing in different countries, the matter is more complex. The greater the degree to which processing must occur within the customs union or free trade area before a good will be deemed to have originated there, the greater the extent to which the preferential arrangement may cause trade diversion. Thus, countries that are not a party to the regional arrangement will prefer less restrictive rules of origin to minimize the impact of preferences on their exports. Countries within the regional arrangement, by contrast, may prefer restrictive rules of origin so that the benefits of the trade preferences do not extend much beyond the borders of regional agreement.

The rules in use within various regional arrangements vary considerably, and have been a source of some concern within GATT through the years. See European Free Trade Association—Examination of the Stockholm Convention, Working Party Report adopted on June 4, 1960, GATT, 9th Supp. BISD 71–73 (1961); European Communities—Agreements With Portugal, Working Party Report adopted on October 19, 1973, GATT, 20th Supp. BISD 177–81 (1974). The WTO Agreement on Rules of Origin aims at harmonization of such rules over time, but is in the main focused on non-preferential rules of origin. See Section 8.3(D) supra.

(9) The GATS analog to Article XXIV is GATS Article V. How does it differ from Article XXIV?

SECTION 11.3   OVERLAPPING OBLIGATIONS IN WTO AND PTA LAW

Preferential trade arrangements typically embody legal obligations that are similar in many respects to WTO obligations. A measure that violates WTO law, therefore, may well violate the law of some PTA. PTAs may also contain their own dispute resolution mechanisms. Hence, the possibility arises that a measure can be challenged under the dispute process of either the WTO or some PTA, affording the complainant a choice of forum. Indeed, one can imagine that a complainant might wish to pursue a claim in both forums.

At one time under MERCOSUR, for example, pursuant to the Protocol of Brasilia, a MERCOSUR member could bring cases in both forks. In Argentina—Definitive Antidumping Duties on Poultry from Brazil, WT/DS241/R, adopted May 19, 2003, Brazil brought a WTO complaint challenging certain measures imposed by Argentina even though it had previously brought a claim (and lost) relating to the same measures in a MERCOSUR dispute settlement proceeding. Argentina argued that Brazil was not acting in good faith, and that estoppel should be applied to bar its claim in the WTO. A third party (Paraguay) argued that the principle of res judicata should bar Brazil's claim. The panel rejected all of these arguments on the facts of the case before it, but seemed open to the possibility that such principles might be applied in appropriate cases. See id., paras. 7.17–7.42. The panel report was not appealed.

The situation under NAFTA has been different from its inception. The basic dispute settlement provisions are contained in Chapter 20. Article 2005 provides that a NAFTA member may pursue its rights under NAFTA law or WTO law "in either forum at the discretion of the complaining party," subject to a few exceptions noted later in this chapter. Putting aside those exceptions, the so-called exclusion clause in Article 2005.6 states that "the forum selected shall be used to the exclusion of the other." Suppose, hypothetically, that a NAFTA member were to file a case in the WTO after losing the same case before a NAFTA panel. Would a WTO panel be obliged to decline jurisdiction on the basis of the above-quoted provision of NAFTA? To what extent are NAFTA obligations binding for purposes of WTO law? The following case provides some insight into these and related issues.

MEXICO—TAX MEASURES ON SOFT DRINKS AND OTHER BEVERAGES

WT/DS308/AB/R.
Appellate Body Report adopted March 24, 2006.

[Mexico imposed various taxes on soft drinks sweetened with substances other than cane sugar and on the distribution of such products, along with various "bookkeeping requirements" on the sellers of such products. Mexico had imposed the measures, targeting products exported in substantial quantity by the United States, because of a dispute over Mexico's access to the US sugar market under NAFTA. Mexico had requested a NAFTA panel to hear that dispute, but the United States had "blocked" the establishment of a panel. (Although NAFTA provides for the creation of a roster of panelists so as to permit the automatic composition of a panel on the request of any party, the roster has never been agreed. Thus, in practice, NAFTA is similar to the old GATT dispute resolution system in allowing a disputant to block panel formation.) The United States challenged the Mexican measures before the WTO under GATT Article III (national treatment), claiming that the taxes and bookkeeping requirements impermissibly discriminated between domestic products and imported like or directly competitive products (we take up the details of national treatment in Chapter 12). Mexico all but conceded that its measures violated Article III—the panel so found and its findings in that regard were not appealed. But Mexico further argued that the panel should have declined to hear the case given the circumstances prevailing in NAFTA, or that in the alternative its violations of Article III could be justified under one of the general exceptions to GATT obligations contained in GATT Article XX(d). Thus ensued the following appeal.]

* * *

IV.   THE PANEL'S EXERCISE OF JURISDICTION

40.   In its first written submission to the Panel, Mexico requested that the Panel decide, as a preliminary matter, to decline to exercise jurisdiction "in favour of an Arbitral Panel under Chapter Twenty of the North American Free Trade Agreement (NAFTA)." In a preliminary ruling, the Panel rejected Mexico's request and found instead that, "under the DSU, it had no discretion to decide whether or not to exercise its jurisdiction in a case properly before it." The Panel added that even if it had such discretion, it "did not consider that there were facts on record that would justify the Panel declining to exercise its jurisdiction in the present case."

* * *

44.   [W]e note that "Mexico does not question that the Panel has jurisdiction to hear the United States' claims." Moreover, Mexico does not claim "that there are legal obligations under the NAFTA or any other international agreement to which Mexico and the United States are both parties, which might raise legal impediments to the Panel hearing this case". Instead, Mexico's position is that, although the Panel had the authority to rule on the merits of the United States' claims, it also had the "implied power" to abstain from ruling on them, and "should have exercised this power in the circumstances of this dispute." Hence, the issue before us in this appeal is not whether the Panel was legally precluded from ruling on the United States' claims that were before it, but, rather, whether the Panel could decline, and should have declined, to exercise jurisdiction with respect to the United States' claims under Article III of the GATT 1994 that were before it.

45.   Turning to Mexico's arguments on appeal, we note, first, Mexico's argument that WTO panels, like other international bodies and tribunals, "have certain implied jurisdictional powers that derive from their nature as adjudicative bodies", and thus have a basis for declining to exercise jurisdiction. We agree with Mexico that WTO panels have certain powers that are inherent in their adjudicative function. Notably, panels have the right to determine whether they have jurisdiction in a given case, as well as to determine the scope of their jurisdiction. In this regard, the Appellate Body has previously stated that "it is a widely accepted rule that an international tribunal is entitled to consider the issue of its own jurisdiction on its own initiative, and to satisfy itself that it has jurisdiction in any case that comes before it." Further, the

Appellate Body has also explained that panels have "a margin of discretion to deal, always in accordance with due process, with specific situations that may arise in a particular case and that are not explicitly regulated." For example, panels may exercise judicial economy, that is, refrain from ruling on certain claims, when such rulings are not necessary "to resolve the matter in issue in the dispute". The Appellate Body has cautioned, nevertheless, that "[t]o provide only a partial resolution of the matter at issue would be false judicial economy."

46. In our view, it does not necessarily follow, however, from the existence of these inherent adjudicative powers that, once jurisdiction has been validly established, WTO panels would have the authority to decline to rule on the entirety of the claims that are before them in a dispute. To the contrary, we note that, while recognizing WTO panels' inherent powers, the Appellate Body has previously emphasized that:

> Although panels enjoy some discretion in establishing their own working procedures, this discretion does not extend to modifying the substantive provisions of the DSU. ... Nothing in the DSU gives a panel the authority either to disregard or to modify ... explicit provisions of the DSU.

47. With these considerations in mind, we examine the scope of a panel's jurisdictional power as defined, in particular, in Articles 3.2, 7.1, 7.2, 11, 19.2, and 23 of the DSU. Mexico argues that "[t]here is nothing in the DSU ... that explicitly rules out the existence of" a WTO panel's power to decline to exercise its jurisdiction even in a case that is properly before it.

[The Appellate Body then reviewed the text of these sections, and concluded, *inter alia*, that the use of the phrase "shall address" in Article 7.2, "should make an objective assessment of the matter before it" in Article 11, and "shall have recourse" to the DSU in Article 23 imply that panels have an obligation to address matters within their terms of reference.]

53. A decision by a panel to decline to exercise validly established jurisdiction would seem to "diminish" the right of a complaining Member to "seek the redress of a violation of obligations" within the meaning of Article 23 of the DSU, and to bring a dispute pursuant to Article 3.3 of the DSU. This would not be consistent with a panel's obligations under Articles 3.2 and 19.2 of the DSU. We see no reason, therefore, to disagree with the Panel's statement that a WTO panel "would seem ... not to be in a position to choose freely whether or not to exercise its jurisdiction."

54. Mindful of the precise scope of Mexico's appeal, we express no view as to whether there may be other circumstances in which legal impediments could exist that would preclude a panel from ruling on the merits of the claims that are before it. In the present case, Mexico argues that the United States' claims under Article III of the GATT 1994 are inextricably linked to a broader dispute, and that only a NAFTA panel could resolve the dispute as a whole. Nevertheless, Mexico does not take issue with the Panel's finding that "neither the subject matter nor the

respective positions of the parties are identical in the dispute under the NAFTA . . . and the dispute before us." Mexico also stated that it could not identify a legal basis that would allow it to raise, in a WTO dispute settlement proceeding, the market access claims it is pursuing under the NAFTA. It is furthermore undisputed that no NAFTA panel as yet has decided the "broader dispute" to which Mexico has alluded. Finally, we note that Mexico has expressly stated that the so-called "exclusion clause" of Article 2005.6 of the NAFTA had not been "exercised". We do not express any view on whether a legal impediment to the exercise of a panel's jurisdiction would exist in the event that features such as those mentioned above were present. In any event, we see no legal impediments applicable in this case.

55.   Finally, as we understand it, Mexico's position is that the "applicability" of its WTO obligations towards the United States would be "call[ed] into question" as a result of the United States having prevented Mexico, by an illegal act (namely, the alleged refusal by the United States to nominate panelists to the NAFTA panel), from having recourse to the NAFTA dispute settlement mechanism to resolve a bilateral dispute between Mexico and the United States regarding trade in sweeteners. Specifically, Mexico refers to the ruling of the Permanent Court of International Justice (the "PCIJ") in the *Factory at Chorzów* case, and "calls into question the 'applicability' of its WTO obligations towards the United States in the context of this dispute".[114]

56.   Mexico's arguments, as well as its reliance on the ruling in *Factory at Chorzów*, is misplaced. Even assuming, arguendo, that the legal principle reflected in the passage referred to by Mexico is applicable within the WTO dispute settlement system, we note that this would entail a determination whether the United States has acted consistently or inconsistently with its NAFTA obligations.[115] We see no basis in the DSU for panels and the Appellate Body to adjudicate non-WTO disputes. Article 3.2 of the DSU states that the WTO dispute settlement system "serves to preserve the rights and obligations of Members under the covered agreements, and to clarify the existing provisions of those agreements". (emphasis added) Accepting Mexico's interpretation would imply that the WTO dispute settlement system could be used to determine rights and obligations outside the covered agreements. In light of

---

114.   * * * The passage of the ruling that Mexico refers to reads as follows:

   . . . one party cannot avail himself of the fact that the other has not fulfilled some obligation, or has not had recourse to some means of redress, if the former party has, by some illegal act, prevented the latter from fulfilling the obligation in question, or from having recourse to the tribunal which would have been open to him.

(Permanent Court of International Justice, *Factory at Chorzów (Germany v. Poland)*

(Jurisdiction), 1927, PCIJ Series A, No. 9, p. 31).

115.   We also note that the ruling of the PCIJ in the *Factory at Chorzów* case relied on by Mexico was made in a situation in which the party objecting to the exercise of jurisdiction by the PCIJ was the party that had committed the act alleged to be illegal. In the present case, the party objecting to the exercise of jurisdiction by the Panel (Mexico) relies instead on an allegedly illegal act committed by the other party (the United States).

the above, we do not see how the PCIJ's ruling in *Factory at Chorzów* supports Mexico's position in this case. * * *

V.   ARTICLE XX(d) OF THE GATT 1994

* * *

66.   Article XX(d) of the GATT 1994 reads:

General Exceptions

Subject to the requirement that such measures are not applied in a manner which would constitute a means of arbitrary or unjustifiable discrimination between countries where the same conditions prevail, or a disguised restriction on international trade, nothing in this Agreement shall be construed to prevent the adoption or enforcement by any contracting party of measures:

. . .

(d) necessary to secure compliance with laws or regulations which are not inconsistent with the provisions of this Agreement, including those relating to customs enforcement, the enforcement of monopolies operated under paragraph 4 of Article II and Article XVII, the protection of patents, trade marks and copyrights, and the prevention of deceptive practices[.]

67.   The Appellate Body explained, in *Korea–Various Measures on Beef*, that two elements must be shown "[f]or a measure, otherwise inconsistent with GATT 1994, to be justified provisionally under paragraph (d) of Article XX". The first element is that "the measure must be one designed to 'secure compliance' with laws or regulations that are not themselves inconsistent with some provision of the GATT 1994", and the second is that "the measure must be 'necessary' to secure such compliance." The Appellate Body also explained that "[a] Member who invokes Article XX(d) as a justification has the burden of demonstrating that these two requirements are met."

68.   In our view, the central issue raised in this appeal is whether the terms "to secure compliance with laws or regulations" in Article XX(d) of the GATT 1994 encompass WTO-inconsistent measures applied by a WTO Member to secure compliance with another WTO Member's obligations under an international agreement.

69.   In order to answer this question, we consider it more helpful to begin our analysis with the terms "laws or regulations" in Article XX(d) (which we consider to be pivotal here) rather than to begin with the analysis of the terms "to secure compliance", as did the Panel. The terms "laws or regulations" are generally used to refer to domestic laws or regulations. As Mexico and the United States note, previous GATT and WTO disputes in which Article XX(d) has been invoked as a defence have involved domestic measures. Neither disputes that the expression "laws or regulations" encompasses the rules adopted by a WTO Member's legislative or executive branches of government. We agree with the

United States that one does not immediately think about international law when confronted with the term "laws" in the plural. Domestic legislative or regulatory acts sometimes may be intended to implement an international agreement. In such situations, the origin of the rule is international, but the implementing instrument is a domestic law or regulation. In our view, the terms "laws or regulations" refer to rules that form part of the domestic legal system of a WTO Member. Thus, the "laws or regulations" with which the Member invoking Article XX(d) may seek to secure compliance do not include obligations of another WTO Member under an international agreement.

70.   The illustrative list of "laws or regulations" provided in Article XX(d) supports the conclusion that these terms refer to rules that form part of the domestic legal system of a WTO Member. This list includes "[laws or regulations] relating to customs enforcement, the enforcement of monopolies operated under paragraph 4 of Article II and Article XVII, the protection of patents, trade marks and copyrights, and the prevention of deceptive practices". These matters are typically the subject of domestic laws or regulations, even though some of these matters may also be the subject of international agreements. The matters listed as examples in Article XX(d) involve the regulation by a government of activity undertaken by a variety of economic actors (e.g., private firms and State enterprises), as well as by government agencies. For example, matters "relating to customs enforcement" will generally involve rights and obligations that apply to importers or exporters, and matters relating to "the protection of patents, trade marks and copyrights" will usually regulate the use of these rights by the intellectual property right holders and other private actors. Thus, the illustrative list reinforces the notion that the terms "laws or regulations" refer to rules that form part of the domestic legal system of a WTO Member and do not extend to the international obligations of another WTO Member.

71.   Our understanding of the terms "laws or regulations" is consistent with the context of Article XX(d). As the United States points out, other provisions of the covered agreements refer expressly to "international obligations" or "international agreements". For example, paragraph (h) of Article XX refers to "obligations under any intergovernmental commodity agreement". The express language of paragraph (h) would seem to contradict Mexico's suggestion that international agreements are implicitly included in the terms "laws or regulations". The United States and China also draw our attention to Article X:1 of the GATT 1994, which refers to "[l]aws, regulations, judicial decisions and administrative rulings" and to "[a]greements affecting international trade policy which are in force between a government . . . of any Member and the government . . . of any other Member". Thus, a distinction is drawn in the same provision between "laws [and] regulations" and "international agreements". Such a distinction would have been unnecessary if, as Mexico argues, the terms "laws" and "regulations" were to encompass international agreements that have not been incorporated, or do not have direct effect in, the domestic legal system of the respective WTO

Member. Thus, Articles X:1 and XX(h) of the GATT 1994 do not lend support to interpreting the terms "laws or regulations" in Article XX(d) as including the international obligations of a Member other than that invoking the provision.

72. We turn to the terms "to secure compliance", which were the focus of the Panel's reasoning and are the focus of Mexico's appeal. The terms "to secure compliance" speak to the types of measures that a WTO Member can seek to justify under Article XX(d). They relate to the design of the measures sought to be justified. There is no justification under Article XX(d) for a measure that is not designed "to secure compliance" with a Member's laws or regulations. Thus, the terms "to secure compliance" do not expand the scope of the terms "laws or regulations" to encompass the international obligations of another WTO Member. Rather, the terms "to secure compliance" circumscribe the scope of Article XX(d).

73. Mexico takes issue with several aspects of the Panel's reasoning related to the interpretation of the terms "to secure compliance". We recall that, according to the Panel, "[t]he context in which the expression is used makes clear that 'to secure compliance' is to be read as meaning to enforce compliance." The Panel added that, in contrast to enforcement action taken within a Member's legal system, "the effectiveness of [Mexico's] measures in achieving their stated goal—that of bringing about a change in the behaviour of the United States—seems ... to be inescapably uncertain." Thus, the Panel concluded that "the outcome of international countermeasures, such as those adopted by Mexico, is inherently unpredictable".

74. It is Mexico's submission that the Panel erred in requiring a degree of certainty as to the results achieved by the measure sought to be justified. Mexico also asserts that the Panel, in its reasoning, incorrectly relied on the Appellate Body Report in *US–Gambling*. We agree with Mexico that the *US–Gambling* Report does not support the conclusion that the Panel sought to draw from it. The statement to which the Panel referred was made in the context of the examination of the "necessity" requirement in Article XIV(a) of the General Agreement on Trade in Services, and did not relate to the terms "to secure compliance". As the Appellate Body has explained previously, "the contribution made by the compliance measure to the enforcement of the law or regulation at issue" is one of the factors that must be weighed and balanced to determine whether a measure is "necessary" within the meaning of Article XX(d). A measure that is not suitable or capable of securing compliance with the relevant laws or regulations will not meet the "necessity" requirement. We see no reason, however, to derive from the Appellate Body's examination of "necessity", in *US–Gambling*, a requirement of "certainty" applicable to the terms "to secure compliance". In our view, a measure can be said to be designed "to secure compliance" even if the measure cannot be guaranteed to achieve its result with absolute certainty. Nor do we consider that the "use of coercion" is a necessary component of a measure designed "to secure

compliance". Rather, Article XX(d) requires that the design of the measure contribute "to secur[ing] compliance with laws or regulations which are not inconsistent with the provisions of" the GATT 1994.

75. Nevertheless, while we agree with Mexico that the Panel's emphasis on "certainty" and "coercion" is misplaced, we consider that Mexico's arguments miss the point. Even if "international countermeasures" could be described as intended "to secure compliance", what they seek "to secure compliance with"—that is, the international obligations of another WTO Member—would be outside the scope of Article XX(d). This is because "laws or regulations" within the meaning of Article XX(d) refer to the rules that form part of the domestic legal order of the WTO Member invoking the provision and do not include the international obligations of another WTO Member.

* * *

77. We observe, furthermore, that Mexico's interpretation of Article XX(d) disregards the fact that the GATT 1994 and the DSU specify the actions that a WTO Member may take if it considers that another WTO Member has acted inconsistently with its obligations under the GATT 1994 or any of the other covered agreements. As the United States points out, Mexico's interpretation of the terms "laws or regulations" as including international obligations of another WTO Member would logically imply that a WTO Member could invoke Article XX(d) to justify also measures designed "to secure compliance" with that other Member's WTO obligations. By the same logic, such action under Article XX(d) would evade the specific and detailed rules that apply when a WTO Member seeks to take countermeasures in response to another Member's failure to comply with rulings and recommendations of the DSB pursuant to Article XXIII:2 of the GATT 1994 and Articles 22 and 23 of the DSU. Mexico's interpretation would allow WTO Members to adopt WTO-inconsistent measures based upon a unilateral determination that another Member has breached its WTO obligations, in contradiction with Articles 22 and 23 of the DSU and Article XXIII:2 of the GATT 1994.

78. Finally, even if the terms "laws or regulations" do not go so far as to encompass the WTO agreements, as Mexico argues, Mexico's interpretation would imply that, in order to resolve the case, WTO panels and the Appellate Body would have to assume that there is a violation of the relevant international agreement (such as the NAFTA) by the complaining party, or they would have to assess whether the relevant international agreement has been violated. WTO panels and the Appellate Body would thus become adjudicators of non-WTO disputes. As we noted earlier, this is not the function of panels and the Appellate Body as intended by the DSU.

Notes and Questions

(1) Consider the hypothetical raised earlier, in which a nation brings a WTO case in violation of some rule in a PTA requiring the case to be

resolved there. How would that case come out? How should it? Suppose, as was alleged by Mexico here, that the other disputant has blocked the PTA process from going forward and made it impossible to resolve it under the PTA?

(2) Are you persuaded that "laws or regulations" under Article XX(d) should be limited to laws or regulations in the domestic legal order of the nation that imposes the measure at issue, and that an extension of the concept to matters of international law (other than WTO law) would place an unacceptable burden on panels to adjudicate such issues? What about a situation in which the international law at issue has direct effect in the domestic legal system of the WTO member imposing the measure (see paragraph 71)—should such a case be treated differently? Is there a good answer to the suggestion in paragraph 77 that if Mexico's argument were accepted, it would logically imply that WTO members could unilaterally take measures to enforce their WTO rights and justify them under Article XX(d)?

(3) The panel had emphasized the apparent ineffectiveness of Mexico's measures at inducing the United States to fulfill its purported NAFTA obligations, and thus found that the measures were not measures "to secure compliance" under Article XX(d). The Appellate Body backed away from this interpretation (see paragraph 74). Who had the better of the argument?

(4) Note that the provision on NAFTA Chapter 20 requiring the parties to choose between the NAFTA and WTO dispute forums does not apply to disputes that enter the binational panel process under Chapter 19. Thus, a complainant in an antidumping or countervailing duty proceeding under NAFTA can take its case to a binational panel as well as to the WTO, and the possibility of inconsistent judgments arises. In the softwood dispute between the United States and Canada, for example, a binational panel held that the US International Trade Commission's finding of injury was unsustainable under NAFTA, while a WTO panel upheld it. The matter has been settled for now by the Softwood Lumber Agreement between the United States and Canada.

(5) Article XX is discussed generally in Chapter 13.

SECTION 11.4   U.S. PARTICIPATION IN REGIONAL ARRANGEMENTS

(A) HISTORY PRIOR TO NAFTA

The United States remained outside the global trend toward customs unions and free trade areas until 1985, when it entered into a free trade agreement with Israel.[1] Under that agreement all duties would be eliminated in four stages by January 1, 1995.[2] The agreement also covers

---

1. Negotiation of the agreement was authorized in 1984. Trade and Tariff Act of 1984, title IV; 19 U.S.C.A. sec. 2112. Under the trade agreement negotiating authority of the 1974 Trade Act, as modified in the 1984 Act for application to a US–Israel trade agreement, congressional approval of legislation implementing the agreement was required. Such legislation was handled under the "fast-track" procedures and was approved in June 1985. Pub.L. No. 99–47, 99 Stat. 82. See House Rep. No. 99–64, 99th Cong., 1st Sess. (1985).

2. Agreement on the Establishment of a Free Trade Area Between the Government of the United States of America and the

nontariff barriers. For example, Israel committed to eliminate export subsidy programs on industrial products and processed agricultural products within six years. In a number of other respects, such as import licensing and government procurement, the agreement establishes more stringent rules than did the Tokyo Round agreements.[3]

The US–Israel agreement was no doubt motivated more by political and military concerns than economic concerns. It provides a way for the United States to encourage economic growth and investment in Israel without the need for direct, on-budget subsidization. But while negotiations with Israel were proceeding, the United States was also exploring the possibility of a free trade arrangement with its largest trading partner—Canada. The 1974 Trade Act stated that it was the sense of Congress that the United States should enter into a free trade agreement with Canada, and the President was authorized to initiate negotiations with Canada.[4] The result was the Canada–United States Free Trade Agreement (CUSFTA), which was signed on January 2, 1988 and came into effect on January 1, 1989.

The CUSFTA was a sweeping accord, reducing or eliminating most duties between the two nations over a period of years. It contained additional provisions relating to rules of origin, technical barriers to trade, agricultural market access and subsidization, safeguards measures, government procurement, trade in services, investment and temporary migration for business persons. Its coverage was substantially broader than that of GATT prior to the end of the Uruguay Round, particularly as to its provisions on services, investment, agriculture and rules of origin. With respect to services and investment in particular, the cornerstone of the CUSFTA commitments was national treatment—in general, the United States and Canada were to afford the same treatment to each other as to their own citizens, with some exceptions.

Some of the most important innovations of the CUSFTA were found in Part VI, which contained the institutional provisions. A Canada–United States Trade Commission was established, with its principal functions relating to dispute settlement. In the event of disputes arising under the agreement (with certain exceptions, i.e. those involving financial services, safeguards and antidumping and countervailing duties), the Commission would undertake to resolve the disputes through consultations and negotiations. If that proved unsuccessful, a dispute settlement panel would be appointed from a list of potential panelists to consider the dispute and issue a ruling promptly. If the Commission was unable

Government of Israel, signed April 22, 1985.

3. Id., arts. 12, 15. The minimum limit for contracts subject to the government procurement provisions is $50,000, about one-third of that of the Tokyo Round Agreement on Government Procurement.

4. Trade Act of 1974, sec. 612, 19 U.S.C.A. sec. 2486(a). In 1979, Congress ordered the President to study the desira-

bility of entering into trade agreements with countries in the northern portion of the Western hemisphere. Trade Agreements Act of 1979, sec. 1104, 19 U.S.C.A. sec. 2486(b). See US Intl.Trade Commn., Background Study of the Economies and International Trade Patterns of the Countries of North America, Central America and the Caribbean (Inv. No. 332–119, 1981).

to agree on the settlement of the dispute after the panel's ruling, the aggrieved party was authorized to suspend concessions under the CUSF-TA to offset its claimed disadvantage. The procedure was modeled somewhat on the GATT system and the grounds for invoking the process included the GATT-based concept of nullification or impairment of benefits (art. 2011). But the system sought to avoid the problems of the GATT system that became evident prior to the Uruguay Round, such as delays, inexperienced panelists and blockage by one party, through imposition of strict deadlines (the process should be completed in 8 or 9 months), the use of a roster from which panelists would be selected and the authorization of compensatory action if no final agreement was reached on the implementation of the panel's decision. In addition to the process described above, the CUSFTA provided for the possibility of binding arbitration (in safeguard disputes). This binding arbitration procedure was similar to the general dispute settlement process except that only the prevailing party was authorized to take compensatory action in the event no settlement was reached.

Chapter 19 established special dispute settlement procedures for antidumping and countervailing duty issues. Under its provisions, so-called binational panels considered claims that amendments to existing antidumping and countervailing duty laws were inconsistent with the relevant GATT Codes and heard appeals from administrative decisions under such laws when requested by an affected party from the other country. Thus, the panels replaced judicial review in such cases. This provision was considered absolutely essential by the Canadians, who felt that the procedure would discourage US administrative authorities from deciding cases on essentially political grounds.

(B) THE NORTH AMERICAN FREE TRADE AGREEMENT (NAFTA)

In 1990, President Bush informed Congress of his intention to enter into negotiations with Mexico toward a free trade agreement, pursuant to negotiating authority contained in the Omnibus Trade and Competitiveness Act of 1988.[5] Since the agreement was intended to include Canada, it would be known as the North American Free Trade Agreement (NAFTA). The NAFTA negotiations were concluded in 1992 and the agreement was signed on December 17, 1992. Political opposition in the United States subsequently led to the negotiation of three "side agreements" covering environmental issues, labor issues and import surges. After a heated political battle, the agreement was approved in Congress and came into effect in 1994.

NAFTA is similar to the CUSFTA, although it goes beyond it in a number of respects. Effectively, the CUSFTA is merged into NAFTA,

---

5. See Pub. L. 100–418, secs. 1102–03, 102 Stat. 1107 (1988), 19 U.S.C. secs. 2902–03.

although formally NAFTA replaces the CUSFTA and the bilateral obligations of the CUSFTA are "suspended."[6]

Part One (Chapters One and Two) of NAFTA lays out objectives and general definitions. Part Two deals with trade in goods. Chapter Three establishes a general requirement of national treatment and provides for the phased elimination of tariffs over a ten year period, with most tariffs eliminated within five years and subject to a fifteen year period in a few cases. Quotas and licensing requirements are also to be eliminated. Chapter Four contains the rules of origin, which generally confer NAFTA origin on a product if (i) it is wholly obtained or produced entirely within the territory of NAFTA, (ii) each of the non-originating components of the product changes tariff heading or (iii) a minimum value added test is met (e.g., 50% of net cost consists NAFTA regional value). Among the many special cases under the origin rules are those that effectively subject automobiles to a 62.5% value added requirement and require most apparel to be sewn from NAFTA origin yarn or fibers. These two rules are somewhat controversial and are more difficult to meet than the analogous rules under the US–Canada FTA. Part Two also contains special provisions for customs procedures (Chapter Five), energy (Chapter Six), agriculture (Chapter Seven) and emergency safeguards (Chapter Eight).

Part Three (Chapter Nine) contains rules governing the use of technical barriers to trade. This provision, along with similar rules in respect of sanitary and phytosanitary measures in Chapter Seven, has been controversial because of a fear by some US environmental and consumer groups that the rules would force the United States to relax health, safety and other standards. Article 906(2) provides, however, that harmonization efforts will be undertaken "[w]ithout reducing the level of safety or of protection of human, animal or plant life or health, the environment or consumers."

Part Four (Chapter Ten) deals with procurement by specified government agencies of specified goods and services. The threshold for coverage is $50,000 ($6.5 million for construction services). Unlike the CUSFTA, which mainly incorporated the provisions of the GATT Government Procurement Code, NAFTA has detailed rules on procurement practices.

Part Five contains provisions on investment (Chapter Eleven), Services (Chapter Twelve), telecommunications (Chapter Thirteen), financial services (Chapter Fourteen), competition policy (Chapter Fifteen) and temporary entry of business persons (Chapter Sixteen). Among the more interesting differences relative to the CUSFTA are in the investment chapter and govern disputes between one of the parties and an investor of another party. They allow a US investor, for example, to seek arbitration of an investment dispute with Mexico. The disputes covered

6. See North American Free Trade Agreement Implementation Act, sec. 107, Pub. L. 103–182, 107 Stat. 2057 (1993).

are those arising out of a violation of NAFTA's rules on investment and certain rules in Chapter Fifteen on monopolies and state enterprises. Thus, a US investor could seek arbitration if it claimed that it did not receive the required compensation on expropriation of its investment, or if the expropriation was not for a public purpose, or if one of the other rules (e.g., national/MFN treatment) of Chapter Eleven were not followed. We consider arbitral decisions under this provision in Chapter 23 infra.

Part Six (Chapter Seventeen) establishes detailed rules with respect to intellectual property, a subject not treated in the CUSFTA to any significant degree. Essentially, the provisions are aimed at ensuring that Mexico provides the sort of protection that the US and Canada provide to intellectual property. Consequently, this chapter contains specific rules on what kinds of intellectual property are to be protected and what protections are to be afforded. In addition, it requires the parties to provide effective domestic law remedies for violations of intellectual property rights, and specifies in some detail procedural and remedial rules.

Part Seven contains institutional provisions that are similar to those of the CUSFTA, adjusted to take account of the existence of three parties. Chapter Nineteen carries over the system of binational panel review of antidumping and countervailing duty decisions reached by administrative agencies. NAFTA provides for a number of changes to the current process. Perhaps the most interesting are the inclusion of a requirement that "[t]he roster * * * include judges or former judges to the fullest extent practicable" (Annex 1901.2), the specification that a panel's failure to apply the appropriate standard of review is grounds for an extraordinary challenge committee to overrule the panel's decision (Article 1904(13)(a)(iii)), and a provision for safeguarding the panel review system (Article 1905), pursuant to which one of the three parties may claim that another party has thwarted the operation of the panel review system and, if the claim is upheld by a special committee, suspend the operation of the binational review process or take certain other action. The first two provisions seem to be designed to make panels less likely to reverse the rulings of administrative agencies, something that they have done relatively often, most often to the displeasure of US industry. Their impact is uncertain since it may be difficult to find judges willing to serve and a recent extraordinary challenge committee has already effectively implemented the second change, but still declined to reverse the panel, despite its disagreement with the panel's intensive review. The third provision was apparently included because of concerns about Mexico's judicial system.

Chapter Twenty provides for the establishment of the Free Trade Commission and the secretariat, and contains NAFTA's general dispute resolution procedures, which are similar to those under Article 18 of the CUSFTA. The parties are generally free to invoke their rights under either GATT dispute settlement procedures or NAFTA procedures, except that a defending party may insist on using the NAFTA procedures in cases involving health or environmental measures that raise factual issues concerning the environment, health, safety or conservation or in cases subject to Article 104, which provides that certain environmental agreements prevail over NAFTA. In addition, Annex 2004 places some limits on nullification or impairment claims in the absence of a technical violation.

As noted, three side agreements were negotiated prior to the approval of NAFTA by the US Congress. The agreement on import surges relates to safeguards measures. The other two agreements address environmental and labor matters. Both of these agreements are structured similarly, in that they create a bureaucracy with the capacity to investigate matters of concern under the side agreement and to promote cooperative activity toward improvement in labor and environmental standards. They also obligate each party to NAFTA to enforce its own laws respecting labor and the environment, and to provide private parties with an opportunity to enforce their rights under national laws. Further, if another party believes that a government is not enforcing its domestic law, a procedure is established through which a complaint may be filed. Should an accord not be reached after such a complaint, a dispute resolution process may be pursued with the possibility of monetary penalties against the recalcitrant government. It is noteworthy that neither side agreement obligates parties to follow any particular labor or environmental standards or to change existing national laws; rather, parties simply covenant to enforce whatever standards have already been enacted or will be enacted in the future in the ordinary course.[7] Consequently, one might question whether the side agreements will prove to be of much consequence in practice.[8]

In 2001, the General Accounting Office compiled a study of the environmental and labor side agreements. It noted that a number of submissions had been made to the NAFTA Secretariat pursuant to both agreements, but only a few of them had resulted in a completed factual investigation, and none had proceeded to the dispute settlement phase. It summarized the experience to date as follows:[9]

> [In the case of the environmental side agreement,] to date, 31 submissions have been filed with the Secretariat. Of these submissions, 8 were against the United States, 13 were against Mexico, and 10 were against Canada. These submissions have raised a wide range of concerns, from narrow questions of a government's failure to effectively enforce environmental laws in a particular instance, to

---

7. Texts of the side agreements are in the Documents Supplement. The labor agreement text may be found in BNA, 1993 Daily Rep. Executives 177 d92 (September 15, 1993), and the environment agreement may be found in BNA, 1993 Daily Rep. Executives 175 d70 (September 13, 1993). A summary of both agreements, prepared by USTR, may be found in BNA, 1993 Daily Rep. Executives 156 d54 (August 16, 1993).

8. See Taylor, NAFTA's Green Accords: Sound and Fury Signifying Little, CATO Policy Analysis No. 198 (November 17, 1993).

9. US General Accounting Office, North American Free Trade Agreement: U.S. Experience With Environment, Labor, and Investment Dispute Settlement Cases, Report No. GAO–01–933 (July 20, 2001).

broader concerns about enforcement in general. The submission process can lead to the publication of a "factual record," a report that outlines the history of the issue, a Party's obligations under the law in question, and the facts relevant to assertions made in the submission. Of the submissions made to date, only two have resulted in completed factual records, and neither of those completed factual records has involved the United States.

[In the case of the labor side agreement,] to date, 23 submissions have been filed, with 7 against the United States, 14 against Mexico, and 2 against Canada. Although these submissions have covered a broad range of issues, a majority of them have raised concerns about freedom of association. Thus far, no submission has reached the dispute settlement phase.

(C) RECENT DEVELOPMENTS

The United States has pursued an aggressive policy of negotiating free trade agreements in recent years. Since 2000, FTAs have come into force with Jordan (2001), Chile (2004), Singapore (2004), Australia (2005), Morocco (2006) and Bahrain (2006). In addition, the Central American Dominican Republic Free Trade Agreement (CAFTA) has come into force with El Salvador (2006), Guatemala (2006), Honduras (2006), Nicaragua (2006), and the Dominican Republic (2007), but not yet with Costa Rica. FTAs with Oman and Peru have been signed and approved by Congress, but have not yet come into force. FTAs have been signed, but not yet approved by Congress, with Colombia, Korea and Panama. In recent years, FTA negotiations have also occurred with Ecuador, Malaysia, the Southern African Customs Union, Thailand and the United Arab Emirates, but for various reasons they were not concluded prior to the expiration of President Bush's negotiating authority.

To persuade the new Democratic majorities in Congress to consider the then pending FTAs, the Bush Administration negotiated an understanding with the Chair of the House Ways and Means Committee on certain changes that would be made to those FTAs. The understanding required a strengthening of the provisions on labor and the environment and some limitations on the provisions dealing with pharmaceuticals and investment. See Inside US Trade, "Schwab, Congress Announce ... FTA Deal", May 11, 2007. The four pending FTAs were subsequently modified, but it remains unclear whether all will be approved.

(D) SELECTED ISSUES IN NAFTA DISPUTE RESOLUTION

We conclude this chapter with brief attention to the dispute resolution system of NAFTA, as well as its predecessor under the CUSFTA, and the interface of this transnational dispute resolution process with the national legal system of the United States.

(1) Use of the Dispute Resolution Process

By far the most active part of the NAFTA dispute resolution system has been the binational panel review process for antidumping and countervailing duty cases, a process that produced 97 dispute settlement reports through the end of 2007. Three of these binational panel decisions were further appealed to extraordinary challenge committees. Dispute settlement reports under Chapter 20, by contrast, which covers all other provisions of NAFTA (except the private actions pursuant to Chapter 11 on investment) have been few and far between, with only three completed reports by the end of 2007, covering cross-border trucking services from Mexico to the United States, certain Canadian agricultural tariffs, and a corn broom safeguard measure applied by the United States

Private actions by investors pursuant to NAFTA Chapter 11 have also been quite significant in number, although systematic information about those actions can be difficult to obtain. The NAFTA Claims website, http://www.naftaclaims.com/, lists a total of 50 disputes that have proceeded through some stage of the arbitration process, a number of which are ongoing at this writing. We will return to the investor rights provisions briefly in Chapter 23.

(2) Constitutional Concerns

Article 19 of the NAFTA, like Article 19 of the CUSFTA, provides that appeals from administrative determinations in antidumping and countervailing duty cases may be taken to a "binational panel." Appellate review by the panel replaces ordinary judicial review—in the United States, the Court of International Trade would otherwise have jurisdiction. The decisions of a binational panel are reviewable on limited grounds by an "extraordinary challenge committee,"[10] but are never appealable to a US court. As such, the operation of these binational panels is quite different than WTO dispute settlement. The panels are substituting for national courts, they are applying national law and their decisions are virtually self executing.

Both the binational panel and the extraordinary challenge committee consist of individuals appointed by the involved nations. A panel consists of five members, two appointed by each disputant nation, and the fifth by agreement of the disputant nations or, failing such agreement, by one of them chosen by lot. The extraordinary challenge committee is similarly constructed, except that it consists of only three individuals. NAFTA requires that panel members be judges or former judges "to the extent practicable." Members of an extraordinary challenge committee must be judges or former judges.

In the United States, the institution of binational panel review raises some constitutional questions. First, the "transfer" of appellate jurisdiction from the Court of International Trade and the Court of Appeals for the Federal Circuit—both Article III courts—to a binational panel, has led some commentators to argue that the panel mechanism

---

10. See NAFTA, Article 1904(13) and Annex 1904.13.

impermissibly deprives litigants of judicial review by an Article III court. Second, the "Appointments Clause" vests the power to appoint "officers of the United States" with the President, subject to Senate confirmation, except for "inferior officers" who may be appointed by Department heads. As noted, members of binational panels are appointed by both parties to the dispute. If such panelists are "officers of the United States," as some commentators have argued on the grounds that they provide appellate review under US law, then the fact that some are appointed by a foreign government could be of some constitutional concern. Likewise, the fact that the US panelists are appointed by USTR rather than by the President may be of constitutional concern unless they may be viewed as "inferior officers."[11] Thus far, however, the NAFTA panel mechanism has survived constitutional challenge, although the merits of the issues are not yet resolved.[12]

(3) Extraordinary Challenges and the Standard of Review

The binational panel review process was included in the CUSFTA at the insistence of Canada, which felt that agency decisions in the United States were politicized and that existing appellate review was too deferential to provide foreign respondents with much protection against agency politics. But similar concerns arise with binational panel review—will the panels undertake to follow the law carefully in accordance with their obligations, or will political factors intrude, perhaps causing panel decisions to turn on which country has the panel majority?

The primary check on panels that go astray is the extraordinary challenge process, itself potentially imperfect because the members of the extraordinary challenge committee are appointed in much the same way as those of the binational panel. The extraordinary challenge committee may review the actions of panels for misconduct or conflict of

11. Much was written on these issues after the entry into force of the CUSFTA. The NAFTA panel review mechanism differs from that of the CUSFTA in some respects that might have constitutional significance, such as in the capacity of a party to suspend it and revert to ordinary judicial review under certain exceptional conditions. Nevertheless, the constitutional concerns about the CUSFTA panels might also be raised, in slightly modified form, about the NAFTA panels.

Among the numerous papers on this set of issues, all written with particular reference to the CUSFTA, are Christenson & Gambrel, Constitutionality of Binational Panel Review in Canada–U.S. Free Trade Agreement, 23 Intl.Law. 401 (1989); Davey, The Appointments Clause and International Dispute Settlement Mechanisms: A False Conflict, 49 Wash. & Lee L.Rev. 1315 (1992); Morrison, Appointments Clause Problems in the Dispute Resolution Provisions of the United States–Canada Free

Trade Agreement, 49 Wash. & Lee L.Rev. 1299 (1992); Note, The Binational Panel Mechanism for Reviewing United States–Canadian Antidumping and Countervailing Duty Determinations: A Constitutional Dilemma?, 29 Va.J.Intl.L. 681 (1989); Note, Chapter 19 of the Canada–United States Free Trade Agreement: An Unconstitutional Preclusion of Article III Review, 5 Conn. J.Intl.L. 317 (1989); Note, The Constitutionality of Chapter 19 of the United States–Canada Free Trade Agreement: Article III and the Minimum Scope of Judicial Review, 89 Colum.L.Rev. 897 (1989).

12. Challenges to the constitutionality of binational review under the CUSFTA were mounted prior to NAFTA, but dismissed on jurisdictional grounds. See, e.g., National Council for Industrial Defense v. United States, 827 F.Supp. 794 (D.D.C. 1993). A similar case after NAFTA dismissed on standing grounds was American Coalition for Competitive Trade v. Clinton, 128 F.3d 761 (D.C.Cir.1997).

interest on the part of a panelist, for failure to follow appropriate procedures, or for exceeding their authority as by failing to apply the correct standard of review.[13] NAFTA attempts to reduce the degree to which the extraordinary challenge committee may be influenced by politics by requiring that all committee members have judicial experience. Whether these provisions will suffice to ensure a reality and a perception of fairness and lack of bias remains to be seen.

IN RE LIVE SWINE FROM CANADA

Panel No. ECC–93–1904–01USA.
1993 WL 566371 (1993).

This memorandum opinion and order arises from the extraordinary challenge proceeding conducted pursuant to Article 1904.13 and Annex 1904.13 of the United States–Canada Free–Trade Agreement ("FTA") in the matter of Live Swine From Canada. The proceeding followed a Request For An Extraordinary Challenge Committee ("Request") filed by the Office of the United States Trade Representative ("USTR"). * * *

An Extraordinary Challenge Committee ("ECC") does not serve as an ordinary appellate court. Article 1904.13 provides that a Party may avail itself of the extraordinary challenge procedure only if it satisfies each prong of a three-part threshold test.[14] If the USTR fails to meet its burden, we must affirm the Panel's decision. The ECC should be perceived as a safety valve in those extraordinary circumstances where a challenge is warranted to maintain the integrity of the binational panel process. * * * The exceptional nature of an extraordinary challenge was accentuated by the drafters of the FTA by limiting extraordinary challenges to the United States and Canadian governments, and not to other Participants in the Panel's proceedings. * * *

III. ALLEGATION OF ERROR BY THE USTR

The USTR on behalf of the Government of the United States argues that the Panel Majority in Decision II manifestly exceeded its jurisdiction by failing to apply the appropriate standard of judicial review, and in particular by reversing Commerce's specificity determination and "supplanting it" with "the appropriate test" announced by the Panel Majority in its opinion. The USTR asserts that such error materially

---

13. NAFTA, art. 1904(13).

14. Article 1904.13 reads:

Where, within a reasonable time after the panel decision is issued, a Party alleges that:

a) i) a member of the panel was guilty of gross misconduct, bias, or a serious conflict of interest, or otherwise materially violated the rules of conduct,

    ii) the panel seriously departed from a fundamental rule of procedure, or

iii) the panel manifestly exceeded its powers, authority or jurisdiction set forth in this Article, and

b) any of the actions set out in subparagraph (a) has materially affected the panel's decision and threatens the integrity of the binational panel review process,

that Party may avail itself of the extraordinary challenge procedure set out in Annex 1904.13.

affected the Panel's decision and thereby threatened the integrity of the binational panel review process. Based on the oral and written record, the Committee is not persuaded that the USTR has sustained its burden of proving that the Panel manifestly exceeded its jurisdiction by failing to apply the correct standard of judicial review.

The North American Free Trade Agreement ("NAFTA") makes explicit what was implicit in the FTA, that if a panel fails to apply the appropriate standard of review, it manifestly exceeds "its powers, authority or jurisdiction," the first prong of our three-part test, FTA Article 1904.13(a)(iii). The equivalent provision in the NAFTA reads: "the panel manifestly exceeded its powers, authority or jurisdiction set out in this Article, for example, by failing to apply the appropriate standard of review ...."

During oral argument, Counsel for the Canadian government argued that it was required that a Panel "expressly refuse" to apply a standard of review prescribed in applicable domestic law in order to conclude that the Panel "manifestly exceeded its ... jurisdiction." Expressed rejection is not required. The appropriate test is whether the Panel accurately articulated the scope of review and * * * whether it "has been conscientiously applied." Although we cannot say here, based upon the record before us, that the Panel did not conscientiously apply the appropriate standard of review, that is not to say that in another case if a panel simply cites the correct standard of review and the record does not reflect the conscientious application of it, that panel would not be manifestly exceeding its jurisdiction.

The Panel correctly cited the standard of review it had to follow under US law. The Panel appropriately looked first to section 516A(b)(1)(B) of the Tariff Act of 1930, as amended, (19 U.S.C. § 1516A(b)(1)(B) (1992)) for its scope of review. Section 516A(b)(1)(B) provides that the Panel "shall hold unlawful any determination by Commerce found * * * to be unsupported by substantial evidence on the record, or otherwise not in accordance with law."

In addition, both Parties and the Panel correctly recognized that the "Special Rule," 19 U.S.C. § 1677(5)(B) (1992), applied to the underlying dispute. This provision requires that Commerce determine whether a "bounty, grant or subsidy" was provided to a "specific enterprise or industry ... " but is silent as to how Commerce should do so (emphasis added). 19 U.S.C. § 1677(5)(B) (1992). Because this statutory provision is silent, the Panel properly recognized that it was required to give deference to Commerce's statutory interpretation. The Panel appropriately cited Chevron, U.S.A. v. Natural Res. Def. Council, 467 U.S. 837 (1984) through its progeny in support of this proposition. The panel stated: "In the absence of clearly discernible legislative intent, panels must limit their inquiry to whether Commerce's statutory interpretations are 'sufficiently reasonable.' In this regard, '[t]he agency's interpretation need not be the only reasonable construction or the one the court would adopt had the question initially arisen in a judicial proceeding.' Id. ...." The Panel also recognized that "under [its standard of review], binational panels may not engage in de novo review or simply impose their constructions of the statute upon the agency."

Not only did the Panel accurately articulate its standard of review * * * [it]concluded after a brief discussion of the specificity test that Commerce's determination was not in accordance with law, nor based on substantial evidence. Although we need not and will not reach a decision on the merits of these conclusions, the Committee felt the Panel may have erred. Nonetheless, on balance, the Committee was not persuaded that the Panel failed to apply the properly articulated standard of review. Because the Committee was not persuaded that the Panel manifestly exceeded the appropriate standard of review, the Committee need not address the second and third prongs of our test as set forth in FTA Article 1904.13(b).

Notes and Questions

(1) Does the extraordinary challenge committee do enough here to verify that the proper standard of review was "conscientiously applied?" What more should it do, if anything?

(2) Note that the *Live Swine* case was a pre-NAFTA decision pursuant to the Canada–US Free Trade Agreement, although the standards that it applied were the same as those now applicable under NAFTA. In the three extraordinary challenge cases filed to date under NAFTA, the committee has upheld the binational panel each time, although panels have been strongly criticized at times. See Pure Magnesium from Canada, ECC 2003–1904–01USA, October 17, 2004.

Chapter 12

THE NATIONAL TREATMENT CLAUSE

SECTION 12.1 INTRODUCTION

The national treatment obligation of the General Agreement on Tariffs and Trade, like the MFN obligation, is a rule of nondiscrimination.[1] In the case of MFN, the obligation prohibits discrimination as between the same goods from different exporting countries. The national treatment clause, in contrast, imposes the principle of nondiscrimination as between domestically produced goods and the same imported goods. It is a central feature of international trade rules and policy,[2] and exists within the WTO/GATT system to prevent government practices that evade tariff and other market access obligations.

Article III is the central national treatment obligation of the General Agreement. Paragraph 1 establishes the general principle that internal taxes and regulations "should not be applied * * * so as to afford protection to domestic production." In some cases, this principle is specifically incorporated into the obligations established in the other provisions of Article III. Paragraph 2 of Article III requires national treatment in respect of internal taxation (such as sales, excise or value added taxes), while paragraph 4 requires it in respect of regulations affecting the sale and use of goods generally. The other paragraphs of Article III deal with particular situations, including paragraph 8, which carves out important exceptions for government procurement and subsidization.

Article III is closely related to a number of other GATT provisions, particularly Articles I, II, XI, XVII and XX, and it is helpful at this point

---

1. Many trade treaties negotiated prior to the General Agreement on Tariffs and Trade included a clause which imposed a "national treatment" obligation upon the parties. See John H. Jackson, World Trade and the Law of GATT 277 & nn. 7 & 8 (1969).

2. In addition to the references in the text of this chapter, the reader may find the following references useful in further re-

search on the national treatment obligation: Jackson, supra note 1, ch. 12; US Tariff Commn., Trade Barriers, pts. 1–4, Report to the Committee on Finance of the United States Senate and its Subcomm. on International Trade (USTC Pub. No. 665 1974); Kenneth W. Dam, The GATT: Law and International Economic Organization ch. 7 (1970).

to preview those interactions. For example, the subject matter of Article III, paragraphs 2 and 4 (internal taxation and sales regulations), is incorporated into Article I. Thus, in respect of those matters, both GATT nondiscrimination principles are applicable.

Article III acts to reinforce the tariff bindings made pursuant to Article II by limiting the circumstances in which it is permissible for a nation to provide treatment for domestic goods in its national legislation and programs which is more favorable than that for imported goods. Such treatment will tend to disfavor the importation and purchase of imported goods, and consequently it is a form of protection, which can be even more severe than tariffs. A GATT binding to limit a tariff on a particular commodity would be valueless if there were not some limitations on the types of internal taxation or regulation which a country could impose to afford protection against such imports. To cite one easy example: Suppose tariffs on widgets were bound at 10%, but a country imposed an internal excise or sales tax on all widgets, in an amount of 5% for domestic goods and 10% for imported goods. The effect would be similar to adding 5% to the tariff. Such a practice is proscribed by Article III. This result underlines the philosophy of the General Agreement: protection should be transparent and in the form of tariffs.

The interaction of Articles III and XI was explored in Section 9.1. As noted there, it has been said that Article XI applies to measures that affect the actual importation of products, while Article III deals with measures affecting imported products. This line may sometimes be hard to draw. A note to Article III provides that measures applied to domestic products, which are applied to imported products at the time of importation, may be analyzed under Article III.

There is also a complex relationship between Article III and XVII, which was examined in Section 9.4. Article XVII deals with state trading enterprises and imposes certain obligations on them. It has sometimes been claimed to impose a sort of national treatment obligation, although as noted above some interpretative material suggests the contrary.

The interrelationship of Article III and Article XX, GATT's general exceptions clause, sometimes presents extremely difficult problems. Article XX, which itself contains language that imposes a kind of loose national treatment obligation, allows government actions that violate GATT obligations but that are justifiable on health, safety and similar grounds. There are broad policy issues raised by the interaction of the trade liberalization function of Article III and the exceptions established by Article XX. A nation may have a wide variety of domestic programs and legislation designed to promote health, welfare and various economic goals. It may regulate the sale of goods, so as to assure their reasonable safety when used by the public. It may regulate the production of goods in order to prevent pollution of the atmosphere or of water. It may design a tax structure to assist depressed areas of the country or to redistribute wealth from the rich to the poor. Few would advocate a system of international economic rules that would prevent nations from exercising their sovereignty to promote domestic policy goals in these various ways. But to the extent that these policies tend to disfavor imports, there may be a conflict between the liberal trade goals of international economic policy and national policy goals embodied in a wide variety of local and national laws and regulations.

The more the international economic system imposes rules to limit such hidden protectionism, however, the less freedom there is for national or local governmental units to pursue even their legitimate domestic policies. These same issues arise in any federal system—such as that of the United States or the EU—where there are different levels of government with overlapping responsibilities and powers over some subject matters. The question is which level of government should appropriately have the authority to make certain types of decisions. If too much decision-making is centralized at the federal level, then local governments cannot use initiative and cannot respond to constituents, even though they may be closer to the particular problems of those constituents. Some central control may be necessary, however, as there seems to be a natural tendency for local government units to establish policies which favor their constituents at the expense of constituents located in other government units, to the general detriment of the federal system. We have already examined some aspects of this issue in Sections 3.6 (US federal-state relations) and 4.5 (the subsidiarity issue in the EU).

We will consider the Article XX exceptions in some detail in Chapter 13. In Chapter 14, we will examine the problems of technical barriers to trade and the applicable WTO rules at the international level. One interesting question will be whether differing degrees of integration (economic, political, social) within an entity necessitate different approaches to these problems. In this regard, recall the discussion of the economic integration of Europe in Section 4.5 supra.

In the next sections of this chapter, we first take up the national treatment obligation generally, with excerpts from two of the most important GATT panel reports on Article III. We then consider in Section 12.3 the prohibition on discriminatory internal taxes found in Article III:2. In analyzing this provision, close attention is given to the text and interpretative notes of Article III. A key issue is distinguishing like products, directly competitive or substitutable products, and other products. In Section 12.4, we turn to an examination of Article III:4, which requires that imported products be given no less favorable treatment than like domestic products in respect of certain internal regulations. The concept of like product is crucial here too, but different considerations apply. Finally, we take a quick look at the exceptions contained in Article III:8, and specifically the one for government procurement. We will revisit the issue of national treatment in Chapter 19 on trade in services since one of the major questions that arose in negotiating the General Agreement on Trade in Services was the extent to which a national treatment obligation should apply to banking, insurance and other services.

SECTION 12.2   THE NATIONAL TREATMENT OBLIGATION: THE BASIC RULE

Numerous GATT and WTO panel and Appellate Body decisions have addressed the interpretation of Article III. Historically, the following two decisions are probably the most important, with the first decision giving a broad reading to paragraph 4 in the early days of GATT dispute settlement and the second one building on it 20 years later in 1979. In reading these cases, the student should focus on the scope of Article III. Exactly how far does it go in preventing discriminatory treatment of imports? Might it require comparatively favorable treatment of imports?

ITALIAN DISCRIMINATION AGAINST IMPORTED AGRICULTURAL MACHINERY

GATT Panel Report adopted October 23, 1958.
7th Supp. BISD 60 (1959).

[The United Kingdom challenged an Italian law (no. 949) pursuant to which the Italian Government had established a fund, used to grant special credit terms for the purchase of Italian agricultural machinery. The loans were granted at 3 per cent; purchasers of foreign agricultural machinery on credit would receive less favorable terms. During the period 1952–1957 the purchasers of about half of the Italian tractors sold in Italy (i.e., about one-third of all tractors sold in the country) benefited from these credit facilities. In 1949, before the entry into force of Law No. 949, Italian import duties on various types of tractors and other agricultural machinery had been bound under GATT Article II.]

5.   The United Kingdom delegation noted that Article III:4 of the General Agreement provided that products imported into the territory of any contracting party "shall be accorded treatment no less favourable than that accorded to like products of national origin in respect of all laws, regulations and requirements affecting their internal sale, offering for sale, purchase, transportation * * * "etc. As the credit facilities provided under the Italian Law were not available to the purchasers of imported tractors and other agricultural machinery these products did not enjoy the equality of treatment which should be accorded to them. The fact that these credit facilities were reserved exclusively to the purchasers of Italian tractors and other agricultural machinery represented a discrimination and the operation of the Law involved an inconsistency with the provisions of Article III of the General Agreement which provides that laws, regulations and requirements affecting internal sale should not be applied to imported products so as to afford protection to domestic producers. The United Kingdom would not challenge the consistency with the General Agreement of subsidies which the Italian Government might wish to grant to domestic producers of tractors and other agricultural machinery in accordance with the terms of paragraph 8(b) of Article III. However, in the case of the Italian Law the

assistance by the State was not given to producers but to the purchasers of agricultural machinery; a case which is not covered by the provisions of paragraph 8(b). Even in the case of subsidies granted to producers the rights of the United Kingdom under Article XXIII of the General Agreement would be safeguarded as was recognized by the CONTRACT-ING PARTIES in paragraph 13 of the Report on Other Barriers to Trade which they approved during the course of the Review Session.[1]

6. The Italian delegation considered that the General Agreement was a trade agreement and its scope was limited to measures governing trade; thus the text of paragraph 4 of Article III applied only to such laws, regulations and requirements which were concerned with the actual conditions for sale, transportation, etc., of the commodity in question and should not be interpreted in an extensive way. In particular, the Italian delegation stated that the commitment undertaken by the CONTRACTING PARTIES under that paragraph was limited to qualitative and quantitative regulations to which goods were subjected, with respect to their sale or purchase on the domestic market.

7. It was clear in their view that the Law No. 949 which concerned the development of the Italian economy and the improvement in the employment of labour was not related to the questions of sale, purchase or transportation of imported and domestically produced products which were the only matters dealt with in Article III.

8. Moreover the Italian delegation considered that the text of Article III:4 could not be construed in such a way as to prevent the Italian Government from taking the necessary measures to assist the economic development of the country and to improve the conditions of employment in Italy.

9. Finally, the Italian delegation, noting that the United Kingdom delegation recognized that the Italian Government would be entitled to grant subsidies exclusively to domestic producers, stressed it would not be logical to exclude this possibility in the case of credit facilities which had a far less pronounced effect on the terms of competition.

10. In the view of the Italian delegation it would be inappropriate for the CONTRACTING PARTIES to construe the provisions of Article III in a broad way since this would limit the rights of contracting parties in the formulation of their domestic economic policies in a way which was not contemplated when they accepted the terms of the General Agreement.

11. The Panel agreed that the question of the consistency of the effects of the Italian Law with the provisions of the General Agreement raised a problem of interpretation. It had the impression that the contention of the Italian Government might have been influenced in part by the slight difference of wording which existed between the French

---

1. [original note] Third Supplement, Basic Instruments and Selected Documents, page 224. [This refers to the possibility of a bringing a non-violation case on the grounds that a tariff concession had been nullified by domestic subsidies. See Section 7.4(A) supra.]

and the English texts of paragraph 4 of Article III. The French text which had been submitted to the Italian Parliament for approval provided that the imported products "ne seront pas soumis à un traitement moins favorable" whereas the English text read "the imported product shall be accorded treatment no less favourable". It was clear from the English text that any favourable treatment granted to domestic products would have to be granted to like imported products and the fact that the particular law in question did not specifically prescribe conditions of sale or purchase appeared irrelevant in the light of the English text. It was considered, moreover, that the intention of the drafters of the Agreement was clearly to treat the imported products in the same way as the like domestic products once they had been cleared through customs. Otherwise indirect protection could be given.

12.   In addition, the text of paragraph 4 referred both in English and French to laws and regulations and requirements *affecting* internal sale, purchase, etc., and not to laws, regulations and requirements governing the conditions of sale or purchase. The selection of the word "affecting" would imply, in the opinion of the Panel, that the drafters of the Article intended to cover in paragraph 4 not only the laws and regulations which directly governed the conditions of sale or purchase but also any laws or regulations which might adversely modify the conditions of competition between the domestic and imported products on the internal market.

13.   The Italian delegation alleged that the provisions of paragraph 8(b) which exempted the granting of subsidies to producers from the operation of this Article showed that the intention of the drafters of the Agreement was to limit the scope of Article III to laws and regulations directly related to the conditions of sale, purchase, etc. On the other hand, the Panel considered that if the Italian contention were correct and if the scope of Article III was limited in this way (which would, of course, not include any measure of subsidization) it would have been unnecessary to include the provisions contained in paragraph 8(b) since they would be excluded *ipso facto* from the scope of Article III. The fact that the drafters of Article III thought it necessary to include this exemption for production subsidies would indicate that the intent of the drafters was to provide equal conditions of competition once goods had been cleared through customs.

14.   Moreover, the Panel agreed with the contention of the United Kingdom delegation that in any case the provisions of paragraph 8(b) would not be applicable to this particular case since the credit facilities provided under the Law were granted to the purchasers of agricultural machinery and could not be considered as subsidies accorded to the producers of agricultural machinery.

15.   The Panel also noted that if the Italian contention were correct, and if the scope of Article III were limited in the way the Italian delegation suggested to a specific type of laws and regulations, the value of the bindings under Article II of the Agreement and of the general

rules of non-discrimination as between imported and domestic products could be easily evaded.

16. The Panel recognized and the United Kingdom delegation agreed with this view that it was not the intention of the General Agreement to limit the right of a contracting party to adopt measures which appeared to it necessary to foster its economic development or to protect a domestic industry, provided that such measures were permitted by the terms of the General Agreement. The GATT offered a number of possibilities to achieve these purposes through tariff measures or otherwise. The Panel did not appreciate why the extension of the credit facilities in question to the purchasers of imported tractors as well as domestically produced tractors would detract from the attainment of the objectives of the Law, which aimed at stimulating the purchase of tractors mainly by small farmers and co-operatives in the interests of economic development. If, on the other hand, the objective of the Law, although not specifically stated in the text thereof, were to protect the Italian agricultural machinery industry, the Panel considered that such protection should be given in ways permissible under the General Agreement rather than by the extension of credit exclusively for purchases of domestically produced agricultural machinery.

* * *

25. In the light of the considerations set out above the Panel suggests to the CONTRACTING PARTIES that it would be appropriate for them to make a recommendation to the Italian Government in accordance with paragraph 2 of Article XXIII. The Panel considers that the recommendation should draw the attention of the Italian Government to the adverse effects on United Kingdom exports of agricultural machinery, particularly tractors, of those provisions of Law 949 limiting the prescribed credit facilities to purchasers of Italian produced machinery and suggest to the Italian Government that it consider the desirability of eliminating within a reasonable time the adverse effects of the Law on the import trade of agricultural machinery by modifying the operation of that Law or by other appropriate means.

UNITED STATES—SECTION 337 OF THE TARIFF ACT OF 1930

GATT Panel Report adopted November 7, 1989.
36th Supp. BISD 345 (1990).

[This case arose out of a complaint by the European Community that Section 337 of the US Tariff Act of 1930 violated Article III.]

2.2 Under Section 337 of the United States Tariff Act of 1930 unfair methods of competition and unfair acts in the importation of articles into the United States, or in their sale, are unlawful if these unfair acts or methods of competition have the effect or tendency to (i) destroy or to substantially injure an industry efficiently and economically operated in the United States, (ii) prevent the establishment of such an industry, or (iii) restrain or monopolise trade and commerce in the United States. The unfair acts and methods of competition in question include the importation or sale of goods that infringe valid United States patents. * * * Since it was revised in the Trade Act of 1974, the majority of investigations under the Section 337 have concerned alleged infringements of patents. * * *

2.3   Remedies available under Section 337, in the event of a violation of the Section, consist of orders excluding the articles concerned from importation into the United States (exclusion orders) and/or cease and desist orders directing parties violating Section 337 to stop the act or method of competition found to be unfair. The exclusion order may be a general order covering all imports that, in a patent-based case, infringe the United States patent in question, or may be limited to goods produced by a respondent in the case.

2.4   Investigations under Section 337 are carried out by the United States International Trade Commission (USITC). The USITC is an independent administrative agency of the United States Government. The USITC is not created as a court under Article III of the United States Constitution, but is authorised and directed by Congress to conduct proceedings under Section 337 which are similar to court proceedings. Section 337 proceedings are subject to the Administrative Procedure Act, which governs similar "quasi-judicial proceedings" conducted by numerous agencies of the United States Federal Government.

* * *

V.   Findings

[Although Section 337 applies to more than patent disputes, the Panel noted that the complaint in this case and the submissions of the parties concentrated on the application of Section 337 to patent-based cases, and the Panel's findings and conclusions are limited to such cases.]

5.4   The central and undisputed facts before the Panel are that, in patent infringement cases, proceedings before the USITC under Section 337 are only applicable to imported products alleged to infringe a United States patent; and that these proceedings are different, in a number of respects, from those applying before a federal district court when a product of United States origin is challenged on grounds of patent infringement. The [European] Community maintained that the differences between the two proceedings are such that the treatment accorded to imported products is less favorable than that accorded to like products of United States origin, inconsistently with Article III:4 of the General Agreement, and that this less favorable treatment cannot be justified under Article XX(d) of the General Agreement. The United States maintained that Section 337 is justifiable under Article XX(d) and, in any event, is not inconsistent with Article III:4 since it does not accord imported products less favorable treatment than that accorded to like products of United States origin.

* * *

(iii) Relation of Article III to Article XX(d)

5.8　The parties to the dispute agreed that Article III:4 applies to substantive patent law, since such law affects the "internal sale, offering for sale, purchase, transportation or use" of imported and domestic products. They also agreed that the consistency of the substantive provisions of United States patent law with the General Agreement is not at issue. Further, the parties agreed that Section 337, when applied in cases of alleged patent infringement, is a means to secure compliance with United States patent law in respect of imported products. They disagreed, however, on the question of whether a measure to secure compliance with patent laws—in contrast to the substantive patent law itself—is covered by Article III:4. * * *

5.9　The Panel noted that Article XX is entitled "General Exceptions" and that the central phase in the introductory clause reads: "nothing in this Agreement shall be construed to prevent the adoption or enforcement ... of measures ...". Article XX(d) thus provides for a limited and conditional exception from obligations under other provisions. The Panel therefore concluded that Article XX(d) applies only to measures inconsistent with another provision of the General Agreement, and that, consequently, the application of Section 337 has to be examined first in the light of Article III:4. If any inconsistencies with Article III:4 were found, the Panel would then examine whether they could be justified under Article XX(d).

(iv) Article III:4

(a) Meaning of "Laws, Regulations and Requirements" in Article III:4

5.10　The Panel then examined Section 337 in the light of Article III:4. The Panel first addressed the issue of whether only substantive laws, regulations and requirements or also procedural laws, regulations and requirements can be regarded as "affecting" the internal sale of imported products. * * * The Panel noted that the text of Article III:4 makes no distinction between substantive and procedural laws, regulations or requirements and it was not aware of anything in the drafting history that suggests that such a distinction should be made. A previous Panel had found that "the selection of the word 'affecting' would imply ... that the drafters of the Article intended to cover in paragraph 4 not only the laws and regulations which directly governed the conditions of sale or purchase but also any laws or regulations which might adversely modify the conditions of competition between the domestic and imported products on the internal market," [citing para. 12 of the *Italian Agricultural Machinery* case, excerpted earlier in this section]. In the Panel's view enforcement procedures cannot be separated from the substantive provisions they serve to enforce. If the procedural provisions of internal law were not covered by Article III:4, contracting parties could escape the national treatment standard by enforcing substantive law, itself meeting the national treatment standard, through procedures less favorable to imported products than to like products of national origin. The interpretation suggested by the United States would therefore defeat the purpose of Article III, which is to ensure that internal measures "not be applied to imported or domestic products so as to afford protection to domestic production" (Article III:1). The fact that Section 337 is used as a means for the enforcement of United States patent law at the *border* does not provide an escape from the applicability of Article III:4; the interpretative note to Article III states that any law, regulation or requirement affecting the internal sale of products that is enforced in the case of the imported product at the time or point of importation is nevertheless subject to the provisions of Article III. Nor could the applicability of Article III:4 be denied on the ground that most of the procedures in the case before the Panel are applied to persons rather than products, since the factor determining whether persons might be susceptible to Section 337 proceedings or federal district court procedures is the source of the challenged products, that is whether they are of United States origin or imported. For these reasons, the Panel found that the procedures under Section 337 come within the concept of "laws, regulations and requirements" affecting the internal sale of imported products, as set out in Article III of the General Agreement.

(b) The "No Less Favorable" Treatment Standard of Article III:4

5.11 The Panel noted that, as far as the issues before it are concerned, the "no less favorable" treatment requirement set out in Article III:4, is unqualified. These words are to be found throughout the General Agreement and later agreements negotiated in the GATT framework as an expression of the underlying principle of equality of treatment of imported products as compared to the treatment given either to other foreign products, under the most favored nation standard, or to domestic products, under the national treatment standard of Article III. The words "treatment no less favorable" in paragraph 4 call for effective equality of opportunities for imported products in respect of the application of laws, regulations and requirements affecting the internal sale, offering for sale, purchase, transportation, distribution or use of products. This clearly sets a minimum permissible standard as a basis. On the one hand, contracting parties may apply to imported products different formal legal requirements if doing so would accord imported products more favorable treatment. On the other hand, it also has to be recognised that there may be cases where application of formally identical legal provisions would in practice accord less favorable treatment to imported products and a contracting party might thus have to apply different legal provisions to imported products to ensure that the treatment accorded them is in fact no less favorable. For these reasons, the mere fact that imported products are subject under Section 337 to legal provisions that are different from those applying to products of national origin is in itself not conclusive in establishing inconsistency with Article III:4. In such cases, it has to be assessed whether or not such differences in the legal provisions applicable do or do not accord to imported products less favorable treatment. Given that the underlying objective is to guarantee equality of treatment, it is incumbent on the contracting party applying differential treatment to show that, in spite of such differences, the no less favorable treatment standard of Article III is met.

5.12   The Panel noted the differing views of the parties on how an assessment should be made as to whether the differences between Section 337 and federal district court procedures do or do not accord imported products less favorable treatment than that accorded to products of United States origin. In brief, the United States believed that this determination could only be made on the basis of an examination of the *actual results* of past Section 337 cases. It would follow from this reasoning that any unfavorable elements of treatment of imported products could be offset by more favorable elements of treatment, provided that the results, as shown in past cases, have not been less favorable. The Community's interpretation of Article III:4 would require that Section 337 not be *capable* of according imported products less favorable treatment; elements of less and more favorable treatment could thus only be offset against each other to the extent that they always would arise in the same cases and necessarily would have an offsetting influence on each other.

5.13   The Panel examined these arguments carefully. It noted that a previous Panel had found that the purpose of the first sentence of Article III:2, dealing with internal taxes and other internal charges, is to protect "expectations on the competitive relationship between imported and domestic products".[2] Article III:4, which is the parallel provision of Article III dealing with the "non-charge" elements of internal legislation, has to be construed as serving the same purpose. Article III:4 would not serve this purpose if the United States interpretation were adopted, since a law, regulation or requirement could then only be challenged in GATT after the event as a means of rectifying less favorable treatment of imported products rather than as a means of forestalling it. In any event, the Panel doubted the feasibility of an approach that would require it to be demonstrated that differences between procedures under Section 337 and those in federal district courts had actually caused, in a given case or cases, less favorable treatment. The Panel therefore considered that, in order to establish whether the "no less favorable" treatment standard of Article III:4 is met, it had to assess whether or not Section 337 in itself may lead to the application to imported products of treatment less favorable than that accorded to products of United States origin. It noted that this approach is in accordance with previous practice of the CONTRACTING PARTIES in applying Article III, which has been to base their decisions on the distinctions made by the laws,

---

2. [original note] Report of Panel on United States—Taxes on Petroleum and Certain Imported Substances (L/6175, para-graph 5.1.9), adopted by the Council on June 17, 1987.

regulations or requirements themselves and on their potential impact rather than on the actual consequences for specific imported products.

5.14   The Panel further found that the "no less favorable" treatment requirement of Article III:4 has to be understood as applicable to each individual case of imported products. The Panel rejected any notion of balancing more favorable treatment of some imported products against less favorable treatment of other imported products. If this notion were accepted, it would entitle a contracting party to derogate from the no less favorable treatment obligation in one case, or indeed in respect of one contracting party, on the ground that it accords more favorable treatment in some other case, or to another contracting party. Such an interpretation would lead to great uncertainty about the conditions of competition between imported and domestic products and thus defeat the purposes of Article III.

(c) Appraisal of Section 337 in Terms of Article III:4

5.15   The United States contended that Section 337 accords imported products more favorable treatment than that accorded to domestic products in district court proceedings because of [several factors.] The Panel examined whether these elements of claimed more favorable treatment could within the meaning of Article III:4 offset any elements of less favorable treatment of imported products alleged by the Community.

5.16   As has already been stated above, an element of more favorable treatment would only be relevant if it would always accompany and offset an element of differential treatment causing less favorable treatment. * * *

5.17   The Panel noted that some of the procedural advantages that, according to the United States, are given to respondents could operate in all cases. The Panel also recognised that the substantive economic requirements put procedural burdens not only on the respondent but also on the complainant, which has the burden of proof on these matters, and that these procedural burdens could operate in all cases. The Panel took these factors into account to the extent that they might be capable of exerting an offsetting influence in each individual case of less favorable treatment resulting from an element cited by the Community.

5.18   In cases concerning imported products over which both federal district courts and the USITC have jurisdiction, the complainant has the choice of which forum to use, or possibly to initiate a complaint in both fora; no equivalent choice of forum is available to a plaintiff in a case concerning products of United States origin. This option was referred to on numerous occasions by the Community and by third contracting parties making submissions. The Panel found that, given the differences between the proceedings of the USITC and of federal courts, to provide the complainant with the choice of forum where imported products are concerned and to provide no corresponding choice where domestically-produced products are concerned is in itself less favorable treatment of imported products and is therefore inconsistent with Article

III:4. It is also a reason why in practice Section 337 is more likely to be employed in those cases where the specific elements that might accord less favorable treatment to imported products are significant. The complainant will tend to avoid recourse to Section 337 in cases where elements of more favorable treatment of the respondent than that accorded in federal district court litigation might play a role, for example where public interest or policy considerations might be expected to intervene.

5.19　The Panel considered the specific differences between Section 337 proceedings and those in federal district courts referred to by the Community to assess whether they accord less favorable treatment to imported products than that accorded to products of United States origin in patent-based cases: * * *

(d) Summary of Findings Under Article III:4

5.20　The Panel found that Section 337, inconsistently with Article III:4 of the General Agreement, accords to imported products alleged to infringe United States patents treatment less favorable than that accorded under federal district court procedures to like products of United States origin as a result of the following factors:

(i) the availability to complainants of a choice of forum in which to challenge imported products, whereas no corresponding choice is available to challenge products of United States origin.

(ii) the potential disadvantage to producers or importers of challenged products of foreign origin resulting from the tight and fixed time-limits in proceedings under Section 337, when no comparable time-limits apply to producers of challenged products of United States origin;

(iii) the non-availability of opportunities in Section 337 proceedings to raise counterclaims, as is possible in proceedings in federal district court;

(iv) the possibility that general exclusion orders may result from proceedings brought before the USITC under Section 337, given that no comparable remedy is available against infringing products of United States origin.

(v) the automatic enforcement of exclusion orders by the United States Customs Service, when injunctive relief obtainable in federal court in respect of infringing products of United States origin requires for its enforcement individual proceedings brought by the successful plaintiff;

(vi) the possibility that producers or importers of challenged products of foreign origin may have to defend their products both before the USITC and in federal district court, whereas no corresponding exposure exists with respect to products of United States origin.

5.21 The Panel considered whether all these differences of treatment could be traced back to one common cause, this being the structure of the USITC which is fundamentally not a court of law but an administrative agency, and whether this structural difference could be said to entail in itself treatment incompatible with the requirements of Article III. The Panel however reached no conclusion in this respect, as this question had not been raised in such general terms by the Community.

[The panel then rejected the US defense based on Article XX(d), which permits measures necessary to secure compliance with law relating to, inter alia, the protection of patents. We consider the Article XX exceptions in Chapter 13.]

Notes and Questions

(1) The *Section 337* case is unusual in that it effectively overruled a prior panel decision. In United States—Imports of Certain Automotive Spring Assemblies, GATT, 30th Supp. BISD 107 (Panel report adopted May 26, 1983), the use of Section 337 had been upheld in a specific case, but when the GATT Council adopted the panel report it did so in light of an understanding that adoption of the report "shall not foreclose future examination of the use of Section 337 to deal with patent infringement cases from the point of view of consistency with Articles III and XX of the General Agreement." GATT Doc. C/M/168, item 7. We examine Section 337 and the US implementation of the panel's findings in Chapter 20 infra.

(2) The broad scope of Article III:4 is underscored by these panel decisions. The concluding lines of paragraphs 11 and 12 of the *Italian Agricultural Machinery* case are particularly noteworthy, as they stress the role of Article III in (i) limiting protective measures to border measures (mainly tariffs) and (ii) preventing evasion of tariff bindings. How does the Section 337 decision build on these conclusions of the *Italian Agricultural Machinery* case? See, in particular, paragraph 5.11. What does it mean to say

> that the words "treatment no less favorable" in paragraph 4 call for *effective equality of opportunities* for imported products in respect of the application of laws, regulations and requirements affecting the internal sale, offering for sale, purchase, transportation, distribution or use of products (emphasis added)?

Suppose that the market for cigarettes in a country had been closed to imports and dominated by a domestic monopoly. If the market is opened to imports, but at the same time advertising of cigarettes is banned, could the exporting countries claim that in order to provide effective equality of opportunities, they must be allowed some freedom to advertise their products? See Thailand—Restrictions on Importation of and Internal Taxes on Cigarettes, GATT, 37th Supp. BISD 200, 224 (1991) (Panel report adopted Nov. 7, 1990) (panel suggested that even if an advertising restriction were found to violate Article III, the restriction might be justified as necessary under Article XX(b)).

(3) The *Italian Agricultural Machinery* panel's rejection of Italy's paragraph 8(b) defense is typical. If interpreted broadly, any discrimination

against imports could be characterized as a government subsidy to domestic producers and therefore exempt under paragraph 8(b). This would obviously completely eviscerate the substantive provisions of Article III. See also United States—Measures Affecting Alcoholic and Malt Beverages, 39th Supp. BISD 206 (Panel report adopted June 19, 1992)(rejected US attempt to justify lower taxes on domestic products and tax credits available only in respect of domestic products by reference to Article 8(b)). Yet, does it make much sense to distinguish a subsidy to sellers from a subsidy to purchasers? How are they different in their economic impact?

(4) How does the *Section 337* panel deal with the problem of measuring the effect of a violation? Did it focus on the actual impact of Section 337 or the potential impact? Over time, it has become accepted in GATT that a mandatory law that might result in a GATT violation violates the General Agreement on its face and no negative impact need be shown. The explanation for this expansive interpretation is in part given in paragraph 5.13, where it is noted that Article III is aimed at protecting expectations on competitive relationships between imports and domestic products. We previously discussed aspects of this issue in Section 7.4(A) on dispute settlement.

(5) Note that the panel did not rule out the possibility that a party could treat imported and domestic products differently without violating Article III (para. 5.11). Who would have the burden of proving the different treatment afforded no less favorable treatment? How easy do you think it would be to meet this burden? Note also that the panel rejected the notion of balancing more favorable and less favorable aspects of a law. (para. 5.14) This is consistent with the interpretation that has been given to Article I, as we saw in Section 9.2(B)(2). We examine the question of what constitutes less favorable treatment in Section 12.4(B) infra.

(6) What does national treatment mean in a federal system? Suppose that Michigan favors its own citizens over those of neighboring US states. If a national treatment obligation applies to Michigan, does Michigan owe Canadians the treatment it gives its own citizens or only the most favorable treatment that it gives noncitizens?

SECTION 12.3 DISCRIMINATORY TAXES: ARTICLE III:2

In this section, we look at the problem of discriminatory taxation. While most product-based taxes are applied uniformly across a broad range of products (such as general sales taxes or value added taxes), certain excise or registration taxes may vary greatly depending on product definitions. In particular, various national systems for taxing alcoholic beverages have often been alleged to provide protection to domestic products, whether intentionally or otherwise. As we will see, Article III:2 can be used to attack these systems in two ways: First, it can be claimed that the products involved are all like products and that only one tax rate can be applied. Second, even if the beverages are not like products, Article III:2, second sentence, can be invoked to claim that the tax system is being used to protect some domestic products, in contravention of Article III:1 and 2. In reading the following Appellate Body report, consider the following questions: How does the Appellate Body's analysis of the like product issue compare to the *SPF* and *Spanish Coffee* cases in Section 10.2? If different, are the differences justified? How does the second sentence of Article III:2 affect, if at all, the like-product issue? Does it justify (or obviate the need for) a broad definition of like product? What differences are there in the way that the two sentences of Article III:2 operate?

JAPAN—TAXES ON ALCOHOLIC BEVERAGES

WT/DS8, 10 & 11/AB/R.
Appellate Body Report adopted November 1, 1996.

[Canada, the EC and the United States challenged the Japanese law on liquor taxation on the grounds that it violated Article GATT III:2 by taxing a Japanese product—shochu—less heavily than certain like or competitive imported products (including vodka, gin, whisky, brandy, rum and liqueurs). The Panel concluded that (i) shochu and vodka were like products and Japan, by taxing the latter in excess of the former, violated Article III:2, first sentence and (ii) shochu and the other products were "directly competitive or substitutable products" and Japan, by not taxing them similarly, violated Article III:2, second sentence. A 1987 GATT case had found the prior Japanese liquor tax system to violate Article III.

At issue in the WTO case was the proper interpretation of Article III:2, the second sentence of which specifically refers to Article III:1 and is the subject of an interpretative note. These provisions should be reviewed before studying the Appellate Body's report. After setting out the provisions of Articles 31 and 32 of the Vienna Convention on the Law of Treaties, the Appellate Body noted that "A fundamental tenet of treaty interpretation flowing from the general rule of interpretation set out in Article 31 is the principle of effectiveness (*ut res magis valeat quam pereat*).[1] In *US—Gasoline*, we noted that '[o]ne of the corollaries of the general rule of interpretation' in the Vienna Convention is that interpretation must give meaning and effect to all the terms of the treaty. An interpreter is not free to adopt a reading that would result in reducing whole clauses or paragraphs of a treaty to redundancy or inutility." It then turned to an examination of Article III in general and Article III:2 in particular.]

The broad and fundamental purpose of Article III is to avoid protectionism in the application of internal tax and regulatory measures. More specifically, the purpose of Article III "is to ensure that internal measures 'not be applied to imported or domestic products so as to afford

---

1. [original note 21] See also (1966) Yearbook of the International Law Commission, Vol. II, p. 219: "When a treaty is open to two interpretations one of which does and the other does not enable the treaty to have appropriate effects, good faith and the objects and purposes of the treaty demand that the former interpretation should be adopted."

protection to domestic production' ''. Toward this end, Article III obliges Members of the WTO to provide equality of competitive conditions for imported products in relation to domestic products. "[T]he intention of the drafters of the Agreement was clearly to treat the imported products in the same way as the like domestic products once they had been cleared through customs. Otherwise indirect protection could be given". Moreover, it is irrelevant that "the trade effects" of the tax differential between imported and domestic products, as reflected in the volumes of imports, are insignificant or even non-existent; Article III protects expectations not of any particular trade volume but rather of the equal competitive relationship between imported and domestic products. Members of the WTO are free to pursue their own domestic goals through internal taxation or regulation so long as they do not do so in a way that violates Article III or any of the other commitments they have made in the WTO Agreement.[2]

The broad purpose of Article III of avoiding protectionism must be remembered when considering the relationship between Article III and other provisions of the WTO Agreement. Although the protection of negotiated tariff concessions is certainly one purpose of Article III, the statement in paragraph 6.13 of the Panel Report that "one of the main purposes of Article III is to guarantee that WTO Members will not undermine through internal measures their commitments under Article II" should not be overemphasized. The sheltering scope of Article III is not limited to products that are the subject of tariff concessions under Article II. The Article III national treatment obligation is a general prohibition on the use of internal taxes and other internal regulatory measures so as to afford protection to domestic production. This obligation clearly extends also to products not bound under Article II. This is confirmed by the negotiating history of Article III.[3]

ARTICLE III:1

The terms of Article III must be given their ordinary meaning—in their context and in the light of the overall object and purpose of the WTO Agreement. Thus, the words actually used in the Article provide the basis for an interpretation that must give meaning and effect to all its terms. The proper interpretation of the Article is, first of all, a textual interpretation. Consequently, the Panel is correct in seeing a distinction between Article III:1, which "contains general principles", and Article III:2, which "provides for specific obligations regarding internal taxes and internal charges". Article III:1 articulates a general principle that internal measures should not be applied so as to afford protection to domestic production. This general principle informs the rest of Article III. The purpose of Article III:1 is to establish this general principle as a guide to understanding and interpreting the specific obligations con-

---

2. Quoting *Italian Agricultural Machinery*, para. 11; *Section 337*, para. 5.10; and *Superfund*, para. 5.1.9 (which was quoted in *Section 337*, para. 5.13.).

3. Quoting statements by two delegates to the 1947 GATT negotiations. EPCT/TAC/PV.10, pp. 3 and 33.

tained in Article III:2 and in the other paragraphs of Article III, while respecting, and not diminishing in any way, the meaning of the words actually used in the texts of those other paragraphs. In short, Article III:1 constitutes part of the context of Article III:2, in the same way that it constitutes part of the context of each of the other paragraphs in Article III. Any other reading of Article III would have the effect of rendering the words of Article III:1 meaningless, thereby violating the fundamental principle of effectiveness in treaty interpretation. Consistent with this principle of effectiveness, and with the textual differences in the two sentences, we believe that Article III:1 informs the first sentence and the second sentence of Article III:2 in different ways.

ARTICLE III:2, FIRST SENTENCE

Article III:1 informs Article III:2, first sentence, by establishing that if imported products are taxed in excess of like domestic products, then that tax measure is inconsistent with Article III. Article III:2, first sentence does not refer specifically to Article III:1. There is no specific invocation in this first sentence of the general principle in Article III:1 that admonishes Members of the WTO not to apply measures "so as to afford protection". This omission must have some meaning. We believe the meaning is simply that the presence of a protective application need not be established separately from the specific requirements that are included in the first sentence in order to show that a tax measure is inconsistent with the general principle set out in the first sentence. However, this does not mean that the general principle of Article III:1 does not apply to this sentence. To the contrary, we believe the first sentence of Article III:2 is, in effect, an application of this general principle. The ordinary meaning of the words of Article III:2, first sentence leads inevitably to this conclusion. Read in their context and in the light of the overall object and purpose of the WTO Agreement, the words of the first sentence require an examination of the conformity of an internal tax measure with Article III by determining, first, whether the taxed imported and domestic products are "like" and, second, whether the taxes applied to the imported products are "in excess of" those applied to the like domestic products. If the imported and domestic products are "like products", and if the taxes applied to the imported products are "in excess of" those applied to the like domestic products, then the measure is inconsistent with Article III:2, first sentence.

This approach to an examination of Article III:2, first sentence, is consistent with past practice under the GATT 1947. Moreover, it is consistent with the object and purpose of Article III:2, which the panel in the predecessor to this case dealing with an earlier version of the Liquor Tax Law, rightly stated as "promoting non-discriminatory competition among imported and like domestic products [which] could not be achieved if Article III:2 were construed in a manner allowing discriminatory and protective internal taxation of imported products in excess of like domestic products".

(a) "Like Products"

Because the second sentence of Article III:2 provides for a separate and distinctive consideration of the protective aspect of a measure in examining its application to a broader category of products that are not "like products" as contemplated by the first sentence, we agree with the Panel that the first sentence of Article III:2 must be construed narrowly so as not to condemn measures that its strict terms are not meant to condemn. Consequently, we agree with the Panel also that the definition of "like products" in Article III:2, first sentence, should be construed narrowly.

How narrowly is a matter that should be determined separately for each tax measure in each case. We agree with the practice under the GATT 1947 of determining whether imported and domestic products are "like" on a case-by-case basis. The Report of the Working Party on Border Tax Adjustments, adopted by the CONTRACTING PARTIES in 1970, set out the basic approach for interpreting "like or similar products" generally in the various provisions of the GATT 1947:

> ... the interpretation of the term should be examined on a case-by-case basis. This would allow a fair assessment in each case of the different elements that constitute a "similar" product. Some criteria were suggested for determining, on a case-by-case basis, whether a product is "similar": the product's end-uses in a given market; consumers' tastes and habits, which change from country to country; the product's properties, nature and quality.[4]

This approach was followed in almost all adopted panel reports after *Border Tax Adjustments*. This approach should be helpful in identifying on a case-by-case basis the range of "like products" that fall within the narrow limits of Article III:2, first sentence in the GATT 1994. Yet this approach will be most helpful if decision makers keep ever in mind how narrow the range of "like products" in Article III:2, first sentence is meant to be as opposed to the range of "like" products contemplated in some other provisions of the GATT 1994 and other Multilateral Trade Agreements of the *WTO Agreement*. In applying the criteria cited in *Border Tax Adjustments* to the facts of any particular case, and in considering other criteria that may also be relevant in certain cases, panels can only apply their best judgement in determining whether in fact products are "like". This will always involve an unavoidable element of individual, discretionary judgement. * * *

No one approach to exercising judgement will be appropriate for all cases. The criteria in *Border Tax Adjustments* should be examined, but there can be no one precise and absolute definition of what is "like". The concept of "likeness" is a relative one that evokes the image of an accordion. The accordion of "likeness" stretches and squeezes in different places as different provisions of the *WTO Agreement* are applied. The

---

4. [original note 45] Report of the Working Party on *Border Tax Adjustments*, BISD 18S/97, para. 18.

width of the accordion in any one of those places must be determined by the particular provision in which the term "like" is encountered as well as by the context and the circumstances that prevail in any given case to which that provision may apply. We believe that, in Article III:2, first sentence of the GATT 1994, the accordion of "likeness" is meant to be narrowly squeezed.

The Panel determined in this case that shochu and vodka are "like products" for the purposes of Article III:2, first sentence. We note that the determination of whether vodka is a "like product" to shochu under Article III:2, first sentence, or a "directly competitive or substitutable product" to shochu under Article III:2, second sentence, does not materially affect the outcome of this case.

* * *

(b) "In Excess Of"

The only remaining issue under Article III:2, first sentence, is whether the taxes on imported products are "in excess of" those on like domestic products. If so, then the Member that has imposed the tax is not in compliance with Article III. Even the smallest amount of "excess" is too much. "The prohibition of discriminatory taxes in Article III:2, first sentence, is not conditional on a 'trade effects test' nor is it qualified by a *de minimis* standard."[5] * * *

ARTICLE III:2, SECOND SENTENCE

Article III:1 informs Article III:2, second sentence, through specific reference. Article III:2, second sentence, contains a general prohibition against "internal taxes or other internal charges" applied to "imported or domestic products in a manner contrary to the principles set forth in paragraph 1". As mentioned before, Article III:1 states that internal taxes and other internal charges "should not be applied to imported or domestic products so as to afford protection to domestic production". Again, Ad Article III:2 states as follows:

> A tax conforming to the requirements of the first sentence of paragraph 2 would be considered to be inconsistent with the provisions of the second sentence only in cases where competition was involved between, on the one hand, the taxed product and, on the other hand, a directly competitive or substitutable product which was not similarly taxed.

Article III:2, second sentence, and the accompanying Ad Article have equivalent legal status in that both are treaty language which was negotiated and agreed at the same time. The Ad Article does not replace or modify the language contained in Article III:2, second sentence, but, in fact, clarifies its meaning. Accordingly, the language of the second

5. [original note 51] *United States— Measures Affecting Alcoholic and Malt Beverages*, BISD 39S/206, para 5.6. * * *

sentence and the Ad Article must be read together in order to give them their proper meaning.

Unlike that of Article III:2, first sentence, the language of Article III:2, second sentence, specifically invokes Article III:1. The significance of this distinction lies in the fact that whereas Article III:1 acts implicitly in addressing the two issues that must be considered in applying the first sentence, it acts explicitly as an entirely separate issue that must be addressed along with two other issues that are raised in applying the second sentence. Giving full meaning to the text and to its context, three separate issues must be addressed to determine whether an internal tax measure is inconsistent with Article III:2, second sentence. These three issues are whether:

(1) the imported products and the domestic products are *"directly competitive or substitutable products" which are in competition with each other*;

(2) the directly competitive or substitutable imported and domestic products are *"not similarly taxed"*; and

(3) the dissimilar taxation of the directly competitive or substitutable imported domestic products is *"applied ... so as to afford protection to domestic production"*.

Again, these are three separate issues. Each must be established separately by the complainant for a panel to find that a tax measure imposed by a Member of the WTO is inconsistent with Article III:2, second sentence.

(a) *"Directly Competitive or Substitutable Products"*

If imported and domestic products are not "like products" for the narrow purposes of Article III:2, first sentence, then they are not subject to the strictures of that sentence and there is no inconsistency with the requirements of that sentence. However, depending on their nature, and depending on the competitive conditions in the relevant market, those same products may well be among the broader category of "directly competitive or substitutable products" that fall within the domain of Article III:2, second sentence. How much broader that category of "directly competitive or substitutable products" may be in any given case is a matter for the panel to determine based on all the relevant facts in that case. As with "like products" under the first sentence, the determination of the appropriate range of "directly competitive or substitutable products" under the second sentence must be made on a case-by-case basis.

In this case, the Panel emphasized the need to look not only at such matters as physical characteristics, common end-uses, and tariff classifications, but also at the "market place". This seems appropriate. The GATT 1994 is a commercial agreement, and the WTO is concerned, after all, with markets. It does not seem inappropriate to look at competition in the relevant markets as one among a number of means of identifying the broader category of products that might be described as "directly competitive or substitutable".

Nor does it seem inappropriate to examine elasticity of substitution as one means of examining those relevant markets. The Panel did not say that cross-price elasticity of demand is "*the* decisive criterion" for determining whether products are "directly competitive or substitutable". The Panel stated the following:

> In the Panel's view, the decisive criterion in order to determine whether two products are directly competitive or substitutable is whether they have common end-uses, *inter alia*, as shown by elasticity of substitution.

We agree. And, we find the Panel's legal analysis of whether the products are "directly competitive or substitutable products" in paragraphs 6.28–6.32 of the Panel Report to be correct.

* * *

(b) "Not Similarly Taxed"

To give due meaning to the distinctions in the wording of Article III:2, first sentence, and Article III:2, second sentence, the phrase "not similarly taxed" in the Ad Article to the second sentence must not be construed so as to mean the same thing as the phrase "in excess of" in the first sentence. On its face, the phrase "in excess of" in the first sentence means any amount of tax on imported products "in excess of" the tax on domestic "like products". The phrase "not similarly taxed" in the Ad Article to the second sentence must therefore mean something else. It requires a different standard, just as "directly competitive or substitutable products" requires a different standard as compared to "like products" for these same interpretive purposes.

* * *

* * * Thus, in any given case, there may be some amount of taxation on imported products that may well be "in excess of" the tax on domestic "like products" but may not be so much as to compel a conclusion that "directly competitive or substitutable" imported and domestic products are "not similarly taxed" for the purposes of the Ad Article to Article III:2, second sentence. * * * We agree with the Panel that this amount of differential taxation must be more than *de minimis* to be deemed "not similarly taxed" in any given case. And, like the Panel, we believe that whether any particular differential amount of taxation is *de minimis* or is not *de minimis* must, here too, be determined on a case-by-case basis. Thus, to be "not similarly taxed", the tax burden on imported products must be heavier than on "directly competitive or substitutable" domestic products, and that burden must be more than *de minimis* in any given case.

In this case, the Panel applied the correct legal reasoning in determining whether "directly competitive or substitutable" imported and domestic products were "not similarly taxed". However, the Panel erred in blurring the distinction between that issue and the entirely separate issue of whether the tax measure in question was applied "so as to afford protection". Again, these are separate issues that must be addressed individually. * * *

(c) "So As To Afford Protection"

This third inquiry under Article III:2, second sentence, must determine whether "directly competitive or substitutable products" are "not similarly taxed" in a way that affords protection. This is not an issue of intent. It is not necessary for a panel to sort through the many reasons legislators and regulators often have for what they do and weigh the relative significance of those reasons to establish legislative or regulatory intent. If the measure is applied to imported or domestic products so as to afford protection to domestic production, then it does not matter that there may not have been any desire to engage in protectionism in the minds of the legislators or the regulators who imposed the measure. It is irrelevant that protectionism was not an intended objective if the particular tax measure in question is nevertheless, to echo Article III:1, "*applied* to imported or domestic products so as to afford protection to domestic production". This is an issue of how the measure in question is *applied*.

* * *

Although it is true that the aim of a measure may not be easily ascertained, nevertheless its protective application can most often be discerned from the design, the architecture, and the revealing structure of a measure. The very magnitude of the dissimilar taxation in a particular case may be evidence of such a protective application, as the Panel rightly concluded in this case. Most often, there will be other factors to be considered as well. In conducting this inquiry, panels should give full consideration to all the relevant facts and all the relevant circumstances in any given case.

* * *

[As noted earlier], having stated the correct legal approach to apply with respect to Article III:2, second sentence, the Panel then equated dissimilar taxation above a *de minimis* level with the separate and distinct requirement of demonstrating that the tax measure "affords protection to domestic production". * * * [I]n every case, a careful, objective analysis, must be done of each and all relevant facts and all the relevant circumstances in order to determine the existence of protective taxation. Although the Panel blurred its legal reasoning in this respect, nevertheless we conclude that it reasoned correctly that in this case, the Liquor Tax Law is not in compliance with Article III:2. As the Panel did, we note that:

> ... the combination of customs duties and internal taxation in Japan has the following impact: on the one hand, it makes it difficult for foreign-produced shochu to penetrate the Japanese market and, on the other, it does not guarantee equality of competi-

tive conditions between shochu and the rest of white and brown spirits. Thus, through a combination of high import duties and differentiated internal taxes, Japan manages to "isolate" domestically produced shochu from foreign competition, be it foreign produced shochu or any other of the mentioned white and brown spirits.

Our interpretation of Article III is faithful to the "customary rules of interpretation of public international law". WTO rules are reliable, comprehensible and enforceable. WTO rules are not so rigid or so inflexible as not to leave room for reasoned judgements in confronting the endless and ever-changing ebb and flow of real facts in real cases in the real world. They will serve the multilateral trading system best if they are interpreted with that in mind. In that way, we will achieve the "security and predictability" sought for the multilateral trading system by the Members of the WTO through the establishment of the dispute settlement system.

Notes and Questions

(1) The Appellate Body report is particularly interesting for the interpretative method that it lays out. For those familiar with the arguments in the case, however, the report was unusual in the way it dealt with those arguments. While the views of the Appellate Body on meaning of "like product" are clear, it does not specifically discuss the alternative meaning put forward by both Japan and the United States (and opposed by the EC and Canada). While there were subtle differences in their approach, Japan and the US had essentially argued that in determining the likeness of products it is necessary to consider the aims and effect of the measure at issue to determine whether the tax or regulatory distinction made by the measure is "so as to afford protection," in the words of Article III:1. If there were no such aim or effect, then the products would not be like and would not be subject to Article III:2, first sentence. The policy justification for such an interpretation would be to avoid a mechanical application of the like products test of Article III that could lead to a finding that a non-protectionist measure designed to achieve legitimate policy goals denied national treatment in violation of Article III. The so-called aims and effect test had been used in one adopted GATT panel report,[6] along with more traditional factors, in defining product likeness and had been used as the sole basis for determining likeness in one unadopted report.[7]

The panel in the instant case declined to follow the aims and effect test on the grounds that it lacked a textual basis in Article III. After all, even if Article III:1 provides context for interpretation of Article III:2, how can it justify changing an examination of the likeness of products into an examination of the purpose or effect of legislation? Moreover, application of such a test could have the effect of converting an Article XX defense that a respondent would normally have the burden of establishing (e.g., the safety exception of Article XX(b)) into an element of the complainant's case (e.g.,

6. Panel Report on United States–Measures Affecting Alcoholic and Malt Beverages, BISD 39/206, 294–295 (adopted on June 19, 1992).

7. Panel Report on United States–Taxes on Automobiles, GATT Doc. DS31/R (Sept. 29, 1994)(not adopted).

the products are like because there is a protectionist aim and effect to the measure and not a safety rationale), thereby making it more difficult to establish an Article III violation.

In your view, should the aims and effect test have been accepted by the Appellate Body? If Article III:1 is the context for all of Article III, why shouldn't it be necessary in order to establish a violation of any part of Article III to show that a measure is applied so as to afford protection? How does the Appellate Body deal with the relationship between Article III:1 and the two sentences of Article III:2? To the extent that the policy justification for that test is to avoid invalidating legitimate regulations, do you see how a narrow view of the scope of the phrase "like products" in Article III:2 largely accomplishes that goal? Different considerations may apply in the case of Article III:4, which we consider in the next section.

(2) There have been two other WTO alcohol tax cases—one involving Korea and the other Chile. Those cases follow the outlines established in the Japan case, but they also examine in more detail the definitions of "competitive or substitutable products" and "not similarly taxed". Korea—Taxes on Alcoholic Beverages, WT/DS75 & 84/R & AB/R, adopted by the DSB on February 17, 1999; Chile—Taxes on Alcoholic Beverages, WT/DS87 & 110/R & AB/R, adopted by the DSB on January 12, 2000.

(3) What are the key factors in determining the third element of a violation of Article III:2, second sentence? In other words, how does one establish that a measure is applied so as to afford protection? Do you think that the existence of domestic production should suffice to establish the lack of protection (or discrimination)? If so, how much domestic production should be necessary?

(4) More generally, what are the stakes in applying Article III:2? Is it simply a matter of protecting expectations generated during tariff negotiations? If so, does that imply that changes in domestic policies are the real problem? Why does the national treatment article not then "grandfather" certain pre-existing discriminatory policies? Should "like product" be defined primarily with reference to what the negotiators understood or would have reasonably understood to be its scope? Might tariff classification headings not be quite helpful on this point? Is discrimination among reasonably close substitutes problematic for reasons other than a possible frustration of expectations? Are MacIntosh computers "like" IBM computers? Are minivans "like" passenger sedans?

(5) In the drafting history of Article III:2, the following example is given of the type of protection that the Article III:2, second sentence, is designed to prevent. Suppose that a country produces apples and imports oranges, which it cannot produce. An internal tax on oranges, but not on fruits grown domestically (such as apples), could operate to protect the domestic apple industry. The drafting history suggests that the orange exporting country could rely on Article III:2, second sentence, in attacking the tax on oranges in GATT. The tariff on oranges, as a practical matter, would have to be bound in order to make this argument attractive. Why?

(6) Article 90 of the EC Treaty provides:

No Member State shall impose, directly or indirectly, on the products of other Member States any internal taxation of any kind in excess of that imposed directly or indirectly on similar domestic products. Furthermore, no Member State shall impose on the products of other Member States any internal taxation of such a nature as to afford indirect protection to other products.

In applying it, the EC Court of Justice has concluded that significantly different tax rates on wine versus beer and grain-based spirits versus wine- or fruit-based spirits violate Article 90. The court has not always made it clear whether it relied on the first sentence or second sentence of Article 90. See Commission v. France (Alcohol excise tax), Case 168/78, [1980] ECR 347; Commission v. United Kingdom (Wine and Beer Taxes), Case 170/78, [1983] ECR 2265. Would you expect such a result to be reached in GATT under Article III under the reasoning of the *Japanese Alcoholic Beverages* case?

(7) Suppose a country applies a tax on the purchase of new cars. Suppose further that the tax due increases progressively as the car's horsepower increases, up to a maximum of 1100 francs, but that there is a special 5000 franc tax on high horsepower cars, all of which are imported. These facts gave rise to an EC Court of Justice ruling that the French tax system violated Article 90 of the EC Treaty, which is set out in Note 6 above.

In HUMBLOT v. DIRECTEUR DES SERVICES FISCAUX, Case 112/84, [1985] ECR 1367, the court ruled:

[13] Such a system of domestic taxation is, however, compatible with Article [90] only in so far as it is free from any discriminatory or protective effect.

[14] That is not true of a system like the one at issue in the main proceedings. Under that system there are two distinct taxes: a differential tax which increases progressively and is charged on cars not exceeding a given power rating for tax purposes and a fixed tax on cars exceeding that rating which is almost five times as high as the highest rate of the differential tax. Although the system embodies no formal distinction based on the origin of products it manifestly exhibits discriminatory or protective features contrary to Article [90], since the power rating determining liability has been fixed at a level such that only imported cars, in particular from other Member States, are subject to the special tax whereas all cars of domestic manufacture are liable to the distinctly more advantageous differential tax.

[15] In the absence of considerations relating to the amount of the special tax, consumers seeking comparable cars as regards such matters as size, comfort, actual power, maintenance costs, durability, fuel consumption and price would naturally choose from among cars above and below the critical power rating laid down by French law. However, liability to the special tax entails a much larger increase in taxation than passing from one category of car to another in a system of progressive taxation embodying balanced differentials like the system on which the differential tax is based. The resultant additional taxation is liable to cancel out the

advantages which certain cars imported from other Member States might have in consumers' eyes over comparable cars of domestic manufacture, particularly since the special tax continues to be payable for several years. In that respect the special tax reduces the amount of competition to which cars of domestic manufacture are subject and hence is contrary to the principle of neutrality with which domestic taxation must comply.

The US claimed in 1956 that the French tax violated Article III, but no GATT panel examined it. In 1994, a GATT panel examined an EU challenge to several US auto measures: a "gas guzzler" tax,[8] a luxury tax[9] and the Corporate Average Fuel Efficiency (CAFE) rules.[10] The EU claimed that although EU-origin cars hold only four percent of the US market, 88% of the revenue collected from these levies is from EU cars. The panel upheld the luxury and gas guzzler taxes, but found certain averaging formulae in the CAFE rules violated Article III:4 by treating domestic and foreign cars differently, in a manner not acceptable under Article XX(g). GATT Doc. DS31/R (Sept. 29, 1994). The report was never adopted.

(8) Assume that the United States adopts legislation that imposes (i) a tax on certain chemicals sold or imported into the United States and (ii) a tax on certain imported substances containing chemicals subject to the first tax. The tax on imported substances is set so that a substance would bear the same tax as it would if it had been made in the US from chemicals subject to the first tax. The taxes are used to fund the so-called Superfund, which is used to cleanup hazardous waste sites in the United States. Is the tax on imported substances permissible under Article III?

An affirmative answer was given by a GATT panel in UNITED STATES—TAXES ON PETROLEUM AND CERTAIN IMPORTED SUBSTANCES, GATT, 34th Supp. BISD 136 (1988)(Panel report adopted June 17, 1987), which was also excerpted in Section 7.4(A)(dispute settlement):

> 5.2.3 The Panel noted that the United States justified the tax on certain imported substances as a border tax adjustment corresponding in its effect to the internal tax on certain chemicals from which these substances were derived. The Panel further noted that the EEC considered the tax on certain chemicals not to be eligible for border tax adjustment because it was designed to tax polluting activities that occurred in the United States and to finance environmental programs benefiting only United States producers. Consistent with the Polluter–Pays Principle, the United States should have taxed only products of domestic origin because only their production gave rise to environmental problems in the United States. * * *
>
> 5.2.4 The report of the Working Party on Border Tax Adjustments, adopted by the CONTRACTING PARTIES in 1970, concluded the

8. 26 U.S.C.A. sec. 4064 (taxes range from $1000 for cars with fuel efficiency rating of less than 22.5 miles per gallon to $7700 for cars below 12.5 MPG).

9. 26 U.S.C.A. sec. 4001 (to be phased out in 2002).

10. 49 U.S.C.A. secs. 32901–32919 (civil penalties payable based on the extent to which an automaker's product line fails to achieve average fuel economy standards specified by Secretary of Transportation).

following on the rules of the General Agreement relating to tax adjustments applied to goods entering into international trade:

"There was convergence of views to the effect that taxes directly levied on products were eligible for tax adjustment. Examples of such taxes comprised specific excise duties, sales taxes and cascade taxes and the tax on value added ... Furthermore, the Working Party concluded that there was convergence of views to the effect that certain taxes that were not directly levied on products were not eligible for tax adjustment. Examples of such taxes comprised social security charges whether on employers or employees and payroll taxes" (BISD 18S/100–101).

As these conclusions of the CONTRACTING PARTIES clearly indicate, the tax adjustment rules of the General Agreement distinguish between taxes on products and taxes not directly levied on products; they do not distinguish between taxes with different policy purposes. Whether a sales tax is levied on a product for general revenue purposes or to encourage the rational use of environmental resources, is therefore not relevant for the determination of the eligibility of a tax for border tax adjustment. For these reasons the Panel concluded that the tax on certain chemicals, being a tax directly imposed on products, was eligible for border tax adjustment independent of the purpose it served. The Panel therefore did not examine whether the tax on chemicals served environmental purposes and, if so, whether a border tax adjustment would be consistent with these purposes.

Note the distinction made by the GATT Working Party between taxes imposed on products and taxes imposed on income. As is brought out in the review problems which follow, it is generally accepted that Article III applies to the former, and not the latter. But what if an income tax benefit (e.g., deduction or credit) is tied to the purchase of a domestic product?

Review Problems

Consider whether each situation described below is consistent or inconsistent with GATT Article III:

(1) Suppose the United States imposed a tax on automobiles which cannot operate more efficiently than 15 miles per gallon of gasoline, but rebates 50% of that tax to any domestic automobile company for use solely in research on auto energy conservation. See United States—Measures Affecting Alcoholic and Malt Beverages, GATT, 39th Supp. BISD 206 (1993)(Panel report adopted June 19, 1992)(excise tax credits available only to domestic brewers violate Article III).

(2) A special accelerated depreciation income tax deduction is granted to domestic manufacturing companies, but not to foreign manufacturers, even when they derive locally taxable income from sales of imported goods.

(3) Suppose US purchasers of automobiles are granted a gasoline tax rebate of $300 for the year in which they purchased a new *domestically produced* automobile.

(4) Suppose US law imposes a 10% excise tax on the sale of domestically produced or imported cars, but provides that such excise tax shall be one

percentage point less than 10% for each 5% improvement in the officially rated gas mileage of each particular current year's make and model, over the model's rating for 1990. That is, if a car was rated at 20 miles-per-gallon in 1990, and 22 miles-per-gallon in 1992, then the 10% improvement would result in an 8% excise tax on the 1993 model, rather than a 10% tax. Suppose further, that it can be established that the best selling imported cars in 1990 had miles-per-gallon ratings of 30% to 50% over most American domestically made models (and that therefore much improvement would be more difficult for the imported makes). Would such a law be consistent with US WTO obligations?

(5) More generally, would the border tax adjustment rules be relevant to the design of a carbon tax? See generally Joost Pauwelyn, *U.S. Federal Climate Policy and Competitiveness Concerns: The Limits and Options of International Trade Law*, Working Paper, Nicolas Institute for Environmental Policy Solutions, Duke University, available at http://www.nicholas.duke.edu/institute/internationaltradelaw.pdf.

SECTION 12.4 DISCRIMINATORY REGULATIONS: ARTICLE III:4

Article III:4 requires that imported products receive no less favorable treatment than domestic like products in respect of laws, regulations and requirements affecting their internal sale, offering for sale, purchase, transportation, distribution or use. We have already examined two older Article III:4 cases—*Italian Agricultural Machinery* and *Section 337*—and seen that it has been interpreted broadly. In this section, we focus on the actual terms of Article III:4. First, we examine how the concept of "like product" should be interpreted. Does the phrase have the same meaning that it does in Article III:2? What considerations argue for a different scope? Second, what is treatment "no less favorable"? We saw that the *Section 337* panel concluded that identical treatment may not be required, but when is non-identical treatment less favorable? For both of the foregoing issues—like product and less favorable treatment—what role should Article III:1, which is not mentioned in Article III:4, play in their interpretation? Third, while the definition of "laws" and "regulations" may be relatively clear, what are "requirements" for purposes of Article III:4?

(A) LIKE PRODUCTS

EUROPEAN COMMUNITIES—MEASURES AFFECTING ASBESTOS AND ASBESTOS–CONTAINING PRODUCTS

WT/DS135/AB/R.
Appellate Body Report adopted by the DSB on April 5, 2001.

[This case involved a Canadian challenge of a French regulation that prohibits the manufacture, processing, sale, import, marketing and transfer of all varieties of asbestos fibres, regardless of whether these substances have been incorporated into materials, products or devices, subject to a limited exception in cases where no substitute product exists. Canada claimed that the regulation is inconsistent with GATT Articles III and XI and Article 2 of the TBT Agreement, and that under GATT Article XXIII:1(b), it nullified or impaired advantages accruing to Canada directly or indirectly under WTO Agreement (a non-violation claim). The panel ruled that in general the TBT Agreement did not apply to the regulation (a finding reversed by the Appellate Body), that like products were involved such that Article III:4 was violated (also reversed), but that the regulation fell within the exception of GATT Article XX(b) and did not nullify or impair advantages accruing to Canada. We discuss the TBT issue in Section 14.3, the "like product" issue in this section and the Article XX(b) exception in Section 13.2.

The panel found that chrysotile asbestos fibres are "like" polyvinyl alcohol, cellulose and glass fibres ("PCG fibres") and that cement-based products containing chrysotile asbestos fibres are "like" cement-based products containing one of the PCG fibres. The Panel also concluded that all these cement-based products are "like".]

88. [After noting that the term "like products" appears in a number of different provisions in several WTO agreements, the Appellate Body noted:] [T]he term must be interpreted in light of the context, and of the object and purpose, of the provision at issue, and of the object and purpose of the covered agreement in which the provision appears. * * *

89. It follows that, while the meaning attributed to the term "like products" in other provisions of the GATT 1994, or in other covered agreements, may be relevant context in interpreting Article III:4 of the GATT 1994, the interpretation of "like products" in Article III:4 need not be identical, in all respects, to those other meanings.

90. Bearing these considerations in mind, we turn now to the ordinary meaning of the word "like" in the term "like products" in Article III:4. According to one dictionary, "like" means:

Having the same characteristics or qualities as some other . . . thing; of approximately identical shape, size, etc., with something else; similar.[1]

91. This meaning suggests that "like" products are products that share a number of identical or similar characteristics or qualities. The reference to "similar" as a synonym of "like" also echoes the language of the French version of Article III:4, *produits similaires*, and the Spanish version, *productos similares*, which, together with the English version, are equally authentic.

92. However, as we have previously observed, "dictionary meanings leave many interpretive questions open." In particular, this definition does not resolve three issues of interpretation. First, this dictionary

---

1. [original note 61] *The New Shorter Oxford English Dictionary*, Lesley Brown   (ed.) (Clarendon Press, 1993), Vol. I, p. 1588.

definition of "like" does not indicate *which characteristics or qualities are important* in assessing the "likeness" of products under Article III:4. For instance, most products will have many qualities and characteristics, ranging from physical properties such as composition, size, shape, texture, and possibly taste and smell, to the end-uses and applications of the product. Second, this dictionary definition provides no guidance in determining the *degree or extent to which products must share qualities or characteristics* in order to be "like products" under Article III:4. Products may share only very few characteristics or qualities, or they may share many. Thus, in the abstract, the term "like" can encompass a spectrum of differing degrees of "likeness" or "similarity". Third, this dictionary definition of "like" does not indicate *from whose perspective* "likeness" should be judged. For instance, ultimate consumers may have a view about the "likeness" of two products that is very different from that of the inventors or producers of those products.

93. To begin to resolve these issues, we turn to the relevant context of Article III:4 of the GATT 1994. In that respect, we observe that Article III:2 of the GATT 1994, which deals with the internal tax treatment of imported and domestic products, prevents Members, through its first sentence, from imposing internal taxes on imported products "in excess of those applied ... to *like* domestic products." (emphasis added) In previous Reports, we have held that the scope of "*like*" products in this sentence is to be construed "narrowly". This reading of "like" in Article III:2 might be taken to suggest a similarly narrow reading of "like" in Article III:4, since both provisions form part of the same Article. However, both of these paragraphs of Article III constitute specific expressions of the overarching, "general principle", set forth in Article III:1 of the GATT 1994. As we have previously said, the "general principle" set forth in Article III:1 "informs" the rest of Article III and acts "as a guide to understanding and interpreting the specific obligations contained" in the other paragraphs of Article III, including paragraph 4. Thus, in our view, Article III:1 has particular contextual significance in interpreting Article III:4, as it sets forth the "general principle" pursued by that provision. Accordingly, in interpreting the term "like products" in Article III:4, we must turn, first, to the "general principle" in Article III:1, rather than to the term "like products" in Article III:2.

94. In addition, we observe that, although the obligations in Articles III:2 and III:4 both apply to "like products", the text of Article III:2 differs in one important respect from the text of Article III:4. Article III:2 contains *two separate* sentences, each imposing *distinct* obligations: the first lays down obligations in respect of "like products", while the second lays down obligations in respect of "directly competitive or substitutable" products. By contrast, Article III:4 applies only to "like products" and does not include a provision equivalent to the second sentence of Article III:2. * * *

95. For us, this textual difference between paragraphs 2 and 4 of Article III has considerable implications for the meaning of the term

"like products" in these two provisions. In *Japan–Alcoholic Beverages*, we concluded, in construing Article III:2, that the two separate obligations in the two sentences of Article III:2 must be interpreted in a harmonious manner that gives meaning to *both* sentences in that provision. We observed there that the interpretation of one of the sentences necessarily affects the interpretation of the other. Thus, the scope of the term "like products" in the first sentence of Article III:2 affects, and is affected by, the scope of the phrase "directly competitive or substitutable" products in the second sentence of that provision. * * *

96.   In construing Article III:4, the same interpretive considerations do not arise, because the "general principle" articulated in Article III:1 is expressed in Article III:4, not through two distinct obligations, as in the two sentences in Article III:2, but instead through a single obligation that applies solely to "like products". Therefore, the harmony that we have attributed to the two sentences of Article III:2 need not and, indeed, cannot be replicated in interpreting Article III:4. Thus, we conclude that, given the textual difference between Articles III:2 and III:4, the "accordion" of "likeness" stretches in a different way in Article III:4.

[After recalling its statement of the purpose of Article III in *Japan Alcoholic Beverages*, quoted in Section 12.3 supra, the Appellate Body continued:]

98.   As we have said, although this "general principle" is not explicitly invoked in Article III:4, nevertheless, it "informs" that provision. Therefore, the term "like product" in Article III:4 must be interpreted to give proper scope and meaning to this principle. In short, there must be consonance between the objective pursued by Article III, as enunciated in the "general principle" articulated in Article III:1, and the interpretation of the specific expression of this principle in the text of Article III:4. This interpretation must, therefore, reflect that, in endeavouring to ensure "equality of competitive conditions", the "general principle" in Article III seeks to prevent Members from applying internal taxes and regulations in a manner which affects the competitive relationship, in the marketplace, *between the domestic and imported products involved*, "so as to afford protection to domestic production."

99.   As products that are in a competitive relationship in the marketplace could be affected through treatment of *imports* "less favourable" than the treatment accorded to *domestic* products, it follows that the word "like" in Article III:4 is to be interpreted to apply to products that are in such a competitive relationship. Thus, a determination of "likeness" under Article III:4 is, fundamentally, a determination about the nature and extent of a competitive relationship between and among products. In saying this, we are mindful that there is a spectrum of degrees of "competitiveness" or "substitutability" of products in the marketplace, and that it is difficult, if not impossible, in the abstract, to indicate precisely where on this spectrum the word "like" in Article III:4 of the GATT 1994 falls. We are not saying that *all* products which are in

some competitive relationship are "like products" under Article III:4. In ruling on the measure at issue, we also do not attempt to define the precise scope of the word "like" in Article III:4. Nor do we wish to decide if the scope of "like products" in Article III:4 is co-extensive with the combined scope of "like" and "directly competitive or substitutable" products in Article III:2. However, we recognize that the relationship between these two provisions is important, because there is no sharp distinction between fiscal regulation, covered by Article III:2, and non-fiscal regulation, covered by Article III:4. Both forms of regulation can often be used to achieve the same ends. It would be incongruous if, due to a significant difference in the product scope of these two provisions, Members were prevented from using one form of regulation—for instance, fiscal—to protect domestic production of certain products, but were able to use another form of regulation—for instance, non-fiscal—to achieve those ends. This would frustrate a consistent application of the "general principle" in Article III:1. For these reasons, we conclude that the scope of "like" in Article III:4 is broader than the scope of "like" in Article III:2, first sentence. Nonetheless, we note, once more, that Article III:2 extends not only to "like products", but also to products which are "directly competitive or substitutable", and that Article III:4 extends only to "like products". In view of this different language, and although we need not rule, and do not rule, on the precise product scope of Article III:4, we do conclude that the product scope of Article III:4, although broader than the *first* sentence of Article III:2, is certainly not broader than the *combined* product scope of the *two* sentences of Article III:2 of the GATT 1994.

100.   We recognize that, by interpreting the term "like products" in Article III:4 in this way, we give that provision a relatively broad product scope—although no broader than the product scope of Article III:2. In so doing, we observe that there is a second element that must be established before a measure can be held to be inconsistent with Article III:4. Thus, even if two products are "like", that does not mean that a measure is inconsistent with Article III:4. A complaining Member must still establish that the measure accords to the group of "like" *imported* products "less favourable treatment" than it accords to the group of "like" *domestic* products. The term "less favourable treatment" expresses the general principle, in Article III:1, that internal regulations "should not be applied ... so as to afford protection to domestic production". If there is "less favourable treatment" of the group of "like" imported products, there is, conversely, "protection" of the group of "like" domestic products. However, a Member may draw distinctions between products which have been found to be "like", without, for this reason alone, according to the group of "like" *imported* products "less favourable treatment" than that accorded to the group of "like" *domestic* products. In this case, we do not examine further the interpretation of the term "treatment no less favourable" in Article III:4, as the Panel's findings on this issue have not been appealed or, indeed, argued before us.

101.   We turn to consideration of how a treaty interpreter should proceed in determining whether products are "like" under Article III:4. As in Article III:2, in this determination, "[n]o one approach . . . will be appropriate for all cases." Rather, an assessment utilizing "an unavoidable element of individual, discretionary judgement" has to be made on a case-by-case basis. The Report of the Working Party on *Border Tax Adjustments* outlined an approach for analyzing "likeness" that has been followed and developed since by several panels and the Appellate Body. This approach has, in the main, consisted of employing four general criteria in analyzing "likeness": (i) the properties, nature and quality of the products; (ii) the end-uses of the products; (iii) consumers' tastes and habits—more comprehensively termed consumers' perceptions and behaviour—in respect of the products; and (iv) the tariff classification of the products. We note that these four criteria comprise four categories of "characteristics" that the products involved might share: (i) the physical properties of the products; (ii) the extent to which the products are capable of serving the same or similar end-uses; (iii) the extent to which consumers perceive and treat the products as alternative means of performing particular functions in order to satisfy a particular want or demand; and (iv) the international classification of the products for tariff purposes.

102.   These general criteria, or groupings of potentially shared characteristics, provide a framework for analyzing the "likeness" of particular products on a case-by-case basis. These criteria are, it is well to bear in mind, simply tools to assist in the task of sorting and examining the relevant evidence. They are neither a treaty-mandated nor a closed list of criteria that will determine the legal characterization of products. More important, the adoption of a particular framework to aid in the examination of evidence does not dissolve the duty or the need to examine, in each case, *all* of the pertinent evidence. In addition, although each criterion addresses, in principle, a different aspect of the products involved, which should be examined separately, the different criteria are interrelated. For instance, the physical properties of a product shape and limit the end-uses to which the products can be devoted. Consumer perceptions may similarly influence—modify or even render obsolete—traditional uses of the products. Tariff classification clearly reflects the physical properties of a product.

103.   The kind of evidence to be examined in assessing the "likeness" of products will, necessarily, depend upon the particular products and the legal provision at issue. When all the relevant evidence has been examined, panels must determine whether that evidence, as a whole, indicates that the products in question are "like" in terms of the legal provision at issue. We have noted that, under Article III:4 of the GATT 1994, the term "like products" is concerned with competitive relationships between and among products. Accordingly, whether the *Border Tax Adjustments* framework is adopted or not, it is important under Article III:4 to take account of evidence which indicates whether, and to

what extent, the products involved are—or could be—in a competitive relationship in the marketplace.

[The Appellate Body then examined the Panel's findings that the products at issue were like, considering what the Panel had said with respect to each of the four *Border Taxes* criteria. With respect to the "properties, nature and quality of the products", it noted that the Panel found that it was not decisive that the products "do not have the same structure or chemical composition", nor that asbestos is "unique". Instead, the Panel focused on "market access" and whether the products have the "same applications" and can "replace" each other for some industrial uses. In its examination of this criterion, the Panel declined to consider health risks of the products.

In respect of "end-use", the Appellate Body noted that the Panel stated that it had already found, under the first criterion, that the products have "certain identical or at least similar end-uses" and that it did not, therefore, consider it necessary to elaborate further on this criterion. The Panel declined to "take a position" on "consumers' tastes and habits", the third criterion, "[b]ecause this criterion would not provide clear results". Finally, the Panel did not regard as "decisive" the different "tariff classification" of the fibres.

The Appellate Body then considered in detail the Panel's evaluation of likeness under the four criteria. In this regard, it stated:]

111.   We believe that physical properties deserve a separate examination that should not be confused with the examination of end-uses. Although not decisive, the extent to which products share common physical properties may be a useful indicator of "likeness". Furthermore, the physical properties of a product may also influence how the product can be used, consumer attitudes about the product, and tariff classification. It is, therefore, important for a panel to examine fully the physical character of a product. We are also concerned that it will be difficult for a panel to draw the appropriate conclusions from the evidence examined under each criterion if a panel's approach does not clearly address each criterion separately, but rather entwines different, and distinct, elements of the analysis along the way.

112.   In addition, we do not share the Panel's conviction that when two products can be used for the same end-use, their "*properties* are then *equivalent*, if not identical." (emphasis added) Products with quite different physical properties may, in some situations, be capable of performing similar or identical end-uses. Although the *end-uses* are then "*equivalent*", the physical properties of the products are not thereby altered; they remain different. Thus, the physical "uniqueness" of asbestos that the Panel noted does not change depending on the particular use that is made of asbestos.

* * *

114.   [As to the appropriateness of considering the health risks of the products, the Appellate Body stated that this] carcinogenicity, or

toxicity, constitutes, as we see it, a defining aspect of the physical properties of chrysotile asbestos fibres. The evidence indicates that PCG fibres, in contrast, do not share these properties, at least to the same extent. We do not see how this highly significant physical difference *cannot* be a consideration in examining the physical properties of a product as part of a determination of "likeness" under Article III:4 of the GATT 1994.

115.   We do not agree with the Panel that considering evidence relating to the health risks associated with a product, under Article III:4, nullifies the effect of Article XX(b) of the GATT 1994. Article XX(b) allows a Member to "adopt and enforce" a measure, *inter alia*, necessary to protect human life or health, even though that measure is inconsistent with another provision of the GATT 1994. Article III:4 and Article XX(b) are distinct and independent provisions of the GATT 1994 each to be interpreted on its own. The scope and meaning of Article III:4 should not be broadened or restricted beyond what is required by the normal customary international law rules of treaty interpretation, simply because Article XX(b) exists and may be available to justify measures inconsistent with Article III:4. The fact that an interpretation of Article III:4, under those rules, implies a less frequent recourse to Article XX(b) does not deprive the exception in Article XX(b) of *effet utile*. Article XX(b) would only be deprived of *effet utile* if that provision could not serve to allow a Member to "adopt and enforce" measures "necessary to protect human ... life or health". Evaluating evidence relating to the health risks arising from the physical properties of a product does not prevent a measure which is inconsistent with Article III:4 from being justified under Article XX(b). We note, in this regard, that, different inquiries occur under these two very different Articles. Under Article III:4, evidence relating to health risks may be relevant in assessing the *competitive relationship in the marketplace* between allegedly "like" products. The same, or similar, evidence serves a different purpose under Article XX(b), namely, that of assessing whether a *Member* has a sufficient basis for "adopting or enforcing" a WTO-inconsistent measure on the grounds of human health.

116.   We, therefore, find that the Panel erred in excluding the health risks associated with chrysotile asbestos fibres from its examination of the physical properties of that product.

117.   Before examining the Panel's findings under the second and third criteria, we note that these two criteria involve certain of the key elements relating to the competitive relationship between products: first, the extent to which products are capable of performing the same, or similar, functions (end-uses), and, second, the extent to which consumers are willing to use the products to perform these functions (consumers' tastes and habits). Evidence of this type is of particular importance under Article III of the GATT 1994, precisely because that provision is concerned with competitive relationships in the marketplace. If there is—or could be—*no* competitive relationship between products, a Member cannot intervene, through internal taxation or regulation, to protect

domestic production. Thus, evidence about the extent to which products can serve the same end-uses, and the extent to which consumers are—or would be—willing to choose one product instead of another to perform those end-uses, is highly relevant evidence in assessing the "likeness" of those products under Article III:4 of the GATT 1994.

118. We consider this to be especially so in cases where the evidence relating to properties establishes that the products at issue are physically quite different. In such cases, in order to overcome this indication that products are *not* "like", a higher burden is placed on complaining Members to establish that, despite the pronounced physical differences, there is a competitive relationship between the products such that *all* of the evidence, taken together, demonstrates that the products are "like" under Article III:4 of the GATT 1994. In this case, where it is clear that the fibres have very different properties, in particular, because chrysotile is a known carcinogen, a very heavy burden is placed on Canada to show, under the second and third criteria, that the chrysotile asbestos and PCG fibres are in such a competitive relationship.

119. [The Appellate Body then concluded] that the Panel did not adequately examine the evidence relating to end-uses.

120. The Panel declined to examine or make any findings relating to the third criterion, consumers' tastes and habits, "[b]ecause this criterion would not provide clear results". There will be few situations where the evidence on the "likeness" of products will lend itself to "clear results". In many cases, the evidence will give conflicting indications, possibly within each of the four criteria. For instance, there may be some evidence of similar physical properties and some evidence of differing physical properties. Or the physical properties may differ completely, yet there may be strong evidence of similar end-uses and a high degree of substitutability of the products from the perspective of the consumer. A panel cannot decline to inquire into relevant evidence simply because it suspects that evidence may not be "clear" or, for that matter, because the parties agree [according to Canada] that certain evidence is not relevant. In any event, we have difficulty seeing how the Panel could conclude that an examination of consumers' tastes and habits "would not provide clear results", given that the Panel did not examine *any* evidence relating to this criterion.

121. Furthermore, in a case such as this, where the fibres are physically very different, a panel cannot conclude that they are "like products" if it *does not examine* evidence relating to consumers' tastes and habits. In such a situation, if there is *no* inquiry into this aspect of the nature and extent of the competitive relationship between the products, there is no basis for overcoming the inference, drawn from the different physical properties of the products, that the products are not "like".

122. In this case especially, we are also persuaded that evidence relating to consumers' tastes and habits would establish that the health

risks associated with chrysotile asbestos fibres influence consumers' behaviour with respect to the different fibres at issue. We observe that, as regards *chrysotile asbestos and PCG fibres*, the consumer of the fibres is a *manufacturer* who incorporates the fibres into another product, such as cement-based products or brake linings. We do not wish to speculate on what the evidence regarding these consumers would have indicated; rather, we wish to highlight that consumers' tastes and habits regarding *fibres*, even in the case of commercial parties, such as manufacturers, are very likely to be shaped by the health risks associated with a product which is known to be highly carcinogenic.[2] A manufacturer cannot, for instance, ignore the preferences of the ultimate consumer of its products. If the risks posed by a particular product are sufficiently great, the ultimate consumer may simply cease to buy that product. This would, undoubtedly, affect a manufacturer's decisions in the marketplace. Moreover, in the case of products posing risks to human health, we think it likely that manufacturers' decisions will be influenced by other factors, such as the potential civil liability that might flow from marketing products posing a health risk to the ultimate consumer, or the additional costs associated with safety procedures required to use such products in the manufacturing process.

* * *

124.   We observe also that the Panel did not regard as decisive the different tariff classifications of the chrysotile asbestos, PVA, cellulose and glass fibres, each of which is classified under a different tariff heading. In the absence of a full analysis, by the Panel, of the other three criteria addressed, we cannot determine what importance should be attached to the different tariff classifications of the fibres.

125.   In sum, in our view, the Panel reached the conclusion that *chrysotile asbestos and PCG fibres* are "like products" under Article III:4 of the GATT 1994 on the following basis: the Panel disregarded the quite different "properties, nature and quality" of chrysotile asbestos and PCG fibres, as well as the different tariff classification of these fibres; it considered no evidence on consumers' tastes and habits; and it found that, for a "small number" of the many applications of these fibres, they are substitutable, but it did not consider the many other end-uses for the fibres that are different. Thus, the only evidence supporting the Panel's finding of "likeness" is the "small number" of shared end-uses of the fibres.

[Accordingly, the Appellate Body reversed the panel's conclusion that chrysotile and PCG fibres are "like products". It reached the same result in respect of the Panel's finding that cement products containing

---

2. [original note 103] We recognize that consumers' reactions to products posing a risk to human health vary considerably depending on the product, and on the consumer. Some dangerous products, such as tobacco, are widely used, despite the known health risks. The influence known dangers have on consumers' tastes and habits is, therefore, unlikely to be uniform or entirely predictable.

asbestos and those containing PCG fibres are like. It then made its own examination of likeness:]

134.   We address first the "likeness" of *chrysotile asbestos fibres* and *PCG fibres*. As regards the physical properties of these fibres, we recall that the Panel stated that:

> * * * The parties agree that none of the substitute fibres mentioned by Canada in connection with Article III:4 has the same structure, either in terms of its form, its diameter, its length or its potential to release particles that possess certain characteristics. Moreover, they do not have the same chemical composition, which means that, in purely physical terms, none of them has the same nature or quality.
> . . .

135.   We also see it as important to take into account that, since 1977, chrysotile asbestos fibres have been recognized internationally as a known carcinogen because of the particular combination of their molecular structure, chemical composition, and fibrillation capacity. * * * In contrast, the Panel found that the PCG fibres "are not classified by the WHO at the same level of risk as chrysotile." The experts also confirmed, as the Panel reported, that current scientific evidence indicates that PCG fibres do "not present the same risk to health as chrysotile" asbestos fibres.

136.   It follows that the evidence relating to properties indicates that, physically, chrysotile asbestos and PCG fibres are very different. As we said earlier, in such cases, in order to overcome this indication that products are *not* "like", a high burden is imposed on a complaining Member to establish that, despite the pronounced physical differences, there is a competitive relationship between the products such that, *all* of the evidence, taken together, demonstrates that the products are "like" under Article III:4 of the GATT 1994.

137.   The Panel observed that the end-uses of chrysotile asbestos and PCG fibres are the same "for a small number" of applications. The Panel simply adverted to these overlapping end-uses and offered no elaboration on their nature and character. We note that Canada argued before the Panel that there are some 3,000 commercial applications for asbestos fibres. Canada and the European Communities indicated that the most important end-uses for asbestos fibres include, in no particular order, incorporation into: cement-based products; insulation; and various forms of friction lining. Canada noted that 90 percent, by quantity, of French imports of chrysotile asbestos were used in the production of cement-based products. This evidence suggests that chrysotile asbestos and PCG fibres share a small number of similar end-uses and, that, as Canada asserted, for chrysotile asbestos, these overlapping end-uses represent an important proportion of the end-uses made of chrysotile asbestos, measured in terms of quantity.

138.   There is, however, no evidence on the record regarding the nature and extent of the many end-uses for chrysotile asbestos and PCG fibres which are *not* overlapping. Thus, we do not know what proportion

of all end-uses for chrysotile asbestos and PCG fibres overlap. Where products have a wide range of end-uses, only some of which overlap, we do not believe that it is sufficient to rely solely on evidence regarding the overlapping end-uses, without also examining evidence of the nature and importance of these end-uses in relation to all of the other possible end-uses for the products. In the absence of such evidence, we cannot determine the significance of the fact that chrysotile asbestos and PCG fibres share a small number of similar end-uses.

139.   As we have already stated, Canada took the view, both before the Panel and before us, that consumers' tastes and habits have no relevance to the inquiry into the "likeness" of the fibres. We have already addressed, and dismissed, the arguments advanced by Canada in support of this contention. We have also stated that, in a case such as this one, where the physical properties of the fibres are very different, an examination of the evidence relating to consumers' tastes and habits is an indispensable—although not, on its own, sufficient—aspect of any determination that products are "like" under Article III:4 of the GATT 1994. If there is no evidence on this aspect of the nature and extent of the competitive relationship between the fibres, there is no basis for overcoming the inference, drawn from the different physical properties, that the products are not "like". However, in keeping with its argument that this criterion is irrelevant, Canada presented *no* evidence on consumers' tastes and habits regarding chrysotile asbestos and PCG fibres.

140.   Finally, we note that chrysotile asbestos fibres and the various PCG fibres all have different tariff classifications. While this element is not, on its own, decisive, it does tend to indicate that chrysotile and PCG fibres are not "like products" under Article III:4 of the GATT 1994.

141.   Taken together, in our view, all of this evidence is certainly far from sufficient to satisfy Canada's burden of proving that chrysotile asbestos fibres are "like" PCG fibres under Article III:4 of the GATT 1994. Indeed, this evidence rather tends to suggest that these products are not "like products" for the purposes of Article III:4 of the GATT 1994.

* * *

149.   One Member of the Division hearing this appeal wishes to make a concurring statement. * * *

151.   In paragraph 113 of the Report, we state that "[w]e are very much of the view that evidence relating to the health risks associated with a product may be pertinent in an examination of 'likeness' under Article III:4 of the GATT 1994." We also point out, in paragraph 114, that "[p]anels must examine fully the physical properties of products. In particular, ... those physical properties of products that are likely to influence the competitive relationship between products in the market place. In the cases of chrysotile asbestos fibres, their molecular structure, chemical composition, and fibrillation capacity are important be-

cause the microscopic particles and filaments of chrysotile asbestos fibres are carcinogenic in humans, following inhalation." This carcinogenicity we describe as "a defining aspect of the physical properties of chrysotile asbestos fibres", which property is not shared by the PCG fibres, "at least to the same extent." We express our inability to "see how this highly significant physical difference *cannot* be a consideration in examining the physical properties of a product as part of a determination of 'likeness' under Article III:4 of the GATT 1994." (emphasis in the original) We observe also that the Panel, after noting that the carcinogenicity of chrysotile asbestos fibres has been acknowledged by international bodies and confirmed by the experts the Panel consulted, ruled that it "[has] sufficient evidence that *there is in fact a serious carcinogenic risk associated with the inhalation of chrysotile fibres.*" (emphasis added) In fact, the scientific evidence of record for this finding of carcinogenicity of chrysotile asbestos fibres is so clear, voluminous, and is confirmed, a number of times, by a variety of international organizations, as to be practically overwhelming.

152.   In the present appeal, considering the nature and quantum of the scientific evidence showing that the physical properties and qualities of chrysotile asbestos fibres include or result in carcinogenicity, my submission is that there is ample basis for a definitive characterization, on completion of the legal analysis, of such fibres as *not* "like" PCG fibres. PCG fibres, it may be recalled, have not been shown by Canada to have the same lethal properties as chrysotile asbestos fibres. That definitive characterization, it is further submitted, may and should be made even in the absence of evidence concerning the other two *Border Tax Adjustments* criteria (categories of "potentially shared characteristics") of end-uses and consumers' tastes and habits. It is difficult for me to imagine what evidence relating to economic competitive relationships as reflected in end-uses and consumers' tastes and habits could outweigh and set at naught the undisputed deadly nature of chrysotile asbestos fibres, compared with PCG fibres, when inhaled by humans, and thereby compel a characterization of "likeness" of chrysotile asbestos and PCG fibres.

153.   The suggestion I make is not that *any* kind or degree of health risk, associated with a particular product, would *a priori* negate a finding of the "likeness" of that product with another product, under Article III:4 of the GATT 1994. The suggestion is a very narrow one, limited only to the circumstances of this case, and confined to chrysotile asbestos fibres as compared with PCG fibres. To hold that these fibres are not "like" one another in view of the undisputed carcinogenic nature of chrysotile asbestos fibres appears to me to be but a small and modest step forward from mere reversal of the Panel's ruling that chrysotile asbestos and PCG fibres are "like", especially since our holding in completing the analysis is that Canada failed to satisfy a complainant's burden of proving that PCG fibres are "like" chrysotile asbestos fibres under Article III:4. That small step, however, the other Members of the Division feel unable to take because of their conception of the "funda-

mental", perhaps decisive, role of economic competitive relationships in the determination of the "likeness" of products under Article III:4.

154. My second point is that the necessity or appropriateness of adopting a "fundamentally" economic interpretation of the "likeness" of products under Article III:4 of the GATT 1994 does not appear to me to be free from substantial doubt. Moreover, in future concrete contexts, the line between a "fundamentally" and "exclusively" economic view of "like products" under Article III:4 may well prove very difficult, as a practical matter, to identify. It seems to me the better part of valour to reserve one's opinion on such an important, indeed, philosophical matter, which may have unforeseeable implications, and to leave that matter for another appeal and another day, or perhaps other appeals and other days. I so reserve my opinion on this matter.

Notes and Questions

(1) The concurring statement is the first in the history of the Appellate Body. Is it really a dissent? What about the substantive point? Does the majority put too much emphasis on the view of the market?

(2) In light of the Appellate Body decisions in the *Japan–Alcoholic Beverages* and the *Asbestos* cases, it would seem that a panel would always be well advised to consider the *Border Tax Adjustments* criteria carefully in any analysis of product likeness. It also seems clear that a panel should examine any other relevant factors. What other factors are relevant in determining likeness? To what extent are those other factors secondary in importance to a market analysis?

(3) It has often been assumed in GATT/WTO discussions that determining the likeness of products cannot be based on an analysis of the way in which the products were made. Otherwise, countries would be tempted to discriminate against products from countries following policies or in a state of development below their own. Thus, it has been argued that it would be inappropriate to distinguish between products on the grounds of whether they are produced in an environmentally friendly way or by workers benefiting from certain labor rights or wage levels. For example, in BELGIAN FAMILY ALLOWANCES, 1st Supp. BISD 59–62 (1953)(Panel report adopted Nov. 7, 1952), a GATT panel was faced with a Belgian law that levied a charge on foreign goods purchased by public authorities when those goods originated in a country whose system of family allowances did not meet specific requirements. The panel noted that some countries had been exempted from the charge and concluded that if the General Agreement were definitively in force "it is clear that that exemption would have to be granted unconditionally to all other contracting parties (including [the complaining countries of] Denmark and Norway). The consistency or otherwise of the system of family allowances in force in the territory of a given contracting party with the requirements of the Belgian law would be irrelevant in this respect."

Under the Appellate Body's *Asbestos* decision, would it be appropriate to consider such distinctions in making a likeness determination? Would it be necessary to show that the market recognized the distinctions? How significant would that market differentiation have to be? Given that products come with histories and origins and distinctions can be made on those bases, why couldn't those distinctions offer a basis for calling some products unlike other products? In this connection, does GATT ever allow discrimination on the basis of how a product is produced? See Article XX(e) (prison labor). More generally, could a distinction based on how a product is produced— even if found to violate Article III—be justified under other provisions of Article XX? We examine Article XX in Chapter 13.

(4) In *Asbestos*, the Appellate Body suggests that the breadth of the definition of like products for purposes of Article III:4 includes products that would be considered to be directly competitive or substitutable for purposes of Article III:2 (para. 99). To establish a violation of Article III:2 in respect of such products, it would be necessary to show that the taxation at issue was dissimilar and applied so as to afford protection. For purposes of establishing a violation of Article III:4, less favorable treatment need be shown, but not protection. Does this suggest that Article III:4 in practice restricts government discretion much more than Article III:2? Or does the need to show less favorable treatment in practice mean that protection must be shown? The next sub-section explores the concept of less favorable treatment.

(5) Given the broader coverage of Article III:4 would it make sense to consider whether the "aims and effect" test mentioned in the preceding section should be used for purposes of defining likeness in Article III:4?

(6) Would you say that the emphasis on markets and the competitiveness of products is likely to lead to fewer or more findings of product likeness?

(B) LESS FAVORABLE TREATMENT

In most Article III:4 cases, the question of whether a measure affords less favorable treatment has not been a major issue. However, it worth remembering that not all different treatment is necessarily less favorable. Thus, there are occasions when it is necessary to decide precisely what this aspect of Article III:4 means.

KOREA—MEASURES AFFECTING IMPORTS OF FRESH, CHILLED AND FROZEN BEEF

WT/DS161 & 169/AB/R.
Appellate Body Report adopted January 10, 2001.

[Australia and the United States challenged a number of aspects of Korean treatment of imported beef, including the so-called dual retail system, which required that imported and domestic beef be sold in different stores (or, in the case of large stores, in different sections). The Panel found that the dual retail system accords treatment less favorable to imported beef than to like Korean beef, and is, thus, inconsistent with Article III:4 of the GATT 1994. This finding was based on the Panel's view that any measure based exclusively on criteria relating to the origin of a product is inconsistent with Article III:4 and on the Panel's assessment of how the dual retail system modifies the conditions of competition between imported and like domestic beef in the Korean market. Korea argued on appeal that the system does not accord treatment less favorable to imported beef than to like domestic beef and therefore does not violate Article III:4.

[The Appellate Body began by recalling its description of the purpose of Article III, as set out earlier in this chapter in *Japan–Alcoholic Beverages*, and the analysis of the *Section 337* panel in paragraph 5.11 of its report, also set out above. It then continued:]

137.   A formal difference in treatment between imported and like domestic products is thus neither necessary, nor sufficient, to show a violation of Article III:4. Whether or not imported products are treated "less favourably" than like domestic products should be assessed instead by examining whether a measure modifies the *conditions of competition* in the relevant market to the detriment of imported products.

138.   We conclude that the Panel erred in its general interpretation that "[a]ny regulatory distinction that is based exclusively on criteria relating to the nationality or the origin of the products is incompatible with Article III."

139.   The Panel went on, however, to examine the conditions of competition between imported and like domestic beef in the Korean market. The Panel gave several reasons why it believed that the dual retail system alters the conditions of competition in the Korean market in favour of domestic beef. First, it found that the dual retail system would "limit the possibility for consumers to compare imported and domestic products", and thereby "reduce opportunities for imported products to compete directly with domestic products". Second, the Panel found that, under the dual retail system, "the only way an imported product can get on the shelves is if the retailer agrees to substitute it, not only for one but for all existing like domestic products." This disadvantage would be more serious when the market share of imports (as is the case with imported beef) is small. Third, the Panel found that the dual retail system, by excluding imported beef from "the vast majority of sales outlets", limits the potential market opportunities for imported beef. This would apply particularly to products "consumed on a daily basis", like beef, where consumers may not be willing to "shop around". Fourth, the Panel found that the dual retail system imposes more costs on the imported product, since the domestic product will tend to continue to be sold from existing retail stores, whereas imported beef will require new stores to be established. Fifth, the Panel found that the dual retail system "encourages the perception that imported and domestic beef are different, when they are in fact like products belonging to the same market", which gives a competitive advantage to domestic beef, "based on criteria not related to the products themselves". Sixth, the Panel found that the dual retail system "facilitates the maintenance of a price differential" to the advantage of domestic beef.

* * *

141. It will be seen below that we share the ultimate conclusion of the Panel in respect of the consistency of the dual retail system for beef with Article III:4 of the GATT 1994. Portions, however, of the Panel's analysis *en route* to that conclusion appear to us problematic. For instance, while limitation of the ability to compare visually two products, local and imported, at the point of sale may have resulted from the dual retail system, such limitation does not, in our view, necessarily reduce the opportunity for the imported product to compete "directly" or on "an equal footing" with the domestic product. Again, even if we were to accept that the dual retail system "encourages" the perception of consumers that imported and domestic beef are "different", we do not think it has been demonstrated that such encouragement necessarily implies a competitive advantage for domestic beef. Circumstances like limitation of "side-by-side" comparison and "encouragement" of consumer perceptions of "differences" may be simply incidental effects of the dual retail system without decisive implications for the issue of consistency with Article III:4.

142. We believe that a more direct, and perhaps simpler, approach to the dual retail system of Korea may be usefully followed in the present case. In the following paragraphs, we seek to focus on what appears to us to be the fundamental thrust and effect of the measure itself.

143. Korean law in effect requires the existence of two distinct retail distribution systems so far as beef is concerned: one system for the retail sale of domestic beef and another system for the retail sale of imported beef. A small retailer (that is, a non-supermarket or non-department store) which is a "Specialized Imported Beef Store" may sell any meat *except domestic beef*; any other small retailer may sell any meat *except imported beef*. A large retailer (that is, a supermarket or department store) may sell both imported and domestic beef, as long as the imported beef and domestic beef are sold in separate sales areas. A retailer selling imported beef is required to display a sign reading "Specialized Imported Beef Store".

144. Thus, the Korean measure formally separates the selling of imported beef and domestic beef. However, that formal separation, *in and of itself*, does not necessarily compel the conclusion that the treatment thus accorded to imported beef is less favourable than the treatment accorded to domestic beef.[3] To determine whether the treatment given to imported beef is less favourable than that given to domestic beef, we must, as earlier indicated, inquire into whether or not the Korean dual retail system for beef modifies the *conditions of competition* in the Korean beef market to the disadvantage of the imported product.

145. When beef was first imported into Korea in 1988, the new product simply entered into the pre-existing distribution system that had

---

3. [original note 85] Apart from the display sign requirement, dealt with in para. 151. [See Note (5).]

been handling domestic beef. The beef retail system was a unitary one, and the conditions of competition affecting the sale of beef were the same for both the domestic and the imported product. In 1990, Korea promulgated its dual retail system for beef. Accordingly, the existing small retailers had to choose between, on the one hand, continuing to sell domestic beef and renouncing the sale of imported beef or, on the other hand, ceasing to sell domestic beef in order to be allowed to sell the imported product. Apparently, the vast majority of the small meat retailers chose the first option. The result was the virtual exclusion of imported beef from the retail distribution channels through which domestic beef (and until then, imported beef, too) was distributed to Korean households and other consumers throughout the country. Accordingly, a new and separate retail system had to be established and gradually built from the ground up for bringing the imported product to the same households and other consumers if the imported product was to compete at all with the domestic product. Put in slightly different terms, the putting into legal effect of the dual retail system for beef meant, in direct practical effect, so far as imported beef was concerned, the sudden cutting off of access to the normal, that is, the previously existing, distribution outlets through which the domestic product continued to flow to consumers in the urban centers and countryside that make up the Korean national territory. The central consequence of the dual retail system can only be reasonably construed, in our view, as the imposition of a drastic reduction of commercial opportunity to reach, and hence to generate sales to, the same consumers served by the traditional retail channels for domestic beef. In 1998, when this case began, eight years after the dual retail system was first prescribed, the consequent reduction of commercial opportunity was reflected in the much smaller number of specialized imported beef shops (approximately 5,000 shops) as compared with the number of retailers (approximately 45,000 shops) selling domestic beef.

146.   We are aware that the dramatic reduction in number of retail outlets for imported beef followed from the decisions of individual retailers who could choose freely to sell the domestic product or the imported product. The legal necessity of making a choice was, however, imposed by the measure itself. The restricted nature of that choice should be noted. The choice given to the meat retailers was *not* an option between remaining with the pre-existing unified distribution set-up or going to a dual retail system. The choice was limited to selling domestic beef only or imported beef only. Thus, the reduction of access to normal retail channels is, in legal contemplation, the effect of that measure. In these circumstances, the intervention of some element of private choice does not relieve Korea of responsibility under the GATT 1994 for the resulting establishment of competitive conditions less favourable for the imported product than for the domestic product.

147.   We also note that the reduction of competitive opportunity through the restriction of access to consumers results from the imposition of the dual retail system for beef, notwithstanding [what Korea

describes as] "perfect regulatory symmetry" of that system, and is not a function of the limited volume of foreign beef actually imported into Korea. The fact that the WTO-consistent quota for beef has, save for two years, been fully utilized does not detract from the lack of equality of competitive conditions entailed by the dual retail system.

148. We believe, and so hold, that the treatment accorded to imported beef, as a consequence of the dual retail system established for beef by Korean law and regulation, is less favourable than the treatment given to like domestic beef and is, accordingly, not consistent with the requirements of Article III:4 of the GATT 1994.

149. It may finally be useful to indicate, however broadly, what we are not saying in reaching our above conclusion. We are *not* holding that a dual or parallel distribution system that is *not* imposed directly or indirectly by law or governmental regulation, but is rather solely the result of private entrepreneurs acting on their own calculations of comparative costs and benefits of differentiated distribution systems, is unlawful under Article III:4 of the GATT 1994. What is addressed by Article III:4 is merely the *governmental* intervention that affects the conditions under which like goods, domestic and imported, compete in the market within a Member's territory.

Notes and Questions

(1) Korea invoked the exception in Article XX(d) to justify the dual retail system and we examine that issue in the next chapter.

(2) In contrast to its analysis in the *Asbestos* case, the Appellate Body does not emphasize (or even mention) the role of Article III:1 in interpreting the second element of Article III:4. Should it have done so? Does an examination of whether conditions of competition have been modified to the detriment of imports necessarily address whether a measure has been applied so as to afford protection to domestic production?

(3) More generally, could the no-less-favorable-treatment requirement be interpreted with reference to Article III:1 in order to achieve the goal sought by the proponents of the "aims and effect" test for like products that we have previously examined in this chapter? That is, could (or should) the requirement of no less favourable treatment be read to include an element of protection, such that the lack of protection could be used as a defense to a claim of less favorable treatment?

(4) Dominican Republic—Measures Affecting the Importation and Internal Sale of Cigarettes, WT/DS302/AB/R, adopted May 19, 2005, involved a requirement that the tax stamp required on packages of cigarettes sold in the Dominican Republic had to be affixed in the Dominican Republic under the supervision of its tax authorities. The panel found this requirement violated Article III:4 because, although applicable to both domestic and imported cigarettes, it modified the conditions of competition in the market place to the detriment of the imports. In the panel's view, it resulted in additional processes and costs for the imports and caused them to be presented in a less appealing manner. The panel's ruling on Article III:4 was not appealed, although its rejection of an Article XX(d) defense was appealed.

See Section 13.3 infra. The case also involved a requirement that importers and domestic producers of cigarettes post a bond to secure payment of taxes. The panel found that this requirement did not violate Article III:4. On appeal, the Appellate Body stated:

> 96.   The Appellate Body indicated in *Korea–Beef* that imported products are treated less favourably than like products if a measure modifies the conditions of competition in the relevant market *to the detriment of imported products*. However, the existence of a detrimental effect on a given imported product resulting from a measure does not necessarily imply that this measure accords less favourable treatment to imports if the detrimental effect is explained by factors or circumstances unrelated to the foreign origin of the product, such as the market share of the importer in this case. In this specific case, the mere demonstration that the per-unit cost of the bond requirement for imported cigarettes was higher than for some domestic cigarettes during a particular period is not, in our view, *sufficient* to establish "less favourable treatment" under Article III:4 of the GATT 1994. Indeed, the difference between the per-unit costs of the bond requirement alleged by Honduras is explained by the fact that the importer of Honduran cigarettes has a smaller market share than two domestic producers (the per-unit cost of the bond requirement being the result of dividing the cost of the bond by the number of cigarettes sold on the Dominican Republic market). In this case, the difference between the per-unit costs of the bond requirement alleged by Honduras does not depend on the foreign origin of the imported cigarettes.

Do you agree? Are there subtle differences in approach between this case and others we have examined in this chapter?

(5) As part of the dual retail system, Korea required that stores selling imported beef display a sign declaring "Specialized Imported Beef Store". The Panel found that the requirement was ancillary to the dual retail system and as that violated Article III:4, so did the sign requirement. The Appellate Body did not review that finding, noting that "[w]hen considered independently from a dual retail system, a sign requirement might or might not be characterized legally as consistent with Article III:4." (para. 151) Suppose Korea abolished the dual retail system, but kept the sign requirement. How would you analyse a challenge to that requirement under Article III:4?

Consider the following cases. TERRITORY OF HAWAII v. HO, 41 Hawaii 565 (1957) involved a law making it unlawful for any person to sell imported eggs unless a placard bearing the words "WE SELL FOREIGN EGGS" was displayed in a conspicuous place. The court concluded that such a requirement violated Article III:4 since a similar requirement was not imposed on domestic eggs. As to Article XX, the Court found it inapplicable because deceptive practices could better be prevented by a straightforward origin-marking requirement. Moreover, "[w]e think that the additional requirement of a placard of origin only in the case of foreign eggs constitutes a disguised restriction on international trade." Do you agree?

An April, 1967 order of the United States Federal Trade Commission changed its labeling rules concerning fur products, by requiring an animal formerly designated as "Mink, Japanese" to be henceforth designated as

"Japanese Weasel." A Wall Street Journal article of May 8, 1967, entitled "FTC Labels a 'Mink' from Japan a Weasel—and the Fur Flies," notes that all mink whether Asian or American are members of the weasel family, and implies that the desire of the FTC to require Japanese mink to be labeled weasel may stem from a desire to protect US mink ranchers from competition of the Japanese fur. The rule is still in force. 16 C.F.R. sec. 301.0 (2007). Did the FTC action violate Article III:4?

In dealing with a similar issue, the EC Court of Justice once held that an origin-marking requirement applicable to domestic and imported products violates Article 28 of the EC Treaty, which prohibits quantitative restrictions and measures having equivalent effect. In Commission v. United Kingdom (Marks of origin), Case 207/83, [1985] ECR 1201, it wrote:

> [I]t has to be recognized that the purpose of indications of origin or origin-marking is to enable consumers to distinguish between domestic and imported products and that this enables them to assert any prejudices which they may have against foreign products. * * * [The EC Treaty] seeks to unite national markets in a single market having the characteristics of a domestic market. Within such a market, the origin-marking requirement * * * makes the marketing in a Member State of goods produced in other Member States * * * more difficult.

For all of the foregoing situations, how does GATT Article IX impact your analysis?[4]

(6) The Agreement on Trade–Related Investment Measures (TRIMs Agreement) contains a list of examples of measures that violate Article III:4. The list includes measures which require "the purchase or use by an enterprise of products of domestic origin * * *, whether specified in terms of particular products, in terms of volume or value of products, or in terms of a proportion of volume or value of its local production; or that an enterprise's purchases or use of imported products be limited to an amount related to the volume of value of local products that it exports." Do you see why these measures violate the terms of Article III:4, and, in particular, the no less favorable treatment requirement?

(C) LAWS, REGULATIONS AND REQUIREMENTS

Article III:4 applies to laws, regulations and requirements affecting the internal sale, etc. of imported goods. We saw at the outset of this chapter that the term "affecting" has been interpreted broadly. This has also been true of the term "requirements". For example, a measure that conditions a governmental benefit on certain action is viewed as a requirement, although in fact there is not obligation to take action. For example, the TRIMs Agreement's illustrative list of investment measures related to trade in goods (TRIMs) that are inconsistent with Article III:4 includes measures "compliance with which is necessary to obtain an advantage".

In the *Japan–Film* case (para. 10.376), the panel assumed for purposes of its analysis of the Article III claims that the phrase "laws, regulations and requirements" should be given a broad reading, basically

4. John H. Jackson, World Trade and the Law of GATT 461 (1969).

equivalent to the term "measures" in Article XXIII:1(b). The *Film* panel's broad reading of the term "measures" for purposes of Article XXIII had been based in part on the Article XI cases, such as *Japan— Semiconductors* discussed in Section 9.2 supra, that had concluded that so-called administrative guidance fell within the definition of "other measures" for purposes of Article XI.

SECTION 12.5 GOVERNMENT PURCHASES

Because of the explicit exception in paragraph 8(a), government purchases are not limited by Article III's national treatment obligation, and because of the language of Article I, it is generally considered that the MFN obligation also does not apply to government purchases,[1] although Article XVII contains a modest constraint on purchases of state enterprises. Consequently, prior to the Tokyo Round, governments were generally free in their procurement policies to discriminate in favor of domestic goods, or in favor of the goods of one country over another, and they often did.

The existence of statutes or policies favoring domestic suppliers was a source of considerable aggravation, particularly to those industries (e.g., aircraft and electric turbines) whose products are often purchased by governments. Moreover, in some countries it seemed that the government owned or operated sector of the economy represented an increasing percentage of the whole economy, with the result that an increasing amount of economic activity was escaping the discipline of the international trade rules. This was a significant part of the motivation which led major nations to undertake, in the Tokyo Round, to negotiate a code on government purchases.[2] Prior to the Tokyo Round, government procurement policies had been the subject of considerable work in the OECD. This work was made available to the Tokyo Round negotiators and the result of the negotiations was a side agreement on government procurement, which entered into force in 1981. It was amended in 1987.

(A) THE 1994 AGREEMENT ON GOVERNMENT PROCUREMENT

Concurrently with the Uruguay Round, a new Agreement on Government Procurement (GPA) was negotiated, and it entered into force on January 1, 1996.[3] The GPA is attached to the WTO Agreement as a plurilateral agreement in Annex 4. As such, it is not part of the "single undertaking" to which all WTO members must subscribe, and its membership is limited mainly to more industrialized WTO members. As of

1. See John H. Jackson, World Trade and the Law of GATT 291 (1969).

2. See generally Report of the Director–General of GATT, The Tokyo Round of Multilateral Trade Negotiations 76–77 (1979); Senate Report No. 96–249, 96th Cong., 1st Sess. 128 (1979).

3. Bernard M. Hoekman & Petros C. Mavroidis, eds., Law and Policy in Public Purchasing: The WTO Agreement on Government Procurement (1997); Arie Reich, International Public Procurement Law: The Evolution of International Regimes on Public Purchasing (1999).

January 2008, the parties to the GPA were Canada, the EC and its member states, Hong Kong China, Iceland, Israel, Japan, Korea, Liechtenstein, Netherlands on behalf of Aruba, Norway, Singapore, Switzerland and the United States. Albania, China, Georgia, Jordan, Kyrgyz Republic, Moldova, Oman, Panama and Chinese Taipei were negotiating accession. As of December 2006, a tentative agreement had been reached on certain revisions to the GPA (available in WTO document GPA/W/297), but negotiations on expanded coverage were still ongoing as of January 2008.

With respect to government procurement covered by the GPA, the GPA requires that a party give no less favorable treatment to products, services and suppliers of another GPA party than it gives (i) to its own domestic products, services and suppliers and (ii) to the products, services and suppliers of any other GPA party (Article III:1). In other words, the GPA imposes national treatment and MFN obligations in respect of government procurement. In addition, Article III:2 bans discrimination against locally-established suppliers on the basis of their foreign ownership or affiliation or on the basis of the foreign source of their goods or services (provided the source is a GPA party).

The coverage of the GPA extends to central government entities, sub-central government entities and other entities (such as utilities) that are listed in annexes 1 to 3 of a party's schedule. It covers procurement above certain thresholds by those entities of goods, services (to the extent specified in annex 4) and construction services (to the extent specified in annex 5). There is variation in the thresholds, which are expressed in terms of IMF special drawing rights (1 SDR was equivalent to $1.58 on January 25, 2008). For the US, federal entities are covered for goods and services procurement in excess of SDR 130,000 and in excess of SDR 5 million for construction services. Sub-federal entities have a higher threshold for goods and services (SDR 355,000), as do other entities (SDR 400,000). In the case of the EC, the thresholds are generally the same, except that sub-federal entities are subject to a SDR 200,000 threshold. There are, however, various exceptions found in the annexes and in the general notes to each party's schedule. For example, the US notes provide that its obligations are subject to continuation of set asides for minority and small businesses. More generally, the GPA has exceptions similar to those found in GATT Articles XX and XXI.

In addition to the non-discrimination requirements, the GPA contains transparency requirements designed to ensure that the rules governing procurement are published and requires parties to report statistics annually on procurement covered by the agreement (Article XIX). In addition, it contains detailed rules on procurement procedures, aimed at ensuring that foreign supplies and suppliers are given an equal opportunity to compete for covered procurement contracts. For example, in cases of limited tenders, where bids are accepted only from qualified suppliers, the agreement has rules on how suppliers are qualified. The GPA also requires parties to establish so-called challenge procedures under which interested suppliers have a right of recourse to an impartial and independent review body before which they may argue that the requirements of the GPA were not met in a specific case (Article XX).

The GPA contains a couple of specific substantive provisions that ban certain policies. First, the use of offsets (e.g., domestic content or counter-trade requirements) is prohibited (Article XVI). Second, Article VI aims at ensuring that technical specifications are not used to discriminate against foreign products or services.

Finally, it should be noted that the GPA contains a number of special provisions for developing countries, designed to encourage their accession.

Notes and Questions

(1) The basic US statute providing a procurement preference for national goods is the Buy American Act of 1933.[4] Subject to exceptions, such as resulted from implementing the GPA, the law essentially requires federal agencies to buy domestically produced goods unless the price is unreasonable or such purchase is otherwise not in the public interest. Under the Federal Acquisition Regulations, domestic suppliers are generally favored if their offer price is not more than six percent above that offered by foreign suppliers.[5] The preference is 50 percent in the case of the Defense Department.[6] The US law implementing the 1979 and 1994 Agreements is Sections 301–308 of the Trade Agreements Acts of 1979, as amended (Documents Supplement).

(2) There were three dispute panel reports issued under the Tokyo Round Code. In the first case, it was determined that VAT and applicable taxes and duties should be included in determining whether a contract met the Code's minimum threshold.[7] In a 1992 report, a panel concluded that the US had violated the Code by excluding an EU supplier from bidding on a sonar mapping system for Antarctica.[8] The US, which never permitted the adoption of the panel report, claimed that the contract was not subject to the Code because it involved the provision of services, as well as goods. Also in 1992, in response to a US complaint, a panel concluded that Norway had violated the Code in connection with procurement of toll collection equipment for the City of Trondheim.[9] The basic issue in the case was whether the contract fell within the Code's research and development/prototype exception. The panel concluded that it did not, essentially because it resulted in the procurement by Trondheim of a complete toll collection system. As we saw in Chapter 7 on dispute settlement, this case highlights the problem of

---

4. 41 U.S.C.A. secs. 10a–10d.

5. 48 CFR sec. 25.105 (2007)(12 percent, if the domestic offer is from a small business concern).

6. 48 CFR sec. 225.502 (2007).

7. See GATT, 29th Supp. BISD 41 (1983); GATT, 30th Supp. BISD 36 (1984); GATT, 31st Supp. BISD 247 (1985); GATT, 34th Supp. BISD 177, 179 (1988); Eur. Comm. O.J. C 25/2 (Jan. 30, 1988)(EU lowered threshold applicable to it by 13% to reflect VAT applied in EU).

8. GATT Doc. GPR.DS1/R (Apr. 23, 1992).

9. Norway–Procurement of Toll Collection Equipment for the City of Trondheim, GATT Doc. GPR.DS2/R (April 28, 1992)(Panel report adopted May 13, 1992, by the Committee on Government Procurement). The US later decided that Norway had adequately implemented the decision. 57 Fed. Reg. 46232 (1992).

effective remedies: To what relief is an aggrieved foreign bidder entitled? The GPA requires that challenge procedures must provide for the possibility of obtaining rapid interim relief (e.g., suspension of the procurement process), but it does not require that such relief must necessarily be given (e.g., the tribunal may take into account "overriding adverse consequences for the interests concerned, including the public interest") (Article XX(7)). What are the advantages and disadvantages of requiring interim relief?

(3) As permitted by the Dispute Settlement Understanding, the GPA provides that the DSU will apply to GPA disputes, subject to certain specific rules (Article XXII). For purposes of such disputes, the DSB consists of only GPA parties. As of 2008, dispute settlement panels had been established in two cases brought under the GPA. One involved a challenge by the EC and Japan to the Massachusetts law that was the subject of the *Crosby* case, excerpted in Section 3.6 supra. After the panel had been composed but before any submissions had been made to it, the proceeding was suspended and later abandoned when the law was struck down by US federal courts. The second case involved a US challenge to Korean procurement in connection with the new Seoul airport at Inchon. The case turned on whether the Korean schedule included the entity responsible for the airport and the panel concluded that it did not. It also rejected a non-violation claim brought by the US in the alternative. The US did not appeal the decision. Korea— Measures Affecting Government Procurement, WT/DS163/R (adopted June 19, 2000).

(4) The WTO has estimated that government procurement represents 10–15% of GDP. According to statistics collected under the Tokyo Round Code for the period 1990–1994, it applied to roughly $30 billion in annually procurement. The GPA was expected to increase that number by a factor of ten. GPA parties are required to report statistics annually that indicate the extent of the coverage of the GPA, but the parties have not done so on a systematic basis.

(5) A multilateral working group on transparency in government procurement practices was established at the 1996 Singapore Ministerial with the aim of developing elements for inclusion in a future agreement on the subject. This work has been on hold since 2004.

(6) Government procurement was treated in both the US–Canada Free Trade Agreement and the North American Free Trade Agreement. In the FTA, the provisions of the GATT Agreement were incorporated by reference, with the threshold being lowered to US$25,000. FTA, arts. 1303–1304. In addition, there were some expanded procedural and reporting obligations agreed to. Id., arts. 1305–1306. Since Mexico was not a signatory to the GATT Agreement (and did not subsequently become a party to the GPA), NAFTA contains detailed provisions on government procurement. NAFTA, ch. 10. Its provisions expand the number of covered entities and the type of contract covered (e.g., $50,000 for contracts for goods, services or any combination; $6.5 million for construction services), subject in each case to various specific exceptions.

(B) SUB–FEDERAL GOVERNMENT PROCUREMENT PREFERENCES

The desire to favor local suppliers is found at all levels of government. In the United States, as we saw in Section 3.6 supra, many states and localities give some form of preferential treatment to local, state or national bidders.[10] It was estimated in 1990 that all but a very few states had some form of domestic preference policy. The form of preference varies widely. They have been categorized as comprehensive, product-specific, flexible, absolute, buy-state or buy-local.[11] A comprehensive law is one that applies to all government procurement; a product-specific law is one that applies only to a specified product or group of products. In the United States, the steel industry has managed to have a number of states adopt Buy–American statutes for steel.[12] A flexible law gives procurement officials discretion to take into account such factors as quality and price differences. Many of the state statutes are buy-national statutes, which means that there is no discrimination against other states. But some statutes give preferences to state or local producers.

Prior to the GPA, US state and local preferences in government procurement were not subject to US international obligations. That remains largely true, although some procurement by most states is now covered by the GPA. While state and local restrictions can be attacked as interfering with the federal government's exclusive foreign affairs powers, such as we saw in the *Bethlehem* case in Section 3.6 supra, other cases have rejected that claim, as we saw in the *Trojan Technologies* case in the same section. Moreover, the Supreme Court has permitted states to discriminate against interstate commerce in procurement matters under the market participant doctrine, which was also discussed in Chapter 3.

---

10. See generally Robert Fraser Miller, Buy–American Statutes: An Assessment of Validity Under Present Law and a Recommendation for Preemption, 23 Rutgers L.J. 137 (1991).

11. See id. at 140–41.

12. We have already seen one such example in the *Trojan Technologies* case, discussed in Section 3.6(D) supra.

Chapter 13

ARTICLE XX: THE GENERAL EXCEPTIONS

SECTION 13.1 INTRODUCTION

In this chapter, we will examine the general exceptions to GATT rules that are contained in Article XX.[1] In particular, we will examine the exceptions for health (Article XX(b)), enforcement (Article XX(d)) and conservation measures (Article XX (g)). There are, of course, other provisions containing exceptions to GATT rules, but we will focus on Article XX and these three exceptions because they are frequently invoked and have been the subject of an extraordinarily detailed Appellate Body jurisdiction developed during the first seven years of the WTO's existence.

The general exceptions clause of Article XX is of particular importance to one of the most controversial subjects that the WTO has had to confront in recent years—the relationship between trade rules and environmental measures. Insofar as the charge is made that the WTO's rules inappropriately find fault with environmental measures, the extent to which the exceptions to those rules permit the maintenance of the challenged environmental measures is critical. Indeed, the trade-environment conflict first burst on the scene in a case involving US rules banning imports of tuna not taken with dolphin-friendly methods. While the results of the two cases dealing with that issue were never adopted by the GATT Council, the cases received widespread attention and caused many to view GATT in a very unfavorable light. In this chapter, we will treat extensively a case similar to the so-called *Tuna–Dolphin* case, involving US rules banning imports of shrimp not taken with turtle-friendly methods. The difference in approach between the two sets of cases has led some to argue that the trade-environment conflict may not be so deep after all. Nonetheless, we will conclude this chapter with a section raising the question of whether GATT needs a general exception for environmental measures.

At the outset of our examination of Article XX, it is useful to consider its structure. It consists of two parts: an introductory clause

1. See generally John H. Jackson, World Trade and the Law of GATT, ch. 28 (1969).

(often referred to as the chapeau) and a list of types of measures that fall within its scope. That list includes measures:

(a) necessary to protect public morals;

(b) necessary to protect human, animal or plant life or health;

(c) relating to the importation or exportation of gold or silver;

(d) necessary to secure compliance with laws or regulations which are not inconsistent with GATT rules themselves;

(e) relating to the products of prison labor;

(f) imposed for the protection of national treasures;

(g) relating to the conservation of exhaustible natural resources;

(h) undertaken pursuant to obligations of certain international commodity agreements;

(i) involving restrictions on exports necessary to ensure domestic supplies when the domestic price is held below the world price by the government for price stabilization reasons; and

(j) essential to the acquisition or distribution of products in short supply.

As noted above, there is detailed jurisprudence on clauses (b), (d) and (g), but not in respect of the others. It is worth noting that while the scope of these other clauses is for the most part fairly well defined, the scope of clause (a), which permits measures necessary to protect public morals, has not been interpreted in dispute settlement and is potentially quite far-reaching. Could it, for example, justify measures taken to protest an exporter's human rights policies? The issue of linking trade to non-trade policies is considered generally in Chapter 21. GATS contains a similar list of exceptions in its Article XIV. The GATS provision analogous to Article XX(a) covers measures necessary to protect public morals or maintain public order. GATS, art. XIV(a). Does the difference in wording affect the scope of the exception significantly? The only GATS case to address Article XIV(a) found that measures aimed at regulating gambling could fall within its scope. The case—*US Gambling*—is excerpted in Chapter 19.

The Appellate Body has stressed that a proper analysis of an Article XX defense must in all cases begin with a consideration of whether the measure at issue is a type covered by Article XX.[2] For example, is it a measure necessary to protect human health (clause (b)) or one that is related to conservation of exhaustible natural resources (clause (g))? If the measure falls under one of the enumerated clauses, such that it can be "provisionally justified," then it is necessary to see if the measure complies with the requirements of the chapeau, which provides that the exceptions of Article XX are only available if the measure at issue is "not

---

2. United States—Import Prohibition of Certain Shrimp and Shrimp Products, WT/DS58/AB/R, paras. 118–121, Appellate Body Report adopted by the DSB on November 6, 1998; United States—Standards for Reformulated and Conventional Gasoline, WT/DS2 & 4/AB/R, p. 22, Appellate Body Report adopted by the DSB on May 20, 1996.

applied in a manner which would constitute a means of arbitrary or unjustifiable discrimination between countries where the same conditions prevail, or a disguised restriction on international trade." Consequently, in this chapter we will first examine WTO cases that consider whether a measure falls within the list of measures covered by Article XX and then consider how the requirements of the chapeau have been interpreted.

SECTION 13.2 ARTICLE XX(B)— HEALTH MEASURES

Article XX(b) covers measures "necessary to protect human, animal or plant life or health". Two WTO agreements are related to Article XX(b). First, the Agreement on Sanitary and Phytosanitary Measures (the SPS Agreement) applies in general to measures taken to protect human, animal and plant life or health from certain specified risks. The SPS Agreement explicitly provides that measures conforming to its provisions "shall be presumed to be in accordance with * * * GATT 1994 * * *, in particular the provisions of Article XX(b)" (SPS art. 2(4)). Second, the Agreement on Technical Barriers to Trade (the TBT Agreement) applies to technical regulations and standards, which often have a safety or health basis, although the overlap with Article XX(b) is more limited than in the case of the SPS Agreement. The TBT Agreement does not specify how it relates to Article XX, which has lead to some interpretative uncertainties. These two agreements are analyzed in Chapter 14.

Our consideration of Article XX(b) starts with the Appellate Body's decision in the *Asbestos* case. Although the Appellate Body ruled that the products at issue were not like (see Section 12.4(A) supra), which meant that the EC had not violated any WTO rules, the Appellate Body examined the panel's conclusion that even though the measure violated Article III, it could be justified under Article XX(b).

EUROPEAN COMMUNITIES—MEASURES AFFECTING ASBESTOS AND ASBESTOS–CONTAINING PRODUCTS

WT/DS135/AB/R.
Appellate Body Report adopted April 5, 2001.

[The underlying facts of this case are set out in Section 12.4(A) supra.]

155.   Under Article XX(b) of the GATT 1994, the Panel examined, first, whether the use of chrysotile-cement products poses a risk to human health and, second, whether the measure at issue is "necessary to protect human . . . life or health". * * *

* * *

157.   On the issue of whether the use of chrysotile-cement products poses a risk to human health sufficient to enable the measure to fall

within the scope of application of the phrase "to protect human . . . life or health" in Article XX(b), the Panel stated that it "considers that the evidence before it *tends to show* that handling chrysotile-cement products constitutes a risk to health rather than the opposite." (emphasis added) On the basis of this assessment of the evidence, the Panel concluded that:

> "the EC has made a prima facie case for the existence of a health risk in connection with the use of chrysotile, in particular as regards lung cancer and mesothelioma in the occupational sectors downstream of production and processing and for the public in general in relation to chrysotile-cement products. This prima facie case has not been rebutted by Canada. Moreover, the Panel considers that the comments by the experts confirm the health risk associated with exposure to chrysotile in its various uses. *The Panel therefore considers that the EC have shown that the policy of prohibiting chrysotile asbestos implemented by the Decree falls within the range of policies designed to protect human life or health. . . .*" (emphasis added)

Thus, the Panel found that the measure falls within the category of measures embraced by Article XX(b) of the GATT 1994.

* * *

162.   * * * [W]e have examined the seven factors on which Canada relies in asserting that the Panel erred in concluding that there exists a human health risk associated with the manipulation of chrysotile-cement products. We see Canada's appeal on this point as, in reality, a challenge to the Panel's assessment of the credibility and weight to be ascribed to the scientific evidence before it. Canada contests the conclusions that the Panel drew both from the evidence of the scientific experts and from scientific reports before it. As we have noted, we will interfere with the Panel's appreciation of the evidence only when we are "satisfied that the panel has *exceeded the bounds of its discretion*, as the trier of facts, in its appreciation of the evidence." (emphasis added) In this case, nothing suggests that the Panel exceeded the bounds of its lawful discretion. To the contrary, all four of the scientific experts consulted by the Panel concurred that chrysotile asbestos fibres, and chrysotile-cement products, constitute a risk to human health, and the Panel's conclusions on this point are faithful to the views expressed by the four scientists. In addition, the Panel noted that the carcinogenic nature of chrysotile asbestos fibres has been acknowledged since 1977 by international bodies, such as the International Agency for Research on Cancer and the World Health Organization. In these circumstances, we find that the Panel remained well within the bounds of its discretion in finding that chrysotile-cement products pose a risk to human life or health.

* * *

164.   On the issue of whether the measure at issue is "necessary" to protect public health within the meaning of Article XX(b), the Panel stated:

> In the light of France's public health objectives as presented by the European Communities, the Panel concludes that the EC has made a prima facie case for the non-existence of a reasonably available alternative to the banning of chrysotile and chrysotile-cement products and recourse to substitute products. Canada has not rebutted the presumption established by the EC. We also consider that the EC's position is confirmed by the comments of the experts consulted in the course of this proceeding.

165.   Canada argues that the Panel erred in applying the "necessity" test under Article XX(b) of the GATT 1994 "by stating that there is a high enough risk associated with the manipulation of chrysotile-cement products that it could in principle justify strict measures such as the Decree." Canada advances four arguments in support of this part of its appeal. First, Canada argues that the Panel erred in finding, on the basis of the scientific evidence before it, that chrysotile-cement products pose a risk to human health. Second, Canada contends that the Panel had an obligation to "quantify" itself the risk associated with chrysotile-cement products and that it could not simply "rely" on the "hypotheses" of the French authorities. Third, Canada asserts that the Panel erred by postulating that the level of protection of health inherent in the Decree is a halt to the spread of asbestos-related health risks. According to Canada, this "premise is false because it does not take into account the risk associated with the use of substitute products without a framework for controlled use." Fourth, and finally, Canada claims that the Panel erred in finding that "controlled use" is not a reasonably available alternative to the Decree.

166.   With respect to Canada's first argument, we note simply that we have already dismissed Canada's contention that the evidence before the Panel did not support the Panel's findings. We are satisfied that the Panel had a more than sufficient basis to conclude that chrysotile-cement products do pose a significant risk to human life or health.

167.   As for Canada's second argument, relating to "quantification" of the risk, we consider that, as with the *SPS Agreement*, there is no requirement under Article XX(b) of the GATT 1994 to *quantify*, as such, the risk to human life or health. A risk may be evaluated either in quantitative or qualitative terms. In this case, contrary to what is suggested by Canada, the Panel assessed the nature and the character of the risk posed by chrysotile-cement products. The Panel found, on the basis of the scientific evidence, that "no minimum threshold of level of exposure or duration of exposure has been identified with regard to the risk of pathologies associated with chrysotile, except for asbestosis." The pathologies which the Panel identified as being associated with chrysotile are of a very serious nature, namely lung cancer and mesothelioma, which is also a form of cancer. Therefore, we do not agree with Canada

that the Panel merely relied on the French authorities' "hypotheses" of the risk.

168. As to Canada's third argument, relating to the level of protection, we note that it is undisputed that WTO Members have the right to determine the level of protection of health that they consider appropriate in a given situation. France has determined, and the Panel accepted, that the chosen level of health protection by France is a "halt" to the spread of *asbestos*-related health risks. By prohibiting all forms of amphibole asbestos, and by severely restricting the use of chrysotile asbestos, the measure at issue is clearly designed and apt to achieve that level of health protection. Our conclusion is not altered by the fact that PCG fibres might pose a risk to health. The scientific evidence before the Panel indicated that the risk posed by the PCG fibres is, in any case, *less* than the risk posed by chrysotile asbestos fibres, although that evidence did *not* indicate that the risk posed by PCG fibres is non-existent. Accordingly, it seems to us perfectly legitimate for a Member to seek to halt the spread of a highly risky product while allowing the use of a less risky product in its place. In short, we do not agree with Canada's third argument.

169. In its fourth argument, Canada asserts that the Panel erred in finding that "controlled use" is not a reasonably available alternative to the Decree. This last argument is based on Canada's assertion that, in *United States—Gasoline* [see Section 13.4], both we and the panel held that an alternative measure "can only be ruled out if it is shown to be impossible to implement." We understand Canada to mean by this that an alternative measure is only excluded as a "reasonably available" alternative if implementation of that measure is "impossible". We certainly agree with Canada that an alternative measure which is impossible to implement is not "reasonably available". But we do not agree with Canada's reading of either the panel report or our report in *United States—Gasoline*. In *United States—Gasoline*, the panel held, in essence, that an alternative measure did not cease to be "reasonably" available simply because the alternative measure involved *administrative difficulties* for a Member. The panel's findings on this point were not appealed, and, thus, we did not address this issue in that case.

170. Looking at this issue now, we believe that, in determining whether a suggested alternative measure is "reasonably available", several factors must be taken into account, besides the difficulty of implementation. In *Thailand—Restrictions on Importation of and Internal Taxes on Cigarettes*, the panel made the following observations on the applicable standard for evaluating whether a measure is "necessary" under Article XX(b):

> The import restrictions imposed by Thailand could be considered to be "necessary" in terms of Article XX(b) only if there were no alternative measure consistent with the General Agreement, or less

inconsistent with it, which Thailand could *reasonably be expected to employ to achieve its health policy objectives.*[1] (emphasis added)

171. In our Report in *Korea—Beef* [see Section 13.3], we addressed the issue of "necessity" under Article XX(d) of the GATT 1994. In that appeal, we found that the panel was correct in following the standard set forth by the panel in *United States—Section 337 of the Tariff Act of 1930*:

> It was clear to the Panel that a contracting party cannot justify a measure inconsistent with another GATT provision as "necessary" in terms of Article XX(d) if an alternative measure which it could reasonably be expected to employ and which is not inconsistent with other GATT provisions is available to it. By the same token, in cases where a measure consistent with other GATT provisions is not reasonably available, a contracting party is bound to use, among the measures reasonably available to it, that which entails the least degree of inconsistency with other GATT provisions.[2]

172. We indicated in *Korea–Beef* that one aspect of the "weighing and balancing process . . . comprehended in the determination of whether a WTO-consistent alternative measure" is reasonably available is the extent to which the alternative measure "contributes to the realization of the end pursued". In addition, we observed, in that case, that "[t]he more vital or important [the] common interests or values" pursued, the easier it would be to accept as "necessary" measures designed to achieve those ends. In this case, the objective pursued by the measure is the preservation of human life and health through the elimination, or reduction, of the well-known, and life-threatening, health risks posed by asbestos fibres. The value pursued is both vital and important in the highest degree. The remaining question, then, is whether there is an alternative measure that would achieve the same end and that is less restrictive of trade than a prohibition.

173. Canada asserts that "controlled use" represents a "reasonably available" measure that would serve the same end. The issue is, thus, whether France could reasonably be expected to employ "controlled use" practices to achieve its chosen level of health protection—a halt in the spread of asbestos-related health risks.

174. In our view, France could not reasonably be expected to employ *any* alternative measure if that measure would involve a continuation of the very risk that the Decree seeks to "halt". Such an alternative measure would, in effect, prevent France from achieving its chosen level of health protection. On the basis of the scientific evidence before it, the Panel found that, in general, the efficacy of "controlled use" remains to be demonstrated. Moreover, even in cases where "controlled use" practices are applied "with greater certainty", the scientific evi-

---

1. [original note 163] Adopted 20 February 1990, BISD 37S/200, para. 75.

2. [original note 165] Adopted 7 November 1989, BISD 36S/345, para. 5.26; we

expressly affirmed this standard in our Report in *Korea–Beef*, para. 166.

dence suggests that the level of exposure can, in some circumstances, still be high enough for there to be a "significant residual risk of developing asbestos-related diseases." The Panel found too that the efficacy of "controlled use" is particularly doubtful for the building industry and for DIY [do-it-yourself] enthusiasts, which are the most important users of cement-based products containing chrysotile asbestos. Given these factual findings by the Panel, we believe that "controlled use" would not allow France to achieve its chosen level of health protection by halting the spread of asbestos-related health risks. "Controlled use" would, thus, not be an alternative measure that would achieve the end sought by France.

175. For these reasons, we uphold the Panel's finding * * * that the European Communities has demonstrated a *prima facie* case that there was no "reasonably available alternative" to the prohibition inherent in the Decree. As a result, we also uphold the Panel's conclusion * * * that the Decree is "necessary to protect human ... life or health" within the meaning of Article XX(b) of the GATT 1994.

Notes and Questions

(1) Part of Canada's appeal of the panel's findings on Article XX(b) was cast as a failure by the panel to make an "objective assessment" of the evidence it had presented, as required by DSU article 11. In responding to that argument, the Appellate Body stated:

> 178. * * * [I]n the context of the SPS Agreement, we have said previously, in *European Communities—Hormones*, that "responsible and representative governments may act in good faith on the basis of what, at a given time, may be a divergent opinion coming from qualified and respected sources." (emphasis added) In justifying a measure under Article XX(b) of the GATT 1994, a Member may also rely, in good faith, on scientific sources which, at that time, may represent a divergent, but qualified and respected, opinion. A Member is not obliged, in setting health policy, automatically to follow what, at a given time, may constitute a majority scientific opinion. Therefore, a panel need not, necessarily, reach a decision under Article XX(b) of the GATT 1994 on the basis of the "preponderant" weight of the evidence.

The *Hormones* case is discussed in Chapter 14 infra. In light of this statement and the Appellate Body's foregoing analysis of Article XX(b), how would you characterize the extent of a WTO member's discretion in imposing health-related product measures? To what extent did the seriousness of the health threat play a role in the *Asbestos* decision? For example, would a decision by a member to "halt" a less significant, non-life threatening health risk be afforded the same deference in a determination of necessity? What factors should be taken into account in deciding this issue?

(2) The *Thai Cigarettes* case referred to by the Appellate Body in paragraph 170 above involved an attempt by Thailand to invoke Article XX(b) to defend discriminatory taxes it imposed on foreign cigarettes in violation of Article III:2. The panel in that case concluded that such measures were not necessary in that Thailand could accomplish its claimed

health goal through nondiscriminatory taxes that were consistent with GATT rules.

(3) On the question of the burden of proof rules in respect of reasonable alternatives, the Appellate Body noted in *US Gambling*, which is excerpted in Chapter 19:

> 310. [I]t is for a responding party to make a *prima facie* case that its measure is "necessary" by putting forward evidence and arguments that enable a panel to assess the challenged measure in the light of the relevant factors to be "weighed and balanced" in a given case. The responding party may, in so doing, point out why alternative measures would not achieve the same objectives as the challenged measure, but it is under no obligation to do so in order to establish, in the first instance, that its measure is "necessary". * * *

> 311. If, however, the complaining party raises a WTO-consistent alternative measure that, in its view, the responding party should have taken, the responding party will be required to demonstrate why its challenged measure nevertheless remains "necessary" in the light of that alternative or, in other words, why the proposed alternative is not, in fact, "reasonably available". If a responding party demonstrates that the alternative is not "reasonably available", in the light of the interests or values being pursued and the party's desired level of protection, it follows that the challenged measure must be "necessary" within the terms of Article XIV(a) of the GATS.

In *Gambling*, the Appellate Body also clarified the scope of reasonable availability by noting that "an alternative measure may be found not to be 'reasonably available', however, where it is merely theoretical in nature, for instance where the responding Member is not capable of taking it, or where the measure imposes an undue burden on that Member, such as prohibitive costs or substantial technical difficulties." WT/DS285/AB/R, para. 308. Does this suggest that poorer countries may have more leeway in invoking Article XX than others?

(4) In Brazil—Measures Affecting Imports of Retreaded Tires, WT/DS332/AB/R, adopted December 17, 2007, Brazil invoked Article XX(b) to justify its ban on imports of retreaded tires. In considering the necessity of the ban, the Appellate Body concluded:

> 210. [I]t may be useful to recapitulate our views on the issue of whether the Import Ban is necessary within the meaning of Article XX(b) of the GATT 1994. This issue illustrates the tensions that may exist between, on the one hand, international trade and, on the other hand, public health and environmental concerns arising from the handling of waste generated by a product at the end of its useful life. In this respect, the fundamental principle is the right that WTO Members have to determine the level of protection that they consider appropriate in a given context. Another key element of the analysis of the necessity of a measure under Article XX(b) is the contribution it brings to the achievement of its objective. A contribution exists when there is a genuine relationship of ends and means between the objective pursued and the

measure at issue. To be characterized as necessary, a measure does not have to be indispensable. However, its contribution to the achievement of the objective must be material, not merely marginal or insignificant, especially if the measure at issue is as trade restrictive as an import ban. Thus, the contribution of the measure has to be weighed against its trade restrictiveness, taking into account the importance of the interests or the values underlying the objective pursued by it. As a key component of a comprehensive policy aiming to reduce the risks arising from the accumulation of waste tires, the Import Ban produces such a material contribution to the realization of its objective. Like the Panel, we consider that this contribution is sufficient to conclude that the Import Ban is necessary, in the absence of reasonably available alternatives.

211. The European Communities proposed a series of alternatives to the Import Ban. Whereas the Import Ban is a preventive non-generation measure, most of the proposed alternatives are waste management and disposal measures that are remedial in character. We consider that measures to encourage domestic retreading or to improve the retreadability of tires, a better enforcement of the import ban on used tires, and a better implementation of existing collection and disposal schemes, are complementary to the Import Ban; indeed, they constitute mutually supportive elements of a comprehensive policy to deal with waste tires. Therefore, these measures cannot be considered real alternatives to the Import Ban. As regards landfilling, stockpiling, co-incineration of waste tires, and material recycling, these remedial methods carry their own risks or, because of the costs involved, are capable of disposing of only a limited number of waste tires. The Panel did not err in concluding that the proposed measures or practices are not reasonably available alternatives.

Does the Appellate Body's summary strike the right balance in evaluating the Import Ban compared to the alternatives? Do you agree with the distinction it drew between preventative and remedial measures? How would you contrast its overall approach in *Tires* (health risk) with its approaches in *Asbestos* (severe health risk) and in the following case—*Korea Beef* (consumer deception risk)?

SECTION 13.3 ARTICLE XX(D)— ENFORCEMENT MEASURES

Article XX(d) provides an exception to GATT rules for measures "necessary to secure compliance with laws or regulations which are not inconsistent with the provisions of this Agreement, including those relating to customs enforcement, the enforcement of monopolies operated under paragraph 4 of Article II and Article XVII, the protection of patents, trade marks and copyrights, and the prevention of deceptive practices." The following case examines the criteria for establishing this exception.

KOREA—MEASURES AFFECTING IMPORTS OF FRESH, CHILLED AND FROZEN BEEF

WT/DS161 & 169/AB/R.
Appellate Body Report adopted January 10, 2001.

[The Panel was established to consider a complaint by Australia and the United States with respect to Korean measures that affected the importation of certain beef products. We have already considered in Section 12.4(B) the finding of the Appellate Body that Korea's separate retail distribution channels for imported and domestic beef products (the so-called "dual retail system") violated GATT Article III. Here we examine Korea's invocation of Article XX(d).]

157. For a measure, otherwise inconsistent with GATT 1994, to be justified provisionally under paragraph (d) of Article XX, two elements must be shown. First, the measure must be one designed to "secure compliance" with laws or regulations that are not themselves inconsistent with some provision of the GATT 1994. Second, the measure must be "necessary" to secure such compliance. A Member who invokes Article XX(d) as a justification has the burden of demonstrating that these two requirements are met.

158. The Panel examined these two aspects one after the other. The Panel found, "despite ... troublesome aspects, ... that the dual retail system was put in place, at least in part, in order to secure compliance with the Korean legislation against deceptive practices to the extent that it serves to prevent acts inconsistent with the *Unfair Competition Act*." It recognized that the system was established at a time when acts of misrepresentation of origin were widespread in the beef sector. It also acknowledged that the dual retail system "does appear to reduce the opportunities and thus the temptations for butchers to misrepresent [less expensive] foreign beef for [more expensive] domestic beef". The parties did not appeal these findings of the Panel.

159. We turn, therefore, to the question of whether the dual retail system is "necessary" to secure compliance with the *Unfair Competition Act*. Once again, we look first to the ordinary meaning of the word "necessary", in its context and in the light of the object and purpose of Article XX, in accordance with Article 31(1) of the *Vienna Convention*.

160. The word "necessary" normally denotes something "that cannot be dispensed with or done without, requisite, essential, needful". We note, however, that a standard law dictionary cautions that:

[t]his word must be considered in the connection in which it is used, as it is a word susceptible of various meanings. It may import absolute physical necessity or inevitability, or it may import that which is only convenient, useful, appropriate, suitable, proper, or conducive to the end sought. It is an adjective expressing degrees,

and may express mere convenience or that which is indispensable or an absolute physical necessity.[1]

161. We believe that, as used in the context of Article XX(d), the reach of the word "necessary" is not limited to that which is "indispensable" or "of absolute necessity" or "inevitable". Measures which are indispensable or of absolute necessity or inevitable to secure compliance certainly fulfil the requirements of Article XX(d). But other measures, too, may fall within the ambit of this exception. As used in Article XX(d), the term "necessary" refers, in our view, to a range of degrees of necessity. At one end of this continuum lies "necessary" understood as "indispensable"; at the other end, is "necessary" taken to mean as "making a contribution to." We consider that a "necessary" measure is, in this continuum, located significantly closer to the pole of "indispensable" than to the opposite pole of simply "making a contribution to".

162. In appraising the "necessity" of a measure in these terms, it is useful to bear in mind the context in which "necessary" is found in Article XX(d). The measure at stake has to be "necessary to ensure compliance with laws and regulations ..., *including* those relating to customs enforcement, the enforcement of [lawful] monopolies ..., the protection of patents, trade marks and copyrights, and the prevention of deceptive practices". (emphasis added) Clearly, Article XX(d) is susceptible of application in respect of a wide variety of "laws and regulations" to be enforced. It seems to us that a treaty interpreter assessing a measure claimed to be necessary to secure compliance of a WTO-consistent law or regulation may, in appropriate cases, take into account the relative importance of the common interests or values that the law or regulation to be enforced is intended to protect. The more vital or important those common interests or values are, the easier it would be to accept as "necessary" a measure designed as an enforcement instrument.

163. There are other aspects of the enforcement measure to be considered in evaluating that measure as "necessary". One is the extent to which the measure contributes to the realization of the end pursued, the securing of compliance with the law or regulation at issue. The greater the contribution, the more easily a measure might be considered to be "necessary". Another aspect is the extent to which the compliance measure produces restrictive effects on international commerce, that is, in respect of a measure inconsistent with Article III:4, restrictive effects on *imported goods*. A measure with a relatively slight impact upon imported products might more easily be considered as "necessary" than a measure with intense or broader restrictive effects.

164. In sum, determination of whether a measure, which is not "indispensable", may nevertheless be "necessary" within the contemplation of Article XX(d), involves in every case a process of weighing and balancing a series of factors which prominently include the contribution made by the compliance measure to the enforcement of the law or regulation at issue, the importance of the common interests or values

---

1. [original note 103] Black's Law Dictionary, (West Publishing, 1995), p. 1029.

protected by that law or regulation, and the accompanying impact of the law or regulation on imports or exports.

165.   The panel in *United States—Section 337* described the applicable standard for evaluating whether a measure is "necessary" under Article XX(d) in the following terms:

> It was clear to the Panel that a contracting party cannot justify a measure inconsistent with another GATT provision as "necessary" in terms of Article XX(d) if an alternative measure which it could reasonably be expected to employ and which is not inconsistent with other GATT provisions is available to it. By the same token, in cases where a measure consistent with other GATT provisions is not reasonably available, a contracting party is bound to use, among the measures reasonably available to it, that which entails the least degree of inconsistency with other GATT provisions.

166.   The standard described by the panel in *United States—Section 337* encapsulates the general considerations we have adverted to above. In our view, the weighing and balancing process we have outlined is comprehended in the determination of whether a WTO-consistent alternative measure which the Member concerned could "reasonably be expected to employ" is available, or whether a less WTO-inconsistent measure is "reasonably available".

167.   The Panel followed the standard identified by the panel in *United States—Section 337*. It started scrutinizing whether the dual retail system is "necessary" under paragraph (d) of Article XX by stating:

> Korea has to convince the Panel that, contrary to what was alleged by Australia and the United States, no alternative measure consistent with the WTO Agreement is reasonably available at present in order to deal with misrepresentation in the retail market as to the origin of beef.

168.   The Panel first considered a range of possible alternative measures, by examining measures taken by Korea with respect to situations involving, or which could involve, deceptive practices similar to those which in 1989–1990 had affected the retail sale of foreign beef. The Panel found that Korea does not require a dual retail system in *related product areas*, but relies instead on traditional enforcement procedures. There is no requirement, for example, for a dual retail system separating domestic Hanwoo beef from domestic dairy cattle beef. Nor is there a requirement for a dual retail system for any other meat or food product, such as pork or seafood. Finally, there is no requirement for a system of separate restaurants, depending on whether they serve domestic or imported beef, even though approximately 45 per cent of the beef imported into Korea is sold in restaurants. Yet, in all of these cases, the Panel found that there were numerous cases of fraudulent misrepresentation. For the Panel, these examples indicated that misrepresentation of origin could, in principle, be dealt with "on the basis of basic

methods ... such as normal policing under the Korean *Unfair Competition Act*.''

169.   Examining enforcement measures applicable to the same illegal behavior relating to like, or at least similar, products does not necessarily imply the introduction of a ''consistency'' requirement into the ''necessary'' concept of Article XX(d). Examining such enforcement measures may provide useful input in the course of determining whether an alternative measure which could ''reasonably be expected'' to be utilized, is available or not.

170.   For Korea, alternative measures must not only be reasonably available, but must also *guarantee* the level of enforcement sought which, in the case of the dual retail system, is the *elimination* of fraud in the beef retail market. With respect to investigations, Korea argues that this tool can only reveal fraud *ex post*, whereas the dual retail system can combat fraudulent practices *ex ante*. Korea contends that *ex post* investigations do not *guarantee* the level of enforcement that Korea has chosen, and therefore should not be considered. With respect to policing, Korea believes that this option is not ''reasonably available'', because Korea lacks the resources to police thousands of shops on a round-the-clock basis.

171.   We share the Panel's conclusion. We are not persuaded that Korea could not achieve its desired level of enforcement of the *Unfair Competition Act* with respect to the origin of beef sold by retailers by using conventional WTO-consistent enforcement measures, if Korea would devote more resources to its enforcement efforts on the beef sector. It might also be added that Korea's argument about the lack of resources to police thousands of shops on a round-the-clock basis is, in the end, not sufficiently persuasive. Violations of laws and regulations like the Korean *Unfair Competition Act* can be expected to be routinely investigated and detected through selective, but well-targeted, controls of potential wrongdoers. The control of records will assist in selecting the shops to which the police could pay particular attention.

172.   There is still another aspect that should be noted relating to both the method actually chosen by Korea—its dual retail system for beef—and alternative traditional enforcement measures. Securing through conventional, WTO-consistent measures a higher level of enforcement of the *Unfair Competition Act* with respect to the retail sale of beef, could well entail higher enforcement costs for the national budget. It is pertinent to observe that, through its dual retail system, Korea has in effect shifted all, or the great bulk, of these potential costs of enforcement (translated into a drastic reduction of competitive access to consumers) to imported goods and retailers of imported goods, instead of evenly distributing such costs between the domestic and imported products. In contrast, the more conventional, WTO-consistent measures of enforcement do not involve such onerous shifting of enforcement costs which ordinarily are borne by the Member's public purse.

Notes and Questions

(1) Do you see any differences between the Appellate Body's view of the "necessity" requirement under Article XX(d) as compared to it view of the requirement under Article XX(b), which we examined in the *EC Asbestos* case in Section 13.2 supra. For example, in light of paragraph 163, should there have been a consideration of the impact of the French regulation on imported goods? Or is that irrelevant in the case of a health measure?

(2) How does the fact that there are "numerous cases" of origin fraud in other contexts suggest that the enforcement mechanisms used in those contexts are adequate (para. 168)? Despite its protest to the contrary (para. 169), does the Appellate Body effectively endorse a consistency test? What problems do you see in relying on such a test?

(3) Is the Appellate Body's rejection of Korea's argument that it wished to guarantee a specific, high level of enforcement consistent with its acceptance of the French desire to halt exposure to asbestos? How does a panel or the Appellate Body judge how "vital or important * * * common interests or values are" (para. 162)? How much should be left to the discretion of the government concerned?

(4) In Mexico—Tax Measures on Soft Drinks and Other Beverages, WT/DS308/AB/R, adopted March 24, 2006, the Appellate Body ruled that Article XX(d) is not available to justify WTO-inconsistent measures that seek to secure compliance by another WTO member with that other member's international obligations. In that case, Mexico had defended its tax measures as being necessary to cause the United States to comply with its NAFTA obligations. The case is excerpted in Chapter 11.

(5) Dominican Republic—Measures Affecting the Importation and Internal Sale of Cigarettes, WT/DS302/AB/R, adopted May 19, 2005, involved a requirement that the tax stamp required on packages of cigarettes sold in the Dominican Republic had to be affixed in the Dominican Republic under the supervision of its tax authorities. The panel's finding that the requirement violated Article III:4 was not appealed, but its rejection of the respondent's Article XX(d) justification was. The panel had (i) recognized that the tax collection function of tax stamps was an important state concern and that the measure did not have "intense" trade effects, but (ii) concluded that the requirement at issue was of limited effectiveness in preventing forgery of the stamps, tax evasion and smuggling, which were the reasons cited by the Dominican Republic as justifying the requirement. In the panel's view, use of security feature in the tax stamps and police controls would play a more important role in achieving those goals. Finally, the panel was of the view that allowing the tax stamps to be affixed at the point of production would be as effective and WTO-consistent as well. The Appellate Body upheld the panel result.

SECTION 13.4   ARTICLE XX(G)— CONSERVATION MEASURES

Article XX(g) contains an exception to general GATT rules for measures "relating to the conservation of exhaustible natural resources if such measures are made effective in conjunction with restrictions on domestic production or consumption." This clause has been interpreted in two landmark Appellate Body decisions, including the following decision, which was the first issued by the Appellate Body.

UNITED STATES—STANDARDS FOR REFORMULATED AND CONVENTIONAL GASOLINE
WT/DS2/AB/R, pp. 13–20.
Appellate Body Report adopted May 20, 1996.

[This case involved a dispute between the United States and Venezuela, later joined by Brazil. The dispute related to the implementation by the US Environmental Protection Agency (EPA) through its so-called Gasoline Rule of provisions of the US Clean Air Act of 1990 (CAA), which were designed to ensure (i) that pollutants in major population centres were reduced and (ii) that pollution from gasoline combustion did not exceed 1990 levels. To achieve the first goal, the Rule provided that only so-called reformulated gasoline could be sold in certain large metropolitan (and some other) areas that had experienced significant summertime ozone pollution in the past. Conventional gasoline could only be sold outside of these areas. To achieve the second goal, the Gasoline Rule relied on the use of 1990 baselines as described below.

The CAA required reformulated gasoline to meet certain specifications. In addition, it imposed "non-degradation" rules, which required that certain quality aspects of reformulated gasoline not fall below 1990 baseline levels for gasoline generally. In order to prevent the dumping of pollutants extracted from reformulated gasoline into conventional gasoline, the CAA required that conventional gasoline remain as clean as 1990 baseline levels. Consequently, in respect of both reformulated and conventional gasoline, the 1990 baselines were an integral element of the Gasoline Rule, and it contained detailed baseline establishment rules. Baselines could be either individual (established on the basis of the records of the individual) or statutory (established by the EPA and intended to reflect average 1990 US gasoline quality). Any domestic refiner which was in operation for at least six months in 1990 was required to establish an individual baseline representing the quality of gasoline produced by that refiner in 1990. In contrast, the Gasoline Rule did not provide for individual baselines for foreign refiners. Although the EPA at one time proposed allowing limited use by importers of such baselines, Congress enacted legislation specifically denying the funding necessary to implement the proposal.

The Panel Report concluded that the above described rules violated Article III:4, essentially because imported gasoline was required to meet the statutory baseline (with effectively no option to benefit from an individual baseline) while domestic gasoline needed only to meet the applicable individual baseline. In fact, the vast majority of domestic gasoline did not meet the statutory baseline. It should be noted that after January 1, 1998, all reformulated gasoline had to meet the same specified standard, so the Gasoline Rule in respect of individual baselines for reformulated gasoline was essentially a transitional provision for the benefit of US refiners.

The US did not appeal the Panel's finding that Article III:4 had been violated, nor did it appeal the Panel's finding that the Gasoline Rule could not be justified as a health measure under Article XX(b). It did, however, appeal the Panel's rejection of its Article XX(g) defense. While the Panel found that clean air was an exhaustible natural resource for purposes of Article XX(g), it concluded that the less favourable baseline establishment methods at issue were not "primarily aimed" at the conservation of exhaustible natural resources and thus fell outside the justifying scope of Article XX(g).]

The Panel, addressing the task of interpreting the words "relating to", quoted with approval the following passage from the panel report in the 1987 *Herring and Salmon* case:[1]

> as the preamble of Article XX indicates, the purpose of including Article XX:(g) in the General Agreement was not to widen the scope for measures serving trade policy purposes but merely to ensure that the commitments under the General Agreement do not hinder the pursuit of policies aimed at the conservation of exhaustive natural resources. The Panel concluded for these reasons that, while a trade measure did not have to be necessary or essential to the conservation of an exhaustible natural resource, it had to be *primarily aimed* at the conservation of an exhaustible natural resource to be considered as "relating to" conservation within the meaning of Article XX:(g). (emphasis added by the Panel)

The Panel Report then went on to apply the 1987 *Herring and Salmon* reasoning and conclusion to the baseline establishment rules of the Gasoline Rule in the following manner:

> The Panel then considered whether the precise aspects of the Gasoline Rule that it had found to violate Article III—the less favourable baseline establishment methods that adversely affected the conditions of competition for imported gasoline—were primarily aimed at the conservation of natural resources. The Panel saw no direct connection between less favourable treatment of imported gasoline that was chemically identical to domestic gasoline, and the US objective of improving air quality in the United States. Indeed, in the view of the Panel, being consistent with the obligation to provide no less favourable treatment would not prevent the attainment of the desired level of conservation of natural resources under the Gasoline Rule. Accordingly, it could not be said that the baseline establishment methods that afforded less favourable treatment to imported gasoline were primarily aimed at the conservation of natural resources. In the Panel's view, the above-noted lack of connection was underscored by the fact that affording treatment of

---

1. [original note 30] *Canada—Measures Affecting Exports of Unprocessed Herring and Salmon*, BISD 35S/98, para. 4.6; adopted on 22 March 1988.

imported gasoline consistent with its Article III:4 obligations would not in any way hinder the United States in its pursuit of its conservation policies under the Gasoline Rule. Indeed, the United States remained free to regulate in order to obtain whatever air quality it wished. The Panel therefore concluded that the less favourable baseline establishment methods at issue in this case were not primarily aimed at the conservation of natural resources.

It is not easy to follow the reasoning in the above paragraph of the Panel Report. In our view, there is a certain amount of opaqueness in that reasoning. The Panel starts with positing that there was "no direct connection" between the baseline establishment rules which it characterized as "less favourable treatment" of imported gasoline that was chemically identical to the domestic gasoline and "the US objective of improving air quality in the United States." Shortly thereafter, the Panel went on to conclude that "*accordingly, it could not be said that* the baseline establishment rules that afforded less favourable treatment to imported gasoline *were primarily aimed at* the conservation of natural resources" (emphasis added). The Panel did not try to clarify whether the phrase "direct connection" was being used as a synonym for "primarily aimed at" or whether a new and additional element (on top of "primarily aimed at") was being demanded.

One problem with the reasoning in that paragraph is that the Panel asked itself whether the "less favourable treatment" of imported gasoline was "primarily aimed at" the conservation of natural resources, rather than whether the "measure", i.e. the baseline establishment rules, were "primarily aimed at" conservation of clean air. In our view, the Panel here was in error in referring to its legal conclusion on Article III:4 instead of the measure in issue. The result of this analysis is to turn Article XX on its head. Obviously, there had to be a finding that the measure provided "less favourable treatment" under Article III:4 before the Panel examined the "General Exceptions" contained in Article XX. That, however, is a conclusion of law. The chapeau of Article XX makes it clear that it is the "measures" which are to be examined under Article XX(g), and not the legal finding of "less favourable treatment."

* * *

A principal difficulty, in the view of the Appellate Body, with the Panel Report's application of Article XX(g) to the baseline establishment rules is that the Panel there overlooked a fundamental rule of treaty interpretation [i.e., Article 31 of the Vienna Convention on the Law of Treaties].

* * * That general rule of interpretation has attained the status of a rule of customary or general international law. As such, it forms part of the "customary rules of interpretation of public international law" which the Appellate Body has been directed, by Article 3(2) of the DSU, to apply in seeking to clarify the provisions of the *General Agreement* and the other "covered agreements" of the Marrakesh Agreement Establishing the World Trade Organization (the "WTO Agreement"). That direction reflects a measure of recognition that the *General Agreement* is not to be read in clinical isolation from public international law.

Applying the basic principle of interpretation that the words of a treaty, like the *General Agreement*, are to be given their ordinary meaning, in their context and in the light of the treaty's object and purpose, the Appellate Body observes that the Panel Report failed to take adequate account of the words actually used by Article XX in its several paragraphs. In enumerating the various categories of governmental acts, laws or regulations which WTO Members may carry out or promulgate in pursuit of differing legitimate state policies or interests outside the realm of trade liberalization, Article XX uses different terms in respect of different categories:

"necessary"—in paragraphs (a), (b) and (d);

"relating to"—in paragraphs (c), (e) and (g);

"for the protection of"—in paragraph (f);

"in pursuance of"—in paragraph (h);

"involving"—in paragraph (i); and

"essential"—in paragraph (j).

It does not seem reasonable to suppose that the WTO Members intended to require, in respect of each and every category, the same kind or degree of connection or relationship between the measure under appraisal and the state interest or policy sought to be promoted or realized.

At the same time, Article XX(g) and its phrase, "relating to the conservation of exhaustible natural resources," need to be read in context and in such a manner as to give effect to the purposes and objects of the *General Agreement*. The context of Article XX(g) includes the provisions of the rest of the *General Agreement*, including in particular Articles I, III and XI; conversely, the context of Articles I and III and XI includes Article XX. Accordingly, the phrase "relating to the conservation of exhaustible natural resources" may not be read so expansively as seriously to subvert the purpose and object of Article III:4. Nor may Article III:4 be given so broad a reach as effectively to emasculate Article XX(g) and the policies and interests it embodies. The relationship between the affirmative commitments set out in, e.g., Articles I, III and XI, and the policies and interests embodied in the "General Exceptions" listed in Article XX, can be given meaning within the framework of the *General Agreement* and its object and purpose by a treaty interpreter only on a case-to-case basis, by careful scrutiny of the factual and legal context in a given dispute, without disregarding the words actually used by the WTO Members themselves to express their intent and purpose.

The 1987 *Herring and Salmon* report, and the Panel Report itself, gave some recognition to the foregoing considerations of principle. As earlier noted, the Panel Report quoted the following excerpt from the *Herring and Salmon* report:

as the preamble of Article XX indicates, the purpose of including Article XX(g) in the General Agreement was not to widen the scope for measures serving trade policy purposes but merely *to ensure that the commitments under the General Agreement do not hinder the pursuit of policies* aimed at the conservation of exhaustible natural resources. (emphasis added)

All the participants and the third participants in this appeal accept the propriety and applicability of the view of the *Herring and Salmon* report and the Panel Report that a measure must be "primarily aimed at" the conservation of exhaustible natural resources in order to fall within the scope of Article XX(g). Accordingly, we see no need to examine this point further, save, perhaps, to note that the phrase "primarily aimed at" is not itself treaty language and was not designed as a simple litmus test for inclusion or exclusion from Article XX(g).

Against this background, we turn to the specific question of whether the baseline establishment rules are appropriately regarded as "primarily aimed at" the conservation of natural resources for the purposes of Article XX(g). We consider that this question must be answered in the affirmative.

The baseline establishment rules, taken as a whole (that is, the provisions relating to establishment of baselines for domestic refiners, along with the provisions relating to baselines for blenders and importers of gasoline), need to be related to the "non-degradation" requirements set out elsewhere in the Gasoline Rule. Those provisions can scarcely be understood if scrutinized strictly by themselves, totally divorced from other sections of the Gasoline Rule which certainly constitute part of the context of these provisions. The baseline establishment rules whether individual or statutory, were designed to permit scrutiny and monitoring of the level of compliance of refiners, importers and blenders with the "non-degradation" requirements. Without baselines of some kind, such scrutiny would not be possible and the Gasoline Rule's objective of stabilizing and preventing further deterioration of the level of air pollution prevailing in 1990, would be substantially frustrated. The relationship between the baseline establishment rules and the "non-degradation" requirements of the Gasoline Rule is not negated by the inconsistency, found by the Panel, of the baseline establishment rules with the terms of Article III:4. We consider that, given that substantial relationship, the baseline establishment rules cannot be regarded as merely incidentally or inadvertently aimed at the conservation of clean air in the United States for the purposes of Article XX(g).

[The Appellate Body then considered the third clause of Article XX(g), i.e., whether the baseline establishment rules were "made effective in conjunction with restrictions on domestic production or consumption", an issue that the Panel had not considered. In that connection, the Appellate Body noted that it viewed that clause] as a requirement that the measures concerned impose restrictions, not just in respect of imported gasoline but also with respect to domestic gasoline. The clause is a requirement of *even-handedness* in the imposition of restrictions, in the name of conservation, upon the production or consumption of exhaustible natural resources.

There is, of course, no textual basis for requiring identical treatment of domestic and imported products. Indeed, where there is identity of treatment—constituting real, not merely formal, equality of treatment—it is difficult to see how inconsistency with Article III:4 would have arisen in the first place. On the other hand, if no restrictions on domestically-produced like products are imposed at all, and all limitations are placed upon imported products *alone*, the measure cannot be accepted as primarily or even substantially designed for implementing conservationist goals. The measure would simply be naked discrimination for protecting locally-produced goods.

In the present appeal, the baseline establishment rules affect both domestic gasoline and imported gasoline, providing for—generally speaking—individual baselines for domestic refiners and blenders and statutory baselines for importers. Thus, restrictions on the consumption or depletion of clean air by regulating the domestic production of "dirty" gasoline are established jointly with corresponding restrictions with respect to imported gasoline. That imported gasoline has been determined to have been accorded "less favourable treatment" than the domestic gasoline in terms of Article III:4, is not material for purposes of analysis under Article XX(g). * * *

We do not believe, finally, that the clause * * * was intended to establish an empirical "effects test" for the availability of the Article XX(g) exception. * * *

[The Appellate Body then considered whether the requirements of the chapeau to Article XX had been met and concluded that they had not been. Its reasoning on that issue is considered in the notes following the principal case in Section 13.5, where we examine the meaning of the chapeau to Article XX.]

Notes and Questions

(1) Although the United States ultimately lost its appeal, it expressed great satisfaction with the Appellate Body's analysis of Article XX(g). Past GATT panels had focused, as had the *Gasoline* panel, on whether the GATT-inconsistent aspect of a measure was "primarily aimed at" conservation. The Appellate Body's decision that it was necessary to look at the broader measure—the baseline establishment rules generally—and examine whether they were aimed at conservation significantly expanded the scope of Article XX(g). Do you agree with the Appellate Body's approach?

(2) The Appellate Body had the occasion to consider again the scope of Article XX(g) in the *Shrimp* case, which we examine in detail in the next section of this chapter dealing with the chapeau to Article XX. In respect of Article XX(g), one of the issues in the *Shrimp* case was a claim that the phrase "exhaustible natural resources" referred only to minerals and not to living things. Not surprisingly, the Appellate Body rejected that argument;

there was ample GATT and WTO authority finding other fish and clean air to be exhaustible natural resources. Significantly, however, the Appellate Body scarcely mentioned the prior cases, but rather undertook a wide-ranging analysis of the words at issue in light of contemporary understanding:

> 128. Textually, Article XX(g) is *not* limited to the conservation of "mineral" or "non-living" natural resources. * * * "[E]xhaustible" natural resources and "renewable" natural resources are [not] mutually exclusive. One lesson that modern biological sciences teach us is that living species, though in principle, capable of reproduction and, in that sense, "renewable", are in certain circumstances indeed susceptible of depletion, exhaustion and extinction, frequently because of human activities. Living resources are just as "finite" as petroleum, iron ore and other non-living resources.

> 129. The words of Article XX(g), "exhaustible natural resources", were actually crafted more than 50 years ago. They must be read by a treaty interpreter in the light of contemporary concerns of the community of nations about the protection and conservation of the environment. While Article XX was not modified in the Uruguay Round, the preamble attached to the *WTO Agreement* shows that the signatories to that Agreement were, in 1994, fully aware of the importance and legitimacy of environmental protection as a goal of national and international policy. The preamble of the *WTO Agreement*—which informs not only the GATT 1994, but also the other covered agreements—explicitly acknowledges "the objective of *sustainable development*": * * *

> 130. From the perspective embodied in the preamble of the *WTO Agreement*, we note that the generic term "natural resources" in Article XX(g) is not "static" in its content or reference but is rather "by definition, evolutionary".[2] It is, therefore, pertinent to note that modern international conventions and declarations make frequent references to natural resources as embracing both living and non-living resources. [The Appellate Body then referred to, inter alia, the 1982 United Nations Convention on the Law of the Sea; the Convention on Biological Diversity; Agenda 21; the Resolution on Assistance to Developing Countries, adopted in conjunction with the Convention on the Conservation of Migratory Species of Wild Animals; and the Convention on International Trade in Endangered Species of Wild Fauna and Flora ("CITES")].

United States—Restrictions on Importation of Certain Shrimp and Shrimp Products, WT/DS58/AB/R, Appellate Body Report adopted by the DSB on November 6, 1998. Exactly how does the Preamble to the WTO Agreement

---

2. [original note 109] See *Namibia (Legal Consequences) Advisory Opinion* (1971) I.C.J. Rep., p. 31. The International Court of Justice stated that where concepts embodied in a treaty are "by definition, evolutionary", their "interpretation cannot remain unaffected by the subsequent development of law.... Moreover, an international instrument has to be interpreted and applied within the framework of the entire legal system prevailing at the time of the interpretation." See also *Aegean Sea Continental Shelf Case*, (1978) I.C.J. Rep., p. 3; Jennings and Watts (eds.), *Oppenheim's International Law*, 9th ed., Vol. I (Longman's, 1992), p. 1282 and E. Jimenez de Arechaga, "International Law in the Past Third of a Century", (1978–I) 159 *Recueil des Cours* 1, p. 49.

make the term "natural resources" "by definition, evolutionary"? Of what importance is the establishment of a new organization under a new agreement as of January 1, 1995? Does the Appellate Body's reasoning on the evolutionary nature of generic terms apply to all parts of the WTO Agreement? If not, to which parts does it apply? Does this interpretation suggest that there is a "constitutional", as opposed to a mere contractual, aspect to the WTO Agreement? Is it consistent with the notion of looking to the "ordinary meaning" of the terms of a treaty?

(3) The Appellate Body also considered in *Shrimp*, whether the US statute was "related to" conservation. It expressed itself as follows:

> 141.   In its general design and structure, therefore, Section 609 is not a simple, blanket prohibition of the importation of shrimp imposed without regard to the consequences (or lack thereof) of the mode of harvesting employed upon the incidental capture and mortality of sea turtles. Focusing on the design of the measure here at stake, it appears to us that Section 609, *cum* implementing guidelines, is not disproportionately wide in its scope and reach in relation to the policy objective of protection and conservation of sea turtle species. The means are, in principle, reasonably related to the ends. The means and ends relationship between Section 609 and the legitimate policy of conserving an exhaustible, and, in fact, endangered species, is observably a close and real one, a relationship that is every bit as substantial as that which we found in *United States—Gasoline* between the EPA baseline establishment rules and the conservation of clean air in the United States.

> 142.   In our view, therefore, Section 609 is a measure "relating to" the conservation of an exhaustible natural resource within the meaning of Article XX(g) of the GATT 1994.

Does the Appellate Body simply apply its approach in *Gasoline* here? Or do the phrases "not disproportionately wide in its scope" and "means * * * reasonably related to the ends" suggest additional tests for determining whether a measure is one "relating" to conservation? Should there be such tests? Note that the phrase "primarily aimed at" is not used.

(4) There were inconsistent, but unadopted panel reports that addressed the question of whether Article XX(g) could be invoked to justify measures effectively applicable beyond the territory of a Member. Compare United States—Restrictions on Imports of Tuna (Mexico), DS21/R (September 3, 1991), BISD 39S/155 (not adopted) with United States—Restrictions on Imports of Tuna (EC), DS29/R (May 20, 1994) (not adopted). In the *Shrimp* case, the Appellate Body wrote the following on that issue:

> 133.   The sea turtle species here at stake, i.e., covered by Section 609, are all known to occur in waters over which the United States exercises jurisdiction. Of course, it is not claimed that *all* populations of these species migrate to, or traverse, at one time or another, waters subject to United States jurisdiction. Neither the appellant nor any of the appellees claims any rights of exclusive ownership over the sea turtles, at least not while they are swimming freely in their natural habitat—the oceans. We do not pass upon the question of whether there is an implied jurisdictional limitation in Article XX(g), and if so, the nature or extent of that limitation. We note only that in the specific circumstances of the

case before us, there is a sufficient nexus between the migratory and endangered marine populations involved and the United States for purposes of Article XX(g).

Should there be "an implied jurisdictional limitation" in Article XX(g)?

SECTION 13.5 THE CHAPEAU TO ARTICLE XX

The introductory clause to Article XX, which is commonly referred to as the chapeau, conditions the availability of the Article XX exception for measures listed in the specific clauses as follows:

> Subject to the requirement that such measures are not applied in a manner which would constitute a means of arbitrary or unjustifiable discrimination between countries where the same conditions prevail, or a disguised restriction on international trade, nothing in this Agreement shall be construed to prevent the adoption or enforcement by any Member of measures: [(a)-(j)].

The most detailed consideration of the meaning of the chapeau is found in the following case:

UNITED STATES—IMPORT PROHIBITION OF CERTAIN SHRIMP AND SHRIMP PRODUCTS

WT/DS58/AB/R.
Appellate Body Report adopted November 6, 1998.

[This case involved a prohibition imposed by the United States on the importation of certain shrimp and shrimp products. The roots of the case go back to 1987, when the US issued regulations, pursuant to the 1973 Endangered Species Act, that in their final form required all US shrimp trawlers to use turtle excluder devices ("TEDs") in areas where there is a likelihood that shrimp trawling will interact with sea turtles, subject to certain limited exceptions. The regulations became fully effective in 1990.

In 1989, Section 609 of Public Law 101–162 was enacted (16 USC sec. 1537). Among other things, Section 609(b) imposed, not later than 1 May 1991, an import ban on shrimp harvested with commercial fishing technology which may adversely affect sea turtles. It also provided that the import ban would not apply to harvesting nations that are certified as (i) having a fishing environment (e.g., lack of sea turtles or use of artisanal harvesting methods) which does not pose a threat of the incidental taking of sea turtles in the course of shrimp harvesting or (ii) providing documentary evidence of a regulatory program governing the incidental taking of sea turtles in the course of shrimp trawling comparable to the US program and having an average rate of incidental taking of sea turtles comparable to that of US vessels.

The State Department's 1991 Guidelines limited the geographical scope of the import ban imposed by Section 609 to countries in the wider Caribbean/western Atlantic region, and granted these countries a three-year phase-in period. In December 1995, the US Court of International Trade (CIT) found that this geographical limitation violated Section 609 and directed the State Department to extend the ban worldwide not later than May 1, 1996. On April 19, 1996, the State Department issued its 1996 Guidelines, extending Section 609 to all foreign countries effective May 1, 1996.

The 1996 Guidelines provided that all shrimp imported into the US must be accompanied by a form attesting that the shrimp was harvested either in the waters of a certified nation or under conditions that do not adversely affect sea turtles. In late 1996, the CIT ruled that the 1996 Guidelines were in violation of Section 609 in allowing the import of shrimp from non-certified countries (except where taken manually by methods not harming sea turtles). In 1998, the US Court of Appeals vacated the CIT ruling. In practice, however, import of TED-caught shrimp from non-certified countries was not possible while the dispute was pending.

The panel report concluded that the measures at issue violated Article XI and that they were not covered by Article XX. The US had not contested that the measures violated GATT rules but rather claimed they were permitted by Article XX(g), and it appealed the panel's rejection of that defense. The Appellate Body concluded that the measure fell within the scope of Article XX(g), as explained in Notes 2 and 3 to the preceding section.

Then, before turning to a detailed analysis of whether the measures satisfied the terms of the chapeau, the Appellate Body underlined that the Uruguay Round negotiators had effectively qualified the original objectives of GATT 1947 by adding a clause to the preamble to the WTO Agreement on the objective of sustainable development and the protection and preservation of the environment. It went on to note "that this language demonstrates a recognition by WTO negotiators that optimal use of the world's resources should be made in accordance with the objective of sustainable development. As this preambular language reflects the intentions of negotiators of the *WTO Agreement*, we believe it must add color, texture and shading to our interpretation of the agreements annexed to the *WTO Agreement*, in this case, the GATT 1994" (para. 153). It then recalled other more recent developments that in its view helped to elucidate the objectives of WTO members with respect to the relationship between trade and the environment, highlighting in particular the establishment of a permanent Committee on Trade and Environment (the "CTE").]

150. We commence the second tier of our analysis with an examination of the ordinary meaning of the words of the chapeau. The precise language of the chapeau requires that a measure not be applied in a manner which would constitute a means of "arbitrary or unjustifiable discrimination between countries where the same conditions prevail" or a "disguised restriction on international trade." * * * In order for a measure to be applied in a manner which would constitute "arbitrary or

unjustifiable discrimination between countries where the same conditions prevail'', three elements must exist. First, the application of the measure must result in *discrimination*. As we stated in *United States— Gasoline*, the nature and quality of this discrimination is different from the discrimination in the treatment of products which was already found to be inconsistent with one of the substantive obligations of the GATT 1994, such as Articles I, III or XI. Second, the discrimination must be *arbitrary* or *unjustifiable* in character. We will examine this element of *arbitrariness* or *unjustifiability* in detail below. Third, this discrimination must occur *between countries where the same conditions prevail*. In *United States—Gasoline*, we accepted the assumption of the participants in that appeal that such discrimination could occur not only between different exporting Members, but also between exporting Members and the importing Member concerned. Thus, the standards embodied in the language of the chapeau are not only different from the requirements of Article XX(g); they are also different from the standard used in determining that Section 609 is violative of the substantive rules of Article XI:1 of the GATT 1994.

* * *

156.   Turning then to the chapeau of Article XX, we consider that it embodies the recognition on the part of WTO Members of the need to maintain a balance of rights and obligations between the right of a Member to invoke one or another of the exceptions of Article XX, specified in paragraphs (a) to (j), on the one hand, and the substantive rights of the other Members under the GATT 1994, on the other hand. Exercise by one Member of its right to invoke an exception, such as Article XX(g), if abused or misused, will, to that extent, erode or render naught the substantive treaty rights in, for example, Article XI:1, of other Members. Similarly, because the GATT 1994 itself makes available the exceptions of Article XX, in recognition of the legitimate nature of the policies and interests there embodied, the right to invoke one of those exceptions is not to be rendered illusory. The same concept may be expressed from a slightly different angle of vision, thus, a balance must be struck between the *right* of a Member to invoke an exception under Article XX and the *duty* of that same Member to respect the treaty rights of the other Members. To permit one Member to abuse or misuse its right to invoke an exception would be effectively to allow that Member to degrade its own treaty obligations as well as to devalue the treaty rights of other Members. If the abuse or misuse is sufficiently grave or extensive, the Member, in effect, reduces its treaty obligation to a merely facultative one and dissolves its juridical character, and, in so doing, negates altogether the treaty rights of other Members. The chapeau was installed at the head of the list of "General Exceptions" in Article XX to prevent such far-reaching consequences.

157.   In our view, the language of the chapeau makes clear that each of the exceptions in paragraphs (a) to (j) of Article XX is a *limited and conditional* exception from the substantive obligations contained in

the other provisions of the GATT 1994, that is to say, the ultimate availability of the exception is subject to the compliance by the invoking Member with the requirements of the chapeau. This interpretation of the chapeau is confirmed by its negotiating history * * * [which] confirms that the paragraphs of Article XX set forth *limited and conditional* exceptions from the obligations of the substantive provisions of the GATT. Any measure, to qualify finally for exception, must also satisfy the requirements of the chapeau. This is a fundamental part of the balance of rights and obligations struck by the original framers of the GATT 1947.

158. The chapeau of Article XX is, in fact, but one expression of the principle of good faith. This principle, at once a general principle of law and a general principle of international law, controls the exercise of rights by states. One application of this general principle, the application widely known as the doctrine of *abus de droit*, prohibits the abusive exercise of a state's rights and enjoins that whenever the assertion of a right "impinges on the field covered by [a] treaty obligation, it must be exercised bona fide, that is to say, reasonably." An abusive exercise by a Member of its own treaty right thus results in a breach of the treaty rights of the other Members and, as well, a violation of the treaty obligation of the Member so acting. Having said this, our task here is to interpret the language of the chapeau, seeking additional interpretative guidance, as appropriate, from the general principles of international law.

159. The task of interpreting and applying the chapeau is, hence, essentially the delicate one of locating and marking out a line of equilibrium between the right of a Member to invoke an exception under Article XX and the rights of the other Members under varying substantive provisions (e.g., Article XI) of the GATT 1994, so that neither of the competing rights will cancel out the other and thereby distort and nullify or impair the balance of rights and obligations constructed by the Members themselves in that Agreement. The location of the line of equilibrium, as expressed in the chapeau, is not fixed and unchanging; the line moves as the kind and the shape of the measures at stake vary and as the facts making up specific cases differ.

160. With these general considerations in mind, we address now the issue of whether the *application* of the United States measure, although the measure itself falls within the terms of Article XX(g), nevertheless constitutes "a means of arbitrary or unjustifiable discrimination between countries where the same conditions prevail" or "a disguised restriction on international trade". We address, in other words, whether the application of this measure constitutes an abuse or misuse of the provisional justification made available by Article XX(g). We note, preliminarily, that the application of a measure may be characterized as amounting to an abuse or misuse of an exception of Article XX not only when the detailed operating provisions of the measure prescribe the arbitrary or unjustifiable activity, but also where a measure, otherwise fair and just on its face, is actually applied in an arbitrary or unjustifia-

ble manner. The standards of the chapeau, in our view, project both substantive and procedural requirements.

161. We scrutinize first whether Section 609 has been applied in a manner constituting "unjustifiable discrimination between countries where the same conditions prevail". Perhaps the most conspicuous flaw in this measure's application relates to its intended and actual coercive effect on the specific policy decisions made by foreign governments, Members of the WTO. Section 609, in its application, is, in effect, an economic embargo which requires *all other exporting Members*, if they wish to exercise their GATT rights, to adopt *essentially the same* policy (together with an approved enforcement program) as that applied to, and enforced on, United States domestic shrimp trawlers. As enacted by the Congress of the United States, the statutory provisions of Section 609(b)(2)(A) and (B) do not, in themselves, require that other WTO Members adopt *essentially the same* policies and enforcement practices as the United States. Viewed alone, the statute appears to permit a degree of discretion or flexibility in how the standards for determining comparability might be applied, in practice, to other countries. However, any flexibility that may have been intended by Congress when it enacted the statutory provision has been effectively eliminated in the implementation of that policy through the 1996 Guidelines promulgated by the Department of State and through the practice of the administrators in making certification determinations.

162. According to the 1996 Guidelines, certification "shall be made" under Section 609(b)(2)(A) and (B) if an exporting country's program includes a requirement that all commercial shrimp trawl vessels operating in waters in which there is a likelihood of intercepting sea turtles use, at all times, TEDs comparable in effectiveness to those used in the United States. Under these Guidelines, any exceptions to the requirement of the use of TEDs must be comparable to those of the United States program. Furthermore, the harvesting country must have in place a "credible enforcement effort". The language in the 1996 Guidelines is mandatory: certification "shall be made" if these conditions are fulfilled. However, we understand that these rules are also applied in an *exclusive* manner. That is, the 1996 Guidelines specify the *only* way that a harvesting country's regulatory program can be deemed "comparable" to the United States' program, and, therefore, they define the *only* way that a harvesting nation can be certified under Section 609(b)(2)(A) and (B). Although the 1996 Guidelines state that, in making a comparability determination, the Department of State "shall also take into account other measures the harvesting nation undertakes to protect sea turtles", in practice, the competent government officials only look to see whether there is a regulatory program requiring the use of TEDs or one that comes within one of the extremely limited exceptions available to United States shrimp trawl vessels.

163. The actual *application* of the measure, through the implementation of the 1996 Guidelines and the regulatory practice of administrators, *requires* other WTO Members to adopt a regulatory program that is

not merely *comparable*, but rather *essentially the same*, as that applied to the United States shrimp trawl vessels. Thus, the effect of the application of Section 609 is to establish a rigid and unbending standard by which United States officials determine whether or not countries will be certified, thus granting or refusing other countries the right to export shrimp to the United States. Other specific policies and measures that an exporting country may have adopted for the protection and conservation of sea turtles are not taken into account, in practice, by the administrators making the comparability determination.

164. We understand that the United States also applies a uniform standard throughout its territory, regardless of the particular conditions existing in certain parts of the country. * * * It may be quite acceptable for a government, in adopting and implementing a domestic policy, to adopt a single standard applicable to all its citizens throughout that country. However, it is not acceptable, in international trade relations, for one WTO Member to use an economic embargo to require other Members to adopt essentially the same comprehensive regulatory program, to achieve a certain policy goal, as that in force within that Member's territory, *without* taking into consideration different conditions which may occur in the territories of those other Members.

165. Furthermore, when this dispute was before the Panel and before us, the United States did not permit imports of shrimp harvested by commercial shrimp trawl vessels using TEDs comparable in effectiveness to those required in the United States if those shrimp originated in waters of countries not certified under Section 609. In other words, *shrimp caught using methods identical to those employed in the United States* have been excluded from the United States market solely because they have been caught in waters of *countries that have not been certified by the United States*. The resulting situation is difficult to reconcile with the declared policy objective of protecting and conserving sea turtles. This suggests to us that this measure, in its application, is more concerned with effectively influencing WTO Members to adopt essentially the same comprehensive regulatory regime as that applied by the United States to its domestic shrimp trawlers, even though many of those Members may be differently situated. We believe that discrimination results not only when countries in which the same conditions prevail are differently treated, but also when the application of the measure at issue does not allow for any inquiry into the appropriateness of the regulatory program for the conditions prevailing in those exporting countries.

166. Another aspect of the application of Section 609 that bears heavily in any appraisal of justifiable or unjustifiable discrimination is the failure of the United States to engage the appellees, as well as other Members exporting shrimp to the United States, in serious, across-the-board negotiations with the objective of concluding bilateral or multilateral agreements for the protection and conservation of sea turtles, before enforcing the import prohibition against the shrimp exports of those other Members. The relevant factual finding of the Panel reads:

... However, *we have no evidence that the United States actually undertook negotiations on an agreement on sea turtle conservation techniques which would have included the complainants before the imposition of the import ban as a result of the CIT judgement.* From the replies of the parties to our question on this subject, in particular that of the United States, we understand that the United States did not propose the negotiation of an agreement to any of the complainants until after the conclusion of negotiations on the Inter–American Convention for the Protection and Conservation of Sea Turtles, in September 1996, i.e. well after the deadline for the imposition of the import ban of 1 May 1996. Even then, it seems that the efforts made merely consisted of an exchange of documents. We therefore conclude that, in spite of the possibility offered by its legislation, the United States did not enter into negotiations before it imposed the import ban. As we consider that the measures sought by the United States were of the type that would normally require international cooperation, we do not find it necessary to examine whether parties entered into negotiations in good faith and whether the United States, absent any result, would have been entitled to adopt unilateral measures. (emphasis added)

167. *A propos* this failure to have prior consistent recourse to diplomacy as an instrument of environmental protection policy, which produces discriminatory impacts on countries exporting shrimp to the United States with which no international agreements are reached or even seriously attempted, a number of points must be made. First, the Congress of the United States expressly recognized the importance of securing international agreements for the protection and conservation of the sea turtle species in enacting this law. Section 609(a) *directs* the Secretary of State to:

(1) *initiate negotiations as soon as possible for the development of bilateral or multilateral agreements with other nations* for the protection and conservation of such species of sea turtles;

(2) *initiate negotiations as soon as possible* with all foreign governments which are engaged in, or which have persons or companies engaged in, commercial fishing operations which, as determined by the Secretary of Commerce, may affect adversely such species of sea turtles, *for the purpose of entering into bilateral and multilateral treaties with such countries to protect such species of sea turtles*;
* * *

Apart from the negotiation of the Inter–American Convention for the Protection and Conservation of Sea Turtles (the "Inter–American Convention") which concluded in 1996, the record before the Panel does not indicate any serious, substantial efforts to carry out these express directions of Congress.

168. Second, the protection and conservation of highly migratory species of sea turtles, that is, the very policy objective of the measure, demands concerted and cooperative efforts on the part of the many

countries whose waters are traversed in the course of recurrent sea turtle migrations. The need for, and the appropriateness of, such efforts have been recognized in the WTO itself as well as in a significant number of other international instruments and declarations. As stated earlier, the Decision on Trade and Environment, which provided for the establishment of the CTE and set out its terms of reference, refers to both the Rio Declaration on Environment and Development and Agenda 21. Of particular relevance is Principle 12 of the Rio Declaration on Environment and Development, which states, in part:

> Unilateral actions to deal with environmental challenges outside the jurisdiction of the importing country should be avoided. *Environmental measures addressing transboundary or global environmental problems should, as far as possible, be based on international consensus.* (emphasis added)

[The Appellate Body then quoted analogous language calling for multilateral cooperation from Agenda 21 (para, 2.22(i)); the Convention on Biological Diversity (art. 5); and the Convention on the Conservation of Migratory Species of Wild Animals.] Furthermore, we note that WTO Members in the Report of the CTE, forming part of the Report of the General Council to Ministers on the occasion of the Singapore Ministerial Conference, endorsed and supported:

> ... *multilateral solutions based on international cooperation and consensus as the best and most effective way for governments to tackle environmental problems of a transboundary or global nature.* WTO Agreements and multilateral environmental agreements (MEAs) are representative of efforts of the international community to pursue shared goals, and in the development of a mutually supportive relationship between them, *due respect must be afforded to both.* (emphasis added)

169.   Third, the United States did negotiate and conclude one regional international agreement for the protection and conservation of sea turtles: The Inter–American Convention. This Convention was opened for signature on 1 December 1996 and has been signed by five countries, in addition to the United States, and four of these countries are currently certified under Section 609. This Convention has not yet been ratified by any of its signatories. The Inter–American Convention provides that each party shall take "appropriate and necessary measures" for the protection, conservation and recovery of sea turtle populations and their habitats within such party's land territory and in maritime areas with respect to which it exercises sovereign rights or jurisdiction. Such measures include, notably,

> [t]he reduction, to the greatest extent practicable, of the incidental capture, retention, harm or mortality of sea turtles in the course of fishing activities, through the appropriate regulation of such activities, as well as the development, improvement and use of appropriate gear, devices or techniques, including the use of turtle excluder

devices (TEDs) pursuant to the provisions of Annex III [of the Convention].

Article XV of the Inter–American Convention also provides, in part:

ARTICLE XV

Trade Measures

1. *In implementing this Convention, the Parties shall act in accordance with the provisions of the Agreement establishing the World Trade Organization* (WTO), as adopted at Marrakesh in 1994, including its annexes.

2. In particular, and *with respect to the subject-matter of this Convention, the Parties shall act in accordance with the provisions of* the Agreement on Technical Barriers to Trade contained in Annex 1 of the WTO Agreement, as well as *Article XI of the General Agreement on Tariffs and Trade of 1994. . . .* (emphasis added)

170.   The juxtaposition of (a) the *consensual* undertakings to put in place regulations providing for, inter alia, use of TEDs *jointly determined* to be suitable for a particular party's maritime areas, with (b) the reaffirmation of the parties' obligations under the *WTO Agreement*, including the *Agreement on Technical Barriers to Trade* and Article XI of the GATT 1994, suggests that the parties to the Inter–American Convention together marked out the equilibrium line to which we referred earlier. The Inter–American Convention demonstrates the conviction of its signatories, including the United States, that consensual and multilateral procedures are available and feasible for the establishment of programs for the conservation of sea turtles. Moreover, the Inter–American Convention emphasizes the continuing validity and significance of Article XI of the GATT 1994, and of the obligations of the *WTO Agreement* generally, in maintaining the balance of rights and obligations under the *WTO Agreement* among the signatories of that Convention.

171.   The Inter–American Convention thus provides convincing demonstration that an alternative course of action was reasonably open to the United States for securing the legitimate policy goal of its measure, a course of action other than the unilateral and non-consensual procedures of the import prohibition under Section 609. It is relevant to observe that an import prohibition is, ordinarily, the heaviest "weapon" in a Member's armory of trade measures. The record does not, however, show that serious efforts were made by the United States to negotiate similar agreements with any other country or group of countries before (and, as far as the record shows, after) Section 609 was enforced on a world-wide basis on May 1, 1996. Finally, the record also does not show that the appellant, the United States, attempted to have recourse to such international mechanisms as exist to achieve cooperative efforts to protect and conserve sea turtles[1] before imposing the import ban.

---

1.   [original note 174] While the United States is a party to CITES, it did not make any attempt to raise the issue of sea turtle mortality due to shrimp trawling in the

172.   Clearly, the United States negotiated seriously with some, but not with other Members (including the appellees), that export shrimp to the United States. The effect is plainly discriminatory and, in our view, unjustifiable. The unjustifiable nature of this discrimination emerges clearly when we consider the cumulative effects of the failure of the United States to pursue negotiations for establishing consensual means of protection and conservation of the living marine resources here involved, notwithstanding the explicit statutory direction in Section 609 itself to initiate negotiations as soon as possible for the development of bilateral and multilateral agreements. The principal consequence of this failure may be seen in the resulting unilateralism evident in the application of Section 609. As we have emphasized earlier, the policies relating to the necessity for use of particular kinds of TEDs in various maritime areas, and the operating details of these policies, are all shaped by the Department of State, without the participation of the exporting Members. The system and processes of certification are established and administered by the United States agencies alone. The decision-making involved in the grant, denial or withdrawal of certification to the exporting Members, is, accordingly, also unilateral. The unilateral character of the application of Section 609 heightens the disruptive and discriminatory influence of the import prohibition and underscores its unjustifiability.

173.   The application of Section 609, through the implementing guidelines together with administrative practice, also resulted in other differential treatment among various countries desiring certification. Under the 1991 and 1993 Guidelines, to be certifiable, fourteen countries in the wider Caribbean/western Atlantic region had to commit themselves to require the use of TEDs on all commercial shrimp trawling vessels by 1 May 1994. These fourteen countries had a "phase-in" period of three years during which their respective shrimp trawling sectors could adjust to the requirement of the use of TEDs. With respect to all other countries exporting shrimp to the United States (including the appellees, India, Malaysia, Pakistan and Thailand), on December 29, 1995, the United States Court of International Trade directed the Department of State to apply the import ban on a world-wide basis not later than May 1, 1996. On April 19, 1996, the 1996 Guidelines were issued by the Department of State bringing shrimp harvested in all foreign countries within the scope of Section 609, effective May 1, 1996. Thus, all countries that were not among the fourteen in the wider Caribbean/western Atlantic region had only four months to implement the requirement of compulsory use of TEDs. We acknowledge that the greatly differing periods for putting into operation the requirement for use of TEDs resulted from decisions of the Court of International Trade. Even so, this does not relieve the United States of the legal consequences

CITES Standing Committee as a subject requiring concerted action by states. In this context, we note that the United States, for example, has not signed the Convention on the Conservation of Migratory Species of Wild Animals or UNCLOS, and has not ratified the Convention on Biological Diversity.

of the discriminatory impact of the decisions of that Court. The United States, like all other Members of the WTO and of the general community of states, bears responsibility for acts of all its departments of government, including its judiciary.

174. The length of the "phase-in" period is not inconsequential for exporting countries desiring certification. That period relates directly to the onerousness of the burdens of complying with the requisites of certification and the practical feasibility of locating and developing alternative export markets for shrimp. The shorter that period, the heavier the burdens of compliance, particularly where an applicant has a large number of trawler vessels, and the greater the difficulties of reorienting the harvesting country's shrimp exports. The shorter that period, in net effect, the heavier the influence of the import ban. The United States sought to explain the marked difference between "phase-in" periods granted to the fourteen wider Caribbean/western Atlantic countries and those allowed the rest of the shrimp exporting countries. The United States asserted that the longer time-period was justified by the then undeveloped character of TED technology, while the shorter period was later made possible by the improvements in that technology. This explanation is less than persuasive, for it does not address the administrative and financial costs and the difficulties of governments in putting together and enacting the necessary regulatory programs and "credible enforcement effort", and in implementing the compulsory use of TEDs on hundreds, if not thousands, of shrimp trawl vessels.

175. Differing treatment of different countries desiring certification is also observable in the differences in the levels of effort made by the United States in transferring the required TED technology to specific countries. Far greater efforts to transfer that technology successfully were made to certain exporting countries—basically the fourteen wider Caribbean/western Atlantic countries cited earlier—than to other exporting countries, including the appellees. The level of these efforts is probably related to the length of the "phase-in" periods granted—the longer the "phase-in" period, the higher the possible level of efforts at technology transfer. Because compliance with the requirements of certification realistically assumes successful TED technology transfer, low or merely nominal efforts at achieving that transfer will, in all probability, result in fewer countries being able to satisfy the certification requirements under Section 609, within the very limited "phase-in" periods allowed them.

176. When the foregoing differences in the means of application of Section 609 to various shrimp exporting countries are considered in their cumulative effect, we find, and so hold, that those differences in treatment constitute "unjustifiable discrimination" between exporting countries desiring certification in order to gain access to the United States shrimp market within the meaning of the chapeau of Article XX.

* * *

185. In reaching these conclusions, we wish to underscore what we have *not* decided in this appeal. We have *not* decided that the protection and preservation of the environment is of no significance to the Members of the WTO. Clearly, it is. We have *not* decided that the sovereign nations that are Members of the WTO cannot adopt effective measures to protect endangered species, such as sea turtles. Clearly, they can and should. And we have *not* decided that sovereign states should not act together bilaterally, plurilaterally or multilaterally, either within the WTO or in other international fora, to protect endangered species or to otherwise protect the environment. Clearly, they should and do.

186. What we *have* decided in this appeal is simply this: although the measure of the United States in dispute in this appeal serves an environmental objective that is recognized as legitimate under paragraph (g) of Article XX of the GATT 1994, this measure has been applied by the United States in a manner which constitutes arbitrary and unjustifiable discrimination between Members of the WTO, contrary to the requirements of the chapeau of Article XX. For all of the specific reasons outlined in this Report, this measure does not qualify for the exemption that Article XX of the GATT 1994 affords to measures which serve certain recognized, legitimate environmental purposes but which, at the same time, are not applied in a manner that constitutes a means of arbitrary or unjustifiable discrimination between countries where the same conditions prevail or a disguised restriction on international trade. As we emphasized in *United States—Gasoline*, WTO Members are free to adopt their own policies aimed at protecting the environment as long as, in so doing, they fulfill their obligations and respect the rights of other Members under the *WTO Agreement*.

Notes and Questions

(1) The Appellate Body also found that Section 609 had been applied in a manner constituting "arbitrary discrimination". First, it noted that there was little or no flexibility in how officials made the certification determinations and that this rigidity and inflexibility constituted "arbitrary discrimination" within the meaning of the chapeau. Second, it found that the certification process was not transparent or predictable. It highlighted that there was no formal opportunity for an applicant country to be heard, or to respond to any arguments that might be made against it, in the course of the certification process before a decision to grant or to deny certification is made. Countries whose applications are denied also do not receive notice of such denial (other than by omission from the list of approved applications) or of the reasons for the denial. No procedure for review of, or appeal from, a denial of an application is provided. "It appears to us that, effectively, exporting Members applying for certification whose applications are rejected are denied basic fairness and due process, and are discriminated against, *vis-à-vis* those Members which are granted certification" (para. 181). The Appellate Body also noted that these procedural defects were "contrary to the spirit, if not the letter, of Article X:3 of the GATT 1994" (para. 183). The potential scope (and, indeed, the precise source) of this due process require-

ment remains somewhat unclear, but it could obviously have major ramifications over time.

(2) The panel in *Shrimp* had been particularly concerned with the unilateral nature of the US measure and the fact that it was designed to force other countries to change conservation policy across the board (as opposed simply to meet US production standards in respect of products exported to the United States). In the panel's view, this broader purpose was simply not permitted by the chapeau. In commenting on this view, the Appellate Body stated:

> 121. * * * The Panel, in effect, constructed an *a priori* test that purports to define a category of measures which, *ratione materiae*, fall outside the justifying protection of Article XX's chapeau. In the present case, the Panel found that the United States measure at stake fell within that class of excluded measures because Section 609 conditions access to the domestic shrimp market of the United States on the adoption by exporting countries of certain conservation policies prescribed by the United States. It appears to us, however, that conditioning access to a Member's domestic market on whether exporting Members comply with, or adopt, a policy or policies unilaterally prescribed by the importing Member may, to some degree, be a common aspect of measures falling within the scope of one or another of the exceptions (a) to (j) of Article XX. Paragraphs (a) to (j) comprise measures that are recognized as *exceptions to substantive obligations* established in the GATT 1994, because the domestic policies embodied in such measures have been recognized as important and legitimate in character. It is not necessary to assume that requiring from exporting countries compliance with, or adoption of, certain policies (although covered in principle by one or another of the exceptions) prescribed by the importing country, renders a measure *a priori* incapable of justification under Article XX. Such an interpretation renders most, if not all, of the specific exceptions of Article XX inutile, a result abhorrent to the principles of interpretation we are bound to apply.

(3) In the *Gasoline* case (see Section 13.4 supra), the Appellate Body concluded that the US measures at issue did not meet the terms of the chapeau for the following reasons (p. 27):

> We have above located two omissions on the part of the United States: to explore adequately means, including in particular cooperation with the governments of Venezuela and Brazil, of mitigating the administrative problems relied on as justification by the United States for rejecting individual baselines for foreign refiners; and to count the costs for foreign refiners that would result from the imposition of statutory baselines [in contrast to its view that application of the statutory baseline to domestic producers in 1995 would have been physically and financially impossible]. In our view, these two omissions go well beyond what was necessary for the Panel to determine that a violation of Article III:4 had occurred in the first place. The resulting discrimination must have been foreseen, and was not merely inadvertent or unavoidable. In the light of the foregoing, our conclusion is that the baseline establishment rules in the Gasoline Rule, in their application, constitute "unjust-

ifiable discrimination" and a "disguised restriction on international trade."

There was no explanation of why these two shortcomings constituted a disguised restriction on international trade in addition to being discriminatory. The lack of consultations or negotiations with foreign governments was a major factor in the *Shrimp* case. Where else in this chapter has a failure to consider the excessive costs imposed on imports (as opposed to domestic products) been a factor in determining the applicability of Article XX?

(4) In Brazil—Measures Affecting Imports of Retreaded Tires, WT/DS332/AB/R, adopted December 17, 2007, Brazil invoked Article XX(b) to justify its ban on imports of retreaded tires. However, as a result of a MERCOSUR dispute settlement ruling, Brazil did not apply the ban to other MERCOSUR countries, raising the question of whether the ban satisfied the nondiscrimination requirements of the chapeau. The Appellate Body analyzed the issue as follows:

> 229.   The Panel considered that the MERCOSUR exemption resulted in discrimination between MERCOSUR countries and other WTO Members, but that this discrimination would be "unjustifiable" only if imports of retreaded tires entering into Brazil "were to take place in such amounts that the achievement of the objective of the measure at issue would be significantly undermined". [The panel found that such imports had not been significant.] The Panel's interpretation implies that the determination of whether discrimination is unjustifiable depends on the quantitative impact of this discrimination on the achievement of the objective of the measure at issue. As we indicated above, analyzing whether discrimination is "unjustifiable" will usually involve an analysis that relates primarily to the cause or the rationale of the discrimination. By contrast, the Panel's interpretation of the term "unjustifiable" does not depend on the cause or rationale of the discrimination but, rather, is focused exclusively on the assessment of the effects of the discrimination. The Panel's approach has no support in the text of Article XX and appears to us inconsistent with the manner the Appellate Body has interpreted and applied the concept of "arbitrary or unjustifiable discrimination" in previous cases.

> 230.   Having said that, we recognize that in certain cases the effects of the discrimination may be a relevant factor, among others, for determining whether the cause or rationale of the discrimination is acceptable or defensible and, ultimately, whether the discrimination is justifiable. The effects of discrimination might be relevant, depending on the circumstances of the case, because * * * the chapeau of Article XX deals with the manner of application of the measure at issue. Taking into account as a relevant factor, among others, the effects of the discrimination for determining whether the rationale of the discrimination is acceptable is, however, fundamentally different from the Panel's approach, which focused exclusively on the relationship between the effects of the discrimination and its justifiable or unjustifiable character.

It is not clear why Brazil did not raise the MERCOSUR equivalent of Article XX in the MERCOSUR dispute settlement proceedings.

(5) Precisely why did the Appellate Body find that the US actions in *Shrimp* constituted unjustifiable or arbitrary discrimination? In respect of each of these reasons, what would the US have to do to bring its measure into conformity with its WTO obligations? Consider how the Appellate Body dealt with these issues:

UNITED STATES—IMPORT PROHIBITION OF CERTAIN SHRIMP AND SHRIMP PRODUCTS (RECOURSE TO ARTICLE 21.5 BY MALAYSIA)

WT/DS58/AB/RW.
Appellate Body Report adopted November 21, 2001.

[Malaysia brought an Article 21.5 action claiming that the United States had failed to bring Section 609 into conformity with its WTO obligations within the agreed-upon reasonable period of time for implementation. Thus, the compliance panel focused on the actions taken by the United States subsequent to the original *Shrimp* decision. The panel described the US implementing measures as (i) the adoption of the 1999 Guidelines and (ii) US efforts to negotiate an agreement on the conservation of sea turtles with the Governments of the Indian Ocean region and to provide technical assistance on the use of TEDs.

According to the 1999 Guidelines,[2] Section 609 does not apply to shrimp or products of shrimp harvested under specified conditions in which harvesting does not adversely affect sea turtles. These conditions include shrimp harvested in aquaculture; shrimp harvested by trawlers using TEDs comparable in effectiveness to those required in the United States; shrimp harvested exclusively by artisanal means; and shrimp harvested in any other manner that the State Department determines does not pose a threat of the incidental taking of sea turtles.

Under the 1999 Guidelines, importation of shrimp into the US must be accompanied by a declaration attesting that the shrimp at issue were harvested (i) under the conditions defined above or (ii) in waters subject to the jurisdiction of a nation currently certified pursuant to Section 609.

The 1999 Guidelines provide for certification on the basis that the particular fishing environment of the harvesting nation does not pose a threat of incidental taking of sea turtles (e.g., the relevant species of sea turtles are not found in its waters; shrimp are harvested exclusively by means that do not pose a threat to sea turtles, e.g., artisanal means; shrimp trawling takes place exclusively in waters in which sea turtles do not occur). The Guidelines also provide for certification on the basis that a government has adopted and credibly enforced a TEDs program. Moreover, they also allow for the possibility that a country may be certified on the basis of having a regulatory programme not involving the use of TEDs if it demonstrates that it has implemented and is enforcing a comparably effective regulatory program to protect sea

---

2. 64 Fed. Reg. 36949 (1999).

turtles in the course of shrimp trawl fishing without the use of TEDs. In making the latter determination, the State Department is required to take fully into account any demonstrated differences between the shrimp fishing conditions in the United States and in the country in question. In either case, there is also a requirement that the rate of incidental taking of sea turtles must be comparable to the US rate.

The Revised Guidelines also revise the procedures under which the certification process operates. They also indicate that they may be revised in the future to take into consideration additional information on the interaction between sea turtles and shrimp fisheries, changes in the US program and in light of the results of pending litigation in US courts.

The Article 21.5 panel found that the US had made adequate efforts to negotiate an agreement with South East Asia nations. It also concluded that the US had satisfactorily dealt with the other aspects of the unjustifiable discrimination found by the Appellate Body, which it noted were agreed by the parties to be: (i) the insufficient flexibility of the 1996 Guidelines, in particular the absence of consideration of the different conditions that may exist in the exporting nations; (ii) the prohibition of importation of shrimp caught in uncertified countries, even when that shrimp had been caught using TEDs; (iii) the length of the "phase-in" period; and (iv) the differences in the level of efforts made by the United States to transfer successfully TED technology to exporting countries. Similarly, it found that the US had corrected the problems of arbitrary discrimination found by the Appellate Body through the adoption of new procedures.

On appeal Malaysia's arguments concerned (i) the nature and extent of the duty of the United States to pursue international cooperation in protecting and conserving endangered sea turtles and (ii) the flexibility of the Revised Guidelines.]

The Nature and the Extent of the Duty of the United States to Pursue International Cooperation in the Protection and Conservation of Sea Turtles

119.   * * * In *United States—Shrimp*, we stated that the measure at issue there resulted in "unjustifiable discrimination", in part because, as applied, the United States treated WTO Members differently. The United States had adopted a cooperative approach with WTO Members from the Caribbean/Western Atlantic region, with whom it had concluded a multilateral agreement on the protection and conservation of sea turtles, namely the Inter–American Convention. Yet the United States had not, we found, pursued the negotiation of such a multilateral agreement with other exporting Members, including Malaysia and the other complaining WTO Members in that case.

* * *

122.   We concluded in *United States—Shrimp* that, to avoid "arbitrary or unjustifiable discrimination", the United States had to provide all exporting countries "similar opportunities to negotiate" an interna-

tional agreement. Given the specific mandate contained in Section 609, and given the decided preference for multilateral approaches voiced by WTO Members and others in the international community in various international agreements for the protection and conservation of endangered sea turtles that were cited in our previous Report, the United States, in our view, would be expected to make good faith efforts to reach international agreements that are comparable from one forum of negotiation to the other. The negotiations need not be identical. Indeed, no two negotiations can ever be identical, or lead to identical results. Yet the negotiations must be *comparable* in the sense that comparable efforts are made, comparable resources are invested, and comparable energies are devoted to securing an international agreement. So long as such comparable efforts are made, it is more likely that "arbitrary or unjustifiable discrimination" will be avoided between countries where an importing Member concludes an agreement with one group of countries, but fails to do so with another group of countries.

123.   Under the chapeau of Article XX, an importing Member may not treat its trading partners in a manner that would constitute "arbitrary or unjustifiable discrimination". With respect to this measure, the United States could conceivably respect this obligation, and the conclusion of an international agreement might nevertheless not be possible despite the serious, good faith efforts of the United States. Requiring that a multilateral agreement be *concluded* by the United States in order to avoid "arbitrary or unjustifiable discrimination" in applying its measure would mean that any country party to the negotiations with the United States, whether a WTO Member or not, would have, in effect, a veto over whether the United States could fulfill its WTO obligations. Such a requirement would not be reasonable. For a variety of reasons, it may be possible to conclude an agreement with one group of countries but not another. The conclusion of a multilateral agreement requires the cooperation and commitment of many countries. In our view, the United States cannot be held to have engaged in "arbitrary or unjustifiable discrimination" under Article XX solely because one international negotiation resulted in an agreement while another did not.

124.   As we stated in *United States—Shrimp*, "the protection and conservation of highly migratory species of sea turtles ... demands concerted and cooperative efforts on the part of the many countries whose waters are traversed in the course of recurrent sea turtle migrations". Further, the "need for, and the appropriateness of, such efforts have been recognized in the WTO itself as well as in a significant number of other international instruments and declarations". For example, Principle 12 of the Rio Declaration on Environment and Development states, in part, that "[e]nvironmental measures addressing transboundary or global environmental problems should, as far as possible, be based on international consensus". Clearly, and "as far as possible", a multilateral approach is strongly preferred. Yet it is one thing to *prefer* a multilateral approach in the application of a measure that is provisionally justified under one of the subparagraphs of Article XX of the GATT

1994; it is another to require the *conclusion* of a multilateral agreement as a condition of avoiding "arbitrary or unjustifiable discrimination" under the chapeau of Article XX. We see, in this case, no such requirement.

* * *

130. * * * The Panel compared the efforts of the United States to negotiate the Inter–American Convention with one group of exporting WTO Members with the efforts made by the United States to negotiate a similar agreement with another group of exporting WTO Members. The Panel rightly used the Inter–American Convention as a factual reference in this exercise of comparison. It was all the more relevant to do so given that the Inter–American Convention was the only international agreement that the Panel could have used in such a comparison. As we read the Panel Report, it is clear to us that the Panel attached a relative value to the Inter–American Convention in making this comparison, but did not view the Inter–American Convention in any way as an absolute standard. Thus, we disagree with Malaysia's submission that the Panel raised the Inter–American Convention to the rank of a "legal standard". The mere use by the Panel of the Inter–American Convention *as a basis for a comparison* did not transform the Inter–American Convention into a "legal standard". Furthermore, although the Panel could have chosen a more appropriate word than "benchmark" to express its views, Malaysia is mistaken in equating the mere use of the word "benchmark", as it was used by the Panel, with the establishment of a legal standard.

131. The Panel noted that while "factual circumstances may influence the duration of the process or the end result, . . . any effort alleged to be a 'serious good faith effort' must be assessed against the efforts made in relation to the conclusion of the Inter–American Convention." Such a comparison is a central element of the exercise to determine whether there is "unjustifiable discrimination". The Panel then analyzed the negotiation process in the Indian Ocean and South–East Asia region to determine whether the efforts made by the United States in those negotiations were serious, good faith efforts comparable to those made in relation with the Inter–American Convention. In conducting this analysis, the Panel referred to the following elements:

— A document communicated on 14 October 1998 by the United States Department of State to a number of countries of the Indian Ocean and the South–East Asia region. This document contained possible elements of a regional convention on sea turtles in this region.

— The contribution of the United States to a symposium held in Sabah on 15–17 July 1999. The Sabah Symposium led to the adoption of a Declaration calling for the negotiation and implementation of a regional agreement throughout the Indian Ocean and South–East Asia region.

— The Perth Conference in October 1999, where participating governments, including the United States, committed themselves to developing an international agreement on sea turtles for the Indian Ocean and South–East Asia region.

— The contribution of the United States to the Kuantan round of negotiations, 11–14 July 2000. This first round of negotiations towards the conclusion of a regional agreement resulted in the adoption of the Memorandum of Understanding on the Conservation and Management of Marine Turtles and their Habitats of the Indian Ocean and South–East Asia (the "South–East Asian MOU"). The Final Act of the Kuantan meeting provided that before the South–East Asian MOU can be finalized, a Conservation and Management Plan must be negotiated and annexed to the South–East Asian MOU. At the time of the Panel proceedings, the Conservation and Management Plan was still being drafted.

132.   On this basis and, in particular, on the basis of the "contribution of the United States to the steps that led to the Kuantan meeting and its contribution to the Kuantan meeting itself", the Panel concluded that the United States had made serious, good faith efforts that met the "standard set by the Inter–American Convention." In the view of the Panel, whether or not the South–East Asian MOU is a legally binding document does not affect this comparative assessment because differences in "factual circumstances have to be kept in mind". Furthermore, the Panel did not consider as decisive the fact that the final agreement in the Indian Ocean and South–East Asia region, unlike the Inter–American Convention, had not been concluded at the time of the Panel proceedings. According to the Panel, "at least until the Conservation and Management Plan to be attached to the MOU is completed, the United States efforts should be judged on the basis of its active participation and its financial support to the negotiations, as well as on the basis of its previous efforts since 1998, having regard to the likelihood of a conclusion of the negotiations in the course of 2001."

133.   We note that the Panel stated that "any effort alleged to be a 'serious good faith effort' must be assessed against the efforts made in relation to the conclusion of the Inter–American Convention." In our view, in assessing the serious, good faith efforts made by the United States, the Panel did not err in using the Inter–American Convention as an *example*. In our view, also, the Panel was correct in proceeding then to an analysis broadly in line with this principle and, ultimately, was correct as well in concluding that the efforts made by the United States in the Indian Ocean and South–East Asia region constitute serious, good faith efforts comparable to those that led to the conclusion of the Inter–American Convention. We find no fault with this analysis.

134.   In sum, Malaysia is incorrect in its contention that avoiding "arbitrary and unjustifiable discrimination" under the chapeau of Article XX requires the *conclusion* of an international agreement on the

protection and conservation of sea turtles. Therefore, we uphold the Panel's finding that, in view of the serious, good faith efforts made by the United States to negotiate an international agreement, "Section 609 is now applied in a manner that no longer constitutes a means of unjustifiable or arbitrary discrimination, as identified by the Appellate Body in its Report".

The Flexibility of the Revised Guidelines

* * *

136.   Malaysia disagrees with the Panel that a measure can meet the requirements of the chapeau of Article XX if it is flexible enough, both in design and application, to permit certification of an exporting country with a sea turtle protection and conservation programme "comparable" to that of the United States. According to Malaysia, even if the measure at issue allows certification of countries having regulatory programs "comparable" to that of the United States, and even if the measure is applied in such a manner, it results in "arbitrary or unjustifiable discrimination" because it conditions access to the United States market on compliance with policies and standards "unilaterally" prescribed by the United States. * * *

* * *

140.   In *United States—Shrimp*, we concluded that the measure at issue there did not meet the requirements of the chapeau of Article XX relating to "arbitrary or unjustifiable discrimination" because, through the application of the measure, the exporting members were faced with "a single, rigid and unbending requirement" to adopt *essentially the same* policies and enforcement practices as those applied to, and enforced on, domestic shrimp trawlers in the United States. In contrast, in this dispute, the Panel found that this new measure is more flexible than the original measure and has been applied more flexibly than was the original measure. In the light of the evidence brought by the United States, the Panel satisfied itself that this new measure, in design and application, does not condition access to the United States market on the adoption by an exporting Member of a regulatory programme aimed at the protection and the conservation of sea turtles that is *essentially the same* as that of the United States.

141.   As the Panel's analysis suggests, an approach based on whether a measure requires "essentially the same" regulatory programme of an exporting Member as that adopted by the importing Member applying the measure is a useful tool in identifying measures that result in "arbitrary or unjustifiable discrimination" and, thus, do *not* meet the requirements of the chapeau of Article XX. However, this approach is not sufficient for purposes of judging whether a measure does meet the requirements of the chapeau of Article XX. * * *

* * *

143. Given that the original measure in that dispute required "essentially the same" practices and procedures as those required in the United States, we found it necessary in that appeal to rule only that Article XX did not allow such inflexibility. Given the Panel's findings with respect to the flexibility of the new measure in this dispute, we find it necessary in this appeal to add to what we ruled in our original Report. The question raised by Malaysia in this appeal is whether the Panel erred in inferring from our previous Report, and thereby finding, that the chapeau of Article XX permits a measure which requires only "comparable effectiveness".

144. In our view, there is an important difference between conditioning market access on the adoption of essentially the same programme, and conditioning market access on the adoption of a programme *comparable in effectiveness*. Authorizing an importing Member to condition market access on exporting Members putting in place regulatory programmes *comparable in effectiveness* to that of the importing Member gives sufficient latitude to the exporting Member with respect to the programme it may adopt to achieve the level of effectiveness required. It allows the exporting Member to adopt a regulatory programme that is suitable to the specific conditions prevailing in its territory. As we see it, the Panel correctly reasoned and concluded that conditioning market access on the adoption of a programme *comparable in effectiveness*, allows for sufficient flexibility in the application of the measure so as to avoid "arbitrary or unjustifiable discrimination". We, therefore, agree with the conclusion of the Panel on "comparable effectiveness".

* * *

146. We note that the Revised Guidelines contain provisions that permit the United States authorities to take into account the specific conditions of Malaysian shrimp production, and of the Malaysian sea turtle conservation programme, should Malaysia decide to apply for certification. The Revised Guidelines explicitly state that "[if] the government of a harvesting nation demonstrates that it has implemented and is enforcing a comparably effective regulatory program to protect sea turtles in the course of shrimp trawl fishing without the use of TEDs, that nation will also be eligible for certification." Likewise, the Revised Guidelines provide that the "Department of State will take fully into account any demonstrated differences between the shrimp fishing conditions in the United States and those in other nations as well as information available from other sources."

147. Further, the Revised Guidelines provide that the import prohibitions that can be imposed under Section 609 do not apply to shrimp or products of shrimp "harvested in any other manner or under any other circumstances that the Department of State may determine, following consultations with the [United States National Marine Fisheries Services], does not pose a threat of the incidental taking of sea turtles." * * * Additionally, Section II.B(c)(iii) states that "[i]n making certifica-

tion determinations, the Department shall also take fully into account other measures the harvesting nation undertakes to protect sea turtles, including national programmes to protect nesting beaches and other habitat, prohibitions on the direct take of sea turtles, national enforcement and compliance programmes, and participation in any international agreement for the protection and conservation of sea turtles." * * *

148.　These provisions of the Revised Guidelines, on their face, permit a degree of flexibility that, in our view, will enable the United States to consider the particular conditions prevailing in Malaysia if, and when, Malaysia applies for certification. As Malaysia has not applied for certification, any consideration of whether Malaysia would be certified would be speculation.

149.　We need only say here that, in our view, a measure should be designed in such a manner that there is sufficient flexibility to take into account the specific conditions prevailing in *any* exporting Member, including, of course, Malaysia. Yet this is not the same as saying that there must be specific provisions in the measure aimed at addressing specifically the particular conditions prevailing in *every individual* exporting Member. Article XX of the GATT 1994 does not require a Member to anticipate and provide explicitly for the specific conditions prevailing and evolving in *every individual* Member.

150.　We are, therefore, not persuaded by Malaysia's argument that the measure at issue is not flexible enough because the Revised Guidelines do not explicitly address the specific conditions prevailing in Malaysia.

151.　Malaysia argues, finally, that the Panel should have scrutinized the decision of the CIT in the *Turtle Island* case and assessed, in the light of that decision, the likelihood and consequences of the Revised Guidelines being modified in the future. According to Malaysia, the Panel should have come to the conclusion that the Revised Guidelines are not flexible enough because the CIT ruled that the part of the Revised Guidelines allowing TED-caught shrimp from non-certified harvesting countries to be imported into the United States is contrary to Section 609. As we have already ruled, we are of the view that, when examining the United States measures, the Panel took into account the status of municipal law at the time, and reached the correct conclusion. The CIT decision in the *Turtle Island* case has not modified the legal effect or the application of the Revised Guidelines; hence, we are not persuaded by this argument of Malaysia. [Eds. Note: The CIT decision was reversed on appeal.]

153.　For all these reasons, we uphold the finding of the Panel, in paragraph 6.1 of the Panel Report, that "Section 609 of Public Law 101–162, as implemented by the Revised Guidelines of 8 July 1999 and as applied so far by the [United States] authorities, is justified under Article XX of the GATT 1994 as long as the conditions stated in the findings of this Report, in particular the ongoing serious, good faith efforts to reach a multilateral agreement, remain satisfied".

Notes and Questions

(1) In respect of the condition in paragraph 153, the Appellate Body noted that the United States had negotiated and concluded a Memorandum of Understanding with certain countries in the Indian Ocean and South–East Asia region, the South–East Asian MOU, which took effect on September 1, 2001.

(2) On the key issue of negotiations, do you agree with the Appellate Body? Does it let the US off too easily? What of the fact that the negotiations took place while the US measure remained in effect? The panel in fact noted (in para. 5.73) "that, in that context, negotiators may have found themselves constrained to accept conditions that they may not have accepted had Section 609 not been applied. Even if Section 609 as currently applied takes more into account the existence of different conservation programs, it can still influence the outcome of negotiations. This is why the Panel feels it is important to take the reality of international relations into account and considers that the standard of review of the efforts of the United States on the international plane should be expressed as follows: whether the United States made serious good faith efforts to negotiate an international agreement, taking into account the situations of the other negotiating countries."

(3) The stress on negotiations should remind one that are many multilateral agreements dealing with environmental issues. How should a conflict between a WTO requirement and a requirement of a multilateral environmental agreement (MEA) be resolved? By whom? Suppose the MEA authorizes, but does not require, an action that is inconsistent with WTO requirements? To what extent can Article XX be used to excuse compliance with WTO requirements in such a situation? Interestingly, the preamble to the Cartegena Protocol to the Convention on Biological Diversity provides that the Protocol shall not be interpreted as implying a change in the rights and obligations of a party under any existing international agreements, but that this statement is not intended to subordinate the protocol to other international agreements. The negotiations on environmental issues, including the relationship between MEAs and the WTO, that were agreed upon at the Doha Ministerial are described in more detail in Section 13.6 infra.

(4) In *US Gambling*, which is excerpted in Chapter 19, the Appellate Body indicated that the necessity requirement in the GATS Article XIV(a) exception did not require a respondent to demonstrate that it had consulted with trading partners before imposing a WTO-inconsistent measure. Appellate Body Report, WT/DS285/AB/R, para. 317. The panel had viewed such consultations as needed so that a respondent would to be able to show that it had considered all reasonably available WTO-compatible measures before imposing an incompatible measure. Panel Report, para. 6.526.

(5) In light of the *Shrimp* decisions, how would you characterize the extent of the discretion that WTO members have to take unilateral action for the protection of the environment? What are the limits on that discretion? What is the relevance of the product-process distinction (noted in connection with the discussion of like products in Chapter 12) in an analysis under the chapeau of Article XX?

SECTION 13.6　SHOULD ARTICLE XX BE EXPANDED TO COVER ENVIRONMENTAL MEASURES GENERALLY?

Protecting the environment was not a major international concern when the General Agreement on Tariffs and Trade was drafted in 1947. In recent years, however, it has become an issue of great importance to many countries. For developing countries, there are concerns that environmental regulations may be used for protectionist purposes to bar their imports or to offset their comparative advantages. For environmental organizations and developed countries, there are concerns that WTO rules may limit the effectiveness of multilateral environmental agreements (MEAs), that WTO dispute settlement will privilege WTO rules over fundamental environmental principles such as the precautionary principle, and that competitive pressures exacerbated by liberalized trade regimes will make it difficult to enact stricter environmental rules and will promote the movement of polluting industries to jurisdictions with less strict rules. There is also a concern that growth and development promoted by liberalized trade will inevitably worsen the world environment.

Some observers believe that the WTO agreements need to be modified to take account of some of these concerns. In fact, however, compared to GATT 1947, the WTO has taken greater account of environmental issues. For example, while the GATT Preamble called for "developing the full use of the resources of the world", the comparable language in the Preamble to the WTO Agreement provides for expanding trade

> while allowing for the optimal use of the world's resources in accordance with the objective of sustainable development, seeking both to protect and preserve the environment and to enhance the means for doing so in a manner consistent with [WTO members'] respective needs and concerns at different levels of economic development.

While no changes were made to GATT provisions to reflect the new importance attached to the environment and sustainable development in the Preamble, it was decided at Marrakesh to establish a WTO Committee on Trade and Environment. The committee was charged with examining, inter alia, (i) the relationship between the provisions of the multilateral trading system and trade measures for environmental purposes; (ii) the relationship between the provisions of the multilateral trading system and (a) charges and taxes for environmental purposes and (b) requirements for environmental purposes relating to products, including standards and technical regulations, packaging, labeling and recycling; and (iii) the relationship between the dispute settlement mechanisms in the multilateral trading system and those found in MEAs.

One issue that arises in considering these topics is whether the WTO needs an explicit exception permitting certain kinds of measures taken for environmental reasons. In this section, we first briefly recount the controversial history of the trade and environment issue. We then examine the underlying policy considerations involved in the issue. Finally, we consider the extent to which current WTO provisions are adequate or not to the task of allowing member governments to take appropriate environmental measures.

(A) TRADE AND ENVIRONMENT: FROM DOLPHINS TO TURTLES

The potential trade-environment conflict was brought to the forefront in dramatic fashion in September 1991 by the GATT panel decision in the so-called *Tuna–Dolphin* case, which ruled that a US embargo on tuna from countries that did not follow US rules on protecting dolphins during tuna fishing violated GATT and could not be justified under Article XX. The panel report was never adopted by the Contracting Parties, and the panel's reasoning is only of historical interest given the Appellate Body's decisions in the so-called *Shrimp–Turtle* case (see Section 13.5). Nonetheless for almost a decade after its announcement, the case received much attention and at the time was the subject of critical full-page newspaper advertisements in the United States, taken out by environmental and other public interest groups.[1]

The *Tuna–Dolphin* case was decided at a time of heightened international interest in the environment. In the summer of 1992, the United Nations Conference on the Environment and Development (UNCED) met in Rio de Janeiro, Brazil, and was attended by 178 nations. The conference adopted a number of instruments, including a declaration of environmental principles known as the Rio Principles, treaties on global warming and biological diversity, a nonbinding declaration on forest conservation principles and a document known as Agenda 21, which addressed many aspects of the environment and development.[2] UNCED had been preceded by the 1972 Stockholm Conference on the Human Environment, which was sponsored by the United Nations and led to the creation of the United Nations Environment Programme. The OECD has also been active in the past in discussing environmental issues.

A number of the Rio Principles are important for the trade and the environment debate. The basic theme of the Rio conference was sustainable development and a number of the Rio Principles are concerned with that theme. In order to allow states to achieve sustainable development, Principle 8 provides that "states should reduce and eliminate unsustainable patterns of production and consumption." While Principle 2 recognized that "[s]tates have, in accordance with the Charter of the United Nations and the principles of international law, the sovereign right to exploit their own resources pursuant to their own environmental and

---

1. See, e.g., N.Y.Times, Apr. 20, 1992, at A9 (natl. ed.).

2. 31 Int'l Legal Matls. 818 et seq. (1992). The Rio Principles are set out following page 874.

developmental policies," Principle 3 noted that the "right to development must be fulfilled so as to equitably meet developmental and environmental needs of present and future generations." Two other important principles found in the Rio Principles are the "polluter pays" principle, which holds that those responsible for pollution should pay for its consequences and elimination (Principle 16), and the precautionary principle, which provides that "[w]here there are threats of serious or irreversible damage, lack of full scientific certainty shall not be used as a reason for postponing cost-effective measures to prevent environmental degradation." (Principle 15)

(B) THE EFFECT OF EXPANDED INTERNATIONAL TRADE ON ENVIRONMENTAL QUALITY

Much of the trade and environment debate is fueled by concerns over the effects that the multilateral trading system may have on attempts to address appropriately environmental concerns. Even if the system does not preclude adoption of such regulations, there is concern that it may indirectly retard their adoption and undermine their effectiveness. The following WTO study address these issues in a relatively balanced fashion.

HAKAN NORDSTROM & SCOTT VAUGHAN, WTO SECRETARIAT SPECIAL STUDIES NO. 4, TRADE AND ENVIRONMENT 1–7 (1999)[3]

Several key questions are addressed in this study. First, is economic integration through trade and investment a threat to the environment? Second, does trade undermine the regulatory efforts of governments to control pollution and resource degradation? * * *

* * *

* * * [E]nvironmental repercussions of economic integration depend on three interacting elements: a composition effect, a scale effect, and a technique effect.

The *composition effect* refers to the industrial restructuring that takes place when a country exposes itself to the world market. The repercussions on the local environment will be positive if expanding export sectors are less polluting than contracting import-competing sectors, and vice versa. Since one country's exportables are another country's importables, all countries cannot specialize in clean industries. Trade is therefore associated with a relocation of pollution problems in the world. The *scale effect* arises from the boost of economic activity stimulated by trade. Economic growth is harmful for the environment unless production becomes cleaner and less resource consuming at the same time, and consumers become more willing to recycle waste instead of merely jettisoning it. The silver lining of the scale effect is the

---

3. Reprinted with permission.

associated income growth that drives a countervailing demand for a cleaner environment. Provided that governments respond to public demands, environmental policies will be upgraded as income grows, thereby offsetting or perhaps more than offsetting the scale effect. This effect is called the *technique effect*. The net outcome of these interacting elements is theoretically ambiguous, and is therefore ultimately an empirical question.

* * * In the public debate it is often assumed that polluting industries are likely to migrate from developed to developing countries to take advantage of lax regulations, thereby shifting the pollution problems from richer to poorer countries, and also increasing overall emissions in the world. However, this assertion does not seem to be supported by standard trade theory, nor by empirical evidence. Polluting industries tend to be capital intensive, including such industries as chemical industries, ferrous and non-ferrous metals, pulp and paper, and oil refining. According to classical trade theory based on differences in factor endowments, these industries are more likely to conglomerate in capital-abundant developed countries, and to a lesser extent, in economies in transition and newly industrialized countries. What complicates the analysis is that the pattern of trade is determined not just by "natural" comparative advantage, but also by government policies, including environmental regulations. However, pollution abatement costs in developed countries are no more than 1 per cent of production costs for the average industry, rising to perhaps 5 per cent for the worst polluters. It is questionable, although ultimately an empirical issue, if a regulatory cost-disadvantage of a few percentage points can turn comparative advantage around. If not, trade liberalization would tend to shift capital-intensive polluting industries towards developed countries in spite of tougher environmental regulations, and not the other way round.

Indeed, data seem to reject the assertion that polluting industries are migrating from developed to developing countries, although there are of course exceptions. Developed countries' share of polluting industries has remained more or less constant (at around 75–80 per cent) in recent decades, and has even increased marginally in the 1990s. * * *

What is more interesting, perhaps, is that the income gain associated with trade could *in principle* pay for the necessary abatement costs and still leave an economic surplus. This has been shown in various economic simulations. * * *

* * *

[W]e have divided the issue of ["does economic integration undermine environmental policies?"] into four parts: Do stringent environmental regulations undermine the competitiveness of developed countries? Do polluting industries relocate from developed to developing countries to take advantage of lax environmental standards? Are environmental standards being bid down in accordance with the "race-to-the-bottom" hypothesis? Or, if not, has the globalization of the world economy been followed by increased political reluctance to address environmental problems, as suggested by the "regulatory chill" hypothesis?

As far as the consequences of competition under regulatory diversity are concerned, we conclude that these have been somewhat overstated in the public debate. As noted above, the direct cost of pollution control is minor, just a few percentage points of production costs for most industries. No corresponding estimates are available for developing countries, but unless the regulatory cost is zero, the cost savings of moving offshore are less than suggested above. Moreover, some observers have noted that these numbers are in any event exaggerated. The "Porter hypothesis" holds that regulatory pressure, just like competitive pressure, encourages industrial innovations that make production both leaner (less energy and resource demanding) and cleaner at the same time, thereby offsetting the direct compliance costs. The empirical evidence partly supports this hypothesis, although it would be wrong to conclude that environmental regulations do not cost anything. They do cost, but they also bring significant benefit to society and the quality of life. How much they cost depends also on the kind of instruments used to regulate an industry. * * * What is more, while the public debate has focused on the cost side, studies that have compared the profitability of firms in the same industry have not found much evidence that environmental leaders pay a price in terms of reduced profitability. For several reasons, environmental leaders can often recoup costs in the marketplace. Firstly, a growing number of consumers are willing to pay a premium for "green labels." Secondly, firms that accord with the environmental management standards promulgated by the International Organization for Standardization (ISO 14000) seem to enjoy certain competitive advantages, including lower liability insurance, less regulatory oversight, and increased access to customers (including the public sector) that care about their own environmental reputation. Nor is there much evidence that polluting industries are migrating from developed to developing countries to reduce environmental compliance costs, although there are of course exceptions. While it is certainly true that developing countries are net recipients of foreign direct investment, the composition of investments they receive is not biased towards polluting industries, but rather to labor-intensive industries that are less polluting on average. What the data tell us is that, to the extent developed countries are exporting their dirty industries, they are exporting them to each other, not to less developed economies. This suggests that environmental regulations are at most of secondary importance for international investment decisions.

It should also be noted that many multinational firms are moving towards a policy of standardized technologies for all their production plants in the world. The reason is simple. It is less costly to duplicate the home technology than to modify the process in each country. What is more, the choice of technology is not just based on current standards, but on what is expected in the future. It makes commercial sense to install state-of-the-art technology at the time an investment is made rather than retrofitting abatement equipment at a later stage at a much greater expense. Finally, multinationals are becoming more sensitive to the reputation they earn in the market place, at least those multinational firms that are based in countries with an active environmental community. Market forces often reward good environmental performance rather than cost savings at any price, including financial markets that react negatively to environmental mishaps. It has not always been this way, but the tide has changed in recent years. Much of this advance is thanks to the relentless efforts of non-governmental organizations around the world that have made consumers sensitive to the environmental profile of products and producers. In short, when consumers care, producers care.

This is not to say that market forces can be entrusted to solve all problems themselves. Governments must do their part by regulating polluting and resource degrading activities appropriately. And here we seem to have a difficult political dilemma. If policy makers and voters think that domestic industry is crumbling under environmental regulations at the expense of domestic investments and jobs, it may be difficult to forge the necessary political support for new regulatory initiatives. And this problem may become worse still when trade and investment barriers are removed, since industries then become more mobile and more difficult to regulate.

Indeed, some evidence suggests that industries often appeal to competitiveness concerns when lobbying against environmental regulations, and on occasion with some success. How serious is this problem? It would clearly be a serious problem if competitiveness concerns prevented environmental standards from being raised to appropriate levels, or if governments were compelled to build in protectionist elements in environmental regulations to "compensate" industry for alleged adverse competitive effects. However, competitiveness concerns could potentially be a positive force if governments that find it difficult to act individually for political reasons seek cooperative solutions to environmental problems. The growing number of multilateral environmental agreements (currently some 216) may be one indication of the trend in that direction. The lasting effect of the "regulatory chill" may then be more procedural than substantial. That is, initiative may have to shift from the national to the supranational level, just as we saw a shift from the local to the central level in federal states in the 1970s to overcome environmental policy foot-dragging at the local level. Admittedly, however, international cooperation in these matters is not easy to achieve unless governments are convinced of its urgency.

* * *

It should also be kept in mind that not all kinds of growth are equally benign for the environment. Economic growth requiring ever more inputs of natural resources is obviously not as benign for the environment as economic growth driven by technological progress that saves inputs and reduces emissions per unit of output. This kind of growth will not necessarily emerge spontaneously, but may require economic incentives that steer development in a sustainable direction.

Trade could play a positive role in this process by facilitating the diffusion of environment-friendly technologies around the world. Of course, this would require that countries be ready to scrap trade barriers on modern technologies and suppliers of environmental services. A new round of trade liberalization negotiations could make a contribution here. Another potential contribution of such a round would be to address subsidies that harm the environment, including energy, agricultural and fishing subsides. This would yield a double dividend by benefiting the environment and the world economy at the same time.

(C) TENSIONS BETWEEN INTERNATIONAL TRADE RULES AND ENVIRONMENTAL MEASURES: IS A NEW EXCEPTION NEEDED?

We now examine a number of areas where it might be argued that stricter environmental measures are needed and consider whether existing WTO rules can accommodate such measures. In considering the following problems,[4] bear in mind the implications of the WTO cases we have studied, as well as the policy discussion put forward by Nordstrom and Vaughan. Regarding the cases, the particularly relevant decisions include *EC Asbestos* and *Brazil Tires* (French asbestos and Brazil retreaded tire bans found justified under Article XX(b), Section 13.2 supra); *US Gasoline* (discriminatory US regulation found to violate Article III, without Article XX justification, Section 13.4 supra); *US Shrimp* (US embargo on shrimp imports from countries not adopting US rules on turtle protection found to violate Article XI, without Article XX justification; but slightly revised US rules upheld on compliance review under Article XX, section 13.5 supra); and one case in the following chapter: *EC Hormones* (EC rules on use of growth hormones in cattle found not to be based on risk assessment, section 14.2 infra).

(1) Suppose that a country (ENV) wants to regulate the sale of a polluting or unsafe product in a way that could severely curtail imports from developing countries. Should such countries have a right to special and differential treatment (e.g., a transitional period; technical assistance for compliance)? Do they under current rules?

(2) ENV prohibits the importation of tropical hardwoods on the ground that imports of tropical hardwood products tend to induce deforestation in important tropical forest areas, and that such deforestation damages the world environment. ENV is a temperate zone nation with temperate forests, but does not apply any rule limiting the use of temperate forest products, domestic or imported. Should ENV's actions be permitted by WTO rules? Are they? Alternatively, suppose ENV does not ban importation of tropical hardwoods, but requires them to come

---

4. Some of the following problems have been adapted from John H. Jackson, World Trade and Environmental Policies: Congru-ence or Conflict?, 49 Wash. & Lee L. Rev. 1227 (1992).

from sustainably managed forests and/or be so labeled by an internationally recognized certification agency?

(3) ENV bans the use of a certain polluting production process in ENV. May it, consistently with WTO rules, also ban imported goods made using the polluting process? How is the like-product issue relevant to this? Can a measure discriminating among like products in violation of Article III nonetheless benefit from an Article XX exception, assuming that it falls within one of the specific subsections (e.g., XX(a) or XX(g))?

(4) ENV imposes a countervailing duty on any product that is imported from a country that does not have environmental rules as strict as those imposed by ENV. ENV argues that the lack of such a rule is in effect a subsidy and that the subsidy should be off-set by a countervailing duty. Do current WTO rules on subsidies and countervailing duties permit such action? See Chapter 18.

The NAFTA environmental side agreement (see Documents Supplement) permits imposition of fines in the event that a party fails to enforce its own environmental rules. This provision was designed to discourage US companies from moving to Mexico to take advantage of Mexico's lax enforcement of environmental rules, thereby retaining access to the US market, but avoiding US environmental controls. How does the NAFTA provision differ from using countervailing duties as described in the preceding paragraph? Is the situation of a country that has agreed to follow a standard, but failed to, fundamentally different from that of a country that fails to meet standards unilaterally determined by someone else? Suppose that "someone else" is an international organization with broad membership?

(5) Suppose ENV subsidizes the purchase of environmental protection devices, such as smoke stack cleaners. When products from plants benefiting from the subsidy are exported, may an importing country impose a countervailing duty on ENV's exports to offset the benefits of the subsidy? Is it, or should it be, a defense that the subsidy was for a good purpose? What is the relevance of the "polluter pays" principle, which is generally recognized internationally and is one of the Rio Principles? See Chapter 18 and SCM Agreement, art. 8 (no longer in force).

(6) ENV establishes a rule that requires any business firm which sells a product in the ENV market to establish a center that will recycle, or appropriately dispose of, the product when the ENV consumer is finished with it or at the end of the product's useful life. Such centers are relatively easy for domestic producers to establish, but by their very nature are inherently much more difficult for importers or exporters, and particularly difficult for exporters of small quantities to establish. Should this requirement be permitted by WTO rules? Is it? What about rules limiting the use of packaging materials, which impact some imported products more than similar domestic products?

(7) ENV bans importation of a product, justifying its action by reference to an MEA authorizing such action. How would such an action

be judged under WTO rules? What if the MEA required the ban or if ENV claimed that its action facilitated achievement of the MEA's goals? Would it make a difference whether the WTO member challenging the ban was a party to the MEA? Consider the relevance of the interpretative rules discussed in Section 7.4(C) supra.

The North American Free Trade Agreement specifies in Article 104 that the trade obligations of certain specified international environmental agreements prevail over NAFTA, "provided that where a Party has a choice among equally effective and reasonably available means of complying with such obligations, the Party chooses the alternative that is least inconsistent with the other provisions of [NAFTA]." The agreements initially specified were (i) the Convention on International Trade in Endangered Species of Wild Fauna and Flora; (ii) the Montreal Protocol on Substances that Deplete the Ozone Layer; (iii) the Basel Convention on the Control of Transboundary Movements of Hazardous Wastes and Their Disposal; (iv) the US–Canada Agreement Concerning the Transboundary Movement of Hazardous Waste; and (v) the US–Mexico Agreement on Cooperation for the Protection and Improvement of the Environment in the Border Area. Should WTO members agree on a similar list? Is the "least-inconsistent" test a workable one?

(8) In light of its concerns about global warning, ENV wants to impose a carbon tax on products to reflect the environmental costs of their production processes. To address the competitiveness concerns of its domestic industries, it wants to impose a similar charge on imported products. Would the GATT rules on border tax adjustments permit this? Recall note 8 and the review problems in Section 12.2. Is there a product vs. process distinction that is relevant here? In any event, could ENV defend its import charge under Article XX?

Given your answers to the foregoing problems, do the WTO agreements need to be changed to take account of environmental concerns? Can it be argued that the various Appellate Body decisions excerpted in this and other chapters give governments all the flexibility that they need to address such problems? Even if they seem to do so currently, is it appropriate to rely on judicial interpretations, as opposed to negotiated solutions in this area? Unfortunately, the environment negotiations in the Doha Round appear unlikely to produce significant results.

If a new environmental exception is needed in your view, how should such an exception be worded. It could be general and based on the wording of the WTO Agreement preamble—measures necessary to protect and preserve the environment—or it could be more focused. For example, the exception could be limited to specific environmental problems defined in the exception. Or, the exception could establish a framework under which measures meeting a specified standard would be permitted, such as, for example, measures taken pursuant to an MEA that has been ratified by some defined percentage of WTO members. An alternative approach to adding an exception would be to approve waivers in specific cases where existing exceptions are not broad enough to cover desired measures. This latter approach was followed in the so-called Kimberley Process, whereby a waiver was adopted in 2003 to allow WTO members to ban the import and export of rough diamonds to non-participants in the Kimberley Process. The aim of ban was to break the link between armed conflict and trade in rough diamonds. The detailed waiver request is contained in G/C/W/431 (November 12, 2002).

Chapter 14

TECHNICAL BARRIERS TO TRADE: THE SPS AND TBT AGREEMENTS

In this chapter, we examine the problems that arise from the application of technical regulations and standards, including measures taken for health reasons. We first consider why these issues are important in international trade. We then examine the two WTO agreements specifically addressing these problems—the Agreement on Sanitary and Phytosanitary Measures (the SPS Agreement), which applies in general to measures taken to protect human, animal and plant life or health from certain specified risks; and the Agreement on Technical Barriers to Trade (the TBT Agreement), which applies to the use of technical regulations and standards.

SECTION 14.1 INTRODUCTION

We begin with an overview of the problems associated with technical regulations and product standards, followed by a discussion of why the use of such measures for protectionist purposes may be a particularly worrisome type of practice.

ALAN O. SYKES, PRODUCT STANDARDS FOR INTERNATIONALLY INTEGRATED GOODS MARKETS 1–9 (1995)[1]

As tariffs have diminished pursuant to the GATT and other international agreements, the significance of non-tariff impediments to international trade has increased relatively and in some instances absolutely. Diverse standards and regulations governing the sale of products in national markets are a potential source of these non-tariff impediments, and in modern parlance may become "technical barriers to trade."

---

1. © 1995 The Brookings Institution. Reprinted with the permission of The Brookings Institution.

It is ironic that product standards and regulations should create trade barriers, as many of them evolved for the purpose of promoting trade. Familiar weights and measures developed to facilitate the description of goods in commerce and to obviate problems of fraud. Voltage standards allow electrical products to operate satisfactorily in different geographic areas. Standardized television broadcast formats enable programs of varying origin to be viewed on receivers of varying manufacture, a similar function being performed by standard operating systems for microcomputers. Regulations governing the wholesomeness of foodstuffs serve in part to reassure consumers of their safety and thereby to expand the market of willing buyers. Innumerable other examples might be offered.

Yet, it is not difficult to appreciate how these same measures can diverge across national markets and become trade impediments. Standards and regulations may be deliberately crafted to impose a cost disadvantage on foreign competitors. They may also differ across jurisdictions as a result of divergent tastes, because of variations in technology, income or resource endowments, or even by chance. It is thus common for goods that conform to all pertinent standards and regulatory requirements in their country of origin to fail to conform elsewhere. And, even when conformity to foreign standards and regulations is not difficult, the burden of *demonstrating* conformity to the satisfaction of consumers or regulators abroad can still be considerable. "Technical barriers" thus arise both from the divergence of standards and regulations across nations, and from the burden of establishing conformity with them whether or not they are divergent.

It is useful to begin with some terminology. I define a product "standard" as a specification or set of specifications that relates to some characteristic of a product or its manufacture. It may relate to its size, its dimensions, its weight, its design, its function, its ingredients, or any number of other product attributes. It may or may not be formally promulgated by a private or public standard-setting entity. The distinguishing feature of a "standard" is that compliance is *voluntary*. Thus, products that do not conform to a standard are legally permitted to be sold and any penalty for non-conformity is a market one. A "regulation" differs from a standard only in this key respect—it too may relate to any aspect of product characteristics or manufacture, but compliance with a regulation is legally *mandatory*. It is not uncommon for standards to be converted into regulations by government fiat.

* * *

* * * [T]he trading community needs more information about technical barriers. Their importance sector by sector is generally unknown, as is their impact on economic welfare. Additional, systematic research into their incidence and magnitude would be immensely beneficial. And, because information about the problem is so scant, my remaining conclusions must be viewed as quite tentative.

In brief, I conclude that many problems of potential technological *incompatibility* are handled adequately by existing institutions. Decentralized market forces suffice to avoid unproductive incompatibilities (not all are undesirable) in a considerable percentage of cases. Other problems are averted through the work of international standardizing bodies such as the International Organization for Standardization (ISO), which facilitate cooperative activity among national standardizers and do much to avoid unproductive incompatibilities that might otherwise arise by accident.

Nevertheless, some notable compatibility problems have arisen that market forces and international standardizing bodies have not averted, the bulk of which fall into two categories. The first involves incompatibilities that predate extensive international trade or modern international standardization efforts, such as those due to differences between the imperial and metric systems. The second involves incompatibilities associated with new, proprietary technologies, where the selection of a standard necessarily favors one producer group over another and national or sub-national interest groups may block the consensus needed for the adoption of an international (or even national) standard. Historical controversies over television broadcast format standards are illustrative here.

Little can be done at the global level about most problems that fall into the first category. At bottom, the question is whether the nations that adhere to a minority standard would benefit on balance from switching given all of the costs involved, a question that is not always easy to answer (consider the debate in the United States over metric conversion). If the answer is yes, government action will be necessary to make the change for a variety of reasons. But these are primarily matters of national rather than international policy, and I do not dwell on them at length.

As for the second group of incompatibility problems, it is not easy to imagine any reform of international institutions that would eliminate them, and that would also be politically feasible. Outside of the European Community, nations have shown no willingness to cede sovereignty to a central authority with the power to compel them to follow a particular technological standard. Treaty covenants to utilize international standards such as those in the GATT system are also unlikely to be effective, either because the adoption of an international standard is blocked by a lack of consensus or because nations will opt out (as GATT allows). Consequently, when divergence of producer interests threatens to create inefficient incompatibilities in global markets, the best hope for solution may lie in explicit or implicit side payments among producers, as through joint ventures or mergers.

Turning to matters of product *quality*, I find it helpful to distinguish between technical barriers that result from a divergence of national goals and preferences regarding quality, and barriers that result from a divergence in the means selected to achieve similar goals and preferences. I recognize that this line is not always easy to draw, but it can be operationalized easily in many cases and is quite a useful analytical construct.

Legal constraints upon national sovereigns such as those in the GATT system—an approach that I term "policed decentralization"—can respond fairly well in principle to the barriers that result from divergent means to the same end. The most important legal constraint here is the "least restrictive means principle." Related or corollary principles include nondiscrimination requirements, generality requirements, an obligation to employ existing international standards and to afford mutual recognition where adequate to meet domestic objectives, an obligation to justify a refusal of mutual recognition, and others. Adherence to these principles can readily avert technical barriers that result from chance differences in national standards and regulations, and to a lesser extent can police problems of capture by exposing them and subjecting nations that use quality measures for protectionist purposes to reputational penalties or retaliation. In the end, however, the effectiveness of the GATT system or any other legal system for policing these technical barriers also depends upon diligence in enforcement and compliance efforts. On this score, the GATT is apparently less successful to date (though systematic information is again lacking). Recent improvements in GATT dispute resolution as a result of the Uruguay Round have the potential to considerably strengthen the effectiveness of the system, as does the extension of GATT obligations to matters not previously covered (such as process and production standards). * * *

When technical barriers result from genuine differences in national goals and objectives regarding quality, general legal obligations such as those in the GATT system can accomplish much less. Indeed, it is precisely here that "technical barriers" may be economically efficient, and it becomes difficult to know whether anything ought be done about them at all. The reduction of technical barriers in this category will likely come primarily from international cooperation to achieve complete or partial harmonization. * * *

ALAN O. SYKES, REGULATORY PROTECTIONISM AND THE LAW OF INTERNATIONAL TRADE[2]

Government regulation of product markets can increase the costs of production for firms outside of the regulating jurisdiction ("foreign firms") more than it increases costs for firms inside the regulating jurisdiction ("domestic firms") and thereby confer a competitive advantage on domestic firms. I define "regulatory protectionism" as any cost disadvantage imposed on foreign firms by a regulatory policy that discriminates against them or that otherwise disadvantages them in a manner that is unnecessary to the attainment of some genuine, nonpro-

2. 66 U.Chi.L.Rev. 1, 3–6 (1999), ©1999,   ed with permission.
University of Chicago Law Review, reprint-

tectionist regulatory objective. Regulatory protectionism can result either from substantive regulatory requirements or from the mechanisms used by regulators to ensure compliance with substantive requirements (the "conformity assessment" process). It need not be deliberate and may result simply from regulators' failure to appreciate the trade impact of their policies.

To give a few examples, a nation may regulate the pharmaceutical market by requiring government approval of new drugs before they may be sold. If, however, the regulatory authorities require foreign pharmaceutical manufacturers to engage in more testing and clinical trials than domestic manufacturers with no apparent health justification for this difference in treatment, regulatory protectionism arises. Similarly, a policy prohibiting the use of some food preservative in imported foodstuffs, but allowing its use domestically, would constitute regulatory protectionism.

Such cases of overt discrimination provide the clearest examples, but, as the beef hormones case illustrates, facially nondiscriminatory policies may also constitute regulatory protectionism. The European regulation at issue in the beef hormones case imposes a cost disadvantage on foreign suppliers from nations that permit the use of growth hormones, because it requires them to undertake costly measures to certify their exports as hormone-free. European beef producers, however, need not concern themselves with the measures, because hormones are purportedly not used at all in Europe. And because this cost disadvantage results from a regulation that is not necessary to attain any legitimate public health objective (according to WTO findings), it constitutes "regulatory protectionism" as defined in this Article.

It is easy to imagine other examples of facially neutral regulatory protectionism. Transportation regulators might require that all new automobiles sold in the domestic market be equipped with a particular type of airbag that is only manufactured domestically, even though other types of airbags manufactured abroad (and available more cheaply to foreign automobile manufacturers) are just as safe and effective. Or regulators might require all products of a certain type to be tested at a particular laboratory that surreptitiously expedites the processing of domestic goods, even though other laboratories could perform the job adequately.

By contrast, some regulations have a protective effect (raising the costs of foreign firms more than the costs of domestic firms), but are nondiscriminatory and necessary to attain a genuine, nonprotectionist regulatory objective. In legal parlance, they might be called the "least restrictive means" to obtain that objective. For example, a nation may wish to attain a higher level of air quality than others and may require all automobiles sold in the domestic market to meet comparatively stringent hydrocarbon emissions standards. Foreign manufacturers may have higher unit costs of compliance—perhaps they sell few vehicles into the country in question and thus are unable to reap the same scale economies or learning-by-doing economies in regulatory compliance that accrue to domestic firms with larger sales volumes. But if the regulation is nondiscriminatory and no less restrictive alternative is available to meet air quality goals, then the measure does not constitute regulatory protectionism as defined in this Article.

So defined, regulatory protectionism is economically inefficient, in part for the same reasons that protectionism of any sort is inefficient. Protectionism draws high cost domestic firms into the market while excluding low cost foreign firms, and it prices out of the market some consumers who would be willing to purchase goods at a price exceeding the marginal cost of production of efficient suppliers. What previous work has not appreciated, however, is that in most cases regulatory protectionism causes additional deadweight losses that make it considerably more inefficient than other instruments of protection such as tariffs, quotas, and subsidies. Accordingly, the societal returns to legal constraints on regulatory protectionism are greater, other things being equal, than the societal returns to constraints on other protectionist instruments. * * *

[F]rom a political standpoint, regulatory protectionism is an inferior form of protectionism for nations that are unconstrained in their trade policies. But after a nation enters into a trade agreement, circumstances may arise that tempt political officials to employ regulatory protectionism due to constraints on their ability to use other preferred protectionist instruments. It is in the mutual interest of political actors who bind themselves to trade agreements to disable themselves from behaving in this fashion if possible and to encourage renegotiation of the agreed-upon constraints on the politically "efficient" instruments of protection instead. Further, the degree of trade protection afforded by regulatory measures may be difficult to quantify, and the transaction costs of reciprocal trade negotiations can be lowered if protectionism is restricted to more transparent instruments such as tariffs. This line of reasoning affords a "political economy" explanation for the fact that regulatory protectionism is prohibited under the treaty creating the WTO even though various other forms of protectionism are permissible (albeit subject to constraint). The lesson here is but a special case of a more general insight developed in the literature on public choice and regulation—where the self-interest of political actors requires an inefficient transfer of rents to well-organized interest groups (here, domestic industries that seek insulation from foreign competition), it is often best to make that inefficient transfer as efficiently as possible.

Notes and Questions

(1) Why is regulatory protection a potentially greater source of economic inefficiency than other protectionist policies such as tariffs, quotas, and subsidies? Compare, for example, the tariff. A tariff yields revenue to the government equal to the product of the tariff times the quantity (specific tariff) or value (ad valorem tariff) of imports. This government revenue is part of economic surplus for the importing nation (recall the analysis of

tariffs in Chapter 2). What happens to this surplus when regulatory protection is used instead? On your own, consider the same comparison between quotas and subsidies on the one hand, and regulatory protection on the other.

(2) Consider a government that wishes to protect a domestic industry that faces competition from imported goods subject to an unbound tariff. Is it clear why that government would prefer to use the tariff to achieve that objective rather than some protectionist regulatory measure? Once the tariff is bound, by contrast, and the tariff is already at its maximum, the government must turn to some other instrument. This observation suggests one reason why, as tariffs were lowered through the years under GATT, non-tariff barriers such as regulatory protection became more important.

(3) The original GATT discipline on regulatory barriers was simply the national treatment principle of Article III. As you proceed through this chapter, reflect on the question of why the national treatment obligation alone came to be perceived as inadequate. The first technical barriers agreement emerged as a plurilateral agreement during the Tokyo Round, and was ultimately supplanted by the TBT Agreement and the SPS Agreement as part of the single undertaking that established the WTO.

SECTION 14.2   THE SPS AGREEMENT

One of the major goals of the Uruguay Round negotiations was to bring agricultural trade back within GATT disciplines. As noted earlier (Section 9.3), for most of GATT's existence its disciplines were not very effective in the agricultural sector because of waivers, lack of tariff bindings and the widespread use of some questionable non-tariff barriers. Among the non-tariff barriers that concerned negotiators were measures ostensibly taken for sanitary or phytosanitary (SPS) purposes. The attention given this subject ultimately resulted in a separate WTO agreement—the Agreement on Sanitary and Phytosanitary Measures, better known as the SPS Agreement.[1]

The basic obligations of the SPS Agreement are set out in article 2. In essence, while article (2)1 recognizes the right of WTO members to take SPS measures necessary to protect life or health, article 2(2) requires them to apply such measures only to the extent necessary to protect life or health, to base them on scientific principles and not to maintain them without sufficient scientific evidence (subject to a precautionary principle exception). In addition, article 2(3) requires that SPS measures not arbitrarily or unjustifiably discriminate between WTO members where identical or similar conditions prevail and not be applied in a manner that would constitute a disguised restriction on international trade.

Article 3(1) of the SPS Agreement requires WTO members to base their SPS measures on international standards where they exist and if they do so, they are presumed to be in compliance with the agreement

---

1. See generally Joanne Scott, The WTO Agreement on Sanitary and Phyto-sanitary Measures: A Commentary (Oxford University Press, 2007).

(article 3(2)). However, article 3(3) allows them to introduce SPS measures that result in a higher level of SPS protection than would be achieved by measures based on international standards, so long as they are scientifically justified, i.e., based on a risk assessment conducted pursuant to article 5 of the agreement. As a result, it can be said that the SPS Agreement promotes international harmonization, but does not require it.

The SPS Agreement has been the subject of several disputes that have resulted in panel and Appellate Body decisions—dealing with measures to protect human, animal and plant health. The following is perhaps the best known and most controversial of the cases—"beef hormones." The dispute dates back to the 1980's, and resulted in retaliatory tariffs by the United States in the waning years of GATT when the dispute settlement process in the case was at impasse. With the creation of the WTO, the dispute quickly found it way into the WTO dispute settlement system.

EC MEASURES CONCERNING MEAT AND MEAT PRODUCTS (HORMONES)

WT/DS26 & 48AB/R.
Appellate Body Report adopted February 13, 1998.

2.   The Panel dealt with a complaint against the European Communities relating to an EC prohibition of imports of meat and meat products derived from cattle to which either the natural hormones: oestradiol–17ß, progesterone or testosterone, or the synthetic hormones: trenbolone acetate, zeranol or melengestrol acetate ("MGA"), had been administered for growth promotion purposes.

[In reversing the Panel's interpretation of Article 3 of the SPS Agreement, the Appellate Body expressed important views on treaty interpretation generally. It stated in paragraph 164:

"We cannot lightly assume that sovereign states intended to impose upon themselves the more onerous, rather than the less burdensome, obligation by mandating conformity or compliance with such standards, guidelines and recommendations."

In footnote 154 attached to this sentence, the Appellate Body elaborated:

"The interpretative principle of *in dubio mitius*, widely recognized in international law as a 'supplementary means of interpretation', has been expressed in the following terms: 'The principle of *in dubio mitius* applies in interpreting treaties, in deference to the sovereignty of states. If the meaning of a term is ambiguous, that meaning is to be preferred which is less onerous to the party assuming an obligation, or which interferes less with the territorial and personal supremacy of a party, or involves less general restrictions upon the parties.' R. Jennings and A. Watts (eds.), Oppenheim's International Law, 9th ed., Vol. I (Longman, 1992), p. 1278."]

* * *

179. Article 5.1 of the *SPS Agreement* provides:

> Members shall ensure that their sanitary or phytosanitary measures are <u>based on an assessment, as appropriate to the circumstances,</u> of <u>the risks to human,</u> animal or plant <u>life or health,</u> taking into account risk assessment techniques developed by the relevant international organizations. (underlining added)

180. At the outset, two preliminary considerations need to be brought out. The first is that the Panel considered that Article 5.1 may be viewed as a specific application of the basic obligations contained in Article 2.2 of the *SPS Agreement*, which reads as follows:

> Members shall ensure that any sanitary or phytosanitary measure is applied only <u>to the extent necessary to protect</u> human, animal or plant life or health, is <u>based on scientific principles</u> and is not maintained without <u>sufficient scientific evidence,</u> except as provided for in paragraph 7 of Article 5. (underlining added)

We agree with this general consideration and would also stress that Articles 2.2 and 5.1 should constantly be read together. Article 2.2 informs Article 5.1: the elements that define the basic obligation set out in Article 2.2 impart meaning to Article 5.1.

181. The second preliminary consideration relates to the Panel's effort to distinguish between "risk assessment" and "risk management". The Panel observed that an assessment of risk is, at least with respect to risks to human life and health, a "scientific" examination of data and factual studies; it is not, in the view of the Panel, a "policy" exercise involving social value judgments made by political bodies. The Panel describes the latter as "non-scientific" and as pertaining to "risk management" rather than to "risk assessment". We must stress, in this connection, that Article 5 and Annex A of the *SPS Agreement* speak of "risk assessment" only and that the term "risk management" is not to be found either in Article 5 or in any other provision of the *SPS Agreement*. Thus, the Panel's distinction, which it apparently employs to achieve or support what appears to be a restrictive notion of risk assessment, has no textual basis. The fundamental rule of treaty interpretation requires a treaty interpreter to read and interpret the words actually used by the agreement under examination, and not words which the interpreter may feel should have been used.

182. Paragraph 4 of Annex A of the *SPS Agreement* sets out the treaty definition of risk assessment: This definition, to the extent pertinent to the present appeal, speaks of:

> ... the evaluation of the <u>potential for adverse effects on human</u> or animal <u>health</u> arising from the presence of additives, contaminants, toxins or disease-causing organisms in food, beverages or feedstuffs. (underlining added)

183. Interpreting the above definition, the Panel elaborates risk assessment as a two-step process that "should (i) *identify* the *adverse effects* on human health (if any) arising from the presence of the

hormones at issue when used as growth promoters *in meat* . . ., and (ii) if any such adverse effects exist, *evaluate* the *potential* or probability of occurrence of such effects".

184.   The European Communities appeals from the above interpretation as involving an erroneous notion of risk and risk assessment. Although the utility of a two-step analysis may be debated, it does not appear to us to be substantially wrong. What needs to be pointed out at this stage is that the Panel's use of "probability" as an alternative term for "potential" creates a significant concern. The ordinary meaning of "potential" relates to "possibility" and is different from the ordinary meaning of "probability". "Probability" implies a higher degree or a threshold of potentiality or possibility. It thus appears that here the Panel introduces a quantitative dimension to the notion of risk.

185.   In its discussion on a statement made by Dr. Lucier at the joint meeting with the experts in February 1997, the Panel states the risk referred to by this expert is an estimate which " . . . only represents a statistical range of 0 to 1 in a million, not a scientifically identified risk". The European Communities protests vigorously that, by doing so, the Panel is in effect requiring a Member carrying out a risk assessment to quantify the potential for adverse effects on human health.

186.   It is not clear in what sense the Panel uses the term "scientifically identified risk". The Panel also frequently uses the term "identifiable risk", and does not define this term either. The Panel might arguably have used the terms "scientifically identified risk" and "identifiable risk" simply to refer to an ascertainable risk: if a risk is not ascertainable, how does a Member ever know or demonstrate that it exists? In one part of its Reports, the Panel opposes a requirement of an "identifiable risk" to the uncertainty that theoretically always remains since science can *never* provide *absolute* certainty that a given substance will not *ever* have adverse health effects. We agree with the Panel that this theoretical uncertainty is not the kind of risk which, under Article 5.1, is to be assessed. In another part of its Reports, however, the Panel appeared to be using the term "scientifically identified risk" to prescribe implicitly that a certain *magnitude* or threshold level of risk be demonstrated in a risk assessment if an SPS measure based thereon is to be regarded as consistent with Article 5.1. To the extent that the Panel purported to require a risk assessment to establish a minimum magnitude of risk, we must note that imposition of such a quantitative requirement finds no basis in the *SPS Agreement*. A panel is authorized only to determine whether a given SPS measure is "based on" a risk assessment. As will be elaborated below, this means that a panel has to determine whether an SPS measure is sufficiently supported or reasonably warranted by the risk assessment.

187.   Article 5.2 of the *SPS Agreement* provides an indication of the factors that should be taken into account in the assessment of risk. Article 5.2 states that:

> In the assessment of risks, Members shall take into account available scientific evidence; relevant processes and production methods; relevant inspection, sampling and testing methods; prevalence of specific diseases or pests; existence of pest- or disease-free areas; relevant ecological and environmental conditions; and quarantine or other treatment.

The listing in Article 5.2 begins with "available scientific evidence"; this, however, is only the beginning. We note in this connection that the Panel states that, for purposes of the EC measures in dispute, a risk assessment required by Article 5.1 is "a *scientific* process aimed at establishing the *scientific* basis for the sanitary measure a Member intends to take". To the extent that the Panel intended to refer to a process characterized by systematic, disciplined and objective enquiry and analysis, that is, a mode of studying and sorting out facts and opinions, the Panel's statement is unexceptionable. However, to the extent that the Panel purports to exclude from the scope of a risk assessment in the sense of Article 5.1, all matters not susceptible of quantitative analysis by the empirical or experimental laboratory methods commonly associated with the physical sciences, we believe that the Panel is in error. Some of the kinds of factors listed in Article 5.2 such as "relevant processes and production methods" and "relevant inspection, sampling and testing methods" are not necessarily or wholly susceptible of investigation according to laboratory methods of, for example, biochemistry or pharmacology. Furthermore, there is nothing to indicate that the listing of factors that may be taken into account in a risk assessment of Article 5.2 was intended to be a closed list. It is essential to bear in mind that the risk that is to be evaluated in a risk assessment under Article 5.1 is not only risk ascertainable in a science laboratory operating under strictly controlled conditions, but also risk in human societies as they actually exist, in other words, the actual potential for adverse effects on human health in the real world where people live and work and die.

188. Although it expressly recognizes that Article 5.1 does *not* contain any specific procedural requirements for a Member to base its sanitary measures on a risk assessment, the Panel nevertheless proceeds to declare that "there is a minimum procedural requirement contained in Article 5.1". That requirement is that "the Member imposing a sanitary measure needs to submit evidence that at least it actually *took into account* a risk assessment when it enacted or maintained its sanitary measure in order for that measure to be considered as *based on* a risk assessment". The Panel goes on to state that the European Communities did not provide any evidence that the studies it referred to or the scientific conclusions reached therein *"have actually been taken into account by the competent EC institutions* either when it *enacted* those measures (in 1981 and 1988) or *at any later point in time"*. (emphasis added) Thereupon, the Panel holds that such studies could not be considered as part of a risk assessment on which the European Communities based its measures in dispute. Concluding that the Europe-

an Communities had not met its burden of proving that it had satisfied the "minimum procedural requirement" it had found in Article 5.1, the Panel holds the EC measures as inconsistent with the requirements of Article 5.1.

189. We are bound to note that, as the Panel itself acknowledges, no textual basis exists in Article 5 of the *SPS Agreement* for such a "minimum procedural requirement". The term "based on", when applied as a "minimum procedural requirement" by the Panel, may be seen to refer to a human action, such as particular human individuals "taking into account" a document described as a risk assessment. Thus, "take into account" is apparently used by the Panel to refer to some subjectivity which, at some time, may be present in particular individuals but that, in the end, may be totally rejected by those individuals. We believe that "based on" is appropriately taken to refer to a certain *objective relationship* between two elements, that is to say, to an *objective situation* that persists and is observable between an SPS measure and a risk assessment. Such a reference is certainly embraced in the ordinary meaning of the words "based on" and, when considered in context and in the light of the object and purpose of Article 5.1 of the *SPS Agreement*, may be seen to be more appropriate than "taking into account". We do not share the Panel's interpretative construction and believe it is unnecessary and an error of law as well.

190. Article 5.1 does not insist that a Member that adopts a sanitary measure shall have carried out its own risk assessment. It only requires that the SPS measures be "based on an assessment, as appropriate for the circumstances ...". The SPS measure might well find its objective justification in a risk assessment carried out by another Member, or an international organization. The "minimum procedural requirement" constructed by the Panel, could well lead to the elimination or disregard of available scientific evidence that rationally supports the SPS measure being examined. This risk of exclusion of available scientific evidence may be particularly significant for the bulk of SPS measures which were put in place before the effective date of the *WTO Agreement* and that have been simply maintained thereafter.

191. In the course of demanding evidence that EC authorities actually "took into account" certain scientific studies, the Panel refers to the preambles of the EC Directives here involved. The Panel notes that such preambles did not mention any of the scientific studies referred to by the European Communities in the panel proceedings. Preambles of legislative or quasi-legislative acts and administrative regulations commonly fulfil requirements of the internal legal orders of WTO Members. Such preambles are certainly not required by the *SPS Agreement*; they are not normally used to demonstrate that a Member has complied with its obligations under international agreements. The absence of any mention of scientific studies in the preliminary sections of the EC Directives does not, therefore, prove anything so far as the present case is concerned.

192. Having posited a "minimum procedural requirement" of Article 5.1, the Panel turns to the "substantive requirements" of Article 5.1 to determine whether the EC measures at issue are "based on" a risk assessment. In the Panel's view, those "substantive requirements" involve two kinds of operations: first, identifying the scientific conclusions reached in the risk assessment and the scientific conclusions implicit in the SPS measures; and secondly, examining those scientific conclusions to determine whether or not one set of conclusions matches, i.e. conforms with, the second set of conclusions. Applying the "substantive requirements" it finds in Article 5.1, the Panel holds that the scientific conclusions implicit in the EC measures do not conform with any of the scientific conclusions reached in the scientific studies the European Communities had submitted as evidence.

193. We consider that, in principle, the Panel's approach of examining the scientific conclusions implicit in the SPS measure under consideration and the scientific conclusion yielded by a risk assessment is a useful approach. The relationship between those two sets of conclusions is certainly relevant; they cannot, however, be assigned relevance to the exclusion of everything else. We believe that Article 5.1, when contextually read as it should be, in conjunction with and as informed by Article 2.2 of the *SPS Agreement*, requires that the results of the risk assessment must sufficiently warrant—that is to say, reasonably support—the SPS measure at stake. The requirement that an SPS measure be "based on" a risk assessment is a substantive requirement that there be a rational relationship between the measure and the risk assessment.

194. We do not believe that a risk assessment has to come to a monolithic conclusion that coincides with the scientific conclusion or view implicit in the SPS measure. The risk assessment could set out both the prevailing view representing the "mainstream" of scientific opinion, as well as the opinions of scientists taking a divergent view. Article 5.1 does not require that the risk assessment must necessarily embody only the view of a majority of the relevant scientific community. In some cases, the very existence of divergent views presented by qualified scientists who have investigated the particular issue at hand may indicate a state of scientific uncertainty. Sometimes the divergence may indicate a roughly equal balance of scientific opinion, which may itself be a form of scientific uncertainty. In most cases, responsible and representative governments tend to base their legislative and administrative measures on "mainstream" scientific opinion. In other cases, equally responsible and representative governments may act in good faith on the basis of what, at a given time, may be a divergent opinion coming from qualified and respected sources. By itself, this does not necessarily signal the absence of a reasonable relationship between the SPS measure and the risk assessment, especially where the risk involved is life-threatening in character and is perceived to constitute a clear and imminent threat to public health and safety. Determination of the presence or absence of that relationship can only be done on a case-to-case basis, after account

is taken of all considerations rationally bearing upon the issue of potential adverse health effects.

195. We turn now to the application by the Panel of the substantive requirements of Article 5.1 to the EC measures at stake in the present case. The Panel lists the following scientific material to which the European Communities referred in respect of the hormones here involved [list omitted].

196. Several of the above scientific reports appeared to the Panel to meet the minimum requirements of a risk assessment, in particular, the Lamming Report [commissioned by the EC] and the 1988 and 1989 JECFA Reports [prepared for Codex Alimentarius—a FAO–WHO body]. The Panel assumes accordingly that the European Communities had demonstrated the existence of a risk assessment carried out in accordance with Article 5 of the *SPS Agreement*. At the same time, the Panel finds that the conclusion of these scientific reports is that the use of the hormones at issue (except MGA) for growth promotion purposes is "safe". The Panel states:

> .... none of the scientific evidence referred to by the European Communities which specifically addresses the safety of some or all of the hormones in dispute when used for growth promotion, indicates that an identifiable risk arises for human health from such use of these hormones if good practice is followed. All of the scientific studies outlined above came to the conclusion that the use of the hormones at issue (all but MGA, for which no evidence was submitted) for growth promotion purposes is safe; most of these studies adding that this conclusion assumes that good practice is followed.

197. Prescinding from the difficulty raised by the Panel's use of the term "identifiable risk", we agree that the scientific reports listed above do not rationally support the EC import prohibition.

198. With regard to the scientific opinion expressed by Dr. Lucier at the joint meeting with the experts, and as set out in paragraph 819 of the Annex to the US and Canada Panel Reports[2], we should note that this opinion by Dr. Lucier does not purport to be the result of scientific studies carried out by him or under his supervision focusing specifically on residues of hormones in meat from cattle fattened with such hormones. Accordingly, it appears that the single divergent opinion expressed by Dr. Lucier is not reasonably sufficient to overturn the contrary conclusions reached in the scientific studies referred to by the European Communities that related specifically to residues of the hor-

---

2. This paragraph reads in relevant part: "For every million women alive in the United States, Canada, Europe today, about 110,000 of those women will get breast cancer. This is obviously a tremendous public health issue. Of those 110,000 women [who] get breast cancer, maybe several thousand of them are related to the total intake of exogenous oestrogens from every source, including eggs, meat, phyto-oestrogens, fungal oestrogens, the whole body burden of exogenous oestrogens. And by my estimates one of those 110,000 would come from eating meat containing oestrogens as a growth promoter, if used as prescribed." [Note that Dr. Lucier was explaining here his earlier expressed view that the risk was between zero and one in a million–see para. 185.]

mones in meat from cattle to which hormones had been administered for growth promotion.

199.   The European Communities laid particular emphasis on the 1987 IARC [International Agency for Research on Cancer] Monographs and the articles and opinions of individual scientists referred to above. The Panel notes, however, that the scientific evidence set out in these Monographs and these articles and opinions relates to the carcinogenic potential of entire *categories* of hormones, or of the hormones at issue *in general*. The Monographs and the articles and opinions are, in other words, in the nature of general studies of or statements on the carcinogenic potential of the named hormones. The Monographs and the articles and opinions of individual scientists have not evaluated the carcinogenic potential of those hormones when used specifically *for growth promotion purposes*. Moreover, they do not evaluate the specific potential for carcinogenic effects arising from the presence *in "food"*, more specifically, "meat or meat products" of residues of the hormones in dispute. The Panel also notes that, according to the scientific experts advising the Panel, the data and studies set out in these 1987 Monographs have been taken into account in the 1988 and 1989 JECFA Reports and that the conclusions reached by the 1987 IARC Monographs are complementary to, rather than contradictory of, the conclusions of the JECFA Reports. The Panel concludes that these Monographs and these articles and opinions are insufficient to support the EC measures at issue in this case.

200.   We believe that the above findings of the Panel are justified. The 1987 IARC Monographs and the articles and opinions of individual scientists submitted by the European Communities constitute general studies which do indeed show the existence of a general risk of cancer; but they do not focus on and do not address the particular kind of risk here at stake—the carcinogenic or genotoxic potential of the residues of those hormones found in meat derived from cattle to which the hormones had been administered for growth promotion purposes—as is required by paragraph 4 of Annex A of the *SPS Agreement*. Those general studies, are in other words, relevant but do not appear to be sufficiently specific to the case at hand.

201.   With regard to risk assessment concerning MGA, the European Communities referred to the 1987 IARC Monographs. These Monographs deal with, *inter alia*, the category of progestins of which the hormone progesterone is a member. The European Communities argues that because MGA is an anabolic agent which mimics the action of progesterone, the scientific studies and experiments relied on by the 1987 IARC Monographs were highly relevant. However, the Monographs and the articles and opinions of the individual scientists did not include any study that demonstrated how closely related MGA is chemically and pharmacologically to other progestins and what effects MGA residues would actually have on human beings when such residues are ingested along with meat from cattle to which MGA has been administered for growth promotion purposes. It must be recalled in this connection that

none of the other scientific material submitted by the European Communities referred to MGA, and that no international standard, guideline or recommendation has been developed by Codex relating specifically to MGA. The United States and Canada declined to submit any assessment of MGA upon the ground that the material they were aware of was proprietary and confidential in nature. In other words, there was an almost complete absence of evidence on MGA in the panel proceedings. We therefore uphold the Panel's finding that there was no risk assessment with regard to MGA.

202.   The evidence referred to above by the European Communities related to the biochemical risk arising from the ingestion by human beings of residues of the five hormones here involved in treated meat, where such hormones had been administered to the cattle in accordance with good veterinary practice. The European Communities also referred to distinguishable but closely related risks—risks arising from failure to observe the requirements of good veterinary practice, in combination with multiple problems relating to detection and control of such abusive failure, in the administration of hormones to cattle for growth promotion.

203.   The Panel considers this type of risk and examines the arguments made by the European Communities but finds no assessment of such kind of risk. Ultimately, the Panel rejects those arguments principally on *a priori* grounds. First, to the Panel, the provisions of Article 5.2 relating to "relevant inspection, sampling and testing methods":

> . . . do not seem to cover the general problem of control (such as the problem of ensuring the observance of good practice) which can exist for any substance. The risks related to the general problem of control do not seem to be specific to the substance at issue but to the economic or social incidence related to a substance or its particular use (such as economic incentives for abuse). These non-scientific factors should, therefore not be taken into account in a risk assessment but in *risk management*. (underlining added)

Moreover, the Panel finds that, assuming these factors could be taken into account in a risk assessment, the European Communities has not provided convincing evidence that the control or prevention of abuse of the hormones here involved is more difficult than the control of other veterinary drugs, the use of which is allowed in the European Communities. Further, the European Communities has not provided evidence that control would be more difficult under a regime where the use of the hormones in dispute is allowed under specific conditions than under the current EC regime of total prohibition both domestically and in respect of imported meat. The Panel concludes by saying that banning the use of a substance does not necessarily offer better protection of human health than other means of regulating its use.

204.   The European Communities appeals from these findings of the Panel principally on two grounds: firstly, that the Panel has misin-

terpreted Article 5.2 of the *SPS Agreement*; secondly, that the Panel has disregarded and distorted the evidence submitted by the European Communities.

205. In respect of the first ground, we agree with the European Communities that the Panel has indeed misconceived the scope of application of Article 5.2. It should be recalled that Article 5.2 states that in the assessment of risks, Members shall take into account, in addition to "available scientific evidence", "relevant processes and production methods; [and] relevant inspection, sampling and testing methods". We note also that Article 8 requires Members to "observe the provisions of Annex C in the operation of control, inspection and approval procedures . . .". The footnote in Annex C states that "control, inspection and approval procedures include, *inter alia*, procedures for sampling, testing and certification". We consider that this language is amply sufficient to authorize the taking into account of risks arising from failure to comply with the requirements of good veterinary practice in the administration of hormones for growth promotion purposes, as well as risks arising from difficulties of control, inspection and enforcement of the requirements of good veterinary practice.

206. Most, if not all, of the scientific studies referred to by the European Communities, in respect of the five hormones involved here, concluded that their use for growth promotion purposes is "safe", if the hormones are administered in accordance with the requirements of good veterinary practice. Where the condition of observance of good veterinary practice (which is much the same condition attached to the standards, guidelines and recommendations of Codex with respect to the use of the five hormones for growth promotion) is *not* followed, the logical inference is that the use of such hormones for growth promotion purposes may or may not be "safe". The *SPS Agreement* requires assessment of the potential for adverse effects on human health arising from the presence of contaminants and toxins in food. We consider that the object and purpose of the *SPS Agreement* justify the examination and evaluation of all such risks for human health whatever their precise and immediate origin may be. We do not mean to suggest that risks arising from potential abuse in the administration of controlled substances and from control problems need to be, or should be, evaluated by risk assessors in each and every case. When and if risks of these types do in fact arise, risk assessors may examine and evaluate them. Clearly, the necessity or propriety of examination and evaluation of such risks would have to be addressed on a case-by-case basis. What, in our view, is a fundamental legal error is to exclude, on an *a priori* basis, any such risks from the scope of application of Articles 5.1 and 5.2. We disagree with the Panel's suggestion that exclusion of risks resulting from the combination of potential abuse and difficulties of control is justified by distinguishing between "risk assessment" and "risk management". As earlier noted, the concept of "risk management" is not mentioned in any provision of the *SPS Agreement* and, as such, cannot be used to sustain a more restrictive interpretation of "risk assessment" than is justified by

the actual terms of Article 5.2, Article 8 and Annex C of the *SPS Agreement*.

207.   The question that arises, therefore, is whether the European Communities did, in fact, submit a risk assessment demonstrating and evaluating the existence and level of risk arising in the present case from abusive use of hormones and the difficulties of control of the administration of hormones for growth promotion purposes, within the United States and Canada as exporting countries, and at the frontiers of the European Communities as an importing country. Here, we must agree with the finding of the Panel that the European Communities in fact restricted itself to pointing out the condition of administration of hormones "in accordance with good practice" "without further providing an assessment of the potential adverse effects related to non compliance with such practice". The record of the panel proceedings shows that the risk arising from abusive use of hormones for growth promotion combined with control problems for the hormones at issue, may have been examined on two occasions in a scientific manner. The first occasion may have occurred at the proceedings before the Committee of Inquiry into the Problem of Quality in the Meat Sector established by the European Parliament, the results of which constituted the basis of the Pimenta Report of 1989. However, none of the original studies and evidence put before the Committee of Inquiry was submitted to the Panel. The second occasion could have been the 1995 EC Scientific Conference on Growth Promotion in Meat Production. One of the three workshops of this Conference examined specifically the problems of "detection and control". However, only one of the studies presented to the workshop discussed systematically some of the problems arising from the combination of potential abuse and problems of control of hormones and other substances. The study presented a theoretical framework for the systematic analysis of such problems, but did not itself investigate and evaluate the actual problems that have arisen at the borders of the European Communities or within the United States, Canada and other countries exporting meat and meat products to the European Communities. At best, this study may represent the beginning of an assessment of such risks.

208.   In the absence of any other relevant documentation, we find that the European Communities did not actually proceed to an assessment, within the meaning of Articles 5.1 and 5.2, of the risks arising from the failure of observance of good veterinary practice combined with problems of control of the use of hormones for growth promotion purposes. The absence of such a risk assessment, when considered in conjunction with the conclusion actually reached by most, if not all, of the scientific studies relating to the other aspects of risk noted earlier, leads us to the conclusion that no risk assessment that reasonably supports or warrants the import prohibition embodied in the EC Directives was furnished to the Panel. We affirm, therefore, the ultimate conclusion of the Panel that the EC import prohibition is not based on a risk assessment within the meaning of Articles 5.1 and 5.2 of the *SPS*

Agreement and is, therefore, inconsistent with the requirements of Article 5.1.

Notes and Questions

(1) The Appellate Body dealt with many other issues on this appeal. In particular, it ruled that the burden of proof to show a violation of Article 5 was on the complainants. It upheld a number of important procedural rulings made by the panel, in particular in respect of the selection and use of experts under DSU article 13. It also established a standard for determining whether a panel had failed to meet its obligation under DSU article 11 to make an objective assessment of the matter before it (see Section 7.3 infra). In that respect, it engaged in a searching and often critical examination of how the panel had evaluated certain evidence.

(2) The EC measures at issue were adopted and came into effect before 1995, the effective date of the WTO Agreement. Why were they subject to the risk assessment requirements of the SPS Agreement at all?

(3) Article 5.7 of the SPS Agreement contains a version of what is known as the precautionary principle. To be specific, it provides:

> In cases where scientific evidence is insufficient, a [WTO] Member may provisionally adopt [SPS] measures on the basis of available pertinent information, including that from the relevant international organizations as well as from [SPS] measures applied by other Members. In such circumstances, Members shall seek to obtain the additional information necessary for a more objective assessment of risk and review the [SPS] measure accordingly within a reasonable period of time.

In response to a question from the panel, the EC declined to invoke this provision. On appeal, however, it argued that there was the precautionary principle had become a general customary rule of international law or at least a general principle of law on which it could rely to justify its measures. In response, the US suggested that the precautionary principle was more an "approach" than a "principle". Canada took the view that the principle had not yet been incorporated into the corpus of public international law, even though it might in the future crystallize as a general principle of law. The Appellate Body addressed the argument as follows:

> 123.   The status of the precautionary principle in international law continues to be the subject of debate among academics, law practitioners, regulators and judges. The precautionary principle is regarded by some as having crystallized into a general principle of customary international *environmental* law. Whether it has been widely accepted by Members as a principle of *general* or *customary international law* appears less than clear. We consider, however, that it is unnecessary, and probably imprudent, for the Appellate Body in this appeal to take a position on this important, but abstract, question. We note that the Panel itself did not make any definitive finding with regard to the status of the precautionary principle in international law and that the precautionary principle, at least outside the field of international environmental law, still awaits authoritative formulation.

124. It appears to us important, nevertheless, to note some aspects of the relationship of the precautionary principle to the *SPS Agreement*. First, the principle has not been written into the *SPS Agreement* as a ground for justifying SPS measures that are otherwise inconsistent with the obligations of Members set out in particular provisions of that Agreement. Secondly, the precautionary principle indeed finds reflection in Article 5.7 of the *SPS Agreement*. We agree, at the same time, with the European Communities, that there is no need to assume that Article 5.7 exhausts the relevance of a precautionary principle. It is reflected also in the sixth paragraph of the preamble and in Article 3.3. These explicitly recognize the right of Members to establish their own appropriate level of sanitary protection, which level may be higher (i.e., more cautious) than that implied in existing international standards, guidelines and recommendations. Thirdly, a panel charged with determining, for instance, whether "sufficient scientific evidence" exists to warrant the maintenance by a Member of a particular SPS measure may, of course, and should, bear in mind that responsible, representative governments commonly act from perspectives of prudence and precaution where risks of irreversible, e.g. life-terminating, damage to human health are concerned. Lastly, however, the precautionary principle does not, by itself, and without a clear textual directive to that effect, relieve a panel from the duty of applying the normal (i.e. customary international law) principles of treaty interpretation in reading the provisions of the *SPS Agreement*.

125. We accordingly agree with the finding of the Panel that the precautionary principle does not override the provisions of Articles 5.1 and 5.2 of the *SPS Agreement*.

Japan invoked the SPS Agreement's precautionary principle in the so-called *Agricultural Products II* case, but was found not to have shown that it had taken any action to comply with the second sentence of article 5.7. Japan— Measures Affecting Agricultural Products, WT/DS76/AB/R, paras. 86–94 (Appellate Body Report adopted March 19, 1999).

(4) The panel in *EC Hormones* found that the EC also violated article 5.5 of the SPS Agreement, which provides as follows:

With the objective of achieving consistency in the application of the concept of appropriate level of [SPS] protection against risks to human life or health, or to animal and plant life or health, each Member shall avoid arbitrary or unjustifiable distinctions in the levels it considers to be appropriate in different situations, if such distinctions result in discrimination or a disguised restriction on international trade.

In particular, the panel concluded that the EC had made an arbitrary or unjustifiable distinction in banning the use of hormones for growth promotion purposes in meat production, but not regulating their natural occurrence in meat and other foods (and that such distinction had resulted in discrimination or a disguised restriction on trade). On appeal, the Appellate Body reversed the panel's finding of an arbitrary or unjustifiable distinction, noting:

221. We do not share the Panel's conclusions that the above differences in levels of protection in respect of added hormones in treated

meat and in respect of naturally-occurring hormones in food, are merely arbitrary and unjustifiable. To the contrary, we consider there is a fundamental distinction between added hormones (natural or synthetic) and naturally-occurring hormones in meat and other foods. In respect of the latter, the European Communities simply takes no regulatory action; to require it to prohibit totally the production and consumption of such foods or to limit the residues of naturally-occurring hormones in food, entails such a comprehensive and massive governmental intervention in nature and in the ordinary lives of people as to reduce the comparison itself to an absurdity. The other considerations cited by the Panel, whether taken separately or grouped together, do not justify the Panel's finding of arbitrariness in the difference in the level of protection between added hormones for growth promotion and naturally-occurring hormones in meat and other foods.

Do you agree? Are Dr. Lucier's comments, in footnote 2 supra, on the cancer-causing impact of "exogenous oestrogens" relevant? How does one decide what situations are comparable? How many health measures could be justified if they were compared to toleration of smoking?

(5) Consider the obligations in article 2.3 of the SPS Agreement. How do those obligations relate to the obligations in article 5.5? Could there be a violation of article 5.5 without there being a violation of article 2.3? In particular, what does the "distinctions" requirement of article 5.5 add?

(6) A violation of article 5.5 was found in the *Australia Salmon* case. Australia—Measures Affecting the Importation of Salmon, WT/DS18 (Appellate Body Report and Panel Report as modified adopted November 6, 1998; Compliance Panel Report adopted March 20, 2000). In respect of that case, Professor Davey has written:

> In the *Salmon* case, the panel looked at three warning signals (the arbitrariness and unjustifiability of the distinctions in the level of protection provided by different, but comparable, Australian SPS measures; the substantial size of those distinctions; the inconsistency of the Australian measure with SPS Articles 5.1 and 2.2) and three additional factors (the substantial difference in the SPS measures applied by Australia in comparable situations; the change in the conclusions between the draft risk assessment and the final risk assessment; and the absence of measures controlling internal fish movements within Australia) that it cumulated to find discrimination or a disguised restriction. Panel Report, paras. 8.146–8.160. The panel's analysis was upheld by the Appellate Body, although it found that the first additional factor was equivalent to the first warning signal. Appellate Body Report, paras. 159–178. The compliance panel, in examining the new Australian measure implemented in response to the panel/Appellate Body reports, found that there was no longer an unjustifiable or arbitrary distinction between comparable situations. It also noted the absence of two of the three warning signals and of all of the additional factors noted in the original case. Accordingly, no violation of Article 5.5 was found. Compliance Panel Report, paras. 7.86–7.108.

The use of "warning signals" and "additional factors" to determine whether Article 5.5 has been violated is not very satisfactory. Perhaps it is only a matter of language, but there is a suggestion by using those two categories that there is a missing third category—"factors establishing a violation". In other words, the warning signals cause you to be suspicious that there might be a violation (but by definition cannot establish it) and the additional factors support your finding that there is a violation, but do not themselves establish the violation. In the future, more precise standards for the application of Article 5.5 need to be established with respect to this third factor. In doing so, it needs to be considered what, if anything, Article 5.5 adds to what is already covered by Article 2.3.

William J. Davey, Has the WTO Dispute Settlement System Exceeded Its Authority?: A Consideration of Deference Shown by the System to Member Government Decisions and Its Use of Issue–Avoidance Techniques, 4 JIEL 79, 91–92 (2001).

(7) A recent and well-publicized dispute involving the sale of products involving genetically modified organisms (GMOs) is European Communities—Measures Affecting the Approval and Marketing of Biotech Products, WT/DS291, 292 & 293/R, panel report adopted November 21, 2006. The panel report was not appealed. The case involved a challenge to what the complainants characterized as a "moratorium" on the approval of applications for the sale of such products within the EC, as well as certain product-specific national "safeguard" measures that prevented the sale of particular products in certain EC countries even though they had been approved by EC regulators in Brussels. The panel report contains thousands of paragraphs and is far too lengthy and intricate to include here, but the case essentially turned on a handful of core issues. First, the panel concluded that the EC had indeed maintained a *de facto* moratorium on the approval of applications for the sale of GMO products from 1999 to 2003. The *de facto* moratorium on approvals was not itself a "law, decree, regulation, requirement or procedure," and hence did not constitute an SPS "measure" as defined in Annex A(1) of the SPS Agreement. Many of the rules regarding such "measures" were thus inapplicable. The moratorium did, however, result in "undue delay" in the approval procedures for the products at issue, resulting in a violation of Annex C(1)(a) of the Agreement, and accordingly of Article 8. With respect to the national safeguard measures, the panel also found violations. For example, with respect to an Austrian measure on T25 maize, the panel rejected the claim that the measure was a "provisional measure" justified under Article 5.7, because it was not adopted under circumstances where "scientific evidence is insufficient." The panel based this conclusion on the fact that the product had been approved for sale at the Community level by Community regulators pursuant to their own risk assessment, that those regulators had conducted further review of the product's safety in response to the Austrian safeguard measure, and that in the course of this further review the regulators determined that Austria had submitted no new evidence to raise serious doubt about the product's safety.

Before the panel, the EC defended its moratorium in part on its need to fashion new comprehensive rules on GMOs, an argument that the panel held was insufficient to avoid a finding that the moratorium caused "undue delay." In July 2003, new EC rules were completed with the adoption of specific rules on the labeling and tracing of GMO products. Under the rules, retailers will be required to label food consisting of or containing GMOs, including food produced from GMOs. Food produced from GMOs is defined as food derived in whole or part from GMOs but not consisting of or containing GMOs. The label will have to indicate "This product contains genetically modified organisms" or "This product produced from genetically modified [name of organism]". Because it is impossible to be sure that products do not contain minute traces of GMOs, the presence of GMO material in conventional food does not have to be labeled if it is below 0.9% and if its presence is adventitious and technically unavoidable. The new rules also require that the movement of GMO products be tracked through production and distribution. At some point, the US may request new consultations on labeling and traceability, although it has not yet done so. Would the EC rules, as described above, violate the SPS or TBT Agreement or GATT itself? The US has expressed concern about the cost and practicality of the tracing requirement and sees no reason for labeling products that it views as safe.

(8) The hormones saga continues to this day. The United States and Canada both retaliated against the EU for failure to comply with the above ruling. The EU later modified its measure and its ostensible justification without changing its substance from a trade impact standpoint. Canada and the United States considered the changes to be unacceptable and maintained retaliatory measures. Europe insists that it is now in compliance and has challenged the maintenance of the retaliatory measures, as well as the refusal of the United States and Canada to take the matter to an Article 21.5 compliance panel (WT/DS320). A March 2008 panel decision (appealed in May) accepted the latter argument, but also stated that the new EC measure was not SPS–consistent.

(9) The SPS Agreement establishes a committee to administer the agreement. It consists of all WTO members and meets regularly to discuss issues that have arisen under the SPS Agreement. Since members are obligated to notify new and proposed SPS measures, the committee often has occasion to discuss such measures. In 2000, the committee issued "Guidelines to Further the Practical Implementation of Article 5.5" (G/SPS/15, July 18, 2000). The committee has played a useful role in resolving disputes among WTO members concerning SPS measures. See Scott, supra note 1.

SECTION 14.3   THE TBT AGREEMENT

The TBT agreement deals with technical regulations and standards. Annex 1.1 defines a "technical regulation" as follows:

> Document which lays down product characteristics or their related processes and production methods, including the applicable administrative provisions, with which compliance is mandatory. It may also include or deal exclusively with terminology, symbols, packaging, marking or labeling requirements as they apply to a product, process or production method.

A "standard" is defined in Annex 1.2 as a "[d]ocument approved by a recognized body, that provides for repeated use, rules, guidelines or characteristics for products or related processes and production methods, with which compliance is not necessary."

To date, the TBT Agreement has been a subject of less litigation in the WTO than the SPS Agreement. The following case, however, begins to address some of the core issues.

EUROPEAN COMMUNITIES—TRADE DESCRIPTION OF SARDINES

WT/DS231/AB/R.
Appellate Body Report adopted October 23, 2002.

2. This dispute concerns the name under which certain species of fish may be marketed in the European Communities. The measure at issue is Council Regulation (EEC) 2136/89 (the "EC Regulation"), which * * * sets forth common marketing standards for preserved sardines.

3. Article 2 of the EC Regulation provides that:

Only products meeting the following requirements may be marketed as preserved sardines and under the trade description referred to in Article 7:

— they must be covered by CN codes 1604 13 10 and ex 1604 20 50;

— they must be prepared exclusively from fish of the species *"Sardina pilchardus Walbaum"*;

— they must be pre-packaged with any appropriate covering medium in a hermetically sealed container;

— they must be sterilized by appropriate treatment. (emphasis added)

4. *Sardina pilchardus Walbaum* (*"Sardina pilchardus"*), the fish species referred to in the EC Regulation, is found mainly around the coasts of the Eastern North Atlantic Ocean, in the Mediterranean Sea, and in the Black Sea.

5. In 1978, the Codex Alimentarius Commission (the "Codex Commission"), of the United Nations Food and Agriculture Organization and the World Health Organization, adopted a world-wide standard for preserved sardines and sardine-type products, which regulates matters such as presentation, essential composition and quality factors, food additives, hygiene and handling, labelling, sampling, examination and analyses, defects and lot acceptance. This standard, CODEX STAN 94–1981, Rev.1–1995 ("Codex Stan 94"), covers preserved sardines or sardine-type products prepared from the following 21 fish species:

— Sardina pilchardus

— Sardinops melanostictus, S. neopilchardus, S. ocellatus, S. sagax[,] S. caeruleus

— Sardinella aurita, S. brasiliensis, S. maderensis, S. longiceps, S. gibbosa

— Clupea harengus

— Sprattus sprattus

— Hyperlophus vittatus

— Nematalosa vlaminghi

— Etrumeus teres

— Ethmidium maculatum

— Engraulis anchoita, E. mordax, E. ringens

— Opisthonema oglinum.

6.   Section 6 of Codex Stan 94 provides as follows:

6.   LABELLING

In addition to the provisions of the Codex General Standard for the Labelling of Prepackaged Foods (CODEX STAN 1–1985, Rev. 3–1999) the following special provisions apply:

6.1   NAME OF THE FOOD

The name of the product shall be:

6.1.1 (i) "Sardines" (to be reserved exclusively for *Sardina pilchardus* (Walbaum)); or

      (ii) "X sardines" of a country, a geographic area, the species, or the common name of the species in accordance with the law and custom of the country in which the product is sold, and in a manner not to mislead the consumer.

6.1.2 The name of the packing medium shall form part of the name of the food.

6.1.3 If the fish has been smoked or smoke flavoured, this information shall appear on the label in close proximity to the name.

6.1.4 In addition, the label shall include other descriptive terms that will avoid misleading or confusing the consumer. (emphasis added)

7.   Peru exports preserved products prepared from *Sardinops sagax sagax* ("*Sardinops sagax*"), one of the species of fish covered by Codex Stan 94. This species is found mainly in the Eastern Pacific Ocean, along the coasts of Peru and Chile.

8.   *Sardina pilchardus* and *Sardinops sagax* both belong to the *Clupeidae* family and the *Clupeinae* subfamily. As their scientific name suggests, however, they belong to different genus. *Sardina pilchardus* belongs to the genus *Sardina*, while *Sardinops sagax* belongs to the genus *Sardinops*. * * *

* * *

10.   In the Panel Report circulated to Members of the World Trade Organization (the "WTO") on 29 May 2002, the Panel found that the EC Regulation is inconsistent with Article 2.4 of the TBT Agreement, and

exercised judicial economy in respect of Peru's claims under Articles 2.2 and 2.1 of the TBT Agreement and III:4 of the GATT 1994. * * *

* * *

V. THE CHARACTERIZATION OF THE EC REGULATION AS A "TECHNICAL REGULATION"

171. We now turn to whether the Panel erred by finding that the EC Regulation is a "technical regulation" for purposes of Article 2.4 of the TBT Agreement. We recall that we have described the measure at issue—the EC Regulation—earlier in this Report.

172. The Panel found that:

... the EC Regulation is a technical regulation as it lays down product characteristics for preserved sardines and makes compliance with the provisions contained therein mandatory.

173. The European Communities does not contest that the EC Regulation is a "technical regulation" per se. Instead, on appeal, the European Communities reiterates two arguments that the Panel rejected. First, the European Communities argues that the product coverage of the EC Regulation is limited to preserved *Sardina pilchardus*. The European Communities contends that the EC Regulation does not regulate preserved fish made from *Sardinops sagax* or from any other species, and that, accordingly, *Sardinops sagax* is not an identifiable product under the EC Regulation. The European Communities concludes that, in the light of our ruling in *EC–Asbestos* that a "technical regulation" must apply to identifiable products, the EC Regulation is not a "technical regulation" for *Sardinops sagax*.

174. Second, the European Communities contends that a "naming" rule is distinct from a labelling requirement. The European Communities argues that, "[t]he requirement to state a certain name on the label ... involves not only a labelling requirement but also a substantive naming rule, which is not subject to the TBT Agreement." Thus, according to the European Communities, even if it were determined that the EC Regulation relates to *Sardinops sagax*, the "naming" rule set out in Article 2 of the EC Regulation—the provision challenged by Peru—is not a product characteristic. On this basis, the European Communities argues that Article 2 of the EC Regulation—which the European Communities contends sets out a "naming" rule and not a labelling requirement—does not meet the definition of the term "technical regulation" provided in the TBT Agreement.

175. As we explained in *EC–Asbestos*, whether a measure is a "technical regulation" is a threshold issue because the outcome of this issue determines whether the TBT Agreement is applicable. If the measure before us is not a "technical regulation", then it does not fall within the scope of the TBT Agreement. The term "technical regulation" is defined in Annex 1.1 to the TBT Agreement as follows:

1. Technical Regulation

Document which lays down product characteristics or their related processes and production methods, including the applicable administrative provisions, with which compliance is mandatory. It may also include or deal exclusively with terminology, symbols, packaging, marking or labelling requirements as they apply to a product, process or production method.

176. We interpreted this definition in *EC–Asbestos*. In doing so, we set out three criteria that a document must meet to fall within the definition of "technical regulation" in the TBT Agreement. First, the document must apply to an identifiable product or group of products. The identifiable product or group of products need not, however, be expressly identified in the document. Second, the document must lay down one or more characteristics of the product. These product characteristics may be intrinsic, or they may be related to the product. They may be prescribed or imposed in either a positive or a negative form. Third, compliance with the product characteristics must be mandatory. As we stressed in *EC–Asbestos*, these three criteria are derived from the wording of the definition in Annex 1.1. * * *

* * *

182. In our view, the Panel correctly found that the EC Regulation is applicable to an identified product, and that the identified product is "preserved sardines". This is abundantly clear from a plain reading of the EC Regulation itself. The EC Regulation is entitled "Council Regulation (EEC) 2136/89 of 21 June 1989 Laying Down Common Marketing Standards for Preserved Sardines". Article 1, which sets forth the scope of the EC Regulation, states that "[t]his Regulation defines the standards governing the marketing of preserved sardines in the Community." Article 2 states that "[o]nly products meeting the following requirements may be marketed as preserved sardines".

183. This alone, however, does not dispose of the European Communities' argument, as the European Communities reproaches the Panel for failing to acknowledge that the EC Regulation uses the term "preserved sardines" to mean—exclusively—preserved *Sardina pilchardus*. We observe that the EC Regulation does not expressly identify *Sardinops sagax*. However, this does not necessarily mean that *Sardinops sagax* is not an identifiable product. As we stated in *EC–Asbestos*, a product need not be expressly identified in the document for it to be identifiable.

184. Even if we were to accept, for the sake of argument, the European Communities' contention that the term "preserved sardines" in the EC Regulation refers exclusively to preserved *Sardina pilchardus*, the EC Regulation would still be applicable to a range of identifiable products beyond *Sardina pilchardus*. This is because preserved products made, for example, of *Sardinops sagax* are, by virtue of the EC Regulation, prohibited from being identified and marketed under an appellation including the term "sardines".

185. As we explained in *EC–Asbestos*, the requirement that a "technical regulation" be applicable to identifiable products relates to aspects of compliance and enforcement, because it would be impossible to comply with or enforce a "technical regulation" without knowing to what the regulation applied. As the Panel record shows, the EC Regulation has been enforced against preserved fish products imported into Germany containing *Sardinops sagax*. This confirms that the EC Regulation is applicable to preserved *Sardinops sagax*, and demonstrates that preserved *Sardinops sagax* is an identifiable product for purposes of the EC Regulation. Indeed, the European Communities admits that the EC Regulation is applicable to *Sardinops sagax*, when it states in its appellant's submission that "[t]he only legal consequence of the [EC] Regulation for preserved *Sardinops sagax* is that they may not be called 'preserved sardines'."

186. Therefore, we reject the contention of the European Communities that preserved *Sardinops sagax* is not an identifiable product under the EC Regulation.

187. Next, we examine whether the EC Regulation meets the second criterion of a "technical regulation", which is that it must be a document that lays down product characteristics. According to the European Communities, Article 2 of the EC Regulation does not lay down product characteristics; rather, it sets out a "naming" rule. The European Communities argues that, although the definition of "technical regulation" in the TBT Agreement covers labelling requirements, it does not extend to "naming" rules. Therefore, the European Communities asserts that Article 2 of the EC Regulation is not a "technical regulation".

* * *

189. In *EC–Asbestos*, we examined what it means to lay down product characteristics, and concluded that:

> The heart of the definition of a "technical regulation" is that a "document" must "lay down"—that is, set forth, stipulate or provide—"product characteristics". The word "characteristic" has a number of synonyms that are helpful in understanding the ordinary meaning of that word, in this context. Thus, the "characteristics" of a product include, in our view, any objectively definable "features", "qualities", "attributes", or other "distinguishing mark" of a product. Such "characteristics" might relate, inter alia, to a product's composition, size, shape, colour, texture, hardness, tensile strength, flammability, conductivity, density, or viscosity. In the definition of a "technical regulation" in Annex 1.1, the TBT Agreement itself gives certain examples of "product characteristics"—"terminology, symbols, packaging, marking or labelling requirements". These examples indicate that "product characteristics" include, not only features and qualities intrinsic to the product itself, but also related "characteristics", such as the means of identification, the presentation and the appearance of a product. In addition, according to the definition in Annex 1.1 of the TBT Agreement, a "technical regula-

tion'' may set forth the ''applicable administrative provisions'' for products which have certain ''characteristics''. Further, we note that the definition of a ''technical regulation'' provides that such a regulation ''may also include or deal exclusively with terminology, symbols, packaging, marking or labelling requirements''. The use here of the word ''exclusively'' and the disjunctive word ''or'' indicates that a ''technical regulation'' may be confined to laying down only one or a few ''product characteristics''.

Accordingly, product characteristics include not only ''features and qualities intrinsic to the product'', but also those that are related to it, such as ''means of identification''.

190. We do not find it necessary, in this case, to decide whether the definition of ''technical regulation'' in the TBT Agreement makes a distinction between ''naming'' and labelling. This question is irrelevant to the issue before us. As we stated earlier, the EC Regulation expressly identifies a product, namely ''preserved sardines''. Further, Article 2 of the EC Regulation provides that, to be marketed as ''preserved sardines'', products must be prepared exclusively from fish of the species *Sardina pilchardus*. We are of the view that this requirement—to be prepared exclusively from fish of the species *Sardina pilchardus*—is a product characteristic ''intrinsic to'' preserved sardines that is laid down by the EC Regulation. Thus, we agree with the Panel's finding in this regard that:

> . . . one product characteristic required by Article 2 of the EC Regulation is that preserved sardines must be prepared exclusively from fish of the species *Sardina pilchardus*. This product characteristic must be met for the product to be ''marketed as preserved sardines and under the trade description referred to in Article 7'' of the EC Regulation. We consider that the requirement to use exclusively *Sardina pilchardus* is a product characteristic as it objectively defines features and qualities of preserved sardines for the purposes of their ''market[ing] as preserved sardines and under the trade description referred to in Article 7'' of the EC Regulation.

191. In any event, as we said in *EC–Asbestos*, a ''means of identification'' is a product characteristic. A name clearly identifies a product; indeed, the European Communities concedes that a name is a ''means of identification''. * * *

* * *

194. The third and final criterion that a document must fulfil to meet the definition of ''technical regulation'' in the TBT Agreement is that compliance must be mandatory. The European Communities does not contest that compliance with the EC Regulation is mandatory. We also find that it is mandatory.

195. We, therefore, uphold the Panel's finding, in paragraph 7.35 of the Panel Report, that the EC Regulation is a ''technical regulation'' for purposes of the TBT Agreement, because it meets the three criteria

we set out in *EC–Asbestos* as necessary to satisfy the definition of a "technical regulation" under the TBT Agreement.

* * *

VIII.   WHETHER CODEX STAN 94 WAS USED "AS A BASIS FOR" THE EC REGULATION

234.   We turn now to whether Codex Stan 94 has been used "as a basis for" the EC Regulation. It will be recalled that Article 2.4 of the TBT Agreement requires Members to use relevant international standards "as a basis for" their technical regulations under certain circumstances. The Panel found that "the relevant international standard, i.e., Codex Stan 94, was not used as a basis for the EC Regulation". The European Communities appeals this finding.

* * *

242.   The question before us, therefore, is the proper meaning to be attributed to the words "as a basis for" in Article 2.4 of the TBT Agreement. In *EC–Hormones*, we addressed a similar issue, namely, the meaning of "based on" as used in Article 3.1 of the SPS Agreement, which provides:

Harmonization

1.   To harmonize sanitary and phytosanitary measures on as wide a basis as possible, Members shall base their sanitary or phytosanitary measures on international standards, guidelines or recommendations, where they exist, except as otherwise provided for in this Agreement, and in particular in paragraph 3.

In *EC–Hormones*, we stated that "based on" does not mean the same thing as "conform to". In that appeal, we articulated the ordinary meaning of the term "based on", as used in Article 3.1 of the SPS Agreement in the following terms:

A thing is commonly said to be "based on" another thing when the former "stands" or is "founded" or "built" upon or "is supported by" the latter.[150]

[150]L. Brown (ed.), The New Shorter Oxford English Dictionary on Historical Principles (Clarendon Press), Vol. I, p. 187.

The Panel here referred to this conclusion in its analysis of Article 2.4 of the TBT Agreement. In our view, the Panel did so correctly, because our approach in *EC–Hormones* is also relevant for the interpretation of Article 2.4 of the TBT Agreement.

243.   In addition, as we stated earlier, the Panel here used the following definition to establish the ordinary meaning of the term "basis":

The word "basis" means "the principal constituent of anything, the fundamental principle or theory, as of a system of knowledge".[90]

[90][Webster's New World Dictionary, (William Collins & World Publishing Co., Inc., 1976)], p. 117.

Informed by our ruling in *EC–Hormones*, and relying on this meaning of the term "basis", the Panel concluded that an international standard is used "as a basis for" a technical regulation when it is used as the principal constituent or fundamental principle for the purpose of enacting the technical regulation.

244. We agree with the Panel's approach. In relying on the ordinary meaning of the term "basis", the Panel rightly followed an approach similar to ours in determining the ordinary meaning of "based on" in *EC–Hormones*. In addition to the definition of "basis" in Webster's New World Dictionary that was used by the Panel, we note, as well, the similar definitions for "basis" that are set out in the The New Shorter Oxford English Dictionary, and also provide guidance as to the ordinary meaning of the term:

> **3** [t]he main constituent.__....__**5** [a] thing on which anything is constructed and by which its constitution or operation is determined; a determining principle; a set of underlying or agreed principles.

245. From these various definitions, we would highlight the similar terms "principal constituent", "fundamental principle", "main constituent", and "determining principle"—all of which lend credence to the conclusion that there must be a very strong and very close relationship between two things in order to be able to say that one is "the basis for" the other.

246. The European Communities, however, seems to suggest the need for something different. The European Communities maintains that a "rational relationship" between an international standard and a technical regulation is sufficient to conclude that the former is used "as a basis for" the latter. According to the European Communities, an examination based on the criterion of the existence of a "rational relationship" focuses on "the qualitative aspect of the substantive relationship that should exist between the relevant international standard and the technical regulation". In response to questioning at the oral hearing, the European Communities added that a "rational relationship" exists when the technical regulation is informed in its overall scope by the international standard.

247. Yet, we see nothing in the text of Article 2.4 to support the European Communities' view, nor has the European Communities pointed to any such support. Moreover, the European Communities does not offer any arguments relating to the context or the object and purpose of that provision that would support its argument that the existence of a "rational relationship" is the appropriate criterion for determining whether something has been used "as a basis for" something else.

248. We see no need here to define in general the nature of the relationship that must exist for an international standard to serve "as a

basis for" a technical regulation. Here we need only examine this measure to determine if it fulfils this obligation. In our view, it can certainly be said—at a minimum—that something cannot be considered a "basis" for something else if the two are contradictory. Therefore, under Article 2.4, if the technical regulation and the international standard contradict each other, it cannot properly be concluded that the international standard has been used "as a basis for" the technical regulation.

249.   Thus, we need only determine here whether there is a contradiction between Codex Stan 94 and the EC Regulation. If there is, we are justified in concluding our analysis with that determination, as the only appropriate conclusion from such a determination would be that the Codex Stan 94 has not been used "as a basis for" the EC Regulation.

* * *

256.   We accept the European Communities' contention that the EC Regulation contains the prescription set out in section 6.1.1(i) of Codex Stan 94. However, as we have just explained, the analysis must go beyond section 6.1.1(i); it must extend also to sections 6.1.1(ii) and 2.1.1 of Codex Stan 94. And, a comparison between, on the one hand, sections 6.1.1(ii) and 2.1.1 of Codex Stan 94 and, on the other hand, Article 2 of the EC Regulation, leads to the inevitable conclusion that a contradiction exists between these provisions.

257.   The effect of Article 2 of the EC Regulation is to prohibit preserved fish products prepared from the 20 species of fish other than *Sardina pilchardus* to which Codex Stan 94 refers—including *Sardinops sagax*—from being identified and marketed under the appellation "sardines", even with one of the four qualifiers set out in the standard. Codex Stan 94, by contrast, permits the use of the term "sardines" with any one of four qualifiers for the identification and marketing of preserved fish products prepared from 20 species of fish other than *Sardina pilchardus*. Thus, the EC Regulation and Codex Stan 94 are manifestly contradictory. To us, the existence of this contradiction confirms that Codex Stan 94 was not used "as a basis for" the EC Regulation.

258.   We, therefore, uphold the finding of the Panel, in paragraph 7.112 of the Panel Report, that Codex Stan 94 was not used "as a basis for" the EC Regulation within the meaning of Article 2.4 of the TBT Agreement.

IX.   THE QUESTION OF THE "INEFFECTIVENESS OR
INAPPROPRIATENESS" OF CODEX STAN 94

259.   We turn now to the second part of Article 2.4 of the TBT Agreement, which provides that Members need not use international standards as a basis for their technical regulations "when such international standards or relevant parts would be an ineffective or inappropriate means for the fulfilment of the legitimate objectives pursued".

* * *

266. The European Communities appeals the Panel's assignment of the burden of proof under Article 2.4 of the TBT Agreement. The European Communities disputes the Panel's conclusion that the burden rests with the European Communities to demonstrate that Codex Stan 94 is an "ineffective or inappropriate" means to fulfil the "legitimate objectives" of the EC Regulation. The European Communities maintains that the burden of proof rests rather with Peru, as Peru is the party claiming that the measure at issue is inconsistent with WTO obligations.

267. The European Communities also appeals the finding of the Panel that Codex Stan 94 is not "ineffective or inappropriate" to fulfil the "legitimate objectives" of the EC Regulation. In particular, the European Communities argues that the Panel erred in founding its analysis on the factual premise that consumers in the European Communities associate "sardines" exclusively with *Sardina pilchardus*. Furthermore, the European Communities contends that the Panel erred in concluding that the term "sardines", either by itself or when combined with the name of a country or geographic area, is a common name for *Sardinops sagax* in the European Communities. The European Communities also objects to the decision by the Panel to take this conclusion into account in its assessment of whether consumers in the European Communities associate the term "sardines" exclusively with *Sardina pilchardus*.

268. In considering these claims of the European Communities, we will address, first, the question of the burden of proof, and, next, the substantive content of the second part of Article 2.4 of the TBT Agreement.

A. The Burden of Proof

269. Before the Panel, the European Communities asserted that Codex Stan 94 is "ineffective or inappropriate" to fulfil the "legitimate objectives" of the EC Regulation. The Panel was of the view that the European Communities was thus asserting the affirmative of a particular claim or defence, and, therefore, that the burden of proof rests with the European Communities to demonstrate that claim. The Panel justified its position as follows: first, it reasoned that the complainant is not in a position to "spell out" the "legitimate objectives" pursued by a Member through a technical regulation; and, second, it reasoned "that the assessment of whether a relevant international standard is 'inappropriate' . . . may extend to considerations which are proper to the Member adopting or applying a technical regulation.

* * *

275. * * * [T]he circumstances envisaged in the second part of Article 2.4 are excluded from the scope of application of the first part of Article 2.4. Accordingly, * * * there is no "general rule-exception" relationship between the first and the second parts of Article 2.4. Hence, in this case, it is for Peru—as the complaining Member seeking a ruling on the inconsistency with Article 2.4 of the TBT Agreement of the

measure applied by the European Communities—to bear the burden of proving its claim. This burden includes establishing that Codex Stan 94 has not been used "as a basis for" the EC Regulation, as well as establishing that Codex Stan 94 is effective and appropriate to fulfil the "legitimate objectives" pursued by the European Communities through the EC Regulation.

276.   The TBT Agreement acknowledges the right of every WTO Member to establish for itself the objectives of its technical regulations while affording every other Member adequate opportunities to obtain information about these objectives. That said, part of the reason why the Panel concluded that the burden of proof under Article 2.4 is on the respondent is because, in the Panel's view, the complainant cannot "spell out" the "legitimate objectives" of the technical regulation. In addition, the Panel reasoned that the assessment of the appropriateness of a relevant international standard involves considerations which are properly the province of the Member adopting or applying a technical regulation.

277.   In our opinion, these two concerns are not justified. The TBT Agreement affords a complainant adequate opportunities to obtain information about the objectives of technical regulations or the specific considerations that may be relevant to the assessment of their appropriateness. A complainant may obtain relevant information about a technical regulation from a respondent under Article 2.5 of the TBT Agreement, which establishes a compulsory mechanism requiring the supplying of information by the regulating Member. This Article provides in relevant part:

> A Member preparing, adopting or applying a technical regulation which may have a significant effect on trade of other Members shall, upon the request of another Member, explain the justification for that technical regulation in terms of the provisions of paragraphs 2 to 4.

278.   Peru expresses doubts about the usefulness and efficacy of this obligation in the TBT Agreement. Peru argues that a Member may not respond fully or adequately to a request for information under Article 2.5, and that, therefore, it is inappropriate to rely on this obligation to support assigning the burden of proof under Article 2.4 to the complainant. We are not persuaded by this argument. We must assume that Members of the WTO will abide by their treaty obligations in good faith, as required by the principle of pacta sunt servanda articulated in Article 26 of the Vienna Convention. And, always in dispute settlement, every Member of the WTO must assume the good faith of every other Member.

279.   Another source of information for the complainant is the "enquiry point" that must be established by the respondent under [Article 10.1 of] the TBT Agreement. * * *

280.   Indeed, the dispute settlement process itself also provides opportunities for the complainant to obtain the necessary information to

build a case. Information can be exchanged during the consultation phase, and additional information may well become available during the panel phase itself. On previous occasions, we have stated that the arguments of a party "are set out and progressively clarified in the first written submissions, the rebuttal submissions and the first and second panel meetings with the parties", and that "[t]here is no requirement in the DSU or in GATT practice for arguments on all claims relating to the matter referred to the DSB to be set out in a complaining party's first written submission to the panel." Thus, it would not be necessary for the complainant to have all the necessary information about the technical regulation before commencing an action under the DSU. A complainant could collect information before and during the early stages of the panel proceedings and, on the basis of that information, develop arguments relating to the objectives or to the appropriateness that may be put forward during subsequent phases of the proceedings.

281.   The degree of difficulty in substantiating a claim or a defence may vary according to the facts of the case and the provision at issue. For example, on the one hand, it may be relatively straightforward for a complainant to show that a particular measure has a text that establishes an explicit and formal discrimination between like products and is, therefore, inconsistent with the national treatment obligation in Article III of the GATT 1994. On the other hand, it may be more difficult for a complainant to substantiate a claim of a violation of Article III of the GATT 1994 if the discrimination does not flow from the letter of the legal text of the measure, but rather is a result of the administrative practice of the domestic authorities of the respondent in applying that measure. But, in both of those situations, the complainant must prove its claim. There is nothing in the WTO dispute settlement system to support the notion that the allocation of the burden of proof should be decided on the basis of a comparison between the respective difficulties that may possibly be encountered by the complainant and the respondent in collecting information to prove a case.

282.   We, therefore, reverse the finding of the Panel, in paragraph 7.52 of the Panel Report, that, under the second part of Article 2.4 of the TBT Agreement, the burden rests with the European Communities to demonstrate that Codex Stan 94 is an "ineffective or inappropriate" means to fulfil the "legitimate objectives" pursued by the European Communities through the EC Regulation. Accordingly, we find that Peru bears the burden of demonstrating that Codex Stan 94 is an effective and appropriate means to fulfil the "legitimate objectives" pursued by the European Communities through the EC Regulation.

283.   We turn now to consider whether Peru effectively discharged its burden of proof under the second part of Article 2.4 of the TBT Agreement.

B. Whether Codex Stan 94 is an Effective and Appropriate Means to
    Fulfil the "Legitimate Objectives" Pursued by the European Com-
    munities Through the EC Regulation

284. We recall that the second part of Article 2.4 of the TBT
Agreement reads as follows:

> ... except when such international standards or relevant parts
> would be an ineffective or inappropriate means for the fulfilment of
> the legitimate objectives pursued ...

Before ruling on whether Peru met its burden of proof in this case, we
must address, successively, the interpretation and the application of the
second part of Article 2.4.

285. The interpretation of the second part of Article 2.4 raises two
questions: first, the meaning of the term "ineffective or inappropriate
means"; and, second, the meaning of the term "legitimate objectives".
As to the first question, we noted earlier the Panel's view that the term
"ineffective or inappropriate means" refers to two questions—the question of the effectiveness of the measure and the question of the appropriateness of the measure—and that these two questions, although closely
related, are different in nature. The Panel pointed out that the term
"ineffective" "refers to something which is not 'having the function of
accomplishing', 'having a result', or 'brought to bear', whereas [the
term] 'inappropriate' refers to something which is not 'specially suitable', 'proper', or 'fitting' ". The Panel also stated that:

> Thus, in the context of Article 2.4, an ineffective means is a means
> which does not have the function of accomplishing the legitimate
> objective pursued, whereas an inappropriate means is a means
> which is not specially suitable for the fulfilment of the legitimate
> objective pursued. ... The question of effectiveness bears upon the
> results of the means employed, whereas the question of appropriate-
> ness relates more to the nature of the means employed.

We agree with the Panel's interpretation.

286. As to the second question, we are of the view that the Panel
was also correct in concluding that "the 'legitimate objectives' referred
to in Article 2.4 must be interpreted in the context of Article 2.2", which
refers also to "legitimate objectives", and includes a description of what
the nature of some such objectives can be. Two implications flow from
the Panel's interpretation. First, the term "legitimate objectives" in
Article 2.4, as the Panel concluded, must cover the objectives explicitly
mentioned in Article 2.2, namely: "national security requirements; the
prevention of deceptive practices; protection of human health or safety,
animal or plant life or health, or the environment." Second, given the
use of the term "inter alia" in Article 2.2, the objectives covered by the
term "legitimate objectives" in Article 2.4 extend beyond the list of the
objectives specifically mentioned in Article 2.2. Furthermore, we share
the view of the Panel that the second part of Article 2.4 implies that
there must be an examination and a determination on the legitimacy of
the objectives of the measure.

287. With respect to the application of the second part of Article
2.4, we begin by recalling that Peru has the burden of establishing that

Codex Stan 94 is an effective and appropriate means for the fulfilment of the "legitimate objectives" pursued by the European Communities through the EC Regulation. Those "legitimate objectives" are market transparency, consumer protection, and fair competition. To satisfy this burden of proof, Peru must, at least, have established a prima facie case of this claim. If Peru has succeeded in doing so, then a presumption will have been raised which the European Communities must have rebutted in order to succeed in its defence. If Peru has established a prima facie case, and if the European Communities has failed to rebut Peru's case effectively, then Peru will have discharged its burden of proof under Article 2.4. In such an event, Codex Stan 94 must, consistent with the European Communities' obligation under the TBT Agreement, be used "as a basis for" any European Communities regulation on the marketing of preserved sardines, because Codex Stan 94 will have been shown to be both effective and appropriate to fulfil the "legitimate objectives" pursued by the European Communities. Further, in such an event, as we have already determined that Codex Stan 94 was not used "as a basis for" the EC Regulation, we would then have to find as a consequence that the European Communities has acted inconsistently with Article 2.4 of the TBT Agreement.

288.   This being so, our task is to assess whether Peru discharged its burden of showing that Codex Stan 94 is appropriate and effective to fulfil these same three "legitimate objectives". In the light of our reasoning thus far, Codex Stan 94 would be effective if it had the capacity to accomplish all three of these objectives, and it would be appropriate if it were suitable for the fulfilment of all three of these objectives.

289.   We share the Panel's view that the terms "ineffective" and "inappropriate" have different meanings, and that it is conceptually possible that a measure could be effective but inappropriate, or appropriate but ineffective. This is why Peru has the burden of showing that Codex Stan 94 is both effective and appropriate. We note, however, that, in this case, a consideration of the appropriateness of Codex Stan 94 and a consideration of the effectiveness of Codex Stan 94 are interrelated—as a consequence of the nature of the objectives of the EC Regulation. The capacity of a measure to accomplish the stated objectives—its effectiveness—and the suitability of a measure for the fulfilment of the stated objectives—its appropriateness—are both decisively influenced by the perceptions and expectations of consumers in the European Communities relating to preserved sardine products.

290.   We note that the Panel concluded that "Peru has adduced sufficient evidence and legal arguments to demonstrate that Codex Stan 94 is not ineffective or inappropriate to fulfil the legitimate objectives pursued by the EC Regulation." We have examined the analysis which led the Panel to this conclusion. We note, in particular, that the Panel made the factual finding that "it has not been established that consumers in most member States of the European Communities have always associated the common name 'sardines' exclusively with *Sardina pilchar-*

dus". We also note that the Panel gave consideration to the contentions of Peru that, under Codex Stan 94, fish from the species *Sardinops sagax* bear a denomination that is distinct from that of *Sardina pilchardus*, and that "the very purpose of the labelling regulations set out in Codex Stan 94 for sardines of species other than *Sardina pilchardus* is to ensure market transparency". We agree with the analysis made by the Panel. Accordingly, we see no reason to interfere with the Panel's finding that Peru has adduced sufficient evidence and legal arguments to demonstrate that Codex Stan 94 meets the legal requirements of effectiveness and appropriateness set out in Article 2.4 of the TBT Agreement.

291. We, therefore, uphold the finding of the Panel, in paragraph 7.138 of the Panel Report, that Peru has adduced sufficient evidence and legal arguments to demonstrate that Codex Stan 94 is not "ineffective or inappropriate" to fulfil the "legitimate objectives" of the EC Regulation.
* * *

Notes and Questions

(1) Do you agree with the Appellate Body's discussion of the burden of proof? Given that the Appellate Body has ruled that the respondent has the burden of proof when it invokes what the Appellate Body has characterized as the exceptions of Article XX or XXIV, why is the assignment of the burden not on the respondent under Article 2.4 of the TBT Agreement?

(2) The key issue in the case was whether Codex Stan 94 was an "ineffective or inappropriate means" for fulfilment of the EC legitimate objectives. The Appellate Body had little to say on the substance of that issue, which it treated as being determined by a factual finding of the panel. The following is an excerpt of the panel's discussion of the issue:

> 7.113 The European Communities contends that Codex Stan 94, by allowing for the use of the word "sardines" for products other than *Sardina pilchardus*, is ineffective or inappropriate to fulfil the objectives of consumer protection, market transparency and fair competition. The European Communities argues that its consumers expect that products of the same nature and characteristics will always have the same trade description, and that consumers in most member States of the European Communities have always, and in some member States have for at least 13 years, associated "sardines" exclusively with *Sardina pilchardus*.
> * * *

>   * * *

> 7.124 Under Codex Stan 94, if a hermetically sealed container contains fish of species *Sardina pilchardus*, the product would be labelled "sardines" without any qualification. A product containing preserved *Sardinops sagax*, however, would be labelled "X sardines" with the "X" representing the name of a country, the name of a geographic area, the name of the species or the common name in accordance with the law and custom of the country in which the product is sold. If a hermetically sealed container is labelled simply as "sardines" without any qualification, the European consumer would know that it contains European

sardines. However, if the product is labelled, for example, "Pacific sardines", the European consumer would be informed that the product does not contain sardines originating from Europe. * * *

7.125   The European Communities, however, argued that "X sardines" is ineffective or inappropriate to fulfil the legitimate objectives pursued by the EC Regulation because European consumers associate the term "sardines" exclusively with *Sardina pilchardus* and even if "sardines" is combined with a qualification, it would suggest to European consumers that the products are the same but come from different countries or geographic areas. * * *

7.126   Thus, the European Communities asserted, on the one hand, that in most member States the term "sardines" has historically responded to the particular consumer expectations which in its view underlie its Regulation, and acknowledged, on the other hand, that in some member States, it is the Regulation which "created" those "uniform" consumer expectations. * * *

7.127   The European Communities acknowledged that it is the Regulation which in certain member States "created" the consumer expectations which it now considers require the maintenance of that same Regulation. Thus, through regulatory intervention, the European Communities consciously would have "created" consumer expectations which now are claimed to affect the competitive conditions of imports. If we were to accept that a WTO Member can "create" consumer expectations and thereafter find justification for the trade-restrictive measure which created those consumer expectations, we would be endorsing the permissibility of "self-justifying" regulatory trade barriers. Indeed, the danger is that Members, by shaping consumer expectations through regulatory intervention in the market, would be able to justify thereafter the legitimacy of that very same regulatory intervention on the basis of the governmentally created consumer expectations. Mindful of this concern, we will proceed to examine whether the evidence and legal arguments before us demonstrate that consumers in most member States of the European Communities have always associated the common name "sardines" exclusively with *Sardina pilchardus* and that the use of "sardines" in conjunction with "Pacific", "Peruvian" or "*Sardinops sagax*" would therefore not enable European consumers to distinguish between products made from *Sardinops sagax* and *Sardina pilchardus*.

* * *

7.129   [With respect to the evidence submitted by the EC concerning pre–1989 versions of national regulations on "sardines" (i.e., Spanish, French and United Kingdom regulations)], we consider that these do indeed demonstrate that the legislative or regulatory authorities in those countries considered that the common name "sardines" without any qualification was to be reserved for products made from *Sardina pilchardus*, even before the EC Regulation entered into force. We note, however, that these documents, which concern three European Communities' member States, are not probative of the assertion that the use of a qualifying term, such as "Pacific", "Peruvian" or "*Sardinops sagax*", in combination with "sardines" would not enable European consumers to distinguish products made from *Sardinops sagax* as opposed to *Sardina pilchardus*.

7.130   We also note that in the United Kingdom, which imports 97% of all Peruvian exports of preserved *Sardinops sagax* to the European Communities, the 1981 Food Labelling Regulations also allowed for the use of the common name "pilchards" for *Sardina pilchardus* and prescribed the common name "Pacific pilchards" for *Sardinops sagax*. Thus, United Kingdom consumers did not associate *Sardina pilchardus* exclusively with the common name "sardines", and were able to distinguish *Sardinops sagax* from *Sardina pilchardus* by the simple indication of a geographical region (i.e., "Pacific"). If the insertion of the geographic area "Pacific" with the word "pilchard" was used in the United Kingdom to distinguish between *Sardina pilchardus* and *Sardinops sagax*, we fail to see why the inclusion of the name of a country, name of a geographic area, name of the species or the common name with the term "sardines" to refer to *Sardina sagax* would be ineffective or inappropriate to fulfil the legitimate objectives pursued by the EC Regulation.

7.131   Contrary to the European Communities' assertion, Peru submitted evidence to demonstrate that European consumers do not associate "sardines" exclusively with *Sardina pilchardus*. It did so by demonstrating that the term "sardines" either by itself or combined with the name of a country or the geographic area, is a common name for *Sardinops sagax* in the European Communities. In support of its assertion that "sardines" by itself or combined with the name of a country or geographic region is a common name for *Sardinops sagax* in the European Communities, Peru referred to the *Multilingual Illustrated Dictionary of Aquatic Animals and Plants*, published in close cooperation with the European Commission and the member States of the European Communities for the purpose of, *inter alia, improving market transparency*, which lists the common name of *Sardinops sagax* in nine European languages as "sardines" or the equivalent thereof in the national language combined with the country or geographic area of origin. Similarly, Peru submitted copies of the electronic publication, *Fish Base*, produced with the support of the European Commission, which indicates that a common name for *Sardinops sagax* in Italy, the Netherlands, Germany, France, Sweden and Spain is "sardines" or its equivalent in the national language combined with the country or geographical area of origin. In addition, Peru relied on the *Multilingual Dictionary of Fish and Fish Products* prepared by the Organisation for Economic Cooperation and Development ("OECD") which indicates that a common name of *Sardinops sagax* is "sardines", either by itself or combined with the name of a country or geographic area. According to this *Multilingual Dictionary of Fish and Fish Products*, one of the common names in English is "Pacific Sardine", or "Sardine du Pacifique" in French. Even the European Communities acknowledged that one of the common names for *Sardinops sagax* is "sardines" or its equivalent thereof in the national language combined with the country or geographical area of origin.

7.132 According to the Consumers' Association, "a wide array of sardines were made available to European consumers for many decades prior to the imposition of this restrictive Regulation". Canada submitted evidence showing that a Canadian company exported *Clupea harengus harengus* under the trade description "Canadian sardines" to the Netherlands for thirty years, until 1989. Canada also submitted evidence showing that there have been exports of *Clupea harengus harengus* under the trade description "[company name] sardines in hot tabasco" to the United Kingdom for forty years, until 1989. We note in this regard that with respect to the objective of promoting fair competition, the aim of which is to prevent producers of one product from benefitting from the reputation associated with another product, the underlying premise is that the term "sardines" is associated only with *Sardina pilchardus*. However, as species other than *Sardina pilchardus* also contributed to the reputation of the term "sardines" and in light of the fact that "sardines", either by itself or combined with the name of a country or a geographic area, is a common name for *Sardinops sagax* in the European Communities, we do not consider that only *Sardina pilchardus* developed the reputation associated with the term "sardines".

7.133 Even if we were to assume that the consumers in the European Communities associate the term "sardines" exclusively with *Sardina pilchardus*, the concern expressed by the European Communities, in our view, was taken into account when Codex Stan 94 was adopted. By establishing a precise labelling requirement "in a manner not to mislead the consumer", the Codex Alimentarius Commission considered the issue of consumer protection in countries producing preserved sardines from *Sardina pilchardus* and those producing preserved sardines from species other than *Sardina pilchardus* by reserving the term "sardines" without any qualification for *Sardina pilchardus* only. The other species enumerated in Codex Stan 94 are to be labelled as "X sardines" with the "X" denoting the name of a country, name of a geographic area, name of the species or the common name in accordance with the law and custom of the country in which the product is sold. Thus, Codex Stan 94 allows Members to provide precise trade description of preserved sardines which promotes market transparency so as to protect consumers and promote fair competition.

* * *

7.136 Moreover, a 1969 Synopsis of Governments Replies on the Questionnaire on "Canned Sardines", prepared by the Codex Committee on Fish and Fishery Products, demonstrates that the governments of several current European Communities' member States, such as Denmark, Sweden and the United Kingdom, responded affirmatively to the question "[i]s it accepted that existing practices whereby sardine-type products are often labelled as sardines but with an appropriate qualifying phrase should be fully taken into account and provided for so long as the consumer is not deceived?". These governments considered "that this way of designating the sardine-type products as sardines has been in use for about one century in many countries". France was recorded as stating that "only the species recognized as sufficiently near to *Sardina pilchardus* might be designated as 'sardine' followed or preceded by a qualifying term", adding that "a geographic qualifying term could be acceptable on the condition that the consumer is not deceived (i.e., Atlantic sardine can mean either *Sardina pilchardus*, or another species caught in the Atlantic Ocean)". Of all current European Communities' members States, only the Federal Republic of Germany, Portugal and Spain stated that their domestic legislation did "not accept any designation of 'sardines' even with a qualifying term for species other than *Sardina pilchardus* (Walbaum)".

7.137 In light of our considerations above and based on our review of the available evidence and legal arguments, we find that <u>it has not been established that consumers in most member States of the European Communities have always associated the common name "sardines" exclusively with *Sardina pilchardus* and that the use of "X sardines" would therefore not enable the European consumer to distinguish preserved *Sardina pilchardus* from preserved *Sardinops sagax*.</u> We also find that Codex Stan 94 allows Members to provide precise trade description for preserved sardines and thereby promote market transparency so as to protect consumers and promote fair competition.

7.138 We therefore conclude that it has not been demonstrated that Codex Stan 94 would be an ineffective or inappropriate means for the fulfilment of the legitimate objectives pursued by the EC Regulation, i.e., consumer protection, market transparency and fair competition. We conclude that Peru has adduced sufficient evidence and legal arguments to demonstrate that Codex Stan 94 is not ineffective or inappropriate to fulfil the legitimate objectives pursued by the EC Regulation.

Are you convinced by the panel's analysis of the evidence? Is the test underscored in paragraph 7.137 correct? Does it suggest that the EC loses even if many consumers would be confused? Overall, did the panel give appropriate deference to the EC's determinations? What other kinds of evidence might the EC or Peru have presented that would have been probative of whether the EC regulation is necessary to achieve its legitimate objectives?

(3) In the *Asbestos* case (excerpted in Sections 12.4 and 13.2 supra), the panel had ruled that a prohibition on the marketing of a product would not fall within the definition of technical regulation as set out above. The Appellate Body reversed, noting (para. 75):

Viewing the measure as an integrated whole [including both the basic prohibition and exceptions], we see that it lays down "characteristics" for all products that might contain asbestos, and we see also that it lays down the "applicable administrative provisions" for certain products containing chrysotile asbestos fibres which are excluded from the prohibitions in the measure. Accordingly, we find that the measure is a "document" which "lays down product characteristics ... including the applicable administrative provisions, with which compliance is mandatory."

(4) How do the provisions of article 2 of the TBT Agreement compare to GATT Article III? Note in article 2.1, there is a MFN and national treatment

obligation. As in the case of Article III, the obligation is based on according most favorable treatment to "like products." This means that the controversy we noted in respect of Article III over whether identical products produced by different processes or under different conditions must be treated as like products will arise under the TBT Agreement. Suppose a violation of article 2.1 is found because a technical regulation fails to accord no less favorable treatment to the imported like product at issue. Could the exceptions of GATT Article XX be invoked?

(5) Labeling rules are subject to the TBT Agreement. Would it be possible to impose a labeling rule that differentiated products on the basis of the process or production method by which they were made? Would it matter whether the difference was revealed in the product itself?

(6) The heart of the TBT Agreement's obligations on trade barriers is contained in articles 2.2–2.5. Consider, in particular, the language of article 2.2:

> Members shall ensure that technical regulations are not prepared, adopted or applied with a view to or with the effect of creating unnecessary obstacles to international trade. For this purpose, technical regulations shall not be more trade-restrictive than necessary to fulfil a legitimate objective, taking account of the risks non-fulfillment would create. Such legitimate objectives are, *inter alia*, national security requirements; the prevention of deceptive practices; protection of human health or safety, animal or plant life or health, or the environment. In assessing such risks, relevant elements of consideration are, *inter alia*, available scientific and technical information, related processing technology or intended end-uses of products.

A key question presented is how to interpret the word "necessary." How much freedom do parties have to choose their own level of protection for human health? To what extent is the jurisprudence under GATT Article XX(b) and (d) relevant? Should national authorities be given more deference on the issue of what is "necessary" if their objective is, say, the protection of human health or national security on the one hand, versus the avoidance of consumer confusion over the species of sardines or the wheat content of pasta on the other? Can one fashion an economic argument for greater deference to national authorities in the former types of cases because the costs of error by a WTO panel are greater? See Alan O. Sykes, The Least Restrictive Means, 70 *U. Chi. L. Rev.* 403 (2003).

(7) The question of to what extent national regulators must rely on international standards also arises in the SPS setting. Consider SPS article 3.3.

(8) Why do you think that the TBT Agreement establishes a preference for performance characteristics rather than design or descriptive characteristics? See TBT article 2.8.

(9) To what extent does the TBT Agreement apply to local governments and nongovernment organizations? See TBT article 3. What is the extent of the US obligation under article 3.1? Compare GATT Article XXIV:12, as interpreted by the Understanding on the Interpretation of Article XXIV.

(10) To what extent does the TBT Agreement limit the ability of a country to insist on proof that imported products comply with its national standards? To what extent must it accept proof of tests conducted outside the country? See articles 5 and 6.

(11) One of the main goals of the TBT Agreement is transparency, to ensure that those who will be affected by new regulations and standards are informed in time to participate in the drafting process, and that foreign suppliers can readily obtain information about the regulations with which they must comply. How well do its provisions achieve this goal?

(12) The US implementing legislation for the technical barriers agreements can be found as amendments to the Trade Agreements Act of 1979, secs. 401–453.

Chapter 15

SAFEGUARD MEASURES (THE "ESCAPE CLAUSE") AND ADJUSTMENT POLICIES

SECTION 15.1 INTRODUCTION

(A) SCOPE OF THE CHAPTER

Traditionally, international trade rules have distinguished between the ways in which an importing nation can respond to "fair" trade practices on the one hand, and "unfair" trade practices on the other hand. "Safeguard measures" are available under certain conditions to respond to fairly traded imports, while more extensive counter-measures are permitted to respond to imports that are "dumped," subsidized, or otherwise considered to be in violation of international rules of conduct. We discuss safeguard measures in response to fair trade in this chapter, with discussion of unfair trade practices to follow.

Prior to the Uruguay Round, safeguard measures were governed solely by Article XIX of GATT—often referred to as GATT's escape clause. It specifies standards that are supposed to be met before safeguard measures can be imposed. Such measures were to be used only when, "as a result of unforeseen developments and of the effect of obligations incurred" under the GATT, "increased imports" caused or threatened "serious injury" to a domestic industry.

Over time, GATT members began to ignore aspects of these standards in their safeguards policies, and also turned to other techniques for protecting domestic industries such as "voluntary" export restraints and orderly marketing agreements in place of formal actions under Article XIX. Such arrangements came to be known as "gray area measures." Although they technically violated the legal requirements of GATT, they nevertheless embodied government-to-government accords. A rough consensus arose prior to the Uruguay Round, however, that their proliferation was undermining GATT commitments, and that their effects were quite discriminatory. The result was a strong initiative to bring them under GATT discipline, and the Uruguay Round Agreement on Safeguards requires that virtually all gray area measures be eliminated. The result has been increased formal reliance upon Article XIX within the WTO. Between 1995 and 2007, 159 safeguard investigations under national law were notified to the Committee on Safeguards, resulting in over 82 new safeguard measures.[1]

In addition to the prohibition on gray area measures, the Safeguards Agreement also adds substantial clarification and tightening to the rules of safeguards, and has spawned an interesting set of WTO cases. Safeguard measures imposed by the United States and Europe have routinely met with legal challenges, and in every safeguard case that has resulted in a panel or Appellate Body ruling, the challenged measures have been found illegal on multiple grounds. At present, neither the United States nor Europe has any safeguard measures in place, although quite a number are in place in smaller countries that have not been challenged in the dispute settlement process. This chapter will focus on the WTO disputes to date, and on related questions raised under national law.

We are also concerned briefly in this chapter with measures that do not interfere directly in trade, but that nevertheless serve to aid firms or workers harmed by import competition. Subsidies to firms to adapt their product mix to changing competitive conditions, for example, or aid to workers for retraining, may serve as a substitute for or supplement to traditional safeguards measures. These types of programs are often termed "adjustment assistance," and will be the subject of the last section of the chapter.

(B) THE POLICIES OF SAFEGUARDS

What is the logic of affording protection to domestic industries "seriously injured" by import competition? A variety of economic and non-economic arguments for safeguards have been advanced through the years.

(1) Compensation and Adjustment Costs

One theory of safeguards actions is that they might serve to "compensate" those who suffer from trade liberalization. Even granting that increased imports may promote productive efficiency and give the consumer more choice at less expense, the argument runs, the domestic producers of import-competing products may find that they can no longer compete successfully. Businesses may be forced to change their product lines or to go out of business entirely, workers may become unemployed, and communities that were heavily dependent on such businesses may find their tax bases eroded and their local economies in shambles. The injured businesses and workers can argue that they have been made to bear an undue proportion of the costs for society's general gains and that society through government action should help them "adjust" to their new situation. They may urge an analogy here between compensation for trade-related injury and the governmental obligation to

---

1. Source: Annual Reports of the Committee on Safeguards to the Council for Trade in Goods, 1995–2007, compiled through 2005 in Alan O. Sykes, The Agreement on Safeguards: A Commentary (Oxford University Press, 2006).

compensate property owners when property is taken for governmental purposes.

(2) Restoring Competitiveness

It is often claimed by proponents of safeguard measures that they will provide ailing firms with an increase in profits, enabling them to invest in new technology and modern equipment, which will later allow them to compete successfully in the international marketplace. The purported source of net gains to the international community (and to the importing nation) lies with the eventual emergence of efficient competitors. The premise is that the protected industry will in time lower its costs of production to the point that protection is no longer necessary to its survival, and that the eventual savings in production costs (or perhaps the elimination of distortions attributable to monopoly power that would otherwise exist) will more than offset the short-term inefficiencies that arise during the period of protection.

(3) The Safety Valve Hypothesis

"Policymakers need safety valves to pursue a long-term strategy of free trade. * * * [P]olitical pressures for protecting special interests can overwhelm the consensus favoring free trade. The dangers are greatest during periods of general economic distress, which can produce legislated quotas * * * or voluntary restraint agreements or more formal agreements negotiated by the executive branch but motivated by congressional pressure (as in the case of quotas on automobiles, steel and textiles). Safety valves that relieve protectionist pressure, diverting it from the purely political arena, can therefore be extremely useful. They can facilitate trade liberalization and better enable lawmakers to withstand demands for protectionist policies."[2]

(4) The Public Choice/Contractarian Perspective

"Note that the revocation of a particular [trade] concession benefits import-competing firms in the revoking country but hurts exporters abroad. Those exporters will complain to their political officials about the loss of access to their overseas market, and likely withdraw some political support from the officials who were responsible for obtaining the original concession. Indeed, depending upon the form of government, a loss of export earnings may directly reduce the welfare of officials in power. A [politically sophisticated trade] agreement will nevertheless permit 'escape' in states of the world in which the attendant political gains to officials in the importing country 'outweigh' the costs to the officials in the exporting country. Suppose, for example, that in some state of the world, the concession by one country is highly disadvantageous to its officials, and the costs to officials in the other country if the concession is revoked would be modest. The parties may then benefit from an agreement to allow the first country to escape its concession in that state of the world. The quid pro quo from the perspective of officials

2. Robert Lawrence & Robert Litan, Saving Free Trade 23–24 (1986).

in the other country is an agreement to let them escape their concessions in the same or some other state of the world in which they would gain considerably and the costs to officials in their trading partner would be modest."[3] Sykes proceeds to argue, drawing on ideas in the economic literature, that "seriously injured" industries may be especially likely to exert strong pressures on their political officials for protection, while prosperous exporters—those whose exports are increasing—may accept temporary export restrictions without great political resistance. If so, the conditions set out in the GATT escape clause may correspond roughly to circumstances in which safeguard measures benefit officials in the importing country more than they harm officials in exporting countries. All officials may then benefit on average because all know that they can avail themselves of safeguard measures under appropriate circumstances.

How convincing are these various arguments? The literature on the logic and wisdom of safeguards policy is extensive—in addition to the sources noted above, see Paul R. Krugman, Competitiveness: A Dangerous Obsession, Foreign Affairs, Mar./Apr. 1994; Kyle Bagwell and Robert W. Staiger, Enforcement, Private Political Pressure, and the General Agreement on Tariffs and Trade/World Trade Organization Escape Clause, 34 J. Legal Stud. 471 (2005); B. Peter Rosendorff and Helen V. Milner, The Optimal Design of International Trade Institutions: Uncertainty and Escape, 55 Int'l Org. 829 (2001).

SECTION 15.2 RULES AND PROCEDURES FOR SAFEGUARDS CASES

(A) WTO RULES

WTO members undertake safeguard measures pursuant to their own national laws on the subject. The details of the national legal arrangements vary considerably, but they are all subject to certain constraints imposed by the Safeguards Agreement. In this section, we briefly describe key requirements of the Safeguards Agreement, and then consider how the United States has implemented these requirements in its own national legislation.

GATT Article XIX(1)(a) states: "If, as a result of unforeseen developments and of the effect of the obligations incurred by a Member under this Agreement, including tariff concessions, any product is being imported into the territory of that Member in such increased quantities and under such conditions as to cause or threaten serious injury to domestic producers in that territory of like or directly competitive

---

3. Alan O. Sykes, Protectionism as a "Safeguard": A Positive Analysis of the GATT "Escape Clause" With Normative Speculations, 58 U.Chi.L.Rev. 255, 281–82 (1991).

products, the Member shall be free, in respect of such product, and to the extent and for such time as may be necessary to prevent or remedy such injury, to suspend the obligation in whole or in part or to withdraw or modify the concession.''

The parallel provision in the Safeguards Agreement is Article 2.1: ''A Member may apply a safeguard measure to a product only if that Member has determined, pursuant to the provisions set out below, that such product is being imported into its territory in such increased quantities, absolute or relative to domestic production, and under such conditions as to cause or threaten to cause serious injury to the domestic industry that produces like or directly competitive products.''

The essential prerequisites for a safeguard measure in both texts may be broken into the following four elements:

(i) imports in ''such increased quantities'' and ''under such conditions'' as to

(ii) cause or threaten

(iii) serious injury

(iv) to domestic producers of like or directly competitive products.

We may refer to these elements as the ''increased imports'' element (i), the element of actual or threatened ''serious injury'' (iii), the industry definition element (iv), and the causation element (ii).

There are also some obvious differences between the two texts. The Safeguards Agreement indicates that the increased imports requirement can be met by either an absolute increase in imports or an increase relative to domestic production (increased market share). This interpretation is consistent with GATT practice as it evolved prior to the WTO. The other striking difference is the omission from the Safeguards Agreement of any required linkage between ''increased quantities'' on the one hand, and ''unforeseen developments and... the effects of the obligations incurred...under this Agreement'' on the other. This difference has been a source of legal controversy within the WTO as shall be seen.

In addition to the basic prerequisites set out above, the Safeguards Agreement elaborates a number of other requirements.[1] Safeguard measures may only be applied only following an investigation conducted by competent authorities pursuant to previously published procedures. Although the Agreement does not contain detailed procedural requirements, it does require reasonable public notice of the investigation, and that interested parties (importers, exporters, producers, etc.) be given the opportunity to present their views and to respond to the views of others. The relevant authorities are obligated to publish a report presenting and explaining their findings on all pertinent issues, including a demonstration of the relevance of the factors examined.

---

1. This summary borrows heavily from the summary provided by the WTO at http://www.wto.org/english/tratop_e/safeg_e/safeint.htm.

The Agreement defines "serious injury" as significant impairment in the position of a domestic industry. "Threat of serious injury" is threat that is clearly imminent as shown by facts, and not based on mere allegation, conjecture or remote possibility. A "domestic industry" is defined as the producers as a whole of the like or directly competitive products operating within the territory of a Member, or producers who collectively account for a major proportion of the total domestic production of those products.

In determining whether serious injury or threat is present, investigating authorities are to evaluate all relevant factors having a bearing on the condition of the industry, and are not to attribute to imports injury caused by other factors. Factors that must be analyzed are the absolute and relative rate and amount of increase in imports, the market share taken by the increased imports, and changes in level of sales, production, productivity, capacity utilization, profits and losses, and employment of the domestic industry.

Safeguard measures may only be applied to the extent necessary to remedy or prevent serious injury and to facilitate adjustment, within certain limits. If the measure takes the form of a quantitative restriction, the level must not be below the actual import level of the most recent three representative years, unless there is clear justification for doing otherwise. Rules also apply as to how quota shares are to be allocated among supplier countries, as to compensation to Members whose trade is affected, and as to consultations with affected Members.

The maximum duration of any safeguard measure is four years, unless it is extended consistent with the Agreement's provisions. In particular, a measure may be extended only if its continuation is found to be necessary to prevent or remedy serious injury, and only if evidence shows that the industry is adjusting.

The initial period of application plus any extension normally cannot exceed eight years. In addition, safeguard measures in place for longer than one year must be progressively liberalized at regular intervals during the period of application. If a measure is extended beyond the initial period of application, it can be no more restrictive during this period than it was at the end of the initial period, and it should continue to be liberalized. Any measure of more than three years duration must be reviewed at mid-term. If appropriate based on that review, the Member applying the measure must withdraw it or increase the pace of its liberalization.

In applying a safeguard measure, the Member must maintain a substantially equivalent level of concessions and other obligations with respect to affected exporting Members. To do so, any adequate means of trade compensation may be agreed with the affected Members. Absent such agreement, the affected exporting Members individually may suspend substantially equivalent concessions and other obligations. This latter right cannot be exercised during the first three years of application of a safeguard measure if the measure is taken based on an absolute increase in imports, and otherwise conforms to the provisions of the Agreement. This limitation on the right to suspend concessions encourages the use of short term safeguards and diminishes the temptation to resort to gray area measures.

(B) SAFEGUARD MEASURES UNDER U.S. LAW

In the United States, the procedures for obtaining escape clause relief have varied significantly over time, often reflecting general Congressional attitudes towards the desirability of free trade. Existing law is found in title II of the Trade Act of 1974 (sections 201 et seq.), and safeguard cases are sometimes known domestically as "Section 201" cases. Title II is codified at 19 U.S.C. §§ 2251 et seq. Currently under US law, an escape clause proceeding begins with a petition to the International Trade Commission (ITC) by representatives of the allegedly injured domestic industry (such as a trade association, individual firm, union or group of workers), or with a request to the ITC by the President, the US Trade Representative, the Senate Finance Committee, or the House Ways and Means Committee, or upon initiation by the ITC itself. The ITC, formerly known as the Tariff Commission, consists of six Commissioners, not more than three of whom belong to the same political party. A petition for relief must give information justifying relief, including extensive data on imports, domestic production and injury, as well as an explanation of how the industry is making an effort to compete with the imports and how it will adjust if relief is granted.

The initial prerequisites for a safeguard measure under US law are to be found in Section 201 of the 1974 Act, which asks whether "an article is being imported into the United States in such increased quantities as to be a substantial cause of serious injury, or the threat thereof, to the domestic industry producing an article like or directly competitive with the imported article." The term "substantial cause" is later defined as "a cause which is important and not less than any other cause." Plainly, this text differs in some significant ways from the WTO treaty text set out above, a matter that we will take up below. The ITC determines whether these prerequisites of US law are fulfilled. Its investigation and report must be completed within six months.

Interested parties typically submit written materials and present testimony at ITC hearings. Decisions of the ITC are generally reviewable in the Court of International Trade or (in some cases) the Court of Appeals for the Federal Circuit. In escape clause cases, however, in large part because of the involvement of the President, judicial review is extremely limited—essentially to questions of procedural regularity. See Maple Leaf Fish Co. v. United States, 762 F.2d 86 (Fed.Cir.1985).

If the ITC makes an affirmative determination (including a tie vote), those Commissioners voting in the affirmative recommend a remedy and pass the matter on to the President, who must usually act within 60 days. Under Section 203 of the 1974 Trade Act, the remedies open to the President include a range of options. The President can increase duties, impose quotas or tariff rate quotas, or enter into "agreements" with exporting nations (but recall the WTO prohibition that now exists on many such "gray area" measures). The President also has broad discretion to impose as large a trade restriction as he considers necessary to achieve the purposes of Section 201.

One of the significant legislative issues in the drafting of the 1974 Act was how much discretion to give to the President to depart from findings or recommendations of the ITC. Some urged that the ITC determination and remedy be final; while others urged that for foreign policy reasons as well as broader economic policy reasons, the President should have the final say in all of these cases. In the Act as passed, there was a large but not complete measure of discretion for the President,[2] which can be contrasted with the US laws regarding dumping and subsidies, where there is almost no discretion in the executive. The 1974 Act tried to achieve a balance between those who wanted more and those who wanted no presidential discretion, and sections 202 and 203 reflected this objective. The 1988 amendments struck the balance slightly differently, and Section 203 now states that that the President "shall take all appropriate and feasible action within his power which the President determines will facilitate efforts by the domestic industry to make positive adjustment to import competition and provide greater economic and social benefits than costs." Later clauses give the President the right to consider, for example, the impact of relief upon consumers and competition, the burden on the economy of any compensation that may be required to trading partners under GATT, and national security.

Thus, the President considers a substantially broader set of interests than the ITC, and it is not surprising that the President has with some regularity elected not to grant the relief recommended by the ITC. In the original Section 203, a legislative veto was included to allow the Congress by concurrent resolution to force the President to follow the ITC recommendation. After the US Supreme Court's decision in *Chadha*, discussed in Section 3.3 supra, the validity of this congressional veto provision was in doubt. In the 1984 Trade and Tariff Act, Congress amended Section 203 to eliminate this veto, and provided that Congress may override the President and cause the recommendation of the ITC to come into effect by adopting a joint resolution to that effect. This change eliminates the problems raised by *Chadha* since the President may veto any such resolution. Neither the concurrent resolution procedure before 1984 nor the joint resolution procedure in effect since has ever been successfully invoked, however, so that the President's decisions have in practice proven final.

If the President chooses to grant relief in the form of trade restrictions, US law provides that protection shall ordinarily be phased down during the period of relief. It also provides in Section 203 for a four-year

2. As noted, the courts have not attempted to control this discretion. See, e.g., Maple Leaf Fish Co. v. United States, 762 F.2d 86 (Fed.Cir.1985).

period of relief in accordance with the Safeguards Agreement, which can be extended to a total of eight years if the ITC makes a determination that an extension is needed to prevent injury and that a positive adjustment is occurring. The result is that the ITC must undertake a scaled down version of the original investigation after a few years, known as a "203 review" (a review of the President's action taken under Section 203). Respondents have the opportunity to appear and to argue anew that protection is not necessary or that its costs exceed its benefits.

Notes and Questions

(1) The role of the attorney in the ITC phase of a Section 201 proceeding is that of an administrative litigator, submitting briefs and presenting witnesses for or against the findings that the ITC must make if safeguard measures are to be imposed. During the Presidential phase of the escape clause investigation, by contrast, the role of the attorney resembles that of the typical Washington lobbyist, striving to build a political coalition for or against import relief. The potential members of the coalition on the petitioners' side are to a great degree obvious—the beneficiaries of protection, typically the petitioning industry itself. How does one proceed on the respondents' side, given that foreign exporters have no vote in US elections? In reflecting on this issue, it is perhaps instructive to recall what happened after the ITC determinations in the *Automobiles* case and the *Unwrought Copper* case in the 1970's and 1980's. In the *Automobiles* case, President Carter eventually secured a voluntary restraint arrangement with Japan (which lasted, at least on paper, until 1994) despite the negative vote by the ITC. Such a "gray area" measure would now be clearly illegal under WTO rules. In the *Unwrought Copper* case, by contrast, President Reagan declined to grant relief despite a unanimous affirmative vote at the ITC. Of what significance is the fact that the burden of auto restraints fell upon individual American consumers, while the burden of restrictions on refined copper imports would have also fallen on industrial consumers such as the wire and brass industries?

(2) The lobbyists for respondents' interests are retained and paid in many cases by foreign companies or governments. Such "foreign agents" (to use the language of the federal statute that requires them to register their activities with the Justice Department) are regularly the target of criticism and derision by domestic interests, even to the point of suggesting that they are unpatriotic. Should lawyers have any qualms about such representation? Suppose, for example, that respondents' domestic representatives purchase a number of tickets to a $1,000 a plate fundraiser for the Chairman of the Ways and Means Committee. Undue influence, or government as usual?

(3) Given limited space, we focus on issues raised by WTO and US law in this chapter. Additional issues arise under national laws in force elsewhere. The key provisions of European law, in particular, may be found in Council Regulation (EC) No. 3285/94 of 22 December 1994.

SECTION 15.3   CRITICAL ISSUES
IN SAFEGUARDS CASES

In this section, we focus on the issues that have been the most contentious in safeguards cases under both WTO and US law. By and large, these issues concern the basic prerequisites for safeguard measures identified in GATT Article XIX:1(a) and in article 2.1 of the Safeguards Agreement. The discussion is organized by issue rather than by cases, and thus excerpts from certain WTO decisions will appear under more than one heading.

(A) UNFORESEEN DEVELOPMENTS

Recall the difference in language between GATT Article XIX:1(a) and article 2.1 of the Agreement on Safeguards, with only the former requiring a linkage between increased imports and "unforeseen developments." Did article 2.1 effectively "amend" WTO rules to eliminate that requirement?

UNITED STATES—SAFEGUARD MEASURES ON IMPORTS OF FRESH, CHILLED OR FROZEN LAMB MEAT FROM NEW ZEALAND AND AUSTRALIA
WT/DS177 & 178/AB/R.
Appellate Body Report adopted May 16, 2001.

2. On 7 October 1998, the United States International Trade Commission (the "USITC") initiated a safeguard investigation into imports of lamb meat. By Proclamation of the President of the United States, dated 7 July 1999, the United States imposed a definitive safeguard measure, in the form of a tariff-rate quota, on imports of fresh, chilled and frozen lamb meat, effective as of 22 July 1999. * * *

* * *

4. * * * [T]he Panel concluded:

(a) that the United States has acted inconsistently with Article XIX:1(a) of GATT 1994 by failing to demonstrate as a matter of fact the existence of "unforeseen developments";

* * *

Unforeseen Developments

65. Before the Panel, Australia and New Zealand claimed that the United States failed to comply with the requirements of Article XIX:1(a) of the GATT 1994 regarding "unforeseen developments". The Panel found:

Article XIX:1 read in the context of SG Article 3.1 requires the competent national authority, in its determination, to reach a conclusion demonstrating the existence of "unforeseen developments" in the sense of GATT Article XIX:1.

* * *

68.   We begin by noting that the claim made by both Australia and New Zealand before the Panel was that the United States acted inconsistently with its obligation in Article XIX:1(a) of the GATT 1994 relating to "unforeseen developments". Article XIX:1(a) of the GATT 1994 reads:

> If, as a result of unforeseen developments and of the effect of the obligations incurred by a Member under this Agreement, including tariff concessions, any product is being imported into the territory of that Member in such increased quantities and under such conditions as to cause or threaten serious injury to domestic producers in that territory of like or directly competitive products, the Member shall be free, in respect of such product, and to the extent and for such time as may be necessary to prevent or remedy such injury, to suspend the obligation in whole or in part or to withdraw or modify the concession.

69.   In our Reports in *Argentina—Footwear Safeguard* and *Korea— Dairy Safeguard*, we examined the relationship between Article XIX of the GATT 1994 and the Agreement on Safeguards and, in particular, whether, with the entry into force of the Agreement on Safeguards, Article XIX continues to impose obligations on WTO Members when they apply safeguard measures. We observed in those two appeals that "the provisions of Article XIX of the GATT 1994 *and* the provisions of the Agreement on Safeguards are *all* provisions of one treaty, the WTO Agreement", and we said that these two texts must be read "harmoniously" and as "an inseparable package of rights and disciplines". We derived support for this interpretation from Articles 1 and 11.1(a) of the Agreement on Safeguards. We observed, in both the Reports, that:

> Article 1 states that the purpose of the Agreement on Safeguards is to establish "rules for the application of safeguard measures which shall be understood to mean *those measures provided for in* Article XIX of GATT 1994." (emphasis added) The ordinary meaning of the language in Article 11.1(a)—"unless such action conforms with the provisions of that Article applied in accordance with this Agreement"—is that any safeguard action *must conform* with the provisions of Article XIX of the GATT 1994 *as well as* with the provisions of the Agreement on Safeguards. Thus, any safeguard measure imposed after the entry into force of the WTO Agreement must comply with the provisions of *both* the Agreement on Safeguards and Article XIX of the GATT 1994.

70.   We reiterate: Articles 1 and 11.1(a) of the Agreement on Safeguards express the full and continuing applicability of Article XIX of the GATT 1994, which no longer stands in isolation, but has been clarified and reinforced by the Agreement on Safeguards.

71.   Based on this interpretation of the relationship between Article XIX of the GATT 1994 and the Agreement on Safeguards, we found in both these previous Reports:

> The first clause in Article XIX:1(a)—"as a result of unforeseen developments and of the obligations incurred by a Member under

the Agreement, including tariff concessions . . ."—is a dependent clause which, in our view, is linked grammatically to the verb phrase "is being imported" in the second clause of that paragraph. Although we do not view the first clause in Article XIX:1(a) as establishing independent *conditions* for the application of a safeguard measure, additional to the *conditions* set forth in the second clause of that paragraph, we do believe that the first clause describes certain *circumstances* which must be demonstrated as a matter of fact in order for a safeguard measure to be applied consistently with the provisions of Article XIX of the GATT 1994. In this sense, we believe that there is *a logical connection* between the circumstances described in the first clause—"as a result of unforeseen developments and of the effect of the obligations incurred by a Member under this Agreement, including tariff concessions . . ."—and the conditions set forth in the second clause of Article XIX:1(a) for the imposition of a safeguard measure.

72.   Although we stated in these two Reports that, under Article XIX:1(a) of the GATT 1994, unforeseen developments "must be demonstrated as a matter of fact", we did not have occasion, in those two appeals, to examine when, where or how that demonstration should occur. In conducting such an examination now, we note that the text of Article XIX provides no express guidance on this issue. However, as the existence of unforeseen developments is a prerequisite that must be demonstrated, as we have stated, "in order for a safeguard measure to be applied" consistently with Article XIX of the GATT 1994, it follows that this demonstration must be made *before* the safeguard measure is applied. Otherwise, the legal basis for the measure is flawed. We find instructive guidance for where and when the "demonstration" should occur in the "logical connection" that we observed previously between the two clauses of Article XIX:1(a). The first clause, as we noted, contains, in part, the "circumstance" of "unforeseen developments". The second clause, as we said, relates to the three "conditions" for the application of safeguard measures, which are also reiterated in Article 2.1 of the Agreement on Safeguards. Clearly, the fulfilment of these conditions must be the central element of the report of the competent authorities, which must be published under Article 3.1 of the Agreement on Safeguards. In our view, the logical connection between the "conditions" identified in the second clause of Article XIX:1(a) and the "circumstances" outlined in the first clause of that provision dictates that the demonstration of the existence of these circumstances must also feature in the same report of the competent authorities. Any other approach would sever the "logical connection" between these two clauses, and would also leave vague and uncertain how compliance with the first clause of Article XIX:1(a) would be fulfilled.

73.   In this case, we see no indication in the USITC Report that the USITC addressed the issue of "unforeseen developments" at all. It is true that the USITC Report identifies two changes in the type of lamb meat products imported into the United States. These were: the propor-

tion of imported fresh and chilled lamb meat increased in relation to the proportion of imported frozen lamb meat; and, the cut size of imported lamb meat increased. The USITC Report mentions the first of these changes in examining the "like products" at issue, and mentions both changes under the heading "causation" while describing the substitutability of domestic and imported lamb meat in the domestic marketplace. However, we observe that the USITC Report does not discuss or offer any explanation as to why these changes could be regarded as "unforeseen developments" within the meaning of Article XIX:1(a) of the GATT 1994. It follows that the USITC Report does not *demonstrate* that the safeguard measure at issue has been applied, *inter alia*, ". . . as a result of unforeseen developments . . .".

74.   The USITC's failure to address the existence of unforeseen developments, in the USITC Report of April 1999, is not surprising, as the USITC is not obliged by any United States legislation, regulation, or other domestic rule, to examine the existence of unforeseen developments in its investigation into the situation of a domestic industry. Although the United States has subsequently modified its position on this issue,[1] we recall that, as a third participant in both *Korea—Dairy Safeguard* and *Argentina—Footwear Safeguard*, the United States argued that the omission of unforeseen developments from the Agreement on Safeguards meant that it was no longer necessary to demonstrate the existence of unforeseen developments. Our Reports in *Korea—Dairy Safeguard* and *Argentina—Footwear Safeguard*, in which we found that unforeseen developments must be demonstrated as a matter of fact, were circulated on 14 December 1999, that is to say, more than seven months *after* the report of the USITC on the domestic lamb meat industry was published in April 1999. Our two Reports were, therefore, not known to the USITC when it rendered its report in the present case.

75.   Accordingly, although we do not agree with every aspect of the Panel's reasoning, we uphold the Panel's conclusion, in paragraphs 7.45 and 8.1(a) of the Panel Report, "that the United States has failed to demonstrate as a matter of fact the existence of unforeseen developments as required by Article XIX:1(a) of GATT 1994". * * *

76.   We emphasize that neither Australia nor New Zealand has claimed that the United States acted inconsistently with Article 3.1 of the Agreement on Safeguards with respect to unforeseen developments. We do not, therefore, rule on whether the USITC, and, hence, the United States, acted inconsistently with Article 3.1 of the Agreement on Safeguards because the USITC failed to "set[] forth . . . findings and reasoned conclusions" on this issue. Nonetheless, we observe that Article 3.1 requires competent authorities to set forth findings and reasoned conclusions on "all pertinent issues of fact and law" in their published report. As Article XIX:1(a) of the GATT 1994 requires that "unforeseen

---

1.   [original note 40] At the oral hearing, the United States indicated that it is no longer of the view that it is unnecessary to demonstrate the existence of unforeseen developments.

developments" must be demonstrated, as a matter of fact, for a safeguard measure to be applied, the existence of "unforeseen developments" is, in our view, a "pertinent issue[] of fact and law", under Article 3.1, for the application of a safeguard measure, and it follows that the published report of the competent authorities, under that Article, must contain a "finding" or "reasoned conclusion" on "unforeseen developments".

Notes and Questions

(1) The "unforeseen developments" language in GATT Article XIX was largely ignored by GATT members for many decades, which no doubt explains why US law makes no reference to it in its instructions to the ITC. The Appellate Body has now clearly resurrected the requirement. Are you persuaded that GATT Article XIX and the Safeguards Agreement create cumulative obligations as the Appellate Body has concluded? Would it be permissible to conclude that a settled "practice" of ignoring the unforeseen developments requirement in the later decades of GATT warrants the conclusion that this clause of Article XIX was effectively eliminated by the Agreement on Safeguards? Note that other aspects of Article XIX, such as the authority for retaliatory suspension of concessions in XIX:3(a), were explicitly modified in the Agreement on Safeguards (which suspends the retaliation right for three years under specified conditions). Given an obvious intention to amend the safeguards rules in certain respects, why not presume that the omission of the unforeseen developments requirement is yet another such amendment? Or must one presume that no amendment was intended unless it is explicit?

(2) How does a nation comply with the unforeseen developments requirement as a practical matter? The developments in question must have been unforeseen—but by whom? At what point in time? Suppose that the last tariff concession on a particular product was during the Kennedy Round. Can anything that happens today be said to have been "foreseen" by negotiators that long ago? Did the creation of the WTO "reset the clock" so that expectations are measured as of 1994?

(3) What do you see as the purpose of the "unforeseen developments" requirement in GATT Article XIX? Can an understanding of its purpose aid in its interpretation?

(4) In the well-publicized WTO dispute involving a US safeguard measure on various categories of steel imports, the unforeseen developments issue again raised its head. The United States argued, based on a hastily prepared supplemental ITC report on the matter, that US imports had increased because of events such as the Asian financial crisis and the collapse of the former Soviet Union. The panel accepted that these events might have been unforeseen, but concluded that the United States had not done an adequate job of tracing through their effects on US imports and thereby on the domestic industry. The Appellate Body affirmed the panel's findings. See United States—Definitive Safeguard Measures on Imports of Certain Steel Products, WT/DS248–49, 251–54, 258–59/AB/R, adopted December 10, 2003. How are such effects to be established? Would anything sort of a global

econometric model of steel trade, incorporating supply and demand conditions in every major trading nation or region, be sufficient?

(5) Article XIX:1(a) also makes reference to the "effect of the obligations incurred...under this Agreement." The Appellate Body's reading of the treaty text also resurrects this element. What is required to satisfy it? Is it enough for a member to say that, but for a tariff binding or some other GATT obligation, it would have taken protective measures against imports, so that any increase in imports is due to the "obligations incurred?"

(6) For a review of WTO case law on these issues to date, see Alan O. Sykes, The Agreement on Safeguards: A Commentary (Oxford University Press, 2006), chapter 5.

(B) INCREASED IMPORTS

Another prerequisite for safeguard measures is the existence of "such increased quantities" of imports, either in absolute terms or in market share. In determining whether this test is met, perhaps the thorniest issue, on which neither the WTO text nor the US statute provides much guidance, concerns the time period over which the existence of an increase is measured (the "baseline"). For example, what if imports have increased in absolute terms over a one-or two-year period, but are below their absolute and relative peaks, which occurred several years earlier?

ARGENTINA—SAFEGUARD MEASURES ON IMPORTS OF FOOTWEAR

WT/DS121/AB/R.
Appellate Body Report adopted January 12, 2000.

1.   Argentina and the European Communities appeal certain issues of law and legal interpretation in the Panel Report, *Argentina—Safeguard Measures on Imports of Footwear* (the "Panel Report"). The Panel was established to consider a complaint by the European Communities with respect to the application by Argentina of certain safeguard measures on imports of footwear.

* * *

5.   The Panel concluded that "the definitive safeguard measure on footwear based on Argentina's investigation and determination is inconsistent with Articles 2 and 4 of the Agreement on Safeguards" and, therefore, "that there is nullification or impairment of the benefits accruing to the European Communities under the Agreement on Safeguards within the meaning of Article 3.8 of the DSU." * * *

Increased Imports

125.   With respect to the requirement relating to "increased imports", the Panel stated as follows:

The Agreement on Safeguards requires an increase in imports as a basic prerequisite for the application of a safeguard measure. The relevant provisions are in Articles 2.1 and 4.2(a).

* * *

Thus, to determine whether imports have increased in "such quantities" for purposes of applying a safeguard measure, these two provisions require an analysis of the rate and amount of the increase in imports, in absolute terms and as a percentage of domestic production.

126.   In its evaluation of whether the investigation by the Argentine authorities demonstrated the required increase in imports under Articles 2.1 and 4.2(a), the Panel stated the following:

> ... *the Agreement requires not just an increase (i.e., any increase) in imports, but an increase in "such ... quantities" as to cause or threaten to cause serious injury.* The Agreement provides no numerical guidance as to how this is to be judged, nor in our view could it do so. But this does not mean that this requirement is meaningless. To the contrary, we believe that it means that the increase in imports must be judged in its full context, in particular with regard to its "rate and amount" as required by Article 4.2(a). Thus, considering the changes in import levels over the entire period of investigation, as discussed above, seems unavoidable when making a determination of whether there has been an increase in imports "in such quantities" in the sense of Article 2.1 (emphasis added).

127.   [Eds. note: Argentina had examined imports over a five-year period of investigation from 1991 through 1995.] The Panel concluded that Argentina did not adequately consider the "intervening trends in imports, in particular the steady and significant declines in imports beginning in 1994, as well as the sensitivity of the analysis to the particular end points of the investigation period used." For these reasons, the Panel concluded that "Argentina's investigation did not demonstrate that there were increased imports within the meaning of Articles 2.1 and 4.2(a)". The Panel, though, rejected an argument made by the European Communities "that only a 'sharply increasing' trend in imports at the end of the investigation period can satisfy this requirement."

128.   Argentina maintains that, in its interpretation and application of the requirement of "increased imports" in Articles 2.1 and 4.2 of the Agreement on Safeguards, the Panel "impose[d] a variety of methodological hurdles which must be overcome before a finding of 'increased imports' can be justified." In particular, Argentina argues that the Panel misinterpreted the word "rate" in Article 4.2(a) to include "direction", and found that there could only be "increased imports" if: (i) a change in the base year from 1991 to 1992 would still result in an increase; (ii) the analysis of end points and interim periods is mutually reinforcing; and (iii) it is found that the decrease in imports in 1994 and 1995 was

temporary. Argentina also asserts that the Panel "collapsed" the "increased imports" requirement "with the other qualitative requirements of Article" and wrongly treated it as a *"qualitative,* rather than a separate *quantitative* requirement." The ordinary meaning of "increased imports", in Argentina's view, is that imports have become greater, and Argentina argues that there is no factual or contextual support for any additional requirements in the Agreement on Safeguards.

129.   We agree with the Panel that Articles 2.1 and 4.2(a) of the Agreement on Safeguards require a demonstration not merely of *any* increase in imports, but, instead, of imports "in such increased quantities ... and under such conditions as to cause or threaten to cause serious injury." In addition, we agree with the Panel that the specific provisions of Article 4.2(a) require that "the rate *and amount* of the increase in imports ... in absolute and relative terms" (emphasis added) must be evaluated. Thus, we do not dispute the Panel's view and ultimate conclusion that the competent authorities are required to consider the *trends* in imports over the period of investigation (rather than just comparing the end points) under Article 4.2(a). As a result, we agree with the Panel's conclusion that "Argentina did not adequately consider the intervening trends in imports, in particular the steady and significant declines in imports beginning in 1994, as well as the sensitivity of the analysis to the particular end points of the investigation period used."

130.   All the same, while we do not find that the Panel erred in its application of the requirement in Article 2.1 of the Agreement on Safeguards that the *"product is being imported* ... in such increased quantities", we do find the Panel's interpretation of that requirement somewhat lacking. We note that the Panel characterized this condition in Article 2.1 on several occasions in the Panel Report simply as "increased imports". However, the actual requirement, and we emphasize that this requirement is found in both Article 2.1 of the Agreement on Safeguards and Article XIX:1(a) of the GATT 1994, is that "such product *is being imported* ... in such increased quantities", "and under such conditions as to cause or threaten to cause serious injury to the domestic industry" (emphasis added). Although we agree with the Panel that the "increased quantities" of imports cannot be just *any* increase, we do not agree with the Panel that it is reasonable to examine the trend in imports over a five-year historical period. In our view, the use of the present tense of the verb phrase "is being imported" in both Article 2.1 of the Agreement on Safeguards and Article XIX:1(a) of the GATT 1994 indicates that it is necessary for the competent authorities to examine recent imports, and not simply trends in imports during the past five years—or, for that matter, during any other period of several years. In our view, the phrase "is being imported" implies that the increase in imports must have been sudden and recent.

131.   * * * We also believe that the phrase "in *such* increased quantities" in Article 2.1 of the Agreement on Safeguards and Article XIX:1(a) of the GATT 1994 is meaningful to this determination. In our

view, the determination of whether the requirement of imports "in such increased quantities" is met is not a merely mathematical or technical determination. In other words, it is not enough for an investigation to show simply that imports of the product this year were more than last year—or five years ago. Again, and it bears repeating, not just *any* increased quantities of imports will suffice. There must be "*such* increased quantities" as to cause or threaten to cause serious injury to the domestic industry in order to fulfil this requirement for applying a safeguard measure. And this language in both Article 2.1 of the Agreement on Safeguards and Article XIX:1(a) of the GATT 1994, we believe, requires that the increase in imports must have been recent enough, sudden enough, sharp enough, and significant enough, both quantitatively and qualitatively, to cause or threaten to cause "serious injury".

Notes and Questions

(1) Does the Appellate Body in paragraph 130 impliedly accept the European argument that "only a 'sharply increasing' trend in imports at the end of the investigation period can satisfy the [increased imports] requirement?" Is it wise to focus so heavily on the immediate past, or will trends over a larger window of time be more informative as to the competitive position of a domestic industry in relation to imports?

(2) Does the case give enough guidance to members for them to be able to select a baseline for the increased imports inquiry that will withstand scrutiny in the dispute settlement process?

(3) Argentina's choice of a five-year window within which to examine the question of increased imports was perhaps unsurprising given that such an approach had by then become the standard practice of the United States at the ITC. What alternative ways might one use to select the baseline? Are the alternatives subject to such a degree of manipulation that a simple rule of thumb becomes preferable?

With regard to these questions, consider how the ITC wrestled with them during an earlier era in Stainless Steel and Alloy Tool Steel, US Intl. Trade Commn., Inv. No. TA–201–5, Pub. No. 756, 1 ITRD 5404 (1976):

VIEWS OF COMMISSIONERS MOORE AND BEDELL

* * *

We consider the increased imports requirement satisfied because imports increased between 1964 and 1975. We have used this time frame to avoid a determination based solely on a time period in which abnormal economic conditions existed. For example, the time period 1968–74 was not only one of unusual market conditions, but one in which unique governmental actions distorted stainless steel and alloy tool steel import levels. During this period the domestic industry was adversely affected by the Voluntary Restraint Agreement (VRA) and its subsequent changes, a world-wide nickel strike, two recessions, and domestic price controls.

Since 1964, total imports of stainless steel and alloy tool steel have tripled, imports of stainless sheets and strip have more than doubled, and other stainless steel and alloy tool steel articles have increased threefold to tenfold.

The act also states that the Commission should examine whether imports increased relative to domestic production. Imports increased from 116,000 tons in 1973 to 151,000 tons in 1974. During January–September 1975, imports increased to 120,000 tons, compared with 95,000 tons entered during the corresponding period in 1974. The ratio of imports to US production has more than doubled, rising from 9.9 percent in 1973 to 23.1 percent during the most recent period, January–September 1975. Facts developed during the Commission's investigation indicate that imports will continue their upward trend.

* * *

VIEWS OF VICE CHAIRMAN MINCHEW

* * *

It is my view that, in the absence of extraordinary circumstances, the Commission should look at the increase in imports resulting from only the most recent trade concessions, so that the injury considered would be a new and continuing injury from increased imports as opposed to an "old" injury. The Senate Finance Committee Report at page 120 states:

> The increase in imports referred to would generally be such increases as have occurred since the effectiveness of the most recent trade-agreement concessions proclaimed by the President, i.e., as of now, the effectiveness of the Kennedy Round concessions beginning in 1968.

In certain circumstances in the past I have been willing to look at a shorter time frame to determine the trend of increasing imports, as I feel is my prerogative under the statute, but to look back beyond the last trade-agreement concessions would require extraordinary circumstances. In the present case, despite some out-of-the-ordinary occurrences since 1968, I do not feel that these occurrences warrant my looking beyond the 1968 trade-agreement concessions for purposes of determining increased import trends.

* * *

VIEWS OF COMMISSIONER ABLONDI

* * *

Increased Imports

Inseparably connected to the issue of "increased" imports is the selection of a time period over which imports are to be measured. In my judgment the relevant measuring period in the instant case is confined to the period since 1968.

Section 201(b)(1) of the act requires the Commission to determine "whether an article is being imported into the United States in such increased quantities as to be a substantial cause of serious injury, or the threat thereof, to the domestic industry * * * " (emphasis added). By using the present tense, Congress clearly intended that the Commission consider only imports which have occurred during a period relative to the alleged injury. The act requires that imports be related to the injury claimed, and that the injury be current, or "new" injury. The relevant period of importation, then, must necessarily be close to the time of the injury (that is, to the present time) rather than during earlier periods of importation having little or no impact on present industry conditions.

* * *

It has been argued that the period since 1968 is unrepresentative and that the Commission should therefore consider imports which occurred prior to that time. I disagree. The factors cited by advocates of a longer measuring period are insufficient to warrant a departure from the measuring period outlined by Congress.

Many of the factors which are asserted to be the cause of unusual market conditions during the period 1968–74 have been encountered in each investigation conducted by this Commission under section 201. The effects of recessions, dollar devaluations, and price controls were national in scope and not confined to the specialty steel industry. Furthermore, market factors which related specifically to specialty steel during the period 1968–74 did not so distort market conditions as to necessitate the adoption of an alternate measuring period. The nickel strike of 1969 was clearly a temporary condition which served merely to delay imports until the following year. The two affirmative determinations of this Commission under the Antidumping Act each affected only one product from one exporting country. Finally, although the Voluntary Restraint Agreement (VRA) did affect import levels, its impact was limited by several factors, including the voluntary nature of the agreement—which in many instances caused imports to vary both above and below quota levels—and the fact that a substantial number of specialty steel exporters were not parties to the agreement. Clearly, the aforementioned factors are neither unique to the subject industry nor so pervasive as to substantially distort market conditions. Accordingly, there is no basis on which to adopt a measuring period extending before 1968.

In selecting the appropriate measuring period, it has been the established practice of this Commission under section 301 of the Trade Expansion Act as well as under section 201 of the 1974 Trade Act to analyze imports over a period of time of sufficient length to establish trends and thereby put aberrant or temporary conditions into proper perspective. Generally, the period of time selected by the Commission has been 5 years or so. On the basis of such a period, it can be seen that since 1970 total imports of stainless steel and alloy tool steel have declined absolutely and relative to domestic production. In 1974 total imports were over 7,000 tons less than in 1970. During 1970–74, annual US production of stainless and alloy tool steel increased steadily from 700,000 tons to more than 1,325,000 tons. In the same period, the ratio of imports to domestic production was nearly halved, dropping from 24.4 percent to 12.3 percent.

During the recessionary period of 1974 and the first part of 1975, imports did increase relative to domestic production. However, a substantial part of the increase can be attributed to importers' lead times, which at the end of the third quarter of 1974 were roughly twice as long as domestic lead times. Such a differential meant that deliveries on orders placed with foreign producers during the boom period of 1974 continued through the fourth quarter of 1974 and the first and second quarters of 1975—a period during which domestic production fell almost 50 percent below 1974 levels. Clearly, these increases were inconsistent with the general downward trend evidenced during the period 1970–74 and, as such, are not sufficient to satisfy the requirement of "increased" imports.

The ITC proceeded to render a mixed determination in the case, depending on the particular steel product at issue.

(4) Commissioner's Minchew's suggested baseline in the preceding excerpt—the date of the most recent trade concessions—perhaps maps well with the requirement in GATT Article XIX:1(a) that increased imports be linked to "the effect of obligations incurred." Does that baseline make sense? Would the Appellate Body accept it? What if the most recent trade concession was 30 years ago? Did the creation of the WTO reset the clock?

(5) Suppose that imports have declined in absolute terms, but increased in relative terms. Can it fairly be said that "increased imports" are causing injury, or would it be more accurate to say that something else is injuring both the suppliers of imports and their domestic competitors? Likewise, with reference to the paragraph 131 of the Appellate Body report in *Argentina— Footwear*, what is meant by the suggestion that there must be " '*such* increased quantities' as to cause or threaten to cause serious injury to the domestic industry... the increase in imports must have been recent enough, sudden enough, sharp enough, and significant enough, both quantitatively and qualitatively, to cause or threaten to cause 'serious injury' '"? Has the Appellate Body conflated the increased imports requirement with the causation requirement? We will consider such issues further in the materials on causation.

(C) INDUSTRY DEFINITION

Before the market share of imports can be measured, and before the "serious injury" analysis can be undertaken, it is necessary to identify the domestic "industry" that competes with the imports under investigation. GATT Article XIX and the Agreement on Safeguards look to the producers of "like or directly competitive products" for this purpose, language that carries over into US law. The concept of like products is of course found in other GATT provisions (e.g., Arts. I, III, VI), but the addition of the words "directly competitive" suggests that a more expansive definition is intended here. Indeed, it could be argued that if an industry is seriously injured by imports, that is evidence that it produces "directly competitive products."[2]

2. See J. Jackson, World Trade and the
Law of GATT 561 n. 16 (1969).

UNITED STATES—SAFEGUARD MEASURES ON IMPORTS OF FRESH, CHILLED OR FROZEN LAMB MEAT FROM NEW ZEALAND AND AUSTRALIA

WT/DS177 & 178/AB/R.
Appellate Body Report adopted May 16, 2001.

4. * * * [T]he Panel concluded:

(b) that the United States has acted inconsistently with Article 4.1(c) of the Agreement on Safeguards because the USITC, in the lamb meat investigation, defined the domestic industry as including input producers (i.e., growers and feeders of live lamb) as producers of the like product at issue (i.e. lamb meat);

Domestic Industry

77. The USITC defined the domestic industry in this case to include growers and feeders of live lambs, as well as packers and breakers of lamb meat. The USITC did so because it considered that there was a "continuous line of production from the raw to the processed product", and that there was a "substantial coincidence of economic interests" between and among the growers and feeders of live lambs, and the packers and breakers of lamb meat.

* * *

81. The United States ... argues that the USITC's determination of "domestic industry" is correct, in particular, in its reliance on the criteria of a "continuous line of production" and a "coincidence of economic interests" to assess which producers make up the domestic industry. The United States argues that the Agreement on Safeguards allows Members some discretion when defining the term "producers" in the light of the facts and circumstances of each case. Moreover, the United States argues that the Panel's own criteria for determining the scope of the domestic industry are devoid of a textual basis. In this respect, the United States asserts that the Panel incorrectly stated that the USITC had found growers and feeders to be producers of a product separate and distinct from lamb meat. The United States maintains that the USITC's approach in this case is appropriate in order to capture in full the affected domestic industry.

82. As a preliminary matter, we note that the USITC clearly stated in its report that the issue of whether the producers of an input product could be included in the domestic industry producing the processed product is not addressed in the United States safeguard statute. In response to questioning at the oral hearing, the United States confirmed that the two-pronged test applied by the USITC in deciding this issue is not mandated either by the United States safeguard statute or by any provision of the United States Code of Federal Regulations that applies to safeguard investigations and determinations. The United States also confirmed, at the oral hearing, that the USITC has adopted this test for

defining a "domestic industry" in safeguard actions as a matter of practice in the evolution of its own case law; for safeguard actions, the test has not been enacted into law or promulgated as a regulation.

83.   We begin our analysis with the definition of the term "domestic industry" in Article 4.1(c) of the Agreement on Safeguards, which reads:

> (c) in determining injury or threat thereof, a "domestic industry" shall be understood to mean the *producers* as a whole *of the like or directly competitive products* operating within the territory of a Member, or those whose collective output *of the like or directly competitive products* constitutes a major proportion of the total domestic production of *those products*. (emphasis added)

84.   The definition of "domestic industry" in this provision refers to two elements. First, the industry consists of "producers". As the Panel indicated, "producers" are those who grow or manufacture an article; "producers" are those who bring a thing into existence. This meaning of "producers" is, however, qualified by the second element in the definition of "domestic industry". This element identifies the particular products that must be produced by the domestic "producers" in order to qualify for inclusion in the "domestic industry". According to the clear and express wording of the text of Article 4.1(c), the term "domestic industry" extends solely to the "producers ... *of the like or directly competitive* products". (emphasis added) The definition, therefore, focuses exclusively on the producers of a very specific group of products. Producers of products that are *not* "like or directly competitive products" do not, according to the text of the treaty, form part of the domestic industry.

* * *

87.   Accordingly, the first step in determining the scope of the domestic industry is the identification of the products which are "like or directly competitive" with the imported product. Only when those products have been identified is it possible then to identify the "producers" of those products.

88.   There is no dispute that in this case the "like product" is "lamb meat", which is the imported product with which the safeguard investigation was concerned. The USITC considered that the "domestic industry" producing the "like product", lamb meat, includes the growers and feeders of live lambs. The term "directly competitive products" is not, however, at issue in this dispute as the USITC did not find that there were any such products in this case.[3]

---

3. [original note 50] We note that two Commissioners (Askey and Crawford) did not join in the findings of the USITC on this point. These two Commissioners both found that *live lambs*, produced by growers and feeders, are directly competitive with lamb *meat* and that, accordingly, the "do-mestic industry" includes the producers of these competing products. The United States has not argued, before the Panel or before us, that *live lambs* are directly competitive with lamb *meat*, and that issue as we stated earlier, does not form part of this appeal.

89.   The United States argues, nevertheless, that it is permissible, on the facts and circumstances of this case, to include in the "domestic industry" the growers and feeders of live lambs because, as the USITC has found: (1) there is a "continuous line of production" from the raw product, live lambs, to the end-product, lamb meat; and (2) there is a "substantial coincidence of economic interests" between the producers of the raw product and the producers of the end-product.

90.   This interpretation may well have a basis in the USITC case law, but there is no basis for this interpretation in the Agreement on Safeguards. The text of Article 4.1(c) defines the "domestic industry" exclusively by reference to the "producers ... of the like or directly competitive product". There is no reference in that definition to the two criteria relied upon by the United States. In our view, under Article 4.1(c), input products can only be included in defining the "domestic industry" if they are "like or directly competitive" with the end-products. If an input product and an end-product are not "like" or "directly competitive", then it is irrelevant, under the Agreement on Safeguards, that there is a continuous line of production between an input product and an end-product, that the input product represents a high proportion of the value of the end-product, that there is no use for the input product other than as an input for the particular end-product, or that there is a substantial coincidence of economic interests between the producers of these products. In the absence of a "like or directly competitive" relationship, we see no justification, in Article 4.1(c) or any other provision of the Agreement on Safeguards, for giving credence to any of these criteria in defining a "domestic industry".

91.   In this respect, we are not persuaded that the words "as a whole" in Article 4.1(c), appearing in the phrase "producers as a whole", offer support to the United States' position. These words do not alter the requirement that the "domestic industry" extends only to producers of "like or directly competitive products". The words "as a whole" apply to "producers" and, when read together with the terms "collective output" and "major proportion" which follow, clearly address the *number* and the *representative nature* of producers making up the domestic industry. The words "as a whole" do not imply that producers of *other* products, which are *not* like or directly competitive with the imported product, can be included in the definition of domestic industry. Like the Panel, we see the words "as a whole" as no more than "a *quantitative* benchmark for the proportion of producers ... which a safeguards investigation has to cover." (emphasis added)

Notes and Questions

(1) Could the United States properly include growers in the industry by making the move embraced by two ITC Commissioners, namely, holding that lamb meat and live lambs are "directly competitive?" Does it make sense to exclude producers at prior stages of processing from the "industry" that is injured or threatened with injury by imports? If they are to be included in

some cases, why limit those cases to the agricultural sector (as had largely been ITC practice)?

(2) If the ITC overstepped in the *Lamb* case, what is the proper way to assess which products are "like or directly competitive?" Consider the following excerpt from the decision in Wood Shakes and Shingles, US Intl. Trade Commn., Inv. No. TA 201–56, (1986).

VIEWS OF CHAIRWOMAN STERN, COMMISSIONER ECKES, COMMISSIONER LODWICK AND COMMISSIONER ROHR

* * *

Section 201(b)(1) defines the term "industry" in terms of the producers of articles "like or directly competitive" with the imported articles at issue. The statute does not define the terms "like" or "directly competitive." However, the legislative history of the Trade Act of 1974 discusses them as follows: "The words 'like' and 'directly competitive' as used previously and in this bill, are not to be regarded as synonymous or explanatory of each other . . . 'like' articles are those which are substantially identical in inherent or intrinsic characteristic (i.e., materials from which made, appearance, quality, texture, and etc.), and 'directly competitive' articles are those which, although not substantially identical in their inherent or intrinsic characteristics, are substantially equivalent for commercial purposes, that is, are adapted to the same uses and are essentially interchangeable therefore."

* * *

In addition, section 601(5) of the Trade Act of 1974 specifies that the term "directly competitive with" a domestic article may include an imported article at an earlier or later stage of processing if the importation of the article has an economic effect on producers of the domestic article comparable to the effect of the importation of an article at the same stage of processing as the domestic article.

The imported articles at issue in this investigation are wood shakes and shingles. The respondents in this investigation, producers and importers of wood shakes and shingles from Canada, argued that the Commission should conclude that there are four domestic industries. They argued that the imports are properly disaggregated into shakes of western red cedar, shingles of western red cedar, remanufactured shingles of western red cedar, and shingles of northern white cedar, and that a separate industry produces each of these articles.

It is clear that there are both similarities and differences between the various shakes and shingles at issue in this investigation. Western red cedar shakes and shingles are manufactured from the same raw material, frequently in the same facility, and may be manufactured by the same persons, although using somewhat different equipment. Similarly, northern white cedar shingles are manufactured in the same manner, using the same type of equipment, as western red cedar shingles, and can be used for the same purposes, but are manufactured from a different species of tree and are generally produced and marketed in different geographical areas of the United States. Furthermore, the choice of whether to use shakes or shingles in a particular building application appears to be dictated by factors other than the inherent characteristics of the articles, such as consumer preferences and geography.

In determining which producers constitute the domestic industry, the Commission generally considers the productive facilities, manufacturing processes, and the markets for the products at issue in the investigation. In this investigation, approximately 50 percent of the domestic mills produce both shakes and shingles. In addition, both shakes and shingles are marketed for the most part through wholesale distributors and sold to the construction industry.

The various articles at issue here are, to a greater or lesser extent, interchangeable. The choice between western red cedar and northern white cedar shingles, for instance, appears to be largely a function of geographical region (northern white cedar is most popular in the northeast and the Atlantic seaboard, while western red cedar is most popular in the west and southwest), and the particular appearance desired (northern white cedar ages to a silvery grey, while western red cedar ages to a deep reddish brown). In addition, shakes have a more rustic appearance than do shingles. However, both shakes and shingles are used for fundamentally the same purpose, the outside covering of buildings, particularly in residential applications. In this investigation, we conclude that it is appropriate to find a single domestic industry, devoted to the production of wood shakes and shingles.

Respondents suggested that if the Commission were to determine that there is a single industry producing wood shakes and shingles, it should expand the industry definition to include other roofing and siding products, such as asphalt shingles, clay title, and aluminum siding, which they argue are directly competitive with wood shakes and shingles. While it is true that these products have some common ultimate uses as the outside covering of a structure, they are not necessarily equivalent for commercial purposes. The analysis of "like or directly competitive" under section 201 focuses on the question of whether products are essentially interchangeable in the sense of being substantially equivalent for commercial purposes. A contractor or homeowner is not likely to consider products of such fundamentally different appearance as asphalt shingles or clay tiles as the commercial equivalent of wood shakes and shingles. Moreover, roofing products such as asphalt shingles or clay tiles are not suitable for use as siding. In addition, the productive facilities and manufacturing processes for these other roofing and siding products are significantly different from those of wood shakes and shingles. Moreover pricing of these other products appears to be more responsive to forces other than those significant to the pricing of wood shakes and shingles. For instance, the price of asphalt shingles appears to be primarily responsive to the price of oil, a primary input in the manufacture of asphalt shingles.

Is the Commission's analysis convincing? For example, can you isolate the basis for treating white cedar shingles as part of the same industry as red cedar products? If builders in the principal markets for red cedar products in the Western United States often choose between red cedar shakes and tile for the roofs of high-end homes, but virtually never consider white cedar shingles as an option (which are instead popular mainly in East Coast markets), does it make sense to say that white cedar products are part of the industry but tile products are not?

(3) Reflect on the strategic choices in the industry definition battle. Petitioners will typically propose a definition of industry that gives them as much protection as possible against competing imports, without broadening the industry so much that they fear they cannot meet the requirements of increased imports, serious injury and causation. Respondents may pursue a strategy of dividing the proposed industry into several, hoping that at least some of their exports will remain free of restraint even if others do not, or of proposing a broader industry that would cause the petitioners to be aggregated with other domestic firms that are doing well. We see elements of both approaches in the preceding excerpt from *Shakes and Shingles*.

(4) The phrase "like or directly competitive products" on its face seemingly emphasizes the degree of substitutability between products from the perspective of purchasers. If data are available, this "demand side" substitutability can be analyzed econometrically by efforts to estimate the "cross-price elasticity" of demand between two products—the degree to which the demand for one product changes with the price of the other. A large, positive cross-price elasticity (i.e., an increase in the price of one product increases greatly the demand for the other) suggests that the products are close substitutes for consumers.

(5) As the materials above make clear, the ITC also looks closely at the "supply side," to see whether the products are made by the same firms or in the same facilities. What is the logic of this attention to the "supply side?"

(6) Consider an industry with two domestic firms. One is doing well because it imports semi-finished products from abroad and completes their manufacture in the United States, perhaps allowing much of the work that is intensive in relatively unskilled labor to be done overseas. The other firm is doing poorly because it tries to do all of its manufacturing domestically. If the two firms are aggregated, the issue of serious injury becomes a close call; if only the second is included in the domestic "industry," the criteria for relief are more easily met. Which is the proper way to proceed? For a suggestion that only the portion of a manufacturing operation that occurs in the United States should be deemed part of the domestic industry (only the US "value-added" should count), see Certain Cameras, US Intl. Trade Commn., Inv. No. TA 201–62 (1990) (additional Views of Acting Chairman Anne E. Brunsdale). Is that approach permissible under WTO law?

(D) SERIOUS INJURY

Escape clause relief is only permissible under WTO and US law if the increased imports cause or threaten to cause serious injury to the domestic industry. (Later in the book we will see that for relief in dumping and subsidies cases, the domestic industry must be "materially" injured—a test thought to be easier to meet than "serious" injury.) With rare exception, domestic petitioners allege that serious injury exists already and do not rely solely on threat.

ARGENTINA—SAFEGUARD MEASURES ON IMPORTS OF FOOTWEAR

WT/DS121/AB/R.

Appellate Body Report adopted January 12, 2000.

SERIOUS INJURY

132. With respect to the requirement relating to "serious injury", Article 4.2(a) of the Agreement on Safeguards provides, in relevant part:

> In the investigation to determine whether increased imports have caused or are threatening to cause serious injury to a domestic industry under the terms of this Agreement, the competent authorities *shall evaluate all relevant factors* of an objective and quantifiable nature *having a bearing on the situation of that industry, in particular*, ... the share of the domestic market taken by increased imports, changes in the level of sales, production, productivity, capacity utilization, profits and losses, and employment.

133. The Panel stated that the requirements of Article 4.2(a) obliged it to:

> ... consider, first, whether all injury factors listed in the Agreement were considered by Argentina, as the text of Article 4.2(a) of the Agreement ("all relevant factors ... including ... changes in the level of sales, production, productivity, capacity utilisation, profits and losses, and employment") is unambiguous that at a minimum each of the factors listed, in addition to all other factors that are "relevant", must be considered.

The Panel also concluded that, pursuant to the provisions of Article 4.2(c) and, by reference, Article 3 of the Agreement on Safeguards, it was required to examine whether Argentina's findings and conclusions on "serious injury" were supported by the evidence before the Argentine authorities.

134. The Panel read Article 4.2(a) literally to mean that all the listed factors: "changes in the level of sales, production, productivity, capacity utilisation, profits and losses, and employment"—must be evaluated in every investigation. In addition, the Panel stated that all other relevant factors having a bearing on the situation of the industry must also be evaluated. As the Panel found that Argentina had not evaluated two of the listed factors, capacity utilization and productivity, the Panel concluded that Argentina's investigation was not consistent with the requirements of Article 4.2(a).

135. Argentina submits that the Panel erred in its analysis of Argentina's determination of "serious injury". According to Argentina, Article 4.2(c) of the Agreement on Safeguards requires only a demonstration of the relevance of the factors examined, rather than an examination of all the listed factors as relevant. In response to the Panel's finding that Argentina had not properly evaluated the factors of capacity

utilization and productivity, Argentina replies by maintaining that the factor of productivity is explicitly mentioned in Act 338 and that data sufficient to calculate capacity utilization was available to the Argentine authorities. Furthermore, Argentina argues that neither capacity utilization nor productivity was a principal or a significant issue in the investigation. Argentina also takes issue with the Panel's view that the available data for 1996 should have been examined by Argentina in its investigation of "serious injury". Here, Argentina responds that the record clearly shows that the data for 1996 was incomplete, and Argentina submits that it was appropriate and reasonable to use a single review period for which all the data was available as a basis for its determination of "serious injury". In addition, Argentina argues that the Panel erred in several aspects of its examination of the evidence considered by the Argentine authorities.

136.   We agree with the Panel's interpretation that Article 4.2(a) of the Agreement on Safeguards requires a demonstration that the competent authorities evaluated, at a minimum, each of the factors listed in Article 4.2(a) as well as all other factors that are relevant to the situation of the industry concerned. Furthermore, we do not dispute the Panel's finding that Argentina did not evaluate all of the listed factors, in particular, capacity utilization and productivity. We consider the other points that Argentina has raised in this appeal, relating to the availability of data for 1996 and to the Panel's evaluation of the evidence considered by the Argentine authorities, to relate to matters of fact which are not within our mandate, under Article 17.6 of the DSU, to examine on appeal.

137.   For these reasons, we uphold the Panel's conclusion that Argentina did not evaluate "all relevant factors of an objective and quantifiable nature having a bearing on the situation of that industry" as required by Article 4.2(a) of the Agreement on Safeguards.

138.   However, although it was not necessary for the Panel to go beyond where it did in this case, as the Panel found that Argentina had *not* evaluated all of the required listed factors, we do not believe that an evaluation of the listed factors in Article 4.2(a) is all that is required to justify a determination of "serious injury" under the Agreement on Safeguards. We note, in this respect, that there is a definition of "serious injury" in Article 4.1(a) of the Agreement on Safeguards, which reads as follows:

> "serious injury" shall be understood to mean a *significant overall impairment* in the position of a domestic industry. (emphasis added)

And we note that, in its legal analysis of "serious injury" under Article 4.2(a), the Panel made no use whatsoever of this definition.

139.   In our view, it is only when the *overall position* of the domestic industry is evaluated, in light of all the relevant factors having a bearing on a situation of that industry, that it can be determined whether there is "a significant overall impairment" in the position of that industry. Although Article 4.2(a) technically requires that certain

listed factors must be evaluated, and that all other relevant factors must be evaluated, that provision does not specify what such an evaluation must demonstrate. Obviously, any such evaluation will be different for different industries in different cases, depending on the facts of the particular case and the situation of the industry concerned. An evaluation of each listed factor will not necessarily have to show that each such factor is "declining". In one case, for example, there may be significant declines in sales, employment and productivity that will show "significant overall impairment" in the position of the industry, and therefore will justify a finding of serious injury. In another case, a certain factor may not be declining, but the overall picture may nevertheless demonstrate "significant overall impairment" of the industry. Thus, in addition to a technical examination of whether the competent authorities in a particular case have evaluated all the listed factors and any other relevant factors, we believe that it is essential for a panel to take the definition of "serious injury" in Article 4.1(a) of the Agreement on Safeguards into account in its review of any determination of "serious injury".

Notes and Questions

(1) In its analysis of "serious injury," has the Appellate Body done more than merely create hoops for national authorities to jump through in their discussion of the issue—could Argentina have avoided the problems it encountered simply by reciting that it had duly "considered" all the factors listed in the Safeguards Agreement or raised during the investigation? See paragraph 139. How exactly is a panel to "take the definition of serious injury...into account?"

(2) In *US Lamb*, excerpted earlier, the Appellate Body stated that "the standard of 'serious injury' set forth in Art. 4.1(a) is, on its face, very high. In *United States–Wheat Gluten*, we referred to this standard as 'exacting.'" Id., paragraph 124. What is the basis in the treaty text for this "very high" and "exacting" standard? What does it imply about the standard of review before a WTO panel on the question of "serious injury?"

(3) Both WTO and US law provide a list of factors to be considered in assessing the existence of "serious injury." US law further provides that no single factor is "dispositive." Is there any principled way to attach relative weight to the various factors? For example, might it be argued that if the purpose of the escape clause is to address economic dislocation, then unemployment or underemployment ought to be the center of attention, while a loss of profits (especially when firms are owned by diversified shareholders) is of little interest? Or are profits important because shareholders are at least as likely to contribute to national political campaigns as workers, and safeguard measures are more about political pressures for protection than anything else? What about a factor like "capacity utilization"—should it receive any weight if profits are healthy and employment is stable? In short, what is the concept of "serious injury" really trying to capture?

(4) Does the basis for a finding of "serious injury" have any implications for the proper remedy? For example, if unemployment is the most serious problem facing the industry, might that argue for worker adjustment

assistance rather than protective tariffs or quotas? We discuss adjustment assistance briefly in the last section of this chapter.

(E) CAUSATION

Under WTO law, a causal linkage must be established between increased import quantities and serious injury or threat of such injury. This "causation" requirement has proven extraordinarily difficult to satisfy and, indeed, the question of what it even means is conceptually problematic.

The US statutory provisions on the causation issue have changed over time. In the 1951 law, the imports in question had to "cause" or threaten serious injury. The 1955 amendment provided that it was enough that such imports "contributed substantially" to causing or threatening serious injury, while the 1962 Trade Expansion Act provided that imports had to be "the major factor" in causing, or threatening to cause, serious injury. At present, Section 201 requires that the increased imports be a "substantial cause" of serious injury, with substantial cause defined as an "important" cause that is "not less than" any other cause. By contrast, GATT Article XIX and the Safeguards Agreement require simply that increased imports "cause or threaten to cause" serious injury. Among the issues to consider in this section is the degree of consistency between the WTO and US formulations.

You should also reflect on the following conundrum, present under both the WTO and US law formulations of the causation inquiry. Suppose that consumers in the United States lose interest in domestically produced video games, and shift their purchases to games produced abroad simply because they find them more entertaining. As a result, imports of video games increase dramatically, contemporaneously with a decline in the fortunes of US manufacturers. Here, although increased imports arise at a time of industrial decline domestically, both phenomena are "caused" by something else in the ordinary sense of that word—namely, a change in consumer tastes. Likewise, suppose that the domestic steel industry experiences a crippling strike. Domestic production and employment plummets, and imports skyrocket to fill the void. Again, increased imports occur contemporaneously with industrial decline domestically. But it seems that both the injury to the domestic industry, and the increase in imports, are the *result* of a third phenomenon—the strike.

More generally, reflect back on the simple supply and demand diagram in Chapter 2 from the Kenen textbook on international economics. The *quantity* of imports in the diagram is determined by the excess demand for the good in the domestic market at the world price. In economic parlance, import quantity is an "endogenous" variable. It depends on the determinants of domestic demand (such as consumer tastes and income), the determinants of domestic supply (such as input prices and technology) and the determinants of the world price (or more generally the "import supply" curve). Yet, both the US and WTO rules treat "increased quantities" of imports as a causal variable. To an economist, this formulation makes little sense because the quantity of imports is always an "effect" not a "cause." How is someone charged with administering the law to make sense of increased imports as a "cause" in light of this observation?

ARGENTINA—SAFEGUARD MEASURES ON IMPORTS OF FOOTWEAR
WT/DS121/AB/R.
Appellate Body Report adopted January 12, 2000.

* * *

CAUSATION

140.   With respect to the requirement of causation, Article 4.2(b) of the Agreement on Safeguards provides that a determination of serious injury:

... shall not be made unless this investigation demonstrates, on the basis of objective evidence, the existence of the causal link between increased imports of the product concerned and serious injury or threat thereof. When factors other than increased imports are causing injury to the domestic industry at the same time, such injury shall not be attributed to increased imports.

141.   The Panel interpreted the requirements of Article 4.2(b) as follows:

... we will consider whether Argentina's causation analysis meets these requirements on the basis of (i) whether an upward trend in imports coincides with downward trends in the injury factors, and if not, whether a reasoned explanation is provided as to why nevertheless the data show causation; (ii) whether the conditions of competition in the Argentine footwear market between imported and domestic footwear as analysed demonstrate, on the basis of objective evidence, a causal link of the imports to any injury; and (iii) whether other relevant factors have been analysed and whether it is established that injury caused by factors other than imports has not been attributed to imports.

142.   On causation, the Panel stated:

... the *trends*—in both the injury factors and the imports—matter as much as their absolute levels. In the particular context of a causation analysis, we also believe that this provision means that it is the *relationship* between the movements in imports (volume and market share) and the movements in injury factors that must be central to a causation analysis and determination.

In practical terms, we believe therefore that this provision means that if causation is present, an increase in imports normally should coincide with a decline in the relevant injury factors. While such a coincidence by itself cannot *prove* causation (because, *inter alia*,

Article 3 requires an explanation—i.e., "findings and reasoned conclusions"), its absence would create serious doubts as to the existence of a causal link, and would require a *very* compelling analysis of why causation still is present.

143. Argentina argues on appeal that the Panel erred in establishing and applying three "standards" in its analysis of causation. First, Argentina maintains that the Panel required that an upward trend in imports must *coincide* with a *downward* trend in the injury factors. On this point, Argentina maintains that Article 4.2(c) of the Agreement on Safeguards refers to "changes" and not to "downward trends", so that there is no requirement that there be a "downward trend" in each year of the period of investigation. Moreover, Argentina maintains that the Panel's requirement of "coincidence" in time is not implied by the term "cause". Second, Argentina asserts that the Panel used the phrase "under such conditions" to develop a requirement that the "conditions of competition" between imported and domestic footwear in the Argentine market demonstrate a causal link between the increased imports and injury. Argentina asserts that there is no basis in the Agreement on Safeguards for this requirement. Third, Argentina maintains that the Panel required the Argentine authorities to establish that other relevant factors had been analyzed, and that injury caused by factors other than imports is not evidence of serious injury caused by imports. In Argentina's opinion, this requirement goes far beyond what is actually required in Article 4.2(b) of the Agreement on Safeguards.

144. We note that Article 4.2(a) requires the competent authorities to evaluate "the rate and amount of the increase in imports", "the share of the domestic market taken by increased imports", as well as the "changes" in the level of factors such as sales, production, productivity, capacity utilization, and others. We see no reason to disagree with the Panel's interpretation that the words "rate and amount" and "changes" in Article 4.2(a) mean that "the *trends*—in both the injury factors and the imports—matter as much as their absolute levels." We also agree with the Panel that, in an analysis of causation, "it is the *relationship* between the *movements* in imports (volume and market share) and the *movements* in injury factors that must be central to a causation analysis and determination." (emphasis added) Furthermore, with respect to a "coincidence" between an increase in imports and a decline in the relevant injury factors, we note that the Panel simply said that this should "normally" occur if causation is present. The Panel qualified this statement, however, in the following sentence:

> While such a coincidence by itself cannot *prove* causation (because, *inter alia*, Article 3 requires an explanation—i.e., "findings and reasoned conclusions"), its absence would create serious doubts as to the existence of a causal link, and would require a *very* compelling analysis of why causation still is present.

145. We are somewhat surprised that the Panel, having determined that there were no "increased imports", and having determined

that there was no "serious injury", for some reason went on to make an assessment of causation. It would be difficult, indeed, to demonstrate a "causal link" between "increased imports" that did not occur and "serious injury" that did not exist. Nevertheless, we see no error in the Panel's interpretation of the causation requirements, or in its interpretation of Article 4.2(b) of the Agreement on Safeguards. Rather, we believe that Argentina has mischaracterized the Panel's interpretation and reasoning. Furthermore, we agree with the Panel's conclusions that "the conditions of competition between the imports and the domestic product were not analysed or adequately explained (in particular, price); and that 'other factors' identified by the CNCE in the investigation were not sufficiently evaluated, in particular, the tequila effect."

146.   For all these reasons, we uphold the Panel's conclusion that "Argentina's findings and conclusions regarding causation were not adequately explained and supported by the evidence."

Notes and Questions

(1) Is it fair to characterize the Appellate Body's discussion of causation as suggesting that the contemporaneous correlation (or absence of correlation) between increased imports and indicators of industrial decline must be the centerpiece of the analysis? Is correlation the same as causation? Is the absence of correlation evidence of a lack of causation as suggested in paragraph 144? Does the decision in *Footwear* simply sweep under the rug the fundamental problem that inheres in treating an endogenous variable— the quantity of imports—as a causal variable?

(2) Take the example set out at the beginning of this section—imports increase and domestic production and unemployment decline because of a domestic strike in the steel industry. Is correlation between increased imports and industrial decline present? Is that an appropriate case for safeguard measures? What in the Appellate Body's approach to the issue helps us with such issues, if anything?

(3) Before proceeding to the next Appellate Body opinion, consider the following excerpt from the ITC decision that was the subject of that dispute. In Lamb Meat, US Intl. Trade Commn., Inv. No. TA–201–68, Pub. No. 3176 (1999), the ITC had the following to say about the causation question:

> [W]e find that increased imports of lamb meat are a "substantial cause" of the threat of serious injury to the domestic lamb meat industry under section 202(b)(1)(B). * * *

> Imports reached record levels in 1996, and increased another 19.2 percent in 1997. Imports will exceed even those record levels based on annualized data from interim 1998. Australian and New Zealand firms submitting questionnaire responses to the Commission themselves project that their exports to the United States will increase further in 1999. These firms' 1999 projections were 21 percent above projections for full year 1998. * * * As of the time of the Commission's vote on injury, the Australian Government had projected a 6 percent increase in exports to the United States. * * *

Increases in import volume are likely to have further negative effects on the domestic industry's prices, shipment volumes, and financial condition in the imminent future. With regard to prices, given the inability of domestic growers and feeders to reduce production in the short run, the increase in imports has caused prices to fall in the short run. The unit value of domestic, Australian, and New Zealand lamb meat dropped in interim 1998 as compared to interim 1997; over the same period imports (on an annualized basis) increased by the greatest amount of any year during the period of investigation. Moreover, US, Australian, and New Zealand lamb meat prices were in most cases lower for the products surveyed in the second half of 1997 and the first 3 quarters of 1998 than in comparable quarters in 1996 and the first half of 1997. Any further increases in the volume of imports would be expected to put further downward pressure on prices in the US market.

With regard to market share, the share of the domestic market held by imports, as measured both in quantity and value, more than doubled during the period of investigation, from 11.2 percent in 1993 (as measured in quantity) to 23.3 percent in January–September 1998, and from 11.9 percent in 1993 (as measured in share of value) to 30.7 percent in January–September 1998. Most of this increase occurred in 1997 and 1998. The 1997 increase in imports of 9.7 million pounds was mirrored by a decline in US lamb shipments of 8.4 million pounds, suggesting that imports captured market share directly from US producers.

With regard to the domestic industry's financial condition, we found above that financial performance of the various segments worsened due to declining sales and falling prices, a result of the increase in imports. In addition, the increased imports directly captured market share from the domestic producers. Thus, the increase in imports is likely to have a negative impact on the industry's shipments, prices, and financial performance.

As required by the statute, we considered whether any other causes might be a more important cause of the threat of serious injury than increased imports. First, we examined whether termination of payments under the National Wool Act of 1954 ("Wool Act") might be a more important cause. Congress enacted legislation ending the Wool Act in 1993, and the support payments were phased out largely in 1994 and 1995, before the increase in imports that began in 1996. Petitioners claim that the loss of the payments had been largely absorbed by the growers and feeders before the increase in imports. Respondents assert that the industry cannot be expected to absorb so quickly the effects of the loss of such a longstanding payment program.

We have no doubt that the loss of Wool Act payments hurt lamb growers and feeders and caused some to withdraw from the industry. We also believe that it is unrealistic to conclude that the effects of the termination of Wool Act payments had completely disappeared as of 1997. However, the industry had experienced some recovery since full termination in 1996, and the effects of termination of Wool Act payments can be expected to recede further with each passing month. In addition, the termination of the Wool Act could only have had an indirect effect on the financial condition of the packers and breakers, who never received payments under the Wool Act. We find that in the imminent future, the recent loss of Wool Act payments is a less important cause of the threat of serious injury than imports of lamb meat.

We also considered whether competition from other meat products, such as beef, pork, and poultry, might be a more important cause of the threat of serious injury. Although such products appear to compete with lamb to a certain extent, we find no evidence that such competition is a more important cause of future imminent serious injury than imports of lamb meat. As noted above, per capita consumption of lamb meat has been relatively steady since 1995. We also considered whether increased input costs, alleged overfeeding of lambs, and increased concentration in the packer segment might individually be more important causes of the threat of serious injury than the increased imports. We find that they are not. Expenses for growers rose at a modest rate and then fell in January–September 1998. Expenses for feeders increased at a faster pace but not at a dramatic pace. Similarly, costs of inputs for packers and breakers rose moderately in line with production. Thus, there has been no significant increase in input costs that explains the sharp decline in industry profits, and no increase is predicted in the imminent future.

Respondents allege that some US feeders in 1997 held lambs unduly long in feed lots in order to maximize revenue while prices were high, and that these lambs went to slaughter on the heavy side and sold at lower prices, which pulled down other domestic prices. Petitioners disagree, pointing out that the percentage of domestic lamb carcasses with higher fat content as measured by the USDA grading system was lower in 1997 than in 1993 and 1994. Even if we accept respondents' arguments, these "fat" lambs would have accounted for no more than a small share of total domestic lamb production. In any event, respondents do not allege that overfeeding is currently taking place or represents a future threat.

We also considered whether concentration in the packer segment of the industry might be a more important cause of the threat of serious injury. USDA data indicate that nine domestic packing plants accounted for 85 percent of the sheep and lambs slaughtered in 1997. However, petitioners claim that packer concentration has actually decreased over the past 5 years. An undue level of concentration among packers would have suggested that they would have been sheltered from the effects of low-priced imports and would have been able to pass through lower prices more readily to feeders and growers. However, packers, like other segments of the lamb meat industry, experienced deteriorating profits in the latter part of the period of investigation and operated at a loss in January–September 1998. Thus, we conclude that concentration in the packer segment of the industry is a less important cause of the threat of serious injury than increased imports.

Finally, we considered whether the failure to develop and implement an effective marketing program for lamb meat was a more important cause of the threat of serious injury, particularly in light of the

repeal of the longstanding Wool Act payment program. While an effective marketing program to bolster domestic demand could have had an important impact on the industry, in view of the foregoing discussion, we do not find that failure to implement such a program is a more important cause of the threat of serious injury than increased imports.
* * *

The Appellate Body discussion of causation in *US Lamb* follows immediately. Before reading what the Appellate Body has to say, ask yourself whether you are convinced by the ITC's reasoning. Does the ITC do enough to rule out other possible causes of threatened injury, or is its discussion too conclusory? What more should it do, if anything?

UNITED STATES—SAFEGUARD MEASURES ON IMPORTS OF FRESH, CHILLED OR FROZEN LAMB MEAT FROM NEW ZEALAND AND AUSTRALIA

WT/DS177 & 178/AB/R.
Appellate Body Report adopted May 16, 2001.

4.   * * * [T]he Panel concluded:

* * *

(f) that the United States has acted inconsistently with Article 4.2(b) of the Agreement on Safeguards because the USITC's determination in the lamb meat investigation in respect of causation did not demonstrate the required causal link between increased imports and threat of serious injury, in that the determination did not establish that increased imports were by themselves a necessary and sufficient cause of threat of serious injury, and in that the determination did not ensure that threat of serious injury caused by "other factors" was not attributed to increased imports;

* * *

Causation

162.   In assessing the claims made by Australia and New Zealand relating to causation, the Panel began with a "[g]eneral interpretative analysis" of the relevant provisions of the Agreement on Safeguards, before turning to the application of that interpretation to the facts of this dispute. The Panel took note of the terms of Articles 4.2(a) and 4.2(b) of that Agreement and, after examining the ordinary meaning of the word "cause", stated:

> It is not enough that increased imports cause just some injury which may then be intensified to a "serious" level by factors other than increased imports. In our view, therefore, the ordinary meaning of these phrases describing the Safeguards Agreement's causation standard indicates that <u>increased imports must not only be *necessary*, but also *sufficient* to cause or threaten a degree of injury that is *"serious"* enough to constitute a significant overall impairment in the situation of the domestic industry</u>. (underlining added)

163.   The Panel added that:

... the second sentence of SG Article 4.2(b) also makes clear ... that increased imports need *not* be the *sole* or exclusive causal factor present in a situation of serious injury or threat thereof, as the requirement not to attribute injury caused by other factors by implication recognises that *multiple* factors may be present in a situation of serious injury or threat thereof.

* * *

... where a number of factors, one of which is increased imports, are sufficient *collectively* to cause a significant overall impairment of the position of the domestic industry, but increased imports *alone* are not causing injury that achieves the threshold of "seriousness" set up by SG Article 4.2(a) and 4.2(b), the conditions for imposing a safeguard measure are not satisfied. While we believe that a Member remains free to determine any appropriate method of assessing causation, any method that it selects would need to ensure that the injury caused by increased imports, considered alone, is "serious injury", i.e., causing a significant overall impairment in the situation of the domestic industry. Moreover, we cannot see how a causation standard that does not examine whether increased imports are both a *necessary* and *sufficient* cause for serious injury or threat thereof would ensure that injury caused by factors other than increased imports is not attributed to those imports. (underlining added)

164.   The United States appeals the Panel's finding that the USITC's causation analysis was inconsistent with the Agreement on Safeguards. According to the United States, there is no basis in Article 4.2(b) of that Agreement to support the Panel's interpretation that increased imports must be a "necessary and sufficient cause" of, or must, "considered alone", cause, serious injury or a threat thereof. The United States asserts that the Panel's approach is indistinguishable from the approach of the panel in *United States—Wheat Gluten Safeguard*, which we reversed on appeal. The United States concludes that, for the reasons we gave in that appeal, we must also reverse the Panel's findings on causation in this dispute.

165.   We agree with the United States that the Panel's interpretation of the causation requirements in Articles 4.2(a) and 4.2(b) of the Agreement on Safeguards is very similar to the interpretation of the same provisions by the panel in *United States—Wheat Gluten Safeguard*. Both panels reasoned that increased imports, considered on their own, must be capable of causing, or threatening to cause, injury which is "serious". Both panels stated that increased imports must be "sufficient" to cause serious injury. Moreover, both panels accepted that the situation of the domestic industry may be aggravated by other factors which are also contributing to the injury and, therefore, that increased imports need not be the sole cause of injury, but may be one of several causes. Furthermore, we note that, in this case, the Panel relied on the

interpretation of the causation requirements given by the panel in *United States—Wheat Gluten Safeguard* and stated that its interpretation of causation is *consistent* as well with the findings of the Panel in *US—Wheat Gluten* ... (emphasis added) As the United States points out, we did indeed reverse those findings on appeal in our own Report in *United States—Wheat Gluten Safeguard.*

166. In that appeal, in examining the causation requirements in the Agreement on Safeguards, we observed that the first sentence of Article 4.2(b) of the Agreement on Safeguards provides that a determination "shall not be made unless [the] investigation demonstrates ... the existence of *the causal link* between increased imports ... and serious injury or threat thereof." (emphasis added) In interpreting this phrase, we said:

> ... the term "the causal link" denotes, in our view, a relationship of cause and effect such that increased imports contribute to "bringing about", "producing" or "inducing" the serious injury. Although that contribution must be sufficiently clear as to establish the existence of "the causal link" required, the language in the first sentence of Article 4.2(b) does *not* suggest that increased imports be *the sole* cause of the serious injury, or that *"other* factors" causing injury must be excluded from the determination of serious injury. To the contrary, the language of Article 4.2(b), as a whole, suggests that "the causal link" between increased imports and serious injury may exist, *even though other factors are also contributing, "at the same time", to the situation of the domestic industry.*

167. We also noted in that appeal the crucial significance of the second sentence of Article 4.2(b), which states that competent authorities "shall not ... attribute" to increased imports injury caused by other factors, and we found that:

> Clearly, the process of attributing "injury", envisaged by this sentence, can only be made following a separation of the "injury" that must then be properly "attributed". What is important in this process is separating or distinguishing the *effects* caused by the different factors in bringing about the "injury".

168. We emphasized there that the non-attribution language in the second sentence of Article 4.2(b) means that the effects of increased imports, as separated and distinguished from the effects of other factors, must be examined to determine whether the effects of those imports establish a "genuine and substantial relationship of cause and effect" between the increased imports and serious injury.

169. We also addressed, in that appeal, the language in Articles 2.1 and 4.2(a) of the Agreement on Safeguards, which we found to support our reading of the non-attribution language in the second sentence of Article 4.2(b). By way of conclusion, we:

> ... reverse[d] the Panel's interpretation of Article 4.2(b) of the Agreement on Safeguards that increased imports "alone", "in and of

themselves", or *"per se"*, must be capable of causing injury that is "serious".

170.   In view of the close similarity between the respective interpretations of the causation requirements in the Agreement on Safeguards given by this Panel and by the panel in *United States—Wheat Gluten Safeguard*, we are of the view that, for the reasons we gave in *United States—Wheat Gluten Safeguard*, the Panel in this dispute erred in its interpretation of the causation requirements in the Agreement on Safeguards. As we held in *United States—Wheat Gluten Safeguard*, the Agreement on Safeguards does not require that increased imports be "sufficient" to cause, or threaten to cause, serious injury. Nor does that Agreement require that increased imports "alone" be capable of causing, or threatening to cause, serious injury.

171.   Accordingly, we reverse the Panel's interpretation of the causation requirements in the Agreement on Safeguards.

172.   Having reversed the Panel's "[g]eneral interpretative analysis" of "causation", we go on to consider whether the Panel was correct nonetheless in concluding that the United States acted inconsistently with the causation requirements in Article 4.2 of the Agreement on Safeguards. Our own examination of this issue is based *exclusively* on the facts presented in the USITC Report, which form part of the Panel record and are uncontested. Furthermore, notwithstanding the findings we have made previously in this appeal, we must *assume* in our examination: first, that the definition of the domestic industry given by the USITC is correct, *and*, second, that the USITC correctly found that the domestic industry is threatened with serious injury. On this basis, we must examine whether the USITC properly established, in accordance with the Agreement on Safeguards, the existence of the required "causal link" between increased imports and threatened serious injury.

173.   At the outset, we note that this appeal does *not* involve any claim relating to the causation standard set forth in the United States statute. The Panel issued a preliminary ruling that the United States statute *as such* does not fall within the Panel's terms of reference, and this ruling has not been appealed. Therefore, like the Panel, our task on this issue is confined to examining the *application* of the United States' statutory causation standard by the USITC in its determination in the lamb meat investigation for its consistency with the Agreement on Safeguards.

174.   The claims by Australia and New Zealand relating to causation focus principally on the requirement, in Article 4.2(b) of the Agreement on Safeguards, that injury caused by factors other than increased imports should not be "attributed" to those imports. In the view of Australia and New Zealand, it is uncontested that the USITC acknowledged that other factors were having injurious effects on the domestic industry. However, Australia and New Zealand argue that the USITC failed to explain what the injurious effects of the other factors were, and, therefore, that the United States failed to demonstrate compliance with

the "non-attribution" requirement in the second sentence of Article 4.2(b) of the Agreement on Safeguards.

175. Accordingly, we must consider whether the USITC properly ensured that injury caused, or threatened, by factors other than increased imports was not attributed to increased imports, as required by Article 4.2(b). In so considering, we recall that, as we have already elaborated at some length in this Report, when examining a claim under Article 4.2 of the Agreement on Safeguards, panels must review whether the competent authorities have acted consistently with the obligations in Article 4.2 by examining whether those authorities have given a reasoned and adequate explanation as to how the facts support their determination.

176. Article 4.2(b) of the Agreement on Safeguards provides:

(b) The determination referred to in [Article 4.2(a)] shall not be made unless this investigation demonstrates, on the basis of objective evidence, the existence of the causal link between increased imports of the product concerned and serious injury or threat thereof. *When factors other than increased imports are causing injury to the domestic industry at the same time, such injury shall not be attributed to increased imports.* (emphasis added)

177. In our Report in *United States—Wheat Gluten Safeguard*, we said:

Article 4.2(b) presupposes, therefore, as a first step in the competent authorities' examination of causation, that the injurious effects caused to the domestic industry by increased imports are *distinguished from* the injurious effects caused by other factors. The competent authorities can then, as a second step in their examination, attribute to increased imports, on the one hand, and, by implication, to other relevant factors, on the other hand, "injury" caused by all of these different factors, including increased imports. Through this two stage process, the competent authorities comply with Article 4.2(b) by ensuring that any injury to the domestic industry that was *actually* caused by factors other than increased imports is not "attributed" to increased imports and is, therefore, not treated as if it were injury caused by increased imports, when it is not. In this way, the competent authorities determine, as a final step, whether "the causal link" exists between increased imports and serious injury, and whether this causal link involves a genuine and substantial relationship of cause and effect between these two elements, as required by the Agreement on Safeguards.

178. We emphasize that these three steps simply describe a logical process for complying with the obligations relating to causation set forth in Article 4.2(b). These steps are not legal "tests" mandated by the text of the Agreement on Safeguards, nor is it imperative that each step be the subject of a separate finding or a reasoned conclusion by the competent authorities. Indeed, these steps leave unanswered many

methodological questions relating to the non-attribution requirement found in the second sentence of Article 4.2(b).

179. The primary objective of the process we described in *United States—Wheat Gluten Safeguard* is, of course, to determine whether there is "a genuine and substantial relationship of cause and effect" between increased imports and serious injury or threat thereof. As part of that determination, Article 4.2(b) states expressly that injury caused to the domestic industry by factors other than increased imports "shall not be attributed to increased imports." In a situation where *several factors* are causing injury "at the same time", a final determination about the injurious effects caused by *increased imports* can only be made if the injurious effects caused by all the different causal factors are distinguished and separated. Otherwise, any conclusion based exclusively on an assessment of only one of the causal factors—increased imports—rests on an uncertain foundation, because it *assumes* that the other causal factors are *not* causing the injury which has been ascribed to increased imports. The non-attribution language in Article 4.2(b) precludes such an assumption and, instead, requires that the competent authorities assess appropriately the injurious effects of the other factors, so that those effects may be disentangled from the injurious effects of the increased imports. In this way, the final determination rests, properly, on the genuine and substantial relationship of cause and effect between increased imports and serious injury.

180. As we said in our Report in *United States—Wheat Gluten Safeguard*, the non-attribution language in Article 4.2(b) indicates that, logically, the final identification of the injurious effects caused by increased imports must follow a prior separation of the injurious effects of the different causal factors. If the effects of the different factors are not separated and distinguished from the effects of increased imports, there can be no proper assessment of the injury caused by that single and decisive factor. As we also indicated, the final determination about the existence of "the causal link" between increased imports and serious injury can only be made *after* the effects of increased imports have been properly assessed, and this assessment, in turn, follows the separation of the effects caused by all the different causal factors.

181. We emphasize that the method and approach WTO Members choose to carry out the process of separating the effects of increased imports and the effects of the other causal factors is not specified by the Agreement on Safeguards. What the Agreement requires is simply that the obligations in Article 4.2 must be respected when a safeguard measure is applied.

182. In this case, the USITC Report states that the "worsen[ing]" financial situation of the domestic industry, as defined by the USITC, had occurred as "a result of the increase in imports." The USITC identified six factors other than increased imports which were alleged to be contributing to the situation of the domestic industry at the same time. Applying the statutory standard established in United States law,

the USITC considered whether, individually, each of these six factors was a "more important cause" of the threat of serious injury than the increased imports. The USITC concluded that each of these factors was not a more important cause than the increased imports. The USITC then concluded, echoing the United States statutory standard, that "the increased imports are an important cause, and a cause no less important than any other cause, of the threat of serious injury".

183. According to Australia and New Zealand, the USITC's determination on this issue is inconsistent with Article 4.2(b) of the Agreement on Safeguards because the methodology used by the USITC did not ensure that injury caused by the six other factors was not attributed to increased imports. Our examination, therefore, focuses on the issue of non-attribution. As we have just stated, in a situation such as this, where there are several causal factors, the process of ensuring that injury caused by other causal factors is not attributed to increased imports must include a separation of the effects of the different causal factors.

184. By examining the *relative* causal importance of the different causal factors, the USITC clearly engaged in some kind of process to separate out, and identify, the effects of the different factors, including increased imports. Although an examination of the *relative* causal importance of the different causal factors may satisfy the requirements of United States law, such an examination does not, for that reason, satisfy the requirements of the Agreement on Safeguards. On the record before us in this case, a review of whether the United States complied with the non-attribution language in the second sentence of Article 4.2(b) can only be made in the light of the explanation given by the USITC for its conclusions on the relative causal importance of the increased imports, as distinguished from the injurious effects of the other causal factors.

185. In that respect, we see nothing in the USITC Report to indicate how the USITC complied with the obligation found in the second sentence of Article 4.2(b) and, therefore, we see no basis for either the Panel or us to assess the adequacy of the USITC process with respect to the "non-attribution" requirement of Article 4.2(b) of the Agreement on Safeguards. The USITC Report, on its face, does not explain the process by which the USITC separated the injurious effects of the different causal factors, nor does the USITC Report explain how the USITC ensured that the injurious effects of the other causal factors were not included in the assessment of the injury ascribed to increased imports. The USITC concluded only that each of four of the six "other factors" was, relatively, a less important cause of injury than increased imports. As Australia and New Zealand argue, and as the Panel expressly found, in doing so, the USITC acknowledged implicitly that these factors were actually causing injury to the domestic industry at the same time. But, to be certain that the injury caused by these other factors, whatever its magnitude, was not attributed to increased imports, the USITC should also have assessed, to some extent, the injurious effects of these other factors. It did not do so. The USITC did not explain, in any

way, what injurious effects these other factors had on the domestic industry. For instance, of the six "other factors" examined, the USITC focused most on the cessation of the payments under the National Wool Act of 1954 (the "Wool Act") subsidy. The USITC recognized that the Wool Act subsidies represented an important contribution to the profits of the growers and feeders of live lambs. Yet the USITC's analysis of the injurious effects of this "factor" is confined largely to the statement that "the loss of Wool Act payments *hurt* lamb growers and feeders and caused some to withdraw from the industry." (emphasis added) This explanation provides no insight into the nature and extent of the "hurt" caused to the domestic industry by this factor. The USITC stated also that "the effects of termination of the Wool Act payments can be expected to recede further with each passing month." The USITC, thereby, acknowledged that the Wool Act will have on-going effects, but it did not elaborate on what these effects are likely to be nor how quickly they will disappear. In varying degree, the same is true as well for the remaining "other factors" examined. Thus, although the USITC acknowledged that these other factors were having *some* injurious effects, it did not explain what these effects were, nor how those injurious effects were separated from the threat of serious injury caused by increased imports.

186.   In the absence of any meaningful explanation of the nature and extent of the injurious effects of these six "other" factors, it is impossible to determine whether the USITC properly separated the injurious effects of these other factors from the injurious effects of the increased imports. It is, therefore, also impossible to determine whether injury caused by these other factors has been attributed to increased imports. In short, without knowing anything about the nature and extent of the injury caused by the six other factors, we cannot satisfy ourselves that the injury deemed by the USITC to have been caused by increased imports does not include injury which, in reality, was caused by these factors.

187.   In this respect, we also recall that, on this issue, the Panel concluded:

> . . . that the USITC's application of the "substantial cause" test in the lamb meat investigation as reflected in the USITC report did not ensure that threat of serious injury caused by other factors has not been attributed to increased imports.

188.   For the foregoing reasons, we find that the USITC, in its Report, did not adequately explain how it ensured that injury caused to the domestic industry by factors other than increased imports was not attributed to increased imports. In the absence of such an explanation, we uphold, albeit for different reasons, the Panel's conclusions that the United States acted inconsistently with Article 4.2(b) of the Agreement on Safeguards, and, hence, with Article 2.1 of that Agreement.

Notes and Questions

(1) Do you concur that, according to the treaty text, increased quantities of imports need not in themselves be sufficient to cause serious injury (putting aside, of course, how to make sense of import quantities as a casual variable in any setting)?

(2) How is the ITC to ensure that injury caused by other factors is not "attributed" to imports? Is anything short of a multiple regression study acceptable? What if the data for such a study are unavailable?

(3) The *Lamb* decision carefully states that it does not rule on the legality of the "substantial cause" test under US law, and no decision to date has reached that issue. If a challenge were to be brought to it, how would it fare?

(4) In the course of administering the substantial cause test, a few ITC Commissioners through the years have engaged in "shift-share" analysis, asking whether the decline in domestic consumption of a good was a more important reason for diminished domestic production than an increase in import market share. Consider the following excerpt from Commissioner Alberger's opinion in Certain Motor Vehicles, US Intl. Trade Commn., Inv. No. TA–201–44, Pub. No. 1110, 2 ITRD 5241 (1980):

> At the most fundamental level, then, it is useful to allocate the decline in domestic producers' shipments in 1979 and 1980 into two basic components: that portion accounted for by the reduced overall consumption of autos and light trucks because of general economic conditions, and that portion attributable to the increasing market share of import vehicles. The relative magnitude of these two causes can be assessed by comparing the actual decline in domestic shipments to the decline that might have occurred if imports had not increased their market share in 1979–80, i.e., if imports and domestic vehicles had shared equally in the overall decline in sales. The difference between these two figures represents the maximum potential loss in sales due to increased imports. This amount can then be compared to the volume of loss attributable *solely* to reduced demand.

* * *

> [Such analysis suggests] that declining demand accounted for over 80 percent of the net decline in US producers' domestic shipments of both automobiles and trucks from 1978 to 1979, as compared with less than 20 percent of the decline in US producers' domestic shipments being attributable to imports' increasing share of US consumption. Between January–June 1979 and January–June 1980, about two-thirds of the decline in US producers' domestic shipments was attributable to declining demand and only a third was due to the increased share of the US market accounted for by imports. Thus, even if the import share had been held constant during these critical 18 months, and even if all of those sales which went into the increased import share had instead gone to US producers, domestic firms' sales still would have fallen by over 80 percent of their actual decline in 1979 and by over 60 percent of their actual decline in January–June 1980.

Petitioners would perhaps dispute the conclusions I draw [because they] fail to allow for the theory that an import increase in the earlier period of 1976–78 could be accountable for injury which did not become manifest until 1979. However, even if average imports, consumption and domestic shipments for 1976–78 are compared to the 1979 figures, the decline in demand is still greater than the import factor.

Is the logic of Commissioner Alberger's approach clear? Is it appropriate to treat declining domestic "consumption" as a causal variable distinct from increased imports (or, more precisely, the increased market share of imports)? Is it appropriate to treat decreased consumption a single alternative cause of injury under US law for purposes of the substantial cause test? How would you attack this method if you were a petitioner today? How would you attack this method as a respondent?

(5) In the 1970's and 80's, one of the central issues in US escape clause proceedings was whether a domestic recession could be treated as a single, distinct cause of injury under the substantial cause test. If the answer was yes, the effects of recession tended to swamp the effects of imports in the view of many Commissioners. But if recession had to be "disaggregated" into a multitude of underlying causes, increased imports might then appear to be the "substantial cause" of serious injury. On this question, see especially Heavyweight Motorcycles, US Intl. Trade Commn., Inv. No. TA–201–47 (1983) (views of Commissioner Eckes), arguing that if a recession is viewed as a single cause of injury, US industries would be denied relief precisely when they need it most. Persuasive? Section 202(c)(2)(A) of the Trade Act of 1974 was amended in 1988 to read: "the Commission shall consider the condition of the domestic industry over the course of the relevant business cycle, but may not aggregate the causes of declining demand associated with a recession or economic downturn in the United States into a single cause of serious injury or threat."

(6) Suppose that consumer tastes change, such that consumers now prefer imported goods to domestic goods. Are imports the cause of injury, or are consumer tastes the cause of injury? Consider another excerpt from the 1980 *Certain Motor Vehicles* case at the ITC, this time from the views of Commissioner Calhoun:

I have found two factors which seem to be more important causes of the industry's problems than are increased imports...First, the demand for the type of automobile desired by a significant portion of the buying public is shifting from a product line roughly described as larger, less fuel-efficient automobiles to smaller, more fuel-efficient automobiles.
* * *

With regard to the shift in consumer preference from one type of automobile to another, petitioners argued that if such a shift exists it is nothing more than a shift from the purchase of domestic cars to the purchase of imported cars with a resulting increase in imported automobiles. The reason for the increase in imports, they argued, is unimportant to our determination under section 201. Moreover, their view continued, section 201 is specifically designed to provide a remedy in precisely those circumstances in which domestic sales are displaced by sales of imports. While I do not refute this view of the policy underlying section 201 I must take exception, both in concept and in fact, with the view that in this case the shift in consumer preference merely explains why imports might have increased and is not cognizable as an independent source of injury to the domestic industry.* * *

For me the decisive precedent for the integrity of demand shift as a concept distinct from a shift to imports in a circumstance of increasing and competitive imports is *Wrapper Tobacco,* Investigation No. TA–201–3, USITC Pub. No. 746 (1975). *Wrapper Tobacco* has a particular precedential appeal because the behavior of imports in the marketplace was especially strong. First, imports had more than tripled their market penetration over a four-year period while domestic production and total consumption were in decline. Second, the prices of the bulk of the imported articles tended to be below the price of the domestic articles, but certain high-grade imports were priced considerably higher than the domestic product. Third, while some of the imports were considered to be of higher quality than the domestic article, most of the imports were used to produce product lines that competed with those using the domestic product.

In the face of this extremely competitive position of imports, the Commission in *Wrapper Tobacco* made a unanimous negative determination. Four Commissioners relied upon the change in consumer tastes from larger cigars to smaller cigars and other tobacco products as the primary reason for the decline in demand they viewed as a cause of injury more important than increasing imports. Thus, the majority of the Commission had no difficulty in concept or in fact in differentiating between a shift from the domestic article and a shift to imports. * * *

Moreover, where in both concept and in fact a shift in demand is distinguishable from a shift to imports, not to make it a factor in the consideration of causality transforms section 201 from an import relief provision to an industrial relief provision. Under such a view, whenever an industry is in decline because of internal structural changes or exogenous occurrences in the society independent of imports, an industry need only show that imports are increasing concomitant with its difficulty and it could receive relief. While one could make very good arguments supporting the need for an industrial policy which would provide assistance to worthy industries suffering generalized difficulty unassociated with imports, section 201 cannot be so construed. It is plainly and simply an import relief provision and, therefore, our fundamental task on the face of it and from the legislative history is to determine that *imports* are an important cause of the injury and to determine that no other cause is more important than imports. Thus, any other factors that may have contributed to injury must be measured against the contribution made by imports.

Contrast the analysis of Commissioner Calhoun with the position of the United States in the early GATT dispute known as the *Hatter's Fur* case, which followed a decision by the United States to invoke Article XIX and impose restrictions on imports of hat parts. (Sales No. GATT/1951–3 (Nov. 1951.)) In the course of defending its position, the United States contended that a change in fashion had led consumers to prefer imports to domestic products. Could the United States prevail with this argument under current WTO law?

(7) In Unwrought Copper, US Intl. Trade Commn., Inv. No. TA–201–52, 6 ITRD 1708 (1984), the ITC made the following statement:

> During the period of investigation world copper prices fell from 85 cents per pound to 63 cents per pound while average US production costs have decreased from 88 cents to 82 cents. In our view market pressures resulting from this relatively low world price have had a significant negative impact on the domestic copper industry's ability to compete with foreign copper producers. The world price, however, cannot be viewed as an isolated cause of injury existing independent of the overall world supply and demand picture as well as factors of comparative advantage. Indeed, (s)uch a line of reasoning would result in the entire US market being taken over by imports. * * * It must be clearly understood that imports are the vehicle by which the effects of low world prices are transmitted to the US industry. Increased imports in particular are the cause of those negative effects previously detailed.

Does this passage suggest a way to conceive of increased imports as causal—to equate the effects of increased imports with the effects of fluctuations in world prices?

(8) Also in *Unwrought Copper*, the ITC remarked:

> We reject the notion that the Commission must determine whether the domestic industry has a comparative advantage in a product before making an affirmative recommendation. Such a requirement would thwart the purpose of section 201. It would also ignore the reality that costs and conditions of production change and that section 201 is intended to enable an industry to use a period of shelter in order to adjust to shifts in these costs and conditions.

The ITC seems to be suggesting that if the domestic industry lacks comparative advantage and its competitive position is thereby weak on world markets, that fact does not "count" as a cause of injury distinct from imports.

On this general issue, consider also the views expressed in Extruded Rubber Thread, US Intl. Trade Commn. Inv. No. TA–201–63, (1992) (views of Chairman Newquist and Commissioners Rohr and Nuzum):

> The cost advantage arguments raised by respondents help explain why increasing imports are an important cause of serious injury to the domestic industry. Imports may enjoy a cost advantage which, particularly in the case of products that are relatively fungible, enables them to displace sales of competing domestically produced product. This advantage often is one of lower labor or raw material costs. These types of underlying factors, however, cannot constitute "alternative causes" under the Act. Rather, Congress directed the Commission to consider whether alternative causes in the US market or among US producers, such as changes in technology or in consumer tastes, domestic competition from substitute products, plant obsolescence, or poor management were a more important cause of injury than increased imports. Thus, it is the entry of these imports in increased quantities, irrespective of any

competitive attributes of those imports derived from their home market, that the Commission must consider.

Contrast the analysis in *Extruded Rubber Thread* with that in Certain Cameras, US Intl. Trade Commn., Inv. No. TA–201–62, (1990) (views of the Commission):

> In our view, several decisions of [petitioner] Keystone's prior management are more important than increased imports in explaining the serious injury or threat of serious injury. The brief investment by a wholly owned subsidiary of Keystone in the videocassette business was a disaster with long-term financial consequences for the camera company. Keystone's management also seemed unable to adapt to changes in the camera market. In particular, Keystone was not able to gain a strong foothold in the market for 35mm cameras where demand has been growing rapidly. Keystone's management failed to pursue a consistent and effective plan to develop brand name recognition or to develop a distinctive market niche. In a market where brand names command significant price premiums and where new models, features, and concepts rapidly capture market share, Keystone followed no consistent approach to expand its sales and profits. Instead, it sporadically invested in advertising and developed primarily cheaper versions of existing models. In this particular industry, such an approach has not proven to be effective or profitable. Perhaps most telling is Keystone's adjustment plan, which suggests a number of revised management strategies ...Whether we view the videocassette venture and the camera-related business decisions of Keystone as two independent causes or, alternatively, as a single cause, namely "poor management," we conclude that other causes are more important than increased imports. Accordingly, we render a negative determination.

Putting the last two cases together, is it fair to say that when imports have a cost advantage, that is not a distinct cause of injury? But when domestic firms suffer from a cost disadvantage, the situation is different? Does the distinction lie in the reason *why* imports have a cost advantage—if the foreign industry has comparative advantage, imports are to blame for the woes of the domestic industry, but if the domestic industry has "poor management," domestic factors are to blame? Is that the right way to sort cases? For example, in which setting is temporary relief from import competition more likely to allow the domestic industry to restore its competitiveness?

(9) An approach to causation analysis that has particular appeal to economists was embraced briefly by some ITC Commissioners in the 1980s. They posited that in each case, there are three possible cause of injury—shifts in domestic demand, shifts in domestic supply, and shifts in import supply. Under the US substantial cause test, the question then becomes which of these shifts is a more important cause of injury. Consider the following excerpt from Wood Shakes And Shingles, US Intl. Trade Commn., Inv. No. TA 201–56 (1986) (views of Vice Chairman Susan W. Liebeler and Commissioner Anne E. Brunsdale):

> Section 201 requires that increased imports be a substantial cause of serious injury or threat of serious injury to the domestic industry.

* * * The ordinary meaning of the term cause is "anything producing an effect or result." Thus, to begin with, it is important to distinguish causes from effects. The fact that the quantity of imports has increased and that the domestic industry is injured does not necessarily mean that imports are a cause of injury, much less a substantial cause of injury. The coincidence of increases in imports and injury to the domestic industry may be due entirely to changes in other factors. For example, an increase in the domestic industry's costs could cause a reduction in domestic production and an increase in domestic price that could attract increased imports. Injury to the domestic industry would be caused by these higher costs, not by the increase in imports; that is, the increase in imports would be an effect rather than a cause of the injury. Under these conditions, were the Commission to find a positive association between the imports and the injury, it would be making a decision based on a spurious correlation—i.e., a correlation suggesting a causal relationship that does not in fact exist. * * *

Our approach to analyzing causation is guided by the principle that it is imperative to be able to distinguish between cause and effect. In addition, it is important to select a method of analysis that not only incorporates the specific variables cited by Congress as relevant to escape clause cases, but does so in a manner that is coherent and internally consistent. We sought a framework that makes it possible to distinguish situations where "increased imports" are a substantial cause of serious injury from situations where the increase in imports is an effect of changes in other factors operating in the domestic market.

Economic analysis is very useful when examining cause and effect. The framework we adopt is a traditional demand and supply analysis that explains how the price and quantity of a product are determined in a market. This framework has three general components: (1) the domestic demand for the product, (2) the domestic supply of US producers, and (3) the import supply of foreign producers. Each component incorporates the influence of (or depends on) a different collection of specific variables. Indeed, this framework is particularly useful because it enables us to consider the influence of any particular variable deemed relevant to the study of a market.

For example, such things as consumer tastes, construction activity, and prices of substitute products (like asphalt shingles, clay tile, aluminum siding, and slate) each influence the domestic demand for shakes and shingles. Consumer tastes and construction activity affect the market for shakes and shingles only in so far as they affect demand; they do not directly affect either domestic supply or import supply, although both the quantity of domestic shipments and the quantity of imports will in general change in response to the change in demand.

Domestic supply depends on a different collection of variables, including production technology and the supply conditions in the United States of production input like labor and red cedar logs. Similarly, import supply depends on yet another collection of variables, comprised of foreign demand and input supply conditions that are found abroad. * * *

By defining "substantial cause" as a cause "which is important and not less than any other cause," the statute requires the Commission to compare and weigh causes. We believe that it is important to examine causes at a comparable level of aggregation and generality and to do so in a consistent manner from case to case so that all participants in escape clause investigations are fully aware of what is involved. We are mindful of the concern of Congress that escape clause cases "provide a fair and reasonable test for any industry which is being injured by imports. . . ." We believe such a test is possible with a causation analysis framed in terms of the three basic components (domestic demand, domestic supply, and import supply), since they are at a comparable level of aggregation and generality. * * *

The evidence before us suggests that domestic supply did not shift adversely (e.g., domestic technology and input prices did not change significantly). Therefore, we confine our attention to changes in domestic demand and in import supply. * * * To find out how domestic demand and import supply have changed, we examined the data for domestic consumption, quantity of imports, and domestic price. Consumption was about 20 percent lower in 1984 and 1985 than it was in 1978 and approximately equal to the level in 1980. The quantity of imports increased by 20 percent between 1978 and 1984 and 17 percent between 1980 and 1984. An index for deflated composite US prices for western red cedar shakes and shingles shows that the real price dropped about 50 percent between 1978 and 1985 and about 30 percent since 1980. It is clear from these results that an increase in imports cannot be the only cause of injury to domestic producers of shakes and shingles. If domestic supply and demand had not changed, an increase in import supply would have caused an increase in domestic consumption as well as a decrease in price. Since consumption has either fallen or remained constant (depending on the base period used for comparison), domestic demand must have decreased. Therefore, even if the level of imports had remained constant, the domestic shakes and shingles industry would nevertheless be injured by the lower prices necessary to keep cedar shakes and shingles competitive with other products.

At the same time, the evidence on the change in domestic prices and domestic production, together with the increase in imports from Canada, shows that the fall in domestic demand for cedar shakes and shingles is not the only adverse change affecting this industry. The increased quantity of imports at lower prices could only have occurred with an increase in Canadian supply to the US market.

The statute requires that we determine which of these two factors, decreased demand or increased import supply, is more important in causing injury to the domestic shake and shingle industry. The answer to this question turns on the sensitivity or responsiveness of domestic demand and import supply to changes in the domestic price. As explained below, we find that domestic demand is highly sensitive to price while import supply is relatively insensitive to price. Under these conditions, an increase in import supply does not and cannot exert a significant depressing effect on the domestic price. Rather, the primary effect is to increase the quantity of imports and also to increase domestic consumption. Because the effect on the price was minor, the effect on domestic producers was also minor. Hence the increase in import supply cannot be a cause of serious injury to the domestic industry. In contrast, when domestic demand falls and supply is relatively insensitive to changes in price, the result is a sharp decline in market price. As a consequence, there is also a substantial adverse effect on the domestic industry. Therefore, the contraction in domestic demand is a greater cause of injury to the domestic industry than the increase in imports.

Is the approach urged by Commissioners Liebeler and Brunsdale in the *Shakes and Shingles* case permissible under US law after the 1988 amendment that prohibits aggregating the causes of declining demand into a single cause of injury? Can their approach be adapted to the inquiry to be made under GATT Article XIX and article 2.1 of the Agreement on Safeguards? With respect to this last question, suppose that a shift in import supply has contributed to some degree to "serious injury." Is that enough to justify a safeguard measure under WTO law, given that "increased quantities" need not be solely responsible for serious injury according to *US Lamb*? Must the shift in import supply also be linked clearly to "unforeseen developments?" If it could be, how much of a remedy would be permissible—enough to alleviate the "serious injury," enough to alleviate the portion of serious injury attributable to the import supply shift, or only enough to alleviate the serious injury attributable to the portion of the import supply shift caused by unforeseen developments? Finally, suppose that unforeseen developments in the domestic market, such as a shift in consumer tastes toward imports, are responsible for serious injury (as the United States alleged in *Hatter's Fur*)— in other words, unforeseen developments have led to a shift in domestic demand and concurrently to increased imports. Who wins under WTO law? For more on these issues, and for the argument that the Appellate Body has so confused matters as to make it entirely unclear what is legal and what is not, see Alan O. Sykes, The Agreement on Safeguards: A Commentary (Oxford University Press, 2006).

The general approach favored by Liebeler and Brunsdale has received endorsement from some prominent international economists. See, e.g., Gene M. Grossman, Imports as a Cause of Injury: The Case of the U.S. Steel Industry, 20 J. Int'l Econ, 201 (1986); Douglas Irwin, Causing Problems? The WTO Review of Causation and Injury Attribution in U.S. Section 201 Cases, 2 World Trade Rev. 297 (2003).

(10) A somewhat different approach to causal analysis was put forward by the respondents in the *Unwrought Copper* case (to no avail at the ITC as it turned out). That study, which concluded that a recession and rising labor costs were a more important cause of decline in the US industry than imports, is discussed in Robert Pindyck & Julio Rotemberg, Are Imports to Blame? Attribution of Injury Under the 1974 Trade Act, 30 J. L. & Econ. 101 (1987). The approach discussed in that paper asks how much better off the domestic industry would have been had there been a quota in place freezing imports at their base period level. Do you understand how that differs from the approach that equates the injury caused by a shift in import supply with the injury due to increased imports? Which approach is better?

(11) Suppose petitioners argue that the declining price of imports during the period of investigation is the substantial cause of their injury. Respondents contend, correctly, that the price decline is entirely attributable to a general appreciation of the dollar relative to foreign currencies, making imports cheaper in dollar terms. Who wins under US law? Under WTO law? Does it matter what caused the exchange rate movement?

(12) In the *Wheat Gluten* case, mentioned by the Appellate Body in the course of its *Lamb* opinion, the EU claimed that the ITC had neglected to analyze a "relevant factor" under article 4.2(a) of the Safeguards Agreement, namely, whether the depressed price of wheat gluten in the United States might be due to unusually high protein content in domestic wheat gluten that reduced demand for it (rather than primarily to increased imports, as the ITC had found). The Panel Report in the case held that it was unnecessary for the ITC to consider that issue because it was not "clearly raised" by the parties to the ITC proceeding. The Appellate Body disagreed, holding that the obligation to consider all "relevant factors" extended to matters not clearly raised by interested parties to the safeguards investigation. Sound? Is that not an invitation to strategic behavior by respondents, who will raise arguments in a WTO proceeding that they suppressed before national authorities?

(13) Having now seen multiple Appellate Body decisions in safeguards cases, how would you characterize the standard of review being applied by the Appellate Body? Recall the discussion of standards of review in Section 7.4(D)(1), which quotes an earlier part of the *US Lamb* opinion.

(F) REMEDIAL ISSUES

Is it permissible under WTO law for a nation to apply an escape clause remedy on a basis other than MFN? For many years, this issue of "selectivity" was among the most controversial aspects of safeguards policy. The next excerpt from the *Wheat Gluten* case addresses one important dimension of the matter—safeguard preferences for members of customs unions and free trade areas.

UNITED STATES—DEFINITIVE SAFEGUARD MEASURES ON IMPORTS OF WHEAT GLUTEN FROM THE EUROPEAN COMMUNITIES

WT/DS166/AB/R.
Appellate Body Report adopted January 19, 2001.

1. The United States and the European Communities appeal certain issues of law and legal interpretations in the Panel Report, *United States–Definitive Safeguard Measures on Imports of Wheat Gluten from the European Communities* (the "Panel Report"). The Panel was established to consider a complaint by the European Communities with respect to a definitive safeguard measure imposed by the United States on certain imports of wheat gluten.

2. On 1 October 1997, the United States International Trade Commission (the "USITC") initiated a safeguard investigation into

certain imports of wheat gluten. By Proclamation of the President of the United States, dated 30 May 1998, the United States imposed a definitive safeguard measure, in the form of a quantitative restriction on imports of wheat gluten, effective as of 1 June 1998. Products from Canada, a partner with the United States in the North American Free–Trade Agreement ("NAFTA"), and certain other countries were excluded from the application of the safeguard measure. * * *

* * *

93.   Before the Panel, the European Communities claimed that the United States' treatment of imports of wheat gluten from Canada, its partner in the North American Free Trade Agreement ("NAFTA"), was inconsistent with Articles 2.1 and 4.2 of the Agreement on Safeguards. On this issue, the Panel concluded that:

> ... in this case, the United States has acted inconsistently with Articles 2.1 and 4.2 SA by excluding imports from Canada from the application of the safeguard measure (following a separate and subsequent inquiry concerning whether imports from Canada accounted for a "substantial share" of total imports and whether they "contributed importantly" to the "serious injury" caused by total imports) after including imports *from all sources* in its investigation of "increased imports" of wheat gluten into its territory and the consequent effects of such imports on its domestic wheat gluten industry. (emphasis in original)

94.   On appeal, the United States challenges the Panel's interpretation of Articles 2.1 and 4.2 of the Agreement on Safeguards, and argues that the Panel failed to take sufficient account of the fact that, in this case, following its determination that imports from all sources were causing serious injury, the USITC conducted a "separate and subsequent examination", as part of the same investigation, concerning Canadian imports alone. In that examination, the USITC found that, although "imports from Canada account for a substantial share of total imports", those imports were "not contributing importantly to the serious injury caused by imports". On the basis of this examination, the USITC recommended that imports from Canada be excluded from any safeguard measure adopted. The United States considers that, for these reasons, it was justified in excluding imports of wheat gluten from Canada from the scope of application of the safeguard measure. The United States adds that the Panel erred in failing to assess the legal relevance of footnote 1 to the Agreement on Safeguards and Article XXIV of the GATT 1994 to this issue.

95.   In considering the appeal of the United States on this point, we turn first to Article 2.1 of the Agreement on Safeguards, which provides that a safeguard measure may only be applied when "such increased quantities" of a *"product* [are] *being imported* into its territory ... under such conditions as to cause or threaten to cause serious injury to the domestic industry". As we have said, this provision, as elaborated in Article 4 of the Agreement on Safeguards, sets forth the *conditions* for

imposing a safeguard measure. Article 2.2 of the Agreement on Safeguards, which provides that a safeguard measure "shall be applied to a *product being imported* irrespective of its source", sets forth the rules on the *application* of a safeguard measure.

96.   The same phrase—"product . . . being imported"—appears in *both* these paragraphs of Article 2. In view of the identity of the language in the two provisions, and in the absence of any contrary indication in the context, we believe that it is appropriate to ascribe the *same* meaning to this phrase in both Articles 2.1 and 2.2. To include imports from all sources in the determination that increased imports are causing serious injury, and then to exclude imports from one source from the application of the measure, would be to give the phrase "product being imported" a *different* meaning in Articles 2.1 and 2.2 of the Agreement on Safeguards. In Article 2.1, the phrase would embrace imports from *all* sources whereas, in Article 2.2, it would exclude imports from certain sources. This would be incongruous and unwarranted. In the usual course, therefore, the imports included in the determinations made under Articles 2.1 and 4.2 should correspond to the imports included in the application of the measure, under Article 2.2.

97.   In the present case, the United States asserts that the exclusion of imports from Canada from the scope of the safeguard measure was justified because, following its investigation based on imports from *all* sources, the USITC conducted an additional inquiry specifically focused on imports from Canada. The United States claims, in effect, that the scope of its initial investigation, *together with its subsequent and additional inquiry* into imports from Canada, did correspond with the scope of application of its safeguard measure.

98.   In our view, however, although the USITC examined the importance of imports from Canada separately, it did not make any explicit determination relating to increased imports, *excluding imports from Canada*. In other words, although the safeguard measure was applied to imports from all sources, *excluding* Canada, the USITC did not establish explicitly that imports from these *same* sources, excluding Canada, satisfied the conditions for the application of a safeguard measure, as set out in Article 2.1 and elaborated in Article 4.2 of the Agreement on Safeguards. Thus, we find that the separate examination of imports from Canada carried out by the USITC in this case was not a sufficient basis for the safeguard measure ultimately applied by the United States.

99.   Lastly, we note that the United States has argued that the Panel erred in failing to address Article XXIV of the GATT 1994, and in failing to set out a "basic rationale" for finding that footnote 1 to the Agreement on Safeguards did not affect its reasoning on this issue. In this case, the Panel determined that this dispute does not raise the issue of whether, as a general principle, a member of a free-trade area can exclude imports from other members of that free-trade area from the application of a safeguard measure. The Panel also found that it could rule on the claim of the European Communities without having recourse

to Article XXIV or footnote 1 to the Agreement on Safeguards. We see no error in this approach, and make no findings on these arguments.

100.   We, therefore, uphold the Panel's finding, in paragraph 8.182 of the Panel Report, that the United States acted inconsistently with its obligations under Articles 2.1 and 4.2 of the Agreement on Safeguards.

Notes and Questions

(1) The notion that the imports covered by the remedy imposed must be co-extensive with the imports determined to have caused injury is known as the requirement of "parallelism." Are you persuaded that it has adequate support in the treaty text?

(2) Recall Article 2.2 of the Agreement on Safeguards: "Safeguard measures shall be applied to a product being imported irrespective of its source." The Appellate Body avoids the question whether, assuming that parallelism is satisfied, GATT Article XXIV can justify an exemption to this obligation for the imports of a trading partner in a preferential trade agreement. Can Article XXIV be read to create exceptions to the Agreement on Safeguards, or only to GATT? If the former reading is permissible, think back to the *Turkey Textiles* case in Chapter 11—what implications does the Appellate Body's analysis there have for the issue here?

(3) Selectivity is not limited to situations in which imports from a trading partner are completely exempted, but arises also when quantitative limits are allocated among trading partners. The Agreement on Safeguards provides in Article 5 that the "allocation of shares" in any quota system may be worked out "by agreement" with nations having a "substantial interest" in the matter. When agreement is not "practicable," shares are to be allocated based on the shares of trading partners in trade with the importing nation "during a previous representative period," with due account taken of any "special factors" that may have been affecting trade during that period. Likewise, an importing nation may depart even from these principles in allocating shares after prior consultation with the Committee on Safeguards—it must make a showing that departure is justified because imports from certain nations have "increased in disproportionate percentage," and that departure from the principles above is "justified" and "equitable." In short, the Agreement leaves some room for quantitative measures that are more restrictive of imports from nations that have recently increased their market shares. Does it make sense to place stricter limits on exporters that have been expanding their exports most rapidly?

(4) When a nation suspends concessions as a "safeguard", what is the law regarding compensation to affected countries? Article XIX of GATT, paragraphs 2 and 3, requires negotiations over compensation, followed by a withdrawal of equivalent concessions by the nations affected by safeguards if the parties cannot agree on compensation. But in the period leading up to the Uruguay Round, there was a feeling that the compensation requirement of Article XIX discouraged the use of formal safeguards measures and encouraged resort to less-disciplined voluntary restraint and orderly marketing agreements. The final Uruguay Round Agreement weakens the commitment to compensation in an important way. In article 8.1, it provides that countries proposing to apply a safeguards measure "shall endeavour to

maintain a substantially equivalent level of concessions," and must negotiate over the provision of trade compensation. Article 8.2 then provides for the withdrawal of substantially equivalent concessions in the event that agreement fails. But in article 8.3, however, this right of withdrawal is restricted—it is not to be exercised during the first three years of safeguards measures *if* those measures are a response to an *absolute* increase in imports and otherwise conform to the Agreement.

This structure raises a number of issues. First, who decides whether the conditions in article 8.3 are satisfied? In the event of dispute, must a complaining nation go through dispute resolution before taking any retaliation? If dispute resolution takes three years, does that not imply that retaliation will be impossible for three years, even if the conditions in article 8.3 are not met? Exactly this issue arose following the US safeguard measures on steel products in 2001. Ultimately, the EU agreed not to retaliate before the conclusion of dispute resolution, even though it claimed the requirements of article 8.3 had not been met.

Now suppose, arguendo, that the conditions in article 8.3 are clearly met. The nation imposing the safeguard measure knows that it cannot be the target of retaliation for three years, but it still has an obligation to "endeavour to maintain a substantially equivalent level of concessions." What does this mean as a practical matter? Must it negotiate over compensation in "good faith?" Why should it offer anything more than token compensation when retaliation is impossible if negotiations break down?

SECTION 15.4 ADJUSTMENT ASSISTANCE

The Department of Labor administers a program of trade-related adjustment assistance for workers,[1] while the Department of Commerce, Economic Development Administration administers a program of technical assistance for firms and industries. The Labor Department program is by far the larger of the two. In a typical year of late, appropriations for the Labor program have been on the order of $1 billion.

U.S. COMMISSION ON INTERNATIONAL TRADE AND INVESTMENT POLICY (THE WILLIAMS COMMISSION), REPORT 47–49 (1971)

CHOOSING AMONG OPTIONS

Adjustment assistance and [import restrictions] differ importantly in their impact on the economy. While adjustment assistance is focused on the particular firms or workers injured by increased imports, the impact of tariff relief or "voluntary" export restraints cannot be confined to those firms actually suffering injury. All producers of the protected

---

1. See generally M. Trebilcock, M. Chandler & R. Howse, Trade and Transitions: A Comparative Analysis of Adjustment Policies (1990); Richardson, Worker Adjustment to U.S. International Trade: Programs and Prospects, in W. Cline (ed.), Trade Policy in the 1980s, at 393 (1983) (with bibliography); Bratt, Issues in Worker Certification and Questions of Future Direction in the Trade Adjustment Assistance Program, 14 Law & Pol.Intl.Bus. 819, 823 (1982).

product, whether or not they have been injured, benefit from lessened competition.

As opposed to adjustment assistance, both escape-clause relief and orderly marketing agreements would also impose in differing degrees the various costs that are associated with increased protection against imports. * * *

Adjustment assistance, unlike import restriction, would impose direct monetary costs on the taxpayer. But by creating more flexible industries and more highly skilled workers—thus benefiting the entire economy—successful programs of adjustment assistance should offset part or all of their tax cost.

Use of adjustment assistance also avoids the adverse effects on costs of US–produced goods in both domestic and foreign markets, the restriction on access for those goods to markets abroad, and the strains on US foreign relations that may arise when the escape clause is used or when pressure is applied in an effort to obtain "voluntary" export restraints. Hence the Commission feels that in general the government should encourage adjustment rather than impose restrictions—except in those circumstances, outlined below, where protection may be more appropriate.

Under some circumstances, adjustment assistance will be difficult to apply. An industry may require only a brief period of protection, say five years, but no other aid from government programs to improve its competitive position. Or the industry may be so large that a program of adjustment assistance might need an extraordinarily high budgetary appropriation. As a general principle, therefore, in instances where an entire industry—not simply certain of its firms—is seriously injured, temporary import restrictions, coupled with maximum possible adjustment assistance, would be appropriate.

FORMER EMPLOYEES OF COMPUTER SCIENCES CORPORATION v. UNITED STATES SECRETARY OF LABOR

United States Court of International Trade, 2005.
366 F.Supp.2d 1365.

The Trade Act provides for TAA [Trade Adjustment Assistance] benefits to workers who have lost their jobs as a result of increased imports or shifts of production out of the United States. See 19 U.S.C. § 2272. Such benefits include training, re-employment services and various allowances including income support, job search and relocation allowances.

Plaintiffs are former employees of Computer Sciences Corporation's (CSC's) financial services group [FSG] who were separated from their employment as information technology professionals * * *. Plaintiffs petitioned Labor to obtain certification of eligibility for TAA benefits. Labor initiated an investigation and determined that Plaintiffs did not produce an article within the meaning of section 222(c)(3) of the Trade Act and, therefore, were not eligible for TAA benefits. Labor agreed to reconsider its determination and found that the "workers did produce widely marketed software components on CD ROM and tapes, and thus did produce an article within the meaning of the Trade Act." Labor, however, again denied Plaintiffs request for certification because "although [CSC] did report that some 'source coding' did shift to India in the relevant period, [CSC] does not import completed software on physical media that is like or directly competitive with that which was produced at the subject facility. Business development, design, testing, and packaging remain in the United States."

* * *

The Court finds that Labor's determinations are based on incomplete factual findings and its rulings derived from those findings do not demonstrate a reasoned analysis. Labor is required to certify a group of workers as eligible to apply for TAA benefits if "a significant number or proportion of the workers in such workers' firm, or appropriate subdivision of the firm, have become totally or partially separated [from employment]," and if one of two further sets of conditions are satisfied. 19 U.S.C. § 2272(a). First, such workers may qualify if:

> (i) the sales or production, or both, of such firm or subdivision have decreased absolutely; (ii) imports of articles like or directly competitive with articles produced by such firm or subdivision have increased; and (iii) the increase in imports ... contributed importantly to such workers' separation or threat of separation and to the decline in the sales or production of such firm or subdivision.

19 U.S.C. § 2272(a)(2)(A). Second, the workers may qualify if there has been a shift in production to a foreign country by the firm or subdivision of articles like or directly competitive with articles produced by the firm or subdivision, and if any of the following conditions are satisfied: (1) the shift in production was to a country which is a party to a free trade agreement with the United States; (2) the shift in production was to a country that is a beneficiary under one of the various trade preference programs; or (3) there had been or is likely to be an increase in imports of articles like or directly competitive with articles produced by the subject firm or subdivision. See 19 U.S.C. § 2272(a)(2)(B). Labor concedes that a significant number of workers were separated from their jobs in CSC's FSG during the relevant period, thus satisfying the first requirement of 19 U.S.C. § 2272(a).

* * *

Labor's determination that Plaintiffs are not eligible for TAA benefits turns on its determination that the imported code from India is not "like or directly competitive" with the completed software produced by Plaintiffs while employed by CSC. Labor found Plaintiffs ineligible for TAA benefits because CSC "does not import completed software on physical media that is like or directly competitive with that which was produced at the subject facility." Labor contends that "nothing in the administrative record . . . supports the inference that 'code,' for example, constitutes a 'software component' or an article." Furthermore, Labor argues that whether Plaintiffs produced a software component is not relevant. Labor notes that "the storing of completed software onto physical media, the copying of the completed software onto physical media, and the delivery of the software continue to take place at the subject facility." Labor insists that the central basis for its determination is whether the code imported from India is an article like or directly competitive with the completed software produced by Plaintiffs. The Court does not agree.

While Labor may be correct that the code from India is not like or directly competitive with the completed software on physical media produced in the United States, it does not follow that the code from India is not like or directly competitive with a function used in producing the completed software in the United States. Labor notes that "coding is only one function or process in the development of a complete 'article.' " Labor, however, asserts that code is not a software component. Labor's conclusion is counterintuitive because, if code is a process in the development of completed software, then code must also be considered a component of such software.

Labor also contends that code is not an article. Plaintiffs respond that they were engaged in the production of software components which are articles under the Trade Act. Plaintiffs argue that an item does not have to be tangible in order to be an article. Nonetheless, Plaintiffs contend that code is tangible and therefore an article because it "is something 'capable of being possessed or realized' and not simply the contribution of labor, skill, or advice." The Court finds that the record supports neither Labor's nor Plaintiffs' contentions. The Trade Act requires Labor to examine the articles produced by petitioners and compare them to the articles imported from abroad. See 19 U.S.C. § 2272(a)(2). Based on the administrative record, Labor has failed to satisfy its obligation to compare the domestic product with the foreign made product. Consequently, the Court finds that Labor's investigation failed to meet the threshold requirement of reasonable inquiry. * * *

Whether Plaintiffs produced software components is highly relevant to determining whether Plaintiffs are eligible for TAA benefits. Accordingly, the Court remands this matter to Labor with instructions to investigate whether Plaintiffs produced code and if they did, whether the production of code shifted to India. Without further investigation, it is uncertain whether the code from India is like or directly competitive with the article or component of such article produced by Plaintiffs in the United States. Moreover, the Court finds that Labor's contention that code is not a software component nor an article is not supported by substantial evidence. Upon consideration of Plaintiffs' motion for judgment upon the agency record and Labor's response thereto and the administrative record, it is hereby ORDERED * * * that this matter is remanded to Labor with instructions to: (1) explain why code, which is used to create completed software, is not a software component; (2) examine whether Plaintiffs were engaged in the production of code; (3) investigate whether there was a shift in production of code to India; (4) investigate whether code imported from India is like or directly competitive with the completed software or any component of software formerly produced by Plaintiffs; and (5) investigate whether there has been or is likely to be an increase in imports of like or directly competitive articles by entities in the United States.

* * *

Notes and Questions

(1) What is the logic of conditioning adjustment assistance in part on whether the petitioning workers are producers of an "article?" If code is written in India, and then transmitted to the US software manufacturer over the internet, does that constitute the importation of an "article" within the Act? Is there any reason to restrict adjustment assistance to workers who produce goods rather than services?

(2) At this writing, the trade adjustment assistance program is up for renewal in Congress. Among the proposals for renewal is an extension of the program to service industries.

(3) Is there any principled justification for providing more safety net benefits to workers displaced by changes in trade patterns than by changes in, say, technology or domestic consumer tastes?

(4) The economic argument for trade adjustment assistance rather than trade protection is a simple one—adjustment assistance can be targeted more directly to needy workers who suffer from trade-related dislocation, and it can facilitate the movement of those workers from declining sectors into competitive sectors. By contrast, trade protection confers benefits on all stakeholders in protected firms, and may thus benefit to a great degree diversified shareholders who are no sense needy. Likewise, it retards rather than facilitates the movement of resources into more productive uses. Is there another side to this story? Is it realistic to imagine that senior workers who have spent their careers in one industry can retrain themselves for different types of jobs in another industry, and hope to achieve comparable incomes within a reasonable time frame?

(5) What role should the availability of adjustment assistance play in the decision to afford an industry import relief under the escape clause? If sufficient adjustment assistance is available, should import restraints ever be imposed? If so, when?

Chapter 16

THE REGULATION OF DUMPING

SECTION 16.1 INTRODUCTION

(A) RESPONSES TO UNFAIR ACTS IN INTERNATIONAL TRADE

The eight preceding chapters have dealt primarily with the substantive obligations of international trade rules and the exceptions to those rules. In this and the two following chapters, the focus shifts to mechanisms that WTO members are permitted to use to offset "unfair" trade practices of firms or other governments. In particular, we examine WTO rules dealing with dumping by firms and subsidization by government.

It is sometimes said that the safeguard actions studied in Chapter 15 are taken for purposes of adjustment to fairly traded imports, which result naturally from liberal trade policies; whereas the responses to dumping and subsidies considered in Chapters 16–18 are designed to counteract foreign measures which are "unfair" or "market distorting." This distinction between "fair" and "unfair" trade, such as is reflected in the differences between titles II and III of the Trade Act of 1974, is not airtight. Arguments about "unfairness" are sometimes made in escape clause proceedings, where fairness is not technically relevant, and the difficulty of defining "unfairness" leads to suspicions that some proceedings alleging unfairness are really disguised attempts to obtain escape clause type relief.

One of the rationales behind the unfair trade rules we will examine is similar to that behind the antitrust and unfair competition laws that exist to a greater or lesser degree in every country. Just as it is believed that certain domestic activities, such as monopolization, price fixing or market sharing are undesirable, it is thought that certain international trade practices are undesirable and should be regulated. The basic idea behind such rules is sometimes expressed as a desire to create a level playing field where the producers of the world all have an equal chance to compete.

While GATT rules have always permitted countries to take actions to offset injury caused by dumped and subsidized goods, there is considerable controversy within the WTO over how to define the precise scope

752

of permitted actions. Moreover, even to the extent that the rules embodied in the WTO agreements reflect the views of the international trading community as to what is unfair, economists have challenged the underlying premises of certain of those rules. In the case of subsidies, some governments and economists consider them to be an essential tool, useful to correct market failures, reduce income disparities or help disadvantaged groups or regions. With respect to dumping, it is argued that such a practice, a form of "price discrimination," actually has beneficial effects on world and national prosperity, by encouraging competition. The rules for responding to dumped and subsidized imports allow use of import restrictions, such as added duties, which some argue can be anticompetitive and can reduce world welfare.

The problems we will consider in this chapter and the following chapters can be seen in the following situations:

(1) Tractor producers in Bavonia export to Avaly and sell their tractors in the Avaly market for less than they sell the same product in the home market of Bavonia. Competing Avaly tractor manufacturers complain that this import competition is unfair and that the tractors are being "dumped" in Avaly.

(2) Caldonia manufacturers produce watches, and the Caldonia government grants to each producer a subsidy of the equivalent of $20 for each watch. Because of the subsidy, Caldonia watchmakers are able to sell their products in the Avaly market for up to $20 less than Avaly-made watches and the Avaly watch producers cannot compete in Caldonia. The Avaly watchmakers cry "foul."

(3) Duglavsky producers of electronic calculators produce and use a special integrated circuit which is patented in Avaly, but refuse to obtain a patent license or to pay royalties to the Avaly patent holder. Nevertheless, they attempt to export some of these calculators to Avaly where they compete with Avaly-made calculators, whose producers pay royalties to the patent holder. The patent holder, as well as the Avaly producers, seeks to prevent those imports.

These cases involve a variety of problems. For example, it has already been noted that some actions affect a country's *exports* in a way which makes other nations feel aggrieved, while other actions affect a country's *imports* in a way which aggrieves others. In some cases the action is by private firms or manufacturers, (e.g., dumping), in others it is by governments (e.g., subsidies). In some cases an action may breach an international obligation, but in other cases there may be no such breach (or there may be no existing international norm on the subject), yet a trading partner will still feel aggrieved and seek a response.

We will consider each of these problems. First, in Chapters 16 and 17, we will consider the policy issues, US laws and international rules applicable to dumping. In Chapter 18, we will examine the same questions in respect of subsidies. Additionally, in Chapter 20, where our focus will be on international rules in respect of intellectual property, we will also consider Section 337 of the Tariff Act of 1930, which has been invoked to protect US industry from patent infringement and similar actions. More generally, recall that in Chapter 7, we considered Section 301 of the Trade Act of 1974, a statute giving the US President broad authority to take retaliatory measures against what he determines to be unfair trade practices.

Before turning to these detailed discussions, however, there are two general issues affecting all of them that should be considered at the outset. One is sometimes referred to as the problem of interface: How should the world trading system handle problems arising from the fact that different nations have different philosophies of organizing and directing economic activities? The second is the question of how rules on international trade practices should be applied—in a legalistic manner with frequent recourse to courts to establish precise rules of conduct or more flexibly with a view toward government or industry negotiated settlements of disputes?

(B) THE INTERFACE THEORY OF ECONOMIC RELATIONS

Many of the "unfair" trading practices that we will examine have been considered unfair because they interfere with or distort free market economy principles. The WTO, of course, is largely based upon such principles. It is not surprising, therefore, that it is often difficult to apply its trading rules to nonmarket economies. Recall in that regard, our discussion of the rules on state trading enterprises in Chapter 9. In addition, even between the relatively similar western industrial market economies, there are wide differences regarding the degree of government involvement in the economy, by regulation or by ownership. As world economic interdependence has increased, it has become more difficult to manage relationships between various economies. This problem can be analogized to the difficulties involved in trying to get two computers of different makes to work together. To do so, one needs an "interface" mechanism to mediate between the two computers. Likewise in international economic relations, and particularly trade, some interface mechanism may be necessary to allow different economic systems to trade together harmoniously.

These problems can be easily seen in the chapters on dumping and subsidies. We will see that part of the definition of dumping is selling for export at below home-market prices or costs. But for nonmarket economies, are there meaningful costs and prices? In the case of subsidies, it may be easy to identify cash payments to an exporter, but there are a myriad of government policies that affect the competitiveness of a business. If the goal is really to achieve a "level playing field," does that imply that the world's governments must adopt uniform policies? If not, how will it be humanly possible to analyze (or in these days, to program a computer to analyze) the effect of different policies? Besides, isn't trade to some degree based on differences between countries?

A less obvious example of the interface problem and the difficulties of defining unfairness can be seen in the following problem, which focuses on so-called variable cost analysis. It may arise in the context of two economies that differ only slightly in respect of their acceptance of basic free market economic principles. As the problem demonstrates, even given such similarities, there may be differences in the way the respective economies operate over the course of the business cycle that may create situations that are considered unfair by some, even though these differences may not have resulted from any conscious unfair policies or practices.

Take an industrial sector (such as steel) in two economies (such as the United States and Japan) with the following characteristics:

Society A

Worker tenure (no layoffs of workers)

Capitalization with a high debt-equity ratio (e.g., 90% debt)

Society B

No worker tenure (wages for workers are therefore variable costs)

Capitalization with low debt-equity ratio (e.g., less than 50%) (dividends can be skipped)

In times of slack demand, economists note that it is rational for a firm to continue to produce as long as it can sell its product at or above its short-term variable costs. This is true because it must in any event pay its fixed costs. Of course, this is true only for limited periods; presumably over the regular course of the business cycle, the firm must not incur losses in the long term.

An analysis of the short-term variable costs of firms in Societies A and B can be done as follows:

Costs of a Firm (per unit of production)	Society A	Society B
Plant Upkeep	20 fixed	20 fixed
Debt Service	90 fixed	50 fixed
Dividends (cost of capital)	10 variable	50 variable
Worker Costs	240 fixed	240 variable
Cost of Materials	240 variable	240 variable
Total Costs (per unit of production)	600	600
Fixed	350	70
Variable	250	530

As noted above, it will be rational for producers in Society A to continue production so long as they can obtain a price of 250, while producers in Society B need to receive a price of 530. Thus, in a period of falling prices and demand, the producers in Society A can be expected to garner, through exports to Society B, an increasing share of the Society B market. Suppose this happens, and the firms in Society B close. Are Society A's exports to Society B unfair?

There are no easy answers to the questions raised above. Indeed, they are in fact probably more complicated than the foregoing would indicate because whatever general rules exist, it is argued that special considerations should apply to developing countries (see Chapter 24).

(C) THE PROBLEM OF LEGALIZATION

As we proceed through the next few chapters, the reader will note that application of the major statutes on unfair trade practices, such as dumping and subsidization, is characterized, particularly in the United States, by complex rules and proceedings and by extensive involvement of lawyers and courts. While our examination of other legal systems will not be extensive, it is fair to say that proceedings in those systems are more informal, and therefore less costly. It can be argued that the added expense of the US approach is worth its cost, a matter we will discuss in more detail in Chapter 25. More frequent judicial review leads to more detailed rules and allows parties to tailor their conduct to avoid violations. Of course, at the same time it may lead to the creation of unintended loopholes that allow certain conduct because it is considered to be technically outside the rules, even though an unbiased observer would probably conclude that the rules were meant to apply to such conduct, and vice versa.

The lack of precisely defined rules leaves considerable discretion in the hands of those officials who apply the rules. They may as a result be in a position to use the rules only when appropriate to effectuate the real purpose of the rules. Their exercise of discretion will be difficult to review, however, and this, of course, presents serious problems of potential abuse, problems which may be magnified since those seeking protection from the officials are constituents of sorts of the officials, while those who will be adversely affected are foreigners.

The reader should consider, as we proceed through these chapters, whether the US system has struck the proper balance between flexibility and reasonable cost, on the one hand, and predictability and "over legalization," on the other hand.

SECTION 16.2   ANTIDUMPING LAWS: THE UNDERLYING POLICY ISSUES[1]

(A) INTRODUCTION

Dumping is broadly defined as exporting goods at prices below those charged on the domestic market (or, if none, on a third-country market) or at prices insufficient to cover the cost of the goods sold. For example, if a US industry sells its product in the US market for $10/unit and sells the same product on the same terms for export to the EU at an equivalent price of $9/unit, it would be dumping the product in the EU market. Under the rules discussed below, if the dumping caused material

---

1. There are numerous books and articles on dumping, and space constraints preclude listing more than a few. A particularly useful book that compares US, EC, Canadian and Australian antidumping laws and contains an extensive bibliography, as well as comments by many experts, is John H. Jackson & Edwin A. Vermulst, eds., Anti-

dumping Law and Practice: A Comparative Study (1989). See also Bernard M. Hoekman, Free Trade and Deep Integration: Antidumping and Antitrust in Regional Agreements (1998); Richard Boltuck & Robert E. Litan, eds., Down in the Dumps (1991); Jacob Viner, Dumping: A Problem in International Trade (1923).

injury to the EU industry (or threatened it), the EU would be permitted to impose antidumping duties of $1/unit to offset the dumping. In addition, if it cost an EU company $20/unit to produce its product and it sold the product in the US and EU at $18/unit, it would be engaged in dumping in the US in the amount of $2/unit. The former case involves what is sometimes referred to as international price discrimination; the latter as below-cost sales.

Whether dumping should be controlled through the use of offsetting, antidumping (AD) duties is a matter of some controversy within the world of international trade specialists, so we begin with an examination of the underlying policy issues raised by AD laws. Then, we undertake a detailed analysis of US AD rules, followed by a consideration of a particularly controversial WTO case on dumping.

Part of the reason for the controversy over the use of AD duties stems from the fact that they are imposed frequently, which has raised concerns that they may have become a disguised form of protectionism. WTO statistics indicate that in the 1980s, the average number of AD investigations initiated per year was around 140 cases and four countries—the US, the EU, Canada and Australia were by far the major users of AD measures. Since the formation of the WTO, WTO statistics indicate that the following countries have been the most frequent users and/or targets of such laws:

Antidumping actions (January 1, 1995 to June 30, 2007)

Country	Investigations initiated (50+)	Measures imposed	Measures in force	Measures imposed on (25+)
Argentina	220	157	62	14
Australia	189	72	46	8
Brazil	138	67	50	70
Canada	141	87	40	12
China	138	97	103	397
Chinese Taipei	13	4	7	110
Egypt	59	43	31	4
EC	363	237	149	[335]*
India	474	347	178	78
Indonesia	65	29	n/a	76
Japan	6	3	2	99
Korea	93	54	29	139
Malaysia	43	25	16	45
Mexico	94	82	69	26
New Zealand	53	19	10	3
Peru	63	45	33	0
Russia	n/a	n/a	n/a	84
South Africa	203	121	61	35
Thailand	37	27	24	80
Turkey	109	110	99	22
United States	375	242	229	106

Country	Investigations initiated (50+)	Measures imposed	Measures in force	Measures imposed on (25+)
Overall total	3097	1997	n/a	1997

*EU (45) and individual member states

While there are some apparent discrepancies in the data, it is clear that use of AD measures is significant. The average number of annual initiations for the period grew to almost 250, although since January 1, 2005, the average annual number of initiations has only been 180. In terms of measures imposed, the major users of AD laws are (in order): India, US, EU, Argentina, South Africa and Turkey. Indeed, in terms of measures imposed since January 1, 2005, the top two users are India and China. In terms of targets, China is by far the main target. In terms of product sectors, the main targets have been base metals (610), chemicals (395), plastics (257), textiles (169) and machinery and electrical equipment (151).

(B) THE POLICY DEBATE OVER ANTIDUMPING LAWS

As noted above, dumping can be broadly defined as selling for export at prices below (i) those prevailing in the home market (international price discrimination) or (ii) those necessary to cover production costs (below cost sales). In each case, some international trade scholars question the desirability of using AD duties to offset such behavior. Nevertheless, the laws have strong supporters.

ALAN O. SYKES, INTERNATIONAL LAW[2]

"Dumping" refers to certain pricing practices by private firms engaged in international trade. Although its precise meaning has changed through the years, dumping occurs under modern trade laws when an exporting firm's prices satisfy (roughly) one of three conditions: (a) its F.O.B. price to the complaining export market is below its F.O.B. price to its home market for the same goods (or for similar goods adjusted for cost and quality differences); (b) in the absence of substantial home market sales of identical or similar goods, its F.O.B. price to the complaining export market is below the F.O.B. export price to some third country market; or (c) its F.O.B. price to the complaining export market is below the fully allocated cost of production for the good in question (including an allocation of fixed costs, general selling and administrative expenses, and so on). * * *

---

2. Excerpted from A. Mitchell Polinsky and Steven Shavell (eds.), Handbook of Law and Economics, vol. I (2007). Reprinted with permission. See also Wılliam J. Davey, Antidumping Laws: A Time for Restriction,1988 Fordham Corp. L. Inst. 8–1; Alan V. Deardorff, Economic Perspectives on Antidumping Law, in Robert M. Stern (ed.), The Multilateral Trading System: Analysis and Options for Change ch. 6 (1993).

GATT Article VI provides that dumping "is to be condemned," but does not prohibit it or impose any obligation on WTO members to prevent or punish it. Instead, importing nations are permitted to take countermeasures against dumping, in the form of an "antidumping duty" that may not exceed the "margin" of dumping found to exist on the goods in question. That margin is equal to the difference between the "fair value" of the goods computed using one of the three benchmarks above, and the F.O.B. export price to the country imposing the duty. For example, under the first criterion for dumping, the margin would be computed as the F.O.B. price to the home market minus the F.O.B. price to the export market. GATT does not permit antidumping duties in all instances of dumping, however, but limits them to cases in which the dumping is causing or threatening to cause "material injury" to the import-competing industry, a requirement known as the "injury test." These requirements were elaborated, along with the procedures for the conduct of antidumping investigations, in the WTO Antidumping Agreement, the successor to the Tokyo Round Antidumping Code.

Antidumping laws first emerged in Canada in the early 1900's, and quickly spread to the United States. Their proponents put them forward as an adjunct to antitrust statutes, plugging a purported "loophole" that would otherwise allow foreign firms to engage in monopolization through aggressive pricing. A moment's reflection on the standards for dumping above, however, suggests that they are radically different from the variable cost-based standards for predatory pricing that have evolved under modern antitrust law. Price discrimination dumping, reflected in possibilities (a) and (b) above, can assuredly occur at prices above variable cost. And possibility (c) above involves not a comparison between price and some measure of variable cost, but a comparison between price and (roughly) a measure of long run average cost. Further, although the material injury test requires that some harm befall import-competing firms as a prerequisite to antidumping duties, it falls far short of a structural analysis of the industry to determine whether monopolization is a plausible outcome, and antidumping duties are routinely observed in industries producing such items as steel products, potatoes, textiles and footwear—all industries that are highly unconcentrated on a global level and where a danger of monopolization is utterly implausible as a basis for antidumping measures.

The connection between antidumping policy and sensible antitrust policy is thus a tenuous one at best. [In a 1998 study for the Brookings Institution,] Sykes reviews the economic and political history of antidumping laws at considerable length, and concludes that their proponents were well aware that antidumping measures were not a necessary part of antitrust policy. Instead, the goal was to provide additional tariff protection to troubled industries plagued by import competition, an objective akin to the rationale behind the GATT escape clause discussed earlier.

Nevertheless, early economic writing on antidumping policy took a favorable view of it. [The prominent economist Jacob Viner argued in

1923] that low prices attributable to dumping are transitory, and asserted that they may impose adjustment costs on the importing nation that exceed the benefits of temporarily cheaper imports. The basis for Viner's analysis, however, was shaky. Dumping need not be transitory at all (the price discrimination form of dumping arises because different markets have different demand elasticities, a fact that may well persist over time). Even when dumping prices are transitory, nothing in Viner's work (or since) demonstrates that temporarily cheap imports systematically impose adjustment costs that exceed the welfare gains to the importing country from temporarily cheaper imports. If actors in import-competing industries have rational expectations, one would expect them to incur adjustment costs only to the extent that they are cost-justified from a social standpoint.

Not surprisingly, therefore, economic commentators eventually began to question the wisdom of antidumping policy. The lack of any connection between antidumping policy and sensible anti-predation measures has now been noted by commentators too numerous to mention. Others have noted that an antidumping duty may prove beneficial to an importing nation under special circumstances, as when it has not yet imposed the "optimal tariff" to exploit its monopsony power, or where it protects a "strategic industry" with positive spillovers, but in such cases the economic benefits of the antidumping duty are purely coincidental because a duty would be useful regardless of the pricing practices of the targeted exporters. It is fair to say that an academic consensus now exists to the effect that antidumping law is welfare-reducing in general.

Notes and Questions

(1) In an attempt to counter economic critiques of antidumping laws, the European Commission once asserted that there are three types of dumping which are particularly damaging:

> *state trade dumping* from economies whose main aim may not be cost efficiency but to earn hard currency at any price. In these cases the margins by which the prices of the Community producers are undercut may be unusually high. Because the exporters in question often do not follow normal business behaviour, this type of dumping in unpredictable in view of its occurrence, volume, price and duration;

> *"cyclical" dumping* occurs in industries subject to periodic excess supply and capacity in which there is an incentive to export during the period of shrinking domestic demand to dump the excess production at prices below full cost, thus exporting unemployment. Cyclical dumping can be expected in industries with high investment and consequently high fixed costs, like the steel or chemical industry, and has the effect of exacerbating the difficulties facing an industrial sector in the importing country which is already affected by economic recession;

> *strategic dumping* aimed at achieving, through an aggressive export strategy, a strong position on important export markets. The long-term character of such dumping usually stems from the fact that the dumper

operates from a home market base where foreign competition is weak or non-existent. This strategy has as its main aim the expansion of production to benefit from scale and learning economies for products such as in the electronics sector.

EC Commission, Eleventh Annual Report on the Community's Anti-dumping and Anti-subsidy Activities para. 2.3 (1993). Dumping by state trading companies has become much less significant as the nations of the former Communist bloc have adopted market economies (and as many have joined the EU). Professor Sykes deals with the issue of cyclical dumping (see also note 4 below), but what about strategic dumping? Would it justify AD measures? Is the key issue whether one focuses on (i) the overall effect on the global or national economies; (ii) the benefit to national consumers; or (iii) the health of the companies that make up a specific national industry?

(2) AD laws have strong supporters in the US Congress, and it seems unlikely that they will disappear in the near future, no matter how the economic policy debate evolves. First, members of Congress find it convenient to deflect complaints about import competition by referring constituents to the AD procedures, and second, many people, particularly in import sensitive industries, feel strongly that dumping is unfair. It has sometimes been speculated that congressional support may ebb in the future if the spread of AD laws leads to increased complaints by US exporters about the need to protect US industry by toughening the international rules on dumping to reduce the use of AD laws against them. To date, no such shift in attitudes has been detectable, although the US is a major target of AD measures, as noted above.

(3) The fundamental complaint about dumping is that it is an unfair business practice, one "condemned" in GATT Article VI when it causes injury. But how unfair is dumping? One way to evaluate whether and to what extent dumping is unfair is to consider how domestic legal systems treat dumping-like behavior. We have seen that dumping consists of price discrimination and below-cost sales. The question then becomes: What rules limit price discrimination and below-cost sales by domestic firms in the domestic market? In the case of the United States, domestic price discrimination is regulated by the Robinson–Patman Act.[3] How does that law compare with the US AD statute? As a general rule, it would seem that US AD laws are applied in a much more restrictive manner than the Robinson–Patman Act. There are, for example, a number of defenses to price discrimination under Robinson–Patman, but virtually none to dumping. Court decisions interpreting the Robinson–Patman Act state that ultimately its purpose is to protect competition, not individual competitors,[4] while the AD laws seem designed to protect domestic competitors whatever the effect on overall domestic competition.[5] These differences in the rules applied to price

3. 15 U.S.C.A. sec. 13. See Stephen F. Ross, Principles of Antitrust Law ch. 7 (1993).

4. Brooke Group Ltd. v. Brown & Williamson Tobacco Corp., 509 U.S. 209, 113 S.Ct. 2578, 125 L.Ed.2d 168 (1993).

5. See Ronald A. Cass, Price Discrimination and Predation Analysis in Antitrust

and International Trade: A Comment, 61 U. Cincinnati L.Rev. 877 (1993); Report of the Ad Hoc Committee on Antitrust and Antidumping of the American Bar Association Section on Antitrust Law, 46 Antitrust L.J. 653, 691–693 (1974).

discrimination domestically and internationally, which allow more price discrimination domestically, suggest that price discrimination is perhaps not so unfair. In the case of below-cost sales, there is acceptance of that practice in the United States, so long as it is not predatory.[6] Indeed, in a recession where all steel producing companies are losing money, US steelmakers do not sue each other for making below-cost sales, but they do bring AD actions against imports. In light of this, would you say that the existence of AD laws is consistent with the WTO's general philosophy of requiring national treatment? Should the scope of AD laws be limited to the scope of domestic rules against price discrimination and below-cost sales? What might justify differential treatment of imports?

(4) A second aspect of the unfairness argument is that AD laws are appropriate in times of recession because without them the country with the most open markets will suffer most because it will become a dumping ground for producers in other countries who have protected markets. (The EC Commission's defense of AD laws is based on the existence of such a protected market, although imposition of AD duties is not conditional on showing that the exporter's home market is protected.) AD laws in such circumstances can ensure that the burdens of recession are equitably shared. One can argue, however, that the safeguard procedures described in Chapter 15 offer a better method for dealing with this problem. The relief afforded by US AD rules is based on the amount (margin) of dumping and is not adjusted to reflect the extent of injury suffered by domestic industry. Since there is no necessary relationship between the margin of dumping and that injury, are AD laws well suited as an adjustment mechanism? Would your answer differ if available safeguard procedures were more expensive than AD procedures and rarely invoked successfully?

(5) On the unfairness issue more generally, one study concluded, after examining all 174 final affirmative injury findings of the International Trade Commission in antidumping and countervailing duty cases between 1980 and 1988, that

in 84% of the countervailing duty cases, 59% of the antidumping cases, and 67% of the joint antidumping/countervailing duty cases, the dumping (or subsidy) margin and the market share of unfair imports were too small (less than 5%) to expect that unfair imports have a significant impact on competing domestic industries.[7]

In the words of the authors, "Despite the importance of the fairness issue, there is surprisingly little information about the extent to which [dumped and subsidized] imports actually harm domestic producers."[8]

(6) As noted above, to some extent AD laws seem inconsistent with the philosophy of antitrust laws because they focus on the protection of individual competitors rather than overall competition. This concern is underscored

6. See Brooke Group Ltd. v. Brown & Williamson Tobacco Corp., 509 U.S. 209, 113 S.Ct. 2578, 125 L.Ed.2d 168 (1993).

7. Morris E. Morkre & Kenneth Kelly, Perspectives on the Effects of Unfair Imports on Domestic Industries, 61 U. Cincinnati L. Rev. 919, 944 (1993).

8. Id. at 920, citing as a "notable exception" one study of four industries: brass sheet, unfinished mirrors, candles and oil country tubular goods.

by studies that show that the most frequent users of AD actions are concentrated industries,[9] and by concerns raised when AD cases are "settled" by agreements to raise prices or cease exporting. Do you think that AD laws should be modified to include a consideration of consumer and/or competitive interests? How could this be done? The EU AD rules call for consideration of "Community interest" in deciding whether to impose AD duties, but the provision has seldom been invoked to reduce AD duty levels.

(7) Some argue that the WTO system should expand the scope of AD laws to cover "social" or "exchange rate" dumping. "Social" dumping occurs when import prices are low because of comparatively lower wages and less strict environmental rules and factory safety rules in the exporting countries. "Exchange rate" dumping occurs when import prices decline because of shifts in exchange rates. Would such an expansion be appropriate in your view? If there were to be such an expansion, what sort of definitional issues would have to be addressed? We explore the issue of linkages between international trade and worker rights generally in Chapter 21.

(8) AD laws tend to be replaced by rules on competition (antitrust laws) in respect of trade between members of advanced free trade areas (integrated markets), such as the EU, the European Economic Area, and the Australia–New Zealand pact, but they continue to be used often in looser free trade areas, such as NAFTA. As noted in Chapter 11, NAFTA rules allow private parties affected by AD decisions of national authorities to appeal those decisions to binational panels of independent experts in lieu of normal judicial review.

SECTION 16.3   UNITED STATES ANTIDUMPING LAW[1]

Antidumping rules are generally quite complex and the WTO dispute settlement cases on dumping mirror that complexity. In order to comprehend the WTO cases, it is essential first to have an understanding of how a simple antidumping case unfolds and what the basic issues are in such a case. Thus, we will first examine US antidumping rules and a simple US case before considering the applicable WTO rules in the next section.

Since 1980, the administration of the US AD law has been split between the Import Administration of the International Trade Administration of the US Department of Commerce (typically referred to as the "IA" or the "ITA" or "Commerce" or "DOC" or "USDOC"), which determines whether dumping has occurred, and the International Trade Commission (typically referred to as the "ITC" or the "Commission"),

---

9. Davey, supra note 2, at 8–33 to 8–36.

1. The current US antidumping statute was enacted by the Trade Agreements Act of 1979, which added a new title VII to the Tariff Act of 1930 (see Documents Supplement). Those sections of title VII that are particularly relevant to AD actions are Sections 731–39 (AD investigations), Sections 751–52 (reviews) and Sections 771–83 (definitions and procedures). Those sections are codified, as amended, at 19 U.S.C.A. secs. 1673–73h; 1675–75a, 1677–77n. The basic statute governing appeals from administrative decisions in AD cases is Section 516A of the Tariff Act, 19 U.S.C.A. sec. 1516a.

which determines whether US industry has demonstrated material injury.[2] Prior to 1980 administration of the AD rules had been in the hands of the Treasury Department, which was criticized by some in Congress for too often exercising its considerable discretion so as avoid the imposition of AD duties.

In this section, we will first focus on the procedural aspects of US law and then examine the substantive issues of AD law. Injury issues will be treated in Chapter 17. Since 1980, AD proceedings in the United States have become very formalized and are played out according to a complex set of rules, largely designed to minimize administrative discretion. The notes following our description of US procedures will contrast US practices with those of the EU and Canada.

(A) PROCEDURAL ASPECTS OF US ANTIDUMPING LAW

JOHN H. JACKSON & WILLIAM J. DAVEY, REFORM OF THE ADMINISTRATIVE PROCEDURES USED IN US ANTIDUMPING AND COUNTERVAILING DUTY CASES[3]

* * * There are three distinct stages in US AD and CVD [countervailing duty] cases: First, the initial investigation, which determines whether or not an AD/CVD order will be issued. Second, the annual review procedure, in which the actual amount of AD/CV duties to be collected is established. Third, the revocation procedures, by which cases are finally terminated. In addition, there is judicial review of all final determinations in these three stages.

1. Initial Investigations

An AD or CVD proceeding is typically commenced by the filing of a petition in respect of a specific product on behalf of the US domestic industry producing that product. Thereafter, the statute establishes strict deadlines for completion by the ITA and the ITC of the various phases of the initial investigation. Once an investigation is opened, the ITA is responsible for determining the extent of dumping or subsidization, while the ITC determines whether US industry has suffered material injury. The order of their determinations is as follows: First, the ITC makes a preliminary injury determination; then the ITA makes both its preliminary and final dumping/subsidy determination; and finally the ITC makes its final injury determination. The time limits established by Congress for these determinations are as follows:

2. The AD rules of the ITA are found at 19 C.F.R. pt. 351 (2007). Those of the ITC are at 19 C.F.R. pt. 207 (2007). As to basic source material, actions taken by the ITA are published in the Federal Register and the available on the ITA website. Notices of determinations by the ITC are also published in the Federal Register and the decisions are available on the ITC website.

3. This report to the Administrative Conference of the United States was published in Administrative Conference of the United States: Recommendations and Reports 909 (1991) and reprinted in a slightly revised version in 6 The Admin.L.J.Am.U. 399 (1992).

Action	Days After Petition Filed	
	AD	CVD
ITA decision to initiate investigation	20	20
ITC preliminary injury determination	45	45
ITA preliminary dumping/subsidy determination	160	85
ITA final dumping/subsidy determination	235	160
ITC final injury determination	280	205

[These deadlines are subject to extension in certain cases, which means that AD cases usually take longer than 280 days to complete.]

The decision by the ITA on whether to initiate an investigation is largely pro forma. At this stage, the ITA determines whether the petition properly alleges the basis for an action, contains information reasonably available to the petitioner in support thereof and is filed by an appropriate party.[4] The ITA does not permit arguments against initiation to be made by respondents.

If the ITA initiates an investigation, the ITC determines whether there is a reasonable indication that US industry has been materially injured by the allegedly dumped or subsidized imports. To make that determination, the ITC collects information from the US industry and others through questionnaires and uses other information available to it about the industry. * * *

If the ITC preliminary determination is affirmative, the ITA continues its preliminary investigation (which goes forward in any event during the ITC's preliminary investigation). The ITA sends questionnaires to the exporters, importers and other parties known to be involved in the case, including the relevant foreign government in a CVD case. The questionnaires aim to establish the information needed to determine whether dumping or subsidization has occurred, i.e. information on domestic and export prices, information concerning adjustments needed to make those prices "comparable," information about costs if there are allegations of below-cost sales, information about government programs and information about receipt of government benefits by individual companies. On the basis of the questionnaire responses, or, in the absence of adequate information from a respondent, the best information available to it (which may be information supplied by the petitioner), the ITA determines on a preliminary basis whether the

---

4. [original note 41] 19 C.F.R. sec. [351.203]. Petitions may be filed by a manufacturer, producer or wholesaler in the United States of a like product; a certified union or recognized union or group of workers representative of an industry in the United States engaged in the manufacture, production or wholesale of a like product; a trade or business association a majority of whose members manufacture, produce or wholesale a like product in the United States; and an association, a majority of whose members is composed of the foregoing. There is a special rule for processed agricultural products. Tariff Act of 1930, sec. 771(9)(C)-(G); 19 U.S.C. sec. 1677(9)(C)-(G).

foreign goods are being sold in the United States at less than fair value or have been subsidized. It does so by calculating the preliminary subsidy margin or dumping margin, i.e. the difference between the [export] price and the [normal] value of the goods in question. In the case of an affirmative determination, the Customs Service is directed to "suspend liquidation" of all subsequent imports of the product in question and to collect a deposit or bond thereon equal to the preliminary margin. Suspension of liquidation means that the final amount of duty owed on the imported goods is held open for later determination. A preliminary negative decision does not end the case, however, as the ITA is required to proceed to a final determination.

Between its preliminary and final determinations, the ITA verifies the questionnaire responses, typically by sending ITA personnel to conduct an on-site examination of the books and records of the respondent. In addition, both the respondent and the petitioner typically file comments in respect of the preliminary determination. In its final determination, the ITA responds to these comments and revises its preliminary determination in light of those comments that it accepts and whatever additional relevant information has come to its attention.

* * *

If the ITA makes an affirmative preliminary dumping or subsidy determination, the ITC commences a further investigation into the injury issue. * * * In the final ITC investigation, * * * a hearing is typically scheduled, at which the parties can present witnesses and legal arguments. * * *

Assuming that the ITC makes an affirmative injury finding, an AD or CVD order is issued. * * * With respect to imports of the merchandise made after the issuance of an AD or CVD order, a duty equal to the final dumping or subsidy margin is collected provisionally as an estimated AD or CV duty. This provisional amount must normally be deposited with the US government in cash. The final amount of duty owing on these imports is determined in the annual review procedure discussed below.

It is possible under the AD and CVD statutes for the foreign exporters or government to "settle" a case by agreeing to cease dumping, to cease subsidization or to revise their prices so as to eliminate the injury to US industry. Such settlements are known as price undertakings in the GATT Codes and suspension agreements in US law. * * *

* * *

Finally, one important procedural aspect of US AD/CVD proceedings must be highlighted. Much of the information collected by the ITA and ITC is viewed by the suppliers as highly sensitive commercial information, such as detailed data on costs, prices and customers. While such information is treated as confidential by the agencies and is not available to the public or parties generally, it is available to attorneys for the parties under protective orders. This practice allows attorneys for the parties to participate much more effectively in the proceedings than would be the case if there was no access to such confidential information.

2. Administrative Reviews

As explained above, the dumping or subsidy margin determined by the ITA in its final determination in an investigation is used to set the amount that must be deposited on importation of products subject to an AD or CVD order. The ITA, at the request of an interested party, will conduct a review each year to establish the exact extent of dumping or subsidization, and the importer either receives a refund if the amount deposited was too high (plus interest) or pays an additional sum (plus interest) if it was too low. Commerce Department officials told us that such a request is received in approximately 50–60% of the cases. In those cases where no review is requested, the amount deposited as the estimated duty is collected as the definitive amount due. In the other cases, reviews are held.

* * * Essentially the same sort of information is collected in a review as in the initial investigation. * * *

3. Revocation

AD and CVD orders remain in effect until they are revoked. Even if an annual review finds no dumping or subsidization, which means that no amount is required to be deposited on future importations, the AD/CVD order remains in effect and it is possible that a subsequent review could result in the assessment of AD or CV duties.

* * *

[There are several statutory procedures that can lead to revocation, but] revocation is relatively rare unless there is no opposition from US industry. * * * This means that the unsettling effect on international trade inherent in a US AD or CVD order typically continues for a considerable period of time.

[As required by the WTO AD Agreement, the United States added a sunset review provision, to implement article 11.3 of the WTO AD Agreement, which provides for the revocation of AD orders after five years unless there is a determination that "the expiry of the duty would be likely to lead to continuation or recurrence of dumping and injury." Existing orders were deemed to have been imposed on January 1, 1995. During 2000, more than 100 AD orders were revoked following sunset reviews. More recently, revocations as a result of sunset reviews have been much less common.]

4. Judicial Review

US law provides for appeals from final determinations of the ITA or ITC to the Court of International Trade (CIT). * * * Decisions by the ITA not to initiate an investigation and negative preliminary decisions by the ITC are reviewed to see if they are "arbitrary, capricious, or an abuse of discretion, or otherwise not in accordance with law." Final determinations by the ITA and the ITC are reviewed to see if they are "unsupported by substantial evidence on the record, or otherwise not in accordance with law." From the CIT, cases are appealable to the Court of Appeals for the Federal Circuit, and to the Supreme Court on writ of certiorari. Decisions involving Canadian [or Mexican] products may instead be "appealed" to binational panels under the [NAFTA].

Prior to 1979, the law relating to judicial review in AD/CVD cases was different and there was relatively little judicial review of such cases. Now, judicial review is much more common, and it appears that most AD and CVD final determinations are appealed to the CIT. * * *

Notes and Questions

(1) Although AD proceedings are administrative proceedings, the typical pattern of US administrative proceedings—the use of administrative law judges and reliance on adversarial hearings—is not used in AD cases. Contested issues are resolved by the ITA staff; hearings are not used to any significant degree in the fact-finding process. Although this makes the US system more informal than one might normally expect in the US, the US system seems in general to be more formal than those of other countries. Generally, the EU, Canadian and Australian systems seem to afford more discretion to administrators and operate more informally. Judicial review seems more intrusive in the United States than the other three jurisdictions. All of this means that AD proceedings in the US are relatively expensive, so much so that their expense is sometimes cited as a trade barrier in itself. We discuss the cost of trade law remedies generally in Chapter 25.

Judicial review in the United States can be particularly time-consuming because the CIT often remands a decision to the ITA or the ITC for further proceedings. Appeals to the Federal Circuit are generally not permitted as long as remands are ordered. The result is that some very important issues to the administration of the AD/CVD laws go unresolved for many years when judges of the CIT (or the CIT and the ITA) disagree. For example, the first Federal Circuit opinion dealing with the key issue of the 1979 CVD law—the definition of countervailable subsidy—was not rendered until 1991.

(2) Article 5.4 of the WTO AD Agreement specifies that the investigating authorities must determine the degree of support within domestic industry for opening an investigation. The minimum level of acceptable support is set at those who account for 25% of total production. See Section 732(c)(4).

(3) As noted in the foregoing excerpt, confidential information submitted by the parties to US authorities in AD/CVD cases is usually available under court protective order to attorneys for the opposing parties. This allows counsel to monitor the decisions of the authorities much more effectively. In contrast, under EU rules confidential information is generally not subject to review by the parties or their attorneys, although summaries of the information must be provided. As a result, attorneys are less able to argue their clients' cases effectively. Canadian agencies also make confidential information available to attorneys under rules similar to those used in the US. It appears that there have been relatively few (and largely inadver-

tent) violations of US protective orders. Given that the information requested by the US authorities often concerns very sensitive commercial information on customers, prices and costs, one might wonder why parties are willing to supply it if there is any risk at all of disclosure. The answer is that if the information requested is not submitted, the authorities are permitted to use the best information available, which may be the allegations of the opposing parties and which is likely to be very unfavorable.

(4) The results of dumping cases in the EU are much different than in the United States. The amount of the duty imposed in the EU is not necessarily the amount of the dumping margin. The EU authorities have the discretion to impose a lesser duty if it would be sufficient to eliminate the injury to EU industry, a practice endorsed but not required by the WTO AD Agreement, article 9.1. This practice is referred to in the EU as using "injury margins" or the "lesser duty rule" and a significant proportion of EU AD duties are reduced on the basis of such analysis. Moreover, the EU is required to take into account the "Community interest" in imposing duties, although this provision is not typically applied to reduce duties as the EU authorities seem to equate Community interest with complainant (and not consumer) interests in most cases. Likewise in Canada, the Canadian International Trade Tribunal may consider whether an AD duty would be in the public interest and may recommend to the relevant Minister that duties should not be imposed or should be reduced. It appears that such recommendations have been made only rarely.

Should the US adopt some form of lesser duty rule? What would the advantages and disadvantages of such a rule be? In particular, consider such issues as (i) is it appropriate to grant protection to an industry in excess of its injury, (ii) could the discretion of administrative agencies in setting the lesser duty be effectively monitored by courts, (iii) which US agency would set the duty rate, and (iv) how would the US annual review process be affected? US law gives users a hearing, but their views need not be considered. Section 777(h).

(5) If duties are ultimately imposed in the EU, they are imposed on a prospective basis. There is no annual review to determine the precise amount of the dumping margins. While there is the possibility of obtaining a refund if no dumping in fact occurred in a given transaction, refunds are not common because of procedural and substantive impediments in the applicable EU rules. After one year has passed, it is possible to ask the EU authorities to review and, if appropriate, revise the duty rate.

In Canada, if dumping and injury are found, Revenue Canada usually sets the normal value for the product in question by establishing a so-called benchmark price. Future imports at less than the benchmark price are subject to a duty in the amount of the shortfall. Thus, as in the EU system, there is a prospective duty, but like the US system, if the exporter stops dumping, there is usually no duty due.

Which of those systems would you say is superior? On what basis? Do you think that any one system is significantly more protectionist or expensive to administer than the others?

One problem with imposing a prospective duty as the EU does is that a dumper might choose to absorb the duty itself in order to maintain the same market price. To avoid this problem, the EU added a new provision to its AD regulation in 1988, which is designed to prevent the absorption of AD duties by the exporter or related parties. If the EU finds that they have absorbed the AD duty, an additional AD duty may be imposed. Is this consistent with the WTO AD Agreement?

(6) Generally speaking, the prospect of a fixed prospective duty such as imposed in the EU is disturbing for exporters. Even if one stops dumping, the duty may continue to be payable. To avoid this kind of duty, companies subject to EU investigations typically have made so-called price undertakings, pursuant to which they settle the case by agreeing to respect certain price levels in their exports to the EU and to report their prices to the EU regularly. From 1980 to 1989, of those cases in which dumping and injury were found, 183 cases (66%) were concluded by undertakings. However, although they continue to be used, undertakings seem to have been used less often by the EU in recent years. Similarly, the use of undertakings in Canada also seems to have declined.

The US statute (section 734) arguably discourages the use of undertakings (called suspension agreements in US law) by imposing various conditions on their use. Is this consistent with the letter of the WTO AD Agreement? With its spirit? Should the US make more extensive use of undertakings? What are the risks of using them? For example, do you see the potential for antitrust problems? For enforcement problems?

(B) THE SUBSTANTIVE RULES: DETERMINATIONS OF DUMPING

As noted earlier, dumping is broadly defined as exporting goods at prices below those charged on the domestic market (or, if none, on a third-country market) or at prices insufficient to cover the cost of the goods sold. Thus, the basic substantive determination in an antidumping case is whether the export price is less than the domestic/third country price or the cost of production. If it is, and if the relevant domestic industry has been materially injured as a result (an issue we treat in Chapter 17), then antidumping duties may be imposed.

The determination of whether the export price is less than the domestic price is quite complex, but the logic of the exercise is simple. First, it is necessary to ensure that the prices used are reliable and have not been manipulated (e.g., through related-party transactions). Second, the prices compared must be truly comparable, i.e., the prices must be for the same merchandise sold on the same terms and be charged at the same level of distribution. In other words, it is necessary to ensure that it is an "apples to apples" comparison. Typically, invoice prices are the starting point. Various adjustments are then made because export sales may be made on quite different terms than sales on the home market, thereby making inappropriate a simple comparison of invoice prices. To take an example, exports may be sold on a CIF basis for cash and with a limited warranty, while domestic sales may be made on an FOB basis on 60 days credit and with full warranty. The adjustment process tries to compensate for such differences. It essentially attempts to arrive at comparable "ex factory" prices for the exports and for the similar products sold in the home market.

Much work is involved in this effort to establish comparable values. Often, accountants and economic consultants work with the lawyers in these cases, and since comparisons with foreign markets are involved, not only are language skills essential, but analysts must have knowledge of different accounting standards. The adjustment process can be very confusing, but the key is to focus on whether a proposed adjustment expands the difference (called the dumping margin) between the export price and the normal value or decreases it. Generally speaking, the petitioners (domestic industry) will want to minimize the export price and maximize the normal value, while the respondents (exporters) will want to do the opposite.

The following case and notes focus only on some of the more basic issues raised in AD cases. We cannot in this book do more than introduce these intricate and complex matters.

(1) Calculating the Dumping Margin

We start by examining a recent, relatively straightforward AD case involving hot-rolled steel products from India. While AD cases may be much more complex, involving many exporters and a multitude of product models, this case provides a useful introduction to the basic issues in an AD proceeding. Note the terminology used in the US antidumping statute, which provides that if imports occur at "less than fair value", i.e., they are dumped, and are causing or threatening material injury, then an antidumping duty will be assessed equal to the amount by which the "normal value" exceeds the "export price."[5] "Normal value" is the WTO and US term used to refer, depending on the relevant comparison, to the domestic price, the third country price or the constructed value of the product, which is derived from its cost of production.

Following the Commerce Department's determination are notes and questions that focus on the key aspects of each of the subdivisions of this case. It may be helpful to refer to the corresponding note after reading each section of Commerce's determination.

CERTAIN HOT–ROLLED CARBON STEEL FLAT PRODUCTS FROM INDIA[6]

We preliminarily determine that certain hot-rolled carbon steel flat products (HRS) from India are being sold, or are likely to be sold, in the United States at less than fair value (LTFV), as provided in section 733

5. The relevant statutory sections are 731 (imposition of AD duties), 772 (definition of export price) and 773 (definition of normal value). 19 U.S.C.A. secs. 1673, 1677a, 1677b.

6. US Department of Commerce, International Trade Administration, Notice of Preliminary Determination of Sales at Less Than Fair Value and Postponement of Final Determination, 66 Fed.Reg. 22157 (May 3, 2001).

of the Act. The estimated margins of sales at LTFV are shown in the Suspension of Liquidation section of this notice.

Case History [Note 2]

This investigation was initiated on December 4, 2000. * * * On December 28, 2000, the United States International Trade Commission (ITC) preliminarily determined that there is a reasonable indication that imports of the products subject to this investigation from Argentina, China, India, Indonesia, Kazakhstan, the Netherlands, Romania, South Africa, Taiwan, Thailand, and Ukraine, are materially injuring an industry in the United States producing the domestic like product.

The Department issued antidumping questionnaires to the two mandatory respondents in India on January 11, 2001. [Section A of the questionnaire requests general information concerning a company's corporate structure and business practices, the merchandise under investigation that it sells, and the manner in which it sells that merchandise in all of its markets. Section B requests a complete listing of all home market sales, or, if the home market is not viable, of sales in the most appropriate third-country market (this section is not applicable to respondents in non-market economy (NME) cases). Section C requests a complete listing of US sales. Section D requests information on the cost of production (COP) of the foreign like product and the constructed value (CV) of the merchandise under investigation. Section E requests information on further manufacturing.] We received responses to our questionnaire from both mandatory respondents, Ispat Industries Ltd. (Ispat) and Essar Steel Ltd. (Essar). We issued supplemental questionnaires, pertaining to sections A, B, C, and D of the antidumping questionnaire, to Ispat and Essar in March 2001. Ispat and Essar responded to these supplemental questionnaires in April 2001.

* * *

Period of Investigation

The period of investigation (POI) for this investigation is October 1, 1999, through September 30, 2000. This period corresponds to the four most recent fiscal quarters prior to the month of the filing of the petition (i.e., November 2000).

Scope of Investigation

For purposes of these investigations, the products covered are certain hot-rolled carbon steel flat products * * * .

Selection of Respondents

Section 777A(c)(1) of the Act directs the Department to calculate individual dumping margins for each known exporter and producer of the subject merchandise. Where it is not practicable to examine all known producers/exporters of subject merchandise, section 777A(c)(2) of the Act permits the Department to investigate either (1) a sample of exporters, producers, or types of products that is statistically valid based on the information available at the time of selection, or (2) exporters and producers accounting for the largest volume of the subject merchandise that can reasonably be examined. Using company-specific export data for the POI, which we obtained from the American Embassy in New Delhi, India, we found that four Indian exporters shipped HRS to the United States during the POI. Due to limited resources we determined that we could investigate only the two largest producers/Exporters, accounting for more than 60 percent of total exports to the United States. Therefore, we designated Ispat and Essar as mandatory respondents and sent them the antidumping questionnaire.

Product Comparisons

In accordance with section 771(16) of the Act, all products produced by the respondents covered by the description in the Scope of Investigation section, above, and sold in India during the POI are considered to be foreign like products for purposes of determining appropriate product comparisons to US sales. Where there were no sales of identical merchandise in the home market to compare to US sales, we compared US sales to the next most similar foreign like product on the basis of the characteristics listed above.

Fair Value Comparisons [Note 3]

To determine whether sales of HRS from India were made in the United States at LTFV, we compared the export price (EP) to the normal value (NV), as described in the Export Price and Normal Value sections of this notice. In accordance with section 777A(d)(1)(A)(i) of the Act, we calculated weighted-average EPs. We compared these to weighted-average home market prices.

* * *

Export Price [Note 4]

For the price to the United States, we used EP, in accordance with section 772(a) of the Act, because Ispat and Essar sold the merchandise directly to unaffiliated US customers or sold the merchandise to unaffiliated trading companies, with knowledge that these companies in turn sold the merchandise to US customers, and constructed export price was not otherwise warranted. For both Ispat and Essar, we calculated EP using the packed prices charged to the first unaffiliated customer in the United States (the starting price).

We deducted from the starting price, where applicable, amounts for discounts and rebates, and movement expenses in accordance with section 772(c)(2)(A) of the Act. In this case, movement expenses include foreign inland freight, international freight, foreign and US brokerage and handling charges, insurance, US duties and US inland freight.

* * *

Normal Value [Note 5]

A. Selection of Comparison Market

Section 773(a)(1) of the Act directs that NV be based on the price at which the foreign like product is sold in the home market, provided that the merchandise is sold in sufficient quantities (or has sufficient aggregate value, if quantity is inappropriate) and that there is no particular market situation in the home market that prevents a proper comparison with the EP transaction. The statute contemplates that quantities (or value) will normally be considered insufficient if they are less than five percent of the aggregate quantity (or value) of sales of the subject merchandise to the United States.

For this investigation, we found that Ispat and Essar each had a viable home market for HRS. Thus, the home market is the appropriate comparison market in this investigation, and we used the respondents' submitted home market sales data for purposes of calculating NV.

In deriving NV, we made adjustments as detailed in the Calculation of NV Based on Home Market Prices and Calculation of NV Based on CV, sections below.

B. Affiliated–Party Transactions and Arm's-Length Test

* * * Ispat reported that it made home market sales to other affiliated companies. We applied the arm's-length test to sales from Ispat to these affiliated companies by comparing them to sales of identical merchandise from Ispat to unaffiliated home market customers. If these affiliated party sales satisfied the arm's-length test, we used them in our analysis. Sales to affiliated customers in the home market which were not made at arm's-length prices were excluded from our analysis because we considered them to be outside the ordinary course of trade.

* * *

C. Cost of Production [COP] Analysis [Note 6]

Concurrent with the filing of the original petition, the petitioners alleged that sales of HRS in the home market of India were made at prices below the fully absorbed COP, and accordingly, requested that the Department conduct a country-wide sales-below-COP investigation. Based upon the comparison of the adjusted prices from the petition for the foreign like product to its COP, and in accordance with section 773(b)(2)(A)(i) of the Act, we found reasonable grounds to believe or suspect that sales of HRS manufactured in India were made at prices below the COP. As a result, the Department has conducted an investigation to determine whether Ispat and Essar made sales in the home market at prices below their respective COPs during the POI within the meaning of section 773(b) of the Act. We conducted the COP analysis described below.

1. Calculation of COP. In accordance with section 773(b)(3) of the Act, we calculated a weighted-average COP for each respondent based on the sum of the cost of materials and fabrication for the foreign like product, plus amounts for the home market general and administrative (G & A) expenses and interest expenses. We relied on the COP data submitted by Ispat and Essar in their cost questionnaire responses,

except, as noted below, in specific instances where Ispat's submitted costs were not appropriately quantified or valued.

a. Changes to Ispat's Cost of Production. Based on the information on the record, it appears that Ispat reached commercial levels of production prior to the POI. Therefore, we disallowed the start-up adjustment claimed by Ispat. We adjusted the reported costs to include depreciation expenses and certain raw material costs that were omitted. We recalculated Ispat's G & A expense ratio using its company-wide G & A costs from its fiscal year 2000 audited financial statements. We adjusted Ispat's financial expense ratio to include the net exchange rate difference and loss on cancellation of forward contract per its audited financial statements.

2. Test of Home Market Sales Prices. On a model-specific basis, we compared the revised COP to the home market prices, less any applicable discounts and rebates, movement charges, selling expenses, commissions, and packing. We then compared the adjusted weighted-average COP to the home market sales of the foreign like product, as required under section 773(b) of the Act, in order to determine whether these sales had been made at prices below the COP within an extended period of time (i.e., a period of one year) in substantial quantities and whether such prices were sufficient to permit the recovery of all costs within a reasonable period of time.

3. Results of the COP Test. Pursuant to section 773(b)(2)(C) of the Act, where less than 20 percent of a respondent's sales of a given product were at prices less than the COP, we did not disregard any below-cost sales of that product because we determined that the below-cost sales were not made in "substantial quantities." Where 20 percent or more of a respondent's sales of a given product during the POI were at prices less than the COP, we determined such sales to have been made in "substantial quantities" within an extended period of time in accordance with section 773(b)(2)(B) or the Act. In such cases, because we compared prices to POI average costs, we also determined that such sales were not made at prices that would permit recovery of all costs within a reasonable period of time, in accordance with section 773(b)(2)(D) of the Act. Therefore, we disregarded the below-cost sales.

We found that, for certain models of HRS, more than 20 percent of the home market sales by Ispat and Essar were made within an extended period of time at prices less than the COP. Further, the prices did not provide for the recovery of costs within a reasonable period of time. We therefore disregarded these below-cost sales and used the remaining sales as the basis for determining NV, in accordance with section 773(b)(1) of the Act.

D. Calculation of NV Based on Home Market Prices [Note 7]

We based home market prices on the packed prices to unaffiliated purchasers in India. We adjusted, where applicable, the starting price for discounts and rebates. We made adjustments for any differences in packing, in accordance with section 773(a)(6)(A) and 773(a)(6)(B)(i) of the Act, and we deducted movement expenses and domestic brokerage and handling, pursuant to section 773(a)(6)(B)(ii) of the Act. In addition, where applicable, we made adjustments for differences in circumstances of sale (COS) pursuant to section 773(a)(6)(C)(iii) of the Act * * * . We also made COS adjustments, where applicable, by deducting direct selling expenses incurred for home market sales (credit expense and warranty) and adding US direct selling expenses. We also made adjustments, pursuant to 19 CFR 351.410(e), for indirect selling expenses incurred on comparison-market or US sales where commissions were granted on sales in one market but not in the other (the commission offset). No other adjustments to NV were claimed or allowed.

E.   Calculation of NV Based on CV [Constructed Value] [Note 8]

Section 773(a)(4) of the Act provides that, where NV cannot be based on comparison-market sales, NV may be based on CV. Accordingly, for those models of HRS for which we could not determine the NV based on comparison-market sales, either because there were no sales of a comparable product or all sales of the comparison products failed the COP test, we based NV on CV.

F.   Level of Trade (LOT)

In accordance with section 773(a)(1)(B) of the Act, to the extent practicable, we determine NV based on sales in the comparison market at the same LOT as the US transaction (in this case EP transactions). The NV LOT is that of the starting-price sales in the comparison market or, when NV is based on CV, that of the sales from which we derive selling, general, and administrative (SG & A) expenses and profit. For EP sales, the US LOT is also the level of the starting-price sale, which is usually from exporter to importer.

To determine whether NV sales are at a different LOT than EP transactions, we examine stages in the marketing process and selling functions along the chain of distribution between the producer and the unaffiliated customer. If the comparison market sales are at a different LOT and the difference affects price comparability, as manifested in a pattern of consistent price differences between the sales on which NV is based and comparison market sales at the LOT of the export transaction, we make a LOT adjustment under section 773(a)(7)(A) of the Act.

In implementing these principles in this investigation, we obtained information from the respondents about the marketing stages involved in the reported US and home market sales, including a description of the selling activities performed by the respondents for each channel of distribution. In identifying LOTs for EP and home market sales, we considered the selling functions reflected in the starting price before any adjustments. In this investigation, neither Ispat nor Essar requested a LOT adjustment [and we made none in light of the facts.]

Currency Conversions [Note 9]

We made currency conversions into US dollars in accordance with section 773A of the Act based on exchange rates in effect on the dates of the US sales, as obtained from the Federal Reserve Bank (the Department's preferred source for exchange rates).

Verification

In accordance with section 782(i) of the Act, we intend to verify all information relied upon in making our final determination.

All Others Rate

Recognizing the impracticality of examining all producers and exporters in all cases, section 735(c)(5)(A) of the Act provides for the use of an "all others" rate, which is applied to non-investigated firms. See SAA at 873. This section states that the all others rate shall generally be an amount equal to the weighted average of the weighted-average dumping margins established for exporters and producers individually investigated, excluding any zero and de minimis margins, and any margins based entirely upon the facts available. Therefore, we have preliminarily assigned to all other exporters of Indian HRS, an "all others" margin that is the weighted average of the margins calculated for Ispat and Essar.

Suspension of Liquidation

In accordance with section 733(d) of the Act, we are directing the US Customs Service (Customs Service) to suspend liquidation of all entries of HRS from India that are entered, or withdrawn from warehouse, for consumption on or after the date of publication of this notice in the Federal Register. We will instruct the Customs Service to require a cash deposit or the posting of a bond equal to the weighted-average amount by which NV exceeds EP, as indicated in the chart below. We will adjust the deposit requirements to account for any export subsidies found in the companion countervailing duty investigation. These suspension-of-liquidation instructions will remain in effect until further notice. The weighted-average dumping margins are as follows:

Manufacturer/exporter	Margin (percent)
Ispat Industries Ltd	39.36
Essar Steel Ltd	34.55
All Others	34.75

Notes and Questions

The following notes and questions relate for the most part to issues considered in the *India HRS* case.

(1) The foregoing decision is a preliminary determination. During the next phase of the investigation, Commerce receives comments from the parties on its preliminary determination and verifies the information submitted by respondents by sending Commerce officials to examine their books and records. It is not unusual for there to be significant changes in the dumping calculation as a result of the comments and verification.

(2) As the foregoing decision makes clear, respondents were required on short notice to submit detailed information on their domestic and export

sales and their production costs. While it is not made clear in the parts of the decision that are excerpted, Commerce requires the information to be supplied in specific formats so that it can be easily processed. The information supplied by exporters is made available to petitioners' attorneys under protective orders forbidding disclosure to the petitioners. This enables the attorneys to comment meaningfully on the Commerce decision. One might legitimately ask why would a foreign company supply such detailed and sensitive information? As noted earlier, the answer is that a failure to provide the information would result in a decision by Commerce to use the "information available," which might well be the allegations of the petitioners and which might lead to the imposition of very high duties. See Section 782(d). Annex II to the WTO AD Agreement sets standards for the use of best information available. Certain US practices regarding information available were found to violate WTO rules in United States—Anti–Dumping Measures on Certain Hot–Rolled Steel Products from Japan, WT/DS184/AB/R, adopted by the DSB on August 24, 2001.

(3) *Fair Value Comparisons.* The traditional method of calculating a dumping margin is somewhat unusual and raises serious fairness questions in the minds of some. Take the following example: In the home market, seven sales are shown to occur, one each at a price of 20, 21, 22, 23, 24, 25 and 26. Seven imports into the United States are also made, at the same time, one at each of those prices. Obviously the average price in both cases is 23. But this does not mean that there is no dumping. The normal value has typically been calculated as an average, i.e. 23. But each shipment to the US has been compared to that average, so three of the imports (those made at 20, 21 and 22) would have been made at a price below the average and would be viewed as having been dumped, with dumping margins of 3, 2, and 1. The other four imports would be viewed as not having been dumped and would be assigned a dumping margin of "zero". When the dumping margins are averaged $(3+2+1+0+0+0+0/7 = 0.86)$, the result would be a finding of dumping.

Some countries urged in the Uruguay Round that the GATT Antidumping Code be amended to require that the export and home market prices be established by the use of average prices over the same time period. In the example given above, this would mean that no dumping would be found, as the average price would be the same in both markets, i.e., 23. Ultimately, a compromise was reached that provided that in AD investigations average-to-average comparisons should be the normal calculation method, unless the authorities find "a pattern of export prices which differ significantly among different purchasers, regions or time periods," which cannot be taken into account appropriately by an average-to-average comparison. WTO AD Agreement, art. 2.4.2. Note that average-to-average comparisons were used in the India HRS case. The extent to which the WTO rules generally prohibit the above-described practice—known as "zeroing"—has been the subject of several controversial WTO cases, which we examine in the next section.

Should there be a dumping margin so small that no duties should be imposed? Prior to the Uruguay Round, the US used a 0.5% cutoff, but in the Uruguay Round it was agreed that a margin of less than 2% should be deemed de minimis. WTO AD Agreement, art. 5.8. Sections 733(b)(3), 735(a)(4). If an AD order is issued because of non de minimis margins, would the de minimis rule apply in the annual reviews to set the actual amount of duties collected? The Appellate Body found that the analogous provision in the WTO Subsidies Agreement did not apply to reviews. US Carbon Steel, WT/DS213/AB/R, paras. 67–69.

(4) *Export Price.* The calculation of export price is relatively straightforward when sales are made to unrelated parties prior to importation into the US, as was the case in India HRS. The main adjustment that is made to the invoice price is to eliminate transportation and related "movement" expenses so as to arrive at an ex-factory price.

When the goods have not been sold to an unrelated party before importation into the US, US law provides for the use of a constructed export price. A typical example of such a situation would be a foreign manufacturer that sells goods to a US distribution subsidiary, which imports the products into the United States and then resells them to unrelated parties. If the constructed export price is used to establish the export price, then any US distribution costs (and any additional US manufacturing costs) are factored out of the price charged to the first unrelated party. The rules also provide for an adjustment to normal value to the extent that it includes indirect selling expenses that are comparable to indirect selling expenses that are deducted from the constructed export price because they were incurred in the US. This adjustment, known as the constructed export price offset, cannot exceed the amount of indirect selling expenses deducted from the constructed export price. 19 C.F.R. sec. 351.412(f) (2007). What explains the special rules applicable in the constructed export price situation?

(5) *Normal Value.* The calculation of normal value is more complex. In the first instance, Commerce determines whether there are sufficient sales in the home market, defined as at least 5% of sales to the US, to serve as a basis for normal value. See Section 773(a). If there are not adequate sales in the home market, then Commerce has a choice of establishing normal value through the use of export prices to third countries or constructed value, which is discussed below. Although the regulations indicate a preference for using third-country sales, constructed value is often used. 19 C.F.R. sec. 351.404(f) (2007). What might explain the preference for using third-country exports instead of constructed value for setting normal value?

(6) *Cost of Production.* As explained in India HRS, Commerce may exclude below-cost sales from consideration in calculating normal value in certain circumstances. If the volume of the remaining above-cost sales is inadequate, constructed value is used to set normal value. Section 773(b)(1) provides that "sales made at less than the cost of production * * * within an extended period of time in substantial quantities, and * * * not at prices which would permit recovery of all costs within a reasonable period of time" may be disregarded in determining normal value. A number of questions are presented. What is an extended period of time? What are substantial quantities? What is a reasonable period of time? How does Commerce answer these questions in the India HRS case? Do you agree with its answers? See WTO AD Agreement, art. 2.2.1 (including the footnotes!).

As noted in the first section of this chapter, economists would expect a profit-maximizing firm to produce at a loss, at least in the short run, if it was recovering its marginal, as opposed to average, costs. Does the Commerce rule reflect that expectation? How should end-of-season sales be treated under Section 773(b)? How should sales of perishable products be treated? What about sales of airplanes that had incurred such massive development costs that those costs will be recovered only after several years of sales?

(7) *Price-to-Price Comparisons.* In order to make the export price and the normal value comparable, certain non-movement adjustments must also be made. The basic rules are laid out in Sections 772(c)–(f) and 773(a)(6)–(7), and, in particular, in specific Commerce regulations on adjustments for quantities,[7] different physical characteristics,[8] and different circumstances of sale.[9] Adjustments for quantity differences are relatively unusual. Adjustments for physical differences are usually based on cost differences. The most common and controversial adjustments are for differences in the circumstances of sale. The regulation provides:[10]

(b) *In general.* * * * [T]he Secretary will make circumstances of sale adjustments under Section 773(a)(6)(C)(iii) of the Act only for direct selling expenses and assumed expenses.

(c) *Direct selling expenses.* "Direct selling expenses" are expenses, such as commissions, credit expenses, guarantees, and warranties, that result from, and bear a direct relationship to, the particular sale in questions.

(d) *Assumed expenses.* Assumed expenses are selling expenses that are assumed by the seller on behalf of the buyer, such as advertising expenses.

The way in which Commerce treats advertising and technical services is elaborated in the following excerpt from its Antidumping Manual, ch. 8, pp. 26–30 (1998):

Advertising and Sales Promotion

Most advertising expenses are aimed at the customer of the producer or exporter and as such they are not adjusted for as COS adjustments because they are considered indirect in nature. Advertising and sales promotion expenses can, however, be "assumed" by the producer or exporter on behalf of its customer. If this is the case, a COS adjustment is warranted. The most common types of assumed advertising expenses are consumer advertising costs paid for totally by the producer and cooperative (co-op) consumer advertising which is paid for jointly by the producer and first unrelated purchaser and aimed at customers of the first purchaser.

* * *

Technical Services

Another area of claims for adjustments for differences in COS is technical service expenses. These claims are particularly common in cases where the merchandise under investigation or review is sold to an industrial user. Such claims are usually made for services involving the use of an industrial material in a manufacturing process or the opera-

---

7. 19 CFR sec. 351.409 (2007).

8. 19 CFR sec. 351.411 (2007).

9. 19 CFR sec. 351.410 (2007).

10. Id.

tion of machinery. Where technical services are rendered as part of a sales agreement, all, or some portion of them, may constitute COS expenses. Many claims, however, relate to services provided for purposes of determining new uses for a product in future production. Such services are considered to constitute goodwill or sales promotion and as such the expenses are not considered directly related to the sales under consideration.

Claims for technical services rendered in assisting the customer in solving problems with products purchased are adjusted for as COS to the extent that the variable costs can be segregated from the fixed costs. The allowable variable costs are usually travel expenses and contracted services by unrelated technicians as these expenses would not have been incurred if the sales in question had not been made. Salaries of technicians employed by the exporter usually would not be allowed as a COS adjustment because they are usually fixed costs which are incurred whether or not the sales are made. Therefore, they are usually indirect selling expenses.

(8) *Constructed Value.* Constructed value is based on the cost of manufacture of a product, plus selling, general and administrative expenses allocable to it, plus an appropriate profit. If constructed value is used, there have been two noteworthy problems under US law. First, there has been the question of how to allocate research and development and start-up costs. For some products, these costs may be substantial and whether or not there is dumping found may turn on how they are allocated. If these costs are spread over a short time period, the constructed value of the product (i.e. its normal value) will be much higher. See Section 773(f)(1)(C). Second, prior to the 1994 Act, the US statute required a minimum of 10% to be added for "administrative costs," and 8% for "profits." Particularly as to the latter figure, questions were raised whether the US requirement was consistent with US international obligations under GATT and the Antidumping Code, because often in times of recession, or for certain types of products, profits are not nearly so high as 8%. The current rule is in Section 773(e)(2). See WTO AD Agreement, art. 2.2.2.

(9) *Currency Conversion.* Suppose a Swedish exporter establishes price lists annually and adheres strictly to them. When the prices are set on January 1, the ex-factory price to Swedish customers is 50SK/kg. For US customers, it is a CIF price of $6/kg, where $1/kg represents the cost of shipping and insurance. On January 1, the SK:US$ exchange rate is 10:1. Is the US price a dumping price? On February 1, the rate is 9:1. Is the US price a dumping price? For six months, the rate remains at 9:1. Is there dumping? On September 1, the rate falls to 10:1, but shipping costs have increased $0.25/kg. Is the US price a dumping price? Should it be? See WTO AD Agreement, art. 2.4.1; Section 773A.

(10) *Critical Circumstances.* Suppose you are a foreign exporter bent on dumping. You decide the best approach is to dump a massive amount of goods into the United States within a short time period and then stop for several months. If an investigation is opened, there will be no imports on which duties can be applied. If one is not opened for a year, you plan to do

the same thing again. Are you safe from duties? Consider Section 733(e). See also WTO AD Agreement, art. 10.

(11) *Suspension of Liquidation.*[11] AD investigations are opened in respect of a specific product from a specific country. It is not unusual, however, for the same imports from several countries to be investigated simultaneously. Commerce issues a decision in respect of imports from each country investigated, although the ITC may issue one report on injury covering several countries. In its decision, Commerce calculates a specific AD duty rate for each manufacturer or exporter investigated. Subsequent exports by an entity not specifically mentioned in the Commerce decision will be required to deposit estimated duties at the "all others" rate. There are procedures by which a new exporter can obtain a specific rate.

Problems

(1) Firm E in Country X has sold 500,000 pairs of sunglasses to M, a United States importer, at a price of $5.00 per unit. Included in this price are the following: $.40 per unit for extra packaging and handling costs in preparing the sunglasses for a transoceanic voyage; a $15,000 shipment charge for the entire lot (delivery will be in five installments); $.50 per unit to cover the export tax imposed by X. E and M have no particular commercial ties.

Firm E also sells this line of sunglasses in X, at a price of $4.75 a pair. Using only the information here provided, will the Commerce Department find the sunglasses to be sold at less than fair value if a complaint is brought by a United States manufacturer of sunglasses? If so, how much additional duty will be imposed?

(2) Assuming the information in Problem (1), will any of the following factors change your answer?

(a) E has no advertising costs in the United States, but it spends approximately $.12 per unit sold for advertising in X.

(b) Although E offers discount quantity sales to buyers in X, no buyer has ordered more than 500 pairs at one time. All sunglasses sold are produced in the same plant in X, and are stored in the same warehouse before shipment.

(c) M paid in advance for the entire lot, whereas buyers in X always choose to be billed after shipment. The cost of insuring against default and of handling the extra paperwork averages out to $.05 per pair in X.

(d) E offers to refund the purchase price to any consumer in X who is unhappy, for any reason, with the sunglasses. In the past few years, the cost of such refunds (often unreasonably requested) has averaged $.03 on each pair actually sold.

---

11. "Liquidation" is the process of settling the duty due on an import into the United States. That process is suspended in AD cases because the duty due is not finally determined until completion of the administrative review process described in Section 16.3(A).

(2) Nonmarket Economies and Antidumping Rules

In an economy where the government exercises complete control over price and allocation decisions, it is difficult to apply AD rules. The government control means that the home market price is not a real price in the sense that term is used in market economies. Consequently, an interpretative note to Article VI notes that special difficulties in applying AD rules arise when the allegedly dumped imports come from an economy where all prices are fixed by the state and there is a state monopoly of foreign trade. In such cases, the note states that a strict comparison of prices may not be appropriate.

In practice, the US, the EU and others have applied AD duties on products from state-controlled economies on the basis of surrogate market prices and costs. Under a definition added by the 1988 Trade Act, nonmarket economies are defined in Section 771(18) as those that do "not operate on market principles of cost or pricing structures, so that sales of merchandise in such country do not reflect the fair value of the merchandise." The factors to be considered by the ITA in determining nonmarket economy status include (i) the convertability of the currency, (ii) the extent to which wage rates are set by free bargaining, (iii) the extent to which foreign ventures are permitted to operate in the country, (iv) the extent of government ownership of the means of production and (v) the extent of government control over resource allocation. Id. Determinations by the ITA of nonmarket economy status are not appealable.

For nonmarket economies, normal value is to be based on constructed value, where the costs are derived from a market economy country or countries considered to be appropriate by the ITA, or, if such information is inadequate, on the basis of sales prices of comparable merchandise from a market economy country. In each case, the market economy country chosen is to be at a level of development comparable to that of the nonmarket economy country. Section 773(c). For example, under the US statute, the inputs of a product are determined (so many pounds of steel, so many hours of labor) and then the cost of those inputs in a comparable, market-economy country is used to arrive at a minimum appropriate price for the imports from the state-controlled economy. If the actual export price is below that price, AD duties may be applied, assuming injury has been found. An alternative method is to compare the export price of the allegedly dumped product with the price for a comparable product produced in a surrogate country. This is the typical EU approach and is a possible, but not the preferred approach, under the US statute.

Notes and Questions

(1) Would you cooperate with a US AD investigation by supplying price and cost information if you were a producer in a proposed surrogate country? What advantages might result for you? What disadvantages? For example, would you risk an AD proceeding if data you provided showed sales at dumping prices? For whatever reasons, it is not always possible to obtain cooperation.

(2) The US statute specifies that the surrogate country is to be at about the same level of development, which the regulations indicate is normally determined by considering comparative per capita GDP. 19 C.F.R. sec. 351.408(b) (2007). Is there any real reason to believe that prices and costs in the surrogate country accurately reflect what prices and costs would have been in a nonmarket economy if it were a market economy? Given the importance of the choice of the surrogate country—it essentially determines whether dumping will be found—should there be more precise standards for selecting such a country? What standards would you propose? In respect of wages, the ITA has adopted a methodology that does not rely on comparable wages in a single surrogate country.

(3) How should the recent economic reforms in Communist countries be handled? US practices takes account of these reforms in two ways. First, it is possible to establish that a specific industry is sufficiently market-oriented such that the normal rules are applied. To establish this requires a showing that (i) there is virtually no government involvement in setting prices or production quantities; (ii) the industry is characterized by private or collective ownership; and (iii) market-determined prices are paid for all significant inputs. Second, it is possible to establish that an individual firm is sufficiently independent of government control (both de jure and de facto) that it is entitled to a separate rate, as opposed to being subject to the country-wide rate. ITA, Antidumping Manual, ch. 8, pp. 90–92 (1998). As of January 2008, the ITA continues to treat China as a non-market economy.

(C) ANTICIRCUMVENTION MEASURES

In the late 1980's, there was considerable concern in the US and the EU that AD duties were being circumvented and that it was necessary to take action to prevent such circumvention. How might AD duties be circumvented? First, since the duties are applicable to goods coming from a specific country, it may be possible to change the origin of the goods by shifting production to a third country. Second, since the duties apply to imports of a specific product, it may be possible to change the characteristics of that product so that it is no longer the product specified in the order imposing AD duties. Third, it may be possible to import components of the product (assuming they are not subject to AD duties themselves) and assemble the product in the country imposing the AD duties.

In June 1987, the EU amended its AD regulation to provide that AD duties could be imposed on products assembled in the EU if (i) an AD duty had previously been imposed on similar products when imported, (ii) the products were assembled in substantially increased quantities in the EU by a company related to one subject to such AD duty and (iii) the value of the parts and materials from the country subject to AD duties that were contained in the product assembled in the EU exceeded by 50% the value of all other parts and materials used in the product.[12] Following a complaint by Japan in GATT, this provision was found by a

---

12. EC Regulation 2423/88, art. 13 (10)(a), in Eur.Comm.O.J., L 209 (Aug. 2, 1988).

GATT dispute settlement panel to violate GATT Article III.[13] In the view of the panel, the charges imposed by the EU rules were internal taxes subject to Article III:2, not duties under Article II:1(b), because they were imposed on the assembled products, not the imported parts and components, and they were collected when the assembled products were introduced into EU commerce, not at the EU border. Do you agree? Since the EU did not impose such taxes on domestic producers of the like products, the panel concluded that the measures violated Article III:2.

The United States addressed the circumvention issue in the 1988 Trade Act, which added a series of anticircumvention provisions as Section 781 of the 1930 Tariff Act. For example, Section 781, as amended in 1994, allows the ITA to expand the scope of an AD order to cover components of a product subject to the order if those components are imported into the United States for assembly where the US assembly process is minor or insignificant and the value of the components is a significant portion of the total value of the product. In making its decision, the ITA is to consider whether there was an increase in component imports into the United States after the AD order was issued and whether the exporter of the components is related to the assembler. A related provision with similar rules would cover the situation where the components are exported to a third country, assembled and then exported to the United States. These two provisions are designed to prevent circumvention of an AD order by importing disassembled or unfinished merchandise into the United States (or a third country) for assembly in the United States (or that third country). The Act also allows the ITA to expand the scope of an AD order to include (i) later developed, but essentially similar merchandise and (ii) merchandise that has been altered in a minor way.

The 1988 Act established a procedure by which US parties can apply to have a product category created with respect to "short life cycle merchandise" if the merchandise has been subject to at least two antidumping determinations. Short life cycle merchandise is merchandise that is likely to be outmoded within four years. Such merchandise is then subject to shorter investigation deadlines. Tariff Act of 1930, Section 739.

Some of the US anticircumvention provisions are somewhat similar to the EU provision, which was found to violate GATT Article III. However, because the US measures would be applied as duties, at the border, at the time of entry, the reasoning of the GATT panel in the EU case would not seem to apply to the US provisions. Could those provisions be attacked on other grounds? For example, could it be argued that under Article VI and the WTO AD Agreement a new injury investigation in respect of the different product must be conducted before imposing duties? The WTO AD Agreement does not deal with anticircumvention measures because no agreement could be reached on their scope.

---

13. EEC—Regulation on Imports of Parts and Components, 37th Supp. BISD 132 (1990)(Panel report adopted May 16, 1990).

SECTION 16.4 THE WTO RULES ON DUMPING

(A) THE EVOLUTION OF THE INTERNATIONAL OBLIGATIONS

Beginning with Canada in 1904, nations started unilaterally to legislate against dumping in order to protect domestic industries from a perceived threat of predatory behavior from abroad. When the preliminary ITO–GATT work began, the United States offered a proposal for standards modeled upon its own 1921 Antidumping Act. The need for such standards seems to have been generally accepted, and the result was GATT Article VI, which deals with both antidumping and countervailing duties.[1] Article VI does not require governments to forbid dumping. Rather, it condemns injurious dumping and authorizes the imposition of AD duties to offset dumping if the dumping causes material injury to a domestic industry. Article VI is relatively brief and says little about the many procedural and substantive issues that arise in AD cases.

As the use of AD laws grew over time, there were efforts in GATT to reach agreement on more specific standards for AD cases. These efforts culminated in 1967 with the negotiation of the 1967 Antidumping Code by the United States and 17 other nations.[2] In addition to specifying minimal procedural standards for AD cases, the Code also required that dumping be the "principal" cause of the material injury to domestic industry. Unfortunately, the US President had received no authorization from Congress to negotiate and enter into such an agreement.[3] As a consequence, even though it is arguable that the Code was consistent with the wording of the then effective US statute,[4] certain congressional leaders were incensed at the President's action, and took action that, according to then Senate Finance Committee Chairman Russell B. Long, meant that "Congress has forbidden the Executive Branch and the Tariff Commission to interpret the Antidumping Act more narrowly in the future than in the past by virtue of the negotiation of the [1967] Antidumping Code."[5]

There were extensive negotiations during the Tokyo Round concerning a code on subsidies, which we will discuss in Chapter 18. When those negotiations were completed, it was agreed that provisions in the 1967 Antidumping Code should be conformed to their analogues in the Subsi-

---

1. See generally John J. Jackson, World Trade and the Law of GATT 403–424 (1969), for a discussion of the development and meaning of both Article VI and the 1967 Antidumping Code.

2. GATT, 15th Supp. BISD 74 (1968).

3. The Senate Finance Committee Report on the Trade Expansion Act of 1962, which provided authorization for Kennedy Round negotiations, explicitly stated that the then current antidumping statute was "not intended to be affected." S.Rep. No. 2059, 87th Cong., 2d Sess. 19 (1962).

4. See generally John J. Barcelo, III, Antidumping Laws as Barriers to Trade: The United States and the International Antidumping Code, 57 Cornell L.Rev. 491 (1972).

5. Russell B. Long, United States Law and the International Anti-dumping Code, 3 Intl. Lawyer 464, 486 (1969).

dies Code.[6] In addition, the requirement that dumping be the principal cause of injury was omitted. The result was a new Agreement on Implementation of Article VI, which effectively replaced the 1967 Antidumping Code.[7] The US Congress had authorized these negotiations and the 1979 Code was implemented by the United States through the 1979 Trade Agreements Act.

In the Uruguay Round, it was not initially expected that the 1979 Code would be a major subject of negotiations. But as the negotiations unfolded, it turned out that many contracting parties were dissatisfied with GATT regulation of AD procedures and substance. On the one hand, the US and the EU were concerned about gaining GATT acceptance of the use of certain devices to prevent the circumvention of AD duties. They were also interested in regulating more closely the procedures used in AD actions in light of the increased use by Mexico and other developing countries of AD laws. On the other hand, many of the countries commonly targeted by AD actions, including countries in East Asia and Scandinavia, pressed for changes in the substantive rules applied in AD cases so as to make them less susceptible to use for protectionist purposes. The ensuing negotiations were among the more hotly contested in the Round. The result of the negotiations was a bit of a compromise: Both the procedural and substantive rules were tightened. No agreement was reached, however, on use of anticircumvention measures.

AD rules continue to be controversial in the WTO. There have been many AD cases brought to the dispute settlement system and, in particular, there have been quite a few successful challenges of US AD practices. AD rules are one of the more difficult subjects under discussion in the Doha negotiations, where a number of countries are supporting more restrictions on their use. The US initially generally opposed including AD rules in the negotiations.

(B) THE WTO RULES ON DUMPING[8]

The basic WTO provision on dumping is GATT Article VI. As noted earlier, it condemns injurious dumping, but does not require WTO members to make unlawful. Article VI:1 sets out the basic definition of dumping:

> [A] product is to be considered as being introduced into the commerce of an importing country at less than its normal value, if the price of the product exported from one country to another
>
> (a) is less than the comparable price, in the ordinary course of trade, for the like product when destined for consumption in the exporting country, or,

---

6. GATT, The Tokyo Round of Multilateral Trade Negotiations, Report by the Director–General of GATT 181 (1979).

7. GATT, 26th Supp. BISD 171 (1980).

8. E. Vermulst, The WTO Anti-dumping Agreement: A Commentary (Oxford University Press, 2006); J. Czako et al, A Handbook of Anti-dumping Investigations (WTO, 2003).

(*b*) in the absence of such domestic price, is less than either

> (i) the highest comparable price for the like product for export to any third country in the ordinary course of trade, or

> (ii) the cost of production of the product in the country of origin plus a reasonable addition for selling cost and profit.

Due allowance shall be made in each case for differences in conditions and terms of sale, for differences in taxation, and for other differences affecting price comparability.

Where the situation described exists, Article VI:2 provides:

> In order to offset or prevent dumping, a member may levy on any dumped product an anti-dumping duty not greater in amount than the margin of dumping in respect of such product. For the purposes of this Article, the margin of dumping is the price difference determined in accordance with the provisions of paragraph 1.

In order to impose AD duties, Article VI:6 requires that "the effect of the dumping * * * is such as to cause or threaten material injury" to domestic industry, an issue we consider in Chapter 17.

While Article VI does not further define dumping or contain any rules on the procedures to be followed in AD investigations, the WTO Antidumping Agreement does. In particular, article 2 specifies in considerable detail how dumping is to be determined, and several of the detailed rules were referenced in the preceding section. Of considerable importance is the statement in article 2.4 that "[a] fair comparison shall be made between the export price and normal value". This is expanded upon in article 2.4.2, which requires average-to-average comparisons in certain situations. We examine that provision in more detail below in the "zeroing" cases.

Articles 3 and 4 of the agreement relate to the determination of injury and the definition of domestic industry. Most of the rest of the agreement is focused on procedures. For example, article 5 specifies in detail the information that the authorities must have before an investigation may be initiated. Article 6 requires certain rights to be afforded to those accused of dumping, such as a full opportunity throughout the investigations to defend their interests and notice of the essential facts on which definitive action is to be taken, in sufficient time to respond. It also contains specific rules (elaborated in annexes) on verification inspections and the use of available facts when parties refuse to provide information. Article 12 requires public notice of the initiation of investigations and of determinations to impose AD duties. The latter notice is to include a report setting forth in sufficient detail the findings and conclusions reached on all issues of fact and law considered material by the investigative authorities. Article 13 requires the maintenance of judicial, arbitral or administrative tribunals or procedures to review administrative actions relating to final determinations.

The agreement also has provisions regulating the use of provisional AD duties (art. 7), retroactive duties (art. 10) and undertakings (art. 8).

The collection of AD duties is dealt with in article 9 (e.g., annual reviews, refund procedures, rates for non-investigated exporters, new shipper reviews). The periodic review of measures, including the five-year sunset review, is treated in article 11. Article 16 of the agreement establishes a Committee on AD Practices, which has issued a number of recommendations on AD procedures.

(C) THE WTO CASE LAW ON DUMPING

There have been many AD cases brought to the WTO dispute settlement system. Indeed, since 2000, roughly one-third of the Appellate Body's reports have concerned dumping actions. These cases typically are too complex to be usefully examined in an introductory international law trade class. However, we include two cases below on particularly notable issues: "zeroing" and the Byrd Amendment.

Overall, AD cases in dispute settlement tend to be characterized by a multiplicity of claims and often result in very detailed panel reports. See, e.g., Guatemala—Cement II, WT/DS156/R, adopted November 17, 2000 (14 violations of articles 5, 6 and 12 found, highlighting the difficulty that developing countries may face in complying with the detailed procedural requirements of the AD Agreement); EC—Salmon (Norway), WT/DS337/R, adopted January 15, 2008 (22 violations found, particularly in respect of articles 2.2 (cost of production calculations); 6 (use of available facts and disclosure obligations); and 9 (treatment of non-investigated companies), with 15 claims rejected and 10 not decided on judicial economy grounds). There have also been a number of cases challenging US practices in respect of the five-year, sunset review requirement in article 11.3 of the AD Agreement. It appears that of some 291 US sunset reviews, the relevant AD order was revoked in the 74 cases where the domestic industry did not appear, but continued in the other 217 cases. However, in most of those cases (80–85%), the foreign respondents did not appear. US—OCTG Sunset Reviews, WT/DS268, para. 206. Thus, the sunset review requirement may not have had a significant impact on revocations, at least in US practice.

(1) The Zeroing Controversy

The practice of zeroing is described in Note 3 to the India HRS case in Section 16.3. The practice had been challenged under the Tokyo Round AD Code, as violation of its article 2.6, which is the predecessor to article 2.4 of the current AD Agreement. The challenges were rejected, in part because the article did not deal with averaging techniques. See, e.g., US—Salmon (Norway), 41 BISD 229, paras. 474–486 (1994); EEC—Cotton Yarn (Brazil), 42 BISD 17, paras. 498–502 (1995). Article 2.4.2 of the AD Agreement explicitly does deal with such techniques. It provides that

> Subject to the provisions governing fair comparison in paragraph 4, the existence of margins of dumping during the investigation phase shall normally be established on the basis of a comparison of a weighted average normal value with a weighted average of prices of

all comparable export transactions or by a comparison of normal value and export prices on a transaction-to-transaction basis. [There is an exception for targeted dumping, which is discussed in the following case.]

It has been argued, principally by the United States, that this provision does not prohibit the use of zeroing techniques in three instances. First, in an AD investigation involving several models of a product, it is argued that the weighted-average-to-weighted-average [W-W] requirement applies only to the calculation of a dumping margin for each model and that zeroing may be used in aggregating the model-by-model dumping margins in order to obtain an overall dumping margin for the product under investigation. Essentially, the argument is that the average-to-average requirement of article 2.4.2 only applies in calculating margins for "comparable export transactions", which means that it applies in calculating dumping margins for each model (i.e., only they are comparable transactions) but not for calculating margins for the product overall. This argument was first rejected in EC—Bed Linen, WT/DS141/AB/R, adopted March 12, 2001. The Appellate Body was of the view that all transactions involving one like product were comparable. This result has been accepted by the EU and the US.

Second, the US has argued that the dumping margins found using a transaction-by-transaction (T-T) methodology may be aggregated into one overall dumping margin by using zeroing techniques. Third, the US has argued that article 2.4.2 is limited by its terms to "the investigation phase", which means that zeroing techniques may be used in reviews. At the time of the panel decision in the following case, zeroing in both of these situations appeared to have been rejected by the Appellate Body. The panel nonetheless upheld the use of zeroing in both situations.

In the initial zeroing cases, the Appellate Body focused its analysis on the language of article 2.4.2. It also stated in EC—Bed Linen, without any analysis or consideration of the meaning of "fair", that zeroing was inconsistent with article 2.4's requirement that a "fair comparison" be made between the export price and normal value. In its more recent cases, it seems to place much more emphasis on the concepts of dumping and dumping margins and has expanded upon its view of zeroing and the "fair comparison" requirement.

UNITED STATES—MEASURES RELATING TO ZEROING AND SUNSET REVIEWS

WT/DS322/AB/R.
Appellate Body Report adopted January 23, 2007.

98. * * * Before the Panel, Japan referred to both "model zeroing"[9] and "simple zeroing"[10] procedures, and claimed that the [US

---

9. [original note 13] The Panel used the term "model zeroing" to refer to the methodology whereby the USDOC "makes

[weighted] average-to-[weighted] average [('W–W')] comparisons of export price and normal value within individual 'averaging

Department of Commerce's (USDOC's)] "zeroing procedures", as they relate, inter alia, to original investigations, periodic reviews, and new shipper reviews, are inconsistent, as such, with certain provisions of the Anti–Dumping Agreement and the GATT 1994.

* * *

107. Our analysis begins with a discussion of the fundamental disciplines that apply under the Anti–Dumping Agreement and the GATT 1994 to all anti-dumping proceedings. * * *

A. *The Concepts of "Dumping" and "Margins of Dumping"*

108. First, we recall that dumping is defined in Article VI:1 of the GATT 1994 as occurring when a "product" of one country is introduced into the commerce of another country at less than the normal value of the "product". Consistent with this definition, Article VI:2 provides for the levying of anti-dumping duties in respect of a "dumped product" in order to offset or prevent the injurious effect of dumping.

109. This definition of dumping is carried over into the Anti–Dumping Agreement by Article 2.1. Furthermore, by virtue of the opening phrase of Article 2.1—"[f]or the purposes of this Agreement"— this definition applies throughout the Agreement. Thus, the terms "dumping", as well as "dumped imports", have the same meaning in all provisions of the Agreement and for all types of anti-dumping proceedings, including original investigations, new shipper reviews, and periodic reviews. In each case, they relate to a product because it is the product that is introduced into the commerce of another country at less than its normal value in that country.

110. Article VI:2 defines "margin of dumping" as the difference between the normal value and the export price and establishes the link between "dumping" and "margin of dumping". The margin of dumping reflects the magnitude of dumping. It is also one of the factors to be taken into account to determine whether dumping causes or threatens material injury. Article VI:2 lays down that "[i]n order to offset or prevent dumping, a Member may levy on any dumped product an anti-dumping duty not greater in amount than the margin of dumping in respect of such product." Thus, the margin of dumping also is defined in relation to a "product".

111. Secondly, the Anti–Dumping Agreement prescribes that dumping determinations be made in respect of each exporter or foreign

---

groups' established on the basis of physical characteristics ('models') and disregards any amounts by which average export prices for particular models exceed normal value in aggregating the results of these multiple comparisons to calculate a weighted average margin of dumping."

10. [original note 14] The Panel used the term "simple zeroing" to refer to the methodology whereby the USDOC "deter-

mines a weighted average margin of dumping based on [weighted] average-to-transaction [('W–T')] or transaction-to-transaction [('T–T')] comparisons between export price and normal value and disregards any amounts by which export prices of individual transactions exceed normal value in aggregating the results of these multiple comparisons."

producer examined. This is because dumping is the result of the pricing behaviour of individual exporters or foreign producers. Margins of dumping are established accordingly for each exporter or foreign producer on the basis of a comparison between normal value and export prices, both of which relate to the pricing behaviour of that exporter or foreign producer. In order to assess properly the pricing behaviour of an individual exporter or foreign producer, and to determine whether the exporter or foreign producer is in fact dumping the product under investigation and, if so, by which margin, it is obviously necessary to take into account the prices of all the export transactions of that exporter or foreign producer.

112.   Other provisions of the Anti–Dumping Agreement also make it clear that "dumping" and "margins of dumping" relate to the exporter or foreign producer. Article 6.10 requires, "as a rule", that investigating authorities determine "an individual margin of dumping for each known exporter or producer". * * * Article 9.5 indicates that the purpose of new shipper reviews is to determine "individual margins of dumping for any exporters or producers in the exporting country in question who have not exported the product" and refers to a "determination of dumping in respect of such producers or exporters".

113.   Thirdly, the Anti–Dumping Agreement and the GATT 1994 are not concerned with dumping per se, but with dumping that causes or threatens to cause material injury to the domestic industry. Article 3.1 stipulates that a determination of injury shall be based on an objective examination of both the volume of the dumped imports and the effect of the dumped imports on prices in the domestic market for like products, and the consequent impact of these imports on domestic producers of such products. * * *

114.   Thus, it is evident from the design and architecture of the Anti–Dumping Agreement that: (a) the concepts of "dumping" and "margins of dumping" pertain to a "product" and to an exporter or foreign producer; (b) "dumping" and "dumping margins" must be determined in respect of each known exporter or foreign producer examined; (c) anti-dumping duties can be levied only if dumped imports cause or threaten to cause material injury to the domestic industry producing like products; and (d) anti-dumping duties can be levied only in an amount not exceeding the margin of dumping established for each exporter or foreign producer. These concepts are interlinked. They do not vary with the methodologies followed for a determination made under the various provisions of the Anti–Dumping Agreement.

115.   A product under investigation may be defined by an investigating authority. But "dumping" and "margins of dumping" can be found to exist only in relation to that product as defined by that authority. They cannot be found to exist for only a type, model, or category of that product. Nor, under any comparison methodology, can "dumping" and "margins of dumping" be found to exist at the level of an individual transaction. Thus, when an investigating authority calcu-

lates a margin of dumping on the basis of multiple comparisons of normal value and export price, the results of such intermediate comparisons are not, in themselves, margins of dumping. Rather, they are merely "inputs that are [to be] aggregated in order to establish the margin of dumping of the product under investigation for each exporter or producer."

* * *

B. *Determination of Margins of Dumping Based on Transaction-to-Transaction Comparisons in Original Investigations*

* * *

118. Article 2.4.2 sets out three comparison methodologies that investigating authorities may use to calculate margins of dumping. The first sentence of Article 2.4.2 provides for two comparison methodologies (W–W and T–T) involving symmetrical comparisons of normal value and export price. Article 2.4.2 stipulates that these two methodologies "shall normally" be used by investigating authorities to establish margins of dumping. As an exception to the two normal methodologies, the second sentence of Article 2.4.2 sets out a third comparison methodology which involves an asymmetrical comparison between weighted average normal value and prices of individual export transactions. This methodology may be used only if the following two conditions are met: (i) that the authorities find a pattern of export prices that differ significantly among different purchasers, regions, or time periods; and (ii) that an explanation is provided as to why such differences cannot be taken into account appropriately by the use of a W–W or T–T comparison.

119. Under the T–T comparison methodology at issue in this appeal, the margin of dumping is established by a comparison between the normal value and the export price in individual transactions. The issue before us is whether zeroing procedures are, as such, inconsistent with the first sentence of Article 2.4.2 in the context of T–T comparisons in original investigations.

120. Recently, in *US–Softwood Lumber V (Article 21.5–Canada)*, the Appellate Body dealt for the first time with a determination of margins of dumping based on T–T comparisons in an original investigation. For the Appellate Body, the reference in the first sentence of Article 2.4.2 to " 'a comparison' in the singular suggest[ed] an overall calculation exercise involving aggregation of these multiple transactions." Therefore, "[t]he transaction-specific results are mere steps in the comparison process" and the "individual transaction comparisons are not the final results of the calculation, but, rather, are inputs for the overall calculation exercise." Thus, the text of Article 2.4.2 indicates that the calculation of a margin of dumping using the T–T comparison methodology is a "multi-step exercise in which the results of transaction-specific comparisons are inputs that are [to be] aggregated in order to establish the margin of dumping of the product under investigation for each exporter or producer." The Appellate Body found that, in aggregat-

ing the results of transaction-specific comparisons, "an investigating authority must consider the results of all of the comparisons and may not disregard the results of comparisons in which export prices are above normal value." The Appellate Body concluded, therefore, that zeroing, as applied in the determination made on the basis of the T–T comparison methodology at issue in that case, was inconsistent with Article 2.4.2 of the Anti–Dumping Agreement.

121. We see no reason to depart from the Appellate Body's reasoning in [US–Softwood Lumber V (Article 21.5) and US–Softwood Lumber V]. In the latter case, the Appellate Body held that, "[i]f an investigating authority has chosen to undertake multiple comparisons, the investigating authority necessarily has to take into account the results of all those comparisons in order to establish margins of dumping for the product as a whole under Article 2.4.2." The Appellate Body addressed there the issue of model zeroing under the W–W comparison methodology in an original investigation. That methodology involved the division of the product under investigation into sub-groups of identical, or similar, product types. In aggregating the results of the sub-group comparisons to calculate the dumping margin for the product under investigation, the USDOC had treated as zero the results of the sub-groups in which weighted average normal value was equal to or less than the weighted average export price. Thus, zeroing did not occur within the sub-groups but occurred across the sub-groups in the process of aggregating the results of the sub-group comparisons.

122. The Appellate Body held that dumping and margins of dumping can be found to exist only for the product under investigation as a whole, and that they cannot be found to exist for a type, model, or category of that product. The comparisons at the sub-group level are not margins of dumping within the meaning of Article 2.4.2. It is only on the basis of aggregating all these "intermediate values" that an investigating authority can establish margins of dumping for the product under investigation as a whole. The Appellate Body therefore found that the model zeroing was inconsistent with Article 2.4.2 of the Anti–Dumping Agreement.

123. We fail to see why, if, for the purpose of establishing a margin of dumping, such a product is dealt with under the T–T comparison methodology in an original investigation, zeroing would be consistent with Article 2.4.2 of the Anti–Dumping Agreement. If anything, zeroing under the T–T comparison methodology would inflate the margin of dumping to an even greater extent as compared to model zeroing under the W–W comparison methodology. This is because zeroing under the T–T comparison methodology disregards the result of each comparison involving a transaction in which the export price exceeds the normal value, whereas under the W–W comparison methodology, zeroing occurs, as noted above, only across the sub-groups in the process of aggregation.

124. We do not consider that the absence of the phrase "all comparable export transactions" in the context of the T–T comparison

methodology suggests that zeroing should be permissible under that methodology. Because transactions may be divided into groups under the W–W comparison methodology, the phrase "all comparable export transactions" requires that each group include only transactions that are comparable and that no export transaction may be left out when determining margins of dumping under that methodology. Furthermore, the W–W comparison methodology involves the calculation of a weighted average export price. By contrast, under the T–T comparison methodology, all export transactions are taken into account on an individual basis and matched with the most appropriate transactions in the domestic market. Therefore, the phrase "all comparable export transactions" is not pertinent to the T–T comparison methodology. Consequently, no inference may be drawn from the fact that these words do not appear in relation to this methodology.

125. We acknowledge that the W–W and T–T comparison methodologies are distinct and may not produce identical results. However, as the Appellate Body stated in *US–Softwood Lumber V (Article 21.5–Canada)*, the W–W and T–T comparison methodologies "fulfil the same function", they are "alternative means for establishing margins of dumping", and "there is no hierarchy between them". It would therefore be "illogical to interpret the [T–T] comparison methodology in a manner that would lead to results that are systematically different from those obtained under the [W–W] methodology". Indeed, if zeroing is prohibited under the W–W comparison methodology and permitted under the T–T comparison methodology, the application of the T–T methodology would lead to results that are systematically different from those obtained through the application of the W–W methodology. Moreover, by systematically disregarding comparison results involving export transactions occurring at prices above the normal value, the zeroing methodology fails to establish margins of dumping for the product under investigation properly, as required under Article 2.4.2.

126. We recall that the Anti–Dumping Agreement requires the determination of an individual margin of dumping for each known exporter or foreign producer. If it is permissible to determine a separate margin of dumping for each transaction, the consequence would be that several margins of dumping could be found to exist for each known exporter or foreign producer. The larger the number of export transactions, the greater the number of such transaction-specific margins of dumping for each exporter or foreign producer. This would create uncertainty and divergences in determinations to be made in original investigations and subsequent stages of anti-dumping proceedings.

127. As we have stated, the Anti–Dumping Agreement does not contemplate the determination of dumping or a margin of dumping at the model-or transaction-specific level. The Anti–Dumping Agreement contemplates the aggregation of all the comparisons made at the transaction-specific level in order to establish an individual margin of dumping for each exporter or foreign producer examined. As we understand it, the position of the United States is that Article 2.4.2 does not address the

issue of aggregation of transaction-specific comparison results, but if aggregation is performed, the results of comparisons where the export transactions occurred above normal value may be disregarded in the calculation of the margin of dumping, because such transactions do not involve dumping.

128. In this respect, we recall that the Anti–Dumping Agreement deals with injurious dumping and that the "volume of dumped imports" is a critical factor in injury determination. As we understand it, under United States law, if an exporter or foreign producer is found to be dumping, the USITC may include all imports from that exporter or foreign producer in the volume of dumped imports for purposes of determining injury. If, as a consequence of zeroing, the results of certain comparisons are disregarded only for purposes of calculating margins of dumping, but taken into consideration for determining injury, this would mean that the same transactions are treated as "non-dumped" for one purpose, and as "dumped" for another purpose. This is not in consonance with the need for consistent treatment of a product in an anti-dumping investigation.

129. For these reasons, we disagree with the Panel that dumping may be determined at the level of individual transactions, and that multiple comparison results are margins of dumping in themselves. We also disagree with the Panel that the terms "product" and "products" can apply to individual transactions and do not require an examination of export transactions at an aggregate level. Nor can we agree with the Panel that "a Member may treat transactions in which export prices are less than normal value as being more relevant than transactions in which export prices exceed normal value." Accordingly, we disagree with the Panel's finding that, "in the context of the [T–T] methodology in the first sentence of Article 2.4.2, the term 'margins of dumping' can be understood to mean the total amount by which transaction-specific export prices are less than transaction-specific normal values."

130. We turn next to the second sentence of Article 2.4.2 of the Anti–Dumping Agreement from which the Panel drew contextual support for its finding that zeroing is permitted under the T–T comparison methodology in original investigations. This sentence reads:

> A normal value established on a weighted average basis may be compared to prices of individual export transactions if the authorities find a pattern of export prices which differ significantly among different purchasers, regions or time periods, and if an explanation is provided as to why such differences cannot be taken into account appropriately by the use of a weighted average-to-weighted average or transaction-to-transaction comparison.

131. We recall that, under the first sentence of Article 2.4.2, an investigating authority is "normally" required to use either of the two symmetrical comparison methodologies provided for in that sentence. The second sentence of Article 2.4.2 provides an asymmetrical comparison methodology to address a pattern of "targeted" dumping found

among certain purchasers, in certain regions, or during certain time periods. By its terms, this methodology may be used if two conditions are met: first, that the investigating authorities "find a pattern of export prices which differ significantly among different purchasers, regions or time periods"; and secondly, that an "explanation" be provided as to why such differences in export prices cannot be taken into account appropriately by the use of either of the two symmetrical comparison methodologies set out in the first sentence of Article 2.4.2. The second requirement thus contemplates that there may be circumstances in which targeted dumping could be adequately addressed through the normal symmetrical comparison methodologies. The asymmetrical methodology in the second sentence is clearly an exception to the comparison methodologies which normally are to be used.

132.   In its reasoning, the Panel assumed that there was a "logical impossibility of reconciling a general prohibition of zeroing with the express provision for the use of a [W–T comparison methodology] in the second sentence of Article 2.4.2." According to the Panel, if zeroing were prohibited under all comparison methodologies, application of the second sentence of Article 2.4.2 would always yield results that would be "mathematically equivalent" to those obtained by applying the W–W comparison methodology, thereby rendering the second sentence of Article 2.4.2 inutile. The Panel further assumed that, if zeroing were permitted under the W–T comparison methodology, it should, by logical implication, be permitted under the T–T comparison methodology as well.

133.   We recall that the Appellate Body had occasion to discuss this "mathematical equivalence" argument in *US–Softwood Lumber V (Article 21.5–Canada)*, but rejected it for several reasons. The Appellate Body said, inter alia, that "[o]ne part of a provision setting forth a methodology is not rendered inutile simply because, in a specific set of circumstances, its application would produce results that are equivalent to those obtained from the application of a comparison methodology set out in another part of that provision." The Appellate Body also found that the mathematical equivalence argument is based on certain assumptions that may not hold good in all situations. The Appellate Body further observed that the second sentence provides for an "exception", and as such, "the comparison methodology in the second sentence of Article 2.4.2 ([W–T]) alone cannot determine the interpretation of the two methodologies provided in the first sentence, that is, [T–T] and [W–W]." In addition, the Appellate Body noted that, even if W–W and W–T methodologies were to yield equivalent results in certain situations, this would not be sufficient to compel a finding that zeroing is permissible under the T–T comparison methodology, because the mathematical equivalence argument does not relate to this methodology. The Appellate Body added that it could be argued, in reverse, that "the use of zeroing under the two comparison methodologies set out in the first sentence of Article 2.4.2 would enable investigating authorities to capture pricing

patterns constituting 'targeted dumping', thus rendering the third methodology inutile.''

134. As regards the relationship between the T–T comparison methodology and the W–T comparison methodology of the second sentence of Article 2.4.2, the Panel's reasoning appears to assume that the universe of export transactions to which these two comparison methodologies apply is the same, and that these two methodologies differ only in that, under the W–T comparison methodology, a normal value is established on a weighted average basis, while it is established on a transaction-specific basis under the T–T comparison methodology. Thus, according to the Panel, if zeroing is permitted under the W–T comparison methodology in the second sentence of Article 2.4.2, it should logically be permitted under the T–T comparison methodology as well.

135. We disagree with the assumption underlying the Panel's reasoning. The emphasis in the second sentence of Article 2.4.2 is on a ''pattern'', namely a ''pattern of export prices which differs significantly among different purchasers, regions or time periods.'' The prices of transactions that fall within this pattern must be found to differ significantly from other export prices. We therefore read the phrase ''individual export transactions'' in that sentence as referring to the transactions that fall within the relevant pricing pattern. This universe of export transactions would necessarily be more limited than the universe of export transactions to which the symmetrical comparison methodologies in the first sentence of Article 2.4.2 would apply. In order to unmask targeted dumping, an investigating authority may limit the application of the W–T comparison methodology to the prices of export transactions falling within the relevant pattern.

136. For these reasons, we are unable to agree with the Panel that the second sentence of Article 2.4.2 provides contextual support for a finding that zeroing is permissible under the T–T comparison methodology. We wish to emphasize, however, that our analysis of the second sentence of Article 2.4.2 is confined to addressing the contextual arguments drawn by the Panel from that provision.

137. In the light of our analysis of Article 2.4.2 of the Anti-Dumping Agreement, we conclude that, in establishing ''margins of dumping'' under the T–T comparison methodology, an investigating authority must aggregate the results of all the transaction-specific comparisons and cannot disregard the results of comparisons in which export prices are above normal value.

* * *

141. Next, we examine whether zeroing is inconsistent with the ''fair comparison'' requirement in Article 2.4 of the Anti-Dumping Agreement.

* * *

146.   The Appellate Body has previously made it clear that the use of zeroing under the T–T comparison methodology distorts the prices of certain export transactions because the "prices of [certain] export transactions [made] are artificially reduced." In this way, "the use of zeroing under the [T–T] comparison methodology artificially inflates the magnitude of dumping, resulting in higher margins of dumping and making a positive determination of dumping more likely." The Appellate Body has further stated that "[t]his way of calculating cannot be described as impartial, even-handed, or unbiased." As the Appellate Body has previously found, under the first sentence of Article 2.4.2, "an investigating authority must consider the results of all the comparisons and may not disregard the results of comparisons in which export prices are above normal value." Therefore, we consider that zeroing in T–T comparisons in original investigations is inconsistent with the fair comparison requirement in Article 2.4.

* * *

C.   *Zeroing As Such in Periodic Reviews and New Shipper Reviews*

[As to the US practice of using "zeroing" in reviews, the Appellate Body noted that its previous analysis compelled the conclusion that the practice violated the Anti–Dumping Agreement. But it noted an additional contextual argument made in respect of Article 9 reviews.]

152.   We examine next the "important considerations specific to Article 9" identified by the Panel as supporting its view that it is permissible to interpret Article VI of the GATT 1994 and relevant provisions of the Anti–Dumping Agreement "to mean that there is no general requirement to determine dumping and margins of dumping for the product as a whole, which, by itself or in conjunction with a requirement to establish margins of dumping for exporters or foreign producers, entails a general prohibition of zeroing."

153.   The "important considerations" identified by the Panel relate to the operation of retrospective and prospective duty assessment systems under Articles 9.3.1 and 9.3.2 of the Anti–Dumping Agreement. The Panel noted that these provisions specify how to implement the requirement in Article 9.3 "that the amount of anti-dumping duty not exceed the margin of dumping". The Panel's interpretative approach also relies on Article 9.4(ii), which refers to the calculation of the "liability for payment" of anti-dumping duties "on the basis of a prospective normal value".

154.   The Panel stated that, under Articles 9.3.1 and 9.3.2, a margin of dumping is calculated for determining the final liability for payment of anti-dumping duties in a retrospective duty assessment system, and for determining the amount of anti-dumping duty that must be refunded in a prospective duty assessment system. The Panel added that "the obligation to pay an anti-dumping duty is incurred on an importer-and import-specific basis." For the Panel, "the importer-and import-specific character of the payment of anti-dumping duties must be

taken into account in interpreting the meaning of 'margin of dumping.' "
Under the Panel's rationale, if certain export sales to a given importer
are made at prices above normal value, those sales do not need to be
taken into account in determining the margin of dumping for the
relevant exporter that has made the sale to the importer.

155.   We are unable to agree with the reasoning of the Panel. As
the Appellate Body has stated previously, under Article 9.3 of the Anti–
Dumping Agreement and Article VI:2 of the GATT 1994, investigating
authorities "are required to ensure that the total amount of antidumping duties collected on the entries of a product from a given
exporter shall not exceed the margin of dumping established for that
exporter", in accordance with Article 2. Put differently, "the margin of
dumping established for an exporter or foreign producer operates as a
ceiling for the total amount of anti-dumping duties that can be levied on
the entries of the subject product (from that exporter) covered by the
duty assessment proceeding." The Appellate Body has further emphasized that "[a]lthough Article 9.3 sets out a requirement regarding the
amount of the assessed anti-dumping duties, it does not prescribe a
specific methodology according to which the duties should be assessed."
In particular, the Appellate Body has underscored that "a reading of
Article 9.3 of the Anti–Dumping Agreement and Article VI:2 of the
GATT 1994 does not suggest that final anti-dumping duty liability
cannot be assessed on a transaction-or importer-specific basis, or that
the investigating authorities may not use specific methodologies that
reflect the distinct nature and purpose of proceedings governed by these
provisions, for purposes of assessing final anti-dumping duty liability,
provided that the total amount of anti-dumping duties that are levied
does not exceed the exporters' or foreign producers' margins of dumping."

156.   Finally, the Panel expresses its concern that, if a Member
applies a retrospective duty assessment system, it "may be precluded
from collecting anti-dumping duties in respect of particular export transactions at prices less than normal value to a particular importer at a
particular point of time because of prices of export transactions to other
importers at a different point in time that exceed normal value." This
concern is not well founded. The concept of dumping relates to the
pricing behaviour of exporters or foreign producers; it is the exporter,
not the importer, that engages in practices that result in situations of
dumping. At the time of importation, an administering authority may
collect duties, in the form of a cash deposit, on all export sales, including
those occurring at above the normal value. However, in a review proceeding under Article 9.3.1, the authority is required to ensure that the
total amount of anti-dumping duties collected from all the importers of
that product does not exceed the total amount of dumping found in all
sales made by the exporter or foreign producer, calculated according to
the margin of dumping established for that exporter or foreign producer
without zeroing. The same "ceiling" applies in review proceedings under

Article 9.3.2, because the introductory clause of Article 9.3 applies equally to prospective and retroactive duty assessment systems.

157.   Next, we examine the Panel's reasoning relating to Article 9.4(ii) of the Anti–Dumping Agreement, which deals with the calculation of the liability for payment of anti-dumping duties on the basis of a so-called "prospective normal value".[11]

158.   Before the Panel, Japan argued that the collection of a variable duty on an entry-by-entry basis under a prospective normal value system does not involve the establishment of margins of dumping with respect to individual export transactions, because the actual margin of dumping in such a system is only determined in a review under Article 9.3.2. Moreover, according to Japan, in a prospective normal value system, "the final liability for duties must be assessed in a review under Article 9.3.2".

159.   The Panel disagreed, noting that Japan's argument was "inconsistent with the prospective nature of such a system". The Panel added that "[i]t is clear from the text of Article 9.4(ii) of the [Anti–Dumping] Agreement that in a prospective normal value system 'liability for payment of anti-dumping duties is calculated on the basis of a prospective normal value'." Moreover, "[a]lthough Article 9.3.2 provides for a refund procedure when the amount of anti-dumping duties is assessed on a prospective basis, a requirement that arguably also applies to prospective normal value systems referred to in Article 9.4(ii), a refund procedure in a prospective duty assessment system is not a determination of final liability for payment of anti-dumping duties." The Panel further noted that "[t]he phrase 'determination of the final liability for payment of anti-dumping duties' is used in Article 9.3.1 in connection with retrospective duty assessment procedures but does not figure in Article 9.3.2."

160.   The Panel stated that, "notwithstanding the possibility of a refund, liability for payment of anti-dumping duties is final in a prospective normal value system at the time of importation of a product." This may be so, but it does not mean that the anti-dumping duty collected at the time of importation represents a "margin of dumping". Nor does it mean that the total amount of anti-dumping duties that are levied can exceed the exporter's or foreign producer's "margin of dumping". Under a prospective normal value system, exporters may choose to raise their export prices to the level of the prospective normal value in order to avoid liability for payment of anti-dumping duties on each export transaction. However, under Article 9.3.2, the amount of duties collected is subject to review so as to ensure that, pursuant to Article 9.3 of the Anti–Dumping Agreement, the amount of the anti-dumping duty collected does not exceed the margin of dumping as established under Article 2.

11.   [original note 367] In a prospective normal value system, the authorities announce in advance a prospective normal value that applies to future entries of a given product and anti-dumping duties are assessed on the basis of the difference between this "prospective normal value" and the prices of individual export transactions for that product.

It is open to an importer to request a refund if the duties collected exceed the exporter's margin of dumping. Whether a refund is due or not will depend on the margin of dumping established for that exporter.

161. The Panel stated that, in a prospective normal value system, "liability for payment of anti-dumping duties is incurred only to the extent that prices of individual export transactions are below normal value." Therefore, Article 9.4(ii) "confirms that the concept of dumping can apply on a transaction-specific basis to prices of individual export transactions below the normal value." The Panel also stated that "[i]f in a prospective normal value system individual export transactions at prices less than normal value can attract liability for payment of anti-dumping duties, without regard to whether or not prices of other export transactions exceed normal value", there is no reason why duties may not be similarly assessed under the United States' retrospective duty assessment system.

162. We are unable to agree. Under any system of duty collection, the margin of dumping established in accordance with Article 2 operates as a ceiling for the amount of anti-dumping duties that could be collected in respect of the sales made by an exporter. To the extent that duties are paid by an importer, it is open to that importer to claim a refund if such a ceiling is exceeded. Similarly, under its retrospective system of duty collection, the United States is free to assess duty liability on a transaction-specific basis, but the total amount of anti-dumping duties that are levied must not exceed the exporters' or foreign producers' margins of dumping.

163. The Anti–Dumping Agreement is neutral as between different systems for levy and collection of anti-dumping duties. The Agreement lays down the "margin of dumping" as the ceiling for collection of duties regardless of the duty assessment system adopted by a WTO Member, and provides for a refund if the ceiling is exceeded. It is therefore incorrect to say that the Anti–Dumping Agreement favours one system, or places another system at a disadvantage.

Notes and Questions

(1) Why such controversy over zeroing? It is probably accurate to say that the technique tends to strike those who are new to AD rules as unfair, and traditional targets of dumping actions have long felt aggrieved by the practice. For the United States and some others, the controversy probably stems from a belief that the Appellate Body's decisions are not consistent with what was negotiated in the Uruguay Round and are not soundly reasoned. At the time the Uruguay Round implementing legislation was drafted, it was the view of the US that it had to forego simple zeroing in investigations, but that it was permitted to continue to zero in annual reviews. See Ways & Means Memo on AD/CVD Provisions, May 24, 1994, in Special Report, Inside US Trade, June 3, 1994. Thus, the Appellate Body's failure to analyze or give any weight to the words "during the investigation phase" in article 2.4.2 upsets the US, especially since the Appellate Body has held that the *de minimis* rules of Article 11.9 of the SCM Agreement (similar

to Article 5.8 of the Antidumping Agreement) apply only to investigations and not reviews. More generally, the current view of the Appellate Body on zeroing seems grounded in its view of the definition of ''dumping'' and ''margins of dumping'' in GATT Article VI, which suggests that zeroing has always been a violation, notwithstanding the fact that it has long been the subject of negotiations. In addition, the Appellate Body's conclusion that zeroing violates the ''fair comparison'' language of article 2.4 would seem to make article 2.4.2 mostly superfluous. How would you defend the Appellate Body from these criticisms? Panels have been sympathetic to the US position. As noted above, the panel in this case did not follow prior Appellate Body case law on zeroing; nor did the panel in US–Stainless Steel (Mexico), WT/DS344/R, which was excerpted in Section 7.4(C)(2). These zeroing cases are the only ones to date where panels have explicitly refused to follow clear Appellate Body precedents that were directly on point.

(2) In respect of the ''fairness'' of zeroing, how would you respond to the classic argument of zeroing defenders that zeroing practices resemble commonly accepted traffic law: drivers are ticketed when they exceed the speed limit (say, by 10 miles per hour) and it is irrelevant that yesterday they drove much more slowly (say, 11 miles per hour under the speed limit)?

(3) Note the US argument that the Appellate Body's rationale means that prospective normal values or benchmarks, which have been traditionally use by a number of countries (see Section 16.3), are no longer permitted. How does the Appellate Body response to that argument? Are you convinced? It would seem that the administrative attraction of such systems would decline significantly if refund procedures had to be implemented.

(4) As noted in Chapter 7, there is a special standard of review applicable to AD cases—article 17.6 of the AD Agreement. In the *US—Zeroing (Japan)* case, the Appellate Body's complete discussion of that provision was as follows (para. 189):

> In our analysis, we have been mindful of the standard of review provided in Article 17.6(ii). However, we consider that there is no room for recourse to the second sentence of Article 17.6(ii) in this appeal. This is because, in our view, Articles 2.4, 2.4.2, 9.3, 9.5, and 11.3 of the *Anti-Dumping Agreement* and Articles VI:1 and VI:2 of the GATT 1994, when interpreted in accordance with customary rules of interpretation of public international law, as required by the first sentence of Article 17.6(ii), do not admit of another interpretation of these provisions as far as the issue of zeroing before us is concerned.

Does this adequately address the substance of article 17.6(ii)? In the Uruguay Round, the US pushed strongly for a provision limiting panel review of AD administrative decisions. It now feels that the Appellate Body is ignoring what it negotiated for.

(5) The ultimate impact of prohibiting the use of zeroing in calculating AD margins is not yet clear. There may well be more use made of the so-called ''targeted dumping'' exception in article 2.4.2. Moreover, AD investigating authorities have considerable discretion over margin calculations and may be able to offset the impact of not zeroing by using other techniques. See Brink Lindsey & Dan Ikenson, Antidumping 101: The Devilish Details of

"Unfair Trade" Law, Center for Trade Policy Studies No. 20 (Cato Institute, 2002).

(2) *The Byrd Amendment*

In this section, we consider an important Appellate Body decision concerning the WTO-consistency of a US law that created a right of private entities harmed by dumping to receive a share of antidumping duties collected by the US government. The Appellate Body had previously considered in *United States—Anti–Dumping Act of 1916*, WT/DS136/AB/R, adopted September 26, 2000, an old US law that allowed, under certain conditions, civil actions and criminal proceedings to be brought against importers who have sold foreign-produced goods in the United States at prices which are "substantially less" than the prices at which the same products are sold in a relevant foreign market. Private parties were permitted under the law to recover treble damages in such cases. The Appellate Body found the 1916 Act to violate WTO rules, and it was repealed in late 2004.[12] The Appellate Body's reasoning was explained in the *Byrd Amendment* case, which is set out below.

UNITED STATES—CONTINUED DUMPING AND SUBSIDY OFFSET ACT OF 2000 ("BYRD AMENDMENT")

WT/DS217/AB/R.
Appellate Body Report adopted January 27, 2003.

[The case was brought by Australia, Brazil, Canada, Chile, the European Communities, India, Indonesia, Japan, Korea, Mexico and Thailand. They challenged the United States Continued Dumping and Subsidy Offset Act of 2000 (the "CDSOA"), known in the United States as the "Byrd Amendment" as being in violation of various provisions of AD Agreement, the SCM Agreement, GATT 1994 and the WTO Agreement. This excerpt focuses on the provisions of the AD Agreement; references to the provisions of the SCM Agreement and subsidies have been edited out without indication. The AD and SCM provisions were treated as being identical for purposes of the case.]

12.   The CDSOA provides that the United States Commissioner of Customs ("Customs") shall distribute, on an annual basis, duties assessed pursuant to [an anti-dumping duty order] to "affected domestic producers" for "qualifying expenditures". An "affected domestic produc-

---

12. The repeal did not affect pending cases. To date, only one successful 1916 Act action has been reported, although several cases have reportedly been settled. The one successful action was brought by Goss International Corporation, which obtained a jury verdict in excess of $10 million, trebled to over $30 million, plus attorneys' fees. Goss Intl. Corp. v. Tokyo Kikai Seisakusho, Ltd., 321 F.Supp.2d 1039 (N.D. Iowa), affd. (2–1), 434 F.3d 1081 (8th Cir. 2006), cert. denied, 547 U.S. 1180, 126 S.Ct. 2363, 165 L.Ed.2d 280 (2006). Japan has a "clawback" statute that would enable the defendant to sue to recover damages paid by it. The Eighth Circuit later decided for reasons, inter alia, of international comity that the defendant should not be enjoined from invoking that statute. Goss Intl. Corp. v. Man Roland Druckmaschinen AG, 491 F.3d 355 (8th Cir. 2007), cert. pending, Goss Intl. Corp. v. Tokyo Kikai Seisakusho Ltd.

er" is defined as a domestic producer that: (a) was a petitioner or interested party in support of the petition with respect to which an anti-dumping duty order has been entered; and (b) remains in operation. The term "qualifying expenditures" refers to expenditures on specific items identified in the CDSOA, which were incurred after the issuance of the anti-dumping duty order. Those expenditures must relate to the production of the same product that is subject to the anti-dumping order, with the exception of expenses incurred by associations which must relate to the same case.

13. The CDSOA, together with its implementing regulations issued by Customs, provides that Customs shall establish a special account and a clearing account with respect to each anti-dumping duty order. All anti-dumping duties assessed under such orders are first deposited into a "clearing account". Transfers from "clearing accounts" to "special accounts" are made by Customs throughout the fiscal year. Such transfers are made only after the entries in question that are subject to an anti-dumping order have been properly "liquidated". Thus, when, and only when, the entries have been liquidated, will the proceeds be transferred to a special account. Only once there are funds in a special account (not a clearing account), can distributions to domestic producers under the CDSOA be made. Therefore, if liquidation of entries has been enjoined, for instance, by a court—perhaps pending judicial review of the determination of dumping—or if liquidation of entries has been suspended due to an administrative review of those entries, the relevant special account will be empty and no distribution can be made to domestic producers under the CDSOA.

14. Pursuant to the CDSOA, Customs shall distribute all funds (including all interest earned on the funds) from the assessed duties received in the preceding fiscal year (and contained in the special accounts) to each affected domestic producer based on a certification by the affected domestic producer that it is eligible to receive the distribution and desires to receive a distribution for qualifying expenditures incurred since the issuance of the order or finding. * * *

* * *

VII. ARTICLE 18.1 OF THE ANTI-DUMPING AGREEMENT

* * *

234. * * * Article 18.1 of the Anti–Dumping Agreement reads as follows:

No specific action against dumping of exports from another Member can be taken except in accordance with the provisions of GATT 1994, as interpreted by this Agreement.[24]

---

[24] This is not intended to preclude action under other relevant provisions of GATT 1994, as appropriate.

* * *

236.   Looking to the ordinary meaning of the words used in these provisions, we read them as establishing two conditions precedent that must be met in order for a measure to be governed by them. The first is that a measure must be "specific" to dumping. The second is that a measure must be "against" dumping. These two conditions operate together and complement each other. If they are not met, the measure will not be governed by Article 18.1. If, however, it is established that a measure meets these two conditions, and thus falls within the scope of the prohibitions in those provisions, it would then be necessary to move to a further step in the analysis and to determine whether the measure has been "taken in accordance with the provisions of GATT 1994", as interpreted by the AD Agreement. * * *

A.   The Term "Specific" in the Phrase "Specific Action Against" Dumping

* * *

238.   [I]n *US–1916 Act*, we interpreted the phrase "specific action against dumping" in Article 18.1. We said:

In our view, the ordinary meaning of the phrase "specific action against dumping" of exports within the meaning of Article 18.1 is action that is taken in response to situations presenting the constituent elements of "dumping". "Specific action against dumping" of exports must, at a minimum, encompass action that may be taken only when the constituent elements of "dumping" are present.[66]

---

[66] We do not find it necessary, in the present cases, to decide whether the concept of "specific action against dumping" may be broader.

239.   We recall that, in *US–1916 Act*, the United States argued that the 1916 Act did not fall within the scope of GATT Article VI because it targeted predatory pricing, as opposed to dumping. We disagreed, and determined that the 1916 Act was a "specific action against dumping" because the constituent elements of dumping were "built into" the essential elements of civil and criminal liability under the 1916 Act. We also found that the "wording of the 1916 Act . . . makes clear that these actions can be taken only with respect to conduct which presents the constituent elements of 'dumping'." Accordingly, a measure that may be taken only when the constituent elements of dumping or a subsidy are present, is a "specific action" in response to dumping within the meaning of Article 18.1. In other words, the measure must be inextricably linked to, or have a strong correlation with, the constituent elements of dumping. Such link or correlation may, as in the 1916 Act, be derived from the text of the measure itself.

240.   This leads to the question of how to determine what are the constituent elements of dumping or a subsidy. We recall that, in *US–1916 Act*, we said the constituent elements of dumping are found in the definition of dumping in GATT Article VI:1, as elaborated in Article 2 of the AD Agreement.

* * *

242.   In our view, the Panel was correct in finding that the CDSOA is a specific action related to dumping or a subsidy within the meaning of Article 18.1. It is clear from the text of the CDSOA, in particular from Section 754(a) of the Tariff Act, that the CDSOA offset payments are inextricably linked to, and strongly correlated with, a determination of dumping, as defined in GATT Article VI:1 and in the AD Agreement. The language of the CDSOA is unequivocal. First, CDSOA offset payments can be made only if anti-dumping duties have been collected. Second, such duties can be collected only pursuant to an anti-dumping duty order. Third, an anti-dumping duty order can be imposed only following a determination of dumping, as defined in GATT Article VI:1 and in the AD Agreement. In the light of the above elements, we agree with the Panel that "there is a clear, direct and unavoidable connection between the determination of dumping and CDSOA offset payments". In other words, it seems to us unassailable that CDSOA offset payments can be made only following a determination that the constituent elements of dumping are present. Therefore, consistent with the test established in *US–1916 Act*, we find that the CDSOA is "specific action" related to dumping within the meaning of Article 18.1.

243.   [T]he United States argues that the CDSOA is not specific action related to dumping subsidy because, contrary to the 1916 Act examined in a previous appeal, the language of the CDSOA does not refer to the constituent elements of dumping and dumping is not the trigger for application of the CDSOA. The United States suggested at the oral hearing that the CDSOA is not "specific" because the constituent elements of dumping do not form part of the essential components of the CDSOA. In addition, the United States submits that, according to the Panel's reasoning, any expenditure of collected anti-dumping duties, including expenditure for international emergency relief, would be characterized as specific action against dumping. For the United States, the Panel's approach "cannot withstand scrutiny."

244.   We disagree with these arguments. The criterion we set out in *US–1916 Act* for specific action in response to dumping is not whether the constituent elements of dumping are explicitly referred to in the measure at issue, nor whether dumping triggers the application of the action, nor whether the constituent elements of dumping form part of the essential components of the measure at issue. Our analysis in *US–1916 Act* focused on the strength of the link between the measure and the elements of dumping. In other words, we focused on the degree of correlation between the scope of application of the measure and the constituent elements of dumping. In noting that the "wording of the

1916 Act also makes clear that these actions can be taken *only* with respect to conduct which presents the constituent elements of 'dumping' ", we did not require that the language of the measure include the constituent elements of dumping. This is clear from our use of the word "also", which suggests that this aspect of the 1916 Act was a supplementary reason for our finding, and not the basis for it. Indeed, we required that the constituent elements of dumping be "present", which in our view can include cases where the constituent elements of dumping are implicit in the measure. Thus, * * * the "test" established in *US–1916 Act* "is met not only when the constituent elements of dumping are 'explicitly built into' the action at issue, but also where ... they are implicit in the express conditions for taking such action." In fact, the presence of the constituent elements of dumping is implied by the very words of the CDSOA, which refer to "[d]uties assessed pursuant to a countervailing duty order, an antidumping duty order, or a finding under the Antidumping Act of 1921 ...".

245. We also disagree with the submission of the United States that, under the Panel's reasoning, any expenditure of the collected antidumping duties would be characterized as a specific action against dumping. This submission does not take into account the express terms of Article 18.1, which, as we said earlier, contain two conditions precedent, namely that the action be "specific" to dumping, and that it be "against" dumping. To refer to the example given by the United States, international emergency relief financed from collected anti-dumping would not, in our opinion, be subject to the prohibitions of Article 18.1, because such action would have no effect whatsoever on dumping and, therefore, could not be characterized as operating "against" dumping. * * *

B. The Term "Against" in the Phrase "Specific Action Against" Dumping or a Subsidy

* * *

247. We agree with the Panel that our statement in *US–1916 Act*— to the effect that "the ordinary meaning of the phrase 'specific action against dumping' of exports within the meaning of Article 18.1 is action that is taken in response to situations presenting the constituent elements of 'dumping' "—is not conclusive as to the nature of the condition flowing from the term "against". The Panel took the position that an action operates "against" dumping or a subsidy within the meaning of Article 18.1 if it has an adverse bearing on dumping. The United States criticizes this approach, contending that an action is "against" dumping if it is "in hostile/active opposition" to dumping. The United States puts emphasis on the argument that an action, in order to be characterized as being "against" dumping, must "come into contact with" dumping, in the sense of "operating directly" on the imported good, or the entity responsible for the dumped good. In the view of the United States, the Panel erred by finding that the term "against" in Article 18.1 encompasses any form of adverse bearing, whether it be direct or indirect, and

by finding that this term does not imply a requirement that the action applies directly to the imported good or an entity responsible for it, and is burdensome. The United States contends that such a requirement derives from the ordinary meaning of the term "against". Specifically, the United States relies on a definition found in the New Shorter Oxford English Dictionary, according to which "against" means "in contact with". In order to identify the ordinary meaning of the term "against" as used in Article 18.1, the United States posits three definitions of that term: (1) "of motion or action in opposition"; (2) "in hostility or active opposition to"; and (3) "in contact with".

248.   In our view, the first and second definitions invoked by the United States could, arguably, have some relevance in identifying the ordinary meaning of the term "against" as used in Article 18.1. However, we do not believe the third definition is appropriate given the substance of Articles 18.1. Indeed, the third definition refers to physical contact between two objects and, thus, in our view, is irrelevant to the idea of opposition, hostility or adverse effect that is conveyed by the word "against" as used in Article 18.1. It should be remembered that dictionaries are important guides to, not dispositive statements of, definitions of words appearing in agreements and legal documents.

* * *

251.   A textual analysis of Article 18.1 supports, rather than defeats, the finding of the Panel that these provisions are applicable to measures that do not come into direct contact with the imported good, or entities responsible for the dumped good. We note that Article 18.1 refers only to measures that act against "dumping", and that there is no express requirement that the measure must act against the imported dumped product, or entities responsible for that product. * * *

252.   Turning to considerations of object and purpose, we do not consider that the object and purpose of the AD Agreement, as reflected in Article 18.1, support the incorporation into these provisions, through the term "against", of a requirement that the measure must come into direct contact with the imported good, or the entity responsible for it. * * * Excluding from Article 18.1 actions that do not come into direct contact with the imported good or the entity responsible for the dumped subsidized good, would undermine that function [of limiting the range of actions that a Member may take unilaterally to counter dumping].

* * *

254.   Recalling the other two elements of the definition of "against" from the New Shorter Oxford Dictionary relied upon by the United States, namely "of motion or action in opposition" and "in hostility or active opposition to", to determine whether a measure is "against" dumping, we believe it is necessary to assess whether the design and structure of a measure is such that the measure is "opposed to", has an adverse bearing on, or, more specifically, has the effect of dissuading the practice of dumping, or creates an incentive to terminate

such practices. In our view, the CDSOA has exactly those effects because of its design and structure.

255.   The CDSOA effects a transfer of financial resources from the producers/exporters of dumped goods to their domestic competitors. This is demonstrated by the following elements of the CDSOA regime. First, the CDSOA offset payments are financed from the anti-dumping duties paid by the foreign producers/exporters. Second, the CDSOA offset payments are made to an "affected domestic producer", defined in Section 754(b) of the Tariff Act as "a petitioner or interested party in support of the petition with respect to which an anti-dumping duty order * * * has been entered" and that "remains in operation". * * * [T]he "affected domestic producers" which are eligible to receive payments under the CDSOA, are necessarily competitors of the foreign producers/exporters subject to an anti-dumping order. Third, * * * the "qualifying expenditures" of the affected domestic producers, for which the CDSOA offset payments are made, "must be related to the production of the same product that is the subject of the related order or finding, with the exception of expenses incurred by associations which must relate to a specific case." Fourth, * * * there is no statutory or regulatory requirement as to how a CDSOA offset payment to an affected domestic producer is to be spent, thus indicating that the recipients of CDSOA offset payments are entitled to use this money to bolster their competitive position vis-à-vis their competitors, including the foreign competitors subject to anti-dumping duties.

256.   All these elements lead us to conclude that the CDSOA has an adverse bearing on the foreign producers/exporters in that the imports into the United States of the dumped products (besides being subject to anti-dumping duties) result in the financing of United States competitors—producers of like products—through the transfer to the latter of the duties collected on those exports. Thus, foreign producers/exporters have an incentive not to engage in the practice of exporting dumped products or to terminate such practice. Because the CDSOA has an adverse bearing on, and, more specifically, is designed and structured so that it dissuades the practice of dumping, and because it creates an incentive to terminate such practice, the CDSOA is undoubtedly an action "against" dumping, within the meaning of Article 18.1.

* * *

C.   Footnote 24 of the Anti–Dumping Agreement

260.   The United States * * * contends that [footnote 24] permits actions involving dumping consistent with GATT 1994 provisions and not addressed by GATT Article VI, and that these actions are not encompassed by the prohibitions against "specific action" in Article 18.1. In other words, according to the United States, an action that falls within footnote 24 cannot be characterized as a "specific action" within the meaning of Article 18.1, and such action would, therefore, not be WTO-inconsistent.

261. We disagree with this argument. We note, first, that, in *US–1916 Act*, we commented on footnote 24 as follows:

> Footnote 24 to Article 18.1 of the Anti–Dumping Agreement states:
>
> This is not intended to preclude action under other relevant provisions of GATT 1994, as appropriate.
>
> We note that footnote 24 refers generally to "action" and not, as does Article 18.1, to "specific action against dumping" of exports. "Action" within the meaning of footnote 24 is to be distinguished from "specific action against dumping" of exports, which is governed by Article 18.1 itself.

262. The US reasoning is tantamount to treating footnote 24 as the primary provision, while according Article 18.1 residual status. This not only turns the normal approach to interpretation on its head, but it also runs counter to our finding in *US–1916 Act*. In that case, we provided guidance for determining whether an action is specific to dumping: an action is specific to dumping when it may be taken only when the constituent elements of dumping are present, or, put another way, when the measure is inextricably linked to, or strongly correlates with, the constituent elements of dumping. This approach is based on the texts of Article 18.1, and not on the accessory footnotes. Footnote 24 is a clarification of the main provision, added to avoid ambiguity; it confirms what is implicit in Article 18.1, namely, that an action that is not "specific" within the meaning of Article 18.1, but is nevertheless related to dumping, is not prohibited by Article 18.1.

D. Whether the CDSOA is in Accordance with the WTO Agreement

263. Having determined that the CDSOA is a "specific action against" dumping within the meaning of Article 18.1, we move to the next step of our analysis, which is to determine whether the action is "in accordance with the provisions of the GATT 1994, as interpreted by" the AD Agreement.

264. We interpreted "provisions of GATT 1994" as referred to in Article 18.1 in *US–1916 Act*. In particular, we stated that the "provisions" are, in fact, the provisions of GATT Article VI concerning dumping:

> We recall that footnote 24 to Article 18.1 refers to "other relevant provisions of GATT 1994". These terms can only refer to provisions other than the provisions of Article VI concerning dumping. Footnote 24 thus confirms that the "provisions of GATT 1994" referred to in Article 18.1 are in fact the provisions of Article VI of the GATT 1994 concerning dumping.

265. We also stated in that appeal that "Article VI, and, in particular, Article VI:2, read in conjunction with the AD Agreement, limit the permissible responses to dumping to definitive anti-dumping duties, provisional measures and price undertakings." As CDSOA offset payments are not definitive anti-dumping duties, provisional measures or price undertakings, we conclude, in the light of our finding in *US–1916*

Act, that the CDSOA is not "in accordance with the provisions of the GATT 1994, as interpreted by" the Anti–Dumping Agreement. It follows that the CDSOA is inconsistent with Article 18.1 of that Agreement.

Notes and Questions

(1) Are you convinced that the AD Agreement precludes legislation such as the 1916 Act and the Byrd Amendment? In particular, are you satisfied with the analysis of the meaning of "against"?

(2) Is it possible for the US government to subsidize industries hurt by dumping or foreign subsidies without running afoul of the ruling in the *Byrd Amendment* case? How would you structure such a program? If it is not possible, has the Appellate Body added a new form of prohibited subsidy to the WTO Agreement? Is that appropriate? In that regard, it is noteworthy that the panel stated in its conclusion: "If Members are of the view that subsidization is a permitted response to unfair trade practices, we suggest that they clarify this matter through negotiation." Panel Report, para. 8.3.

(3) The panel in the *Byrd Amendment* case found that the US legislation falsified the degree of support for antidumping/countervail actions by giving an incentive for members of an industry to support a petition, whether or not they really did, so as to qualify themselves for any potential payments under the Byrd Amendment. In the panel's view, this constituted a violation of article 5.4 of the AD Agreement. The Appellate Body disagreed. What is your view?

(4) The Byrd Amendment was repealed in February 2006, effective as of October 1, 2007. Duties collected before that date will be available for distribution at some later date. While the complainants welcomed the repeal, their view is that the US is not yet in compliance because of the transitional provisions. Several of the complainants—including the EU and Japan—are currently applying retaliatory measures pursuant to DSU article 22.

(5) Because the imposition of AD duties tends to disrupt trade flows, relatively few US companies have benefited from Byrd Amendment payments. Indeed, the Government Accountability Office (GAO) found that, in money terms, about one-half of all Byrd disbursements were received by only 5 of 770 recipient companies, and 80 percent of all disbursements went to 39 companies. Moreover, three of the five top recipients are currently under common ownership. GAO, "Issues and Effects of Implementing the Continued Dumping and Subsidy Offset Act," GAO–05–979. The repeal effort may have been aided by the fact that so few benefited.

Chapter 17

INJURY ANALYSIS IN ANTIDUMP-ING AND COUNTERVAILING DUTY CASES

SECTION 17.1   INTRODUCTION

(A) WTO RULES: AN OVERVIEW

Before antidumping or countervailing duties may be imposed under WTO law, the importing nation must determine that "the effect of the dumping or subsidization, as the case may be, is such as to cause or threaten material injury to an established domestic industry, or is such as to retard materially the establishment of a domestic industry," GATT Article VI:6(a). This requirement is known as the "injury test." The requirements of the injury test have been elaborated in Article 3 of the WTO Agreement on Implementation of Article VI (the Antidumping Agreement) and in Article 15 of the WTO Agreement on Subsidies and Countervailing Measures.

Aside from the references to dumping or subsidization, the provisions in the two WTO Agreements relating to injury are virtually identical. Each requires that a determination of injury be based on "positive evidence" and an "objective examination" regarding the volume of the unfairly traded imports, their effect on "prices in the domestic market of like products," and the consequent impact of the imports on domestic producers of such products. Each requires the investigating authorities to consider whether there has been a "significant increase" in the unfairly traded imports, whether there has been "significant price undercutting" by the unfairly traded imports, and whether the imports have otherwise depressed prices or prevented price increases. Each requires an evaluation of "all relevant economic factors and indices" having a bearing on the state of the domestic industry, and provides a non-exhaustive list of such factors. Each requires "the demonstration of a causal relationship between the [unfairly traded] imports and the injury to the domestic industry." Moreover, it must be determined that the unfairly traded imports, "through the effects of (dumping or subsidization)," are causing injury. Investigating authorities must examine "any known factors" in addition to the unfairly traded imports that are causing injury, and must not attribute injury caused by those factors to unfairly traded imports. A finding of a threat of injury (as distinguished from current injury) must be based on "facts" and not "allegation, conjecture or remote possibility." The threatened injury must also be "clearly foreseen and imminent." In delineating the domestic industry, the general rule (subject to some exceptions) is that the industry consists of the "domestic producers as a whole of the like products."

It is perhaps useful to note some distinctions and similarities between the injury analysis here and that in safeguards cases. The requisite degree of injury here is "material" injury as distinguished from "serious" injury, the former being understood to imply a weaker standard. The injury analysis here does not strictly require "increased quantities" of imports, although the requisite examination of the volume of unfairly traded imports implies that an increase in unfairly traded imports will usually be present in practice for an affirmative finding of injury. The industry here is also defined more narrowly, to include only the "like" products and not the broader category of "directly competitive" products, although the practical importance of this distinction is unclear. Finally, there is no requirement here of any linkage to "unforeseen developments."

As in the safeguards area, a causal linkage is required between the imports and the injury, and a "non-attribution" analysis is required to ensure that injury caused by other factors is not attributed to imports. Other aspects of the causation inquiry are somewhat different. For example, in the safeguards area, the question is whether "increased quantities" of imports have caused or threatened injury. Because import quantities are endogenous from an economic perspective as discussed in Chapter 15, this phrasing poses a difficult interpretive problem in safeguards cases. The inquiry here, by contrast, is whether the dumped or subsidized imports, "through the effects" of the unfair trade practice, are causing injury. This distinction suggests a different type of counterfactual inquiry for the assessment of causation, as shall be seen below.

Another important distinction between injury analysis in the safeguards area and the injury analysis here relates to the amount and scope of litigation within the WTO. Although the Appellate Body has addressed a number of the central interpretive questions for safeguards cases (how well they have been addressed is another matter), the case law regarding the injury test in antidumping and countervailing duty cases is spotty. Accordingly, we will rely much more heavily on US materials in this chapter to draw out some of the central issues.

(B) U.S. LAW

The injury test has long existed under US antidumping law. US countervailing duty law, by contrast, did not contain an injury requirement for many years, an omission that was "grandfathered" into GATT by the Protocol of Provisional Application. With time, an injury test was added to US countervailing duty law for otherwise non-dutiable imports, and then after the Tokyo Round for all imports from Subsidies Code signatories. Under the Uruguay Round Subsidies Agreement, the United States at last extended the injury test to all countervailing duty cases involving a member of the WTO.

The relevant portions of US law follow the requirements of the WTO Agreements closely and are found in the Tariff Act of 1930, as amended. See Sections 701–705 (countervailing duties); Sections 731–35 (dumping); Section 771 (definitional section applicable to both). Because the injury analysis in dumping and countervailing duty cases is so similar, we will treat them together in this chapter.

As under WTO law, the injury investigation in a US dumping or countervailing duty case is simpler than the injury analysis in a US escape clause proceeding. In addition to the differences noted above, US antidumping and countervailing duty law has nothing akin to the "substantial cause" test that applies in US escape clause cases. Rather, the question is simply whether the unfairly traded imports cause or threaten material injury, or retard the establishment of a new industry. Concurrent causes of injury, even causes that may be more important than the unfair imports, do not preclude countermeasures unless those other causes are solely responsible for whatever injury has been suffered. To be sure, the question of how to distinguish the effects of various possible causes coherently (the "non-attribution" analysis in WTO parlance) can remain a difficult one.

Given these distinctions from the safeguards context, the application of the injury test in antidumping and countervailing duty cases requires only two or perhaps three steps in the analysis. First, the relevant domestic industry must be "defined" so that the impact of imports on it can be assessed. Second, under what has sometimes been termed the "bifurcated" or "trends" version of the injury test, the domestic industry must be examined for signs of "material injury" or threat of such injury. If none are present under the bifurcated approach, analysis of causation is unnecessary. If material injury or threat is present, however, the question of its cause must be reached as the third stage of analysis. An alternative approach, sometimes termed "unitary," combines these two steps—it seeks to identify the effect on the domestic industry of unfair imports, and makes a judgment whether that effect amounts to material injury. At one time, US ITC Commissioners were quite divided over the question whether to apply a "bifurcated" or "unitary" method of analysis. More recently, the issue seems quiescent as the structure of ITC opinions tracks more closely the structure of WTO law, presumably because of a desire to make the determinations more robust to possible WTO challenges. The approach of the WTO Codes does not include an inquiry into the existence of "material injury" as a distinct stage of analysis prior to an assessment of "causation," and in that respect is closer to what has been termed "unitary" analysis in the United States.

An examination of injury under US law can occur at three different points during a dumping or countervailing duty proceeding. A "preliminary" injury investigation occurs after a case has been filed but before the Commerce Department (ITA) has made a determination whether the alleged unfair trade practice actually exists. In this preliminary investigation, the ITC decides whether there is a "reasonable indication" that the injury test can be satisfied. See Tariff Act of 1930, Sections 703, 733. If the answer is no, the investigation terminates—the idea is to "weed out" some cases early without the need for a full-blown ITA investigation or a complete injury investigation by the ITC. The "reasonable indication" standard is understood to be only a modest hurdle for petitioners.

Following an affirmative preliminary determination, the ITA investigation will proceed to conclusion. If dumping or subsidization is ultimately determined to exist, the parties return to the ITC for the "final" injury investigation. Here, the injury test is applied more stringently and the petitioners' standard of proof is higher. An affirmative determination at this stage results in the issuance of an antidumping or countervailing duty "order," with duties to be collected by Customs.

An injury analysis may also be required after a final order is issued. Prior to the Uruguay Round, exporters subject to an order could, after a time, petition for a review of the injury finding on grounds of "changed circumstances." The Uruguay Round agreements add a further requirement that antidumping and countervailing duty orders be terminated within five years of the last injury finding unless a new finding is made that they are needed to prevent the recurrence of injury (in a so-called "sunset review").

When fully staffed, the ITC has six sitting Commissioners. In any ITC vote on injury, a tie vote is considered a victory for the US petitioners.

Injury investigations under US law are not governed by the Administrative Procedure Act (though some would argue that they should be), and they are typically much less formal and structured than proceedings before many other federal regulatory agencies. Nevertheless, hearings are held, and an opportunity to present briefs and witnesses is afforded to all interested parties.

The materials that follow emphasize the substantive rather than procedural aspects of injury proceedings, and are divided between the industry definition issue and the material injury/causation issues. We omit any further consideration of the "material retardation" variant of injury because reliance on that standard is quite unusual in practice, perhaps because there is no established domestic industry to petition for relief. A rare discussion of that standard may be found in BMT Commodity Corp. v. United States, 667 F.Supp. 880 (CIT 1987).

Notes and Questions

(1) Before proceeding to the details of injury analysis, it is useful to reflect on its function. Why are the ostensibly "unfair" practices of dumping

and subsidization only "unfair" if injury results? Take the subsidies case in particular—might it be argued that if the purpose of WTO discipline on subsidies is to discourage governments from distorting the allocation of resources in the global marketplace, countermeasures ought be taken (indeed encouraged) whether or not producers in a particular importing nation are "injured?"

(2) Alternatively, suppose that dumping and subsidies are thought objectionable because of the adjustment costs that must be incurred by import-competing industries, costs that the injury test was conceived to detect. Which approach to injury analysis does this theory support—the bifurcated or the unitary approach?

(3) Recall that the injury test under the escape clause requires "serious injury," understood to be a greater level of injury than "material injury." Why not require "serious injury" here as well?

SECTION 17.2   INDUSTRY DEFINITION

Both WTO and US law define the "industry" similarly as, in most cases, "the producers as a whole of a domestic like product" or those whose output constitutes a "major proportion" of the domestic production of the like products. See, e.g., Tariff Act of 1930, Section 771(4)(A). This last proviso is designed to permit investigations to go forward even when data from a few producers are lacking. An exception to this definition of industry, invoked on occasion, is that the industry may be limited to producers in a particular geographic area. In addition, it is permissible to exclude from the industry domestic producers that are "related" to the exporters under investigation, on the grounds that they may benefit from the unfair trade in a way that masks injury to domestic producers as a whole. We will not focus on these exceptions, and instead consider the industry definition exercise for the standard case.

CERTAIN ORANGE JUICE FROM BRAZIL

USITC Inv. No. 731–TA–1089 (Final), March, 2006.
Views of the Commission.

Based on the record in this investigation, we find that an industry in the United States is materially injured by reason of imports of certain orange juice from Brazil found to be sold in the United States at less than fair value ("LTFV") [three Commissioners dissenting].

I.   Domestic Like Product

A.   In General

In determining whether an industry in the United States is materially injured or threatened with material injury by reason of imports of the subject merchandise, the Commission first defines the "domestic like product" and the "industry." Section 771(4)(A) of the Tariff Act of 1930, as amended ("the Act"), defines the relevant domestic industry as the "producers as a [w]hole of a domestic like product, or those producers whose collective output of a domestic like product constitutes a major proportion of the total domestic production of the product." In turn, the Act defines "domestic like product" as "a product which is like, or in the absence of like, most similar in characteristics and uses with, the article subject to an investigation . . ."

The decision regarding the appropriate domestic like product(s) in an investigation is a factual determination, and the Commission has applied the statutory standard of "like" or "most similar in characteristics and uses" on a case-by-case basis. No single factor is dispositive, and the Commission may consider other factors it deems relevant based on the facts of a particular investigation. The Commission looks for clear dividing lines among possible like products and disregards minor variations. Although the Commission must accept the determination of the Department of Commerce ("Commerce") as to the scope of the imported merchandise allegedly sold at LTFV, the Commission determines what domestic product is like the imported articles Commerce has identified. * * *

B. Product Description

In its final determination, Commerce defined the imported merchandise within the scope of the investigation as follows: Certain orange juice for transport and/or further manufacturing produced in two different forms: (1) Frozen orange juice in a highly concentrated form, sometimes referred to as frozen concentrated orange juice for further manufacturing (FCOJM); and (2) pasteurized single-strength orange juice which has not been concentrated, referred to as Not–From–Concentrate (NFC). Commerce expressly excluded from the scope reconstituted and retail orange juice as follows: Excluded from the scope of the investigation are reconstituted orange juice and frozen orange juice for retail (FCOJR). Reconstituted orange juice is produced through further manufacture of FCOJM, by adding water, oils and essences to the orange juice concentrate. FCOJR is concentrated typically at 42 degrees Brix, in a frozen state, packed in retail size containers ready for sale to consumers. FCOJR is a finished consumer product, and is produced through manufacture of FCOJM, a bulk manufacturer's product.

C. Analysis

Petitioners, as well as Respondents Coca–Cola, Louis Dreyfus and Cutrale, argue that the Commission should find a single domestic like product that includes conventional FCOJM and NFC and organic FCOJM and NFC, coextensive with Commerce's scope. Respondents Citrosuco and Tropicana contend that FCOJM and NFC are two separate like products. Respondent Montecitrus urges the Commission to find four separate like products: (1) organic FCOJM, (2) organic NFC, (3) conventional FCOJM, and (4) conventional NFC.

1. Whether Conventional FCOJM and Conventional NFC Are Separate Domestic Like Products

Physical Characteristics and Uses: FCOJM and NFC are both made from the same types of "round" oranges and therefore bear a substantial degree of similarity in terms of physical characteristics. FCOJM is six or seven times more concentrated than NFC. The differing degrees of concentration of FCOJM and NFC are reflected in the amount of sugar they contain by weight. The sugar content of a solution is measured on the Brix scale, which indicates the percentage by weight of sugar contained in a solution at a particular temperature. FCOJM typically has a Brix of about 65 whereas NFC generally has a Brix of almost 12.17. Despite this difference in Brix levels, purchasers generally found both forms comparable. Twelve out of 18 US purchasers reported that FCOJM and NFC are comparable with regard to shelf life. With respect to purchasers who reported purchasing both forms of the product, 8 out of 9 purchasers reported that FCOJM and NFC are comparable in terms of color and ingredients, 7 out of 9 purchasers reported them comparable for viscosity, packaging, and vitamin content, 6 out of 9 purchasers reported comparable shelf-life, and 6 out of 8 reported comparable Brix levels. FCOJM and NFC are both bulk intermediate products predominantly used to produce single-strength orange juice for retail consumption. * * *

Interchangeability: At the bulk level, conventional FCOJM and NFC are interchangeable in the sense that either can be used to produce single-strength retail orange juice. We recognize that NFC is rarely, if ever, used to produce FCOJM and FCOJM cannot be "unconcentrated" and converted into NFC. However, while there are physical differences, the predominant use of both FCOJM and NFC is still the production of single-strength retail juice. Furthermore, almost all purchasers who purchase both FCOJM and NFC reported that the bulk level products are comparable when specific factors are considered. Accordingly, we do not view the fact that FCOJM and NFC are different physical forms of the same wholesale product as detracting from their essential interchangeability in the manufacture of retail orange juice.

Channels of Distribution: FCOJM and NFC are generally sold in bulk to distributors, remanufacturers, and packagers. The questionnaire responses received by the Commission show that conventional FCOJM and NFC have significant overlap in the channels of distribution, particularly in the remanufacturers and repackagers channel. In addition, the largest US purchasers of bulk orange juice buy both FCOJM and NFC and reported that they further process or repackage both at the same facilities.

Common Manufacturing Facilities, Employees, and Methods: The manufacturing processes, employees, and facilities used to make FCOJM and NFC demonstrate a significant degree of overlap. The record indicates that domestic producers accounting for [confidential] percent of US production in crop year 2004/05 manufacture FCOJM and NFC at the same plant facility using the same employees. Data on the record also show that in the manufacturing facilities which produce both FCOJM and NFC, a significant majority of the production costs of both products are incurred during the same manufacturing process and on shared equipment, particularly when the expense of the raw material used in both products (i.e., round oranges) is considered in the overall cost. During the manufacturing process, oranges used for FCOJM and NFC are all sized, graded, washed, and stored in bins until the point of juice extraction. The equipment used to extract juice from the oranges is the same for FCOJM and NFC. The extractor and finisher pressures used on the equipment depend upon the ripeness of the orange, regardless of whether FCOJM or NFC is produced.

After juice extraction, the production processes for FCOJM and NFC diverge. Juice made into FCOJM is sent to an evaporator where most of the water is taken out by vacuum and heat to obtain a base concentration level, typically 65 degrees Brix. Juice made into NFC is sent to a pasteurizer and is processed by flash-heating without removing any water content from the juice. Following these separate processes, both products enter storage until they are needed for production of retail orange juice. * * *

Producer and Customer Perceptions: Petitioners and three Respondents argue that FCOJM and NFC are perceived to be similar products, whereas two other Respondents insist that NFC is perceived to be superior to FCOJM. The questionnaire responses addressing customer perceptions held by the immediate purchasers (e.g., remanufacturers, packers, grocery stores, and food service establishments) suggest that these customers perceive NFC as superior to FCOJM not because they find NFC has superior handling or quality features at the wholesale level, but because NFC single-strength orange juice is marketed downstream as a premium product at the retail level.

Price: Throughout the period examined, domestically produced conventional NFC carried a price premium at the wholesale level over domestically produced conventional FCOJM with a $0.25 per pound (or [confidential] percent) price premium in crop year 2001/02, a $0.25 per pound (or 24 percent) price premium in crop year 2002/03, a $0.38 per pound (or [confidential] percent) price premium in crop year 2003/04, and a $0.36 per pound (or [confidential] percent) price premium in crop year 2004/05. The responses to the Commission's questionnaires confirm that, on average, NFC carries a price premium over FCOJM at the wholesale level. Petitioners and certain of the Respondents agree, however, that the wholesale price premium for NFC is driven primarily by its higher storage and transportation costs. This is distinct from pricing at the retail level where brand names and advertising strongly affect pricing. Furthermore, the wholesale price premium for NFC overstates any price premium at the retail level. While NFC may have a wholesale price premium over FCOJM, the processing of NFC for retail does not require the reconstitution costs that FCOJM must incur (i.e., the addition of water, oil, and essences which had been removed during the evaporation process). These reconstitution costs are passed along to retail FCOJ purchasers at the next level of trade.

Conclusion: On balance, we find that the six like product factors discussed above weigh in favor of finding a single domestic like product. We also find it significant that, unlike in the preliminary phase, three Respondents (i.e., Coca–Cola, Cutrale, and Louis Dreyfus) have urged the Commission to find a single domestic like product in this final phase investigation. Absent any clear dividing line based upon the above analysis, we find that conventional FCOJM and NFC are a single domestic like product.

2. Whether Organic FCOJM and Organic NFC Are Separate Domestic Like Products

Physical Characteristics and Uses: Organic FCOJM and organic NFC are produced from the same types of "round" oranges used to produce conventional FCOJM and NFC. Under the US Department of Agriculture ("USDA")'s national organic production ("NOP") Regulations, which were implemented in October 2002, organic groves may be separate from conventional groves, with enough of a "buffer zone" between the two to make sure synthetic pesticides and fertilizers do not reach an organic grove. However, the same tree can produce organic and non-organic oranges during its life cycle. While organic oranges typically yield a higher Brix level, we have already established that purchasers view different forms of juice as comparable despite differences in Brix level. Like conventional FCOJM and NFC, organic FCOJM and NFC predominantly are used to produce single-strength orange juice for retail.

Interchangeability: USDA implemented NOP Regulations in October 2002. These NOP Regulations are the governing standards with respect to domestically produced organic FCOJM and NFC. Because of NOP Regulations, purchasers of organic FCOJM and/or NFC intending to produce an organic retail product cannot substitute conventional FCOJM and/or NFC. On the other hand, purchasers of conventional FCOJM do not typically substitute organic FCOJM and NFC because of the price premium associated with organic FCOJM and NFC.

Channels of Distribution: Organic-specific distributors typically sell their oranges to smaller juice processing plants, and organic orange juice is distributed to organic-certified retail warehouses. Some firms reported in their questionnaire responses that conventional and organic FCOJM and NFC have similar distribution channels while other firms reported that they do not. It is clear, however, that just like conventional bulk orange juice, bulk organic orange juice is used to produce a single-strength consumer product that is then predominantly distributed for retail sale in grocery stores that also sell conventional orange juice. We find that, on balance, organic orange juice and conventional orange juice are sold in overlapping channels of distribution.

Common Manufacturing Facilities, Employees, and Methods: As explained above, while organic oranges must be grown on segregated trees according to special procedures, the same tree can produce organic and conventional oranges during its life cycle. It is true that under the NOP Regulations, organic groves must be kept separate from conventional orange groves by at least 50 feet, and those same regulations prohibit grove owners from using any synthetic pesticides or fertilizers for at least three years before they are permitted to market their fruit using the organic label. But organic orange juice processors use the same production equipment as conventional FCOJM and NFC processors, and produce both conventional and organic orange juice on that equipment, albeit on different production runs. Because of this, and the fact that organic and conventional oranges can be grown on the same tree during the tree's life cycle, we find, on balance, that organic and conventional FCOJM and NFC orange juice use common manufacturing equipment, employees, and methods.

Producer and Customer Perceptions: With respect to organic FCOJM and NFC, the record on producer and customer perceptions is very limited. Although some responding purchasers to the Commission's questionnaire reported that organic orange juice is perceived as healthier than conventional FCOJM and NFC, these perceptions apply to the retail product rather than the wholesale product.

Price: Organic NFC carries a substantial price premium over conventional NFC, which was confirmed by the purchaser questionnaire responses received by the Commission.

Conclusion: With respect to organic FCOJM and NFC, the Commission received questionnaire responses from one domestic producer of organic orange juice and a small number of US purchasers. Thus, the information on the record in this investigation is rather limited with respect to organic orange juice. We have considered the six like product factors discussed above based on the available evidence, and we find that they weigh in favor of finding a single domestic like product. Absent any clear dividing line between conventional and organic orange juice, we find a single domestic like product consisting of conventional FCOJM, conventional NFC, organic FCOJM, and organic NFC, coextensive with Commerce's scope. Throughout the remainder of this opinion, we will call this domestic like product "certain orange juice."

Notes and Questions

(1) FCOJM is different from NFC in the sense that the former must be reconstituted before it can be consumed, while the latter is ready for ultimate consumption and simply needs to be repackaged for retail sale. Can products different in this fashion nevertheless be "like?"

(2) Why should "channels of distribution" be relevant to the inquiry? Toilets and shingles are both sold in building materials stores like Home Depot. Does that make them "like?"

(3) Likewise, why focus on "common manufacturing facilities, employees and methods?" Imagine that a woodworker uses a lathe to make a wooden table leg in a furniture factory. He then uses the same lathe to make a wooden doorknob. Like products?

(4) In discussing "producer and consumer perceptions," the ITC notes that a number of purchasers seem to regard the not from concentrate orange

juice as a premium product. It then dismisses this observation on the grounds that "these customers perceive NFC as superior to FCOJM not because they find NFC has superior handling or quality features at the wholesale level, but because NFC single-strength orange juice is marketed downstream as a premium product at the retail level." Persuasive?

(5) In discussing price, the ITC acknowledges that NFC carries a price premium at the retail level, and an even greater premium at the wholesale level because of the further processing that must be done on FCOJM. Likewise, the ITC acknowledges a "substantial price premium" for organic orange juice products. Are such price differentials not compelling evidence that the products are unlike? Would it make sense to look deeper into the relationship between these prices, such as to inquire whether changes in the prices of the two goods are highly correlated? Would it be appropriate to deem a generic product and a premium product to be "like" if the latter carried a large premium, but the ratio of the two prices, or perhaps the absolute differential between them, was always about the same?

(6) A related set of issues comes up in cases involving both finished and semi-finished goods. It may be quite clear that the semi-finished product (say, a partially manufactured steel flange) is not a viable substitute for the finished product. Yet, with a bit of further manufacturing, the semi-finished product becomes a finished product. Moreover, imports of finished products can most certainly affect the fortunes of domestic manufacturers of semi-finished products. Should the domestic producers of the semi-finished products be included in the "industry?" Is it permissible to do so under the law? Recall the similar issue that arose in the safeguards context in *US Lamb*, in which it was held by the WTO Appellate Body that growers of live lambs could not be deemed to produce a product "like" the imported lamb meat at issue there.

(7) As indicated earlier, the ITC can base its findings on harm to a regional industry. The key factors are that the regional producers must sell all or almost all of their production in the region, the regional market must not be supplied to any substantial degree by US producers from outside the region and all or almost all of the regional producers must be materially injured. Those requirements are discussed in a series of opinions in which the Court of International Trade found the ITC had erred in its application of the statute. Atlantic Sugar, Ltd. v. United States, 519 F.Supp. 916 (CIT 1981); 553 F.Supp. 1055 (CIT 1982); 573 F.Supp. 1142 (CIT 1983).

(8) The concept of "like product" appears at many points in GATT. How does the like product analysis of the ITC compare to the analysis in GATT and WTO cases earlier in this book, such as *EC Asbestos*?

SECTION 17.3   MATERIAL INJURY OR THREAT BY REASON OF UNFAIRLY TRADED IMPORTS

The definition of "material injury" is set out in Section 771(7) of the Tariff Act of 1930, along with the factors to be considered by the ITC in its analysis. These provisions should be reviewed at this time, along with the relevant parts of Article 3 of the Antidumping Agreement and Article 15 of the Subsidies and Countervailing Measures Agreement.

As noted earlier, WTO case law in this area is spotty. In one of the earliest rulings, Thailand—Anti–Dumping Duties on Angles, Shapes and Sections of Iron or Non–Alloy Steel and H–Beams from Poland, WT/DS122/AB/R, adopted April 5, 2001, the Appellate Body held, inter alia, that the factors enumerated in article 3.4 of the Antidumping Agreement *must* be considered during the course of injury analysis by national authorities. The same rule presumably applies in countervailing duty cases.

The question of how much data investigating authorities must gather has also arisen. In Guatemala—Definitive Antidumping Measures on Grey Portland Cement from Mexico, WT/DS156/R, adopted November 17, 2000 (not appealed), the panel held that a single year's worth of data on imports and industry conditions could be adequate (Id., para. 8.266). The Committee on Antidumping Practices, however, has issued a non-binding recommendation urging members to base their analysis on data for at least three years. Id.

The question has also arisen as to whether, when imports from a particular country are found to be dumped, the investigating authorities must base their injury analysis exclusively on the dumped imports from that country or may instead treat all imports from the country in question as dumped (when assessing, for example, the "volume of dumped imports"). In European Communities—Antidumping Duties on Imports of Cotton–Type Bed Linen from India, WT/DS141/R, panel report adopted March 12, 2001, the panel ruled that all imports from a country that is a source of dumped imports may be treated as dumped for purposes of the injury analysis. Id., para. 6.136. That issue was not addressed in the appeal of the case.

We excerpt one other WTO ruling below concerning causation and non-attribution analysis, but will develop a broader overview of how injury analysis proceeds using two ITC cases.

FRESH CUT ROSES FROM COLOMBIA AND ECUADOR
USITC Inv. No. 731–TA–684–85 (Final), 1995.
Views of the Commission.

[W]e determine that an industry in the United States is neither materially injured nor threatened with material injury by reason of imports of fresh cut roses from Colombia and Ecuador that are sold in the United States at less than fair value (LTFV).

* * *

[W]e reaffirm our preliminary determination that there is a single like product in these investigations consisting of all fresh cut roses regardless of variety or size. Consequently, we determine that the domestic industry consists of all producers of fresh cut roses.

* * *

Because only a reasonable overlap of competition is required, we cumulatively assess the volume and price effects of all subject imports in determining whether there is material injury by reason of those imports.

IV.   No Material Injury by Reason of LTFV Imports

* * * For the reasons discussed below, we determine that the domestic industry producing fresh cut roses is not materially injured by reason of LTFV imports from Colombia and Ecuador.

A.   *The Volume of Subject Imports*

The volume of imports from Colombia and Ecuador on a cumulated basis increased by quantity from 380.4 million stems in 1991 to 438.2 million stems in 1992 to 534.8 million stems in 1993, and was 413.2 million stems in interim 1993 compared with 467.2 million stems interim 1994. In value terms, subject imports increased from $92.6 million in 1991 to $94.4 million in 1992 to $109.2 million in 1993. In interim 1994, subject imports were valued at $101.6 million compared with $86.3 million in interim 1993. The volume of US shipments of cumulated subject imports followed similar trends, increasing in absolute terms throughout the period of investigation.

Market share of cumulated subject imports increased by quantity throughout the period of investigation from 46.1 percent in 1991 to 56.0 percent in 1993; the market share of cumulated subject imports was 60.6 percent in interim 1994 compared with 57.0 percent in interim 1993. By value, the market share of cumulated subject imports increased from 39.8 percent in 1991 to 46.6 percent in 1993, and was 52.1 percent in interim 1994 compared with 47.6 percent in interim 1993. As noted above, the data for apparent US consumption based on Commission questionnaire data is derived from a smaller base of domestic producers than data obtained from USDA. Based on apparent consumption derived from USDA data, the market share of cumulated subject imports was lower, increasing from 37.7 percent in 1991 to 41.6 percent in 1992 to 47.5 percent in 1993 by quantity.

Despite the absolute volume and market share of cumulated subject imports, and the increases in their volume and market share that occurred during the period, we do not find the volume of subject imports to be significant for several reasons. First, while absolute volume of cumulated subject imports increased by 40.6 percent from 1991 to 1993, and by 13.1 percent between interim periods, the rate of increase in their market share did not rise commensurately, increasing by 9.9 percentage points from 1991 to 1993 and by 3.6 percentage points between interim periods. This is due to the 15.6 increase in overall apparent US consumption by quantity between 1991 and 1993 and the 6.3 percent increase between interim periods. This fact suggests that the subject imports were sold into important new markets and did not significantly displace domestic fresh cut roses in their existing markets.

Second, the fact that subject imports served largely to satisfy increases in demand in the mass merchandiser market further supports the conclusion that the volume of subject imports is not significant. Importers of roses from Colombia and Ecuador aggressively targeted and developed the mass merchandiser market over the period of investigation. With few exceptions, US growers do not appear to have aggressively targeted this market, but rather focused primarily on their traditional retail customer base. Moreover, domestic producers reportedly would not be able to provide consistently the large quantities of roses that mass merchandisers require. Because there is substantial evidence that the mass merchandiser market is the fastest growing segment of the market, and there is no evidence that the retail florist segment is growing, we believe that the mass merchandiser market accounted for most of the growth in US consumption over the period of investigation and a large proportion of subject imports served this market.

In addition, US growers are unable to satisfy demand during times of peak demand, especially during the Valentine's Day season, which accounts for the largest volume of rose sales for any given period. During this period of high demand, US growers in many instances can only supply partial allocations of red roses to purchasers. In addition, growers will many times force purchasers to purchase other types of flowers (e.g., non-red roses) in order to obtain the sought after red roses. For purchasers, availability of supply is an important factor in purchasing considerations. Also, due to the limits on their ability to increase production in the short term, US growers cannot sufficiently increase their rose production to meet Valentine's Day demand. Therefore, fresh cut roses have been imported to meet domestic demand both for the mass merchandiser segment of the market throughout the year, as well as other segments (e.g., retail florist segment) during periods of peak demand.

Moreover, the limited substitutability of domestic roses and subject imports, as discussed in the next section, diminishes the volume impact of the subject imports. Non-price factors have a significant impact on purchasers' decisions.

For these reasons, we find that the volumes of subject imports are not significant.

B.   The Effect of Subject Imports on Domestic Prices

In evaluating the effect of LTFV imports on prices, the Commission considers whether there has been significant price underselling of imports and whether the imports depress prices to a significant degree or prevent price increases that otherwise would have occurred, to a significant degree.

A number of factors are relevant to our determination of the price effect of subject imports on domestic producers' prices including the limited degree of substitutability between the domestic and subject roses, the nature of demand for roses, and the availability of supply.

The more substitutable products are, the more likely that potential purchasers will make their relative purchasing decisions based upon price differences between the products. Conversely, where there is a high degree of product differentiation, products are less substitutable, and price is less likely to be a determining factor in purchasing decisions. Several non-price factors reduce the substitutability between domestic roses and roses from Colombia and Ecuador. As noted previously, domestic producers and producers of roses in Colombia and Ecuador grow different varieties of roses. In general, long, thick stems, large blooms, and vibrant colors are characteristics of Colombian and Ecuadorean roses that distinguish them from domestic roses. Freshness and longevity are favored characteristics of domestic roses.

We find that price plays a subordinate role to other factors such as product quality, variety, and the seasonality of demand. Most purchasers reported that domestic roses were inferior in quality to subject imports. For purchasers, product quality—which includes physical attributes such as stem length and thickness, bloom size, color, freshness, and durability (vase-life)—was more important than price. Purchasers designated bloom size and availability of particular quantities and types of roses as the two most important factors they consider when making purchases. The Commission contacted specific purchasers named in the domestic industry's lost sales allegations. Many of these purchasers confirmed that subject imports were purchased in lieu of domestic roses for non-price reasons, such as product quality and availability.

In many instances, despite the availability of lower-priced roses, sales of more expensive rose varieties increased. This further confirms that price plays a subordinate role to non-price factors such as product quality. For example, sales of the Kardinal rose, a premium quality and relatively expensive domestic rose variety, increased at a faster rate than lower-priced domestic rose varieties such as sweetheart and Cara Mia roses. The product comparisons also show that large quantities of the premium imported Madame del Bard rose (the highest rated imported rose) were sold even when they were priced higher than the domestic Kardinal rose (the highest rated domestic rose) in the same periods. In other instances, the domestic Kardinal rose oversold the Madame del Bard rose.

Because prices of roses sold on a spot basis tend to fluctuate widely, often changing several times per day, the usefulness of the pricing comparisons in these investigations is limited. In addition, certain comparisons were based on sales of significantly different quantities, which could have affected the relative prices. Due to these factors, as well as the limited substitutability of the domestic and imported products, we find that the pricing comparisons have less probative value.

Nevertheless, a consideration of the price comparisons in these investigations showed mixed underselling and overselling by the subject imports with no consistent trend across channels of distribution (e.g., sales to wholesalers versus sales to mass merchandisers) or by type of sale (e.g., spot sales versus standing order sales). For example, in most comparisons, the Madame del Bard roses from Colombia and Ecuador oversold the domestic Royalty on standing order sales to wholesalers and spot sales to mass merchandisers, but undersold the Royalty in spot sales to wholesalers. For non-red roses, on an aggregate basis, there was also mixed underselling and overselling by subject imports showing no consistent pattern. We find the low degree of substitutability and the relative importance of non-price factors discussed above diminishes the significance of any underselling.

We find little or no evidence of price depression. The pricing data we collected show that, based on quarterly f.o.b. prices, the prices for Colombian, Ecuadorean and US fresh cut roses fluctuated over the period of investigation. Prices for red roses generally peaked in the first quarter of each year of the investigation, falling to lower levels during the remaining quarters and reaching their nadir in the third quarter. Prices of non-red roses also demonstrated some seasonal fluctuation, although not as dramatic. Taking into account seasonal fluctuations, prices of domestic fresh cut red roses were generally steady, decreasing only slightly during the period of investigation, despite the fact that prices for subject imports of red roses fluctuated downward. Moreover, annual unit values for red roses were relatively stable during the period of investigation. There were no consistent trends for non-red roses, which supports our conclusion that there is limited substitutability between subject imports and the domestic like product. Even if price trends are similar, however, this would not necessarily warrant a conclusion that any lower-priced Colombian and Ecuadorean fresh cut roses depressed prices of domestic fresh cut roses. Rather, we find that seasonal demand shifts are driving pricing patterns.

We also do not find that subject imports suppressed domestic fresh cut rose prices to a significant degree. Petitioners argued that they were unable to raise prices sufficiently to cover costs, but we do not find that domestic growers could have raised prices sufficiently to cover their costs even in the absence of LTFV imports from Colombia and Ecuador. Most purchasers stated that the current price of Colombian and Ecuadorean roses would have to be more than ten percent higher to cause them to shift to purchases of domestic roses. Indeed, a significant number of purchasers stated that price was not really a factor at all in their purchasing decisions, which further supports the finding of limited substitutability between subject imports and the domestic like product and minimizes the possibility of any significant adverse price effects from the subject imports. In addition, most importers stated that despite antidumping duties, their purchases of subject imports would remain unchanged. This reflects the significant influence of non-price factors in purchasing decisions and confirms our conclusion that there is limited substitutability between domestic roses and subject imports.

Given the importance of non-price factors and the lack of correlation between the prices of domestic and subject roses, we do not find that subject imports have depressed or suppressed domestic rose prices to a significant degree.

C.   The Impact of Subject Imports on the Domestic Industry

We conclude that subject imports did not have an adverse impact on the domestic industry sufficient to warrant an affirmative determination. Many US producers reported that they were facing difficulties due to increased production costs and reduced volumes of rose sales, and an inability to increase rose prices. We determine, however, that any failure by the domestic industry to raise prices sufficiently, or increase their rose production to cover their costs was not due to LTFV imports to any significant degree. Although cumulated subject imports increased in volume and market share, we find that these increases, and the level of market share, have not adversely impacted the domestic industry. The growth in volume of subject imports served largely to supplement demand during peak seasons. In addition, subject imports satisfied increases in US demand in the expanding mass merchandiser market, a segment of the market that domestic growers have failed to supply to any significant degree.

Further, as discussed in the previous section, purchasers tend to base their rose purchasing decisions not on price but on a variety of non-price factors, and they find subject imports and roses sold by the domestic industry are differentiated. We find that the low substitutability between imports and domestic products, as well as the inability of the domestic industry to increase production in the short term in response to any price increase, indicates that subject imports have not had an adverse impact on the domestic industry. The COMPAS (Commercial Policy Analysis System) output further supports the conclusion that domestic prices, shipment volumes, and overall revenues would not have been significantly different from their 1993 levels in the absence of unfairly traded fresh cut roses from Colombia and Ecuador. This, together with the mixed evidence of underselling and the tendency of pricing trends to track seasonal fluctuation in demand, support the conclusion that the imports had no significant impact.

Accordingly, we conclude that the domestic industry is not materially injured by reason of LTFV imports of fresh cut roses from Colombia and Ecuador.

Notes and Questions

(1) What is the ITC's response to the observation that the volume and market share of imports has risen rapidly during the period of investigation? Does it persuade you? Can one truly say that the volume of imports is "insignificant" with a market share of 50–60%? Suppose it is true that many imports sell through mass outlets such as Sam's Club and Costco. Can it fairly be said that such products do not much affect domestic firms that sell through traditional florists? What of the notion that domestic growers have difficulty meeting periods of peak demand, and imports fill the gap—does it follow that imports do not cause injury?

(2) The ITC in *Fresh Roses* "cumulates" the imports from Ecuador and Colombia. It has long been settled that when an investigation covers several producers from a single country, those producers may be aggregated in the analysis of whether the unfair imports cause injury—a separate analysis for each producer is not required. Many cases involve allegations against producers in a number of countries, however, and the question arises as to when "cumulation" is also permissible across countries. A provision to authorize cumulation was added to US law in 1984, though the ITC had cumulated on its own authority previously. See Section 771(7)(G) of the Tariff Act of 1930. After the Uruguay Round, cumulation is permitted under WTO law as long as the extent of the unfair practice in each country is not "de minimis" and "a cumulative assessment of the effects of the imports is appropriate in light of the conditions of competition between imported products and the conditions of competition between the imported products and the like domestic product." See AD Agreement, Art. 3.3; Agreement on Subsidies, Art. 15.3. The result of cumulation, of course, is that producers in a nation with a small market share, and perhaps declining exports to the United States, may be found to be a cause of material injury because they have been aggregated with larger or more successful exporters from other nations. Is this reasonable?

(3) The reference at the end of the excerpt to COMPAS (Commercial Policy Analysis System) pertains to a type of simulation model that has been used by staff economists of the ITC in dumping and countervailing duty investigations. The inputs into the simulation include baseline information on price and output, and estimates of such factors as: the elasticity of demand for domestic and imported goods; the cross-elasticity of demand (degree of substitutability) between imported and domestic goods; the elasticity of supply of domestic production, the imports under investigation, and "non-subject" imports; and the margins of dumping or subsidization. The model then estimates the impact on domestic prices and output that would result from a cessation of dumping or subsidization, or from a withdrawal of the unfair imports from the market altogether. As the *Roses* case indicates, Commissioners often pay some attention to the results of these simulations, but rarely rely on them as the primary basis for their determination. For further discussion of these more explicitly "economic" approaches to injury analysis, see Richard Boltuck, Assessing the Effects on the Domestic Industry of Price Dumping, *in* Policy Implications of Antidumping Measures 99 (P.M. Tharakan ed., 1991); Michael Knoll, An Economic Approach to the Determination of Injury Under United States Antidumping and Countervailing Duty Law, 22 N.Y.U.J.Intl.L. & Pol. 37 (1989). A survey of five "approaches" to causation analysis at the ITC may be found in Seth Kaplan, Injury and Causation in USITC Antidumping Determinations: Five Recent Approaches, *in* Policy Implications of Antidumping Measures, supra. A critical discussion of ITC practice is that of Ronald Cass & Warren Schwartz, Causality, Coherence and Transparency in the Implementation of International Trade Laws, *in* Fair Exchange: Reforming Trade Remedy Laws (Michael Trebilcock & Robert York eds., 1990). The argument that "injury" should not include a loss of monopoly profit is put forward in Diane Wood, "Unfair" Trade Injury: A Competition–Based Approach, 41 Stan.L.Rev. 1153 (1989).

CERTAIN ORANGE JUICE FROM BRAZIL

USITC Inv. No. 731–TA–1089 (Final), March, 2006.
Views of the Commission.

[The ITC found in favor of the petitioners on the basis of a 3–3 vote. The analysis of the three Commissioners voting in favor of the injury finding follows.]

III. Material Injury By Reason of the Subject Imports

A. General Legal Standards

In the final phase of antidumping or countervailing duty investigations, the Commission determines whether an industry in the United States is materially injured by reason of the imports under investigation. In making this determination, the Commission must consider the volume of subject imports, their effect on prices for the domestic like product, and their impact on domestic producers of the domestic like product, but only in the context of US production operations. The statute defines "material injury" as "harm which is not inconsequential, immaterial, or unimportant." In assessing whether the domestic industry is materially injured by reason of subject imports, we consider all relevant economic factors that bear on the state of the industry in the United States. No single factor is dispositive, and all relevant factors are considered "within the context of the business cycle and conditions of competition that are distinctive to the affected industry."

For the reasons stated below, we determine that the domestic industry producing certain orange juice is materially injured by reason of subject imports from Brazil.

B. Conditions of Competition

Several conditions of competition inform our analysis of whether the domestic industry is materially injured by reason of subject imports from Brazil.

1. Supply Conditions

There are currently 20 extractor-processors producing certain orange juice in the United States. Because there is no economical way to import oranges, domestic processors are wholly dependent on US (mostly Florida) growers for their supply of oranges. Orange juice processors face significant year-to-year fluctuations in the supply of their primary input, round oranges. These fluctuations result from both weather conditions (e.g., freezes, hurricanes, and droughts) and other factors including citrus diseases (e.g., Citrus Canker and Citrus Greening). During the period examined, the Florida orange crop declined from 230 million boxes in crop year 2001/02 to 203 million boxes in crop year 2002/03, and increased to 242 million boxes in crop year 2003/04, the second largest Florida orange crop in history. However, in the aftermath of Hurricanes Charley, Frances, and Jeanne, which struck Florida's orange groves in the late summer and early fall of 2004, the Florida orange crop declined to 149.6 million boxes in crop year 2004/05. Florida orange growers reported that the 2004 and 2005 Florida hurricanes resulted in both significant crop damage and the spread of citrus diseases, making it necessary to replant a substantial number of orange trees. In the aftermath of Hurricane Wilma, which struck Florida in the fall of 2005, it is projected that the size of the Florida orange crop will recover only moderately to 190 million boxes in crop year 2005/06. * * *

2. Demand Conditions

The United States is the largest consumer of orange juice in the world. Domestic demand for certain orange juice is primarily a function of demand for downstream products using FCOJM and NFC, predominantly retail orange juice. The parties all agreed that the popularity of low carbohydrate diets during the period examined reduced demand for orange juice. Nevertheless, record data indicate that apparent US consumption of the domestic like product increased modestly over the period examined. Apparent US consumption fell from 1.45 billion gallons single-strength equivalent (SSE) in crop year 2001/02 to 1.43 billion gallons SSE in crop year 2002/03 before increasing slightly to 1.44 billion gallons SSE in crop year 2003/04, and increasing to 1.50 billion gallons SSE in crop year 2004/05, for an overall increase of 3.5 percent. * * *

C. Volume of Subject Imports

Section 771(7)(C)(i) of the Act provides that the "Commission shall consider whether the volume of imports of the merchandise, or any increase in that volume, either in absolute terms or relative to production or consumption in the United States, is significant." For the reasons discussed below, we find the absolute volume of subject imports to be significant and we also find the overall increase in subject import volume over the period examined, both in absolute terms and relative to production and consumption in the United States, to be significant.

By quantity, subject imports increased by 122.0 million gallons SSE[1] or 111.2 percent during the period examined.[2] The parties agree, and the

---

1. SSE gallons are a standard volume measurement for orange juice at a ready-to-drink concentration level of 11.8 Brix. One gallon of SSE orange juice of 11.8 degrees Brix is equivalent to 1.029 pounds solids.

2. [original note 133] The quantity of subject imports increased from 109.7 million gallons SSE in crop year 2001/02 to 227.3 million gallons SSE in crop year 2002/03, dropped to 154.2 million gallons SSE in crop year 2003/04, and increased to 231.7 million gallons SSE in crop year 2004/05. By value, subject imports increased from $99.2 million in crop year 2001/02 to $242.3 million in crop year 2002/03, dropped to $142.7 million in crop year 2003/04, and increased to $232.5 million in crop year 2004/05. CR/PR at Table IV–2.

Respondents argue that the Commission should use a three-year period of investigation between crop year 2002/03 and crop year 2004/05 rather than a four-year period of investigation between crop year 2001/02 and crop year 2004/05. Respondents state that it is customary Commission practice for the Commission to use a three-year period of investigation and they also argue that the Commission should not use crop year 2001/02 as the starting period for the period examined because (according to Respondents) that crop year was "an aberrational year for imports from Brazil" with historically low levels. Respondents also contend that the Commission's selection of a four-year period of investigation is arbitrary and that the Commission could have used an even longer period of investigation such as five years.

record confirms, that imports of orange juice are necessary to meet domestic demand. It is not surprising, therefore, that the greatest annual increases in subject imports occurred in crop years 2002/03 and 2004/05, when US shipments were at their lowest levels during the period examined.

Subject imports' share of the US market more than doubled during the period examined, increasing by 7.9 percentage points overall. Subject imports' share of the US market climbed from 7.6 percent in crop year 2001/02 to 15.9 percent in crop year 2002/03, dropped to 10.7 percent in crop year 2003/04, and climbed to 15.4 percent in crop year 2004/05. * * *

Regardless of the period examined, we find the volume of subject imports to be significant. Although we examined the longer-term data supplied by Respondents, our finding that the volume of subject imports is significant does not depend upon an "arbitrary" selection of crop year 2001/02 as the start date for the period examined, but rather upon our assessment that Brazilian subject imports increasingly exceeded residual demand throughout the period examined. Furthermore, we note that subject imports rose sharply in the most recent crop years from 154.2 million pounds solids in crop year 2003/04 to 231.7 million pounds solids in crop year 2004/05. * * *

For the above reasons, we find that subject import volume is significant, both in absolute terms and relative to domestic production and consumption.

D.   Price Effects of the Subject Imports

Section 771(C)(ii) of the Act provides that, in evaluating the price effects of subject imports,

> the Commission shall consider whether—(I) there has been significant price underselling by the imported merchandise as compared with the price of domestic like products of the United States, and (II) the effect of imports of such merchandise otherwise depresses prices to a significant degree or prevents price increases, which otherwise would have occurred, to a significant degree.

The Commission has discretion to set its period of investigation. While the Commission typically gathers data for the most recent three full years, plus the most recent interim period, it has on occasion deviated from doing so, when, for example, conditions of competition for the industry warrant such a deviation. The Commission has examined longer time periods where it found that an examination of the longer time period would better allow it to understand the conditions in the market, the cyclical nature of an industry, or generally provide it with a broader perspective of the market.

We found that in this industry, which is subject to unpredictable domestic production cycles due to natural factors such as hurricanes, frost, and disease, there does not appear to be a "normal" baseline year for import levels. Agricultural products (including certain orange juice) often face natural production cycles.

Consequently, the Commission found it more reliable to gather industry data for crop years October 2001 through September 2002, October 2002 through September 2003, October 2003 through September 2004, and October 2004 through September 2005 in order to assess any apparent cyclicality and the unpredictable nature of domestic production. * * *

The domestic market for certain orange juice is competitive and price-sensitive. Eleven out of 18 US purchasers reported in their questionnaire responses that subject imports and the domestic like product are either "always" or "frequently" interchangeable. Other market participants reported almost evenly in their questionnaire responses that subject imports and the domestic like product are "frequently" or "always" or "sometimes" interchangeable. Although most US purchasers ranked quality as the most important factor in purchasing decisions, available data do not suggest significant quality distinctions between the domestic like product and subject imports. Most US purchasers ranked price as the second most important factor in their purchasing decisions.

The pricing data in this final phase of the investigation were requested for one conventional FCOJM product, one conventional NFC product, and one organic FCOJM product. * * *

The pricing data indicate significant underselling of the domestic like product by the subject merchandise. FCOJM (Product 1) accounted for the overwhelming majority of subject imports, by volume, during the period examined and totaled more than 90 percent of subject imports in each year. FCOJM subject imports undersold domestically produced FCOJM in 41 out of 48 quarterly comparisons, with margins of underselling averaging 8.2 percent. Although we note that the comparisons for NFC (Product 2) show numerous instances of overselling, we find the overall underselling to be significant because FCOJM subject imports dwarfed NFC subject imports, which accounted for less than 10 percent of subject imports by volume during the period examined. We also find this underselling to be significant because domestically produced FCOJM represented a substantial volume of domestic sales during the period examined.

Respondents argue that this underselling is not significant because it is attributable to certain long-term contracts. However, the fact that an importer contracted in advance for a price that then undersells the domestic like product over a long period does not mean underselling is not occurring or has no adverse effects on US market prices. Moreover, while Respondents assert that Brazilian juice sells at a modest discount compared to the highest-quality, 100–percent Valencia domestic product, there is no record evidence that the Brazilian certain orange juice for which pricing data were reported is of lower quality and value than the domestic product for which we collected pricing data. We therefore conclude that the underselling is significant.

We also find that subject import prices are suppressing domestic price increases, which otherwise would have occurred, to a significant degree. While the unit cost of goods sold ("COGS") for domestic processors has risen slightly, the domestic industry's ratio of COGS to net sales has steadily increased throughout the period examined. This indicates that the domestic industry has been unable to recoup its rising production costs through higher prices on its sales of the domestic like product. Respondents concede that, in light of the hurricanes and citrus diseases that have significantly reduced domestic production in crop years 2004/05 and 2005/06, prices in the US market should be rising. They contend, however, that it is not reasonable for the Commission to find that domestic prices would have been even higher than they are, absent the current volume and lower prices of Brazilian imports, because any greater price increases would raise retail prices to the point where US consumers begin to reduce their orange juice purchases. This theory is not supported by the record, because Respondents are confusing wholesale and retail prices. The record indicates a growing gap between wholesale prices (i.e., prices for the domestic like product) and retail orange juice prices over the period examined. In general, the former have declined while the latter have increased somewhat. We therefore find that prices for the domestic like product could be considerably higher without impacting retail prices at all.

Rather than looking to demand factors to explain the domestic industry's inability to raise prices commensurate with rising production costs, we find that this cost-price squeeze is attributable to the volume of Brazilian imports entering the US at lower than market prices. In fact, the domestic industry's cost-price squeeze accelerated in the final year of the period examined, when Brazilian subject imports were at their highest levels. Between 2003 and 2004, the cost-price squeeze resulted in a 7.8 percentage point decline in the domestic industry's operating margin, which was more accelerated than the 1.8 percentage point drop in the domestic industry's operating margin between 2002 and 2003, when the domestic industry also experienced a cost-price squeeze.

The increase in subject imports in crop year 2004/05 did not simply meet demand and make up for the reduced US supply. Table C–3 of the Staff's Confidential Final Report shows that subject imports increased from 154.2 million gallons SSE in crop year 2003/04 to 231.7 million gallons SSE in crop year 2004/05. This was an increase of 77.5 million gallons. As noted previously, inventories of subject imports increased from 26.6 million gallons at year end 2003/04 to 51.3 million gallons at year end 2004/05, an increase of 24.7 million gallons. This evidence shows that 32 percent of the increase in subject imports in crop year 2004/05 went into inventories rather than being used to meet US demand and replace decreased domestic supplies caused by the 2004 hurricanes. This inventory-related increase in available supply supports our finding that subject imports are suppressing prices and negatively impacting the domestic industry. Absent the increasing inventories of Brazilian subject imports in the US market, particularly in the final full year of the period examined, overall ending stocks would have been significantly lower. We find that lower inventories would have created upward pressure on domestic prices of certain orange juice, allowing domestic processors an opportunity to more fully recover cost increases.
* * *

Based on the overall pricing data, and the available data indicating interchangeability between the domestic like product and subject imports, we find that the increasing volumes of lower-priced subject imports prevented increases in domestic prices for certain orange juice, which otherwise would have occurred, to a significant degree.

E.   Impact of the Subject Imports[3]

Section 771(7)(C)(iii) provides that the Commission, in examining the impact of the subject imports on the domestic industry, "shall evaluate all relevant economic factors which have a bearing on the state of the industry." These factors include output, sales, inventories, capacity utilization, market share, employment, wages, productivity, profits, cash flow, return on investment, ability to raise capital, research and development, and factors affecting domestic prices. No single factor is dispositive and all relevant factors are considered "within the context of the business cycle and conditions of competition that are distinctive to the affected industry."

By most measures, the domestic industry's condition worsened over the period examined despite increasing apparent US consumption. While the absolute volume of subject imports rose sharply over the period examined, domestic shipments of certain orange juice declined dramatically overall during the period examined. Domestic producers' market share declined from 87.2 percent in crop year 2001/02 to 79.9 percent in crop year 2002/03, increased to 84.8 percent in crop year 2003/04, and fell to 76.5 percent in crop year 2004/05. Although domestic processors' capacity increased by 2.7 percent overall during the period examined, domestic processors' capacity utilization dropped by 28.3 percentage points between crop year 2001/02 and crop year 2004/05. Domestic production fell by 31.3 percent between crop year 2001/02 and crop year 2004/05. US producers' end-of-period inventories of certain orange juice fell by 2.0 percent overall during the period examined declining from 423.7 million pounds solids in crop year 2001/02 to 415.2 million pounds solids in crop year 2004/05, with a decline between crop year 2003/04 and crop year 2004/05. However, as discussed above, the amount of Brazilian subject imports held in US inventory increased during the period examined. Relative to production, US shipments and total shipments, US producers' inventories increased between crop year 2001/02 and crop year 2004/05. Similarly, on a relative basis, reported inventories of subject merchandise grew from 2.3 percent of total available supply in crop year 2001/02 to 3.4 percent of total available supply in crop year 2004/05. This is an increase of 52 percent in the relative amounts of subject imports held in inventories. The number of production workers employed by processors and hours worked declined from crop year 2001/02 to crop year 2004/05. Wages paid to workers employed by US processors also declined during the period examined.

3.   [original note 170] The Act instructs the Commission to consider the "magnitude of the dumping margin" in an antidumping proceeding as part of its consideration of the impact of imports. 19 U.S.C. sec. 1677(7)(C)(iii)(V). In its final affirmative determination, Commerce found a weighted-average dumping margin of 9.73 percent for Fisher, 19.19 percent for Cutrale, 60.29 percent for Montecitrus, and 15.42 percent for all other Brazilian subject producers. 71 F. R. 2183 (January 13, 2006).

The domestic processors' financial indicators worsened substantially over the period examined. The combined data for toll and non-toll operations for domestic processors show an overall decline in their operating performance for the period examined. By quantity, net sales for domestic processors on their combined toll and non-toll processing operations declined from 985.0 million pounds solids in 2002 to 975.0 million pounds solids in 2003 to 904.5 million pounds solids in 2004, and fell from 788.0 million pounds solids in interim 2004 to 695.5 million pounds solids in interim 2005. By value, net sales for domestic processors on their combined toll and non-toll processing operations declined from $852.0 million in 2002 to $781.9 million in 2003 to $718.7 million in 2004, although they increased slightly from $576.1 million in interim 2004 to $603.8 million in interim 2005. For combined toll and non-toll operations for domestic processors, the ratio of operating income to net sales declined from 8.4 percent in 2002 to 6.6 percent in 2003 to a negative 1.2 percent in 2004, and dropped from 7.8 percent in interim 2004 to 2.5 percent in interim 2005. Even when viewed separately rather than combined, domestic processors also experienced deteriorating profitability and operating losses in non-toll and toll operations during the period examined. Cash flow and return on investment for domestic processors both show a similar overall decline during the period examined. Capital expenditures for domestic processors also declined during the period examined.

Domestic growers also experienced declining operating profitability during the period examined. Domestic growers' operating income declined irregularly over the period examined from $12.7 million in 2002 to $3.9 million in 2004. Domestic growers' ratio of operating income to net sales declined from 6.6 percent in 2002 and 2003 to 2.3 percent in 2004. Net sales (by value) for domestic growers declined irregularly over the period examined from $190.7 million in 2002 to $170.0 million in 2004. Domestic growers' experienced all of this deteriorating profitability even as they received approximately $5.7 million in US government financial assistance in 2003 and 2004.

We have considered Respondents' arguments that injury to the domestic industry was attributable to factors other than subject imports. These other factors alleged by Respondents include: the Atkins diet and other low-carbohydrate diets, supply shortages in domestic production of certain orange juice in the aftermath of the 2004 Florida hurricanes, US inventory levels, the necessity of subject imports for blending and duty drawback, and the growing presence of nonsubject imports in the US market. As explained above, the record shows that subject imports contributed importantly to the domestic industry's injury, and, as further discussed below, these alleged "other causes" were not sufficient to sever the causal nexus that we have found between subject imports and the domestic industry's weakened state.

Although apparent consumption did dip somewhat during the period examined, any demand-dampening effects of low-carbohydrate diets (i.e. Atkins diet) were clearly wearing off as apparent consumption rose during the latter part of the period examined. Moreover, while the volume of nonsubject imports rose over the period examined, they grew at a slower rate and represented a smaller share of apparent consumption than Brazilian subject imports. As noted above, we do not find that blending or duty drawback demonstrate that subject imports are not having adverse volume or price effects on the domestic industry.

We recognize that some of the declining trends experienced by domestic processors and growers, including trends in production, shipments, capacity utilization, and employment, in part reflect the after-effects of hurricanes and the related spread of citrus diseases, and we do not attribute such effects to the subject imports. Rather, as noted in our volume analysis, we conclude that the record demonstrates a causal nexus between subject imports and material injury to the domestic industry independent of these other factors, based on the extent to which the total volume of Brazilian subject merchandise present in the US market exceeds any supply shortage and the effect of low prices of such volumes on the domestic industry's pricing and financial performance.

At a time of steady or rising demand, the domestic industry has lost market share to the subject imports. While the hurricanes and other factors limiting the domestic industry's ability to meet demand may account for some of the sales of subject imports in the United States, they do not detract from the fact that subject imports have significantly undersold the domestic like product for a product where price is an important factor for purchasers and quality differences do not create a meaningful premium for the domestic like product. For non-toll operations, while both COGS and net sales on a per pound basis decreased each year between 2002/03 and 2004/05, the decline in net sales unit values was greater than the decline in the domestic industry's COGS. * * * The domestic industry exhibits a classic cost/price squeeze and has been unable to raise its prices sufficiently to cover its production costs even in what Respondents' characterize as a short-supply market. We therefore find that the subject imports have significantly and adversely affected the domestic industry through their increased sales at the expense of the domestic industry and through the extent to which the subject imports suppressed domestic prices to a significant degree, as indicated above.

In sum, we conclude that subject imports had a significant adverse impact on the condition of the domestic industry during the period examined. As discussed above, we find the volume of subject imports to be significant and that the subject imports had significant price-suppressing effects. We also find that the volume and price effects of the subject imports adversely affected the performance of the domestic industry during the period examined. Therefore, we find that the domestic industry producing certain orange juice is materially injured by reason of subject imports of certain orange juice from Brazil that are sold in the United States at less than fair value.

Notes and Questions

(1) In many investigations, the ITC uses a three-year window for its analysis—that is, it gathers annual data on the domestic industry and imports for the last three full calendar years. It may then also use data for the most recent "interim" or part years. For example, for an investigation conducted in the Summer of 2008, the ITC would typically gather annual data for 2005, 2006 and 2007, and might add data comparing the first quarter of 2007 with the first quarter of 2008. In *Orange Juice*, however, the ITC used data for the last four full crop years. Were you persuaded by its explanation in original note 133 as to why it chose this approach? How might the case have appeared different if the ITC had used data for only the three most recent crop years? Can you appreciate why respondents were arguing for the shorter period?

(2) Consider the relationship between the domestic orange crop and the volume of imports. If you were representing respondents, could you fashion a helpful argument based on that relationship?

(3) Does the information in the opinion give you some insight into why respondents argued that NFC should be treated as a separate "like product?" See Section 17.2.

(4) It is evident from the analysis that the ITC is considering the condition of orange growers as part of its analysis, not simply processors of orange juice. Permissible under WTO law?

(5) How useful is evidence of "underselling"—essentially, a comparison between the prices of imported and domestic goods? If the imported good is commonly cheaper, does that prove it is causing injury, or might it simply show that it is of lower quality? Likewise, if the imported good is more expensive than the domestic good, does that suggest an absence of injury, or just that the import is a premium product? Did the ITC respond persuasively to the suggestion that much of the underselling by FCOJM was due to the prices established by long-term contracts?

(6) The ITC argues that domestic growers have been unable to raise prices in response to increases in cost of goods sold despite a period of "rising demand." What is the evidence of rising demand? Is consumption the same as demand?

(7) What consideration did the Commission give to the "magnitude of the margin of dumping" as required by US and WTO law? Was it adequate?

This issue has been a matter of considerable controversy through the years. The argument for considering the magnitude of the unfair trade practice is straightforward—the greater the degree of dumping or subsidization, the more harm it is likely to cause. But the US statute refers to injury "by reason of [dumped or subsidized] imports," not "by reason of" dumping or subsidization, and for many years ITC Commissioners often took the view that the magnitude of the unfair trade practice is irrelevant. The Uruguay Round Antidumping Agreement addressed this issue obliquely by requiring that the margin of dumping be considered (see art. 3.4); the new Subsidies Agreement does not explicitly require the magnitude of subsidization to be considered. US law was accordingly amended for antidumping cases but not countervailing duty cases. Both WTO agreements require, however, that unfairly traded imports be found to cause injury "through the effects of [dumping or subsidies]." Yet, where that text appears, a footnote also appears cross-referencing earlier paragraphs that do not refer to the size of the unfair trade practice. In your judgment, to what extent does WTO law require a clear linkage between the unfair trade practice and material injury? Is a statutory requirement that the margin be "considered" equivalent to requiring that "dumping" be established as the cause of injury, as opposed to the "dumped imports?"

(8) Related, some Commissioners at times have employed an analytical technique termed "margins analysis." They would compare the "margin" or magnitude of dumping or subsidization calculated by the ITA to the price difference between imported and domestic goods, and then decide whether the unfair trade practice was large enough to cause injury. Thus, for example, suppose that the "fair value" of imported goods (the margin of dumping) is 10% higher than their actual price. The imports undersell domestic goods, however, by an average of 15%. "Margins analysis" would then conclude that dumping was not the cause of any injury on the grounds that the elimination of dumping would still leave the imports with a price advantage. Sound?

(9) Were you satisfied with the analysis by the ITC regarding the other possible causes of injury put forward by respondents? In that regard, consider the following excerpt from the Appellate Body report in United States—Antidumping Measures on Certain Hot–Rolled Steel Products from Japan, WT/DS184/AB/R, adopted August 23, 2001:

> 216. In the Panel proceedings, Japan claimed that the USITC acted inconsistently with the causation requirements in Article 3.5 of the Anti–Dumping Agreement, first, because it did not adequately examine factors, other than dumped imports, which were also causing injuries to the domestic industry and, second, because, the USITC failed to ensure that injuries caused by these other factors were not attributed to the dumped imports. Japan's arguments focused on four other factors, the importance of which, it said, had been recognized by the USITC. These factors were: the increase in production capacity of mini-mills; the effects of a strike at General Motors ('GM') in 1998; declining demand for hot-rolled steel from the United States' pipe and tube industry; and the effects of prices of non-dumped imports.

> 217. The Panel examined each of these factors in turn and concluded that the USITC did not fail adequately to examine them. The Panel went on to address Japan's claim regarding the proper attribution of injury. The Panel interpreted the non-attribution language in Article 3.5 of the Anti–Dumping Agreement to mean that:

>> ... the authority is to examine and ensure that these other factors do not break the causal link that appeared to exist between dumped imports and material injury on the basis of an examination of the volume and effects of the dumped imports under Articles 3.2 and 3.4 of the AD Agreement. * * *

> 220. On appeal, Japan argues that the Panel erred because it did not correctly interpret the non-attribution language in Article 3.5 of the Anti–Dumping Agreement. According to Japan, that provision means

that the effects of the "other" causal factors must be "separated" and "distinguished", and that their "bearing" on the domestic industry must be assessed. Japan cites as support the Appellate Body Reports in *United States—Wheat Gluten Safeguard* and *United States—Lamb Safeguard*.

221.   We observe that the issue raised on appeal is confined to the Panel's interpretation and application of the non-attribution language in Article 3.5 of the Anti–Dumping Agreement, and does not relate to the Panel's finding that there is no requirement that dumped imports alone be capable of causing injury. The relevant part of Article 3.5 reads:

> It must be demonstrated that the dumped imports are, through the effects of dumping, as set forth in paragraphs 2 and 4, causing injury within the meaning of this Agreement. The demonstration of a causal relationship between the dumped imports and the injury to the domestic industry shall be based on an examination of all relevant evidence before the authorities. The authorities shall also examine any known factors other than the dumped imports which at the same time are injuring the domestic industry, and the injuries caused by these other factors must not be attributed to the dumped imports. * * *

223.   The non-attribution language in Article 3.5 of the Anti–Dumping Agreement applies solely in situations where dumped imports and other known factors are causing injury to the domestic industry at the same time. In order that investigating authorities, applying Article 3.5, are able to ensure that the injurious effects of the other known factors are not "attributed" to dumped imports, they must appropriately assess the injurious effects of those other factors. Logically, such an assessment must involve separating and distinguishing the injurious effects of the other factors from the injurious effects of the dumped imports. If the injurious effects of the dumped imports are not appropriately separated and distinguished from the injurious effects of the other factors, the authorities will be unable to conclude that the injury they ascribe to dumped imports is actually caused by those imports, rather than by the other factors. Thus, in the absence of such separation and distinction of the different injurious effects, the investigating authorities would have no rational basis to conclude that the dumped imports are indeed causing the injury which, under the Anti–Dumping Agreement, justifies the imposition of anti-dumping duties.

224.   We emphasize that the particular methods and approaches by which WTO Members choose to carry out the process of separating and distinguishing the injurious effects of dumped imports from the injurious effects of the other known causal factors are not prescribed by the Anti–Dumping Agreement. What the Agreement requires is simply that the obligations in Article 3.5 be respected when a determination of injury is made. * * *

228.   * * * [W]e agree with the United States that the different causal factors operating on a domestic industry may interact, and their effects may well be inter-related, such that they produce a combined effect on the domestic industry. We recognize, therefore, that it may not

be easy, as a practical matter, to separate and distinguish the injurious effects of different causal factors. However, although this process may not be easy, this is precisely what is envisaged by the non-attribution language. If the injurious effects of the dumped imports and the other known factors remain lumped together and indistinguishable, there is simply no means of knowing whether injury ascribed to dumped imports was, in reality, caused by other factors. Article 3.5, therefore, requires investigating authorities to undertake the process of assessing appropriately, and separating and distinguishing, the injurious effects of dumped imports from those of other known causal factors. * * *

234. The Panel's examination of Japan's claim under Article 3.5 was based on an erroneous interpretive approach. In view of the Panel's consequential failure to verify whether the USITC separated and distinguished the injurious effects of dumped imports from those of the other known factors, there was no means by which the Panel could properly satisfy itself, in examining Japan's claim, that the injurious effects of the other factors had not, in fact, been attributed by the USITC to the dumped imports, inconsistently with the Anti–Dumping Agreement. We must, therefore, reverse the Panel's findings in paragraphs 7.257, 7.261 and 8.2(c) of its Report as they are bereft of legal basis.

With reference to the analysis in *Orange Juice*, what exactly does the ITC do to "separate and distinguish" the effects of other possible causes of injury, so as to ensure that their effects are not "attributed" to dumped imports as required by WTO law? Would its non-attribution analysis withstand a WTO challenge?

Like the panel in *US Hot–Rolled Steel*, the tendency of panels confronted with challenges to the causal analysis of national authorities in these unfair trade cases to date has been to accept the non-attribution analysis of investigating authorities without great scrutiny. See also Egypt—Definitive Antidumping Duties on Steel Rebar from Turkey, WT/DS211/R, adopted October 1, 2002, paras. 7.107–7.126. The Appellate Body, by contrast, in line with its position in safeguards cases, seems to demand a more exacting approach in *Hot-Rolled Steel*. At this writing it remains unclear whether the non-attribution requirement will become a major stumbling block for nations seeking to employ antidumping and countervailing duties.

We conclude with another issue relating to causation that has become quite controversial under US law.

GERALD METALS, INC. v. UNITED STATES

United States Courts of Appeals, Federal Circuit, 1997.
132 F.3d 716.

[A] plurality of three [ITC] commissioners found material injury to the domestic industry by reason of LTFV imports of pure magnesium from Russia, Ukraine, and China; the remaining three commissioners dissented from this determination. Because the commissioners were evenly divided on the question of material injury by reason of the pure magnesium imports, the views of the plurality finding material injury constitute the determination of the Commission, pursuant to 19 U.S.C. sec. 1677(11) (1994).

* * *

Much of the record features information about imports from Russia. Specifically, the record shows, in the words of Vice Chairman Nuzum, that "a sizeable portion of the imports from Russia were fairly-traded. These imports undersold domestic product almost as frequently as did LTFV imports." Similarly the record shows, in the words of Commissioner Crawford, that "dumped Russian imports and fairly-traded Russian imports are very close, if not perfect, substitutes for each other."

All pure magnesium from Russia originates with one of two producers—Avisma Titanium–Magnesium Works (Avisma) and Solikamsk Magnesium Works (SMW). Although trading companies can import Russian pure magnesium from only these two sources, Commerce assigned zero percent dumping margins to some companies, such as Gerald Metals, while assigning margins of 100.25% to other companies. Commerce assigned to all trading companies importing pure magnesium from Ukraine margins greater than zero, ranging from 36.05% to 104.27%. Commerce assigned a margin of 108.26% to all Chinese imports.

Gerald Metals imported both fairly-traded Russian pure magnesium and LTFV Ukrainian pure magnesium. Gerald Metals reasons that because fairly-traded Russian imports are substitutes for LTFV Russian imports, domestic purchasers of magnesium products could fill their demand without resort to LTFV imports. Thus, Gerald Metals argues, the LTFV goods did not cause the injury to domestic industry. Instead, the injury was the result of market forces other than unfair trading.

The Court of International Trade found substantial evidence to support the Commission's determination. * * *

* * *

Applying an analytical framework outlined in Title 19, the Commission determines whether LTFV imports materially injure a domestic industry. Section 1677(7)(A) defines "material injury" as a "harm which is not inconsequential, immaterial, or unimportant." When determining whether imports have caused material injury to a domestic industry, the Commission evaluates:

(I) the volume of imports of the merchandise that is the subject of the investigation,

(II) the effect of imports of that merchandise on prices in the United States for domestic like products, and

(III) the impact of imports of such merchandise on domestic producers of domestic like products, but only in the context of production operations within the United States. . . .

Additionally, the Commission "may consider such other economic factors as are relevant to the determination."

However, a showing that economic harm to domestic industry occurred when LTFV imports are also on the market is not enough to show that the imports caused a material injury. See United States Steel Group v. United States, 96 F.3d 1352, 1358 (Fed.Cir.1996) ("To claim that the temporal link between these events proves that they are causally related is . . . fallacy. . . ."). An affirmative injury determination requires both (1) present material injury and (2) a finding that the material injury is "by reason of" the subject imports. Hence, the anti-dumping statute mandates a showing of causal—not merely temporal—connection between the LTFV goods and the material injury.

Because this appeal hinges on whether the subject imports caused the injury, this court reviews the record evidence to determine whether substantial evidence supports the Commission's determination that the domestic industry was injured by reason of the subject imports. Substantial evidence is " 'such relevant evidence as a reasonable mind might accept as adequate to support a conclusion.' " * * *

The central dispute in this case is the Commission's asserted failure to incorporate the undisputed facts about fairly-traded Russian imports into its analysis of the harm caused by reason of the cumulated LTFV imports. Although the record contained surveys of purchaser comparisons of domestic product to the subject imports, there is no similar evidence of product differentiation, non-price differences, or differences in terms and conditions between the two classes of Russian imports—fairly traded and LTFV.

Indeed, only two producers were responsible for all Russian imports. The primary difference in the price and treatment of Russian pure magnesium depended on which trading company imported the product. Pricing by different trading companies, which had dumping margins of either zero percent or 100.25%, determined whether the magnesium arrived as fairly-traded or LTFV. Therefore, only one reasonable conclusion can be drawn from the record: other than differences in the trading company, the Russian imports—both fairly-traded and LTFV—were perfect substitutes for each other, if not the exact same product.

Similarly, Russian and Ukrainian pure magnesium products compete with one another. The Commission noted that the parties to the investigation did not dispute that LTFV imports from Russia and Ukraine competed with one another. Although there was some evidence of product quality differences between these imports, the Commission nonetheless concluded that its supposition was confirmed by other purchasers who stated that they did not differentiate between Russian or Ukrainian magnesium when dealing with the Commonwealth of Independent States (the association of former Soviet Union republics). Thus, the record supports the inference that Russian imports, either fairly-traded or LTFV, are substitutes for LTFV Ukrainian imports.

* * *

These aspects of the record point to a gap in the causal nexus between the LTFV Ukrainian imports and material harm to domestic industry. The Court of International Trade acknowledged this causation problem, but, without citing adequate record support, dismissed this evidence.

First, the Court of International Trade found no evidence supporting Gerald Metals' claim that fairly-traded Russian imports would have replaced all or the greater part of the subject imports. The court stated that Gerald Metals had premised this argument on the false assumption that producers would switch to different importers trading at fair value in the same way that domestic consumers switch to different trading companies when buying pure magnesium. According to the court, domestic consumers use non-price factors to select a trading partner.

A more reasonable view of the record, however, contradicts these conclusions. At the beginning of the period of investigation, the cumulated LTFV imports had a greater market share than the Russian fairly-traded imports; however, by the end of the period, the market share of the fairly-traded Russian imports was greater than that of the LTFV imports. Comparing the quantities purchased by domestic consumers during the entire period reveals that the sales of Russian LTFV product just slightly exceeded that of the fairly-traded Russian product. In fact, the quantity of all Russian pure magnesium sales—including both fairly-traded and LTFV—was three times the combined quantity of sales of LTFV imports from Ukraine and China.

The Court of International Trade apparently failed to evaluate this data in conjunction with the fact that all Russian magnesium originated from only two producers. As previously indicated, the importer, not the producer, set the price and determined whether Russian magnesium was fairly-traded or LTFV. The domestic consumption and market penetration data reveal that Russian producers sold to fairly-trading importers almost as often as to unfairly trading importers and that domestic purchasers acquired Russian imports from both types of importers in roughly similar amounts.

Indeed, this evidence demonstrates that, contrary to the Court of International Trade's analysis, domestic purchasers were not repelled from the LTFV imports as compared to fairly-traded imports because of non-price factors. This inference is underscored by the fact that the same importer, Gerald Metals, sold fairly-traded Russian product as well as LTFV Ukrainian product to domestic purchasers. Without further explanation, this court cannot adequately review the Court of International Trade's dismissal of the prospect that fairly-traded goods would have replaced LTFV goods.

The Court of International Trade also reasoned that the Commission's injury determination did not rest upon the purported shift of all domestic purchasers of LTFV magnesium to domestic product. In fact, the domestic industry framed its material injury case not in terms of lost sales but in terms of the inability of domestic producers to raise prices without suffering lost sales volume.

After the suspension of LTFV imports of pure magnesium from Canada in 1991–92, the domestic industry apparently expected to raise prices for its pure magnesium. At this time, imports—both LTFV and fairly-traded—entered the United States due in part to liquidation of stockpiles in the former Soviet Union. These imports apparently disrupted the expectation of higher prices for domestic products. The enhanced availability on the world market of magnesium from the former Soviet Union is one of the relevant economic factors influencing both the finding of injury and causation.

Determining the accurate causation of a disrupted market expectation, however, requires careful economic evidence and analysis. The anti-dumping statute requires that the Commission consider all relevant economic factors "within the context of the business cycle and conditions of competition that are distinctive to the affected industry." Generally, a sudden increase in world supply in the face of a relatively stable demand results in lower prices. While the statute protects domestic magnesium producers from injury caused by LTFV imports, its scope of protection does not reach so far as to support artificially inflated prices when fairly-traded imports are underselling the domestic product and LTFV imports are readily convertible to fairly-traded product by merely changing importers.

The Court of International Trade erred by applying an incorrect legal test for the amount of contribution to material harm by LTFV goods necessary to satisfy the "by reason of" standard. The court stated that "even though fairly-priced imports may have been another cause of injury, the Commission has a statutory obligation not to weigh causes," and "thus . . . correctly did not compare the impact of subject imports to the impact of other factors, like the fairly-traded imports." Thus, the court followed the reasoning that any contribution constitutes sufficient causation to satisfy the "by reason of" test.

To the contrary, the statute requires the injury to occur "by reason of" the LTFV imports. This language does not suggest that an importer of LTFV goods can escape countervailing duties by finding some tangential or minor cause unrelated to the LTFV goods that contributed to the harmful effects on domestic market prices. By the same token, this language does not suggest that the Government satisfies its burden of proof by showing that the LTFV goods themselves contributed only minimally or tangentially to the material harm.

* * *

Accordingly, this court concludes that the Court of International Trade failed to consider properly the presence of fairly-traded Russian imports in affirming the Commission's determination of material injury by reason of the LTFV goods.

Notes and Questions

(1) On remand, the ITC determined that imports of pure magnesium at less than fair value had not caused or threatened material injury, and the Court of International Trade affirmed.

(2) Even if Russian imports traded at fair value are perfectly substitutable with dumped Ukrainian imports, does it follow that dumped imports can cause no material harm? What more must be shown before that conclusion can be reached?

(3) Similar issues arose in Bratsk Aluminium Smelter v. United States, 444 F.3d 1369 (Fed. Cir. 2006), in which the Federal Circuit once again remanded a case because the ITC failed to consider whether non-subject imports would have replaced the dumped imports to such a degree that the domestic industry would not have benefited from the elimination of the dumped imports. The ITC currently interprets Bratsk as requiring it to make a specific finding on this issue whenever the investigation involves a "commodity product," and when price competitive non-subject imports are a significant factor in the market. It thus inquires whether this two-part test is met and, if so, whether non-subject imports could supplant the dumped imports to such a degree that the dumped imports cannot be deemed to cause injury. If the two-part test is not met, however, it does not consider itself bound to make a specific finding with respect to non-subject imports. See, e.g., Certain Activated Carbon from China, USITC Inv. No. 731–TA–1103, April 2007. Is it correct to suppose that these issues only arise for "commodity products?"

Chapter 18

SUBSIDIES AND
COUNTERVAILING DUTIES

SECTION 18.1   INTRODUCTION

Disputes over government subsidies that affect trade predate the original GATT agreement, and the area remains divisive and contentious. The most difficult issues relate to the problem of distinguishing between "legitimate" government activities, on the one hand, and trade-distorting subsidies, on the other. Some progress was made during the Uruguay Round, but the problems of definition have by no means been solved. The governments of the major western trading nations continue to maintain divergent views on the role of government involvement with industry, and even more disagreement is found when the policies of developing countries are considered. This chapter surveys the legal and policy issues relating to international and national discipline of subsidies. This section introduces the basic rules under WTO law and the core policy questions pertaining to subsidies in international trade. Section 18.2 then considers a variety of specific issues that have arisen in the WTO. Section 18.3 affords a brief introduction to US countervailing duty proceedings.

(A) INTERNATIONAL DISCIPLINES ON SUBSIDIES AND COUNTERVAILING MEASURES

In international trade parlance, there are two types of subsidies: the "domestic" subsidy; and the "export" subsidy. The domestic subsidy is granted to an industry on all of its production of a product, regardless of whether that production is exported. It can have effects similar to those of a tariff. For example, if the domestic industry produces widgets at a cost of $1.00 each, while the foreign industry can produce and deliver widgets at a price of $.90 each, the foreign goods should compete successfully against the domestic product. But if the domestic government grants a subsidy to the widget industry of 20 cents for each widget produced, it should be able to sell the widget for 20 cents less than otherwise. Thus, it can reduce its price to a level below that of the imports, and effectively drive out the import competition. In this sense, the subsidy is protectionist, although unlike a tariff, it lowers the prices of the products concerned rather than raises them, and is thus favorable to consumers. The subsidy is also like a tariff in another sense; it can distort resource allocation by drawing resources into the production of a good or service where production would be uneconomic but for the subsidy.

An export subsidy, by contrast, is paid to an industry only on products that are exported. Thus, if the domestic industry produced widgets at a dollar each, and received a 20 cent subsidy for each widget exported, it could sell its widgets abroad for about 80 cents each. The widgets that are sold in the domestic market, however, would cost a dollar each, and presumably would be priced at or above that level. Consequently, with an export subsidy, goods tend to be sold abroad at a price below that of the goods sold in the domestic market. Like the domestic subsidy, an export subsidy can distort resource allocation by inducing production and exportation that is otherwise uneconomic.

Despite the ability of subsidies to distort the allocation of resources, it is not immediately obvious why the nations that *import* subsidized goods or services should object to them. More will be said about that issue below. Nevertheless, WTO rules allow an importing nation to respond to certain foreign subsidies by imposing "countervailing duties." These duties are set equal to the amount of the foreign subsidy, ostensibly to offset its effects on trade. The WTO system also imposes significant constraints upon the ability of governments to use both domestic and export subsidies.

GATT Article XVI contains the original obligations on subsidies. It consisted originally of one paragraph (XVI:1), with a loose obligation to report all subsidies which operate to increase exports or decrease imports. The article was amended extensively during the GATT 1954–55 review session. Four paragraphs were added to Article XVI, containing two key obligations: one obligation (paragraph 3) prohibits using an export subsidy on primary products which results in obtaining more than "an equitable share of world export trade in that product;" a second obligation (paragraph 4) prohibits a subsidy on the export of non-primary products which results in an export price lower than the comparable price for like goods which are not exported (the so-called "bi-level pricing" condition).[1] These Article XVI amendments, however, were accepted only by certain industrialized nations of GATT. Developing countries objected to the differential treatment of primary and other goods.

It will be recalled that introduction of a new domestic subsidy on a product which is bound in a country's GATT schedule has been termed a "prima facie nullification or impairment" for purposes of Article XXIII complaints.[2]

---

1. For a complete discussion of this subject, see John H. Jackson, World Trade and the Law of GATT 372–74 (1969).

2. See discussion of the *EC Oilseeds* and the *Australia/Chile fertilizer* cases in Section 7.4(A).

Apart from obligations concerning the use of subsidies, the original GATT authorized unilateral government responses in the form of countervailing duties. Article VI of GATT governs such measures, prohibiting the use of both antidumping and countervailing duties for the same situation, and imposing a "material injury" requirement as a prerequisite to the use of countervailing duties. If these conditions are met, a government is authorized to apply a countervailing duty on imported goods (in excess of regular bound duty rates), in an amount "equal to the estimated bounty or subsidy" granted directly or indirectly on the "manufacture, production or export."

In 1960, the GATT Contracting Parties adopted a report of a working party which included an "illustrative list" of practices that would be considered as "export subsidies" for purposes of GATT Article XVI, paragraph 4.[3] This list has been very important for the interpretation of GATT subsidy obligations.

In the Tokyo Round, a Subsidies Code was negotiated, and accepted by about two dozen signatories. Among other things, it tightened the restrictions on export subsidies; elaborated the procedures to be utilized by importing nations in their countervailing duty investigations; set forth criteria to be examined in the assessment of injury under the injury test; and established a Subsidies Code Committee to resolve disputes.

The Uruguay Round Subsidies Agreement is an important step forward over the Tokyo Round Code for a number of reasons. Unlike the Code, it is binding on all WTO members. It also significantly extends WTO discipline over domestic subsidies, provides some guidance on what domestic subsidies are "unfair," and encourages greater resort to WTO dispute resolution rather than unilateral countervailing measures. Its principal innovations were summarized by the GATT Secretariat as follows:[4]

> Unlike its predecessor, the [Agreement on Subsidies and Countervailing Measures] contains a definition of subsidy and introduces the concept of a "specific" subsidy—for the most part, a subsidy available only to an enterprise or industry or group of enterprises or industries within the jurisdiction of the authority granting the subsidy. Only specific subsidies would be subject to the disciplines set out in the agreement.

> The agreement established three categories of subsidies. First, it deems the following subsidies to be "prohibited": those contingent, in law or in fact, whether solely or as one of several other conditions, upon export performance; and those contingent, whether solely or as one of several other conditions, upon the use of domestic over imported goods. Prohibited subsidies are subject to new dispute settlement procedures. The main features include an expedited timetable for action by the Dispute Settlement body, and if it is

---

3. GATT, 9th Supp. BISD 185 (1961); see also Jackson, supra note 1, at 385.

4. GATT Focus Newsletter, Dec. 1993, at 10–11.

found that the subsidy is indeed prohibited, it must be immediately withdrawn. If this is not done within the specified time period, the complaining member is authorized to take countermeasures.

The second category is "actionable" subsidies. The agreement stipulates that no member should cause, through the use of subsidies, adverse effects to the interests of other signatories, i.e. injury to domestic industry of another signatory, nullification or impairment of benefits accruing directly or indirectly to other signatories under the General Agreement (in particular the benefits of bound tariff concessions), and serious prejudice to the interests of another member. "Serious prejudice" shall be presumed to exist for certain subsidies included when the total *ad valorem* subsidization of a product exceeds 5 per cent. In such a situation, the burden of proof is on the subsidizing member to show that the subsidies in question do not cause serious prejudice to the complaining member. Members affected by actionable subsidies may refer the matter to the Dispute Settlement Body. In the event that it is determined that such adverse effects exist, the subsidizing member must withdraw the subsidy or remove the adverse effects.

The third category involves non-actionable subsidies, which could either be non-specific subsidies, or specific subsidies involving assistance to industrial research and pre-competitive development activity, assistance to disadvantaged regions, or certain type of assistance for adapting existing facilities to new environmental requirements imposed by law and/or regulations. * * * [The provisions defining non-actionable research-and environment-related subsidies expired after five years, however, and have not been renewed. Eds.]

One part of the agreement concerns the use of countervailing measures on subsidized imported goods. It sets out disciplines on the initiation of countervailing cases, investigations by national authorities and rules of evidence to ensure that all interested parties can present information and argument. Certain disciplines on the calculation of the amount of a subsidy are outlined as is the basis for the determination of injury to the domestic industry. The agreement would require that all relevant economic factors be taken into account in assessing the state of the industry and that a causal link be established between the subsidized imports and the alleged injury. Countervailing investigations shall be terminated immediately in cases where the amount of the subsidy is *de minimis* (the subsidy is less than 1 per cent *ad valorem*) or where the volume of subsidized imports, actual or potential, or the injury is negligible. Except under exceptional circumstances, investigations shall be concluded within one year after their initiation and in no case more than 18 months. All countervailing duties have to be terminated within 5 years of their imposition unless the authorities determine on the basis of a review that the expiry of the duty would be likely to lead to continuation or recurrence of subsidization and injury.

The agreement recognizes that subsidies may play an important role in economic development programmes of developing countries, and in the transformation of centrally-planned economies to market economies. Least-developed countries and developing countries that have less than $1,000 per capita GNP are thus exempted from disciplines on prohibited export subsidies, and have a time-bound exemption from other prohibited subsidies. For other developing countries, the export subsidy prohibition would take effect 8 years after the entry into force of the agreement establishing the WTO, and they have a time-bound agreement (though fewer years than for poorer developing countries) exemption from the other prohibited subsidies. Countervailing investigation of a product originating from a developing-country member would be terminated if the overall level of subsidies does not exceed 2 per cent (and from certain developing countries 3 per cent) of the value of the product, or if the volume of the subsidized imports represents less than 4 per cent of the total imports for the like product in the importing signatory. For countries in the process of transformation from a centrally-planned into a market economy, prohibited subsidies shall be phased out within a period of seven years from the date of entry into force of the agreement."

––––––––––

The new Subsidies or SCM Agreement to an important degree exempts agricultural subsidies, leaving them to the Agreement on Agriculture. In that Agreement, both export subsidies and domestic subsidies to agriculture are subject to a complex set of commitments for their reduction over a period of years. It treats agricultural subsidies much like bound tariffs, with country-by-country schedules indicating what is permissible, coupled with formulas for the phase down of permissible subsidies. Article 13 of the Agriculture Agreement also creates certain "safe harbor" provisions during its implementation period for measures that conform to the Agreement, exempting them from countervailing duties in some cases, and generally exempting them from the "prohibited" and "actionable" categories under the Subsidies Agreement.

(B) POLICY CONSIDERATIONS

Much has been written about the wisdom of WTO/GATT subsidy policies and the use of countervailing measures. The following materials provide the reader with a flavor of the literature. Very roughly, the issues divide into two categories: What is the appropriate scope of restrictions on subsidization by member nations, and when should an importing nation respond to foreign subsidies with some form of countervailing measure?[5]

–––––––

5. See also Barcelo, Subsidies and Countervailing Duties—Analysis and a Proposal, 9 L. & Pol.Intl.Bus. 779 (1977); Schwartz, Zenith Radio Corp. v. United States: Countervailing Duties and the Regulation of International Trade, 1978 Sup.Ct.Rev. 297;

GARY C. HUFBAUER & JOANNA SHELTON ERB, SUBSIDIES IN INTERNATIONAL TRADE
5–6 (1984)[6]

THE RATIONALE FOR DISCIPLINING SUBSIDIES

Sovereign governments are free to adopt whatever macroeconomic, industrial, or social policies, including the use of subsidies, that they deem necessary to achieve their overall goals. Politicians, producers, and taxpayers may debate the relative merits of supporting one industry versus another, and whether the cost of government financial support is worth the drain on public resources. But in a representative government, the costs and benefits of public policies presumably are settled more or less to the satisfaction of the key interested parties.

An economist might, therefore, ask why the international community should concern itself with the subsidy practices of its member nations. * * *

The answer is * * * simple: unbridled and competing national subsidies can undermine world prosperity. Whatever the analytic merits of a purist free trade, turn-the-other-cheek approach, the Great Depression taught the world that protective policies can quickly and destructively spread from nation to nation. Because the concentrated interests of producers command greater political support than the diffuse interests of consumers, national governments find it much easier to emulate the vices of protection than the virtues of free trade. This lesson has prompted the international community to fashion guidelines that distinguish between acceptable and unacceptable national subsidy measures and to codify those guidelines both in bilateral treaties and in multilateral agreements. In fact, a major purpose of the General Agreement on Tariffs and Trade (GATT) is to discipline protective import policies. Robert E. Baldwin has ably summarized negotiating history since the 1930s:

> The 1930s experience with export subsidies as well as with competitive devaluation, which has the effect of a general export subsidy and import surcharge, apparently convinced the GATT founders that export subsidies exacerbate international political tensions and should be eliminated. Though consumers in the importing country gain from export subsidization by other nations, domestic-producer groups in the importing countries are forced to curtail output and incur a producer-surplus loss.... The view that domestic producers

Alan O. Sykes, The Economics of WTO Rules on Subsidies and Countervailing Measures, *in* A. Appleton, P. Macrory & M. Plummer (eds.), The World Trade Organization: Legal, Economic and Political Analysis, vol. II (Springer Verlag 2005); Kyle Bagwell & Robert W. Staiger, Will International Rules on Subsidies Disrupt the World Trading System?, 96 Am.Econ.Rev. 877 (2006).

6. © 1984, Institute for International Economics. Reproduced by permission. See also D. Wallace, F. Loftus & V. Krikorian, Interface Three: Legal Treatment of Domestic Subsidies (1984).

are somehow more entitled to domestic compared to foreign markets is still widely held by the general public. Thus, in the case of export subsidies, it was not necessary for the founders of GATT to implement their international political objective with regard to this distortion only gradually (as with tariffs) and export subsidies were banned outright.

WARREN F. SCHWARTZ & EUGENE W. HARPER, JR., THE REGULATION OF SUBSIDIES AFFECTING INTERNATIONAL TRADE[7]

A subsidy is treated in the GATT framework as a "distortion" of international trade, that is, as creating a disparity between the actual costs incurred in producing a particular good and those which must be borne by the firm undertaking its production. In fact, however, much (perhaps all) government support can be defended as being a "correction" rather than a "distortion" of the market process. The need for correction is said to derive from the existence of "externalities," that is, costs or benefits that are borne or reaped by nonparties to a transaction and are not therefore taken into account in the market process.

As a result, the issue is not that of identifying and remedying "distortions" but rather of determining if a particular measure on balance "corrects" or "distorts" the market process, that is whether it increases or decreases the efficiency with which resources are allocated. Resolution of this question turns upon theoretical and empirical judgments about how well the domestic political system performs the tasks of deciding what intervention should be undertaken and implementing the program that is adopted.

* * *

There are only a few ways in which [an international] standard could conceivably contribute to dealing with the question of subsidies. First, it could implement the notion that particular preferences, which are in fact held by the people of a country, should not be given weight by legislators in deciding whether to institute subsidies. Thus, for example, the desire to have a certain portion of the population engage in agriculture could be said to be "less important" than "efficient" agricultural production (by which is meant, of course, "efficient" in terms of all production possibilities and preferences exclusive of wanting people to engage in agriculture). However, we know of no objective basis for adopting such a standard.

The second basic notion that could be embodied in an international standard is that the domestic measure is inefficient in terms of the preferences actually held in the country. This judgment could be made on three bases.

7. 70 Mich.L.Rev. 831 (1972). Reprinted by permission.

First, it could be asserted that the structure of the domestic political process is calculated to lead to oversubsidization. There are empirical and theoretical grounds for believing that oversubsidization is likely to result under existing systems. * * *

The second respect in which it might be said that a domestic measure is inefficient is that there are better ways to accomplish its objectives. If, for example, the purpose of the measure is to increase the level of research and development in an industry rather than the output of the industry, a subsidy geared to output would be inefficient. * * *

The final respect in which the domestic process could be said to be inefficient is that implementation has been faulty. We have talked, for example, about subsidies for infant export industries. Justification for these subsidies is found in the externalities that accompany the introduction of new goods of a certain type originating in a particular country. But any effort to devise and implement a scheme of subsidies that reflects, with substantial accuracy, the externalities actually created will encounter great difficulties. The program may easily degenerate into an indiscriminate grant of subsidies, involving the risk of political corruption and adding an element of uncertainty that makes intelligent decision-making about resource allocation extremely difficult. It may be, moreover, that alternative measures, such as the government's providing information about foreign markets to domestic producers and all domestic products to foreign buyers, are better calculated to deal with the basic problem. We do not believe, however, that an international body could be empowered to make a judgment of this kind. What really must be said after all is that a domestic measure has been badly, if not corruptly, administered.

Thus we are not very sanguine that a useful international standard can be devised.

ALAN O. SYKES, COUNTERVAILING DUTY LAW: AN ECONOMIC CRITIQUE[8]

Subsidies arise for a variety of reasons and have a variety of consequences for the subsidizing country. Subsidies can correct market failures and enhance economic welfare in the subsidizing country, or can distort resource allocation and reduce the subsidizing country's economic welfare. They can also enhance or reduce worldwide economic welfare. Much of the existing literature on the international discipline of subsidy practices devotes considerable attention to the question whether these various categories of subsidies can be reliably distinguished. From the perspective of a country that imports the subsidized merchandise, however, these distinctions are often of no consequence. Specifically, if product and input markets in the importing country are perfectly competitive and adjust quickly to any disequilibrium, a subsidy will enhance the economic welfare of the importing country whatever the

8. 89 Colum.L.Rev. 199 (1989). Reprinted by permission.

effect of the subsidy on the welfare of the subsidizing country or on the welfare of the world as a whole.

In contrast, countervailing duties will often reduce the welfare of the importing country. The principal caveat to this last proposition is that duties may improve the "terms of trade" for the importing country. A second caveat relates to the question whether countervailing duties may deter subsidization altogether and thereby confer benefits on producers in the importing country who must compete with subsidized goods in their *export* markets.

The cases in which countervailing duties might in theory generate a net benefit to the economy, however, are difficult to identify in practice. Moreover, even if the cases of potential benefit could be reliably identified, a systematic effort to impose duties in those cases might well result in a retaliatory or strategic response by trading partners that would eliminate the gains. Finally, the costs to the government of administering the countervailing duty laws, as well as the rent-seeking expenditures of domestic producer groups seeking to avail themselves of protection, can be considerable. These costs weigh further against any type of countervailing duty policy.

It is even more clear that the *existing* U.S. countervailing duty laws cannot be explained or justified as a mechanism for the imposition of welfare-enhancing duties in competitive markets. Existing law largely ignores the factors that would be essential to ascertain the welfare consequences of duties, and the central features of existing law—the special treatment of export subsidies, the specificity test, the injury test, and so on—have little or no bearing on the welfare effects of duties in a competitive setting. Thus, a net gain to the economy under existing law can arise only by chance. In short, the economic case for applying any type of countervailing duty policy in competitive markets, let alone existing U.S. policy, appears quite weak.

JOHN H. JACKSON, THE WORLD TRADING SYSTEM 282 (2d ed. 1997)[9]

The basic problem with all of these views, however, is that they focus on too narrow a perspective—that of the importing country. When one moves to a worldwide perspective—that is, in order to explore which actions will enhance or decrease worldwide net welfare—then a stronger case can be made for providing some kind of international or national disciplines on the use of subsidies of internationally traded goods. The economists would apparently admit that in such circumstances some subsidies tend to distort international production and trading patterns, and reduce efficiency and thus reduce world welfare. This is, however, a rather peculiar argument to use within an importing nation for the

9. © 1997 by The Massachusetts Institute of Technology. Reprinted by permission of The MIT Press.

application of countervailing duties. It is certainly not the basis of most of the arguments heard. Most of the arguments originate from competing producer groups, and they are most interested in their own welfare, and not in that of the world in general. On the other hand, it can be argued that if such relatively parochial or selfish motivations result in the use of measures, such as countervailing duties, that coincidentally in the long run tend to inhibit a practice (subsidization) that reduces world welfare, then why not take advantage of such parochial/selfish motivations? This argument would support the use of countervailing duties.

Notes and Questions

(1) How does one distinguish a subsidy that distorts resource allocation from one that corrects a market failure? Is there an answer to Schwartz and Harper, who doubt that a principled distinction can be drawn between them? Take the case of farm subsidies—is it impossible to tell whether a farm subsidy distorts agricultural production on the one hand, or is an economically desirable response to a national preference for the preservation of family farms on the other?

(2) Are export subsidies more worrisome or objectionable than domestic subsidies? Might one argue yes on the grounds that it is difficult to imagine a market failure that is best addressed by an export subsidy? Or might one argue no on the grounds that trade is often inefficiently restricted by trade barriers, and export subsidies may then move the volume of trade closer to its efficient level?

(3) Suppose that a firm benefits from a subsidy program that seems to distort resource allocation. But suppose that it also operates in an environment where it must comply with expensive regulations that its competitors in other countries do not face, or perhaps it is subject to higher corporate taxes or taxes on its labor inputs. Is such a firm really advantaged in a "net" sense by the activities of its government? Should the answer to that question factor into a determination whether the firm is "subsidized?" Could one ever hope to measure reliably the "net" effect of governments on the competitive position of their firms?

(4) Even if some subsidies distort resource allocation, and even if reliable rules to identify them can be fashioned, will the uncoordinated, unilateral use of countervailing duties by importing nations do much to police the problem as Jackson imagines? Consider a subsidizing country confronted with a prospect of a countervailing duty in one of the export markets for its subsidized goods. Is the rational response to that prospect to terminate the subsidy program, or something else?

SECTION 18.2   WTO RULES

(A) "FINANCIAL CONTRIBUTION" AND "BENEFIT"

Under article I.1 of the SCM Agreement, a "subsidy" entails a "financial contribution" by a government that confers a "benefit" on the recipient. The next two cases address the concept of "benefit."

CANADA—MEASURES AFFECTING THE EXPORT OF CIVILIAN AIRCRAFT

WT/DS70/AB/R.

Appellate Body Report adopted on August 20, 1999.

2. The Panel considered claims made by Brazil relating to the activities of the Export Development Corporation (the "EDC"); the operation of Canada Account; * * * The Panel found "that Canada Account debt financing since 1 January 1995 for the export of Canadian regional aircraft" and "TPC assistance to the Canadian regional aircraft industry" constitute prohibited export subsidies inconsistent with Articles 3.1(a) and 3.2 of the SCM Agreement. * * *

* * *

V. INTERPRETATION OF "BENEFIT" IN ARTICLE 1.1(b) OF THE SCM AGREEMENT

149. In interpreting the term "benefit" in Article 1.1(b) of the SCM Agreement, the Panel found that:

.... the ordinary meaning of "benefit" clearly encompasses some form of advantage.... In order to determine whether a financial contribution (in the sense of Article 1.1(a)(i)) confers a "benefit", *i.e.*, an advantage, it is necessary to determine whether the financial contribution places the *recipient* in a *more advantageous position than would have been the case but for the financial contribution*. In our view, the only logical basis for determining the position the recipient would have been in absent the financial contribution is the *market*. Accordingly, a financial contribution will only confer a "benefit", *i.e.*, an advantage, if it is *provided on terms that are more advantageous than those that would have been available to the recipient on the market*. (emphasis added)

150. The Panel concluded that the notion of "cost to government" is not relevant to the interpretation and application of the term "benefit", within the meaning of Article 1.1(b) of the SCM Agreement. The Panel found contextual support for this reading of "benefit" in Article 14 of the SCM Agreement. It also found that Annex IV of that Agreement does not form part of the relevant context of "benefit" in Article 1.1(b).

151. Canada appeals the Panel's legal interpretation of the term "benefit" in Article 1.1(b) of the SCM Agreement. In Canada's view, the Panel erred in its interpretation of "benefit" by focusing on the commercial benchmarks in Article 14 "to the exclusion of cost to government", and by rejecting Annex IV as relevant context. Canada maintains that Annex IV of the SCM Agreement supports the view that "cost to government", which is mentioned in Annex IV, is a legitimate interpretation of the term "benefit". In its appellee's submission, Brazil agrees fully with the Panel's interpretation.

152. Under the heading *"Definition of a Subsidy"*, Article 1.1 of the SCM Agreement provides, in relevant part:

1.1 For the purpose of this Agreement, a subsidy shall be deemed to exist if:

(a)(1) there is a financial contribution by a government or any public body within the territory of a Member (referred to in this Agreement as "government") . . .

. . .

and

(b) *a benefit is thereby conferred.* (emphasis added)

153. In addressing this issue, we start with the ordinary meaning of "benefit". The dictionary meaning of "benefit" is "advantage", "good", "gift", "profit", or, more generally, "a favourable or helpful factor or circumstance". Each of these alternative words or phrases gives flavour to the term "benefit" and helps to convey some of the essence of that term. These definitions also confirm that the Panel correctly stated that "the ordinary meaning of 'benefit' clearly encompasses some form of advantage." Clearly, however, dictionary meanings leave many interpretive questions open.

154. A "benefit" does not exist in the abstract, but must be received and enjoyed by a beneficiary or a recipient. Logically, a "benefit" can be said to arise only if a person, natural or legal, or a group of persons, has in fact received something. The term "benefit", therefore, implies that there must be a recipient. This provides textual support for the view that the focus of the inquiry under Article 1.1(b) of the SCM Agreement should be on the recipient and not on the granting authority. The ordinary meaning of the word "confer", as used in Article 1.1(b), bears this out. "Confer" means, *inter alia*, "give", "grant" or "bestow". The use of the past participle "conferred" in the passive form, in conjunction with the word "thereby", naturally calls for an inquiry into *what was conferred on the recipient.* Accordingly, we believe that Canada's argument that "cost to government" is one way of conceiving of "benefit" is at odds with the ordinary meaning of Article 1.1(b), which focuses on the *recipient* and not on the *government* providing the "financial contribution".

155. We find support for this reading of "benefit" in the context of Article 1.1(b) of the SCM Agreement. Article 14 sets forth guidelines for calculating the amount of a subsidy in terms of "the benefit to the recipient". Although the opening words of Article 14 state that the guidelines it establishes apply "[f]or the purposes of Part V" of the SCM Agreement, which relates to "countervailing measures", our view is that Article 14, nonetheless, constitutes relevant context for the interpretation of "benefit" in Article 1.1(b). The guidelines set forth in Article 14 apply to the calculation of the "benefit *to the recipient* conferred *pursuant to paragraph 1 of Article 1".* (emphasis added) This explicit textual

reference to Article 1.1 in Article 14 indicates to us that "benefit" is used in the same sense in Article 14 as it is in Article 1.1. Therefore, the reference to "benefit *to the recipient*" in Article 14 also implies that the word "benefit", *as used in Article 1.1*, is concerned with the "benefit *to the recipient*" and not with the "cost to government", as Canada contends.

156.   The structure of Article 1.1 as a whole confirms our view that Article 1.1(b) is concerned with the "benefit" to the recipient, and not with the "cost to government". The definition of "subsidy" in Article 1.1 has two discrete elements: "a financial contribution by a government or any public body" and "a benefit is thereby conferred". The first element of this definition is concerned with whether the *government* made a "financial contribution", as that term is defined in Article 1.1(a). The focus of the first element is on the action of the government in making the "financial contribution". That being so, it seems to us logical that the second element in Article 1.1 is concerned with the "benefit ... conferred" on the *recipient* by that governmental action. Thus, subparagraphs (a) and (b) of Article 1.1 define a "subsidy" by reference, first, to the action of the granting authority and, second, to what was conferred on the recipient. Therefore, Canada's argument that "cost to *government*" is relevant to the question of whether there is a "benefit" to the *recipient* under Article 1.1(b) disregards the overall structure of Article 1.1.

157.   We also believe that the word "benefit", as used in Article 1.1(b), implies some kind of comparison. This must be so, for there can be no "benefit" to the recipient unless the "financial contribution" makes the recipient "better off" than it would otherwise have been, absent that contribution. In our view, the marketplace provides an appropriate basis for comparison in determining whether a "benefit" has been "conferred", because the trade-distorting potential of a "financial contribution" can be identified by determining whether the recipient has received a "financial contribution" on terms more favourable than those available to the recipient in the market.

158.   Article 14, which we have said is relevant context in interpreting Article 1.1(b), supports our view that the marketplace is an appropriate basis for comparison. The guidelines set forth in Article 14 relate to equity investments, loans, loan guarantees, the provision of goods or services by a government, and the purchase of goods by a government. A "benefit" arises under each of the guidelines if the recipient has received a "financial contribution" on terms more favourable than those available to the recipient in the market.

159.   Canada has argued that the Panel erred in failing to take account of paragraph 1 of Annex IV as part of the relevant context of the term "benefit". We fail to see the relevance of this provision to the interpretation of "benefit" in Article 1.1(b) of the SCM Agreement. Annex IV provides a method for calculating the total *ad valorem* subsidization of a product under the "serious prejudice" provisions of Article 6

of the SCM Agreement, with a view to determining whether a subsidy is used in such a manner as to have "adverse effects". Annex IV, therefore, has nothing to do with whether a *"benefit"* has been conferred, nor with whether a measure constitutes a subsidy within the meaning of Article 1.1. We agree with the Panel that Annex IV is not useful context for interpreting Article 1.1(b) of the SCM Agreement.

160. Canada insists that the concept of "cost to government" is relevant in the interpretation of "benefit". We note that this interpretation of "benefit" would exclude from the scope of that term those situations where a "benefit" is conferred by a private body under the direction of government. These situations cannot be *excluded* from the definition of "benefit" in Article 1.1(b), given that they are specifically *included* in the definition of "financial contribution" in Article 1.1(a)(iv). We are, therefore, not persuaded by this argument of Canada.

161. In light of the foregoing, we find that the Panel has not erred in its interpretation of the word "benefit", as used in Article 1.1(b) of the SCM Agreement.

Notes and Questions

(1) Both US and WTO law generally value subsidies as the benefit to the recipient rather than the cost to the government. Thus, for example, if a government borrows at 8% and lends at 10%, the recipient of the loan will still be subsidized if that recipient would otherwise have to pay 12%. In general, is the cost to the government or the benefit to the recipient the proper standard as an economic matter? How is the benefit to the recipient measured? In particular, how is *the* market interest rate determined if it is shown, as is often the case, that different banks and other financing entities offer varying rates for similar transactions?

(2) An exception to this principle under WTO law may be found in item k of the Illustrative List of Export Subsidies contained in Annex I to the SCM Agreement. It provides that the value of an export credit subsidy is to be measured against the cost of the funds to the entity that grants the subsidy. Why the distinction? Another exception arises via paragraph 1 of Annex IV, regarding serious prejudice. Again, why the difference?

(3) Suppose that a government restricts the exportation of an essential input product for an industry. For example, suppose that the government of Canada restricts the exportation of logs, an essential input into the production of lumber. The economic effect of the restriction is to increase the domestic supply of logs, and thus to lower their price to domestic purchasers. Can such a policy be deemed a "subsidy?" If the price of the input product is indeed reduced, it seems that a "benefit" is present. But is there a "financial contribution by a government" within article 1.1(a)(1) of the SCM Agreement? The government itself does not provide a direct transfer of funds, forego revenue otherwise due, or provide goods and services. Might it be said that the government has implicitly "direct[ed] a private body" to supply goods to the domestic industry, in that if the sellers of logs cannot export them they have no choice but to sell them domestically? An unappealed panel decision answers this question in the negative, and holds that export

restrictions cannot constitute a subsidy to a downstream industry. Sound? See United States—Measures Treating Export Restraints as Subsidies (Softwood I), WT/DS194/R, adopted August 23, 2001.

UNITED STATES—IMPOSITION OF COUNTERVAILING DUTIES ON CERTAIN HOT–ROLLED LEAD AND BISMUTH CARBON STEEL PRODUCTS ORIGINATING IN THE UNITED KINGDOM

WT/DS138/AB/R.
Appellate Body Report adopted June 7, 2000.

2.   The alleged subsidies countervailed relate principally to equity infusions granted by the British Government to a state-owned company, British Steel Corporation ("BSC"), between 1977 and 1986. In 1986, BSC and Guest, Keen and Nettlefolds ("GKN"), a privately-owned company, created United Engineering Steels Limited ("UES") as a joint venture. Both BSC and GKN provided assets to UES, in return for equal shares in the joint venture. In particular, BSC spun-off its leaded bar-producing assets to UES. Negotiations concerning the spin-off were conducted at arm's length, consistent with commercial considerations. BSC ceased producing leaded bars after the spin-off of its leaded bar-producing assets to UES. In preparation for the privatization of BSC, British Steel plc ("BSplc") assumed, in September 1988, the property, rights and liabilities of BSC, including BSC's holding in UES. In December 1988, the British government completed the privatization through a sale of BSplc shares on the stock market. The United States Department of Commerce ("USDOC") found that the sale of BSplc shares was at arm's length, for fair market value and consistent with commercial considerations. On 20 March 1995, BSplc purchased GKN's holding in UES, whereupon UES was renamed British Steel Engineering Steels ("BSES").

3.   Countervailing duties on imports of leaded bars were originally imposed in 1993. Since then, the USDOC has undertaken a number of annual reviews of the countervailing duties applied to imports of leaded bars originating in the United Kingdom. The European Communities' claims in this case relate to the countervailing duties imposed following administrative reviews initiated in 1995, 1996 and 1997, which dealt with leaded bar imports in the calendar years 1994, 1995 and 1996, respectively. In each of these reviews, the USDOC applied its allocation methodology for untied, non-recurring subsidies to determine the amount of the benefit from the pre–1986 subsidies to BSC allocable to the relevant period of review. The USDOC also applied its "change-in-ownership" methodology to determine the extent to which the pre–1986 subsidies granted to BSC "travelled" to UES and/or BSplc/BSES. The USDOC imposed countervailing duties on the basis that a certain proportion of the subsidies granted to BSC had "passed through" to UES and BSplc/BSES. * * *

* * *

52. The principal question before the Panel in this case was whether the countervailing duties at issue were inconsistent with the obligations of the United States under the SCM Agreement. The Panel concluded:

> ... the countervailing duties imposed as a result of the USDOC's 1995, 1996 and 1997 administrative reviews are not in accordance with the premise underlying Articles 19.1, 19.4 and 21.2 of the SCM Agreement, Article VI:3 of the GATT 1994, and the object and purpose of countervailing duties as expressed in footnote 36 to Article 10. . . .

> Accordingly, we conclude that the countervailing duties imposed as a result of the USDOC's 1995, 1996 and 1997 administrative reviews are inconsistent with Article 10 of the SCM Agreement.

In reaching this conclusion, the Panel found:

> . . . . the USDOC should have examined the continued existence of "benefit" already deemed to have been conferred by the pre–1985/86 "financial contributions" to BSC, and it should have done so from the perspective of UES and BSplc/BSES respectively, and not BSC.

> . . .

> . . . . fair market value was paid for all productive assets, goodwill etc. employed by UES and BSplc/BSES in the production of leaded bars imported into the United States in 1994, 1995 and 1996. In these circumstances, we fail to see how pre–1985/86 "financial contributions" bestowed on BSC could subsequently be considered to confer a "benefit" on UES and BSplc/BSES during the relevant periods of review.

The United States appeals the above findings of the Panel.

53. Before we begin our analysis, we note that the measures at issue in this case are the duties imposed as a result of the 1995, 1996 and 1997 *administrative reviews*, not the duties imposed as a result of the original 1993 final countervailing duty determination. Nevertheless, the Panel based its reasoning in part on Articles 19.1 and 19.4 of the SCM Agreement, which are provisions dealing with the imposition of counter-vailing duties as a result of a final determination. We believe that Articles 19.1 and 19.4 provide useful context in interpreting the obligations regarding administrative reviews, but that the applicable provision covering administrative reviews is Article 21, which provides in paragraph 2:

> The authorities shall review the need for the continued imposition of the duty, where warranted, on their own initiative or, provided that a reasonable period of time has elapsed since the imposition of the definitive countervailing duty, upon request by any interested party which submits positive information substantiating the need for a review. Interested parties shall have the right to request the authorities to examine whether the continued imposition of the duty is necessary to offset subsidization, whether the injury would be likely

to continue or recur if the duty were removed or varied, or both. If, as a result of the review under this paragraph, the authorities determine that the countervailing duty is no longer warranted, it shall be terminated immediately.

Pursuant to this paragraph, the authorities of a Member applying a countervailing duty must, where warranted, "review the need for the continued imposition of the duty". In carrying out such a review, the authorities must "examine whether the continued imposition of the duty is necessary to offset subsidization" and/or "whether the injury would be likely to continue or recur if the duty were removed or varied". Article 21.2 provides a review mechanism to ensure that Members comply with the rule set out in Article 21.1 of the SCM Agreement, which stipulates:

A countervailing duty shall remain in force only as long as and to the extent necessary to counteract subsidization which is causing injury.

54.   Setting aside the issue of injury, which does not arise in this case, we note that in order to establish the continued need for countervailing duties, an investigating authority will have to make a finding on *subsidization*, i.e., whether or not the subsidy continues to exist. If there is no longer a subsidy, there would no longer be any need for a countervailing duty.

55.   Article 1.1 of the SCM Agreement defines a "subsidy" as follows:

For the purpose of this Agreement, a subsidy shall be deemed to exist if:

(a)(1) there is a financial contribution by a government or any public body within the territory of a Member . . .

and

(b) a benefit is thereby conferred.

The existence of a "financial contribution" is not at issue in this appeal. The principal issue in this appeal concerns the interpretation of the term "benefit" in Article 1.1 above.

56.   The United States argues, on the basis of footnote 36 to Article 10 of the SCM Agreement and Article VI:3 of the GATT 1994, that the relevant "benefit" is a benefit to a company's *productive operations*, rather than, as the Panel held, a benefit to *legal or natural persons*. It is true, as the United States emphasizes, that footnote 36 to Article 10 of the SCM Agreement and Article VI:3 of the GATT 1994 both refer to subsidies bestowed or granted directly or indirectly "upon the manufacture, production or export of any merchandise". In our view, however, it does not necessarily follow from this wording that the "benefit" referred to in Article 1.1(b) of the SCM Agreement is a benefit to *productive operations*.

57.   In our Report in *Canada–Aircraft,* we stated, with regard to the term "benefit" in Article 1.1(b):

A "benefit" does not exist in the abstract, but must be received and enjoyed by a beneficiary or a recipient. Logically, a "benefit" can be said to arise only if a person, natural or legal, or a group of persons, has in fact received something. The term "benefit", therefore, implies that there must be a recipient. . . .

* * *

58. We, therefore, agree with the Panel's findings that benefit as used in Article 1.1(b) is concerned with the "benefit to the recipient", that such recipient must be a natural or legal person, and that in the present case:

> . . . . in order to determine whether any subsidy was bestowed on the production by UES and BSplc/BSES respectively of leaded bars imported into the United States in 1994, 1995 and 1996, it is necessary to determine whether there was any "benefit" to UES and BSplc respectively (*i.e.*, the producers of the imported leaded bars at issue).

59. The United States also appeals the Panel's finding that the investigating authority must demonstrate the existence, during the relevant period of investigation or review, of a continued "benefit" from a prior "financial contribution". The United States argues that the use of the present tense of the verb "is conferred" in Article 1.1 of the SCM Agreement shows that an investigating authority must demonstrate the existence of "benefit" only at the time the "financial contribution" was made. The United States also relies on the context of Article 1.1, in particular Articles 14 and 27.13 of the SCM Agreement, in support of this interpretation.

60. Article 1.1 sets out the definition of a subsidy for the purposes of the SCM Agreement. However, Article 1.1 does not address the *time* at which the "financial contribution" and/or the "benefit" must be shown to exist. We therefore consider that Article 1.1 does not provide a basis for the argument made by the United States. We also find nothing in Articles 14 or 27.13 of the SCM Agreement that supports the United States' position.

61. We have already stated that in a case involving countervailing duties imposed as a result of an administrative review, Articles 21.1 and 21.2 of the SCM Agreement are relevant. As discussed above, Article 21.1 allows Members to apply countervailing duties "only as long as and to the extent necessary to counteract subsidization . . .". Article 21.2 sets out a review mechanism to ensure that Members comply with this rule. In an administrative review pursuant to Article 21.2, the investigating authority may be presented with "positive information" that the "financial contribution" has been repaid or withdrawn and/or that the "benefit" no longer accrues. On the basis of its assessment of the information presented to it by interested parties, as well as of other evidence before it relating to the period of review, the investigating authority must determine whether there is a continuing need for the application of counter-

vailing duties. The investigating authority is not free to ignore such information. If it were free to ignore this information, the review mechanism under Article 21.2 would have no purpose.

62.   Therefore, we agree with the Panel that while an investigating authority may presume, in the context of an administrative review under Article 21.2, that a "benefit" continues to flow from an untied, non-recurring "financial contribution", this presumption can never be "irrebuttable". In this case, given the changes in ownership leading to the creation of UES and BSplc/BSES, the USDOC was *required* under Article 21.2 to examine, on the basis of the information before it relating to these changes, whether a "benefit" accrued to UES and BSplc/BSES. We thus agree with the Panel's finding that:

> .... the changes in ownership leading to the creation of UES and BSplc/BSES should have caused the USDOC to examine whether the production of leaded bars by UES and BSplc/BSES respectively, and not BSC, was subsidized. In particular, the USDOC should have examined the continued existence of "benefit" already deemed to have been conferred by the pre–1985/86 "financial contributions" to BSC, and it should have done so from the perspective of UES and BSplc/BSES respectively, and not BSC.

63.   The Panel, however, also stated:

> .... when an investigation or review takes place, the investigating authority must establish the existence of a "financial contribution" and "benefit" during the relevant period of investigation or review. Only then will that investigating authority be able to conclude, to the satisfaction of Article 1.1 (and Article 21), that there **is** a "financial contribution", and that a "benefit" **is** thereby conferred.

We do not agree with the Panel's implied view that, in the context of an administrative review under Article 21.2, an investigating authority must *always* establish the existence of a "benefit" during the period of review *in the same way as* an investigating authority must establish a "benefit" in an original investigation. We believe that it is important to distinguish between the original investigation leading to the imposition of countervailing duties and the administrative review. In an original investigation, the investigating authority must establish that *all* conditions set out in the SCM Agreement for the imposition of countervailing duties are fulfilled. In an administrative review, however, the investigating authority must address those issues which have been raised before it by the interested parties or, in the case of an investigation conducted on its own initiative, those issues which warranted the examination.

64.   Having found that, in the particular circumstances of this case, the USDOC, in its 1995, 1996 and 1997 administrative reviews, should have examined the continued existence of a "benefit" to UES and BSplc/BSES, the Panel subsequently examined whether the "financial contributions" bestowed on BSC between 1977 and 1986 could be considered to confer a "benefit" on UES and BSplc/BSES. The Panel found that:

... fair market value was paid for all productive assets, goodwill etc. employed by UES and BSplc/BSES in the production of leaded bars imported into the United States in 1994, 1995 and 1996. In these circumstances, we fail to see how pre–1985/86 "financial contributions" bestowed on BSC could subsequently be considered to confer a "benefit" on UES and BSplc/BSES during the relevant periods of review.

The United States also appeals this finding.

65. In examining this issue, we note that, according to the Panel:

The United States has not denied that the BSC spin-off was negotiated for fair market value.

and that:

Both parties agree that the privatization of British Steel plc was "at arm's length, for fair market value and consistent with commercial considerations".

* * *

67. Therefore, the issue before us is whether, given these factual findings, the Panel erred in finding that the "financial contributions" bestowed on BSC could not be considered to confer a "benefit" on UES and BSplc/BSES. We note that in our Report in *Canada–Aircraft*, we stated:

.... the word "benefit", as used in Article 1.1(b), implies some kind of comparison. This must be so, for there can be no "benefit" to the recipient unless the "financial contribution" makes the recipient "better off" than it would otherwise have been, absent that contribution. In our view, the marketplace provides an appropriate basis for comparison in determining whether a "benefit" has been "conferred", because the trade-distorting potential of a "financial contribution" can be identified by determining whether the recipient has received a "financial contribution" on terms more favourable than those available to the recipient in the market.

68. The question whether a "financial contribution" confers a "benefit" depends, therefore, on whether the recipient has received a "financial contribution" on terms more favourable than those available to the recipient in the market. In the present case, the Panel made factual findings that UES and BSplc/BSES paid fair market value for all the productive assets, goodwill, etc., they acquired from BSC and subsequently used in the production of leaded bars imported into the United States in 1994, 1995 and 1996. We, therefore, see no error in the Panel's conclusion that, in the specific circumstances of this case, the "financial contributions" bestowed on BSC between 1977 and 1986 could not be deemed to confer a "benefit" on UES and BSplc/BSES.

Notes and Questions

(1) Are you persuaded that the transfer of assets to new owners at "fair market value" cleanses them of any subsidy? Suppose that a government

builds a plant at a cost of $1 million. It then auctions the plant off to the highest bidder and receives $500,000, which is the most that any rational buyer would pay. Has resource allocation been distorted? Could one argue that the buyer receives a "benefit" in being able to purchase something that costs $1 million for a price of only $500,000?

(2) In response to this case and others, the US Department of Commerce has changed its methodology for analyzing subsidization following a change in ownership of assets. See 66 Fed. Reg. 37125 (June 23, 2003). It now employs a presumption that a privatization sale extinguishes any subsidy, if and only if the sale occurs at "fair market value" and in an "arm's-length transaction." The presumption of extinguishment can be rebutted, however, if "the broader market conditions necessary for the transaction price to reflect fairly and accurately the subsidy benefit were not present, or were severely distorted by government action." Examples of the latter situation would be circumstances where the market participants did not have "equal access to information," where there were no safeguards against "collusive behavior," or where the government accompanied privatization transactions with other incentives such as exemptions from environmental remediation obligations. Do the new rules pass muster under the Appellate Body's analysis? Suppose the United States were to conclude that the "broader market conditions" had been distorted by a government that had constructed excess capacity in the relevant industry, thereby depressing the sale price of the assets?

UNITED STATES—FINAL COUNTERVAILING DUTY DETERMINATION WITH RESPECT TO CERTAIN SOFTWOOD LUMBER FROM CANADA (SOFTWOOD IV)

WT/DS257/AB/R.
Appellate Body Report, adopted February 17, 2004.

[The United States imposed countervailing duties based on a finding that Canadian provinces sold timber harvesting rights (or "stumpage" rights) to Canadian lumber companies for a price that did not reflect their fair market value. Canada argued that no subsidy existed because private timber in Canada was sold at the same price as government timber. The United States argued that the low government prices caused private timber sellers to reduce their prices as well, and that they were thus not a reliable benchmark. The amount of the subsidy was then calculated based on "cross-border comparisons," whereby timber prices in neighboring US border states were used to measure the fair market value of the Canadian timber on provincial lands. A further set of issues in the case involved "pass through," whereby the United States at times presumed that subsidies received by timber harvesters were passed through to unrelated sawmills and lumber remanufacturers.]

V.   CALCULATION OF BENEFIT

A.   *Introduction*

77.   * * * In the countervailing duty investigation underlying this dispute, USDOC determined that there were "no useable market-deter-

mined prices between Canadian buyers and sellers'' that could be used to determine whether provincial stumpage programmes provide goods for less than adequate remuneration. Therefore, USDOC used as a benchmark prices of stumpage in certain bordering states in the northern United States, making adjustments purportedly to account for differences in conditions between those states and Canadian provinces.

78. Before the Panel, Canada claimed that, by rejecting private prices in Canada, and using instead adjusted cross-border prices, USDOC acted inconsistently with Articles 10, 14, 14(d), 19.1, 19.4, and 32.1 of the SCM Agreement and Article VI:3 of the GATT 1994. The United States responded that the ''appropriate benchmark for measuring benefit in this case would normally have been the fair market value of timber in Canada'', but that private timber sales in Canada did not represent a ''commercial'' market because they were distorted by government intervention. Therefore, according to the United States, USDOC was entitled to use prices for comparable stumpage from alternative sources, in this case from the bordering states in the northern United States, which were then adjusted to reflect market conditions in Canada, in accordance with Articles 1 and 14(d) of the SCM Agreement.

79. The Panel agreed with Canada and found that:

In light of the fact that the USDOC acknowledged the existence of a private stumpage market in Canada, we find that the resort to US prices as the benchmark for the determination of benefit on grounds that private prices in Canada were distorted is inconsistent with Article 14 (d) [of the] SCM Agreement.

* * *

B. *Whether Article 14(d) of the SCM Agreement Permits Investigating Authorities to Use a Benchmark Other Than Private Prices in the Country of Provision*

* * *

83. Article 14 of the SCM Agreement provides:

* * *

(d) the provision of goods or services or purchase of goods by a government shall not be considered as conferring a benefit unless the provision is made for less than adequate remuneration, or the purchase is made for more than adequate remuneration. The adequacy of remuneration shall be determined in relation to prevailing market conditions for the good or service in question in the country of provision or purchase (including price, quality, availability, marketability, transportation and other conditions of purchase or sale).

* * *

85. The question then becomes how to determine whether adequate remuneration was paid for the goods provided by the government.

This is dealt with in the second sentence of Article 14(d), which provides that "[t]he adequacy of remuneration shall be determined in relation to prevailing market conditions for the good or service in question in the country of provision or purchase (including price, quality, availability, marketability, transportation and other conditions of purchase or sale)".

86. * * * From this, the Panel reasoned that:

Therefore, according to Article 14 (d), the price of the good provided, its quality, availability, marketability, transportation and other conditions of purchase or sale which are used as the benchmark for determining the adequacy of the remuneration have to be such as are prevailing in the country of provision. In sum, a plain reading of the text of Article 14 (d) leads us to the initial conclusion that the market which is to be used as the benchmark for determining benefit to the recipient is the market of the country of provision, in this case Canada.

The Panel then went on to reject the United States' contention that the term "market" means "fair market value" or a market "undistorted by government intervention". * * *

* * *

88. We now examine the meaning of the phrase "in relation to" in Article 14(d). We are of the view that the Panel failed to give proper meaning and effect to the phrase "in relation to" as it is used in Article 14(d). The Panel reasoned that the phrase "in relation to" in the context of Article 14(d) means "in comparison with". Hence, the Panel concluded that the determination of the adequacy of remuneration has to be made "in comparison with" prevailing market conditions for the goods in the country of provision, and thus no other comparison will do when private market prices exist. We do not agree.

89. As we see it, the phrase "in relation to" implies a comparative exercise, but its meaning is not limited to "in comparison with". The phrase "in relation to" has a meaning similar to the phrases "as regards" and "with respect to". These phrases do not denote the rigid comparison suggested by the Panel, but may imply a broader sense of "relation, connection, reference". Thus, the use of the phrase "in relation to" in Article 14(d) suggests that, contrary to the Panel's understanding, the drafters did not intend to exclude any possibility of using as a benchmark something other than private prices in the market of the country of provision. This is not to say, however, that private prices in the market of provision may be disregarded. Rather, it must be demonstrated that, based on the facts of the case, the benchmark chosen relates or refers to, or is connected with, the conditions prevailing in the market of the country of provision.

90. Although Article 14(d) does not dictate that private prices are to be used as the exclusive benchmark in all situations, it does emphasize by its terms that prices of similar goods sold by private suppliers in the country of provision are the primary benchmark that investigating

authorities must use when determining whether goods have been provided by a government for less than adequate remuneration. In this case, both participants and the third participants agree that the starting-point, when determining adequacy of remuneration, is the prices at which the same or similar goods are sold by private suppliers in arm's length transactions in the country of provision. This approach reflects the fact that private prices in the market of provision will generally represent an appropriate measure of the "adequacy of remuneration" for the provision of goods. However, this may not always be the case. As will be explained below, investigating authorities may use a benchmark other than private prices in the country of provision under Article 14(d), if it is first established that private prices in that country are distorted because of the government's predominant role in providing those goods.

* * *

C. When May Investigating Authorities Use a Benchmark Other Than Private Prices in the Country of Provision?

97. Having established that prices in the market of the country of provision are the primary, but not the exclusive, benchmark for calculating benefit, we come to the next question that arises in our analysis, namely, when an investigating authority may use a benchmark other than private prices in the country of provision for purposes of calculating the benefit under Article 14(d).

98. Despite the Panel's finding that Article 14(d) requires the use of private prices in the country of provision as the benchmark whenever they exist, the Panel nevertheless acknowledged that "it will in certain situations not be possible to use in-country prices" as a benchmark, and gave two examples of such situations, neither of which it found to be present in the underlying countervailing duty investigation: (i) where the government is the only supplier of the particular goods in the country; and, (ii) where the government administratively controls all of the prices for those goods in the country. In these situations, the Panel reasoned that the "only remaining possibility would appear to be the construction of some sort of a proxy for, or estimate of, the market price for the good in that country".

99. The United States claims, on appeal, that the Panel erred in not recognizing that Article 14(d) also allows investigating authorities to use a benchmark other than private prices in a third situation: where private prices are "substantially influenced" or "effectively determined" by the government's financial contribution. We understand that by "substantially influenced" or "effectively determined", the United States refers to a situation where the government has such a predominant role in the market, as a provider of certain goods, that private suppliers will align their prices with those of the government-provided goods; in other words, a situation where the government effectively acts as a "price-setter" and private suppliers are "price-takers". Considering that the situation of government predominance in the market, as a

provider of certain goods, is the only one raised on appeal by the United States, we will limit our examination to whether an investigating authority may use a benchmark other than private prices in the country of provision in that particular situation.

100. In analyzing this question, we have some difficulty with the Panel's approach of treating a situation in which the government is the sole supplier of certain goods differently from a situation in which the government is the predominant supplier of those goods. In terms of market distortion and effect on prices, there may be little difference between situations where the government is the sole provider of certain goods and situations where the government has a predominant role in the market as a provider of those goods. Whenever the government is the predominant provider of certain goods, even if not the sole provider, it is likely that it can affect through its own pricing strategy the prices of private providers for those goods, inducing the latter to align their prices to the point where there may be little difference, if any, between the government price and the private prices. This would be so even if the government price does not represent adequate remuneration. The resulting comparison of prices carried out under the Panel's approach to interpreting Article 14(d) would indicate a "benefit" that is artificially low, or even zero, such that the full extent of the subsidy would not be captured, as the Panel itself acknowledged. As a result, the subsidy disciplines in the SCM Agreement and the right of Members to countervail subsidies could be undermined or circumvented when the government is a predominant provider of certain goods.

* * *

D. Alternative Benchmarks

104. Having reached this conclusion, the question thus arises what alternative benchmark, consistent with Article 14(d), could be available in such situations, for purposes of determining whether the goods have been provided by the government for less than adequate remuneration.

* * *

106. We agree with the submissions of the participants and third participants that alternative methods for determining the adequacy of remuneration could include proxies that take into account prices for similar goods quoted on world markets, or proxies constructed on the basis of production costs. We emphasize, however, that where an investigating authority proceeds in this manner, it is under an obligation to ensure that the resulting benchmark relates or refers to, or is connected with, prevailing market conditions in the country of provision, and must reflect price, quality, availability, marketability, transportation and other conditions of purchase or sale, as required by Article 14(d). At any rate, we are not called upon, in this appeal, to suggest alternative methods that would be available to investigating authorities upon a determination that private prices in the country of provision are distorted due to the

government's predominant role in the market as provider of the same or similar goods. Nor are we required to determine the consistency with Article 14(d) of all the alternative methods mentioned by the participants and third participants; such assessment will depend on how any such method is applied in a particular case. We, therefore, make no findings on the WTO-consistency of any of these methods in the abstract.

107. Rather, it is only the specific alternative method used by USDOC in the underlying countervailing duty investigation for determining the adequacy of remuneration that is at issue in this appeal. The benchmark used by USDOC consisted of prices of stumpage in bordering states of the northern United States. The United States explained before the Panel that cross-border stumpage prices were duly adjusted to take into account market conditions prevailing in Canada. We turn to this method used by USDOC next.

E. The Consistency of the Alternative Benchmark Used by USDOC with Article 14(d)

* * *

112. [T]he Panel's ultimate finding that USDOC failed to determine benefit consistently with Articles 10, 14, 14(d) and 32.1 of the SCM Agreement is predicated exclusively on its interpretation of Article 14(d), which we have already reversed above. Thus, we must also reverse the Panel's consequential finding, in paragraph 7.65 of the Panel Report, that USDOC failed to determine benefit consistently with Articles 14 and 14(d) of the SCM Agreement and that the imposition of countervailing duties based on that determination was inconsistent with Articles 10 and 32.1 of that Agreement. It does not necessarily follow, however, that we find that USDOC's determination of benefit in the underlying countervailing duty investigation is consistent with Article 14(d), as we have interpreted this provision in the preceding paragraphs.

* * *

114. Both participants acknowledged during the oral hearing that, if we were to modify or reverse the Panel's interpretation of Article 14(d), there would be insufficient findings of fact by the Panel or undisputed facts in the Panel record to enable us to complete the legal analysis of this issue. We agree. * * *

* * *

122. * * * Having found that there is an insufficient factual basis to complete the legal analysis, we do not make findings on whether USDOC's determination of the existence and amount of benefit in the underlying countervailing duty investigation is consistent or inconsistent with Articles 14 and 14(d) of the SCM Agreement and whether the imposition of countervailing duties based on that determination is consistent or inconsistent with Articles 10 and 32.1 of that Agreement.

VI. PASS-THROUGH

* * *

127. The United States notes that it "does not appeal the Panel's finding that, where the subsidy is received by independent harvesters, i.e., entities that do not produce [softwood lumber] product[s] under investigation and operate at arm's length, a pass through analysis would be required to determine if the subsidy received by the independent harvesters was indirectly bestowed on production of softwood lumber". Thus, the situation where tenured timber harvesters do not process logs into softwood lumber and sell at arm's length all the logs they harvest to unrelated sawmills is not before us in this appeal. We also note that Canada does not argue that a pass-through analysis is required in the absence of arm's length transactions between tenured timber harvesters, sawmills and remanufacturers. Hence, the situation where vertically integrated enterprises, not operating at arm's length, harvest timber under stumpage contracts, produce softwood lumber and remanufacture lumber, is also not before us.

128. * * * This appeal thus concerns the situations where: (i) a tenured timber harvester owns a sawmill and processes some of the logs it harvests into softwood lumber, but at the same time sells at arm's length some of the logs it harvests to unrelated sawmills for processing into lumber; and (ii) a tenured timber harvester processes logs it harvests into lumber, and sells at arm's length some, or all, of the lumber it produces to lumber remanufacturers for further processing.
* * *

* * *

135. * * * Article VI:3 of the GATT 1994 reads:

[n]o countervailing duty shall be levied on any product of the territory of a Member imported into the territory of another Member in excess of an amount equal to the estimated bounty or subsidy determined to have been granted, directly or indirectly, on the manufacture, production or export of such product in the country of origin or exportation... The term "countervailing duty" shall be understood to mean a special duty levied for the purpose of offsetting any bounty or subsidy bestowed, directly, or indirectly, upon the manufacture, production or export or any merchandise.

* * *

138. We note that, if we were to find that USDOC's final determination and the imposition of countervailing duties on Canadian imports of softwood lumber products contravene the requirements of Article VI:3 of the GATT 1994, the United States necessarily would not have "take[n] all necessary steps to ensure that the imposition of a countervailing duty ... is in accordance with the provisions of Article VI of GATT 1994", as required by Article 10 of the SCM Agreement. The "specific action against a subsidy" taken by the United States would also

not, as required by Article 32.1 of the SCM Agreement, be "in accordance with the provisions of GATT 1994, as interpreted by the [SCM] Agreement". Consequently, any inconsistency of the United States' imposition of countervailing duties on Canadian imports of softwood lumber products with Article VI:3 of the GATT 1994, would necessarily render this measure inconsistent also with Articles 10 and 32.1 of the SCM Agreement.

139. The Panel described the pass-through problem as follows: "[w]here the subsidies at issue are received by someone other than the producer of the investigated product, the question arises whether there is subsidization in respect of that product." In addressing this question, we note that Article VI:3 prohibits levying countervailing duties on an imported product "in excess of an amount equal to the estimated ... subsidy determined to have been granted, directly or indirectly, on the manufacture, production or export of such product". According to Article VI:3, countervailing duties are "levied for the purpose of offsetting ... subsid[ies] bestowed, directly or indirectly, upon the manufacture, production or export of any merchandise". The definition of the term "countervailing duties" in footnote 36 to Article 10 of the SCM Agreement is along the same lines.

140. The phrase "subsid[ies] bestowed ... indirectly", as used in Article VI:3, implies that financial contributions by the government to the production of inputs used in manufacturing products subject to an investigation are not, in principle, excluded from the amount of subsidies that may be offset through the imposition of countervailing duties on the processed product. Where the producer of the input is not the same entity as the producer of the processed product, it cannot be presumed, however, that the subsidy bestowed on the input passes through to the processed product. In such case, it is necessary to analyze to what extent subsidies on inputs may be included in the determination of the total amount of subsidies bestowed upon processed products. For it is only the subsidies determined to have been granted upon the processed products that may be offset by levying countervailing duties on those products.

141. In our view, it would not be possible to determine whether countervailing duties levied on the processed product are in excess of the amount of the total subsidy accruing to that product, without establishing whether, and in what amount, subsidies bestowed on the producer of the input flowed through, downstream, to the producer of the product processed from that input. Because Article VI:3 permits offsetting, through countervailing duties, no more than the "subsidy determined to have been granted ... directly or indirectly, on the manufacture [or] production ... of such product", it follows that Members must not impose duties to offset an amount of the input subsidy that has not passed through to the countervailed processed products. It is only the amount by which an indirect subsidy granted to producers of inputs flows through to the processed product, together with the amount of subsidy bestowed directly on producers of the processed product, that may be offset through the imposition of countervailing duties. The

definition of "countervailing duties" in footnote 36 to Article 10 of the SCM Agreement supports this interpretation of the requirements of Article VI:3 of the GATT 1994.

* * *

157. As we mentioned above, the United States acknowledges that a pass-through analysis is required where a tenured "independent" harvester, which does not own a sawmill and thus does not produce softwood lumber, sells logs at arm's length to unrelated sawmills. We do not see why the mere fact that a tenured harvesters owns—or does not own—a sawmill, should affect whether a pass-through analysis is necessary with respect to logs sold at arm's length. We understand the United States to argue that benefits, initially attached to logs, but retained by a harvester/sawmill when the logs are sold in arm's length transactions to unrelated buyers, may be used by such a vendor to "cross-subsidize" its own production of softwood lumber processed in-house from other logs. We agree, in the abstract, that a transfer of benefits from logs sold in arm's length transactions to lumber produced in-house from different logs is possible for a harvester that owns a sawmill. But whether, in fact, this occurs depends on the particular case under examination. In any event, these arm's length sales at issue concern logs, which are not products subject to the investigation. Accordingly, in cases where logs are sold by a harvester/sawmill in arm's length transactions to unrelated sawmills, it may not be assumed that benefits attaching to the logs (non-subject products) automatically pass through to the lumber (the subject product) produced by the harvester/sawmill. A pass-through analysis is thus required in such situations.

158. Indeed, we disagree with the proposition that, as long as an enterprise produces products subject to an investigation, any benefits accruing to the same enterprise from subsidies conferred on any different products it produces (which are not subject to that investigation), could be included, without need of a pass-through analysis, in the total amount of subsidization found to exist for the investigated product, and that may be offset by levying countervailing duties on that product. We conclude that the pass-through of the benefit cannot be presumed with respect to arm's length sales of logs by harvesters, who own sawmills, to unrelated sawmills, for further processing.

* * *

160. We turn now to the second pass-through situation at issue, which concerns tenured timber harvesters that own or are related to sawmills, process the logs they harvest into softwood lumber, and sell lumber to unrelated remanufacturers for further processing. The question here is whether a pass-through analysis is required in respect of these arm's length sales of softwood lumber.

161. In this situation, the products of both the harvesters/sawmills and the remanufacturers are subject to the investigation. It is uncontested that "certain softwood lumber" includes "primary" lumber produced

by sawmills and "remanufactured" lumber produced by remanufacturers. We also note that USDOC chose to conduct this investigation on an aggregate basis. Canada accepts that aggregate investigations are contemplated by Article 19 of the SCM Agreement, but takes issue with how USDOC calculated the total amount of the subsidy and the countervailing duty rate in the investigation at issue. We have confirmed above that performing investigations on an aggregate basis is permitted under the SCM Agreement and the GATT 1994, and we have observed that calculation issues are beyond the scope of this appeal.

162. The Panel reasoned in this respect:

> . . . some portion of any subsidy from stumpage is attributable to the harvester/sawmill's production of the lumber for re-manufacturing and some is attributable to the other products (including lumber) that the harvester/sawmill produces. Here, if the subsidies attributable to the lumber for re-manufacturing are not passed through to the re-manufacturer that purchases it, then those subsidies should not be included in the numerator of the subsidization equation, as in this situation it is the re-manufactured product, not the upstream lumber product, that is the subject merchandise under investigation.

163. In our view, the Panel's reasoning confuses pass-through questions that may arise when individual enterprises are investigated, with questions arising in the calculation of the total amount and the rate of subsidization on an aggregate basis. The question before us is whether it is necessary to analyze whether benefits have been passed through from one product subject to the investigation (primary softwood lumber) to another product subject to that investigation (remanufactured softwood lumber). Once it has been established that benefits from subsidies received by producers of non-subject products (that is, inputs) have passed through to producers of subject products (primary and remanufactured softwood lumber), we do not see why a further pass-through analysis between producers of subject products should be required in an investigation conducted on an aggregate basis. In this situation, it is not necessary to calculate precisely how subsidy benefits are divided up between the producers of subject products in order to calculate, on an aggregate basis, the total amount of subsidy and the country-wide countervailing duty rate for those subject products.

164. It is true, as pointed out by the Panel, that a particular shipment of remanufactured softwood lumber entering the United States might not be subsidized at all, especially if the remanufacturer purchased the primary lumber it processed at arm's length. It is also far from certain that every single shipment of primary lumber will, in fact, be subsidized, or, even if it is, that it is subsidized at the average ad valorem country-wide rate determined in an aggregate investigation. Nevertheless, as we indicated above, Article 19 of the SCM Agreement contemplates the imposition of a country-wide countervailing duty rate, even when a specific exporter is not subsidized, or when that country-wide rate does not match the precise amount of subsidization benefiting

a specific shipment. And as mentioned above, the possibility for an exporter not investigated individually to request, pursuant to Article 19.3, an expedited review to establish an individual countervailing duty rate for that exporter, also confirms that a country-wide duty rate may, in principle, be imposed. However, the pass-through question would not be the same when determining, through the review procedure provided for in Article 19.3, an individual countervailing duty rate for the exporter that requested the review. In such a review, it is likely that a pass-through analysis would be required to determine whether input subsidies on logs, having passed through to the production of softwood lumber inputs, have passed through also to remanufactured lumber produced from those inputs by the particular exporter.

165.   For these reasons, we reverse the Panel's finding, in paragraph 7.99 of the Panel Report, that USDOC's failure to conduct a pass-through analysis in respect of arm's length sales of lumber by tenured harvesters/sawmills to unrelated remanufacturers is inconsistent with Articles 10 and 32.1 of the SCM Agreement and Article VI:3 of the GATT 1994.

Notes and Questions

(1) The long running softwood dispute was settled, at least for now, by the Softwood Lumber Agreement in late 2006.

(2) If one accepts the premise that timber sales by the Canadian government suppress the prices received by private sellers, what sort of alternative benchmark makes the most sense? Is there any principled way to choose between, say, an estimated cost of production benchmark, and a price established in another jurisdiction?

(3) Do you understand the distinction being drawn as to the pass through issue between situations in which the subsidy is bestowed on a non-subject product, and situations in which it is bestowed on a subject product? Do you concur that no pass through analysis is required when the subsidy on the non-subject product is received by a vertically integrated firm that also produces the subject product? The US rules on the subject of "upstream subsidies" are to be found in Section 771A of the Tariff Act of 1930 and in 19 C.F.R. sec. 351.523.

(4) The notion that timber or "stumpage" pricing can confer a subsidy has been challenged by various economic experts during the history of the softwood dispute. Their argument has sometimes been termed the "economic rent" argument, and is summarized in the following excerpt from a NAFTA binational panel review of a US countervailing duty on softwood imports in 1993:

> No one in this case challenged the principles of classical Ricardian economic theory regarding natural resources. According to this 150–year old theory, the market for natural resources does not exhibit the normal elasticities in supply and demand whereby if prices go up (or down), purchase and production of the good will correspondingly go down (or up). Rather, because of the fact that natural resources have a basically fixed supply and strictly limited alternative uses, no such output and

downstream price effects will flow from movements in resource prices, at least within what is called the "normal range." No matter how high the price charged by the owner within that range, as long as the purchaser of the right to harvest the natural resource can sell the product downstream for a higher price, the producer will harvest and sell as much of the resource as it can while making a profit on each unit sold. By the same token, no matter how low the price charged by the owner, the producer will not be able to harvest and sell more of this resource because the fixed (i.e., inelastic) supply of the latter means there is no more of the resource available for that purpose. The price set for the natural resource does play a key role in determining how the financial value—the economic rent—of the resource will be divided between owner and purchaser. It does not, however, have any market distorting impact on the output of the resource and thence on the amount and price of downstream products.

There are two important qualifications to this thesis. One concerns the situation in which the price charged for the resource is or becomes "excessive" for some reason. The resource price is excessive if, when added to the costs of harvesting and transporting the resource, it makes the total cost of production greater than the price that will be paid by downstream users. In such a case, where the producer will incur a loss on extraction and sale of each unit, reduction in price of the resource does permit an increase in levels of production. However, such a resource price effect is not market "distorting". The price has simply been moved to the normal range one would expect in a competitive market in which owners of a resource try to set their prices at a level where they can make some sales and profits, rather than leave the resource lie fallow.

A different qualification must be made at the other end of the price range. Here, rather than charge a positive price for the resource, the owners enter into a contractual arrangement whereby producers actually secure a "net benefit" from purchase and harvesting of the resource. For example, the resource may be located in a remote region where costs of extraction and transportation are themselves higher than the sale price of the same resource located in more accessible locations. If the owner (in particular, a government) has other social and political reasons for wanting to see this region developed, it may charge a nominal price for the resource, but pursuant to a contract whereby the owner makes considerably greater expenditures on extraction and transportation of the resource. This is done in order to lower the ultimate cost to producers sufficiently to make production in this location profitable. Such an in-kind net benefit will have an impact on output of the resource in question, precisely because it alters the normal market signals regarding this particular resource location. It is at this level, and only at this level, that government decisions about pricing natural resources can constitute a countervailable "subsidy" if one adopts the market distortion analysis of the legislation.

We conclude that, in this case, Commerce should have considered whether or not these provincial programs could and did have a distorting effect on the operation of normal competitive markets before concluding that these governmental policies involve the type of "preferential" pricing that constitutes a countervailable subsidy within the meaning of the Tariff Act. Accordingly, we remand this part of the stumpage decision back to Commerce for review of all the evidence regarding the natural resource market for standing timber in light of the legal principles formulated in this decision.

Certain Softwood Lumber Products From Canada, United States–Canada Free Trade Agreement Binational Panel Review, Panel No. U.S.A.–92–1904–02, Report of May 6, 1993.

Do you find the economic rent argument persuasive? If, indeed, stumpage prices below fair market value do not affect prices in the downstream log market, then is it clear that they will have any effect on the prices charged for timber on neighboring private lands in Canada—can private owners not charge what the market will bear, based on the same downstream log price, that they could if the government timber were sold for full value?

(5) A related, more general set of issues, involves the question whether a "subsidy" should only be found where the governmental measure at issue can be shown to have had a cross-border effect. Suppose, for purposes of illustration, that the government of Japan decides to give each Japanese automaker a billion yen on a one time basis. Suppose further that the auto companies respond by distributing the money to their shareholders as an extra dividend. By hypothesis, there is no expansion of Japanese auto production in response to the government's largesse, and thus no adverse impact of the "subsidy" on US competitors. Is it nevertheless countervailable in the event of a complaint by the US industry? Is it actionable under WTO law? Various commentators have argued through the years that a "subsidy" should only be found where the program in question can be shown to have stimulated production or exports and thus had an effect on prices abroad. See the symposium beginning at 21 L. & Pol.Intl.Bus. 503 (1990); Goetz, Granet & Schwartz, The Meaning of "Subsidy" and "Injury" in the Countervailing Duty Law, 6 Intl.Rev.L. & Econ. 17 (1986).

(B) SPECIFICITY

Article 1.2 of the SCM Agreement provides that a subsidy is subject to the disciplines of Part II of the Agreement (prohibited subsidies), Part III (actionable subsidies), or Part V (countervailable subsidies) only if the subsidy is "specific." Article 2 further provides that export subsidies and import substitution subsidies are automatically "specific." Otherwise, specificity arises if the subsidy is "specific to an enterprise or industry or group of enterprises or industries" including situations in which subsidies are limited to "certain enterprises located within a designated geographical region within the jurisdiction of the granting authority." Thus, before "domestic subsidies" are subject to the disciplines of the Agreement, they must in effect be sufficiently "targeted."

The specificity test originated in US law, and its rationale is plainly to afford some basis for distinguishing legitimate functions of government from functions that are somehow unfair or trade-distorting. A

NAFTA panel[1] explained its understanding of the rationale for the specificity test as follows: "Specificity analysis is required because it has long been recognized that the reach of the countervailing duty law should not extend to benefits and services, like highways, law enforcement and education, that governments routinely provide to their population at large. The statutory basis for drawing the distinction between such widely used and specific domestic subsidies is found in the definition of 'subsidy,' [which] includes domestic subsidies only if 'provided to a specific enterprise or industry, or group of enterprises or industries.' Legislative history of this law provides two rationales for this specificity test. First, Congress recognized that every export benefits from some general government assistance (e.g., public roads, utilities, education), and therefore, every import would arguably be subject to countervailing duties without such a test. Second, government programs which do not confer benefits selectively do not upset the free market forces that countervailing duties are meant to offset."

To date, specificity rulings have received virtually no attention in the WTO dispute process. Accordingly, we offer the following excerpt from a US countervailing duty case to give a flavor of how the test applies in practice.

OIL COUNTRY TUBULAR GOODS FROM AUSTRIA

Preliminary Determination, 50 Fed. Reg. 23334.
Intl.Trade Admin. (1985).

[The ITA determined that the exporter, Voest–Alpine AG, benefited from subsidies in the form of equity infusions from the Austrian government (0.08%), grants by the Austrian government (1.60%) and subsidized export financing (0.08%), all of which are typical forms of subsidization. The ITA also examined a number of other government programs:]

D. Various Cash Grant Programs

Petitioners alleged that the Federal government provides cash grants, equal to 100,000 Schillings per job created, to companies relocating to, or expanding plants in the special development and coal-mining areas.

The government response stated that a 100,000 Schilling Action program was established by joint resolution between Austria's federal and state governments. Funds from this program are granted (by both the federal and the applicable state government) as a premium in an amount no greater than 100,000 Schillings for each newly created job. To receive these cash grants, a company must meet the following requirements: (1) The recipient must have invested at least 400,000 Schillings in a newly estimated plant or 200,000 Schillings in the expansion of an

1. Pure and Alloy Magnesium From Canada, Panel No. USA–92–1904–03. Report of August 16, 1993.

old plant; (2) the character of the investment must be innovative; and (3) the recipient must make an employment guarantee of at least three years.

Under this program, Voest–Alpine AG was awarded a cash grant for the construction of its new seamless tube mill in Kindberg, Styria. Accordingly, 50 percent of any grant awarded is to be paid by the state (Styria) government and 50 percent by the federal government. The grant was approved in 1981 with payment to be made in two equal installments. The first installment was paid in May, 1983; the second installment is still outstanding. We have no information on the record that the rate of federal support does not vary from state to state and/or that the support is available in all parts of Austria. Because this program may be limited to companies located in specific regions, we preliminarily determine this grant to be countervailable.

II.   Programs Determined Not to Confer a Subsidy

We preliminarily determine that subsidies are not being provided to manufacturers, producers, or exporters in Austria of oil country tubular goods under the following programs:

* * *

B.   *Labor Subsidies*

Petitioners alleged that Voest–Alpine AG has received benefits from labor programs sponsored by the Austrian government.

1.   *Government-Funded Labor Training.* The government response stated that under the Labor Market Promotion Act, Law No. 31/1969, companies in Austria may receive funds from the Austrian government for the establishment of in-house training programs to improve worker skills or to teach workers new vocations. In addition, under this law companies in Austria with low levels of capacity utilization may receive funds to be paid to the workers involved in training combined with reduced hours of work. Employees whose working hours are reduced receive support payments compensating them for the loss in earnings sustained. Workers receiving benefits under this program spend the difference between their reduced working hours and their normal working hours in training programs. The government's response stated that funding for these labor training programs is available to all sectors of Austrian industry and not just to the iron and steel industry or to export-related industries. Because this program is not limited to a specific enterprise or industry, or group of enterprises or industries, we preliminarily determine that the program does not constitute a subsidy.

2.   *Special Assistant Act.* The Special Assistant Act of 1973, Law No. 642/1973, provides enhanced unemployment benefits for former employees of sectors of the economy hit by the downturn which have been let go and are at least 55 years old for men or 50 years old for women. The Federal Minister of Social Affairs is empowered to determine by decree which sectors of the economy warrant application of the

provisions of the law. In a decree issued on March 21, 1983, the iron and steel industry was included within the provisions of this law. The government of Austria's response stated that payments under this law are made directly to the workers who have been laid off by an employer. The employer itself is not entitled to any support or subsidies under this law and is not relieved from payment of any expenses otherwise the obligation of such employer. Because this program provides assistance to workers and does not relieve Voest–Alpine AG of any expenses or obligations, we preliminarily determine that the company does not receive a subsidy under this program.

* * *

D. Loan Guaranty Program

Petitioners alleged that Voest–Alpine AG has received substantial loan guarantees from the Austrian government. The Austrian government's response stated that loans issued by insurance companies in Austria must meet certain strict requirements for investment security according to section 77 of the Insurance Supervisory Law of October 18, 1976. Because of these requirements, commercial loans by insurance companies must be guaranteed by the government or secured by a pledge of a real estate. The government guarantees insurance company loans to Voest–Alpine AG to enable the insurance companies to find larger-scale legally eligible investments for placement of their investment portfolios, rather than to enable Voest–Alpine AG to raise funds, which it is able to do through other sources. Accordingly, we preliminarily determine that this program does not provide subsidies to Voest–Alpine AG.

Notes and Questions

(1) To what degree can the specificity test serve to identify foreign government practices that distort the market? Might subsidies widely available to the agricultural sector create distortions even if they are not legally "specific?" Might a subsidy directed to a single industry that produces a positive external benefit to the economy, such as a research and development spillover, not correct rather than create a distortion? What about targeted subsidies that help firms to comply with expensive government regulations?

(2) Are you persuaded that a firm receives no "subsidy" when its workers receive payments but not the firm itself? Should the law distinguish between situations in which subsidies are given to the producers of a product, versus equal subsidies to the product's purchasers? Recall the *Italian Farm Machinery* case under GATT, excerpted in Section 12.2.

(3) Is there any analytically sound basis for deciding when the number of recipients is small enough that the program becomes "specific to an enterprise or industry or group of enterprises or industries"? Does Section 771(5A) of the US Tariff Act of 1930 add any greater clarity or predictability? Consider the following scenarios:

(i) A government makes grants to companies that train workers for certain electronic or "hi-tech" jobs.

(ii) A government makes grants to laid-off workers, which relieve firms of legal obligations to make severance payments.

(iii) A government makes grants to firms to enable the closing of unprofitable facilities.

(iv) Government-owned timber is sold at prices below fair market value. The timber is harvested by both lumber producers and paper producers. The resulting lumber and paper in turn is used by a wide range of downstream industries.

(v) A government provides income support to all farmers who produce fruits or vegetables.

(vi) Same scenario, but the income support is limited to a depressed agricultural region within the granting jurisdiction.

(C) PROHIBITED (EXPORT AND IMPORT SUBSTITUTION) SUBSIDIES

Brazil and Canada have engaged in a lengthy and complex series of cases in which each has accused the other of providing export subsides to producers of small commercial or "regional" aircraft. Two of the resulting decisions are excerpted here.

CANADA—MEASURES AFFECTING THE EXPORT OF CIVILIAN AIRCRAFT—RECOURSE BY BRAZIL TO ARTICLE 21.5 OF THE DSU

WT/DS70/AB/RW.
Appellate Body Report adopted August 4, 2000.

2.   The original panel found, *inter alia*, that "Canada Account debt financing since 1 January 1995 for the export of Canadian regional aircraft" and "[TPC—Technology Partnerships Canada] assistance to the Canadian regional aircraft industry [constitute] export subsidies inconsistent with Article[s] 3.1(a) and 3.2 of the SCM Agreement". The original panel concluded that "Canada shall withdraw [these] subsidies.... within 90 days."

* * *

4.   Canada took steps to implement the recommendations and rulings of the DSB with respect to both the Canada Account and TPC. Taking the view that these measures were not consistent with Article 3.1(a) of the SCM Agreement, Brazil requested that the matter be referred to the original panel, pursuant to Article 21.5 of the *Understanding on Rules and Procedures Governing the Settlement of Disputes* (the "DSU"). * * *

* * *

34.   Canada restructured the TPC programme by amending TPC's operating documentation, with effect from 18 November 1999. In that respect, Canada introduced, *inter alia*, the following new TPC documents: "Special Operating Agency Framework Document"; "Terms and

Conditions"; "Investment Application Guide"; and, "Investment Decision Document". The new TPC "Terms and Conditions" document states that the "granting of contributions will not be contingent, either in law or in fact, upon actual or anticipated export performance" (Section 6.1). This is repeated in the TPC Investment Application Guide (Section 5). Section 5 of that Guide also states that "administering officials will not request or consider information concerning the extent to which applicant or recipient enterprises do or may export."

* * *

39. In conducting its review under Article 21.5 of the DSU, the Article 21.5 Panel declined to examine Brazil's argument that "the Canadian regional aircraft industry continues to be 'specifically targeted' for TPC assistance because of its undisputed export orientation." The Article 21.5 Panel stated that this argument "did not form part" of the reasoning of the original panel and was "not relevant to the present dispute, which concerns the issue of whether or not Canada *has implemented the DSB recommendation* ...". (emphasis added)

40. We have already noted that these proceedings, under Article 21.5 of the DSU, concern the "consistency" of the revised TPC programme with Article 3.1(a) of the SCM Agreement. Therefore, we disagree with the Article 21.5 Panel that the scope of these Article 21.5 dispute settlement proceedings is limited to "the issue of whether or not Canada *has implemented the DSB recommendation*". The recommendation of the DSB was that the measure found to be a prohibited export subsidy must be withdrawn within 90 days of the adoption of the Appellate Body Report and the original panel report, as modified—that is, by 18 November 1999. That recommendation to "withdraw" the prohibited export subsidy did not, of course, cover the new measure—because the new measure did not exist when the DSB made its recommendation. It follows then that the task of the Article 21.5 Panel in this case is, in fact, to determine whether the new measure—the revised TPC programme—is consistent with Article 3.1(a) of the SCM Agreement.

* * *

42. Consequently, in these proceedings, the task of the Article 21.5 Panel was not limited solely to determining whether the revised TPC programme had been rid of those aspects of the original measure—the TPC programme, as previously constituted—that had been identified in the original proceedings, in the context of all of the facts, as not being consistent with Canada's WTO obligations. Rather, the Article 21.5 Panel was obliged to examine the revised TPC programme for its consistency with Article 3.1(a) of the SCM Agreement. The fact that Brazil's argument in these Article 21.5 proceedings "did not form part" of the original panel's reasoning relating to the *previous* TPC programme does not necessarily mean that this argument is "not relevant" to the Article 21.5 proceedings, which relate to the *revised* TPC programme. In our view, the Article 21.5 Panel should have examined the

merits of Brazil's argument as it relates to the *revised* TPC programme. We conclude, therefore, that the Article 21.5 Panel erred by declining to examine Brazil's argument that the revised TPC programme "specifically targeted" the Canadian regional aircraft industry for assistance because of its export-orientation.

43. With a view to resolving this dispute, and considering that the undisputed facts on the record are adequate for this purpose, we believe that we should complete the Article 21.5 Panel's analysis by examining this argument. In so doing, we observe that the essence of Brazil's argument is that the Canadian regional aircraft industry is "specifically targeted" for assistance in two different ways under the revised TPC programme.

44. First, Brazil notes that the "Eligible Areas" for TPC assistance include "Aerospace and Defence", and that these industrial sectors are the sole such sectors to be identified expressly as eligible for TPC assistance. The other two "Eligible Areas" are "Environmental Technologies" and "Enabling Technologies", which could involve projects drawn from any industrial sector, including "Aerospace and Defence". In Brazil's view, the express identification of "Aerospace and Defence" as "Eligible Areas" puts these industrial sectors, which include the Canadian regional aircraft industry, in a privileged position and represents "specific targeting" of the Canadian regional aircraft industry. Second, Brazil maintains that the Canadian regional aircraft industry is also "specifically targeted", in practice, through the allocation of TPC funding assistance. According to Brazil, 65 per cent of TPC funding has, in the past, "gone to the [Canadian] aerospace industry".

45. Brazil maintains that the reason for these two types of "targeting" is the high export-orientation of the industry. In support of this argument, Brazil relies on a series of statements made by Canadian Government Ministers, Members of Parliament, other government officials, and by the TPC itself, regarding the objectives of TPC. Brazil acknowledges that the statements it relies upon were made in connection with the *old* TPC. programme, as *previously* constituted. Brazil argues, nevertheless, that the "specific targeting" is a fact that tends to establish that the revised TPC programme involves subsidies which are *de facto* export contingent.

46. Canada does not contest any of the factual assertions made by Brazil in presenting its "specific targeting" argument. However, Canada emphasizes that the statements Brazil relies upon were made in relation to the *old* TPC programme, not to the *revised* programme. Canada also states that no TPC assistance has been granted or committed under the *revised* TPC programme to the Canadian regional aircraft industry. In other words, Canada asserts that there have been, thus far, no transactions involving the Canadian regional aircraft industry under this new measure. Brazil does not contest this assertion.

47. It is worth recalling that the granting of a subsidy is not, in and of itself, prohibited under the SCM Agreement. Nor does granting a

"subsidy", without more, constitute an inconsistency with that Agreement. The universe of subsidies is vast. Not all subsidies are inconsistent with the SCM Agreement. The only "prohibited" subsidies are those identified in Article 3 of the SCM Agreement; Article 3.1(a) of that Agreement prohibits those subsidies that are "contingent, in law or in fact, upon export performance". We have stated previously that "a subsidy is prohibited under Article 3.1(a) if it is 'conditional' upon export performance, that is, if it is 'dependent for its existence on' export performance." We have also emphasized that a "relationship of conditionality or dependence", namely that the granting of a subsidy should be "tied to" the export performance, lies at the "very heart" of the legal standard in Article 3.1(a) of the SCM Agreement.

48. To demonstrate the existence of this "relationship of conditionality or dependence", we have also stated that it is *not* sufficient to show that a subsidy is granted in the knowledge, or with the anticipation, that exports will result. Such knowledge or anticipation does not, taken alone, demonstrate that the granting of the subsidy is "contingent upon" export performance. The second sentence of footnote 4 of the SCM Agreement stipulates, in this regard, that the *"mere fact* that a subsidy is granted to enterprises which export shall not *for that reason alone* be considered to be an export subsidy ...". (emphasis added) That fact, by itself, does not, therefore, compel the conclusion that there is a "relationship of conditionality or dependence", such that the granting of a subsidy is "tied to" export performance. However, we have also said that the export-orientation of a recipient "may be taken into account as *a* relevant fact, provided it is one of several facts which are considered and is not the only fact supporting a finding" of export contingency. (underlining added)

49. Recalling all this, at its core, we see Brazil's argument about "specific targeting" essentially as a contention that the SCM Agreement precludes the two types of targeting Brazil identifies simply because of the high export-orientation of the Canadian regional aircraft industry. However, in our view, the fact that an industrial sector has a high export-orientation is not, by itself, sufficient to preclude that sector from being expressly identified as an eligible or privileged recipient of subsidies. Nor does the high export-orientation of an industry limit, in principle, the amount of subsidies that may be granted to that industry. As we have said, granting subsidies, in itself, is not prohibited. Under Article 3.1(a) of the SCM Agreement, the subsidy must be *export contingent* to be prohibited. The two "targeting" factors *may* very well be relevant to an inquiry under Article 3.1(a) of the SCM Agreement, but they do not necessarily provide conclusive evidence that the granting of a subsidy is *"contingent"*, *"conditional"* or *"dependent"* upon export performance. In these proceedings, we do not see the two "targeting" factors, by themselves, as adequate proof of prohibited export *contingency.*

50. Moreover, the evidence that Brazil relies upon in seeking to demonstrate that the Canadian regional aircraft industry is "specifically

targeted" *because of* its high export-orientation relates to the TPC as *previously* constituted, and not to the *revised* TPC programme. In particular, Brazil relies upon evidence of the high proportion of TPC funding allocated to the Canadian regional aircraft industry under the *old* TPC programme and on statements made in connection with that programme by Canadian Government Ministers, Members of Parliament, officials, and by TPC itself. The burden of explaining the relevance of the evidence, in proving the claim made, naturally rests on whoever presents that evidence. Brazil has not offered any convincing explanation as to why the evidence relating to the *old* TPC programme continues to be relevant to the *revised* TPC programme. We do not believe we should simply assume that this particular evidence is relevant in respect of the revised TPC programme.

51.   For all these reasons, we find that Brazil has not sufficiently established that the Canadian regional aircraft industry is "specifically targeted" *because of* its high export-orientation.

52.   We conclude that Brazil has failed to establish that the revised TPC programme is inconsistent with Article 3.1(a) of the SCM Agreement. We also conclude that Brazil has failed to establish that Canada has not implemented the recommendations and rulings of the DSB. The outcome of the present proceedings does not, of course, preclude possible subsequent dispute resolution proceedings regarding the WTO-consistency of the revised TPC programme, or of specific instances of assistance actually granted under that programme.

BRAZIL—EXPORT FINANCING PROGRAMME FOR AIRCRAFT

WT/DS46/AB/R.
Appellate Body Report adopted August 20, 1999.

3.   PROEX is administered by the Comit de Crédito as Exportaçes (the "Committee"), an inter-agency group within the Ministry of Finance in Brazil. Day-to-day operations of PROEX are conducted by the Bank of Brazil. Under PROEX, the Government of Brazil provides interest rate equalization subsidies for sales by Brazilian exporters, including Embraer.

4.   For sales of regional aircraft, PROEX interest rate equalization subsidies amount to 3.8 percentage points of the actual interest rate on any particular transaction. The lending bank charges its normal interest rate for the transaction, and receives payment from two sources: the purchaser, and the Government of Brazil. Of the total interest rate payments, the Government of Brazil pays 3.8 percentage points, and the purchaser pays the rest. In this way, PROEX reduces the financing costs of the purchaser and, thus, reduces the overall cost to the purchaser of purchasing an Embraer aircraft.

* * *

7. The Panel considered claims by Canada that PROEX is inconsistent with the prohibition on export subsidies under Article 3.1(a) of the Agreement on Subsidies and Countervailing Measures (the "SCM Agreement"). * * * The Panel reached the conclusion that PROEX interest rate equalization payments are subsidies within the meaning of Article 1 of the SCM Agreement, and are contingent upon export under Article 3.1(a) of that Agreement. In reaching this conclusion, the Panel found that the PROEX interest rate equalization payments were not "permitted" under the first paragraph of item (k) of the Illustrative List of Export Subsidies in Annex I of the SCM Agreement (the "Illustrative List"). The Panel also found that Brazil failed to comply with certain of the conditions of Article 27.4 of the SCM Agreement, and that, therefore, the prohibition in Article 3.1(a) of the SCM Agreement applied to Brazil. Having found that PROEX payments are inconsistent with Article 3.1(a), the Panel recommended that Brazil withdraw the subsidies within 90 days pursuant to Article 4.7 of the SCM Agreement.

[The Appellate Body held that Brazil, as a developing country, was not exempt from the prohibition on export subsidies because it had increased its subsidies in contravention of Article 27.4 of the SCM Agreement.]

* * *

VIII. Are PROEX Interest Rate Equalization Payments Used "To Secure a Material Advantage in the Field of Export Credit Terms"?

165. Having determined that Brazil has not complied with the provisions of Article 27.4, we conclude that the prohibition of Article 3.1(a) applies to Brazil in this case. We must therefore examine Brazil's appeal of the finding of the Panel relating to Brazil's alleged "affirmative defence" under item (k) of the Illustrative List.

* * *

168. Item (k) of the Illustrative List provides as follows:

(k) The grant by governments (or special institutions controlled by and/or acting under the authority of governments) of export credits at rates below those which they actually have to pay for the funds so employed (or would have to pay if they borrowed on international capital markets in order to obtain funds of the same maturity and other credit terms and denominated in the same currency as the export credit), or the payment by them of all or part of the costs incurred by exporters or financial institutions in obtaining credits, *in so far as they are used to secure a material advantage in the field of export credit terms.*

Provided, however, that if a Member is a party to an international undertaking on official export credits to which at least twelve original Members to this Agreement are parties as of 1 January 1979 (or a successor undertaking which has been adopted by those original Members), or if in practice a Member applies the interest rates provisions of the relevant undertaking, an export credit practice which is in conformity with those provisions shall not be considered an export subsidy prohibited by this Agreement. (emphasis added)

169.   Before the Panel, Brazil contended that, although PROEX payments are export subsidies, they are nevertheless "permitted" by item (k) of the Illustrative List. The Panel noted that to rule in favour of Brazil on this issue, it would need to find for Brazil on all of the following three points: first, that PROEX payments are "the payment by [governments] of all or part of the costs incurred by exporters or financial institutions in obtaining credits"; second, that PROEX payments are not "used to secure a material advantage in the field of export credit terms"; and, third, that a "payment" within the meaning of item (k) which is not "used to secure a material advantage in the field of export credit terms" is "permitted" by the SCM Agreement even though it is a subsidy which is contingent upon export performance within the meaning of Article 3.1(a) of that Agreement. The Panel also noted that Brazil had explicitly acknowledged that the "material advantage" clause in item (k) constitutes an "affirmative defence", and, therefore, that the burden of establishing that "defence" was on Brazil.

170.   The Panel concluded as follows:

In conclusion, we consider that an item (k) payment is "used to secure a material advantage" where the payment has resulted in the availability of export credit on terms which are more favourable than the terms that would otherwise have been available to the purchaser with respect to the transaction in question. Even if we were to assume, as argued by Brazil, that PROEX payments are the "payment by [a government] of all or part of the costs incurred by exporters or financial institutions in obtaining credits", and that such payments can be deemed to be "permitted" by item (k) where they are not "used to secure a material advantage in the field of export credit terms"—issues we need not here decide—Brazil has failed to demonstrate the PROEX payments are not "used to secure a material advantage in the field of export credit terms". Accordingly, we reject Brazil's affirmative defense based on item (k) of the Illustrative List.

* * *

177.   As always, we examine the terms of the provision at issue, in this case, the "material advantage" clause of item (k). We look first to the ordinary meaning of the language used. We agree with the Panel's statement that the ordinary meaning of the word "advantage" is "a more favorable or improved position" or a "superior position". However, we note that item (k) does not refer simply to "advantage". The word "advantage" is qualified by the adjective "material". As mentioned before, in its ultimate interpretation of the phrase "used to secure a material advantage" which the Panel finally adopted and applied to the

export subsidies for regional aircraft under PROEX, the Panel read the word "material" out of item (k). This, we consider to be an error.

178. We also note that in two of its interpretive statements, the Panel used the "marketplace" as the benchmark for comparing the subsidies on sales of regional aircraft under PROEX. However, in two other statements, the Panel made no reference to the "marketplace" as the basis for comparison. In one of those two statements, it referred, instead, more generally, to "the terms that would have been available in the absence of the payment." For the purposes of our analysis, we will assume that the Panel meant to use the "marketplace" as the benchmark for determining whether the PROEX subsidies were "used to secure a material advantage".

179. We note that the Panel adopted an interpretation of the "material advantage" clause in item (k) of the Illustrative List that is, in effect, the same as the interpretation of the term "benefit" in Article 1.1(b) of the SCM Agreement adopted by the panel in *Canada–Aircraft*. If the "material advantage" clause in item (k) is to have *any* meaning, it must mean something different from "benefit" in Article 1.1(b). It will be recalled that for any payment to be a "subsidy" within the meaning of Article 1.1, that payment must consist of both a "financial contribution" and a "benefit". The first paragraph of item (k) describes a type of subsidy that is deemed to be a prohibited export subsidy. Obviously, when a payment by a government constitutes a "financial contribution" and confers a "benefit", it is, a "subsidy" under Article 1.1. Thus, the phrase in item (k), "in so far as they are used to secure a material advantage", would have no meaning if it were simply to be equated with the term "benefit" in the definition of "subsidy". As a matter of treaty interpretation, this cannot be so. Therefore, we consider it an error to interpret the "material advantage" clause in item (k) of the Illustrative List as meaning the same as the term "benefit" in Article 1.1(b) of the SCM Agreement.

180. We note that there are two paragraphs in item (k), and that the "material advantage" clause appears in the first paragraph. Furthermore, the second paragraph is a proviso to the first paragraph. The second paragraph applies when a Member is "a party to an international undertaking on official export credits" which satisfies the conditions of the proviso, or when a Member "applies the interest rates provisions of the relevant undertaking". In such circumstances, an "export credit practice" which is in conformity with the provisions of "an international undertaking on official export credits" shall not be considered an export subsidy prohibited by the SCM Agreement. The OECD Arrangement is an "international undertaking on official export credits" that satisfies the requirements of the proviso in the second paragraph in item (k). However, Brazil did not invoke the proviso in the second paragraph of item (k) in its defence. Brazil argued before the Panel that it "has concluded that conformity to the OECD provisions is too expensive."

181.   Thus, this case falls under the first paragraph, and not under the proviso of the second paragraph, of item (k) of the Illustrative List. Consequently, the issue here is whether the export subsidies for regional aircraft under PROEX "are used to secure" for Brazil "a material advantage in the field of export credit terms". Nevertheless, we see the second paragraph of item (k) as useful context for interpreting the "material advantage" clause in the text of the first paragraph. The OECD Arrangement establishes minimum interest rate guidelines for export credits supported by its participants ("officially-supported export credits"). Article 15 of the Arrangement defines the minimum interest rates applicable to officially-supported export credits as the Commercial Interest Reference Rates ("CIRRs"). Article 16 provides a methodology by which a CIRR, for the currency of each participant, may be determined for this purpose. We believe that the OECD Arrangement can be appropriately viewed as one example of an international undertaking providing a specific market benchmark by which to assess whether payments by governments, coming within the provisions of item (k), are "used to secure a material advantage in the field of export credit terms". Therefore, in our view, the appropriate comparison to be made in determining whether a payment is "used to secure a material advantage", within the meaning of item (k), is between the actual interest rate applicable in a particular export sales transaction after deduction of the government payment (the "*net* interest rate") and the relevant CIRR.

182.   It should be noted that the commercial interest rate with respect to a loan in any given currency varies according to the length of maturity as well as the creditworthiness of the borrower. Thus, a potential borrower is not faced with a single commercial interest rate, but rather with a range of rates. Under the OECD Arrangement, a CIRR is the *minimum* commercial rate available in that range for a particular currency. In any given case, whether or not a government payment is used to secure a "*material* advantage", as opposed to an "advantage" that is not "material", may well depend on where the *net* interest rate applicable to the particular transaction at issue in that case stands in relation to the range of commercial rates available. The fact that a particular *net* interest rate is below the relevant CIRR is a positive indication that the government payment in that case has been "used to secure a material advantage in the field of export credit terms".

183.   Brazil has conceded that it has the burden of proving an alleged "affirmative defence" under item (k). In light of our analysis, it was for Brazil to establish a *prima facie* case that the export subsidies for regional aircraft under PROEX do not result in net interest rates below the relevant CIRR. We note, however, that Brazil did not provide *any information* to the Panel on this point. We also note that Brazil declined to provide this information, even when specifically requested to do so by the Panel. Because Brazil provided *no information* on the net interest rates paid by purchasers of Embraer aircraft in actual export sales transactions, we have no basis on which to compare the net

interest rates resulting from the interest rate equalization payments made under PROEX with the relevant CIRR.

184. Accordingly, we find that Brazil has failed to meet its burden of proving that export subsidies for regional aircraft under PROEX are not "used to secure a material advantage in the field of export credit terms" within the meaning of item (k) of the Illustrative List.

185. We are aware that the OECD Arrangement allows a government to "match", under certain conditions, officially-supported export credit terms provided by another government. In a particular case, this could result in net interest rates below the relevant CIRR. We are persuaded that "matching" in the sense of the OECD Arrangement is not applicable in this case. Before the Panel, Brazil argued for an interpretation of the clause "in the field of export credit terms" that would include as an "export credit term" the price at which a product is sold, and maintained that, therefore, Brazil was entitled to "offset" *all the subsidies* provided to Bombardier by the Government of Canada. The Panel rejected Brazil's argument, finding instead that "[w]e see nothing in the ordinary meaning of the phrase to suggest that 'the field of export credit terms' generally encompasses the price at which a product is sold." We note that this finding was *not* appealed by either Brazil or Canada. Even if we were to assume that the "matching" provisions of the OECD Arrangement apply in this case (an argument Brazil did not make), those provisions clearly do not allow a comparison to be made between the net interest rates applied as a consequence of subsidies granted by a particular Member and the total amount of subsidies provided by another Member. We also note that under PROEX, the interest rate equalization subsidies for regional aircraft are provided at an "across-the-board" rate of 3.8 per cent for *all* export sales transactions. That rate is fixed, and does not vary depending on the total amount of subsidies provided by another Member to its regional aircraft manufacturers. Thus, we cannot accept Brazil's argument that the export subsidies for regional aircraft under PROEX should be "permitted" because they "match" the total subsidies provided to Bombardier by the Government of Canada.

186. For all these reasons, we do not agree with the Panel's interpretation of the phrase "used to secure a material advantage in the field of export credit terms" in item (k) of the Illustrative List. We do, however, agree with the Panel's conclusion that "Brazil has failed to demonstrate the PROEX payments are not 'used to secure a material advantage in the field of export credit terms'." We, therefore, uphold the Panel's rejection of the "affirmative defence" claimed by Brazil on the basis of item (k) of the Illustrative List.

187. In so doing, we do not rule on whether the export subsidies for regional aircraft under PROEX are "the payment by [governments] of all or part of the costs incurred by exporters or financial institutions in obtaining credits". Nor do we opine on whether a "payment" within

the meaning of item (k) which is not "used to secure a material advantage within the field of export credit terms" is, *a contrario*, "permitted" by the SCM Agreement, even though it is a subsidy which is contingent upon export performance within the meaning of Article 3.1(a) of that Agreement. The Panel did not rule on these issues, and the lack of Panel findings on these issues was not appealed.

Notes and Questions

(1) Suppose that the new Canadian TPC program continues to provide support primarily to aircraft production, and perhaps to one or two other export-oriented industries. Would it then be WTO illegal?

(2) Brazil went another round with Canada on Canadian aircraft-related programs, resulting in a decision that payments under certain other programs amounted to prohibited export subsidies. See Canada—Export Credits and Loan Guarantees for Regional Aircraft, WT/DS222/R, adopted February 19, 2002.

(3) What if the Brazilian PROEX payments result in net interest rates of 0.5% below the pertinent CIRR benchmark. Would a violation of WTO law be proven? On this set of issues, see the Appellate Body report in the subsequent compliance panel proceeding, Brazil—Export Financing Programme for Aircraft, Recourse by Canada to Article 21.5 of the DSU, WT/DS46/AB/RW, adopted August 4, 2000. The saga continued as Brazil revised the PROEX program, and Canada continued to challenge it. See Brazil—Export Financing Programme for Aircraft, Second Recourse by Canada to Article 21.5 of the DSU, WT/DS46/RW/2, adopted August 23, 2001 (holding that PROEX III, *as such*, did not violate Art. 3.1 of the SCM Agreement).

(4) What was the issue left undecided regarding whether PROEX involved "the payment by [governments] of all or part of the costs incurred by exporters or financial institutions in obtaining credits?"

(5) The OECD Arrangement permits parties to match an offer by another party that is not in conformity with the Arrangement. Would such an offer fall within the terms of item (k) as quoted in paragraph 168 above? Two panels have said no, because when a party matches a derogation, it is not "in conformity with [the interest rate] provisions" of the Arrangement. Do you agree? See Canada—Measures Affecting the Export of Civilian Aircraft–Recourse to Article 21.5 by Brazil, WT/DS70/RW, para. 5.114, panel report adopted August 4, 2000; Brazil—Export Financing Programme for Aircraft—Second Recourse to Article 21.5 by Canada, WT/DS46/RW/2, para. 5.118, panel report adopted August 23, 2001. The issue was not appealed in either case.

(6) Which is the purpose of the second paragraph of item (k) of the Illustrative List? From an economic standpoint, why is an export subsidy any more acceptable if it is part of an international undertaking?

UNITED STATES—TAX TREATMENT FOR "FOREIGN SALES CORPORATIONS"

WT/DS108/AB/R.
Appellate Body Report adopted March 20, 2000.

A. Overview of Relevant United States Tax Laws

6. For United States citizens and residents, the tax laws of the United States generally operate "on a worldwide basis". This means that, generally, the United States asserts the right to tax all income earned "worldwide" by its citizens and residents. A corporation organized under the laws of one of the fifty American states or the District of Columbia is a "domestic", or United States, corporation, and is "resident" in the United States for purposes of this "worldwide" taxation system. Under United States tax law, "foreign" corporations are defined as all corporations that are *not* incorporated in one of the fifty states or the District of Columbia.

7. The United States generally taxes any income earned by foreign corporations within the territory of the United States. The United States generally does not tax income that is earned by foreign corporations outside the United States. However, such "foreign-source" income of a foreign corporation generally will be subject to United States taxation when such income is "effectively connected with the conduct of a trade or business within the United States". United States tax laws and regulations provide for the tax authorities to conduct a factual inquiry to determine whether a foreign corporation's income is "effectively connected" income.

8. Many foreign corporations are related to United States corporations. Generally, a United States parent corporation is only subject to taxation on income earned by its foreign subsidiary when such income is transferred to the United States parent in the form of a dividend. The period between the earning of such income by the subsidiary and the transfer to the United States parent company of a dividend is called "deferral" under the United States tax system, because the payment of tax on that income is deferred until the income is repatriated to the United States.

9. The United States has also adopted a series of "anti-deferral" regimes that depart from the principle of deferral and that, in general, respond to specific policy concerns about potential tax avoidance by United States corporations through foreign affiliates. One of these regimes is Subpart F of the United States Internal Revenue Code (the "IRC"), which limits the availability of deferral for certain types of income earned by certain controlled foreign subsidiaries of United States corporations. Under Subpart F, certain income earned by a foreign subsidiary can be imputed to its United States parent corporation even though it has not yet been repatriated to the parent in the form of a dividend. The effect of Subpart F is that a United States parent corpora-

tion is immediately subject to United States taxation on such imputed income even while the income remains with the foreign subsidiary.

10.   These generally prevailing United States tax rules are altered for FSCs [Foreign Sales Corporations] by the FSC measure.

B.   The FSC Measure

11.   FSCs are foreign corporations responsible for certain sales-related activities in connection with the sale or lease of goods produced in the United States for export outside the United States. The FSC measure essentially exempts a portion of an FSC's export-related foreign-source income from United States income tax. * * *

12.   A corporation must satisfy several conditions to qualify as an FSC. To qualify, a corporation must be a foreign corporation organized under the laws of a country that shares tax information with the United States, or under the laws of a United States possession other than Puerto Rico. The corporation must satisfy additional requirements relating to its foreign presence, to the keeping of records, and to its shareholders and directors. The corporation must also elect to be an FSC for a given fiscal year. There is no statutory requirement that an FSC be affiliated with or controlled by a United States corporation. The FSC measure is, however, such that the benefit to both FSCs and the United States corporations that supply goods for export will, as a practical matter, often be greater if the United States supplier is related to the FSC. As a result, many FSCs are controlled foreign subsidiaries of United States corporations.

13.   The foreign-source income of an FSC may be broadly divided into "foreign trade income" and all other foreign-source income. "Foreign trade income" is essentially the foreign-source income attributable to an FSC from qualifying transactions involving the export of goods from the United States. An FSC's other foreign-source income may include *inter alia* "investment income", such as interest, dividends and royalties, and active business income not deriving from qualifying export transactions. This appeal raises a number of issues with respect to the taxation of an FSC's *foreign trade income*. Foreign trade income is in turn divided into *exempt* foreign trade income and *non-exempt* foreign trade income. As explained below, the United States tax treatment of an FSC's *exempt* foreign trade income differs from the United States tax treatment of an FSC's *non-exempt* foreign trade income.

14.   An FSC's foreign trade income is its "foreign trading gross receipts" generated in qualifying transactions. Qualifying transactions involve the sale or lease of "export property" or the performance of services "related and subsidiary" to such sale or lease. "Export property" is property manufactured or produced in the United States by a person other than an FSC, sold or leased by or to an FSC for use, consumption or disposition outside the United States, and of which no more than 50 per cent of its fair market value is attributable to imports. In addition, for FSC income to be foreign trade income, certain economic

processes relating to qualifying transactions must take place outside the United States, and the FSC must be managed outside the United States.

15. Under the FSC measure, an FSC may, at its option, choose to apply one of three transfer pricing rules in order to calculate its foreign trade income from qualifying transactions. These pricing rules serve two purposes. First, the transfer pricing rules allocate the income from transactions involving United States export property as between an FSC and its United States supplier. The part of this income attributable to the FSC is its foreign trade income (i.e. exempt and non-exempt foreign trade income). The second purpose of the transfer pricing rules is to determine how much of the income from transactions involving United States export property that is allocated to the FSC as foreign trade income is *exempt* foreign trade income, and how much of it is *non-exempt* foreign trade income. The transfer pricing rule applied to determine the amount of the FSC's foreign trade income must also be applied to determine the division of that foreign trade income into exempt and non-exempt foreign trade income.

C. EXEMPTIONS PROVIDED BY THE FSC MEASURE

16. The FSC measure establishes three main exemptions which affect the United States tax liability of the FSC, of its United States supplier and, possibly United States shareholders. The first exemption relates to the United States tax treatment of the foreign-source income of a foreign corporation. Under United States law generally, the foreign-source income of a foreign corporation engaged in trade or business in the United States is taxable only to the extent that it is "effectively connected with the conduct of a trade or business within the United States". This rule applies whether or not a foreign corporation is controlled by a United States corporation. To determine whether the foreign-source income of a foreign corporation is "effectively connected with the conduct of a trade or business within the United States", a factual inquiry is undertaken by the tax authorities. Under the FSC measure, however, the exempt portion of an FSC's foreign trade income is "treated as foreign source income which is not effectively connected with the conduct of a trade or business within the United States". In other words, the exempt portion of the FSC's foreign trade income is not subject to a factual inquiry to determine if it is "effectively connected with the conduct of a trade or business within the United States". Thus, under this first exemption, a portion of an FSC's foreign-source income is *legislatively determined not to be* "effectively connected" and, therefore, is not taxable in the hands of the FSC—without regard to what conclusion an administrative factual inquiry might come to in the absence of the FSC measure.

17. The second exemption relates to the United States tax treatment of certain income earned by a foreign corporation that is controlled by a United States corporation. Under United States law generally, a United States shareholder in a controlled foreign corporation must include in his gross income each year a *pro rata* share of certain forms of

income of the foreign controlled corporation which has not yet been distributed to its United States parent. Such income is known as "Subpart F income". The United States shareholder corporation is immediately subject to United States tax on its Subpart F income, even though it has not yet received the income from its foreign affiliate. Under the FSC measure, however, the foreign trade income of an FSC is generally exempted from Subpart F. Thus, under this second exemption, the parent of an FSC is *not* required to declare its *pro rata* share of the undistributed income of an FSC that is derived from the foreign trade income of the FSC, and is *not* taxed on such income.

18. The third exemption deals with the tax treatment of dividends received by United States corporations from foreign corporations. Under United States law generally, dividends received by a United States corporation which are derived from the foreign-source income of a foreign corporation are taxable, unless such income has already been taxed under the Subpart F rules. Under the FSC measure, however, United States corporate shareholders of an FSC generally may deduct 100 per cent of dividends received from distributions made out of the foreign trade income of an FSC. Thus, under the third exemption, the parent of an FSC is generally not taxed on dividends received that are derived from the foreign trade income of the FSC.

* * *

ARTICLE 1.1(a) OF THE SCM AGREEMENT

90. We turn now to the definition of the term "subsidy" and, in particular, to Article 1.1(a)(1)(ii) [of the SCM Agreement], which provides that there is a "financial contribution" by a government, sufficient to fulfil that element in the definition of a "subsidy", where "government revenue that is *otherwise due* is foregone or not collected". (emphasis added) In our view, the *"foregoing"* of revenue *"otherwise* due" implies that less revenue has been raised by the government than would have been raised in a different situation, or, that is, "otherwise". Moreover, the word "foregone" suggests that the government has given up an entitlement to raise revenue that it could "otherwise" have raised. This cannot, however, be an entitlement in the abstract, because governments, in theory, could tax *all* revenues. There must, therefore, be some defined, normative benchmark against which a comparison can be made between the revenue actually raised and the revenue that would have been raised "otherwise". We, therefore, agree with the Panel that the term "otherwise due" implies some kind of comparison between the revenues due under the contested measure and revenues that would be due in some other situation. We also agree with the Panel that the basis of comparison must be the tax rules applied by the Member in question. To accept the argument of the United States that the comparator in determining what is "otherwise due" should be something other than the prevailing domestic standard of the Member in question would be to imply that WTO obligations somehow compel Members to choose a

particular kind of tax system; this is not so. A Member, in principle, has the sovereign authority to tax any particular categories of revenue it wishes. It is also free *not* to tax any particular categories of revenues. But, in both instances, the Member must respect its WTO obligations. What is "otherwise due", therefore, depends on the rules of taxation that each Member, by its own choice, establishes for itself.

91. The Panel found that the term "otherwise due" establishes a "but for" test, in terms of which the appropriate basis of comparison for determining whether revenues are "otherwise due" is "the situation that would prevail but for the measures in question". In the present case, this legal standard provides a sound basis for comparison because it is not difficult to establish in what way the foreign-source income of an FSC would be taxed "but for" the contested measure. However, we have certain abiding reservations about applying any legal standard, such as this "but for" test, in the place of the actual treaty language. Moreover, we would have particular misgivings about using a "but for" test if its application were limited to situations where there actually existed an alternative measure, under which the revenues in question would be taxed, absent the contested measure. It would, we believe, not be difficult to circumvent such a test by designing a tax regime under which there would be *no* general rule that applied formally to the revenues in question, absent the contested measures. We observe, therefore, that, although the Panel's "but for" test works in this case, it may not work in other cases. We note, however, that, in this dispute, the European Communities does not contest either the Panel's interpretation of the term "otherwise due" or the Panel's application of that term to the facts of this case. The United States also accepts the Panel's interpretation of that term as a general proposition.

92. The United States does, however, argue that the Panel erred because the general interpretation of the term "otherwise due" "must yield" to the standard the United States perceives in footnote 59 of the SCM Agreement, which the United States contends, is the "controlling legal provision" for interpretation of the term "otherwise due" with respect to a measure of the kind at issue. In the view of the United States, footnote 59 means that the FSC measure is not a "subsidy" under Article 1.1 of the SCM Agreement. Thus, the United States does not read footnote 59 as providing context for the general interpretation of the term "otherwise due"; rather, the United States views footnote 59 as a form of exception to that general interpretation. * * *

93. Article 1.1 sets forth the general definition of the term "subsidy" which applies "for the purpose of this Agreement". This definition, therefore, applies wherever the word "subsidy" occurs throughout the SCM Agreement and conditions the application of the provisions of that Agreement regarding *prohibited* subsidies in Part II, *actionable* subsidies in Part III, *non-actionable* subsidies in Part IV and countervailing measures in Part V. By contrast, footnote 59 relates to one item in the Illustrative List of Export Subsidies. Even if footnote 59 means—as the United States also argues—that a measure, such as the FSC measure, is

not a prohibited *export* subsidy, footnote 59 does not purport to establish an exception to the general definition of a *"subsidy"* otherwise applicable throughout the entire SCM Agreement. Under footnote 5 of the SCM Agreement, where the Illustrative List indicates that a measure is not a prohibited *export* subsidy, that measure is *not* deemed, for that reason alone, not to be a "subsidy". Rather, the measure is simply *not prohibited* under the Agreement. Other provisions of the SCM Agreement may, however, still apply to such a "subsidy". We note, moreover, that, under footnote 1 of the SCM Agreement, "the exemption of an exported *product* from duties or taxes *borne by the like product* when destined for domestic consumption . . . shall not be deemed to be a subsidy". (emphasis added) The tax measures identified in footnote 1 as not constituting a *"subsidy"* involve the exemption of exported *products* from *product-based* consumption taxes. The tax exemptions under the FSC measure relate to the taxation of *corporations* and not *products*. Footnote 1, therefore, does *not* cover measures such as the FSC measure.

94. In light of the above, we do not accept the United States' argument that footnote 59 qualifies the general interpretation of the term "otherwise due". That being so, it is not necessary for us to examine, at this point, the United States' arguments on the interpretation of footnote 59. * * *

95. The United States' appeal from the Panel's findings under Article 1.1 of the SCM Agreement is limited to its contention that the general interpretation of the term "otherwise due" is qualified by footnote 59. As we do not accept that sole ground of appeal, we uphold the Panel's finding that, under the FSC measure, the government of the United States foregoes revenue that is "otherwise due" under Article 1.1(a)(1)(ii) of the SCM Agreement. We note, in this respect, that the United States acknowledges that the FSC measure represents a departure from the rules of taxation that would "otherwise" apply to FSCs. We note also that the United States does not contest that, absent the FSC measure, the tax liability of the FSCs would be higher.

Article 3.1(a) of the SCM Agreement

96. The United States' appeal from the Panel's findings under Article 3.1(a) is limited to its contention that footnote 59 * * * means that the FSC measure is not an "export subsidy". Footnote 59 reads:

> The Members recognize that deferral need not amount to an export subsidy where, for example, appropriate interest charges are collected. *The Members reaffirm the principle that prices for goods in transactions between exporting enterprises and foreign buyers under their or under the same control should for tax purposes be the prices which would be charged between independent enterprises acting at arm's length.* Any Member may draw the attention of another Member to administrative or other practices which may contravene this principle and which result in a significant saving of direct taxes in export transactions. In such circumstances the Members shall

normally attempt to resolve their differences using the facilities of existing bilateral tax treaties or other specific international mechanisms, without prejudice to the rights and obligations of Members under GATT 1994, including the right of consultation created in the preceding sentence.

Paragraph (e) is not intended to limit a Member from taking measures to avoid the double taxation of foreign-source income earned by its enterprises or the enterprises of another Member. (emphasis added)

97.   We need to examine footnote 59 sentence by sentence. The first sentence of footnote 59 is specifically related to the statement in item (e) of the Illustrative List that the "full or partial exemption remission, or deferral specifically related to exports, of direct taxes" is an export subsidy. The first sentence of footnote 59 qualifies this by stating that "deferral need not amount to an export subsidy where, for example, appropriate interest charges are collected." Since the FSC measure does not involve the *deferral* of direct taxes, we do not believe that this sentence of footnote 59 bears upon the characterization of the FSC measure as constituting, or not, an "export subsidy".

98.   The second sentence of footnote 59 "reaffirms" that, in allocating export sales revenues, for tax purposes, between exporting enterprises and controlled foreign buyers, the price for the goods shall be determined according to the "arm's length" principle to which that sentence of the footnote refers. Like the Panel, we are willing to accept, for the sake of argument, the United States' position that it is "implicit" in the requirement to use the arm's length principle that Members of the WTO are not obliged to tax foreign-source income, and also that Members may tax such income less than they tax domestic-source income. We would add that, even in the absence of footnote 59, Members of the WTO are *not* obliged, by WTO rules, to tax *any* categories of income, whether foreign- or domestic-source income. The United States argues that, since there is no requirement to tax export-related foreign-source income, a government cannot be said to have "foregone" revenue if it elects not to tax that income. It seems to us that, taken to its logical conclusion, this argument by the United States would mean that there could *never* be a foregoing of revenue "otherwise due" because, in principle, under WTO law generally, *no* revenues are ever due and *no* revenue would, in this view, ever be "foregone". That cannot be the appropriate implication to draw from the requirement to use the arm's length principle.

99.   Furthermore, we do not believe that the requirement to use the arm's length principle resolves the issue that arises here. That issue is *not*, as the United States suggests, whether a Member is or is not obliged to tax a particular category of foreign-source income. As we have said, a Member is not, in general, under any such obligation. Rather, the issue in dispute is whether, *having decided to tax a particular category of foreign-source income*, namely foreign-source income that is "effectively connected with a trade or business within the United States", the

United States is *permitted to carve out an export contingent exemption from the category of foreign-source income that is taxed under its other rules of taxation.* Unlike the United States, we do not believe that the second sentence of footnote 59 addresses this question. It plainly does not do so expressly; neither, as far as we can see, does it do so by necessary implication. As the United States indicates, the arm's length principle operates when a Member chooses not to tax, or to tax less, certain categories of foreign-source income. However, the operation of the arm's length principle is unaffected by the choice a Member makes as to *which* categories of foreign-source income, if any, it will not tax, or will tax less. Likewise, the operation of the arm's length principle is unaffected by the choice a Member might make to grant exemptions from the generally applicable rules of taxation of foreign-source income that it has selected for itself. In short, the requirement to use the arm's length principle does not address the issue that arises here, nor does it authorize the type of export contingent tax exemption that we have just described. Thus, this sentence of footnote 59 does not mean that the FSC subsidies are not export subsidies within the meaning of Article 3.1(a) of the SCM Agreement.

100.   The third and fourth sentences of footnote 59 set forth rules that relate to remedies. In our view, these rules have no bearing on the substantive obligations of Members under Articles 1.1 and 3.1 of the SCM Agreement. So, we turn to the fifth and final sentence of footnote 59. That sentence provides:

> Paragraph (e) is not intended to limit a Member from taking measures to avoid the double taxation of foreign-source income earned by its enterprises or the enterprises of another Member.

101.   On appeal, the United States maintains that the FSC measure is a measure "to avoid double taxation of foreign-source income" *under footnote 59.* As a consequence, the United States further contends that the FSC measure is excluded from the prohibition against export subsidies in Article 3.1(a) of the SCM Agreement. During the oral hearing, we asked the United States to identify where it had asserted before the Panel that the FSC measure is a measure "to avoid double taxation of foreign-source income" under footnote 59. That is, we asked the United States to tell us specifically where it had invoked the fifth sentence of footnote 59 as a means of justifying the FSC measure. In reply, the United States pointed to its first written submission to the Panel. In that submission, in describing the FSC measure and before setting forth its legal arguments, the United States stated that "the FSC is designed to prevent double taxation of export income earned outside the United States by exempting a portion of the FSC's income from taxation." The United States pointed also to certain general arguments it made before the Panel concerning the fifth sentence of footnote 59. However, the United States did not indicate that, in its substantive arguments to the Panel, it had justified the FSC measure as a measure "to avoid double taxation" under footnote 59. Nor do we find any indication in the Panel Record that the United States ever invoked this justification. We, there-

fore, conclude that the United States did not assert, far less argue, before the Panel that the FSC measure is a measure "to avoid double taxation of foreign-source income" under footnote 59. Our conclusion is confirmed by the Panel's statement, in footnote 682 of the Panel Report, that the United States had not asserted that the fifth sentence of footnote 59 was "relevant to this dispute". It follows, therefore, that this issue was not properly litigated before the Panel and that the Panel was not asked to examine whether the FSC measure is a measure "to avoid double taxation of foreign-source income" under footnote 59.

* * *

121. In light of all the foregoing, we uphold the Panel's conclusion, in paragraph 8.1 of the Panel Report, that the FSC tax exemptions involve subsidies contingent upon export performance that are prohibited under Article 3.1(a) of the SCM Agreement.

Notes and Questions

(1) A subsidy exists if tax revenue "otherwise due" is not collected, yet there is no obligation to tax any particular type of income in the first instance. Why define "subsidy" in this fashion? Does it make any economic sense?

(2) With reference to paragraph 91, when would the panel's "but for" test become problematic? What would the Appellate Body substitute for it?

(3) If the United States had properly pleaded its "double taxation" argument based on footnote 59 before the panel, what result?

(4) The *FSC* case has a long history. GATT disputes involving the United States, Belgium, France and the Netherlands arose in the mid–1970's, which included a challenge before a GATT panel to the US tax law creating Domestic International Sales Corporations (DISC's). The panel ruled that the DISC legislation was an export subsidy. See DISC—United States Tax Legislation, GATT Doc. No. L/4422, GATT 23d Supp. BISD 98 (1977). The United States blocked adoption of the report until a compromise was reached in 1981 that resulted in a declaration that tracked closely the language of footnote 59 of the SCM Agreement. Three years later the FSC measure was enacted, which the United States insisted was consistent with the principles of the 1981 declaration. In an omitted part of the *FSC* case, the Appellate Body held that the 1981 declaration of the GATT Council had not been incorporated into GATT 1994 as an "other decision" (see definition of GATT 1994 in Annex 1A to the WTO Agreement) and did "not provide useful interpretative 'guidance' in resolving the legal issue relating to the FSC measure that is raised in this appeal" (para. 120). The US FSC measure was repealed and replaced in the Extraterritorial Income Exclusion Act of 2000 (ETI), which was itself the subject of an DSU article 21.5 challenge by the European Community on the grounds that it too was an export subsidy. The challenge was successful—the ETI was also found to forego revenue otherwise due, to be contingent on export performance, and not to represent an appropriate response to double taxation under footnote 59. See United States—Tax Treatment for "Foreign Sales Corporations", Recourse to Article 21.5 of the DSU by the European Communities, WT/DS108/AB/RW,

adopted January 29, 2002. Thereafter followed a period of European retaliation, and the United States again amended its legislation. The new legislation resolved the basic problems, but "grandfathered" some aspects of the FSC and ETI systems, leading to yet another European complaint before a compliance panel, resulting in a ruling that the grandfather provisions in the new legislation violated the SCM Agreement. See United States—Tax Treatment for "Foreign Sales Corporations", Second Recourse to Article 21.5 of the DSU by the European Communities, WT/DS108/AB/RW2, adopted March 14, 2006. The US then repealed the grandfather provisions to avoid further EU retaliatory measures.

(5) In Canada—Certain Measures Affecting the Automotive Industry, WT/DS139 & 142/AB/R, adopted June 19, 2000, a challenge was brought to the Canadian Motor Vehicle Tariff Order (MVTO). The pertinent details of that order were summarized as follows:

> 9.   Under the MVTO 1998, [an] import duty exemption is available to manufacturers of motor vehicles on imports [of vehicles] "from any country entitled to the Most–Favoured–Nation Tariff", if the manufacturer meets the following three conditions: (1) it must have produced in Canada, during the designated "base year", motor vehicles of the class imported; (2) the ratio of the net sales value of the vehicles *produced in Canada* to the net sales value of all vehicles of that class *sold* for consumption *in Canada* in the period of importation must be "equal to or higher than" the ratio in the "base year", and the ratio shall not in any case be lower than 75:100 (the "ratio requirements"); and (3) the amount of Canadian value added in the manufacturer's local production of motor vehicles must be "equal to or greater than" the amount of Canadian value added in the local production of motor vehicles of that class during the "base year" (the "CVA requirements").

The Appellate Body upheld that finding that the duty exemption amounted to revenue "otherwise due" that is foregone. The more subtle issue concerned the question whether the system conferred prohibited subsidies under article 3 of the SCM Agreement. With regard to the ratio requirements, the Appellate Body found:

> 104.   We agree with the Panel that "[i]n cases where the production-to-sales ratio is 100:100, the only way to import any motor vehicles duty-free is to export, and the amount of import duty exemption allowed is directly dependent upon the amount of exports achieved." Like the Panel, we fail to see how a manufacturer with a production-to-sales ratio of 100:100 could obtain access to the import duty exemption—and still maintain its required production-to-sales ratio—without exporting. A manufacturer producing motor vehicles in Canada with a sales value of 100 that does not export must sell all those motor vehicles in Canada. That manufacturer's production-to-sales ratio becomes 100:100, but without the benefit of importing duty-free one single motor vehicle. Only if that manufacturer exports motor vehicles produced in Canada does it become entitled to import motor vehicles free of duty. The value of motor vehicles which can be imported duty-free is strictly limited to the value of motor vehicles exported. In our view, as the import duty exemption is simply not available to a manufacturer unless it exports

motor vehicles, the import duty exemption is clearly conditional, or dependent upon, exportation and, therefore, is contrary to Article 3.1(a) of the SCM Agreement. * * *

108. Even where the ratio requirement for a particular manufacturer is set at less than 100:100, in our view, there is contingency "in law" upon export performance because, as a result of the operation of the MVTO 1998 and the SROs themselves, the granting of, or the entitlement to, the import duty exemption is tied to the exportation of motor vehicles by the manufacturer beneficiaries. By the very operation of the measure, the more motor vehicles that a manufacturer exports, the more motor vehicles it can import duty-free. In other words, a clear relationship of dependency or conditionality exists between the granting of the import duty exemption and the exportation of motor vehicles by manufacturer beneficiaries. We find, therefore, that, even when the ratio requirements are less than 100:100, the measure is "contingent . . . in law . . . upon export performance".

With respect to the CVA requirements, the issue was whether the measure was "contingent on the use of domestic over imported goods." On this question, the Appellate Body remarked:

128. * * * In its examination, however, the Panel did not conduct an analysis of how the CVA requirements under the MVTO 1998 * * * actually work. The Panel began its legal analysis by stating that "a value-added requirement is in no sense synonymous with a condition to use domestic over imported goods." The Panel apparently reached this conclusion without any inquiry into the specific CVA requirements for specific manufacturer beneficiaries. Although the Panel did explain what *types* of costs could be used to satisfy the CVA requirements, the Panel did not, for any MVTO manufacturer * * * make any findings as to the *actual level* of CVA required. The Panel's statement that "value-added requirements" are "not synonymous" with a condition to use domestic over imported goods seems to have been based on "value-added requirements" considered *in the abstract* as opposed to the actual CVA requirements. * * *

129. * * * The Panel simply speculated that "depending upon the factual circumstances", a manufacturer "*might well be* willing and *able* to satisfy a CVA requirement *without using any domestic goods whatsoever*". (emphasis added) The Panel did not, however, scrutinize the actual CVA requirements for MVTO and SRO manufacturers to see whether they could indeed be satisfied without using domestic goods.

130. The Panel's reasoning implies that under no circumstances could *any* value-added requirement result in a finding of contingency "in law" upon the use of domestic over imported goods. We do not agree. We noted that the definition of "Canadian value added" in the MVTO 1998 *requires* a manufacturer to report to the Government of Canada the *aggregate* of certain listed costs of its production of motor vehicles, and that the first such cost item specified is the cost of Canadian parts and materials *used* in the production of motor vehicles in its factory in Canada. It seems to us that whether or not a particular manufacturer is able to satisfy its specific CVA requirements without using any Canadi-

an parts and materials in its production depends very much on the *level* of the applicable CVA requirements. For example, if the level of the CVA requirements is very high, we can see that the use of domestic goods may well be a necessity and thus be, in practice, required as a *condition* for eligibility for the import duty exemption. By contrast, if the level of the CVA requirements is very low, it would be much easier to satisfy those requirements *without* actually using domestic goods; for example, where the CVA requirements are set at 40 per cent, it might be possible to satisfy that level simply with the aggregate of other elements of Canadian value added, in particular, labour costs. The multiplicity of *possibilities* for compliance with the CVA requirements, when these requirements are set at low levels, may, depending on the specific level applicable to a particular manufacturer, make the use of domestic goods only one *possible* means (means which might not, in fact, be utilized) of satisfying the CVA requirements.

The Appellate Body then held that it could not complete the analysis of the CVA requirements given the incomplete record.

(6) The Illustrative List of Export Subsidies contained in Annex I to the SCM Agreement notes many practices that are not addressed in the preceding cases. Consider, for example, the following measures—which are prohibited export subsidies?

i. "Tariff drawbacks," by which a firm that exports goods receives a refund of the tariffs that were imposed upon imported raw materials, or component parts, utilized in the production of the goods for export.

ii. An exemption for goods for exportation of the obligation to pay a value-added tax.

iii. A pro rata corporate income tax rebate for goods exported, calculated by applying the ratio of the value of goods exported over the total value of goods produced, multiplied by the amount of corporate income tax paid.

iv. Government intervention in the foreign exchange market whereby the central bank purchases foreign currency with domestic currency for the purpose of keeping the value of domestic currency low so that domestic exports will be more competitive on world markets.

(7) Suppose a government provides a one-time grant to a company that enables it to build a new manufacturing facility. The grant is later found to confer an illegal export subsidy. What is the remedy under WTO law? Such an issue arose in a dispute involving Australian subsidies to exporters of automotive leather. The panel concluded that in the circumstances of that case, repayment of the subsidy was necessary in order for the subsidy to be withdrawn as required by the SCM Agreement. Do you agree? See Australia—Subsidies Provided to Producers and Exporters of Automotive Leather, Recourse to Article 21.5 of the DSU by the United States, WT/DS126/RW, adopted February 11, 2000.

(D) A NOTE ON AGRICULTURAL SUBSIDIES

The WTO Agreement on Agriculture established distinct rules for agricultural subsidies, within a framework that contemplates negotiated reductions in agricultural support programs. For example, the Agreement on Agriculture permits export subsidies consistent with commitments (amounts) specified in individual member's schedules (see article 8). In article 9, the agreement specifies the subsidies that are subject to the scheduled commitments. Article 10(1) then provides that the "[e]xport subsidies not listed in [article 9] shall not be applied in a manner which results in, or threatens to lead to, circumvention of export subsidy commitments; nor shall non-commercial transactions be used to circumvent such commitments." The only case examining these provisions in detail is the original and compliance proceedings in Canada—Measures Affecting the Importation of Milk and the Exportation of Dairy Products, WT/DS103 & 113. Following an adverse compliance decision in 2002, Canada eventually withdrew the programs at issue.

The Agreement on Agriculture also contains the so-called "peace clause" in article 13. It insulated subsidies (both export and domestic) granted in conformity with the Agreement from being challenged under the SCM Agreement. Subsidies not in conformity with the Agreement, by contrast, were subject to challenge under both the Agriculture Agreement and the SCM Agreement. The most celebrated case challenging subsidies on the grounds that they did not conform to the Agriculture Agreement was the upland cotton case. See United States—Subsidies on Upland Cotton, WT/DS267/AB/R, adopted March 21, 2005. The case held that a variety of programs benefiting US cotton producers were not protected by the peace clause, and violated various provisions of the Agriculture and SCM Agreements. A recent Appellate Body report finds that the United States remains in violation of its commitments. United States—Subsidies on Upland Cotton, Recourse by Brazil to Article 21.5 of the DSU, WT/DS267/AB/RW, June 2, 2008.

The "peace clause" expired in 2004 (after the upland cotton case was filed). Given the extensive subsidization in the agricultural sector, the expiration of the peace clause may have dramatic consequences, although it has yet to unleash a flood of new litigation. For the moment, WTO members seem to be awaiting the outcome of the Doha Round before pursuing new cases.

(E) ACTIONABLE SUBSIDIES AND "SERIOUS PREJUDICE"

The SCM Agreement, in article 5, provides that an "actionable subsidy" exists if one of three circumstances arise: injury to the domestic industry of another member, nullification or impairment of benefits under GATT, especially the Article II bindings, or "serious prejudice." Article 6 then proceeds to define the concept of serious prejudice in some detail. The first case to address the concept in the dispute process follows.

INDONESIA—CERTAIN MEASURES AFFECTING THE AUTOMOBILE INDUSTRY

WT/DS54, 55, 59 & 64/R.
Panel Report adopted July 23, 1998.

2.15 Two sets of measures have been identified by all parties under the 1996 National Car programme:

2.16 The first set of measures—the February 1996 Programme—provides for the grant of "pioneer" or National Car company status to Indonesian car companies that meet specified criteria as to ownership of facilities, use of trademarks, and technology. Maintenance of pioneer status is dependent on the National Cars' meeting increasing local content requirements over a three year period. The benefits provided are exemption from luxury tax on sales of National Cars, and exemption from import duties on parts and components.

2.17 The second set of measures—the June 1996 Programme—provides that National Cars manufactured in a foreign country by Indonesian nationals and which fulfil the local content requirements prescribed by the Minister of Industry and Trade, shall be treated the same as National Cars manufactured in Indonesia, i.e. exempt from import duties and luxury tax. In accordance with Decree 142/96, imported National Cars are deemed to comply with the 20 per cent local content requirement for the end of the first production year if the overseas producer manufacturing the National Cars "counter-purchases" Indonesian parts and components that account for at least 25 per cent of the C & F value of the imported cars.

* * *

CLAIMS OF SERIOUS PREJUDICE UNDER PART III OF THE SCM AGREEMENT

14.153 * * * The European Communities and the United States contend that the tariff and luxury sales tax exemptions provided by Indonesia through the National Car programme are specific subsidies which have caused serious prejudice to their interests within the meaning of Article 5(c) of the Agreement on Subsidies and Countervailing Measures ("SCM Agreement"). Specifically, the complainants allege that the effect of alleged subsidies for the national car is (a) to displace or impede imports of like products of the European Communities and the United States into the Indonesian market and (b) a significant price undercutting by the subsidized national car as compared with like EC and US products in the Indonesian market. * * *

* * *

14.155 As with any analysis under the SCM Agreement, the first issue to be resolved is whether the measures in question are subsidies within the meaning of Article 1 that are specific to an enterprise or industry or group of enterprises or industries within the meaning of

Article 2. It is to be recalled that the measures in question are: import duty and luxury sales tax exemptions on CBU [completely built-up, i.e., finished] Timors [a model of compact car] imported by PT TPN [an Indonesian company] from Korea, import duty exemptions on parts and components used or to be used in the assembly of the Timor in Indonesia, and luxury sales tax exemptions on Timors assembled in Indonesia. In this case, the European Communities, the United States and Indonesia agree that these measures are specific subsidies within the meaning of those articles. * * *

14.156 Article 27 of the SCM Agreement provides significant special and differential treatment for developing country Members of the WTO, including with respect to claims of serious prejudice arising from subsidies provided by developing country Members. Thus, Article 27.9 provides that

> Regarding actionable subsidies granted or maintained by a developing country Member other than those referred to in paragraph 1 of Article 6, action may not be authorized or taken pursuant to Article 7 unless nullification or impairment of tariff concessions or other obligations under GATT 1994 is found to exist as a result of such subsidy, in such a way as to displace or impede imports of a like product into the market of the subsidizing developing country Member or unless injury to a domestic industry in the market of an importing Member occurs.

In other words, Article 27.9 provides that, *in the usual case*, developing country Members may not be subject to a claim that their actionable subsidies have caused serious prejudice to the interests of another Member. Rather, a Member may only bring a claim that benefits under GATT have been nullified or impaired by a developing country Member's subsidies or that subsidized imports into the complaining Member have caused injury to a domestic industry.

14.157 The complainants do not contest that Indonesia is a developing country Member entitled to the special and differential treatment provided by Article 27.9. Rather, they contend that Article 27.9 is not applicable in this case because the subsidies in question fall under the provisions of Article 6.1(a), i.e., that the *ad valorem* subsidization of the Timor exceeds 5 per cent. * * *

14.158 We agree that Article 27.8 allows a WTO Member to bring a serious prejudice claim with respect to subsidies provided by a developing country Member which fall within the scope of Article 6.1. Article 27.8 provides that:

> There shall be no presumption in terms of paragraph 1 of Article 6 that a subsidy granted by a developing country Member results in serious prejudice, as defined in this Agreement. Such serious prejudice, where applicable under the terms of paragraph 9, shall be demonstrated by positive evidence, in accordance with the provisions of paragraphs 3 through 8 of Article 6.

In other words, while a subsidy falling within the terms of Article 6.1 generally is presumed to cause serious prejudice to the interests of another Member, that presumption is not applicable where the subsidizing country is a developing country Member. Instead, while such a subsidy by a developing country Member may be subject to a serious prejudice challenge, a complainant does not benefit from a presumption of serious prejudice; rather, a complainant must demonstrate the existence of serious prejudice by positive evidence.

14.159   The question remains whether the subsidization challenged in this dispute satisfies the requirements of Article 6.1(a). That provision states that "[s]erious prejudice shall be deemed to exist in the case of . . . the total *ad valorem* subsidization of a product exceeding five per cent. . . . " * * *

* * *

14.161   The calculations provided by the European Communities and the United States present a variety of issues under Article 6.1(a) and Annex IV. However, we do not need in this case to calculate the precise level of *ad valorem* subsidization. Rather, we need only determine whether the *ad valorem* rate of subsidization exceeds 5 per cent. This question is not in dispute here, since Indonesia calculates that the *ad valorem* subsidization conferred by the exemption from the luxury sales tax alone is 29.54 per cent for Timors imported from Korea, 26.20 per cent for Timors assembled at the Tambun plant, and 18.68 per cent for Timors to be assembled at the Karawang plant. * * *

14.162   For the foregoing reasons, we find that the complainants are not precluded by Article 27 from seeking to demonstrate, by positive evidence, that Indonesia has caused, through the effects of the subsidies at issue in this case, serious prejudice to their interests.

* * *

Like Product Analysis

14.164   Article 6.3 provides in relevant parts as follows:

Serious prejudice in the sense of paragraph (c) may arise in any case where one or several of the following may apply:

(a) the effect of the subsidy is to displace or impede the exports of a *like product* of another Member into the Market of the subsidizing Member;

. . .

(c) the effect of the subsidy is a significant price undercutting by the subsidized product as compared with the price of a *like product* of another Member in the same market or significant price suppression, price depression or lost sales in the same market(emphasis added).

It is clear from the text of Article 6.3 that any analysis of displacement or impedance or of price undercutting must focus on the effects of the subsidy vis B vis the like product to the subsidized product. * * *

* * *

14.175   Turning first to the argument of the European Communities that all passenger cars should be considered "like products" to the Timor, we consider that such a broad approach is not appropriate in this case. While it is true that all passenger cars "share the same basic physical characteristics and share an identical end-use", we agree with Indonesia that passenger cars are highly differentiated products. * * * Viewed from the perspective of the SCM Agreement, it is almost inconceivable that a subsidy for Timors could displace or impede imports of Rolls Royces, or that any meaningful analysis of price undercutting could be performed between these two models. In short, we do not consider that a Rolls Royce can reasonably be considered to have "characteristics closely resembling" those of the Timor.

14.176   The European Communities contend that we must consider all passenger cars to be "like" because any effort to differentiate between passenger cars with a multitude of differing characteristics would inevitably result in arbitrary divisions. We are aware that there are innumerable differences among passenger cars and that the identification of appropriate dividing lines between them may not be a simple task. However, this does not in our view justify lumping all such products together where the differences among the products are so dramatic. * * *

14.177   One reasonable way for this panel to approach the "like product" issue is to look at the manner in which the automotive industry itself has analyzed market segmentation. The United States and the European Communities have submitted information regarding the market segmentation approach taken by DRI's Global Automotive Group, a company whose clients include all major auto manufacturers, including KIA, PT TPN's national car partner. * * *

14.178   * * * DRI has in its analysis considered the physical characteristics of the cars in question when designing its segmentation. It has used as an initial filter the size of the vehicle, but it has then divided cars of a given size into upper and lower end categories, and has moved luxury cars, regardless of size, from lower segments to the E segment. We consider such an approach, which segments the market based on a combination of size and price/market position, to be a sensible one which is consistent with the criteria relevant to "like product" analysis under the SCM Agreement.

* * *

14.181   In our view, the DRI market segmentation analysis presented by the European Communities and the United States supports the view that all vehicles in the C1 Segment—including the 306, Optima and Escort—are "like products" to the Timor within the meaning of the

SCM Agreement. By contrast, the DRI analysis places the Vectra and the Neon in different market segments (D1 and C2 respectively), and this in our view weakens the complainants' view that these products should be considered to be "like" the Timor.

* * *

Treatment of Cars Imported Unassembled

14.194 Indonesia maintains a duty of 200 per cent on imports of passenger cars, and as a result imports of CBU passenger cars (that is, completely-built-up cars) into Indonesia are very small. In fact, almost all passenger cars imported into Indonesia, including the 306 and the Optima, are imported as CKD (completely knocked-down) kits and assembled in Indonesia. The complainants have stated that the Escort and Neon would have been imported in CKD kit form and assembled in Indonesia as well. Article 6.3 provides that serious prejudice may arise where the effect of the subsidy is "to displace or impede the imports of a like product of another Member into the market of the subsidizing Member" or is "a significant price undercutting by the subsidized product as compared with the price of a like product of another Member." Thus, in the context of a displacement or impedance claim, the question arises whether imports of CKD kits are "imports of a like product [to the Timor] of another Member" where the final passenger car assembled in Indonesia is a "like product" to the Timor. In the case of price undercutting, the related question is whether a passenger car assembled in Indonesia from an imported CKD kit is a "like product of another Member."

* * *

14.197 We do not consider that an unassembled product *ipso facto* is not a like product to that product assembled. Recalling the view of the Appellate Body that tariff classification may be a useful tool in like product analysis, we note that, under the General Rules for the Interpretation of the Harmonized System:

> Any reference in a heading to an article shall be taken to include a reference to that article incomplete or unfinished, provided that, as presented, the incomplete or unfinished article has the essential character of the complete or finished article.

We think that a comparable approach to the relation between assembled and unassembled products makes good sense in the context of this dispute. It appears that, in order to avoid paying 200 per cent duties on CBU passenger cars, EC and US car producers ship to Indonesia virtually complete CKD kits that are effectively "cars in a box." Accordingly, we believe that they can properly be considered to have characteristics closely resembling those of a completed car.

Products Not Originating in a Complaining Member

14.198 Before turning to an analysis of adverse effects, we must first consider whether the United States may claim that it has suffered serious prejudice as a result of displacement/impedance or of price undercutting with respect to a product which does not originate in the United States solely on the basis that the producer of that product is a "US company".

* * *

14.200 In considering this issue, our starting point is that both Article XVI of GATT and the SCM Agreement are Annex 1A multilateral agreements on trade in goods. It comes as no surprise, therefore that in its discussion of serious prejudice, Article XVI:1 focuses on the effects of subsidization on trade in goods. That article provides as follows:

> If any contracting party grants or maintains any subsidy, including any form of income or price support, which operates directly or indirectly *to increase exports of any product from, or to reduce imports of any product* into, its territory, it shall notify the CONTRACTING PARTIES in writing of the extent and nature of the subsidization, of the estimated effect of the subsidization *on the quantity of the affected product or products imported into or exported from* its territory and of the circumstances making the subsidization necessary. In any case in which it is determined that serious prejudice to the interests of any other contracting party is caused or threatened by any *such subsidization*, the contracting party granting the subsidy shall, upon request, discuss with the other contracting party or parties concerned, or with the CONTRACTING PARTIES, the possibility of limiting the subsidization. (emphasis added).

This focus on the trade effects of subsidization is carried over into Part III of the SCM Agreement. Article 5 provides that no Member should cause, through the use of any subsidy, "adverse effects to the interests of other Members." One such adverse effect is "serious prejudice to the interests of another Member," which the SCM Agreement indicates is used in the same sense as in Article XVI:1. Article 6.3 provides that serious prejudice may arise where one or several of four listed situations exist. As we have seen, the United States alleges two such situations, i.e., (i) that "the effect of the subsidy is to displace or impede the *imports of a like product of another Member* into the market of the subsidizing Member"; and (ii) that "the effect of the subsidy is a significant price undercutting by the subsidized product as compared with the price of *a like product of another Member* in the same market or significant price suppression, price depression or lost sales in the same market" (emphasis added).

14.201 In our view, the text of Article XVI and of Part III of the SCM Agreement make clear that serious prejudice may arise where a Member's trade interests have been affected by subsidization. We see nothing in Article XVI or in Part III that would suggest that the United States may claim that it has suffered adverse effects merely because it believes that the interests of US *companies* have been harmed where US *products* are not involved. The United States has cited no language in Article XVI:1 or Part III suggesting that the nationality of producers is relevant to establishing the existence of serious prejudice. Accordingly, given that serious prejudice may only arise in the case at hand where there is "displacement or impedance of imports of a like product from another Member" or price undercutting "as compared with the like product of another Member", we do not consider that the United States can convert such effects on products from the European Communities into serious prejudice to US interests merely by alleging that the products affected were produced by US companies.

14.202   In light of our view that the existence of alleged harm to US *companies* is not a basis for a claim of serious prejudice to the interests to the United States, the question remains whether one Member may bring a claim that another Member has suffered serious prejudice as a result of subsidization. In our view the answer is no. It will be recalled that Article 7 of the SCM Agreement sets forth the steps to be taken by a Member which believes that it has suffered adverse effects within the meaning of Part III. Article 7.2 provides that:

> A request for consultations under paragraph 1 shall include a statement of available evidence with regard to *(a)* the existence and nature of the subsidy in question, and *(b)* the injury caused to the domestic industry, or the nullification or impairment, or serious prejudice [footnote omitted] caused to the interests of the Member requesting consultations.

It is clear from Article 7.2 that the dispute settlement procedures set forth in Article 7 may only be invoked by a Member where that Member believes that it has itself suffered serious prejudice as a result of subsidization.

* * *

Displacement and Impedance

14.207   Having determined that certain EC and US passenger car models are (or, in the case of the Neon, may be) like products to the Timor, we must next examine whether the complainants have demonstrated that the effect of the subsidies provided pursuant to the National Car programme has been to displace or impede the exports of those models from the Indonesian market.

(a) Market Share Data

14.208   Before proceeding to an examination of the market share data submitted by complainants, we must consider the threshold legal issue of whether Article 6.4 of the SCM Agreement is relevant to a dispute, such as this, where the adverse effects alleged by the complainants relate to displacement or impedance of a like product into the market of the subsidizing Member under Article 6.3(a). That Article provides as follows:

> *For the purpose of paragraph 3(b),* the displacement or impeding of exports shall include any case in which, subject to the provisions of

paragraph 7, it has been demonstrated that there has been a change in relative shares of the market to the disadvantage of the non-subsidized like product (over an appropriately representative period sufficient to demonstrate clear trends in the development of the market for the product concerned, which, in normal circumstances, shall be at least one year). "Change in relative shares of the market" shall include any of the following situations: *(a)* there is an increase in the market share of the subsidized product; *(b)* the market share of the subsidized product remains constant in circumstances in which, in the absence of the subsidy, it would have declined; *(c)* the market share of the subsidized product declines, but at a slower rate than would have been the case in the absence of the subsidy. (emphasis added).

The European Communities and the United States acknowledge that Article 6.4 on its face does not apply to the displacement and impedance claims in this dispute, as their claims are based on Article 6.3(a) (effect in the market of the subsidizing Member) while Article 6.4 only applies "for the purpose of" Article 6.3(b) (effects in the market of a third country). The complainants argue, however, that there is no reason why the type of analysis set forth in Article 6.4 should not be appropriate also in the case of claims of displacement and impedance of imports from the market of the subsidizing country. Indonesia, by contrast, contends that Article 6.4 is not relevant to this dispute.

14.209 The significance of this issue in terms of the obligations on the complainants is considerable. If the type of analysis set forth in Article 6.4 is appropriate in this case, then the complainants arguably could make a *prima facie* case of displacement or impedance simply by demonstrating that the market share of a subsidized product has increased over an appropriately representative period. If, on the other hand, the type of analysis set forth in Article 6.4 is not appropriate in this case, then the complainants must demonstrate that *"the effect of the subsidy"* is to displace or impede imports into Indonesia, that is, that they have lost export sales to Indonesia that they would otherwise have made and that those export sales were lost as a result of the subsidies provided pursuant to the National Car programme.

14.210 We agree with Indonesia that Article 6.4 is not relevant in this case. The drafting of the provision is unambiguous, and the specific reference to Article 6.3(b) creates a strong inference that an Article 6.4 type of analysis is *not* appropriate in the case of Article 6.3(a) claims. The complainants have identified nothing in the context of the provision or the object and purpose of the SCM Agreement that would suggest a different conclusion.

14.211 Our conclusion does not of course mean that market share data are irrelevant to the analysis of displacement or impedance into a subsidizing Member's market. To the contrary, market share data may be highly relevant evidence for the analysis of such a claim. However, such data are no more than evidence of displacement and impedance caused by subsidization, and a demonstration that the market share of the subsidized product in the subsidizing Member has increased does not *ipso facto* satisfy the requirements of Article 6.3(a).

14.212   Having determined that the EC and US models in the C1 Segment (and arguably those in the C2 Segment) are "like" the subsidized Timor, we consider it appropriate to analyze market shares for the C Segment. A review of the data provided by Indonesia under the Annex V procedure demonstrates that the Timor quickly gained a very substantial share of the Indonesian C Segment passenger car market upon its introduction. [T]he Timor was not sold in 1995 and thus had a zero share of the C Segment market. In 1996, the year of introduction, the Timor captured a 16.9 per cent share of the Indonesian C Segment, while during the period January–May 1997 (the latest period for which we have been provided with data), that market share had climbed to 42.4 percent. Table 2 breaks this market share data down on a quarterly basis. These data indicate that Timor had no sales until the fourth quarter of 1996. In that quarter, its market share in the C Segment reached 40.9 per cent. It dropped to 38.8 per cent for the first quarter of 1997 but during the partial second quarter for which we have data (April–May) that share had climbed to 47.7 per cent.

14.213   In assessing whether this change in market share in fact amounted to a displacement or impedance of imports of EC and US origin products into Indonesia, our starting point is actual market shares for the three EC models we have found to be like products, and for the one US model which we assume *arguendo* to be a like product, to the Timor. The Neon was never introduced into the Indonesia market (allegedly because of the National Car programme), and the market share of US-origin passenger cars in the C Segment of the Indonesian passenger car market was therefore zero. Because the Escort also was never introduced into the Indonesian market, the EC market share data are based solely on sales of the 306 and the Optima. [T]he European Communities in 1995 had an Indonesian market share in the C Segment of 2.4 per cent. The EC share climbed to 5.7 per cent in 1996, but dropped to 3.7 per cent for the period for which we have data (January–May 1997). Table 2, *infra* at p. 386, breaks down these data on a quarterly basis. This analysis shows that in the first three quarters of 1996, EC market share in the C Segment ranged from 6.9 to 7.8 per cent. In the fourth quarter of 1996 (the quarter in which the Timor first entered the market), EC market share dropped to 3.7 per cent. In the first quarter of 1997, EC market share fell even further to 3.3 per cent, and remained at a relatively low 4.2 per cent in the partial second quarter for which we have data (April–May 1997).

14.214   Focusing on market shares alone, the data before us show a potentially significant correlation between the introduction of the subsidized Timor and the decline in EC market share in the C Segment of the Indonesian market. The quarterly data show that the EC market share for C Segment cars in Indonesia increased substantially during the first three quarters of 1996, but that, in the fourth quarter of 1996, coincident with the introduction of the Timor, the European models' market share dropped to 3.7 per cent, where it remained on average during the first five months of 1997. Thus, there seems to be little question that the EC market share in the C Segment dropped substantially relative to that of the subsidized Timor, and the close correlation in time between the introduction of the Timor and the drop in EC market share suggests a causal link between the two.

14.215   If Article 6.4 of the SCM Agreement applied in this dispute, this showing of a change in relative market shares to the disadvantage of the non-subsidized like product might well have been sufficient to establish the European Communities' *prima facie* case of displacement or impedance. In the absence of that article, however, it is not enough for the European Communities to demonstrate a decline in relative market share; rather, the European Communities must demonstrate that "the effect of the subsidy is to displace or impede the imports" of an EC-origin "like product" into the Indonesian market, i.e., that some imports that would have occurred did not occur as a result of the subsidies. While declining market share may be relevant to establishing such a situation, we consider that we must proceed further with the analysis and look at actual sales figures for the products in question.

14.216   In spite of their declines in market share, the absolute volume of sales of the relevant EC models did not significantly decline after the introduction of the Timor. Rather, sales of C Segment vehicles from the EC were 419 units in 1995 and 1,445 units in 1996. For 1997 we have full data from the Annex V process on the C Segment only for January–May, and this shows EC sales of 611 units, which amounts to 1,466 units on an annualized basis. We also have sales figures for the Optima (257 units) and 306 (656 units) for the period January–August 1997 from the European Communities. These figures, totalled and annualized, show sales of 1,370 units for 1997. On a quarterly basis, sales of the Optima and 306 remained relatively constant during the period from the fourth quarter of 1996 through May 1997 at between 300 and 400 units per quarter.

14.217   The explanation for the loss of market share with no decline in absolute sales volume is that the size of the Indonesian market expanded after the introduction of the Timor. What is particularly relevant here is that the increase in the size of the market was largely attributable to sales of the Timor. In particular, between the third and fourth quarters of 1996, the market for C Segment cars increased by 6,326 units, of which the Timor accounted for 4,278 units (68%). A similar pattern was evident during the first five months of 1997. Thus, relatively stable EC sales volumes in a rapidly expanding market resulted in market share declines but not in declines in absolute volumes.

14.218   We agree with the European Communities that a complainant need not demonstrate a decline in sales in order to demonstrate displacement or impedance. This is inherent in the ordinary meaning of those terms. Thus, displacement relates to a situation where sales volume has declined, while impedance relates to a situation where sales which otherwise would have occurred were impeded. The question before us is therefore whether the market share and sales data above would support a view that, but for the introduction of the subsidized Timor, sales of EC C Segment passenger cars would have been greater than they were.

14.219 In a usual case, a decline in market share in a stable or growing market, corresponding in time with the introduction of a subsidized product, might suggest that sales would have been higher but for the introduction of the subsidized product. This would be particularly the case where, in the period prior to the introduction of the subsidized product, the market share of the non-subsidized product had been rising. In this case, however, Indonesia contends that the introduction of the subsidized Timor was itself responsible for the rapid expansion of the market through the introduction of a new, highly affordable passenger car within the reach of first-time buyers. While the European Communities dismisses this argument as "purely speculative," the sales data in terms of volume of sales discussed above provide some support for this view. Thus, one possible interpretation of the data is that, if the subsidized Timor had not been introduced, the Indonesian C Segment market would have remained relatively stable or in any event would have posted during the last quarter of 1996 and the first eight months of 1997 more gradual increases, comparable to those experienced during the period between the first quarter of 1995 and the second quarter of 1996.

14.220 Assuming that, had the subsidized Timor not been introduced, the Indonesian C Segment market would have remained stable or grown at a more moderate rate during the period for which we have data, the question is whether sales of EC C Segment models in absolute terms would have been higher than those actually achieved. Here, the data are inconclusive. While the European Communities contend that its market share had been steadily increasing and that this trend would have continued but for the introduction of the subsidized Timor, actual sales consisted of only two models, the Optima and 306. As Table 2 shows, quarterly sales data for the Optima do not demonstrate any clear upward trend in the six quarters prior to the introduction of the subsidized Timor. Rather, the increase in EC sales was a result of the introduction of the 306 in the first quarter of 1996. While the European Communities state that 1996 sales of the 306 (1,086 units) were 400 units lower than planned, we have no knowledge of the basis for those sales forecasts. Sales of the 306 for partial year 1997 were at an annualized rate of between 984 units (January–August data) and 1,070 units (January to May data), down slightly from the annualized rate in the first half of 1996 of 1,214 units. Thus, if we assume that in the absence of the Timor the market would have remained stable or continued a more gradual increase through August 1997, and that the 306 would have maintained the market share it had achieved in the first half of 1996, these sales might have been expected to increase at most slightly. Such a conclusion is, in any event, highly speculative based on the facts available.

* * *

14.222 In short, the dramatic fall in EC market share in the C Segment is not in this case decisive evidence of displacement or impedance, as the data lend some credence to the Indonesian view that the introduction of the subsidized Timor actually created much of the market growth. Thus, we are required to speculate as to how the market would have performed in the absence of the introduction of the Timor, and as to the share of the market which EC models could have been expected to obtain in that hypothetical situation. It is quite possible that the Indonesian market would have remained stable or increased somewhat in late 1996 and early 1997, even without the introduction of the subsidized Timor, and that EC models would have at least maintained their market share, such that EC sales would have increased slightly. This conclusion is however highly tentative, and does not in our view satisfy the requirement, in the present case, that serious prejudice be demonstrated by positive evidence.

* * *

Price Undercutting

14.237 In addition to arguing that serious prejudice has been caused to their interests through displacement or impedance of their exports to Indonesia, the complainants assert that the subsidized Timor significantly undercuts the prices of EC and US like products in the Indonesian market.

14.238 In determining whether serious prejudice within the meaning of Article 5(c) arises from price undercutting, we must first consider Article 6.3(c) of the SCM Agreement. That provision states that

"serious prejudice in the sense of paragraph 5(c) may arise in any case where one or several of the following apply:

. . .

(c) the effect of the subsidy is a significant price undercutting by the subsidized product as compared with the price of a like product of another Member in the same market or significant price suppression, price depression or lost sales in the same market; . . .

Further elaboration on the application of Article 6.3(c) is provided in Article 6.5 of the SCM Agreement, which provides as follows:

For the purpose of paragraph 3(c), price undercutting shall include any case in which such price undercutting has been demonstrated through a comparison of prices of the subsidized product with prices of a non-subsidized like product supplied to the same market. The comparison shall be made at the same level of trade and at comparable times, due account being taken of any other factor affecting price comparability. However, if such a direct comparison is not possible, the existence of price undercutting may be demonstrated on the basis of export unit values.

14.239   As noted in paragraph 14.213, no U.S.-origin passenger car that is a "like product" to the subsidized Timor currently is sold in Indonesia. In the absence of any such sales in the Indonesian market, the United States by definition cannot demonstrate that the effect of the subsidies provided pursuant to the National Car programme was a significant price undercutting by the subsidized product as compared with the price of a like product of the United States in the Indonesian market. In any event, we note that the United States did not present any information regarding the price at which the Neon, the sole US-origin passenger car allegedly planned for sale in Indonesia, would have been sold in that market. Rather, the United States merely made the unsubstantiated statement that, if Chrysler had gone ahead with its plans to sell the Neon in Indonesia, the Timor would have undercut the price of the least expensive model of the Neon by more than US$5000. We do not consider that such a conclusory statement, unbacked by any supporting explanation, calculations or documentation, is sufficient to meet the United States' burden to demonstrate the existence of a significant price undercutting by positive evidence.

* * *

14.241   We now turn to the EC argument that the prices of the subsidized National Cars significantly undercut the prices of like passengers cars imported from the European Communities. In support of their price undercutting arguments, the European Communities rely on data regarding the list and market prices for passenger cars sold in Indonesia which show that the Timor has both a list and a market price which are much lower than the list and market prices for the 306 and the Optima, which we have determined to be like products (of another Member) to the Timor.

14.242   With respect to list prices, data submitted by Indonesia during the Annex V process show that the Timor had the lowest list price of any passenger car in the Indonesian market except the Mazda MR–90 as of November 1996 and March 1997. * * *

* * *

14.254   We note that under Article 6.3(c) serious prejudice may arise only where the price undercutting is "significant." Although the term "significant" is not defined, the inclusion of this qualifier in Article 6.3(c) presumably was intended to ensure that margins of undercutting so small that they could not meaningfully affect suppliers of the imported product whose price was being undercut are not considered to give rise to serious prejudice. This clearly is not an issue here. To the contrary, it is our view that, even taking into account the possible effects of . . . physical differences on price comparability, the price undercutting by the Timor of the Optima and 306 cannot reasonably be deemed to be other than significant.

14.255 Finally, we note that serious prejudice may arise under Article 6.3(c) only where the price undercutting is "the effect of the subsidy." In this case, we agree with the European Communities that Indonesia, in information that it provided in the Annex V process effectively concedes that the tariff and tax subsidies under the National Car programme are responsible for the significant level of price undercutting. * * *

14.256 For the foregoing reasons, we find that the effect of the subsidies to the Timor pursuant to the National Car programme is to cause serious prejudice to the interests of the European Communities in the sense of Article 5(c) of the SCM Agreement through a significant price undercutting as compared with the price of EC-origin like products in the Indonesian market.

Notes and Questions

(1) The decision in the *Indonesia Autos* case was not appealed. The violation of the SCM Agreement was only one of the grounds for a finding against Indonesia.

(2) Was the panel faithful to the definition of "like product" in the SCM Agreement? Plainly, cars were deemed "like" despite important physical differences between them. Is the panel's approach consistent with the *EC Asbestos* interpretation of GATT Article III:4 by the Appellate Body (see Section 12.4 supra)?

(3) Why limit "standing" to bring a claim to nations whose exports are curtailed, and to exclude nations whose investors' are importantly injured?

(4) Given the physical differences between the products, and any actual or perceived quality differences, how persuasive is the existence of "price undercutting" as a basis for a finding of "serious prejudice?"

(5) An extended discussion of "serous prejudice" may also be found in United States—Subsidies on Upland Cotton, WT/DS267/AB/R, adopted March 21, 2005, paras. 395–512.

SECTION 18.3 UNITED STATES COUNTERVAILING DUTY LAW

Countervailing duties are less common than antidumping duties, and were for many years imposed primarily by the United States. According to WTO statistics, at the end of 1995 the United States imposed 71 countervailing measures, almost two-thirds of the 111 measures then in place for WTO members. The use of countervailing measures has broadened somewhat, however, under the auspices of the WTO. From 1995–2007, 117 new measures were notified. Of that total, 47 were imposed by the United States, 23 by the EU, 11 by Canada, and 36 by a group of 11 other countries.

The United States has had some form of countervailing duty legislation in place since 1897. It was strengthened and elaborated in the Tariff

Act of 1930, section 303, which authorized the Treasury Department to impose duties on imported merchandise to offset any "bounty or grant" bestowed upon it. This applied only to dutiable imports, but in 1974 was extended to non-dutiable imports. At the same time, an injury test was added covering non-dutiable imports, as required by Article VI of the GATT. Prior to the 1974 amendments, the absence of any injury test was protected by the "grandfather clause" in the Protocol of Provisional Application.

Neither prior law nor the 1930 Act defined the term "bounty or grant." The Treasury Department, which administered the statute until 1980, struggled with the term continually. Administrative practice failed to resolve many of the obvious issues, in part because countervailing duty actions were fairly uncommon.

Although it is difficult to compare records during the period from the first countervailing duty law in 1897 to mid–1973, it appears that there were approximately 84 countervailing duties applied under US law over this 76–year span. From 1897 to 1934, there were approximately 35 duties imposed. From 1935 to 1940 there were 24, while from 1941 to 1945 there were none. The 20–year period from 1946 to 1966 saw only 13 duties imposed (3 in 1951, 2 in 1953, no more than 1 in any other year). After 1967, however, activity increased. From 1967 to 1973 there were 12 countervailing duties imposed.[1]

In 1973, the Treasury Department issued a countervailing duty order of considerable importance. The order imposed countervailing duties on tires imported from Canada and made by Michelin Tire Manufacturing Co. of Canada, Ltd.[2] The order was significant because the subsidies countervailed were domestic subsidies of the sort often granted by governmental units in the United States. Specifically, the following were held to be subsidies: Grants to Michelin by the Canadian federal and Nova Scotia governments; a special accelerated depreciation provision of the Canadian income tax law made available to Michelin; low-interest loans provided to Michelin by Nova Scotia; and property tax concessions provided by municipalities. These grants and concessions had been made available as part of programs to bolster the relatively weak economy of Nova Scotia. The imposition of a countervailing duty in these circumstances was apparently the first time that the US statute had been applied to such subsidies.[3] Although the grants and concessions were indeed designed to help Nova Scotia's economy, a significant proportion (75%) of the tires produced needed to be exported. Since the US market was the only logical export destination, is it arguable that the

1.   These statistics were compiled from the reports issued in Treasury Decisions. The figures from 1897 through 1934 are difficult to compile with precision, inasmuch as the method of reporting the imposition of countervailing duties was not very systematic during those years.

2.   38 Fed.Reg. 1018 (1973); 7 Customs Bull. 24 (1973).

3.   See generally Guido & Morrone, The Michelin Decision: A Possible New Direction for U.S. Countervailing Duty Law, 6 L. & Pol.Intl.Bus. 237 (1974).

subsidies were in large part export subsidies because they were intended to be used to construct a plant to produce exports.

The Trade Act of 1974 made a number of additional changes in the statute. The principal changes were to require the Treasury Department to make a preliminary decision within six months of the filing date of a petition and a final decision within 12 months. The Act also required the publication of determinations by the Treasury Department and gave disappointed petitioners the right to appeal negative determinations. By so limiting the discretion of the Treasury Department as to the procedural aspects of countervailing investigations, it appeared likely that there would be a significant increase in the number of petitions filed. But Congress also realized the need for a new international agreement on subsidies and the need for the President to have some flexibility in negotiating such an agreement. The result was that the Secretary of the Treasury was given the right in Section 331(a) of the 1974 Act to waive imposition of countervailing duties if certain conditions were met. As a consequence, the 1974 Act did not lead to increased imposition of countervailing duties.

The Trade Agreements Act of 1979 implemented the Tokyo Round Subsidies Code under US law. It changed the law dramatically and created procedures much like those applicable to antidumping cases. The authority to investigate allegations of subsidization was transferred from the Treasury Department to the Commerce Department, International Trade Administration (ITA). ITA was to conduct both a preliminary inquiry and a final inquiry separated by a public hearing and a process of "verification" during which the information provided by the foreign government(s) under investigation was to be audited for accuracy. Investigations were to be subjected to tight time limits, and the authority under the 1974 Act for the President to waive the imposition of countervailing duties under certain circumstances was abolished. Further, the statute directed the International Trade Commission to conduct an injury investigation in every countervailing duty case involving a signatory to the Subsidies Code, a non-signatory entitled to the same treatment by virtue of other treaty obligations, or any non-dutiable import. As with the ITA proceeding, the ITC proceeding was separated into a preliminary inquiry—to occur prior to the ITA investigation—and a final inquiry to occur after the completion of the ITA investigation. Affirmative determinations by both agencies result in the issuance of a countervailing duty "order" to be enforced by Customs. Both the ITA and ITC determinations were made appealable to the new Court of International Trade, and subsequently to the Federal Circuit. The removal of political discretion from the process had a dramatic effect in increasing the number of cases filed.

The 1979 Act also introduced some new concepts to clarify what subsidies are countervailable. Consistent with the harsh treatment of export subsidies in GATT, the Act provided that all such subsidies would be countervailable. As for domestic subsidies, the Act added the "specificity test," which provided that a countervailable "subsidy" would be found in the event that a foreign government program provided benefits to a "specific enterprise or group of enterprises." See Tariff Act of 1930 (as amended), section 771(5). The act also included a non-exhaustive list of government programs that might be deemed to constitute subsidies if specific, such as direct payments, the forgiveness of debts, or the provision of services on terms inconsistent with commercial considerations.

The implementing legislation for the Uruguay Round preserves the same basic structure of US countervailing duty law. Because all WTO members are parties to the Uruguay Round accord, the injury test applies in every countervailing duty investigation involving a WTO member. US law is modified to accord with the "green light" category of non-actionable subsidies, and modified slightly to comply with the "sunset" requirement in Article 21 of the SCM Agreement. Provisions are also added to facilitate the enforcement of US rights under the SCM Agreement, and to authorize company specific countervailing duties.

The injury test was discussed in the preceding chapter. The materials that follow focus on the ITA portion of the countervailing duty investigation. Because the issues before the ITA overlap heavily with issues under WTO law, the materials here are brief.

BRITISH STEEL CORP. v. UNITED STATES

United States Court of International Trade, 1986.
632 F.Supp. 59.

The central issue presented, having significant international trade implications for foreign governments that make "equity infusions" in state-owned enterprises in poor financial health, is: Under what circumstances are such companies "uncreditworthy" thereby making the government's investments commercially unreasonable and hence countervailable subsidies under 19 U.S.C. sec. 1677(5)(B)(i)?

* * *

Section 771(5) of the Tariff Act of 1930, as amended, 19 U.S.C. sec. 1677(5), embraces any subsidy "bestowed directly or indirectly on the manufacture, production, or export of any class or kind of merchandise" including: "[t]he provision of capital, loans or loan guarantees on terms inconsistent with commercial considerations". [Previously,] this Court construed the commercial considerations test concluding that an investment is consistent with commercial considerations if a reasonable investor could expect a reasonable rate of return on his investment within a reasonable period of time.

* * *

ITA applied the same "reasonable investor" criterion in determining [that] the British government's equity infusions in FY 1977/78—the year at issue in the present review—were "inconsistent with commercial considerations" within the meaning of the statute.

ITA reviewed BSC's financial history, commencing with its establishment in 1967. The review covered such fundamental indicia of financial condition as net income of BSC, net income before interest and taxes, cash flow from operations, coverage of interest expenses, return on equity, return on sales and current assets and liabilities.

ITA also considered such additional pertinent factors as the substantial cost of forming BSC, leading to unfavorable financial results for the first few years of the company's existence; the enormous social costs borne by BSC because of the British government's policy decisions, such as keeping high-cost plants open to preserve jobs; BSC's massive losses; the extremely bleak prospects of the company expressed by its own chairman in BSC's 1976–77 annual report; and the dismal outlook for the world steel market in general.

Based on its analysis of the foregoing factors, ITA reached the following conclusion:

> After considering the results for fiscal years 1975–76 and 1976–77 and the outlook for the world steel market in general, a reasonable investor in 1977 would not have considered British Steel with its large losses, poor return on equity, and other signs of structural problems, to be a reasonable commercial investment.

* * *

Plaintiffs argue that ITA's "reasonable investor" test is irrelevant to the commercial reasonableness of the British government's equity infusions and contrary to law. According to plaintiffs, the British government, unlike an outside investor, could not simply abandon BSC and incur no further losses if it decided to close the firm, and therefore the steps the British government took as the sole investor in the corporation were reasonably taken to minimize its prospective losses. In short, plaintiffs contend that the overall operating results and financial ratios of a loss-incurring company are irrelevant to the issue of whether the British government's equity infusions were inconsistent with commercial considerations within the purview of the statute. [The court disagreed.]

* * *

[BSC] also urges that the Net Present Value (NPV) test be utilized in determining the commercial reasonableness of the British government's investments in BSC. [BSC] observes that under standard principles of economic analysis, the commercial reasonableness of capital expenditures by BSC on new projects must properly be judged against an evaluation of the NPV of each project. Thus, projects whose discounted cash flows show a positive NPV are commercially justified; projects whose cash flow show a negative NPV are not. According to plaintiffs, NPV analysis focuses upon whether investment in a new project is commercially worthwhile (positive), and it is irrelevant whether a capital project (or some combination of projects) returns the corporation to overall profitability. In support of NPV analysis, plaintiffs make reference to "concrete market examples" of private companies that had suffered heavy losses in successive years and nevertheless continued to make new capital investments.

Defendants, however, correctly observe that NPV analysis is largely predicated upon long-term earnings and interest-rate assumptions, which at best would be tenuous; and that BSC furnished analyses only of individual projects without any evaluation of those projects in terms of their effect upon BSC's overall operations and income-producing prospects.

While unquestionably NPV analyses were of importance to BSC's management, they were relevant to an outside investor only to the extent that the analyses showed how the investments in the individual projects would affect the overall operations and future profitability of BSC. Stated differently, from the investor's point of view, an investment would not be commercially reasonable if overall the company may still constantly lose money and never provide a reasonable return no matter how justifiable a company's decision respecting individual projects analyzed on the basis of NPV.

* * *

In sum, the court finds ITA's determination that the British government's investments in BSC in FY 1977/78 were inconsistent with commercial considerations, predicated upon its reasonable investor test, is supported by substantial evidence and otherwise in accordance with law.

Notes and Questions

(1) Is the "reasonable investor test" in *British Steel* a sensible one? Is it not the case that firms teetering on the brink of bankruptcy still have some positive value in the capital markets? What difference does it make whether the company is already wholly owned by the government? Why not let a government take account of the costs that it would incur if a company shuts down and the workers collect unemployment benefits? What if it can be shown that the government equity infusion was used for a project that was expected to have positive net present value, and that the project was indeed profitable after the fact?

(2) Suppose the equity infusion involves a large, publicly traded company. Can one not simply compare the price paid for shares by the government and the prevailing market price? For some variations along these lines, see the ITA regulations on equity infusions, 19 C.F.R. sec. 351.507.

(3) The calculation of benefits under the countervailing duty laws can become quite complicated for a variety of reasons. For example, suppose that the firm receiving an equity infusion produces a wide range of products—how is the subsidy to be allocated among them? A further issue concerns the timing of the benefit stream. If a company receives a $50 million grant to build a factory with a useful life of 20 years, for example, how is the benefit from that grant to be allocated over the 20-year period? For some insight into such issues, see the ITA regulations on the calculation of countervailing duties in the documents supplement.

(4) Take a look at section 771(6) of the Tariff Act of 1930, defining "net countervailable subsidy," and observe that the permissible deductions from an otherwise countervailable benefit are quite limited—application fees and the like. Thus, it is not permissible for a foreign government to argue that a countervailable benefit is offset by some unusual tax burden or costly regulation to which the beneficiary of the subsidy program has been subjected. The desire to limit such deductions is perhaps quite understandable for administrative reasons. But does this mean that US law cannot really hope to identify the *net* effect of foreign governments on the competitive positions of their industries? And, if so, what does the law accomplish?

(5) Do you understand how duties are calculated? Suppose that Company X produces a single product, and has one million dollars per year in total worldwide sales. Of that total, $800,000 in sales are domestic, $100,000 in sales are to the United States, and $100,000 in sales are to Europe. The company receives export subsidies of $10,000 pertaining to its US sales and $20,000 pertaining to its European sales. In addition the company receives $100,000 per year in countervailable domestic subsidies. What is the appropriate countervailing duty on imports into the United States? [Hint: the answer is 20%.]

(6) Bear in mind that the countervailing duty rate at the conclusion of an ITA investigation is based on historical information, but will be applied prospectively. As in an antidumping case, therefore, the duty may not reflect the actual degree of subsidization over the period to which it applies. Consequently, the ITA periodically conducts "administrative reviews" to reassess the level of countervailable subsidies and adjust the duty accordingly. Overpayments are refunded (with interest), and the importer of record is liable to Customs for any underpayments (with interest).

(7) Note the regulations applicable to remissions or exemptions from direct and indirect taxes. (19 C.F.R. secs. 351.509–510, 517–519) A remission of or exemption from direct taxes is always a countervailable export subsidy. A remission of or exemption from indirect taxes is not a subsidy if it is contingent on exportation, but the remission or exemption of indirect taxes constitutes a subsidy when the remission or exemption is *not* contingent on exportation. Duty drawbacks contingent on exportation that refund duties paid on physically incorporated inputs are not a subsidy, and so forth. Among other things, this structure implies that countries which rely heavily on value-added (a type of indirect) taxes to raise revenue have more freedom to issue rebates on exportation than countries which rely on direct taxes (payroll, income). See Executive Branch GATT Studies No. 1, Tax Adjustments in International Trade: GATT Provisions and EEC Practices (1973). Does the difference in treatment make sense? Are the US regulations consistent with the SCM Agreement?

(8) In Certain Free Sheet Paper from the People's Republic of China, Final Affirmative Countervailing Duty Determination, 72 Fed. Reg. 60646 (2007), the ITA reversed its longstanding policy of declining to apply the countervailing duty laws to non-market economies. ITA argues that the Chinese economy is different from the old Soviet style economies that were the basis for ITA's prior policy. The issue was mooted in that case by a final negative injury vote at the ITC, but it is likely that a countervailing duty order will soon issue against China. At that point we may expect challenges to the new ITA policy both in US court and in the WTO.

Chapter 19

INTERNATIONAL TRADE
IN SERVICES

SECTION 19.1 INTRODUCTION

Trade in services is of substantial and growing importance to the world and national economies. A 1991 report to the US Congress estimated that such trade accounted for 25% of all world trade, for $90 billion in US exports, for 60% of total US output and for 90% of the growth in US employment since 1980.[1] A year later, another report put US services exports at $164 billion.[2] For the year 2000, the WTO reports that US services exports have risen to $274 billion, and that total world trade in commercial services has reached $1.4 trillion.[3]

USTR, International Trade in Services[4]

Today, services are the essential infrastructure of a modern economy. Telecommunication networks, computer networks, distribution networks, and other technology-rich inputs underpin a new kind of business reality. Services businesses are "force multipliers" that expand opportunities and increase productivity across other sectors of the economy.

- In 2005, services industries accounted for 68 percent of U.S. GDP and 79 percent of real GDP growth. * * *

- The size of the U.S. economy has doubled since 1990, driven mainly by the growth of the services sector.

Despite its importance, trade in services was slow to come under multilateral discipline. The Treaty of Rome afforded some constraints on

1. See Report to the Congress on the Extension of Fast Track Procedures, March 1, 1991, at 51.

2. Office of the U.S. Trade Representative, The North American Free Trade Agreement Source Book, August 14, 1992.

3. WTO, 2001 Annual Report, Table II.4.

4. Office of the United States Trade Representative, "Trade and Services, Services Trade Fuels Growth of U.S. Economy", January 2007, available at: www.ustr. gov.

service sector protectionism in Europe, various friendship, commerce and navigation treaties contained limited bilateral commitments on services, and some efforts were made to discipline trade in services through the OECD.[5] The United States also pursued service sector liberalization in its free trade agreements, achieving important breakthroughs with the services provisions of the US–Canada FTA and subsequently NAFTA. But global discipline was lacking until the conclusion of the General Agreement on Trade in Services (GATS) as part of the Uruguay Round. GATS for the first time brings world trade in services within a legal framework broadly analogous to that governing trade in goods, and it is surely among the most notable achievements of the Uruguay Round.

Why did it take so long for trade in services to be incorporated into the WTO/GATT system? One possible response is that barriers to trade in services rarely resemble the usual border measures that affect trade in goods (tariffs and quotas). Instead, domestic regulatory policies, investment restrictions and migration restrictions tend to be the principal trade impediments. As a result, agreements on trade in services tend to be more complex and perhaps more intrusive on entrenched domestic policies. The following materials provide some background on the distinction between goods and services and the special issues that international agreements on trade in services must address.

After this introductory Section 19.1, this chapter proceeds as follows: Section 19.2 presents a brief overview of the GATS system, including the relevant documents and the structure of the GATS obligations. The next section turns to the WTO case law on GATS, but it recognizes that so far there have been very few such cases. In fact, of the five cases resulting in adopted reports, four (*Canada Autos, Canada Periodicals, EC Bananas III* and *Mexico Telecoms*) do not really get into many aspects of a true services case, either because they are a peripheral part of cases relating to goods, or are centrally focused on an ancillary document (*Telecoms*) rather than on GATS itself. Section 19.3 briefly surveys those four cases. The first "real" services case is the *US Gambling* case, which actually requires wending through the major issues involved in the treaty language of GATS. Consequently, Section 19.4 is devoted to the *Gambling* case, which is extensive, complex and comprises many procedural steps.

---

5. Discussion of pre-Uruguay Round agreements respecting services may be found in Geza Feketekuty, Trade in Professional Services: An Overview, in 1 U.Chi.Leg.Forum 1 (1986); John H. Jack-son, International Competition in Services: A Constitutional Framework (1988); and Phedon Nicolaides, Economic Aspects of Services: Implications for a GATT Agreement, 23 J. World Trade 125 (1989).

GEZA FEKETEKUTY, TRADE IN PROFESSIONAL SERVICES: AN OVERVIEW[6]

THE DESIRABILITY OF LIBERALIZING TRADE IN SERVICES

When goods are traded, economic principles of comparative advantage apply. Similarly, specialization and international trade in services can lead to the same economic gains as trade in goods. When imported services can be acquired more cheaply or are of higher quality than services produced at home, both economies benefit.

It is argued that gains from specialization on the basis of comparative advantage are not relevant in the service sector because services are essential to the functioning of a country and therefore must be under local control. Yet it is difficult to see a fundamental distinction between autos and insurance in this respect. Both are essential to the functioning of a country. Moreover, governments have regulatory means for assuring that broader social objectives are achieved. The argument for free service trade is not an argument for the non-observance of local regulations designed to protect the public against abuses by either local or foreign service providers. Just as an auto sold in a foreign market must meet that country's safety or environmental regulations, so must an insurance policy sold in a foreign market meet domestic regulations designed to protect the interests of policy holders.

It is also argued that service industries in many countries have not been able to develop the means to compete with foreign firms. It is suggested that if they were given enough time to invest in up-to-date equipment and management techniques, they could compete effectively. Trade in such services, therefore, should not be liberalized—at least not until local firms have become competitive.

This is the same infant-industry argument that has been applied to trade in goods. As with goods, it is valid only up to a point. Some level of protection can give local industry more time to prepare itself for international competition; however, without some competition at the outset, and with no definite prospects for more competition in the future, local industry will not have sufficient incentive to become competitive. Moreover, by protecting its service industries, a country deprives itself of efficient, up-to-date, and moderately-priced service inputs for the production of its goods and other services. This deprivation will become increasingly detrimental to the country's ability to compete internationally as service inputs become more important to production processes.

JAGDISH BHAGWATI, ECONOMIC PERSPECTIVE ON TRADE IN PROFESSIONAL SERVICES[7]

I. THE DISTINCTION BETWEEN GOODS AND SERVICES

[T]he interest in service trade is very recent. One byproduct of this is that the relevant data are both unreliable and far too limited. The

---

6. 1 U.Chi.Leg.Forum 1, 3–4 (1986). Reprinted by permission.

7. 1 U.Chi.Leg.Forum 45, 45–53 (1986). Reprinted with permission. More technical

limitations on data now available are a function not only of logistical problems in data collection, but also of unresolved conceptual questions which impair our present ability to generate meaningful and adequate statistics on the matter at hand. It is still not clear, for example, how services are to be defined, or how they are different from goods.

A. Non–Storability

Perhaps the earliest useful attempt to define the distinction between services and goods was made by T. Hill only one decade ago. Hill focused on the non-storability of services, stressing that services must be consumed as they are produced and cannot be put into stock by producers. This key characteristic does not cover all items which we customarily report as services; "answering services," for example, do store messages nowadays. Such exceptions, however, do not detract from the usefulness of a definition of services that characterizes them as non-storable because they require simultaneous provision and use.

B. User–Producer Interaction

If services must be used as they are produced, there must be *interaction* between the user and the provider of the service. A producer of goods, by contrast, can generally store the finished product and transact with users at any subsequent time. This interaction, in turn, implies that we can contemplate two essential categories of services: those that necessarily require the physical proximity of the user and the provider, and those that do not though such physical proximity may indeed be useful even in the second category. * * *

1. *Physical Proximity Essential.* The class of services where physical proximity between provider and user is essential is usefully thought of as consisting of three categories.

Category A: Immobile–User, Mobile–Provider. There is an important class of services which requires that the provider go to the user, where the reverse mobility is simply impossible. For example, when the Connecticut Turnpike was being built, an Indian or South Korean construction firm bidding for the contract could perhaps have provided the designs and skilled inputs from home base. But such a firm simply could not have supplied the labor services, except by moving Indian or South Korean labor to Connecticut where the turnpike was to be built. Services of this sort are aptly referred to as "temporary-factor-relation-requiring" services.

Category B: Mobile–User, Immobile–Provider. There is another important class of services where the user really must move to the provider

treatments of possible differences between trade in goods and trade in services include Wilfred Ethier & Henrik Horn, Services in International Trade, *in* International Trade and Trade Policy 223 (Elhanan Helpman & Assaf Razin eds., 1991); Alan Deardorff, Comparative Advantage and International Trade and Investment in Services, *in* Trade and Investment in Services: Canada/U.S. Perspectives (Robert Stern ed., 1985); and James Melvin, Trade in Producer Services: A Heckscher–Ohlin Approach, 97 J.Pol. Econ. 1180 (1989).

rather than the provider to the user. This location-specificity of the provider arises from the fact that the service provider is a vector of characteristics, some key elements of which are simply not transferable geographically to the user's location. Complex neurosurgery for example, simply cannot be done in Gabon because, even though the Massachusetts General Hospital can fly their surgeons over there, there is no way the necessary support services and hospital care can be duplicated or even approximated.

Category C: Mobile–User, Mobile–Provider. Finally, there is a range of services where mobility is symmetrically possible. For example, hair-cuts and lectures are in principle transmittable between user and provider in the location of either, the only difference being the cost of providing the service in one location rather than the other.

2. *Physical Proximity Inessential: The "Long–Distance" Services.* In the second broad class of services, physical proximity between providers and users may be useful, but it is not, strictly speaking, necessary. These are basically "long-distance" services, in the sense that the transactions do not require the immediacy of geographical proximity. Traditional banking and insurance services would fall into this category, because loans and insurance policies can be secured by mail or phone. The type of legal services here discussed, however, presumably require continual contact with the client. Because an attorney serving a corporation may have to interact face-to-face with many of the corporation's employees, legal services could be provided long-distance only in an extremely inefficient and hence expensive fashion. This applies equally to a large class of other professional services such as accounting or management consulting.

II. THE IMPLICATIONS OF THIS TAXONOMY FOR SERVICE TRADE NEGOTIATIONS

The above taxonomy of the service sector has significant implications for the optimal structure of international negotiations in service trade. I will focus here on the special considerations relevant to trade in temporary-factor-relocation-requiring services, which require the provider to move to the user.

First, because it requires factor relocation, trade in such services simultaneously implies *either* direct foreign investment *or* labor migration *or* both. Permitting trade in services, therefore, is tantamount to permitting such factor flows. It is thus inappropriate to think of such service trade in the customary category of trade as distinguished from the category of factor flows: the two are inextricably tied together. For this reason, it is preferable to think of service *transactions* rather than of service *trade*.

Second, the opening up of such service transactions between nations creates immediate difficulties stemming from the differences between what has traditionally been considered acceptable with regard to factor flows as against trade, differences which often reflect political sensitivities as well as economic considerations. Thus, Frank Rossi, in his excellent contribution regarding the restraints on the operations of international accounting organizations, cites as one obstacle possible restrictions on the repatriation of earnings encountered in several developing countries. Yet these are precisely the kind of restraints that apply to all direct foreign investment in these countries. Moreover, domestic enterprises in the same service sectors are subjected to the very same restrictions arising from exchange control.

Yet analyzed as a trade issue, rather than as a transactional issue, such restraints look totally unreasonable: the trade access is not meaningful unless profits can be repatriated. * * *

The third implication of this two-sided nature of service transactions is that attention must be paid to factor-mobility restrictions. Because they are in essence factor flows, service transactions can be readily impeded simply by preventing the requisite factor flows, rather than by establishing trade tariffs or prohibitions. * * *

Restraints on factor mobility can arise simply from visa restrictions, or, as with legal services, from the restrictions imposed by regulatory bodies such as the Bar or the Bench on the foreign nationals desiring to provide such services. In the case of the United States, complications also arise from the difficulty of getting all states to adopt uniform policies, thus making the question of reciprocity as a way of opening access even more intractable than it is otherwise.

Fourth, it is important to understand why I keep emphasizing the *temporary* aspect of "factor-relocation-requiring" services. * * * * "[M]igratory" (or permanent) as distinct from "transient" (or temporary) labor flows raise a different, and more difficult, set of issues which, if brought into the discussion, would compromise the possibility of making significant progress on the issue. Two critical reasons underlie this judgment.

[The first is the effects of the "brain drain" on the nations from which emigration occurs. The migrants gain from leaving, but those left behind suffer as the services provided by the migrants become more scarce and the price rises.]

* * *

The second reason for distinguishing temporary from permanent immigration is that permanent immigration is generally judged by moral-philosophical principles very different from the utilitarian calculus that underlies the economic case for free trade and free investment flows. The "right to exclude" is simply not consistent, in general, with the efficient allocation of world resources, because it prevents some labor inputs from being put to their highest valued use. Instead, a country's exclusion of immigrants is often defended on the basis of "communitarian" ideas such as those developed by philosophers such as Michael Walzer. Such communitarian arguments flatly reject efficiency as the standard against which government policy is to be judged; they are based instead on other moral judgments.

An added reason for concern is that the professional groups that fear substantial loss of earnings are exceptionally well organized, and can often adduce attractive arguments to support their protectionist goals. The American Medical Association, for example, can invoke the possibility of deleterious impact on public health to reject an open-ended services compact permitting free and permanent immigration. It is important therefore that the *temporary* nature of factor relocation, designed to permit service transactions to transpire, be made explicit in negotiations on service trade regulation. If it is not, the possibility of negotiating anything worthwhile will be lost.

U.S. NATIONAL STUDY ON TRADE IN SERVICES, A SUBMISSION BY THE UNITED STATES GOVERNMENT TO THE GENERAL AGREEMENT ON TARIFFS AND TRADE 37–39 (1982)

CONCEPTUAL ISSUES RELATED TO TRADE IN SERVICES

In examining issues surrounding services and trade in services, a number of generic issues common to many service sectors call for specific attention. Discussion of these issues may help conceptualize general principles, rules and procedures as they relate to trade in services.

Three questions regarding generic issues are considered in this section. First, how should competition between private service firms and public service monopolies be managed? This problem arises much more in services than in goods because many countries provide services through public monopolies in order to regulate service industries. Second, to what extent can trade in services and investment in services be distinguished and how important is it to be able to make that distinction clear? The answer to this question is significant as service firms may find it necessary to establish operations (i.e. invest) in the countries to which they export. In order to properly manage issues that affect service exports, countries must determine whether they should be dealt with as investment or trade problems. Third, to what extent is it necessary for countries to allow the movement of labor in order to make it possible for service companies to export? Because services are closely linked to people and the knowledge and experience they possess and because countries are sensitive to the movement of people across their borders, appropriate, balanced treatment of conflicting goals concerning immigration, employment, and trade in services is desirable.

A. *Competition Between Private Firms and Government Monopolies*

Many important service industries are highly regulated by national governments because the services they supply are perceived as vital to national sovereignty, well-being, and security. Indeed, many countries provide such critical services through government-owned or controlled monopolies. * * *

There are three main issues concerning competition between public and private service firms. The first concerns competition between public service monopolies and private service firms outside the national borders of the country involved. Problems arise, in particular, in transborder services between one country and another. The monopoly position at home inevitably gives public service monopolies an unequal advantage vis-à-vis private competitors from other countries in transborder services such as aviation and telecommunications. The monopolies can use their dominant position in their home market to disadvantage their foreign private competitors. Also, the allocation of rates or fees for international services are frequently established through negotiations between domestic and foreign carriers. Where this results in a negotiation between a monopoly on one side and competing foreign firms on the other side, questions can arise concerning the equity of the outcome.

Another type of issue concerns the supply of services by a public service monopoly to foreign firms. In some cases, domestic monopolies have charged foreign firms higher fees for services rendered, or have provided foreign firms a lower quality service than that provided domestic firms. These types of issues become particularly acute when the domestic monopoly also happens to be a competitor. For example, a national airline which owns the ground servicing monopoly can put competing foreign airlines at a distinct disadvantage through a variety of discriminatory practices.

A third type of issue concerns competition between public service monopolies and private foreign firms in service activities outside the scope of the domestic monopoly. There has been a growing tendency to allow public service monopolies to compete with other firms in providing services not covered by the monopoly. In such competition, the public service monopolies can use their inherent power to disadvantage foreign private competition.

In each of these areas, the issue is whether monopolies should be required to adopt an arms-length relationship between its monopoly activities and its activities as a competitor internationally, as a competitor domestically in other services, and as a supplier of services.

B.　Distinguishing Trade in Services From Investment in Services

Governments have traditionally separated trade issues from investment issues, developing separate disciplines in each area. Trade rules, covering "the right to sell" abroad, have tended to be more comprehensive than investment rules. If countries are to embark on the formulation of rules for trade in services, they must know whether this can be done in a meaningful way without dealing with the more sensitive issue of investment in services.

In order to separate trade and investment issues, countries must be capable of distinguishing between the services, or the component of services, which is traded (i.e., produced abroad) and the services, or the component of a service which can only be produced locally. Thus, for example, data processing services provided by a foreign computer center through long-distance communication links is clearly trade. Data processing services provided locally by a foreign-owned computer processing facility is an investment activity.

An important issue with respect to the distinction between trade and investment concerns the distribution system. Under traditional trade concepts the question of access to the distribution system or to service/maintenance facilities is a trade issue, while ownership of the distribution system is an investment issue. Under the principles of the GATT, a product which has overcome the legitimate barriers at the border is entitled to full national treatment, i.e., there is an obligation to treat a foreign producer in the same manner as a domestic producer. Thus, a foreign producer is entitled to the same access to the domestic distribution system as a domestic producer. For example, a foreign manufacturer of autos, who has paid the tariff at the border, is entitled to have the same access to the domestic distribution system as a domestic manufacturer.

The existing GATT approach to the distribution system could be applied to trade in services. Thus, access to a local distribution system would be treated as a trade issue, while ownership of the distribution system would be treated as an investment issue. Access to the distribution system would include the right of a foreign supplier of services to negotiate a contract with local businesses to provide distribution or servicing facilities. Thus, for example, if the national treatment principle were adopted for trade in services, a foreign insurance company that was able to overcome the agreed restrictions at the border, would have a right to sign a contract with local insurance brokers or claims adjusters to sell their policies and to handle claims.

A somewhat different issue arises with respect to some service industries, such as insurance, over the matter of establishment. In a number of countries, domestic regulatory authorities require insurance companies to fully establish themselves legally before they are given a right to sell insurance to local residents. Establishment, in this case, is a requirement imposed in order to protect domestic policyholders; it is no different from any other regulatory requirement imposed by governments for the protection of local citizens, such as health, safety or environmental regulations. Under current trade rules covering trade in goods, the national treatment principle ensures that foreign producers of goods receive the same treatment under domestic regulations as domestic producers. If the national treatment principle were adopted for trade in services, a domestic regulation requiring legal establishment for insurance companies should be treated in the same way as any other domestic regulation. In other words, foreign insurance companies granted access to the local market under trade rules, would have a right to establish themselves legally under the national treatment principle.

A still different issue arises in the context of professional services, in particular professional services that require a local presence. The sale of professional services which are to be provided locally is not a trade issue as such, while the sale of professional services produced outside the importing country is clearly a trade issue. Thus, the purchase of engineering services produced outside the importing country by a foreign engineering firm would clearly be a trade issue. The establishment of a local engineering practice by a foreign engineer would not be a trade issue. Locally delivered professional services, however, could have a trade component as well as a non-trade component and trade rules would apply to the traded component. A fully accredited local engineer could, for example, establish a contractual relationship with a foreign engineering firm whereby that engineering firm would agree to provide certain engineering drawings or technical information. The drawings or information provided by the foreign engineering firm would clearly be trade. Or if the issue is put the other way, foreign suppliers of services given access to the local market under trade rules would have the right to contract with fully accredited local professionals to deliver the service. In other words, local professionals, as local businessmen, could have the right under trade rules to buy expertise, support services from a foreign firm. Issues concerning a foreign-owned professional practice or the admission of foreign professionals to a domestic practice would not be covered by international trade rules.

While it is important for trade negotiating purposes to make a distinction between trade issues and investment issues, this does not imply that investment barriers are irrelevant to trade. Indeed, in many cases, the ability to invest in elements of the distribution system or in local enterprises can substantially enhance a firm's ability to export its services. In order to exploit these trade opportunities, parallel efforts need to be pursued in other fora to reduce foreign investment barriers. The OECD Code of Liberalization of Capital Movements, one such parallel effort, has expanded investment opportunities among developed countries. Furthermore, the Code is about to be amended to include those aspects of the right of establishment most closely related to direct investment. Another effort has been the negotiation of Bilateral Investment Treaties, particularly with developing countries. These treaties cover many areas of services; though here too, efforts will need to be undertaken to improve coverage.

C. *Immigration, Labor and Trade in Services*

The ability of a company to conduct service business internationally depends, in many instances, on the ability of salesmen or professionals with specific skills to move across national borders. This is the case for trade in services, as it has been the case for trade in goods.

International trade depends on some movement of people. Those engaged in international sales and financing of goods frequently travel abroad to market their products, to locate sources of supply and to arrange transactions. Trade in services may depend even more heavily on the movement of people than trade in merchandise. Service professionals may have special expertise that is not available locally. For example, services industries have complained that foreign personnel that are needed to set up data processing systems, to audit financial records, to train or supervise workers and to transmit or use other special knowledge, skills, expertise or talent required for commercial activities are frequently unavailable.

These industries have expressed concern about personnel-type and professional-practice problems that exist in banking, insurance, law, engineering and construction, hotels/motels, telecommunications, data processing, accounting, advertising, franchising and health care. Among the complaints listed are work permit requirements for professional and technical personnel; minimum percentages of local nationals to be employed; hiring restrictions or quotas; citizenship or licensing requirements for foreign engineers, lawyers and other professionals.

* * *

Immigration laws that restrict the availability of many types of workers exist in many countries including the United States. * * *

The United States feels that it is unlikely that a general approach to visa or professional practice problems would be either feasible or desirable over the foreseeable future. Few, if any, countries are likely to be willing to open their borders to face international movement of people in a general way. Thus, while governments are willing to accommodate individual salesmen or professionals and while mechanisms have been developed through bilateral agreements to establish appropriate ground rules, no government has been willing to undertake generalized obligations vis-a-vis the world as a whole. This reluctance is due to a variety of political, social and cultural concerns which dominate national policy-making in this area, and which inevitably override trade concerns.

The United States does not believe that it would be useful or appropriate to negotiate immigration problems in a trade forum such as GATT nor does it believe that immigration rules should be subordinated to trade rules. Efforts to deal with disputes over the legitimacy of the rules governing the movement of labor should be dealt with under existing consular mechanisms.

Notes and Questions

(1) If an American law firm opens a branch office in Brussels, staffed in part by American citizens, is there any "trade" in services, or is it an "investment" in services? What about the services provided by a Japanese manager of a Honda plant in Kentucky—are they a "Japanese export?" The Hondas produced in that plant, of course, would not be considered an export of Japan but rather part of US domestic production. In the remainder of this chapter, you should be sensitive to the fuzzy distinctions between trade in services and investment in services, to the treatment for international trade accounting purposes of earnings abroad by temporary migrants, and to the legal significance of such matters in GATS and elsewhere.

(2) Are there domestic policies at stake in services sectors that are not at stake in goods sectors? Fiduciary, solvency and prudential concerns?

Professional competence concerns? How does the WTO/GATT system handle their closest analogs in goods sectors? Among other things, the Agreements on Technical Barriers and Sanitary and Phytosanitary Measures appear quite relevant.

SECTION 19.2   STRUCTURE AND DOCUMENTS OF THE GATS SYSTEM FOR SERVICES

The services obligations of the WTO Agreement are primarily set forth in the General Agreement on Trade in Services (GATS), thus examination of the GATS text is a good way to begin understanding these obligations. The full text of GATS is in the Documents Supplement. There are also various treaty clauses relevant to services distributed in many other WTO agreements, most notably those relating to dispute settlement, government procurement, etc. However, here we focus on GATS.

(A) KEY GATS DOCUMENTS

There are a number of documents apart from the WTO agreements themselves that can be relevant to an analysis or understanding of GATS obligations. Some general lists usually include the following:

Decision on Trade in Services and the Environment

Decision on Negotiations on Movement of Natural Persons

Decision on Financial Services

Decision on Negotiations on Maritime Transport Services

Decision on Negotiations on Basic Telecommunications

Decision on Professional Services

Various Annexes and Understandings on some of these subjects

Procedures for the Implementation of GATS Article XXI (Schedules)

Telecommunications Reference Paper

Services Sectoral Classification Lists

Provisional UN Central Product Classification (CPC)

Guidelines for Scheduling Specific GATS Commitments in the Doha Round

Most significantly, two post-Uruguay Round negotiations resulted in additional services commitments for many WTO members. These negotiations are interesting because they did not involve all WTO members, but rather were concluded by a "critical mass" of WTO members, representing the vast majority of the participants in the service sector at issue. This deviation from the single undertaking of the Uruguay Round—through this approach known as "variable geometry"—may have interesting implications for the conclusion of the Doha Round negotiations. Under this approach, those members participating in the negotiations agreed to modify their GATS schedules to incorporate their additional commitments on market access. The schedules are, of course, generally applied on an MFN basis (see GATS Article II). Thus, even WTO members who did not agree to additional commitments can take advantage of their benefits. In other words, they can "free ride" without reciprocal responsibilities. The two negotiations resulted in the following protocols:

> Fourth Protocol to the General Agreement on Trade in Services (adopted April 30, 1996; entry into force February 5, 1998). This document provided the legal basis for the annexation of new basic telecommunications schedules to the Uruguay Round services schedules. It included commitments from 69 governments accounting for more than 90 percent of global telecoms revenues. Particularly notable is a "telecoms reference paper" setting forth competition policy rules regarding how obligated members should regulate their telecoms markets, including opening the markets which had been traditionally dominated by government monopolies.[1]

> Fifth Protocol to the General Agreement on Trade in Services (adopted November 14, 1997, entered into force March 1, 1999). The Fifth Protocol provided for the annexation of new financial services schedules to the Uruguay Round services schedules. In included commitments from 70 countries. In all, 102 WTO members had commitments in this sector by the end of 1997. These nations represented over 95% of trade in banking, insurance, securities and financial information.[2]

As demonstrated by these post Uruguay Round negotiations, GATS operates more in the nature of an "umbrella" agreement, fostering future negotiation of service sector commitments pursuant to the modalities set forth in GATS. So far (as of early 2008), however, governments have not been able to achieve much further success in opening market access in service sectors, even in the context of the Doha Development Agenda.

Two sectors targeted for further market opening have been accounting and legal services. Negotiations on the accounting sector have developed an interesting document (set forth below in this section) providing rules for "good governance" related to regulatory actions of member states, and it has been suggested that this document could be a sort of "template" for other sectoral developments.

(B) AN OVERVIEW OF THE GATS STRUCTURE

Part I of GATS contains its "Scope and Definition", with explanations of the four modes of services delivery, namely: a) from the territory of one WTO member into another member; b) in the territory of one

---

1. Report of the Basic Group of Telecommunications, WTO Doc. S/GBT/4, Available at: http://www.wto.org/english/news_e/pres97_e/finalrep.htm, 15 February 1997.

2. The Results of the Financial Services Negotiation under the General Agreement on Trade in Services (GATS), Link Available at: http://www.wto.org/English/tratop_e/serv_e/finance_e/finance_fiback_e.htm, 12 December 1997.

member to a service consumer of another member; c) by a service supplier of one member through its commercial presence in the territory of another; d) by a service supplier of one member through the presence of natural persons from it into the territory of another member. (See GATS Article I for detail.) The fourth mode is perhaps the most controversial, involving visitation by workers into another member's territory.

Part II of GATS contains general obligations (as contrasted with schedules). These include:

Article II: MFN (Most Favored Nation) treatment (more limited than the GATT version)

Article III: Obligations on transparency and disclosure

Article IV: Obligations relating to the treatment of developing countries

Article V: Regarding economic integration (e.g., regional arrangements)

Article VI: regarding domestic regulation. The GATS text, especially Article VI, paragraph 4, has a potentially strong authority for developing measures which could obligate WTO members to observe certain regulatory behavior in service sectors. However, not much success has occurred in the Doha Round, or otherwise.

Articles VIII and IX: relating to competition policy and business practices

Article XIII on government procurement

Article XIV: General Exceptions (similar to GATT Article XX)

Notable is the absence of any text regarding dumping or antidumping. Also notable is that both safeguards and subsidies are dealt with only as a matter for future negotiation (not yet resulting in any operating measures).This can be contrasted with the GATT rules, which have extensive obligations on these two subjects. On the other hand, GATS has a stronger position on competition policy, especially in Articles VIII and IX.

Part III of GATS contains "specific commitments" generally focusing on market access. This includes:

Article XVI, which concerns market access (to be negotiated and carried out through schedules of commitments). The schedules, which are a requirement of WTO membership similar in operation to goods tariff schedules in GATT, but with some differences, such as providing six specific commitments relating to various barrier practices, unless the schedule explicitly negates these commitments. These six rules against measures (unless otherwise specified in the schedules) include: a) limits on number of suppliers; b) limits on value of services; c) limits on number of service operations; d) limits on number of natural persons employed in a service sector; e) measures restricting specific types of legal entity used; and f) limits on the participation of foreign capital. (See GATS Article XVI for detail.)

Article XVII is even more notable since it specifies that national treatment applies only to scheduled service obligations (and even then can be constrained in scope and definition). This is a strong contrast to GATT, in which national treatment applies regardless of scheduling. This manifests what is often referred to as a "bottom up" approach to national treatment obligations, while GATT (and also NAFTA) is deemed "top down".

The rest of the GATS treaty text is mostly about institutional provisions and some further encouragements for market opening negotiations. The following article goes into more detail on the structure and operation of GATS.

BERNARD HOEKMAN, THE GENERAL AGREEMENT ON TRADE IN SERVICES[3]

II. THE FRAMEWORK

The GATS contains two sets of obligations: (1) a set of *general* concepts, principles and rules that create obligations that apply to *all* measures affecting trade in services; and (2) *specific* negotiated obligations that constitute commitments that apply to those service sectors and subsectors that are listed in a member country's schedule. The architecture of the GATS therefore differs significantly from that of the GATT. The Agreement also contains a set of attachments that include annexes that take into account sectoral specificities and various institutional decisions and understandings. Services are defined to include any service in any sector except those supplied in the exercise of governmental functions. The Agreement applies to four "modes of supply:" (1) cross-border supply of a service (that is, not requiring the physical movement of supplier or consumer); (2) provision of services implying movement of the consumer to the location of the supplier; (3) services sold in the territory of a Member by (legal) entities that have established a presence there but originate in the territory of another Member; and (4) provision of services requiring the *temporary* movement of *natural* persons (service suppliers or persons employed by a service supplier who is a national of a country that is a party to the agreement).

Article II on unconditional MFN is a core general obligation of the Agreement: each service or service supplier from a Member must be treated no less favorably than any other foreign service or service supplier. MFN applies to all trade in services as defined in Article I. Because the level of market openness varies among countries, a binding requirement to apply unconditional MFN was resisted by service indus-

---

3. Paper prepared for presentation at an OECD Workshop on The New World Trading System, Paris, April 25–26, 1994. Reprinted with permission. See also Harry G. Broadman, GATS: The Uruguay Round Accord on International Trade and Investment in Services, 17 The World Economy, May 1994, at 281.

try representatives in a number of industrialized countries. They argued that unconditional MFN would allow countries with restrictive policies to main their status quo and "free ride" in the markets of more open countries. Financial service industries from G–7 countries and U.S. telecommunications providers successfully lobbied for MFN exemptions as a way to force sectoral reciprocity. An Annex allowing for MFN exemptions was included in the GATS. It specifies that MFN exemptions should in principle be time-bound (lasting no longer than ten years) and are subject to periodic review and negotiation in subsequent trade liberalizing rounds. Although the Annex does allow pressure to be exerted on countries with more restrictive regimes, invocation of MFN exemptions clearly will reduce the value of the GATS as a whole, especially as "domino effects" are likely to occur.

In the final days of the Uruguay Round it became clear that a number of participants were ready to invoke the Annex on Article II exceptions for financial services, basic telecommunications, maritime transport, and/or audio-visual services. Rather than allow a situation to develop where countries would withdraw conditional offers in these areas and exempt them from the MFN obligation, a compromise solution was reached under which negotiations on a number of these sectors could continue without endangering the establishment of the GATS. A second Annex on financial services was included, providing for negotiations on financial services to be concluded within six months of the entry into force of the agreement establishing the WTO. If negotiations are not successful—i.e., the market access offers made by a certain countries are not satisfactory to other, demandeur, countries—Members are free to withdraw conditional offers in this area (invoke an MFN exemption). During the six month period those countries that have listed exemptions conditional upon the level of commitments taken by other Members will not apply them. A Ministerial Decision was also taken to allow negotiations on basic telecommunications to start in early 1994. These are to be concluded by end-April 1996. Until then, both the MFN requirement and the possibility of invoking an exemption will not enter into force for these services, except to the extent that a Member has made a specific commitment for the sector. Maritime and audio-visual services were taken off the agenda altogether, with the agreement to initiate negotiations on these sectors within three years of the entry into force of the agreement establishing the WTO. Much depends therefore on ongoing or imminent negotiations.

There are three articles in Part III of the GATS on Specific Commitments, entitled Market Access, National Treatment, and Additional Commitments (Articles XVI, XVII and XVIII respectively). *Market access* is not defined in the GATS. Instead, agreement was reached on a list of six measures that in principle are prohibited. These consist of limitation on: (i) the number of service suppliers allowed; (ii) the value of transactions or assets; (iii) the total quantity of service output; (iv) the number of natural persons that may be employed; (v) the type of legal entity through which a service supplier is permitted to supply a service (e.g., branches vs. subsidiaries for banking); and (vi) participation of foreign capital in terms of a maximum percentage limit of foreign shareholding or the absolute value of foreign investment. *National treatment* for foreign services and service suppliers is defined as treatment no less favorable than that accorded to like domestic services and service suppliers. Such treatment may or may not be identical to that applying to domestic firms, in recognition of the fact that in some instances identical treatment may actually worsen the conditions of competition for foreign-based firms (e.g., a requirement for insurance firms that reserves be held locally). Although the measures that are prohibited under the market access article are mostly non-discriminatory, they also include discriminatory policies. The latter will also violate national treatment [e.g., number (vi)].

Table 1

Format for Country Schedules of Specific Commitments

Sector or sub-sector	Mode of supply	Conditions and limitations on market access	Conditions and qualifications on national treatment	Additional commitments
	Cross-border			
	Commercial presence			
	Movement of consumer			
	Movement of personnel			

Specific commitments are scheduled by modes of supply and apply *only* to listed service sectors and subsectors (i.e., a positive list approach was taken towards sectoral coverage), subject to sector-specific qualifications, conditions and limitations that may continue to be maintained, either across all modes of supply or for a specific mode (i.e., a negative list approach for policies that violate national treatment or market access). Any or all of the six types of measures that are prohibited in the market access article may continue to be applied to a sector that is listed by a country as long as these measures are scheduled. Table 1 illustrates the rather confusing format of country schedules of specific commitments used in the GATS. A consequence of the decisions to distinguish between general and specific obligations, to schedule specific commitments by mode of supply, and to allow for MFN exemptions is that very much depends on the content of the country schedules and the extent to which MFN exemptions are invoked. In comparison to the GATT, general rules and principles are much less important (binding). As discussed further below, this can be expected to have consequences for the operation of the agreement, in particular dispute settlement.

Why did this structure emerge? An admittedly greatly oversimplified synopsis of initial negotiating stances is helpful in understanding the structure of the GATS. Before and during the 1986 Ministerial meeting at Punta del Este establishing the agenda of the Uruguay round, many developing countries defended the view that GATT negotiations should not address services. While these countries did not manage to block the inclusion of services on the round's agenda, they did succeed in putting services on a separate track in an attempt to establish the principle that no cross-issue linkages be possible between traditional GATT issues and services. Moreover, at their insistence economic development and growth were agreed to be an objective of any agreement. Many developing countries argued that the lack of comprehensive statistical information was a justification for excluding service transactions involving establishment by foreign providers from the coverage of an agreement. Great emphasis was put on the need for governments to be able to address restrictive business practices, impose conditions of inward FDI, and support infant industries. A consequence of this was that a generally applicable national treatment obligation was considered to be unacceptable.

The EU's initial negotiating position was that trade should be defined so as to include all types of transactions necessary in a sector in order to achieve "effective" market access. A "regulations committee" was proposed that would determine the "appropriateness" of regulation, criteria to determine this to be negotiated. Inappropriate measures were to be subject to liberalization over time, the goal being to achieve "comparable" market access on a sector-by-sector basis for all participating countries. Any framework agreement was to involve only limited obligations of a generally binding nature. In particular, national treatment was to be only an *objective*. The implication of this was that any binding commitments were to apply on a sector-specific level. The United States' initial proposal was the most liberal: MFN was to apply to all signatories and national treatment was to be a binding, general obligation. While the existence of national monopolies was accepted, the U.S. proposed that services should by such entities be provided to foreign-based users on a non-discriminatory basis. Trade was to be defined broadly, including FDI (commercial presence). All measures limiting market access for foreign service providers were to be put on the table.

Thus, both the EU and major developing countries expressed an early preference for an agreement with "soft" obligations—the EU arguing that national treatment should only apply to specific sectors, major developing countries opposing even that. Only the U.S. and certain small open economies—both OECD members and newly industrialized countries like Singapore—were in favor of a "hard" agreement along GATT lines from the start, with generally binding obligations and universal sectoral coverage. At the end of the day the original EU/developing country preference for a "soft" framework agreement prevailed. In return for acceptance that trade in services be defined to include the four possible "modes of supply," and agreement that certain non-discriminatory measures restricting market access were in principle negotiable, national treatment became a specific commitment, and it was agreed that scheduling of specific commitments would be on a sector-by-sector and modes-of-supply basis. The positive list approach to determining the sectoral coverage of specific commitments emerged in large part because many developing countries apparently felt they did not have the administrative resources required to determine all the measures that currently applied to each sector and decide which they would want to exempt. As many of these countries did not have the intention of making very substantial commitments to liberalize access to their service markets in any event, they much preferred a positive list approach. This then put the administrative burden on those countries that did intend to schedule the majority of their market services (i.e., mostly OECD countries and the NICs).

III. COUNTRY SCHEDULES OF SPECIFIC COMMITMENTS

The structure of the GATS implies that negotiations in the services area were (and will be) sectoral, and can be expected to be driven very much by the concerns and interests of the major players in each industry. Thus, although restrictions on inward FDI and non-discriminatory barriers to market access were agreed to be legitimate objects of negotiation, this is on a sector-by-sector basis. Two issues related to the specific commitments can be identified as having possible implications for the functioning of the GATS: (1) the design of the country schedules (see Table 1); and (2) the content of the country schedules. Several problems can be identified with respect to the design of the scheduling of specific commitments under the GATS, all of which may prove detrimental to the functioning of the agreement, and could affect the prospects for future multilateral liberalization by increasing the incentive to pursue regional options (more on the latter below). First, the *hybrid approach to scheduling* (i.e. a positive list of commitments requiring the negative listing of non-conforming measures to be maintained) yields a mostly unsatisfactory outcome from a transparency point of view. The GATS generates no information on sectors, sub-sectors and activities in which no commitments are scheduled—most often the sensitive ones where restrictions and discriminatory practices abound. This is a serious shortcoming when one considers the nature and origin of impediments to trade in the services area (i.e. regulatory barriers at both the national and subnational levels). The top-down "list it or lose it" approach used in the NAFTA or Australia–New Zealand agreement on trade in services would have significantly enhanced transparency. Second, the *à la carte approach to liberalization* foreseen under the GATS' hybrid approach to scheduling allows countries to schedule commitments whilst maintaining significant degrees of regulatory discretion (i.e. as potential departures from otherwise bound non-discriminatory undertakings). Thus, commitments relating to commercial presence may be subject to the right to maintain or impose authorization and/or screening procedures, and the criteria or specific measures that underpin such procedures may not necessarily be clearly defined or specified in the schedule. Third, the *scheduling of commitments according to modes of supply* creates incentives to offer fewer commitments on the cross-border movement of services and service providers (i.e. labor). Somewhat ironically, given the early resistance to discussing investment-related matters in the GNS, the bulk of commitments lodged under the GATS, especially by developing countries, relate to the commercial presence mode of supply. The decision to schedule by modes of supply has meant that commitments on commercial presence may be disguised trade-related investment measures (TRIMs) for services. That is, by only scheduling commercial presence as a mode of supply, foreign service providers may be compelled to establish as a prerequisite for market access, even if cross-border trade is feasible.

Nothing in the GATS compels Members to schedule commitments by mode of supply. What is useful from a definitional point of view may not be a good idea from an operational point of view. This appears to have been the conclusion drawn in the NAFTA context, where the concept of modes of supply was only used to define trade in services. The fact that the GATS itself does not mandate any particular scheduling methodology suggests that a more rational approach could be followed in future negotiations. Given that a sectoral approach has been chosen, the needs of service providers could be factored into specific commitments in any given sector (e.g. access to capital information, telecoms networks (public and private), or accompanying labor mobility). Much will depend in this connection on the experience that is obtained with the GATS in the coming years, and on the "case law" that will be developed through the functioning of the dispute settlement process.

As noted earlier, market access is not defined in the GATS, there being instead a closed list of in principle prohibited measures. The measures that are prohibited will frequently reflect a country's regulatory regime. For example, governments may impose limitations in the context of "natural monopolies" or public utilities. What matters then are not the limitations *per se*, but how contestable markets are. If a government periodically auctions licenses, are the limitations on the number of firms (licenses) a market access barrier? As it is worded that market access article gives a foreign firm the opportunity to use Article XVI as the justification for a complaint to the WTO independent of the degree of contestability of a regulated market. This is because the article focuses on the *form* of measures, not on their *effect*. The scope for disputes (i.e., need for interpretation by panels) appears great in this connection. The same applies with respect to allegations that national treatment commitments have been violated. Many sectors will continue to be subject to scheduled measures that violate national treatment but that may be worded somewhat ambiguously, again complicating dispute settlement. More generally, in the services context it is not possible to point to a bound tariff level, and argue that a policy nullifies or impairs an earlier concession. In comparison to the GATT, therefore, dispute settlement in the GATS will rely less on fundamental principles/concepts. Instead, interpretation of country schedules can be expected to form the main part of the panel process. This in itself will increase the number of cases as it reduces the scope for one panel finding to have a general impact in terms of interpreting the rules. Finally, the history of GATT dispute settlement cases relating to disciplines that were less than clearcut (e.g., subsidies) suggests that there is the potential for some controversy ...

IV. DISCIPLINES ON PREFERENTIAL (REGIONAL) LIBERALIZATION

The GATS is similar to GATT in permitting signatories to pursue preferential liberalization arrangement, subject to a number of conditions that are intended to minimize potential adverse effect on non-members as well as on the multilateral trading system as a whole. Two issues are of particular interest in this connection: (1) the rules that were negotiated in the GATS with respect to regional agreements; and (2) the effect that the GATS is likely to have on the incentive to pursue regional options.

Analogous to Article XXIV of the GATT, Article V of the GATS imposes three conditions on economic integration agreements involving GATS Members. First, they must have "substantial sectoral coverage" (Art. V:1(a)). An interpretive note states that this should be understood in terms of the number of sectors, volume of trade affected, and that no mode of supply should be excluded on an *a priori* basis. Substantial sectoral coverage is not the same as "substantially *all* trade" (the language of the GATT), suggesting that the intention of the drafters of GATS was perhaps to be less restrictive than those drafting Article XXIV of the GATT. This conclusion can also be drawn with respect to the other two conditions. Thus, the second requirement is that integration agreements are to eliminate substantially all discrimination between or among the parties to the agreement in sectors subject to multilateral commitments. More precisely, what is required is the elimination of existing discriminatory measures *and/or* the prohibition of new or more discriminatory measures (Art. V:1(b)). A mere *standstill* agreement may therefore be sufficient. Third, such agreements are not to raise the *overall* level of barriers to trade in services originating in other GATS member *within the respective sectors or subsectors* compared to the level applicable prior to such an agreement. As no distinction is made between customs unions and free trade areas in Article V, countries participating in a free trade area may be permitted to raise some barriers against non-members, as long as the overall level of barriers of all the members of the agreement vis-à-vis non-members, for each of the relevant sectors or sub-sectors, does not increase. This is a significant difference with the GATT, which prohibits such "rebalancing" for members of a free trade area, unless compensation is offered to affected GATT contracting parties.

Articles V:2 and V:3(a) of the GATS respectively allow for consideration to be given to the relationship between a particular regional agreement and the wider process of economic integration among member countries, and give developing countries flexibility regarding the realization of the internal liberalization requirements (i.e., Art. V:1). Given that a standstill may already be sufficient, presumably this flexibility applies to sectoral coverage. It is also worth noting that Article V:3(a) does not speak of agreements *between* developing countries, but of agreements that have developing countries as parties. Thus, in principle, this "flexibility" extends to agreements that have both developed and developing country signatories.

The conditions imposed by Article V are relatively weak. The requirements regarding the extent of internal liberalization that must occur under Article V imply only a limited constraint on "strategic" violations of the MFN obligation and the specific commitments on market access and national treatment made under the GATS. The absence of any requirement in Article V that integration agreements be "open" in principle (i.e., contain an accession clause) is an important shortcoming. Article V appears to have been worded primarily with a view to ensuring that existing regional agreements would be consistent with the GATS. Weak multilateral disciplines, in conjunction with the rather convoluted structure of the GATS and the resulting lack of transparency and significant scope for governments to determine the conditions of competition for foreign service suppliers, suggests that the net effect of the GATS may well be to increase the marginal incentive for Members to pursue regional options.

V.   GATS AND DEVELOPING COUNTRIES

A final issue is the helpfulness of the GATS to countries seeking to enhance the economic efficiency of their service industries. Participation in a multilateral agreement imposing certain disciplines and constraints on national policy formation key may help a government in pursuing or implementing desired changes in domestic policies. Membership in the GATS may increase both the credibility of initial reform and help governments resist demands from politically influential interest groups for altering policies in the future. The GATS imposes costs on "backsliding," reflected in Article XXI on Modification of Schedules. This provision allows parties to withdraw concessions subject to negotiation with— and compensation of—affected parties. In the event bilateral negotiations result in inadequate offers of compensation for affected parties, the GATS foresees an arbitration. If the Member state withdrawing a concession does not comply with the suggestions of the arbitration panel, retaliation may be authorized. The existence of Article XXI will help governments to oppose attempts by domestic industries and other interest groups desiring to restrict market access at some point after liberalization has occurred.

But, this is all conditional upon significant liberalization taking place. Will membership of the GATS help governments pursue liberalization efforts? The standard rationale for the pursuit of multilateral (reciprocal) liberalization efforts is that increased access to foreign markets is likely to be of interest to domestic export-oriented industries, and that these are then given an incentive to oppose lobbying by import-competing industries against the opening of domestic markets. This political dynamic is arguably less strong in the GATS context because developing countries tend to have less of an interest in service exports (or, more accurately, many of the services where they are likely to have or develop a comparative advantage require movement of labor, and this is a mode of supply that has mostly been kept off the table). The main need for most developing countries is to liberalize access to their service markets, thereby reaping efficiency gains as firms and consumers obtain access to lower priced, higher quality services. The issue is what the GATS does to help a government liberalize in the face of opposition by powerful domestic lobbies. The non-generality of national treatment is an important negative factor in this connection, as is the sector-specificity of market access commitments. A government cannot tell its lobbies that it must join the GATS, and that this means it must automatically abide by the national treatment principle for all sectors to ensure that national treatment and market access obligations will apply. This clearly makes matters much more difficult for governments that "need" an external justification for resisting protectionist pressures. Another weakness of the GATS in this regard is Article XIX which allows for "appropriate flexibility for individual developing countries for opening fewer sectors, liberalizing fewer types of transactions, progressively extending market access in line with their development situation and, when making access to their markets available to foreign service suppliers, attaching to it conditions aimed at achieving the objectives" of increasing the participation of developing countries in world trade. This is a guideline for the conduct of future trade liberalizing rounds rather than "obligations" to be undertaken. But it does give developing countries substantial scope to limit the sectoral coverage of their offers.

More generally, GATS imposes few limitations on national policy, leaving a Member pretty much free to do as it likes in the policy domain, subject to the constraint that no discrimination across alternative sources of supply occurs. It allows parties to implement policies that are detrimental to—or inconsistent with—economic efficiency. A good example is the article specifying the conditions under which measures to safeguard the balance-of-payments may be taken, such measures rarely being efficient. It can also be noted that the GATS does not require a participating country to alter the regulatory structure of certain service sectors, or to pursue an active antitrust or competition policy. Liberalization of trade and investment may need to be augmented by regulatory change (frequently deregulation) and an effective competition policy in order to increase the efficiency of service sectors such as finance, transportation, and telecommunications. If liberalization is simply equated with increased market access for (certain) foreign suppliers, this may have little effect in markets that are characterized by a lack of competition. The main result will then simply be to redistribute rents across firms.

Notes and Questions

(1) Look at the definition of trade in services in GATS. Does it encompass the sale of insurance by a US company to a foreign national by mail? Does it encompass the opening of an insurance sales office abroad by a US firm? Does it encompass the purchase of an insurance policy by a foreign national during a visit to the United States? Does it encompass the receipt of a television signal off a satellite? Does it encompass the acquisition of a foreign insurer by a US company? Pay particular attention to Article I:2 of GATS.

(2) Focus on Article II:2 of GATS, allowing reservations from the most-favored-nation obligation. Are there principled justifications for such reservations? To pressure another country to open its market? Other reasons?

(3) Suppose that an American bank desires to open an office in Japan. Assume that Japan has promised national treatment for banking in its national schedule. The American firm applies for permission to operate, much as would a Japanese firm. The response to the application takes a long time. Finally, the application is denied on the grounds that the American firm does not meet the solvency criteria that Japanese firms must meet. Is there any argument that Japan has violated the GATS? Focus on Article VI.

(4) Are preferences among NAFTA members consistent with the GATS? What must the NAFTA members show here in the event of a challenge?

(5) The details of the GATS system remain to be worked out in a number of areas, as a quick perusal of the agreement will suggest. Among the uncertainties are the standards for applying measures to guard against import surges and "unfair" trade. To what extent should the rules governing safeguards, subsidies and dumping differ for service sectors? For some thoughts on such issues, see the discussion in John H. Jackson, International Competition in Services: A Constitutional Framework (1988).

(6) Note that GATS is in many ways an agreement respecting investment in services as well as trade in services. See, for example, Article XVI:2(f).

(7) Some of the service sector restrictions in play in GATS involve arguably anticompetitive practices by professional and trade associations, especially when they are enforced by government regulation. How well will GATS perform when the issue is, say, whether a licensing restriction is a legitimate consumer protection measure or a mere restriction on competitive entry?

(8) GATS negotiations are ongoing and new, sector-specific disciplines may be expected. An example with respect to trade in accounting services, is the following:

DISCIPLINES ON DOMESTIC REGULATION
IN THE ACCOUNTANCY SECTOR

S/WPPS/W/21.
Adopted by WTO Council on Trade in Services, December 14, 2000.

I. OBJECTIVES

1. Having regard to the Ministerial Decision on Professional Services, Members have agreed to the following disciplines elaborating upon the provisions of the GATS relating to domestic regulation of the sector. The purpose of these disciplines is to facilitate trade in accountancy services by ensuring that domestic regulations affecting trade in accountancy services meet the requirements of Article VI:4 of the GATS. The disciplines therefore do not address measures subject to scheduling under Articles XVI and XVII of the GATS, which restrict access to the domestic market or limit the application of national treatment to foreign suppliers. Such measures are addressed in the GATS through the negotiation and scheduling of specific commitments.

II. GENERAL PROVISIONS

2. Members shall ensure that measures not subject to scheduling under Articles XVI or XVII of the GATS, relating to licensing requirements and procedures, technical standards and qualification requirements and procedures are not prepared, adopted or applied with a view to or with the effect of creating unnecessary barriers to trade in accountancy services. For this purpose, Members shall ensure that such measures are not more trade-restrictive than necessary to fulfil a legitimate objective. Legitimate objectives are, inter alia, the protection of consumers (which includes all users of accounting services and the public generally), the quality of the service, professional competence, and the integrity of the profession.

III. TRANSPARENCY

3. Members shall make publicly available, including through the enquiry and contact points established under Articles III and IV of the GATS, the names and addresses of competent authorities (i.e. governmental or non-governmental entities responsible for the licensing of professionals or firms, or accounting regulations).

4. Members shall make publicly available, or shall ensure that their competent authorities make publicly available, including through the enquiry and contact points:

(a) where applicable, information describing the activities and professional titles which are regulated or which must comply with specific technical standards;

(b) requirements and procedures to obtain, renew or retain any licences or professional qualifications and the competent authorities' monitoring arrangements for ensuring compliance;

(c) information on technical standards; and

(d) upon request, confirmation that a particular professional or firm is licensed to practise within their jurisdiction.

5. Members shall inform another Member, upon request, of the rationale behind domestic regulatory measures in the accountancy sector, in relation to legitimate objectives as referred to in paragraph 2.

6. When introducing measures which significantly affect trade in accountancy services, Members shall endeavour to provide opportunity for comment, and give consideration to such comments, before adoption.

7. Details of procedures for the review of administrative decisions, as provided for by Article VI:2 of the GATS, shall be made public, including the prescribed time-limits, if any, for requesting such a review.

IV. Licensing Requirements

8. Licensing requirements (i.e. the substantive requirements, other than qualification requirements, to be satisfied in order to obtain or renew an authorization to practice) shall be pre-established, publicly available and objective.

9. Where residency requirements not subject to scheduling under Article XVII of the GATS exist, Members shall consider whether less trade restrictive means could be employed to achieve the purposes for which these requirements were set, taking into account costs and local conditions.

10. Where membership of a professional organisation is required, in order to fulfil a legitimate objective in accordance with paragraph 2, Members shall ensure that the terms for membership are reasonable, and do not include conditions or pre-conditions unrelated to the fulfilment of such an objective. Where membership of a professional organization is required as a prior condition for application for a licence (i.e. an authorization to practice), the period of membership imposed before the application may be submitted shall be kept to a minimum.

11. Members shall ensure that the use of firm names is not restricted, save in fulfilment of a legitimate objective.

12. Members shall ensure that requirements regarding professional indemnity insurance for foreign applicants take into account any existing insurance coverage, in so far as it covers activities in its territory or the relevant jurisdiction in its territory and is consistent with the legislation of the host Member.

13. Fees charged by the competent authorities shall reflect the administrative costs involved, and shall not represent an impediment in themselves to practising the relevant activity. This shall not preclude the recovery of any additional costs of verification of information, processing and examinations. A concessional fee for applicants from developing countries may be considered.

V.   Licensing Procedures

14. Licensing procedures (i.e. the procedures to be followed for the submission and processing of an application for an authorization to practise) shall be pre-established, publicly available and objective, and shall not in themselves constitute a restriction on the supply of the service.

15. Application procedures and the related documentation shall be not more burdensome than necessary to ensure that applicants fulfil qualification and licensing requirements. For example, competent authorities shall not require more documents than are strictly necessary for the purpose of licensing, and shall not impose unreasonable requirements regarding the format of documentation. Where minor errors are made in the completion of applications, applicants shall be given the opportunity to correct them. The establishment of the authenticity of documents shall be sought through the least burdensome procedure and, wherever possible, authenticated copies should be accepted in place of original documents.

16. Members shall ensure that the receipt of an application is acknowledged promptly by the competent authority, and that applicants are informed without undue delay in cases where the application is incomplete. The competent authority shall inform the applicant of the decision concerning the completed application within a reasonable time after receipt, in principle within six months, separate from any periods in respect of qualification procedures referred to below.

17. On request, an unsuccessful applicant shall be informed of the reasons for rejection of the application. An applicant shall be permitted, within reasonable limits, to resubmit applications for licensing.

18. A licence, once granted, shall enter into effect immediately, in accordance with the terms and conditions specified therein.

VI.   Qualification Requirements

19. A Member shall ensure that its competent authorities take account of qualifications acquired in the territory of another Member, on the basis of equivalency of education, experience and/or examination requirements.

20. The scope of examinations and of any other qualification requirements shall be limited to subjects relevant to the activities for which authorization is sought. Qualification requirements may include education, examinations, practical training, experience and language skills.

21. Members note the role which mutual recognition agreements can play in facilitating the process of verification of qualifications and/or in establishing equivalency of education.

VII.   Qualification Procedures

22. Verification of an applicant's qualifications acquired in the territory of another Member shall take place within a reasonable time-

frame, in principle within six months and, where applicants' qualifications fall short of requirements, shall result in a decision which identifies additional qualifications, if any, to be acquired by the applicant.

23.   Examinations shall be scheduled at reasonably frequent intervals, in principle at least once a year, and shall be open for all eligible applicants, including foreign and foreign-qualified applicants. Applicants shall be allowed a reasonable period for the submission of applications. Fees charged by the competent authorities shall reflect the administrative costs involved, and shall not represent an impediment in themselves to practising the relevant activity. This shall not preclude the recovery of any additional costs of verification of information, processing and examinations. A concessional fee for applicants from developing countries may be considered.

24.   Residency requirements not subject to scheduling under Article XVII of the GATS shall not be required for sitting examinations.

VIII.   TECHNICAL STANDARDS

25.   Members shall ensure that measures relating to technical standards are prepared, adopted and applied only to fulfill legitimate objectives.

26.   In determining whether a measure is in conformity with the obligations under paragraph 2, account shall be taken of internationally recognized standards of relevant international organizations applied by that Member.

Note on Accounting and Legal Services

(1) Of particular interest to law students is international trade in legal services. To what extent should the rules applicable to accountants also be applied in the legal area? For comparison, the EC treatment of legal services is examined in George A. Bermann, Roger J. Goebel, Eleanor M. Fox & William J. Davey, European Community Law, ch. 18 (2d ed. 2002).

(2) Do the disciplines contained in the accountancy measure go far enough? Again, perhaps it is useful to think about their application in the legal context. Nations have a reasonable basis for insisting that licensed attorneys possess a working knowledge of domestic law. They can also claim an interest in protecting the consumers of legal services, some of whom may be unable to judge the quality of their representation very well, against incompetence. Yet, Bar Associations are also effective interest groups in the political process, and may be expected to pursue protectionist measures disguised as rules for the protection of consumers. For example, is there any reason to prohibit the formation of partnerships between domestic and foreign lawyers that could give advice on both domestic and foreign law? Is there any reason to restrict the way that revenues are shared in such an arrangement? Is it acceptable to prohibit foreign law firms from entering the domestic market on the grounds that some of their partners are non-lawyers (e.g., accountants), violating domestic rules against multidisciplinary practice? Is it reasonable to require that applicants for licenses to practice domestic law must have a J.D. degree from a domestic institution, even if

they have foreign law degrees from excellent schools and have no difficulty passing the domestic bar exam? If the accountancy rules above applied to legal services, what would they have to say about these issues?

(3) Legal services were on the agenda during the Uruguay Round negotiations, with the key issues relating to the commitments in the national schedules. The United States, in particular, had hoped to obtain substantially greater access to the Japanese market. But in the end, the Japanese offered only a "joint enterprise scheme." According to the *American Lawyer*, "under that arrangement, Japanese lawyers can only share revenue and profits that foreign firms generate from their Tokyo offices, not from the firm as a whole. Further * * * [t]he foreign firm and the Japanese lawyer can not even use the same office space without following strict cost accounting rules." The joint enterprise could give only limited advice on Japanese law, the Japanese lawyer could not be a partner in the foreign firm, and the joint enterprise could not employ Japanese lawyers as associates. The history of the negotiations, and their outcome, is recounted in Karen Dillon, Unfair Trade, The American Lawyer, April, 1994, at 53–56. For a discussion of the barriers to trade in legal services and how GATS might best address them, see the concluding section of Alan O. Sykes, "Efficient Protection" Through WTO Rulemaking, *in* Efficiency, Equity and Legitimacy: The Multilateral Trading System at the Millennium (Pierre Sauvé et. al. eds.) (Brookings Institution: 2001).

Note About Services in NAFTA

The North American Free Trade Agreement (NAFTA, see history and overview in Section 11.3) contains interesting and some say innovative treaty obligations regarding services. It is interesting to note that the NAFTA services approach on MFN and National Treatment is (unlike GATS) a "top down" approach, with obligations which apply to all relevant activity without scheduling, (see NAFTA articles 1202 and 1203). NAFTA has its own dispute settlement system (in fact several different systems) and some cases have dealt with service issues. The following is a very brief abstract from one of those cases about a troublesome dispute between the United States and Mexico regarding trucking:

IN THE MATTER OF CROSS–BORDER TRUCKING SERVICES

USA–MEX–98–2008–01.
2001 FTAPD LEXIS 2 (2001).

1.   The Panel in this proceeding must decide whether the United States is in breach of Articles 1202 (national treatment for cross-border services) and/or 1203 (most-favored-nation treatment for cross-border services) of NAFTA by failing to lift its moratorium on the processing of applications by Mexican-owned trucking firms for authority to operate in the U.S. border states. Similarly, the Panel must decide whether the United States breached Articles 1102 (national treatment) and/or 1103 (most-favored-nation treatment) by refusing to permit Mexican investment in companies in the United States that provide transportation of

international cargo. Given the expiration on December 17, 1995 of the Annex I reservation that the United States took to allowing cross-border trucking services and investment, the maintenance of the moratorium must be justified either under the language of Articles 1202 or 1203, or by some other provision of NAFTA, such as those found in Chapter Nine (standards) or by Article 2101 (general exceptions).

* * *

77. * * * [O]n December 18, 1995, [U.S. Transportation] Secretary Pena issued a press release which stated that although Mexico and the United States were working to improve Mexican truck safety, because it was not yet a completed process, the United States would accept and process applications from Mexican trucking firms, but the applications would not be finalized. Therefore, no Mexican trucks have been allowed to pass out of the pre-existing commercial zones until the United States concludes consultations with the Mexican government. Through this refusal to finalize Mexican applications, the United States essentially continued the moratorium on Mexican trucks that had been in place prior to December 18, 1995.

78. The United States explained its actions were based on the alleged lack of safety in Mexican trucks, and referred to two alleged incidents involving Mexican trucks, one in November 1995 and the other in Fall 1995, where spillages of hazardous material had occurred. In the latter alleged incident, the driver of the Mexican truck was 16 years old, carried no insurance or shipping papers and the truck involved had faulty brakes and a number of bald tires. Mexico contends that these alleged incidents are not relevant to this dispute, because Mexico could have presented information on several incidents in which U.S. truck operators caused accidents while acting in breach of U.S. law.

* * *

214. [T]he Panel declines to examine the motivation for the U.S. decision to continue the moratorium on cross-border trucking services and investment; it confines its analysis to the consistency or inconsistency of that action with NAFTA. The Panel notes that this approach is fully consistent with the practice of the WTO Appellate Body, which in *Japan—Taxes on Alcoholic Beverages*, at 28, and in *Chile—Taxes on Alcoholic Beverages*, para. 62, has declined to inquire into the subjective motivations of government decision-makers, or examine their intent. As the Appellate Body observed in analogous circumstances, in *Chile–Alcoholic Beverages*, "The subjective intentions inhabiting the minds of individual legislators or regulators do not bear upon the inquiry, if only because they are not accessible to treaty interpreters."

* * *

Services

278. Based on these considerations, and noting the previously discussed objectives of NAFTA in facilitating increased trade in services,

the Panel is of the view that the U.S. refusal to consider applications is not consistent with the obligation to provide national treatment. Thus, the continuation of the moratorium beyond December 18, 1995, was a violation of the national treatment and most-favored-nation provisions of Articles 1202 and 1203, respectively, in that there is no legally sufficient basis for interpreting "in like circumstances" as permitting a blanket moratorium on all Mexican trucking firms. Nor is the departure from national treatment and most-favored-nation treatment under these Articles justified under Article 2101 (general exceptions).

Notes and Questions Regarding Trucking Case

(1) The panel seems to suggest that case-by-case evaluation of the applications of Mexican truckers to provide cross-border trucking services is required. Is it possible in such a process to address US safety concerns adequately? Can the United States plausibly take the position that its licensing process for operators does little to ensure that their trucks are properly maintained and that their drivers are properly trained? That such matters are the province primarily of domestic drivers' licensing and safety inspection authorities, which are inadequate in Mexico? Thus, unless every truck crossing North at the border is to be given a thorough safety inspection and every driver a driver's examination by US authorities, is a denial of approval to operate "reasonably necessary?"

(2) Suppose that the United States had made a better factual showing, based on a sizable sample of inspections at the border, that Mexican trucks are much less likely to meet US safety standards than US or Canadian trucks, or that a significant percentage of Mexican operators are unable to pass the road test given in the United States for commercial driver's licenses. Could it then justify a continued moratorium?

(3) What sort of "case-by-case" analysis will pass muster? Could the United States take the position that since the safety of Mexican trucks is in greater doubt due to the deficiencies of its domestic regulatory system, operating licenses will be granted only to those operators who post a million dollar bond or otherwise establish that they have substantial assets in the United States to satisfy civil liability judgments against them in the event of an accident?

(4) Suppose the United States responded to the panel ruling by approving most applications for operating licenses from Mexico, but put in place a system of safety inspection at the border that put every Mexican truck through a lengthy inspection process (not applicable to US trucks returning from Mexico), and that required every entering Mexican driver to take a driving test or prove that they had passed the test previously. The result was huge lines at the border, delaying transit by many hours and placing Mexican truckers at a competitive disadvantage. Would NAFTA afford Mexican operators any relief? Would additional facts be relevant?

(5) This issue remains controversial. While the US administration has committed itself to expand the scope for Mexican trucking service providers in the US, congressional and union opposition has made such expansion

difficult to achieve. Even as recently as March 12, 2008, a report concerning the Mexican Truck Program had this to say[4]:

> Transportation Secretary Mary E. Peters released a report that found not allowing Mexican trucks to operate in the United States could cost nearly 41,000 jobs—a direct result of Mexican retaliation toward US exports for not complying with the North American Free Trade Agreement.
>
> Shortly after Peters' announcement, International Brotherhood of Teamsters General President James P. Hoffa said allowing the Mexican trucks into the nation would further the "hemorrhaging" of US jobs by the thousands.
>
> Peters told reporters that a coalition of more than 69 US companies and organizations supports the program "because of the benefits it provides to US exporters who every year ship billions worth of products and produce into Mexico."
>
> "Should Congress choose to end the project, Mexico has the right under the rules of NAFTA to impose fees and tariffs on US goods that would surely result in lost business and lost jobs," Peters said. "Whatever their reason, this is no time to let the politics of pessimism dim the promise of prosperity for hundreds of thousands of American drivers, growers and manufacturers."

SECTION 19.3   OVERVIEW OF WTO CASE LAW ON SERVICES

The reader will recall that in Section 19.2, there was a brief introduction to the obligations for services under WTO rules, and notable was the fact that the number of WTO cases regarding services is quite small.

This section takes up four of the five cases, all four of which occurred before the US Gambling case (subject of the next section 19.4), and all four of which do not provide much analysis of GATS. Section 19.4 will, through an examination of procedures and results of the Gambling case, be much more revealing about the scope and interpretation of GATS.

CANADA—CERTAIN MEASURES AFFECTING THE AUTOMOTIVE INDUSTRY

WT/DS139 & 142/R.
Appellate Body Report adopted June 19, 2000.

[In Section 10.2(B)(2), we considered whether certain import duty exemptions on motor vehicles, accorded to particular automobile manufacturers in Canada that met the requisite "ratio requirements" and value-added requirements violated GATT Article I's MFN requirement

---

4. BNA, International Trade Daily, 12 March 2008, Supporters, Critics Debate Effect of Mexican Truck Program on Jobs, (p. 1350).

and in Section 18.2(C), we considered whether they constituted prohibited subsidies under the SCM Agreement. In another part of the case, it was urged that such measures discriminated among providers of wholesale selling services in violation of Article II of GATS.]

147.   Canada appeals the Panel's conclusion that the import duty exemption is inconsistent with Article II:1 of the GATS. Canada first appeals the Panel's finding that the measure is one "affecting trade in services" within the scope of Article I:1 of the GATS.

* * *

155.   With GATS, arts. I:1–2 & XXVIII(a), (b), (c), (d), (f) and (g)] in mind, we believe that at least two key legal issues must be examined to determine whether a measure is one "affecting trade in services": first, whether there is "trade in services" in the sense of Article I:2; and, second, whether the measure in issue "affects" such trade in services within the meaning of Article I:1.

156.   We look first at whether there is "trade in services" in this case. For the purposes of the GATS, "trade in services" is defined in Article I:2 as the "supply of a service" in any one of four listed modes of supply. At issue here is the supply of a service under mode (c) of Article I:2, that is, the supply of a service "by a service supplier of one Member, through *commercial presence* in the territory of any other Member". (emphasis added) "Commercial presence" is, in turn, defined in Article XXVIII(d) as "any type of business or professional establishment, including through (i) the constitution, acquisition or maintenance of a juridical person . . .".

157.   The complainants in this case allege that the "trade in services" here relevant is "wholesale trade services of motor vehicles", which is a category of services recognized in the Central Product Classification.[1] Canada does not dispute that there are service suppliers of the United States, the European Communities and Japan which are established in Canada and which provide wholesale trade services of motor vehicles. Accordingly, we hold that the "trade in services" here in issue is wholesale trade services of motor vehicles supplied by service suppliers of certain Members through commercial presence in Canada.

158.   Having concluded that there is, in fact, "trade in services" in this case, we consider next whether the measure at issue "affects" trade in services. In *European Communities–Bananas*, we said:

> In our view, the use of the term "affecting" reflects the intent of the drafters to give a broad reach to the GATS. The ordinary meaning of the word "affecting" implies a measure that has "an effect on", which indicates a broad scope of application. This interpretation is

---

1.   [original note 157] Provisional Central Product Classification, United Nations Statistical Papers, Series M, No. 77, 1991, Subclass 61111, p. 189. This was replaced in 1997 by the Central Product Classification (CPC) Version 1.0 (United Nations Statistical Papers, Series M, No. 77, 1998, Subclass 61281, p. 363), which continues to recognize wholesale trade services of motor vehicles as a category of services.

further reinforced by the conclusions of previous panels that the term "affecting" in the context of Article III of the GATT is wider in scope than such terms as "regulating" or "governing".

159.   We also found in that case that, although the subject matter of the GATT 1994 and that of the GATS are different, particular measures "could be found to fall within the scope of both the GATT 1994 and the GATS", and that such measures include those "that involve a service relating to a particular good or a service supplied in conjunction with a particular good." We further stated, in that case, that:

> Whether a certain measure affecting the supply of a service related to a particular good is scrutinized under the GATT 1994 or the GATS, or both, is a matter that can only be determined on a case-by-case basis.

160.   In cases where the same measure can be scrutinized under *both* the GATT 1994 and the GATS, however, the focus of the inquiry, and the specific aspects of the measure to be scrutinized, under each agreement, will be different because the subjects of the two agreements are different. Under the GATS, as we stated in *European Communities–Bananas*, "the focus is on how the measure affects the supply of the service or the service suppliers involved."

161.   We note that Canada argues that the import duty exemption is not a measure "affecting trade in services" within the meaning of Article I of the GATS, because it is a tariff measure that affects the *goods* themselves and not the supply of distribution services. As such, Canada maintains, the measure at issue does not "affect" a service supplier in its *capacity as a service supplier* and in its *supply of a service.* Canada relies on our report in *European Communities–Bananas* to support its argument that the import duty exemption falls exclusively within the scope of the GATT 1994, as it affects trade in goods as goods, and does *not* involve a service *relating to a particular good* or a service *supplied in conjunction with a particular good.*

162.   The Panel, however, determined that:

> Like the measures at issue in the *EC–Bananas III* case, the import duty exemption granted only to manufacturer beneficiaries bears upon conditions of competition in the supply of distribution services, regardless of whether it directly governs or indirectly affects the supply of such services. In our view, therefore, the import duty exemption falls in the third category of measures, identified by the Appellate Body in *EC–Bananas III*, as involving "a service relating to a particular good or a service supplied in conjunction with a particular good", which "could be scrutinized under both the GATT 1994 and the GATS".

163.   In *European Communities–Bananas*, we agreed with the panel that "the operators as defined under the relevant regulations of the European Communities are, indeed, suppliers of 'wholesale trade ser-

vices' within the definition set out in the Headnote to Section 6 of the CPC." Although the operators in that case were engaged in certain activities that were not, strictly speaking, within the definition of "distributive trade services" in the Headnote to Section 6 of the Central Product Classification, we concluded there that "there is no question that they are also engaged in other activities involving the wholesale distribution of bananas that are within that definition." With respect to the fact that the operators were vertically integrated with producers, ripeners and retailers, we stated, in that case, that "even if a company is vertically-integrated, and even if it performs other functions related to the production, importation, distribution and processing of a product, *to the extent that it is also engaged in providing 'wholesale trade services'* and is therefore *affected in that capacity* by a particular measure of a Member *in its supply of those 'wholesale trade services'*, that company *is a service supplier* within the scope of the GATS." (emphasis added)

164.   In this case, the Panel did not examine any evidence relating to the provision of wholesale trade services of motor vehicles within the Canadian market and, as a result, did not make any factual findings as to the structure of the market for motor vehicles in Canada, nor as to which companies actually provide wholesale trade services of motor vehicles. As a result, the Panel also never examined whether or how the import duty exemption affects *wholesale trade service suppliers in their capacity as service suppliers*. Rather, the Panel simply stated:

> Like the measures at issue in the *EC–Bananas III* case, the import duty exemption granted only to *manufacturer beneficiaries* bears upon conditions of competition in the supply of distribution services, regardless of whether it directly governs or indirectly affects the supply of such services. (emphasis added)

165.   We do not consider this statement of the Panel to be a sufficient basis for a legal finding that the import duty exemption "affects" wholesale trade services of motor vehicles *as services*, or wholesale trade service suppliers *in their capacity as service suppliers*. The Panel failed to analyze the evidence on the record relating to the provision of wholesale trade services of motor vehicles in the Canadian market. It also failed to articulate what it understood Article I:1 to require by the use of the term "affecting". Having interpreted Article I:1, the Panel should then have examined all the relevant facts, including *who* supplies wholesale trade services of motor vehicles through commercial presence in Canada, and *how* such services are supplied. It is not enough to make assumptions. Finally, the Panel should have applied its interpretation of "affecting trade in services" to the facts it should have found.

166.   The European Communities and Japan may well be correct in their assertions that the availability of the import duty exemption to certain manufacturer beneficiaries of the United States established in Canada, and the corresponding unavailability of this exemption to manufacturer beneficiaries of Europe and of Japan established in Canada, has

an effect on the operations in Canada of wholesale trade service suppliers of motor vehicles and, therefore, "affects" those wholesale trade service suppliers in their capacity as service suppliers. However, the Panel did not examine this issue. The Panel merely asserted its conclusion, without explaining how or why it came to its conclusion. This is not good enough.

167. For these reasons, we believe that the Panel has failed to examine whether the measure is one "affecting trade in services" as required under Article I:1 of the GATS. The Panel did not show that the measure at issue affects wholesale trade services of motor vehicles, as services, or wholesale trade service suppliers of motor vehicles, in their capacity as service suppliers. [The Appellate Body went on to hold that the Panel had also done an inadequate job of examining whether discrimination among service suppliers existed in violation of Article II:1 of GATS.]

EUROPEAN COMMUNITIES—REGIME FOR THE IMPORTATION, SALE AND DISTRIBUTION OF BANANAS

WT/DS27/AB/R.
Appellate Body Report adopted September 25, 1997.

[Eds. note: The following description of the factual background to the dispute is taken from the Report of the Panel:

4.600 The Complaining parties claimed that the EC's banana regime went beyond WTO-inconsistent treatment of imported Latin American bananas. The regime's import licensing provisions directly targeted North and South American firms that distributed bananas. These licensing provisions provided definite competitive advantages to EC-and ACP-owned firms that wholesaled bananas vis-à-vis their competitors based in Latin America and the United States. [Eds. note: The acronym ACP refers to Asian, Caribbean and Pacific countries, parties to the Lomé Convention and beneficiaries of European banana preferences.] * * *

4.601 The Complaining parties claimed further that the Latin American and US firms that imported and sold bananas in the EC market were in the wholesaling business. Wholesale and retail trade services made up the larger category of distributive trade services. Distribution of goods was a huge service sector, on which millions of service jobs depended worldwide. In the GATS, the EC had undertaken specific commitments that covered both cross-border wholesaling activities and wholesaling activities based on a commercial presence within the EC. The combination of cross-border and commercial presence activities encompassed the entire process of wholesaling products from abroad into and through the EC. All of the main Latin American and US companies supplied wholesale trade services to the EC on a cross-border and commercial presence basis. Each such company provided wholesale services by acting as a middleman, purchasing bananas from other companies and reselling them to other wholesalers or retailers. This was in addition to the activities these companies performed in marketing their own bananas to and in the EC.

4.602 The United States argued that the EC banana regime employed discrete but compounding measures to reconfigure the Latin American banana service market in favour of EC and ACP suppliers, including through the use of: (i) operator category allocations, which granted the right to import 30 per cent of the Latin American banana tariff quota predominantly to EC and ACP firms; * * * and (iv) activity function allocations, which took the Latin American banana import rights that remained after the removal of 30 per cent under (i), and granted over 40 per cent of those remaining rights to predominantly EC firms that had ripened (but had not necessarily ever imported) bananas, or that had a role in importing bananas that was limited only to the administrative, frequently "paper-only" task of customs clearance. * * *

4.608 According to the Complaining parties, the EC thus manipulated these two features of the banana regime (the operator categories and activity functions) to strip opportunities for Latin American banana distribution business away from the firms that had traditionally supplied nearly all Latin American bananas into the EC market and award these opportunities to their competitors, which were EC or ACP-owned companies. By drastically altering competitive conditions in this manner, these aspects of the regime violated the principles of MFN and national treatment of Articles II and XVII of GATS. * * *

4.609 The EC noted that the measures contested under the GATS remained the same as those contested under the GATT, i.e. the licensing system and, in particular, the allocation. In the opinion of the EC, these were measures directed at goods and except for some broad allegations on competitive conditions, the Complainants concerned did not substantiate that these measures related to trade in services. * * *]

[Eds. note: In a section of the opinion that was referenced in our excerpt from the *Canada Autos* case, the Appellate Body rejected the argument of the European Communities that importers of bananas were not involved with trade in services. As it did in *Autos*, it found that a company involved with trade in goods could also be engaged in the service of wholesale or retail selling, and upheld the Panel's finding that some of the "operators" affected by the European banana import licensing scheme were indeed providing such services. It further noted "that the European Communities has made a full commitment for wholesale trade services (CPC 622), with no conditions or qualifications, in its Schedule of Specific Commitments under the GATS. Although these operators, as defined in the relevant EC regulations, are engaged in some activities that are not strictly within the definition of "distributive trade services" in the Headnote to Section 6 of the CPC, there is no question that they are also engaged in other activities involving the wholesale distribution of bananas that are within that definition." In addition, the Appellate Body concluded that the non-discrimination obligations in GATS Article II and XVII applied to both *de jure*, or formal, discrimination, and *de facto* discrimination. In the case of GATS Article XVII and the activity function rules, it concluded as follows:]

246. As indicated earlier, we do not accept the argument by the European Communities that the aims or effects of the activity function rules are relevant in determining whether they provide less favourable conditions of competition to services and service suppliers of foreign origin. In this respect, we note the Panel's factual conclusions that:

> . . . even the EC statistics suggest that 74 to 80 per cent of ripeners are EC controlled. Thus, we conclude that the vast majority of the ripening capacity in the EC is owned or controlled by natural or juridical persons of the EC and that most of the bananas produced in or imported to the EC are ripened in EC owned or controlled ripening facilities.

* * * Given these factual findings, we see no reason to reverse the Panel's legal conclusion that the allocation to ripeners of a certain proportion of the Category A and B licences allowing the importation of third-country and non-traditional ACP bananas at in-quota tariff rates creates less favourable conditions of competition for like service suppliers of Complainants' origin, and is therefore inconsistent with the requirements of Article XVII of GATS.

Notes and Questions

(1) Under what circumstances would importers of goods *not* also be involved in the supply of services?

(2) What information is required to determine whether trade in services is "affected" by the measures at issue? Contrast the *Bananas* case with the *Autos* case—why was it clear that the measures involved in *Bananas* were "affecting trade in services" but not the measures involved in *Autos*? With reference to the *Autos* case, assume that the automakers who benefited from the import duty exemption had integrated wholesale operations, and that those operations were engaged in selling the vehicles that had been imported duty free. Does that give those wholesaling operations a competitive edge over wholesaling operations that do not have access to duty free imports? Is that enough to establish that trade in services is "affected?" Is it enough to establish a violation of GATS Article I:1 or II:1? What more information would you want to have, if any?

(3) Was the discrimination among operators in Bananas *de jure* or *de facto*, and why?

(4) Under any quota scheme, the rights to import under the quota must be allocated somehow. Consider the common situation in which importers are also wholesalers. What systems of allocating the quota rights will pass muster under national treatment and most-favored-nation principles of GATS (assuming they both apply under a Member's schedules)? Should a nation distribute quota rights in accordance with pre-quota market shares? Is it acceptable to let in the imports that show up first at the border, and exclude those that arrive later? Even if domestic importers seem to end up first in line with regularity? If the quota rights are allocated in a manner

that complies with the requirements of GATT, can they still be challenged under GATS?

(5) The two preceding cases involved arguments by respondent countries to the effect that GATT governed the measures in question, but not GATS. The reverse situation may also arise.

CANADA—CERTAIN MEASURES CONCERNING PERIODICALS

WT/DS31/AB/R.
Appellate Body Report adopted July 30, 1997.

[Eds. note: The following description of the measure at issue in this excerpt is taken from the panel report in the case:]

2.6 In 1995, Bill C–103, which added Part V.I—Tax on Split-run Periodicals to the Excise Tax Act, became law. The amendment calls for the imposition, levy and collection, in respect of each split-run edition of a periodical, a tax equal to 80 per cent of the value of all the advertisements contained in the split-run edition. The tax is levied on a per issue basis. The value of all advertisements in a split-run edition of a periodical is the total of all the gross fees for all the advertisements contained in the edition. The term "periodical" means printed material that is published in a series of issues that appear not less than twice a year and not more than once a week. Where an issue of a periodical is published in several versions, each version is an edition of the issue. Each edition of the issue must be considered separately when determining whether an edition is a split-run edition. The definition of "periodical" explicitly excludes a catalogue which is substantially made up of advertisements.

2.7 The amendment defines a split-run edition as an edition of an issue of a periodical that:

(i) is distributed in Canada;

(ii) in which more than 20 per cent of the editorial material is the same or substantially the same as editorial material that appears in one or more excluded editions of one or more issues of one or more periodicals; and

(iii) contains an advertisement that does not appear in identical form in all the excluded editions.

There are two exclusionary provisions. Under the first, the particular edition is not a split-run edition if it is an edition that is primarily circulated outside Canada. In effect, this is an exemption for editions that are distributed in Canada, but are mainly distributed outside Canada. Under the second, a particular edition of an issue of a periodical that would otherwise be a split-run edition is not a split-run edition if all the advertisements in the particular edition appear in identical form in one or more editions of that issue that are primarily distributed outside Canada and that have a combined circulation outside Canada that is greater than the circulation in Canada of the particular edition. The purpose is to prevent a publisher from qualifying for this exemption by having all the advertisements in its Canadian split-run edition also appear in one of its excluded editions that has a very small circulation.]

The Panel Report * * * contains the following conclusions: * * * Part V.1 of the Excise Tax Act is inconsistent with Article III:2, first sentence, of GATT 1994 * * *

* * *

Canada submits that the Panel erred in law when it applied Article III:2, first sentence, of the GATT 1994 to a measure affecting advertising services. Canada asserts that the GATT 1994 applies, as the GATT 1947 had always applied previously, to measures affecting trade in goods, but it has never been a regime for dealing with services in their own right. In Canada's view, if the GATT 1994 applied to all aspects of services measures on the basis of incidental, secondary or indirect effects on goods, the GATT 1994 would effectively be converted into a services agreement. More precisely, the GATT 1994 should not apply merely on the ground that a service makes use of a good as a tangible medium of communication. Assuming that the measure at issue is designed essentially to restrict access to the services market, the mere fact that a service makes use of a good as a vehicle or a medium is an insufficient ground on which to base a challenge under the GATT 1994.

Canada asserts that the Panel's decision to consider Part V.1 of the Excise Tax Act as a measure subject to Article III of the GATT 1994 was based largely upon an unwarranted generalization of the terms of Article III:4, as well as a misconstruction of the word "indirectly" in Article III:2, first sentence. Canada argues that it is evident from its text that Article III:4 of the GATT 1994 governs only services measures that affect the ability of foreign goods to compete on an equal footing with domestic goods. Canada submits that advertising services are only subject to Article III:4 to the extent that they affect the "internal sale or offering for sale, purchase, transportation, distribution or use" of a product that is entitled to national treatment under Article III of the GATT 1994. The inference that advertising services in general are covered by Article III:2 of the GATT 1994 is without foundation.

Canada stresses that the concept of "indirectly" in Article III:2 of the GATT 1994 is intended to capture taxes which apply to "inputs" that contribute to the production or distribution of a good, such as raw materials, services inputs and intermediate inputs. It is important to distinguish services inputs that are directly involved in the production or marketing of a good from services that are "end-products" in their own right. In Canada's view, the advertising services of a publisher are not, like labour in the production of a car, an input into the production of a good. Canada asserts that services are often delivered by means of a good, and that the taxation of services that are associated with goods in this way does not "subject" those goods "indirectly" to the tax, because the tax does not affect the costs of the production, distribution and marketing of the goods. Canada argues that, although magazines serve as a tangible medium in which advertising is incorporated, this association, however close, does not meet the tests appropriate to the interpretation of Article III:2 of the GATT 1994. Canada maintains that advertising is not an input or a cost in the production, distribution or use of magazines as physical products. Therefore, the taxation of magazine advertising services is not indirect taxation of magazines as goods within the meaning of Article III:2.

Canada asserts that the Panel mischaracterized Part V.1 of the Excise Tax Act as a measure affecting trade in goods. It is a measure regulating access to the magazine advertising market. Most magazines represent two distinct economic outputs, that of a good and an advertising medium for providing a service, depending on the perspective of the purchaser. According to Canada, the tax is not applied to the consumer good because it is not based on, nor applied to, the price of a magazine. Instead, the tax is calculated using the value of advertising carried in a split-run edition of a magazine and is assessed against the publisher of each split-run magazine as the seller of the advertising service.

In Canada's view, since the provision of magazine advertising services falls within the scope of the General Agreement on Trade in Services (the "GATS"), and Canada has not undertaken any commitments in respect of the provision of advertising services in its Schedule of Specific Commitments, Canada is not bound to provide national treatment to Members of the WTO with respect to the provision of advertising services in the Canadian market.

* * *

We are unable to agree with Canada's proposition that the GATT 1994 is not applicable to Part V.1 of the Excise Tax Act. First of all, the measure is an excise tax imposed on split-run editions of periodicals. We note that the title to Part V.1 of the Excise Tax Act reads, "TAX ON SPLIT–RUN PERIODICALS", not "tax on advertising". Furthermore, the "Summary" of An Act to Amend the Excise Tax Act and the Income Tax Act, reads: "The Excise Tax Act is amended to impose an excise tax in respect of split-run editions of periodicals". Secondly, a periodical is a good comprised of two components: editorial content and advertising content. Both components can be viewed as having services attributes, but they combine to form a physical product—the periodical itself.

The measure in this appeal, Part V.1 of the Excise Tax Act, is a companion to Tariff Code 9958, which is a prohibition on imports of special edition periodicals, including split-run or regional editions that contain advertisements primarily directed to a market in Canada and that do not appear in identical form in all editions of an issue distributed in that periodical's country of origin. Canada agrees that Tariff Code 9958 is a measure affecting trade in goods, even though it applies to split-run editions of periodicals as does Part V.1 of the Excise Tax Act. As Canada stated in the oral hearing during this appeal:

> Tariff Code 9958 is basically an import prohibition of a physical good, i.e., the magazine itself. In that sense the entire debate was as

to whether or not there was a possible defence against the application of Article XI of the GATT. In that case, therefore, there were direct effects and Canada recognized that there were effects on the physical good—the magazine as it crossed the border.

The Panel found that Tariff Code 9958 is an import prohibition, although it applies to split-run editions of periodicals which are distinguished by their advertising content directed at the Canadian market. Canada did not appeal this finding of the Panel. It is clear that Part V.1 of the Excise Tax Act is intended to complement and render effective the import ban of Tariff Code 9958. As a companion to the import ban, Part V.1 of the Excise Tax Act has the same objective and purpose as Tariff Code 9958 and, therefore, should be analyzed in the same manner.

An examination of Part V.1 of the Excise Tax Act demonstrates that it is an excise tax which is applied on a good, a split-run edition of a periodical, on a "per issue" basis. By its very structure and design, it is a tax on a periodical. It is the publisher, or in the absence of a publisher resident in Canada, the distributor, the printer or the wholesaler, who is liable to pay the tax, not the advertiser.

Based on the above analysis of the measure, which is essentially an excise tax imposed on split-run editions of periodicals, we cannot agree with Canada's argument that this internal tax does not "indirectly" affect imported products. It is a well-established principle that the trade effects of a difference in tax treatment between imported and domestic products do not have to be demonstrated for a measure to be found to be inconsistent with Article III. The fundamental purpose of Article III of the GATT 1994 is to ensure equality of competitive conditions between imported and like domestic products. We do not find it necessary to look to Article III:1 or Article III:4 of the GATT 1994 to give meaning to Article III:2, first sentence, in this respect. In *Japan—Alcoholic Beverages*, the Appellate Body stated that "Article III:1 articulates a general principle" which "informs the rest of Article III". However, we also said that it informs the different sentences in Article III:2 in different ways. With respect to Article III:2, second sentence, we held that "Article III:1 informs Article III:2, second sentence, through specific reference".

Article III:2, first sentence, uses the words "directly or indirectly" in two different contexts: one in relation to the application of a tax to imported products and the other in relation to the application of a tax to like domestic products. Any measure that indirectly affects the conditions of competition between imported and like domestic products would come within the provisions of Article III:2, first sentence, or by implication, second sentence, given the broader application of the latter.

The entry into force of the GATS, as Annex 1B of the *WTO Agreement*, does not diminish the scope of application of the GATT 1994. Indeed, Canada concedes that its position "with respect to the inapplicability of the GATT would have been exactly the same under the GATT 1947, before the GATS had ever been conceived".

We agree with the Panel's statement:

The ordinary meaning of the texts of GATT 1994 and GATS as well as Article II:2 of the WTO Agreement, taken together, indicates that obligations under GATT 1994 and GATS can co-exist and that one does not override the other.

We do not find it necessary to pronounce on the issue of whether there can be potential overlaps between the GATT 1994 and the GATS, as both participants agreed that it is not relevant in this appeal. Canada stated that its

. . . principal argument is not based . . . on the need to avoid overlaps and potential conflicts. On the contrary it is based on a textual interpretation of the provision, on the plain meaning of the words in Article III:2—more precisely the word 'indirectly' interpreted in its legal context and in light of the object and purpose of the provision.

We conclude, therefore, that it is not necessary and, indeed, would not be appropriate, in this appeal to consider Canada's rights and obligations under the GATS. The measure at issue in this appeal, Part V.1 of the Excise Tax Act, is a measure which clearly applies to goods—it is an excise tax on split-run editions of periodicals . . .

Notes and Questions

(1) Think through the pertinent comparisons under GATT Article III:2—which imported products are purportedly "like" which domestic products? Note that in a later part of the opinion, the Appellate Body determined that the excise tax was inconsistent with Article III:2, second sentence, but reversed the finding of inconsistency with Article III:2, first sentence.

(2) Suppose a nation wanted to encourage the development of its insurance industry. One type of insurance covers damage to goods in transit from abroad. The nation enacts a law providing that importers who buy their insurance coverage from foreign insurance carriers must pay a "foreign insurance tax" equal to 50% of the premiums paid to foreign insurers. Same case or different?

Note on Mexico—Measures Affecting Telecommunication Services, WT/DS204/R, Panel Report, adopted June 1, 2004

In 2002 the United States brought a WTO case against Mexico arguing that the Mexican government operated its telecommunications monopoly "Telemex" in a manner that was inconsistent with the obligations of the "Reference Paper" attached to the GATS Annex on Telecommunications (embodied in the schedules of Mexico pursuant to the WTO Telecommunications Agreement of 15 February 1997.) The reference paper set forth obligations which concerned competition policies for government policies on regulations. The panel concluded in favor of the United States. No appeal was taken so the panel report was adopted. The reference paper did not engage much with the rest of GATS.

The panel ruled that telecom interconnection rates changed by Telemex were not "cost oriented" as required by the reference paper, and also concluded that Mexico acted inconsistently with the GATS Annex on Telecommunication by "failing to ensure that commercially present commercial agencies of the United States have access to and use of private leased circuits and are permitted to interconnect these circuits to public telecommunications transport networks and services or with circuits of other service suppliers."

The panel report is lengthy and detailed, discussing the complex facts of the Telemex measures, and interpreting various words of the reference paper, including "cost oriented." In addition, the panel considered the GATS definition of cross-border supply of services.

According to the United States, the services at issue are supplied from the United States into Mexico, within the meaning of GATS Article I:2(a), which defines what is commonly referred to as "cross-border" trade in services, as follows: "from the territory of one Member into the territory of any other Member." Specifically the United States argued, "facilities-based operators in the territory of the United States deliver traffic consisting of the services at issue from United States customers to the Mexican border where, under Mexican law, the traffic is transferred to Mexican operators, who then terminate the United States operators' traffic, consisting of the services at issue, in Mexico." In doing so, US service suppliers "link their network at the border to that of a Mexican operator." Furthermore, "non-facilities-based operators" (i.e., commercial agencies) would do the same if permitted under Mexican law. (paras. 7.25–26) In response, Mexico argued that the services at issue are not supplied "cross-border" because "[i]n order to transmit customer data cross-border 'from' one Member 'into' another Member, the supplier must *itself transmit* the customer data within the territory of that other Member." Thus, an operator who simply "hands off" traffic at the border to another operator would not be supplying cross-border; only "full circuit" or "end-to-end" provision by the same operator constitutes cross-border supply. (para. 7.27).

According to the panel, Mexico's argument implies that cross-border supply can only occur "if the supplier operates, or is present in some way, on the other side of the border." The issue, the panel said, "is therefore whether, with respect to the telecommunications services at issue, cross-border supply between two Members under Article I:2(a) occurs only if the supplier *itself* operates, or is present, on the other side of the border, or if cross-border supply can occur also if a supplier simply 'hands off' traffic at the border." (para. 7.28).

The panel used an "Explanatory Note" issued by the GATT Secretariat to confirm its view that the services at issue, in which US suppliers "link their networks at the border with those of Mexican suppliers for termination within Mexico," "are services which are supplied cross-border within the meaning of Article I:2(a) of the GATS." (para 7.45).

The case presents interesting considerations of competition policy ideas which may in the future become more significant in the WTO context.

SECTION 19.4   *U.S. GAMBLING*

(A) INTRODUCTION

This case began with a request for consultations by Antigua and Barbuda dated March 27, 2003 (WTO document WT/DS285/1). It followed with the request for the establishment of a panel on June 13, 2003 (WT/DS285/2). The panel reported on April 30, 2004 (WT/DS285/R). This was then appealed by both sides on 7 and 19 January 2005. The Appellate Body report was adopted April 20, 2005 (WT/DS285/AB/R).

The following outline will help the reader to understand the *Gambling* case (and indeed generally to understand the way the service commitments operate). The linked issues in the *Gambling* case can be charted as follows:

1) What obligations of GATS are raised by the complaint? These could be general obligations (particularly those of GATS Part II), but more specifically in the *Gambling* case they were schedule commitments (GATS Part III).

2) If a schedule commitment is demonstrated, then the question is has it been breached? GATS Article XVI is key in this case.

3) Next assuming that respondent's (US) action was inconsistent with its scheduled commitment, can it invoke an exception, particularly an exception in GATS Article XIV (general exceptions, similar to GATT Article XX). The panel concluded no, but the Appellate Body reversed and ruled that Article XIV(a) (the public morals exception) applied.

4) Since Article XIV(a) includes the word "necessary", i.e., it only covers measures *necessary* to protect public morals, the necessity test must be and was discussed.

5) Once a GATS Article XIV exception is deemed to apply, then it is necessary to determine if the requirements of the "chapeau" of Article XIV have been complied with.

6) Ultimately, the Appellate Body concluded that the respondent (US) had violated its scheduled commitments and could not have recourse to the exception in Article XIV(a) because its measure was applied inconsistently with the requirements of the chapeau.

This case has some contextual facts that are unusual, so it is appropriate to include brief notes about those since they can provide some background to understand the case, even though they may not have direct relevance to the WTO legal positions. One such context is the belief by some US persons closely involved with the case that the US government made a mistake in drafting its schedule for services, and that the US government never would have consciously committed the US to open its market to such a controversial and morally debated practice as internet gambling services. Some persons therefore designate this case as an "oops" case, and raise the policy question whether the WTO rules in general should accommodate such errors as this one, at least where no other WTO member has been harmed because of reliance on what some would claim is obviously an error. In the notes below after this case text, added context will be mentioned.

The following is the text of the Appellate Body *Gambling* report, extensively abridged for classroom use. After that text, the authors follow with some notes about the extensive and interesting "post appellate" actions taken, and a second brief note about other "context" circumstances.

UNITED STATES—MEASURES AFFECTING THE CROSS–BORDER SUPPLY OF GAMBLING AND BETTING SERVICES

WT/DS285/AB/R.
Appellate Body Report adopted April 20, 2005.

1.   The United States, and Antigua and Barbuda ("Antigua"), each appeals certain issues of law and legal interpretations developed in the Panel Report, United States—Measures Affecting the Cross–Border Supply of Gambling and Betting Services (the "Panel Report"). The Panel was established to consider a complaint by Antigua concerning certain measures of state and federal authorities that allegedly make it unlawful for suppliers located outside the United States to supply gambling and betting services to consumers within the United States.

2.   Before the Panel, Antigua claimed that certain restrictions imposed by the United States through federal and state laws resulted in a "total prohibition" on the cross-border supply of gambling and betting services from Antigua. Antigua contended that such a "total prohibition" was contrary to obligations of the United States under the General Agreement on Trade in Services (the "GATS"). In particular, Antigua asserted that the GATS Schedule of the United States includes specific commitments on gambling and betting services. Antigua argued that, because the United States made full market access and national treatment commitments (that is, inscribed "None" in the relevant columns of its GATS Schedule), the United States, in maintaining the measures at issue, is acting inconsistently with its obligations under its GATS Schedule, as well as under Articles VI, XI, XVI, and XVII of the GATS.

* * *

[The United States included within its scheduled GATS market access commitments the cross-border provision of "other recreational services (except sporting)". At issue initially in this case was whether or not this commitment included gambling services. The Appellate Body found that, after applying the interpretative rules of Article 31 of the Vienna Convention on the Law of Treaties, the quoted phrase was ambiguous and that recourse to Article 32 on supplementary means of interpretation was necessary. In that regard, inter alia, it found that the GATS scheduling preparatory work indicated that "gambling and betting services" were included under the heading "sporting and other recreational services", but in the subcategory of "other recreational services" and not the subcategory of "sporting services". Accordingly, even though the US did not follow the classification scheme of the preparatory work, the US commitment was found to cover gambling and betting services. Since the three challenged US laws—the Wire Act (18 USC 1084), the Travel Act (18 USC 1952) and the Illegal Gambling Business Act (IGBA) (18 USC 1955)—prohibit the supply of gambling and betting services, the US was found to have measures inconsistent with GATS Articles XVI:1, XVI:2(a) and XVI:2(c).

The Panel also examined eight state laws. Ultimately, the Appellate Body did not uphold any violations with respect to those laws.

Both the panel and the Appellate Body reports contain lengthy analyses of the meaning of the US schedule and whether it included internet gambling so as to obligate the US to allow the cross-border supply of gambling services to its territory. The Appellate Body analysis deeply engaged a variety of interpretation techniques mostly guided by the language of Articles 31 and 32 of the Vienna Convention on the Law of Treaties, as noted above. These techniques included careful textual (and dictionary) approaches ("ordinary wording"), consideration of the role of context, the fact that the US schedule provided that only the English version of the schedule is authentic, use of a 1993 GATT document and other documents regarding scheduling guidelines (as context), and consideration of the object and purpose of GATS, subsequent practice, preparatory work, and other interpretative techniques.

This lengthy analysis seems to reinforce the Appellate Body's "Vienna Convention" approach to interpretation, and also to suggest that interpretation of schedule commitments should also follow this approach and not necessarily be different than interpretation methods for other treaty language.

The following includes a small selection of the Appellate Body analysis of whether the US schedule bound it regarding gambling services. Then the Appellate Body turns to the other important arguments (especially relating to GATS Article XIV(a), the "morals" exception) and here too establishes important new jurisprudence. While aimed at GATS XIV, this jurisprudence will also have effects on the nearly identical language of GATT Article XX.]

V.   Interpretation of the Specific Commitments Made by the United States in its GATS Schedule

* * *

[Article 31 of the Vienna Convention on the Law of Treaties]

161.   The contentious issues in this appeal concern whether the Panel erred in the way that it used the Vienna Convention principles of interpretation in determining the scope of the specific commitments made by the United States in subsector 10.D of its GATS Schedule, and

whether the Panel erred in the conclusions it drew on the basis of its approach.

162. The United States' appeal focuses on the Panel's interpretation of the word "sporting" in subsector 10.D of the United States' GATS Schedule. According to the United States, the ordinary meaning of "sporting" includes gambling and betting and the Panel erred in finding otherwise. We observe first that the interpretative question addressed by the Panel was a broader one, namely "whether the US Schedule includes specific commitments on gambling and betting services notwithstanding the fact that the words 'gambling and betting services' do not appear in the US Schedule." In tackling this question, the Panel turned to Sector 10 of the United States' Schedule to the GATS, which Antigua claimed included a specific commitment on gambling and betting services, and the United States claimed did not. The relevant part of the United States' Schedule provides:

Sector or subsector	Limitations on market access
10. RECREATIONAL, CULTURAL, & SPORTING SERVICES	
A. ENTERTAINMENT SERVICES (INCLUDING THEATRE, LIVE BANDS AND CIRCUS SERVICES)	1) None 2) None 3) None 4) Unbound, except as indicated in the horizontal section
B. NEWS AGENCY SERVICES	1) None 2) None 3) None 4) Unbound, except as indicated in the horizontal section
C LIBRARIES, ARCHIVES, MUSEUMS AND OTHER CULTURAL SERVICES	1) None 2) None 3) None 4) Unbound, except as indicated in the horizontal section
D. OTHER RECREATIONAL SERVICES (except sporting)	1) None 2) None 3) The number of concessions available for commercial operations in federal, state and local facilities is limited 4) Unbound, except as indicated in the horizontal section

* * *

187. The above examination leads us to the view that an examination of the term "Other recreational services (except sporting)" in its context does not clearly reveal whether, in the United States' Schedule to the GATS, gambling and betting services fall within the category of "other recreational services" or within the category of "sporting services". Accordingly, we turn to the object and purpose of the GATS to obtain further guidance for our interpretation.

188. The Panel referred to the requirement of "transparency" found in the preamble to the GATS, as supporting the need for precision and clarity in scheduling, and underlining the importance of having Schedules that are "readily understandable by all other WTO Members, as well as by services suppliers and consumers". The Panel also referred to the Appellate Body Report in *EC–Computer Equipment* as follows:

> The Appellate Body found that "the security and predictability of 'the reciprocal and mutually advantageous arrangements directed to the substantial reduction of tariffs and other barriers to trade' is an object and purpose of the WTO Agreement, generally, as well as of GATT 1994." This confirms the importance of the security and predictability of Members' specific commitments, which is equally an object and purpose of the GATS. (footnote omitted)

* * *

195. The above reasoning leads us to the conclusion—contrary to the Panel—that application of the general rule of interpretation set out in Article 31 of the Vienna Convention leaves the meaning of "other recreational services (except sporting)" ambiguous and does not answer the question whether the commitment made by the United States in subsector 10.D of its Schedule includes a commitment in respect of gambling and betting services. Accordingly, we are required, in this case, to turn to the supplementary means of interpretation provided for in Article 32 of the Vienna Convention.

[Article 32 of the Vienna Convention on the Law of Treaties]

196. We observe, as a preliminary matter, that this appeal does not raise the question whether W/120 and the 1993 Scheduling Guidelines constitute "supplementary means of interpretation, including the preparatory work of the treaty and the circumstances of its conclusion". Both participants agree that they do, and we see no reason to disagree.

* * *

203. The Scheduling Guidelines thus underline the importance of using a common format and terminology in scheduling, and express a clear preference for parties to use W/120 and the CPC classifications in their Schedules. At the same time, the Guidelines make clear that parties wanting to use their own subsectoral classification or definitions—that that is, to disaggregate in a way that diverges from W/120 and/or the CPC—were to do so in a "sufficiently detailed" way "to avoid any ambiguity as to the scope of the commitment."

* * *

208. In our view, therefore, the relevant entry in the United States' Schedule, "Other recreational services (except sporting)", must be interpreted as excluding from the scope of its specific commitment services corresponding to CPC class 9641, "Sporting services". For the same reasons, the entry must be read as including within the scope of its

commitment services corresponding to CPC 9649, "Other recreational services", including Sub-class 96492, "Gambling and betting services".

* * *

[Article XVI of GATS]

214. Article XVI of the GATS sets out specific obligations for Members that apply insofar as a Member has undertaken "specific market access commitments" in its Schedule. The first paragraph of Article XVI obliges Members to accord services and service suppliers of other Members "no less favourable treatment than that provided for under the terms, limitations and conditions agreed and specified in its Schedule." The second paragraph of Article XVI defines, in six sub-paragraphs, measures that a Member, having undertaken a specific commitment, is not to adopt or maintain, "unless otherwise specified in its Schedule". The first four sub-paragraphs concern quantitative limitations on market access; the fifth sub-paragraph covers measures that restrict or require specific types of legal entity or joint venture through which a service supplier may supply a service; and the sixth sub-paragraph identifies limitations on the participation of foreign capital.

215. The Panel found that the United States' Schedule includes specific commitments on gambling and betting services, and we have upheld this finding. The Panel then considered the consistency of the measures at issue with the United States' obligations under Article XVI of the GATS. The scope of those obligations depends on the scope of the specific commitment made in the United States' Schedule. In this case, the relevant entry for mode 1 supply in the market access column of subsector 10.D of the United States' Schedule reads "None". In other words, the United States has undertaken to provide full market access, within the meaning of Article XVI, in respect of the services included within the scope of its subsector 10.D commitment. In so doing, it has committed not to maintain any of the types of measures listed in the six sub-paragraphs of Article XVI:2.

216. Before the Panel, Antigua claimed that, in maintaining measures that prohibit the cross-border supply of gambling and betting services, the United States is maintaining quantitative limitations that fall within the scope of sub-paragraphs (a) and (c) of Article XVI and that are, therefore, inconsistent with the market access commitment undertaken in subsector 10.D of the United States' Schedule. The Panel took the view that a prohibition on the supply of certain services effectively "limits to zero" the number of service suppliers and number of service operations relating to that service. The Panel reasoned that such a prohibition results in a "zero quota" and, therefore, constitutes a " 'limitation on the number of service suppliers in the form of numerical quotas' within the meaning of Article XVI:2(a)" and "a limitation 'on the total number of service operations or on the total quantity of service

output ... in the form of quotas' within the meaning of Article XVI:2(c)''.

* * *

252. For all of these reasons, we uphold the Panel's finding, in paragraph 6.355 of the Panel Report, that a measure prohibiting the supply of certain services where specific commitments have been undertaken is a limitation:

> ... within the meaning of Article XVI:2(c) because it totally prevents the services operations and/or service output through one or more or all means of delivery that are included in mode 1. In other words, such a ban results in a "zero quota" on one or more or all means of delivery include in mode 1.

* * *

[Application of Article XVI to the Measures at Issue]

257. Having upheld the Panel's interpretation of Article XVI:2(a) and (c), we now consider its application of that interpretation to the measures at issue in this case. In so doing, we consider, for the reasons already explained, only that part of the Panel's analysis relating to the three federal laws, and not its analysis relating to state laws.

258. The Panel's explanation of the three federal laws is set out in paragraphs 6.360 to 6.380 of the Panel Report. It is, in our view, useful to set out briefly the relevant part of each statute, as well as the Panel's finding in respect of that statute. The relevant part of the Wire Act states:

> Whoever being engaged in the business of betting or wagering knowingly uses a wire communication facility for the transmission in interstate or foreign commerce of bets or wagers or information assisting in the placing of bets or wagers on any sporting event or contest, or for the transmission of a wire communication which entitles the recipient to receive money or credit as a result of bets or wagers, or for information assisting in the placing of bets or wagers shall be fined under this title or imprisoned not more than two years, or both.

259. With respect to this provision, the Panel found that "the Wire Act prohibits the use of at least one or potentially several means of delivery included in mode 1", and that, accordingly, the statute "constitutes a 'zero quota' for, respectively, one, several or all of those means of delivery." The Panel reasoned that the Wire Act prohibits service suppliers from supplying gambling and betting services using remote means of delivery, as well as service operations and service output through such means. Accordingly, the Panel determined that "the Wire Act contains a limitation 'in the form of numerical quotas' within the

meaning of Article XVI:2(a) and a limitation 'in the form of a quota' within the meaning of Article XVI:2(c).''

* * *

264. The United States' appeal of the Panel's findings with respect to the consistency of its measures with sub-paragraphs (a) and (c) of Article XVI:2 rests on two pillars: (i) that the Panel erred in interpreting those provisions; and (ii) that the measures at issue do not contain any limitations that explicitly take the form of numerical quotas or designated numerical units. The United States does not appeal the Panel's findings as to the various activities that are prohibited under these statutes. We have upheld the Panel's interpretation of sub-paragraphs (a) and (c) of Article XVI:2 and, in particular, its determination that these provisions encompass measures equivalent to a zero quota. In these circumstances, the fact that the Wire Act, the Travel Act and the IGBA do not explicitly use numbers, or the word "quota", in imposing their respective prohibitions, does not mean, as the United States contends, that the measures are beyond the reach of Article XVI:2(a) and (c). As a result, there is no ground for disturbing the above findings made by the Panel.

265. We have upheld the Panel's finding that the United States' Schedule to the GATS includes a specific commitment in respect of gambling and betting services. In that Schedule, the United States has inscribed "None" in the first row of the market access column for subsector 10.D. In these circumstances, and for the reasons given in this section of our Report, we also uphold the Panel's ultimate finding, in paragraph 7.2(b)(i) of the Panel Report, that, by maintaining the Wire Act, the Travel Act, and the Illegal Gambling Business Act, the United States acts inconsistently with its obligations under Article XVI:1 and Article XVI:2(a) and (c) of the GATS.

* * *

[GATS Article XIV(a)]

291. Article XIV of the GATS sets out the general exceptions from obligations under that Agreement in the same manner as does Article XX of the GATT 1994. Both of these provisions affirm the right of Members to pursue objectives identified in the paragraphs of these provisions even if, in doing so, Members act inconsistently with obligations set out in other provisions of the respective agreements, provided that all of the conditions set out therein are satisfied. Similar language is used in both provisions, notably the term "necessary" and the requirements set out in their respective chapeaux. Accordingly, like the Panel, we find previous decisions under Article XX of the GATT 1994 relevant for our analysis under Article XIV of the GATS.

292. Article XIV of the GATS, like Article XX of the GATT 1994, contemplates a "two-tier analysis" of a measure that a Member seeks to justify under that provision. A panel should first determine whether the

challenged measure falls within the scope of one of the paragraphs of Article XIV. This requires that the challenged measure address the particular interest specified in that paragraph and that there be a sufficient nexus between the measure and the interest protected. The required nexus—or "degree of connection"—between the measure and the interest is specified in the language of the paragraphs themselves, through the use of terms such as "relating to" and "necessary to". Where the challenged measure has been found to fall within one of the paragraphs of Article XIV, a panel should then consider whether that measure satisfies the requirements of the chapeau of Article XIV.

293. Paragraph (a) of Article XIV covers: " ... measures ... necessary to protect public morals or to maintain public order." (footnote omitted)

* * *

296. In its analysis under Article XIV(a), the Panel found that "the term 'public morals' denotes standards of right and wrong conduct maintained by or on behalf of a community or nation." The Panel further found that the definition of the term "order", read in conjunction with footnote 5 of the GATS, "suggests that 'public order' refers to the preservation of the fundamental interests of a society, as reflected in public policy and law." The Panel then referred to Congressional reports and testimony establishing that "the government of the United States consider[s] [that the Wire Act, the Travel Act, and the IGBA] were adopted to address concerns such as those pertaining to money laundering, organized crime, fraud, underage gambling and pathological gambling." On this basis, the Panel found that the three federal statutes are "measures that are designed to 'protect public morals' and/or 'to maintain public order' within the meaning of Article XIV(a)."

297. Antigua contests this finding on a rather limited ground, namely that the Panel failed to determine whether the concerns identified by the United States satisfy the standard set out in footnote 5 to Article XIV(a) of the GATS, which reads:

[t]he public order exception may be invoked only where a genuine and sufficiently serious threat is posed to one of the fundamental interests of society.

298. We see no basis to conclude that the Panel failed to assess whether the standard set out in footnote 5 had been satisfied. As Antigua acknowledges, the Panel expressly referred to footnote 5 in a way that demonstrated that it understood the requirement therein to be part of the meaning given to the term "public order".

* * *

300. In the second part of its analysis under Article XIV(a), the Panel considered whether the Wire Act, the Travel Act, and the IGBA are "necessary" within the meaning of that provision. The Panel found

that the United States had not demonstrated the "necessity" of those measures.

301.　This finding rested on the Panel's determinations that: (i) "the interests and values protected by [the Wire Act, the Travel Act, and the IGBA] serve very important societal interests that can be characterized as 'vital and important in the highest degree' "; (ii) the Wire Act, the Travel Act, and the IGBA "must contribute, at least to some extent", to addressing the United States' concerns "pertaining to money laundering, organized crime, fraud, underage gambling and pathological gambling"; (iii) the measures in question "have a significant restrictive trade impact"; and (iv) "[i]n rejecting Antigua's invitation to engage in bilateral or multilateral consultations and/or negotiations, the United States failed to pursue in good faith a course of action that could have been used by it to explore the possibility of finding a reasonably available WTO-consistent alternative."

* * *

304.　We note, at the outset, that the standard of "necessity" provided for in the general exceptions provision is an *objective* standard. To be sure, a Member's characterization of a measure's objectives and of the effectiveness of its regulatory approach—as evidenced, for example, by texts of statutes, legislative history, and pronouncements of government agencies or officials—will be relevant in determining whether the measure is, objectively, "necessary". A panel is not bound by these characterizations, however, and may also find guidance in the structure and operation of the measure and in contrary evidence proffered by the complaining party. In any event, a panel must, on the basis of the evidence in the record, independently and objectively assess the "necessity" of the measure before it.

305.　In *Korea–Various Measures on Beef*, the Appellate Body stated, in the context of Article XX(d) of the GATT 1994, that whether a measure is "necessary" should be determined through "a process of weighing and balancing a series of factors". The Appellate Body characterized this process as one:

> . . . comprehended in the determination of whether a WTO-consistent alternative measure which the Member concerned could "reasonably be expected to employ" is available, or whether a less WTO-inconsistent measure is "reasonably available".

306.　The process begins with an assessment of the "relative importance" of the interests or values furthered by the challenged measure. Having ascertained the importance of the particular interests at stake, a panel should then turn to the other factors that are to be "weighed and balanced". The Appellate Body has pointed to two factors that, in most cases, will be relevant to a panel's determination of the "necessity" of a measure, although not necessarily exhaustive of factors that might be considered. One factor is the contribution of the measure to the realization of the ends pursued by it; the other factor is the restrictive impact of the measure on international commerce.

307.   A comparison between the challenged measure and possible alternatives should then be undertaken, and the results of such comparison should be considered in the light of the importance of the interests at issue. It is on the basis of this "weighing and balancing" and comparison of measures, taking into account the interests or values at stake, that a panel determines whether a measure is "necessary" or, alternatively, whether another, WTO-consistent measure is "reasonably available".

308.   The requirement, under Article XIV(a), that a measure be "necessary"—that is, that there be no "reasonably available", WTO-consistent alternative—reflects the shared understanding of Members that substantive GATS obligations should not be deviated from lightly. An alternative measure may be found not to be "reasonably available", however, where it is merely theoretical in nature, for instance, where the responding Member is not capable of taking it, or where the measure imposes an undue burden on that Member, such as prohibitive costs or substantial technical difficulties. Moreover, a "reasonably available" alternative measure must be a measure that would preserve for the responding Member its right to achieve its desired level of protection with respect to the objective pursued under paragraph (a) of Article XIV.

309.   It is well-established that a responding party invoking an affirmative defence bears the burden of demonstrating that its measure, found to be WTO-inconsistent, satisfies the requirements of the invoked defence. In the context of Article XIV(a), this means that the responding party must show that its measure is "necessary" to achieve objectives relating to public morals or public order. In our view, however, it is not the responding party's burden to show, in the first instance, that there are *no* reasonably available alternatives to achieve its objectives. In particular, a responding party need not identify the universe of less trade-restrictive alternative measures and then show that none of those measures achieves the desired objective. The WTO agreements do not contemplate such an impracticable and, indeed, often impossible burden.

310.   Rather, it is for a responding party to make a *prima facie* case that its measure is "necessary" by putting forward evidence and arguments that enable a panel to assess the challenged measure in the light of the relevant factors to be "weighed and balanced" in a given case. The responding party may, in so doing, point out why alternative measures would not achieve the same objectives as the challenged measure, but it is under no obligation to do so in order to establish, in the first instance, that its measure is "necessary". If the panel concludes that the respondent has made a *prima facie* case that the challenged measure is "necessary"—that is, "significantly closer to the pole of 'indispensable' than to the opposite pole of simply 'making a contribution to' "—then a panel should find that challenged measure "necessary" within the terms of Article XIV(a) of the GATS.

311. If, however, the complaining party raises a WTO-consistent alternative measure that, in its view, the responding party should have taken, the responding party will be required to demonstrate why its challenged measure nevertheless remains "necessary" in the light of that alternative or, in other words, why the proposed alternative is not, in fact, "reasonably available". If a responding party demonstrates that the alternative is not "reasonably available", in the light of the interests or values being pursued and the party's desired level of protection, it follows that the challenged measure must be "necessary" within the terms of Article XIV(a) of the GATS.

312. In considering whether the United States' measures are "necessary" under Article XIV(a) of the GATS, the Panel began by considering the factors set out by the Appellate Body in *Korea–Various Measures on Beef* as they apply to the Wire Act, the Travel Act, and the IGBA. Antigua claims that the Panel erred in concluding, in the course of its analysis of these factors, that the three federal statutes contribute to protecting the interests raised by the United States.

313. The Panel set out, in some detail, how the United States' evidence established a specific connection between the remote supply of gambling services and each of the interests identified by the United States, except for organized crime. In particular, the Panel found such a link in relation to money laundering, fraud, compulsive gambling, and underage gambling. Considering that the three federal statutes embody an outright prohibition on the remote supply of gambling services, we see no error in the Panel's approach, nor in its finding, in paragraph 6.494 of the Panel Report, that the Wire Act, the Travel Act, and the IGBA "must contribute" to addressing those concerns.

* * *

315. In its "necessity" analysis under Article XIV(a), the Panel appeared to understand that, in order for a measure to be accepted as "necessary" under Article XIV(a), the responding Member must have first *"explored and exhausted"* all reasonably available WTO-compatible alternatives before adopting its WTO-inconsistent measure. This understanding led the Panel to conclude that, in this case, the United States had "an obligation to consult with Antigua before and while imposing its prohibition on the cross-border supply of gambling and betting services". Because the Panel found that the United States had not engaged in such consultations with Antigua, the Panel also found that the United States had not established that its measures are "necessary" and, therefore, provisionally justified under Article XIV(a).

* * *

317. In our view, the Panel's "necessity" analysis was flawed because it did not focus on an alternative measure that was reasonably available to the United States to achieve the stated objectives regarding the protection of public morals or the maintenance of public order. Engaging in consultations with Antigua, with a view to arriving at a

negotiated settlement that achieves the same objectives as the challenged United States' measures, was not an appropriate alternative for the Panel to consider because consultations are by definition a process, the results of which are uncertain and therefore not capable of comparison with the measures at issue in this case.

* * *

322. Having reversed this finding, we must consider whether, as the United States contends, the Wire Act, the Travel Act, and the IGBA are properly characterized as "necessary" to achieve the objectives identified by the United States and accepted by the Panel. The Panel's analysis, as well as the factual findings contained therein, are useful for our assessment of whether these measures satisfy the requirements of paragraph (a) of Article XIV.

323. As we stated above, a responding party must make a *prima facie* case that its challenged measure is "necessary". A Panel determines whether this case is made through the identification, and weighing and balancing, of relevant factors, such as those in *Korea–Various Measures on Beef*, with respect to the measure challenged. In this regard, we note that the Panel: (i) found that the three federal statutes protect "very important societal interests"; (ii) observed that "strict controls may be needed to protect [such] interests"; and (iii) found that the three federal statutes contribute to the realization of the ends that they pursue. Although the Panel recognized the "significant restrictive trade impact" of the three federal statutes, it expressly tempered this recognition with a detailed explanation of certain characteristics of, and concerns specific to, the remote supply of gambling and betting services. These included: (i) "the volume, speed and international reach of remote gambling transactions"; (ii) the "virtual anonymity of such transactions"; (iii) "low barriers to entry in the context of the remote supply of gambling and betting services"; and the (iv) "isolated and anonymous environment in which such gambling takes place". Thus, this analysis reveals that the Panel did not place much weight, in the circumstances of this case, on the restrictive trade impact of the three federal statutes. On the contrary, the Panel appears to have accepted virtually all of the elements upon which the United States based its assertion that the three federal statutes are "indispensable".

324. The Panel further, and in our view, tellingly, stated that

... the United States has legitimate specific concerns with respect to money laundering, fraud, health and underage gambling that are specific to the remote supply of gambling and betting services, which suggests that the measures in question are "necessary" within the meaning of Article XIV(a). (emphasis added)

325. From all of the above, and in particular from the summary of its analysis made in paragraphs 6.533 and 6.534 of the Panel Report, we understand the Panel to have acknowledged that, *but for* the United States' alleged refusal to accept Antigua's invitation to negotiate, the

Panel would have found that the United States had made its *prima facie* case that the Wire Act, the Travel Act, and the IGBA are "necessary", within the meaning of Article XIV(a). We thus agree with the United States that the "sole basis" for the Panel's conclusion to the contrary was its finding relating to the requirement of consultations with Antigua.

326. * * * Because the United States made its *prima facie* case of "necessity", and Antigua failed to identify a reasonably available alternative measure, we conclude that the United States demonstrated that its statutes are "necessary", and therefore justified, under paragraph (a) of Article XIV.

* * *

338. Notwithstanding its finding that the measures at issue are not provisionally justified, the Panel examined whether those measures satisfy the requirements of the chapeau of Article XIV "so as to assist the parties in resolving the underlying dispute in this case." * * *

339. The chapeau of Article XIV provides:

Subject to the requirement that such measures are not applied in a manner which would constitute a means of arbitrary or unjustifiable discrimination between countries where like conditions prevail, or a disguised restriction on trade in services, nothing in this Agreement shall be construed to prevent the adoption or enforcement by any Member of measures [of the type specified in the subsequent paragraphs of Article XIV]. . . .

The focus of the chapeau, by its express terms, is on the application of a measure already found by the Panel to be inconsistent with one of the obligations under the GATS but falling within one of the paragraphs of Article XIV. By requiring that the measure be applied in a manner that does not to constitute "arbitrary" or "unjustifiable" discrimination, or a "disguised restriction on trade in services", the chapeau serves to ensure that Members' rights to avail themselves of exceptions are exercised reasonably, so as not to frustrate the rights accorded other Members by the substantive rules of the GATS.

* * *

346. In examining whether discrimination exists in the United States' application of the Wire Act, the Travel Act, and the IGBA, the Panel found that "some of the concerns the United States has identified are specific only to the remote supply of gambling and betting services." As a result, the Panel determined that it would have been "inappropriate", in the context of determining whether WTO-consistent alternative measures are reasonably available, to compare the United States' treatment of concerns relating to the *remote* supply of gambling services, with its treatment of concerns relating to the *non*-remote supply of such services. Antigua characterizes this approach as an improper "segment[ation]" of the gambling industry, the result of which was to

"exclude[] a substantial portion of gambling and betting services from any analysis at all."

347.   We have already observed that the Panel found, on the basis of evidence adduced by the United States, that the *remote* supply of gambling services gives rise to particular concerns. We see no error in the Panel's maintaining such a distinction for purposes of analyzing any discrimination in the application of the three federal statutes. Such an approach merely reflects the view that the distinctive characteristics of the remote supply of gambling services may call for distinctive regulatory methods, and that this could render a comparison between the treatment of remote and non-remote supply of gambling services inappropriate.

348.   We consider next whether, contrary to the United States' allegations, the Panel accurately described and applied the correct interpretation of the chapeau of Article XIV. On the basis of the arguments advanced by Antigua, the Panel examined certain instances of alleged discrimination in the application of the Wire Act, the Travel Act, and the IGBA. In the course of this analysis, the Panel found that the United States had not prosecuted certain domestic remote suppliers of gambling services, and that a United States statute (the Interstate Horseracing Act) could be understood, on its face, to permit certain types of remote betting on horseracing within the United States. On the basis of these two findings, the Panel concluded that:

> ... the United States has not demonstrated that it applies its prohibition on the remote supply of these services in a *consistent manner* as between those supplied domestically and those that are supplied from other Members. Accordingly, we believe that the United States has not demonstrated that it does not apply its prohibition on the remote supply of wagering services for horse racing in a manner that does not constitute "arbitrary and unjustifiable discrimination between countries where like conditions prevail" and/or a "disguised restriction on trade" in accordance with the requirements of the chapeau of Article XIV. (emphasis added)

349.   The United States contends that the Panel's reasoning, in particular its standard of "consistency", reveals that the Panel, in fact, assessed only whether the United States treats domestic service suppliers differently from foreign service suppliers. Such an assessment is inadequate, the United States argues, because the chapeau also requires a determination of whether differential treatment, or discrimination, is "arbitrary" or "unjustifiable".

350.   The United States based its defence under the chapeau of Article XIV on the assertion that the measures at issue prohibit the remote supply of gambling and betting services by *any supplier*, whether domestic or foreign. In other words, the United States sought to justify the Wire Act, the Travel Act, and the IGBA on the basis that there is *no discrimination* in the manner in which the three federal statutes are applied to the remote supply of gambling and betting services. The

United States could have, but did not, put forward an additional argument that *even if* such discrimination exists, it does not rise to the level of "arbitrary" or "unjustifiable" discrimination.

* * *

352. In the course of examining whether the Wire Act, the Travel Act, and the IGBA are applied consistently with the chapeau of Article XIV, the Panel considered whether these laws are enforced in a manner that discriminates between domestic and foreign service suppliers. Antigua identified four United States firms that it claimed engage in the remote supply of gambling services but have not been prosecuted under any of the three federal statutes: Youbet.com, TVG, Capital OTB, and Xpressbet.com. Antigua contrasted this lack of enforcement with the case of an Antiguan service supplier that "had modelled [its] business on that of Capital OTB" but was nevertheless prosecuted and convicted under the Wire Act. In support of its argument that it applies these statutes equally to domestic and foreign service suppliers, the United States submitted statistical evidence to show that most cases prosecuted under these statutes involved gambling and betting services solely within the United States.

353. The Panel also "note[d] indications by the United States" that prosecution proceedings were pending against one domestic remote supplier of gambling services (Youbet.com), but stated that it had no evidence as to whether any enforcement action was being taken against the other three domestic remote suppliers of gambling services identified by Antigua. As to foreign service suppliers, the Panel observed that it had evidence of the prosecution of one Antiguan operator for violations of the Wire Act. The Panel found this evidence "inconclusive" and concluded that the United States had not shown that it enforces its prohibition against the remote supply of gambling services on the three domestic service suppliers in a manner consistent with the chapeau of Article XIV.

354. We observe, first, that none of the three federal statutes distinguishes, on its face, between domestic and foreign service suppliers. We agree with the Panel that, in the context of facially neutral measures, there may nevertheless be situations where the selective prosecution of persons rises to the level of discrimination. In our view, however, the evidence before the Panel could not justify finding that, notwithstanding the neutral language of the statute, the facts are "inconclusive" to establish "non-discrimination" in the United States' enforcement of the Wire Act. The Panel's conclusion rests, not only on an inadequate evidentiary foundation, but also on an incorrect understanding of the type of conduct that can, as a matter of law, be characterized as discrimination in the enforcement of measures.

355. In this case, the Panel came to its conclusion—that the United States failed to establish non-discrimination in the enforcement of its laws—on the basis of only five cases: one case of prosecution against a foreign service supplier; one case of "pending" prosecution

against a domestic service supplier; and three cases with no evidence of prosecution against domestic service suppliers. From these five cases, the Panel in effect concluded that the United States' defence had been sufficiently rebutted to warrant a finding of "inconclusiveness".

356. In our view, the proper significance to be attached to isolated instances of enforcement, or lack thereof, cannot be determined in the absence of evidence allowing such instances to be placed in their proper context. Such evidence might include evidence on the *overall* number of suppliers, and on *patterns* of enforcement, and on the reasons for particular instances of non-enforcement. Indeed, enforcement agencies may refrain from prosecution in many instances for reasons unrelated to discriminatory intent and without discriminatory effect.

357. Faced with the limited evidence the parties put before it with respect to enforcement, the Panel should rather have focused, as a matter of law, on the wording of the measures at issue. These measures, on their face, do *not* discriminate between United States and foreign suppliers of remote gambling services. * * *

358. * * * We examine [next] Antigua's appeal relating to video lottery terminals and Nevada bookmakers, and then consider the United States' appeal concerning the Interstate Horseracing Act.

359. The Panel examined Antigua's allegations that several states in the United States permit video lottery terminals, and that Nevada permits bookmakers to offer their services over the internet and telephone. The Panel rejected both of these allegations. Antigua contends that the Panel made these findings notwithstanding that Antigua had submitted evidence and the United States had submitted none, and that, by so finding, the Panel effectively "reversed" the burden of proof

360. Antigua is correct that the burden of proof is on the United States, as the responding party invoking the Article XIV defence. Once the United States established its defence with sufficient evidence and arguments, however, it was for Antigua to rebut the United States' defence. In rejecting Antigua's allegations relating to video lottery terminals and Nevada bookmakers, we understand the Panel to have determined that Antigua failed to rebut the United States' asserted defence under the chapeau, namely that its measures do not discriminate at all. Consequently, we do not read the Panel to have reversed the burden of proof in these two instances, and we dismiss this ground of Antigua's appeal.

361. We now turn to the [US] claim relating to the * * * scope of application of the Interstate Horseracing Act ("IHA"). Before the Panel, Antigua relied on the text of the IHA, which provides that "[a]n interstate off-track wager *may be accepted* by an off-track betting system" where consent is obtained from certain organizations. Antigua referred the Panel in particular to the definition given in the statute of "interstate off-track wager":

[T]he term ... 'interstate off-track wager' means a legal wager placed or accepted in one State with respect to the outcome of a horserace taking place in another State and includes pari-mutuel wagers, where lawful in each State involved, *placed or transmitted by an individual in one State via telephone or other electronic media and accepted by an off-track betting system in the same or another State*, as well as the combination of any pari-mutuel wagering pools. (emphasis added)

Thus, according to Antigua, the IHA, on its face, authorizes *domestic* service suppliers, but not *foreign* service suppliers, to offer remote betting services in relation to certain horse races. To this extent, in Antigua's view, the IHA "exempts" domestic service suppliers from the prohibitions of the Wire Act, the Travel Act, and the IGBA.

362.   The United States disagreed, claiming that the IHA—a civil statute—cannot "repeal" the Wire Act, the Travel Act, or the IGBA—which are criminal statutes—*by implication*, that is, merely by virtue of the IHA's adoption *subsequent* to that of the Wire Act, the Travel Act, and the IGBA. Rather, under principles of statutory interpretation in the United States, such a repeal could be effective only if done *explicitly*, which was not the case with the IHA.

* * *

364.   In our view, this aspect of the United States' appeal essentially challenges the Panel's failure to accord sufficient weight to the evidence submitted by the United States with respect to the relationship under United States law between the IHA and the measures at issue. The Panel had limited evidence before it, as submitted by the parties, on which to base its conclusion. This limitation, however, could not absolve the Panel of its responsibility to arrive at a conclusion as to the relationship between the IHA and the prohibitions in the Wire Act, the Travel Act, and the IGBA. The Panel found that the evidence provided by the United States was not sufficiently persuasive to conclude that, as regards wagering on horseracing, the remote supply of such services by *domestic* firms continues to be prohibited notwithstanding the plain language of the IHA. In this light, we are not persuaded that the Panel failed to make an objective assessment of the facts.

* * *

369.   Thus, our conclusion—that the Panel did not err in finding that the United States has not shown that its measures satisfy the requirements of the chapeau—relates solely to the possibility that the IHA exempts only domestic suppliers of remote betting services for horse racing from the prohibitions in the Wire Act, the Travel Act, and the IGBA.

Note Regarding Post Appellate Procedures in the Gambling Case

Pursuant to the Dispute Settlement Understanding rules, once the Appellate Body has determined that a government is acting inconsistently with its WTO obligations, certain follow-up procedures designed to address problems of compliance are applicable. The *Gambling* case has an unusual number of such follow-up actions, and in fact still continues to have more. The following paragraphs briefly summarize some of these procedures:

1) Reasonable period of time: Under DSU article 21.3(c), in the absence of an agreement, the parties to a dispute can submit to arbitration the issue of what should be the reasonable period for compliance. In the *Gambling* case this procedure began June 6, 2005, and resulted in a determination that the reasonable time for the US to comply was 11 months, 2 weeks from April 20, 2005 (date of adoption of the Appellate Body Report). This award was circulated August 19, 2005 (WT/DS285/13).

2) Compliance with Appellate Body report: DSU article 21.5 allows a winning party to refer to the original panel the question of whether the losing party to a dispute has adequately complied with its obligations as defined in the adopted report within the set reasonable period of time for compliance. Since the United States took no action to implement the findings of the report by the expiration of the reasonable period of time (i.e., April 3, 2006), Antigua requested that such a panel be established. The panel determined the US had not complied and its report (WT/DS285/RW)was adopted on May 22, 2007.

3) As noted in Section 7.5(A) supra, DSU articles 21.5 and 22.2 pose a "sequencing problem" for the winning complainant, because logically some argue that an article 21.5 determination of failure to comply should come first, yet article 22.2 rules on retaliatory actions have a time limit that usually does not allow the article 21.5 proceeding (with appeal) to finish. Consequently, a practice has developed pursuant to which many WTO litigating parties enter into a bilateral ad hoc agreement to start both article 21.5 and article 22 proceedings and then suspend the article 22.2 case until completion of the 21.5 process. This was done in this case (WT/DS285/16).

4) Level of retaliatory actions permitted by the dispute winner: If the losing party fails to bring its measure into conformity with its obligations within the reasonable period of time (which the foregoing panel determined to be the case in *Gambling*), DSU article 22.2 allows the winner to request the DSB to approve suspension of concessions it owes to the losing party (i.e. give it authority to take retaliatory measures), and unless the DSB determines negatively by consensus (reverse consensus), such request is deemed approved.

5) When a request is made pursuant to article 22.2, the losing party may request arbitration of the level of the suspension of concessions. In this case, the request to suspend concessions was made June 21, 2007 and referred to arbitration under DSU article 22.6 on July 24, 2007. The arbitration decision, which is extensively excerpted in Section 7.5 supra, was circulated on December 21, 2007. In this case, Antigua argued that the level should be equivalent to all the potential gambling services prohibited by the US, arguing the amount should be $US 3.4 billion. The arbitrators' decision (2 to 1) agreed with the US view that since it had failed to establish its public morals defense only because of discriminatory measures in respect of horseracing, the level should be set on the basis of the loss to Antigua of gambling in respect of horseracing. Thus, the arbitration decision concluded

that the appropriate level of suspension of concessions should be US$21 million (WT/DS285/ARB). The arbitrators also determined that Antigua should be allowed to suspend concessions under the TRIPS Agreement. See Section 7.5 supra.

6) Another interesting facet of this case was the US announcement (May 4, 2007) that pursuant to GATS Article XXI it would modify its GATS schedule to eliminate the commitments on gambling. This process operates even if the schedule is valid and binding on a WTO member, but it requires such member to give compensation to those other WTO members affected. The US has been negotiating with various interested WTO members about appropriate compensation in this regard. Press reports indicate that the US has reached settlements in this regard with most interested parties, except of course, Antigua.[1]

Additional Contextual Note on the Gambling Case

The "public morals" issues in the *Gambling* case are highlighted by the extensive debates going on in the United States about the appropriate extent of legal gambling both at the federal level and in a number of individual states of the United States. At the federal level, there have been some legal officials that argue that even horseracing gambling internet services is prohibited, so that no discrimination against imported services is involved. This legal judgment appears to be controversial and not yet "enforced." In addition, despite proposals to try to obtain congressional changes to either prohibit domestic internal horseracing gambling services, or to permit these services for imports (either which would arguably moot the case as eliminating discrimination), such proposals seem to have made no headway. Indeed, on the other hand, bills have been introduced in the US Congress to open up many types of gambling services. These also seem to be controversial.

In addition, in various states (such as Maryland, and perhaps Kentucky and others) there is vigorous debate about legalizing various gambling services, such as slot machines. These "context facts" illustrate the significance of social attitude differences among nation states. These attitudes reinforce some calls for the WTO to be cautious with reference to imposing mandates which are inconsistent with local mores in respect of such matters as trade in genetically modified organisms or use of hormones in beef production.

Question: Should there be a "social attitudes" exception introduced for WTO norms, analogously to other exceptions or to the safeguards rules?

WTO Director–General Pascal Lamy in speaking on "The Emergence of Collective Preferences in International Trade: Implications for Regulating Globalization" once noted (when he was still a member of the EC Commission):[2]

---

1. "Costa Rica Accepts U.S. Compensation Offer Over Internet Gambling", BNA Intl. Trade Daily, Mar. 17, 2008.

2. Speech available at: http://ec.europa.eu/archives/commission_1999_2004/lamy/ speeches_articles/spla242_en.htm, last visited 17 March 2008. See also Steve Charnovitz, An Analysis of Pascal Lamy's Proposal on Collective Preferences. 8 JIEL 449–472 (2005).

[T]he threat to societal choices has not received proper attention.* * *
Trade is the natural point of intersection for different systems of
collective preferences. * * * The challenge is to design an open trading
system that everyone accepts and that safeguards legitimate social
choices. Every player wants respect for their political autonomy and for
their collective preferences at the same time as gaining access to their
partners' markets. The problem is that the cause of safeguarding
legitimate social choices can be hijacked by protectionist interests.

Chapter 20

TRADE RELATED ASPECTS OF INTELLECTUAL PROPERTY RIGHTS

The growing importance and complexity of intellectual property law requires multiple courses for a thorough treatment, and it is not uncommon to find distinct curricular offerings on patents, copyrights and trademarks and related matters. In this brief survey, therefore, we can only scratch the surface of the issues that arise. Our emphasis will be on matters of special prominence in international trade, leaving the details of US and other domestic laws to another forum.[1]

SECTION 20.1 INTRODUCTION

(A) INTELLECTUAL PROPERTY RIGHTS AND POLICIES

Traditional descriptions of intellectual property law often divide the subject into patent, copyright, trademark and trade dress, and trade secret law. These distinctions can blur at times (is a computer chip a proper subject of patent or should the blueprint for assembling it be copyrightable? what about a computer program?). But these categories provide a serviceable first cut at organizing the subject.

Patent law concerns "inventions," which can take many forms. They may constitute a new product, a new process for making an old product, a new molecule, or even a new organism. Typically, national patent laws require that inventions be "non-obvious," or some similar term, to be patentable, and that they have some actual or potential commercial application. The granting of a patent confers upon the inventor a number of rights, including the right to prevent others from producing or selling the invention for the life of the patent. The inventor may also prevent others from developing products that incorporate the invention without permission. Thus, the patent holder gains an opportunity to

---

1. Leading references on intellectual property law include Donald S. Chisum, Chisum on Patents (looseleaf); J. Thomas McCarthy, Trademarks and Unfair Compe- tition 4th ed. (looseleaf); David Nimer, Nimmer on Copyright (looseleaf); and Paul Goldstein, Goldstein on Copyright (3d ed. 2005).

capture added returns from its time-limited "monopoly" over the production and sale of the product (although many patents in fact confer little monopoly power). Patent holders may also receive a direct monetary reward for invention from the government that grants the patent.

The policy issues associated with patent law, even in a closed economy, are rich and fascinating. Patents are widely considered essential, at least under many circumstances, to provide appropriate incentives for innovation. Inventors typically bear the costs of research, and if others can appropriate the benefits by producing and selling the commercially valuable fruits of research, inventors may have no incentive to invent. But it is equally clear that patents have important social costs. Once an invention exists, it is desirable, other things being equal (such as the rate of inventive activity), that it be made available to all who are willing to pay the marginal costs of reproducing it. Yet, if the patented product has no or few good substitutes, the patent holder will tend to charge a monopoly price over the life of the patent, thus introducing the distortion of monopoly pricing into the economy. Further, because the returns to a patent can be large, the possibility arises that the patent system will induce excessive investment in research. The most widely studied example arises when a number of inventors all know that a patentable invention is just over the horizon, and each rushes to invent it first. The resources devoted to such a "patent race" can significantly exceed the resources that a careful social calculus would suggest appropriate. Additional issues arise when future innovators must build upon prior inventions to create others—how will the patent on an existing invention affect the incentive of another inventor to try and build upon it? The breadth of patent rights is also a matter of great importance. If minor changes to an invention suffice to create a new and different product that does not infringe the patent, then patent rights will have less value, perhaps too little. Yet, if patent rights are defined broadly so that similar but different products are infringing, the scope of monopoly power and the possible distortions associated with it and with patent races will grow.[1]

Taking these considerations together, one principle that emerges is that patent protection makes little sense where it is unnecessary to spur innovation. This observation provides support for one of the most basic and oft-litigated principles of patent law—that patents may not be enforced if the invention is "obvious." But there are many more issues that must be resolved, and it is not at all clear what an ideal patent law should provide. Indeed, the contours of an ideal system are probably to a

---

1. The theoretical literature on patents is voluminous. Seminal papers include Arrow, Economic Welfare and the Allocation of Resources for Invention, in NBER, The Rate and Direction of Inventive Activity: Economic and Social Factors (1962); Kitch, The Nature and the Function of the Patent System, 20 J.L. & Econ. 265 (1977) and Machlup, An Economic Review of the Patent System, Study of the Subcomm. on Pat-ents, Trademarks & Copyrights, Comm. on the Judiciary, 85th Cong., 2d Sess. (Study No. 15, 1958). More recent sources are noted in a symposium in 5 J.Econ. Perspectives 3 (1991). See particularly the papers by Besen & Raskind, Scotchmer and Ordover in that volume. See generally William M. Landes & Richard A. Posner, The Economic Structure of Intellectual Property Law (2003).

great degree unknowable and variable with circumstances, and it is not even clear that patents should exist at all in preference to government rewards for invention that provide innovators with incentive for research but do not introduce the distortions of monopoly after the fact. Nevertheless, the governments of developed countries have for many decades afforded their nationals—and to considerable degree the nationals of other countries—the opportunity to obtain patent rights, usually of significant duration (20 years from date of patent application after the Uruguay Round), and subject to a variety of restrictions on precisely what is patentable and what is not.

Copyright law concerns "literary and artistic expression," which again can take many forms. Books, films, songs and paintings are paradigm examples, but copyright can also extend to computer programs and operating systems, to a blueprint for making a computer chip, or to databases even though the individual bits of data are not themselves copyrightable. To a significant extent the policy issues with copyright are similar to those with patent—absent copyright protection, authors and other creators could not appropriate the returns to their work and would have little incentive to do it in many cases. But the policy concerns regarding the monopoly distortion from patents and patent races carry over to a lesser extent in the copyright context. As popular as Stephen King may be, his copyrights do not confer upon him nearly the degree of market power that, say, a patent on the internal combustion engine would confer, and we need not fear that the existence of copyright will induce someone else to race him to write "Carrie." These distinctions are easy to exaggerate, however, as brief reflection on the use of copyright to protect computer chip designs will suggest. Further, like patent, copyright confers upon creators some rights to control the use of their work by others who might build on it ("derivative uses"), and hence the incentives of other creators are to some extent in play. Indeed, one can imagine those incentives being profoundly affected depending upon what is copyrightable—imagine a world in which anyone who computed a definite integral owed a royalty to Newton's estate! Thus, copyright is conventionally limited to the "expression," and does not extend to the idea that underlies it; we can compute definite integrals at our pleasure and even sell our services for that purpose, but we cannot reproduce and sell our calculus texts to others if the copyright is still in force. Likewise, one cannot copyright a fact merely by writing it down.[2]

Because of these limitations, the grant of a copyright is *in most cases* less likely than a patent to raise concerns about monopoly and the incentives for subsequent creators. It is thus easier for creators to obtain copyright protection (for some purposes they need do nothing to obtain it

---

2. Again the literature is substantial. Many sources are collected in the Journal of Economic Perspectives symposium cited in note 1 supra. Well known papers include Breyer, The Uneasy Case for Copyright: A Study of Copyright in Books, Photocopies and Computer Programs, 84 Harv.L.Rev. 281 (1970) and Landes & Posner, An Economic Analysis of Copyright Law, 18 J. Legal Stud. 325 (1989).

but create), and it usually lasts longer (the life of the author plus 70 years in the United States).

Trademark and trade dress law concern the rights of a seller to market a product or service in a distinctive manner, and to prevent others from passing their goods or services off in misleading fashion. Trademarks enable sellers to use a symbol or name to identify their wares, and in turn enable consumers quickly and readily to identify the good or service as that of a particular manufacturer, franchise system, or the like. They are useful to a seller when they come to symbolize a level of quality or value in existing goods or services or in the introduction of new goods and services. Absent legal restrictions, other sellers might then be tempted to mislead consumers by using the trademark established by another firm. And, even when the trademark itself is not used by another, similar packaging or other aspects of presentation (trade dress) may lead consumers to make mistaken purchases. Misstatements or misleading indications of geographic origin are another source of concern (imagine a beer brewed in Newark with the name "Beck" and a label entirely in German), and the protection of geographical indications is a matter of some current controversy. Thus, the rationale for trademark and trade dress law is in large measure akin to the rationale for sanctioning fraud—misleading statements can cause individuals to enter transactions that are not valuable to them and that they would not enter but for the misinformation. In addition, if sellers can mislead buyers with impunity, buyers will no longer trust trademarks or trade dress as markers of quality. It will then become more difficult for sellers to reap the returns from efforts to produce high quality goods and services, and the incentive to provide quality in the marketplace will diminish.

The dangers of protection for trademarks and trade dress relate primarily to overbreadth. It would be most unfortunate if McDonald's could enjoin the use of an arch for any purpose, or if Levi Strauss & Co. could enjoin the sale by another of any trousers with two legs. Likewise, words that may have proprietary content at some point in time can become a part of ordinary language later, and restrictions on the use of such language can be costly. Thus, in one manner or another, trademark and trade dress law limit the rights of sellers to circumstances in which confusion is a serious risk (trademarks must be "distinctive"), and further limit the scope of words and symbols that may become protected as trademarks (for example, generic words cannot be trademarks). With such restrictions in place, trademark and trade dress law may be understood as promoting quality and lowering consumer search costs while simultaneously endeavoring to avoid undue restrictions on the use of language and symbols in ordinary communication and otherwise.[3]

Trade secret law is most closely related to patent law. Broadly speaking, a trade secret is information that has value to its holder, and that would have less value if generally known. Some trade secrets are

---

3. See Landes & Posner, Trademark Law: An Economic Perspective, 30 J.L. & Econ. 265 (1987); Besen & Raskind, supra note 1.

the appropriate subject of patents, but their holder may elect not to pursue a patent for various reasons, such as the fact that considerable information must be disclosed in the patent application process or that the application process and subsequent litigation may be costly. Other trade secrets are simply not patentable (such as customer lists). Protection for trade secrets is typically limited to a prohibition on the use of "improper means" to acquire them. Corporate espionage is actionable, as may be the disclosure of trade secrets by a former employee. But where a trade secret is discovered through proper means, such as reverse engineering or independent invention, there is usually no protection for it, in stark contrast to the situation with patent rights. These distinctions raise a number of puzzles that are not fully understood. One might wonder why protection for trade secrets is not broader on the one hand or, on the other, why it exists at all if the secret is not patentable.[4] We shall not purport to resolve these puzzles here, but simply note that some form of trade secret law seems to have evolved in most developed nations, although the details of that evolution and the extent of protection under the law has varied considerably.

(B) THE INTERNATIONAL DIMENSION

We cannot hope to address the broad policy issues associated with these various areas of intellectual property rights, and will leave such questions to other courses. Instead, we limit our attention to the primary ways that intellectual property has come to play a role in the international trading system.

Intellectual property has long been a subject of international interest as we shall see. An obvious source of potential tension internationally is the temptation to discriminate against foreign nationals in the provision of intellectual property rights. Discrimination has been prohibited by a number of international agreements through the years, including to a degree the national treatment obligation of GATT Article III, and now the Uruguay Round Agreement on Trade Related Aspects of Intellectual Property (hereafter the WTO TRIPS Agreement).

More difficult questions arise when nations do not pursue facially discriminatory policies, but disagree on the proper scope of intellectual property rights for domestic and foreign citizens alike. The United States has long been among the leading advocates for stronger intellectual property rights in the trading community, based on at least a perception that US inventors and creators lose considerable sums due to lax protection overseas. A 1988 study by the US International Trade Commission (relying mainly on industry-provided estimates) put the total loss to the US economy due to "inadequate" intellectual property protection abroad at roughly $24 billion annually.[5] The accuracy of such estimates is open to some question, and indeed it is very difficult to

---

4. An interesting discussion of these issues is that of Friedman, Landes & Posner, Some Economics of Trade Secret Law, 5 J. Econ. Perspectives 61 (1991).

5. US International Trade Commission, Foreign Protection of Intellectual Property Rights and the Effect on U.S. Industry and Trade, USITC Pub. No. 2065 (1988), at 4–2.

know what the full costs and benefits of varying intellectual property regimes are to different nations. Nevertheless, there can be little doubt that the stakes are considerable.

Disputes have been particularly commonplace through the years between developed and developing nations. Developing countries tend to have lower levels of human capital in the population at large than developed nations, and thus perhaps less capacity in relation to their size to generate commercially valuable innovations. Strict intellectual property laws in developing countries may thus facilitate profit-making by foreigners at the expense of domestic consumers. Weak laws, by contrast, which others may view as permitting "piracy," reduce domestic prices and may even facilitate export sales of the "pirated" items.[6] Hence, it is not unexpected that developing countries might have preferred less restrictive intellectual property regimes than developing nations.[7]

Important disputes have also arisen among developed nations, of course, on matters such as various purported instances of "piracy." These disputes persisted and multiplied despite the existence of a number of long-standing international agreements on intellectual property, such as the Paris Convention for the Protection of Industrial Property (from 1883) and the Berne Convention for the Protection of Literary and Artistic Works (from 1886).[8]

The WTO TRIPS Agreement sought to resolve many of these issues. Our primary focus below will be on the TRIPS Agreement and, in particular, on a few of the disputes that have arisen under it and on some of the ongoing broader policy disputes.

6. Weak intellectual property laws can be a double-edged sword, to be sure, as they stifle domestic innovation and may even have adverse effects on the rate of innovation abroad which will hurt consumers in the developed and developing nations alike. Likewise, if foreigners suspect that direct investment and technology transfer may facilitate piracy, developing nations with weak intellectual property laws may find it difficult to attract assistance that might be valuable for development. A notable effort to develop empirical information on such issues is that of Edwin Mansfield, Unauthorized Use of Intellectual Property: Effects on Investment, Technology Transfer and Innovation, *in* National Research Council, Global Dimensions of Intellectual Property Rights in Science and Technology 107 (1993). The other papers in that volume are also of considerable interest.

7. It does not follow that the policies preferred by developing nations will be worse for the world as a whole than the policies preferred by developed nations. Just as developing nations may prefer to be "pirates," developed nations may delight in exploiting the monopoly power that strict intellectual property rights (particularly in the patent area) may facilitate. The globally

"optimal" policy, therefore, might well lie in between, and in any case there can be no assurance that one side or the other is "right" from the global perspective. The literature on these issues includes Frederick Abbott, Protecting First World Assets in the Third World: Intellectual Property Negotiations in the GATT Multilateral Framework, 22 Vand.J.Transnatl.L. 689 (1989); Judith Chin & Gene Grossman, Intellectual Property Rights and North–South Trade, *in* The Political Economy of International Trade 90 (Ronald Jones & Anne Krueger eds., 1990); Alan Deardorff, Welfare Effects of Global Patent Protection, Economica, February 1992, at 35; Ishac Diwan & Dani Rodrik, Patents, Appropriate Technology and North–South Trade, 30 J.Intl.Econ. 27 (1991); and Arvind Subramanian, The International Economics of Intellectual Property Right Protection: A Welfare–Theoretic Trade Policy Analysis, 19 World Development 945 (1991).

8. These and other international agreements are collected in International Treaties on Intellectual Property (M. Leaffer ed., 1990).

We will also touch on the problem of "infringing imports"—i.e., imported goods that are alleged to infringe the rights of some right holder in the importing country. We will examine in particular the phenomenon of "gray-market" imports, whereby a good that is lawfully produced abroad subject to a patent or trademark license is imported into the territory of another country in a manner that infringes the exclusive license of another for that territory. We also consider the general administrative remedy under US law for "unfair competition" from imports—Section 337 of the Tariff Act of 1930—which as a practical matter is focused heavily on intellectual property issues.

SECTION 20.2 TRIPS AND WTO DEVELOPMENTS

The past two decades have witnessed dramatic developments in the form of new international accords over intellectual property rights. First, the United States, Canada and Mexico reached agreement on the intellectual property provisions of NAFTA, especially significant for the commitment by a developing nation to afford intellectual property rights comparable to those prevalent in developed economies. Next, the Uruguay Round TRIPS Agreement created elaborate substantive and procedural obligations binding on all WTO signatories.

(A) HISTORY

International agreements on intellectual property date back over a century.[1] The Paris Convention for the Protection of Industrial Property was first concluded in 1883, though it has been revised a number of times since. It covers "industrial property" broadly, including patents, trademarks, marks of origin, and methods of unfair competition. The Berne Convention for the Protection of Literary and Artistic Works (focused on copyright) was first concluded in 1886. A number of other accords exist as well, though their membership tends to be considerably smaller. Both the Paris and Berne Conventions, as well as many of the other agreements, are administered by the World Intellectual Property Organization (WIPO), an arm of the United Nations.

The Paris and Berne Conventions (the latter joined only recently by the United States) include commitments to national treatment.[2] GATT Article III also required national treatment in matters affecting the importation of goods, as we saw in Chapter 12. The Conventions also include measures to prevent the appropriation of intellectual property by someone in another country who copies it and then registers, files, or produces it first in that country. For example, if company X files a patent application in country A, company X shall for a period of time be deemed to have filed on the same date in country B, quite important

---

1. A compendium of the more important agreements is International Treaties on Intellectual Property (M. Leaffer ed. 1990).

2. See Article 2 of the Paris Convention and Article 5 of the Berne Convention, reprinted in International Treaties on Intellectual Property, supra.

under a "first to file" system for granting patents.[3] Likewise, if company X has a trademark that is unregistered in country A but is widely recognized by consumers there, company X can for a period of time apply to cancel the registration of another company that registers the mark in country A.[4] To a limited extent, the Conventions also set minimum standards for the protection of intellectual property. The most important examples are perhaps those in the Berne Convention, which requires that most copyrights extend for the life of the author plus 50 years,[5] and that authors have the right to object to any "distortion, mutilation or other modification" of the work (the so-called "droit moral" or "moral rights.")[6]

Notwithstanding the variety of long-standing agreements in this area, many nations complained before the Uruguay Round that intellectual property protection was deficient in other nations. The weaknesses in the existing regime were numerous. Among other things, the membership of the various conventions and treaties was quite incomplete. Many of the newly industrialized and larger developing countries, in particular, were not parties to one or more of them. Also, especially in the area of patents, the substantive restrictions on domestic law were few. Signatories could exclude some categories of inventions from patentability altogether, and give minimal patent duration to others, as long as they did not discriminate against foreign nationals. Finally, as with many international agreements, there were concerns about the level of compliance and the effectiveness of dispute resolution.[7] Attempts by the United States and other countries to address these issues in WIPO had proved unsuccessful, in large part because of the wide divergence of views on intellectual property rights in that organization. Moreover, in a single issue forum, such as WIPO, there was no possibility of securing changes in intellectual property laws in exchange for concessions on other trade issues, as there is in the GATT/WTO system.

(B) THE URUGUAY ROUND NEGOTIATIONS[8]

Because of US dissatisfaction with the existing international intellectual property agreements, the United States was the prime mover to include the subject of intellectual property in the Uruguay Round. Inclusion of this subject was strongly opposed by a number of important

---

3. See Article 4 of the Paris Convention.

4. See Article 6*bis* of the Paris Convention.

5. See Article 7.

6. See Article 6*bis*.

7. A useful review of the pre-Uruguay Round institutions and negotiating positions may be found in Emmert, Intellectual Property in the Uruguay Round—Negotiating Strategies of the Western Industrialized Countries, 11 Mich.J.Intl.L. 1317 (1990), and in Benko, Protecting Intellectual Prop-

erty Rights: Issues and Controversies (1987).

8. For a general description of the negotiations, see The GATT Uruguay Round: A Negotiating History (1986–1992), at 2241–2333 (T. Stewart ed., 1993); Reichman, The TRIPS Component of the GATT's Uruguay Round: Competitive Prospects for Intellectual Property Owners in an Integrated World Market, 4 Fordham Intellectual Prop., Media & Entertainment L.J. 171 (1993).

developing countries. In the end, however, it was agreed to include intellectual property rights as a subject in the negotiations.

At about the same time as a new round of negotiations in GATT was under consideration, the United States began putting considerable pressure on certain of its trading partners to improve their enforcement of intellectual property rights. This pressure resulted in the adoption of new or revised intellectual property laws by a number of countries, including Brazil, Singapore, South Korea, Taiwan and Thailand. Initially this pressure was applied through initiation or threat of Section 301 actions, including actions under Special 301, a provision added to US trade law in 1988. The US has also pressured various developing countries to strengthen their intellectual property laws by threatening to withdraw their benefits under the Generalized System of Preferences.

Because of the initial opposition of many developing countries to including intellectual property as a negotiating topic in the Uruguay Round, it was expected that the negotiations would center on North–South issues. In the end, however, there were many difficult disputes to resolve between developed countries as well. Once it became necessary to define exactly the terms of patent, copyright, trademark and other forms of intellectual property protection, the differences in industrialized country laws became more significant. In fact, developing country opposition to a TRIPS Agreement moderated significantly during the course of the negotiations. This was in part because as more of the advanced developing countries adopted or revised intellectual property laws, the amount of change required by an international agreement became less significant for many of them. Moreover, in a few of those countries, production of valuable intellectual property had started to occur and rules on protection of such property seemed likely to be more beneficial in the long run than they had in the past.

While we cannot trace all of the significant issues that the negotiators discussed, we will highlight some of the more important ones. Thereafter, in the next subsection, we describe the results of the negotiations. In reading the summary of the results, the student should consider how the following issues were resolved. We address the issues in the order they are treated in the TRIPS Agreement.

Copyright. As noted above, the Berne Convention provides for so-called moral rights. Article *6bis* provides that an author has "the right * * * to object to any distortion, mutilation, or other modification of, or other derogatory action in relation to the work that would be prejudicial to his honor or reputation." Thus, an artist controls some aspects of the use of his or her work even after it is sold. Although the US is a party to the Berne Convention, it does not generally provide copyright holders with such moral rights. Many other countries do. Should all countries be required to provide such rights, including the U.S? Why would you think that the US does not provide such rights generally?

The extent to which computer software can be copyrighted (or patented) has been a controversial issue in a number of legal systems and specific statutes have sometimes been introduced to clarify the issue. Consequently, one of the issues faced by the Uruguay Round negotiators was how to treat software. Consider whether distinctions should be made in the types of software that can be protected. And what about data bases? What policy issues do you see regarding whether they should be protected?

Third, there was the question of a copyright holder's right to control use of the work after it has been sold, in particular, the extent to which the holder should be able to prohibit rental of the work. To what extent does this right exist in the US? Why would you expect the holder to want to control rental? Should the holder be able to? Should there be any conditions on exercising such control? Consider the position of libraries and video rental stores.

Finally, there was the question of what are called neighboring rights, so-called because they neighbor on copyright. These rights include the right of performers to control reproduction of their performances and the right of broadcasters to control rebroadcast of their programs. Such rights have been recognized at the international level only recently in a 1961 convention and are not as widely recognized as many other intellectual property rights. The issue was whether they should be more broadly recognized. What arguments can you see for and against such recognition?

Trademarks. One issue with respect to trademarks was whether the US requirement of use as a condition of protection should be permitted. On the question of trademark enforcement, another issue concerned the extent to which countries had to take measures to prevent counterfeiting.

Industrial Designs. The principal dispute here concerned the scope of protection. What sort of products should be protected as industrial designs? Spare parts, for example? Would it be appropriate to let the maker of a product (such as automobiles) control the market for spare parts for its product through protection of industrial designs? What economic effects could be expected?

Patents. Among the important patent issues were whether the United States should be permitted to maintain its "first to invent" rule, which awards a patent to the first person to have invented a product, as opposed to the practice elsewhere in the world, where the first person to file a patent application for an invention is typically awarded the patent. The US system also had a discriminatory element—the first to invent rule did not apply to noncitizens. Their priority was based on the date of their first filing. At issue was how, if at all, the US system would be changed.

Another important issue was the subject matter that could be patented, and the extent to which certain products could be excluded from patent coverage, such as pharmaceutical products or the results of biotechnology research. Should different rules apply to such products?

Finally, there was the question of compulsory licensing. Many developing countries, and some developed ones, have rules requiring that a patent holder must license its patent in certain circumstances, particularly if the patent is not being utilized in the country where the patent exists. Multinational corporations obviously will want to patent a product throughout the world, but they may be less interested in establishing manufacturing facilities in every country where they have patent protection. Under what conditions, if any, should the use of the patent be allowed without the voluntary consent of the holder?

There are, of course, a multitude of other issues. But the foregoing discussion highlights some of the more important ones that were discussed in the TRIPS negotiations. In the next section, we describe the TRIPS Agreement, which is contained in the Documents Supplement. The reader should consider how, if at all, the foregoing issues were resolved.

(C) OVERVIEW OF THE TRIPS AGREEMENT

The Uruguay Round TRIPS Agreement is an extraordinary accomplishment that addresses many (though by no means all) of the concerns that existed prior to the Round. The agreement will include all WTO members, and thus is expected to incorporate virtually all of the major players in the international economy. It also goes well beyond what was in place previously regarding the requirements for substantive rights. Finally, dispute resolution under the TRIPs Agreement will be comparable to that elsewhere in the WTO/GATT system.

The TRIPS Agreement bears considerable similarity to the intellectual property provisions in NAFTA. The NAFTA provisions, aimed largely but not entirely at conforming the policies of Mexico to those of the United States and Canada, encompassed all forms of patent protection, compulsory licensing, copyright, trademark protection, trade secrets, semiconductor mask designs, domestic enforcement, and dispute resolution. Because of their overlap with and similarity to the TRIPS Agreement, we omit detailed discussion.[9] Likewise, amendments to US law necessitated by TRIPS and NAFTA were generally modest, and at a level of detail that need not detain us here.

The following summary of the TRIPS Agreement was prepared by the GATT Secretariat.

GATT FOCUS NEWSLETTER
DECEMBER 1993, at 12–14

The agreement recognizes that widely varying standards in the protection and enforcement of intellectual property rights and the lack of a multilateral framework of principles, rules and disciplines dealing with international trade in counterfeit goods have been a growing source of tension in international economic relations. Rules and disciplines were

---

9. A nice summary of the highlights may be found in Wineburg, NAFTA to Break Down Barriers, Legal Times, October 26, 1992, at 21.

needed to cope with these tensions. To that end, the agreement addresses the applicability of basic GATT principles and those of relevant international intellectual property agreements, the provision of adequate intellectual property rights; the provision of effective enforcement measures for those rights; multilateral dispute settlement; and transitional arrangements.

Part I of the agreement sets out general provisions and basic principles, notably a national-treatment commitment under which the nationals of other parties must be given treatment no less favourable than that accorded to a party's own nationals with regard to the protection of intellectual property. It also contains a most-favoured-nation clause, a novelty in an international intellectual property agreement, under which any advantage a party gives to the nationals of another country must be extended immediately and unconditionally to the nationals of all other parties, even if such treatment is more favourable than that which it gives to its own nationals.

Part II addresses each intellectual property right in succession. With respect to copyright, parties are required to comply with the substantive provisions of the Berne Convention for the protection of literary and artistic works, in its latest version (Paris 1971), though they will not be obliged to protect moral rights as stipulated in Article 6*bis* of that Convention. It ensures that computer programs will be protected as literary works under the Berne Convention and lays down on what basis data bases should be protected by copyright. Important additions to existing international rules in the area of copyright and related rights are the provisions on rental rights. The draft requires authors of computer programmes and producers of sound recordings to be given the right to authorize or prohibit the commercial rental of their works to the public. A similar exclusive right applies to films where commercial rental has led to widespread copying which is materially impairing the right of reproduction. The draft also requires performers to be given protection from unauthorized recording and broadcast of live performances (bootlegging). The protection for performers and producers of sound recordings would be for no less than 50 years. Broadcasting organizations would have control over the use that can be made of broadcast signals without their authorization. This right would last for at least 20 years.

With respect to trademarks and service marks, the agreement defines what types of signs must be eligible for protection as a trademark or service mark and what the minimum rights conferred on their owners must be. Marks that have become well-known in a particular country shall enjoy additional protection. In addition, the agreement lays down a number of obligations with regard to the use of trademarks and service marks, their term of protection, and their licensing or assignment. For example, requirements that foreign marks be used in conjunction with local marks would, as a general rule, be prohibited.

In respect of geographical indications, the agreement lays down that all parties must provide means to prevent the use of any indication which misleads the consumer as to the origin of goods, and any use which would constitute an act of unfair competition. A higher level of protection is provided for geographical indications for wines and spirits, which are protected even where there is no danger of the public's being misled as to the true origin. Exceptions are allowed for names that have already become generic terms, but any country using such an exception must be willing to negotiate with a view to protecting the geographical indications in question. Furthermore, provision is made for further negotiations to establish a multilateral system of notification and registration of geographical indications for wines.

Industrial designs are also protected under the agreement for a period of 10 years. Owners of protected designs would be able to prevent the manufacture, sale or importation of articles bearing or embodying a design which is a copy of the protected design.

As regards patents, there is a general obligation to comply with the substantive provisions of the Paris Convention (1967). In addition, the agreement requires that 20–year patent protection be available for all inventions, whether of products or processes, in almost all fields of technology. Inventions may be excluded from patentability if their commercial exploitation is prohibited for reasons of public order or morality; otherwise, the permitted exclusions are for diagnostic, therapeutic and surgical methods, and for plants and (other than microorganisms) animals and essentially biological processes for the production of plants or animals (other than microbiological processes). Plant varieties, however, must be protectable either by patents or by a *sui generis* system (such as the breeder's rights provided in a UPOV [International Convention for the Protection of New Varieties of Plants] Convention). Detailed conditions are laid down for compulsory licensing or governmental use of patents without the authorization of the patent owner. Rights conferred in respect of patents for processes must extend to the products directly obtained by the process; under certain conditions alleged infringers may be ordered by a court to prove that they have not used the patented process.

With respect to the protection of layout designs of integrated circuits, the agreement requires parties to provide protection on the basis of the Washington Treaty on Intellectual Property in Respect of Integrated Circuits which was opened for signature in May 1989, but with a number of additions: protection must be available for a minimum period of 10 years; the rights must extend to articles incorporating infringing layout designs; innocent infringers must be allowed to use or sell stock in hand or ordered before learning of the infringement against a suitable royalty; and compulsory licensing and government use is only allowed under a number of strict conditions.

Trade secrets and know-how which have commercial value must be protected against breach of confidence and other acts contrary to honest commercial practices. Test data submitted to government in order to obtain marketing approval for pharmaceutical or agricultural chemicals must also be protected against unfair commercial use.

The final section in this part of the agreement concerns anti-competitive practices in contractual licences. It provides for consultations between governments where there is reason to believe that licensing practices or conditions pertaining to intellectual property rights constitute an abuse of these rights and have an adverse effect on competition. Remedies against such abuses must be consistent with the other provisions of the agreement.

Part III of the agreement sets out the obligations of member governments to provide procedures and remedies under their domestic law to ensure that intellectual property rights can be effectively enforced, by foreign right holders as well as by their own nationals. Procedures should permit effective action against infringement of intellectual property rights but should be fair and equitable, not unnecessarily complicated or costly, and should not entail unreasonable time-limits or unwarranted delays. They should allow for judicial review of final administrative decisions. There is no obligation to put in place a judicial system distinct from that for the enforcement of laws in general, nor to give priority to the enforcement of intellectual property rights in the allocation of resources or staff.

The civil and administrative procedures and remedies spelled out in the text include provisions on evidence and proof, injunction, damages and other remedies which would include the right of judicial authorities to order the disposal or destruction of infringing goods. Judicial authorities must also have the authority to order prompt and effective provisional measures, in particular where any delay is likely to cause irreparable harm to the right holder, or where evidence is likely to be destroyed. Further provisions relate to measures to be taken at the border for the suspension by customs authorities of release, into domestic circulation, of counterfeit and pirated goods. Finally, parties should provide for criminal procedures and penalties at least in cases of wilful trademark counterfeiting or copyright piracy on a commercial scale. Remedies should include imprisonment and fines sufficient to act as a deterrent.

The agreement would establish a Council for Trade–Related Aspects of Intellectual Property Rights to monitor the operation of the agreement and governments' compliance with it. Dispute settlement would take place under the integrated GATT dispute-settlement procedures as revised in the Uruguay Round.

With respect to the implementation of the agreement, it envisages a one-year transition period for developed countries to bring their legislation and practices into conformity. Developing countries and countries in the process of transformation from a centrally-planned into a market economy would have a five-year transition period, and least-developed countries 11 years. Developing countries which do not at present provide product patent protection in an area of technology would have up to 10 years to introduce such protection. However, in the case of pharmaceutical and agricultural chemical products, they must accept the filing of patent applications from the beginning of the transitional period. Though the patent need not be granted until the end of this period, the novelty of the invention is preserved as of the date of filing the application. If authorization for the marketing of the relevant pharmaceutical or agricultural chemical is obtained during the transitional period, the developing country concerned must offer an exclusive marketing right for the product for five years, or until a product patent is granted, whichever is shorter.

Subject to certain exceptions, the general rule is that the obligations in the agreement would apply to existing intellectual property rights as well as to new ones.

(D) CASES ARISING UNDER THE TRIPS AGREEMENT

As of March, 2008, 23 requests for consultations involving distinct claims of TRIPS violations have been made through the dispute settlement process. The bulk of them have not proceeded beyond the consultation phase, and many have resulted in mutually agreed settlements. Of those that have generated dispute settlement reports, some have involved essentially transitional issues. In Canada—Term of Patent Protection, WT/DS170/AB/R, Appellate Body Report adopted October 12, 2000, the issue was what to do about patents granted before the TRIPS Agreement came into effect that do not conform to the length of patent requirement in TRIPS. In India—Patent Protection for Pharmaceutical and Agricultural Chemical Products, WT/DS50/AB/R, Appellate Body Report adopted January 16, 1998, the issue was whether India had provided an adequate administrative process to preserve the rights of patent applicants regarding subject matter that would not become patentable in India until 2005. Two disputes of more than transitional importance have involved the ability of nations to grant "limited exceptions" to the substantive requirements of the TRIPS Agreement.

CANADA—PATENT PROTECTION OF PHARMACEUTICAL PRODUCTS

WT/DS114/R.
Panel Report adopted April 7, 2000.

7.1 At issue in this dispute is the [EC and its member states' challenge to the] conformity of two provisions of Canada's *Patent Act* with Canada's obligations under the *Agreement on Trade–Related Aspects of Intellectual Property Rights* ("the TRIPS Agreement"). The two provisions in dispute, Sections 55.2(1) and 55.2(2) of the Patent Act, create exceptions to the exclusive rights of patent owners. Under Article 28.1 of the TRIPS Agreement, patent owners shall have the right to exclude others from making, using, selling, offering for sale or importing the patented product during the term of the patent. According to Article 33 of the TRIPS Agreement, the term of protection available shall not end before the expiration of a period of 20 years counted from the filing date of the application against which the patent was granted. Sections 55.2(1) and 55.2(2) allow third parties to make, use or sell the patented product during the term of the patent without the consent of the patent owner in certain defined circumstances.

7.2   Section 55.2(1) provides as follows:

> "It is not an infringement of a patent for any person to make, construct, use or sell the patented invention solely for uses reasonably related to the development and submission of information required under any law of Canada, a province or a country other than Canada that regulates the manufacture, construction, use or sale of any product."

Section 55.2(1) is known as the "regulatory review exception". It applies to patented products such as pharmaceuticals whose marketing is subject to government regulation in order to assure their safety or effectiveness. The purpose of the regulatory review exception is to permit potential competitors of the patent owner to obtain government marketing approval during the term of the patent, so that they will have regulatory permission to sell in competition with the patent owner by the date on which the patent expires. Without the regulatory review exception, the patent owner might be able to prevent potential competitors from using the patented product during the term of the patent to comply with testing requirements, so that competitors would have to wait until the patent expires before they could begin the process of obtaining marketing approval. This, in turn, would prevent potential competitors from entering the market for the additional time required to complete the regulatory approval process, in effect extending the patent owner's period of market exclusivity beyond the end of the term of the patent.

* * *

7.7   Section 55.2(2) of the Patent Act, which is referred to as "the stockpiling exception", reads as follows:

> "It is not an infringement of a patent for any person who makes, constructs, uses or sells a patented invention in accordance with subsection (1) to make, construct or use the invention, during the applicable period provided for by the regulations, for the manufacture and storage of articles intended for sale after the date on which the term of the patent expires."

The provision allows competitors to manufacture and stockpile patented goods during a certain period before the patent expires, but the goods cannot be sold until the patent expires. Without this exception, the patent owner's right to exclude any person from "making" or "using" the patented good would enable the patent owner to prevent all such stockpiling.

7.8   The exception created by Section 55.2(2) does not become effective until implementing regulations are issued. The only regulations issued to date under the stockpiling exception have been regulations making the exception operative with regard to pharmaceutical products.

The period during which pharmaceutical products can be made and stockpiled is six months immediately prior to the expiration of the patent.

7.9　The text of Section 55.2(2) gives permission only to "make, construct or use" the patented product for purposes of stockpiling. In answer to a question from the Panel, however, Canada has taken the position that the exception will be construed also to allow the "sale" of patented ingredients that have been ordered by a producer who is stockpiling the final patented product—for example, with regard to pharmaceuticals, sales by fine chemical producers of active ingredients ordered by the generic producer.

7.10　The stockpiling exception is available only to persons who have invoked the regulatory review exception in Section 55.2(1). This limitation has the effect of limiting the exception to products that are subject to the kind of government marketing regulations referred to in Section 55.2(1). As a practical matter, only persons who have actually obtained regulatory permission to market such regulated products would be able to benefit from the stockpiling exception, because there would be no commercial advantage in having a stock of goods on hand when the patent expires unless one also has regulatory permission to sell those goods as of that date. Conversely, the stockpiling exception does complement the competitive effects of the regulatory review exception. Without the additional permission to stockpile during the term of the patent, competitors who obtain regulatory permission to sell on the day the patent expires would still not be able to enter the market on that day, because they would first have to manufacture a sufficient stock of goods.

* * *

The Stockpiling Exception

7.17　The Panel began by considering the claims of violation concerning Section 55.2(2), the so-called stockpiling provision. It began by considering the EC claim that this measure was in violation of Article 28.1 of the TRIPS Agreement, and Canada's defence that the measure was an exception authorized by Article 30 of the Agreement.

7.18　Article 28.1 provides:

"Rights Conferred

　1.　A patent shall confer on its owner the following exclusive rights:

　(a) Where the subject-matter of a patent is a product, to prevent third parties not having the owner's consent from the acts of making, using, offering for sale, selling, or importing for these purposes that product;"

There was no dispute as to the meaning of Article 28.1 exclusive rights as they pertain to Section 55.2(2) of Canada's Patent Act. Canada acknowledged that the provisions of Section 55.2(2) permitting third parties to "make", "construct" or "use" the patented product during the term of the patent, without the patent owner's permission, would be a violation of Article 28.1 if not excused under Article 30 of the Agreement. The dispute on the claim of violation of Article 28.1 involved whether Section 55.2.(2) of the Patent Act complies with the conditions of Article 30.

7.19   The TRIPS Agreement contains two provisions authorizing exceptions to the exclusionary patent rights laid down in Article 28—Articles 30 and 31. Of these two, Article 30—the so-called limited exceptions provision—has been invoked by Canada in the present case. It reads as follows:

"Exceptions to Rights Conferred

Members may provide limited exceptions to the exclusive rights conferred by a patent, provided that such exceptions do not unreasonably conflict with the normal exploitation of the patent and do not unreasonably prejudice the legitimate interests of the patent owner, taking account of the legitimate interests of third parties."

7.20   Both parties agreed upon the basic structure of Article 30. Article 30 establishes three criteria that must be met in order to qualify for an exception: (1) the exception must be "limited"; (2) the exception must not "unreasonably conflict with normal exploitation of the patent"; (3) the exception must not "unreasonably prejudice the legitimate interests of the patent owner, taking account of the legitimate interests of third parties". The three conditions are cumulative, each being a separate and independent requirement that must be satisfied. Failure to comply with any one of the three conditions results in the Article 30 exception being disallowed.

7.21   The three conditions must, of course, be interpreted in relation to each other. Each of the three must be presumed to mean something different from the other two, or else there would be redundancy. Normally, the order of listing can be read to suggest that an exception that complies with the first condition can nevertheless violate the second or third, and that one which complies with the first and second can still violate the third. The syntax of Article 30 supports the conclusion that an exception may be "limited" and yet fail to satisfy one or both of the other two conditions. The ordering further suggests that an exception that does not "unreasonably conflict with normal exploitation" could nonetheless "unreasonably prejudice the legitimate interests of the patent owner".

* * *

"Limited Exceptions"

7.27   Canada asserted that the word "limited" should be interpreted according to the conventional dictionary definition, such as "confined within definite limits", or "restricted in scope, extent, amount". Canada argued that the stockpiling exception in Section 55.2(2) is restricted in scope because it has only a limited impact on a patent owner's rights.

The stockpiling exception, Canada noted, does not affect the patent owner's right to an exclusive market for "commercial" sales during the patent term, since the product that is manufactured and stockpiled during the final six months of the term cannot be sold in competition with the patent owner until the patent expires. By "commercial sales", Canada clearly meant sales to the ultimate consumer, because it acknowledged that sales of patented ingredients to producers engaged in authorized stockpiling is permitted. Thus, Canada was arguing that an exception is "limited" as long as the exclusive right to sell to the ultimate consumer during the term of the patent is preserved. In addition, Canada also claimed that the exception is further limited by the six-month duration of the exception, and by the fact that it can be used only by persons that have made, constructed or used the invention under Section 55.2(1).

7.28   The EC interpreted the word "limited" to connote a narrow exception, one that could be described by words such as "narrow, small, minor, insignificant or restricted". The EC measured the "limited" quality of the proposed exception by reference to its impact on the exclusionary rights granted to the patent owner under Article 28.1. Applying that measure, the EC contended that the stockpiling exception is not "limited" because it takes away three of the five Article 28.1 rights—the rights to exclude "making", "using" and "importing". The EC argued that the impairment of three out of five basic rights is in itself extensive enough to be considered "not limited". The EC further contended that limitation of the exception to the last six months of the patent term does not constitute a limited impairment of rights when six months is taken as a percentage of the 20–year patent term, and especially not when taken as a percentage of the actual eight to 12–year period of effective market exclusivity enjoyed by most patented pharmaceuticals. In addition, the EC noted, there was no limitation on the quantities that could be produced during this period, nor any limitation on the markets in which such products could be sold. Finally, the EC pointed out that no royalty fees are due for such production, and that the patent holder does not even have a right to be informed of the use of the patent.

7.29   In considering how to approach the parties' conflicting positions regarding the meaning of the term "limited exceptions", the Panel was aware that the text of Article 30 has antecedents in the text of Article 9(2) of the Berne Convention. However, the words "limited exceptions" in Article 30 of the TRIPS Agreement are different from the corresponding words in Article 9(2) of the Berne Convention, which reads "in certain special cases". The Panel examined the documented negotiating history of TRIPS Article 30 with respect to the reasons why negotiators may have chosen to use the term "limited exceptions" in place of "in special circumstances". The negotiating records show only that the term "limited exceptions" was employed very early in the drafting process, well before the decision to adopt a text modelled on

Berne Article 9(2), but do not indicate why it was retained in the later draft texts modelled on Berne Article 9(2).

7.30   The Panel agreed with the EC that, as used in this context, the word "limited" has a narrower connotation than the rather broad definitions cited by Canada. Although the word itself can have both broad and narrow definitions, the narrower being indicated by examples such as "a mail train taking only a limited number of passengers", the narrower definition is the more appropriate when the word "limited" is used as part of the phrase "limited exception". The word "exception" by itself connotes a limited derogation, one that does not undercut the body of rules from which it is made. When a treaty uses the term "limited exception", the word "limited" must be given a meaning separate from the limitation implicit in the word "exception" itself. The term "limited exception" must therefore be read to connote a narrow exception—one which makes only a small diminution of the rights in question.

7.31   The Panel agreed with the EC interpretation that "limited" is to be measured by the extent to which the exclusive rights of the patent owner have been curtailed. The full text of Article 30 refers to "limited exceptions to the exclusive rights conferred by a patent". In the absence of other indications, the Panel concluded that it would be justified in reading the text literally, focusing on the extent to which legal rights have been curtailed, rather than the size or extent of the economic impact. In support of this conclusion, the Panel noted that the following two conditions of Article 30 ask more particularly about the economic impact of the exception, and provide two sets of standards by which such impact may be judged. The term "limited exceptions" is the only one of the three conditions in Article 30 under which the extent of the curtailment of rights as such is dealt with.

7.32   The Panel does not agree, however, with the EC's position that the curtailment of legal rights can be measured by simply counting the number of legal rights impaired by an exception. A very small act could well violate all five rights provided by Article 28.1 and yet leave each of the patent owner's rights intact for all useful purposes. To determine whether a particular exception constitutes a limited exception, the extent to which the patent owner's rights have been curtailed must be measured.

7.33   The Panel could not accept Canada's argument that the curtailment of the patent owner's legal rights is "limited" just so long as the exception preserves the exclusive right to sell to the ultimate consumer during the patent term. Implicit in the Canadian argument is a notion that the right to exclude sales to consumers during the patent term is the essential right conveyed by a patent, and that the rights to exclude "making" and "using" the patented product during the term of the patent are in some way secondary. The Panel does not find any support for creating such a hierarchy of patent rights within the TRIPS Agreement. If the right to exclude sales were all that really mattered, there would be no reason to add other rights to exclude "making" and "using". The fact that such rights were included in the TRIPS Agreement, as they are in most national patent laws, is strong evidence that they are considered a meaningful and independent part of the patent owner's rights.

7.34 In the Panel's view, the question of whether the stockpiling exception is a "limited" exception turns on the extent to which the patent owner's rights to exclude "making" and "using" the patented product have been curtailed. The right to exclude "making" and "using" provides protection, additional to that provided by the right to exclude sale, during the entire term of the patent by cutting off the supply of competing goods at the source and by preventing use of such products however obtained. With no limitations at all upon the quantity of production, the stockpiling exception removes that protection entirely during the last six months of the patent term, without regard to what other, subsequent, consequences it might have. By this effect alone, the stockpiling exception can be said to abrogate such rights entirely during the time it is in effect.

7.35 In view of Canada's emphasis on preserving commercial benefits *before* the expiration of the patent, the Panel also considered whether the market advantage gained by the patent owner in the months after expiration of the patent could also be considered a purpose of the patent owner's rights to exclude "making" and "using" during the term of the patent. In both theory and practice, the Panel concluded that such additional market benefits were within the purpose of these rights. In theory, the rights of the patent owner are generally viewed as a right to prevent competitive commercial activity by others, and manufacturing for commercial sale is a quintessential competitive commercial activity, whose character is not altered by a mere delay in the commercial reward. In practical terms, it must be recognized that enforcement of the right to exclude "making" and "using" during the patent term will necessarily give all patent owners, for all products, a short period of extended market exclusivity after the patent expires. The repeated enactment of such exclusionary rights with knowledge of their universal market effects can only be understood as an affirmation of the purpose to produce those market effects.

7.36 For both these reasons, the Panel concluded that the stockpiling exception of Section 55.2(2) constitutes a substantial curtailment of the exclusionary rights required to be granted to patent owners under Article 28.1 of the TRIPS Agreement. Without seeking to define exactly what level of curtailment would be disqualifying, it was clear to the Panel that an exception which results in a substantial curtailment of this dimension cannot be considered a "limited exception" within the meaning of Article 30 of the Agreement.

7.37 Neither of the two "limitations" upon the scope of the measure are sufficient to alter this conclusion. First, the fact that the exception can only be used by those persons who have utilized the regulatory review exception of Section 55.2(1) does limit the scope of the exception both to those persons and to products requiring regulatory approval. In regard to the limitation to such persons, the Panel considered this was not a real limitation since only persons who satisfy regulatory requirements would be entitled to market the product. In regard to the limitation to such products, the Panel considered that the fact that an exception does not apply at all to other products in no way changes its effect with regard to the criteria of Article 30. Each exception must be evaluated with regard to its impact on each affected patent, independently. Second, the fact that the exception applied only to the last six months of the patent term obviously does reduce its impact on all affected patented products, but the Panel agreed with the EC that six months was a commercially significant period of time, especially since there were no limits at all on the volume of production allowed, or the market destination of such production.

7.38 Having concluded that the exception in Section 55.2(2) of the Canadian Patent Act does not satisfy the first condition of Article 30 of the TRIPS Agreement, the Panel therefore concluded that Section 55.2(2) is inconsistent with Canada's obligations under Article 28.1 of the Agreement. This conclusion, in turn, made it unnecessary to consider any of the other claims of inconsistency raised by the European Communities. Accordingly, the Panel did not consider the claims of inconsistency under the second and third conditions of Article 30, the claim of inconsistency with TRIPS Article 27.1, and the claim of inconsistency with Article 33.

The Regulatory Review Exception
"Limited Exceptions"

* * *

7.41 In the case of the regulatory review exception * * * Canada added two further arguments based on the negotiating history of Article 30 and on the subsequent practices of certain WTO Members. Canada pointed out that in 1984 the United States had enacted a regulatory review exception similar to Section 55.2(1) of Canada's Patent Act, known as the "Bolar exemption". Canada asserted that the United States "Bolar exemption" was well known during the negotiation of Article 30, and that governments were aware that the United States intended to secure an exception that would permit it to retain its "Bolar exemption". Canada further asserts that it was known that the United States agreed to the general language of Article 30 on the understanding that the provision would do so. Canada called attention to subsequent statements by United States officials stating that "[O]ur negotiators ensured that the TRIPS Agreement permits the Bolar exemption to be maintained."

7.42 With regard to subsequent practice, Canada pointed out that after the conclusion of the TRIPS Agreement four other WTO Members (Argentina, Australia, Hungary and Israel) adopted legislation containing similar regulatory review exceptions, and that both Japan and

Portugal adopted interpretations of existing patent law which confirmed exemptions for regulatory review submissions. Canada argued that these actions are subsequent practices by parties to the agreement, within the meaning of Article 31(3)(b) of the Vienna Convention, that confirm its interpretation that regulatory review exceptions are authorized by TRIPS Article 30.

* * *

7.44 In the previous part of this Report dealing with the stockpiling exception of Section 55.2(2), the Panel concluded that the words "limited exception" express a requirement that the exception make only a narrow curtailment of the legal rights which Article 28.1 requires to be granted to patent owners, and that the measure of that curtailment was the extent to which the affected legal rights themselves had been impaired. As was made clear by our conclusions regarding the stockpiling exception, the Panel could not accept Canada's contention that an exception can be regarded as "limited" just so long as it preserves the patent owner's exclusive right to sell to the ultimate consumer during the patent term.

7.45 In the Panel's view, however, Canada's regulatory review exception is a "limited exception" within the meaning of TRIPS Article 30. It is "limited" because of the narrow scope of its curtailment of Article 28.1 rights. As long as the exception is confined to conduct needed to comply with the requirements of the regulatory approval process, the extent of the acts unauthorized by the right holder that are permitted by it will be small and narrowly bounded. Even though regulatory approval processes may require substantial amounts of test production to demonstrate reliable manufacturing, the patent owner's rights themselves are not impaired any further by the size of such production runs, as long as they are solely for regulatory purposes and no commercial use is made of resulting final products.

7.46 The Panel found no basis for believing that activities seeking product approvals under foreign regulatory procedures would be any less subject to these limitations. There is no *a priori* basis to assume that the requirements of foreign regulatory procedures will require activities unrelated to legitimate objectives of product quality and safety, nor has the EC provided any evidence to that effect. Nor is there any reason to assume that Canadian law would apply the exception in cases where foreign requirements clearly had no regulatory purpose. Nor, finally, is there any reason to assume that it will be any more difficult to enforce the requirements of Canadian law when Canadian producers claim exceptions under foreign procedures. With regard to the latter point, the Panel concurred with Canada's point that the government is not normally expected to regulate the actual conduct of third parties in such cases. The enforcement of these conditions, as with other enforcement of patent rights, occurs by means of private infringement actions brought by the patent owner. The patent owner merely has to prove that the challenged conduct is inconsistent with the basic patent rights created by national law. Once that initial case is made, the burden will be on the party accused of infringement to prove its defence by establishing that its conduct with respect to foreign regulatory procedures was in compliance with the conditions of Section 55.2(1).

7.47 In reaching this conclusion, the Panel also considered Canada's additional arguments that both the negotiating history of Article 30 of the TRIPS Agreement and the subsequent practices of certain WTO Member governments supported the view that Article 30 was understood to permit regulatory review exceptions similar to Section 55.2(1). The Panel did not accord any weight to either of those arguments, however, because there was no documented evidence of the claimed negotiating understanding, and because the subsequent acts by individual countries did not constitute "practice in the application of the treaty which establishes the agreement of the parties regarding its interpretation" within the meaning of Article 31.3(b) of the Vienna Convention.

7.48 A final objection to the Panel's general conclusion remains to be addressed. Although the point was raised only briefly in the parties' legal arguments, the Panel was compelled to acknowledge that the economic impact of the regulatory review exception could be considerable. According to information supplied by Canada itself, in the case of patented pharmaceutical products approximately three to six-and-a-half years are required for generic drug producers to develop and obtain regulatory approval for their products. If there were no regulatory review exception allowing competitors to apply for regulatory approval during the term of the patent, therefore, the patent owner would be able to extend its period of market exclusivity, de facto, for some part of that three to six-and-half year period, depending on how much, if any, of the development process could be performed during the term of the patent under other exceptions, such as the scientific or experimental use exception. The Panel believed it was necessary to ask whether measures having such a significant impact on the economic interests of patent owners could be called a "limited" exception to patent rights.

7.49 After analysing all three conditions stated in Article 30 of the TRIPS Agreement, the Panel was satisfied that Article 30 does in fact address the issue of economic impact, but only in the other two conditions contained in that Article. As will be seen in the analysis of these other conditions below, the other two conditions deal with the issue of economic impact, according to criteria that relate specifically to that issue. Viewing all three conditions as a whole, it is apparent that the first condition ("limited exception") is neither designed nor intended to address the issue of economic impact directly.

* * *

"Normal Exploitation"

7.51 The second condition of Article 30 prohibits exceptions that "unreasonably conflict with a normal exploitation of the patent". Canada took the position that "exploitation" of the patent involves the extraction of commercial value from the patent by "working" the patent, either by selling the product in a market from which competitors are excluded, or by licensing others to do so, or by selling the patent rights outright. The European Communities also defined "exploitation" by referring to the same three ways of "working" a patent. The parties differed primarily on their interpretation of the term "normal".

* * *

7.54 The Panel considered that "exploitation" refers to the commercial activity by which patent owners employ their exclusive patent rights to extract economic value from their patent. The term "normal" defines the kind of commercial activity Article 30 seeks to protect. The ordinary meaning of the word "normal" is found in the dictionary definition: "regular, usual, typical, ordinary, conventional". As so defined, the term can be understood to refer either to an empirical conclusion about what is common within a relevant community, or to a normative standard of entitlement. The Panel concluded that the word "normal" was being used in Article 30 in a sense that combined the two meanings.

7.55 The normal practice of exploitation by patent owners, as with owners of any other intellectual property right, is to exclude all forms of competition that could detract significantly from the economic returns anticipated from a patent's grant of market exclusivity. The specific forms of patent exploitation are not static, of course, for to be effective exploitation must adapt to changing forms of competition due to technological development and the evolution of marketing practices. Protection of all normal exploitation practices is a key element of the policy reflected in all patent laws. Patent laws establish a carefully defined period of market exclusivity as an inducement to innovation, and the policy of those laws cannot be achieved unless patent owners are permitted to take effective advantage of that inducement once it has been defined.

7.56 Canada has raised the argument that market exclusivity occurring after the 20-year patent term expires should not be regarded as "normal". The Panel was unable to accept that as a categorical proposition. Some of the basic rights granted to all patent owners, and routinely exercised by all patent owners, will typically produce a certain period of market exclusivity after the expiration of a patent. For example, the separate right to prevent "making" the patented product during the term of the patent often prevents competitors from building an inventory needed to enter the market immediately upon expiration of a patent. There is nothing abnormal about that more or less brief period of market exclusivity after the patent has expired.

7.57 The Panel considered that Canada was on firmer ground, however, in arguing that the additional period of de facto market exclusivity created by using patent rights to preclude submissions for regulatory authorization should not be considered "normal". The additional period of market exclusivity in this situation is not a natural or normal consequence of enforcing patent rights. It is an unintended consequence of the conjunction of the patent laws with product regulatory laws, where the combination of patent rights with the time demands of the regulatory process gives a greater than normal period of market exclusivity to the enforcement of certain patent rights. It is likewise a form of exploitation that most patent owners do not in fact employ. For the vast majority of patented products, there is no marketing regulation of the kind covered by Section 55.2(1), and thus there is no possibility to extend patent exclusivity by delaying the marketing approval process for competitors.

7.58   The Panel could not agree with the EC's assertion that the mere existence of the patent owner's rights to exclude was a sufficient reason, by itself, for treating all gains derived from such rights as flowing from "normal exploitation". In the Panel's view, the EC's argument contained no evidence or analysis addressed to the various meanings of "normal"—neither a demonstration that most patent owners extract the value of their patents in the manner barred by Section 55.2(1), nor an argument that the prohibited manner of exploitation was "normal" in the sense of being essential to the achievement of the goals of patent policy. To the contrary, the EC's focus on the exclusionary rights themselves merely restated the concern to protect Article 28 exclusionary rights as such. This is a concern already dealt with by the first condition of Article 30 ("limited exception") and the Panel found the ultimate EC arguments here impossible to distinguish from the arguments it had made under that first condition.

7.59   In sum, the Panel found that the regulatory review exception of Section 55.2(1) does not conflict with a normal exploitation of patents, within the meaning of the second condition of Article 30 of the TRIPS Agreement. The fact that no conflict has been found makes it unnecessary to consider the question of whether, if a conflict were found, the conflict would be "unreasonable". Accordingly, it is also unnecessary to determine whether or not the final phrase of Article 30, calling for consideration of the legitimate interests of third parties, does or does not apply to the determination of "unreasonable conflict" under the second condition of Article 30.

"Legitimate Interests"

* * *

7.62   The European Communities argued that the regulatory review exception in Section 55.2(1) fails to satisfy the third condition of Article 30. The primary EC argument on this point rested on an interpretation that identified "legitimate interests" with legal interests. The EC asserted that the "legitimate interests" of the patent owner can only be the full enjoyment of his patent rights during the entire term of the patent. Given that starting point, it followed that any exception to Article 28.1 rights would constitute "prejudice" to the legitimate interests of a patent owner. Consequently, the remainder of the EC's argument concentrated on whether the prejudice was "unreasonable", an issue which in turn focused on whether the "legitimate interests of third parties" outweighed the patent owner's interests in full enjoyment of his legal rights. The EC first argued that the only relevant "third parties" for the purpose of Article 30 are the patent owner's competitors—in the case of pharmaceutical patents the generic drug producers, because they were the only parties with interests adverse to those of patent owners. According to the EC's view, the TRIPS Agreement constitutes a recognition that patent systems serve the interest of the society, including the multiple interests of its health policy. That being so, the patent rights granted by that Agreement, being a part of the balance of rights and obligations that governments have agreed to as beneficial, cannot be found to be adverse to, or in conflict with, the interests represented by general social welfare policy. And that, in turn, means that the only adverse third party interests to patent owners are the interests of those firms with whom they compete.

7.63   Then, following its position that "legitimate interests" are essentially legal interests, the EC went on to argue that the legitimate interests of competing producers are essentially the same as those of patent owners—that is, the full enjoyment of their legal rights. The legal rights of the patent owner's competitors, the EC argues, are the rights to make, use or sell the patented product on the day *after* the patent expires. Such competitors, therefore, could have no "legitimate" interest in the rights granted by the regulatory review exception of Section 55.2(1), because they could have no legal right to "make" or "use" (or "sell") the patented product during the term of the patent.

7.64   Given these interpretations of the third condition of Article 30, the EC concluded: (1) that the impairment of the patent owner's Article 28 legal rights by the regulatory review exception amounts to "prejudice" to the patent owner's legitimate interests; and (2) that in the absence of any legitimate third party interest to the contrary, the abrogation of rights authorized by Section 55.2(1) is substantial enough to be characterized as "unreasonable".

* * *

7.68   The word "legitimate" is commonly defined as follows:

(a) Conformable to, sanctioned or authorized by, law or principle: lawful; justifiable; proper;

(b) Normal, regular, conformable to a recognized standard type.

Although the European Communities' definition equating "legitimate interests" with a full respect of legal interests pursuant to Article 28.1 is within at least some of these definitions, the EC definition makes it difficult to make sense of the rest of the third condition of Article 30, in at least three respects. First, since by that definition every exception under Article 30 will be causing "prejudice" to some legal rights provided by Article 28 of the Agreement, that definition would reduce the first part of the third condition to a simple requirement that the proposed exception must not be "unreasonable". Such a requirement could certainly have been expressed more directly if that was what was meant. Second, a definition equating "legitimate interests" with legal interests makes no sense at all when applied to the final phrase of Article 30 referring to the "legitimate interests" of third parties. Third parties are by definition parties who have no legal right at all in being able to perform the tasks excluded by Article 28 patent rights. An exceptions clause permitting governments to take account of such third party legal interests would be permitting them to take account of nothing. And third, reading the third condition as a further protection of legal rights would render it essentially redundant in light of the very similar protection of legal rights in the first condition of Article 30 ("limited exception").

7.69   To make sense of the term "legitimate interests" in this context, that term must be defined in the way that it is often used in legal discourse—as a normative claim calling for protection of interests that are "justifiable" in the sense that they are supported by relevant public policies or other social norms. This is the sense of the word that often appears in statements such as "X has no legitimate interest in being able to do Y". We may take as an illustration one of the most widely adopted Article 30–type exceptions in national patent laws—the exception under which use of the patented product for scientific experimentation, during the term of the patent and without consent, is not an infringement. It is often argued that this exception is based on the notion that a key public policy purpose underlying patent laws is to facilitate the dissemination and advancement of technical knowledge and that allowing the patent owner to prevent experimental use during the term of the patent would frustrate part of the purpose of the requirement that the nature of the invention be disclosed to the public. To the contrary, the argument concludes, under the policy of the patent laws, both society and the scientist have a "legitimate interest" in using the patent disclosure to support the advance of science and technology. While the Panel draws no conclusion about the correctness of any such national exceptions in terms of Article 30 of the TRIPS Agreement, it does adopt the general meaning of the term "legitimate interests" contained in legal analysis of this type.

7.70   The negotiating history of the TRIPS Agreement itself casts no further illumination on the meaning of the term "legitimate interests", but the negotiating history of Article 9(2) of the Berne Convention, from which the text of the third condition was clearly drawn, does tend to affirm the Panel's interpretation of that term. With regard to the TRIPS negotiations themselves, the meaning of several important drafting changes turns out to be equivocal upon closer examination. The negotiating records of the TRIPS Agreement itself show that the first drafts of the provision that was to become Article 30 contemplated authorizing "limited exceptions" that would be defined by an illustrative list of exceptions—private use, scientific use, prior use, a traditional exception for pharmacists, and the like. Eventually, this illustrative list approach was abandoned in favour of a more general authorization following the outlines of the present Article 30. The negotiating records of the TRIPS Agreement give no explanation of the reason for this decision.

7.71   The text of the present, more general version of Article 30 of the TRIPS Agreement was obviously based on the text of Article 9(2) of the Berne Convention. Berne Article 9(2) deals with exceptions to the copyright holder's right to exclude reproduction of its copyrighted work without permission. The text of Article 9(2) is as follows:

> "It shall be a matter for legislation in the countries of the Union to permit the reproduction of [literary and artistic] works in certain special cases, provided that such reproduction does not conflict with a normal exploitation of the work and does not unreasonably prejudice the legitimate interests of the author."

The text of Berne Article 9(2) was not adopted into Article 30 of the TRIPS Agreement without change. Whereas the final condition in Berne Article 9(2) ("legitimate interests") simply refers to the legitimate interests of the author, the TRIPS negotiators added in Article 30 the instruction that account must be taken of "the legitimate interests of third parties". Absent further explanation in the records of the TRIPS negotiations, however, the Panel was not able to attach a substantive meaning to this change other than what is already obvious in the text itself, namely that the reference to the "legitimate interests of third parties" makes sense only if the term "legitimate interests" is construed as a concept broader than legal interests.

7.72   With regard to the meaning of Berne Article 9(2) itself, the Panel examined the drafting committee report that is usually cited as the most authoritative explanation of what Article 9(2) means. The drafting committee report states:

> "If it is considered that reproduction conflicts with the normal exploitation of the work, reproduction is not permitted at all. If it is considered that reproduction does not conflict with the normal exploitation of the work, the next step would be to consider whether it does not unreasonably prejudice the legitimate interests of the author. Only if such is not the case would it be possible in certain special cases to introduce a compulsory license, or to provide for use without payment. A practical example may be photocopying for various purposes. If it consists of producing a very large number of copies, it may not be permitted, as it conflicts with a normal exploitation of the work. If it implies a rather large number of copies for use in industrial undertakings, it may not unreasonably prejudice the legitimate interests of the author, provided that, according to national legislation, an equitable remuneration is paid. If a small number of copies is made, photocopying may be permitted without payment, particularly for individual or scientific use."

The Panel recognized that the drafting committee's examples concern the area of copyright as opposed to patents, and that, even further, they deal with the situation as it was in 1967, and accordingly the Panel was reluctant to read too much into these examples as guides to the meaning of Article 30. But the Panel did find that the concepts of "normal exploitation" and "legitimate interests" underlying the three examples used by the drafting committee were consistent with the Panel's definitions of these concepts and of the differences between them.

7.73 In sum, after consideration of the ordinary meaning of the term "legitimate interests", as it is used in Article 30, the Panel was unable to accept the EC's interpretation of that term as referring to legal interests pursuant to Article 28.1. Accordingly, the Panel was unable to accept the primary EC argument with regard to the third condition of Article 30. It found that the EC argument based solely on the patent owner's legal rights pursuant to Article 28.1, without reference to any more particular normative claims of interest, did not raise a relevant claim of non-compliance with the third condition of Article 30.

7.74 After reaching the previous conclusion concerning the EC's primary argument under the "legitimate interests" condition of Article 30, the Panel then directed its attention to another line of argument raised in statements made by the EC and by one third party. This second line of argument called attention to the fact that patent owners whose innovative products are subject to marketing approval requirements suffer a loss of economic benefits to the extent that delays in obtaining government approval prevent them from marketing their product during a substantial part of the patent term. According to information supplied by Canada, regulatory approval of new pharmaceuticals usually does not occur until approximately eight to 12 years after the patent application has been filed, due to the time needed to complete development of the product and the time needed to comply with the regulatory procedure itself. The result in the case of pharmaceuticals, therefore, is that the innovative producer is in fact able to market its patented product in only the remaining eight to 12 years of the 20–year patent term, thus receiving an effective period of market exclusivity that is only 40–60 per cent of the period of exclusivity normally envisaged in a 20–year patent term. The EC argued that patent owners who suffer a reduction of effective market exclusivity from such delays should be entitled to impose the same type of delay in connection with corresponding regulatory requirements upon the market entry of competing products. According to the EC,

> "[T]here exists no reason why the research based pharmaceutical enterprise is obliged to accept the economic consequence of patent term erosion because of marketing approval requirements which reduce their effective term of protection to 12–8 years while the copy producer should be entirely compensated for the economic consequence of the need of marketing approval for his generic product, and at the expense of the inventor and patent holder".

Applied to the regulatory review exception, this argument called for the removal of such exceptions so that patent owners may use their exclusionary patent rights to prevent competitors from engaging in product development and initiating the regulatory review process until the patent has expired. The result of removing the exception would be to allow patent owners to create a period of further, de facto market exclusivity after the expiration of the patent, for the length of time it would take competing producers to complete product development and obtain marketing approval.

7.75 The normative claim being made in this second argument ultimately rested on a claim of equal treatment for all patent owners. The policy of the patent laws, the argument would run, is to give innovative producers the advantage of market exclusivity during the 20–year term of the patent. Although patent laws do not guarantee that patent owners will obtain economic benefits from this opportunity, most patent owners have at least the legal opportunity to market the patented product during all or virtually all this 20–year period of market exclusivity. Producers whose products are subject to regulatory approval requirements may be deprived of this opportunity for a substantial part of the 20–year period.

7.76 Under the Panel's interpretation of Article 30, this argument could be characterized as a claim of "legitimate interest" under the third condition of Article 30. It was distinct from the claim made under the second condition of Article 30 ("normal exploitation"), because it did not rest on a claim of interest in the "normal" means of extracting commercial benefits from a patent. Instead, it was a distinctive claim of interest, resting on a distinctive situation applicable only to patent owners affected by marketing approval requirements, asking for an additional means of exploitation, above and beyond "normal exploitation," to compensate for the distinctive disadvantage claimed to be suffered by this particular group of claimants.

7.77 The Panel therefore examined whether the claimed interest should be considered a "legitimate interest" within the meaning of Article 30. The primary issue was whether the normative basis of that claim rested on a widely recognized policy norm.

7.78 The type of normative claim put forward by the EC has been affirmed by a number of governments that have enacted de jure extensions of the patent term, primarily in the case of pharmaceutical products, to compensate for the de facto diminution of the normal period of market exclusivity due to delays in obtaining marketing approval. According to the information submitted to the Panel, such extensions have been enacted by the European Communities, Switzerland, the United States, Japan, Australia and Israel. The EC and Switzerland have done so while at the same time allowing patent owners to continue to use their exclusionary rights to gain an additional, de facto extension of market exclusivity by preventing competitors from applying for regulatory approval during the term of the patent. The other countries that have enacted de jure patent term extensions have also, either by legislation or by judicial decision, created a regulatory review exception similar to

Section 55.2(1), thereby eliminating the possibility of an additional de facto extension of market exclusivity.

7.79 This positive response to the claim for compensatory adjustment has not been universal, however. In addition to Canada, several countries have adopted, or are in the process of adopting, regulatory review exceptions similar to Section 55.2(1) of the Canadian Patent Act, thereby removing the de facto extension of market exclusivity, but these countries have not enacted, and are not planning to enact, any *de jure* extensions of the patent term for producers adversely affected by delayed marketing approval. When regulatory review exceptions are enacted in this manner, they represent a decision not to restore any of the period of market exclusivity due to lost delays in obtaining marketing approval. Taken as a whole, these government decisions may represent either disagreement with the normative claim made by the EC in this proceeding, or they may simply represent a conclusion that such claims are outweighed by other equally legitimate interests.

7.80 In the present proceeding, Canada explicitly disputed the legitimacy of the claimed interest. As noted above, Canada appeared to interpret the term "legitimate interests" in accordance with the Panel's view of that term as a widely recognized normative standard. Canada asserted:

> "[N]otwithstanding the private economic advantage that would be obtained by doing so, a patentee can have no legitimate interest deriving from patent law in exercising its exclusive use and enforcement rights within the term of protection to achieve, through exploitation of regulatory review laws, a *de facto* extension of that term of protection beyond the prescribed period, thereby unilaterally altering the bargain between the patentee and society. In this respect, the interests of a patentee of a pharmaceutical invention can be no different from those of patentees in other fields of technology."

7.81 Canada's argument that all fields of technology must be treated the same implicitly rejected the EC's argument that those fields of technology affected by marketing approval requirements should be given certain additional marketing advantages in compensation. Canada was asked by the Panel to explain the distinction between its decision in Section 55.2(1) to remove the delay in obtaining marketing approval for competitive producers seeking to enter the market after the patent expires and its decision not to correct or compensate for the similar delay encountered by the patent owner himself. Canada responded that the de facto diminution of the market exclusivity for patent owners was an unavoidable consequence of the time required to ensure and to demonstrate the safety and efficacy of the product, whereas the delay imposed on competitors by use of the patent rights to block product development and initiation of the regulatory review process during the term of the patent was neither necessary to product safety nor otherwise an appropriate use of patent rights. Canada's answer implied a further question as to the extent to which the marketing delays experienced by patent owners were in fact the result of government regulatory action, as opposed to the normal consequence of the necessary course of product development for products of this kind.

7.82   On balance, the Panel concluded that the interest claimed on behalf of patent owners whose effective period of market exclusivity had been reduced by delays in marketing approval was neither so compelling nor so widely recognized that it could be regarded as a "legitimate interest" within the meaning of Article 30 of the TRIPS Agreement. Notwithstanding the number of governments that had responded positively to that claimed interest by granting compensatory patent term extensions, the issue itself was of relatively recent standing, and the community of governments was obviously still divided over the merits of such claims. Moreover, the Panel believed that it was significant that concerns about regulatory review exceptions in general, although well known at the time of the TRIPS negotiations, were apparently not clear enough, or compelling enough, to make their way explicitly into the recorded agenda of the TRIPS negotiations. The Panel believed that Article 30's "legitimate interests" concept should not be used to decide, through adjudication, a normative policy issue that is still obviously a matter of unresolved political debate.

7.83   Consequently, having considered the two claims of "legitimate interest" put forward by the EC, and having found that neither of these claimed interests can be considered "legitimate interests" within the meaning of the third condition of Article 30 of the TRIPS Agreement, the Panel concluded that Canada had demonstrated to the Panel's satisfaction that Section 55.2(1) of Canada's Patent Act did not prejudice "legitimate interests" of affected patent owners within the meaning of Article 30.

7.84   Having reviewed the conformity of Section 55.2(1) with each of the three conditions for an exception under Article 30 of the TRIPS Agreement, the Panel concluded that Section 55.2(1) does satisfy all three conditions of Article 30, and thus is not inconsistent with Canada's obligations under Article 28.1 of the TRIPS Agreement.

Article 27.1 of the TRIPS Agreement

7.85   The EC claimed that Section 55.2(1) of the Canada Patent Act is also in conflict with the obligations under Article 27.1 of the TRIPS Agreement. Article 27.1 provides:

"Article 27

Patentable Subject Matter

1.   Subject to the provisions of paragraphs 2 and 3, patents shall be available for any inventions, whether products or processes, in all fields of technology, provided that they are new, involve an inventive step and are capable of industrial application. Subject to paragraph 4 of Article 65, paragraph 8 of Article 70 and paragraph 3 of this

Article, *patents shall be available and patent rights enjoyable without discrimination as to the place of invention, the field of technology and whether products are imported or locally produced.*" (emphasis added)

7.86   The EC argued that the anti-discrimination rule stated in the italicized language in the text of Article 27.1 above not only requires that the core patent rights made available under Article 28 be non-discriminatory, but also requires that any exceptions to those basic rights made under Articles 30 and 31 must be non-discriminatory as well. Thus, the EC concluded, Article 27.1 requires that the exception made by Section 55.2(1) must be non-discriminatory. The EC contended that Section 55.2(1) does not comply with the obligations of Article 27.1, because it is limited, both *de jure* and de facto, to pharmaceutical products alone, and thus discriminates by field of technology.

7.87   Canada advanced two defences to the EC's claim of an Article 27.1 violation. First, Canada argued that the non-discrimination rule of Article 27.1 does not apply to exceptions taken under Article 30. Second, Canada argued that Section 55.2(1) does not discriminate against pharmaceutical products. The Panel examined these two defences in order.

7.88   Canada took the position that Article 27.1's reference to "patent rights" that must be enjoyable without discrimination as to field of technology refers to the basic rights enumerated in Article 28.1 subject to any exceptions that might be made under Article 30. In other words, governments may discriminate when making the "limited" exceptions allowed under Article 30, but they may not discriminate as to patent rights as modified by such exceptions.

7.89   In support of this position, Canada argued that the scope of Article 30 would be reduced to insignificance if governments were required to treat all fields of technology the same, for if all exceptions had to apply to every product it would be far more difficult to meet the requirement that Article 30 exceptions be "limited". It would also be more difficult to target particular social problems, as are anticipated, according to Canada, by Articles 7 and 8 of the TRIPS Agreement. Conversely, Canada argued, requiring that exceptions be applied to all products would cause needless deprivation of patent rights for those products as to which full enforcement of patent rights causes no problem.

7.90   Canada acknowledged that there are certain textual difficulties with this position. It acknowledged that two of the primary purposes of Article 27.1 were to eliminate two types of discrimination that had been practised against pharmaceuticals and certain other products— either a denial of patentability for such products, or, if patents were granted, automatic compulsory licences permitting others to manufacture such products for a fee. Canada acknowledged that, in order to preclude discrimination as to compulsory licences, the non-discrimination rule of Article 27 was made applicable to Article 31 of the TRIPS Agreement, which grants a limited exception for compulsory licences under specified conditions. To defend its position, therefore, Canada was required to explain how Article 27.1 could apply to exceptions made under Article 31, but not to exceptions made under its neighbouring exception provision in Article 30. Canada argued that Article 31 was "mandatory" in character while Article 30 was "permissive," and that this distinction made it appropriate to apply the non-discrimination provision to the former but not the latter.

7.91   The Panel was unable to agree with Canada's contention that Article 27.1 did not apply to exceptions granted under Article 30. The text of the TRIPS Agreement offers no support for such an interpretation. Article 27.1 prohibits discrimination as to enjoyment of "patent rights" without qualifying that term. Article 30 exceptions are explicitly described as "exceptions to the exclusive rights conferred by a patent" and contain no indication that any exemption from non-discrimination rules is intended. A discriminatory exception that takes away enjoyment of a patent right is discrimination as much as is discrimination in the basic rights themselves. The acknowledged fact that the Article 31 exception for compulsory licences and government use is understood to be subject to the non-discrimination rule of Article 27.1, without the need for any textual provision so providing, further strengthens the case for treating the non-discrimination rules as applicable to Article 30. Articles 30 and 31 are linked together by the opening words of Article 31 which define the scope of Article 31 in terms of exceptions not covered by Article 30. Finally, the Panel could not agree with Canada's attempt to distinguish between Articles 30 and 31 on the basis of their mandatory/permissive character; both provisions permit exceptions to patent rights subject to certain mandatory conditions. Nor could the Panel understand how such a "mandatory/permissive" distinction, even if present, would logically support making the kind of distinction Canada was arguing. In the Panel's view, what was important was that in the rights available under national law, that is to say those resulting from the basic rights and any permissible exceptions to them, the forms of discrimination referred to in Article 27.1 should not be present.

7.92   Nor was the Panel able to agree with the policy arguments in support of Canada's interpretation of Article 27. To begin with, it is not true that being able to discriminate against particular patents will make it possible to meet Article 30's requirement that the exception be "limited". An Article 30 exception cannot be made "limited" by limiting it to one field of technology, because the effects of each exception must be found to be "limited" when measured against each affected patent. Beyond that, it is not true that Article 27 requires all Article 30 exceptions to be applied to all products. Article 27 prohibits only discrimination as to the place of invention, the field of technology, and whether products are imported or produced locally. Article 27 does not prohibit bona fide exceptions to deal with problems that may exist only in certain product areas. Moreover, to the extent the prohibition of discrimination does limit the ability to target certain products in dealing with certain of the important national policies referred to in Articles 7 and 8.1, that fact may well constitute a deliberate limitation rather than a frustration of purpose. It is quite plausible, as the EC argued, that the TRIPS Agreement would want to require governments to apply exceptions in a nondiscriminatory manner, in order to ensure that governments do not succumb to domestic pressures to limit exceptions to areas where right holders tend to be foreign producers.

7.93   The Panel concluded, therefore, that the anti-discrimination rule of Article 27.1 does apply to exceptions of the kind authorized by Article 30. We turn, accordingly, to the question of whether Section 55.2(1) of the Canadian Patent Act discriminates as to fields of technology.

7.94   The primary TRIPS provisions that deal with discrimination, such as the national treatment and most-favoured-nation provisions of Articles 3 and 4, do not use the term "discrimination". They speak in more precise terms. The ordinary meaning of the word "discriminate" is potentially broader than these more specific definitions. It certainly extends beyond the concept of differential treatment. It is a normative term, pejorative in connotation, referring to results of the unjustified imposition of differentially disadvantageous treatment. Discrimination may arise from explicitly different treatment, sometimes called "*de jure* discrimination", but it may also arise from ostensibly identical treatment which, due to differences in circumstances, produces differentially disadvantageous effects, sometimes called "de facto discrimination". The standards by which the justification for differential treatment is measured are a subject of infinite complexity. "Discrimination" is a term to be avoided whenever more precise standards are available, and, when employed, it is a term to be interpreted with caution, and with care to add no more precision than the concept contains.

* * *

7.99   With regard to the issue of *de jure* discrimination, the Panel concluded that the European Communities had not presented sufficient evidence to raise the issue in the face of Canada's formal declaration that the exception of Section 55.2(1) was not limited to pharmaceutical products. Absent other evidence, the words of the statute compelled the Panel to accept Canada's assurance that the exception was legally available to every product that was subject to marketing approval requirements. In reaching this conclusion, the Panel took note that its legal finding of conformity on this point was based on a finding as to the meaning of the Canadian law that was in turn based on Canada's representations as to the meaning of that law, and that this finding of conformity would no longer be warranted if, and to the extent that, Canada's representations as to the meaning of that law were to prove wrong.

7.100   The Panel then turned to the question of de facto discrimination. Although the EC's response to the Panel's questions indicated that it did intend to raise the issue of de facto discrimination, the EC did not propose a formal definition of de facto discrimination, nor did it submit a systematic exposition of the evidence satisfying the elements of such a concept. Australia and the United States, third parties in the proceedings, referred to previous GATT and WTO legal rulings treating de facto discrimination, but primarily for the purpose of suggesting the mirror image principle—that not all differential treatment is "discrimination". Canada did not associate itself with the Australian and United States positions. Notwithstanding the limited development of the arguments on the issue of de facto discrimination, the Panel concluded that its terms of reference required it to pursue that issue once raised, and accordingly the Panel proceeded to examine the claim of a de facto discrimination violation on the basis of its own examination of the record in the light of the concepts usually associated with claims of de facto discrimination.

7.101   As noted above, de facto discrimination is a general term describing the legal conclusion that an ostensibly neutral measure transgresses a non-discrimination norm because its actual effect is to impose differentially disadvantageous consequences on certain parties, and because those differential effects are found to be wrong or unjustifiable. Two main issues figure in the application of that general concept in most legal systems. One is the question of de facto discriminatory effect— whether the actual effect of the measure is to impose differentially disadvantageous consequences on certain parties. The other, related to the justification for the disadvantageous effects, is the issue of purpose— not an inquiry into the subjective purposes of the officials responsible for the measure, but an inquiry into the objective characteristics of the measure from which one can infer the existence or non-existence of discriminatory objectives.

7.102   With regard to the first issue—the actual effects of the measure, the EC had argued that, despite its potentially broad coverage of many industries, the exception created by Section 55.2(1) had "in effect" applied only to pharmaceutical patents. The Panel received no systematic information on the range of industries that have actually made use of Section 55.2(1). In the absence of such information, the critical question was whether there was some practical reason why the regulatory review exception would in reality work only to the disadvantage of producers of patented pharmaceutical products. The Panel asked the parties for an explanation of any practical considerations that would limit the scope of application of Section 55.2(1) to pharmaceutical products, but no such explanation was provided. Nor was the Panel able to find such a practical reason from the information before it. The Panel concluded that the EC had not demonstrated that Section 55.2(1) had had a discriminatory effect limited to patented pharmaceutical products.

7.103   On the issue of discriminatory purpose, the EC had stressed on several occasions that, in the public discussion of Section 55.2(1), all relevant participants had been exclusively concerned with the impact of the measure on pharmaceutical products, with both support and opposition to the measure being argued in terms of that one dimension. Canada did not contest this characterization of the public debates.

7.104   The Panel did not find this evidence from the debates on Section 55.2(1) to be persuasive evidence of a discriminatory purpose. To be sure, such evidence makes it clear that the primary reason for passing the measure was its effect on promoting competition in the pharmaceutical sector. This is also evident from Canada's justification for the measure presented in this dispute settlement proceeding. But preoccupation with the effects of a statute in one area does not necessarily mean that the provisions applicable to other areas are a sham, or of no actual or potential importance. Individual problems are frequently the driving force behind legislative actions of broader scope. The broader scope of the measure usually reflects an important legal principle that rules being applied in the area of primary interest should also be applied to other areas where the same problem occurs. Indeed, it is a common desideratum in many legal systems that legislation apply its underlying principles as broadly as possible. So long as the broader application is not a sham, the legislation cannot be considered discriminatory. In the absence of any proof that the broader scope was a sham, it must be found that the evident concentration of public attention upon the effects of Section 55.2(1) on the pharmaceutical industry is not, by itself, evidence of a discriminatory purpose.

7.105   In sum, the Panel found that the evidence in record before it did not raise a plausible claim of discrimination under Article 27.1 of the TRIPS Agreement. It was not proved that the legal scope of Section 55.2(1) was limited to pharmaceutical products, as would normally be required to raise a claim of *de jure* discrimination. Likewise, it was not proved that the adverse effects of Section 55.2(1) were limited to the pharmaceutical industry, or that the objective indications of purpose demonstrated a purpose to impose disadvantages on pharmaceutical patents in particular, as is often required to raise a claim of de facto discrimination. Having found that the record did not raise any of these basic elements of a discrimination claim, the Panel was able to find that Section 55.2(1) is not inconsistent with Canada's obligations under Article 27.1 of the TRIPS Agreement. Because the record did not present issues requiring any more precise interpretation of the term "discrimination" in Article 27.1, none was made.

Notes and Questions

(1) Canada did not appeal the decision. It has since amended its patent law to comply with the ruling.

(2) The regulatory review exception allows the manufacturers of generic drugs to enter the market quickly after the patent on the competing drug expires (by securing regulatory approval in advance of the expiration date). Without it, a period of several years might be needed after the expiration of the patent to secure approval of the generic product. By contrast, the stockpiling exception simply allows manufacturing of the generic product starting six months before the expiration of the patent, and thus facilitates generic entry a few months earlier than otherwise at most (assuming that regulatory approval has been secured). As a practical matter, therefore, the

regulatory review exception seems more important to the facilitation of quick generic entry than the stockpiling exception, and can be expected to impose far greater economic costs on the holders of pharmaceutical patents. In light of these facts about their relative economic impact, has the Panel given a coherent explanation of why the regulatory review exception is "limited" but the stockpiling exception is not? What reading of "limited" is to be given if it is uncorrelated with the economic impact of the exception on the patent holder? Would it make more sense to treat the negotiating history presented by Canada, and the proliferation of regulatory review exceptions in national legislation, as the key to the finding on this issue?

(3) Is it not "normal" for patent holders to enforce their rights so as to delay competition as long as possible? Why is it not "legitimate" for pharmaceutical patent holders to enforce their rights to delay generic competition, especially when much of the life of their patent is consumed by the clinical trials and regulatory hurdles that they must surmount before they can obtain regulatory approval and begin to sell the drug?

(4) Were you satisfied with the Panel's response to the claim that the regulatory review exception is *de facto* discriminatory?

(5) A rather similar dispute, involving the "limited exceptions" permitted to copyright protection under Article 13, was the following.

UNITED STATES—SECTION 110(5) OF THE US COPYRIGHT ACT

WT/DS160/R.
Panel Report adopted July 27, 2000.

2.1   The dispute concerns Section 110(5) of the US Copyright Act of 1976, as amended * * *. The provisions of Section 110(5) place limitations on the exclusive rights provided to owners of copyright in Section 106 of the Copyright Act in respect of certain performances and displays.

* * *

2.9   The 1998 Amendment has added a new subparagraph (B) to Section 110(5), to which we, for the sake of brevity, hereinafter refer to as a "business" exemption. It exempts, under certain conditions, communication by an establishment of a transmission or retransmission embodying a performance or display of a nondramatic musical work intended to be received by the general public, originated by a radio or television broadcast station licensed as such by the Federal Communications Commission, or, if an audiovisual transmission, by a cable system or satellite carrier.

2.10   The beneficiaries of the business exemption are divided into two categories: establishments other than food service or drinking establishments ("retail establishments"), and food service and drinking establishments. In each category, establishments under a certain size limit are exempted, regardless of the type of equipment they use. The size limits are 2,000 gross square feet (186 m2) for retail establishments and 3,750 gross square feet (348 m2) for restaurants.

* * *

2.12   In 1999, Dun & Bradstreet, Inc. * * * estimated that 70 per cent of eating establishments and 73 per cent of drinking establishments fell under the 3,750 square feet limit, and that 45 per cent of retail establishments fell under the 2,000 square feet limit.

* * *

2.14   If the size of an establishment is above the limits referred to in paragraph 2.10 above (there is no maximum size), the exemption applies provided that the establishment does not exceed the limits set for the equipment used. The limits on equipment are different as regards, on the one hand, audio performances, and, on the other hand, audiovisual performances and displays. The rules concerning equipment limitations are the same for both retail establishments and restaurants above the respective size limits.

* * *

6.30   A major issue in this dispute is the interpretation and application to the facts of this case of Article 13 of the TRIPS Agreement. The US defense is firmly based upon it. The United States submits that the Article clarifies and articulates the "minor exceptions" doctrine applicable under certain provisions of the Berne Convention (1971) and incorporated into the TRIPS Agreement. * * *

[Eds. note: The panel next proceeds through a lengthy discussion of the Berne Convention and its relationship to the TRIPS Agreement, after which it finds:]

6.94   We conclude that Article 13 of the TRIPS Agreement applies to Articles 11*bis*(1)(iii) and 11(1)(ii) of the Berne Convention (1971) as incorporated into the TRIPS Agreement, given that neither the express wording nor the context of Article 13 or any other provision of the TRIPS Agreement supports the interpretation that the scope of application of Article 13 is limited to the exclusive rights newly introduced under the TRIPS Agreement.

* * *

6.97   Article 13 of the TRIPS Agreement requires that limitations and exceptions to exclusive rights (1) be confined to certain special cases, (2) do not conflict with a normal exploitation of the work, and (3) do not unreasonably prejudice the legitimate interests of the right holder. * * *

* * *

6.103   The United States submits that the fact that the TRIPS Agreement does not elaborate on the criteria for a case to be considered "special" provides Members flexibility to determine for themselves whether a particular case represents an appropriate basis for an exception. But it acknowledges that the essence of the first condition is that the exceptions be well-defined and of limited application.

* * *

6.107   We start our analysis of the first condition of Article 13 by referring to the ordinary meaning of the terms in their context and in the light of its object and purpose. It appears that the notions of "exceptions" and "limitations" in the introductory words of Article 13 overlap in part in the sense that an "exception" refers to a derogation from an exclusive right provided under national legislation in some respect, while a "limitation" refers to a reduction of such right to a certain extent.

6.108   The ordinary meaning of "certain" is "known and particularised, but not explicitly identified", "determined, fixed, not variable; definitive, precise, exact". In other words, this term means that, under the first condition, an exception or limitation in national legislation must be clearly defined. However, there is no need to identify explicitly each and every possible situation to which the exception could apply, provided that the scope of the exception is known and particularised. This guarantees a sufficient degree of legal certainty.

6.109   We also have to give full effect to the ordinary meaning of the second word of the first condition. The term "special" connotes "having an individual or limited application or purpose", "containing details; precise, specific", "exceptional in quality or degree; unusual; out of the ordinary" or "distinctive in some way". This term means that more is needed than a clear definition in order to meet the standard of the first condition. In addition, an exception or limitation must be limited in its field of application or exceptional in its scope. In other words, an exception or limitation should be narrow in quantitative as well as a qualitative sense. This suggests a narrow scope as well as an exceptional or distinctive objective. To put this aspect of the first condition into the context of the second condition ("no conflict with a normal exploitation"), an exception or limitation should be the opposite of a non-special, i.e., a normal case.

* * *

6.113   In the case at hand, in order to determine whether subparagraph (B) * * * Section 110(5) [is] confined to "certain special cases", we first examine whether the exceptions have been clearly defined. Second, we ascertain whether the exemptions are narrow in scope, *inter alia*, with respect to their reach. In that respect, we take into account what percentage of eating and drinking establishments and retail establishments may benefit from the business exemption under subparagraph (B) * * *. On a subsidiary basis, we consider whether it is possible to draw inferences about the reach of the business . . . exemption from the stated policy purposes underlying these exemptions according to the statements made during the US legislative process.

6.114   As noted above, the United States argues that the essence of the first condition of Article 13 of the TRIPS Agreement is that exceptions be well-defined and of limited application. It claims that the business exemption of subparagraph (B) meets the requirements of the first condition of Article 13, because it is clearly defined in Section 110(5) of the US Copyright Act by square footage and equipment limitations.

* * *

6.116   The European Communities contends that the business exemption is too broad in its scope to pass as a "certain special case", given the large number of establishments which potentially may benefit from it. For the European Communities, it is irrelevant that the size of establishments and the type of equipment are clearly defined, when the broad scope of the business exemption turns an exception into the rule.

6.117   It appears that the European Communities does not dispute the fact that subparagraph (B) is clearly defined in respect of the size limits of establishments and the type of equipment that may be used by establishments above the applicable limits. The primary bone of contention between the parties is whether the business exemption, given its scope and reach, can be considered as a "special" case within the meaning of the first condition of Article 13.

* * *

6.133   The factual information presented to us indicates that a substantial majority of eating and drinking establishments and close to half of retail establishments are covered by the exemption contained in subparagraph (B) of Section 110(5) of the US Copyright Act. Therefore, we conclude that the exemption does not qualify as a "certain special case" in the meaning of the first condition of Article 13.

Notes and Questions

(1) The brief excerpt above omits discussion of the other limitations contained in Article 13. The panel found that the business exception also "conflict[s] with a normal exploitation" of the rights of copyright holders, and that it "unreasonably prejudice[s] the legitimate interests of the right holder[s]." By contrast, the "homestyle exemption" under US copyright law, which provides that smaller establishments may expose their customers to certain broadcasts over "homestyle" receiving equipment without having to obtain a license from the copyright holder, was found by the Panel to be permissible under Article 13.

(2) The United States did not appeal the decision, but conforming changes to the US copyright law have not been made at this writing. Instead, the US and the EC arbitrated the level of nullification or impairment under DSU Article 25 and entered into a temporary compensation agreement pursuant to which the US paid the EC $3.3 million to compensate for lost royalties for the three-year period ending December 20, 2004. The case thus represents an interesting use of "monetary compensation" in the system, and leads to the further question whether monetary compensation might usefully play a larger role. See Section 7.5 supra on DSU remedies.

(3) Compare the *Canada Pharmaceutical Patents* case to the *US Section 110(5) Copyright Act* case. Is the difference in the language of Articles 13 and 30 critical to the difference in outcomes (regarding the regulatory review

exception and the business exception)? Are they consistent as a policy matter in your view?

(4) A much publicized dispute, involving a long-running trademark battle between the US company Bacardi and the French company Pernod, is the so-called "Havana Club" case. Havana Club is a brand of rum originally made in Cuba. The Castro regime expropriated the production facilities of the family that produced Havana Club rum, and that family moved to Spain. The production of Havana Club continued under the auspices of a state-owned company, but it could not be sold legally in the United States due to the US embargo on trade with Cuba. Pernod entered a joint venture with the Cuban company for the production of Havana Club, with an eye toward selling it in the United States after the embargo ended. It thus wished to register and protect the trademark in the United States. Meanwhile, Bacardi entered an arrangement with the family living in Spain that had originally held the Havana Club trademark, and began producing Havana Club rum in the Bahamas and exporting it to the United States. An extensive litigation then ensued in US court over who had the right to the Havana Club trademark (and trade name). Among other things, Pernod argued that the trademark had been "abandoned" by the original owners and hence that they had no right to license it to Bacardi.

The US Congress eventually got into the act by passing a statute designed to address some of the issues in the litigation—Section 211 of the Omnibus Appropriations Act of 1998. That statute was the subject of a complaint to the WTO. See United States—Section 211 of the Omnibus Appropriations Act of 1998, WT/DS176/AB/R, adopted January 2, 2002. Both sides claimed victory in the case. From the US perspective, many of the European claims were rejected. The case established that each nation has a right to determine in its domestic law who "owns" a trademark. The mere fact that an entity can register and enforce a mark in one WTO member state (e.g., the EC) does not automatically entitle it to be able to register and enforce it in others (such as the United States). Further, it is permissible for a nation to refuse to register and enforce trademarks that it considers to have been unlawfully expropriated. The EC did succeed in establishing, however, that the TRIPS Agreement extends protection to trade names as well as trademarks. Further, for reasons that are rather complicated, the EC prevailed on the proposition that Section 211 violated the national treatment and most-favored-nation obligations in TRIPS by creating certain additional hurdles to the enforcement of trademark and trade name rights by foreign nationals. As of this writing, the US has yet to revise Section 211.

(5) Two complaints were brought by Australia and the United States regarding EC measures relating to trademarks and geographical indications. A central component of both complaints was the argument that the EC regulations regarding the protection of geographical indications (such as "Idaho potato") violated national treatment obligations because the EC would only afford such protection to products from countries that afforded reciprocal protection to geographical indications on products from the EC. The complaints were consolidated before a single panel that ruled for Australia and the United States on this issue. See EC—Trademarks and Geographical Indications, WT/DS174 & 290/R, adopted April 20, 2005. The panel findings were not appealed.

(E) THE TRIPS AGREEMENT AND PUBLIC HEALTH: ACCESS TO ESSENTIAL MEDICINES

Among the most controversial issues to arise in connection with the TRIPS Agreement, although it has not yielded any litigation within the WTO, has been the effect of TRIPS on the prices of pharmaceuticals in developing countries.[10] The issue has been particularly prominent with regard to HIV/AIDS medications. As TRIPS obligations phased in for developing countries and they were required to give effect to all pharmaceutical patents, including process patents, the prices of certain HIV/AIDS medications either rose or were expected to rise dramatically, raising the concern that poor patients in developing countries affected by the AIDS pandemic would have no hope of affording them.

The debate over the proper response to this problem under TRIPS focused on two possibilities. The one that garnered the most attention is the possibility of "compulsory licenses." Compulsory patent licenses are used for various purposes under the domestic law of WTO members, such as to sanction patent holders who have abused their patents for anticompetitive purposes. Compulsory licenses under TRIPS are governed by Article 31, which contains three provisions of particular relevance here: (i) the prospective issuer of the compulsory license or its licensee must have made efforts (and failed) over a reasonable period of time to obtain authorization to use the patent from the right holder on reasonable commercial terms, except that this requirement may be waived in the case of a "national emergency or other circumstances of extreme urgency;" (ii) the compulsory license must be "predominately for the supply of the domestic market" of the country that grants it; and (iii) the right holder is to receive "adequate remuneration...taking into account the economic value of the authorization." These provisions open up the possibility that a developing country faced with a serious health crisis (such as the HIV/AIDS epidemic) might declare a "national emergency," and issue compulsory licenses for the production of patented pharmaceuticals with little or no prior negotiation with the patent holder. The country or the licensee would still be obliged to pay "adequate remuneration," but could perhaps argue that the appropriate level of remuneration was minimal if the pharmaceuticals were being consumed by poor citizens who could not afford to pay for them.

The requirement that production under a compulsory license be "predominantly" for the domestic market of the country that issues the license, however, poses a potential problem. Developing countries without the technical capacity to manufacture might seem to be foreclosed from the compulsory license option by this principle.

The compulsory licensing process in the pharmaceutical setting was a particular focus of the Doha ministerial meeting in 2001. The meeting

---

10. For additional discussion, see, e.g., Fred Abbott, The WTO Medicines Decision: World Pharmaceutical Trade and the Protection of Public Health, 99 Am. J. Int'l L. 317 (2005); Frederic M. Scherer, Industry Structure, Strategy and Public Policy 362–66 (1996); Alan O. Sykes, TRIPS, Pharmaceuticals, Developing Countries, and the Doha "Solution," 3 Chi. J. Int'l L. 47 (2002).

resulted in a Declaration on the TRIPS Agreement and Public Health, which provides in pertinent part:

> Each member has the right to grant compulsory licences and the freedom to determine the grounds upon which such licences are granted.

> Each member has the right to determine what constitutes a national emergency or other circumstances of extreme urgency, it being understood that public health crises, including those relating to HIV/AIDS, tuberculosis, malaria and other epidemics, can represent a national emergency or other circumstances of extreme urgency.

Thus, the Doha ministerial meeting underscored the notion that compulsory licenses could be used to address pressing public health matters, although it sidestepped the issue of "adequate remuneration" and the problem of developing countries that lack domestic manufacturing capability.

The latter issue was revisited in 2003, resulting in a waiver of the obligation to require the licensee to produce primarily for the domestic market, applicable only in cases involving pharmaceutical products. A member wishing to avail itself of the waiver must notify the WTO, and demonstrate that it lacks domestic manufacturing capacity. The waiver puts in place a number of safeguards designed to ensure that production under the compulsory license is limited to what is needed to supply the market of the member invoking the waiver, and that the production is not diverted to other markets. See General Council Decision on Implementation of Paragraph 6 of the Doha Declaration on the TRIPS Agreement and Public Health, WT/L/540, September 1, 2003. The terms of the waiver have now been converted into an amendment to the TRIPS Agreement that is presently open for ratification. At this writing, only one notification has been provided in accordance with the waiver, involving licenses for production in Canada to supply a drug to the Rwandan market.

"Parallel imports" afford another possible option for lowering pharmaceutical prices in developing countries. Article 28.1 of TRIPS gives the patent holder the exclusive right to control "making, using, offering for sale, selling, or importing" the patented product (or products made directly by a patented process). Standing alone, Article 28 seemingly allows the holder of a valid patent to prevent others from importing the patented product from another nation. If the patent holder could do that effectively, it would be able to engage in price discrimination across national markets—it could charge a higher price in country A than in country B, for example, and prevent anyone from importing the product into country A from country B to undercut the higher price in A (it could prevent price "arbitrage"). Article 6 of TRIPS provides, however, that the agreement does not resolve "the issue of the exhaustion of intellectual property rights." This cryptic statement, cross-referenced in Article 28, means that TRIPS does not dictate to national governments the circumstances under which a right holder may be deemed to have exhausted its rights through, for example, the sale of the patented product. If the initial sale of the product "exhausts" patent rights, then the patent holder would not have the right to prevent another party from reselling the product, including reselling for exportation. Such a situation opens up the possibility of price arbitrage across national markets, so that the patent holder's exports to a particular market might end up in competition with its own products sold initially in another national market at a lower price—a situation of "parallel imports." If the patent holder has no right to prevent parallel imports into a developing country (as long as the country adopts a particular posture toward the "exhaustion" issue in its domestic law), then consumers of pharmaceuticals in that country may import them from the foreign country where they are cheapest.

Notes and Questions

(1) Is there any risk that the prospect of compulsory licenses for medicines to address public health crises in developing countries might importantly dampen the incentives for pharmaceutical innovation? Consider, in particular, the incentives to develop new drugs to treat the so-called "tropical diseases" (such as malaria and sleeping sickness) that are found almost exclusively in the developing world.

(2) If you owned a pharmaceutical company that was faced with a choice between lowering your prices in a developing country or having that country issue a compulsory license to another company for the production of your patented drug, which option would you choose? More generally, would you expect many compulsory licenses to be issued in practice, or is the mere threat of compulsory licenses going to do most of the work?

(3) What is the proper interpretation of the "adequate remuneration" requirement that accompanies compulsory licensing? How does one measure the "economic value of the authorization?" If you owned a company that manufactured a product subject to a compulsory license, and believed that you had not been offered "adequate remuneration," what would your remedy be as a practical matter? Is your government likely to take the matter to the WTO?

(4) If the goal is to lower the price of patented medicines in poorer countries, are parallel imports helpful or harmful? If parallel imports are prohibited and a patent holder can price discriminate across national markets, might it not rationally charge higher prices in wealthy countries and lower prices in poorer countries? Would this pricing strategy continue in the presence of parallel imports?

(5) Consider the following hypothetical. A developing country has a terrible earthquake, and needs a great deal of money to rebuild. Its government declares a national emergency, and issues (or threatens to issue) compulsory licenses for the production of all movies, records, pharmaceuticals, electronics, and all other patented or copyrighted products sold in its territory. The licensees will be required by law to sell everything at a "break-even" price that just covers their costs. Right holders will receive only token remuneration under any compulsory licenses that are granted, and may either lower their prices to match the prices that will be offered by

the compulsory licensees, or lose all sales to the licensees. The government then imposes a tax on each product that results in a price that is identical to the price that was previously charged by the right holder, and uses the tax revenue to fund its rebuilding. In effect, the scheme converts all of the original revenues to right holders in excess of the break-even price of compulsory licensees into tax revenue for the government. Would this arrangement be acceptable under the TRIPS Agreement? Is it acceptable as a policy matter? How would you distinguish it from the use of compulsory licenses to lower the price of "essential medicines?"

SECTION 20.3   INFRINGING IMPORTS

In this section we focus on the remedies that may be available under national law to address the importation of goods that a right holder believes to be infringing its intellectual property. We begin the "gray market" problem as it has been addressed under US law, and proceed to the more generic administrative remedy for unfair import competition under Section 337 of the 1930 Tariff Act.

(A) THE GRAY MARKET PROBLEM

It has long been settled that the holder of a valid US patent can prevent the importation of infringing merchandise from abroad, even if it is lawfully produced and sold abroad. See Boesch v. Graff, 133 U.S. 697, 10 S.Ct. 378, 33 L.Ed. 787 (1890); Griffin v. Keystone Mushroom Farm, Inc., 453 F.Supp. 1283 (E.D.Pa.1978). An issue that was much more controversial for many years, and remains so to an extent, concerns the importation of trademarked goods from a foreign country when they are sold abroad legally in accordance with a valid trademark registration or license. Such goods are commonly termed "gray market" imports.

K–MART CORP. v. CARTIER, INC.

Supreme Court of the United States, 1988.
486 U.S. 281, 108 S.Ct. 1811, 100 L.Ed.2d 313.

KENNEDY, J.: A gray-market good is a foreign-manufactured good, bearing a valid United States trademark, that is imported without the consent of the United States trademark holder. These cases present the issue whether the Secretary of the Treasury's regulation permitting the importation of certain gray-market goods, 19 CFR sec. 133.21 (1987), is a reasonable agency interpretation of sec. 526 of the Tariff Act of 1930 (1930 Tariff Act), 19 U.S.C. sec. 1526.

I

[Joined by REHNQUIST, C.J. & WHITE, BLACKMUN, O'CONNOR & SCALIA, JJ.]

A

The gray market arises in any of three general contexts. The prototypical gray-market victim (case 1) is a domestic firm that purchases from an independent foreign firm the rights to register and use the latter's trademark as a United States trademark and to sell its foreign-manufactured products here. Especially where the foreign firm has already registered the trademark in the United States or where the product has already earned a reputation for quality, the right to use that trademark can be very valuable. If the foreign manufacturer could import the trademarked goods and distribute them here, despite having sold the trademark to a domestic firm, the domestic firm would be forced into sharp intrabrand competition involving the very trademark it purchased. Similar intrabrand competition could arise if the foreign manufacturer markets its wares outside the United States, as is often the case, and a third party who purchases them abroad could legally import them. In either event, the parallel importation, if permitted to proceed, would create a gray market that could jeopardize the trademark holder's investment.

The second context (case 2) is a situation in which a domestic firm registers the United States trademark for goods that are manufactured abroad by an affiliated manufacturer. In its most common variation (case 2a), a foreign firm wishes to control distribution of its wares in this country by incorporating a subsidiary here. The subsidiary then registers under its own name (or the manufacturer assigns to the subsidiary's name) a United States trademark that is identical to its parent's foreign trademark. The parallel importation by a third party who buys the goods abroad (or conceivably even by the affiliated foreign manufacturer itself) creates a gray market. Two other variations on this theme occur when an American-based firm establishes abroad a manufacturing subsidiary corporation (case 2b) or its own unincorporated manufacturing division (case 2c) to produce its United States trademarked goods, and then imports them for domestic distribution. If the trademark holder or its foreign subsidiary sells the trademarked goods abroad, the parallel importation of the goods competes on the gray market with the holder's domestic sales.

In the third context (case 3), the domestic holder of a United States trademark authorizes an independent foreign manufacturer to use it. Usually the holder sells to the foreign manufacturer an exclusive right to use the trademark in a particular foreign location, but conditions the right on the foreign manufacturer's promise not to import its trademarked goods into the United States. Once again, if the foreign manufacturer or a third party imports into the United States, the foreign-manufactured goods will compete on the gray market with the holder's domestic goods.

B

* * * Section 526 of the 1930 Tariff Act, 19 U.S.C. sec. 1526, prohibits importing "into the United States any merchandise of foreign manufacture if such merchandise ... bears a trademark owned by a citizen of, or by a corporation or association created or organized within, the United States, and registered in the Patent and Trademark Office by

a person domiciled in the United States . . ., unless written consent of the owner of such trademark is produced at the time of making entry." 19 U.S.C. sec. 1526(a).

The regulations implementing section 526 for the past 50 years have not applied the prohibition to all gray-market goods. The Customs Service regulation now in force provides generally that "[f]oreign-made articles bearing a trademark identical with one owned and recorded by a citizen of the United States or a corporation or association created or organized within the United States are subject to seizure and forfeiture as prohibited importations." But the regulation furnishes a "common-control" exception from the ban, permitting the entry of gray-market goods manufactured abroad by the trademark owner or its affiliate:

(c) Restrictions not applicable. The restrictions . . . do not apply to imported articles when:

(1) Both the foreign and the U.S. trademark or trade name are owned by the same person or business entity; [or]

(2) The foreign and domestic trademark or trade name owners are parent and subsidiary companies or are otherwise subject to common ownership or control. . . .

The Customs Service regulation further provides an "authorized-use" exception, which permits importation of gray-market goods where

(3) [t]he articles of foreign manufacture bear a recorded trademark or trade name applied under authorization of the U.S. owner. . . .

Respondents, an association of United States trademark holders and two of its members, brought suit in Federal District Court in February 1984, seeking both a declaration that the customs service regulation, 19 CFR secs. 133.21(c)(1)-(3) (1987), is invalid and an injunction against its enforcement. Coalition to Preserve the Integrity of American Trademarks v. United States, 598 F.Supp. 844 (DDC 1984). They asserted that the common-control and authorized-use exceptions are inconsistent with section 526 of the 1930 Tariff Act. Petitioners K–Mart and 47th Street Photo intervened as defendants.

The District Court upheld the Customs Service regulation, but the Court of Appeals reversed, holding that the Customs Service regulation was an unreasonable administrative interpretation of section 526. We granted certiorari to resolve a conflict among the Courts of Appeals.

A majority of this Court now holds that the common-control exception of the Customs Service regulation, section 133.21(c)(1)-(2) is consistent with section 526. See opinion of Brennan, J., below. A different majority, however, holds that the authorized-use exception, section 133.21(c)(3), is inconsistent with section 526. See opinion of Scalia, J., infra. We therefore affirm the Court of Appeals in part and reverse in part.

II

* * *

B

[Joined by WHITE, J.]

I conclude that subsections (c)(1) and (c)(2) of the Customs Service regulation are permissible constructions designed to resolve statutory ambiguities. All Members of the Court are in agreement that the agency may interpret the statute to bar importation of gray-market goods in what we have denoted case 1 and to permit the imports under case 2a. See opinions of Brennan, J. and Scalia, J. As these writings state, "owned by" is sufficiently ambiguous, in the context of the statute, that it applies to situations involving a foreign parent, which is case 2a. This ambiguity arises from the inability to discern, from the statutory language, which of the two entities involved in case 2a can be said to "own" the United States trademark if, as in some instances, the domestic subsidiary is wholly owned by its foreign parent.

A further statutory ambiguity contained in the phrase "merchandise of foreign manufacture," suffices to sustain the regulations as they apply to cases 2b and 2c. This ambiguity parallels that of "owned by," which sustained case 2a, because it is possible to interpret "merchandise of foreign manufacture" to mean (1) goods manufactured in a foreign country, (2) goods manufactured by a foreign company, or (3) goods manufactured in a foreign country by a foreign company. Given the imprecision in the statute, the agency is entitled to choose any reasonable definition and to interpret the statute to say that goods manufactured by a foreign subsidiary or division of a domestic company are not goods "of foreign manufacture."

C

[Joined by REHNQUIST, C.J., & BLACKMUN, O'CONNOR & SCALIA, JJ.]

Subsection (c)(3) of the regulation, however, cannot stand. The ambiguous statutory phrases that we have already discussed, "owned by" and "merchandise of foreign manufacture," are irrelevant to the proscription contained in subsection (3) of the regulation. This subsection of the regulation denies a domestic trademark holder the power to prohibit the importation of goods made by an independent foreign manufacturer where the domestic trademark holder has authorized the foreign manufacturer to use the trademark. Under no reasonable construction of the statutory language can goods made in a foreign country by an independent foreign manufacturer be removed from the purview of the statute.

BRENNAN, J., dissenting, with whom MARSHALL and STEVENS, JJ., join, and with whom WHITE, J., joins as to Part IV, concurring in part and dissenting in part:

* * * There is no dispute that section 526 protects the trademark holder in the first of the three gray-market contexts identified by the Court—the prototypical gray-market situation in which a domestic firm purchases from an independent foreign firm the rights to register and use in the United States a foreign trademark (case 1). The dispute in this litigation centers almost exclusively around the second context, involving a foreign manufacturer that is in some way affiliated with the United States trademark holder, whether the trademark holder is a subsidiary of (case 2a), the parent of (case 2b), or the same as (case 2c), the foreign manufacturer. The Customs Service's common-control exception denudes the trademark holder of section 526's protection in each of the foregoing cases. I concur in the Court's judgment that the common-control exception is consistent with section 526, [though I reach this conclusion for different reasons]. * * *

Also at issue, although the parties and amici give it short shrift, is the third context (case 3), in which the domestic firm authorizes an independent foreign manufacturer to use its trademark abroad. The Customs Service's authorized-use exception deprives the trademark holder of section 526's protection in such a situation. For reasons set forth in Part IV of this opinion, I dissent from the Court's judgment that the authorized-use exception is inconsistent with section 526.

I

* * *

The most blatant hint that Congress did not intend to extend section 526's protection to affiliates of foreign manufacturers (case 2) is the provision's protectionist, almost jingoist, flavor. Its structure bespeaks an intent, characteristic of the times, to protect only domestic interests. A foreign manufacturer that imports its trademarked products into the United States cannot invoke section 526 to prevent third parties from competing in the domestic market by buying the trademarked goods abroad and importing them here: The trademark is not "registered in the Patent and Trademark Office." The same manufacturer cannot protect itself against parallel importation merely by registering its trademark in the United States: It is not "a person domiciled in the United States." Nor can the manufacturer insulate itself by hiring a United States domiciliary to register the trademark: The owner is not "organized within . . . the United States." For the same reason, it will not even suffice for the foreign manufacturer to incorporate a subsidiary here to register the trademark on the parent's behalf, if the foreign parent still owns the trademark.

The barriers that Congress erected seem calculated to serve no purpose other than to reserve exclusively to domestic, not foreign, interests the extraordinary protection that section 526 provides. But they are fragile barriers indeed if a foreign manufacturer might bypass them by the simple device of incorporating a shell domestic subsidiary and transferring to it a single asset—the United States trademark. Such a reading of section 526 seems entirely at odds with the protectionist sentiment that inspired the provision. If a foreign manufacturer could insulate itself so easily from the competition of parallel imports, much of § 526's limiting language would be pointless.

The language of section 526 can reasonably be read, as the Customs Service has, to avoid such an anomaly. Section 526 defines neither "owned by" nor "of foreign manufacture," and both phrases admit of considerable ambiguity when applied to affiliates of foreign manufacturers. More specifically, in each of the disputed gray-market cases involving a domestic affiliate of a foreign manufacturer (case 2), it cannot be confidently discerned either which entity owns the trademark or whether the goods in question are "of foreign manufacture."

* * *

IV

I turn now to my small area of disagreement with the Court's judgment—the Court's conclusion that the authorized-use exception is inconsistent with the plain language of section 526. In my view, section 526 does not unambiguously protect from gray-market competition a United States trademark owner who authorizes the use of its trademark abroad by an independent manufacturer (case 3).

Unlike the variations of corporate affiliation in case 2, the ambiguity in section 526, admittedly, is not immediately apparent in case 3. In that situation, the casual reader of the statute might suppose that the domestic firm still "own[s]" its trademark. Any such supposition as to the meaning of "owned by," however, bespeaks stolid anachronism not solid analysis. It follows only from an understanding of trademark law that established itself long after the 1922 enactment and 1930 reenactment of section 526. * * *

When section 526 was before Congress, the prevailing law held that a trademark's sole purpose was to identify for consumers the product's physical source or origin. See, E.G., Macmahan Pharmacal Co. v. Denver Chemical Mfg. Co., 113 F. 468, 475 (C.A.8 1901). "Under this early 'source theory' of protection, trademark licensing was viewed as philosophically impossible, since licensing meant that the mark was being used by persons not associated with the real manufacturing 'source' in a strict, physical sense of the word." 1 McCarthy, Trademarks and Unfair Competition, at 826. * * *

Nor was it at all obvious then that a trademark owner could authorize the use of its trademark in one geographic area by selling it along with business and goodwill, while retaining ownership of the trademark in another geographic area. * * *

Not until the 1930's did a trend develop approving of trademark licensing—so long as the licensor controlled the quality of the licensee's products—on the theory that a trademark might also serve the function of identifying product quality for consumers. 1 McCarthy, Trademarks and Unfair Competition, at 827–829. And not until the passage of the Lanham Trade–Mark Act in 1946 did that trend become the rule. Similarly, it was not until well after section 526's enactment that it became clear that a trademark owner could assign rights in a particular territory along with goodwill, while retaining ownership in another distinct territory.

Manifestly, the legislators who chose the term "owned by" viewed trademark ownership differently than we view it today. Any prescient legislator who could have contemplated that a trademark owner might license the use of its trademark would almost certainly have concluded that such a transaction would divest the licensor not only of the benefit of section 526's importation prohibition, but of all trademark protection; and anyone who gave thought to the possibility that a trademark holder might assign rights to use its trademark, along with business and goodwill, to an unrelated manufacturer in another territory had good reason to expect the same result. At the very least, it seems to me plain that Congress did not address case 3 any more clearly than it addressed case 2a, 2b, or 2c. To hold otherwise is to wrench statutory words out of their legislative and historical context and treat legislation as no more than a "collection of english words" rather than "a working instrument of government...." United States v. Dotterweich, 320 U.S. 277, 280 (1943).

Justice Scalia's assertion that the foregoing analysis of case 3 is not based on the "resolution of textual 'ambiguity,'" depends on the proposition that an ancient statute is not ambiguous—and judges can never inform their interpretation with reference to legislative purpose—merely because the scope of its language has, by some fortuitous development, expanded to embrace situations that its drafters never anticipated. The proposition is unexceptionable where the postenactment development does not implicate the purpose of the statute, [but] is fallacious, however, when the postenactment development does implicate the statute's purpose.

* * *

Particularly in light of that longstanding agency interpretation, I would uphold the authorized-use exception as reasonable.

SCALIA, J., concurring in part and dissenting in part (joined by REHNQUIST, C.J. & BLACKMUN and O'CONNOR, JJ.):

I agree with the Court's analytic approach to this matter, and with its conclusion that subsection (c)(3) of the regulation is not a permissible construction. I therefore join Parts I, II–A, and II–C of the Court's opinion. In my view, however, subsections (c)(1) and (c)(2) of the regulation are also in conflict with the clear language of section 526(a). * * *

The Court observes that the statutory phrase "owned by" is ambiguous when applied to domestic subsidiaries of foreign corporations (case 2a). With this much I agree. It may be reasonable for some purposes to say that a trademark nominally owned by a domestic subsidiary is "owned by" its foreign parent corporation. This lawsuit would be different if the Customs Service regulation at issue here did no more than resolve this arguable ambiguity, by providing that a domestic subsidiary of a foreign parent could not claim the protection of section 526(a). In fact, however, that has never been asserted to be the theory of the regulation, and is assuredly not its only, or even its principal, effect. The authority to clarify an ambiguity in a statute is not the authority to alter even its unambiguous applications, and section 526(a) unambiguously encompasses most of the situations that the regulation purports to exclude.

Thus, the regulation excludes from section 526(a)'s import prohibition products bearing a domestic trademark that have been manufactured abroad by the trademark owner (case 2c), or by the trademark owner's subsidiary (case 2b). But the statutory requirement that the trademark be "owned by" a United States citizen or corporation is unambiguous with respect to these two cases. A parent corporation may or may not be said to "own" the assets owned by its subsidiary, but no matter how that ambiguity is resolved it is impossible to conclude that a trademark owned by a United States corporation and applied abroad either by the corporation or its foreign subsidiary is "owned by" anyone other than a United States corporation.

Five Members of the Court (hereinafter referred to as "the majority") assert, however, that the regulation's treatment of situations 2b and 2c is attributable to the resolution of yet another ambiguity in section 526(a). The statute excludes only merchandise "of foreign manufacture," which the majority says might mean "manufactured by a foreigner" rather than "manufactured in a foreign country." I think not. Words, like syllables, acquire meaning not in isolation but within their context. While looking up the separate word "foreign" in a dictionary might produce the reading the majority suggests, that approach would also interpret the phrase "I have a foreign object in my eye" as referring, perhaps, to something from Italy. The phrase "of foreign manufacture" is a common usage, well understood to mean "manufactured abroad." Hence, when statutes and regulations intend to describe the universe of manufactured goods, they do not refer to goods "of foreign or citizen manufacture," but to goods "of foreign or domestic manufacture." See, E.G., 19 CFR sec. 133.21(a)(1987). I know of no instance in which anyone, anywhere, has used the phrase with the meaning the majority suggests—and the majority provides no example.

In the particular context of the present statute, however, the majority's suggested interpretation is not merely unusual but inconceivable, since it would have the effect of eliminating section 526(a)'s protection for some trademark holders in case 1—which contains what the Court describes as the "proto-typical" gray-market victims. Not uncommonly a foreign trademark owner licenses an American firm to use its trademark in the United States and also licenses one or more other American firms to use the trademark in other countries. In this situation, the firm with the United States license could not keep out gray-market imports manufactured abroad by the other American firms, since, under the majority's interpretation, the goods would not be "of foreign manufacture." Thus, to save the regulation, the majority proposes an interpretation that undermines even the core of the statute.

* * *

If it were, as Justice Kennedy believes, "the current interpretation of the regulations we are sustaining," one would expect there to be in place some mechanism that enables the Customs Service to identify goods that are not only manufactured abroad but also (as the majority's interpretation requires) manufactured by foreigners. Acquiring this knowledge cannot be easy, since the importer of merchandise will often not know the manufacturer's identity, much less its corporate pedigree. International corporate ownership, not a matter of public record, is often a closely guarded secret. Yet although there is in place a regulation requiring the country of origin (i.e., whether "manufactured abroad") to be plainly indicated on all imports, see 19 CFR secs. 134.0–134.55 (1987), there is none requiring the nationality of the manufacturer to be stated. After today's decision, of course, the Customs Service, if it would not rather amend its regulations, will presumably have to devise means to enforce what we say it has been enforcing.

* * *

I find it extraordinary for this Court, on the theory of deferring to an agency's judgment, to burden that agency with an interpretation that it not only has never suggested, but that is contrary to ordinary usage, to the purposes of the statute, and to the interpretation the agency appears to have applied consistently for half a century.

Notes and Questions

(1) Are "gray market" imports good or bad in general? On the one hand, they increase competition and tend to lower prices to consumers. Some have argued, therefore, that restrictions on gray market imports are anti-competitive. On the other hand, they injure the holder of the domestic trademark, as the imports may "free ride" on advertising and service networks of the domestic trademark holder, thus reducing the returns to such activities and discouraging them. How can one begin to decide which effects are more important? Might the remedy of exclusion be too severe? To what extent is it sufficient or insufficient to require the foreign-made product to disclose its foreign origin so that, for example, consumers will not mistakenly buy it if it is inferior and domestic service facilities can avoid providing uncompensated warranty service? This resolution of the problem is not unfamiliar—US consumers can purchase cameras covered by a Nikon, U.S.A. warranty, for example, or can pay a slightly lower price for an ostensibly identical camera from Japan without the opportunity to obtain warranty service in the United States. Some of the issues are discussed in Michael Knoll, Gray–Market Imports: Causes, Consequences and Responses, 18 L. & Pol.Intl.Bus. 145 (1986).

(2) Reflect briefly on the question of why the gray market problem cannot be adequately addressed by contract. When gray market importation occurs without the consent of the domestic trademark owner, it often occurs because the foreign trademark owner has sold goods to an unaffiliated third party, who then resells them in the domestic market. Thus, even if contractual solutions might be devised to govern the behavior of licensees, licensors and affiliates, resale by third-party purchasers is at issue as well. Yet, might not contractual solutions sometimes be viable there, at least when the third-party purchaser is buying in bulk quantities sufficient to resell substantial numbers of units abroad?

(3) Suppose that the trademarked goods entering the US are made by a subsidiary of the US trademark holder, but have been modified so as to appeal to consumers in the foreign market. In other words, the goods bear the same trademark as the US-made goods, but are materially different. Here, exclusion has been held proper notwithstanding circumstances that fall within the common control exceptions discussed in *K–Mart*. See Lever Bros. Co. v. United States, 981 F.2d 1330 (D.C.Cir.1993).

(B) INFRINGING IMPORTS: THE ADMINISTRATIVE REMEDY

The cases above arose in federal court, which provides one forum for enforcing the rights of US and foreign nationals that are cognizable under federal statutes. But US law has long provided an additional, administrative forum in which domestic firms can seek relief from imports that infringe their intellectual property rights—Section 337 of the 1930 Tariff Act.[1]

On its face, Section 337 applies to any form of "unfair competition," though in practice it is mainly employed in intellectual property disputes. Relief from imports that infringe valid and enforceable patents, copyrights, trademarks, or semiconductor mask works does not require a showing of injury under Section 337 after the 1988 Trade Act, merely a showing that a domestic industry relating to the imported articles "exists or is in the process of being established."[2] Other forms of "unfair competition," however, are only remediable under Section 337 if they are likely to destroy or "substantially injure" a domestic industry, prevent its establishment, or restrain or monopolize trade.[3]

A Section 337 proceeding begins with the filing of a complaint by an aggrieved party.[4] The ITC then decides whether to initiate an investigation, and if it does, the respondent must file a written answer. The case is assigned to an ITC administrative law judge (ALJ), who supervises discovery, rules on any motions and eventually issues a decision in the case. There are broad provisions for discovery, including the use of oral depositions, written interrogatories and inspection of documents. An ITC staff attorney is assigned to the case as well (the Investigating Attorney, or IA). Following discovery, a hearing is held before the ALJ, who then

---

1. 19 U.S.C.A. sec. 1337.

2. 19 U.S.C.A. sec. 1337(a)(1)(B)-(D), (a)(2).

3. 19 U.S.C.A. sec. 1337(a)(1)(A).

4. The general procedures applicable to Section 337 cases are set out in 19 CFR pt. 210 (1993).

provides an initial determination to the ITC. The initial determination becomes the Commission's determination unless the Commission orders a review of it in its entirety or with respect to particular issues. The Commission is required to dispose of cases "at the earliest practicable time." The President then has 60 days to exercise his right to override the Commission decision.[5]

A showing that Section 337 has been violated does not entitle the complainant to relief. The Commission may determine that relief is not in the national interest after examining the public health and welfare, competitive conditions, and effects on consumers.[6] The President also has broad discretion to overrule relief "for policy reasons."[7]

Subject to these constraints, the ITC is authorized to grant two types of relief. First, it may issue an order excluding from entry into the United States any article found to be imported in violation of Section 337, to be enforced by Customs.[8] It may also issue such an exclusion order on a preliminary basis during the course of the investigation, although importation will be permitted on payment of a bond.[9] Under ITC practice, exclusion orders may be "general," addressed to all importations that may violate Section 337, or may be "limited," addressed only to the products of the respondents in the investigation. Second, the Commission may order a person violating Section 337 to cease and desist.[10] Violations of such an order may be punished by a fine equal to the greater of $10,000 a day or the domestic value of the goods entered or sold on such day in violation of the order. Appeals of ITC decisions are made to the US Court of Appeals for the Federal Circuit.[11]

As discussed in Section 12.2 supra, prior procedures under Section 337 could afford considerable advantages to a plaintiff relative to a proceeding in Federal court, and these advantages were found by a GATT panel to deny national treatment. But the Uruguay Round implementing legislation made a number of changes designed to achieve GATT conformity. *Inter alia*, time limits for the completion of investigations were abolished; respondents were given the right to file counterclaims (removed to Federal court); parallel proceedings in Federal court could be stayed at the request of a respondent; and statutory limitations upon general exclusion orders were enacted. Whether these changes will suffice in the view of any future WTO panel remains to be seen.

The substantive issues that arise in Section 337 cases span the issues that arise in ordinary patent, trademark, copyright, and other unfair competition litigation. Hence, we make no effort to provide a survey here, but focus briefly on certain issues relating to remedy, to the "public interest," and to the "industry" requirement of Section 337 cases.

5. 19 U.S.C.A. sec. 1337(j)(2).

6. 19 U.S.C.A. sec. 1337(d).

7. 19 U.S.C.A. sec. 1337(j)(2).

8. 19 U.S.C.A. sec. 1337(d).

9. 19 U.S.C.A. sec. 1337(e).

10. 19 U.S.C.A. sec. 1337(f).

11. 19 U.S.C.A. sec. 1337(f)(2).

CERTAIN BATTERY–POWERED RIDE–ON TOY VEHICLES AND COMPONENTS THEREOF

United States International Trade Commission, 1991.[12]

On May 15, 1990, Kransco filed a complaint with the Commission under section 337 of the Tariff Act of 1930. The complaint alleged that Chien Ti Enterprise Co., Ltd. ("Chien Ti"), a Taiwanese corporation that manufactures and exports children's toys, was violating section 337 by exporting to the United States rideable toy vehicles that infringe claims of five US patents owned by Kransco.

* * *

On December 5, 1990, the presiding administrative law judge (ALJ) issued an initial determination (ID) granting the motion of complainant Kransco for summary determination. The ID concluded that a violation of section 337 had been established in the importation of certain battery-powered ride-on toy vehicles and components thereof by reason of infringement of the five patents at issue.

* * *

(1) We have determined that there has been a sale for importation of infringing battery-powered ride-on toy vehicles by respondent Chien Ti. Accordingly, we affirm the ID's conclusion that a violation of section 337 has been established.

(2) We have issued a general exclusion order directed to products that infringe the '666 or '009 design patents and a limited exclusion order directed to products that infringe the claims at issue of the '958, '263, or '646 product patents.

(3) We have concluded that the public interest considerations articulated in section 337(d) do not preclude issuance of relief in this investigation.

* * *

Kransco's complaint is based on section 337(a)(1)(B)(i). That section proscribes:

> The importation into the United States, the sale for importation, or the sale within the United States after importation by the owner, importer, or consignee, of articles that infringe a valid and enforceable United States patent or a valid and enforceable United States copyright registered under Title 17, United States Code.

The sole issue under review is whether the "importation" requirement of the above provision has been satisfied. We conclude that importation has been demonstrated, because the record shows that Chien Ti made numerous shipments of infringing vehicles to the United

12. Investigation No. 337–TA–314, USITC Pub. No. 2420.

States through a trading company, Qunsan Enterprise Co., Ltd. ("Qunsan").

The pertinent facts concerning the Qunsan shipments are not in dispute. Chien Ti itself admitted that it has sold its Jeep and Racer toy vehicle models to Qunsan and that Qunsan then exported these models to the United States. Chien Ti additionally sent a facsimile to J & L Meyer, Inc. on December 21, 1989, stating that it knew that its toys were being exported to Miami, San Francisco, and Long Beach, among other places.

The ALJ correctly found from this record that "Chien Ti knew that toy vehicles it sold to Qunsan were exported to the United States," but did not determine the legal significance of this finding. The statute itself, however, expressly states that section 337 proscribes "the sale for importation," as well as importation, by the "owner, importer or consignee" of infringing articles. Indeed, longstanding Commission precedent holds that a section 337 violation can be found when a foreign manufacturer sells infringing goods to a foreign trading company with the knowledge that the goods will subsequently be exported to the United States, even if the manufacturer does not itself export or deal directly with U.S. importers.

Consequently, the ALJ's finding that Chien Ti knew that Qunsan was exporting to the United States infringing Jeep and Racer model toy vehicles compels the legal conclusion that section 337's importation requirement has been satisfied with respect to all five Kransco patents at issue. In light of this conclusion and the ID's rulings on validity, infringement, and domestic industry which we determined not to review, we determine that a violation of section 337 has been established.

* * *

Complainant Kransco has requested issuance of a general exclusion order covering each of the five patents at issue. The [ITC investigating attorney] IA, by contrast, supports issuance of a general exclusion order with respect to the '666 and '009 patents and a limited exclusion order with respect to the three product patents.

In considering whether to issue a general exclusion order, we have traditionally balanced complainant's interest in obtaining complete relief against the public interest in avoiding the disruption of legitimate trade that such relief may cause. Thus we determined in Certain Airless Paint Spray Pumps, Inv. No. 337–TA–90, USITC Pub. 1199 at 18 (May 1981), that a complainant seeking a general exclusion order must prove "both a widespread pattern of unauthorized use of its patented invention and certain business conditions from which one might reasonably infer that foreign manufacturers other than the respondents to the investigation may attempt to enter the U.S. market with infringing articles." Factors relevant to demonstrating whether there is a "widespread pattern of unauthorized use" include:

(a) a Commission determination of unauthorized importation into the United States of infringing articles by numerous foreign manufacturers;

(b) the pendency of foreign infringement suits based upon foreign patents which correspond to the domestic patent at issue;

(c) other evidence which demonstrates a history of unauthorized foreign use of the patented invention.

Factors relevant to showing whether "certain business conditions" exist include:

(a) an established market for the patented product in the U.S. market and conditions of the world market;

(b) the availability of marketing and distribution networks in the United States for potential foreign manufacturers;

(c) the cost to foreign entrepreneurs of building a facility capable of producing the patented article;

(d) the number of foreign manufacturers whose facilities could be retooled to produce the patented article; or

(e) the cost to foreign manufacturers of retooling their facility to produce the patented article.

With respect to the criterion of "widespread pattern of unauthorized use," the record contains information suggesting that there is a pattern of use of the design patents at issue. Kransco has submitted documents purporting to show that five foreign manufacturers, in addition to Chien Ti, produce vehicles alleged to infringe the '666 patent, and that two foreign manufacturers, in addition to Chien Ti, produce vehicles that arguably infringe the '009 patent.

By contrast, Kransco has failed to submit evidence purporting to show even a pattern of use for any of the three product patents at issue. With respect to the '958 patent, Kransco has submitted evidence indicating merely that one non-respondent manufacturer produces a vehicle that allegedly infringes the patent.

The record contains considerable information indicating the existence of business conditions that would encourage new foreign entrants to enter the U.S. Market. Confidential information concerning sales revenue and volume furnished by Kransco indicates that there is an established market in the United States for the products utilizing the patents at issue. Additionally, marketing and distribution networks in the United States appear to be available for potential importers and foreign manufacturers of toy vehicles. Kransco has submitted deposition testimony of a toy distributor, who has no apparent pecuniary interest in the outcome of this investigation, indicating that foreign toy manufacturers have ready access to the U.S. market. Moreover, as previously discussed, numerous foreign manufacturers already produce allegedly infringing vehicles, and, according to Kransco, the plants of over ten additional foreign manufacturers could be retooled to produce such vehicles.

With respect to the two design patents at issue, complainant Kransco's strong showing with respect to the "business conditions" prong of the *Spray Pumps* test is not matched for the "widespread pattern of unauthorized use" prong. We have nonetheless determined to issue a general exclusion order with respect to the '666 and '009 design patents for four reasons. First, Kransco has shown that numerous manufacturers worldwide produce vehicles that appear to infringe the design patents, and that many others have the potential for manufacturing infringing vehicles. Second, Kransco's fears of imminent importation of infringing vehicles manufactured by entities other than respondent Chien Ti appear to be well-founded in light of the representations of TCV Industrial Co., Ltd., that its Jeep-like toy vehicles—which allegedly utilize the design of the '666 patent—will soon be marketed in the United States. Consequently, issuance of a limited exclusion order may be insufficient to accord Kransco complete relief against infringing imports. Third, issuing a general exclusion order in this investigation would not subvert the Commission's policy of "encourag[ing] complainants to include in an investigation all those foreign manufacturers which it believes have entered, or are on the verge of entering, the domestic market with infringing articles." There is nothing in the record to suggest that any manufacturer other than Chien Ti had entered or was about to enter the U.S. market with infringing vehicles at the time this investigation was instituted. Fourth, we do not believe that a general exclusion order limited to the design patents will be difficult for the Customs Service to administer, or will unduly restrain trade. Application of the standard for finding legal infringement of a design patent, which, as noted, concerns the similarity of designs in the eyes of an ordinary observer, does not require technical expertise or specialized equipment.

A number of the considerations militating in favor of issuance of a general exclusion order with respect to the design patents are not applicable to the three product patents at issue. Kransco has not made any showing of a "widespread pattern of unauthorized use" with respect to two of the product patents, and its showing with respect to the '958 patent is not strong. Consequently, we believe that the potential that a limited exclusion order will accord Kransco incomplete relief is much less significant with these patents. Buttressing this belief is testimony from Kransco's own official indicating that the vehicles' design, as opposed to their construction or mechanical systems, is a prime reason for their popularity with consumers. We consequently have issued a limited exclusion order with respect to the three product patents at issue.

* * *

Section 337 instructs the Commission to consider the effect of any remedy "upon the public health and welfare, competitive conditions in the United States economy, the production of like or directly competitive articles in the United States, and United States consumers." The legislative history of this provision, added to section 337 by the Trade Act of 1974, indicates that the commission should decline to issue relief when the adverse effect on the public interest would be greater than the interest in protecting the patent holder.[13]

We do not believe that either of these concerns is implicated in the instant investigation. We agree with Kransco and the IA that an adequate supply of ride-on toy vehicles is not necessary to ensure public health, safety, or welfare in the United States. In any event, the record indicates that an adequate supply of such vehicles will exist even upon issuance of an exclusion order. Consequently, we conclude that the public interest does not preclude granting relief.

CERTAIN PLASTIC ENCAPSULATED INTEGRATED CIRCUITS

United States International Trade Commission, 1992.[14]

On July 9, 1990, Texas Instruments Incorporated (TI) filed a complaint under section 337 of the Tariff Act of 1930 (19 U.S.C. § 1337) alleging that respondents * * * had imported and sold within the United States certain plastic encapsulated integrated circuits manufactured by a [patented] process. * * *

On October 15, 1991, the presiding administrative law judge (ALJ) issued a final initial determination (ID) finding a violation of section 337 on the ground that certain of respondents' imported plastic encapsulated integrated circuits were manufactured by a process covered by [the] patent. * * *

After review, the Commission affirmed the ALJ's determination that all respondents had violated section 337. [In so doing, the ITC reversed an ALJ finding that "claim 17" of the patent had not been infringed, and issued a limited exclusion order and cease and desist orders.]

* * *

C.   Domestic Industry

The Omnibus Trade and Competitiveness Act of 1988 (OTCA) amended section 337 of the Tariff Act of 1930 to specify the types of

---

13. [original note 27] See S.Rep. 1298, 93d Cong., 2d Sess. 197 (1974). The Commission has declined to grant relief on public interest grounds in only three cases. See Certain Fluidized Supporting Apparatus, Inv. No. 337–TA–182/188, USITC Pub. 1667 (October 1984) (temporary relief denied when domestic industry could not provide adequate supply of medical product useful to public health); Certain Inclined–Field Acceleration Tubes, Inv. No. 337–TA–67, USITC Pub. 1119 (December 1980) (re-lief denied when exclusion order would have stifled nuclear structure research programs in public interest); Certain Automatic Crankpin Grinders, Inv. No. 337–TA–60, USITC Pub. 1022 (December 1979) (relief denied when domestic industry could not provide adequate supply of product needed for automobiles to satisfy federal energy efficiency requirements).

14. Investigation No. 337–TA–315, USITC Pub. No. 2574.

unfair acts covered by that section.[15] As amended, section 337 explicitly prohibits the importation and sale of imported articles that—

(i) infringe a valid and enforceable United States patent . . . ; or

(ii) are made, produced, processed, or mined under, or by means of, a process covered by the claims of a valid and enforceable United States patent.

In order to prove a violation of section 337 in a patent-based case, a complainant must show that an industry exists in the United States practicing the patent. Specifically, there can be a violation of section 337—

only if an industry in the United States, relating to the articles protected by the patent, . . . exists or is in the process of being established. 19 U.S.C. sec. 1337(a)(2).

In cases involving alleged infringement of statutory intellectual property rights, section 337(a)(3) defines domestic industry as follows:

(a)(3) . . . an industry in the United States shall be considered to exist if there is in the United States, with respect to the articles protected by the patent, copyright, [registered] trademark, or mask work concerned—

(A) significant investment in plant and equipment;

(B) significant employment of labor or capital; or

(C) substantial investment in its exploitation, including engineering, research and development, or licensing.

19 U.S.C. sec. 1337(a)(3). Thus, this section 337 investigation requires a determination as to whether a domestic industry exists, that is, whether the complainant is exploiting or practicing the patent in controversy.

The ALJ applied the domestic industry criteria set out in section 337(a)(3) to find that TI's domestic activities are sufficient to demonstrate the existence of a domestic industry. He found that TI practices the patent at its domestic facility, and that TI is specifically practicing claims 12 and 14 of the * * * patent at its domestic facility. He based this finding on the agreement among witnesses that TI and the respondents use the same or similar processes, coupled with his finding that respondents use an encapsulation process covered by claims 12 and 14. Because the ALJ found no infringement of claim 17, he did not make a finding regarding TI's practice of claim 17.

As noted, the parties agree that the types of plastic encapsulated integrated circuits likely to have all conductors parallel to each other are those with low-pin counts. Respondents argue that because TI did not introduce into evidence any lead frames produced in the United States which include parallel leads and "because TI has never manufactured

---

15. [original note 29] Under the amended statute, there is no requirement to show injury to the domestic industry in cases involving alleged infringement of patents (including process patents), copyrights, registered trademarks, or mask works. 19 U.S.C. sec. 1337(a)(1)(B).

low-pin count integrated circuits (i.e. less than 8 leads) at its domestic facility," TI does not practice claim 17. TI admits that it is does not presently manufacture low-pin count package types at its domestic facility. * * *

In addressing domestic industry, we are mindful that the statute requires only that any one of the three criteria set out in section 337(a)(3) be met in order to satisfy the domestic industry requirement. In this respect, we note that we have adopted, inter alia, the ALJ's factual findings and conclusions regarding the existence of a domestic industry as evidenced by TI's engineering and research and development efforts. As the ALJ found, "it is difficult in situations such as that presented in this investigation to draw a bright line dividing those projects which exploit the patent at issue from those which to not." Likewise, it is equally, if not more difficult to segregate those projects that exploit claims 12 and 14 of the patent, but not claim 17.

Given the close similarity and overlap among these three claims, there is no bright line separating the research and development efforts relating to one of these claims from those relating to the others.

We accordingly find that TI's research and development efforts represent a substantial investment in exploitation of all claims found infringed, including claim 17. By virtue of this finding, it is unnecessary to decide specifically whether the claims that are infringed must be the ones that are practiced by the domestic industry in order for there to be a violation of section 337.[16]

Notes and Questions

(1) A general exclusion order applies to all infringing products, even those of parties not before the ITC, and places in the hands of the Customs Service the task of determining whether a product is infringing. Should these orders be permitted?

16. [original note 37] The IAs [staff investigating attorneys] argue that the language of section 337 and the legislative history of the 1988 amendments support the view that where the domestic industry practices some of the claims of a patent, a respondent's infringement of any of the claims of that patent provides a basis for finding a violation of section 337. The IAs note that the statute emphasizes infringement and practice of the patent, rather than infringement and practice of the individual claims of the patent. Specifically, the IAs quote the language of the statute referring to infringement of a U.S. patent (19 U.S.C. sec. 1337(a)(1)(B)(i)); the requirement that an industry exist in the United States "relating to the articles protected by the patent," (Id. at sec. 1337(a)(2)); and the domestic industry requirements "with respect to the articles protected by the patent" (Id. at sec. 1337(a)(3)).

In making this argument, the IAs question several IDs [initial determinations] or orders in which Commission ALJs have held that there must be "claim correspondence," i.e., that a violation of section 337 can be based on a particular claim only if the domestic industry practices that claim. * * * The claim correspondence requirement was not reviewed by the Commission and was not appealed to the Federal Circuit. The ID did, however, become the Commission's determination by virtue of the Commission's decision not to review it.

In light of our determination that there is a domestic industry meeting each claim at issue we need not determine whether claim correspondence is necessary to establish the existence of a domestic industry. The Commission notes, however, that, in a future investigation, it may be necessary to evaluate the propriety of a claim correspondence approach to the domestic industry analysis.

(2) As noted, the ITC may grant a cease and desist order in addition to an exclusion order. These orders are typically directed at domestic importers or sellers, ordering them to cease and desist from selling the offending merchandise. Why is such an order needed if offending imports are excluded?

(3) When should the "public interest" counsel against relief? Given the statute's reference to "competitive conditions," is it right to say that the mere prospect of increased consumer prices will not preclude relief?

(4) What is the point of the "domestic industry" requirement? Suppose a US citizen holds a valid US patent for something not presently made in the United States, and not likely to be made here in the near future. Should foreign manufacturers nevertheless have to buy a license before exporting to this country a product that infringes the patent?

(5) Among the practices that the ITC has indicated could be unfair under Section 337, in addition to the infringement of patents, trademarks and copyrights, are price fixing, group boycotts, deceptive pricing, combination and conspiracy to restrain and monopolize trade, misrepresentation of the country of origin of the goods, an attempt to monopolize, a refusal to deal, predatory pricing, and trade secret misappropriation.[17] Thus, although most Section 337 cases seem to involve patents, the concept of unfair competition is broad enough to cover actions that violate other US laws, including trade laws. For example, on occasion there have been complaints about an importer's use of predatory pricing, which by its very nature suggests the possibility of dumping. The 1974 Trade Act provided that if the ITC had reason to believe that an investigation might come under the antidumping or countervailing laws, it should notify the authorities administering those laws. In 1979, Section 337(b)(3) was clarified to indicate that the ITC investigation can proceed nevertheless under Section 337 unless it is based solely on alleged dumping or subsidization.

(6) Recall that where a US registered trademark is involved, it is possible to register that trademark with the Customs Service. Entry will thereafter be denied to articles bearing that trademark, subject to the caveats discussed above in connection with gray market imports.

(7) After the GATT panel decision holding that Section 337 violated Article III (see Section 12.2 supra), the use of Section 337 fell significantly for a while, perhaps because complainants feared that relief obtained under it would not last. In recent years, however, the number of new filings has increased. The total number of cases initiated over the past twenty year period is just under 350, and thus Section 337 remains quite an important part of the US trade policy arsenal.

---

17. See US Intl. Trade Commn., Office of the Administrative Law Judges, Compen- dium of Section 337 Decisions sec. 101, at 2 (1981).

Chapter 21

LINKAGES BETWEEN
INTERNATIONAL TRADE POLICY
AND HUMAN RIGHTS,
LABOR STANDARDS
AND NATIONAL SECURITY

SECTION 21.1   INTRODUCTION

(A) OVERVIEW

The linkages between trade policies and non-economic policy objectives pose some of the most perplexing conceptual questions that exist in the subject of international relations. We have explored some of these questions in Chapters 12–14 in respect of trade and the environment. Here, we examine these issues more broadly. On the one hand, what is the relationship between expanded international trade and human rights and labor standards? How do they interact? On the other hand, when a nation (like the United States) has considerable economic power, there is a temptation to use that power to pursue a wide variety of national objectives. Should trade measures be used to pressure other nations to protect human rights? To promote minimum labor standards? To inhibit trafficking in illegal drugs? To discourage or punish assistance to terrorism or weapons sales (especially of missiles or nuclear arms)? To deter or punish aggression? To engage generally in economic warfare against nations viewed as unfriendly?

We cannot here resolve the issue of what is the exact relationship between expanded international trade and human rights and labor standards. Nor can we answer the questions of whether nations should use trade measures to promote human rights and labor standards. We can, however, explore the debates over the relationships and consider what nations have done in the past in such circumstances and attempt to assess the effectiveness of their actions.

We start in this introductory section with an historical overview of the use of trade and other economic sanctions and some reflections on their effectiveness. In Section 21.2, we examine human rights generally and how trade controls have been used to promote them. In Section 21.3 we look more closely at one specific aspect of individual rights—worker rights—and consider US attempts to use the threat of revoking trade preferences to promote such rights. Finally, in Section 21.4, we consider foreign policy and national security goals and their relationship to trade.

(B) HISTORICAL USE OF ECONOMIC SANCTIONS

Economic sanctions have been used regularly throughout history. In recent years, they have typically used by international organizations and powerful countries to try to influence the behavior of other countries. They are used for a wide variety of reasons. The classic study of the use of economic sanctions cites 174 examples of the use of sanctions between World War I and the present day (involving 204 episodes when account is taken of multiple objectives or phases).[1] The objectives of these sanctions include attempts to affect military activities undertaken by other countries; to destabilize countries; to promote protection of human rights; to adopt policies relating to nuclear non-proliferation, the control of drug trafficking and the suppression of terrorism. (The study does not consider trade retaliatory measures taken under WTO rules such as those we considered in Chapter 7.) The predominant user of sanctions is the United States, followed by the United Nations, the United Kingdom, the European Union and Russia. In looking at the use of sanctions over time, the study found that in recent years there has been, if anything, an increase in the use of economic sanctions.[2]

One of the key questions that are raised by the use of economic sanctions is the issue of effectiveness. How often do they succeed in changing behaviors in the direction desired. Overall, the authors found that economic sanctions achieved their purpose about one-third of the time.[3] In analyzing the cases, they rated the success of sanctions based on the type of policy goal that was sought to be achieved, as the following table indicates:[4]

Table 6.1 Success by type of policy goal

Policy goal	Success cases	Failure cases	Success ratio (percentage of total)
Modest policy changes	22	21	51
Regime change and democratization	25	55	31
Disruption of military adventures	4	15	21
Military impairment	10	23	31
Other major policy changes	10	23	30
Totals	70	134	34

Compared to their last study, which examined the use of sanctions through 1989, the authors found that the overall success rate had not

---

1. Kimberly Ann Elliot, Gary Clyde Hufbauer, Jeffrey J. Schott & Barbara Oegg, Economic Sanctions Reconsidered (3d ed. 2007).

2. The list of sanctions studied is found in id. at 20–39.

3. Id. at 158.

4. Id. at 159.

changed. Interestingly, however, they found that the use of sanctions for some purposes was more successful and for other purposes it was less so. In particular, the use of sanctions was not so successful when aimed at regime change or democratization. They also found that the use of economic sanctions by the United States—particularly when acting uni-laterally, was less successful in the post Cold War period, likely because of the decline in the size of the US economy compared to the overall world economy.

The authors of the study list a number of guidelines for policy-makers to follow in order to maximize the chance that sanctions will succeed. For example, they note that (i) major policy changes are difficult to achieve, as are changes in the policies of autocratic regimes; (ii) it is easier to affect the behavior of friendly nations, as opposed to nations perceived as adversaries; (iii) sanctions should imposed all at once, not on a gradual basis and are more effective when imposed by one or a small group of countries; and (iv) that care should be taken in the selection of the sanctions imposed and in considering the impact on domestic constituencies.[5]

Notes and Questions

(1) Is it sensible to place great stress on the question of effectiveness? If a government wishes to show its support of certain principles, such as basic human rights or democracy, why should it not use trade controls to do so? Does the fact that imposing trade controls is by itself unlikely to change a foreign government's policies mean that it should not be done?

(2) As discussed in Chapter 7, the use of economic sanctions is the ultimate remedy in WTO dispute settlement. Are there lessons to be learned for the WTO system from the foregoing material? For example, what do the authors' guidelines suggest for WTO practice?

(3) In light of the fact that economic sanctions often do not work, should the US government be required to make public its determination of the likely effect on the US economy and the likely effectiveness of the sanctions before implementing them?

SECTION 21.2   HUMAN RIGHTS AND INTER-NATIONAL TRADE POLICY: TENSION OF CONFLICTING GOALS

One of the more controversial issues involving linkages has been the question of whether trade sanctions should be used to promote human rights. In the United States, the issue has been most controversial in the case of the People's Republic of China and whether the US should continue to grant China MFN treatment or whether it should deny MFN treatment to Chinese goods in an effort to promote human rights in China. In this section, we first consider the question of defining interna-tional human rights—what does that concept embrace and who decides

---

5. Id. at 160–178.

what are international human rights? We then consider whether trade sanctions should be used to promote them. Finally, we look at a US law—known as the Jackson–Vanik Amendment—that conditions MFN treatment for some countries in some circumstances to human rights.

(A) INTERNATIONAL HUMAN RIGHTS DEFINED

Different people and different organizations have defined human rights in different ways. Indeed, most of international human rights law developed after World War II, in large part in response to Nazi atrocities. Nonetheless, there are some common threads in what are generally considered to be basic human rights.[1]

Probably the most important expression of the concept of human rights is contained in the United Nation's Universal Declaration of Human Rights.[2] The declaration includes a long list of rights, some of which will be mentioned below, and it provides in its preamble that governments and individuals should "strive by teaching and education to promote respect for these rights and freedoms and by progressive measures, national and international, to secure their universal and effective recognition and observance."

The declaration proclaims that all people are born free and equal in dignity and rights and that everyone has the right to life, liberty and the security of person. It bans slavery, torture, and inhuman or degrading punishment. It holds that all are equal before the law. It contains provisions providing rights to accused criminals, as well as establishing rights to found families and own property. It also includes rights to participate in governance and to assemble. It encompasses such rights as the right to work, to education and to an adequate standard of living.

Compared to the US Constitution (including the Bill of Rights), the UN Declaration contains provisions dealing with most of what is in the US Constitution (in general terms), but goes beyond it in several areas, such as the family, education and economic rights mentioned above.

There are other significant, multilateral instruments that establish human rights. In its annual report to Congress, the State Department listed the following "International Human Rights Conventions," the substance of which is often apparent from the title.[3] As of February 2001, the United States was a party to those conventions marked with an asterisk and a signatory to those marked with two asterisks.

— Convention to Suppress the Slave Trade and Slavery (1926)*

— Convention Concerning Forced Labor (ILO, 1930)

---

1. See generally Lori F. Damrosch, Louis Henkin, Richard C. Pugh, Oscar Schachter & Hans Smit, International Law: Cases and Materials 586–683 (4th ed. 2001); Barry E. Carter & Phillip R. Trimble, International Law 844–925 (3rd ed. 1999).

2. Dec. 10, 1948, U.N.G.A. Res. 217A(III), U.N. Doc. A/810 (1948).

3. US Dept. of State, 2006 Country Reports on Human Rights Practices, Appendix D (2007).

— Convention Concerning Freedom of Association and Protection of the Right to Organize (ILO, 1948)

— Convention on the Prevention and Punishment of the Crime of Genocide (1948)*

— Convention Concerning the Application of the Principles of the Right to Organize and Bargain Collectively (ILO, 1949)

— Geneva Convention Relative to Treatment of Prisoners of War (1949)*

— Geneva Convention Relative to the Protection of Civilian Persons in Time of War (1949)*

— Convention for the Suppression of the Traffic in Persons and of the Exploitation of the Prostitution of Others (1950)

— European Convention for the Protection of Human Rights and Fundamental Freedoms (1950)

— Convention on the Political Rights of Women (1953)*

— Supplementary Convention on the Abolition of Slavery, the Slave Trade, and Institutions and Practices Similar to Slavery (1956)*

— Convention Concerning the Abolition of Forced Labor (ILO, 1957)*

— International Convention on the Elimination of All Forms of Racial Discrimination (1965)*

— International Covenant on Civil and Political Rights (1966)*

— International Covenant on Economic, Social and Cultural Rights (1966)**

— United Nations Convention Relating to the Status of Refugees (1951)

— Protocol Relating to the Status of Refugees (1967)*

— American Convention on Human Rights (1969)**

— Convention Concerning Minimum Age for Admission to Employment (ILO, 1973)

— Protocol Additional to the Geneva Conventions of August 12, 1949, and Relating to the Protection of Victims of International Armed Conflicts (Protocol I) (1977)**

— Protocol Additional to the Geneva Conventions of August 12, 1949, and Relating to the Protection of Victims of Non–International Armed Conflicts (Protocol II) (1977)**

— Convention on the Elimination of All Forms of Discrimination Against Women (1979)**

— Convention Against Torture and Other Cruel, Inhuman or Degrading Treatment or Punishment (1984)*

— Convention on the Rights of the Child (1989)**

— Convention on the Worst Forms of Child Labor (1999)*

Notes and Questions

(1) Some scholars question whether the rights listed in the U.N. Declaration and the above conventions are really universal. They suggest that they are derived from Western concepts of government and social structure and that they are not necessarily accepted or appropriately applied in other cultures. For example, there is great stress on individual rights as opposed to group (family, community or state) rights and on freedom of action as opposed to societal order. How would you respond to such arguments? Who should decide such issues?

(2) These issues were presented in a Spring 1994 debate over the question of whether applying several strokes of a cane, which inflicts considerable pain and may lead to scarring, is an appropriate punishment for vandalism (or any other offense). Singapore imposes such a punishment for a number of offenses, including vandalism. The US government urged Singapore not to cane a US youth living in Singapore who had been convicted of vandalism, arguing that his confession may have been coerced and that caning was too severe a punishment.[4] Singapore rejected the US request, although the number of strokes was reduced from six to four. Singapore Senior Minister Lee Kuan Yew, who was prime minister for the three decades prior to 1990, was quoted in the US press as stressing the need for a well-ordered society, "arguing that the Western concept of individual rights had been taken to extremes and left the United States in a crisis." He cited a "list of social ills that plague the United States but scarcely exist in Singapore—street violence, homelessness, unemployment."[5] Is caning an inappropriate punishment? Is it a violation of human rights (the UN declaration bans "inhuman or degrading treatment or punishment")? Who should decide the answer to that question?

(B) LINKING TRADE AND HUMAN RIGHTS: THE JACKSON–VANIK AMENDMENT

The most important link between international human rights and US trade law is found in title IV of the Trade Act of 1974 (the so-called Jackson–Vanik provision), which is described in Section 10.3. This provision establishes a complicated scheme for determining when Communist countries may be given most-favored-nation (now called in US law "normal trade relations") treatment under US trade law and requires annual consideration of whether to renew such treatment. Its most controversial application occurred in the 1990's in connection with China. While the importance of Jackson–Vanik continues to shrink as more and more former Communist countries are removed from its coverage,[6] the controversy over China remains of interest as an example

4. See 30 Weekly Compilation of Presidential Documents 838 (1994).

5. Philip Shenon, To Justify Flogging, Singapore Cites "Chaos" on US Streets, N.Y.Times, Apr. 13, 1994, at A2, col. 3.

6. In 2000, Congress provided for permanent normal trade relations with China, conditional on its entry into the WTO, which occurred in December 2001. See Section 6.6 supra.

of the various issues that may present themselves when a country considers imposing trade sanctions to promote human rights.

The United States began giving MFN treatment to Chinese goods in 1980 and such treatment was relatively non-controversial until 1989 when the Chinese government suppressed pro-democracy demonstrators in Tiananmen Square. This led to calls for non-renewal of MFN treatment. President Bush, however, continued to renew such treatment. In 1993, President Clinton, who had criticized the Bush Administration policy, renewed MFN treatment, subject to specific conditions in respect of granting exit visas to certain individuals, Chinese compliance with the 1992 US–China agreement on prison labor and overall significant progress by China in respect of (i) taking steps to begin adhering to the Universal Declaration of Human Rights, (ii) releasing and providing an acceptable accounting of those imprisoned for the nonviolent expression of their political and religious beliefs, (iii) ensuring humane treatment of prisoners, (iv) protecting Tibet's distinctive religious and cultural heritage and (v) permitting international radio and television broadcasts into China.[7]

In 1994, President Clinton extended MFN treatment despite only limited progress on these issues and announced his intention to break the link between MFN treatment and human rights issues. He did, however, impose restrictions on Chinese munitions exports to the US to record continuing US dissatisfaction with Chinese human rights policies. In his statement announcing his decision, he noted that "serious human rights abuses continue in China." He concluded, however, that[8]

> [t]he question for us now is, given the fact that there has been some progress but that not all of the requirements of the executive order were met, how can we best advance the cause of human rights and other profound interests the United States has in our relationship with China.
>
> I have decided that the United States should renew Most Favored Nation trading status toward China. This decision, I believe, offers us the best opportunity to lay the basis for long-term sustainable progress in human rights and for the advancement of our other interests with China. Extending M.F.N. will avoid isolating China and instead will permit us to engage the Chinese with not only economic contacts but with cultural, educational and other contacts, and with a continuing aggressive effort in human rights—an approach that I believe will make it more likely that China will play a responsible role, both at home and abroad.
>
> I am moving, therefore, to delink human rights from the annual extension of Most Favored Nation trading status for China. That linkage has been constructive during the past year, but I believe, based on our aggressive contacts with China in the past several

---

7.   58 Fed.Reg. 31327, 31329 (1993).   **8.**   1994 Westlaw 209851, #1 (White House).

months, that we have reached the end of the usefulness of that policy, and it is time to take a new path toward the achievement of our constant objectives. We need to place our relationship into a larger and more productive framework.

* * * I am also pursuing a new and vigorous American program to support those in China working to advance the cause of human rights and democracy. This program will include increased broadcasts for Radio Free Asia and the Voice of America, increased support for nongovernmental organizations working on human rights in China, and development, with American business leaders, of a voluntary set of principles for business activity in China.

* * *

* * * [T]he question, therefore, is not whether we continue to support human rights in China but how can we best support human rights in China and advance our other very significant issues and interests. I believe we can do it by engaging the Chinese.

At the time of this announcement, there were at least two other issues between the US and China that were of particular concern. First, the US wanted Chinese assistance in persuading North Korea not to develop nuclear weapons and to permit inspections of its nuclear facilities by the International Atomic Energy Agency. Second, the US did not want to lose large orders placed in the US by the Chinese government and corporations, particularly those for aircraft.

Notes and Questions

(1) The China MFN issue had become more controversial in part because of the large increase in US imports from China in recent years. In 1993, US imports from China were valued at $31.5 billion, making China the fourth largest supplier of goods to the US (trailing only Canada, Japan and Mexico). US exports to China in 1993 totaled only $8.8 billion, which meant a trade deficit in 1993 of $22.8 billion (second only to the US deficit with Japan).[9] In 1988, in contrast, the deficit was only $3.5 billion.[10] The volume of Chinese exports, many of which would probably not have been viable if subjected to the non-MFN (Smoot–Hawley) tariff rates, meant that general denial of MFN would have been quite disruptive for US businesses selling Chinese products in the US, as well as for the Chinese exporters themselves. Making such a large volume of trade dependent on an all-or-nothing, subjective annual evaluation of Chinese human rights practices may not have made good policy sense. But did the decision have to be all-or-nothing? What about withdrawal of MFN treatment for only some products or some (e.g., state- or army-controlled) enterprises? Would such an approach be workable? It was urged by opponents of MFN renewal, who seemed to concede that a complete withdrawal of MFN treatment was too draconian.

9. US Dept. of Commerce, Business America, Apr. 1994, at 39.

10. 1994 Economic Report of the President & Annual Report of the Council of Economic Advisors 216 (1994).

(2) Review the factors that Hufbauer et al. list as the requirements for effective use of sanctions in Section 21.1 supra. In light of those factors, do you think that suspension of MFN treatment of Chinese goods would have likely caused the Chinese government to respect human rights? Is effectiveness an important consideration if the goal is to express strongly held beliefs about the inappropriateness of another country's actions?

(3) The proponents of continuing MFN treatment for China argued that expanding trade with China strengthened its private sector, which would ultimately weaken the authority of the central Communist government and over time lead to more freedom in China. It is, of course, impossible to know if they are right, but what do you think?

(4) Another response that is sometimes made to complaints about a country's failure to respect basic political rights is that in developing countries it is more meaningful for the government to improve living standards than it is to worry about political rights. The suggestion is that over time adequate political rights will develop. Do you agree? Some would argue that an equitable income distribution, not overall GDP levels, is the key factor. Should that be taken into account?

(5) Is it ever appropriate to use trade sanctions to enforce human rights? If so, which human rights should be selected as candidates for such enforcement? Are the concerns listed in President Clinton's memorandum the type of rights that deserve to be so protected? He listed concerns with emigration rights, prison labor, implementation of the UN Declaration, release of nonviolent political and religious prisoners, prisoner rights, treatment of Tibet and allowing radio and TV broadcasts into China. Are all of these human rights? Are they of same importance? Should there have to be a connection with international trade (e.g., exports of prison labor) before it is appropriate to use trade sanctions to promote human rights?

(6) One of GATT's biggest concerns historically was to control discrimination in international trade. Should there be WTO/GATT review of trade sanctions imposed for human rights purposes to ensure that similarly situated countries (in terms of human rights) are treated the same? Should there be WTO/GATT review to ensure that trade sanctions ostensibly for human rights purposes are not really for protectionist purposes? How could such a review be undertaken?

(7) In Section 21.4, we will see that the WTO does not effectively oversee trade actions taken under the GATT Article XXI for national security or political reasons. Should a similar rule apply for human rights?

(8) One of the issues raised by US complaints about human rights practices in other countries is whether it is appropriate for the US to "intervene" in the internal affairs of another country. Needless to say, countries that are the targets of US complaints are quick to raise this argument. What gives the United States the right to tell other sovereign nations how to structure their governments and treat their citizens? At the time that President Clinton was considering the China MFN issue, the Prime Minister of Singapore, Goh Chok Tong, was quoted as suggesting "that the Chinese may one day threaten to withhold most-favored-nation status from the US unless it does more to improve living conditions in

Detroit, Harlem and South Central Los Angeles."[11] Suppose such action was taken by an advanced industrialized country having a more equal income distribution than the US does. How, if at all, would sanctions imposed by that country against the US be fundamentally different than the US taking such action to promote democracy? Again we are led to the question: Who should decide what the important human rights are, whether they are satisfactorily met and what sanctions are appropriate?

SECTION 21.3   LABOR STANDARDS AND INTERNATIONAL TRADE POLICY[1]

(A) LABOR STANDARDS AND THE WTO

At the end of the Uruguay Round, the United States and France proposed that the WTO agenda include consideration of the relationship of trade, on the one hand, and labor standards and social justice, on the other. This proposal was opposed by many developing countries, who saw it as an attempt to restrict their exports to the developed world. In their view, any attempt to label exports from low-wage countries as unfair was an attempt to repeal comparative advantage—the driving force behind international trade. While nothing became of the specific proposal, the issue of labor standards arose again and was probably the most controversial subject at the WTO's first ministerial meeting in Singapore in December 1996.

In paragraph 4 of the Singapore ministerial declaration, WTO Members included the following statement on core labor standards:

> We renew our commitment to the observance of internationally recognized core labour standards. The International Labour Organization (ILO) is the competent body to set and deal with these standards, and we affirm our support for its work in promoting them. We believe that economic growth and development fostered by increased trade and further trade liberalization contribute to the promotion of these standards. We reject the use of labour standards for protectionist purposes, and agree that the comparative advantage of countries, particularly low-wage developing countries, must in no way be put into question. In this regard, we note that the WTO and ILO Secretariats will continue their existing collaboration.

The internationally recognized core labor standards referred to are (i) the right of association, (ii) the right to organize and bargain collectively, (iii) the prohibition of forced labor, (iv) the prohibition of exploitive child labor and (v) nondiscrimination in employment. The rights are specified in more detail in the eight fundamental conventions of the ILO, two conventions on each of the right of association, forced labor, child labor

---

11. Quoted in Karen Elliott House, "... But Asia Holds Us in Contempt," Wall St. J., May 27, 1994, at A–10.

1. See generally Lance Compa, Labor Rights and Labor Standards in Internation-

al Trade, 25 L. & Pol.Intl.Bus. 165 (1993); Steve Charnovitz, The Influence of International Labour Standards on the World Trading Regime: A Historical Overview, 126 Intl. Labor Rev. 565 (1987).

and discrimination. The United States is a party to only two of the conventions (one on forced labor and one on child labor).

The issue of trade and labor standards arose again in the course of the WTO's failed 1999 Seattle ministerial. Initially, the United States had proposed the creation of a WTO working party on labor rights with focus on a range of areas such as social protections and core labor standards, while the EU had proposed the creation of a standing forum on labor involving the WTO and the ILO. While the US and the EU were apparently willing to scale back their proposals, ultimately nothing was agreed at Seattle. According to some observers, the efforts to obtain agreement on some type of discussion of labor issues in the WTO were seriously set back following an interview given by US President Clinton in which he said ultimately he wanted the WTO system to be able to enforce labor standards with sanctions (a position that had been denied by US negotiators).[2] The trade and labor question was not a major issue at Doha.

Notes and Questions

(1) Although the subject of labor standards or worker rights is thought of as a new issue, it is not. There were discussions of the need to have some sort of international trade/minimum labor standard connection in the 1920s.[3] Indeed, Article 7:1 of the ITO Charter provided:

> The Members recognize that measures relating to employment must take into account the rights of workers under inter-governmental declarations, conventions and agreements. They recognize that all countries have a common interest in the achievement and maintenance of fair labour standards related to productivity, and thus in the improvement of wages and working conditions as productivity may permit. The Members recognize that unfair labor conditions, particularly in production for export, create difficulties in international trade, and, accordingly, each Member shall take whatever action may be appropriate and feasible to eliminate such conditions within its territory.

Could this serve as a basis for an addition to the WTO agreements?

(2) GATT Article XX(e) allows a country to ban imports of prison labor. A review of the conventions listed in Section 21.2 supra shows that the only human rights conventions existing in 1947 were those on slavery and forced labor. Thus, the General Agreement arguably reflected the international consensus on worker rights at the time it was drafted. Since that time, however, there have been other conventions recognizing certain worker rights. Is that an argument for "updating" the WTO view of what measures should be included under Article XX?

(3) Section 307 of the Tariff Act of 1930, 19 U.S.C.A. sec. 1307, bars the entry into the United States of goods "mined, produced, or manufactured wholly or in part in any foreign country by convict labor or/and forced labor or/and indentured labor under penal sanctions." "Forced labor" is defined as

---

2. "U.S., EU Back Off From Modest Proposals for Labor Rights–Trade Link, Inside U.S. Trade," December 10, 1999.

3. See generally Charnovitz, supra note 1.

"all work or service which is extracted from any person under the menace of any penalty for its nonperformance and for which the worker does not offer himself voluntarily." See generally 19 CFR secs. 12.42–.45 (2007). As of April 1, 2008, several Mexican products were subject to exclusion under this provision. 19 CFR sec. 12.42(h). In recent years, there has been considerable controversy over the extent to which Chinese exports to the United States include products of forced or prison labor. The US and China entered into an agreement in 1992 dealing with this subject and improved implementation of the agreement was a condition for US renewal of Chinese MFN status.

(4) During the NAFTA negotiations, there were concerns that US industry would move to Mexico to take advantage of low Mexican wages and lax labor laws generally and that Mexican exporters (whether transplanted US companies or others in Mexico) would be able to expand their exports to the United States. In deciding to support NAFTA, President Clinton announced that he would negotiate side agreements on the environment, labor and import surges. In the labor field, the result was the North American Agreement on Labor Cooperation, which is reproduced in the Documents Supplement. Under this agreement, each party recognized the right of the others to establish their own labor standards, but the agreement obligated each party to "promote compliance with and effectively enforce its labor law through appropriate government action." Agreement, art. 3. The parties are also obligated to ensure that "persons with a legally recognized interest under [their] law in a particular matter have appropriate access to administrative, judicial or labor tribunals for the enforcement of [their] labor law." Agreement, art. 4. The agreement also requires certain procedural guarantees be afforded. Agreement, art. 5. In addition, it establishes a procedure under which an Evaluation Committee of Experts (ECE) may analyze patterns of practice by a party in the enforcement of its occupational safety and health or other technical labor standards, which would seem to include child labor and minimum wage laws. Agreement, art. 23. On basis of the ECE's report, one party may claim that "there has been a persistent pattern of failure by [another] to effectively enforce such standards." Agreement, art. 27. If consultations between the parties fail and the NAFTA Labor Council (i.e., the Canadian, Mexican and US labor ministers) cannot agree, then an arbitral panel may be appointed, which will consist of independent experts, to consider whether the persistent pattern of failure is trade-related and covered by mutually recognized labor laws. Agreement, art. 29. If the panel concludes that there has been such a failure, it may ultimately impose a monetary fine if a party fails to adopt and implement an action plan to correct the failure. Agreement, art. 39 and annex 39. If the fine is not paid, NAFTA benefits otherwise owed to the nonpaying party may be suspended. Agreement, art. 41. How would you evaluate this procedure as a means of enforcing labor standards? The GAO indicated in 2001 that no labor disputes under NAFTA had reached the dispute settlement phase. See Section 11.3(B) supra.

(5) The NAFTA Labor Agreement does not specify any minimum labor standards, but in Annex 1 it lists guiding principles that the parties are committed to promote, each in its own way. The eleven principles are:

— Freedom of association and protection of the right to organize

— The right to bargain collectively

— The right to strike

— Prohibition of forced labor

— Labor protections for children and young persons

— Minimum employment standards (e.g., minimum wages and overtime pay)

— Elimination of employment discrimination

— Equal pay for men and women

— Prevention of occupational injuries and illnesses

— Compensation for occupational injuries and illnesses

— Protection of migrant workers

How do these compare to the worker rights listed in the US GSP statute? See Section 24.3(B) infra.

(6) In an effort to defuse opposition to ratification of NAFTA in the United States, President Salinas of Mexico committed Mexico to raise its minimum wage in line with Mexican productivity increases.[4] How could such a commitment be enforced? Note that a similar commitment was contained in the ITO Charter, as quoted above in Note 1.

(7) As of 2008, the most recently negotiated US free trade agreements have contained stricter rules regarding labor rights. These were added at the insistence of congressional Democrats as one of several conditions for approving those agreements pending when they took control of Congress in 2007, although only one of the pending agreements (with Peru) had been approved as of January 2008. The other pending agreements are with Colombia, Korea and Panama. Basically, the agreements require the parties to respect internationally recognized core labor standards and to effectively enforce their labor laws (including those related to the core standards, plus those related to acceptable conditions of work with respect to minimum wages, hours of work, and occupational safety and health). Although there are expanded consultation requirements in the event of a dispute over compliance with the labor rights chapter, the labor rights provisions are ultimately subject to the same dispute settlement procedures and enforcement mechanisms as commercial obligations, unlike other US FTAs such as NAFTA. The following materials suggest that labor rights cases may not be initiated very often.

(B) LABOR STANDARDS AND THE US GSP SCHEME

The concept of "internationally recognized worker rights," is defined in Title V of the Trade Act of 1974, which establishes the US Generalized System of Preferences for developing countries. That program is discussed more generally in Section 24.3(B) infra. Here we will examine the procedure that may lead to the withdrawal of GSP benefits if a beneficiary developing country (BDC) fails to afford such worker

---

4. Keith Bradsher, The Free–Trade Accord: 3 Nations Resolve Issues Holding Up Trade Pact Vote, N.Y.Times, Aug. 14, 1993, sec. 1, at 1, col. 6; Anthony DePalma, Mexico Raises Minimum Wages as Pledged, id., Dec. 12, 1993, sec. 1, at 6, col. 1.

rights. Under the regulations implementing the GSP program, interested parties may ask that a BDC be investigated to determine if it meets the criteria for continued inclusion in the GSP program. The following case highlights the rights at issue and the approach taken by US authorities.

GENERALIZED SYSTEM OF PREFERENCES
SUBCOMMITTEE OF THE TRADE POLICY
STAFF COMMITTEE, 1992 GSP ANNUAL
REVIEW—WORKER RIGHTS REVIEW SUMMARY—
INDONESIA (CASE 007–CP–92, JULY 1993)

INTRODUCTION

In response to petitions filed in June 1992 by Asia Watch and the International Labor Rights Education and Research Fund, the inter-agency Subcommittee on the Generalized System of Preferences (GSP) conducted a review of worker rights laws and practices in Indonesia. The purpose of the review was to determine whether Indonesia is complying with the worker rights provision of Section 502(b) of the US GSP law, which requires beneficiary countries to have taken or be taking steps to afford internationally recognized worker rights.

The GSP program, originally enacted in 1974, provides duty-free entry to eligible products from beneficiary developing countries. [It] defines internationally recognized worker rights as follows:

a) the right of association;

b) the right to organize and bargain collectively;

c) a prohibition against any form of forced or compulsory labor;

d) a minimum age for the employment of children;

e) acceptable conditions of work with respect to minimum wages, hours of work and occupational safety and health.

The legislative history * * * indicates that Congress intended for level of development to be taken into account in assessing whether GSP beneficiary countries meet the "taking steps" standard. The 1984 report of the Committee on Ways and Means on the renewal act states that:

It is not the expectation of the Committee that developing countries come up to the prevailing labor standards of the US and other highly-industrialized countries. It is recognized that acceptable minimum standards may vary from country to country.

The Subcommittee noted that it is established United States policy that basic human rights are universal and that all governments are required to respect basic human rights, which include the first three cited worker rights, irrespective of social systems or state of economic development.

In the course of its review, the Subcommittee examined several submissions from the petitioners and the Government of Indonesia, the Department of State's Country Reports on Human Rights Practices, documents from the International Labor Organization (ILO), and a number of reports from the US Embassy in Jakarta, Indonesia.

PRINCIPAL ISSUES

The GSP Subcommittee identified possible worker rights problems in all five worker rights categories listed in the GSP statute: right of association, the right to organize and bargain collectively, the minimum age for the employment of children, acceptable conditions of work, and forced labor.

Right of Association

The right of association includes the right of workers to establish and join organizations of their own choosing. The right of association also includes the right to strike.

Principal problems identified were 1) a union registration requirement which severely inhibits the formation of worker organizations; 2) a requirement that all unions be members of a single nationwide union structure (the All Indonesian Workers Union (SPSI)) over which the government has a great deal of influence; 3) a prohibition on union formation by civil servants; 4) government harassment of groups and individuals attempting to form new labor unions; 5) harassment of those who risk work action; and 6) police and military intervention between management and workers.

Under the Indonesian labor regulations in force when the review began, a worker organization could register as a "worker union" only if it consisted of a minimum of 1000 workplace level units. These units in turn had to be located in at least 100 districts in at least 20 different provinces. This numerical requirement operated as a significant barrier to union formation, thus impinging on workers' right to establish organizations of their own choosing. In its February 26 submission, the Government of Indonesia provided a draft of a union registration regulation which lowers the registration requirements to 100 workplace level units in 25 districts in 5 provinces. The regulation also requires that a "worker union" have at least 10,000 members.

While lowering the numerical requirements for establishing a "worker union" could result in workers enjoying a greater degree of freedom in establishing organizations of their own choosing, there is a concern that even these new limits may operate as a barrier to union formation. The Subcommittee noted that the 10,000 member requirement is not in conformity with the ILO's standards for freedom of association. On the question of numerical requirements for union formation, the ILO's Freedom of Association Committee has stated:

> Restrictions concerning race, minimum number of members, supervisors and the structure of trade unions
>
> Para. 256. The establishment of a trade union may be considerably hindered, or even rendered impossible, when legislation fixes the minimum number of members of a trade union at obviously too high

a figure, as is the case, for example, where legislation requires that a union must have at least 50 founder members.

Para. 257. The legal requirement that there be a minimum number of 20 members to form a union does not seem excessive and, therefore, does not in itself constitute an obstacle to the formation of a trade union.

Freedom of Association, Digest of Decisions and Principles of the Freedom of Association Committee (3d ed.)

Indonesian law and practice effectively prohibits the formation of organizations as alternatives to the SPSI. By law, all worker organizations wishing to engage in traditional labor union activity (e.g., negotiating collective bargaining agreements) must be part of the SPSI, thus preventing workers from establishing and joining alternative unions. For example, the Government of Indonesia recently promulgated a regulation requiring that when a group of workers in a company wishes to form a union, they must first register with an existing union, of which there is only one—the SPSI. Further, during the review the Subcommittee obtained credible reports of harassment of individuals who attempt to form alternatives to the SPSI. Harassment has taken many forms, including the disruption of meetings and the detainment of individuals involved in efforts to create alternative worker organizations.

This infringement of workers' right of association is exacerbated by the fact that the SPSI is not a truly independent workers' organization. The extent to which it is controlled by the Government of Indonesia was noted in the State Department's 1992 Human Rights Report:

> [T]he government has a great deal of influence over the SPSI, the head of the SPSI is a senior member of GOLKAR [a government-sponsored political organization], two senior SPSI officials are Members of Parliament representing GOLKAR, and the Minister of Manpower is a member of the SPSI's Consultative Council. According to credible reports, the Government interferes in the selection of SPSI officers, especially the placing of retired military officers in mid-level positions.

* * *

In addition, Indonesian law does not allow civil servants to join labor unions. Civil servants must join the civil servants corps (KORPRI), a nonunion association whose leadership council is chaired by the Minister of Home Affairs. Indeed, KORPRI's charter states that its "main duty" is to implement policy as set forth by its central trustees (all of whom are government ministers) as opposed to representing the labor interests of civil servants. Further, KORPRI does not fit the definition of a truly independent labor union because its leadership is dominated by government ministers. The subcommittee noted that workers in some state owned enterprises are covered by collective labor agreements negotiated by SPSI units, but these are rare. The overwhelming majority of civil servants do not enjoy true freedom of association and, as a result, are denied the right to bargain collectively.

The Subcommittee viewed seriously these obstructions to the free formation of independent trade unions. The requirement that union formation is dependent upon participation in an organization heavily influenced by the government not only infringes the workers' right to join organizations of their own choosing, but is contrary to the ILO's standard that workers should be able to create and join unions that are free of government domination and control. Mandatory membership in organizations which do not engage in union activities is not a substitute for true freedom of association. In addition, the ILO has specifically criticized the prohibition on the formation of independent unions by civil servants as incompatible with the principles of freedom of association. The Subcommittee did note, however, that the Government of Indonesia has recently requested input from the ILO as to how to bring its union registration regulation into closer compliance with international norms. Such input could prove to be a valuable asset in any effort to improve the rights of Indonesian workers in this important area.

With respect to the right to strike, the Subcommittee noted several shortcomings when it compared Indonesian law and practice with international norms. One of the more serious concerns regarded the involvement and interference by the police and/or military in strikes, often when there is no threat to property and public order. When this involvement has occurred, it has taken various forms such a significant police or military presence during strikes, or presence during negotiations between workers and management when there is no apparent threat to public order. Plant level union officials have stated that this presence during negotiations is intimidating. In addition, workers assert that the military and police have beaten strike leaders.

Another concern in this area involves the obstacles to workers who wish to conduct a legal strike. In order to comply with the law, disaffected workers must go through a cumbersome and time-consuming dispute settlement process, including intensive mediation by the Ministry of Manpower, before legally being able to engage in strike activity. The process has little credibility with the workers and is therefore mostly ignored. As a result, most strikes are illegal. While leaders of illegal strikes are not usually arrested, they often lose their jobs because of their activities.

The Government of Indonesia is considering amendments to its strike law, and provided the subcommittee with a draft of the new law. The Subcommittee was concerned because the draft law contains inadequate procedures for protecting workers' right to strike. The new law would allow either party to an industrial dispute to request compulsory arbitration. While the matter is being arbitrated, workers would be prohibited from engaging in strike activity. However, the new law does not set forth any deadline for resolution of the dispute. As a result, for an indefinite length of time workers could be effectively denied their right to strike.

The Subcommittee was especially concerned to learn that on February 5, 1993, the Ministry of Manpower issued a directive which constitutes a serious infringement upon workers' right to strike. The directive provides that in the event of "any strike," the local office of the Ministry of Manpower is to invite labor and management to engage in settlement negotiations and that workers are to return to work during the negotiations. The directive further provides that if workers do not return to work, they are to be considered having resigned. By providing advance authorization for employers to retaliate against workers who engage in strike activity, the directive is contrary to the ILO's principles on freedom of association.

A final issue of concern in the area of the right of association is military and police interference in routine labor activities. As noted in the [1992 State Department] Human Rights Report, the Government of Indonesia interferes in the selection of SPSI officers by placing retired military officers in mid-level positions. In addition, the police require any organization to obtain a permit before holding a meeting. While permits are routinely issued to the SPSI, there is concern that other organizations have difficulty obtaining the necessary permits.

Right to Organize and Bargain Collectively

With respect to the right to organize and bargain collectively, the principal problem is the legal requirement that a group of workers can negotiate a collective labor agreement (CLA) only if it is a chapter of a government-recognized union. The only government-recognized union is the SPSI. Therefore, this law effectively limits the right to organize and bargain collectively to SPSI members (who constitute less than 2% of Indonesia's total work force and approximately 6% of the industrial work force). Further, only about one half of the SPSI units have CLAs. Thus, the collective labor agreements in force cover only a small percentage of Indonesian workers.

Workers who are members of organizations that are unable to obtain union status (primarily because of the numerical requirements) are prohibited from negotiating the terms of a CLA with management. These workers can be covered by "company regulations" which define generally the terms and conditions of employment. Company regulations are subject to review by the Ministry of Manpower and are good for a period of two years. However, there are several key respects in which company regulations differ from CLAs:

— CLAs are negotiated between labor and management and signed by representatives of both parties. Company regulations are promulgated by management, albeit after receiving input from labor.

— CLAs set forth the wage scales for the employees. Company regulations do not establish employee's base wages beyond stating that the company will agree to pay the legally mandated minimum wage.

— When an employer violates the provisions of a CLA, an employee can seek redress through the industrial dispute settlement system. It appears that violations of company regulations can only be addressed through an individual breach of contract action in court.

While CLAs cover only a very small percentage of Indonesian workers, the Subcommittee noted that the number of CLAs in force has increased over the past several years.

Prohibition of any form of forced labor

The petitioner alleged that the Government of Indonesia condones the practice of forced labor by logging companies among the Asmat tribe in Irian Jaya, and there were credible reports of forced labor in 1990. There were also reports of girls being sold as domestic workers and men being sold as agricultural workers. In the course of several years, the Government of Indonesia has stated on numerous occasions that it intends to investigate these allegations, but has not provided the results of any investigation.

The petitioners also alleged that forced labor exists with respect to certain East Timorese workers. According to the petition, these workers were lured to Java with the promise of vocational training and high-paying jobs, promises which did not materialize. It remains unclear as to whether these East Timorese workers were the victims of fraud. Regardless, it did not appear to the Subcommittee that the condition of these workers constitutes forced labor as defined by international standards.

Minimum age for employment of children

Child labor is a serious problem in both the formal and informal sectors in Indonesia. A 1987 regulation on child labor legalizes the employment of children under the age of 14, but only under certain circumstances. Because the regulation does not set a minimum age for the employment of children, it has effectively superseded a 1925 government ordinance which set a minimum employment age of 12. The Government of Indonesia has never promulgated implementing regulations for its 1951 labor act which included provisions on child labor. Further, there is no evidence that the Government of Indonesia enforces the existing restrictions on the employment of children. Since the promulgation of the current regulation in 1987, no employers have been taken to court for violating it. The government rarely conducts inspections of workplaces, choosing instead to rely primarily on Ministry of Manpower supervisors who learn of irregularities through other means. In the two inspections which the Government of Indonesia described in its November 16 submission, it claims to have found "very few child workers under 14 years old" in one instance and "no child labor" in another.

Acceptable conditions of work

The regional minimum wage rates in Indonesia are consistently less than the figure needed to enable a single worker or family to meet basic needs of nutrition, clothing and shelter. In addition to being inadequate, the legally-mandated minimum wage is widely ignored by employers. Failure to provide the minimum wage is most common grounds for strikes on the part of Indonesian workers.

Proactive enforcement of the minimum wage law is virtually nonexistent. There are few instances of ministry personnel conducting inspections of workplaces. The supervisors in each provincial office of the Ministry of Manpower instead rely upon reports of violations submitted by others. When the supervisor learns of a violation, he is supposed to issue a warning; only after three warnings can the employer be penalized for failing to comply with the law. When an employer is punished, the most common sanction is a nominal fine. The ineffectiveness of this system appears to contribute to the widespread disregard of the minimum wage laws by employers.

Occupational safety and health laws are likewise ineffectual. The 1992 Human Rights Report describes government enforcement and supervision of these laws as generally "weak." The government's efforts in this area are hampered by a scarcity of trained inspectors. Further, while employees who report unsafe working conditions are protected by law against employer retaliation, ineffective enforcement of this law allows retaliation to occur without sanction.

Positive Actions Noted

The Subcommittee noted favorably that the Government of Indonesia has indicated an interest in amending certain of its laws and practices to bring them into closer compliance with international norms. In particular, the Government of Indonesia has requested input from the International Labor Organization (ILO) on how to bring its regulation on the registration of unions into closer compliance with international standards. The Subcommittee hopes that the Government of Indonesia will, in the near future, act to bring its law and practice into conformity with international standards regarding this fundamental worker right.

The Government of Indonesia has also indicated an interest in reviewing its laws and regulations governing the right to strike. While the draft law presented by the Government of Indonesia in its submission is flawed, the Subcommittee appreciated the fact that Government of Indonesia was reviewing its strike law. The Subcommittee hopes that the Government of Indonesia, with further input regarding international standards in this area, will promulgate a law which will constitute a concrete step towards providing this important worker right. Equally important, the Subcommittee hopes that the Government of Indonesia will show evidence of respecting the exercise of this right in practice. Such an advance could obviate workers' need to engage in illegal strikes.

The Subcommittee also noted that the SPSI is planning a restructuring through which it will decentralize into autonomous sectoral organizations. This restructuring will not be formalized before the next SPSI convention in 1995. The Subcommittee welcomes this move as decentralization may serve to improve the SPSI's efficiency at representing the concerns of its members. It should be noted, however, that decentralization is not a substitute for freedom of association.

RECOMMENDATION

The Subcommittee viewed the Government of Indonesia's positive actions as indicative of interest in bringing its worker rights laws and practices into closer compliance with international norms. Accordingly, the Subcommittee recommended that the review of Indonesian worker rights laws and practices be extended until February 5, 1994 in order to monitor developments in all the areas of concern, and to provide the Government of Indonesia with an opportunity to incorporate ILO advice regarding its labor laws and practices.

While noting the above positive actions, the Subcommittee determined that there were numerous significant deficiencies in Indonesia's labor laws and practices. The Subcommittee's most serious concerns had to do with the right of association, particularly with respect to the right to freely form independent unions and the right to strike. Additional concerns were in the areas of the right to organize and bargain collectively, child labor, and acceptable conditions of work. Questions about the use of forced labor remain unanswered.

The Subcommittee's concerns made it unable to recommend that Indonesia is taking steps to provide internationally recognized worker rights. The Subcommittee particularly noted that there has been little progress to date with respect to the areas of major concern. The Subcommittee believed it important to underline the central importance of the right of association, a basic human right and fundamental right of workers. In the absence of substantial concrete progress in the key issue areas in the future, Indonesia's continued GSP eligibility will be in serious jeopardy.

Notes and Questions

(1) Ultimately, GSP benefits were not withdrawn from Indonesia, presumably because of political concerns. Indonesia is the fourth largest country in the world in terms of population. It is strategically located, and it was to be the 1994 host of the Asia–Pacific Economic Cooperation meeting. As such, it is a country with whom the US wants to maintain good relations.

(2) Other US trade laws also make reference to the same worker rights criteria that are contained in the GSP statute. For example, benefits under the Caribbean Basin Economic Recovery Act and the Andean Trade Preferences Act, both discussed in Section 24.3(B) infra, are also subject to a beneficiary country meeting the worker rights standard. A similar condition is imposed for beneficiaries of the Overseas Private Investment Corporation (OPIC), which insures, reinsures, guarantees and finances projects in devel-

oping countries.[5] Section 301 of the 1974 Trade Act, which is described in Chapter 7 supra, includes in its definition of "unreasonable" acts, a "persistent pattern of conduct" that denies the same worker rights outlined in the GSP statute. Section 301(d)(3)(B)(iii), 19 U.S.C.A. sec. 2411(d)(3)(B)(iii).

(3) Many investigations are requested of BDC labor practices and some are made. For example, according to USTR, in the 2005–2006 period, petitions for worker rights reviews were rejected in respect of Bangladesh, Costa Rica, Dominican Republic, El Salvador, Guatemala, Honduras, Iraq, Oman and Panama. During that same period, an ongoing investigation of Niger continued and investigations were closed in respect of Swaziland and Uganda. Overall, relatively few countries lose GSP benefits. Indeed, an examination of the pattern of suspensions and withdrawals, suggests that countries tend to lose benefits only when they have other political problems in their relationships with the United States. It appears to be true, however, that the investigations do give the United States an opportunity to put some pressure on countries to modify their labor practices. How successful does it appear from the above extract that the United States has been in this regard in the case of Indonesia?

(4) Look again at the five specified worker rights, as listed in the above decision. What does "(e) acceptable conditions of work with respect to minimum wages, hours of work and occupational safety and health" mean? Does the Indonesian decision clarify this standard sufficiently? Would it be possible, or appropriate, under this standard to require a BDC to meet US standards for wages and working conditions?

SECTION 21.4   TRADE CONTROLS FOR NATIONAL SECURITY AND POLITICAL PURPOSES

(A) INTRODUCTION

A classic exception to liberal trade policies and rules is the so-called national security exception. It is generally accepted that the benefits normally associated with free markets, such as efficient allocation of resources, do not outweigh the imperative need to ensure national survival. Thus, if a nation's defense and security depend, or are believed to depend, on the existence of industries such as shipbuilding or steel-making, those industries are likely to be maintained regardless of cost or any other economic considerations. The issue of national security being so important, it has always seemed inevitable that a national security exception would apply to international trade rules. The problem with a national security exception in international agreements, however, is that it is virtually impossible to define its limits. Almost every sector of economic endeavor can and does argue that it is necessary for national security, from shoes to watches, radios to beef production.

---

5.   22 U.S.C.A. sec. 2191a(a)(1) (incorporating GSP statute definition of worker rights).

The basic justification for the national security exception is that it is necessary to provide for national defense by ensuring production of goods essential for defense. That is not, however, the only reason that the exception exists. Nations often wish to use trade controls for political purposes that may have only a tangential relationship to national security. For example, a country may dislike the discriminatory racial policies of another government and therefore exercise controls over trade with that government. Countries may choose to refrain from granting MFN status to other countries, because those countries are viewed as unfriendly or because to grant such status would be politically unpopular and therefore risk the survival of elected officials in their positions. For whatever the reasons, the facts of international economic life are that nations will pursue political goals with economic means.

The materials in this section review the GATT rules applicable to the use of trade controls for national security and political purposes. In subdivision D, we summarize some US laws related to such purposes.

(B) THE GATT EXCEPTION FOR NATIONAL SECURITY TRADE CONTROLS

GATT Article XXI contains a general exception to all GATT obligations for certain measures taken by a member "necessary for the protection of its essential security interests." Although in principle limited to the three specified situations listed in Article XXI(b), the exception is broad enough to be subject to abuse.[1] Essentially the same language appears in GATS Article XIVbis and TRIPS Article 73. In addition, at the time a country becomes a WTO member, WTO Article XIII permits that country or any other member to refuse to apply the WTO Agreement as between themselves (a similar provision was contained in GATT Article XXXV). This authority can be used to prevent WTO rules applying for any reason—political, national security or otherwise.[2]

The question of the scope of Article XXI has only infrequently arisen in GATT. Czechoslovakia complained against the United States in 1949, arguing that the US export controls preventing certain exports to Czechoslovakia were a violation of US GATT obligations. The Czechoslovakian complaint was rejected by the GATT Contracting Parties. During the discussion it was contended that:

> every country must have the last resort on questions relating to its own security. On the other hand, the CONTRACTING PARTIES should be cautious not to take any step which might have the effect of undermining the General Agreement.[3]

As a result of congressional action, the United States suspended MFN treatment in 1951 towards Communist countries, including Czechoslo-

---

1. See generally John H. Jackson, World Trade and the Law of GATT 748–752 (1969).

2. Id. at 100–102.

3. Id. at 749; GATT Doc. CP.3/SR. 22, at 7 (1949).

vakia.[4] Again, the United States–Czechoslovakia relationship was brought to GATT, and the GATT Contracting Parties finally ruled that these two governments "shall be free to suspend, each with respect to the other, the obligations of the General Agreement on Tariffs and Trade."[5] No explicit reference was made in this declaration to any clause of the General Agreement that authorized this action, although it might be termed a "waiver." Other comparably ambiguous cases have included a Peruvian prohibition of Czechoslovakian imports, ultimately lifted after consultation, and a Ghanaian ban on Portuguese products, exercising Article XXXV of GATT.[6] Article XXXV has been invoked in a number of other situations, of course.[7]

More recently, the issue of the scope of the national security exception came before GATT as a result of Nicaragua's protest of US controls on trade between the United States and Nicaragua. In 1983, when the United States cut Nicaragua's sugar import quota from 58,000 to 6,000 short tons, the GATT Council adopted a panel report concluding that the US action violated Article XIII:2 because the United States did not hold negotiations with Nicaragua.[8] The United States did not press an argument that its actions were justified under Article XXI, and it did not attempt to block a decision by the Council on the Nicaraguan complaint. Nonetheless, the United States did not change its policy as a result of the GATT decision.

In 1985, President Reagan prohibited all trade between the United States and Nicaragua.[9] Nicaragua again raised objections in GATT. This time the United States explicitly took the position that its actions were imposed for national security reasons pursuant to Article XXI and that, in the reported words of the US ambassador to GATT, "The GATT is not an appropriate forum for debating political and security issues." According to the US ambassador, the United States "sees no basis for GATT Contracting Parties to question, approve, or disapprove the judgment of each Contracting Party as to what is necessary to protect its national security interests." Reportedly, the US position was supported by Australia, Canada and most European countries, as well as the EU, whose ambassador stated, "while we do not wish to pass judgment before the Council, it is not the role of GATT to resolve disputes in the field of national security." Nicaragua argued that the United States could not credibly claim that Nicaragua was a threat to US security.[10]

---

4. 65 Stat. 73, sec. 5 (1951).

5. Jackson, supra note 1, at 749–750; GATT, II BISD 36 (1952).

6. Jackson, supra note 1, at 750–751; see GATT Doc. SR. 9/27, at 10 (1955), but see also GATT Doc. L/2844 (1967), wherein Peru announced that it had abrogated, as of August 1, 1967, its decree of March 11, 1953, which restricted trade with countries having centrally planned economies. GATT Doc. SR. 19/12, at 196 (1961).

7. See Section 6.6(C) supra.

8. United States—Imports of Sugar from Nicaragua, GATT, 31st Supp. BISD 67 (1985) (Panel report adopted Mar. 13, 1984).

9. Executive Order No. 12513, 50 Fed. Reg. 18629 (1985).

10. 2 BNA Intl. Trade Rptr. 765 (1985); 3 BNA Intl. Trade Rptr. 380 (1986).

In the end, the United States did not block the creation of a panel to consider Nicaragua's complaint. In its report, the panel ultimately concluded that[11]

"as it was not authorized to examine the justification for the US invocation of a general exception to the obligations under the General Agreement, it could find the United States neither to be complying with its obligations under the General Agreement nor to be failing to carry out its obligations under that Agreement."

On the wider task of assisting the Contracting Parties in further action on this matter, the panel noted that "embargoes such as the one imposed by the United States, independent of whether or not they were justified under Article XXI, ran counter to the basic aims of the GATT." The panel also recommended that the Council, in any further consideration of the matter, take into account the following general questions:

If it were accepted that the interpretation of Article XXI was reserved entirely to the contracting party invoking it, how could the Contracting Parties ensure that this general exception to all obligations under the General Agreement is not invoked excessively or for purposes other than those set out in this provision? If the Contracting Parties give a panel the task of examining a case involving in Article XXI invocation without authorizing it to examine the justification of that invocation, do they limit the adversely affected contracting party's right to have its complaint investigated in accordance with Article XXIII:2? Are the powers of the Contracting Parties under Article XXIII:2 sufficient to provide redress to contracting parties subjected to a two-way embargo?

Nicaragua said it was unfortunate that the panel did not answer the fundamental questions raised in the report, and that it had failed to consider the International Court of Justice's ruling that the US embargo was in violation of international law. It then asked the Council to recommend the following: first, the immediate removal of the embargo; second, the authorization of special support measures to that countries could grant trade preferences aimed at re-establishing a balance in Nicaragua's pre-embargo global trade relations and at compensating Nicaragua for the damage caused by the embargo; and finally, to prepare an interpretative note on Article XXI which would reflect the elements in this case.

In the US view, the panel had reached sound conclusions in a difficult situation. It therefore believed that the Council should adopt the report, decline to consider the panel's questions, and remove the matter from its agenda. It added that there had been many instances of trade sanctions imposed by various contracting parties for reasons of national security. Rarely had those been raised

---

11. GATT, GATT Activities 1986, at 58–59 (1987).

in the GATT and never before had a party insisted on establishing a panel. It reiterated the view that GATT was not the proper forum for examining or judging national security disputes. In May 1987, the panel report was still under consideration by the Council.

The US supported adoption of the panel report, but Nicaragua opposed adoption. Consequently, the report was never adopted. US–Nicaragua trade relations were normalized following the electoral defeat of the Sandinista party in 1990.

Notes and Questions

(1) Suppose that imports of watches increase to the point that they threaten to eliminate all US watch production. Could the United States impose import restrictions on watch imports under GATT Article XXI? What if a similar situation existed for bicycles? Shoes? Cotton? Computers? Steel? Foodstuffs? Is there any limiting principle to the national security exception? After all, don't armies need watches and shoes and food and just about everything imaginable at one time or another?

(2) Review GATT Article XXI(b). Can you formulate more precisely defined and limited rules as to when the national security exception may be used? What assumptions must be made for such a formulation?

(C) THE USE OF ECONOMIC SANCTIONS FOR POLITICAL PURPOSES UNDER INTERNATIONAL LAW

The General Agreement does not specifically authorize the use of trade controls for political purposes, except that in Article XXI(c) there is an exemption from GATT obligations in respect of actions taken by a Contracting Party "in pursuance of its obligations under the United Nations Charter for the maintenance of international peace and security."

The United Nations Charter empowers the Security Council to impose economic and military sanctions upon nations which threaten world peace. A prerequisite to the imposition of such sanctions is a Security Council determination of the existence of "any threat to the peace, breach of the peace, or act of aggression."[12] Once such a determi-

---

12. United Nations Charter arts. 25, 39, 41, 42:

Art. 25. The Members of the United Nations agree to accept and carry out the decisions of the Security Council in accordance with the present Charter.

* * *

Art. 39. The Security Council shall determine the existence of any threat to the peace, breach of the peace, or act of aggression and shall make recommendations, or decide what measures shall be taken in accordance with Articles 41 and 42, to maintain or restore international peace and security.

* * *

Art. 41. The Security Council may decide what measures not involving the use of armed force are to be employed to give effect to its decisions, and it may call upon the Members of the United Nations to apply such measures. These may include complete or partial interruption of economic relations and of rail, sea, air, postal, telegraphic, radio, and other means of communication, and the severance of diplomatic relations.

Art. 42. Should the Security Council consider that measures provided for in Article 41 would be inadequate or have proved to be inadequate, it may take such action by air, sea, or land forces as may be necessary to maintain or restore international peace and

nation is made, recourse may be had to either Article 41 or Article 42 of the Charter.

Article 41 provides in a general way for taking measures "not involving the use of armed force." Economic and diplomatic sanctions are suggested, along with interruption of communications. Article 42 permits military action should the Council "consider that measures provided for in Article 41 would be inadequate or have proved to be inadequate." Once the Security Council has made an Article 39 determination and has decided upon sanctions, it may invoke Article 25 of the Charter, which binds member nations "to accept and carry out the decisions of the Security Council."

In the first 40 years of the U.N.'s existence, the Security Council only once called for broad-based economic sanctions to be applied against a country. In that instance, it asked member nations to impose economic sanctions on Rhodesia, after it unilaterally declared independence from the United Kingdom in 1965.[13] The sanctions were lifted after Rhodesia returned to its prior colonial status in 1979. The following year it became independent as Zimbabwe. During this period, the Security Council also adopted resolutions calling for limited sanctions to be applied to the Republic of South Africa to protest its policy of apartheid. For example, in 1977 it called for an arms embargo to be imposed on South Africa and in 1985 it called for the adoption of such measures as suspension of new investment, prohibition of the sale of South African gold coins, suspension of guaranteed export loans, prohibition of new contracts in the nuclear field and prohibition of all sales of computer equipment that might be used by South African army or police units.[14] The U.N. General Assembly had called upon the Security Council to impose broader economic sanctions on South Africa, but the Security Council did not do so.[15] The apartheid system was later abolished and South Africa had free elections in 1994.

Since the late 1980s, the Security Council has been more active in calling for economic sanctions. Many countries (and occasionally companies and individuals) have been targeted. Information on currently effective sanctions is available at www.un.org/sc/committees (sanctions committees). The type of sanctions imposed has ranged from comprehensive economic and trade sanctions to more specific measures such as arms embargoes, travel bans, and financial or diplomatic restrictions.

Notes and Questions

(1) Should the WTO Agreement contain an explicit "political escape clause" to allow any country to "opt out" of trading relationships with any

security. Such action may include demonstrations, blockade, and other operations by air, sea, or land forces of Members of the United Nations.

13. S.C.Res. 232, U.N.Doc. S/Res/232 (1966); 30 U.N. SCOR, Spec.Supp. No. 2, Vol. II, at 100; U.N.Doc. S/11594/Rev. 1 (1975). See also Myres S. McDougall & W.

Michael Riesman, Rhodesia and the United Nations: The Lawfulness of International Concern, 62 Am.J.Intl.L. 1 (1968).

14. S.C.Res. 569, U.N.Doc. S/Res/569 (1985); S.C.Res. 418, U.N.Doc. S/Res/417 (1977).

15. See, e.g., G.A.Res. 35/227, U.N.Doc. A/Res/35/227 (1981).

other country on political grounds (much as WTO Article XIII now allows at the time a country becomes a member)?

(2) Do the GATT responses to the US–Czechoslovakia and US–Nicaragua cases essentially create a political purposes exception to the General Agreement and, by implication, the WTO Agreement?

(D) U.S. NATIONAL SECURITY AND FOREIGN POLICY CONTROLS

As noted in Section 9.2 supra, the United States imposes export controls for national security and foreign policy purposes under the Export Administration Act. Here we look at several other US statutes related to trade and other controls for national security and foreign policy purposes.

(1) National Security Controls Under Section 232

Section 232 of the Trade Expansion Act of 1962 authorizes the imposition of import controls for national security purposes. It provides in the first instance that the President shall not reduce duties or eliminate other import restrictions if such action would threaten to impair national security. In addition, it establishes a procedure by which any interested party can ask that an investigation be conducted to determine if imports of any article into the United States are threatening to impair the national security. Although the wording of Section 232 suggests that it could have broad application, it has not often been applied, particularly in recent years.

(2) Trade and Other Controls Under IEEPA[16]

When the United States wants to impose economic sanctions for national security or foreign policy purposes, it typically acts to control more than just import or export flows. It may ban a range of financial transactions with the target country. Accordingly, it typically acts under the International Emergency Economic Powers Act (IEEPA), which was described in Section 3.3(C)(1) supra and which grants the President very broad discretionary powers to regulate international economic relations with other countries, once he declares a national emergency exists. IEEPA is set out in the Documents Supplement.[17] Formerly, wide-ranging economic sanctions were imposed under the Trading with the Enemy Act and some continue to be applied under that act. Section 3.3(C)(1) supra. US economic sanctions are typically administered by the Treasury Department's Office of Foreign Assets Control. Information about currently effective sanctions, which have been imposed for anti-terrorism, anti-proliferation, anti-drug and other reasons, can be found at http://www.ustreas.gov/offices/enforcement/ofac/.

---

16. See generally Michael P. Malloy, United States Economic Sanctions: Theory and Practice (2001).

17. Executive orders issued under IEEPA appear in the notes to 50 U.S.C.A. sec. 1701.

(3) Foreign Use of Trade Controls: U.S. Antiboycott Rules[18]

Section 8 of the Export Administration Act (EAA) regulates compliance by US persons with a boycott by foreign countries against a country that is friendly to the United States and that is not the object of a boycott pursuant to US law or regulation.[19] Essentially, the purpose of the provision, which was first adopted in 1977, is to make it unlawful for US companies to participate in the Arab boycott of Israel. That boycott, which is followed to varying degrees by the various Arab countries, calls for a ban on imports from and exports to Israel. In addition, it provides for a so-called secondary boycott of Israel, pursuant to which firms that do business with Israel or have certain other relations with it are blacklisted and unable to do business in the Arab world. The US antiboycott rules usually do not, as a practical matter, prevent US businesses from doing business with Arab countries or complying with the terms of the primary Arab boycott, i.e. that part of the boycott prohibiting the importation into Arab countries of Israeli origin goods. They do serve, however, to discourage US businesses from complying too readily with the secondary boycott. As such, the rules seem to have been largely accepted by all concerned, although US business interests cite them as an impediment that costs them business vis-à-vis European and Japanese competitors who do not have to worry about such rules. Moreover, the complexity of the rules creates a trap for the unwary, as the distinction between what is permitted and what is prohibited by the EAA may often seem virtually indistinguishable to the untrained eye.[20] For example, it is permissible to agree to certify that the goods to be supplied to an Arab country are of US, Canadian or whatever origin, but not that the goods are not of Israeli origin.[21]

Section 8 of the EAA applies only to US persons (broadly defined to include controlled foreign subsidiaries) and only with respect to activities in the interstate or foreign commerce of the United States. Obviously, many activities of US controlled subsidiaries would not involve the foreign commerce of the United States. The EAA provides that US persons should not engage in any boycott-related activities listed in Section 8(a)(1), except to the extent permitted by Section 8(a)(2). In addition, the law requires extensive reporting of requests to support boycotts.

Different antiboycott rules are found in the Internal Revenue Code. These provisions, added by the Tax Reform Act of 1976, require US taxpayers to report operations in, with or related to a boycotting country or national thereof and participation in the boycott, including receipt of requests to participate. Participation may lead to a loss of tax benefits.[22]

18. See generally Kennan L. Teslik, Congress, the Executive Branch, and Special Interests: The American Response to the Arab Boycott of Israel (1982).

19. 50 U.S.C.A.App. sec. 2407.

20. The regulations are set out at 15 CFR pt. 760 (2007).

21. 50 U.S.C.A.App. sec. 2407(a)(2)(B).

22. Tax Reform Act of 1976, Pub.L. No. 94–455, sec. 1061–64, 90 Stat. 1520 (adding 26 U.S.C.A. secs. 908, 952(a), 995(b)(1)(F)(ii) and 999). The Treasury Department issued Guidelines explaining the scope of the statute on several occasions between 1976 and 1978. See 1976–2 C.B. 628, 1977–1 C.B. 529, 1977–2 C.B. 505, 1978–1 C.B. 521. See generally Richard L. Kaplan, Income Taxes and the Arab Boycott, 32 Tax Lawyer 313 (1979).

Chapter 22

MONETARY AFFAIRS AND TRADE POLICY

SECTION 22.1   INTRODUCTION

Although the focus of this book is on the regulation of international trade, some attention to international monetary issues is important. In the past few years, for example, the value of the dollar has declined dramatically against the Euro, the yen and the British pound. Such exchange rate movements, whether they result from free market forces or some form of government intervention into exchange markets, can have dramatic effects on trade flows unless they are offset by movements in other prices. In addition, monetary difficulties associated with a "balance of payments" problem may motivate governmental measures that directly interfere with trade. This chapter briefly considers the interface between trade and monetary issues, leaving a more thorough treatment of international monetary law, especially the law of the International Monetary Fund (IMF), to other courses.

We begin with an introduction to trade finance, exchange rate determination and the balance of payments. Section 22.2 then considers the effects of government intervention into foreign exchange markets on trade, with particular reference to the current controversy regarding China's exchange rate policies. Section 22.3 examines trade intervention for balance of payments purposes and the international rules applicable to countries with balance of payments problems.

(A) THE ROLE OF FOREIGN EXCHANGE IN TRADE

Suppose that a US company wants to export its goods to a buyer in country X. How will the buyer pay for them? One possibility is that the buyer will export some other good in exchange for the goods—"barter" in traditional terms, a form of "countertrade" in modern parlance. Or perhaps a trading house will orchestrate a multiparty barter transaction. But barter is often infeasible or at least quite costly to coordinate, and it is much more convenient if the parties to the transaction can employ money (to see its advantages, you need only reflect briefly on how

1088

difficult it would be to go about your own day-to-day transactions on a barter basis).

In domestic transactions, the use of money is routine. The buyer gives domestic currency or its equivalent to the seller, who can then use it to pay workers, buy raw materials, and so on. But in the typical international transaction, the buyer does not have a store of the seller's home currency, and the seller may not have much desire for the buyer's currency because all of the seller's expenses are payable in its own currency. Thus, in our hypothetical example, the need arises for a transaction whereby the buyer's home currency is exchanged for dollars, which can then be used to pay the US exporter. Such transactions are viable as long as there are other parties who desire to exchange dollars for the buyer's home currency. A foreign exchange market brings these parties together directly or indirectly through the intermediation of exchange traders.

The need to purchase foreign exchange can introduce another concern for the parties, termed "exchange risk." Perhaps the buyer obtains a price quote of $100/unit, but knows that the goods will not be shipped for awhile and thus payment will not be due until later. The exchange rate between the buyer's home currency and dollars may change in the interim. If the buyer waits until payment is due to buy dollars, therefore, the effective price may be higher or lower in terms of the buyer's home currency. To a "risk averse" buyer, this uncertainty can be an added cost of the transaction. The buyer can reduce or avoid it by entering the exchange market when the order is placed to buy dollars under a forward contract. The desire to avoid exchange risk thus explains in part the existence of futures markets for foreign exchange in addition to the spot market.

The foreign exchange market serves as a perfectly satisfactory mechanism for the facilitation of many international transactions, but in some instances the demand for a particular currency is too thin to support an active market. With the currencies of smaller developing nations, for example, the number of entities wishing to buy the currency at a point in time may be quite small, and exchange traders may be unwilling to hold onto the currency very long because of economic and political risks affecting its value. Potential buyers in those countries may thus have difficulty obtaining dollars, Euros, yen and the like to make their purchases, because no one wants the home currency that they can offer in exchange. Here, old-fashioned barter and its more sophisticated modern incarnations may take over again.[1] Currencies that are readily traded for others are sometimes termed "hard" currencies, while those that are not are sometimes termed "soft" currencies.

(B) EXCHANGE RATE DETERMINATION

Presently, the prices of the dollar, the Euro, the yen and many other major currencies on foreign exchange markets are determined primarily

---

1. See Jean–Francois Hennart, The Transaction Cost Rationale for Counter- trade, 5 J.L.Econ. & Org. 127 (1989).

by private market forces—so-called "floating" rates. The price of currencies that float will be determined by aggregate supply and demand for the currency. A movement in the price of one currency relative to another will also typically result in an adjustment in third currency prices through a process of arbitrage.

The result of floating rates can be considerable volatility. A small change in relative interest rates, for example, may cause a large shift in the demand for a particular currency to buy financial assets. Exchange rate volatility, in turn, may create variability in the extent to which a nation's exports are competitive on world markets. For political and perhaps economic reasons as well, such variability is sometimes seen as harmful, and central banks may intervene in the exchange markets to try and suppress it, with different degrees of success. Firms may also respond to variability by changing their pricing policies, as by pricing in the currency of the buyer rather than the seller, or by pricing in some third currency that they perceive to be more stable.

Various alternatives to floating rates are imaginable, and indeed for many years the governments of the major trading nations endeavored to maintain "fixed" exchange rates. They did so essentially by having their central banks offer to buy or sell currency as needed to balance supply and demand at the fixed exchange rate, or by offering (at least to other governments) to exchange their currency for gold at a fixed price (the "gold standard"). Such a policy required that central banks hold substantial reserves of foreign currencies or of specie. The United States pegged the dollar to gold, and backed up its commitment by promising to trade dollars for gold with foreign central banks, until 1971.

The International Monetary Fund was originally conceived to help support this system of fixed rates by lending monetary reserves to nations that ran short of them. In the end, however, the availability of IMF lending was not enough to persuade all of the major trading nations that efforts to maintain fixed rates were worthwhile. Periodic "devaluations" put the lie to the notion that rates were really fixed. The global fixed rate system came to an end when, in 1971, the United States indicated that it would no longer exchange dollars for gold and closed the "gold window."[2]

Under the current provisions of the International Monetary Fund Agreement, a country has considerable flexibility in deciding how to manage its exchange rates—from allowing the rate to float freely to tying it to some other rate or to a formula. As noted, the United States has generally elected to let its exchange rate float freely. Most of the members of the European Union have agreed to eliminate exchange fluctuations between them altogether by creating a common currency, the Euro, which also floats (the British have elected to retain the pound

---

2. A nice history of the gold standard years and its connection to the international monetary situation is provided by Kenneth Dam, From the Gold Clause Cases to the Gold Commission: A Half Century of American Monetary Law, 50 U.Chi.L.Rev. 504 (1983).

rather than to join the monetary union). Some major trading nations, however, elect to fix or "peg" their exchange rates, most notably China, a subject to which we return in Section 22.2. The practice of pegging the exchange rate, that is seeking to hold its value constant in relation to some other currency or basket of currencies, is sometimes defended as a way to ensure monetary discipline by a country that might otherwise engage in inflationary policies.

(C) THE BALANCE OF PAYMENTS ACCOUNT AND THE "DEFICIT"

The balance of payments is always in balance (save for a "statistical discrepancy")–it is an accounting identity. Thus, when we hear of a "balance of payments deficit," the implicit claim is that when one or more entries on the balance of payments ledger is ignored, payments outflows exceed inflows.

The balance of payments account includes two principal components–the "current account" and the "capital account." The current account in turn reflects three kinds of transactions: merchandise trade, services trade, and "transfers" (such as foreign aid, remittances to family members, and interest payments to foreign holders of government debt). The capital account reflects purchases from foreigners or sales to foreigners of financial and real assets (bonds, stocks, real estate and so on).

The aggregate of all these transactions will be "in balance," in the sense that payments must equal receipts. But the individual components of the accounts may exhibit "surplus" or "deficit." The United States in recent years has run quite a substantial current account deficit, invariably accompanied by a large merchandise trade deficit. The current account deficit is offset by a capital account surplus, which simply means that the United States is borrowing from abroad (selling capital assets to foreigners). We can think of the situation as one in which US purchases of goods and services from abroad exceed US sales of goods and services abroad because the foreigners who end up with a net dollar surplus from those current account transactions prefer to invest the dollars in US capital assets than to use them to purchase US goods and services.

What causes such a situation to arise, and is it a problem? The answer is complex and we cannot hope to explicate it fully, let alone resolve the normative issue, in this brief introduction. One way to think about the matter is to note that the capital account surplus is equal to the difference between national savings and national investment. If the latter exceeds the former, the nation must of necessity be borrowing from abroad to finance the excess investment. That may occur in part because the domestic savings rate is low relative to the savings rate abroad, or because the borrower nation is viewed as a particularly attractive place to invest. As long as those conditions remain stable, a current account deficit can be run (and has been run) for quite an extended period of time.

If investors begin to question the wisdom of investing in the borrower nation, by contrast, perhaps out of a fear that it will start to "print money" to pay its international debts thus causing inflation and diminishing the value of financial assets denominated in its currency, a large current account deficit may be viewed as unsustainable. The demand for its currency will fall and it will depreciate relative to other currencies. Its exports then become more competitive and its imports more expensive, which will tend to reduce the current account deficit. The sharp, recent decline in the value of the dollar no doubt reflects a view that the current account situation for the United States has become untenable over the long haul. The macroeconomic consequences of that decline, which include record oil prices, remain to be seen.

(D) EXCHANGE RATE FLUCTUATIONS AND THEIR EFFECTS ON TRADE

The recent decline in the value of the dollar highlights the possibility that exchange rates can move fairly rapidly and significantly. The following excerpt forcefully argues that such exchange rate movements can have a substantial impact on trade, potentially outstripping the effects of changes in the traditional instruments of trade policy. It also argues that an important linkage may exist between monetary conditions and the political impetus for trade protection.

C. FRED BERGSTEN & JOHN WILLIAMSON, EXCHANGE RATES AND TRADE POLICY[3]

Trade policy has traditionally been associated with tariffs, quotas, export subsidies, and other nontariff distortions. Relatively little attention has been paid to the impact of exchange rates on trade policy, despite widespread analyses by international monetary economists of their impact on trade flows. This paper argues that the continued failure to link the trade and monetary aspects of international economic exchange is a major mistake, in terms both of diagnosing the policy problems which now confront the trading system and of dealing with those problems in the foreseeable future.

MISALIGNED CURRENCIES AND TRADE PROTECTION

The bifurcation between money and trade, at both the analytical and policy levels, is understandable yet strange. It is understandable for three reasons. First, different officials and, usually, different ministries are responsible for monetary and trade matters in most countries. * * *

Second, there is a legitimate difference between the focus of trade policy on the *level* of trade flows and the focus of exchange rates (and international monetary policy, more broadly) on trade *balances*. As long as trade negotiations are reciprocal in practice as well as in principle, trade policy has a neutral impact on the trade balance. Similarly, the

3. © 1983, Institute for International Economics. Reproduced by permission from   W. Cline (ed.), Trade Policy in the 1980s, at 99–103, 107–09 (1983).

balance of payments adjustment process addresses the problem of the trade balance rather than the trade level. * * *

But the main reason why the money-trade relationship has been so ignored is probably the widespread assumption that the international monetary system will not permit the existence of substantial exchange rate misalignments for prolonged periods. * * *

This bifurcation is strange, however, because exchange rates demonstrably do deviate substantially from their equilibrium paths for substantial periods of time, and because the basic case for liberal trade rests upon the assumption inter alia of balance of payments equilibrium, hence equilibrium exchange rates. If the exchange rate conveys price signals to producers and consumers which are incorrect reflections of the underlying economic relationships, significant distortions can result for production, hence trade.

Persistent overvaluation of a country's exchange rate will, of course, adversely affect the country's price competitiveness in international trade (in both goods and services). Exports will be discouraged and imports will be encouraged. The tradable goods sector of the economy, as a whole, will be disadvantaged with resulting distortions in the distribution of domestic output. The current account will shift adversely, financed via private capital inflows or a decline in the country's external reserves. The amounts of money involved can be quite sizable; for the United States, the typical analysis suggests that the merchandise trade balance declines by about $3 billion for every percentage point decline in US international price competitiveness.

From the standpoint of trade policy, the chief implication is the (additional?) pressure that is generated for protectionist measures. Export-and import-competing firms and workers will tend to seek help from their governments to offset these distortions, which undermine their ability to compete, with some degree of legitimacy since the distortions are accepted—in some cases, even fostered—by those governments. Coalitions in support of trade restrictions will be much easier to form, and much broader in their political clout, because no longer will only the most vulnerable firms and workers be seeking help—and no longer will the countervailing pressures from successful exporters be as effective. As we shall see below, overvaluation of the dollar has proved to be an accurate "leading indicator" of trade policy in the United States— perhaps the most accurate of all such indicators—in the postwar period.

The protectionist impact of an overvalued currency, moreover, may persist beyond the duration of the overvaluation itself. Once adopted, protection is frequently maintained long after its initial cause (or justification) has passed. A return to currency equilibrium, or even "reverse overshooting" to undervalued levels, may not produce elimination of restrictions implemented to offset a previous overvaluation. Exchange rate oscillations may thus produce a ratchet effect on protection, raising it during (the inevitably reversible) periods of overvaluation but failing to undo it when equilibrium is restored.

* * *

The Impact of Misalignments on Trade Flows

* * *

During the 1960s a number of studies attempted to estimate separately "exchange-rate elasticities" and "tariff elasticities," the former representing the impact on trade flows of exchange rate changes and the latter the impact of tariff changes. The stylized fact emerged that tariff elasticities were substantially larger, by a factor of two or three, than exchange rate elasticities. The usual explanation of this empirical regularity was the greater confidence presumably felt by traders that tariff changes would result in "permanent" changes in competitiveness.

In comparing the relative importance of tariff and exchange rate changes, however, it must be recognized that there has been a much greater degree of fluctuation in exchange rates than in tariffs during the postwar period. The celebrated trade liberalization of the Kennedy Round, for example, which is widely referred to as a 35 percent reduction, cut tariffs by an average of only 4–5 percentage points for the United States and European Economic Community (EEC) and about 7 percentage points for Japan and the United Kingdom. By contrast, real effective exchange rates frequently change by such amounts within very short periods of time—and remain further away from their underlying equilibrium paths (by as much as 10–20 percent) for extended episodes ... Hence the economic impact of exchange rate changes may at times substantially exceed the impact of tariff changes, even if tariff elasticities are in fact a good bit higher than exchange rate elasticities.

Notes and Questions

(1) What sense can one make of the notion of "misalignment" when rates are market-determined? What causes "misalignment?" Economist John Williamson, one of the co-authors of the foregoing excerpt, ascribes most misalignment to market inefficiencies and macroeconomic policies, such as those pursued by the United States in the early 1980s, when he claims the use of monetary restraint to reduce inflation led to abnormally high interest rates and an overvalued dollar. See John Williamson, The Exchange Rate System (1983). Do you understand why high interest rates in the United States cause the dollar to appreciate? How is "misalignment" as a result of high interest rates to be distinguished from "equilibrium?"

(2) The authors suggest some effects of misalignment. If a firm's home currency is overvalued, for example, the firm may contract its operations undesirably because its export sales are slow or its import competition is intense, and later have to re-expand them when the exchange rates are properly aligned. This will lead to considerable and unnecessary adjustment costs, it might be argued. But what is to be made of this observation? *Given* the purported misalignment of currencies, is it not better for such adjust-

ments to occur than not? And, if the fear is of an excessive adjustment to a transitory phenomenon, why do private actors not recognize that the phenomenon is transitory and take that into account in deciding how much to adjust?

SECTION 22.2   THE TRADE/EXCHANGE RATE RELATIONSHIP UNDER INTERNATIONAL LAW

The important relationship between exchange rates and trade was recognized at the time of the founding of GATT. Article XV(4) of GATT provides, for example, that members "shall not, by exchange action, frustrate the intent of the provisions of this Agreement."

This issue has recently come to the fore with particular regard to the exchange rate policies of China. China pegged its currency (the RMB[1]) to the dollar for many years and more recently shifted to pegging it against a basket of major currencies. It has been forced to intervene extensively in international exchange markets to prevent the RMB from appreciating. As a result, China has accumulated enormous reserves of foreign exchange. It has also developed large global and bilateral trade surpluses, especially with the United States and the EU. Numerous public officials and commentators argue that the RMB is badly "undervalued" as a result of China's exchange market intervention, and accuse China of "currency manipulation." In the following sections, we briefly sketch some of the legal issues raised by the current rift over China's policies.

(A) IMF SURVEILLANCE

The core functions of the IMF historically related primarily to the management of a system of fixed exchange rates.[2] But it was recognized from the outset that exchange market intervention might have worrisome effects that extend beyond purely monetary issues. Article IV(1)(iii) of the Articles of Agreement of the IMF provides in pertinent part: "each member shall . . . avoid manipulating exchange rates or the international monetary system in order to prevent effective balance of payments adjustment or to gain an unfair competitive advantage over other members." The Articles did not define the term "manipulation," however, or the term "unfair competitive advantage."

To make these obligations effective, Article IV(3) provides that the Fund "shall oversee the international monetary system in order to ensure its effective operation, and shall oversee the compliance of each member with its obligations under [Article IV(1)]." The "surveillance" of each member's policies pursuant to this language is known as "bilateral surveillance." In recent practice, bilateral surveillance involves an

---

1. The Chinese currency is also known as the yuan or the renminbi.

2. See generally Kenneth W. Dam, The Rules of the Game (University of Chicago Press, 1982).

assessment of the policies of each member by the IMF staff, followed by consultations between the IMF and the monetary authorities of the member. The staff will convey to the member the results of its analysis on issues such as whether a fundamental misalignment exists, sometimes on a qualitative and sometimes on a quantitative basis.[3]

For many years, this process proceeded with little official guidance as to the exact content of the obligations under Article IV(1)(iii). In response to calls for more specificity within the IMF, a June 2007 decision of the IMF Executive Board provides some interpretative analysis.[4] Annex IV of that decision defines "manipulation" as "policies that are targeted at—and actually affect—the level of an exchange rate. Moreover, manipulation may cause the exchange rate to move or may prevent such movement." Regarding the concept of unfair advantage, the Annex goes on to state that "a member will only be considered to be manipulating exchange rates in order to gain an unfair advantage over other members if the Fund determines both that: (A) the member is engaged in these policies for the purpose of securing fundamental exchange rate misalignment in the form of an undervalued exchange rate and (B) the purpose of securing such misalignment is to increase net exports." Thus, one touchstone for manipulation is an effort to influence the balance of trade. A determination whether such an effort has been undertaken is to be based on "an objective assessment...based on all available evidence, including consultation with the member concerned. Any representation made by the member regarding the purpose of its policies will be given the benefit of any reasonable doubt."

As noted in the above passages, "manipulation" also requires a "fundamental misalignment." A companion staff paper to the 2007 Board decision describes "fundamental misalignment" as a situation when "the underlying current account" (defined in a footnote as the actual current account stripped of cyclical forces) differs from the "equilibrium current account" and the discrepancy is "significant." That is, the real exchange rate must be such that the balance of payments situation facing a member is significantly at odds with situation that it would face from some longer term macroeconomic equilibrium perspective.[5]

An obvious question arises as to how seriously these obligations are taken and enforced within the system. The "reasonable doubt" principle noted above may make it somewhat difficult for the Fund to conclude that any manipulation is for the purpose of increasing net exports. The interpretative language is also somewhat ambiguous as to situations in which manipulation is undertaken only in part for that reason.

3. See IMF, Treatment of Exchange Rate Issues in Bilateral Surveillance—A Stocktaking, August 30, 2006.

4. IMF, Bilateral Surveillance over Member's Policies, Executive Board Decision, June 15, 2007.

5. IMF, Review of the 1997 Decision–Proposal for a New Decision Supplement, June 13, 2007.

Furthermore, the 2007 Board decision emphasizes that "[d]ialogue and persuasion are key pillars of effective surveillance." The Fund's "assessments and advice are intended to assist that member in making policy choices, and to enable other members to discuss these policy choices with that member." Plainly, the conception of the process is far from that of an adversarial dispute process, and much more grounded on the objectives of persuasion and consensus. In principle, members of the Fund can be punished for violations through a curtailment of their access to the resources of the Fund, suspension from membership or even expulsion[6], but there is no hint in the Board decision that such sanctions will enter the surveillance process in any serious way and no history of them being employed against ostensible violators of Article IV(1)(iii). Moreover, for a country that is accumulating vast reserves of foreign exchange, the threat of being cut off from fund resources will likely be of little moment.

With regard to the recent situation with China, the details of IMF surveillance and staff conversations with China are not public. It does appear that the staff has suggested to China that its currency suffers from misalignment, but it has not attempted to quantify its extent.[7]

(B) TRADE MEASURES AS A RESPONSE TO "MANIPULATION"

Critics of China's exchange rate policies claim that China is manipulating its exchange rate to stimulate exports and retard imports, the former being the equivalent of a prohibited export subsidy and the latter being the equivalent of an across the board tariff increase in violation of China's market access commitments. China, of course, rejects this suggestion and argues that its practice of pegging the RMB is designed to ensure macroeconomic stability and to further other benign objectives. The intent behind China's policy, as well as its economic effects, may well be murky.

The economic welfare effects on trading partners are also hardly straightforward. Furthermore, even if China's policies are perceived as harmful to the interests of trading partners, there is great debate as to what sort of response to the situation makes the most sense.

The current US administration has favored diplomacy and dialogue with China, encouraging it to allow the RMB to float upward much more rapidly than in the past but not forcing the issue through any formal action. Many China critics have favored a more aggressive posture, however, and a number of legislative proposals have been introduced on Capitol Hill. These proposals run the gamut from insisting that the Treasury Department refer the matter to the IMF, requiring the United States Trade Representative to bring a formal complaint to the World

---

6. See IMF Art. XXVI. Such sanctions have played some role historically in cases involving the failure of a member to meet its repayment obligations to the Fund.

7. See IMF, Treatment of Exchange Rate Issues in Bilateral Surveillance—A Stocktaking, August 30, 2006.

Trade Organization (WTO), imposing retaliatory tariffs across the board against Chinese goods, and treating China's supposed "currency manipulation" as source of dumping or countervailable subsidies that would permit the imposition of antidumping or countervailing duties on Chinese imports. Some commentators have also argued for the negotiation of new WTO rules on currency manipulation within the Doha Round.[8]

Notes and Questions

(1) If the emphasis within the IMF is on private consultation and suasion, and if a nation that is "manipulating" its currency proves unresponsive to reform suggestions, is it prudent for the WTO to step in and bring its dispute settlement mechanism to bear on what is arguably an IMF matter?

(2) Is Article XV(4) of GATT precise enough to be enforceable? How would a complainant establish that a member was, "by exchange action, frustrating the intent of GATT?"

(3) Could exchange action be the basis for a nonviolation complaint under GATT Article XXIII:1(b)? Under what circumstances? See Section 7.4(A) supra.

(4) Assume, arguendo, that exchange rate manipulation can have effects equivalent to an export subsidy. Is a countervailing duty permissible under the SCM Agreement? A complaint based on the existence of a prohibited subsidy?

(5) One proposal pending in Washington would allow exchange rate manipulation to be treated as dumping—it would result in a reduction in the export price, and thus in a larger margin of dumping under any method for calculating normal value. Permissible under WTO law?

(6) Is it possible to quantify with any reliability the magnitude of any "manipulation?" If quantification is extremely difficult, does that argue for any particular policy option, or against all of them?

SECTION 22.3   TRADE MEASURES FOR BALANCE OF PAYMENTS REASONS

Nations with balance of payments difficulties may intervene in the exchange market, as we have seen. They may also intervene to discourage or prevent the expenditure of scarce foreign exchange on imports, using the familiar instruments of trade protection. The wisdom of such measures is often in doubt, but their use has been extensive and the WTO/GATT system expressly permits them under certain conditions.

The jurisdiction of WTO/GATT here overlaps with that of the IMF, which has been a source of some tension and confusion through the years. The IMF has general jurisdiction over payments matters and considerable competence regarding balance of payments problems. The

---

8. See Aaditya Mattoo & Arvind Subramanian, Currency Undervaluation and Sovereign Wealth Funds: A New Role for the World Trade Organization, Peterson Inst. For Int'l Economics Working Paper 08–2, January, 2008.

WTO has general jurisdiction over trade matters. The GATT articles dealing with the use of trade restrictions for balance of payments reasons require, among other things, a determination whether balance of payments measures are justified by balance of payments difficulties—information bearing upon that determination is often available only in the IMF. The case involving India below gives some indication of the interplay of the two organizations.[1]

(A) GATT AND TRADE RESTRICTIONS FOR BALANCE OF PAYMENTS REASONS

(1) Legal Background: The Original GATT Agreement

Some of the most elaborate and complex provisions of the General Agreement on Tariffs and Trade are concerned with the use of trade restrictions for balance of payments reasons. (See Articles XII through XV.) These provisions were the result of extensive debates during the preparatory work.[2] In addition, GATT contains obligations relating to exchange rate and currency controls which can operate to restrict imports.

It will be recalled that Article XI of GATT prohibits the use of quotas generally. The principal exceptions to this prohibition are Article XII and XVIII (applying to developing countries), which both contain provisions that authorize the use of quantitative restrictions or quotas against imports in case of balance of payments difficulties. (There is no explicit authorization in the General Agreement for the use of higher tariffs or tariff surcharges for balance of payments reasons.) It will also be recalled that the most-favored-nation obligation is one of the most important features of GATT, contained in Article I. When quotas or quantitative restrictions are utilized, however, the Article I non-discrimination language may not adequately support the MFN principle, and consequently Article XIII of GATT sets forth a "non-discrimination principle" tailored to the use of quotas. It speaks of the need to administer quotas so as not to damage or reduce imports from countries in a way that would change the historical shares of the importing market. But departures from this principle are permitted in certain more difficult balance of payments situations, and Article XIV sets forth this exception. Finally, Article XV of GATT tries to establish a satisfactory relationship between GATT and the IMF, requiring the existence of certain facts to be determined by the IMF. Article XVIII, section B, deals with the special balance of payments problems of developing countries.

---

1. See John H. Jackson, World Trade and the Law of GATT ch. 18 (1969). Concerning some of the institutional aspects of the IMF, see American Society of International Law, Report of Panel on International Monetary Policy: Long–Term International Monetary Reform: A Proposal for an Improved International Adjustment Process, (1972); see also UNCTAD, Money, Finance and Development: Papers on International Monetary Reform, U.N.Doc. TD/B/479 (1974).

2. Jackson, supra note 1, at chs. 18 and 26.

The provisions of Article XVIII differ somewhat, but not drastically, from those of Article XII.[3]

(2) *The Use of Payments Measures Under GATT: Policy and Practice*

At one time, particularly during the period of "fixed" exchange rates prior to 1971, even developed nations invoked the GATT balance of payment provisions with some regularity. The United States imposed a temporary import surcharge[4] in August of 1971, signaling the crisis that led in September of that year to the closing of the "gold window" and the collapse of the fixed exchange rate system. The President's authority to take that action was questioned but withstood court challenge. Later, Section 122 of the Trade Act of 1974, 19 U.S.C.A. sec. 2132, made clear that the President may impose temporary import surcharges for balance of payments purposes, though it has not been invoked since its enactment. The GATT legality of the tariff surcharge is discussed briefly below.

Other major trading nations have from time to time resorted to surcharges even into the 1970s, but in recent years, however, most of the use (and abuse) of the balance of payments provisions in GATT has been by developing nations. The legitimacy of these actions has at times been challenged, both on economic and legal grounds.

ISAIAH FRANK, IMPORT QUOTAS, THE BALANCE OF PAYMENTS AND THE GATT[5]

The exception for dealing with balance-of-payments problems consists of a set of lengthy, complex and rather opaque provisions scattered over several GATT articles (Articles XII to XV and XVIII). The provisions are of three types: (i) the criteria for invoking the exception, (ii) the obligations applying to the use of quantitative restrictions under the exception and (iii) procedural rules relating to review and consultation.

No useful purpose would be served by attempting to recount the detailed articles, but a brief summary is essential. The basic provision is that quantitative restrictions may be used to safeguard a country's "external financial position and its balance of payments", but only to the extent necessary "(i) to forestall the imminent threat of, or to stop, a serious decline in its monetary reserves or (ii), in the case of a contracting party with very low monetary reserves, to achieve a reasonable rate of increase in its reserves" (Article XII [1 and 2]). Determinations as to the adequacy of reserves are left to the IMF.

But the right to impose quantitative restrictions for balance-of-payments reasons is not unlimited. Countries are obliged to relax the

---

3. See a chart of these differences in Jackson, supra note 1, at 689.

4. An import or tariff surcharge refers to a uniform ad valorem tariff in addition to any tariff already imposed.

5. 10 World Economy 307 (1987), reprinted with permission of the author. See also Richard Eglin, Surveillance of Balance of Payments Measures in the GATT, 10 World Economy 1 (1987).

restrictions as conditions permit. Moreover, the restrictions must be applied on a non-discriminatory basis. Since quantitative restrictions are readily open to discrimination in their administration, Article XIII(2) of the GATT calls on countries, in applying such restrictions on any product, to "aim at a distribution of trade in such product approaching as closely as possible the shares which the various contracting parties might be expected to obtain in the absence of such restrictions".

* * *

The focus of the balance-of-payments exception on the adequacy of a country's monetary reserves suggests that the provision is predicated on the existence of a par-value system. Under such a system, an adequate level of reserves is needed to defend the fixed parity without resorting to severe deflationary measures that could result in an abrupt contraction of employment and economic activity. If, however, the level of reserves is low or falling, a second line of defence of the exchange rate is the reduction of imports through trade restrictions. The idea that a less expansionary macro-economic policy might render unnecessary the resort to trade restrictions is specifically rejected in Article XII of the GATT.

It is true that the need for reserves may not have been greatly reduced with the adoption of a system of floating rates of exchange. Under a managed float, countries continue to hold reserves for intervention in foreign-exchange markets, as a precaution against unanticipated disturbances and as a demonstration of creditworthiness. As a means of defending reserve positions, however, countries possess today an alternative to import restrictions in their freedom to let the exchange rate move.

Even if a temporary reduction of imports is deemed necessary to deal with a balance-of-payments problem, it remains something of a mystery as to why it should take the form of quantitative restrictions rather than tariffs. One possible justification under the Bretton Woods system of fixed rates of exchange might be the need for speed in a situation where a country was rapidly losing reserves. But this was precisely the explanation given by the United Kingdom in 1964 for *avoiding* the use of quantitative restrictions and adopting instead an import surcharge to defend its payments position, even though the surcharge was unauthorized by the GATT. In its notification to the GATT, the United Kingdom stated that reduction in its balance-of-payments deficit "required urgent action which would only have been delayed while the elaborate administrative machinery of import licensing was re-established and licences were allocated to importers".

Similarly, when the United States adopted an import surcharge in 1971, it stressed the need "to provide relatively quick benefits to its trade balance" until the problem could be adequately dealt with in other ways. Thus the need for speed in defending the balance of payments through trade measures would appear to argue in favour of the imposition of a uniform tariff rather than inherently selective and discriminatory quantitative restrictions that inevitably carry a heavy administrative load.

An alternative justification for import quotas in cases of balance-of-payments difficulties is the desire to concentrate the import restriction on luxury goods so that scarce foreign exchange would be conserved for imports of more essential products. But the effect of such a restriction is to encourage the domestic production of non-competitive luxury goods and the increased importation of raw materials and intermediate products to support that production. If the intention is to reduce the consumption of luxury goods without diverting fungible domestic resources to their production at home, the preferred method would be a tax on the consumption of luxury goods regardless of whether they are produced at home or abroad. In short, it is difficult to find a defensible rationale for the specification of quantitative restrictions as the preferred trade measure to counter temporary balance-of-payments problems.

Resort to Balance-of-Payments Exception

So far as can be ascertained, no industrial country has invoked balance-of-payments reasons for quantitative restrictions imposed in recent years. When a balance-of-payments justification has been given for trade restrictions, the action has generally taken the form of tariffs which, in turn, have been in the form of across-the-board surcharges rather than selective tariffs that protect particular categories of goods.

Developing countries, however, have resorted extensively to quantitative restrictions for balance-of-payments reasons. For example, in 1983 Brazil notified the GATT that she had in effect 361 quantitative restrictions, the justification for which, according to the IMF, was "balance of payments reasons related to the process of development". The same justification was given for 442 quantitative restrictions by Ghana, 122 by India, 253 by the Republic of Korea, 330 by Nigeria, 434 by Pakistan, 492 by Tunisia and lesser numbers by other developing countries.

In fact the use by developing countries of quantitative restrictions for balance-of-payments reasons may be presumed to be far more extensive than indicated by those self-notifications to the GATT. The table in the IMF report from which the above data were taken showed no notifications for many developing countries—including, for example, Argentina and Colombia, countries which are known to have had wide-ranging systems of import controls.

* * *

Neither the principle nor the practice of the use of quantitative restrictions for balance-of-payments reasons has been seriously examined in the almost forty years of the GATT's existence. But experience over that period has unequivocally demonstrated the essentially protective nature of such restrictions. The most telling evidence is that in the vast majority of cases the quantitative restrictions have been applied to highly selective groups of products rather than across the board. Quantitative restrictions should therefore be recognized for what they are, namely a subterfuge for protection. The best way to deal with the problem would be to eliminate from the GATT the right to impose quantitative restrictions for balance-of-payments reasons.

INDIA—QUANTITATIVE RESTRICTIONS ON IMPORTS OF AGRICULTURAL, TEXTILE AND INDUSTRIAL PRODUCTS
WT/DS90/AB/R.
Appellate Body Report adopted September 22, 1999.

2.   India maintains quantitative restrictions on the importation of agricultural, textile and industrial products falling in 2,714 tariff lines. India invoked balance-of-payments justification in accordance with Article XVIII:B of the GATT 1994, and notified these quantitative restrictions to the Committee on Balance-of-Payments Restrictions (the "BOP Committee"). On 30 June 1997, following consultations in the BOP Committee, India proposed eliminating its quantitative restrictions over a seven-year period. Some of the Members of the BOP Committee, including the United States, were of the view that India's balance-of-payments restrictions could be phased out over a shorter period than that proposed by India.

* * *

110.   India appeals the Panel's interpretation of the Note *Ad* Article XVIII:11 of the GATT 1994 and, in particular, the word "thereupon". India claims that the Panel erred in law in interpreting the word "thereupon" to mean "immediately". According to India, "thereupon":

> ... indicates that there must be a *direct* causal link between the removal of measures imposed [for] balance-of-payments reasons and the recurrence of the conditions defined in Article XVIII:9. (emphasis added)

111.   The Note *Ad* Article XVIII:11 provides:

> The second sentence in paragraph 11 shall not be interpreted to mean that a contracting party is required to relax or remove restrictions if such relaxation or removal *would thereupon produce* conditions justifying the intensification or institution, respectively, of restrictions under paragraph 9 of Article XVIII. (emphasis added)

112.   The conditions which justify the intensification or institution of balance-of-payments restrictions under Article XVIII:9 (a) and (b) are a threat of a serious decline in monetary reserves, a serious decline in monetary reserves, or inadequate monetary reserves.

113.   The Panel found that to maintain balance-of-payments restrictions under the Ad Note:

> ... it must be determined that one of the conditions contemplated in sub-paragraphs (a) and (b) of Article XVIII:9 would appear

immediately after the removal of the measures, and a causal link must be established between the anticipated reoccurrence of the conditions of Article XVIII:9 and the removal. It should be noted that the text requires more than a mere possibility of reoccurrence of the conditions ("would produce"). The Ad Note therefore allows for the maintenance of measures on the basis only of clearly identified circumstances, and not on the basis of a general possibility of worsening of balance-of-payments conditions after the measures have been removed. (underlining added)

114.   We agree with the Panel that the Ad Note, and, in particular, the words "would thereupon produce", require a *causal link of a certain directness* between the removal of the balance-of-payments restrictions and the recurrence of one of the three conditions referred to in Article XVIII:9. As pointed out by the Panel, the Ad Note demands more than a mere possibility of recurrence of one of these three conditions and allows for the maintenance of balance-of-payments restrictions on the basis only of clearly identified circumstances. In order to meet the requirements of the Ad Note, the probability of occurrence of one of the conditions would have to be clear.

115.   We also agree with the Panel that the Ad Note and, in particular, the word "thereupon", expresses a *notion of temporal sequence* between the removal of the balance-of-payments restrictions and the recurrence of one of the conditions of Article XVIII:9. We share the Panel's view that the purpose of the word "thereupon" is to ensure that measures are not maintained because of some distant possibility that a balance-of-payments difficulty may occur.

116.   The Panel considered the various dictionary definitions of the word "thereupon" and came to the conclusion that "the most appropriate meaning should be 'immediately'." The Panel found support for this interpretation in the context in which the word "thereupon" is used, the objective of paragraphs 4 and 9 of Article XVIII and the Ad Note, and the object and purpose of the *WTO Agreement*.

117.   We recall that balance-of-payments restrictions may be maintained under the Ad Note if their removal or relaxation would thereupon produce: (i) a threat of a serious decline in monetary reserves; (ii) a serious decline in monetary reserves; *or* (iii) inadequate monetary reserves. With regard to the first of these conditions, we agree with the Panel that the word "thereupon" means "immediately".

118.   As to the two other conditions, i.e., a serious decline in monetary reserves or inadequate monetary reserves, we note that the Panel, in paragraph 5.198 of its Report, qualified its understanding of the word "thereupon" as follows:

We do not mean that the term "thereupon" should necessarily mean within the days or weeks following the relaxation or removal of the measures; this would be unrealistic even though instances of very rapid deterioration of balance-of-payments conditions could occur.

119.   We agree with the Panel that it would be unrealistic to require that a serious decline or inadequacy in monetary reserves should actually occur within days or weeks following the relaxation or removal of the balance-of-payments restrictions. The Panel was, therefore, correct to qualify its understanding of the word "thereupon" with regard to these two conditions. While not explicitly stating so, the Panel in fact interpreted the word "thereupon" for these two conditions as meaning "soon after". This is also one of the possible dictionary meanings of the word "thereupon". We are of the view that instead of using the word "immediately", the Panel should have used the words "soon after" to express the temporal sequence required by the word "thereupon". However, in view of the Panel's own qualification of the word "thereupon", the use of "immediately" with respect to these two conditions does not amount to a legal error.

120.   We, therefore, uphold the Panel's interpretation of the Ad Note and, in particular, the word "thereupon".

121.   India claims that the Panel erred in law:

> . . . by requiring India to use macro-economic and other development policy instruments to meet balance-of-payments problems caused by the immediate removal of its import restrictions.

India argues that such a requirement amounts to a change in its development policy, and is, therefore, inconsistent with the proviso to Article XVIII:11 of the GATT 1994.

122.   The second sentence of Article XVIII:11 provides that Members:

> . . . shall progressively relax any restrictions applied under this Section as conditions improve, maintaining them only to the extent necessary under the terms of paragraph 9 of this Article and shall eliminate them when conditions no longer justify such maintenance;

and adds the following proviso:

> *Provided* that no contracting party shall be required to withdraw or modify restrictions on the ground that a change in its development policy would render unnecessary the restrictions which it is applying under this Section.

123.   In reply to a question by the Panel, the IMF stated:

> The Fund's view remains . . . that the external situation can be managed using macro-economic policy instruments alone. Quantitative restrictions (QRs) are not needed for balance-of-payments adjustments and should be removed over a relatively short period of time. . . .

124.   In reaching its conclusion that the removal of India's balance-of-payments restrictions will not "immediately" produce the recurrence of any of the conditions of Article XVIII:9 and that the maintenance of these measures is, therefore, not justified under the Note *Ad* Article XVIII:11, the Panel took this statement of the IMF into account.

125.   India argues that the Panel required India to change its development policy in order that the removal of the balance-of-payments restrictions would not produce a recurrence of any of the conditions of Article XVIII:9. We disagree. Nothing in the Panel Report suggests that the Panel imposed this requirement. On the contrary, in paragraph 5.220 of its Report, the Panel stated:

> India had in the past used macroeconomic policy instruments to defend the rupee, suggesting that the use of macroeconomic policy instruments as mentioned by the IMF would not necessarily constitute a change in India's development policy.

126.   Furthermore, we are of the opinion that the use of macroeconomic policy instruments is not related to any particular development policy, but is resorted to by all Members regardless of the type of development policy they pursue. The IMF statement that India can manage its balance-of-payments situation using macroeconomic policy instruments alone does not, therefore, imply a change in India's development policy.

127.   In paragraph 5.209 of the Panel Report, the Panel referred to the following IMF statement:

> The macroeconomic policy instruments would need to be complemented by structural measures such as scaling back reservations on certain products for small-scale units and pushing ahead with agricultural reforms.

128.   We believe structural measures are different from macroeconomic instruments with respect to their relationship to development policy. If India were asked to implement agricultural reform or to scale back reservations on certain products for small-scale units as indispensable policy changes in order to overcome its balance-of-payments difficulties, such a requirement would probably have involved a change in India's development policy.

129.   We note that the Panel did not take a position on the question whether the adoption of the structural measures of the type mentioned by the IMF would entail a change in India's development policy. The Panel concluded in paragraph 5.211 of its Report as follows:

> The IMF's suggestions on "structural measures" should not be taken in isolation from the context in which they are made. We recall that the IMF began its reply to Question 3 by stating that India's "external situation can be managed by using macroeconomic policy instruments alone". Its comments on structural measures appear only at the end of its answer after it has suggested other liberalization measures, such as tariff reductions. The adoption by India of "structural measures" is not suggested as a condition for preserving India's reserve position. Thus, we cannot conclude that the removal of India's balance-of-payment measures would thereupon lead to conditions justifying their reinstitution that could be avoided only by a change in India's development policy.

Clearly, the Panel interpreted the IMF statement to the effect that the implementation of structural measures is not a condition for the preservation of India's external financial position. We consider this interpretation to be reasonable.

130.   We conclude that the Panel did not require India to change its development policy and, therefore, did not err in law with regard to the proviso to Article XVIII:11.

Notes and Questions

(1) A major issue in the *India QR* case was whether the dispute settlement system should consider the US claim at all, or whether it was more appropriately handled in the WTO Balance-of-Payments Committee. Of course, in the committee, India or the United States could have blocked any outcome they did not like under the WTO practice of consensus decision-making. The panel, upheld by the Appellate Body, concluded that it could consider the case on the basis of the Uruguay Round Understanding on the Balance-of-Payments Provisions of GATT 1994, the first footnote of which provides: "The provisions of Articles XXII and XXIII of GATT 1994, as elaborated and applied by the [DSU] may be invoked with respect to any matters arising from the application of restrictive import measures taken for balance-of-payments purposes." India argued that this language did not allow consideration of the justification of balance-of-payments measures.

(2) Is there any plausible justification, even in a country experiencing severe balance of payments difficulties, for import measures that are more restrictive with respect to particular imported goods than others? Should the WTO ban such selective measures outright?

(3) The United States has also resorted to unilateral initiatives to attack import restrictions justified by purported balance of payments concerns. A 1989 "Super 301" case against Brazil resulted in the elimination of a number of quantitative restrictions by the Brazilian government. See Brazil Import Licensing, Inv. No. 301–73, 55 Fed. Reg. 22876 (1990).

(4) Various proposals have been introduced in the US Congress from time to time to require import surcharges to deal with the trade deficit generally or with particular nations. Putting aside their legality under GATT, can such measures work when exchange rates float? Or will reduced demand for imports cause the price of foreign currencies to fall, reducing the price of imports, increasing the price of US exports abroad, and thus accomplishing little or nothing?

(3) Tariff Surcharges and the Uruguay Round Agreement

Most of the tariffs of industrialized countries (particularly those on non-agricultural goods) are "bound" in their GATT schedules as a result of negotiated "concessions." There is no general exception in GATT to these "bindings" for balance of payments reasons. Thus, while the original GATT authorized the use of quantitative restrictions for balance of payments reasons, it did not allow tariff increases to be so used. As Isaiah Frank indicated in the excerpt above, however, a case can be made that "tariff surcharges" are preferable to quantitative restrictions if any trade intervention is to occur at all.[6]

Not surprisingly, import surcharges were used with some regularity despite the absence of legal authorization for them, even to the point that some would argue that GATT had been "amended de facto." The legal force of such arguments need not be tested here, however, in light of the results of the Uruguay Round.

The "Understanding on the Balance of Payments Provisions of the General Agreement on Tariffs and Trade 1994" [Understanding], contained in the Documents Supplement, provides in paragraph 2 that "notwithstanding the provisions of Article II, price-based measures taken for balance of payments purposes may be applied in excess of the duties inscribed in the schedule of a Member." Indeed, in paragraph 3, the Understanding strongly encourages price-based measures (such as import surcharges and import deposit requirements) in preference to new quantitative restrictions unless the price-based measures would prove inadequate. It further indicates in paragraph 4 that measures may only be applied to control the "general level of imports." An exception exists for "essential products," but trade measures that burden particular products greatly relative to others appear to be prohibited.

Other provisions of the Understanding encourage announced time schedules for the removal of balance of payments measures and require notification of all new measures to the WTO/GATT. They also provide for consultations under the auspices of a Committee on Balance of Payments Restrictions, which will make recommendations to the General Council regarding the conformity of measures under review with GATT obligations.

6. A paper by the GATT secretariat written in 1965 elaborates some of the reasons:

2. (i) Surcharges were preferred to quantitative restrictions because they were administratively less cumbersome and were less likely to freeze the pattern of trade.

(ii) The substantial revenues obtained from use of surcharges were essential to the success of the country's stabilization programme.

(iii) The surcharges were placed both on bound and unbound items to avoid unfair discrimination between exporters.

3. (i) The conversion of surcharges to internal measures could aggravate industrial conditions, especially in situations where there are accumulation of stocks. The use of such internal measures in place of surcharges could also cause serious internal political difficulties.

(ii) Internal measures alone were not sufficient to restore equilibrium and balance-of-payments and additional measures to restrict imports were necessary.

(iii) In urgent situations, surcharges could be quickly imposed. Otherwise, there could be disastrous delays in bringing a new law before parliament.

Contracting parties have in various instances noted the following considerations in authorizing the use of surcharges:

(i) In one or two instances, the use of surcharges represented a significant simplification over the system of restrictions previously enforced.

(ii) The effect of the surcharges would be less restrictive than quantitative restrictions permitted under Articles XII or XVIII.

(iii) In addition to its direct effect on the level of reserves, the use of surcharges was in certain instances, necessary to insure success of the government stabilization program.

See GATT Doc.Com.TD/F/W.3, at 1–2.

(B) GATT OBLIGATIONS RELATING TO CURRENCY PAR VALUES AND EXCHANGE CONTROLS

Regardless of the balance of payments condition of a nation, currency par values and exchange controls can be manipulated to defeat the effect of other trade obligations of GATT. The drafters of GATT thus included several obligations relating to these practices. For example, it was well known that a requirement of a license, in order to make a payment in foreign exchange, could effectively prevent the importation of goods or control them through the control exercised in the granting of licenses. In some cases, the obligations of the International Monetary Fund suffice to prevent the abusive practices which would affect trade, and Article XV of GATT recognizes this fact. Some of the parties to GATT are not members of the IMF, however, and consequently it was necessary to include in GATT some substitute for the IMF obligations in these cases. Article XV, paragraph 4, contains such substitutes, and paragraph 6 of that Article provides that a non-Fund member should establish a "special exchange agreement" with the Contracting Parties of GATT, presumably to provide some of the IMF-type obligations.[7] Scattered throughout GATT are various other commitments relating to similar problems.[8] For example, MFN under Article 1 imposes the obligation of nondiscrimination with respect to international transfer of payments; and Article II, paragraphs 3 and 6, limit the possibility of using devaluation or other currency exchange techniques to "impair the value of any of the concessions" under GATT.[9]

---

7. See generally Jackson, supra note 1, at ch. 18.

8. See Jackson, supra note 1, at 492; commitments relating to exchange controls and currency practices occur in Articles I, para. 1; II, paras. 3 and 6; VI, pars. 2 and 3; VII, para. 4(a) and (c); VIII, paras. 1 and 4, and, of course, the elaborate BOP exceptions in Articles XI through XIV and Article XVIII, Section B.

9. The floating exchange rate system has posed some new problems for GATT rules. If a currency increases in value in relation to other currencies, can that be the basis for an adjustment in the tariff under bindings, pursuant to Article II of GATT? See Frieder Roessler, Selective Balance-of-Payment Adjustment Measures Affecting Trade: The Roles of the GATT and the IMF, 9 J.World Trade L. 622 (1975).

Chapter 23

TRADE AND INVESTMENT

SECTION 23.1   INTRODUCTION

The emphasis of this book is on international trade, but we would be remiss to ignore investment. Trade and foreign investment may be substitutes to a degree—if barriers to trade impede the export of finished products, manufacturers may elect instead to invest in a manufacturing facility in the target market. And as we noted in the materials on trade in services, investment and services trade are often inextricably intertwined, especially where services exports require the establishment of a foreign presence in a target market. Barriers to investment, therefore, may have consequences akin to those of trade barriers.

Many of the economic treaties that we have considered directly or indirectly create international rules that bear on investment. We touched briefly in Chapter 5 on the history of Friendship, Commerce and Navigation treaties, and the subsequent Bilateral Investment Treaties (BITs). Among other things, these agreements sought to secure opportunities for foreign investors and to protect prior investments against expropriation. GATT had something to say about investment rules as well—when restrictions on foreign investors had the effect of discouraging the importation of foreign goods, they had the potential to violate the GATT national treatment obligation or other GATT provisions. This principle was embodied formally in the Uruguay Round Agreement on Trade–Related Investment Measures (TRIMs), considered below. The Uruguay Round GATS has profound implications for investment in service sectors, as we noted in Chapter 19 on trade in services.

Nevertheless, broad multilateral disciplines on investment restrictions remain lacking in the trading community. On the premise that considerable economic gains would attend a reduction in international barriers to investment, the OECD undertook during the 1990's to promote the concept of a Multilateral Agreement on Investment (MAI). The proposed MAI would have included general non-discrimination obligations, transparency provisions, provisions governing the migration of investors, provisions affecting state monopolies, and various sector

1110

specific disciplines, among other things.[1] The timing of the MAI initiative proved unfortunate from the perspective of its proponents. It ran squarely into the anti-globalization sentiment of the late 1990s, fueled in large measure by environmental and labor groups. The OECD has for now abandoned the initiative.

Efforts to develop broader investment disciplines within the WTO have met a similar fate. At the 1996 Singapore ministerial meeting, a working group on the relationship between trade and investment was established. That group began to consider ways that investment rules might be developed and applied within the WTO. Support for investment negotiations persisted at the time of the Doha ministerial, resulting in the following paragraph (22) of the Doha Declaration in 2001:

> In the period until the Fifth Session, further work in the Working Group on the Relationship Between Trade and Investment will focus on the clarification of: scope and definition; transparency; non-discrimination; modalities for pre-establishment commitments based on a GATS-type, positive list approach; development provisions; exceptions and balance-of-payments safeguards; consultation and the settlement of disputes between members. Any framework should reflect in a balanced manner the interests of home and host countries, and take due account of the development policies and objectives of host governments as well as their right to regulate in the public interest. The special development, trade and financial needs of developing and least-developed countries should be taken into account as an integral part of any framework, which should enable members to undertake obligations and commitments commensurate with their individual needs and circumstances. Due regard should be paid to other relevant WTO provisions. Account should be taken, as appropriate, of existing bilateral and regional arrangements on investment.

By the time of the Cancun ministerial in 2003 (the "Fifth Session"), however, ministers were unable to agree on an approach to continued negotiations. Nations such as the EU and Japan strongly supported further efforts on investment, but a group of developing countries led by India opposed them. Finally, the General Council decided on August 1, 2004, to drop investment from the Doha work program (along with competition policy and transparency in government procurement).

If global progress on investment issues has been slow, more dramatic developments are visible at the regional level. NAFTA incorporates broad rules on investment within the region, including general obligations to afford MFN and national treatment to NAFTA investors. The "investor rights" provisions of NAFTA are particularly remarkable in that they create private rights of action to enforce their terms (unlike most of the provisions of NAFTA, which can only be enforced by member

1. The 1998 negotiating text for the MAI may be found in the ASIL basic documents of international economic law, 1998 BDIEL AD LEXIS 33.

nations), including a private right of action for damages in the event of "expropriation," a concept that has proved elusive.

The remainder of this chapter is divided into two sections. Section 23.2 considers the limited WTO rules on investment with an emphasis on the TRIMs Agreement. Section 23.3 then considers some important recent developments under NAFTA.

SECTION 23.2   WTO AND TRIMS

Although GATT contains no direct restrictions on the ability of members to regulate foreign investment, it was settled before the Uruguay Round that restrictions on investors might impermissibly encourage the purchase of domestic over imported goods. In Canada—Administration of the Foreign Investment Review Act (FIRA),[1] Canada was accused of conditioning the approval of applications for foreign investment in Canada on commitments by the investor/applicant to use a certain amount of Canadian goods in their manufacturing operations. Such "domestic content" requirements were found to conflict with GATT Article III:4 (the panel did not reach the question whether Article III:5 had also been violated).

The TRIMs Agreement, negotiated during the Uruguay Round, built on the *FIRA* case to prohibit trade-related investment measures that conflict with Article III or Article XI of GATT. Domestic content restrictions are offered as an illustration of such measures in the annex to the TRIMs Agreement, as are certain other restrictions on the ability of investors to import or export. The TRIMs Agreement was one of many provisions of WTO law at issue in a dispute between Indonesia and major automobile exporters (Japan, the European Union and the United States) over Indonesia's programs to encourage the development of its domestic auto industry.

INDONESIA—CERTAIN MEASURES AFFECTING THE AUTOMOBILE INDUSTRY
WT/DS54,55,59 & 64/R.
Panel Report adopted July 23, 1998.

Claims of Local Content Requirements

14.58   The European Communities and the United States claim that the 1993 car programme, by providing for local content requirements linked to tax benefits for finished cars incorporating a certain percentage value of domestic products, and to customs duty benefits for imported parts and components used in cars incorporating a certain percentage value of domestic products, violates the provisions of Article 2 of the TRIMs Agreement, and Article III:4 of the GATT.

14.59   Japan, the European Communities and the United States also claim that the 1996 car programme, by providing for local content

---

1. GATT, 30th Supp. BISD 140 (panel report adopted Feb. 7, 1984).

requirements linked to tax benefits for National Cars (which by definition incorporate a certain percentage value of domestic products), and to
customs duty benefits for imported parts and components used in
National Cars, violates the provisions of Article 2 of the TRIMs Agreement and Article III:4 of the GATT.

* * *

14.63   As to which claims, those under Article III:4 of GATT or
Article 2 of the TRIMs Agreement, to examine first, we consider that we
should first examine the claims under the TRIMs Agreement since the
TRIMs Agreement is more specific than Article III:4 as far as the claims
under consideration are concerned. * * *

THE APPLICATION OF THE TRIMs AGREEMENT

14.64   Article 2.1 of the TRIMs Agreement provides that

"... no Member shall apply any TRIM that is inconsistent with the
provisions of Article III or Article XI of GATT 1994."

By its terms, Article 2.1 requires two elements to be shown to establish a
violation thereof: first, the existence of a TRIM; second, that TRIM is
inconsistent with Article III or Article XI of GATT. No claims have been
raised with reference to a violation of Article XI of GATT.

* * *

14.66   We note also that Article 2.2 of the TRIMs Agreement
provides:

"2.2 An Illustrative List of TRIMs that are inconsistent with the
obligations of national treatment provided for in paragraph 4 of
Article III of GATT 1994 ... is contained in the Annex to this
Agreement."

* * *

Are the Indonesian measures "investment measures"?

14.73   We note that the use of the broad term "investment measures" indicates that the TRIMs Agreement is not limited to measures
taken specifically in regard to *foreign* investment. Contrary to India's
argument, we find that nothing in the TRIMs Agreement suggests that
the nationality of the ownership of enterprises subject to a particular
measure is an element in deciding whether that measure is covered by
the Agreement. We therefore find without textual support in the TRIMs
Agreement the argument that since the TRIMs Agreement is basically
designed to govern and provide a level playing field for foreign investment, measures relating to internal taxes or subsidies cannot be construed to be a trade-related investment measure. We recall in this
context that internal tax advantages or subsidies are only one of many
types of advantages which may be tied to a local content requirement
which is a principal focus of the TRIMs Agreement. The TRIMs Agreement is not concerned with subsidies and internal taxes as such but

rather with local content requirements, compliance with which may be encouraged through providing any type of advantage. Nor, in any case, do we see why an internal measure would necessarily not govern the treatment of foreign investment.

14.74   We next consider whether the Indonesian measures are investment measures. In this regard, we consider the following extracts (emphases added) from the official Indonesian legislation relevant and instructive.

14.75   With regard to the 1993 car programme, we note:

—The "considerations section" of the Decree of the Ministry of Industry announcing the 1993 car programme states:

> "a.   that within the framework of *supporting and promoting the development of the automotive industry and/or the component industry* in the future, it is deemed necessary to regulate the local content levels of domestically produced motor vehicles or components in connection with the grant of incentives in the imposition of import duty rates;
>
> b.   that in order to *further strengthen domestic industrial development* by taking into account the trend of technological advance and the increase of the capability and mastering of industrial design and engineering, it is necessary to improve the relevant existing regulations already laid down;"

—The "considerations section" of the 1995 amendment to the 1993 car programme states:

> "That *in the framework of further promoting of the development of the motor vehicles industry and/or domestically produced components*, it is considered necessary to amend . . ."

14.76   With regard to the February 1996 car programme, we note the following:

—The title of the Presidential Instruction for the National Car programme (No. 2) is "The *Development* of the National Automobile Industry".

—Paragraph a) of the "Considering" section of the Government Regulation No. 20 states:

> "that in the effort *to promote the growth of the domestic automotive industry*, it is deemed necessary to enact regulations concerning the Sales Tax on Luxury Goods upon the delivery of domestically produced motor vehicles".

—In addition, the State Minister for Mobilization of Investment Funds/Chairman of the Investment Coordinating Board issued a decree entitled "Investment Regulations within the Framework of the Realisation of the Establishment of the National Automobile Industry" which emphasized that the new measures were intended to promote investment, stating in its fifth considering:

"5. that it is therefore necessary to issue *a decree for the regulation of investment* in the national automobile industry."

—Article 2 of that same Investment Regulation by the Minister of State for Mobilization of Investment Funds/Chairman of the Investment Coordinating Board provides:

"In order *to realise the development of the national automobile industry* as meant in Article 1:

1. . . .

2. *In the endeavour to realise the development of such national car industry, the investment approval will be issued to the automobile industry sector with tax facilities in accordance with legal provisions enacted specifically for such purpose.*"

—The Decision relating to the investment facilities regarding the Determination of PT. Timor Putra National to Establish and Produce a National Car, entitled "Decision of the State Minister for the Mobilization of Investment Funds/Chairman of the Capital Investment Co-ordinating Board" states:

"1. That *in implementing a national car industry it is deemed necessary to determine investment approval* for a car industry which will build and produce a national car.

2.   That in the framework of investment for the car industry, PT.Timor Putra National has submitted an application and working program to build a national car industry and *has obtained domestic investment approval* (PMDN) NO.607/ PMDN/1995, dated 9 November 1995".

14.77   With regard to the June 1996 car programme, we note that the "Considering" section of the Decree of the President of the Republic No. 4267 on the Extension (June) to the February 1996 car programme provides:

"a. that the *development of the national car is aimed at improving the nation's self-reliance* . . . and to achieve this solid preparations and continuous support are necessary;

b. that the preparation for domestic production of national cars require the *availability of huge financing* and therefore will be carried out in stages;

c. that in connection with the preparations, it is considered necessary to establish a policy on the implementation stage of the production of national cars."

—The "Considering" section of the Government Regulation No. 3667 states:

"That within the *framework of promoting the development of the automotive industry in the increased use of domestically produced automotive components*, it is deemed necessary to grant

Sales Tax on Luxury Goods facilities to the group of luxury goods upon delivery of certain motor vehicles"

—The Elucidation to the Government Regulation No. 36 states:

"Within the *framework of speeding up the realisation of production of national motor vehicles using domestically made automotive components, it is necessary to promote the domestic automotive industry* in order to further its growth particularly in the face of global competition. *One of the endeavours which can be exerted is the provision of a tax incentive in the form of exemption* from the assessment of Sales Tax on Luxury Goods on the delivery of certain motor vehicles which have achieved certain levels of local content."

14.78   We note also that Indonesia indicates that the objectives of the National Car programme include the following:

—To improve the competitiveness of local companies and strengthen overall industrial development;

—To develop the capacity of multiple-source auto parts and components;

—To encourage the development of the automotive industry and the automotive component industry;

—To bring about major structural changes in the Indonesian automobile industry;

—To encourage the transfer of technology and contribute to large-scale job creation;

—To encourage car companies to increase their local content, resulting in a rapid growth of investment in the automobile industry.

14.79   Indonesia has also stated that PT TPN is a "domestic capital investment company".

14.80   On the basis of our reading of these measures applied by Indonesia under the 1993 and the 1996 car programmes, which have investment objectives and investment features and which refer to investment programmes, we find that these measures are aimed at encouraging the development of a local manufacturing capability for finished motor vehicles and parts and components in Indonesia. Inherent to this objective is that these measures necessarily have a significant impact on investment in these sectors. For this reason, we consider that these measures fall within any reasonable interpretation of the term "investment measures". We do not intend to provide an overall definition of what constitutes an investment measure. We emphasize that our characterization of the measures as "investment measures" is based on an examination of the manner in which the measures at issue in this case relate to investment. There may be other measures which qualify as investment measures within the meaning of the TRIMs Agreement because they relate to investment in a different manner.

14.81 With respect to the arguments of Indonesia that the measures at issue are not investment measures because the Indonesian Government does not regard the programmes as investment programmes and because the measures have not been adopted by the authorities responsible for investment policy, we believe that there is nothing in the text of the TRIMs Agreement to suggest that a measure is not an investment measure simply on the grounds that a Member does not characterize the measure as such, or on the grounds that the measure is not explicitly adopted as an investment regulation. In any event, we note that some of the regulations and decisions adopted pursuant to these car programmes were adopted by investment bodies.

Are the Indonesian measures "trade-related"?

14.82 We now have to determine whether these investment measures are "trade-related". We consider that, if these measures are local content requirements, they would necessarily be "trade-related" because such requirements, by definition, always favour the use of domestic products over imported products, and therefore affect trade.

Illustrative List of the TRIMs Agreement

14.83 An examination of whether these measures are covered by Item (1) of the Illustrative List of TRIMs annexed to the TRIMs Agreement, which refers amongst other situations to measures with local content requirements, will not only indicate whether they are trade-related but also whether they are inconsistent with Article III:4 and thus in violation of Article 2.1 of the TRIMs Agreement.

14.84 The Annex to the TRIMs Agreement reads as follows:

"Annex: Illustrative List

1. TRIMs that are inconsistent with the obligation of national treatment provided for in paragraph 4 of Article III of GATT 1994 include those which are mandatory or enforceable under domestic law or under administrative rulings, or compliance with which is necessary to obtain an advantage, and which require:

(a) the purchase or use by an enterprise of products of domestic origin or from any domestic source, whether specified in terms of particular products, in terms of volume or value of products, or in terms of a proportion of volume or value of its local production;"

14.85 We note that all the various decrees and regulations implementing the Indonesian car programmes operate in the same manner. They provide for tax advantages on finished motor vehicles using a certain percentage value of local content and additional customs duty advantages on imports of parts and components to be used in finished motor vehicles using a certain percentage value of local content. We also note that under the June 1996 car programme, the local content envisaged in the February 1996 car programme could be performed through an undertaking by the foreign producer of National Cars to counter-purchase Indonesian parts and components.

14.86   For instance, the Decision to issue the Decree of the Minister of Industry Concerning The Determination of Local Content Levels of Domestically Made Motor Vehicles or Components attached to the Decree of the Ministry of Industry announcing the 1993 car programme states in its Article 2:

> "(1) The Automotive Industry and/or the Components Industry *may obtain certain Incentives* within the framework of importing needed Components, Sub–Components, basic materials and semi-Finished Goods, originating in one source as well as various sources (multi sourcing), *if the production has reached/can achieve certain Local Content levels.* (. . .)

> (3) The *Local Content levels* of domestically made Motor Vehicles and/or Components which are *eligible for Incentives* including their Incentive rates shall be those listed in Attachment I to this decree." (emphasis added)

The Instruction of the President of the Republic of Indonesia No.2 of 1996 of the National Car programme (dated 19 February 1998) states in its "INSTRUCT . . . SECONDLY:

> "WITHIN the framework of establishment of the National Car Industry:

> 1.   The Minister of Industry and Trade will foster, guide and grant facilities in accordance with provisions of laws in effect such that the national car industry:

>> a.   uses a brand name of its own;

>> b.   *uses components produced domestically as much as possible*;

>> c.   is able to export its products." (emphasis added)

More specifically Regulation No. 20/1996 established the following sales tax structure where passenger cars of more than 1600cc and jeeps with local content of less than 60% would pay 35% tax; passenger cars of less than 1600cc, jeeps with local content of more than 60%, and light commercial vehicles (other than jeeps using gas) would pay 20% tax; and National Cars would pay 0% tax. We recall that one of the requirements for designation as a "National Car" is that the local content rate must be 20% at the end of the first year, 40% at the end of the second year and 60% at the end of the third year.

14.87   We also note with reference to the June 1996 car programme, that the Decree of the President of the Republic of Indonesia Number 42 of 1996 on the production of National Cars provides in Article 1:

> "National Cars which are made overseas by Indonesian workers and fulfil the local content stipulated by the Minister of Industry and Trade will be treated equally to those made in Indonesia."

The Decree of the Minister of Industry and Trade adopted pursuant to this Presidential Decree 42 states in Articles 1, 2 and 3:

"Article 1

Within the framework of preparations, the production of national cars can be carried out overseas for a one-time maximum period of 1 (one) year on the condition that Indonesian made parts and components are used.

Article 2

The procurement of Indonesian made parts and components shall be performed through a system of counter purchase of parts and components of motor vehicles by the overseas company carrying out the production and reexporting of national cars to Indonesia.

Article 3

The value of the Counter purchase referred to in Article 2 shall be fixed at the minimum of 25% (twenty-five percent) of the import value of the national cars assembled abroad (C & F value)".

14.88 We believe that under these measures compliance with the provisions for the purchase and use of particular products of domestic origin is necessary to obtain the tax and customs duty benefits on these car programmes, as referred to in Item 1(a) of the Illustrative List of TRIMs.

14.89 We need now to decide whether these tax and customs duty benefits are "advantages" in the meaning of the chapeau of paragraph 1 of that Illustrative List. In the context of the claims under Article III:4 of GATT, Indonesia has argued that the reduced customs duties are not internal regulations and as such cannot be covered by the wording of Article III:4. We do not consider that the matter before us in connection with Indonesia's obligations under the TRIMs Agreement is the customs duty relief as such but rather the internal regulations, i.e. the provisions on purchase and use of domestic products, compliance with which is necessary to obtain an advantage, which advantage here is the customs duty relief. The lower duty rates are clearly "advantages" in the meaning of the chapeau of the Illustrative List to the TRIMs Agreement and as such, we find that the Indonesian measures fall within the scope of the Item 1 of the Illustrative List of TRIMs.

14.90 Indonesia also argues that the local content requirements of its car programmes do not constitute classic local content requirements within the meaning of the *FIRA* panel (which involved a binding contract between the investor and the Government of Canada) because they leave companies free to decide from which source to purchase parts and components. We note that the Indonesian producers or assemblers of motor vehicles (or motor vehicle parts) must satisfy the local content targets of the relevant measures in order to take advantage of the customs duty and tax benefits offered by the Government. The wording of the Illustrative List of the TRIMs Agreement makes it clear that a simple advantage conditional on the use of domestic goods is considered to be a violation of Article 2 of the TRIMs Agreement even if the local content requirement is not binding as such. We note in addition that this argument has also been rejected in the Panel Report on *Parts and Components*.

14.91   We thus find that the tax and tariff benefits contingent on meeting local requirements under these car programmes constitute "advantages". Given this and our earlier analysis of whether these local content requirements are TRIMs and covered by the Illustrative List annexed to the TRIMs Agreement, we further find that they are in violation of Article 2.1 of the TRIMs Agreement.

14.92   We note that a violation of Article 2.1 of the TRIMs Agreement may be justified under Articles 3, 4 or 5 of the TRIMs Agreement. However, Indonesia has not invoked any of the general exceptions of GATT as referred to in Article 3 of the TRIMs Agreement, nor the provisions available to developing countries referred to in Article 4. In addition, Indonesia does not claim that the measures in dispute benefit from the transitional period under Article 5 of the TRIMs Agreement.

Notes and Questions

(1) Numerous other provisions of WTO law were at issue in the case, resulting in several findings of violations by Indonesia. The case was not appealed.

(2) Consider the illustrative list of TRIMs in the annex to the agreement—are you clear on the distinction between TRIMs that conflict with GATT Article III and TRIMs that conflict with GATT Article XI?

(3) Pay attention to the relationship between the TRIMs Agreement and GATS. Suppose Indonesia required that foreign-owned banks must hire 90% of their workforce from the domestic labor force at some minimum wage or above—requirements that do not apply to domestically-owned banks. Does the TRIMs Agreement have any bearing on the permissibility of such policies?

(4) Reflect on the scope of the TRIMs Agreement. Suppose that a government enacts discriminatory corporate tax rates that are higher on corporations whose shareholders are predominantly foreign. Is that measure a TRIM? What about a rule that prohibits foreign investors from bidding on the rights to harvest timber from government lands, where most of the lumber produced therefrom will eventually be exported?

(5) The Canadian *FIRA* case, noted in the introduction to this section, involved a further challenge to Canada's so-called "export performance requirements," whereby commitments were extracted from investors to export some proportion of the output from their manufacturing facilities. The *FIRA* panel determined that such requirements did not violate GATT. Was the panel correct (see GATT Article XVII:1(c))? Does the TRIMs Agreement do anything to condemn export performance requirements?

SECTION 23.3 INVESTOR RIGHTS UNDER NAFTA

Before proceeding, the reader should review the investment provisions contained in NAFTA Chapter 11. Section A contains the substantive obligations. In addition to general non-discrimination principles, note the elaboration of the issues addressed by the TRIMs Agreement in Article 1106 on "Performance Requirements." (In what ways does NAFTA go farther than the TRIMs Agreement in constraining such measures?) Note also Article 1110, which affords investors a right to compensation for "expropriation."

Section B pertains to the settlement of disputes between investors and NAFTA members. It permits investors to submit claims involving the violation of provisions in Section A to arbitration through the international center for the settlement of investment disputes (ICSID, affiliated with the World Bank) or under UNCITRAL arbitration rules. It thus creates a "private right of action" that is quite unusual in the world of trade agreements (the European Union affords private rights of action on "trade issues" to its citizens, however, as do typical BITs). In addition to the private action, Section B allows the arbitrators to award monetary damages.

These investor rights provisions were perhaps expected to be of little moment when NAFTA was negotiated, in part because private rights of action had not been perceived as problematic during the history of BITs. Inspired by modern thinking about "regulatory takings," however, investor plaintiffs under NAFTA have advanced some unexpected claims of "expropriation," which have made the investor rights provisions highly controversial and have led NAFTA members to consider the possibility of changing them. In 2008, for example, presidential candidate Hillary Clinton expressed the view that the NAFTA provisions affording private rights of action to investors should be repealed.

AZINIAN v. UNITED MEXICAN STATES

International Centre for the Settlement of Investment
Disputes (Additional Facility).
Case No. ARB(AF)/97/2.

Award, November 1, 1999.[1]

Before the Arbitral Tribunal constituted under Chapter Eleven of the North American Free Trade Agreement

[The claimants were American citizens and shareholders of DESONA, a Mexican corporation formed for the purpose of providing solid waste disposal services to the city of Naucalpan de Juarez pursuant to a "concession contract" entered in 1993.]

---

1.   39 Intl. Legal Materials 537 (2000).

9. On 15 November, the Concession Contract was signed. Two days later DESONA commenced its commercial and industrial waste collection * * *.

* * *

12. In January and February, there were a number of meetings between the personnel of DESONA and the Ayuntamiento [the City Council] concerning implementation of the Concession Contract. * * *

13. In mid-February, the Ayuntamiento sought independent legal advice about the Concession Contract. It was advised that there were 27 "irregularities" in connection with the conclusion and performance of the Concession Contract.

* * *

17. On 21 March, despite a protest from DESONA on 16 March, the Ayuntamiento decided to annul the Concession Contract. * * *

* * *

21. On 13 July, DESONA appealed to the Superior Chamber of the Administrative Tribunal, which upheld the Ayuntamiento's annulment of the Concession Contract by a judgment dated 17 November. The Superior Chamber held that of the 27 alleged irregularities, nine had been demonstrated. Of these, seven related to various perceived misrepresentations by the Claimants in connection with the conclusion of the Concession Contract.

22. On 10 December, DESONA lodged a further appeal, in the form of a so-called amparo petition, to the Federal Circuit Court.

23. On 18 May 1995, the Federal Circuit Court ruled in favour of the Naucalpan Ayuntamiento, specifically upholding the Superior Chamber's judgment as to the legality of the nine bases accepted for the annulment.

24. On 17 March 1997, the Claimant shareholders of DESONA initiated the present arbitral proceedings against the Government of Mexico under Chapter Eleven of the North American Free Trade Agreement (hereinafter "NAFTA"), by submitting a claim to arbitration pursuant to Article 1137(1)(b) thereof.

* * *

75. The Claimants contend that "the City's wrongful repudiation of the Concession Contract violates Articles 1110 ("Expropriation and Compensation") and 1105 ("Minimum Standard of Treatment") of NAFTA" and accordingly seek the following relief, as articulated in their Prayer for Relief dated 23 June 1999:

"A. With respect to the enterprise, as follows:

1. The value of the concession as an ongoing enterprise on March 21, 1994, the date of the taking based upon the values obtained: * * *

2.   Interest on the amount awarded as the value of the concession as set forth in section A above from the date of the taking at the rate of 10% per annum to the date of the award.

3.   Cost of the proceedings, including but not limited to attorneys fees, experts and accounting fees and administrative fees. * * *

* * *

79.   As this is the first dispute brought by an investor under NAFTA to be resolved by an award on the merits, it is appropriate to consider first principles.

80.   NAFTA is a treaty among three sovereign States which deals with a vast range of matters relating to the liberalisation of trade. Part Five deals with "Investment, Services and Related Matters." Chapter Eleven thereunder deals specifically with "Investment."

81.   Section A of Chapter Eleven establishes a number of substantive obligations with respect to investments. Section B concerns jurisdiction and procedure; it defines the method by which an investor claiming a violation of the obligations established in Section A may seek redress.

82.   Arbitral jurisdiction under Section B is limited not only as to the persons who may invoke it (they must be nationals of a State signatory to NAFTA), but also as to subject matter: claims may not be submitted to investor-state arbitration under Chapter Eleven unless they are founded upon the violation of an obligation established in Section A.

83.   To put it another way, a foreign investor entitled in principle to protection under NAFTA may enter into contractual relations with a public authority, and may suffer a breach by that authority, and still not be in a position to state a claim under NAFTA. It is a fact of life everywhere that individuals may be disappointed in their dealings with public authorities, and disappointed yet again when national courts reject their complaints. It may safely be assumed that many Mexican parties can be found who had business dealings with governmental entities which were not to their satisfaction; Mexico is unlikely to be different from other countries in this respect. NAFTA was not intended to provide foreign investors with blanket protection from this kind of disappointment, and nothing in its terms so provides.

84.   It therefore would not be sufficient for the Claimants to convince the present Arbitral Tribunal that the actions or motivations of the Naucalpan Ayuntamiento are to be disapproved, or that the reasons given by the Mexican courts in their three judgements are unpersuasive. Such considerations are unavailing unless the Claimants can point to a violation of an obligation established in Section A of Chapter Eleven attributable to the Government of Mexico.

85.   The Claimants have alleged violations of the following two provisions of NAFTA:

Article 1110(1)

"No party may directly or indirectly nationalize or expropriate an investment of an investor of another Party in its territory or take a measure tantamount to nationalization or expropriation of such investment ('expropriation') except:

(a) for a public purpose;

(b) on a non-discriminatory basis;

(c) in accordance with due process of law and Article 1105(1); and

(d) on payment of compensation in accordance with paragraphs 2 through 6."

Article 1105(1)

"Each Party shall accord to investments of investors of another Party treatment in accordance with international law, including fair and equitable treatment and full protection and security."

86. Although the parties to the Concession Contract accepted the jurisdiction of the Mexican courts, the Claimants correctly point out that they did not exclude recourse to other courts or arbitral tribunals—such as this one—having jurisdiction on another foundation. Nor is the fact that the Claimants took the initiative before the Mexican courts fatal to the jurisdiction of the present Arbitral Tribunal. The Claimants have cited a number of cases where international arbitral tribunals did not consider themselves bound by decisions of national courts. Professor Dodge, in his oral argument, stressed the following sentence from the well-known ICSID case of Amco v. Indonesia: "An international tribunal is not bound to follow the result of a national court." As the Claimants argue persuasively, it would be unfortunate if potential claimants under NAFTA were dissuaded from seeking relief under domestic law from national courts, because such actions might have the salutary effect of resolving the dispute without resorting to investor-state arbitration under NAFTA. Nor finally has the Respondent argued that it cannot be held responsible for the actions of a local governmental authority like the Ayuntamiento of Naucalpan.

87. The problem is that the Claimants' fundamental complaint is that they are the victims of a breach of the Concession Contract. NAFTA does not, however, allow investors to seek international arbitration for mere contractual breaches. Indeed, NAFTA cannot possibly be read to create such a regime, which would have elevated a multitude of ordinary transactions with public authorities into potential international disputes. The Claimants simply could not prevail merely by persuading the Arbitral Tribunal that the Ayuntamiento of Naucalpan breached the Concession Contract.

88. Understanding this proposition perfectly well, Professor Dodge insisted that the claims are not simply for breach of contract, but involve "the direct expropriation of DESONA's contractual rights" and "the indirect expropriation of DESONA itself."

89. Professor Dodge then argued that a breach of contract constitutes an expropriation "if it is confiscatory," or, quoting Professor Brownlie, Principles of Public International Law, 5th edition at 550, if "the state exercises its executive or legislative authority to destroy the contractual rights as an asset." Specifically, he invoked a "wealth of authority treating the repudiation of concession agreements as an expropriation of contractual rights."

90. Labelling is, however, no substitute for analysis. The words "confiscatory," "destroy contractual rights as an asset," or "repudiation" may serve as a way to describe breaches which are to be treated as extraordinary, and therefore as acts of expropriation, but they certainly do not indicate on what basis the critical distinction between expropriation and an ordinary breach of contract is to be made. The egregiousness of any breach is in the eye of the beholder—and that is not satisfactory for present purposes.

91. It is therefore necessary to examine whether the annulment of the Concession Contract may be considered to be an act of expropriation violating NAFTA Article 1110. If not, the claim must fail. The question cannot be more central.

92. Before examining this crucial issue, it should be recalled that the Claimants originally grounded their claim on an alleged violation of Article 1105 as well as one of Article 1110. While they have never abandoned the ground of Article 1105, it figured very fleetingly in their later pleadings, and not at all in Professor Dodge's final arguments. This is hardly surprising. The only conceivably relevant substantive principle of Article 1105 is that a NAFTA investor should not be dealt with in a manner that contravenes international law. There has not been a claim of such a violation of international law other than the one more specifically covered by Article 1110. In a feeble attempt to maintain Article 1105, the Claimants' Reply Memorial affirms that the breach of the Concession Contract violated international law because it was "motivated by noncommercial considerations, and compensatory damages were not paid." This is but a paraphrase of a complaint more specifically covered by Article 1110. For the avoidance of doubt, the Arbitral Tribunal therefore holds that under the circumstances of this case if there was no violation of Article 1110, there was none of Article 1105 either.

93. The Respondent argues that the Concession Contract came to an end on two independently justified grounds: invalidity and rescission.

94. The second is the more complex. It postulates that the Ayuntamiento was entitled to rescind the Concession Contract due to DESONA's failure of performance. If the Ayuntamiento was not so entitled, its termination of the Concession Contract was itself a breach. Most of the evidence and debate in these proceedings have focused on this issue: was DESONA in substantial non-compliance with the Concession Contract? The subject is complicated by the fact that DESONA was apparently not given the benefit of the 30–day cure period defined in Article 31 of the Concession Contract.

95. The logical starting point is to examine the asserted original invalidity of the Concession Contract. If this assertion was founded, there is no need to make findings with respect to performance; nor can there be a question of curing original invalidity.

96. From this perspective, the problem may be put quite simply. The Ayuntamiento believed it had grounds for holding the Concession Contract to be invalid under Mexican law governing public service concessions. At DESONA's initiative, these grounds were tested by three levels of Mexican courts, and in each case were found to be extant. How can it be said that Mexico breached NAFTA when the Ayuntamiento of Naucalpan purported to declare the invalidity of a Concession Contract which by its terms was subject to Mexican law, and to the jurisdiction of the Mexican courts, and the courts of Mexico then agreed with the Ayuntamiento's determination? Further, the Claimants have neither contended nor proved that the Mexican legal standards for the annulment of concessions violate Mexico's Chapter Eleven obligations; nor that the Mexican law governing such annulments is expropriatory.

97. With the question thus framed, it becomes evident that for the Claimants to prevail it is not enough that the Arbitral Tribunal disagree with the determination of the Ayuntamiento. A governmental authority surely cannot be faulted for acting in a manner validated by its courts unless the courts themselves are disavowed at the international level. As the Mexican courts found that the Ayuntamiento's decision to nullify the Concession Contract was consistent with the Mexican law governing the validity of public service concessions, the question is whether the Mexican court decisions themselves breached Mexico's obligations under Chapter Eleven.

98. True enough, an international tribunal called upon to rule on a Government's compliance with an international treaty is not paralysed by the fact that the national courts have approved the relevant conduct of public officials. As a former President of the International Court of Justice put it: "The principles of the separation and independence of the judiciary in municipal law and of respect for the finality of judicial decisions have exerted an important influence on the form in which the general principle of State responsibility has been applied to acts or omissions of judicial organs. These basic tenets of judicial organization explain the reluctance to be found in some arbitral awards of the last century to admit the extension to the judiciary of the rule that a State is responsible for the acts of all its organs. However, in the present century State responsibility for acts of judicial organs came to be recognized. Although independent of the Government, the judiciary is not independent of the State: the judgment given by a judicial authority emanates from an organ of the State in just the same way as a law promulgated by the legislature or a decision taken by the executive. The responsibility of the State for acts of judicial authorities may result from three different types of judicial decision. The first is a decision of a municipal court clearly incompatible with a rule of international law. The second is what it known traditionally as a 'denial of justice.' The third occurs when, in

certain exceptional and well-defined circumstances, a State is responsible for a judicial decision contrary to municipal law." Eduardo Jimenez de Arechaga, "International Law in the Past Third of a Century," 159–1 Recueil des cours (General Course in Public International Law, The Hague, 1978). (Emphasis added.)

99.   The possibility of holding a State internationally liable for judicial decisions does not, however, entitle a claimant to seek international review of the national court decisions as though the international jurisdiction seised has plenary appellate jurisdiction. This is not true generally, and it is not true for NAFTA. What must be shown is that the court decision itself constitutes a violation of the treaty. Even if the Claimants were to convince this Arbitral Tribunal that the Mexican courts were wrong with respect to the invalidity of the Concession Contract, this would not per se be conclusive as to a violation of NAFTA. More is required; the Claimants must show either a denial of justice, or a pretence of form to achieve an internationally unlawful end.

100.   But the Claimants have raised no complaints against the Mexican courts; they do not allege a denial of justice. Without exception, they have directed their many complaints against the Ayuntamiento of Naucalpan. The Arbitral Tribunal finds that this circumstance is fatal to the claim, and makes it unnecessary to consider issues relating to performance of the Concession Contract. For if there is no complaint against a determination by a competent court that a contract governed by Mexican law was invalid under Mexican law, there is by definition no contract to be expropriated.

101.   The Arbitral Tribunal does not, however, wish to create the impression that the Claimants fail on account of an improperly pleaded case. The Arbitral Tribunal thus deems it appropriate, ex abundante cautela, to demonstrate that the Claimants were well advised not to seek to have the Mexican court decisions characterised as violations of NAFTA.

102.   A denial of justice could be pleaded if the relevant courts refuse to entertain a suit, if they subject it to undue delay, or if they administer justice in a seriously inadequate way. There is no evidence, or even argument, that any such defects can be ascribed to the Mexican proceedings in this case.

103.   There is a fourth type of denial of justice, namely the clear and malicious misapplication of the law. This type of wrong doubtless overlaps with the notion of "pretence of form" to mask a violation of international law. In the present case, not only has no such wrongdoing been pleaded, but the Arbitral Tribunal wishes to record that it views the evidence as sufficient to dispel any shadow over the bona fides of the Mexican judgments. Their findings cannot possibly be said to have been arbitrary, let alone malicious.

Notes and Questions

(1) Suppose an "investor" loses a breach of contract action against a private party in the national courts of a member state. Might that conceivably constitute "expropriation?" Should such a claim be possible?

(2) Must a potential claimant exhaust its remedies under national law before proceeding to NAFTA arbitration? Sensible? As a strategic matter, how should a potential complainant proceed in deciding when to initiate NAFTA arbitration? How should arbitrators approach a case in which no authoritative judicial decision has been rendered in a national court?

(3) What behavior would constitute a "clear and malicious" misapplication of the law? How might a court "administer justice in a seriously inadequate way?" Do these principles mean that the arbitrators should apply a highly deferential standard of review, but may hold for the complainant in cases where the arbitrators find clear legal error? Or must the complainant show that national courts exhibited personal animosity, corruption, or some other impropriety?

(4) Why would the parties to a trade agreement such as NAFTA give investors a private right of action to enforce investor rights provisions, but not allow private parties a right of action to enforce the wide array of other commitments on trade? Is the function of an investment agreement fundamentally different from the function of a trade agreement from the perspective of the "importing" country? See Alan O. Sykes, Public Versus Private Enforcement of International Economic Law: Standing and Remedy, 34 J. Leg. Stud. 631 (2005).

METALCLAD CORP. v. UNITED MEXICAN STATES

40 I.L.M. 36 (2001).
Before the Arbitral Tribunal constituted under Chapter Eleven
of the North American Free Trade Agreement.

1.   This dispute arises out of the activities of the Claimant, Metalclad Corporation (hereinafter "Metalclad"), in the Mexican Municipality of Guadalcazar (hereinafter "Guadalcazar"), located in the Mexican State of San Luis Potosi (hereinafter "SLP"). Metalclad alleges that Respondent, the United Mexican States (hereinafter "Mexico"), through its local governments of SLP and Guadalcazar, interfered with its development and operation of a hazardous waste landfill. Metalclad claims that this interference is a violation of the Chapter Eleven investment provisions of the North American Free Trade Agreement (hereinafter "NAFTA"). * * *

2.   Metalclad is an enterprise of the United States of America, incorporated under the laws of Delaware. EcoMetalclad Corporation (hereinafter "ECO") is an enterprise of the United States of America, incorporated under the laws of Utah. Eco is wholly-owned by Metalclad, and owns 100% of the shares in Ecosistemas Nacionales, S.A. de C.V. (hereinafter "ECONSA"), a Mexican corporation. In 1993, ECONSA purchased the Mexican company Confinamiento Tecnico de Residuos Industriales, S.A. de C.V. (hereinafter "COTERIN") with a view to the acquisition, development and operation of the latter's hazardous waste transfer station and landfill in the valley of La Pedrera, located in Guadalcazar. COTERIN is the owner of record of the landfill property as well as the permits and licenses which are at the base of this dispute.

* * *

28. In 1990 the federal government of Mexico authorized COTE-RIN to construct and operate a transfer station for hazardous waste in La Pedrera, a valley located in Guadalcazar in SLP. * * *

29. On January 23, 1993, the National Ecological Institute (herein-after "INE"), an independent sub-agency of the federal Secretariat of the Mexican Environment, National Resources and Fishing (hereinafter "SEMARNAP"), granted COTERIN a federal permit to construct a hazardous waste landfill in La Pedrera (hereinafter "the landfill").

* * *

31. Shortly thereafter, on May 11, 1993, the government of SLP granted COTERIN a state land use permit to construct the landfill. * * *

32. One month later, on June 11 1993, Metalclad met with Gover-nor of SLP to discuss the project. Metalclad asserts that at this meeting it obtained the Governor's support for the project. In fact, the Governor acknowledged at the hearing that a reasonable person might expect that the Governor would support the project if studies confirmed the site as suitable or feasible and if the environmental impact was consistent with Mexican standards.

33. Metalclad further asserts that it was told by the President of the INE and the General Director of the Mexican Secretariat of Urban Development and Ecology (hereinafter "SEDUE" [the predecessor or-ganization to SEMARNAP]) that all necessary permits for the landfill had been issued with the exception of the federal permit for operation of the landfill. A witness statement submitted by the President of the INE suggests that a hazardous waste landfill could be built if all permits required by the corresponding federal and state laws have been acquired.

34. Metalclad also asserts that the General Director of SEDUE told Metalclad that the responsibility for obtaining project support in the state and local community lay with the federal government.

35. On August 10, 1993, the INE granted COTERIN the federal permit for operation of the landfill. On September 10, 1993, Metalclad * * * purchased COTERIN, the landfill site and the associated permits.

* * *

37. Metalclad asserts that shortly after its purchase of COTERIN, the Governor of SLP embarked on a public campaign to denounce and prevent the operation of the landfill.

38. Metalclad further asserts, however, that in April 1994, after months of negotiation, Metalclad believed that it had secured SLP's agreement to support the project. Consequently, in May 1994, after receiving an eighteen-month extension of the previously issued federal construction permit from the INE, Metalclad began construction of the

landfill. Mexico denies the SLP's agreement or support had ever been obtained.

* * *

45.　Metalclad completed construction of the landfill in March 1995. On March 10, 1995, Metalclad held an "open house," or "inauguration," of the landfill which was attended by a number of dignitaries from the United State and from Mexico's federal, state and local governments.

46.　Demonstrators impeded the "inauguration," blocked the exit and entry of buses carrying guests and workers, and employed tactics of intimidation against Metalclad. Metalclad asserts that the demonstration was organized at least in part by the Mexican state and local governments, and that state troopers assisted in blocking traffic into and out of the site. Metalclad was thenceforth effectively prevented from opening the landfill.

* * *

50.　On December 5, 1995, thirteen months after Metalclad's application for the municipal construction permit was filed, the application was denied. * * *

* * *

52.　Metalclad has pointed out that there was no evidence of inadequacy of performance by Metalclad of any legal obligation, nor any showing that Metalclad violated the terms of any federal or state permit; that there was no evidence that the Municipality gave any consideration to the recently completed environmental reports indicating that the site was in fact suitable for a hazardous waste landfill; that there was no evidence that the site, as constructed, failed to meet specific construction requirements; that there was no evidence that the Municipality ever required or issued a municipal construction permit for any other construction project in Guadalcazar; and that there was no evidence that there was an established administrative process with respect to municipal construction permits in the Municipality of Guadalcazar.

53.　Mexico asserts that Metalclad was aware through due diligence that a municipal permit might be necessary on the basis of the case of COTERIN (1991, 1992), and other past precedents for various projects in SLP.

* * *

58.　From May 1996 through December 1996, Metalclad and the State of SLP attempted to resolve their issues with respect to the operation of the landfill. These efforts failed and, on January 2, 1997, Metalclad initiated the present arbitral proceeding against the Government of Mexico under Chapter Eleven of the NAFTA.

59.　On September 23, 1997, three days before the expiry of his term, the Governor issued an Ecological Decree declaring a Natural Area for the protection of rare cactus. The Natural Area encompasses the area of the landfill. Metalclad relies in part on this Ecological Decree as an additional element in its claim of expropriation, maintaining that the decree effectively and permanently precluded the operation of landfill.

* * *

72. Metalclad contends that Mexico, through its local governments of SLP and Guadalcazar, interfered with and precluded its operation of the landfill. Metalclad alleges that this interference is a violation of Articles 1105 and 1110 of Chapter Eleven of the investment provisions of NAFTA.

73. A threshold question is whether Mexico is internationally responsible for the acts of SLP and Guadalcazar. The issue was largely disposed of by Mexico in paragraph 233 of its post-hearing submission, which stated that "[Mexico] did not plead that the acts of the Municipality were not covered by NAFTA. [Mexico] was, and remains, prepared to proceed on the assumption that the normal rule of state responsibility applies; that is, that the Respondent can be internationally responsible for the acts of state organs at all three levels of government." Parties to that Agreement must ensure that all necessary measures are taken in order to give effect to the provisions of the Agreement, including their observance, except as otherwise provided in this Agreement, by state and provincial governments." (NAFTA Article 105) A reference to a state or province includes local governments of that state or province. (NAFTA Article 201(2)) The exemptions from the requirements of Articles 1105 and 1110 laid down in Article 1108(1) do not extend to states or local governments. This approach accords fully with the established position in customary international law. * * *

74. NAFTA Article 1105(1) provides that "each Party shall accord to investments of investors of another Party treatment in accordance with international law, including fair and equitable treatment and full protection and security." For the reasons set out below, the Tribunal finds that Metalclad's investment was not accorded fair and equitable treatment in accordance with international law, and that Mexico has violated NAFTA Article 1105(1).

75. An underlying objective of NAFTA is to promote and increase cross-border investment opportunities and ensure the successful implementation of investment initiatives. (NAFTA Article 102(1)).

76. Prominent in the statement of principles and rules that introduces the Agreement is the reference to "transparency" (NAFTA Article 102(1)). The Tribunal understands this to include the idea that all relevant legal requirements for the purpose of initiating, completing and successfully operating investments made, or intended to be made, under the Agreement should be capable of being readily known to all affected investors of another Party. There should be no room for doubt or uncertainty on such matters. Once the authorities of the central government of any Party (whose international responsibility in such matters has been identified in the preceding section) become aware of any scope

for misunderstanding or confusion in this connection, it is their duty to ensure that the correct position is promptly determined and clearly stated so that investors can proceed with all appropriate expedition in the confident belief that they are acting in accordance with all relevant laws.

77.   Metalclad acquired COTERIN for the sole purpose of developing and operating a hazardous waste landfill in the valley of La Pedrera, in Guadalcazar, SLP.

78.   The Government of Mexico issued a federal construction and operating permits for the landfill prior to Metalclad's purchase of COTERIN, and the Government of SLP likewise issued a state operating permit which implied its political support for the landfill project.

79.   A central point in this case has been whether, in addition to the above-mentioned permits, a municipal permit for the construction of a hazardous waste landfill was required.

80.   When Metalclad inquired, prior to its purchase of COTERIN, as to the necessity for municipal permits, federal officials assured it that it had all that was needed to undertake the landfill project. Indeed, following Metalclad's acquisition of COTERIN, the federal government extended the federal construction permit for eighteen months.

81.   As presented and confirmed by Metalclad's expert on Mexican law, the authority of the municipality extends only to the administration of the construction permit, "... to grant licenses and permits for constructions and to participate in the creation and administration of ecological reserve zones ...". (Mexican Const. Art. 115, Fraction V). However, Mexico's experts on constitutional law expressed a different view.

82.   Mexico's General Ecology Law of 1988 (hereinafter "LGEEPA") expressly grants to the Federation the power to authorize construction and operation of hazardous waste landfills. Article 5 of the LGEEPA provides that the powers of the Federation extend to:

> V.   the regulation and control of activities considered to be highly hazardous, and of the generation, handling and final disposal of hazardous materials and wastes for the environments of ecosystems, as well as for the preservation of natural resources, in accordance with [the] Law, other applicable ordinances and their regulatory provisions.

83.   LGEEPA also limits the environmental powers of the municipality to issues relating to non-hazardous waste. Specifically, Article 8 of the LGEEPA grants municipalities the power in accordance with the provisions of the law and local laws to apply:

> legal provisions in matters of prevention and control of the effects on the environment caused by generation, transportation, storage, handling treatment and final disposal of solid industrial wastes which are not considered to be hazardous in accordance with the provisions of Article 137 of [the 1988] law.

84. The same law also limits state environmental powers to those not expressly attributed to the federal government. Id., Article 7.

85. Metalclad was led to believe, and did believe, that the federal and state permits allowed for the construction and operation of the landfill. Metalclad argues that in all hazardous waste matters, the Municipality has no authority. However, Mexico argues that constitutionally and lawfully the Municipality has the authority to issue construction permits.

86. Even if Mexico is correct that a municipal construction permit was required, the evidence also shows that, as to hazardous waste evaluations and assessments, the federal authority's jurisdiction was controlling and the authority of the municipality only extended to appropriate construction considerations. Consequently, the denial of the permit by the Municipality by reference to environmental impact considerations in the case of what was basically a hazardous waste disposal landfill, was improper, as was the municipality's denial of the permit for any reason other than those related to the physical construction or defects in the site.

87. Relying on the representations of the federal government, Metalclad started constructing the landfill, and did this openly and continuously, and with the full knowledge of the federal, state, and municipal governments, until the municipal "Stop Work Order" on October 26, 1994. The basis of this order was said to have been Metalclad's failure to obtain a municipal construction permit.

88. In addition, Metalclad asserted that federal officials told it that if it submitted an application for a municipal construction permit, the Municipality would have no legal basis for denying the permit and that it would be issued as a matter of course. The absence of a clear rule as to the requirement or not of a municipal construction permit, as well as the absence of any established practice or procedure as to the manner of handling applications for a municipal construction permit, amounts to a failure on the part of Mexico to ensure the transparency required by NAFTA.

89. Metalclad was entitled to rely on the representations of federal officials and to believe that it was entitled to continue its construction of the landfill. In following the advice of these officials, and filing the municipal permit application on November 15, 1994, Metalclad was merely acting prudently and in the full expectation that the permit would be granted.

90. On December 5, 1995, thirteen months after the submission of Metalclad's application—during which time Metalclad continued its open and obvious investment activity—the Municipality denied Metalclad's application for a construction permit ...

91. Moreover, the permit was denied at a meeting of the Municipal Town Council of which Metalclad received no notice, to which it received no invitation, and at which it was given no opportunity to appear.

92. The Town Council denied the permit for reasons which included, but may not have been limited to, the opposition of the local population, the fact that construction had already begun when the application was submitted, the denial of the permit to COTERIN in December 1991 and January 1992, and the ecological concerns regarding the environmental effect and impact on the site and surrounding communities. None of the reasons included a reference to any problems associated with the physical construction of the landfill or to any physical defects therein.

93. The Tribunal therefore finds that the construction permit was denied without any consideration of, or specific reference to, construction aspects or flaws of the physical facility.

* * *

96. In 1997 SLP re-entered the scene and issued an Ecological Decree in 1997 which effectively and permanently prevented the use by Metalclad of its investment.

97. The actions of the Municipality following its denial of the municipal construction permit, coupled with the procedural and substantive deficiencies of the denial, support the Tribunal's finding, for the reasons stated above, that the Municipality's insistence upon and denial of the construction permit in this instance was improper.

98. This conclusion is not affected by NAFTA Article 1114, which permits a Party to ensure that investment activity is undertaken in a manner sensitive to environmental concerns. The ... issuance of the federal permits show clearly that Mexico was satisfied that this project was consistent with, and sensitive to, its environmental concerns.

99. Mexico failed to ensure a transparent and predictable framework for Metalclad's business planning and investment. The totality of these circumstances demonstrates a lack of orderly process and timely disposition in relation to an investor of a party acting in the expectation that it would be treated fairly and justly in accordance with the NAFTA.

100. Moreover, the acts of the State and the Municipality—and therefore the acts of Mexico—fail to comply with or adhere to the requirements of NAFTA, Article 1105(1) that each Party accord to investments of investors of another Party treatment in accordance with the international law, including fair and equitable treatment. This is so particularly in light of the governing principle that internal law (such as the Municipality's stated permit requirements) does not justify failure to perform a treaty. (Vienna Convention on the Law of Treaties, Arts. 26, 27.)

101. The Tribunal therefore holds that Metalclad was not treated fairly or equitably under the NAFTA and succeeds on its claim under Article 1105.

102. NAFTA Article 1110 provides that "no party shall directly or indirectly ... expropriate an investment ... or take a measure tanta-

mount to ... expropriation ... except: (a) for a public purpose; (b) on a non-discriminatory basis; (c) in accordance with due process of law and Article 1105(1); and (d) on payment of compensation.... "A measure" is defined in Article 201(1) as including "any law, regulation, procedure, requirement or practice."

103.   Thus, expropriation under NAFTA includes not only open, deliberate and acknowledged takings of property, such as outright seizure or formal or obligatory transfer of title in favour of the host State, but also covert or incidental interference with the use of property which has the effect of depriving the owner, in whole or in significant part, of the use or reasonably-to-be-expected economic benefit of property even if not necessarily to the obvious benefit of the host State.

104.   By permitting or tolerating the conduct of Guadalcazar in relation to Metalclad which the Tribunal has already held amounts to unfair and inequitable treatment breaching Article 1105 and by thus participating or acquiescing in the denial to Metalclad of the right to operate the landfill, notwithstanding the fact that the project was fully approved and endorsed by the federal government, Mexico must be held to have taken a measure tantamount to expropriation in violation of NAFTA Article 1110(1).

105.   The Tribunal holds that the exclusive authority for siting and permitting a hazardous waste landfill resides with the Mexican federal government. This finding is consistent with the testimony of the Secretary of SEMARNAP and, as stated above, is consistent with the express language of the LGEEPA.

106.   As determined earlier (see above, para. 92), the Municipality denied the local construction permit in part because of the Municipality's perception of the adverse environmental effects of the hazardous waste landfill and the geological unsuitability of the landfill site. In so doing, the Municipality acted outside its authority. As stated above, the Municipality's denial of the construction permit without any basis in the proposed physical construction or any defect in the site ... effectively and unlawfully prevented the Claimant's operation of the landfill.

107.   These measures, taken together with the representations of the Mexican federal government, on which Metalclad relied, and the absence of a timely, orderly or substantive basis for the denial by the Municipality of the local construction permit, amount to an indirect expropriation.

108.   The present case resembles in a number of pertinent respects that of Biloune, et al. v. Ghana Investment Centre, et al., *95 I.L.R. 183, 207–10 (1993)* (Judge Schwebel, President; Wallace and Leigh, Arbitrators). In that case, a private investor was renovating and expanding a resort restaurant in Ghana. As with Metalclad, the investor, basing itself on the representations of a government affiliated entity, began construction before applying for a building permit. As with Metalclad, a stop work order was issued after a substantial amount of work had been completed. The order was based on the absence of a building permit. An

application was submitted, but although it was not expressly denied, a permit was never issued. The Tribunal found that an indirect expropriation had taken place because the totality of the circumstances had the effect of causing the irreparable cessation of work on the project. The Tribunal paid particular regard to the investor's justified reliance on the government's representations regarding the permit, the fact that government authorities knew of the construction for more than one year before issuing the stop work order, the fact that permits had not been required for other projects and the fact that no procedure was in place for dealing with building permit applications. Although the decision in Biloune does not bind this Tribunal, it is a persuasive authority and the Tribunal is in agreement with its analysis and its conclusion.

109.   Although not strictly necessary for its conclusion, the Tribunal also identifies as a further ground for a finding of expropriation the Ecological Decree issued by the Governor of SLP on September 20, 1997. The Decree covers an area of 188,758 hectares within the "Real de Guadalcazar" that includes the landfill site, and created therein an ecological preserve. This Decree had the effect of barring forever the operation of the landfill.

* * *

111.   The Tribunal need not decide or consider the motivation or intent of the adoption of the Ecological Decree. Indeed, a finding of expropriation on the basis of the Ecological Decree is not essential to the Tribunal's finding of a violation of NAFTA Article 1110. However, the Tribunal considers that the implementation of the Ecological Decree would, in and of itself, constitute an act tantamount to expropriation.

112.   In conclusion, the Tribunal holds that Mexico has indirectly expropriated Metalclad's investment without providing compensation to Metalclad for the expropriation. Mexico has violated Article 1110 of the NAFTA.

113.   In this instance, the damages arising under NAFTA, Article 1105 and the compensation due under NAFTA, Article 1110 would be the same since both situations involve the complete frustration of the operation of the landfill and negate the possibility of any meaningful return on Metalclad's investment. In other words, Metalclad has completely lost its investment.

114.   Metalclad has proposed two alternative methods for calculating damages: the first is to use a discounted cash flow analysis of future profits to establish the fair market value of the investment (approximately $90 million); the second is to value Metalclad's actual investment in the landfill (approximately $20–25 million).

115.   Metalclad also seeks an additional $20–25 million for the negative impact the circumstances are alleged to have had on its other business operations. The Tribunal disallows this additional claim because a variety of factors, not necessarily related to the La Pedrera development, have affected Metalclad's share price. The causal relation-

ship between Mexico's actions and the reduction in value of Metalclad's other business operations are too remote and uncertain to support this claim. This element of damage is, therefore, left aside.

* * *

118.   NAFTA, Article 1135(1)(a), provides for the award of monetary damages and applicable interest where a Party is found to have violated a Chapter Eleven provision. With respect to expropriation, NAFTA, Article 1110(2), specifically requires compensation to be equivalent to the fair market value of the expropriated investment immediately before the expropriation took place. This paragraph further states that "the valuation criteria shall include going concern value, asset value including declared tax value of tangible property, and other criteria, as appropriate, to determine fair market value."

119.   Normally, the fair market value of a going concern which has a history of profitable operation may be based on an estimate of future profits subject to a discounted cash flow analysis. Benvenuti and Bonfant Srl v. The Government of the People's Republic of Congo, 1 ICSID Reports 330; *21 I.L.M. 758;* AGIP SPA v. The Government of the People's Republic of Congo, 1 ICSID Reports 306; *21 I.L.M. 737.*

120.   However, where the enterprise has not operated for a sufficiently long time to establish a performance record or where it has failed to make a profit, future profits cannot be used to determine going concern or fair market value. In Sola Tiles, Inc. v. Iran (1987) (14 Iran–U.S.C.T.R. 224, 240–42; *83 I.L.R. 460, 480–81),* the Iran–U.S. Claims Tribunal pointed to the importance in relation to a company's value of "its business reputation and the relationship it has established with its suppliers and customers." Similarly, in Asian Agricultural Products v. Sri Lanka (4 ICSID Reports 246 (1990) at 292), another ICSID Tribunal observed, in dealing with the comparable problem of the assessment of the value of goodwill, that its ascertainment "requires the prior presence on the market for at least two or three years, which is the minimum period needed in order to establish continuing business connections."

121.   The Tribunal agrees with Mexico that a discounted cash flow analysis is inappropriate in the present case because the landfill was never operative and any award based on future profits would be wholly speculative.

122.   Rather, the Tribunal agrees with the parties that fair market value is best arrived at in this case by reference to Metalclad's actual investment in the project. Thus, in Phelps Dodge Corp. v. Iran (10 Iran–U.S. C.T.R. 121 (1986)), the Iran–U.S. Claims Tribunal concluded that the value of the expropriated property was the value of claimant's investment in that property. In reaching this conclusion, the Tribunal considered that the property's future profits were so dependent on as yet unobtained preferential treatment from the government that any prediction of them would be entirely speculative. (Id. at 132–33.) Similarly, in the Biloune case (see above), the Tribunal concluded that the value of

the expropriated property was the value of the claimant's investment in that property. While the Tribunal recognized the validity of the principle that lost profits should be considered in the valuation of expropriated property, the Tribunal did not award lost profits because the claimants could not provide any realistic estimate of them. In that case, as in the present one, the expropriation occurred when the project was not in operation and had yet to generate revenue. (Biloune, *95 I.L.R. at 228–229*). The award to Metalclad of the cost of its investment in the landfill is consistent with the principles set forth in Chorzow Factory (Claim for Indemnity) (Merits), Germany v. Poland, P.C.I.J. Series A., No. 17 (1928) at p. 47, namely, that where the state has acted contrary to its obligations, any award to the claimant should, as far as is possible, wipe out all the consequences of the illegal act and reestablish the situation which would in all probability have existed if that act had not been committed (the status quo ante).

123.   Metalclad asserts that it invested $20,474,528.00 in the landfill project, basing its value on its United States Federal Income Tax Returns and Auditors' Workpapers of Capitalized Costs for the Landfill reflected in a table marked Schedule A and produced by Metalclad as response 7(a) in the course of document discovery. The calculations include landfill costs Metalclad claims to have incurred from 1991 through 1996 for expenses categorized as the COTERIN acquisition, personnel, insurance, travel and living, telephone, accounting and legal, consulting, interest, office, property, plant and equipment, including $328,167.00 for "other."

* * *

125.   The Tribunal agrees, however, with Mexico's position that costs incurred prior to the year in which Metalclad purchased COTERIN are too far removed from the investment for which damages are claimed. The Tribunal will reduce the Award by the amount of the costs claimed for 1991 and 1992.

* * *

127.   The question remains of the future status of the landfill site, legal title to which at present rests with COTERIN. Clearly, COTERIN's substantive interest in the property will come to an end when it receives payment under this award. COTERIN must, therefore, relinquish as from that moment all claim, title and interest in the site. The fact that the site may require remediation has been borne in mind by the Tribunal and allowance has been made for this in the calculation of the sum payable by the Government of Mexico.

128.   The question arises whether any interest is payable on the amount of the compensation. In providing in Article 1135(1) that a Tribunal may award "monetary damages and any applicable interest," NAFTA clearly contemplates the inclusion of interest in an award. On the basis of a review of the authorities, the tribunal in Asian Agricultural Products v. Sri Lanka (4 ICSID Reports 245) held that "interest

becomes an integral part of the compensation itself, and should run consequently from the date when the State's international responsibility became engaged (ibid., p. 294, para. 114). The Tribunal sees no reason to depart from this view. As has been shown above, Mexico's international responsibility is founded upon an accumulation of a number of factors. In the circumstances, the Tribunal considers that of the various possible dates at which it might be possible to fix the engagement of Mexico's responsibility, it is reasonable to select the date on which the Municipality of Guadalcazar wrongly denied Metalclad's application for a construction permit. The Tribunal therefore concludes that interest should be awarded from that date until the date 45 days from that on which this Award is made. So as to restore the Claimant to a reasonable approximation of the position in which it would have been if the wrongful act had not taken place, interest has been calculated at 6% p.a., compounded annually.

* * *

130. Both parties seek an award of costs and fees. However, the Tribunal finds that it is equitable in this matter for each party to bear its own costs and fees, as well as half the advance payments made to ICSID.

131. For the reasons stated above, the Tribunal hereby decides that, reflecting the amount of Metalclad's investment in the project, less the disallowance of expenses claimed for 1991 and 1992 . . . and less the estimated amount allowed for remediation, plus interest at the rate of 6% compounded annually, the Respondent shall, within 45 days from the date on which this Award is rendered, pay to Metalclad the amount of $16,685,000.00. Following such period, interest shall accrue on the unpaid award or any unpaid part thereof at the rate of 6% compounded monthly.

Notes and Questions

(1) With reference to NAFTA Article 1105, precisely how did Mexico fail to afford to Metalclad "treatment in accordance with international law, including fair and equitable treatment . . . ?" Is the arbitral tribunal saying that the lack of transparency in its system constitutes a violation of Article 1105? Are there any transparency obligations in Chapter 11? Does the reference to transparency in Article 102 create those obligations? Are they simply an inherent part of "international law?" If Mexico has violated its own law, is that a basis for finding a violation of Article 1105?

(2) To what extent does the decision rest on the conclusion that, as a matter of Mexican law, the municipality lacked authority to deny a construction permit, at least on the grounds apparently relied on by the municipality? Mexico disputed this proposition in the arbitration—what standard do the arbitrators apply to resolve the conflict? What standard should they apply? If indeed "the exclusive authority for siting and permitting a hazardous waste landfill resides with the Mexican federal government," (para. 105), why not require Metalclad to pursue its remedy in the Mexican legal system?

(3) Suppose that a proper interpretation of Mexican law would afford the municipality some latitude to deny a permit, notwithstanding the representations of certain Mexican federal officials to the contrary. Would "expropriation" nevertheless exist on grounds akin to promissory estoppel or a lack of "transparency?" Why not put the burden on the investor to obtain authoritative legal guidance before it can "rely?" Suppose that after a landfill is constructed following the issuance of all necessary permits, new information comes to light about its environmental consequences, leading the government to shut it down. Expropriation?

(4) With regard to damages, is Metalclad's investment expense a good measure of the "fair market value" of the expropriated investment? Why disallow its expenses relating to the purchase of COTERIN?

(5) The flurry of investor rights litigation under Chapter 11 has led the NAFTA parties to consider modifying Chapter 11. For now, they have settled on some "clarifications," adopted by the NAFTA Free Trade Commission. Some of them relate to procedural matters involving access to confidential information. The others relate to the interpretation of Article 1105:

> "Minimum Standard of Treatment in Accordance with International Law
>
> 1.   Article 1105(1) prescribes the customary international law minimum standard of treatment of aliens as the minimum standard of treatment to be afforded to investments of investors of another Party.
>
> 2.   The concepts of 'fair and equitable treatment' and 'full protection and security' do not require treatment in addition to or beyond that which is required by the customary international law minimum standard of treatment of aliens.
>
> 3.   A determination that there has been a breach of another provision of NAFTA, or of a separate international agreement, does not establish that there has been a breach of Article 1105(1)."

How would this "clarification" have affected the Metalclad case?

(6) NAFTA investor arbitration decisions are subject to limited judicial review. The general attitude of most courts toward arbitration is to afford only a highly deferential check on the abuse of arbitrators' authority. The following case gives a flavor of the standards employed in the United States and the difficulty that a party to arbitration will face in seeking to overturn the arbitral award.

IN RE ARBITRATION BETWEEN INTERNATIONAL THUNDERBIRD GAMING CORPORATION v. UNITED MEXICAN STATES

United States District Court, District of Columbia, 2007.
473 F.Supp.2d 80,
aff'd, 2007 WL 4165398 (D.C. Cir., Nov. 15, 2007).

Thunderbird, seeking to undertake investment activities in Mexico, sought via a solicitation ("Solicitud") to government officials an opinion ("Opinion") regarding the legality of certain types of entertainment machines. As described in the Solicitud, the machines were stand-alone "skill machines" that tested their users' abilities, without the involvement of luck or betting. In the responsive Opinion, the government opined that so long as the machines functioned as they were described in the Solicitud (that is, without the intervention of luck or gambling), they would be permissible for commercial use and would fall outside the regulatory jurisdiction of the Mexican gaming authority, the Secretariat de Gobernacion.

After receipt of the Opinion, Thunderbird opened gaming facilities where patrons played at a variety of machines. These machines were primarily of two types: video slot machines (where video representations of wheels spun and the player pushed buttons to stop the reels) and video poker machines. Both of these types of machines were equipped with modifiable computerized random number generators that set the machines' payout rates, which rates were neither visible to nor otherwise known by the machine's users. Shortly after establishment of Thunderbird's facilities, Mexican authorities closed them.

Thunderbird responded by filing a request for an arbitration pursuant to the North American Free Trade Agreement ("NAFTA"), which provides protections to foreign investors against discrimination and expropriation without fair compensation. The arbitration hearings were held in Washington, D.C., and the tribunal issued an award in favor of Mexico, with costs and partial fees also assessed in Mexico's favor. The total award amounted to $1,252,862. With this action, Thunderbird petitions the court to vacate the award, arguing that the tribunal acted in manifest disregard of the law. Mexico moves, in turn, for confirmation, recognition, and enforcement of the award pursuant to the Federal Arbitration Act, 9 U.S.C. sec. 1 et seq. (2006), and Article VI of the Convention on the Recognition and Enforcement of Foreign Arbitral Awards ("New York Convention"). See 9 U.S.C. sec. 201 (incorporating the Convention into United States law).

II Analysis

A.   Standard of Review

Courts have long recognized that judicial review of an arbitration award is extremely limited. A court may vacate an award only if there is a showing that one of the limited circumstances enumerated in the Federal Arbitration Act ("FAA") is present, or if the arbitrator acted in manifest disregard of the law. Thunderbird bears the heavy burden of establishing that vacatur of the arbitration award is appropriate. Furthermore, in the absence of a legal basis to vacate, this court has no discretion but to confirm the award.

Thunderbird's primary argument is that the NAFTA panel acted in "manifest disregard of the law" by announcing a particular standard for burdens of proof and then failing to apply that standard. Manifest disregard of the law "means more than error or misunderstanding with respect to the law." Thus, a party seeking to have an arbitration award vacated on this ground must at least establish that "(1) the arbitrators knew of a governing legal principle yet refused to apply it or ignored it altogether and (2) the law ignored by the arbitrators was well defined, explicit, and clearly applicable to the case..." see also Duferco Int'l Steel Trading v. T. Klaveness Shipping A/S, 333 F.3d 383, 390 (2d Cir. 2003) ("Even where explanation for an award is deficient or non-existent, we will confirm it if a justifiable ground for the decision can be inferred from the facts of the case.").

B. Discussion

1. Burdens of Proof

Thunderbird argues that the panel acted in manifest disregard of the law in applying the burden-of-proof standards it adopted. In its award, the panel articulated the following rule:

> The Tribunal shall apply the well-established principle that the party alleging a violation of international law giving rise to international responsibility has the burden of proving its assertion. If said Party adduces evidence that prima facie supports its allegation, the burden of proof may be shifted to the other Party, if the circumstances so justify.

Thunderbird alleges that it provided sufficient evidence of a prima facie case of violations of international law, and that the tribunal erred when it failed to require Mexico to produce any additional evidence of its own to rebut the presumption arising from that showing.

This argument rests, of course, on the assumption that Thunderbird satisfied its burden to prove a prima facie case. Though nowhere in the award does the tribunal articulate in any detail what, precisely, would be required for such a showing to be made, it appears that the tribunal concluded that Thunderbird had not met its initial burden. * * * In any event, for this court to disturb the award, it would have to be plainly manifest that the tribunal both (1) determined that Thunderbird had met its prima facie burden and (2) refused to require Mexico to overcome the resulting presumption of a violation of international law. Otherwise, this court would be asked to improperly assess the factual question of whether that prima facie burden had been met in the first instance.
* * *

Notes and Questions

(1) Note the distinction between "manifest disregard of the law" and mere legal error, the latter being enough to overturn the decision of a lower court in domestic appellate review (or WTO appellate review). If a tribunal acts in disregard of the law, will such behavior ever be "manifest" under the standard articulated here? Would a tribunal ever make a clear statement to the effect that "complainant has met its burden of establishing a prima facie case, but we will not bother to ask respondent for a rebuttal?"

(2) In addition to "manifest disregard of the law," the statutory grounds for vacating an award under the Federal Arbitration Act, 9 U.S.C. sec. 10, are: (1) the award was procured by corruption, fraud, or undue means; (2) there was evident partiality or corruption in the arbitrators, or either of them; (3) the arbitrators were guilty of misconduct in refusing to

postpone the hearing, upon sufficient cause shown, or in refusing to hear evidence pertinent and material to the controversy; or of any other misbehavior by which the rights of any party have been prejudiced; or (4) the arbitrators exceeded their powers, or so imperfectly executed them that a mutual, final, and definite award upon the subject matter submitted was not made.

(3) The standards for overturning an arbitral award elsewhere may differ. Mexico challenged the *Metalclad* award in the Supreme Court of British Columbia (Vancouver being the designated place of arbitration). The relevant BC statute provides for an award to be set aside if the arbitral tribunal makes a decision on matters beyond the scope of the submissions to arbitration. In The United Mexican States v. Metalclad Corp., 2001 BCSC 664 (May 2, 2001), the BC court took a broad view of the scope of review permitted by the statute and ruled that in two instances the arbitral tribunal had decided on matters beyond the scope of the submission to arbitration by relying on ostensible "transparency" obligations. However, the basic finding of the tribunal was not overruled. Thus, the effect of the BC court ruling was limited and only led to a reduction in the period for which interest was due.

(4) A number of recent preferential trade agreements negotiated by the United States also contain investment provisions. The pending US–Columbia Free Trade Agreement, for example, contains investor rights provisions which, like those in NAFTA, permit individual investors to take claims to arbitration. The US–Australia Free Trade Agreement, by contrast, does not afford private rights of action to investors.

(5) NAFTA investor arbitration remains quite active. The NAFTA Claims website, http://www.naftaclaims.com/, lists a total of 50 disputes that have proceeded through some stage of the arbitration process, a number of which are ongoing at this writing. Investor-state arbitration is burgeoning more generally, often pursuant to the provisions of bilateral investment treaties. The Investment Treaty Arbitration website is a useful resource on such matters, http://ita.law.uvic.ca/.

Chapter 24

DEVELOPING COUNTRIES AND THE WTO SYSTEM

SECTION 24.1 INTRODUCTION

One of the more difficult problems that have faced the WTO/GATT system is how developing countries should be integrated into that system. Of course, there are great differences among the countries commonly referred to as developing countries—they include the poorest of the poor nations as well as the so-called newly industrialized countries, they include dictatorships and democracies, state-run economies and free-market economies, and they vary politically from one end of the spectrum to the other. There are nonetheless many issues on which the developing countries seem to take a common position and they often refer to themselves as part of the same group, so despite the differences it is useful to treat them together in this chapter.

Historically, the developing world was dissatisfied with GATT. It felt that it had little influence in GATT decisions, that the dispute settlement system was not particularly useful for its purposes and that some fundamental GATT principles were unsuited for trade involving developing countries. As a consequence, for many years, developing countries pressed for special treatment in GATT and attempted in the United Nations (and related organizations such as UNCTAD) to create new rules, not based on GATT, to embody their concept of how the world economy should operate. In this chapter, after an historical overview of developing country interest in the GATT/WTO system, we examine the special provisions of the WTO agreements that provide for special treatment for developing countries. We then turn to the most ambitious scheme adopted by the developed countries to promote trade with developing countries—the Generalized System of Preferences, with particular attention to US implementation of that system and a major WTO dispute settlement cases addressing the EU's GSP scheme. We conclude by briefly considering the efforts of the developing countries to reorder legal thinking in respect of the international economic system by pressing for the acceptance of a new international economic order.

THE URUGUAY ROUND AND BEYOND: THE FINAL REPORT FROM THE FORD FOUNDATION SUPPORTED PROJECT ON DEVELOPING COUNTRIES AND THE GLOBAL TRADING SYSTEM (COORDINATED BY JOHN WHALLEY, 1989)[1]

THE DEVELOPING COUNTRIES' INTEREST IN THE SYSTEM

The overriding interest that developing countries have traditionally seen themselves as having in the trading system is to use it to speed their growth and development. Their interest in the present-day trading system is a reflection of how important or unimportant they see it in helping to achieve their overriding objective of development.

* * *

For most countries, their approach to the trading system involves a computation of benefits and costs. The benefits developing countries can get from a multilateral trading system depend upon what they can gain from an effective rules-based multilateral system of discipline. The main benefit is to set limits on the trade policy behavior of other countries, particularly more powerful developed countries. Effective discipline provides better assurance of access for developing country exports to developed country markets, and, in addition, limits their ability to distort third-country markets by means of export subsidies. The smaller and weaker the country, the more value there is in multilateral discipline. For it is only through such disciplines that small countries can restrain the behavior of larger and more powerful governments. As a group, therefore, and since they are small, developing countries stand to benefit from multilateral sources of discipline.

The costs to developing countries are somewhat less obvious. There are differences of opinion among developing countries as to whether and to what extent multilateral disciplines may actually help developing countries by assisting governments in eliminating unwanted protection where domestic political support for liberalization is diffuse and weak. There is, however, fairly broad agreement in the developing world that extra freedom from trade policy disciplines for developing countries, over that applying to developed countries, is necessary in order to achieve their growth and development objectives, and beyond a certain point restrictions on their use of trade policy are undesirable.

In understanding what the growth and development objective of developing countries implies for the global trading system, it is important to emphasize how different the circumstances of developed and developing countries typically are. Developing countries are economically small compared to developed countries, and their leverage in global negotiations is correspondingly limited. In addition, exports by individual countries are often concentrated on a few product lines, so that there is typically substantially more volatility in developing country terms of trade compared to developed countries. In general, developing countries

---

1. Reprinted with the permission of John Whalley.

see themselves as more susceptible to external shocks than developed countries.

* * *

The need for special treatment under the rules of the system is however, accepted as being different across countries. Those that have largely achieved their developmental objectives, such as Korea, accept that they have less need to be able to preserve a chosen developmental strategy in the face of trade shocks (and, indeed, will typically face less extreme trade shocks) than would be true for a lower income African country such as Tanzania. Special and Differential treatment does not imply equally special rules in the trading system for all developing countries at all times. Developing countries accept that different rules should apply to different countries at various stages of development. While their aim is to use the system to allow for development to proceed according to the strategies which countries see as in their best interest, it is accepted that the most latitude should be given to the least developed countries.

Given these potential benefits and costs, the interest of the developing countries in any actual or proposed trading system depends on their calculation as to how benefits and costs balance. On the benefit side, they need to know how well the rules of the system protect their particular trading interests, and how effective the enforcement of those rules will be in practice. On the cost side, they have to determine how much freedom from rules they need, and how much freedom the system will give them.

[U]ntil recently developing countries appear to have made a fairly negative calculation about the GATT system, and thus about their interest in participating in it. While one of the benefits of the GATT was supposed to be discipline over trade partners' policies, they noted that the rules of GATT did not cover some of their key trade interests, such as agriculture, and that ad hoc exceptions had been made for other key export interests such as textiles and clothing. They believed, further, that developed countries had not observed the rules that did exist, and that the developing countries had little or no power to achieve better enforcement. With regard to costs, developing countries seem to have concluded that they needed substantial freedom from international disciplines in order to pursue development policies. This view, coupled with a pessimistic view of the benefits offered by the GATT system, had led them to seek a fairly broad interpretation of the principle of Special and Differential treatment. The net result was that developing countries were relatively disinterested in GATT negotiations. There was a willingness to make demands of developed countries but a reluctance to offer participation of their own which would satisfy the requests of the developed countries.

[R]elatively little trade liberalization occurred in developing countries after the formation of GATT in 1947 up to the early to mid–1980s. * * * Over these years, many developing countries considered it to be acceptable and desirable to use high tariffs and quotas to restrain imports, to maintain fixed exchange rates, and to use foreign exchange rationing as a further trade-restricting device. While there are a range of views on import substitution, one view persuasively argued in the 1950s and 1960s and widely associated with Prebisch, held that protection (and induced import substitution) allowed developing countries to achieve more rapid industrialization, which was, in turn, seen as development promoting. As a result, countries following import substitution development strategies argued that they should be free from internationally negotiated disciplines limiting their trade policy actions. * * *

* * *

Prior to the launch of the Uruguay Round, * * * [d]eveloping countries were, generally speaking, opposed to any major trade liberalization in which their trade barriers would fall, either unilaterally or multilaterally, since this was seen as inconsistent with their chosen development strategies. They also felt betrayed by a trading system in which larger developed countries seemed to be allowed to take actions against them with impunity. And they viewed the system as yielding little or no positive benefits for them. Developed countries had not lived up to their promises to help them develop through trade, and they believed themselves to be too small to exercise much leverage to make developed countries change their position.

Developed countries, on the other hand, tended to see disciplines within the system as largely one-sided. They had taken on GATT discipline and liberalized, while developing countries had not. Until developing countries indicated their willingness to participate more fully by taking on further multilateral disciplines, developed countries offered little hope that negotiations could advance.

[D]espite the accumulation of tensions in the trading system documented in the preceding section, thinking on trade matters involving developed and developing countries may be undergoing more change than at any time in the post-war years. Ongoing re-evaluation seems to be present on many fronts in the developing world, including the role that trade plays in development, and how developing countries should participate in global trade negotiations. While perhaps less apparent, a re-evaluation of options also seems to be underway in the developed world.

These developments suggest that what developed countries have been seeking all these years—namely fuller participation by developing countries in the system, including developing countries taking on more disciplines through multilateral negotiations—may be coming within reach. At the same time, what developing countries have been seeking— namely, that developed countries live up to their GATT commitments— may also be something that developing countries can now begin to pursue using their growing leverage within the system.

* * *

What these changes reflect is, in large part, new thinking on trade matters in developing countries. This is, of course, hard to quantify. But as we see the intellectual process now underway, it involves a re-evaluation of the merits of import substitution development strategies in a number of countries, and a growing appreciation of the importance of maintaining as open a trading system as possible. The latter factor has been accentuated by the fear from the early to mid–1980s that developed countries would turn increasingly protectionist.

Recent re-evaluation of the desirability of import substitution strategies in developing countries can be traced to many factors. One has been the perception that import substitution strategies have not worked as well as was hoped; rather than promoting growth, they are now seen in some circles in the developing world as having spawned domestic inefficiency and a bureaucracy administering import controls. Importantly, such policies are also seen as inhibiting export performance. Another has been the increased leverage of multilateral agencies resulting from widespread balance-of-payments problems in developing countries. They usually condition financial assistance on, among other things, greater liberalization of countries' trade and payments regimes.

The allegedly stronger performance of those developing countries which have been more outward-oriented in their trade strategies has been central to debate on these matters. The performance of the Asian NICs, and particularly Korea, has frequently been held up as a prime example of how import substitution trade strategies have failed, while outward-oriented trade strategies have succeeded.

This is somewhat of an oversimplification of, especially, the earlier period of high Korean growth. The statement that growth in exports was crucial to Korean growth seems to us incontrovertible, even though free trade was not the chosen route in the early years. During the period that Korea dramatically increased its growth rate (from the early 1960s through to the late 1970s), it maintained most of its existing protection, using import duty remissions for export industries instead. It was major export promotion programs which moved the economy towards trade neutrality and substantially changed Korea's trade dependency. Only subsequently did reductions in tariffs occur. A pattern of high export growth following a move from trade repressing import substitution towards a more neutral system of incentives also occurred in other developing countries in the 1960s, such as Brazil, which still maintains relatively high levels of protection today.

The crucial issue is whether import substitution helps domestic manufacturing industries grow so they can later become important in world markets, or whether it simply generates inefficient protected domestic industries and the economy is ultimately prevented from obtaining the benefits from access to more efficient foreign products. The comparison between economies in Asia, and Africa and Latin America where growth rates have been low if not negative has been part of the debate. Our sense is that a perception is growing in the developing world that widespread import substitution has not worked as well as was hoped; rather than growth, it is now frequently seen as having spawned domestic inefficiency and a bureaucracy administering import controls.

This feeling is especially strong in the large number of developing countries with major balance-of-payments problems, and which have made high export growth and economic diversification a top policy priority. In these countries, achieving efficient domestic production, as opposed to reducing imports, has become the essential element in industrial policy. Increasingly the view is heard that the solution to their problems lies in more trade involvement rather than less. This represents a fundamental change in the stance of policy towards industrialization and trade policies in the developing world as compared to the views which prevailed previously.

The increased interest of developing countries in the multilateral trading system coincided with a greater desire on the part of the developed countries for encouraging increased developing country participation in the system. In particular, in the Uruguay Round, the developed world wanted the developing world to make commitments to respect intellectual property rights, open their markets to services trade and limit trade-related investment measures. Consequently, the developed world seemed more willing than in the past to address seriously issues of concern to the developing countries. In the next two sections, we consider generally the special rules applicable to developing countries in the WTO agreements and the tariff preferences provided to developing countries under the GSP system.

SECTION 24.2   THE EVOLUTION OF WTO/GATT RULES FOR DEVELOPING COUNTRIES

The debate over whether developing countries should receive special treatment in the WTO/GATT system is not new. In the negotiations on the ITO, the developing countries tried to obtain rules more favorable to them. However, as Professor Jackson has concluded:[1]

The issues at Geneva in 1947 did not, viewed from the perspective of the present day, seem to be free trade versus protectionism, or internationalism versus national sovereignty. Each of the groups in the debate desired international control of some things and not of others. Both sides desired to use certain types of trade protective measures but wanted to limit or restrict others. The controversy seemed to be over *which* trade restrictions would be subjected to international control and which not. From the point of view of the

---

1.   John H. Jackson, World Trade and the Law of GATT 637–38 (1969).

less-developed country, the wealthy countries wanted freedom to use those restrictions that only they were most able to use effectively while banning those restrictions that less-developed countries felt they were most able to use.

Although the developing countries were largely unsuccessful in their early efforts to obtain special treatment, they continued to press their case.

GATT was not oblivious to developing country complaints, and they have been studied by GATT committees of experts on more than one occasion. For example, in 1958, the so-called Haberler Report concluded that the developed countries should lower their barriers to exports of primary products from developing countries.[2] In 1984, a GATT-sponsored group of experts noted the adverse effect that nontariff barriers were having on developing country exports and called for their reduction.[3]

Moreover, it is worth noting that in practice developing countries in GATT were often able in to maintain many trade restrictions, particularly high tariffs and quotas. While GATT Article II requires WTO members to limit tariffs to bound levels, many developing countries historically bound very few tariffs. While they were required to bind tariffs in the Uruguay Round as a condition of WTO membership, many did so at a relatively high level. As to quotas, under GATT rules, they may be imposed to counter balance-of-payments difficulties, a problem of many developing countries. In addition, it is probably true that there was a tendency in GATT to overlook trade policy actions of developing countries which were "technically" inconsistent with GATT obligations.

(A) GATT ARTICLE XVIII

Article XVIII was the original article of GATT designed to grant certain privileges to developing countries. It has not often been formally invoked. The reader will note, in examining Article XVIII, that it first establishes criteria describing those nations entitled to utilize its provisions, and then basically grants four privileges:

Part A: The right to renegotiate tariff bindings so as to raise tariffs on products a developing country desires to produce, thus enabling protection of so-called infant industries;

Part B: The privilege to use quantitative restrictions when in balance-of-payments difficulties (with criteria and actions permitted being slightly different from the general balance-of-payment clause of GATT Article XII);

Part C: A privilege to use any measure necessary to promote a *particular* industry;

2. GATT, Trends in International Trade (1958).

3. GATT, Trade Policies for A Better Future (1985) (Report of Eminent Persons

on Problems Facing the International Trading System).

Part D: Under this part, certain countries with economies in process of development, but not falling within the criteria of low living standards, can apply for permission to deviate from GATT rules so as to establish a particular industry.

What nations are eligible to invoke Article XVIII? By its terms, Article XVIII refers to "contracting parties the economies of which can only support low standards of living and are in the early stages of development." Several interpretative notes clarify these concepts.

(B) PART IV OF GATT

Following the 1958 Haberler Report referred to above, and as a result of developing country initiatives in the early and mid–1960s, Articles XXXVI, XXXVII and XXXVIII were added to GATT as Part IV. These articles are devoted solely to the problems of developing countries. Although it has been suggested that they are primarily "hortatory" in wording, and so without direct legal implications, Article XXXVII, paragraphs 1(b) and 1(c), arguably may have direct legal impact:

1. The developed contracting parties shall to the fullest extent possible—that is, except when compelling reasons, which may include legal reasons, make it impossible—give effect to the following provisions:

                              * * *

(b) refrain from introducing, or increasing the incidence of, customs duties or non-tariff import barriers on products currently or potentially of particular export interest to less-developed contracting parties; and

(c)(i) refrain from imposing new fiscal measures, and (ii) in any adjustments of fiscal policy accord high priority to the reduction and elimination of fiscal measures, which would hamper, or which hamper, significantly the growth of consumption of primary products [produced in less-developed contracting parties].

In fact, developed countries have frequently imposed various trade remedy measures on developing country imports and have not been challenged under Article XXXVII.

(C) THE TOKYO ROUND AND THE ENABLING CLAUSE

An UNCTAD analysis of the Tokyo Round results, excerpted in part below, concluded that they were "modest and wanting in many specific respects". While it noted that there were general provisions on differential and more favorable treatment in a number of the Tokyo Round agreements, it viewed the provisions as vague or inadequate. It also noted that the general tariff cuts agreed by the developed countries were not often of interest to them and that those cuts would in any event reduce the benefits of preferential tariffs that developing countries had been receiving under GSP schemes, which had been authorized in the early 1970s (see next section). It cannot be said, however, that the developing countries obtained nothing of significance in the Tokyo Round. In particular, they obtained the adoption by the GATT Contracting Parties of the so-called Enabling Clause, which is an explicit recognition of the principle that developing countries should receive differential and more favorable treatment in GATT, at least under certain circumstances.

GATT CONTRACTING PARTIES, DECISION OF NOVEMBER 28, 1979 ON DIFFERENTIAL AND MORE FAVORABLE TREATMENT, RECIPROCITY AND FULLER PARTICIPATION OF DEVELOPING COUNTRIES[4]

Following negotiations within the framework of the Multilateral Trade Negotiations, the Contracting Parties *decide* as follows:

1. Notwithstanding the provisions of Article I of the General Agreement, contracting parties may accord differential and more favorable treatment to developing countries, without according such treatment to other contracting parties.

2. The provisions of paragraph 1 apply to the following:

(*a*) Preferential tariff treatment accorded by developed contracting parties to products originating in developing countries in accordance with the Generalized System of Preferences,[5]

(*b*) Differential and more favorable treatment with respect to the provisions of the General Agreement concerning non-tariff measures governed by the provisions of instruments multilaterally negotiated under the auspices of the GATT;

(*c*) Regional or global arrangements entered into amongst less-developed contracting parties for the mutual reduction or elimination of tariffs and, in accordance with criteria or conditions which may be prescribed by the Contracting Parties, for the mutual reduction or elimination of non-tariff measures, on products imported from one another;

(*d*) Special treatment of the least developed among the developing countries in the context of any general or specific measures in favor of developing countries.

3. Any differential and more favorable treatment provided under this clause:

4. GATT, 26th Supp. BISD 203 (1980). See generally Abdulqawi A. Yusuf, "Differential and More Favorable Treatment": The GATT Enabling Clause, 14 J. World Trade L. 488 (1980); Bela Balassa, The Tokyo Round and the Developing Countries, 14 J. World Trade L. 93 (1980); Gerald M. Meier, The Tokyo Round of Multilateral Trade Negotiations and the Developing Countries, 13 Cornell Intl.L.J. 249 (1980).

5. [original footnote 3] As described in the Decision of the CONTRACTING PARTIES of 25 June 1971, relating to the establishment of "generalized, non-reciprocal and non-discriminatory preferences beneficial to the developing countries" (BISD 18S/24).

(a) shall be designed to facilitate and promote the trade of developing countries and not to raise barriers to or create undue difficulties for the trade of any other contracting parties;

(b) shall not constitute an impediment to the reduction or elimination of tariffs and other restrictions to trade on a most-favored-nation basis;

(c) shall in the case of such treatment accorded by developed contracting parties to developing countries be designed and, if necessary, modified, to respond positively to the development, financial and trade needs of developing countries.

4.   Any contracting party taking action to introduce an arrangement pursuant to paragraphs 1, 2 and 3 above or subsequently taking action to introduce modification or withdrawal of the differential and more favorable treatment so provided shall:

(a) notify the Contracting Parties and furnish them with all the information they may deem appropriate relating to such action;

(b) afford adequate opportunity for prompt consultations at the request of any interested contracting party with respect to any difficulty or matter that may arise. The Contracting Parties shall, if requested to do so by such contracting party, consult with all contracting parties concerned with respect to the matter with a view to reaching solutions satisfactory to all such contracting parties.

5.   The developed countries do not expect reciprocity for commitments made by them in trade negotiations to reduce or remove tariffs and other barriers to the trade of developing countries, i.e., the developed countries do not expect the developing countries, in the course of trade negotiations, to make contributions which are inconsistent with their individual development, financial and trade needs. Developed contracting parties shall therefore not seek, neither shall less-developed contracting parties be required to make, concessions that are inconsistent with the latters' development, financial and trade needs.

6.   Having regard to the special economic difficulties and the particular development, financial and trade needs of the least-developed countries, the developed countries shall exercise the utmost restraint in seeking any concessions or contributions for commitments made by them to reduce or remove tariffs and other barriers to the trade of such countries, and the least-developed countries shall not be expected to make concessions or contributions that are inconsistent with the recognition of their particular situation and problems.

7.   The concessions and contributions made and the obligations assumed by developed and less-developed contracting parties under the provisions of the General Agreement should promote the basic objectives of the Agreement, including those embodied in the Preamble and in Article XXXVI. Less-developed contracting parties expect that their capacity to make contributions or negotiated concessions or take other

mutually agreed action under the provisions and procedures of the General Agreement would improve with the progressive development of their economies and improvement in their trade situation and they would accordingly expect to participate more fully in the framework of rights and obligations under the General Agreement.

8.   Particular account shall be taken of the serious difficulty of the least-developed countries in making concessions and contributions in view of their special economic situation and their development, financial and trade needs.

9.   The contracting parties will collaborate in arrangements for review of the operation of these provisions, bearing in mind the need for individual and joint efforts by contracting parties to meet the development needs of developing countries and the objectives of the General Agreement.

1982 REPORT BY THE SECRETARY–GENERAL OF UNCTAD, ASSESSMENT OF THE RESULTS OF THE MULTILATERAL TRADE NEGOTIATIONS[6]

176.   * * * The key provisions of the [Enabling Clause] allow countries parties to the General Agreement to accord differential and more favorable treatment to developing countries without according such treatment to other countries, notwithstanding the MFN provisions of article I of the General Agreement. * * *

178.   The "enabling clause" is counterbalanced by the "graduation" clause in paragraph 7 of the decision. * * *

179.   It may be noted that the results achieved in this area of the negotiations are more a matter of form than of substance. On the one hand, the enabling clause introduces in the GATT legal system differential treatment in four areas where the developing countries already enjoyed it on a *de facto* basis (and to some extent on a legal basis). On the other hand, the clause limits any further enlargement of the scope of differential treatment within the GATT structure by making it subject to approval by the Contracting Parties to the General Agreement. Furthermore, the decision introduces the graduation principle, which, although vaguely worded, establishes a legal precedent within the GATT system by requiring the developing countries to accept greater obligations as their economic situation improves. This concept could have far-reaching consequences for the future world trading system if its implementation were to allow developed countries to discriminate among developing countries in a unilateral and arbitrary manner.

Notes and Questions

(1) The Enabling Clause is analyzed in detail in the *EC Tariff Preferences* case in the next section.

6.   UNCTAD Doc. T/B/778/Rev.1, at 29.

(2) To what extent does the granting of special treatment to developing countries undermine the basic WTO/GATT principle of most-favored-nation treatment? In considering your answer, you should review the materials in Chapter 10 above.

(3) Do you agree with the UNCTAD Report's criticisms, which suggest that developing countries should be disappointed with the results of the Tokyo Round? Is it realistic to complain that falling tariffs harm those benefiting from special tariff preferences?

(4) Should there be a graduation principle applied to developing countries, such as that contained in paragraph 7 of the Decision? How can it be applied? Given the diversity of economic development in the developing countries, should those countries be subdivided according to their level of development, with the more advanced countries being entitled to fewer special privileges than the least developed developing countries? How many subdivisions should there be? What becomes of the most-favored-nation principle if this is done? In this connection, the way in which the US GSP scheme handles the problem of graduation is described in the next section of this chapter.

(5) Would the Enabling Clause permit a developing country to give tariff preferences exclusively to least developed countries? In 1999, the WTO General Council granted a general ten-year waiver for such preferences. WT/L/304 (June 17, 1999). As is the practice in the WTO, the waiver incorporates the UN definition of least developed countries. Developing-country status in the WTO, including for the purposes of the waiver, is self-determined by each member.

(D) THE URUGUAY ROUND AND RULES PROVIDING SPECIAL AND DIFFERENTIAL TREATMENT

The Uruguay Round addressed a number of specific trade issues of interest to developing countries. In particular, there was an agreement on the phasing out over ten years of textile quotas (see Section 9.3(B) supra); a Safeguards Agreement was negotiated (see Chapter 15 supra), which requires the phase out of existing VERs; barriers to agricultural trade were reduced (see Section 9.3(A) supra); and some new disciplines were applied to the application of antidumping and countervailing duties. See Chapters 16–18 supra. In addition, there were significant tariff cuts agreed to, including deep cuts in tariffs on tropical products. The results of the Uruguay Round were not viewed by all as uniformly favorable to the developing world. In addition to accepting WTO discipline over intellectual property, services and some investment measures, the developing countries also agreed to bind many of their tariffs (even if at high levels) and had to accept a continuing erosion of GSP preferences.

As in the case of the Tokyo Round, most Uruguay Round agreements have special provisions applicable to developing countries. While it is not possible to detail all of these provisions, a number can be cited: Agriculture Agreement, arts. 15 (longer phase-in of reduction commitments for developing countries, no commitments required of least developed) & 16 (consideration of effect of agreement on least developed and net-food-importing developing countries); SPS Agreement, arts. 10 (general) & 14 (longer transitional period); Textiles Agreement, art. 6(6) (least developed countries to be treated more favorably in application of transitional safeguards); Antidumping Agreement, art. 15 (other "constructive remedies" to be explored before imposition of antidumping duties); Valuation Agreement, art. 20 (expanded transitional period); TBT Agreement, art. 12 (general); TRIMs Agreement, arts. 4 (exemption for balance-of-payment measures of developing countries) & 5 (expanded transitional period); Subsidies Agreement, art. 27 (least developed developing countries exempted from export subsidy ban; others given longer time to phase-out export subsidies); Safeguards Agreement, art. 9 (special exemption from safeguards in cases of low market share; more freedom to use safeguards); GATS, art. IV (increased participation of developing countries); and TRIPS Agreement, arts. 65 (implementation normally required within one year, but developing countries given up to five years generally and ten years in some cases in respect of patent protection) & 66 (least developed developing countries given 11 years to implement, with possible extensions). There was also a decision taken on measures in favor of least-developed countries, which provides that they will only be required to comply with WTO/GATT obligations "to the extent consistent with their individual development, financial and trade needs, or their administrative and institutional capabilities." Note the extent to which the favorable treatment consists of different rules as compared to longer transition periods.

(E) DEVELOPING COUNTRIES IN THE WTO: THE DOHA DEVELOPMENT AGENDA

(1) In General

Developing countries have played an active and vocal role in the WTO. Given space constraints, it is difficult to describe in detail the many issues of particular concern to developing countries. Nonetheless, a number of issues may be highlighted.

First, as developing countries have become more active in the WTO/GATT system, they have expressed dissatisfaction with the decision-making mechanisms. Often in the WTO, important decisions are first reached by a small group of countries, who then convince the rest of the membership to accept them. While the major developing countries have long been involved in this process, newer and smaller developing country members have felt excluded and that their views are not given adequate consideration. In theory, the small groups are representative and include those with particular concerns about an issue, but there is no doubt that the process of internal decision-making needs to become more inclusive and open.

Second, developing countries undertook very extensive obligations by joining the WTO. In many cases, they needed to reform or adopt new laws and administrative practices. Given their limited resources, they have strongly supported a significant increase in assistance from relevant international organizations and developed countries. Their difficulties in this regard have made some of them reluctant to start or to participate meaningfully in a new round of negotiations that will inevitably lead to even more obligations that they must meet. This reluctance has perhaps made developed countries more interested in providing the necessary technical assistance. The existence of these implementation problems for developing countries has also led to requests for extended transitional periods beyond those provided in the Uruguay Round (e.g., under the TRIMs Agreement) and for more specific and useful special and differential treatment to be provided to developing countries.

Third, developing countries have been concerned that they have yet to receive substantial market access benefits from the Uruguay Round. This is viewed as a particular problem in agriculture, where market access commitments in the Uruguay Round were rather limited, and in textiles, where the major textile importing countries were slow to phase out quotas. The developing countries want improved market access in developed-country markets for goods and services (e.g., low-wage services) that are of interest to them.

Fourth, they want stricter controls on various import restrictions that they perceive are used by developed countries to keep out developing-country exports. These restrictions include those imposed in the form of antidumping or countervailing duties and those that impose unnecessary SPS and product standards that exclude developing country agricultural and other exports.

Finally, some developing countries have also expressed concern that some of the "new" issues for the WTO/GATT system—environment, human rights, labor standards—may lead to disguised protectionism. See Chapters 13.6 and 21 supra.

(2) The Doha Development Agenda

The decision to call the WTO's first negotiating round the Doha Development Agenda was in large part in response to the many developing country complaints outlined in the prior materials. Some of those complaints have been addressed within the context of the regular operation of the WTO—such as those dealing with governance matters, renewal of waivers and extensions of transition periods. But as the name suggests, development is a major theme of the Doha negotiations. We have traced the history and current status of those negotiations in Chapter 6. Here we will simply highlight that there is considerable controversy over whether the Doha negotiations should be focused on development and over whether they are in fact focused thereon.

Among those who question the wisdom of a development round are T.N. Srinivasan who notes that while addressing specific needs of developing countries in negotiations is laudable, there is a danger that calling the negotiations the Doha Development Agenda "carries with it the danger that it may create inappropriate and unrealistic expectations that the successful completion of the Doha Round would also solve the problem of development". In his view, "the problem for many DCs is largely domestic and only marginally related to external constraints of market access and development assistance" as it largely "lies at the center of economic, social and political processes of each developing country". Those processes "are not only deep rooted and complex, but, importantly, vary immensely across the developing world, reflecting, in part, their diverse history". Moreover, he fears that "[a]nother possible consequence of characterizing the Doha Round as the Development Round is that it will inevitably lead to pressure being brought to bear on the WTO to become yet another international development agency", notwithstanding the fact that the "WTO is already overloaded". He notes there are already several such agencies.[8]

Others argue that the Doha agenda is largely of interest to developed countries and perhaps some of the advanced developing countries. They point to the major emphasis of the negotiations on market access and agriculture. For them, the negotiations should reflect the fact that the balance of concessions in the WTO is fundamentally tilted in favor of the developed countries, who have dominated GATT/WTO negotiations in the past. They suggest much more in the way of unilateral market access liberalization by the developed countries and more flexibility—preferential treatment—for the developing world.[9]

The issue of how effective preferential treatment has been is an interesting one that we examine next in the context of the generalized system of tariff preferences.

SECTION 24.3   THE GENERALIZED SYSTEM OF PREFERENCES (GSP)

(A) HISTORY

In 1964, Raul Prebisch, the first Secretary–General of UNCTAD, argued at the UNCTAD I conference that a system of tariff preferences for developing country products would help promote their export of manufactures and free them from their dependence on the export of primary products, which were noted for their price instability. The hope was that this would spur the economic development of developing countries by promoting their export earnings, industrialization and rates of economic growth. The proposal was studied both in UNCTAD and OECD meetings. Ultimately a framework agreement was reached and the GATT contracting parties authorized the creation of the generalized system of preferences (GSP) by a waiver adopted in 1971.[1] The waiver

8. T.N. Srinivasan, Doha Round of Multilateral Negotiations and Development, Stanford Center for International Development, Working Paper No. 252 (September 2005).

9. See, e.g., Joseph E. Stiglitz & Andrew Charlton, Fair Trade for All: How Trade Can Promote Development (2003).

1. Generalized System of Preferences, Decision of the Contracting Parties, June

was for ten years, but the need to extend it was eliminated by the adoption of the Enabling Clause in 1979.

It was clear from the work in the OECD and UNCTAD that it would not be possible to agree on one system applicable to all developed countries. Accordingly, the GSP was understood as system composed of individual national schemes, which shared the goals outlined above. By 1981, eleven OECD members had adopted GSP schemes (counting the EU as one; there were ten EU members at the time). Currently, according to UNCTAD, there are still eleven GSP schemes: Australia, Belarus, Canada, the European Union, Japan, New Zealand, Norway, the Russian Federation, Switzerland, Turkey and the United States, but the EU now has 27 members.

REPORT BY THE SECRETARY–GENERAL OF THE OECD, THE GENERALIZED SYSTEM OF PREFERENCES: REVIEW OF THE FIRST DECADE 9–12, 90–91 (1983)[2]

From the beginning, the OECD preference schemes represented a delicate compromise between the developing countries' desire to have the fewest possible obstacles to market access and the fear in the industrialized countries that a general tariff "disarmament" would create serious disruptions. Initially, the developed countries considered that their preference schemes represented the maximum concession they could give in this field and they consequently looked forward to a period of stability in the operation of the system. * * * However, the beneficiary developing countries continued to press for a broader system corresponding more to their original demands, in terms of product and country coverage and depth of preferential tariff reduction. As time passed, the preference-giving countries came to accept that the system should evolve and be improved. * * *

* * *

It has proved difficult to assess the actual effects of the GSP, due to the unavailability of relevant statistics in certain cases and the problem of isolating the GSP from other factors influencing the rapid overall growth of developing countries' exports since the early 1970s. * * *

In the context of the developed countries' overall trade policies toward developing countries it appears nevertheless that the GSP has been playing an important role in contributing to freer market access and to trade expansion. * * * From 1976 to 1980 OECD imports from developing countries grew at an average annual rate of 21 per cent, compared with 19.6 per cent growth for OECD imports from all sources. The positive influence of the GSP on the evolution of imports from developing countries can be seen from the fact that imports benefiting

25, 1971, in GATT, 18th Supp. BISD 24 **2.** Reprinted by permission of the (1972). OECD.

from GSP treatment grew over the period at an average rate of nearly 27 per cent per year.

Notes and Questions

(1) UNCTAD maintains extensive, up-to-date information concerning GSP systems in various countries on its website (www.unctad.org).

(2) Some WTO members provide preferential treatment to select developing countries under non-GSP schemes as well. Such schemes typically benefit from a WTO waiver.

(3) More recent studies also conclude that the extent of GSP benefits may be limited. For example, Grossman and Sykes concluded in their analysis of the *EC Tariff Preferences* case:

> To summarize, there are no good estimates of the aggregate benefits that developing countries derive from GSP schemes. Economic theory predicts an improvement in the terms of trade on eligible products, which may be smaller than the preference margin if the developing countries collectively are large in the markets for their exports and so depress world prices as they expand their exports. Benefits beyond the pure terms-of-trade gain are possible if the export industries happen to be ones that generate positive learning spillovers, but there is no evidence to suggest that products included in existing GSP schemes are more worthy of encouragement than others. Compliance costs associated with rules of origin and the like surely cut into the potential beneficial effects of GSP as well, and exclusions of products deemed "sensitive" in the donor countries have done so to an even greater extent. Finally, GSP schemes may have encouraged overinvestment in sectors that will prove only temporarily eligible and may have retarded the process of trade liberalization in the eligible countries. For all these reasons, the benefits generated by tariff preference schemes, while perhaps positive, are likely to be reasonably small.

Gene M. Grossman & Alan O. Sykes, European Communities—Conditions for the Granting of Tariff Preferences to Developing Countries, in H. Horn & P. Mavroidis (eds.), The WTO Case Law of 2003, at 267 (2006).

(B) THE U.S. GSP SCHEME

The US GSP scheme was authorized for ten years by Title V of the Trade Act of 1974.[3] It has been revised and renewed several times, most recently through December 31, 2008. The provisions of Title V are very detailed, reflecting congressional desires to exclude certain categories of countries and products from the scheme and to afford protection to US industry in certain cases. The key issues under Title V are the criteria (i) that a country must initially meet to be designated as a beneficiary developing country, (ii) for including products in the scheme, (iii) for removing products from the scheme and (iv) for removing countries from the scheme. The US has special preference programs for Caribbean Basin, Andean and

---

3. Title V is codified at 19 U.S.C.A. secs. 2461–2467.

African countries, which afford more generous treatment to their imports than is given under the US GSP program described below.[4]

(1) Criteria for Inclusion of Countries

The US GSP scheme is potentially applicable to most developing countries. The statutory scheme grants broad discretionary authority to the President to designate countries as beneficiaries. It does, however, direct the President to take a number of factors into account.[5] Some of these factors are simple enough: Has the country in question expressed a desire to be a GSP beneficiary? Is it truly a developing country? Do other major developed countries grant it GSP status? Other factors focus on whether the country follows policies promoted by the United States: Has the country assured the United States of equitable and reasonable access to its markets and commodity resources? Has it assured the United States that it will refrain from engaging in unreasonable export practices? Does the country provide adequate and effective protection of intellectual property rights? Has the country taken action to reduce trade distorting investment policies and to reduce or eliminate barriers to trade in services? Has it taken steps or is it taking steps to afford workers internationally recognized worker rights?

Even if the President is disposed to grant GSP status, there are certain countries that Congress has excluded from receiving GSP status: Communist countries (except in certain instances), certain export cartel members, countries that expropriate US property without compensation, countries that fail to recognize arbitral awards in favor of US citizens, countries that aid and abet international terrorism, countries that do not afford internationally recognized worker rights to workers in the country and countries that have not eliminated the worst forms of child labor.[6] In respect of the last five categories, the President has the power to designate a country as a GSP beneficiary despite the exclusion provisions if he determines that to do so would be in the national economic interest of the United States.

4. These programs are implemented pursuant to the Caribbean Basin Economic Recovery Act (as amended), codified in 19 U.S.C.A. secs. 2701–2707; the Andean Trade Preferences Act, codified in 19 U.S.C.A. secs. 3201–3206; and the African Growth and Opportunity Act, codified in 19 U.S.C.A. secs. 3701–3741. The preferences need to be renewed regularly.

5. Section 502(c); 19 U.S.C.A. sec. 2462(c).

6. Section 502(b); 19 U.S.C.A. sec. 2462(b). The statute also excludes by name the following countries: Australia, Canada, EU member states, Iceland, Japan, Monaco, New Zealand, Norway and Switzerland.

Countries that give preferences to products from developed countries other than the United States are also excluded. In addition, the Narcotics Control Trade Act, codified at 19 U.S.C.A. sec. 2492, provides that the President shall deny GSP treatment to products from major drug producing countries and major drug-transit countries to achieve the purposes of that act if the President considers it necessary to do so. The President has the discretion not to take such action on the grounds that the country is cooperating with the US or because the vital interests of the US require that such action not be taken.

(2) Criteria for Product Coverage

Section 503(b) provides that certain articles are not eligible for GSP treatment: certain textiles and apparel articles; certain watches; import-sensitive electronic articles; import-sensitive steel articles; import-sensitive glass products; and certain articles of footwear, handbags, luggage, flat goods, work gloves and leather wearing apparel. As to articles that are not automatically excluded, the president has fairly broad discretion in selecting articles to receive GSP treatment.[7]

(3) Criteria for Excluding Products from Coverage

There are two provisions in the Act that may result in an otherwise eligible product being denied GSP treatment because it comes from a beneficiary country that is deemed to be sufficiently competitive in the US market such that it does not need preferential treatment any more with respect to that particular product. If these so-called "competitive need" exclusions are applied, a specific product from a specific beneficiary is denied GSP treatment. Imports of the product in question from other not-so-competitive beneficiary countries continue to receive GSP treatment. Moreover, other not-so-competitive products from the beneficiary country subject to the competitive need exclusion remain eligible for GSP treatment.

Section 503(c)(2), which establishes the basic competitive need exclusion, dates from the 1974 Act. It provides that if a GSP beneficiary becomes a significant supplier, in percentage or dollar terms, of a particular product to the US market, it may lose its GSP status in respect of that product. The theory is that if the specified thresholds are exceeded, the country in question has demonstrated its ability to compete in the United States without special treatment and that its GSP benefits should be restricted so as to allow other GSP beneficiaries to have a better chance to compete for the market in question. For 1996, the thresholds were set at 50% or more of the total import value, or $75 million, to be increased annually by $5 million. Section 503(c)(2)(E)-(F) authorizes the President to disregard the 50% threshold if imports from a country are less than a de minimis amount—$13 million as of 1996, to be increased annually by $500,000, or if the product was not produced in the United States as of January 1, 1995. Section 503(d) authorizes the President to waive a competitive need exclusion, subject to a number of conditions such as that the waiver is in the US national economic interest. Section 503(c)(2)(D) provides an exemption from the competitive need rules for the least-developed developing countries.

(4) Criteria for Excluding or Graduating Countries

Section 502(d)(2) requires the President to withdraw or suspend a country's beneficiary status under the US GSP scheme if he determines that, as a result of changed circumstances, the country would be barred by Section 502(b)(2) from designation as a beneficiary country. The US trade representative annually accepts petitions to reconsider the benefi-

---

7. Section 503(a); 19 U.S.C.A. sec. 2463(a).

ciary status of countries for these reasons.[8] The President has very broad discretion in deciding whether to withdraw GSP benefits from a country on these grounds.[9] One of the more common reasons for a review of GSP beneficiary country status is based on a claim that a country has not taken steps to afford internationally recognized rights to its work force. We discuss that issue in detail in Section 21.3(B) supra.

If the President determines that a beneficiary of the US GSP scheme has become a "high income" country, as defined by the World Bank ($10,726 per capita GNI in 2005) then that country is graduated from the US GSP scheme under Section 502(e).

Notes and Questions

(1) Congress has taken a substantial interest in the operation of the GSP system and has placed many limitations on its use. In particular, the statute indicates Congress' penchant for using trade legislation in an attempt to accomplish other US foreign policy goals such as discouraging export cartels, expropriation and terrorism and encouraging protection of worker rights and intellectual property rights. Keep these conditions in mind while reading the *EC–GSP* case in the next subsection.

(2) For a detailed statistical and historical overview of the operation of the US preference programs, including the application of the various statutory conditions and limitations, see Government Accountability Office, U.S. Trade Preference Programs: An Overview of Use by Beneficiaries and U.S. Administrative Reviews, GAO–07–1209 (Sept. 2007).

(3) A key issue in GSP schemes is how to define the origin of goods. If strict definitions are not used, the goal of promoting development may be undermined by exporters performing only minor finishing activities in the developing country. The basic US rule is that for a product to qualify for GSP treatment, (i) the cost or value of materials incorporated in the product that were produced in the beneficiary country, plus (ii) the direct costs of processing operations performed on the product in that country, must amount to at least 35% of the customs value of the product on import into the United States. Preferential and other rules of origin are analyzed in Section 8.3(D) supra.

(C) WTO CASE LAW

EUROPEAN COMMUNITIES—CONDITIONS FOR THE GRANTING OF TARIFF PREFERENCES TO DEVELOPING COUNTRIES

WT/DS246/AB/R.
Appellate Body Report adopted April 20, 2004.

[India challenged provisions of the EC's GSP scheme that granted additional preferences to twelve specified countries because of their need

8. The procedures, which are found in 15 C.F.R., part 2007 (2007), are described in Office of the US Trade Representative, U.S. Generalized System of Preferences Guidebook, February 2007.

9. International Labor Rights Educ. & Research Fund v. Bush, 752 F.Supp. 495 (D.D.C.1990) (Presidential discretion so

broad that challenge is not justiciable), aff'd, 954 F.2d 745 (D.C.Cir.1992) (two judges voted to affirm—one found that only the Court of International Trade could have jurisdiction of such a claim and the other that plaintiffs lacked standing; one judge dissented and found standing and justiciability in respect of one portion of plaintiff's complaint).

to combat drug production and trafficking (the so-called "Drug Arrangements").]

89.   In considering whether the Enabling Clause [which is excerpted in Section 24.2] is an exception to Article I:1 of the GATT 1994, we look, first, to the text of the provisions at issue. Article I:1, which embodies the MFN principle, * * * plainly imposes upon WTO Members the obligation to treat "like products . . . equally, irrespective of their origin".

90.   We turn now to the Enabling Clause, which has become an integral part of the GATT 1994.[10] Paragraph 1 of the Enabling Clause, which applies to all measures authorized by that Clause, provides:

> Notwithstanding the provisions of Article I of the General Agreement, contracting parties may accord differential and more favourable treatment to developing countries, without according such treatment to other contracting parties. (footnote omitted)

The ordinary meaning of the term "notwithstanding" is, as the Panel noted, "[i]n spite of, without regard to or prevention by". By using the word "notwithstanding", paragraph 1 of the Enabling Clause permits Members to provide "differential and more favourable treatment" to developing countries "in spite of" the MFN obligation of Article I:1. Such treatment would otherwise be inconsistent with Article I:1 because that treatment is not extended to all Members of the WTO "immediately and unconditionally". Paragraph 1 thus excepts Members from complying with the obligation contained in Article I:1 for the purpose of providing differential and more favourable treatment to developing countries, provided that such treatment is in accordance with the conditions set out in the Enabling Clause. As such, the Enabling Clause operates as an "exception" to Article I:1.[11]

* * *

129.   * * * [W]e understand India's claim before the Panel to have been limited to the consistency of the Drug Arrangements with the term

---

10.   [original note 192] In response to questioning at the oral hearing, the participants and third participants agreed that the Enabling Clause is one of the "other decisions of the CONTRACTING PARTIES" within the meaning of paragraph 1(b)(iv) of the language of Annex 1A incorporating the GATT 1994 into the *WTO Agreement*. That provision stipulates that: "1. The General Agreement on Tariffs and Trade 1994 ('GATT 1994') shall consist of: . . . (b) the provisions of the legal instruments set forth below that have entered into force under the GATT 1947 before the date of entry into force of the WTO Agreement: . . . (iv) other decisions of the CONTRACTING PARTIES to GATT 1947[.]"

11.   [original note 212] In this regard, we recall the Appellate Body's statement in *EC–Hormones* that: ". . . merely characterizing a treaty provision as an "exception" does not by itself justify a "stricter" or "narrower" interpretation of that provision than would be warranted by examination of the ordinary meaning of the actual treaty words, viewed in context and in the light of the treaty's object and purpose, or, in other words, by applying the normal rules of treaty interpretation." (Appellate Body Report, para. 104)

"non-discriminatory" in footnote 3 to paragraph 2(a) of the Enabling Clause. * * * Therefore, in this Report, we do not rule on whether the Enabling Clause permits *ab initio* exclusions from GSP schemes of countries claiming developing country status, or the partial or total withdrawal of GSP benefits from certain developing countries under certain conditions.

* * *

143. * * * Paragraph 1 of the Enabling Clause authorizes WTO Members to provide "differential and more favourable treatment to developing countries, without according such treatment to other WTO Members". As explained above, such differential treatment is permitted "notwithstanding" the provisions of Article I of the GATT 1994. Paragraph 2(a) and footnote 3 thereto clarify that paragraph 1 applies to "[p]referential tariff treatment accorded by developed contracting parties to products originating in developing countries in accordance with the Generalized System of Preferences", "[a]s described in the [1971 Waiver Decision], relating to the establishment of 'generalized, non-reciprocal and non discriminatory preferences beneficial to the developing countries' ".

144. The Preamble to the 1971 Waiver Decision in turn refers to "preferential tariff treatment" in the following terms:

> * * * *Considering* that mutually acceptable arrangements have been drawn up in the UNCTAD concerning the establishment of general-ized, non-discriminatory, non-reciprocal preferential tariff treatment in the markets of developed countries for products originating in developing countries[.] (original italics; underlining added)

145. Paragraph 2(a) of the Enabling Clause provides, therefore, that, to be justified under that provision, preferential tariff treatment must be "in accordance" with the GSP "as described" in the Preamble to the 1971 Waiver Decision. "Accordance" being defined in the dictionary as "conformity", only preferential tariff treatment that is in conformity with the description "generalized, non-reciprocal and non-discriminatory" treatment can be justified under paragraph 2(a).

146. * * * [W]e do not agree with [the EC's] assertion that * * * the phrase "generalized, non-reciprocal and non discriminatory" in footnote 3 merely refers to the description of the GSP in the 1971 Waiver Decision and, of itself, does not impose any legal obligation on preference-granting countries. * * *

147. We find support for our interpretation in the French version of paragraph 2(a) of the Enabling Clause, requiring that the tariff preferences be accorded *"conformément au Système généralisé de préfér-ences"*. The term "in accordance" is thus *"conformément"* in the French version. In addition, the phrase "[a]s described in [the 1971 Waiver Decision]" in footnote 3 is stated as *"[t]el qu'il est défini dans la décision des PARTIES CONTRACTANTES en date du 25 juin 1971"*. Similarly, the Spanish version uses the terms *"conformidad"* and *"[t]al como lo*

define la Decisión de las PARTES CONTRATANTES de 25 de junio de 1971". In our view, the stronger, more obligatory language in both the French and Spanish texts—that is, using "as defined in" rather than "as described in"—lends support to our view that only preferential tariff treatment that is "generalized, non-reciprocal and non-discriminatory" is covered under paragraph 2(a) of the Enabling Clause.

* * *

151.   We examine now the ordinary meaning of the term "non-discriminatory" in footnote 3 to paragraph 2(a) of the Enabling Clause. As we observed, footnote 3 requires that GSP schemes under the Enabling Clause be "generalized, non-reciprocal and non discriminatory". Before the Panel, the participants offered competing definitions of the word "discriminate". India suggested that this word means " 'to make or constitute a difference in or between; distinguish' and 'to make a distinction in the treatment of different categories of peoples or things'." The European Communities, however, understood this word to mean " 'to make a distinction in the treatment of different categories of people or things, esp. *unjustly* or *prejudicially* against people on grounds of race, colour, sex, social status, age, etc.' "

152.   Both definitions can be considered as reflecting ordinary meanings of the term "discriminate" and essentially exhaust the relevant ordinary meanings. The principal distinction between these definitions, as the Panel noted, is that India's conveys a *"neutral* meaning of making a distinction", whereas the European Communities' conveys a *"negative* meaning carrying the connotation of a distinction that is unjust or prejudicial." Accordingly, the ordinary meanings of "discriminate" point in conflicting directions with respect to the propriety of according differential treatment. Under India's reading, any differential treatment of GSP beneficiaries would be prohibited, because such treatment necessarily makes a distinction between beneficiaries. In contrast, under the European Communities' reading, differential treatment of GSP beneficiaries would not be prohibited *per se*. Rather, distinctions would be impermissible only where the basis for such distinctions was improper. Given these divergent meanings, we do not regard the term "non-discriminatory", on its own, as determinative of the permissibility of a preference-granting country according different tariff preferences to different beneficiaries of its GSP scheme.

153.   Nevertheless, at this stage of our analysis, we are able to discern some of the content of the "non-discrimination" obligation based on the ordinary meanings of that term. Whether the drawing of distinctions is *per se* discriminatory, or whether it is discriminatory only if done on an improper basis, the ordinary meanings of "discriminate" converge in one important respect: they both suggest that distinguishing among similarly-situated beneficiaries is discriminatory. For example, India suggests that all beneficiaries of a particular Member's GSP scheme are similarly-situated, implicitly arguing that any differential treatment of such beneficiaries constitutes discrimination. The European Communi-

ties, however, appears to regard GSP beneficiaries as similarly-situated when they have "similar development needs". Although the European Communities acknowledges that differentiating between similarly-situated GSP beneficiaries would be inconsistent with footnote 3 of the Enabling Clause, it submits that there is no inconsistency in differentiating between GSP beneficiaries with "different development needs". Thus, based on the ordinary meanings of "discriminate", India and the European Communities effectively appear to agree that, pursuant to the term "non-discriminatory" in footnote 3, similarly-situated GSP beneficiaries should not be treated differently. The participants disagree only as to the basis for determining whether beneficiaries are similarly-situated.

154.   Paragraph 2(a), on its face, does not explicitly authorize or prohibit the granting of different tariff preferences to different GSP beneficiaries. It is clear from the ordinary meanings of "non-discriminatory", however, that preference-granting countries must make available identical tariff preferences to all similarly-situated beneficiaries.

155.   We continue our interpretive analysis by turning to the immediate context of the term "non-discriminatory". We note first that footnote 3 to paragraph 2(a) stipulates that, in addition to being "non-discriminatory", tariff preferences provided under GSP schemes must be "generalized". According to the ordinary meaning of that term, tariff preferences provided under GSP schemes must be "generalized" in the sense that they "apply more generally; [or] become extended in application". However, this ordinary meaning alone may not reflect the entire significance of the word "generalized" in the context of footnote 3 of the Enabling Clause, particularly because that word resulted from lengthy negotiations leading to the GSP. In this regard, we note the Panel's finding that, by requiring tariff preferences under the GSP to be "generalized", developed and developing countries together sought to eliminate existing "special" preferences that were granted only to certain designated developing countries. Similarly, in response to our questioning at the oral hearing, the participants agreed that one of the objectives of the 1971 Waiver Decision and the Enabling Clause was to eliminate the fragmented system of special preferences that were, in general, based on historical and political ties between developed countries and their former colonies.

* * *

157.   As further context for the term "non-discriminatory" in footnote 3, we turn next to paragraph 3(c) of the Enabling Clause, which specifies that "differential and more favourable treatment" provided under the Enabling Clause:

> ... shall in the case of such treatment accorded by developed contracting parties to developing countries be designed and, if necessary, modified, to respond positively to the development, financial and trade needs of developing countries.

158.   At the outset, we note that the use of the word "shall" in paragraph 3(c) suggests that paragraph 3(c) sets out an obligation for developed-country Members in providing preferential treatment under a GSP scheme to "respond positively" to the "needs of developing countries". Having said this, we turn to consider whether the "development, financial and trade needs of developing countries" to which preference-granting countries are required to respond when granting preferences must be understood to cover the "needs" of developing countries *collectively*.

159.   * * * Paragraph 3(c) refers generally to "the development, financial and trade needs of developing countries". The absence of an explicit requirement in the text of paragraph 3(c) to respond to the needs of "all" developing countries, or to the needs of "each and every" developing country, suggests to us that, in fact, that provision imposes no such obligation.

160.   Furthermore, as we understand it, the participants in this case agree that developing countries may have "development, financial and trade needs" that are subject to change and that certain development needs may be common to only a certain number of developing countries. We see no reason to disagree. Indeed, paragraph 3(c) contemplates that "differential and more favourable treatment" accorded by developed to developing countries may need to be "modified" in order to "respond positively" to the needs of developing countries. Paragraph 7 of the Enabling Clause supports this view by recording the expectation of "less-developed contracting parties" that their capacity to make contributions or concessions under the GATT will "improve with the progressive development of their economies and improvement in their trade situation". Moreover, the very purpose of the special and differential treatment permitted under the Enabling Clause is to foster economic development of developing countries. It is simply unrealistic to assume that such development will be in lockstep for all developing countries at once, now and for the future.

161.   In addition, the Preamble to the WTO Agreement, which informs all the covered agreements including the GATT 1994 (and, hence, the Enabling Clause), explicitly recognizes the "need for positive efforts designed to ensure that developing countries, and especially the least developed among them, secure a share in the growth in international trade commensurate with the needs of their economic development". The word "commensurate" in this phrase appears to leave open the possibility that developing countries may have different needs according to their levels of development and particular circumstances. The Preamble to the WTO Agreement further recognizes that Members' "respective needs and concerns at different levels of economic development" may vary according to the different stages of development of different Members.

162.   In sum, we read paragraph 3(c) as authorizing preference-granting countries to "respond positively" to "needs" that are *not*

necessarily common or shared by all developing countries. Responding to the "needs of developing countries" may thus entail treating different developing-country beneficiaries differently.

163. However, paragraph 3(c) does not authorize *any* kind of response to *any* claimed need of developing countries. First, we observe that the types of needs to which a response is envisaged are limited to "development, financial and trade needs". * * * [T]he existence of a "development, financial [or] trade need" must be assessed according to an *objective* standard. Broad-based recognition of a particular need, set out in the WTO Agreement or in multilateral instruments adopted by international organizations, could serve as such a standard.

164. Secondly, paragraph 3(c) mandates that the response provided to the needs of developing countries be "positive". "Positive" is defined as "consisting in or characterized by constructive action or attitudes". This suggests that the response of a preference-granting country must be taken with a view to *improving* the development, financial or trade situation of a beneficiary country, based on the particular need at issue. As such, in our view, the expectation that developed countries will "respond positively" to the "needs of developing countries" suggests that a sufficient nexus should exist between, on the one hand, the preferential treatment provided under the respective measure authorized by paragraph 2, and, on the other hand, the likelihood of alleviating the relevant "development, financial [or] trade need". In the context of a GSP scheme, the particular need at issue must, by its nature, be such that it can be effectively addressed through tariff preferences. Therefore, only if a preference-granting country acts in the "positive" manner suggested, in "respon[se]" to a widely-recognized "development, financial [or] trade need", can such action satisfy the requirements of paragraph 3(c).

165. Accordingly, we are of the view that, by requiring developed countries to "respond positively" to the "needs of developing countries", which are varied and not homogeneous, paragraph 3(c) indicates that a GSP scheme may be "non-discriminatory" even if "identical" tariff treatment is not accorded to "all" GSP beneficiaries. Moreover, paragraph 3(c) suggests that tariff preferences under GSP schemes may be "non-discriminatory" when the relevant tariff preferences are addressed to a particular "development, financial [or] trade need" and are made available to all beneficiaries that share that need.

* * *

167. Finally, we note that, pursuant to paragraph 3(a) of the Enabling Clause, any "differential and more favourable treatment . . . shall be designed to facilitate and promote the trade of developing countries and not to raise barriers to or create undue difficulties for the trade of any other contracting parties." This requirement applies, *a fortiori*, to any preferential treatment granted to one GSP beneficiary that is not granted to another. Thus, although paragraph 2(a) does not prohibit *per se* the granting of different tariff preferences to different

GSP beneficiaries, and paragraph 3(c) even contemplates such differentiation under certain circumstances, paragraph 3(a) requires that any positive response of a preference-granting country to the varying needs of developing countries not impose unjustifiable burdens on other Members.

* * *

169. * * * An interpretation of "non-discriminatory" that does not require the granting of "identical tariff preferences" allows not only for GSP schemes providing preferential market access to all beneficiaries, but also the possibility of additional preferences for developing countries with particular needs, provided that such additional preferences are not inconsistent with other provisions of the Enabling Clause, including the requirements that such preferences be "generalized" and "non-reciprocal". We therefore consider such an interpretation to be consistent with the object and purpose of the WTO Agreement and the Enabling Clause.

[The Appellate Body then considered whether its interpretation of paragraph 2(a) rendered paragraph 2(d) redundant. It concluded it did not, noting in paragraph 169 that "pursuant to paragraph 2(d), preference-granting countries need not establish that differentiating between developing and least-developed countries is 'non-discriminatory'. This demonstrates that paragraph 2(d) does have an effect that is different and independent from that of paragraph 2(a), even if the term 'non-discriminatory' does not require the granting of 'identical tariff preferences' to all GSP beneficiaries."]

181. [In examining the consistency of the Drug Amendments with the Enabling Clause, we note that:] By their very terms, the Drug Arrangements are limited to the 12 developing countries designated as beneficiaries in Annex I to the Regulation. * * *

* * *

187. We recall our conclusion that the term "non-discriminatory" in footnote 3 of the Enabling Clause requires that identical tariff treatment be available to all similarly-situated GSP beneficiaries. We find that the measure at issue fails to meet this requirement for the following reasons. First, as the European Communities itself acknowledges, according benefits under the Drug Arrangements to countries other than the 12 identified beneficiaries would require an amendment to the Regulation. Such a "closed list" of beneficiaries cannot ensure that the preferences under the Drug Arrangements are available to all GSP beneficiaries suffering from illicit drug production and trafficking.

188. Secondly, the Regulation contains no criteria or standards to provide a basis for distinguishing beneficiaries under the Drug Arrangements from other GSP beneficiaries. Nor did the European Communities point to any such criteria or standards anywhere else, despite the Panel's request to do so. As such, the European Communities cannot justify the Regulation under paragraph 2(a), because it does not provide a basis for establishing whether or not a developing country qualifies for prefer-

ences under the Drug Arrangements. Thus, although the European Communities claims that the Drug Arrangements are available to all developing countries that are "similarly affected by the drug problem", because the Regulation does not define the criteria or standards that a developing country must meet to qualify for preferences under the Drug Arrangements, there is no basis to determine whether those criteria or standards are discriminatory or not.

189.   For all these reasons, we find that the European Communities has failed to prove that the Drug Arrangements meet the requirement in footnote 3 that they be "non-discriminatory". * * *

Notes and Questions

(1) The EU modified its GSP program in 2005. Council Regulation (EC) 980/2005, OJ L169/1 (June 30, 2005). Additional tariff preferences were made available to countries (i) that applied by October 2005 and (ii) that had implemented (or committed to ratify and implement by 2008) a list of 27 international conventions related to core human and labor rights and to the environment and good governance (including several relating to drug trafficking). All of the countries benefiting from the Drug Arrangements benefit under the new scheme except Pakistan, and there are four additional beneficiaries: Georgia, Sri Lanka, Moldova and Mongolia. Does the new program comply with the Appellate Body's interpretation of the requirements of the Enabling Clause? For an analysis, see Lorand Bartels, The WTO Legality of the EU's GSP+ Arrangement, http://ssrn.com/abstract= 986525.

(2) The Appellate Body approved differential treatment based on the different "development, financial and trade needs" of developing countries. While the control of drug trafficking may be in the EU's interest, how is the control of drug trafficking relevant to the development, financial and trade needs of developing countries? What about compliance with environmental or worker rights rules?

(3) Is there a constraint on the magnitude of the differential treatment that is permitted to address heterogeneous development, financial and trade needs? If differential treatment must be justified by different needs, it would seem to be limited to what is necessary to address those needs adequately. How could one quantify the amount of differentiation needed or other place a principled limit on it?

(4) Are there any constraints on the discretion of donor countries to select the needs in respect of which they give additional preferences? For example, the EU chose seven rather general environmental conventions. Could it have chosen conventions focused on only one environmental problem (e.g., air pollution and not water pollution) or conventions applicable to only one region?

(5) The EU and the US GSP programs do not cover all products of interest to developing countries. Does that raise an issue of whether the programs are "generalized" as required by footnote 3? To the extent that every developing country arguably has different needs, could a GSP scheme

differentiate on a country-by-country basis? What limits does the word "generalized" impose?

(6) The US qualifies access to its GSP program with a number of conditions, which are set out in the preceding subsection. Are those defensible under the Appellate Body's decision? Even if they arguably address development, financial and trade needs, do they effectively impose reciprocity requirements of the sort that footnote 3 would not allow?

(7) There have been no additional WTO challenges to GSP programs. That may reflect the fact that these programs are voluntary and might be eliminated if a donor country felt forced to give more preferences than it wished.

(8) The Enabling Clause was a decision of the GATT Contracting Parties. Does the Appellate Body rule that it is now an integral part of GATT 1994? If so, is it amendable only under the rules of the WTO Agreement? What is the status of other GATT decisions, such as those related to more mundane "housekeeping" issues?

SECTION 24.4   THE NEW INTERNATIONAL ECONOMIC ORDER AND THE CHARTER OF ECONOMIC RIGHTS AND DUTIES OF STATES[1]

The developing countries have attempted in the past to move global negotiations on trade issues into the United Nations and away from the so-called Bretton Woods institutions—the World Bank, the International Monetary Fund and GATT. One aspect of this effort was the creation of UNCTAD—the United Nations Conference on Trade and Employment. Their efforts in this regard have not had great success. In particular, in the area of international trade, UNCTAD's role has been primarily limited to the commodities area. In the 1970s, as part of this effort, UNCTAD promoted the so-called New International Economic Order (NIEO). Although some observers have concluded that the NIEO "no longer exists," having fallen with communism, the problems that gave rise to it and some of the ideas associated with it are still present. For example, some of the ideas found in the Charter can also be found in the Rio Principles adopted in 1992 by the United Nations Conference on Environment and Development. Accordingly, we briefly describe its history and content.

On April 19, 1972, President Echeverria of Mexico proposed to the Third United Nations Conference on Trade and Development that a Charter of Economic Rights and Duties of States should be drafted in order to protect the economic rights of all countries, especially the

1. The text of the charter is found in Report of the Second Committee, U.N. Doc. A/9946, 28 (Dec. 9, 1974) and U.N. Doc. A/RES/3281 (XXIX) (Jan. 15, 1975); see also 14 Intl.Leg. Matls. 251; Charles N. Brower & John B. Tepe, Jr., The Charter of Economic Rights and Duties of States: A Reflection or Rejection of International Law?, 9 Intl.Law. 295 (1975); American Society of International Law, Proceedings of the 68th Annual Meeting 209, 302 (1975).

developing countries. The original intent was to create a document that would be binding upon the signatories and become a part of international law. Given the lukewarm reception the proposal received from most developed countries, however, political reality eventually dictated that this would not be possible.

Many of the countries that refused to accept the Charter did so partly because of its failure to contain either a commitment to follow international law or an acknowledgement of the relevance of international law. A second contested area concerned the legitimacy of cartels. The Charter states in Article 5 that all States have the right to associate in organizations of primary commodity procedures to further their national interests. "Correspondingly all States have the duty to respect that right by refraining from applying economic and political measures that would limit it."

The developed countries also unsuccessfully opposed Article 28 which imposes a duty on all States to adjust the prices of the exports of developing countries in relation to those of their imports.

Article 16 calls for restitution to be made for the economic and social costs of "colonialism, *apartheid*, racial discrimination, neocolonialism and all forms of foreign aggression, occupation and domination." It also provides that States shall not encourage investments that inhibit "the liberation of a territory occupied by force." The United Nations General Assembly adopted the resolution incorporating the Charter on December 12, 1974, by a roll-call vote of 120 to 6, with 10 abstentions. The United States, Belgium, Denmark, the Federal Republic of Germany, Luxembourg, and the United Kingdom voted against. Austria, Canada, France, Ireland, Israel, Italy, Japan, the Netherlands, Norway, and Spain abstained.

Chapter 25

PERSPECTIVES AND CONCLUSIONS: A CHALLENGING FUTURE

SECTION 25.1 INTRODUCTION

There is no dearth of perplexing issues presented in this book. The underlying economic policies involved are themselves intricate, subject to challenge, and often undergoing reappraisal. In a world of dramatically reduced transportation and communication costs, coupled with government tendencies to influence market structures and mechanisms, do the traditional economic theories of comparative advantage really work? To what extent can political leaders and practitioners afford to ignore these economic policies? Why do governments seem to opt often for third or even fourth best measures?

But our concern, as law professionals or prospective lawyers, must also be directed to the jurisprudential and governmental questions of how to make the world system work so as to promote the appropriate economic, political, and social policies. In this book we have faced dozens of difficult conceptual problems related to this broad theme. Is a rule system really appropriate for this endeavor? Are the international institutions adequate to cope with the problems of the next decades or the next century? Are national institutions adequate? Does the U.S. Constitutional system penalize the United States in the context of today's interdependent world and the many international negotiations which occur in it? Do the constitutional and other legal constraints on policy makers nudge them into inferior policy choices? Or do these choices merely reflect compromises which attempt to balance alternative and competing policy goals?

Is the asymmetry of economic power an advantage for the world or does it prevent necessary progress? How can developing countries, non-market economies, or the giant combination of both, be integrated into the system so as to complement the underlying policies of that system? A further detailed inventory of the many problems and issues would take considerably more space.

In this final chapter of this book, we ask the reader to step back from the extensive and elaborate detail of the subject of this book, in order to explore it in a broader way and with regard to the context of broader policies. We include here several scholarly works which are designed to do this. We begin by looking at a pervasive theme of considerable interest to thoughtful legal practitioners: the role of rules (Section 25.2). Then in later sections we discuss some fundamental perspectives and offer some tentative conclusions, and provide a brief look at future prospects as succinctly expressed in an essay by co-author William Davey.

SECTION 25.2 LEGAL RULES OR GOVERNMENT DISCRETION? WHICH IS BEST?

(A) INTRODUCTION

One of the recurring themes of international trade diplomacy and policy is the question of the role of "rule" or "law." To greatly oversimplify the issue, one can observe a sort of dichotomy between a goal of developing and implementing rules of national economic behavior, and a goal of keeping as much freedom or discretion for national political leaders as possible. A great deal has been written on this theme in the broader context of international affairs. Much has also been written on this theme in the particular context of international trade and economic relations. In many of the chapters of this book we have had occasion to refer both to writings of this type, and to particular problems or issues which concern this issue. In some of the published writings about trade policy generally, one can sometimes observe ambivalence and indeed even contradiction within the same work!

In this section we would like explicitly to address this issue of "rule" versus "government discretion." In doing this we will avoid repeating materials on this subject found elsewhere in this book, but we will refer to them as needed.

(B) THE UNITED STATES AND LEGAL PROCEDURES: COSTS AND BENEFITS APPRAISED

JOHN H. JACKSON, PERSPECTIVES ON THE JURISPRUDENCE OF INTERNATIONAL TRADE: COSTS AND BENEFITS OF LEGAL PROCEDURES IN THE UNITED STATES[1]

Both in the United States and abroad the U.S. legal system has been strongly criticized for its handling of international trade regulation. Some of this criticism parallels general statements made about the

---

1. 182 Mich.L.Rev. 1570, 1570, 1574–76, 1578–82, 1587 (1984). Reprinted by permis- sion of the Michigan Law Review Associa- tion.

United States as a litigious society, with too many lawyers and too much attention to "legalism." Despite their serious data faults and some serious misconceptions about comparing the role of a lawyer in the United States to false counterparts in other countries, I feel that it is worthwhile to examine these criticisms more systematically.

* * *

Having given due obeisance to substantive policy, most of the remaining policies that I will mention could be categorized as "procedural." These are the policies that underlie the way that institutions and procedures have been shaped within the United States. Unfortunately, many of these policies are overlooked by important critics of the system. Perhaps it will be easiest for the reader if I enumerate them briefly:

(1) The procedure should maximize the opportunity of government officials to receive all relevant information, arguments, and perspectives. Thus, a procedure that allows all interested parties to present evidence and arguments would enhance the realization of this goal.

(2) The procedure should prevent corruption and ethical *mala fides*, even when the latter fall short of corruption and illegal activity. Another way to express this is that an important policy goal of the procedure is to prevent "back room political deals" that favor special or particular interests while defeating broader policy objectives of the U.S. government.

(3) The procedure should enhance the perception of all parties who will be affected by a decision that they have had their chance to present information and arguments, i.e., that they have had their "day in court." This is an important policy objective, particularly for democratic societies; affected parties must have some confidence in the decision-making process, even when the decision goes against them.

(4) The procedure should be perceived by the citizens at large as fair and tending to maximize the chances for a correct decision. A sense of fairness will include a desire that even weaker interests in a society be treated fairly, i.e., that the ability to get a favorable decision will not depend only on money, political power, status, or other elements deemed unfair.

(5) The procedure should be reasonably efficient, that is, it should allow reasonably quick government decisions and minimize the cost both to government and to private parties of arriving at those decisions. It is this policy goal that is most questioned by the criticisms of the American "legalistic" procedures.

(6) The procedure should tend to maximize the likelihood that a decision will be made on a general national basis (or international basis), not catering particularly to special interests. In other words, the procedure should be designed so that government officials can realistically be assisted in "fending off" special interests that conflict with the general good of the nation.

(7) The procedure must fit into the overall constitutional system of the society concerned and be consistent with policy goals underpinning that constitutional system. For the United States, as stated above, an important policy underpinning the Constitution is the prevention of power monopolies within our society. The system of checks and balances thus creates a constant tension between various branches of the government, which may often appear messy, costly, and inefficient, but which is based on fundamental constitutional principles.

(8) Predictability and stability of decisions are important values. Predictability of decisions, whether based on precedent, statutory formulas, or something else, enables private parties and their counselors (lawyers, economists, and politicians) to calculate generally the potential or lack of potential for a favorable decision under each of a variety of different regulatory schemes. The greater the predictability, the more likely that cases will be brought only if they have a good chance to succeed. The private lawyer often experiences the situation wherein he counsels clients in the privacy of his office in such a way that the client will use her best judgment to decide not to bring a case.

I make no claim that the list of policy objectives enumerated above is exhaustive; I am certain that others can be considered. Likewise, as stated earlier, the policy goals mentioned tend to be related to national procedures rather than to international procedures. However, many of these goals also apply, sometimes with modified weight, to international institutions and procedures.

IV. COSTS OF THE U.S. SYSTEM? QUANTIFIABLE AND NONQUANTIFIABLE

I want to turn now to an attempt to appraise the costs to U.S. society of the U.S. government system of regulating imports. Again, I am only looking at the import side (export regulations could be taken up separately). Furthermore, I am attempting to evaluate the costs of the "legalistic system." There are certain costs that would be incurred no matter what type of import regulation system a government operated, whether it was a system of broad government discretion or a more legalistic system with hearings, statutory criteria, and judicial review. [The original article then presented a chart, based on crude empirical data for the years 1982 and 1983 and thus substantially out of date, estimating the governmental costs of the U.S. trade laws (escape clause, anti-dumping, countervailing duty, Section 337, Section 301, etc.), as well as the private costs (extra-firm, such as lawyers and consultants, and intra-firm such as in-house corporate personnel.)]

* * *

4. Combining the Various Figures

The figures under the three parts above would total approximately $238 million for 1983. To give due allowance to the imprecision of the estimates, we can expand that figure and say that the probability is very high that the total is less than $250 million.

With what can we compare this figure? One obvious comparison is the total value of imports during the year, which for 1983 is estimated to be $254 billion. The result is that the cost of the U.S. import regulation system is 0.0009, or approximately 1/10th of 1 percent of the total annual value of imports. One could conclude that this figure is reasonably insignificant, if it were considered as a sort of "transaction cost" for a regulatory system that had other benefits. It is perhaps not entirely fair, however, to measure or evaluate the cost of the system by dividing those quantifiable costs by the total value of imports. A better cost-benefit approach would be to look at the regulatory system's welfare benefit to society, and I return to that question in the next section of this article. It should also be recognized that this aggregate approach does not answer all relevant questions. For example, the distribution of costs can vary enormously, and may in fact be very unfair (imposing, for example, substantial burdens on certain sectors of the economy, and few burdens on other sectors). Finally, we must remember that there are a number of nonquantifiable costs that need to be weighed in the balance.

B. *Nonquantifiable Costs of the Import Regulatory System*

To focus only on the quantifiable dollar costs of the system would be a major mistake. Some of the most important costs may in fact be non-quantifiable. A few of these should be mentioned.

1. *Foreign Policy Rigidity*

A system that depends on statutory criteria and procedures, allows citizen access, and establishes predictability will inherently diminish the discretion and flexibility of government officials. Indeed, that is exactly what it is designed to do. However, certain types of foreign policy activities may be inhibited by such a system. Secret negotiations are much more difficult and quick decisions are sometimes almost impossible under a "legalistic" system. Indeed, as was demonstrated in the recent countervailing duty case concerning Chinese textiles, as well as in certain portions of the 1982 carbon steel countervailing duty cases, a "legalistic system" tends to give citizen complainants a considerable amount of control over their cases, which in turn risks giving those particular citizens undue advantage to the detriment of broader U.S. foreign policy considerations.

2. *Manipulation or Harassment*

The legalistic type of system that exists in the United States also lends itself to some abuse by special interests that manipulate the system for their own advantage in ways not necessarily contemplated by the Congress when it enacted the relevant statutes. For example, a complainant may be tempted to initiate a proceeding knowing that the procedure will present considerable opportunity to create mischief and difficulty for U.S. foreign policy while the real motive for using the procedure is to negotiate with the government towards some solution that is not contemplated within the statutory or regulatory procedure set up by Congress. A complainant may really desire certain tax benefits or cartel-like quotas dividing up the U.S. market and ensuring domestic interests of a certain portion of that market. It may bring a trade proceeding that contemplates relief through imposition of a certain amount of tariff-like duties at the border solely to try to get the U.S. government to negotiate in a way that would achieve the complainant's true objective of quota-like restraints. In addition, it has been alleged in some commentary and by some foreign observers that the U.S. system tends to result in "multiple harassment," by which domestic industry complainants can bring one procedure after another even though they know that they probably will not succeed in such procedures. The running battle of domestic television interests against imported television sets is often cited as one instance of multiple harassment. The mere institution of such procedures creates considerable uncertainty in the market for the imports and creates costs for the importing firms concerned. Both factors tend to reduce the importation of such challenged goods initially and to increase importers' general costs of penetrating the U.S. market, with attendant effects upon their later price structure and competitiveness in the U.S. market. Although appraisal of the "multiple harassment" charge is not easy, there appear to be few instances in which it can actually be established that such action has occurred. Even the threat of such activity, however, may itself be somewhat inhibiting to foreign exporters who are eyeing the potential of the U.S. market.

3. *Wrong Law Rigidity*

One of the results of the U.S. "legalistic" system of regulating imports is that criteria tend to be embodied in statutes enacted by Congress and then become very hard to change. Because Congress distrusts executive discretion, it tends to establish rather elaborate detail in statutory criteria. But on some occasions the statutory formulas prove later to be inappropriate from a policy or economic point of view. Or an international proceeding will find that the U.S. law violates U.S. international obligations. In these cases it has proved very difficult to get the Congress to change the law, because a variety of special interests tend to be able to block such change. Consequently, the result is that the system has a certain amount of "wrong law rigidity" built into it.

4. *Special Interest Influence on the Formulation of the Statutory Criteria*

The processes by which the Congress writes the statutory criteria and formulates the law are reasonably well known. The system sometimes lends itself to manipulation by special economic interests in the United States that can foresee the results of certain statutory wordings on their potential cases in the future. Thus, an important economic sector can sometimes influence the Congress in developing criteria that will later prove to be very beneficial to it in particular cases, even though such criteria may not be in the overall best interests of the United States. In this respect, however, the process is no different from that of any domestic subject matter. It is perhaps a price one pays for an open democratic system.

5. Big Cases Mishandled

One of the allegations often made is that the United States' elaborate legalistic system of import regulation may operate with reasonable satisfaction only as to the little cases that are generally unimportant in themselves. But when it comes to very big cases that have a broad influence in major sectors of the economy (such as autos, textiles, agriculture, and steel), it is said that the system breaks down and in fact returns, by one subterfuge or another, to a "non-rule system" of extensive executive discretion and "back-room bargaining."

6. The Dilemma of a Legalistic System

As one can begin to surmise from analyzing these various costs, both quantifiable and nonquantifiable, there is to a certain extent a dilemma involved in designing any institutional system for regulating imports. The dilemma is not unique to this subject and is involved in a number of other areas of governmental endeavor also. This dilemma is that the more one maximizes the goals of a legalistic system (predictability, transparency and elimination of corruption and political back-room deals), the more one sacrifices other desirable goals such as flexibility and the ability of government officials to make determinations in the broad national interest as opposed to catering to specific special interests.

V.   The Benefits of the System

The benefits of the legalistic system may be considerable, but they are perhaps harder to appraise. I will discuss them under two categories.

A. Procedural Benefits of the System

Apart from costs and delays, the legalistic system responds well to many of the goals and objectives set out in section III above. Clearly, the more extensive and detailed are the statutory criteria, the public proceedings, the opportunity for judicial review and the like, the more likely that the system will be predictable, corruption-proof and devoid of backroom political deals. An exception to this might be the "big case" question: If the system becomes too rigid, the big cases—those involving considerable political power—will tend to make "end runs" around the system, and thus will not be channeled by the rules and will perhaps be even more vulnerable to flexible executive official discretion than would be the case if the formal procedures were less rigid and could better accommodate the big cases.

B. Substantive Benefits

One of the critical questions, and perhaps the most critical question, is whether this legalistic system, given its costs, in fact provides a substantial measure of benefits (benefits that exceed the costs) to the general welfare of the United States. Here it is necessary to indulge in some assumptions, and to recognize that conclusions are only tentative, in the form of hypotheses that need further testing.

The basic assumption that may be required to justify the legalistic system is that it in fact allows a higher degree of liberal trade access for imports into the U.S. economy. This assumption itself is premised on the assumption that such trade liberalization provides a benefit to the U.S. economy. Most economists believe that trade liberalization does provide such a benefit.

If we can believe (and although it is essentially a "judgment call" many people do believe it) that the U.S. legalistic system, cumbersome, rigid, and costly as it is, in fact provides for an economy more open to imports than virtually any other major industrial economy in the world, then we could count this as a benefit. But measuring that benefit is obviously very difficult. We are measuring it against an unknown— namely, what would be the degree of import restraint in the U.S. economy if the U.S. system were not so legalistic and were more "discretion prone."

One must not forget, however, that there are also a number of non-quantifiable benefits to the system, greater confidence of the citizenry in the operation of its government in this subject matter, the business planning advantage of a higher degree of stability in governmental actions, reduction of corruption, etc.

SECTION 25.3   THE WTO'S "CONSTITUTION" AND ITS WEAKNESSES

JOHN H. JACKSON, THE WTO "CONSTITUTION" AND PROPOSED REFORMS: SEVEN "MANTRAS" REVISITED[1]

II.   The Internal Constitution of the WTO

A.   Mantras

My second subject is the internal constitution. Some of the ideas expressed here can be attributed to ambassadors, governments, or academics. I have not tried to identify authorship for each piece of this puzzle, because usually there have been a number of parallel suggestions. In this part, I will first introduce a series of what I call "mantras." These are phrases that are used commonly, particularly in Geneva and among those who are well experienced as well as some of those who are less experienced. Quite often, these phrases are used in a context in which they do not easily suggest that the content of the phrase should be examined in depth. In other words, the phrases are used to *avoid thinking* certain issues through. Here, I provide a brief overview of seven of these mantras.

(1) The first mantra is that "consensus is great or even sacred." It is said that we must maintain the consensus system of decision making. Often, this is in the context of thinking that there are only two approaches to decision making, that this is a binary choice—one choice is consensus, and the other is voting—and you have to choose between

---

1.   4 JIEL 67, 67–78 (March 2001).

them. However, we do not have to choose between those two. There are a lot of things in between, and there are some real pitfalls about the consensus rule that at least should make us think more about where in between we might focus attention.

(2) Another mantra is that the WTO is an organization that is "government to government." This implies that non-governmental entities have no role here. Once again, we should think this through.

(3) The third mantra is: we must be sure to preserve national or nation-state sovereignty. This mantra is used not only in Geneva, but also in Washington and other capitals. This "mantra" overlooks a good many things. Again, it is not a binary question; it is not a question of all or nothing. The word "sovereignty" has overtones that are totally out of date, but nevertheless the concept of sovereignty probably has some policy merit that we should think about. The policy question really involved in the sovereignty question is: How do you want to allocate power?[2] What decisions do you want made in Geneva, Washington, Sacramento, California, or a neighborhood in Berkeley? By viewing it as a decision about how to *allocate power*, we can disaggregate the question of sovereignty and make people think about how to correctly design that allocation. Some of the policies discussed in Part I suggest directions in this regard. In other words, some of the reasons for going to a higher level of decision making are to solve such questions as the prisoner's dilemma or the race to the bottom.

(4) Another mantra often used is that the organization is "member driven." Member driven means that the members want to keep the WTO Secretariat out of their hair. They do not want to give the Secretariat or the officials or the Director–General any power whatsoever. A totally member driven organization is, in many cases, counterproductive, and most certainly inefficient. Furthermore, if this mantra is used to question the independence of the dispute settlement organs, it undermines the integrity of the adjudicative process of the system.

There are three additional points, which I will call mantras just to put them in sequence, although they are more targeted to current negotiating atmospheres and ideas of structure. Yet, like the other mantras mentioned, these may not have been fully understood or examined.

(5) One is the notion of "single undertaking," a single package idea. I have great concerns and doubts about the single undertaking concept, although I can see its advantages. (Indeed, I can discern the advantages of all these mantras. I do not mean to suggest that they are totally useless.) But I can also perceive certain circumstances where it might be wise to experiment with an approach that would not be part of a single package. There might be different subjects that would require a different time line or a different composition of participants.

---

2. See John H. Jackson, The Great 1994 Sovereignty Debate: United States Acceptance and Implementation of the Uruguay Round Results, in The Jurisprudence of GATT and the WTO: Insights on Treaty Law and Economic Relations 367 (2000).

(6) Similarly, another concept is "MFN" or the most-favored-nation-clause. MFN has enormous strength and advantages in the system, but we should not view it as sacrosanct in its purity, because it has major problems, such as the free-rider problem and the tendency towards the lowest-common-denominator.

(7) Finally, there has been talk about the need for so-called "deliverables". At the outset of discussions regarding a new trade negotiating round, diplomats have worried about the length of time a round often takes (ten years or more) and have spoken of the need to conclude some parts of the round early and have those implemented so that the benefits are "delivered" early.

Indeed, deliverables have advantages, as do these other items. On the other hand, deliverables tend to push policymakers towards sacrificing longer-term institutional strengths for short-term political advantages.

I have raised each of these mantras, and my suggestion is that they can bear examination and should not be off limits from more careful examination.

* * *

B.   The Implications of Seattle

One of the things that the failure of the Seattle ministerial meeting seems to show us is that even the world as recent as 1980 or 1990 is no longer the landscape that we have to deal with today. Part of this change is due to the very fast-moving technology that is influencing trade and everything else. There are two dimensions of this for the internal constitution of the WTO, and there are similar dimensions for external relations of the WTO, which will be discussed in Part III. These two dimensions are: (1) the dispute settlement process and (2) the rest of the decision-making or negotiating process, in other words, the non-dispute settlement process. To some extent, we could think of these dimensions as analogous to political structures at the national level, namely, the relationship of the judiciary to the legislature. One of the questions is: Do we have an effectively working legislature? Do we have an effectively working decision-making or rule-making process? These issues are of considerable importance. Why? Currently, we have a very effective judicial process, certainly more effective than before. It has received lots of credit, and although it is not without some problems, it is well worthwhile. It is a big improvement in things that help to underpin some of the policies mentioned in Part I above. For instance, the rule orientation of the institutions is enhanced by the predictability and stability that the dispute settlement system adds to the implementation of the rules.

However, if the decision-making and rule-making processes fail to produce results, there is a tendency to throw their issues at the dispute settlement process. Therefore, there could be a tendency to ask the dispute settlement process to take on issues that it ought not to. For instance, there could be temptations to put in the hands of the dispute settlement process, issues that are really "rule making" instead of "rule applying."

There are real concerns about the current decision-making structure. This structure developed in the Uruguay Round negotiations, when negotiations focused on a WTO, a World Trade Organization, particularly in the fall of 1993 when major players worked hard to alter some of the previous drafts. While alterations were appropriate in many ways, one of the things that the negotiators did was to constrain and put checks and balances on the decision-making process. They did this by requiring decision by consensus and by super-majorities and through certain other kinds of procedures. Today we realize that those constraints can lead to a lack of effectiveness of the decision-making process. This is one of the issues and one of the dilemmas that we have before us and that requires more examination.

C. Decision Making

There are advantages and disadvantages to a consensus-based decision-making process. One downside of requiring full consensus is that it may be a recipe for impasse, stalemate, and paralysis. In other words, the result may be that things do not get done. We have seen some very interesting examples of that in the last year. There are also examples that often are not easily visible.

For example, there are situations where the participants in this constitution would like to see some evolution and change. These changes may be rather detailed and technical, such as modifying elements of the Dispute Settlement Understanding. Yet, proponents of change may abandon such an effort even before trying, because of their perception that the consensus process makes it impossible to do what they want to do.

What are some alternate methods for decisions? One possibility is to figure out a way to distinguish the more detailed procedural aspects from things that have real substance. There is already a distinction in the amending clause of the WTO between the non-substantive and the more substantive issues. There might be ways to develop a similar distinction in the consensus process. Of course, one of the problems with the consensus process is that in order to change it you must have consensus. Therefore, any country can block a proposed change. This leads us to a search for alternative ways to make changes without amending either the DSU or the WTO as a whole. Often this is a delicate question, and I am not sure the alternatives are workable. If they are not workable, and the parties are without recourse to make changes, we are likely to be in very great trouble.

There are, however, some other possibilities. One possibility is a so-called "critical mass" idea, which has been experimented with. The basic idea is to develop a practice where countries refrain from blocking consensus when a critical mass of countries support a proposed change.

This critical mass of countries could be expressed as an overwhelming majority of countries and an overwhelming amount of the trade weight in the world, such as 90 percent of both of these factors. In addition, there could be other factors. Of course, the proposed change would need to be consistent with the existing treaty obligations, including MFN. One could try to develop a practice, maybe through something called "peer pressure," by encouraging states to refrain from blocking a consensus in certain kinds of decision-making, if these other attributes existed. One parallel or analog to this approach is roughly (but not precisely) the so-called Luxembourg Compromise in the history of the European Communities development.

Another possibility is to use expert or smaller groups attached to a particular committee, such as the Dispute Settlement Body. Such a group would meet with diplomats and perhaps outside experts to draft a proposal that coincided with criteria, such as those mentioned above. Then, when a proposed change is put forward to the final decision makers, the parties could argue that governments should refrain from blocking the consensus in that particular circumstance because of the critical mass argument, the percentage of trade, and so forth.

A third approach is to use a "tariff scheduling" approach. This approach was used in the telecommunications agreement and, to some extent, the financial services agreement. Under this approach, commitments resulting from further negotiations were put in the schedules, which are annexed to the services agreement of those governments that were willing to go along with the measure. Of course, these commitments are usually subject to MFN, depending on some of the aspects of the services agreement. This approach addresses both the difficulties with the consensus rule and the single package. It is analogous to something that was built into the WTO, namely, the Annex 4 Plurilateral Trade Agreements, which are optional.

Unfortunately, it takes a full consensus to add an agreement to Annex 4, so there could well be blocking against that approach. But if there were not blocking, this might also be an approach where certain innovation could occur with smaller groupings than the whole.

Another problem is whether there needs to be some kind of a "steering group," some kind of a small group in the organization, which can help the Director–General and others. Without going into detail, something like this is going to be required. There has been a fair amount of writing, both academic and diplomatic, about how to constitute such a group. There are a number of different proposals, and I would hope that maybe some of them might work. In each of these cases, it is possible to try them for a limited period of time, such as two years. At the end of the two-year period, the provisions could expire. This approach allows the parties to renew negotiations and reach agreement, based on their view of how the provisions played out. If these provisions appear to have been effective, the parties could renew them for an additional period of time.

III.   EXTERNAL RELATIONS IN THE WTO CONSTITUTION

A.   *The Role of Non–Governmental Organizations*

About Seattle, many of us talked about the "inside problem" and the "outside problem." The "inside problem" is what was really going on in the negotiations and the various half a dozen or more factors that prevented success there. The "outside problem" includes the demonstrations, the tensions involved with that, and the organization of NGO and public participation. These are analogous to the structure of this article, with attention to internal problems compared to external. You can look at these problems under both dispute settlement and decision-making dimensions. There are really two parts under each of those, and it may be helpful to view it as a two-by-two matrix. One is the subject or "transparency" and the other is the subject of "participation." Please note that I separate these terms rather dramatically because quite often the word transparency is used in an ambiguous way to cover both. Transparency, as I and others see it, really means information for the public, but it can also mean internal flow of information. Ways of making information available to the public include available documentation, open hearings, and open meetings, at least for the press. Participation, on the other hand, is somewhat more of a problem and is a more delicate issue. Participation by civil society or non-governmental entities means that they have an opportunity to be heard and present their views.

The basic question, and the one most vital here, is the role of NGOs. There are arguments both for and against NGO participation. We should thus recognize both the advantages and disadvantages of NGO participation. The governments are the authorized legitimate representative in the WTO structure. The NGOs sometimes forget that, as we see that in some of their arguments and how they go about their business. In some cases, an NGO may have no legitimate role and no true constituency. Sometimes it is said that some NGOs are part of the so-called "uncivil" society. They are abusive and destructive and can cause various problems, including safety problems. Generally NGOs, even the good ones, can create resource problems. For example, it will involve some resources to open hearings and provide additional documentation, space, and time. On the other hand, there are advantages to NGO participation. First, they can be quite useful. Sometimes they have resources for study and analysis that governments lack. They can bring to the table information that can be very useful in the proceedings. They can also transmit information to concerned and important constituencies in the various countries. They can come to an understanding and then explain the issues to a broader constituency that has not had the time or the information to try to grasp them. In addition, they have real power, as demonstrated by the MAI (Multilateral Agreement on Investment) exercise and the impact of the Internet, and in Seattle, to some extent.

What to do? It is surprising how far behind the WTO is, compared to most of the international organizations in Geneva and other cities, with respect to how it handles NGOs. Other organizations have very elaborate methodologies of accreditation of NGOs based on a variety of criteria, which vary from organization to organization. For example, the United Nations has been doing this for forty or fifty years.[3] In addition, the International Labor Organization (ILO) has fairly elaborate measures, as does the World Intellectual Property Organization (WIPO). WIPO integrates key NGOs that have expertise in some of the technical aspects, such as its "domain name" exercise. UNCTAD also has measures. Why not the WTO? At a minimum, there should be a study, which could be done by a committee reporting to the General Council chairman or one under the supervision of the Director–General.

B. Transparency and Participation

With respect to transparency, there is a problem of documents. To some extent, the very ingenious program of computer documentation in the WTO is quite advanced and can be a real help as part of the outreach, not only to the delegates themselves, but also to civil society and NGOs. There is also a question of whether meetings should be open. I was surprised recently at how willing some experienced diplomats were to see such things as WTO committee meetings made open for public attendance. Even if one is not willing to go that far, because of the negotiating function of at least some of those committee meetings, maybe the Council meetings could be open, or maybe there could be a press gallery for the various Councils, not just the General Council.

Likewise, in the dispute settlement system, some of the same questions arise. For example, there is a problem of the documentation, particularly the panel reports and the delay that is caused in part by translation resource problems, which surely can be overcome.

"Participation" is a different and more difficult question in the context of decision making. There may be grounds to call upon some of the NGOs for assistance as experts, and there certainly is authority to do so. Indeed, the WTO Charter, Article IX, paragraph 2, suggests certain relationships for NGOs. In the dispute settlement system, we have already seen the "amicus curiae" brief as one way to transmit information to the panels. That can be constructive, but it needs to be thought through so as not to cause certain kinds of problems.

IV. CONCLUSION

This article examines the world trading system in its historical context and in light of recent developments. Looking ahead, it is useful to consider how to move forward. By providing leadership, the trade superpowers—the United States, the European Union, and Japan—can play a major role. There are other groups of countries that could get together and try to thrash out ideas, and discuss the pros and cons of

3. United Nations Non–Governmental Liaison Service, The NGLS Handbook of UN Agencies, Programmes and Funds Working for Economic and Social Development (2d ed. 1997).

some of these measures, and then see if there is some in-between measure that tends to maximize the advantages and minimize the disadvantages. Such measures could then be introduced for limited periods of time.

Already suggested by the European Community and the Director–General and others, is an idea of forming a group of parliamentarians to meet at the WTO on a regular basis to exchange information, ideas, and attitudes. Other ideas that have been set forth include the formation of a steering group[3] and an NGO consultative group. There may be a parallel here in the European Community, which has something like an economic and cultural consultation committee that works with it on various subjects. Suggestions for increasing transparency include public sessions and increased access to reports and other documents. Short of amending the agreements, there are many steps that can be taken to strengthen the institution and its agreements. It is worthwhile to focus our efforts on these steps. Clearly, this brief article only touches the surface, so let us hope much further analysis and discussion on these and other WTO "constitutional issues" will occur in the near future.

SECTION 25.4 REFLECTIONS ON THE FUTURE OF THE TRADING SYSTEM

WILLIAM J. DAVEY, THE FUTURE OF INTERNATIONAL ECONOMIC LAW[1]

In celebration of the tenth anniversary of the Journal, the Editors felt that it would be particularly useful and interesting to request members of our Editorial Board to contemplate the future of international economic law. Thus, this third issue of Volume 10 contains a wide-ranging discussion of key issues facing the international economic system in the coming years.

As one contemplates the current scene in international economic relations, there seems to be one over-arching concern that is repeatedly stressed: Are the institutions now in place—and I refer, in particular, to the International Monetary Fund (Fund), the World Bank (Bank), and the World Trade Organization (WTO)—suitable for the 21st century? Certainly, the three institutions have been going through a trying period. The Fund's borrowers have been paying off their loans at a rate such that it cannot currently support itself on the profits of its lending

---

3. *See* Jeffrey J. Schott & Jayashree Watal, Decision-making in the WTO (Institute of International Economics Policy Brief No. 00–2, March 2000) <http://www.iie.com/NEWSLETR/news00–2.htm> (suggesting that "the WTO needs to establish a small, informal steering committee (20 or so in number) that can be delegated responsibility for developing consensus on trade issues among the member countries").

1. 10 JIEL 439, 439–442 (Summer 2007) (Introduction to Special Issue to Celebrate Tenth Year of JIEL).

activities. The Bank has recently been in turmoil over its leadership and alleged conflicts of interest at the very top, a particular embarrassment in light of its recent emphasis on rooting out corruption in developing country governments. The WTO's first wide ranging negotiation—the Doha Development Agenda—was launched only with great difficulty (recall the protests at its failed Seattle ministerial meeting) and little has been accomplished in six years of formal negotiations, despite regular upbeat appraisals emanating from the Secretariat and periodic reports that the four key players (Brazil, the EU, India, and the US) are about to make unspecified progress in bridging their differences over agriculture and market access issues. As this issue goes to press in late June, optimism seems to be in short supply.

Some of the questions raised about these organizations go to the very essence of their existence. For example, are they still needed? As noted above, the Fund seems to be running out of borrowers and alternative official sources of assistance seem to be coming into existence. Even if the institutions are still needed, questions have been raised as to whether they now focus their main efforts on the appropriate activities. Should the Bank, for example, give greater emphasis to concessional lending or outright grants? In the case of each of the institutions, there are difficult and controversial issues involved in integrating the developing world, and particularly such major and fast-growing countries as Brazil, China, India, and Russia, into the governance of the institutions.

The importance of these fundamental issues is reflected in the papers included in this issue. Indeed, the first six papers focus in particular on these issues. In the first paper, Hector Torres analyzes what the Fund must do to regain its legitimacy vis-a-vis its developing country membership. That is followed by Frank Garcia's paper, in which he relies on the thinking of philosopher John Rawls to establish a framework that allows one to analyze whether the activities of the Fund and the Bank are appropriate—in particular in light of the interests of the developing countries and the least developed among them. The following four articles deal specifically with the WTO. Debra Steger notes that the culture of the WTO stems from that of GATT and catalogs a number of problems that it now faces that require changes. She reviews in that regard several proposals for reform—from Russian President Putin's recent call for a new international trade organization to the more detailed analyses on reform contained in the WTO's Sutherland Report and the Atlantic Council's report on transatlantic leadership in the new global economy. In his paper, Thomas Cottier comprehensively sets out a list of the structural issues now facing the WTO and suggests the creation of new fora for consideration of those issues. In particular, he suggests the creation of (i) a consultative committee on structural reform that would consider questions referred to it by the WTO organs and would have non-governmental members (especially from academia) as well as governmental members and (ii) a new standing committee on legal affairs. Dan Esty's paper lays out a framework for assessing good governance in the WTO. He reviews what the critical elements of good governance are, how the WTO rates in respect of those elements and considers what could be done to improve good governance at the WTO. Ernst–Ulrich Petersmann rounds out this group of papers by examining what he characterizes as "judicial governance". In his view, international economic law has increasingly recognized the role of such judicial governance in providing citizens with judicial remedies at various levels for defending their rights and interests as participants in international trade. This trend is one that he argues should be encouraged. All in all, these six papers offer a comprehensive overview of the institutional issues facing the international economic institutions.

The next six papers focus on current problems facing the WTO, which for the most part have arisen in the Doha negotiations or as a result of the limited progress that has been made in those negotiations. The first paper—by Seung–Wha Chang—grapples with the difficult issue of special and differential treatment. The Doha negotiations have been billed from the beginning as a 'development round'. Yet, given the diverse needs and attributes of developing countries, it may be necessary to re-think how special and differential treatment should be incorporated into WTO agreements. Chang reviews the possible alternatives. As the Doha 440 negotiations have faltered, there seems to be increased interest in bilateral or plurilateral preferential trade agreements, even in those areas of the world where they have not been so common in the past (e.g. East Asia). Two papers consider this trend. Fred Abbott's paper suggests that PTAs have become the primary focus of trade negotiators. He finds the way in which the United States and the European Union are able to impose their views on their weaker negotiating partners to be troubling. While he does not find PTAs to be all that threatening to the WTO multilateral system for the time being, he notes that the situation bears watching. Matthew Schaefer argues that perhaps the most effective way to ensure that these new agreements comply with WTO rules is for the United States (and perhaps others) to use their negotiating leverage to promote such compliance—in particular in the areas where compliance with WTO rules is often problematic: coverage of agricultural products, rules of origin and trade remedies. Gary Hufbauer and Sherry Stephenson examine trade in services and how successful the WTO has been to date in liberalizing such trade—both through the commitments undertaken in GATS and in dispute settlement. They also examine the record on services trade liberalization in regional agreements, as well as the difficulties that have been encountered in the ongoing Doha negotiations on services. They also note the relative successes in services liberalization that have been achieved in PTAs.

One of the more controversial types of cases faced by the WTO dispute settlement system is that where the discretion of a member government to regulate within its borders is challenged. Joel Trachtman explores this question by examining three particularly controversial cases—*Helms Burton, Shrimp and Gambling*—as background for examining theoretical bases for allocating regulatory jurisdiction in the WTO.

In WTO dispute settlement, one of the vexing questions concerns remedies. Currently, the basic remedy is the possibility of "retaliation" by the prevailing party if the defaulting party fails to conform to WTO rules. Whether this is the best remedy, or even an effective remedy or usable at all by smaller WTO members are some of the issues that will have to be addressed in the long run. Andrew Green and Michael Trebilcock explore this issue in the context of considering what is the best remedy for a violation of WTO export subsidy rules. While their analysis focuses on that narrow question, their approach and discussion is of great interest to the more general issue as well, since it lays out a framework for systematically considering the remedy issue.

The third group of papers include three that explore issues that are treated to some limited degree in WTO agreements, but which are generally dealt with by other international organizations or agreements. First, Steve Charnovitz reviews the WTO's experience in dealing with environmental issues, particularly in dispute settlement where the WTO Appellate Body has played a major role in reshaping the perceived relationships between WTO rules and member government discretion to act to protect environmental interests. The last two papers deal with issues that were tentatively agreed to be the subject of negotiations in the Doha talks, but which were ultimately not included because of developing country opposition. In respect of competition rules, David Gerber takes a skeptical view of whether the WTO is an appropriate locus for such rules in the near term, citing both the WTO's institutional shortcomings and the difficult substantive question of exactly what might be the basis for agreeing on such rules in light of the diverse approaches taken by various countries for their internal markets. Finally, Won–Mog Choi explores the world of individual-state dispute settlement under investment agreements and what that experience suggests for the WTO. While not every issue facing the WTO and the international economic regime more generally has been treated in this anniversary issue, these 15 papers cover most of the key issues. Of particular note is the concern raised in many of the papers over institutional issues and questions of legitimacy. Certainly that is one area where the international economic organizations and the WTO in particular will have to devote considerable attention in the coming years.

JOHN H. JACKSON, SOVEREIGNTY, THE WTO, AND CHANGING FUNDAMENTALS OF INTERNATIONAL LAW[2]

The evolution of GATT after the ITO failure, and the change of GATT into the WTO, manifested a sense of many nations that an institutional structure was needed for international trade discourse and disciplining constraints on national behavior. Pragmatic accommodation, good practical sense, and important leadership led a weak "birth defected" GATT to become an important part of the world's international economic institutional landscape.

---

2. Cambridge University Press, 2006, at pages 261–262 & 264–265.

Full "sovereignty" was never a prerequisite for participation in GATT or the WTO.

Equality of nations seemed mandated by the GATT treaty text, but in fact the practice veered away from voting and its dilemmas, to a "consensus approach" to decision making developed by practice, and was carried more formally into the WTO, although such approach has a potential for impeding progress on a number of important issues.

Consensus has important values, in promoting full participation and greater transparency at all levels and in all types of participating nations in the institution.

Problems of treaty rigidity clearly diminished the ability of GATT to evolve satisfactorily with the rapidly changing economic environment of the world.

With regard to rule orientation, the objectives of predictability & stability (reducing the risk premium of economic decisions of millions of entrepreneurs) are important, and lead to support for a rule oriented system, with dispute settlement procedures in a "juridical system." Even without explicit treaty rules about this, the GATT DS system evolved and was accepted by the nation-state participants (contracting parties).

Non-government entities (including individuals) are major beneficiaries of the international institutions, particularly in the context of economic subjects, as well as human rights. The practice and jurisprudence has begun to explicitly recognize this, and to reflect understanding of this principle. Important attention to questions about the role of NGOs is also needed, including careful consideration of better procedures for transparency and participation.

Treaty interpretation becomes an important part of the system, and requires an important juridical approach. Questions are developing about whether the traditional "customary" international law approaches to treaty interpretation such as those embodied in the Vienna Convention of the Law of Treaties are adequate for use with treaties which have large membership and are of long duration and thus are more like "constitutions" than a simpler paradigm of bilateral or mini-lateral treaties.

Some treaty interpretation concepts, such as in *dubio mitius* (which is not in the VCLT, but has been urged in some of the advocacy in the WTO), are absurd and destructive of purposes of institutions like the GATT and WTO. This treaty concept represents "consent theory gone amok," and also evokes thoughts about criticism of the famous international law *Lotus Case*, as being "extreme positivism."

There is clearly an important conceptual and juridical relationship between international economic law and general international law. But the relationship is complex, and if misapplied could be destructive. Among the problems is the broad ambiguity of some international law norms, such as "good faith". When juxtaposed with elaborate and reasonably precise sets of procedural norms such as found in parts of the

WTO, a broad or ambiguous rule can offer dangerous latitude to a juridical institution.

Good governance principles need to be applied to international institutions as well as to nation-states. These principles include issues raised above such as transparency and participation, but also need to include checks and balances, and recognition of "subsidiarity" ideas of the importance of local accountability.

The principle of non-interference in the domestic affairs of "sovereign" nations must be balanced with needed international norms to prevent internal government measures from causing harm to other nations, particularly with reference to economic measures which could seriously inhibit economic development and progress in welfare.

* * *

One of the approaches of this book is to respond to the many extensive challenges and criticisms of the concept of "sovereignty" by urging a pause for reflection about the consequences of discarding that concept in broad measure. Since that concept is fundamental to the logical foundations of traditional international law, such discard risks undermining international law, and certain other principles of the international relations system. This could challenge the legitimacy and moral force of international law, part of what Professor Thomas Franck terms the "compliance pull"[3] of norms backed by characteristics of legitimization. It seems clear that the international relations system (including, but not limited to the international legal system) is being forced to reconsider certain sovereignty concepts. But this must be done carefully, because to bury all the sovereignty concepts without adequate replacements could lead to a situation of pure power prevailing, which, in turn, could encourage chaos, misunderstanding, and conflict, almost like Hobbes' state of nature, where life is "nasty, brutish, and short."[4] In the alternative, this vacuum of legitimization principles could lead to greater aggregations of Hegemonic, monopolistic, or "imperial" power that might not always be handled with appropriate principles of good governance or subsidiarity.

As noted in Section 2.3, the search for a *Kelsonian grundnorm* or some other axiomatic legitimation does not seem too productive and can lead to circular logic. So perhaps the best approach is a "pragmatic" one of observing real life circumstances and events to see what "works," in the sense of the "pragmatism" school of American philosophers Charles Sanders Peirce, William James, and John Dewey. This could lead logically to the view that such empirical appraisal might produce varied results for different international law subject matters. It is also a difficult endeavor to undertake the observations required for generalization,

3. Thomas M. Franck, Fairness in International Law and Institutions (Oxford University Press, 1995), at 41.

4. Thomas Hobbes, Leviathan, (orig. 1651) (Viking Press, 1982) ("[In a state of nature] No arts; no letters; no society; and which is worst of all, continual fear and danger of violent death; and the life of man, solitary, poor, nasty, brutish, and short.")

although the opinions and testimony of persons experienced in international relations endeavors can be a short cut, whether through authored works, interviews, testimony on similar evidence. Henkin's famous phrase quoted in Section 2.3 is an example. This process, while derived from varied circumstances, could be viewed as developing some uniform generalizations for international law generally, and if cautiously applied can be seen as similar (but not necessarily congruent) to IL concepts such as *opinio juris,* and "practice under the agreement" (for treaties).

Reflecting on some of these thought currents, one of the recommendations of this book is to disaggregate and to analyze: break down the complex array of "sovereignty" concepts and examine particular aspects in detail and with precision to understand what is really at play. A major part of this approach would be to understand the pragmatic functionalism of allocation of power as between different levels of governance entities in the world. To the extent feasible, this should be done in a manner not tilted either in favor or against international approaches.

Index

References are to Pages

---

†